A History of WESTERN SOCIETY

Sixth Edition

Volume II From Absolutism to the Present

John P. McKay

University of Illinois at
Urbana-Champaign

Bennett D. Hill

Georgetown University

John Buckler

University of Illinois at
Urbana-Champaign

HOUGHTON MIFFLIN COMPANY

Boston   New York

Sponsoring Editor: Andrea Shaw
Development Editor: Dale Anderson
Assistant Editor: Lisa Rothrauff
Senior Project Editor: Christina M. Horn
Editorial Assistant: Leah Y. Mehl
Production/Design Coordinator: Jennifer Meyer Dare
Manufacturing Manager: Florence Cadran
Senior Marketing Manager: Sandra McGuire

Credits   **Page 880:** Parody by Henry Labouchère, quoted in *The Social History of the Machine Gun,* by John Ellis. Copyright © 1975 by John Ellis. Reprinted by permission of Pantheon Books, a division of Random House, Inc.

Volume II Cover Image: *Mlle Dihau at the Piano* (1869–1872), by Edgar Degas. Musée d'Orsay, Paris/Erich Lessing/Art Resource, NY.
Cover Designer: Diana Coe
Photo Researcher: Linda Sykes

Printed in the U.S.A.
Library of Congress Catalog Card Number: 98-72228
ISBN: 0-395-90433-1
 2 3 4 5 6 7 8 9-VH-02 01 00 99

About the Authors

John P. McKay Born in St. Louis, Missouri, John P. McKay received his B.A. from Wesleyan University (1961), his M.A. from the Fletcher School of Law and Diplomacy (1962), and his Ph.D. from the University of California, Berkeley (1968). He began teaching history at the University of Illinois in 1966 and became a professor there in 1976. John won the Herbert Baxter Adams Prize for his book *Pioneers for Profit: Foreign Entrepreneurship and Russian Industrialization, 1885–1913* (1970). He has also written *Tramways and Trolleys: The Rise of Urban Mass Transport in Europe* (1976) and has translated Jules Michelet's *The People* (1973). His research has been supported by fellowships from the Ford Foundation, the Guggenheim Foundation, the National Endowment for the Humanities, and IREX. He has written well over a hundred articles, book chapters, and reviews, which have appeared in numerous publications, including *The American Historical Review, Business History Review, The Journal of Economic History,* and *Slavic Review.* Recently, he contributed extensively to C. Stewart and P. Fritzsche, eds., *Imagining the Twentieth Century* (1997).

Bennett D. Hill A native of Philadelphia, Bennett D. Hill earned an A.B. from Princeton (1956) and advanced degrees from Harvard (A.M., 1958) and Princeton (Ph.D., 1963). He taught history at the University of Illinois at Urbana, where he was department chairman from 1978 to 1981. He has published *English Cistercian Monasteries and Their Patrons in the Twelfth Century* (1968), *Church and State in the Middle Ages* (1970), and articles in *Analecta Cisterciensia, The New Catholic Encyclopaedia, The American Benedictine Review,* and *The Dictionary of the Middle Ages.* His reviews have appeared in *The American Historical Review, Specu-*

lum, The Historian, the *Journal of World History,* and *Library Journal.* He has been a Fellow of the American Council of Learned Societies and served on the editorial board of *The American Benedictine Review,* on committees of the National Endowment for the Humanities, and as Vice President of the American Catholic Historical Association (1995–1996). A Benedictine monk of St. Anselm's Abbey in Washington, D.C., he is also a Visiting Professor at Georgetown University.

John Buckler Born in Louisville, Kentucky, John Buckler received his B.A. (summa cum laude) from the University of Louisville in 1967. Harvard University awarded him the Ph.D. in 1973. From 1984 to 1986 he was an Alexander von Humboldt Fellow at the Institut für Alte Geschichte, University of Munich. He has lectured at the Fondation Hardt at the University of Geneva and at the University of Freiburg. He has also participated in numerous international conferences. He is currently a professor of Greek history at the University of Illinois. In 1980 Harvard University Press published his *Theban Hegemony, 371–362* B.C. He has also published *Philip II and the Sacred War* (Leiden 1989) and co-edited *BOIOTIKA: Vorträge vom 5. Internationalen Böotien-Kolloquium* (Munich 1989). He has contributed articles to *The American Historical Association's Guide to Historical Literature* (Oxford 1995), *The Oxford Classical Dictionary* (Oxford 1996), and *Encyclopedia of Greece and the Hellenic Tradition* (London 1999). His other articles have appeared in journals both here and abroad, including the *American Journal of Ancient History, Classical Philology, Rheinisches Museum für Philologie, Klio, Classical Quarterly, Wiener Studien,* and many others.

Contents in Brief

Contents

✛ Chapter 16

Absolutism and Constitutionalism in Western Europe (ca 1589–1715)   530

✛ Chapter 17

Absolutism in Eastern Europe to 1740   564

✛ Chapter 18

Toward a New World-view   594

❖ **Chapter 19**

The Expansion of Europe in the Eighteenth Century   628

❖ **Chapter 20**

The Changing Life of the People   660

❖ **Chapter 21**

The Revolution in Politics, 1775–1815   690

Maps

❖   ❖   ❖

Timelines

The comparative timeline *A History of Western Society: A Brief Overview* is located at the end of the book.

Listening to the Past

Preface ✤   ✤   ✤

A History of Western Society grew out of the authors' desire to infuse new life into the study of Western civilization. We knew full well that historians were using imaginative questions and innovative research to open up vast new areas of historical interest and knowledge. We also recognized that these advances had dramatically affected the subject of European economic, intellectual, and, especially, social history, while new research and fresh interpretations were also revitalizing the study of the traditional mainstream of political, diplomatic, and religious development. Despite history's vitality as a discipline, however, it seemed to us that both the broad public and the intelligentsia were generally losing interest in the past.

It was our conviction, based on considerable experience introducing large numbers of students to the broad sweep of Western civilization, that a book reflecting current trends could excite readers and inspire a renewed interest in history and our Western heritage. Our strategy was twofold. First, we made social history a core element of our work. We not only incorporated recent research by social historians but also sought to recreate the life of ordinary people in appealing human terms. At the same time we were determined to give great economic, political, cultural, and intellectual developments the attention they unquestionably deserve. We wanted to give individual readers and instructors a balanced, integrated perspective so that they could pursue—on their own or in the classroom—those themes and questions that they found particularly exciting and significant. In an effort to realize fully the potential of our fresh yet balanced approach, we made many changes, large and small, in the editions that followed.

CHANGES IN THE NEW EDITION

In preparing the sixth edition we have worked hard to keep our book up-to-date and to strengthen our distinctive yet balanced approach. Five main lines of revision guided our many changes.

New "Individuals in Society" Feature

First, in each chapter of the sixth edition we have added a short study of a fascinating man or woman or group of people, which is carefully integrated into the main discussion in the text. This new "Individuals in Society" feature grows out of our long-standing focus on people's lives and the varieties of historical experience, and we believe that readers will empathize with these flesh-and-blood human beings as they themselves seek to define their own identities today. The spotlighting of individuals, both famous and obscure, carries forward the greater attention to cultural and intellectual developments that we used to invigorate our social history in the fifth edition, and it reflects changing interests within the historical profession as well as the development of "micro history."

The range of men and women we consider is great. Several are famous historical actors, such as the Roman orator Cicero (Chapter 5), the mystical Saint Teresa of Ávila (Chapter 14), the charismatic Russian rebel Stenka Razin (Chapter 17), the ruthless British imperialist Cecil Rhodes (Chapter 26), and the creator of communist Yugoslavia, Marshal Tito (Chapter 30). Other individuals illuminate aspects of their times but are not well-known: a solid Roman soldier (Chapter 6); a serf who gained freedom and success (Chapter 10); a Jewish businesswoman and mother of thirteen (Chapter 16); a talented midwife in colonial America (Chapter 20); and a pioneering professional woman in nineteenth-century Berlin (Chapter 24). Collective biographies of the Jews of medieval Speyer (Chapter 9) and the Protestant villagers resisting Nazi evil in Le Chambon in southern France (Chapter 29) probe the dimensions of collective identity and social action. Creative artists and intellectuals include the Greek play-wright Menander (Chapter 4), the Italian Renaissance painter Gentile Bellini (Chapter 13), the Jewish philosopher Moses Mendelssohn (Chapter 18), the influential romantic writer Germaine de Staël (Chapter 23), and the left-wing socialist theorist Rosa Luxemburg (Chapter 27).

Expanded Ethnic and Geographic Scope

Second, in this edition we have added significantly more discussion of groups and regions that are frequently shortchanged in the general histories of Europe and Western civilization. This expanded scope is, we feel, an important improvement. It reflects the renewed awareness within the profession of Europe's enormous historical diversity, as well as the efforts of contemporary Europeans to understand the ambivalent and contested meanings of their national, regional, ethnic, and pan-European identities. Examples of this enlarged scope include early Greek influence in the western Mediterranean (Chapter 3) and subsequent developments there (Chapter 4); greatly expanded treatment of Europe's borderlands—Iberia, Ireland, Scotland, eastern Europe, and the Baltic area—in the Middle Ages (Chapters 9, 11, 12); developments in absolutist Sweden and southern Russia (Chapter 17); Spanish urban life (Chapter 24); and completely new and detailed discussion of twentieth-century eastern Europe (Chapters 27, 30, and 31). A broader treatment of Jewish history has been integrated into the text throughout this edition, just as the history of women and gender was integrated in the fifth edition. Examples include anti-Semitism during the Spanish Inquisition (Chapter 13) and in tsarist Russia (Chapter 27); Jewish Enlightenment thought in Germany (Chapter 18); and the unfolding of the Holocaust during the Second World War (Chapter 29).

Organizational Changes

Third, our expanded ethnic and geographic scope is one of several organizational improvements. Chapters 30 and 31 have been completely rewritten in order to present and interpret the historic changes that have transformed Europe and the world in the last fifteen years. Thus Chapter 30 treats the entire cold war era to the mid-1980s, while Chapter 31 analyzes the decline and collapse of communism, the re-emergence and reconstruction of eastern Europe, German unification and its consequences, ethnic conflicts and civil war in

the Balkans, economic and cultural changes, immigration and globalization, the European Union, and the future in the new millennium. Chapter 6 has also been extensively reorganized to include a section on Late Antiquity. Chapters 9, 11, and 12 have been recast to highlight the interactions between English, German, and Spanish colonizers and the peoples they encountered and sometimes conquered. Discussions of politics after 1815 in Chapter 23 and of the public health revolution in Chapter 24 have been sharpened and tightened up.

Incorporation of Recent Scholarship

Fourth, as in all previous revisions we have made a conscientious effort to keep our book up-to-date with new and significant scholarship. Because the authors are committed to a balanced approach that reflects the true value of history, we have continued to incorporate important new findings on political, economic, cultural, and intellectual developments in this edition. Revisions of this nature include Chaldean Babylonia and the Kassites (Chapter 2), the Greek polis (Chapter 3), the Etruscans and the pre-Etruscans (Chapter 5), the Byzantine Empire (Chapter 7), the Merovingian and Carolingian kingdoms (Chapter 8), consumerism in Renaissance Italy (Chapter 13), absolutism in Western Europe (Chapter 16), the Enlightenment in Germany (Chapter 18), women in health care, business, and the liberal professions (Chapters 20, 22, and 24), the social aspects of Italian unification and the consequences of the Franco-Prussian War (Chapter 23), the action of left-wing socialists in Germany (Chapter 27), the causes of the Great Depression and the policies of the New Deal in the United States (Chapter 28), factors influencing Nazi voters in 1932 and Soviet collectivization (Chapter 29), and the collapse of communism (Chapter 31). In short, recent research keeps the broad sweep of our history fresh.

Revised Full-Color Art and Map Programs

Finally, the illustrative component of our work has been carefully revised. We have added many new illustrations to our extensive art program, which includes nearly two hundred color reproductions, letting great art and important events come alive. As in earlier editions, all illustrations have been carefully selected to complement the text, and all carry informative captions based on thorough research that enhance their value. Artwork remains an integral part of our book; the past can speak in pictures as well as in words. The use of full color serves to clarify the maps and graphs and to enrich the textual material. The maps and map captions have been updated to correlate directly to the text, and new maps have been added in Chapters 9 and 31.

DISTINCTIVE FEATURES

In addition to the new "Individuals in Society" study, distinctive features from earlier editions guide the reader in the process of historical understanding. Many of these features also show how historians sift through and evaluate evidence. Our goal is to suggest how historians actually work and think. We want the reader to think critically and to realize that history is neither a list of cut-and-dried facts nor a senseless jumble of conflicting opinions. To help students and instructors realize this goal, we have significantly expanded the discussion of "what is history" in Chapter 1 of this edition.

Revised Primary-Source Feature

In the fifth edition we added a two-page excerpt from a primary source at the end of each chapter. This important feature, entitled "Listening to the Past," extends and illuminates a major historical issue considered in the chapter, and it has been well received by instructors and students. In the new edition we have reviewed our selections and made judicious substitutions. For example, in Chapter 3 Thucydides describes the great plague of Athens and in Chapter 4 Tacitus depicts the meeting of Greek and Egyptian culture. The writings of Godric of Finchdale (Chapter 10) and Christine de Pisan (Chapter 12) shed new light on the Middle Ages, while Calvin outlines his plan for Geneva in Chapter 14. A former African slave details his captivity and sale in Chapter 19, while a Japanese patriot urges military reforms to counter European imperialism in Chapter 26. A soldier and a Viennese woman recount their experiences in the First World War in Chapter 27, and the Solidarity activist Adam Michnik defends nonviolent resistance to communism from prison in Chapter 31.

Each primary source opens with a problem-setting introduction and closes with "Questions for Analysis" that invite students to evaluate the evidence as historians would. Drawn from a range of writings addressing a variety of social, cultural, political, and intellectual issues, these sources promote active involvement and critical interpretation. Selected for their interest and importance and carefully fitted into their historical context, these sources do indeed allow the student to "listen to the past" and to observe how history has been shaped by individual men and women, some of them great aristocrats, others ordinary folk.

Problems of Historical Interpretation

The addition of more problems of historical interpretation in the fifth edition was well received, so we have increased their number again in this edition. We believe that the problematic element helps our readers develop the critical-thinking skills that are among the most precious benefits of studying history. New examples of this more open-ended, interpretive approach include the debate over the transition from Antiquity to the early Middle Ages (Chapter 6), the question of European racism in the Middle Ages (Chapter 12), the issue of gender in the Italian cities of the Renaissance (Chapter 13), the renewed debate on personal and collective responsibilities for the Holocaust (Chapter 29), the dynamics of the great purges in the Soviet Union (Chapter 29), the process of reconstruction in eastern Europe and the debate over globalization (Chapter 31).

Improved Chapter Features

Other distinctive features from earlier editions have been reviewed and improved in the sixth edition. To help guide the reader toward historical understanding, we pose specific historical questions at the beginning of each chapter. These questions are then answered in the course of each chapter, and each chapter concludes with a concise summary of its findings. All of the questions and summaries have been re-examined and frequently revised in order to maximize the usefulness of this popular feature.

In addition to posing chapter-opening questions and presenting more problems in historical interpretation, we have quoted extensively from a wide variety of primary sources in the narrative, demonstrating in our use of these quotations how historians evaluate evidence. Thus primary sources are examined as an integral part of the narrative as well as presented in extended form in the "Listening to the Past" chapter feature. We believe that such an extensive program of both integrated and separate primary source excerpts will help readers learn to interpret and think critically.

Each chapter concludes with carefully selected suggestions for further reading. These suggestions are briefly described to help readers know where to turn to continue thinking and learning about the Western world. Also chapter bibliographies have been thoroughly revised and updated to keep them current with the vast amount of new work being done in many fields.

Revised Timelines

The timelines appearing in earlier editions have been revised in this edition. Once again we provide a unified timeline in an appendix at the end of the book. Comprehensive and easy to locate, this useful timeline allows students to compare simultaneous political, economic, social, cultural, intellectual, and scientific developments over the centuries.

Flexible Format

Western civilization courses differ widely in chronological structure from one campus to another. To accommodate the various divisions of historical time into intervals that fit a two-quarter, three-quarter, or two-semester period, *A History of Western Society* is being published in four versions, three of which embrace the complete work:

- One-volume hardcover edition: A HISTORY OF WESTERN SOCIETY
- Two-volume paperback: A HISTORY OF WESTERN SOCIETY, *Volume I: From Antiquity to the Enlightenment* (Chapters 1–17); *Volume II: From Absolutism to the Present* (Chapters 16–31)
- Three-volume paperback: A HISTORY OF WESTERN SOCIETY, *Volume A: From Antiquity to 1500* (Chapters 1–13); *Volume B: From the Renaissance to 1815* (Chapters 12–21); *Volume C: From the Revolutionary Era to the Present* (Chapters 21–31)
- A HISTORY OF WESTERN SOCIETY, *Since 1300* (Chapters 12–31), for courses on Europe since the Renaissance

Note that overlapping chapters in both the two- and the three-volume sets permit still wider flexibility in matching the appropriate volume with the opening and closing dates of a course term.

ANCILLARIES

Learning and teaching ancillaries, listed below, also contribute to the usefulness of the text.

- *Study Guide*
- *Online Study Guide*
- *Instructor's Resource Manual*
- *Test Items*
- *Computerized Test Items*

- *GeoQuest™: an interactive map CD-ROM*
- *Bibliobase™: custom coursepacks in Western civilization*
- *Power Presentation Manager*
- *Map Transparencies*

The excellent *Study Guide* has been thoroughly revised by Professor James Schmiechen of Central Michigan University. Professor Schmiechen has been a tower of strength ever since he critiqued our initial prospectus, and he has continued to give us many valuable suggestions as well as his warmly appreciated support. His *Study Guide* contains learning objectives, chapter summaries, chapter outlines, review questions, extensive multiple-choice exercises, self-check lists of important concepts and events, and a variety of study aids and suggestions. The sixth edition also retains the study-review exercises on the interpretation of visual sources and major political ideas as well as suggested issues for discussion and essay, chronology reviews, and sections on studying effectively. These sections take the student through reading and studying activities such as underlining, summarizing, identifying main points, classifying information according to sequence, and making historical comparisons. To enable both students and instructors to use the *Study Guide* with the greatest possible flexibility, the guide is available in two volumes, with considerable overlapping of chapters. Instructors and students who use only Volumes A and B of the text have all the pertinent study materials in a single volume, *Study Guide, Volume I* (Chapters 1–21); likewise, those who use only Volumes B and C of the text also have all the necessary materials in one volume, *Study Guide, Volume II* (Chapters 12–31). An *Online Study Guide* is also available for students. Accessible through Houghton Mifflin's @history website (www.hmco.com/college/), it functions as a tutorial, providing rejoinders to all multiple-choice questions that explain why the student's response is or is not correct.

The *Instructor's Resource Manual,* prepared by Professor John Marshall Carter, contains instructional objectives, annotated chapter outlines, suggestions for lectures and discussion, paper and class activity topics, primary-source exercises, map activities, and lists of audio-visual resources. The accompanying *Test Items,* by Professor Charles Crouch of Georgia Southern University, offer identification, multiple-choice, map, and essay questions for a total of approximately two thousand test items. These test items are available to adopters in a Windows version that includes editing capability.

An exciting addition to our map program is a CD-ROM of thirty interactive maps—GeoQuest™, available for both instructors and students.

We are also proud to announce the creation of our on-line primary-source collection, Bibliobase™. This resource will allow instructors to select from over six hundred documents to create their own customized reader for courses in Western civilization. Visit our web site at **www.bibliobase.com** for more information.

To add an exciting multimedia component to lectures, we have created Power Presentation Manager (PPM), a software tool that enables teachers to prepare visual aids for lectures electronically. Using both textual and visual materials, instructors can customize their lectures by incorporating their own material into the PPM and combining it with the electronic resources available. Please contact your Houghton Mifflin Company representative for more information about this innovative and exciting multimedia program.

Finally, a set of full-color Map Transparencies of all the maps in the text is available on adoption.

Acknowledgments   ✛   ✛   ✛

It is a pleasure to thank the many instructors who read and critiqued the manuscript through its development:

Christopher Bellitto
St. Joseph's Seminary

William D. Burgess
East Tennessee State University

Carolyn A. Conley
University of Alabama at Birmingham

Charles Crouch
Georgia Southern University

Robert L. Dise, Jr.
University of Northern Iowa

Greg Eghigian
University of Texas, Arlington

Linda Frey
University of Montana

Mary T. Furgol
Montgomery College

Amy G. Gordon
Denison University

Daniel Gordon
University of Massachusetts, Amherst

Piotr Gorecki
University of Cracow

Jeffrey Herf
Ohio University

David Hudson
California State University, Fresno

Charles Ingrao
Purdue University

David Kammerance
Florence Darlington Technical College

Jonathan Katz
Oregon State University

James K. Kieswetter
Eastern Washington University

Cynthia Kosso
Northern Arizona University

James Lehning
University of Utah

Alex Lichtenstein
Florida International University

Sean Farrell Moran
Oakland University

Ross L. Pattison
Dutchess Community College

Kathleen Paul
University of South Florida

Linda J. Piper
University of Georgia

Norman G. Raiford
Greenville Technical College

Kenneth Schellhage
Northern Michigan University

David S. Sefton
Eastern Kentucky University

Michael Slaven
California University of Pennsylvania

Kay Slocum
Kent State University

Roger P. Snow
University of Great Falls

William Stiebing
University of New Orleans

Bruce M. Taylor
University of Dayton

Thomas Turley
Santa Clara University

Richard D. Weigel
Western Kentucky University

James M. Woods
Georgia Southern University

It is also a pleasure to thank our many editors at Houghton Mifflin for their efforts over many years. To Christina Horn, who guided production in the ever-more intensive email age, and to Dale Anderson, our development editor, we express our special appreciation. And we thank Carole Frohlich for her contributions in photo research and selection.

Many of our colleagues at the University of Illinois and at Georgetown University continued to provide in-formation and stimulation, often without even knowing it. We thank them for it. Bennett Hill wishes to express his appreciation to Ramón de la Fuente for his assistance in the preparation of this sixth edition. John Buckler wishes to thank Professor Nicholas Yalouris, former General Inspector of Antiquities, for his kind permission to publish the newly discovered mosaic from Elis, Greece, in Chapter 3. John McKay happily acknowledges the fine research assistance provided by Camille Monahan and thanks her for it. He also expresses his deep appreciation to Jo Ann McKay for her sharp-eyed editorial support and unfailing encouragement.

Each of us has benefited from the criticism of his co-authors, although each of us assumes responsibility for what he has written. John Buckler has written the first six chapters; Bennett Hill has continued the narrative through Chapter 16; and John McKay has written Chapters 17 through 31. Finally, we continue to welcome the many comments and suggestions that have come from our readers, for they have helped us greatly in this ongoing endeavor.

J. P. M.   B. D. H.   J. B.

Introduction

THE ORIGINS OF MODERN WESTERN SOCIETY

The origins of modern Western society lie in the ancient and medieval past. Through archaeological evidence, scholars trace the roots of Western culture to Mesopotamia, the area in southwest Asia bound by the Tigris and Euphrates Rivers. Each civilization that successfully flourished there between roughly 7000 and 500 B.C.—Mesopotamian, Egyptian, and Hittite—made notable achievements. These achievements became the legacies that were absorbed and utilized by later cultures, Hebraic, Greek, and Roman. The Middle Ages built on the Greek and Roman past. Similarly, the European intellectual and religious movements often called the Renaissance and the Reformation derive from the medieval past. History, the study of change over time, reveals that each age has reinterpreted the cultural legacy of its predecessors in the effort to meet its own demands. The modern world exists as the product of all that has gone before.

THE ANCIENT WORLD

The ancient world provided several cultural elements that the modern world has inherited. First came the beliefs of the Hebrews (Jewish forebears) in one God and in a chosen people with whom God had made a covenant. The book known as the Scriptures, or "sacred writings," embodied Hebraic law, history, and culture. Second, Greek architectural, philosophical, and scientific ideas have exercised a profound influence on Western thought. Rome subsequently gave the West language and law. The Latin language became the instrument of verbal and written communication for more than a

thousand years; Roman concepts of law and government molded Western ideas of political organization. Finally, Christianity, the spiritual faith and ecclesiastical organization that derived from a Palestinian Jew, Jesus of Nazareth (ca 3 B.C.–A.D. 29), also came to condition Western religious, social, and moral values and systems.

The Hebrews

The Hebrews probably originated in northern Mesopotamia. Nomads who tended flocks of sheep, they were forced by drought to follow their patriarch Abraham into the Nile Delta in Egypt according to biblical tradition. The Egyptians enslaved them and put them to work on various agricultural and building projects. In the crucial event of early Jewish history known as "the Exodus," the biblical lawgiver Moses, in response to God's command, led the Hebrews out of Egypt into the Promised Land (Palestine) in the thirteenth century B.C. At that time, the Hebrews consisted of twelve disunited tribes made up of families. They all believed themselves to be descendants of a common ancestor, Abraham. The family was their primary social institution, and most families engaged in agricultural or pastoral pursuits. Under the pressure of a series of wars for the control of Palestine, the twelve independent Hebrew tribes were united into a centralized political force under one king. Kings Saul, David, and especially Solomon (ca 965–925 B.C.) built the Hebrew nation with its religious center at Jerusalem, the symbol of Jewish unity.

The Hebrews developed their religious ideas in the Scriptures, also known as the Hebrew Bible and (to Christians) the Old Testament. In their migration, the Hebrews had come in contact with many peoples, such as the Mesopotamians and the Egyptians, who had many gods. The Hebrews, however, were monotheistic: their God was the one and only God, He had created all things, His presence filled the universe, and He took a strong personal interest in the individual. According to the Scriptures, during the Exodus from Egypt, God had made a covenant with the Hebrews. He promised to protect them as His chosen people and to give them the land; in return, they must worship only Him and obey the Ten Commandments that He had given Moses. The Ten Commandments comprise an ethical code of behavior, forbidding the Hebrews to steal, lie, murder, or commit adultery. This covenant was to prove a constant force in Jewish life. The first five books of the Hebrew Bible constitute the Pentateuch, or the Torah, meaning divine instruction; theoretically, the Torah provides instruction on all activities and social relationships. The Hebrew Bible also contains detailed legal proscriptions, books of history, concepts of social and familial structure, wisdom literature, and prophecies of a Messiah (savior) to come. Parts of the Scriptures show the Hebraic debt to other cultures. For example, the Books of Proverbs and Sirach reflect strong Egyptian influences. The Hebrews developed an emotionally satisfying religion whose ideals shaped not only later faiths, such as Christianity and Islam, but also influenced the modern world.

The Greeks

Whereas ancient Middle Eastern peoples such as the Hebrews interpreted the origins, nature, and end of humanity in religious or theological terms, the Greeks treated these issues in terms of reason. In the fifth century B.C., small independent city-states (poleis) dotted the Greek peninsula. Athens, especially, created a brilliant culture that greatly influenced Western civilization. Athens developed a magnificent architecture whose grace, beauty, and quiet intensity still speak to people. In their comedies and tragedies, the Athenians Aeschylus, Sophocles, and Euripides were the first playwrights to treat eternal problems of the human condition. Athens also experimented with the political system we call democracy. All citizen men participated directly in lawmaking and in the government of the polis. Because a large part of the population—women and slaves—were not allowed to share in the activity of the Assembly, and because aristocrats held most important offices in the polis, Athenian democracy must not be confused with modern democratic practices. The modern form of democracy, moreover, is representative rather than

direct: citizens express their views and wishes through elected representatives. Nevertheless, in their noble experiment in which the people were the government and in their view that the state existed for the good of the citizen, Athenians served to create a powerful political ideal.

Classical Greece of the fifth and fourth centuries B.C. also witnessed an incredible flowering of philosophical ideas. The Greeks were not the first people to speculate about the origins and nature of human beings and the universe. The outstanding achievement of the Greeks, rather, was their interest in treating these questions in rational instead of religious terms. Hippocrates, the "father of medicine," taught that natural means—not magical or religious ones—could be found to fight disease. He based his opinions on observation. Hippocrates also insisted that medicine was a branch of knowledge separate from philosophy. This distinction between natural science and philosophy was supported by the sophists, who traveled the Greek world teaching young men that human beings were the proper subject for study. They laid great emphasis on logic and the meaning of words and criticized traditional beliefs, religion, and even the laws of the polis.

Building on the approach of the sophists, Socrates (ca 470–399 B.C.) spent his life questioning and investigating. Socrates held that human beings and their environments represent the essential subject for philosophical inquiry. He taught that excellence could be learned and, by seeking excellence through knowledge, human beings could find the highest good and ultimately true happiness. Socrates' pupil Plato (427–347 B.C.) continued his teacher's work. Plato wrote down his thoughts, which survive in the form of dialogues. He founded a school, the Academy, where he developed the theory that visible, tangible things are unreal and archetypes of "ideas" or "forms" that are constant and indestructible. In *The Republic*, the first literary description of a utopian society, Plato discusses the nature of justice in the ideal state. In *The Symposium*, he treats the nature and end of love.

Aristotle (384–322 B.C.), Plato's student, continued the philosophical tradition in the next generation. He investigated many subjects, including the nature of government, ideas of matter and motion, outer space, conduct, and language and literature. In all his works, Aristotle emphasizes the importance of directly observing nature; he insisted that theory must follow fact. Aristotle had one of the most inquiring and original minds that Western civilization has ever produced, and his ideas later profoundly shaped both Muslim and Western philosophy and theology.

The Greeks originated medicine, science, philosophy, and other branches of knowledge. They asked penetrating questions and came up with immortal responses. Recent research of Greek historians has focused on two areas: the social and cultural context in which the ideas of Plato and Aristotle flourished and women's experience within that context.

These phenomenal intellectual advances took place against a background of constant warfare. The long and bitter struggle between the cities of Athens and Sparta called the Peloponnesian War (439–404 B.C.), described in the historian Thucydides' classic *The History of the Peloponnesian War,* ended in Athens' defeat. Shortly afterward, Sparta, Athens, and Thebes contested for hegemony in Greece, but no single state was strong enough to dominate the others. Taking advantage of the situation, Philip II (359–336 B.C.) of Macedon, a small kingdom encompassing part of modern Greece and the former Yugoslavia, defeated a combined Theban-Athenian army in 338 B.C. Unable to resolve their domestic quarrels, the Greeks lost their freedom to the Macedonian invader.

In 323 B.C., Philip's son, Alexander of Macedonia, died at the age of 32. During the twelve short years of his reign, Alexander had conquered an empire stretching from Macedonia in the present-day Balkans across the Middle East into Asia as far as India. Because none of the generals who succeeded him could hold together such a vast territory, it disintegrated into separate kingdoms. Scholars label the period dating from ca 800 B.C. to 323 B.C., in which the polis predominated, the Hellenic Age. The time span from Alexander's death in 323 B.C. to the fall of Egypt to Rome in 30 B.C., which was characterized by independent kingdoms, is commonly called the Hellenistic Age.

The Hellenistic period witnessed two profoundly significant developments: the diffusion of Greek culture through Asia Minor and the further advance of science, medicine, and philosophy. As Alexander advanced eastward, he established cities and military colonies in strategic spots. Militarily, these helped secure his supply line and control of the countryside. Culturally, as Greek immigrants poured into the East, they served as powerful instruments in the spread of Hellenism. Though the Greeks were a minority in the East, the dominant language, laws, and institutions became Greek. Thus, a uniform culture spread throughout the East. Greek culture linked the East and the West, and this cultural

bond later helped Roman efforts impose unity on the Mediterranean world.

Hellenistic scientific progress likewise had enormous consequences. Aristarchus of Samos (ca 310–230 B.C.) rejected Aristotle's idea that the earth is the center of the universe, and using only the naked eye, advanced the heliocentric theory that the earth and other planets revolve around the sun. The Alexandrian mathematician Euclid (ca 300 B.C.) compiled a textbook, *Principles of Geometry,* which has proved basic to education in the West. Archimedes of Syracuse studied the principles of mechanics governing instruments such as the lever and invented numerous practical devices, including the catapult and Archimedean screw. Hellenistic physicians dissected the human body, enabling better knowledge of anatomy and improvements in surgery. The mathematician Eratosthenes (285–ca 204 B.C.), who directed the library of Alexandria—the greatest seat of learning in the Hellenistic world—calculated the earth's circumference geometrically at 24,675 miles; it is actually 24,860 miles.

In philosophy, Hellenistic thinkers continued the rational approach of the Greeks. Stoicism, so called from the building where its earliest proponents taught (the *Stoa*), represents the greatest philosophical development of the Hellenistic period. Stressing the value of inner strength, or fortitude, in facing life's difficulties, the Stoics originated the concept of natural law; that is, because all men are brothers and all good men live in harmony with nature (reason) and the universe, one law—the natural law—governs all. The Stoics advocated a universal state government: not a political state but an ethical one based on individual behavior. These ideas strongly attracted the Romans, who used the ideal of a universal state as a rationale for extending their empire over peoples of diverse laws and institutions.

Rome

The city of Rome, situated near the center of the boot-shaped peninsula of Italy, conquered all of what it considered to be the civilized world. Rome's great achievement, however, rested in its ability not only to conquer peoples but also to incorporate them into the Roman way of life. Rome created a world state that embraced the entire Mediterranean basin. It bequeathed to the Middle Ages and the modern world three great legacies: Roman law, the Latin language, and flexible administrative practices.

According to tradition, Rome was founded in the mid-eighth century B.C. Etruscans from the north and waves of Greek immigrants from the south influenced its early history. In 509 B.C., Rome expelled the Etruscan king, Tarquin the Proud, and founded a republic. Scholars customarily divide Roman history into two stages: the republic (ca 509–31 B.C.), during which Rome grew from a small city-state to an empire, and the Empire, the period when the old republican constitution fell to a constitutional monarchy. Between 509 and 290 B.C. Rome subdued all of Italy, and between 282 and 146 B.C. slowly acquired an overseas empire. The dominant feature of the social history of the early Republic was the clash between patrician aristocrats and plebeian commoners.

While the Greeks speculated about the ideal state, the Romans pragmatically developed methods of governing themselves and their empire. Their real genius lay in government and law. Because the Romans continually faced concrete challenges, change was a constant feature of their political life. The senate was the most important institution of the republic. Composed of aristocratic elders, it initially served to advise the other governing group, the magistrates. As the senate's prestige increased, its advice came to have the force of law. Roman law, called the *ius civilis* or "civil law," consisted of statutes, customs, and forms of procedure. The goal of the *ius civilis* was to protect citizens' lives, property, and reputations. As Rome expanded, first throughout Italy and then into the Mediterranean basin, legal devices had to be found to settle disputes among foreigners or between foreigners and Romans. Sometimes magistrates adopted parts of other (foreign) legal systems. On other occasions, they used the law of equity: with no precedent to guide them, they made decisions on the basis of what seemed fair to all parties. Thus, with flexibility the keynote in dealing with specific cases and circumstances, a new body of law, the *ius gentium* or "law of the peoples," evolved. This law was applicable to both Romans and foreigners.

Law was not the only facet of Hellenistic culture to influence the Romans. The Roman conquest of the Hellenistic East led to the wholesale confiscation of Greek sculpture and paintings to adorn Roman temples and homes. Greek literary and historical classics were translated into Latin; Greek philosophy was studied in the Roman schools; Greek plays were adapted to the Roman stage; educated people learned Greek as a matter of course. Public baths based on the Greek model—with exercise rooms, swimming pools, reading rooms, and snack bars—served not only as centers for recreation and exercise but as centers of Roman public life. Rome assimilated the Greek achievement, and Hellenism became an enduring feature of Roman life.

With territorial conquests Romans also acquired serious problems in the control of their vast lands, which surfaced toward the end of the second century B.C. Characteristically, the Romans responded practically, with a system of provincial administration that placed appointed state officials at the head of local provincial governments. The Romans devised an efficient system of tax collecting as well. Overseas warfare required huge armies for long periods of time. A major theme of current historical research has been the changing composition of the Roman army during the republic and the empire. A few army officers gained fabulous wealth, but most soldiers did not and returned home to find their farms in ruins. Those with cash to invest bought up small farms, creating vast estates called *latifundia*. Because the law forbade landless men to serve in the army, most veterans migrated to Rome, seeking work. Victorious armies had already sent tens of thousands of slaves to Rome, and veterans could not compete with slaves in the labor market. A huge unemployed urban population resulted. Its demands for work and political reform were bitterly resisted by the aristocratic senate, and civil war characterized the first century B.C.

Out of the violence and disorder emerged Julius Caesar (100–44 B.C.), a victorious general, shrewd politician, and highly popular figure. He took practical steps to end the civil war, such as expanding citizenship and sending large numbers of the urban poor to found colonies in Gaul, Spain, and North Africa. These settlements spread Roman culture. Fearful that Caesar's popularity and ambition would turn Rome into a monarchy, a group of aristocratic conspirators assassinated him in 44 B.C. Civil war was renewed. Ultimately, in 31 B.C. Caesar's adopted son Octavian, known as Augustus, defeated his rivals and became master of Rome.

The reign of Augustus (31 B.C.–A.D. 14) marked the end of the republic and the beginning of what historians called the empire. Augustus continued Caesar's work. By fashioning a means of cooperation in government among the people, magistrates, senate, and army, Augustus established a constitutional monarchy that replaced the republic. His own power derived from the various magistracies he held and the power granted him by the senate. Thus, as commander of the Roman army, he held the title of *imperator*, which later came to mean "emperor" in the modern sense of sovereign power.

Augustus ended domestic turmoil and secured the provinces. He founded new colonies, mainly in the western Mediterranean basin, which promoted the spread of Greco-Roman culture and the Latin language to the West. Magistrates exercised authority in their regions as representatives of Rome. (Later, after the empire disintegrated, local magnates continued to exercise local power.) Caracalla later extended Roman citizenship to all free men. A system of Roman roads and sea-lanes united the empire. For two hundred years, the Mediterranean world experienced the *pax Romana*—a period of peace, order, harmony, and flourishing culture.

In the third century, this harmony collapsed. Rival generals backed by their troops contested the imperial throne. In the disorder caused by the civil war that ensued, the frontiers were sometimes left unmanned, and Germanic invaders poured across the borders. Throughout the empire, civil war and barbarian invasions devastated towns and farms, causing severe economic depression. The emperors Diocletian (A.D. 285–305) and Constantine (A.D. 306–337) tried to halt the general disintegration by reorganizing the empire, expanding the state of bureaucracy, and imposing heavier taxes. For administrative purposes, Diocletian divided the empire into a western half and an eastern half. Constantine established the new capital city of Constantinople in Byzantium. The two sections drifted further apart throughout the fourth century, when the division became permanent. Diocletian's unrealistic attempt to curb inflation by arbitrarily freezing wages and prices failed. In the early fifth century, the borders collapsed entirely, and various Germanic tribes completely overran the western provinces. In 410 and again in 455, Rome itself was sacked by the barbarians.

After the western Roman Empire's decline, the rich legacy of Greco-Roman culture was absorbed by the medieval world and ultimately the modern world. The Latin language remained the basic medium of communication among educated people for the next thousand years; for almost two thousand years, Latin literature formed the core of all Western education. Roman roads, buildings, and aqueducts remained in use. Rome left its mark on the legal and political systems of most European countries. Rome had preserved the best of ancient culture for later times.

Christianity

The ancient world also left behind a powerful religious legacy, Christianity. Christianity derives from tradition regarding the life, teachings, death, and resurrection of the Galilean Jesus of Nazareth (ca 3 B.C.–A.D. 29). Thoroughly Jewish in his teachings, Jesus preached the coming of the kingdom of God, a "kingdom not of this world," but one of eternal peace and happiness. He urged his followers and listeners to reform their lives according to the commandments, especially those stating, "You shall love the Lord your God with your whole heart, your whole mind, and your whole soul," and "You shall love your neighbor as yourself." Thus, the heart of Christian teaching is love of God and love of neighbor. Some Jews believed that Jesus was the long-awaited Messiah. Others, to whom Jesus represented a threat to ancient traditions, hated and feared him. Though Jesus did not preach rebellion against the Roman governors, the Roman prefect of Judea, Pontius Pilate, feared that the popular agitation surrounding Jesus could lead to revolt against Rome. When Jewish leaders subsequently delivered Jesus to the Roman authorities, Pilate, to avert violence, sentenced him to death by crucifixion—the usual method for common criminals. Jesus' followers maintained that he rose from the dead three days later.

Those followers might have remained a small Jewish sect but for the preaching of a Hellenized Jew, Paul of Tarsus (ca A.D. 5–67). Paul taught that Jesus was the Son of God, that he brought a new law of love, and that Jesus' message was to be proclaimed to all people—Greek and Jew, slave and free, male and female. He traveled among and wrote letters to the Christian communities at Corinth, Ephesus, Thessalonica, and other cities. As the Roman Empire declined, Christianity spread throughout the Roman world. Because it welcomed people of all social classes, offered a message of divine forgiveness and salvation, and taught that every individual has a role to play in the building of the kingdom of God, thereby fostering a deep sense of community in many of its followers, Christianity won thousands of adherents.

Roman efforts to crush Christianity failed. The emperor Constantine legalized Christianity, and in 392, the emperor Theodosius made it the state religion of the empire. Carried by settlers, missionaries, and merchants to Gaul, Spain, North Africa, and Britain, Christianity formed a basic element of Western civilization. Recent scholarly research has stressed that Christianity was a *syncretic* religion; that is, Christianity absorbed aspects of other Middle Eastern religions, such as belief in a savior-god who died and rose again and a sacramental system that included baptism and the Eucharist.

✥ THE MIDDLE AGES

Fourteenth-century writers coined the term *Middle Ages,* meaning a middle period of Gothic barbarism between two ages of enormous cultural brilliance—the Roman world of the first and second centuries, and their own age, the fourteenth century, which these writers thought had recaptured the true spirit of classical antiquity. Recent scholars had demonstrated that the thousand-year period between roughly the fourth and fourteenth centuries witnessed incredible developments: social, political, intellectual, economic, and religious. The men and women of the Middle Ages built on the cultural heritage of the Greco-Roman past and made impressive advances in their own right.

The Early Middle Ages

The time period that historians mark off as the early Middle Ages, extending from about the fifth to the tenth century, saw the emergence of a distinctly Western society and culture. The geographical center of that society shifted northward from the Mediterranean basin to western Europe. Whereas a rich urban life and flourishing trade had characterized the ancient world, the Germanic invasions led to the decline of cities and the destruction of commerce. Early medieval society was rural and local, with the farm or *latifundium* serving as the characteristic social unit.

Several processes were responsible for the development of European culture. First, Europe became Christian. Christian missionary activity led to the slow, imperfect Christianization of the Germanic peoples who had overrun the Roman Empire in the West. Christianity taught the barbarians a higher code of morality and behavior and served as the integrating principle of medieval society. Christian writers played a powerful role in the conservation of Greco-Roman thought. They used Latin as their medium of communication, thereby preserving it. They copied and transmitted classical texts. Writers such as Saint Augustine of Hippo (354–430) used Roman rhetoric and Roman history to defend Christian theology. In so doing, they assimilated classical culture to Christian teaching.

Second, as the Germanic tribes overran the western Roman Empire, they intermarried with the old Gallo-Roman aristocracy. The elite class that emerged held the dominant political, social, and economic power in early—and later—medieval Europe. Germanic custom and tradition, such as ideals of military prowess and bravery in battle, became part of the mental furniture of Europeans.

Third, in the seventh and eighth centuries, Muslim military conquests carried Islam, the religion inspired by the prophet Muhammad (?570–632), from the Arab lands across North Africa, the Mediterranean basin, and Spain into southern France. The Arabs eventually translated many Greek texts. When, beginning in the ninth century, those texts were translated from Arabic into Latin, they came to play a role in the formation of European scientific, medieval, and philosophical thought.

Monasticism, an ascetic form of Christian life first practiced in Egypt and characterized by isolation from the broader society, simplicity of living, and abstention from sexual activity, flourished and expanded in both the Byzantine East and the Latin West. Medieval people believed that the communities of monks and nuns provided an important service: prayer on behalf of the broader society. In a world lacking career opportunities, monasteries also offered vocations for the children of the upper classes. Thus, monks in the West pioneered the clearing of wasteland and forestland; served royal and baronial governments as advisers, secretaries, diplomats, and treasurers; and frequently conducted schools for the education of the young.

In the eighth century, also, the Carolingian dynasty, named after its most illustrious member, Charles the Great, or Charlemagne (768–814), gradually acquired a broad hegemony over much of what is today France, Germany, and northern Italy. Charlemagne's coronation by the pope at Rome in a ceremony filled with Latin anthems represented a fusion of classical, Christian, and Germanic elements. This Germanic warrior-king supported Christian missionary efforts and encouraged both classical and Christian scholarship. For the first time since the decline of the western Roman Empire, western Europe had achieved a degree of political unity. Similarly, the culture of Carolingian Europe blended Germanic, Christian, and Greco-Roman elements.

In the ninth century, a resurgence of aristocratic power provoked chronic civil war among the great magnates of the empire. They resented Carolingian rule and wanted even more lands. These internal conflicts, combined with foreign attacks by Viking (early Scandinavian), Muslim, and Magyar (early Hungarian) marauders, led to the collapse of centralized power. The new invaders wreaked more destruction than had the Germans in the fifth and sixth centuries. Real authority passed into the hands of local strongmen. Political authority was completely decentralized. Scholars describe the society that emerged as feudal and manorial: a small group of military leaders held public political power. They gave such protection as they could to the people living on their estates. They held courts. They coined money. And they negotiated with outside powers. The manor of local estate was the basic community unit. Serfs on the manor engaged in agriculture, which everywhere was the dominant form of economy. Because no feudal lord could exercise authority or provide peace over a very wide area, political instability, violence, and chronic disorder characterized Western society.

The High and Later Middle Ages

By the beginning of the eleventh century, the European world showed distinct signs of recovery, vitality, and creativity. Over the next two centuries that recovery and creativity manifested itself in every facet of culture—economic, social, political, intellectual, and artistic. A greater degree of peace paved the way for these achievements.

The Viking and Magyar invasions gradually ended. Warring knights supported ecclesiastical pressure against violence, and disorder declined. Improvements in farming technology, such as the use of the horse collar, led to an agricultural revolution. Old land was better utilized and new land brought under cultivation. Agricultural productivity increased tremendously. These factors led to considerable population growth.

Increased population contributed to some remarkable economic and social developments. A salient manifestation of the recovery of Europe and of the vitality of the High Middle Ages was the rise of towns and concurrent growth of a new commercial class. Surplus population and the search for new economic opportunities led to the expansion of old towns, such as Florence, Paris, London, and Cologne, and the foundation of completely new ones, such as Munich and Berlin. A new artisan and merchant class, precursor of the later "middle class," appeared. In medieval sociology, three classes existed: the clergy, who prayed; the nobility, who fought; and the peasantry, who tilled the land. The merchant class, engaging in manufacturing and trade, seeking freedom from the jurisdiction of feudal lords, and pursuing wealth with a fiercely competitive spirit, fit none of the standard categories. Townspeople represented a radical force for change.

The period after about 1000 also witnessed the vast migration of peoples from the European heartland (France, western Germany, and England) into frontier regions—Scotland and Ireland, Scandinavia, the Baltic region, eastern Europe, and Spain. Anglo-Norman knights conquered Ireland; Germans settled in the lands between the Oder and the Elbe Rivers; French and Spanish warriors pushed down into Spain. Monks, nuns, and business people followed. With them went ecclesiastical influences, such as the erection of Catholic dioceses and the Roman liturgy. During the next two centuries, these border regions became tied to the Roman papacy and the Latin West.

The twelfth and thirteenth centuries witnessed an enormous increase in the volume of local and international trade. For example, Italian merchants traveled to the regional fairs of France and Flanders to exchange silk from China and slaves from the Crimea for English woolens, French wines, and Flemish textiles. Merchants adopted new business techniques. They had a strongly capitalistic spirit and were eager to invest surplus capital to make more money. These developments added up to what scholars have termed a commercial revolution, a major turning point in the economic and social life of the West. The High Middle Ages saw the transformation of Europe from a rural and agrarian society into an urban and industrial one.

The High Middle Ages also saw the birth of the modern centralized state. Rome had bequeathed to Western civilization the concepts of the state and the law, but for centuries after the disintegration of the western Roman Empire, the state as a reality did not exist. With the possible exception of the Carolingian experience, no early medieval government exercised authority over a wide area; real political power rested in the hands of local strongmen. Beginning in the twelfth century, kings worked to establish means of communication with all their peoples, to weaken the influence of feudal lords and thus to strengthen their own authority, and to build efficient bureaucracies. Kings often created courts of law, which served not only to punish criminals and reduce violence but also to increase royal income. In France, Spain, Italy, and Germany courts applied principles of Roman law. The Roman *ius civilis* was thus preserved through its use in the development of states. The law courts strengthened royal influence. People began to extend their primary loyalty to the king rather than to the "international" church or the local feudal lord. By the end of the thirteenth century, the kings of France and England had achieved a high degree of unity and laid the foundations of modern centralized states. In Italy, Germany, and Spain, however, strong independent local authorities predominated.

In the realm of government and law, the Middle Ages made other powerful contributions to the modern world. The use of law to weaken feudal barons and to strengthen royal authority worked to increase respect for the law itself. Following a bitter dispute with his barons, King John of England (1199–1216) was forced to sign the document known as Magna Carta. Magna Carta contains the principle that there is an authority higher than the king to which even he is responsible: the law. The idea of the "rule of law" became embedded in the Western political consciousness. English kings following John recognized this common law, a law that their judges applied throughout the country. Exercise of common law often involved juries of local people to answer questions of fact. The common law and jury system of the Middle Ages have become integral features of Anglo-American jurisprudence. In the fourteenth century, kings also summoned meetings of the leading classes in their kingdoms, and thus were born representative assemblies, most notably the English parliament.

In their work of consolidation and centralization, kings increasingly used the knowledge of university-trained officials. Universities first emerged in western Europe in the thirteenth century. Medieval universities were educational guilds that produced educated and trained officials for the new bureaucratic states. The universities at Bologna in Italy and Montpellier in France, for example, were centers for the study of Roman law. After Aristotle's works had been translated from Arabic into Latin, Paris became the leading university for the study of philosophy and theology. Medieval Scholastics (philosophers and theologians) sought to harmonize Greek philosophy with Christian teaching. They wanted to use reason to deepen the understanding of what was believed on faith. At the University of Paris, Thomas Aquinas (1225–1274) recorded a brilliant synthesis of Christian revelation and Aristotelian philosophy in his *Summa Theologica*. Medieval universities developed the basic structures familiar to modern students: colleges, universities, examinations, and degrees. Colleges and universities are a major legacy of the Middle Ages to the modern world.

Under the leadership of the Christian church, Christian ideals permeated all aspects of medieval culture. The village priest blessed the fields before the spring planting and the fall harvesting. Guilds of merchants sought the protection of patron saints and held elaborate public celebrations on the saints' feast days. Indeed, the veneration of saints—men and women whose lives contemporaries perceived as outstanding in holiness—and an increasingly sophisticated sacramental system became central features of popular religion. University lectures and meetings of parliaments began with prayers. Kings relied on the services of bishops and abbots in the work of the government. Not only the community's religious life but also its social, political, and often economic life centered around the parish church. The twelfth and thirteenth centuries witnessed a remarkable outburst of Christian piety, as the Crusades (so-called holy wars waged against the Muslims for control of Jerusalem) and Gothic cathedrals reveal. More stone was quarried for churches in medieval France than had been mined in ancient Egypt, where the Great Pyramid alone consumed 40.5 million cubic feet of stone. Churches and cathedrals were visible manifestations of community civic pride. Popular piety also led to the establishment of hospitals and facilities for the homeless and the ill. Recent research has shed light on marriage and the family, pregnancy and childbirth, and literacy in the High and later Middle Ages.

The high level of energy and creativity that characterized the twelfth and thirteenth centuries could not be sustained indefinitely. In the fourteenth century, every conceivable disaster struck Western Europe. Drought and excessive rain each destroyed harvests, causing widespread famine. The bubonic plague (or Black Death) swept across the continent, taking a terrible toll on population. England and France became deadlocked in a long and bitter struggle known as the Hundred Years' War (1337–1453). Schism in the Catholic church resulted in the simultaneous claim by two popes of jurisdiction. Many parts of Europe experienced a resurgence of feudal violence and petty warfare. To protect their economic interests, English settlers in Ireland, German settlers in eastern Europe, and Spanish settlers in reconquered Spain published racist laws that severely discriminated against the indigenous peoples. Out of this misery, disorder, and confusion, a new society gradually emerged.

EARLY MODERN EUROPE

The period frequently labeled early modern Europe, extending from about 1400 to 1600, was an age of great change in European society. But Europe during this period was very different from our modern contemporary world. The Industrial and the French Revolutions, the growth of nationalism, and the profound secularization of culture occurred in the eighteenth and nineteenth centuries; these forces unleashed what we mean when we speak of the "modern world." By late-twentieth-century standards, fifteenth- and sixteenth-century Europe remained—in its class structure, economic life, technology, and methods of communication—closer to imperial Rome than to present-day Europe and America.[1] Our emphasis, therefore, rests on *early* modern Europe, which nevertheless saw phenomenal development. The Renaissance, the Reformation, and the expansion of Europe overseas drastically altered European attitudes, values, and lifestyles.

The Renaissance

While war, famine, disease, and death swept across northern Europe in the fourteenth century, a new culture was emerging in Italy. Italian society underwent great changes. In the fifteenth century, these phenomena spread beyond Italy and gradually influenced northern Europe. Scholars commonly use the French term *renaissance* ("rebirth") to describe the cultural achievements of the fourteenth through sixteenth centuries. The Renaissance evolved in two broad and overlapping stages. In the first period, which dated from about 1050 to 1300, a new economy emerged, based on Venetian and Genoese shipping and long-distance trade and on Florentine banking and cloth manufacturing. At the end of the thirteenth century, Florentine bankers gained control of the papal banking. From this position as tax collectors for the papacy, Florentine mercantile families began to dominate European banking on both sides of the Alps. They had offices in London, Bruges, Barcelona, Tunis, Naples, and Rome. Profits from loans and investments were pumped back into urban industries, especially the woolen industry. Florence bought the highest quality wool from England and Spain, developed techniques for its manufacture, and employed tens of thousands of workers to turn it into cloth. Florentine cloth brought the highest prices in the fairs, markets, and bazaars of Europe, Africa, and Asia.

The wealth so produced brought into existence a new urban and aristocratic class.

In the industrial cities of Venice and Florence, this new aristocratic class governed as oligarchs: they maintained the façade of republican government in which political power theoretically resides in the people and is exercised by their chosen representatives, but, in fact, the oligarchs ruled. In cities with strong agricultural bases, such as Verona, Mantua, and Ferrara, despots predominated. In the fifteenth century, political power and elite culture centered at the princely courts of oligarchs and despots. At his court the Renaissance prince displayed his patronage of the arts and learning.

The second stage of the Renaissance, which lasted from about 1300 to 1600, was characterized by extraordinary manifestations of intellectual and artistic energies. As an intellectual movement the Renaissance possessed certain hallmarks that held profound significance for the evolution of the modern world.

Fourteenth- and fifteenth-century Italians had the self-conscious awareness that they were living in new times. They believed that theirs was a golden age of creativity, an age of rebirth of classical antiquity. They identified with the philosophers and artists of Greek and Roman antiquity, copied the lifestyles of the ancients, and expressed contempt for their immediate medieval past. Second, the Renaissance manifested a new attitude toward humanity and the world, an attitude often described as individualism. Individualism stressed personality, uniqueness, genius—the fullest possible development of human potential. Artist, athlete, sculptor, scholar, whatever—a person's potential should be stretched until fully realized. The thirst for fame and the burning quest for glory were central components of Renaissance individualism.

Closely connected with individualism was a deep interest in the Latin classics. This feature of the Renaissance became known as "the new learning," or simply "humanism." The terms *humanism* and *humanist* derive from the Latin *humanitas,* which the ancient Roman orator Cicero used to describe the literary culture needed by anyone who would be considered educated or civilized. Humanists studied the Latin classics to discover past insights into human nature.

Another basic feature of the Renaissance was a new secular spirit. Secularism involves a greater regard for, and interest in, the things of this world, rather than otherworldly concerns. Medieval people certainly pursued financial profits ruthlessly, and Renaissance men and women had deep spiritual concerns. In the Middle

1. Eugene F. Rice, *The Foundations of Early Modern Europe, 1460–1559.* W. W. Norton & Co., New York, 1970, p. x.

Ages, however, the dominant ideals focused on life after death. The fourteenth and fifteenth centuries witnessed the slow and steady growth of secularism in Italy. Economic changes, preoccupation with money-making, and the rising prosperity of the Italian cities precipitated a fundamental change in the attitudes and values of the urban aristocracy and bourgeoisie.

Renaissance art, which some scholars consider the period's greatest achievement, differed markedly from medieval art. In the Renaissance, the individual portrait emerged as a distinct artistic genre. Whereas medieval artists had depicted the nude human body only in a spiritualizing or moralizing context, Renaissance artists reviewed the classical figure with its balance and self-awareness; in so doing, they revealed the secular spirit of the age. The new style was characterized by greater realism, narrative power, and more effective use of light and shadow. In addition, the Italian artist Brunelleschi (1377–1466) pioneered perspective in painting—the linear representation of distance and space on a flat surface. In the works of Jan van Eyck, Jerome Bosch, and others, northern Europe also witnessed the flowering of an indigenous artistic culture.

The age also saw profound social changes that have enormously influenced the modern world. The invention of the printing press in the mid-fifteenth century revolutionized communication. Printing made governmental propaganda possible, bridged the gap between oral and written cultures, and stimulated the literacy of laypeople. Artists and satirists began to use pornography for political purposes. Women's status in society began to decline. Whereas women in the Middle Ages often had great responsibilities, and, with responsibility, power, in the Renaissance their purpose came to be decorative—to grace the courts of princes and aristocrats. As servants and slaves, black people entered western Europe during the Renaissance in sizable numbers for the first time since the decline of Rome. In northern Europe, urban merchants and rural gentry allied with rising monarchies. With the newly levied taxes paid by business people, kings provided a greater degree of domestic peace and order. In Spain, France, and England, rulers also emphasized royal dignity and authority; they used the tough ideas of the Italian political theorist Machiavelli to ensure the preservation and continuation of their governments. Feudal monarchies gradually evolved in the direction of nation-states.

As the intellectual features of the Renaissance spread outside Italy, they affected the culture of all Europe. A secular attitude toward life has become one of the dominant features of the modern world. Similarly, a strong belief in the realization of individual potential has become an abiding component of our world-view.

The Reformation

The idea of reform is as old as Christianity itself. Jesus had preached the coming of the kingdom of God through the reform of the individual, and through the centuries his cry had been repeated. The need for the reform of the individual Christian and of the institutional church is central to the Christian faith. Christian humanists of the fifteenth and sixteenth centuries urged the reform of the church on the pattern of the early Christian communities.

The sixteenth century was a deeply religious age. Although almost all people were sincere believers and religious practices and observances pervaded their lives, the institutional church showed serious signs of disorder. Clerical immorality, ignorance, and pluralism (the simultaneous holding of two or more church offices by a priest) constituted widespread abuses. The Renaissance princes who ruled the church made only feeble efforts at reform. Informed and intelligent laypeople, especially in the cities, condemned the clergy's tax exempt and privileged social position.

In 1517, Martin Luther (1483–1546), a professor of Scripture at a small German university, launched an attack on clerical abuses. Asked to recant, Luther rejected church authority itself. The newly invented printing press swept Luther's prolific writings across Germany and the rest of Europe. He and other reformers soon won the support of northern German princes who embraced Luther's reforming or "Protestant" ideas. Some of the princes genuinely shared Luther's beliefs, whereas others coveted church lands and revenues. Still others resented the authority of the strongly Catholic Holy Roman emperor Charles V. By accepting Luther's religious ideas—and thereby denying orthodox Catholic doctrine—the princes also rejected the emperor's political authority. In a world that insisted on the necessity of religious unity for political order and social stability, the adoption of the new faith implied political opposition. In England, largely because the papacy would not approve his request for a divorce, King Henry VIII (1509–1547) broke with Rome and established the Church of England. Kings and princes and political and economic issues played the decisive role in the advance of the Reformation.

In the first half of the sixteenth century, perhaps one-fourth of the population of western Europe accepted some version of Protestantism. Besides northern Germany, all of Scandinavia, England, Scotland, and the cities of Geneva and Zurich in Switzerland and Strasbourg in Germany rejected the religious authority of the Roman church and adopted new faiths. The number of Protestant sects proliferated, but the core of Protestant doctrine, consisting of three fundamental ideas, remained. First, Protestants believe that salvation comes by faith alone, not from faith and good works, as Catholic teaching asserts. Second, authority in the Christian church resides in the Scriptures alone, not in tradition or papal authority (which all Protestants rejected). Third, the church itself consists of the community of all believers; medieval churchmen had tended to identify the church with the clergy.

In the later sixteenth century, the Roman church worked to clean up its house. The Council of Trent, meeting intermittently from 1545 to 1563, suppressed pluralism and the sale of church offices, redefined doctrine, and, in a decree with far-reaching social implications, prescribed regulations for valid marriage. The Council also treated the concept of religious vocations, made provision for the education of the clergy, and laid the basis for general spiritual renewal. New religious orders, such as the Society of Jesus (Jesuits), worked to advance that renewal.

The break with Rome and the rise of Lutheran, Anglican, Calvinist, and other faiths shattered the unity of Europe as an organic Christian society. Yet religious belief remained exceedingly strong. In fact, the strength of religious convictions contributed to social and political fragmentation. In the later sixteenth century and throughout most of the seventeenth century, religion and religious issues continued to play a major role in the lives of individuals and in the policies and actions of governments. Religion, whether Protestant or Catholic, decisively influenced the evolution of national states. Though most reformers rejected religious toleration, they helped pave the way for the toleration and pluralism that characterize the modern world.

Overseas Expansion

In the sixteenth and seventeenth centuries, Europeans gained access to large parts of the world for the first time. Overseas expansion broadened Europe's geographical horizons and brought its states into confrontation with ancient civilizations in Africa, Asia, and the Americas. These confrontations led first to conquest, then to exploitation, and finally to profound social changes in both Europe and the conquered territories. At the same time, the consequences of the Renaissance and the Reformation drastically altered intellectual, political, religious, and social life within Europe. War and religious issues dominated the political life of European states. Though religion was commonly used to rationalize international conflicts, wars were fought for power and territorial expansion.

Europeans had a variety of motives for overseas exploration and conquest. Some desired to Christianize the Muslims and pagan peoples. Many others, finding economic and political advancement limited at home, emigrated abroad in search of fresh opportunities. The governments of Portugal, Spain, Holland, and England sponsored and encouraged voyages of exploration. Spices—pepper, nutmeg, mace, cinnamon, ginger— were another incentive. Spices, which added flavor and variety to a monotonous diet, also yielded high profits. The basic reason for European exploration and expansion was the quest for material profit. As the Portuguese navigator Bartholomew Diaz, the first man to round the Cape of Good Hope and open the road to India, put it, his motives were "to serve God and His Majesty, to give light to those who were in darkness, and to grow rich as all men desire to do."

Sixteenth- and seventeenth-century Europeans had the intellectual curiosity, driving ambition, and scientific technology to attempt feats that were as difficult and expensive then as going to the moon is today. The exploration and exploitation of parts of South America, Africa, and Asia increased the standard of living of the colonists, who were now able to enjoy spices and Asian luxury goods; the corresponding influx of South American silver and gold, however, also led to considerable international inflation. Governments, the upper classes, and the peasantry were badly hurt by the inflation. Meanwhile, the middle class of bankers, shippers, financiers, and manufacturers prospered for much of the seventeenth century. European expansion and colonization overseas took place against a background of changing social attitudes, religious conflict, and rising national consciousness. The persecution of thousands of women as "witches" and the beginning of distinctly modern forms of racism reflected people's confusion, ignorance, and uncertainty in an age of great cultural change. Though the medieval religious framework had broken down, most people still thought largely in religious terms. Europeans explained what they did politically and economically in terms of religious doctrine. Religious ideology served as a justification for many goals including the opposition of the French nobility to the Crown and the Dutch struggle for political and economic independence from Spain. In Germany, religious pluralism and the intervention of the French and the Swedes led to the long and devastating Thirty Years' War (1618–1648). After 1648, the divisions between Protestants and Catholics in Germany tended to become permanent.

In France, bitter wars of religion contributed to the rise of absolute monarchy, whereas religious struggle promoted constitutional government in the Netherlands and England. We turn now to these new patterns of government, which have profoundly influenced almost all modern states and societies.

16

Absolutism and Constitutionalism in Western Europe (ca 1589–1715)

✣
The Queen's staircase is among the grandest of the surviving parts of Louis XIV's Versailles. *(© Photo R.M.N.— Mercator)*

The seventeenth century was a period of revolutionary transformation. That century witnessed agricultural and manufacturing crises that had profound political consequences. A colder and wetter climate throughout most of the period meant a shorter farming season. Grain yields declined. In an age when cereals constituted the bulk of the diet for most people everywhere, smaller harvests led to food shortages and starvation. Food shortages in turn meant population decline or stagnation. Industry also suffered. While the evidence does not permit broad generalizations, it appears that the output of woolen textiles, one of the most important manufactures, declined sharply in the first half of the century. This economic crisis was not universal: it struck various sections of Europe at different times and to different degrees. In the middle decades of the century, Spain, France, Germany, and England all experienced great economic difficulties; but these years saw the golden age of the Netherlands.

Meanwhile, governments increased their spending, primarily for state armies; in the seventeenth century, armies grew larger than they had been since the time of the Roman Empire. To pay for these armies, governments taxed. The greatly increased burden of taxation, falling on a population already existing at a subsistence level, triggered revolts. Peasant revolts were extremely common;[1] in France, urban disorders were so frequent an aspect of the social and political landscape as to be "a distinctive feature of life."[2]

Princes struggled to free themselves from the restrictions of custom, powerful social groups, or competing institutions. Spanish and French monarchs gained control of the major institution in their domains, the Roman Catholic church. Rulers of England and some of the German principalities, who could not completely regulate the Catholic church, set up national churches. In the German Empire, the Treaty of Westphalia placed territorial sovereignty in the princes' hands. The kings of France, England, and Spain claimed the basic loyalty of their subjects. Monarchs made laws, to which everyone within their borders was subject. These powers added up to something close to sovereignty.

A state may be termed *sovereign* when it possesses a monopoly over the instruments of justice and the use of force within clearly defined boundaries. In a sovereign state, no system of courts, such as ecclesiastical tribunals, competes with state courts in the dispensation of justice; and private armies, such as those of feudal

lords, present no threat to royal authority because the state's army is stronger. Royal law touches all persons within the country.

Sovereignty had been evolving during the late sixteenth century. Most seventeenth-century governments now needed to address the problem of *which* authority within the state would possess sovereignty—the Crown or privileged groups. In the period between roughly 1589 and 1715, two basic patterns of government emerged in Europe: absolute monarchy and the constitutional state. Almost all subsequent European governments have been modeled on one of these patterns.

- How did these forms of government differ from the feudal and dynastic monarchies of earlier centuries?
- In what sense were these forms "modern"?
- What social and economic factors limited absolute monarchs?
- Which Western countries most clearly illustrate the new patterns of political organization?
- Why is the seventeenth century considered the "golden age of the Netherlands"?

This chapter will explore these questions.

 ABSOLUTISM

In the *absolutist* state, sovereignty is embodied in the person of the ruler. Absolute kings claimed to rule by divine right, meaning they were responsible to God alone. (Medieval kings governed "by the grace of God," but invariably they acknowledged that they had to respect and obey the law.) Absolute monarchs in the seventeenth and eighteenth centuries had to respect the fundamental laws of the land, though they claimed to rule by divine right.

Absolute rulers tried to control competing jurisdictions, institutions, or interest groups in their territories. They regulated religious sects. They abolished the liberties long held by certain areas, groups, or provinces. Absolute kings also secured the cooperation of the one class that historically had posed the greatest threat to monarchy, the nobility. Medieval governments, restrained by the church, the feudal nobility, and their own financial limitations, had been able to exert none of these controls.

In some respects, the key to the power and success of absolute monarchs lay in how they solved their financial problems. Medieval kings frequently had found temporary financial support through bargains with the nobility: the nobility agreed to an ad hoc grant of money in return for freedom from future taxation. In contrast, the absolutist solution was the creation of new state bureaucracies that directed the economic life of the country in the interests of the king, either forcing taxes ever higher or devising alternative methods of raising revenue.

Bureaucracies were composed of career officials appointed by and solely accountable to the king. The backgrounds of these civil servants varied. Absolute monarchs sometimes drew on the middle class, as in France, or utilized members of the nobility, as in Spain and eastern Europe. Where there was no middle class or an insignificant one, as in Austria, Prussia, Spain, and Russia, the government of the absolutist state consisted of an interlocking elite of monarchy, aristocracy, and bureaucracy.

Royal agents in medieval and Renaissance kingdoms had used their public offices and positions to benefit themselves and their families. In England, for example, Crown servants from Thomas Becket to Thomas Wolsey had treated their high offices as their private property and reaped considerable profit from them. The most striking difference between seventeenth-century bureaucracies and their predecessors was that seventeenth-century civil servants served the state as represented by the king. Bureaucrats recognized that the offices they held were public, or state, positions. The state paid them salaries to handle revenues that belonged to the Crown, and they were not supposed to use their positions for private gain. Bureaucrats gradually came to distinguish between public duties and private property.

Absolute monarchs also maintained permanent standing armies. Medieval armies had been raised by feudal lords for particular wars or campaigns, after which the troops were disbanded. In the seventeenth century, monarchs alone recruited and maintained armies—in peacetime as well as wartime. Kings deployed their troops both inside and outside the country in the interests of the monarchy. Armies became basic features of absolutist, and modern, states. Absolute rulers also invented new methods of compulsion. They concerned themselves with the private lives of potentially troublesome subjects, often through the use of secret police.

The word *absolutism* was coined only in 1830, two centuries after the developments it attempts to classify occurred. Some scholars today deny that absolute monarchy was a stage in the evolution of the modern state between medieval feudal monarchies and the constitutional governments of recent centuries. As one student of early modern France writes, "I believe the prevailing historiographical concept of 'absolute monarchy' is a myth promulgated by the royal government and legitimized by historians."[3] Such historians prefer the term *administrative monarchy,* by which they mean that the French state in the seventeenth century became stronger in that it could achieve more of its goals, it was centralized from Paris, and its administrative bureaucracy greatly expanded. Although the administrative monarchy interfered in many aspects of the private individual's daily life, it did not have the consent of the governed, and it especially lacked the idea of the rule of law—law made by a representative body—the administrative monarchy was actually limited, or checked, in ways that traditional interpretations of absolute monarchy did not consider.[4]

The rule of absolute monarchs was not all-embracing because they lacked the financial and military resources and the technology to make it so. Thus the absolutist state was not the same as a totalitarian state. *Totalitarianism* is a twentieth-century phenomenon; it seeks to direct all facets of a state's culture—art, education, religion, the economy, and politics—in the interests of the state. By definition, totalitarian rule is *total* regulation. By twentieth-century standards, the ambitions of absolute monarchs were quite limited: each sought the exaltation of himself or herself as the embodiment of the state. Whether or not Louis XIV of France actually said, "*L'état, c'est moi!*" (I am the state!), the remark expresses his belief that he personified the French nation. Yet the absolutist state did foreshadow recent totalitarian regimes in two fundamental respects: in the glorification of the state over all other aspects of the culture and in the use of war and an expansionist foreign policy to divert attention from domestic ills. All of this is best illustrated by the experience of France, aptly known as the model of absolute monarchy.

The Foundations of French Absolutism: Henry IV, Sully, and Richelieu

In 1589 Henry IV (see page 491) inherited an enormous mess. Civil wars had wracked France since 1561. Catastrophically poor harvests meant that all across France peasants lived on the verge of starvation, fighting off wolves and bands of demobilized soldiers. Some provinces, such as Burgundy, suffered almost complete depopulation. Commercial activity had fallen to one-third its 1580 level. Nobles, officials, merchants, and peasants wanted peace, order, and stability. "Henri le

Procession of the Catholic League   In response to what many French Catholics considered the monarchy's laxness in crushing heresy, nobles, burghers, and friars formed groups or leagues to fight Protestantism at the local level. The resulting chaos, with armed private citizens indiscriminately firing guns, is illustrated in this scene, probably in Paris. *(Musée de Beaux-Arts, Valenciennes/Giraudon/Art Resource, NY)*

Grand" (Henry the Great), as the king was called, promised "a chicken in every pot" and inaugurated a remarkable recovery. Henry may have been the first French ruler since Louis IX, in the thirteenth century, genuinely to care about his people, and he was the only king whose statue the Paris crowd did not tear down in the Revolution of 1789.

Henry converted to Catholicism and sought better relations with the pope. He tried to gain Protestant confidence by issuing the Edict of Nantes in 1598 (see pages 491 and 553) and by appointing the devout Protestant Maximilien de Béthune, duke of Sully, as his chief minister. Aside from a short, successful war with Savoy in 1601, Henry kept France at peace. Maintain-

ing that "if we are without compassion for the people, they must succumb and we all perish with them," Henry sharply lowered taxes on the overburdened peasants. In compensation for the lost revenues, in 1602–1604 he introduced the *paulette,* an annual fee paid by royal officials to guarantee heredity in their offices.

Sully proved to be an effective administrator. He combined the indirect taxes on salt, sales, and transit and leased their collection to financiers. Although the number of taxes declined, revenues increased because of the revival of trade.[5] One of the first French officials to appreciate the possibilities of overseas trade, Sully subsidized the Company for Trade with the Indies.

He started a country-wide highway system and even dreamed of an international organization for the maintenance of peace.

In only twelve years, Henry IV and Sully restored public order in France and laid the foundations for economic prosperity. By the standards of the time, Henry IV's government was progressive and promising. His murder in 1610 by a crazed fanatic led to a severe crisis.

After the death of Henry IV, the queen-regent Marie de' Medici headed the government for the child-king Louis XIII (r. 1610–1643), but in fact feudal nobles and princes of the blood dominated the political scene. In 1624 Marie de' Medici secured the appointment of Armand Jean du Plessis—Cardinal Richelieu (1585–1642)—to the council of ministers. It was a remarkable appointment. The next year, Richelieu became president of the council, and after 1628 he was first minister of the French crown. Richelieu used his strong influence over King Louis XIII to exalt the French monarchy as the embodiment of the French state. One of the greatest servants of that state, Richelieu set in place the cornerstone of French absolutism, and his work served as the basis for France's cultural hegemony of Europe in the later seventeenth century.

Richelieu's policy was the total subordination of all groups and institutions to the French monarchy. The French nobility, with its selfish and independent interests, had long constituted the foremost threat to the centralizing goals of the Crown and to a strong national state. Therefore, Richelieu sought to curb the power of the nobility. In 1624 he succeeded in reshuffling the royal council, eliminating such potential power brokers as the prince of Condé. Thereafter Richelieu dominated the council in an unprecedented way. He leveled castles, long the symbol of feudal independence, and crushed aristocratic conspiracies with quick executions. For example, when the duke of Montmorency, the first peer of France and godson of Henry IV, became involved in a revolt, he was summarily beheaded.

The constructive genius of Cardinal Richelieu is best reflected in the administrative system he established. He extended the use of the royal commissioners called intendants. France was divided into thirty-two *généralités* (districts), in each of which after 1634 a royal intendant held a commission to perform specific tasks, often financial but also judicial and policing. Intendants transmitted information from local communities to Paris and delivered royal orders from the capital to their généralités. Almost always recruited from the newer judicial nobility, the *noblesse de robe,* intendants were appointed directly by the monarch, to whom they were solely responsible. They could not be natives of the districts where they held authority; thus they had no vested interest in their localities. The intendants recruited men for the army, supervised the collection of taxes, presided over the administration of local law, checked up on the local nobility, and regulated economic activities—commerce, trade, the guilds, marketplaces—in their districts. They were to use their power for two related purposes: to enforce royal orders in the généralités of their jurisdiction and to weaken the power and influence of the regional nobility. As the intendants' power increased under Richelieu, so did the power of the centralized French state.

In 1598 Henry IV's lawyers had drawn up the "Law of Concord." It had been published as the Edict of Nantes to create a temporary and provisional situation of religious toleration in order to secure not the permanent coexistence of two religions (the Calvinist, Reformed, or Huguenot faith and Roman Catholicism), but "religious and civil concord"—that is the confessional reunification of all French people under the king's religion, Roman Catholicism. The Edict of Nantes named 150 towns throughout France; the king granted Protestants the right to practice their faith in those towns, and he gave the towns 180,000 écus to support the maintenance of their military garrisons. Huguenots numbered perhaps 10 percent of the total French population, most of them concentrated in the southwest. In 1627 Louis XIII, with the unanimous consent of the royal council, decided to end Protestant military and political independence, because, he said, it constituted "a state within a state." According to Louis, Huguenots demanded freedom of conscience, but they did not allow Catholics to worship in their cities, which he interpreted as *political* disobedience.[6]

Attention focused on La Rochelle, fourth largest of the French Atlantic ports and a major commercial center with strong ties to the northern Protestant states of Holland and England. Louis intended to cut off English aid, and he personally supervised the siege of La Rochelle. The city fell in October 1628. Its municipal government was suppressed, and its walled fortifications were destroyed. Although Protestants retained the right of public worship, the king reinstated the Catholic liturgy, and Cardinal Richelieu himself celebrated the first Mass. The military fall of La Rochelle weakened the influence of aristocratic adherents of Calvinism and was one step in the evolution of a unified French state.

Louis XIII, Richelieu, and later Louis XIV also faced serious urban protests. Real or feared unemployment, high food prices, grain shortages, new taxes, and what ordinary townspeople perceived as oppressive taxation all triggered domestic violence. Major insurrections occurred at Dijon in 1630 and 1668, at Bordeaux in 1635 and 1675, at Montpellier in 1645, in Lyons in 1667–1668 and 1692, and in Amiens in 1685, 1695, 1704, and 1711. Sometimes rumor and misinformation sparked these riots. In any case, they were all characterized by deep popular anger, a vocabulary of violence, and what a recent historian calls "the culture of retribution"—that is, the punishment of royal "outsiders," officials who attempted to announce or to collect taxes. These officials often were seized, beaten, and hacked to death. For example, in 1673 Louis XIV's imposition of new taxes on legal transactions, tobacco, and pewterware provoked a major uprising in Bordeaux.

Municipal and royal authorities responded feebly. They lacked the means of strong action. They feared that stern repressive measures, such as sending in troops to fire on crowds, would create martyrs and further inflame the situation, while forcible full-scale military occupation of a city would be very expensive. Thus authorities allowed the crowds to "burn themselves out," as long as they did not do too much damage. Royal edicts were suspended, prisoners were released, and discussions were initiated. By the end of the century, municipal governments were better integrated into the national structure, and local authorities had the prompt military support of the Paris government. Those who publicly opposed government policies and taxes received swift and severe punishment.[7]

French foreign policy under Richelieu was aimed at the destruction of the fence of Habsburg territories that surrounded France. Consequently, Richelieu supported the Habsburgs' enemies. In 1631 he signed a treaty with the Lutheran king Gustavus Adolphus promising French support against the Catholic Habsburgs in what has been called the Swedish phase of the Thirty Years' War (see page 499). French influence became an important factor in the political future of the German Empire. Richelieu acquired for France extensive rights in Alsace in the east and Arras in the north.

Richelieu's efforts at centralization extended even to literature. In 1635 he gave official recognition to a group of philologists who were interested in grammar and rhetoric. Thus was born the French Academy. With Richelieu's encouragement, the French Academy began the preparation of a dictionary to standardize the French language; it was completed in 1694. The French Academy survives as a prestigious society, and its membership now includes people outside the field of literature.

All of these new policies, especially war, cost money. In his *Political Testament*, Richelieu wrote, "I have always said that finances are the sinews of the state." He fully realized that revenues determine a government's ability to inaugurate and enforce policies and programs. A state secures its revenues through taxation. But the political and economic structure of France greatly limited the government's ability to tax. Seventeenth-century France remained "a collection of local economies and local societies dominated by local elites." The rights of some assemblies in some provinces, such as Brittany, to vote their own taxes; the hereditary exemption from taxation of many wealthy members of the nobility and the middle class; and the royal pension system drastically limited the government's power to tax.

Philippe de Champaigne: Cardinal Richelieu   This portrait, with its penetrating eyes, expression of haughty and imperturbable cynicism, and dramatic sweep of red robes, suggests the authority, grandeur, and power that Richelieu wished to convey as first minister of France. *(Reproduced by courtesy of the Trustees, The National Gallery, London)*

Richelieu and, later, Louis XIV temporarily solved their financial problems by securing the cooperation of local elites. The central government shared the proceeds of tax revenue with local powers. It never gained all the income it needed. Because the French monarchy could not tax at will, it never completely controlled the financial system. In practice, therefore, French absolutism was limited.[8]

In building the French state, Richelieu believed he had to resort to drastic measures against persons and groups within France and to conduct a tough anti-Habsburg foreign policy. He knew also that his approach sometimes seemed to contradict traditional Christian teaching. As a priest and bishop, how did he justify his policies? He developed his own *raison d'état* (reason of state): "Where the interests of the state are concerned, God absolves actions which, if privately committed, would be a crime."[9]

Richelieu persuaded Louis XIII to appoint protégé Jules Mazarin (1602–1661) as his successor. An Italian diplomat of great charm, Mazarin had served on the council of state under Richelieu, acquiring considerable political experience. He became a cardinal in 1641 and a French citizen in 1643. When Louis XIII followed Richelieu to the grave in 1643 and a regency headed by Queen Anne of Austria governed for the child-king Louis XIV, Mazarin became the dominant power in the government. He continued Richelieu's centralizing policies, but his attempts to increase royal revenues led to the civil wars of 1648–1653 known as the "Fronde."

The word *fronde* means "slingshot" or "catapult," and a *frondeur* was originally a street urchin who threw mud at the passing carriages of the rich. But the Fronde originated in the provinces, not Paris, and the term *frondeur* came to be applied to anyone who opposed the policies of the government. Many individuals and groups did so. Influential segments of the nobility resented the increased power of the monarchy under Louis XIII and what they perceived as their diminished role in government. Mazarin could not control them as Richelieu had done. Royal bureaucrats, judges in the parlements, and intendants who considered their positions the means to social and economic advancement felt that they were being manipulated by the Crown and their interests ignored.[10] The state's financial situation steadily weakened because entire regions of France refused to pay taxes. The French defeat of Spanish armies at Rocroi in 1643 marked the final collapse of Spanish military power in Europe; the victory also led the French people to believe that because peace was at hand, taxes were unnecessary. When a desperate government devised new taxes, the Parlement of Paris rejected them. Popular rebellions led by aristocratic factions broke out in the provinces and spread to Paris.[11] As rebellion continued, civil order broke down completely. A vast increase in the state bureaucracy, representing an expansion of royal power, and new means of extracting money from working people incurred the bitter opposition of peasants and urban artisans. Violence continued intermittently for the next twelve years.

The conflicts of the Fronde had three significant results for the future. First, it became apparent that the government would have to compromise with the bureaucrats and social elites that controlled local institutions and constituted the state bureaucracy. These groups were already largely exempt from taxation, and Louis XIV confirmed their privileged social status. Second, the French economy was badly disrupted and would take years to rebuild. Third, the Fronde had a traumatic effect on the young Louis XIV. The king and his mother were frequently threatened and sometimes treated as prisoners by aristocratic factions. On one occasion, a mob broke into the royal bedchamber to make sure the king was actually there; it succeeded in giving him a bad fright. Louis never forgot such humiliations. The period of the Fronde formed the cornerstone of his political education and of his conviction that the sole alternative to anarchy was absolute monarchy. The personal rule of Louis XIV represented the culmination of the process of centralization, but it also witnessed the institutionalization of procedures that would ultimately undermine the absolute monarchy.

The Absolute Monarchy of Louis XIV

According to the court theologian Bossuet, the clergy at the coronation of Louis XIV in Reims Cathedral asked God to cause the splendors of the French court to fill all who beheld it with awe. God subsequently granted that prayer. In the reign of Louis XIV (r. 1643–1715), the longest in European history, the French monarchy reached the peak of absolutist development. In the magnificence of his court, in his absolute power, in the brilliance of the culture that he presided over and that permeated all of Europe, and in his remarkably long life, the "Sun King" dominated his age. No wonder scholars have characterized the second half of the seventeenth century as the "Grand Century," the "Age of Magnificence," and, echoing the eighteenth-century philosopher Voltaire, the "Age of Louis XIV."

In old age, Louis claimed that he had grown up learning very little, but recent historians think he was being modest. True, he knew little Latin and only the rudiments of arithmetic and thus by Renaissance standards was not well educated. Nevertheless, he learned to speak Italian and Spanish fluently, he spoke and wrote elegant French, and he knew some French history and more European geography than the ambassadors accredited to his court. He imbibed the devout Catholicism of his mother, Anne of Austria, and throughout his long life scrupulously performed his religious duties. (Beginning in 1661, Louis attended Mass daily, but rather than paying attention to the liturgy, he said his rosary—to the scorn of his courtiers, who considered this practice "rustic.") Religion, Anne, and Mazarin all taught Louis that God had established kings as his rulers on earth. The royal coronation consecrated Louis to God's service, and he was certain—to use Shakespeare's phrase—that there was a divinity that doth hedge a king. Though kings were a race apart, they could not do as they pleased: they had to obey God's laws and rule for the good of the people.

Louis's education was more practical than formal. Under Mazarin's instruction, he studied state papers as they arrived, and he attended council meetings and sessions at which French ambassadors were dispatched abroad and foreign ambassadors received. He learned by direct experience and gained professional training in the work of government. Above all, the misery he suffered during the Fronde gave him an eternal distrust of the nobility and a profound sense of his own isolation. Accordingly, silence, caution, and secrecy became political tools for the achievement of his goals. His characteristic answer to requests of all kinds became the enigmatic "*Je verrai*" (I shall see).

Louis grew up with an absolute sense of his royal dignity. Contemporaries considered him tall (he was actually five feet five inches) and distinguished in appearance but inclined to heaviness because of the gargantuan meals in which he indulged. A highly sensual man easily aroused by an attractive female face and figure, Louis nonetheless ruled without the political influence of either his wife, Queen Maria Theresa, whom he married as a result of a diplomatic agreement with Spain, or his mistresses. Louis XIV was a consummate actor, and his "terrifying majesty" awed all who saw him. He worked extremely hard and succeeded in being "every moment and every inch a king." Because he so relished the role of monarch, historians have had difficulty distinguishing the man from the monarch.

Historians have often said that Louis XIV introduced significant government innovations, the greatest of which was "the complete domestication of the nobility." By this phrase scholars mean that he exercised complete control over the powerful social class that historically had opposed the centralizing goals of the

Luca Giordano: The Pasta Eater   In the seventeenth century, rich people carried a fork when they dined out, but its use spread very slowly from Italy and came into common use only about 1750. A German preacher damned the fork as a diabolical luxury: "God would not have given us fingers if he wanted us to use forks." So, if King Louis XIV could eat chicken stew with his fingers without spilling it, how can we fault this Neapolitan workingman for enjoying his spaghetti without a fork? *(The Art Museum, Princeton University Museum purchase, John Maclean Magie and Gertrude Magie Fund. Photo: Bruce White)*

French monarchy. Recent research has demonstrated, however, that notions of "domestication" represent an exaggeration. What Louis XIV actually achieved was the cooperation or collaboration of the nobility. Throughout France the nobility agreed to participate in projects that both exalted the monarchy and reinforced the aristocrats' ancient prestige. Thus the relationship between the Crown and the nobility constituted collaboration rather than absolute control.

In the province of Languedoc, for example, Louis and his agents persuaded the notables to support the construction of the Canal des Deux Mers, a waterway linking the Mediterranean Sea and the Atlantic Ocean.

Royal encouragement for the manufacture of luxury draperies in Languedocian towns likewise tied provincial business people to national goals, although French cloths subsequently proved unable to compete with cheaper Dutch ones. Above all, in the campaign for the repression of the Huguenots, the interests of the monarchy and nobility coincided (see page 541). Through mutual collaboration, the nobility and the king achieved goals that neither could have won without the other. For his part, Louis won increased military taxation from the Estates of Languedoc. In return, Louis graciously granted the nobility and dignitaries privileged social status and increased access to his person, which meant access to the enormous patronage the king had to dispense. French government rested on the social and political structure of seventeenth-century France, a structure in which the nobility historically exercised great influence. In this respect, therefore, French absolutism was not so much modern as the last phase of a historical feudal society.[12]

Louis XIV installed his royal court at Versailles, a small town ten miles from Paris. He required all the great nobility of France, at the peril of social, political, and sometimes economic disaster, to come live at Versailles for at least part of the year. Today Versailles stands as the best surviving museum of a vanished society on earth. In the seventeenth century, it became a model of rational order, the center of France, and the perfect symbol of the king's power. (See the feature "Listening to the Past: The Court at Versailles" on pages 562–563.)

Louis XIII had begun Versailles as a hunting lodge, a retreat from a queen he did not like. His son's architects, Le Nôtre and Le Vau, turned what the duke of Saint-Simon called "the most dismal and thankless of sights" into a veritable paradise. Wings were added to the original building to make the palace U-shaped. Everywhere at Versailles the viewer had a sense of grandeur, vastness, and elegance. Enormous staterooms became display galleries for inlaid tables, Italian marble statuary, Gobelin tapestries woven at the state factory in Paris, silver ewers, and beautiful (if uncomfortable) furniture. If genius means attention to detail, Louis XIV and his designers had it: the decor was perfected down to the last doorknob and keyhole. In the gigantic Hall of Mirrors, later to reflect so much of German as well as French history, hundreds of candles illuminated the domed ceiling, where allegorical paintings celebrated the king's victories.

The art and architecture of Versailles served as fundamental tools of state policy under Louis XIV. The king used architecture to overawe his subjects and foreign visitors. Versailles was seen as a reflection of French genius. Thus the Russian tsar Peter the Great imitated Versailles in the construction of his palace, Peterhof, as did the Prussian emperor Frederick the Great in his palace at Potsdam outside Berlin.

As in architecture, so too in language. Beginning in the reign of Louis XIV, French became the language of polite society and the vehicle of diplomatic exchange. French also gradually replaced Latin as the language of international scholarship and learning. The wish of other kings to ape the courtly style of Louis XIV and the imitation of French intellectuals and artists spread the language all over Europe. The royal courts of Sweden, Russia, Poland, and Germany all spoke French. In the eighteenth century, the great Russian aristocrats were more fluent in French than in Russian. In England the first Hanoverian king, George I, spoke fluent French and only halting English. France inspired a cosmopolitan European culture in the late seventeenth century, and that culture was inspired by the king. The French today revere Louis XIV as one of their greatest national heroes because of the culture that he inspired and symbolized.

Against this background of magnificent splendor, Saint-Simon writes, Louis XIV

reduced everyone to subjection, and brought to his court those very persons he cared least about. Whoever was old enough to serve did not dare demur. It was still another device to ruin the nobles by accustoming them to equality and forcing them to mingle with everyone indiscriminately. . . .

Louis XIV took great pains to inform himself on what was happening everywhere, in public places, private homes, and even on the international scene. . . . Spies and informers of all kinds were numberless. . . .

But the King's most vicious method of securing information was opening letters.[13]

Though this passage was written by one of Louis's severest critics, all agree that the king used court ceremonials to undermine the power of the great nobility. By excluding the highest nobles from his councils, he weakened their ancient right to advise the king and to participate in government; they became mere instruments of royal policy. Operas, fetes, balls, gossip, and trivia occupied the nobles' time and attention. Through painstaking attention to detail and precisely calculated showmanship, Louis XIV reduced the major threat to his power. He separated power from status and grandeur: he secured the nobles' cooperation, and the nobles enjoyed the status and grandeur in which they lived.

Louis dominated the court, and in his scheme of things, the court was more significant than the government. In government Louis utilized several councils of state, which he personally attended, and the intendants, who acted for the councils throughout France. A stream of questions and instructions flowed between local districts and Versailles, and under Louis XIV a uniform and centralized administration was imposed on the country. In 1685 France was the strongest and most highly centralized state in Europe.

Councilors of state came from the recently ennobled or the upper middle class. Royal service provided a means of social mobility. These professional bureaucrats served the state in the person of the king, but they did not share power with him. Louis stated that he chose bourgeois officials because he wanted "people to know by the rank of the men who served him that he had no intention of sharing power with them."[14] If great ones were the king's advisers, they would seem to share the royal authority; professional administrators from the middle class would not.

Throughout his long reign and despite increasing financial problems, he never called a meeting of the Estates General. The nobility therefore had no means of united expression or action. Nor did Louis have a first minister; he kept himself free from worry about the inordinate power of a Richelieu. Louis's use of spying and terror—a secret police force, a system of informers, and the practice of opening private letters—foreshadowed some of the devices of the modern state. French government remained highly structured, bureaucratic, centered at Versailles, and responsible to Louis XIV.

Financial and Economic Management Under Louis XIV: Colbert

Finance was the grave weakness of Louis XIV's absolutism. An expanding professional bureaucracy, the court of Versailles, and extensive military reforms (see page 543) cost a great amount of money. The French method of collecting taxes consistently failed to produce enough revenue. Tax farmers, agents who purchased from the Crown the right to collect taxes in a particular district, pocketed the difference between what they raked in and what they handed over to the state. Consequently, the tax farmers profited, while the government got far less than the people paid. In addition, by an old agreement between the Crown and the nobility, the king could freely tax the common people provided he did not tax the nobles. The nobility thereby relinquished a role in government: since nobles did not pay taxes, they could not legitimately claim a say

in how taxes were spent. Louis, however, lost enormous potential revenue. The middle classes, moreover, secured many tax exemptions. With the rich and prosperous classes exempt, the tax burden fell heavily on those least able to pay, the poor peasants.

The king named Jean-Baptiste Colbert (1619–1683), the son of a wealthy merchant-financier of Reims, as controller general of finances. Colbert came to manage the entire royal administration and proved himself a financial genius. Colbert's central principle was that the wealth and the economy of France should serve the state. He did not invent the system called "mercantilism," but he rigorously applied it to France.

Mercantilism is a collection of governmental policies for the regulation of economic activities, especially commercial activities, by and for the state. In seventeenth- and eighteenth-century economic theory, a nation's international power was thought to be based on its wealth, specifically its gold supply. Because, mercantilist theory held, resources were limited, state

Hall of Mirrors, Versailles The grandeur and elegance of the Sun King's reign are reflected in the Hall of Mirrors, where the king's victories were celebrated in paintings on the domed ceiling. Hundreds of candles lit up the dome. *(Michael Holford)*

The Spider and the Fly In reference to the insect symbolism (upper left), the caption on the lower left side of this illustration states, "The noble is the spider, the peasant the fly." The other caption (upper right) notes, "The more people have, the more they want. The poor man brings everything—wheat, fruit, money, vegetables. The greedy lord sitting there ready to take everything will not even give him the favor of a glance." This satirical print summarizes peasant grievances. *(New York Public Library)*

intervention was needed to secure the largest part of a limited resource. To accumulate gold, a country always had to sell more goods abroad than it bought. Colbert believed that a successful economic policy meant more than a favorable balance of trade, however. He insisted that the French sell abroad and buy *nothing* back. France should be self-sufficient, able to produce within its borders everything the subjects of the French king needed. Consequently, the outflow of gold would be halted, debtor states would pay in bullion, and with the wealth of the nation increased, its power and prestige would be enhanced.

Colbert attempted to accomplish self-sufficiency through state support for both old industries and newly created ones. He subsidized the established cloth industries at Abbeville, Saint-Quentin, and Carcassonne. He granted special royal privileges to the rug and tapestry industries at Paris, Gobelin, and Beauvais. New factories at Saint-Antoine in Paris manufactured mirrors

to replace Venetian imports. Looms at Chantilly and Alençon competed with lacemaking at Bruges in the Spanish Netherlands, and foundries at Saint-Étienne made steel and firearms that reduced Swedish imports. To ensure a high-quality finished product, Colbert set up a system of state inspection and regulation. To ensure order within every industry, he compelled all craftsmen to organize into guilds, and within every guild he gave the masters absolute power over their workers. Colbert encouraged skilled foreign craftsmen and manufacturers to immigrate to France, and he gave them special privileges. To improve communications, he built roads and canals, the most famous, the Canal des Deux Mers, linking the Mediterranean and the Bay of Biscay. To protect French goods, he abolished many domestic tariffs and enacted high foreign tariffs, which prevented foreign products from competing with French ones.

Colbert's most important work was the creation of a powerful merchant marine to transport French goods. He gave bonuses to French shipowners and shipbuilders and established a method of maritime conscription, arsenals, and academies for the training of sailors. In 1661 France possessed 18 unseaworthy vessels; by 1681 it had 276 frigates, galleys, and ships of the line. Colbert tried to organize and regulate the entire French economy for the glory of the French state as embodied in the king.

Colbert hoped to make Canada—rich in untapped minerals and some of the best agricultural land in the world—part of a vast French empire. He gathered four thousand peasants from western France and shipped them to Canada, where they peopled the province of Quebec. (In 1608, one year after the English arrived at Jamestown, Virginia, Sully had established the city of Quebec, which became the capital of French Canada.) Subsequently, the Jesuit Jacques Marquette and the merchant Louis Joliet sailed down the Mississippi River and took possession of the land on both sides as far south as present-day Arkansas. In 1684 the French explorer Robert La Salle continued down the Mississippi to its mouth and claimed vast territories and the rich delta for Louis XIV. The area was called, naturally, "Louisiana."

How successful were Colbert's policies? His achievement in the development of manufacturing was prodigious. The textile industry, especially in woolens, expanded enormously, and "France . . . had become in 1683 the leading nation of the world in industrial productivity."[15] The commercial classes prospered, and between 1660 and 1700 their position steadily improved. The national economy, however, rested on agriculture.

Although French peasants did not become serfs, as did the peasants of eastern Europe, they were mercilessly taxed. After 1685 other hardships afflicted them: poor harvests, continuing deflation of the currency, and fluctuation in the price of grain. Many peasants emigrated. With the decline in population and thus in the number of taxable people (the poorest), the state's resources fell. A totally inadequate tax base and heavy expenditure for war in the later years of Louis's reign made Colbert's goals unattainable.

The Revocation of the Edict of Nantes

The absolutist state also attempted to control religion.

We now see with the proper gratitude what we owe to God . . . for the best and largest part of our subjects of the so-called reformed religion have embraced Catholicism, and now that, to the extent that the execution of the Edict of Nantes remains useless, we have judged that we can do nothing better to wipe out the memory of the troubles, of the confusion, of the evils that the progress of this false religion has caused our kingdom . . . than to revoke entirely the said Edict.[16]

Thus in 1685 Louis XIV revoked the Edict of Nantes, by which his grandfather Henry IV had granted liberty of conscience to French Huguenots. The new law ordered the destruction of churches, the closing of schools, the Catholic baptism of Huguenots, and the exile of Huguenot pastors who refused to renounce their faith. Why? There had been so many mass conversions during previous years (many of them forced) that Madame de Maintenon, Louis's second wife, could say that "nearly all the Huguenots were converted." Some Huguenots had emigrated. Richelieu had already deprived French Calvinists of political rights. Why, then, did Louis, by revoking the edict, persecute some of his most loyal and industrially skilled subjects, force others to flee abroad, and provoke the outrage of Protestant Europe?

First, the French monarchy had never intended religious toleration to be permanent (see page 534); religious pluralism was not a seventeenth-century ideal. Although recent scholarship has convincingly shown that Louis XIV was basically tolerant, he considered religious unity politically necessary to realize his goal of "one king, one law, one faith." He hated division within the realm and insisted that religious unity was essential to his royal dignity and to the security of the state.

Second, while France in the early years of Louis's reign permitted religious liberty, it was not a popular policy. Aristocrats had long petitioned Louis to crack down on Protestants. But the revocation was solely the king's decision, and it won him enormous praise. "If the flood of congratulation means anything, it . . . was probably the one act of his reign that, at the time, was popular with the majority of his subjects."[17]

While contemporaries applauded Louis XIV, scholars in the eighteenth century and later damned him for the adverse impact that revocation of the Edict of Nantes had on the economy and foreign affairs. Tens of thousands of Huguenot craftsmen, soldiers, and business people emigrated, depriving France of their skills and tax revenues and carrying their bitterness to Holland, England, Prussia, and Cape Town in southern Africa. Modern scholarship has greatly modified this picture, however. While Huguenot settlers in northern Europe aggravated Protestant hatred for Louis, the revocation of the Edict of Nantes had only minor and scattered effects on French economic development.[18]

French Classicism

Scholars characterize the art and literature of the age of Louis XIV as "French classicism." By this they mean that the artists and writers of the late seventeenth century deliberately imitated the subject matter and style of classical antiquity, that their work resembled that of Renaissance Italy, and that French art possessed the classical qualities of discipline, balance, and restraint. Classicism was the official style of Louis's court. In painting, however, French classicism had already reached its peak before 1661, the beginning of the king's personal government.

Nicholas Poussin (1594–1665) is generally considered the finest example of French classicist painting. Poussin spent all but eighteen months of his creative life in Rome because he found the atmosphere in Paris uncongenial. Deeply attached to classical antiquity, he believed that the highest aim of painting was to represent noble actions in a logical and orderly, but not realistic, way. His masterpiece, *The Rape of the Sabine Women*, exhibits these qualities. Its subject is an incident in Roman history; the figures of people and horses are ideal representations, and the emotions expressed are studied, not spontaneous. Even the buildings are exact architectural models of ancient Roman structures.

Poussin, whose paintings still had individualistic features, did his work before 1661. After Louis's accession to power, the principles of absolutism molded the ideals of French classicism. Individualism was not allowed, and artists' efforts were directed to the glorification of the state as personified by the king. Precise rules

Poussin: The Rape of the Sabine Women (ca 1636) Considered the greatest French painter of the seventeenth century, Poussin in this dramatic work shows his complete devotion to the ideals of classicism. The heroic figures are superb physical specimens, but hardly lifelike. *(The Metropolitan Museum of Art, New York, Harris Brisbane Dick Fund, 1946 [46.160]. Photograph © 1980 The Metropolitan Museum of Art)*

governed all aspects of culture, with the goal of formal and restrained perfection.

Contemporaries said that Louis XIV never ceased playing the role of grand monarch on the stage of his court. If the king never fully relaxed from the pressures and intrigues of government, he did enjoy music and theater and used them as a backdrop for court ceremonials. Louis favored Jean-Baptiste Lully (1632–1687), whose orchestral works combined lively animation with the restrained austerity typical of French classicism. Lully also composed court ballets, and his operatic productions achieved a powerful influence throughout Europe. Louis supported François Couperin (1668–1733), whose harpsichord and organ works possessed the regal grandeur the king loved, and Marc-Antoine

Charpentier (1634–1704), whose solemn religious music entertained him at meals. Charpentier received a pension for the *Te Deums,* hymns of thanksgiving, he composed to celebrate French military victories.

Louis XIV loved the stage, and in the plays of Molière and Racine his court witnessed the finest achievements in the history of the French theater. When Jean-Baptiste Poquelin (1622–1673), the son of a prosperous tapestry maker, refused to join his father's business and entered the theater, he took the stage name "Molière." As playwright, stage manager, director, and actor, Molière produced comedies that exposed the hypocrisies and follies of society through brilliant caricature. *Tartuffe* satirized the religious hypocrite, *Le Bourgeois Gentilhomme* (The Bourgeois Gentleman) attacked the social parvenu, and *Les Femmes Savantes* (The Learned Women) mocked the fashionable pseudo-intellectuals of the day. In structure Molière's plays followed classical models, but they were based on careful social observation. Molière made the bourgeoisie the butt of his ridicule; he stopped short of criticizing the nobility, thus reflecting the policy of his royal patron.

While Molière dissected social mores, his contemporary Jean Racine (1639–1699) analyzed the power of love. Racine based his tragic dramas on Greek and Roman legends, and his persistent theme was the conflict of good and evil. Several plays—*Andromaque, Bérénice, Iphigénie,* and *Phèdre*—bear the names of women and deal with the power of passion in women. Louis preferred *Mithridate* and *Britannicus* because of the "grandeur" of their themes. For simplicity of language, symmetrical structure, and calm restraint, the plays of Racine represent the finest examples of French classicism. His tragedies and Molière's comedies are still produced today.

Louis XIV's Wars

On his deathbed, Louis XIV is reputed to have said, "I have gone to war too lightly and pursued it for vanity's sake." Perhaps he never actually said this. If he did, perhaps it was part of the confessional style of the time, which required that a penitent exaggerate his sins.[19] In any case, the course of Louis's reign suggests that he acted according to his observation that "the character of a conqueror is regarded as the noblest and highest of titles." In pursuit of the title of "conqueror," he kept France at war for thirty-three of the fifty-four years of his personal rule.

It is an axiom of history that war or the preparation for war is always a government's greatest expense. In 1635, when Richelieu became first minister of Louis XIII, the French army consisted of 25,000 men. At Richelieu's death in 1642, the army had 100,000 men. In 1659, at the time of the Treaty of the Pyrenees, which ended the war with Spain, the army theoretically was composed of 250,000 men. These numbers represent a phenomenal expansion of the military and an enormous increase in costs to the state. In 1666 Louis appointed François le Tellier (later marquis de Louvois) secretary of state for war. Under the king's watchful eye, Louvois created a professional army that was modern in the sense that the French state, rather than private nobles, employed the soldiers. The king himself took command and directly supervised all aspects and details of military affairs.

Louis personally appointed not only the marshals of France (the highest rank) but also all officers down to the rank of colonel. Louvois utilized several methods in recruiting troops: dragooning, in which press gangs seized men off the streets, often drunks, bums, and criminals (this method was not popular); conscription; and, after 1688, lottery. Louvois also recruited regiments of foreign mercenaries in Italy, Germany, England, Scotland, Ireland, and Switzerland. Under the strict direction of Jean Martinet (d. 1672), whose name became a byword in the French and English languages for absolute adherence to the rules, the foreign and native-born soldiers were turned into a tough, obedient military machine. A commissariat was established to feed the troops, thereby taking the place of the ancient method of living off the countryside. An ambulance corps was designed to look after the wounded. Uniforms and weapons were standardized. A rational system of training and promotion was imposed. All this added up to a military revolution. A new military machine now existed that gave one national state, France, the potential to dominate the affairs of the continent for the first time in European history.

Louis continued on a broader scale the expansionist policy begun by Cardinal Richelieu. In 1667, using a dynastic excuse, he invaded Flanders, part of the Spanish Netherlands, and Franche-Comté in the east. In consequence, he acquired twelve towns, including the important commercial centers of Lille and Tournai (Map 16.1). Five years later, Louis personally led an army of over 100,000 men into Holland, and the Dutch ultimately saved themselves only by opening the dikes and flooding the countryside. This war, which lasted six years and eventually involved the Holy Roman Empire and Spain, was concluded by the Treaty of Nijmegen (1678). Louis gained additional Flemish towns and all of Franche-Comté.

Encouraged by his successes, by the weakness of the German Empire, and by divisions among the other European powers, Louis continued his aggression. In 1681 he seized the city of Strasbourg, and three years later he sent his armies into the province of Lorraine. At that moment, the king seemed invincible. In fact, Louis had reached the limit of his expansion. The wars of the 1680s and 1690s brought him no additional territories. In 1689 the Dutch prince William of Orange (r. 1689–1702), a bitter foe of Louis XIV, became king of England. William joined the League of Augsburg—which included the Habsburg emperor, the kings of Spain and Sweden, and the electors of Bavaria, Saxony, and the Palatinate. William was the unquestioned leader of the coalition, and he threw the weight of England

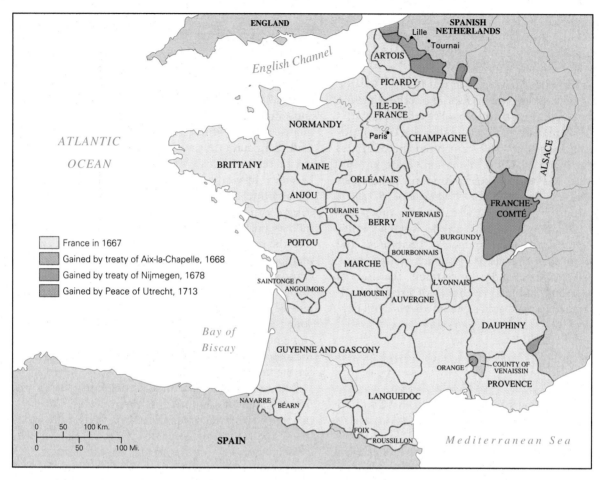

MAP 16.1 The Acquisitions of Louis XIV, 1668–1713 The desire for glory and the weakness of his German neighbors encouraged Louis's expansionist policy, but he paid a high price for his acquisitions.

and the Netherlands into the struggle. Neither the French nor the league won any decisive victories. France lacked the means to win; it was financially exhausted.

Louis was attempting to support an army of 200,000 men in several different theaters of war against the great nations of Europe, the powerful Bank of Amsterdam, and (after 1694) the Bank of England. This task far exceeded French resources, given the very inequitable system of taxation. The military revolution involving the reform and great expansion of the army required funding that the state could not meet. Claude Le Peletier, Colbert's successor as minister of finance, resorted to the devaluation of the currency (which hurt those who hoarded coins) and the old device of selling offices, tax exemptions, and titles of nobility. To raise revenue for the war effort, on December 14, 1689, Louis published

a declaration ordering that all the nation's silverware be handed over to the mint. Setting an example, Louis sent off the silver furniture of Versailles—cabinets, mirrors, tables, armchairs, stools, chimney decorations, *guéridons* (pedestal tables), bowls, urns, vases, candelabra, saltcellars, trays, flowerpots, pails, and spittoons. The royal apartments and the Hall of Mirrors looked like a house repossessed by sheriffs.[20] This action did little good. None of these measures produced enough revenue. So the weight of taxation fell on the already-overburdened peasants. They expressed their frustrations in widespread revolts that hit all parts of France in the 1690s.

A series of bad harvests between 1688 and 1694 brought catastrophe. Cold, wet summers reduced the harvests by an estimated one-third to two-thirds. The price of wheat skyrocketed. The result was widespread starvation, and in many provinces the death rate rose to several times the normal figure. Parish registers reveal that France buried at least one-tenth of its population in those years, perhaps 2 million in 1693 to 1694 alone. Rising grain prices, new taxes for war on top of old ones, a slump in manufacturing and thus in exports, and the constant nuisance of pillaging troops—all these meant great suffering for the French people. France wanted peace at any price. Louis XIV granted a respite for five years while he prepared for the conflict later known as the War of the Spanish Succession (1701–1713).

This war, provoked by the territorial disputes of the previous century, also involved the dynastic question of the succession to the Spanish throne. It was an open secret in Europe that the king of Spain, Charles II (r. 1665–1700), was mentally defective and sexually impotent. In 1698 the European powers, including France, agreed by treaty to partition, or divide, the vast Spanish possessions between the king of France and the Holy Roman emperor, who were Charles II's brothers-in-law. When Charles died in 1700, however, his will left the Spanish crown and the worldwide Spanish empire to Philip of Anjou, Louis XIV's grandson. While the will specifically rejected union of the French and Spanish crowns, Louis was obviously the power in France, not his seventeen-year-old grandson. Louis reneged on the treaty and accepted the will.

The Dutch and the English would not accept French acquisition of the Spanish Netherlands and of the rich trade with the Spanish colonies. The union of the Spanish and French crowns, moreover, would have totally upset the European balance of power. Claiming that he was following both Spanish national interests and French dynastic and national interests, Louis presented Philip of Anjou to the Spanish ambassador saying, "You may salute him as your king." After a Mass of thanksgiving, the Spanish ambassador was heard to say, "What rapture! The Pyrenees no longer exist."[21] The possibility of achieving this goal provoked the long-anticipated crisis.

In 1701 the English, Dutch, Austrians, and Prussians formed the Grand Alliance against Louis XIV. They claimed that they were fighting to prevent France from becoming too strong in Europe, but during the previous half century, overseas maritime rivalry among France, Holland, and England had created serious international tension. The secondary motive of the allied powers was to check France's expanding commercial power in North America, Asia, and Africa. In the ensuing series of conflicts, two great soldiers dominated the alliance against France: Eugene, prince of Savoy, repre-

senting the Holy Roman Empire, and Englishman John Churchill, subsequently duke of Marlborough. Eugene and Churchill inflicted a severe defeat on Louis in 1704 at Blenheim in Bavaria. Marlborough followed with another victory at Ramillies near Namur in Brabant.

The war was finally concluded at Utrecht in 1713, where the principle of partition was applied. Louis's grandson, Philip, remained the first Bourbon king of Spain on the understanding that the French and Spanish crowns would never be united. France surrendered Newfoundland, Nova Scotia, and the Hudson Bay territory to England, which also acquired Gibraltar, Minorca, and control of the African slave trade from Spain. The Dutch gained little because Austria received the former Spanish Netherlands (Map 16.2).

The Peace of Utrecht had important international consequences. It represented the balance-of-power principle in operation, setting limits on the extent to which any one power—in this case, France—could expand. The treaty completed the decline of Spain as a great power. It vastly expanded the British Empire. And it gave European powers experience in international cooperation, thus preparing them for the alliances against France at the end of the century.

The Peace of Utrecht marked the end of French expansionist policy. In Louis's thirty-five-year quest for military glory, his main territorial acquisition was Strasbourg. Even revisionist historians, who portray the aging monarch as responsible in negotiation and moderate in his demands, acknowledge "that the widespread misery in France during the period was in part due to royal policies, especially the incessant wars."[22] To raise revenue for the wars, forty thousand additional offices had been sold, thus increasing the number of families exempt from future taxation. In 1714 France hovered on the brink of financial bankruptcy. Louis had exhausted the country without much compensation. It is no wonder that when he died on September 1, 1715, Saint-Simon wrote, "Those . . . wearied by the heavy and oppressive rule of the King and his ministers, felt a delighted freedom. . . . Paris . . . found relief in the hope of liberation. . . . The provinces . . . quivered with delight . . . [and] the people, ruined, abused, despairing, now thanked God for a deliverance which answered their most ardent desires."[23]

The Decline of Absolutist Spain in the Seventeenth Century

Spanish absolutism and greatness had preceded those of the French. In the sixteenth century, Spain (or, more precisely, the kingdom of Castile) had developed the

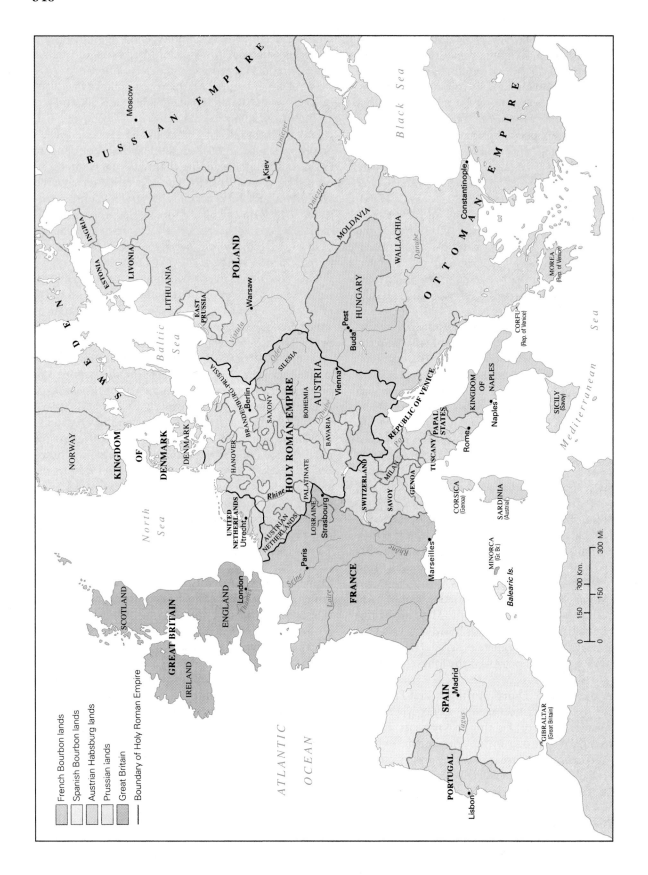

standard features of absolute monarchy: a permanent bureaucracy staffed by professionals employed in the various councils of state, a standing army, and national taxes, the *servicios,* which fell most heavily on the poor.

France depended on financial and administrative unification within its borders; Spain had developed an international absolutism on the basis of silver bullion from Peru. Spanish gold and silver, armies, and glory had dominated the continent for most of the sixteenth century, but by the 1590s the seeds of disaster were sprouting. While France in the seventeenth century was representing the classic model of the modern absolute state, Spain was experiencing steady decline. The lack of a strong middle class, largely the result of the expulsion of the Jews and Moors (see page 445), the agricultural crisis and population decline, the failure to invest in productive enterprises, the intellectual isolation and psychological malaise—all combined to reduce Spain, by 1715, to a second-rate power.

The fabulous and seemingly inexhaustible flow of silver from Mexico and Peru, together with the sale of cloth, grain, oil, and wine to the colonies, greatly enriched Spain. In the early seventeenth century, however, the Dutch and English began to trade with the Spanish colonies, cutting into the revenues that had gone to Spain. Mexico and Peru themselves developed local industries, further lessening their need to buy from Spain. Between 1610 and 1650, Spanish trade with the colonies fell 60 percent.

At the same time, the native Indians and African slaves who worked the South American silver mines under conditions that would have shamed the ancient Egyptian pharaohs suffered frightful epidemics of disease. Moreover, the lodes started to run dry. Consequently, the quantity of metal produced for Spain steadily declined. However, in Madrid royal expenditures constantly exceeded income. The remedies applied in the face of a mountainous state debt and declining revenues were devaluation of the coinage and declarations of bankruptcy. In 1596, 1607, 1627, 1647, and 1680, Spanish kings found no solution to the problem of an empty treasury other than to cancel the national debt. Given the frequency of cancellation, public confidence in the state naturally deteriorated.

Spain, in contrast to the other countries of western Europe, had only a tiny middle class. Disdain for money in a century of increasing commercialism and bourgeois attitudes was a significant facet of Spanish culture. Public opinion, taking its cue from the aristocracy, condemned moneymaking as vulgar and undignified. Those with influence or connections sought titles of nobility and social prestige. Thousands entered economically unproductive professions or became priests, monks, and nuns: there were said to be nine thousand monasteries in the province of Castile alone. The flood of gold and silver had produced severe inflation, pushing the costs of production in the textile industry higher and higher to the point that Castilian cloth could not compete in colonial and international markets. Many businessmen found so many obstacles in the way of profitable enterprise that they simply gave up.[24]

Spanish aristocrats, attempting to maintain an extravagant lifestyle they could no longer afford, increased the rents on their estates. High rents and heavy taxes in turn drove the peasants from the land. Agricultural production suffered, and the peasants departed for the large cities, where they swelled the ranks of unemployed beggars.

Their most Catholic majesties, the kings of Spain, had no solutions to these dire problems. If one can discern personality from pictures, the portraits of Philip III (r. 1598–1622), Philip IV (r. 1622–1665), and Charles II (r. 1665–1700) hanging in the Prado, the Spanish national museum in Madrid, reflect the increasing weakness of the dynasty. Their faces—the small, beady eyes; the long noses; the jutting Habsburg jaws; the pathetically stupid expressions—tell a story of excessive inbreeding and decaying monarchy. The Spanish kings all lacked force of character. Philip III, a pallid, melancholy, and deeply pious man "whose only virtue appeared to reside in a total absence of vice," handed the government over to the lazy duke of Lerma, who used it to advance his personal and familial wealth. Philip IV left the management of his several kingdoms to Gaspar de Guzmán, count-duke of Olivares.

Olivares was an able administrator. He did not lack energy and ideas; he devised new sources of revenue. But he clung to the grandiose belief that the solution to Spain's difficulties rested in a return to the imperial tra-

MAP 16.2 Europe in 1715   The series of treaties commonly called the Peace of Utrecht (April 1713–November 1715) ended the War of the Spanish Succession and redrew the map of Europe. A French Bourbon king succeeded to the Spanish throne on the understanding that the French not attempt to unite the French and Spanish crowns. France surrendered to Austria the Spanish Netherlands (later Belgium), then in French hands, and France recognized the Hohenzollern rulers of Prussia. Spain ceded Gibraltar to Great Britain, for which it has been a strategic naval station ever since. Spain also granted to Britain the *asiento,* the contract for supplying African slaves to America.

Velázquez: Count-Duke Olivares To commemorate a small Spanish victory over the French at the border town of Fuenterrabia in 1638, and to defend Olivares at a time when his policies were being severely criticized, Velázquez depicts him in glistening black armor, gold-embroidered trousers, and with a red sash (ensign of a captain general) over his right shoulder, on a rearing horse as if leading troops into battle in the distance. Although he had sent troops, Olivares was safe in Madrid at the time of the battle. *(Museo del Prado/Institut Amatller d'Art Hispanic)*

dition. Unfortunately, the imperial tradition demanded the revival of war with the Dutch at the expiration of a twelve-year truce in 1622 and a long war with France over Mantua (1628–1659). Spain thus became embroiled in the Thirty Years' War. These conflicts, on top of an empty treasury, brought disaster.

In 1640 Spain faced serious revolts in Catalonia and Portugal; in 1643 the French inflicted a crushing defeat on a Spanish army at Rocroi in what is now Belgium. By the Treaty of the Pyrenees of 1659, which ended the French-Spanish wars, Spain was compelled to surrender extensive territories to France. This treaty marked the end of Spain as a great power.

Seventeenth-century Spain was the victim of its past. It could not forget the grandeur of the sixteenth century and look to the future. The bureaucratic councils

of state continued to function as symbols of the absolute Spanish monarchy. But because those councils were staffed by aristocrats, it was the aristocracy that held the real power. Spanish absolutism had been built largely on slave-produced gold and silver. When the supply of bullion decreased, the power and standing of the Spanish state declined.

The most cherished Spanish ideals were military glory and strong Roman Catholic faith. In the seventeenth century, Spain lacked the finances and the manpower to fight the expensive wars in which it foolishly got involved. Spain also ignored the new mercantile ideas and scientific methods because they came from heretical nations, Holland and England. The incredible wealth of South America destroyed what remained of the Spanish middle class and created contempt for business and manual labor.

The decadence of the Habsburg dynasty and the lack of effective royal councilors also contributed to Spanish failure. Spanish leaders seemed to lack the will to reform. Pessimism and fatalism permeated national life. In the reign of Philip IV, a royal council was appointed to plan the construction of a canal linking the Tagus and Manzanares Rivers in Spain. After interminable debate, the committee decided that "if God had intended the rivers to be navigable, He would have made them so."

In the brilliant novel *Don Quixote,* Spanish writer Miguel de Cervantes (1547–1616) produced one of the great masterpieces of world literature. *Don Quixote* delineates the whole fabric of sixteenth-century Spanish society. The main character, Don Quixote, lives in a world of dreams, traveling about the countryside seeking military glory. From the title of the book, the English language has borrowed the word *quixotic.* Meaning "idealistic but impractical," the term characterizes seventeenth-century Spain. As a leading scholar has written, "The Spaniard convinced himself that reality was what he felt, believed, imagined. He filled the world with heroic reverberations. Don Quixote was born and grew."[25]

CONSTITUTIONALISM

The seventeenth century, which witnessed the development of absolute monarchy, also saw the appearance of the constitutional state. While France and, later, Prussia, Russia, and Austria solved the question of sovereignty with the absolutist state, England and Holland evolved toward the constitutional state. What is constitutionalism? Is it identical to democracy?

Constitutionalism is the limitation of government by law. Constitutionalism also implies a balance between the authority and power of the government, on the one hand, and the rights and liberties of the subjects, on the other. The balance is often very delicate.

A nation's constitution may be written or unwritten. It may be embodied in one basic document, occasionally revised by amendment or judicial decision, like the Constitution of the United States. Or it may be partly written and partly unwritten and include parliamentary statutes, judicial decisions, and a body of traditional procedures and practices, like the English, Canadian, and Dutch constitutions. Whether written or unwritten, a constitution gets its binding force from the government's acknowledgment that it must respect that constitution—that is, that the state must govern according to the laws. Likewise, in a constitutional state, the people look on the laws and the constitution as the protectors of their rights, liberties, and property.

Modern constitutional governments may take either a republican or a monarchial form. In a constitutional republic, the sovereign power resides in the electorate and is exercised by the electorate's representatives. In a constitutional monarchy, a king or queen serves as the head of state and possesses some residual political authority, but again the ultimate, or sovereign, power rests in the electorate.

A constitutional government is not, however, quite the same as a democratic government. In a complete democracy, *all* the people have the right to participate either directly or indirectly (through their elected representatives) in the government of the state. Democratic government, therefore, is intimately tied up with the *franchise* (the vote). Most men could not vote until the late nineteenth century. Even then, women—probably the majority in Western societies—lacked the franchise; they gained the right to vote only in the twentieth century. Consequently, although constitutionalism developed in the seventeenth century, full democracy was achieved only in very recent times.

The Decline of Royal Absolutism in England (1603–1649)

In 1588 Queen Elizabeth I of England exercised very great personal power; by 1689 the English monarchy was severely circumscribed. Change in England was anything but orderly. Seventeenth-century England displayed little political stability. It executed one king, experienced a bloody civil war; experimented with military dictatorship, then restored the son of the murdered king; and finally, after a bloodless revolution, established constitutional monarchy. Political stability came only in the 1690s. How do we account for the fact that after such a violent and tumultuous century, England laid the foundations for constitutional monarchy? What combination of political, socioeconomic, and religious factors brought on a civil war in 1642 to 1649 and then the constitutional settlement of 1688 to 1689?

The extraordinary success of Elizabeth I had rested on her political shrewdness and flexibility, her careful management of finances, her wise selection of ministers, her clever manipulation of Parliament, and her sense of royal dignity and devotion to hard work. The aging queen had always refused to discuss the succession. After her Scottish cousin James Stuart succeeded her as James I (r. 1603–1625), Elizabeth's strengths seemed even greater than they actually had been.

King James was well educated, learned, and, with thirty-five years' experience as king of Scotland, politically shrewd. But he was not as interested in displaying the majesty and mystique of monarchy as Elizabeth had been. He also lacked the common touch. Urged to wave at the crowds who waited to greet their new ruler, James complained that he was tired and threatened to drop his breeches "so they can cheer at my arse." The new king failed to live up to the role expected of him in England. Moreover, James, in contrast to Elizabeth, was a poor judge of character, and in a society already hostile to the Scots and concerned about proper spoken English, James's Scottish accent was a disadvantage.[26]

James was devoted to the theory of the divine right of kings. He expressed his ideas about divine right in his essay "The Trew Law of Free Monarchy." According to James I, a monarch has a divine (or God-given) right to his authority and is responsible only to God. Rebellion is the worst of political crimes. If a king orders something evil, the subject should respond with passive disobedience but should be prepared to accept any penalty for noncompliance.

He went so far as to lecture the House of Commons: "There are no privileges and immunities which can stand against a divinely appointed King." This notion, implying total royal jurisdiction over the liberties, persons, and properties of English men and women, formed the basis of the Stuart concept of absolutism. Such a view ran directly counter to the long-standing English idea that a person's property could not be taken away without due process of law. James's expression of such views before the English House of Commons constituted a grave political mistake.

The House of Commons guarded the state's pocketbook, and James and later Stuart kings badly needed to open that pocketbook. Elizabeth had bequeathed to

James a sizable royal debt. Through prudent management, the debt could have been gradually reduced, but James I looked on all revenues as a happy windfall to be squandered on a lavish court and favorite courtiers. In reality, the extravagance displayed in James's court as well as the public flaunting of his male lovers weakened respect for the monarchy.

Elizabeth had also left to her Stuart successors a House of Commons that appreciated its own financial strength and intended to use that strength to acquire a greater say in the government of the state. The knights and burgesses who sat at Westminster in the late sixteenth and early seventeenth centuries wanted a voice in royal expenditures, religious reform, and foreign affairs. Essentially, the Commons wanted sovereignty.

Profound social changes had occurred since the sixteenth century. The English House of Commons during the reigns of James I and his son Charles I (r. 1625–1649) was very different from the assembly Henry VIII had manipulated into passing his Reformation legislation. A social revolution had brought about the change. The dissolution of the monasteries and the sale of monastic land had enriched many people. Agricultural techniques such as the draining of wasteland and the application of fertilizers had improved the land and its yield. In the seventeenth century, old manorial common land was enclosed and turned into sheep runs, breeding was carefully supervised, and the size of the flocks increased. In these activities, as well as in the renting and leasing of parcels of land, precise accounts were kept.

Many people invested in commercial ventures at home, such as the expanding cloth industry, and through partnerships and joint stock companies engaged in foreign enterprises. Many also made prudent marriages. All these developments led to a great deal of social mobility. Both in commerce and in agriculture, the English in the late sixteenth and early seventeenth centuries were capitalists, investing their profits to make more money. Though the international inflation of the period hit everywhere, in England commercial and agricultural income rose faster than prices. Wealthy country gentry, rich city merchants, and financiers invested abroad.

The typical pattern was for the commercially successful to set themselves up as country gentry, thus creating an elite group that possessed a far greater proportion of land and of the national wealth in 1640 than had been the case in 1540. Small wonder that in 1640 someone could declare in the House of Commons, probably accurately, "We could buy the House of Lords three times over." Increased wealth had also produced a better-educated and more articulate House of Commons.

Many members had acquired at least a smattering of legal knowledge, which they used to search for medieval precedents from which to argue against the king. The class that dominated the Commons wanted political power corresponding to its economic strength.

In England, unlike France, there was no social stigma attached to paying taxes. Members of the House of Commons were willing to tax themselves provided they had some say in the expenditure of those taxes and in the formulation of state policies. The Stuart kings, however, considered such ambitions intolerable presumption and a threat to their divine-right prerogative. Consequently, at every Parliament between 1603 and 1640, bitter squabbles erupted between the Crown and the wealthy, articulate, and legally minded Commons. Charles I's attempt to govern without Parliament (1629–1640) and to finance his government by arbitrary non-parliamentary levies, brought the country to a crisis.

An issue graver than royal extravagance and Parliament's desire to make law also disturbed the English and embittered relations between the king and the House of Commons. That problem was religion. In the early seventeenth century, increasing numbers of English people felt dissatisfied with the Church of England established by Henry VIII and reformed by Elizabeth. Many Puritans (see page 473) believed that the Reformation had not gone far enough. They wanted to "purify" the Anglican church of Roman Catholic elements—elaborate vestments and ceremonials, the position of the altar in the church, even the giving and wearing of wedding rings.

It is very difficult to establish what proportion of the English population was Puritan. According to the present scholarly consensus, the dominant religious groups in the early seventeenth century were Calvinist; their more zealous members were Puritans. It also seems clear that many English men and women were attracted by the socioeconomic implications of John Calvin's theology. Calvinism emphasized hard work, sobriety, thrift, competition, and postponement of pleasure, and it tended to link sin and poverty with weakness and moral corruption. These attitudes fit in precisely with the economic approaches and practices of many (successful) business people and farmers. These values have frequently been called the "Protestant ethic," "middle-class ethic," or "capitalist ethic." While it is hazardous to identify capitalism with Protestantism—there were many successful Catholic capitalists, for example—the "Protestant virtues" represented the prevailing values of members of the House of Commons.

Puritans wanted to abolish bishops in the Church of England, and when James I said, "No bishop, no king," he meant that the bishops were among the chief supporters of the throne. He was no Puritan, but he was Calvinist (see page 467) in doctrine. Yet James and his son Charles I both gave the impression of being sympathetic to Roman Catholicism. Charles supported the policies of William Laud (1573–1645), archbishop of Canterbury, who tried to impose elaborate ritual and rich ceremonials on all churches. Laud insisted on complete uniformity of church services and enforced that uniformity through an ecclesiastical court called the "Court of High Commission." People believed the country was being led back to Roman Catholicism. In 1637 Laud attempted to impose two new elements on the church organization in Scotland: a new prayer book, modeled on the Anglican *Book of Common Prayer,* and bishoprics, which the Presbyterian Scots firmly rejected. The Scots therefore revolted. To finance an army to put down the Scots, King Charles was compelled to summon Parliament in November 1640.

Charles I was an intelligent man, but contemporaries found him deceitful, dishonest, and treacherous. Therefore, they did not trust him. For eleven years, Charles had ruled without Parliament, financing his government through extraordinary stopgap levies considered illegal by most English people. For example, the king revived a medieval law requiring coastal districts to help pay the cost of ships for defense, but he levied the tax, called "ship money," on inland as well as coastal counties. When the issue was tested in the courts, the judges, having been suborned, decided in the king's favor.

Most members of Parliament believed that such taxation without consent amounted to arbitrary and absolute despotism. Consequently, they were not willing to trust the king with an army. Accordingly, this Parliament, commonly called the "Long Parliament" because it sat from 1640 to 1660, proceeded to enact legislation that limited the power of the monarch and made arbitrary government impossible.

In 1641 the Commons passed the Triennial Act, which compelled the king to summon Parliament every three years. The Commons impeached Archbishop Laud and abolished the Court of High Commission. It went further and threatened to abolish the institution of episcopacy. King Charles, fearful of a Scottish invasion—the original reason for summoning Parliament—

Cartoon of 1649: "The Royall Oake of Brittayne"   is chopped down, ending royal authority, stability, Magna Carta (see page 347), and the rule of law. As pigs graze (representing the unconcerned common people), being fattened for slaughter, Oliver Cromwell, with his feet in hell, quotes Scripture. This is a royalist view of the collapse of Charles I's government and the rule of Cromwell. *(Courtesy of the Trustees of the British Museum)*

accepted these measures. Understanding and peace were not achieved, however, partly because radical members of the Commons pushed increasingly revolutionary propositions, partly because Charles maneuvered to rescind those he had already approved. An uprising in Ireland precipitated civil war.

Ever since Henry II had conquered Ireland in 1171, English governors had mercilessly ruled the land, and English landlords had ruthlessly exploited the Irish people. The English Reformation had made a bad situation worse: because the Irish remained Catholic, religious differences became united with economic and political oppression. Without an army, Charles I could neither come to terms with the Scots nor put down the Irish rebellion, and the Long Parliament remained unwilling to place an army under a king it did not trust. Charles thus instigated military action against parliamentary forces. He recruited an army drawn from the nobility and its cavalry staff, the rural gentry, and mercenaries. The parliamentary army was composed of the militia of the city of London, country squires with business connections, and men with a firm belief in the spiritual duty of serving.

The English civil war (1642–1649) tested whether sovereignty in England was to reside in the king or in Parliament. The civil war did not resolve that problem, however, although it ended in 1649 with the execution of King Charles on the charge of high treason—a severe blow to the theory of divine-right monarchy. The period between 1649 and 1660, called the "Interregnum" because it separated two monarchial periods, witnessed England's solitary experience of military dictatorship.

Puritanical Absolutism in England: Cromwell and the Protectorate

The problem of sovereignty was vigorously debated in the middle years of the seventeenth century. In *Leviathan*, English philosopher and political theorist Thomas Hobbes (1588–1679) maintains that sovereignty is ultimately derived from the people, who transfer it to the monarchy by implicit contract. The power of the ruler is absolute, but kings do not hold their power by divine right. This view pleased no one.

When Charles I was beheaded on January 30, 1649, the kingship was abolished. A *commonwealth,* or republican form of government, was proclaimed. Theoretically, legislative power rested in the surviving members of Parliament, and executive power was lodged in a council of state. In fact, the army that had defeated the royal forces controlled the government, and Oliver

Cromwell controlled the army. Though called the "Protectorate," the rule of Cromwell (1653–1658) constituted military dictatorship.

Oliver Cromwell (1599–1658) came from the country gentry, the class that dominated the House of Commons in the early seventeenth century. He himself had sat in the Long Parliament. Cromwell rose in the parliamentary army and achieved nationwide fame by infusing the army with his Puritan convictions and molding it into a highly effective military machine, called the "New Model Army," which defeated the royalist forces.

The army had prepared a constitution, the Instrument of Government (1653), that invested executive power in a lord protector (Cromwell) and a council of state. The instrument provided for triennial parliaments and gave Parliament the sole power to raise taxes. But after repeated disputes, Cromwell tore the document up. He continued the standing army and proclaimed quasi-martial law. He divided England into twelve military districts, each governed by a major general. The major generals acted through the justices of the peace though sometimes overrode them. On the issue of religion, Cromwell favored toleration, and the Instrument of Government gave all Christians, except Roman Catholics, the right to practice their faith. Toleration meant state protection of many different Protestant sects, however, and most English people had no enthusiasm for such a notion; the idea was far ahead of its time. As for Irish Catholicism, Cromwell identified it with sedition. In 1649 he crushed a rebellion in Ireland with merciless savagery, leaving a legacy of Irish hatred for England that has not yet subsided. The state rigorously censored the press, forbade sports, and kept the theaters closed in England.

Cromwell's regulation of the nation's economy had features typical of seventeenth-century absolutism. The lord protector's policies were mercantilist, similar to those Colbert established in France. Cromwell enforced a Navigation Act (1651) requiring that English goods be transported on English ships. The navigation act was a great boost to the development of an English merchant marine and brought about a short but successful war with the commercially threatened Dutch. Cromwell also welcomed the immigration of Jews because of their skills, and they began to return to England after four centuries of absence.

Military government collapsed when Cromwell died in 1658. Fed up with military rule, the English longed for a return to civilian government, restoration of the common law, and social stability. Moreover, the strain of creating a community of puritanical saints proved too psychologically exhausting. Government by military dictatorship was an unfortunate experiment that the English never forgot or repeated. By 1660 they were ready to restore the monarchy.

The Restoration of the English Monarchy

The Restoration of 1660 re-established the monarchy in the person of Charles II (r. 1660–1685), eldest son of Charles I. At the same time, both houses of Parliament were restored, together with the established Anglican church, the courts of law, and the system of local government through justices of the peace. The Restoration failed to resolve two serious problems, however. What was to be the attitude of the state toward Puritans, Catholics, and dissenters from the established church? And what was to be the constitutional position of the king—that is, what was to be the relationship between the king and Parliament?

About the first of these issues, Charles II, a relaxed, easygoing, and sensual man, was basically indifferent. He was not interested in doctrinal issues. The new members of Parliament were, and they proceeded to enact a body of laws that sought to compel religious uniformity. Those who refused to receive the Eucharist of the Church of England could not vote, hold public office, preach, teach, attend the universities, or even assemble for meetings, according to the Test Act of 1673. But these restrictions could not be enforced. When the Quaker William Penn held a meeting of his Friends and was arrested, the jury refused to convict him.

In politics Charles II was determined "not to set out in his travels again," which meant that he intended to get along with Parliament. Charles II's solution to the problem of the relationship between the king and the House of Commons had profound importance for later constitutional development. Generally good rapport existed between the king and the strongly royalist Parliament that had restored him. This rapport was due largely to the king's appointment of a council of five men who served both as his major advisers and as members of Parliament, thus acting as liaison agents between the executive and the legislature. This body—known as the "Cabal" from the names of its five members (Clifford, Arlington, Buckingham, Ashley-Cooper, and Lauderdale)—was an ancestor of the later cabinet system (see page 554). Although its members sometimes disagreed and intrigued among themselves, it gradually came to be accepted that the Cabal was answerable in Parliament for the decisions of the king. This development gave rise to the concept of ministerial responsibility: royal ministers must answer to the Commons.

Harmony between the Crown and Parliament rested on the understanding that Charles would summon frequent parliaments and that Parliament would vote him sufficient revenues. However, although Parliament believed Charles had a virtual divine right to govern, it did not grant him an adequate income. Accordingly, in 1670 Charles entered into a secret agreement with Louis XIV. The French king would give Charles 200,000 pounds annually, and in return Charles would relax the laws against Catholics, gradually re-Catholicize England, support French policy against the Dutch, and convert to Catholicism himself.

When the details of this secret treaty leaked out, a great wave of anti-Catholic fear swept England. This fear was compounded by a crucial fact: although Charles had produced several bastards, he had no legitimate children. It therefore appeared that his brother and heir, James, duke of York, who had publicly acknowledged his Catholicism, would inaugurate a Catholic dynasty. A combination of hatred for the French absolutism embodied in Louis XIV, hostility to Roman Catholicism, and fear of a permanent Catholic dynasty produced virtual hysteria. The Commons passed an exclusion bill denying the succession to a Roman Catholic, but Charles quickly dissolved Parliament, and the bill never became law.

James II (r. 1685–1688) did succeed his brother. Almost at once the worst English anti-Catholic fears, already aroused by Louis XIV's revocation of the Edict of Nantes, were realized. In direct violation of the Test Act, James appointed Roman Catholics to positions in the army, the universities, and local government. When these actions were tested in the courts, the judges, whom James had appointed, decided for the king. The king was suspending the law at will and appeared to be reviving the absolutism of his father and grandfather. He went further. Attempting to broaden his base of support with Protestant dissenters and nonconformists, James issued a declaration of indulgence granting religious freedom to all.

Two events gave the signals for revolution. First, seven bishops of the Church of England petitioned the king that they not be forced to read the declaration of indulgence because of their belief that it was an illegal act. They were imprisoned in the Tower of London but subsequently acquitted amid great public enthusiasm. Second, in June 1688 James's second wife produced a male heir. A Catholic dynasty seemed ensured. The fear of a Roman Catholic monarchy supported by France and ruling outside the law prompted a group of eminent persons to offer the English throne to James's Protestant daughter, Mary, and her Dutch husband,

Prince William of Orange. In December 1688 James II, his queen, and their infant son fled to France and became pensioners of Louis XIV. Early in 1689, William and Mary were crowned king and queen of England.

The Triumph of England's Parliament: Constitutional Monarchy and Cabinet Government

The English call the events of 1688 to 1689 the "Glorious Revolution." The revolution was indeed glorious in the sense that it replaced one king with another with a minimum of bloodshed. It also represented the destruction, once and for all, of the idea of divine-right monarchy. William and Mary accepted the English throne from Parliament and in so doing explicitly recognized the supremacy of Parliament. The revolution of 1688 established the principle that sovereignty, the ultimate power in the state, was divided between king and Parliament and that the king ruled with the consent of the governed.

The men who brought about the revolution quickly framed their intentions in the Bill of Rights, the cornerstone of the modern British constitution. The basic principles of the Bill of Rights were formulated in direct response to Stuart absolutism. Law was to be made in Parliament; once made, it could not be suspended by the Crown. Parliament had to be called at least every three years. Both elections to and debate in Parliament were to be free in the sense that the Crown was not to interfere in them (this aspect of the bill was widely disregarded in the eighteenth century). Judges would hold their offices "during good behavior," a provision that ensured the independence of the judiciary. No longer could the Crown get the judicial decisions it wanted by threats of removal. There was to be no standing army in peacetime—a limitation designed to prevent the repetition of either Stuart or Cromwellian military government. The Bill of Rights granted "that the subjects which are Protestants may have arms for their defense suitable to their conditions and as allowed by law,"[27] meaning that Catholics could not possess firearms because the Protestant majority feared them. Additional legislation granted freedom of worship to Protestant dissenters and nonconformists and required that the English monarch always be Protestant.

The Glorious Revolution found its best defense in political philosopher John Locke's *Second Treatise of Civil Government* (1690). Locke (1632–1704) maintained that people set up civil governments to protect life, liberty, and property. A government that oversteps its proper function—protecting the natural rights of life, liberty, and property—becomes a tyranny. (By

"natural" rights, Locke meant rights basic to all men because all have the ability to reason.) Under a tyrannical government, the people have the natural right to rebellion. Such rebellion can be avoided if the government carefully respects the rights of citizens and if people zealously defend their liberty. Recognizing the close relationship between economic and political freedom, Locke linked economic liberty and private property with political freedom; his defense of property included a justification for a narrow franchise. Locke served as the great spokesman for the liberal English revolution of 1688 to 1689 and for representative government. His idea, inherited from ancient Greece and Rome (see Chapter 4), that there are natural or universal rights equally valid for all peoples and societies played a powerful role in eighteenth-century Enlightenment thought. His ideas on liberty and tyranny were especially popular in colonial America.

The events of 1688 to 1689 did not constitute a *democratic* revolution. The revolution placed sovereignty in Parliament, and Parliament represented the upper classes. The great majority of English people acquired no say in their government. The English revolution established a constitutional monarchy; it also inaugurated an age of aristocratic government, which lasted at least until 1832 and in many ways until 1914.

In the course of the eighteenth century, the cabinet system of government evolved. The term *cabinet* derives from the small private room in which English rulers consulted their chief ministers. In a cabinet system, the leading ministers, who must have seats in and the support of a majority of the House of Commons, formulate common policy and conduct the business of the country. During the administration of one royal minister, Sir Robert Walpole, who led the cabinet from 1721 to 1742, the idea developed that the cabinet was responsible to the House of Commons. The Hanoverian king George I (r. 1714–1727) normally presided at cabinet meetings throughout his reign, but his son and heir, George II (r. 1727–1760), discontinued the practice. The influence of the Crown in decision making accordingly declined. Walpole enjoyed the favor of the monarchy and of the House of Commons and came to be called the king's first, or "prime," minister. In the English cabinet system, both legislative power and executive power are held by the leading ministers, who form the Government.

The Dutch Republic in the Seventeenth Century

In the late sixteenth century, the seven northern provinces of the Netherlands fought for and won their

Jan Vermeer: The Art of Painting or The Artist's Studio   In a typically Dutch interior—black and white marble floor, brass chandelier, map of Holland on the wall—an artist paints an allegory of Clio, the Muse of History (often shown holding a book and a trumpet); the muses, nine goddesses of Greek mythology, were thought to inspire the arts. Considered the second-greatest Dutch painter (after Rembrandt), Vermeer (1632–1675) was a master of scenes of everyday life, but he probably meant his work to be understood on more than one level. *(Kunsthistorisches Museum, Vienna/ Art Resource, NY)*

independence from Spain as the Republic of United Provinces of the Netherlands—an independence that was confirmed by the Peace of Westphalia ending the Thirty Years' War in 1648 (see pages 499–500). The seventeenth century witnessed an unparalleled flowering of Dutch scientific, artistic, and literary achievement. In this period, often called the "golden age of the Netherlands," Dutch ideas and attitudes played a profound role in shaping a new and modern world-view. At the same time, the United Provinces was another model of the development of the modern constitutional state.

Within each province, an oligarchy of wealthy merchants called "regents" handled domestic affairs in the local Estates. The provincial Estates held virtually all the power. A federal assembly, or States General, handled matters of foreign affairs, such as war. But the States General did not possess sovereign authority since all issues had to be referred back to the local Estates for approval. The States General appointed a representative, the *stadholder*, in each province. As the highest execu-

tive there, the stadholder carried out ceremonial functions and was responsible for defense and good order. The sons of William the Silent, Maurice and William Louis, held the office of stadholder in all seven provinces. As members of the House of Orange, they were closely identified with Dutch patriotism. The regents in each province jealously guarded local independence and resisted efforts at centralization. Nevertheless, Holland, which had the largest navy and the most wealth, dominated the republic and the States General. Significantly, the Estates assembled at Holland's capital, The Hague.

The government of the United Provinces fit none of the standard categories of seventeenth-century political organization. The Dutch were not monarchial but fiercely republican. The government was controlled by wealthy merchants and financiers. Though rich, their values were not aristocratic but strongly middle-class, emphasizing thrift, hard work, and simplicity in living. The Dutch republic was not a strong federation but a confederation—that is, a weak union of strong provinces. The provinces were a temptation to powerful neighbors, yet the Dutch resisted the long Spanish effort at reconquest and withstood both French and English attacks in the second half of the century.

The political success of the Dutch rested on the phenomenal commercial prosperity of the Netherlands. The moral and ethical bases of that commercial wealth were thrift, frugality, and religious toleration. John Calvin had written, "From where do the merchant's profits come except from his own diligence and industry?" This attitude undoubtedly encouraged a sturdy people who had waged a centuries-old struggle against the sea.

Alone of all European peoples in the seventeenth century, the Dutch practiced religious toleration. Peoples of all faiths were welcome within their borders. Although there is scattered evidence of anti-Semitism, Jews enjoyed a level of acceptance and absorption in Dutch business and general culture unique in early modern Europe. (See the feature "Individuals in Society: Glückel of Hameln.") It is a testimony to the urbanity of Dutch society that in a century when patriotism was closely identified with religious uniformity, the Calvinist province of Holland under its highest official, Johan van Oldenbarnevelt, allowed Catholics to practice their faith. As long as business people conducted their religion in private, the government did not interfere with them.

Toleration also paid off: it attracted a great deal of foreign capital and investment. Deposits at the Bank of Amsterdam were guaranteed by the city council, and in the middle years of the century, the bank became Europe's best source of cheap credit and commercial intelligence and the main clearing-house for bills of exchange. People of all races and creeds traded in Amsterdam, at whose docks on the Amstel River five thousand ships were berthed. Joost van den Vondel, the poet of Dutch imperialism, exulted:

God, God, the Lord of Amstel cried, hold every conscience free;
And Liberty ride, on Holland's tide, with billowing sails to sea,
And run our Amstel out and in; let freedom gird the bold,
And merchant in his counting house stand elbow deep in gold.[28]

The fishing industry was the cornerstone of the Dutch economy. For half the year, from June to December, fishing fleets combed the dangerous English coast and the North Sea and raked in tiny herring. Profits from herring stimulated shipbuilding, and even before 1600 the Dutch were offering the lowest shipping rates in Europe. The Dutch merchant marine was the largest in Europe. In 1650 contemporaries estimated that the Dutch had sixteen thousand merchant ships,

Room from Het Scheepje (The Little Ship) A retired sea captain who became a successful brewer in Haarlem owned the house (adjacent to his brewery) that included this room. The brass chandelier, plates, tiles, Turkish rug on the table (probably from Transylvania in the then Ottoman Empire), oak mantelpiece, and paneling make this superb example of a Dutch domestic interior during the Golden Age. A bed, built into the wall paneling, was warmed at night by coals in the pan hanging by the fireplace. *(Room from Het Scheepje, Haarlem, The Netherlands, early 17th century. Philadelphia Museum of Art, Gift of Edward W. Bok. 1928-66-1)*

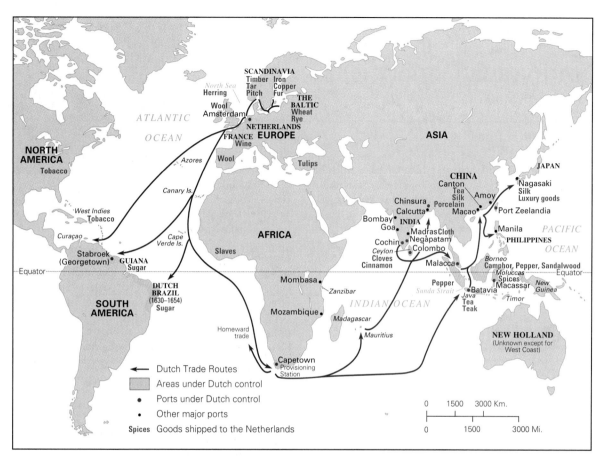

MAP 16.3 Seventeenth-Century Dutch Commerce   Dutch wealth rested on commerce, and commerce depended on the huge Dutch merchant marine, manned by perhaps forty-eight thousand sailors. The fleet carried goods from all parts of the globe to the port of Amsterdam.

half the European total. All the wood for these ships had to be imported: the Dutch bought whole forests from Norway. They also bought entire vineyards from French growers before the grapes were harvested. They controlled the Baltic grain trade, buying entire wheat and rye crops in Poland, east Prussia, and Swedish Pomerania. Because the Dutch dealt in bulk, nobody could undersell them. Foreign merchants coming to Amsterdam could buy anything from precision lenses for the microscope (recently invented by Dutchman Anton van Leeuwenhoek) to muskets for an army of five thousand. Although Dutch cities became famous for their exports—diamonds and linens from Haarlem, pottery from Delft—Dutch wealth depended less on exports than on transport.

In 1602 a group of the regents of Holland formed the Dutch East India Company, a joint stock company. The investors each received a percentage of the profits

proportional to the amount of money they had put in. Within half a century, the Dutch East India Company had cut heavily into Portuguese trading in East Asia. The Dutch seized the Cape of Good Hope, Ceylon, and Malacca and established trading posts in each place. In the 1630s, the Dutch East India Company was paying its investors about a 35 percent annual return on their investments. (See the feature "Individuals in Society: Johan van Oldenbarnevelt" on page 495.) The Dutch West India Company, founded in 1621, traded extensively with Latin America and Africa (Map 16.3).

Trade and commerce brought the Dutch prodigious wealth. In the seventeenth century, the Dutch enjoyed the highest standard of living in Europe, perhaps in the world. Amsterdam and Rotterdam built massive granaries where the surplus of one year could be stored against possible shortages the next. Thus, excepting the 1650s, when bad harvests reduced supplies, food

Individuals in Society

Glückel of Hameln (1646–1724)

In 1690 a Jewish widow in the small German town of Hameln[1] in Lower Saxony sat down to write her autobiography. She wanted to distract her mind from the terrible grief she felt over the death of her husband and to provide her twelve children with a record "so you will know from what sort of people you have sprung, lest today or tomorrow your beloved children or grand-children came and know naught of their family." Out of her pain and heightened consciousness, Glückel produced an invaluable source for scholars.

She was born in Hamburg two years before the end of the Thirty Years' War. In 1649 the merchants of Hamburg expelled the Jews, who moved to nearby Altona, then under Danish rule. When the Swedes overran Altona in 1657–1658, the Jews returned to Hamburg "purely at the mercy of the Town Council." Glückel's narrative proceeds against a background of the constant difficulties (harassment) to which Jews were subjected—special papers, permits, bribes—and in Hamburg she wrote, "And so it has been to this day and, I fear, will continue in like fashion."

When Glückel was "barely twelve," her father betrothed her to Chayim Hameln. She married at age fourteen. She describes him as "the perfect pattern of the pious Jew," a man who stopped his work every day for study and prayer, fasted, and was scrupulously honest in his business dealings. Only a few years older than Glückel, Chayim earned his living dealing in precious metals and in making small loans on pledges (articles held on security). This work required his constant travel to larger cities, markets, and fairs, often in bad weather, always over dangerous roads. Chayim consulted his wife about all his business dealings. As he lay dying, a friend asked if he had any last wishes. "None," he replied. "My wife knows everything. She shall do as she has always done." For thirty years, Glückel had been his friend, full business partner, and wife. They had thirteen children, twelve of whom survived their father, eight then unmarried. As Chayim had foretold, Glückel succeeded in launching the boys in careers and in providing dowries for the girls.

Glückel's world was her family, the Jewish community of Hameln, and the Jewish communities into which her children married. Social and business activities took her to Amsterdam, Baiersdorf, Bamberg, Berlin, Cleves, Danzig, Metz, and Vienna, so her world was not a narrow or provincial one. She took great pride that Prince Frederick of Cleves, later king of Prussia, danced at the wedding of her eldest daughter. The rising prosperity of Chayim's businesses allowed the couple to maintain up to six servants. Jews, however, lived on the margins of Christian society, and traditional sociological categories cannot be applied to them.

Gentleness and deep mutual devotion seem to pervade Rembrandt's *The Jewish Bride. (Rijksmuseum-Stichting Amsterdam)*

Glückel was deeply religious, and her culture was steeped in Jewish literature, legends, and mystical and secular works. Above all, she relied on the Bible. Her language, heavily sprinkled with Scriptural references, testifies to a rare familiarity with the basic book of Western civilization. The Scriptures were her consolation, the source of her great strength in a hostile world.

Students who would learn about business practices, the importance of the dowry in marriage, childbirth, the ceremony of bris, birthrates, family celebrations, even the meaning of life can gain a good deal from the memoirs of this extraordinary woman, who was, in the words of one of her descendants, the poet Heinrich Heine, "the gift of a world to me."

Questions for Analysis

1. Consider the ways in which Glückel of Hameln was an ordinary woman of her times.

2. How was Glückel's life affected by the broad events and issues of the seventeenth century?

1. Town immortalized by the Brothers Grimm. In 1284 the town contracted with the Pied Piper to rid it of rats and mice; he lured them away by playing his flute. When the citizens refused to pay, he charmed away their children in revenge.

Source: The Memoirs of Glückel of Hameln, trans. M. Lowenthal (New York: Schocken Books, 1977).

prices fluctuated very little. By the standards of Cologne, Paris, or London, salaries were high for all workers—except women, and even women's wages were high when compared with those of women in other parts of Europe. All classes of society, including unskilled laborers, ate well. The low price of bread meant that, compared to other places in Europe, a higher percentage of the worker's income could be spent on fish, cheese, butter, vegetables, even meat. A scholar has described the Netherlands as "an island of plenty in a sea of want." Consequently, the Netherlands experienced very few of the food riots that characterized the rest of Europe.[29]

Although the initial purpose of the Dutch East and West India Companies was commercial—the import of spices and silks to Europe—the Dutch found themselves involved in the imperialist exploitation of parts of East Asia and Latin America, with great success. In 1652 the Dutch founded Cape Town on the southern tip of Africa as a fueling station for ships planning to cross the Pacific. But war with France and England in the 1670s hurt the United Provinces. The long War of the Spanish Succession—in which the Dutch prince William of Orange utilized, as King William III of England, English wealth in the Dutch fight against Louis XIV—was a costly drain on Dutch labor and financial resources. The peace signed in 1713 to end the war marked the beginning of Dutch economic decline.

SUMMARY

According to Thomas Hobbes, the central drive in every human is "a perpetual and restless desire of Power, after Power, that ceaseth only in Death." The seventeenth century solved the problem of sovereign power in two fundamental ways: absolutism and constitutionalism. The France of Louis XIV witnessed the emergence of the fully absolutist state. The king commanded all the powers of the state: judicial, military, political, and, to a great extent, ecclesiastical. France developed a centralized bureaucracy, a professional army, and a state-directed economy, all of which Louis personally supervised. For the first time in history, all the institutions and powers of the national state were effectively controlled by a single person. The king saw himself as the representative of God on earth, and it has been said that "to the seventeenth century imagination God was a sort of image of Louis XIV."[30]

As Louis XIV personifies absolutism, so Stuart England exemplifies the evolution of the first modern constitutional state. The conflicts between Parliament and the first two Stuart rulers, James I and Charles I, tested where sovereign power would rest in the state. The resulting civil war did not solve the problem. The Instrument of Government, the document produced in 1653 by the victorious parliamentary army, provided for a balance of government authority and recognition of popular rights; as such, the Instrument has been called the first modern constitution. Unfortunately, it lacked public support. James II's absolutist tendencies brought on the Glorious Revolution of 1688 to 1689, and the people who made that revolution settled three basic issues. Sovereign power was divided between king and Parliament, with Parliament enjoying the greater share. Government was to be based on the rule of law. And the liberties of English people were made explicit in written form in the Bill of Rights. The framers of the English constitution left to later generations the task of making constitutional government work.

The models of governmental power established by seventeenth-century England and France strongly influenced other states then and ever since. As American novelist William Faulkner wrote, "The past isn't dead; it's not even past."

NOTES

1. G. Parker and L. M. Smith, "Introduction," and N. Steensgaard, "The Seventeenth Century Crisis," in *The General Crisis of the Seventeenth Century,* ed. G. Parker and L. M. Smith (London: Routledge & Kegan Paul, 1985), pp. 1–53, esp. p. 12.

2. See W. Beik, *Urban Protest in Seventeenth-Century France: The Culture of Retribution* (New York: Cambridge University Press, 1997), p. 1.

3. J. B. Collins, *The State in Early Modern France* (Cambridge, England: Cambridge University Press, 1995), p. 1.

4. Ibid., p. 3.

5. Ibid., pp. 22–26.

6. See M. Turchetti, "The Edict of Nantes," in *The Oxford Encyclopedia of the Reformation,* ed. H. J. Hillerbrand, vol. 3 (New York: Oxford University Press, 1996), pp. 126–128.

7. See W. Beik, *Urban Protest,* chaps. 1, 2, 3, and 11.

8. J. B. Collins, *Fiscal Limits of Absolutism: Direct Taxation in Early Seventeenth-Century France* (Berkeley and Los Angeles: University of California Press, 1988), pp. 1, 3–4, 215–222.

9. Quoted in J. H. Elliott, *Richelieu and Olivares* (Cambridge: Cambridge University Press, 1984), p. 135; and in W. F. Church, *Richelieu and Reason of State* (Princeton, N.J.: Princeton University Press, 1972), p. 507.

10. D. Parker, *The Making of French Absolutism* (New York: St. Martin's Press, 1983), pp. 146–148.

11. J. B. Collins, *The State in Early Modern France,* pp. 65–78.

12. See W. Beik, *Absolutism and Society in Seventeenth-Century France: State Power and Provincial Aristocracy in Languedoc* (Cambridge: Cambridge University Press, 1985), pp. 279–302.

13. S. de Gramont, ed., *The Age of Magnificence: Memoirs of the Court of Louis XIV by the Duc de Saint Simon* (New York: Capricorn Books, 1964), pp. 141–145.

14. Quoted in J. Wolf, *Louis XIV* (New York: W. W. Norton, 1968), p. 146.

15. Quoted in A. Trout, *Jean-Baptiste Colbert* (Boston: Twayne, 1978), p. 128.

16. Quoted in Wolf, *Louis XIV,* p. 394.

17. Ibid.

18. See W. C. Scoville, *The Persecution of the Huguenots and French Economic Development: 1680–1720* (Berkeley and Los Angeles: University of California Press, 1960).

19. F. Bluche, *Louis XIV,* trans. M. Greengrass (Oxford: Basil Blackwell, 1990), p. 607.

20. Ibid., p. 458.

21. Quoted in Bluche, *Louis XIV,* p. 519.

22. W. F. Church, *Louis XIV in Historical Thought: From Voltaire to the Annales School* (New York: W. W. Norton, 1976), p. 92.

23. Quoted in Gramont, *The Age of Magnificence,* p. 183.

24. J. H. Elliott, *Imperial Spain, 1469–1716* (New York: Mentor Books, 1963), pp. 306–308.

25. B. Bennassar, *The Spanish Character: Attitudes and Mentalities from the Sixteenth to the Nineteenth Century,* trans. B. Keen (Berkeley and Los Angeles: University of California Press, 1979), p. 125.

26. For a revisionist interpretation, see J. Wormald, "James VI and I: Two Kings or One?" *History* 62 (June 1983): 187–209.

27. C. Stephenson and G. F. Marcham, *Sources of English Constitutional History* (New York: Harper & Row, 1937), p. 601.

28. Quoted in D. Maland, *Europe in the Seventeenth Century* (New York: Macmillan, 1967), pp. 198–199.

29. S. Schama, *The Embarrassment of Riches: An Interpretation of Dutch Culture in the Golden Age* (New York: Alfred A. Knopf, 1987), pp. 165–170; quotation is on p. 167.

30. C. J. Friedrich and C. Blitzer, *The Age of Power* (Ithaca, N.Y.: Cornell University Press, 1957), p. 112.

SUGGESTED READING

Students who wish to explore the problems presented in this chapter in greater depth will easily find a rich and exciting literature. The following surveys all provide good background material: H. Kamen, *The Iron Century: Social Change in Europe, 1550–1660* (1971); G. Parker, *Europe in Crisis, 1598–1618* (1980), a sound introduction to the social, economic, and religious tensions of the period; R. S.

Dunn, *The Age of Religious Wars, 1559–1715* (1979), which examines the period from the perspective of the confessional strife between Protestants and Catholics but contains material on absolutism and constitutionalism; and P. Anderson, *Lineages of the Absolutist State* (1974), a Marxist interpretation of absolutism in western and eastern Europe. The classic treatment of constitutionalism remains C. H. McIlwain, *Constitutionalism: Ancient and Modern* (1940), written by a great scholar during the rise of German fascism.

For the period of Louis XIII, Richelieu, and the Fronde, see L. Moote, *Louis XIII: The Just* (1989), an important biography; J. Bergin, *Richelieu: Power and the Pursuit of Wealth* (1989), a detailed study of how Richelieu used his various offices to acquire great wealth for himself and his family; and O. Ranum, *The Fronde* (1994), probably the best work in English on the Fronde. Two important studies of French local administration are J. B. Collins, *Classes, Estates, and Order in Early Modern Brittany* (1994); and R. Schneider, *Public Life in Toulouse, 1463–1789* (1989). Students interested in medical history should find L. Brockless, *The Medical World of Early Modern France* (1997), useful, while G. Calvi, *Histories of a Plague Year: The Social and the Imaginary in Baroque Florence* (1989), offers comparable information on Italian conditions. Those with facility in French might tackle P. Goubert, *Mazarin* (1991), for his administration. K. Norberg, *Rich and Poor in Grenoble, 1600–1815* (1985), provides an interesting case study of the wretched conditions of the poor, while W. Beik, *Urban Protest in Seventeenth-Century France* (1997), explores the cultural significance of the widespread incidence of urban violence.

Louis XIV and his age have predictably attracted the attention of many scholars. Bluche, although hagiographical, is an almost definitive study, and Wolf remains valuable; both are cited in the Notes. The excellent work of P. Burke, *The Fabrication of Louis XIV* (1992), explores the images or representations of the king in stone, bronze, paint, plays, operas, and rituals. Two works of W. H. Lewis, *The Splendid Century* (1957) and *The Sunset of the Splendid Century* (1963), make delightful light reading, especially for the beginning student. For the court of Louis XIV, see also K. A. Hoffmann, *Society of Pleasures: Interdisciplinary Readings in Pleasure and Power During the Reign of Louis XIV* (1997), a sophisticated study of the uses of pleasure as a political tool; R. Chartier, *The Cultural Origins of the French Revolution* (1991); and J.-F. Solnon, *La Cour de France* (1987). The advanced student will want to consult the excellent historiographical analysis by Church mentioned in the Notes. Perhaps the best works of the Annales school on the period are P. Goubert, *Louis XIV and Twenty Million Frenchmen* (1972), and his heavily detailed *The Ancien Régime: French Society, 1600–1750,* 2 vols. (1969–1973), which contains invaluable material on the lives and work of ordinary people. For the French economy and financial conditions, the old study C. W. Cole, *Colbert and a Century of French Mercantilism,* 2 vols.

(1939), is still valuable but should be supplemented by R. Bonney, *The King's Debts: Finance and Politics in France, 1589–1661* (1981), and by the works of Trout and Scoville listed in the Notes. Scoville's book is a significant contribution to revisionist history. For Louis XIV's foreign policy and wars, see P. Sonnino, *Louis XIV and the Origins of the Dutch Wars* (1988); H. Kamen, *The War of Succession in Spain, 1700–1715* (1969); and R. Hatton, ed., *Louis XIV and Europe* (1976), an important collection of essays. R. Hatton, *Europe in the Age of Louis XIV* (1979), is a splendidly illustrated survey of many aspects of seventeenth-century European culture. O. Ranum, *Paris in the Age of Absolutism* (1968), describes the geographical, political, economic, and architectural significance of the cultural capital of Europe, whereas V. L. Tapie, *The Age of Grandeur: Baroque Art and Architecture* (1960), emphasizes the relationship between art and politics and has excellent illustrations.

For Spain and Portugal, in addition to the works in the Notes, see H. Kamen, *Spain in the Later Seventeenth Century, 1665–1700* (1980); M. Defourneaux, *Daily Life in Spain in the Golden Age* (1976), highly useful for an understanding of ordinary people and of Spanish society; and C. R. Phillips, *Ciudad Real, 1500–1750: Growth, Crisis, and Readjustment in the Spanish Economy* (1979), a significant case study. A. Pagden, *Spanish Imperialism and the Political Imagination* (1990), explores Spanish ideas of empire, primarily in Italy and the Americas, and shows that the failure to revise ideas to meet changing circumstances led to the empire's decline.

The following works all offer solid material on English political and social issues of the seventeenth century: M. Ashley, *England in the Seventeenth Century* (1980), and *The House of Stuart: Its Rise and Fall* (1980); J. P. Kenyon, *Stuart England* (1978); and K. Wrightson, *English Society, 1580–1680* (1982). Perhaps the most comprehensive treatments of Parliament are C. Russell, *Crisis of Parliaments, 1509–1660* (1971), and *Parliaments and English Politics, 1621–1629* (1979). On the background of the English civil war, L. Stone, *The Crisis of the Aristocracy* (1965), and *The Causes of the English Revolution* (1972), are standard works; both B. Manning, *The English People and the English Revolution* (1976), and D. Underdown, *Revel, Riot, and Rebellion* (1985), discuss the extent of popular involvement; Underdown's is the more sophisticated treatment. For English intellectual currents, see J. O. Appleby, *Economic Thought and Ideology in Seventeenth-Century England* (1978); and C. Hill, *Intellectual Origins of the English Revolution* (1966). M. J. Braddick, *The Nerves of State: Taxation and the Financing of the English State, 1558–1714* (1996), surveys the evolution of parliamentary taxation as the means of financing state expenses, especially military ones. S. Porter, ed., *London and the Civil War* (1996), treats the city's choice of allegiance and contribution to the war effort.

C. Durston and J. Eales, eds., *The Culture of English Puritanism, 1560–1700* (1996), provides a revisionist definition of the term *Puritan* and explores topics such as Sabbatarianism and iconoclasm. For the several shades of Protestant sentiment in the early seventeenth century, see P. Collinson, *The Religion of Protestants* (1982). C. M. Hibbard, *Charles I and the Popish Plot* (1983), is an important reference work for several religious issues.

For women, see R. Thompson, *Women in Stuart England and America* (1974); and A. Fraser, *The Weaker Vessel* (1985). For Cromwell and the Interregnum, C. Firth, *Oliver Cromwell and the Rule of the Puritans in England* (1956), C. Hill, *God's Englishman* (1972), and A. Fraser, *Cromwell, the Lord Protector* (1973), are all valuable. J. Morrill, *The Revolt of the Provinces* (1980), is the best study of religious neutralism, whereas C. Hill, *The World Turned Upside Down* (1972), discusses radical thought during the period.

For the Restoration and the Glorious Revolution, see R. Hutton, *Charles II: King of England, Scotland and Ireland* (1989), and A. Fraser, *Royal Charles: Charles II and the Restoration* (1979), two highly readable biographies; R. Ollard, *The Image of the King: Charles I and Charles II* (1980), which examines the nature of monarchy; J. Miller, *James II: A Study in Kingship* (1977); J. Childs, *The Army, James II, and the Glorious Revolution* (1980); J. R. Jones, *The Revolution of 1688 in England* (1972); and L. G. Schwoerer, *The Declaration of Rights, 1689* (1981), a fine assessment of that fundamental document. For the continuation of an older system during the rise of the Whigs and Tories, see B. Hill, *The Early Parties and Politics in Britain, 1688–1832* (1996). Other helpful books on the beginning of political parties are J. P. Kenyon, *Revolution Principles: The Politics of Party, 1689–1720* (1977), which also analyzes the ideas of John Locke; and R. Hatton, *The Restoration, 1658–1667* (1985), a thorough but difficult narrative.

On Holland, the starting point for serious study is Schama, mentioned in the Notes, a brilliant and beautifully illustrated achievement. J. L. Price, *Culture and Society in the Dutch Republic During the Seventeenth Century* (1974), is a sound scholarly work. R. Boxer, *The Dutch Seaborne Empire* (1980), and the appropriate chapters of the Maland work cited in the Notes are useful for Dutch overseas expansion and the reasons for Dutch prosperity. The following works focus on the economic and cultural life of the leading Dutch city: V. Barbour, *Capitalism in Amsterdam in the Seventeenth Century* (1950); and D. Regin, *Traders, Artists, Burghers: A Cultural History of Amsterdam in the Seventeenth Century* (1977). J. M. Montias, *Artists and Artisans in Delft: A Socio-economic Study of the Seventeenth Century* (1982), examines another major city. The leading statesmen of the period may be studied in these biographies: H. H. Rowen, *John de Witt, Grand Pensionary of Holland, 1625–1672* (1978); S. B. Baxter, *William the III and the Defense of European Liberty, 1650–1702* (1966); and J. den Tex, *Oldenbarnevelt*, 2 vols. (1973).

Many facets of the lives of ordinary French, Spanish, English, and Dutch people are discussed in P. Burke, *Popular Culture in Early Modern Europe* (1978), an important and provocative study.

LISTENING TO THE
PAST

The Court at Versailles

Although the Duc de Saint-Simon (1675–1755) was a soldier, courtier, and diplomat, his enduring reputation rests on his Memoirs *(1788), an eyewitness account of the personality and court of Louis XIV. A nobleman of ancient lineage, Saint-Simon resented Louis's "domestication" of the nobility and his promotion of the bourgeoisie. The* Memoirs, *excerpted here, remains a monument of French literature and an indispensable historical source, partly for its portrait of the court at Versailles.*

Very early in the reign of Louis XIV the Court was removed from Paris, never to return. The troubles of the minority had given him a dislike to that city; his enforced and surreptitious flight from it still rankled in his memory; he did not consider himself safe there, and thought cabals would be more easily detected if the Court was in the country, where the movements and temporary absences of any of its members would be more easily noticed. . . . No doubt that he was also influenced by the feeling that he would be regarded with greater awe and veneration when no longer exposed every day to the gaze of the multitude.

His love-affair with Mademoiselle de la Vallière, which at first was covered as far as possible with a veil of mystery, was the cause of frequent excursions to Versailles. . . . The visits of Louis XIV becoming more frequent, he enlarged the *château* by degrees till its immense buildings afforded better accommodation for the Court than was to be found at St. Germain, where most of the courtiers had to put up with uncomfortable lodgings in the town. The Court was therefore removed to Versailles in 1682, not long before the Queen's death. The new building contained an infinite number of rooms for courtiers, and the King liked the grant of these rooms to be regarded as a coveted privilege.

He availed himself of the frequent festivities at Versailles, and his excursions to other places, as a means of making the courtiers assiduous in their attendance and anxious to please him; for he nominated beforehand those who were to take part in them, and could thus gratify some and inflict a snub on others. He was conscious that the substantial favours he had to bestow were not nearly sufficient to produce a continual effect; he had therefore to invent imaginary ones, and no one was so clever in devising petty distinctions and preferences which aroused jealousy and emulation. The visits to Marly later on were very useful to him in this way; also those to Trianon [Marly and Trianon were small country houses], where certain ladies, chosen beforehand, were admitted to his table. It was another distinction to hold his candlestick at his *coucher;* as soon as he had finished his prayers he used to name the courtier to whom it was to be handed, always choosing one of the highest rank among those present. . . .

Not only did he expect all persons of distinction to be in continual attendance at Court, but he was quick to notice the absence of those of inferior degree; at his *lever* [formal rising from bed in the morning], his *coucher* [preparations for going to bed], his meals, in the gardens of Versailles (the only place where the courtiers in general were allowed to follow him), he used to cast his eyes to right and left; nothing escaped him, he saw everybody. If any one habitually living at Court absented himself he insisted on knowing the reason; those who came there only for flying visits had also to give a satisfactory explanation; any one who seldom or never appeared there was certain to incur his displeasure. If asked to bestow a favour on such persons he would reply haughtily: "I do not know him"; of such as rarely presented themselves he would say, "He is a man I never see"; and from these judgements there was no appeal.

He always took great pains to find out what was going on in public places, in society, in private houses, even family secrets, and maintained an immense number of spies and tale-bearers. These were of all sorts; some did not know that their reports were carried to him; others did know it; there were others, again, who used to write to him directly, through channels which he prescribed; others who were admitted by the backstairs and saw him in his private room. Many a man in all ranks of life was ruined by these methods, often very unjustly, without ever being able to discover the reason; and when the King had once taken a prejudice against a man, he hardly ever got over it. . . .

No one understood better than Louis XIV the art of enhancing the value of a favour by his manner of bestowing it; he knew how to make the most of a word, a smile, even of a glance. If he addressed any one, were it but to ask a trifling question or make some commonplace remark, all eyes were turned on the person so honored; it was a mark of favour which always gave rise to comment. . . .

He loved splendour, magnificence, and profusion in all things, and encouraged similar tastes in his Court; to spend money freely on equipages [the king's horse carriages] and buildings, on feasting and at cards, was a sure way to gain his favour, perhaps to obtain the honour of a word from him. Motives of policy had something to do with this; by making expensive habits the fashion, and, for people in a certain position, a necessity, he compelled his courtiers to live beyond their income, and gradually reduced them to depend on his bounty for the means of subsistence. This was a plague which, once introduced, became a scourge to the whole country, for it did not take long to spread to Paris, and thence to the armies and the provinces; so that a man of any position is now estimated entirely according to his expenditure on his table and other luxuries. This folly, sustained by pride and ostentation, has already produced widespread confusion; it threatens to end in nothing short of ruin and a general overthrow.

❖ Painting of Louis XIV by Mignard Pierre (1612–1695). *(Galleria Sabauda, Turin/Scala/ Art Resource, NY)*

Questions for Analysis

1. How would you define the French court? Why did Louis XIV move it to Versailles?

2. By what means did Louis control the nobility at Versailles? Why did he use those particular means?

3. Consider the role of ritual and ceremony in some modern governments, such as the U.S. government. How does it compare to Louis XIV's use of ceremony, as portrayed by Saint-Simon?

4. Saint-Simon faulted Louis for encouraging the nobles' extravagance. Is that a justifiable criticism?

Source: F. Arkwright, ed., *The Memoirs of the Duke de Saint-Simon,* vol. 5 (New York: Brentano's, n.d.), pp. 271–274, 276–278.

17
Absolutism in Eastern Europe to 1740

❖
Saint Basil's Cathedral,
Red Square, Moscow.
*(Erroll Rainess/Laurie Platt
Winfrey, Inc.)*

The seventeenth century witnessed a struggle between constitutionalism and absolutism in eastern Europe, as it did in western Europe (see Chapter 16). But with the notable exception of the kingdom of Poland, monarchial absolutism was triumphant in eastern Europe; constitutionalism was decisively defeated. Absolute monarchies emerged in Austria, Prussia, and Russia. This development had significance for at least two reasons. First, these three monarchies exercised enormous influence until 1918, and they created an authoritarian tradition that has remained strong in eastern Europe. Second, the absolute monarchs of eastern Europe had a powerful impact on culture, encouraging a flowering of the baroque style in architecture and the arts.

Although the monarchs of eastern Europe were greatly impressed by Louis XIV and his model of royal absolutism, their states differed in several important ways from that of their French counterpart. Louis XIV built French absolutism on the foundation of a well-developed medieval monarchy and a strong royal bureaucracy. And when Louis XIV came to the throne, the powers of the nobility were already somewhat limited, the French middle class was relatively strong, and the peasants were generally free from serfdom. Eastern absolutism rested on a very different social reality: a powerful nobility, a weak middle class, and an oppressed peasantry composed of serfs.

These different conditions raise three questions:

- Why did the basic structure of society in eastern Europe move away from that of western Europe in the early modern period?

- How and why did the rulers of Austria, Prussia, and Russia, each in a different social environment, manage to build powerful absolute monarchies that proved more durable than that of Louis XIV?

- How did the absolute monarchs' interaction with artists and architects contribute to the splendid achievements of baroque culture?

These are the questions that this chapter will explore.

⚜ LORDS AND PEASANTS IN EASTERN EUROPE

When absolute monarchy took shape in eastern Europe in the seventeenth century, it built on social and economic foundations laid between roughly 1400 and 1650. In those years, the princes and the landed nobility of eastern Europe rolled back the gains made by the peasantry during the High Middle Ages and reimposed a harsh serfdom on the rural masses. The nobility also reduced the importance of the towns and the middle classes. This process differed profoundly from developments in western Europe at the same time. In the west, peasants won greater freedom, and the urban capitalistic middle class continued its rise. Thus the east that emerged contrasted sharply with the west—another aspect of the shattered unity of medieval Latin Christendom.

The Medieval Background

Between roughly 1400 and 1650, nobles and rulers re-established serfdom in the eastern lands of Bohemia, Silesia, Hungary, eastern Germany, Poland, Lithuania, and Russia. The east—the land east of the Elbe River in Germany, which historians often call "East Elbia"—gained a certain social and economic unity in the process. But eastern peasants lost their rights and freedoms. They became bound first to the land they worked and then, by degrading obligations, to the lords they served.

This development was a tragic reversal of trends in the High Middle Ages. The period from roughly 1050 to 1300 had been a time of general economic expansion characterized by the growth of trade, towns, and population. Expansion also meant clearing the forests and colonizing the frontier beyond the Elbe River. Anxious to attract German settlers to sparsely populated lands, the rulers and nobles of eastern Europe had offered potential newcomers economic and legal incentives. Large numbers of incoming settlers obtained land on excellent terms and gained much greater personal freedom. These benefits were also gradually extended to the local Slavic populations, even those of central Russia. Thus by 1300 a very general improvement in peasant conditions had occurred in eastern Europe; serfdom had all but disappeared. Peasants bargained freely with their landlords and moved about as they pleased. Opportunities and improvements east of the Elbe had a positive impact on western Europe, where the weight of serfdom was also reduced between 1100 and 1300.

After about 1300, however, as Europe's population and economy both declined grievously, mainly because of the Black Death, the east and the west went in different directions. In both east and west, a many-sided landlord reaction occurred as lords sought to solve their tough economic problems by more heavily exploiting the peasantry. Yet this reaction generally failed in the west. In many western areas by 1500, almost all of the peasants were free, and in the rest of western Europe serf obligations had declined greatly. East of the Elbe, however, the landlords won. By 1500 eastern peasants were well on their way to becoming serfs again.

Throughout eastern Europe, as in western Europe, the drop in population and prices in the fourteenth and fifteenth centuries caused severe labor shortages and hard times for the nobles. Yet rather than offer better economic and legal terms to keep old peasants and attract new ones, eastern landlords used political and police power to turn the tables on peasants. They did this in two ways.

First, the lords made their kings and princes issue laws that restricted or eliminated the peasants' precious, time-honored right of free movement. Thus a peasant could no longer leave to take advantage of better opportunities elsewhere without the lord's permission, and the lord had no reason to make such concessions. In Prussian territories by 1500, the law required that runaway peasants be hunted down and returned to their lords; a runaway servant was to be nailed to a post by one ear and given a knife to cut himself loose. Until the middle of the fifteenth century, medieval Russian peasants had been free to move wherever they wished and seek the best landlord. Thereafter this freedom was gradually curtailed, so that by 1497 a Russian peasant had the right to move only during a two-week period after the fall harvest. Eastern peasants were losing their status as free and independent men and women.

Second, lords steadily took more and more of their peasants' land and imposed heavier and heavier labor obligations. Instead of being independent farmers paying reasonable, freely negotiated rents, peasants tended to become forced laborers on the lords' estates. By the early 1500s, lords in many territories could command their peasants to work for them without pay as many as six days a week. A German writer of the mid-sixteenth century described peasants in eastern Prussia who "do not possess the heritage of their holdings and have to serve their master whenever he wants them."[1]

The gradual erosion of the peasantry's economic position was bound up with manipulation of the legal system. The local lord was also the local prosecutor, judge, and jailer. As a matter of course, he ruled in his own favor in disputes with his peasants. There were no independent royal officials to provide justice or uphold the common law.

The Consolidation of Serfdom

Between 1500 and 1650, the social, legal, and economic conditions of peasants in eastern Europe continued to decline. Free peasants lost their freedom and became serfs. In Poland, for example, nobles gained complete control over their peasants in 1574, after which they could legally inflict the death penalty on their serfs whenever they wished. In Prussia a long series of oppressive measures reached their culmination in 1653. Not only were all the old privileges of the lords reaffirmed, but peasants were also assumed to be in "hereditary subjugation" to their lords unless they could prove the contrary in the lords' courts, which was practically impossible. Prussian peasants were serfs tied to their lords as well as to the land.

In Russia the right of peasants to move from a given estate was "temporarily" suspended in the 1590s and permanently abolished in 1603. In 1649 a new law code completed the process. At the insistence of the lower nobility, the Russian tsar lifted the nine-year time limit on the recovery of runaways. Henceforth runaway peasants were to be returned to their lords whenever they were caught. The last small hope of escaping serfdom was gone. Control of serfs was strictly the lords' own business, for the new law code set no limits on the lords' authority over their peasants. Although the political development of the various eastern states differed, the legal re-establishment of permanent hereditary serfdom had become the common fate of peasants in the east by the middle of the seventeenth century.

This consolidation of serfdom was accompanied by the growth of estate agriculture, particularly in Poland and eastern Germany. In the sixteenth century, European economic expansion and population growth resumed after the great declines of the late Middle Ages. Prices for agricultural commodities also rose sharply as gold and silver flowed in from the New World. Thus Polish and German lords had powerful economic incentives to increase the production of their estates. And they did.

Lords seized more and more peasant land for their own estates and then demanded and received ever more unpaid serf labor on those enlarged estates. Even when the estates were inefficient and technically backward, as they generally were, the great Polish nobles and middle-rank German lords squeezed sizable, cheap, and thus very profitable surpluses out of their impoverished peasants. Surpluses in wheat and timber were easily sold to big foreign merchants, who exported them to the growing cities of the west. Thus the poor east helped feed the wealthier west.

Punishing Serfs   This seventeenth-century illustration from Olearius's famous *Travels to Moscovy* suggests what eastern serfdom really meant. The scene is set in eastern Poland. There, according to Olearius, a common command of the lord was, "Beat him till the skin falls from the flesh." Selections from Olearius's graphic account are found in this chapter's Listening to the Past. *(University of Illinois Library, Champaign)*

The re-emergence of serfdom in eastern Europe in the early modern period was clearly a momentous human development, and historians have advanced a variety of explanations for it. Some scholars have stressed the economic interpretation. Agricultural depression and population decline in the fourteenth and fifteenth centuries led to a severe labor shortage, they have argued, and thus eastern landlords naturally tied their precious peasants to the land. With the return of prosperity and the development of export markets in the sixteenth century, the landlords finished the job, grabbing the peasants' land and making them work as unpaid serfs on the resulting enlarged estates. This argument by itself is not very convincing, for almost identical economic developments "caused" the opposite result in the west. Indeed, some historians have maintained that labor shortage and economic expansion were key factors in the virtual disappearance of western serfdom.

It seems fairly clear, therefore, that political, rather than economic, factors were crucial in the simultaneous rise of serfdom in the east and decline of serfdom in the west. Specifically, eastern lords enjoyed much greater political power than their western counterparts. In the late Middle Ages, when much of eastern Europe experienced innumerable wars and general political chaos, the noble landlord class greatly increased its political power at the expense of the ruling monarchs. There were, for example, many disputed royal successions, so that weak kings were forced to grant political favors to win the support of the nobility. Thus while strong monarchs were rising in Spain, France, and England and providing effective central government, kings were generally losing power in the east. Such kings could not resist the demands of lords regarding peasants.

Moreover, most eastern monarchs did not want to resist even if they could. The typical king was only first among equals in the noble class. He, too, thought mainly in private, rather than public, terms. He, too, wanted to squeeze as much as he could out of his peasants and enlarge his estates. The western concept and reality of sovereignty, as embodied in a king who protected the interests of all his people, was not well developed in eastern Europe before 1650.

The political power of the peasants was also weaker in eastern Europe and declined steadily after about 1400. Although there were occasional bloody peasant uprisings against the oppression of the landlords, they never succeeded. Nor did eastern peasants effectively resist day-by-day infringements on their liberties by their landlords. Part of the reason was that the lords, rather than the kings, ran the courts—one of the important concessions nobles extorted from weak monarchs. It has also been suggested that peasant solidarity was weaker in the east, possibly reflecting the lack of long-established village communities on the eastern frontier.

Finally, with the approval of weak kings, the landlords systematically undermined the medieval privileges of the towns and the power of the urban classes. Instead of selling products to local merchants in the towns, as required in the Middle Ages, the landlords sold directly to big foreign capitalists. For example, Dutch ships sailed up the rivers of Poland and eastern Germany to the loading docks of the great estates, completely short-circuiting the local towns. Moreover, "town air" no longer "made people free," for the eastern towns had lost their medieval right of refuge and were now compelled to return runaways to their lords. The population of the towns and the importance of the urban middle classes declined greatly. These developments both reflected and promoted the supremacy of noble landlords in most of eastern Europe in the sixteenth century.

 ## THE RISE OF AUSTRIA AND PRUSSIA

Despite the strength of the nobility and the weakness of many monarchs before 1600, strong kings did begin to emerge in many lands in the course of the seventeenth century. War and the threat of war aided rulers greatly in their attempts to build absolute monarchies. There was also an endless struggle for power, as eastern rulers not only fought each other but also battled with armies of Asiatic invaders. In this atmosphere of continual wartime emergency, monarchs reduced the political power of the landlord nobility. Cautiously leaving the nobles the unchallenged masters of their peasants, the would-be absolutist monarchs of eastern Europe gradually gained and monopolized political power in three key areas. First, they imposed and collected permanent taxes without consent. Second, they maintained permanent standing armies, which policed the country in addition to fighting abroad. Third, they conducted relations with other states as they pleased.

As with all general historical developments, there were important variations on the absolutist theme in eastern Europe. The royal absolutism created in Prussia was stronger and more effective than that established in Austria. This advantage gave Prussia a thin edge over Austria in the struggle for power in east-central Europe in the eighteenth century. That edge had enormous long-term political significance, for it was a rising Prussia that unified the German people in the nineteenth century and imposed on them a fateful Prussian stamp.

Austria and the Ottoman Turks

Like all the other peoples and rulers of central Europe, the Habsburgs of Austria emerged from the brutal Thirty Years' War, which lasted from 1618 to 1648, impoverished and exhausted. Their efforts to root out Protestantism in the German lands and to turn the weak Holy Roman Empire into a real state had failed utterly. The Habsburgs did remain the hereditary emperors of the ancient Holy Roman Empire, which was inhabited mainly by German-speakers and was more accurately called the German Empire. But the authority of the empire and its Habsburg emperors had declined almost to the vanishing point. Real power in the German Empire lay in the hands of a bewildering variety of three hundred separate political jurisdictions, which included independent cities, small principalities, medium-size states such as Bavaria and Saxony, and some (but not all) of the territories of Prussia and the Habsburgs.

Defeat in central Europe opened new vistas for the Habsburgs. They were forced to turn inward and eastward in an attempt to fuse their diverse holdings into a strong unified state. An important step in this direction had actually been taken in Bohemia during the Thirty Years' War. Protestantism had been strong among the Czechs, a Slavic people concentrated in Bohemia. Indeed, the lesser Czech nobility was largely Protestant in 1600 and had considerable political power because it dominated the Bohemian Estates—the representative body of the different legal orders in Bohemia. In 1618 the Bohemian Estates had risen up in defense of Protestant rights. This revolt was crushed in 1620 at the Battle of the White Mountain, a momentous turning point in Czech history. The victorious Habsburg king, Ferdinand II (r. 1619–1637), drastically reduced the power of the Bohemian Estates. Ferdinand also confiscated the landholdings of many Protestant nobles and gave them to a few great Catholic nobles who had remained loyal and to a motley band of aristocratic soldiers of fortune who had nothing in common with the Czech-speaking peasants. After 1650 a large portion of the Bohemian nobility was of recent foreign origin and owed everything to the Habsburgs.

With the help of this new nobility, the Habsburgs established strong direct rule over reconquered Bohemia. The condition of the enserfed peasantry worsened substantially: three days per week of unpaid labor—the *robot*—became the norm, and a quarter of the serfs worked for their lords every day but Sundays and religious holidays. Serfs also paid the taxes, which further strengthened the alliance between the Habsburg monarch and the Bohemian nobility. Protestantism was also stamped out, in the course of which a growing unity of religion was brought about. The reorganization of Bohemia was a giant step toward absolutism.

After the Thirty Years' War, Ferdinand III (r. 1637–1657) centralized the government in the hereditary German-speaking provinces, most notably Austria, Styria, and the Tyrol, which formed the core area of the Habsburg holdings. For the first time, Ferdinand III's reign saw the creation of a permanent standing army ready to put down any internal opposition. The Habsburg monarchy was then ready to turn toward the plains of Hungary, which it claimed as the third and largest part of its dominion and which had long been divided and fought over by the Habsburgs and the Ottoman Turks.

The Ottomans had come out of central Asia as conquering warriors, settled in Anatolia, in present-day Turkey, and created one of history's greatest military empires. At their peak in the middle of the sixteenth century under Suleiman the Magnificent (r. 1520–1566), they ruled the most powerful empire in the world. Their possessions stretched from western Persia across North Africa and up into the heart of central Europe (Map 17.1). Followers of Islam, the Ottoman Turks were old and determined foes of the Catholic Habsburgs. Their armies had almost captured Vienna in 1529, and for more than 150 years thereafter the Ottomans ruled the many different ethnic groups living in the Balkans, almost all of Hungary, and part of southern Russia.

The Ottoman Empire was originally built on a fascinating and very non-European conception of state and society. There was an almost complete absence of private landed property. All the agricultural land of the empire was the personal hereditary property of the sultan, who exploited the land as he saw fit according to Ottoman political theory. There was therefore no security of landholding and no hereditary nobility. Everyone was dependent on the sultan.

The top ranks of the bureaucracy were staffed by the sultan's slave corps. Every year the sultan levied a "tax"

Depicting Ottoman Might With his capital Istanbul in the background, this German engraving shows the Turk standing triumphant before the fallen standards of defeated armies in Europe, Africa, and Asia. Crowns and miter caps—symbols of royal and religious authority in Christian Europe—are scattered at his feet. Is this symbolic representation positive or negative? *(Ullstein Bilderdienst)*

of one to three thousand male children on the conquered Christian populations in the Balkans. These and other slaves were raised in Turkey as Muslims and trained to fight and to administer. The most talented slaves rose to the top of the bureaucracy; the less fortunate formed the brave and skillful core of the sultan's army, the so-called janissary corps.

As long as the Ottoman Empire expanded, the system worked well. As the sultan won more territory, he could impose his slave tax on larger populations. Moreover, he could amply reward loyal and effective servants by letting them draw a carefully defined income from conquered Christian peasants on a strictly temporary basis. For a long time, Christian peasants in eastern Europe were economically exploited less by the Muslim Turks than by Christian nobles, and they were not forced to convert to Islam. After about 1570, however, the powerful, centralized Ottoman system slowly began

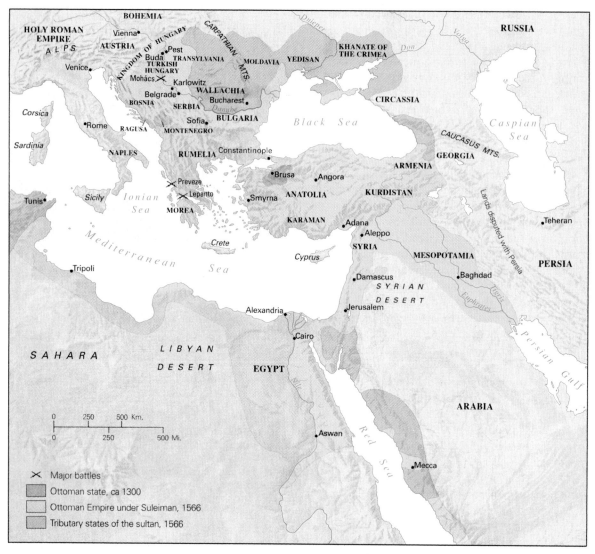

MAP 17.1 The Ottoman Empire at Its Height, 1566 The Ottomans, like their great rivals the Habsburgs, rose to rule a vast dynastic empire encompassing many different peoples and ethnic groups. The army and the bureaucracy served to unite the disparate territories into a single state.

to disintegrate as the Turks' western advance was stopped. Temporary Muslim landholders became hard-to-control permanent oppressors. Weak sultans left the glory of the battlefield for the delights of the harem, and the army lost its dedication and failed to keep up with European military advances.

Yet in the late seventeenth century, under vigorous reforming leadership, the Ottoman Empire succeeded in marshaling its forces for one last mighty attack on the Habsburgs. Building on long-standing support from Protestant nobles in Hungary and reinforced by an alliance with Louis XIV of France, the Turks again marched on Austria. A huge Turkish army surrounded Vienna and laid siege to it in 1683. After holding out against great odds for two months, the city was relieved at the last minute by a mixed force of Habsburg, Saxon, Bavarian, and Polish troops, and the Ottomans were forced to retreat. Soon the retreat became a rout. As Russian and Venetian allies attacked on other fronts, the Habsburgs conquered almost all of Hungary and Transylvania (part of present-day Romania) by 1699 (Map 17.2).

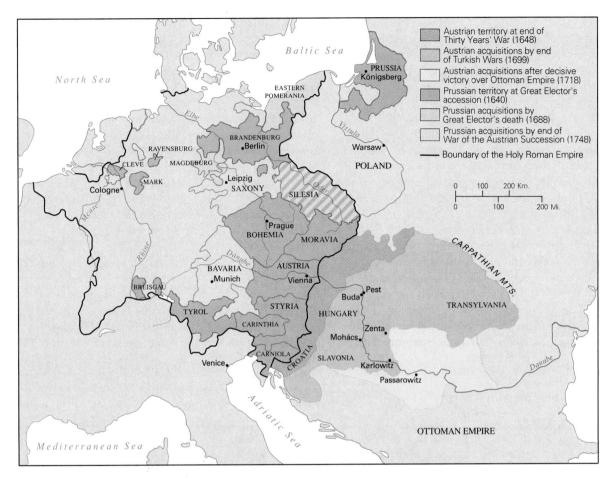

MAP 17.2 The Growth of Austria and Brandenburg-Prussia to 1748   Austria expanded to the southwest into Hungary and Transylvania at the expense of the Ottoman Empire. It was unable to hold the rich German province of Silesia, however, which was conquered by Brandenburg-Prussia.

The Turkish wars and this great expansion strengthened the Habsburg army and promoted some sense of unity in the Habsburg lands. The Habsburgs moved to centralize their power and make it as absolute as possible. But these efforts to create a fully developed, highly centralized, absolutist state were only partly successful.

The Habsburg state was composed of three separate and distinct territories—the old "hereditary provinces" of Austria, the kingdom of Bohemia, and the kingdom of Hungary. These three parts were tied together primarily by their common ruler, the Habsburg monarch. Each part had its own laws and political life, for the three noble-dominated Estates continued to exist, though with reduced powers. The Habsburgs themselves were well aware of the fragility of the union they had forged. In 1713 Charles VI (r. 1711–1740) proclaimed the so-called Pragmatic Sanction, which stated

that the Habsburg possessions were never to be divided and were always to be passed intact to a single heir, who might be female since Charles was the last of all Habsburg males. Charles spent much of his reign trying to get this principle accepted by the various branches of the Habsburg family, by the three different Estates of the realm, and by the states of Europe. His fears turned out to be well founded.

The Hungarian nobility, despite its reduced strength, effectively thwarted the full development of Habsburg absolutism. Time and again throughout the seventeenth century, Hungarian nobles—the most numerous in Europe, making up 5 to 7 percent of the Hungarian population—rose in revolt against Vienna's attempts to impose absolute rule. They never triumphed decisively, but neither were they ever crushed, as the Czech nobility had been in 1620.

The Hungarians resisted because many of them remained Protestants, especially in the area long ruled by the more tolerant Turks, and hated the heavy-handed attempts of the conquering Habsburgs to re-Catholicize everyone. Moreover, until 1683 the lords of Hungary had a powerful military ally in Turkey. Finally, the Hungarian nobility, and even part of the Hungarian peasantry, had become attached to a national ideal long before most of the other peoples of eastern Europe did so. Hungarian nobles were determined to maintain as much independence and local control as possible. Thus when the Habsburgs were bogged down in the War of the Spanish Succession (see page 545), the Hungarians rose in one last patriotic rebellion under Prince Francis Rákóczy in 1703. Rákóczy and his forces were eventually defeated, but this time the Habsburgs had to accept a definitive compromise. Charles VI restored many of the traditional privileges of the Hungarian aristocracy in return for Hungarian acceptance of hereditary Habsburg rule. Thus Hungary, unlike Austria or Bohemia, never came close to being fully integrated into a centralized, absolute Habsburg state.

Prussia in the Seventeenth Century

After 1400 the eastern German princes lost political power and influence, while a revitalized landed nobility became the undisputed ruling class. The Hohenzollern family, which ruled through its senior and junior branches as the imperial electors of Brandenburg and the dukes of Prussia, had little real princely power. The Hohenzollern rulers of Brandenburg and Prussia were nothing more than the first among equals, the largest landowners in a landlord society.

Nothing suggested that the Hohenzollern family and its princely territories would ever play an important role in European or even German affairs. The elector of Brandenburg's right to help choose the Holy Roman emperor with six other electors bestowed prestige, but the elector had no military strength whatsoever. Moreover, geography conspired against the Hohenzollerns. Brandenburg, the area around Berlin and their power base, was completely cut off from the sea (see Map 17.2). A tiny part of the vast north European plain that stretches from France to Russia, Brandenburg lacked natural frontiers and lay open to attack from all directions. The land was poor, a combination of sand and swamp. Contemporaries contemptuously called Brandenburg the "sand-box of the Holy Roman Empire."[2]

Moreover, the territory of the elector's cousin, the duke of Prussia, was totally separated from Brandenburg and was part of Poland. Prussia had originally been conquered in the thirteenth century by the Germanic order of Teutonic Knights as part of a larger struggle between German settlers and the indigenous Slavic populations. However, by 1600 Prussia's German-speaking peasants had much in common with Polish peasants in other provinces, for both ethnic groups had seen most of their freedoms reduced or revoked by their noble landlords. (Poland's numerous lesser nobility also dominated the Polish state, which was actually a constitutional republic headed by an elected king who had little real power.) In 1618 the junior branch of the Hohenzollern family died out, and Prussia reverted to the elector of Brandenburg.

The elector of Brandenburg was a helpless spectator in the Thirty Years' War, his territories alternately ravaged by Swedish and Habsburg armies. Population fell drastically, and many villages disappeared. The power of the Hohenzollerns reached its lowest point. Yet the devastation of Brandenburg and Prussia prepared the way for Hohenzollern absolutism because foreign armies dramatically weakened the political power of the Estates—the representative assemblies of the realm. This weakening of the Estates helped the very talented young elector Frederick William (r. 1640–1688), later known as the "Great Elector," to ride roughshod over traditional representative rights and to take a giant step toward royal absolutism. This constitutional struggle, often unjustly neglected by historians, was the most crucial in Prussian history for hundreds of years, until that of the 1860s.

When he came to power in 1640, the twenty-year-old Great Elector was determined to unify his three quite separate provinces and add to them by diplomacy and war. These provinces were Brandenburg itself; Prussia, inherited in 1618; and completely separate, scattered holdings along the Rhine in western Germany, inherited in 1614 (see Map 17.2). Each of the three provinces was inhabited by Germans, but each had its own Estates, whose power had increased until about 1600 as the power of the rulers declined. Although the Estates had not met regularly during the chaotic Thirty Years' War, they still had the power of the purse in their respective provinces. Taxes could not be levied without their consent. The Estates of Brandenburg and Prussia were dominated by the nobility and the landowning classes, known as the "Junkers." But this was also the case in most European countries that had representative bodies, including the English Parliament before and after the civil war. Had the Estates successfully resisted the absolutist demands of the Great Elector, they, too, might have evolved toward more broadly based constitutionalism.

The struggle between the Great Elector and the provincial Estates was long, complicated, and intense. After the Thirty Years' War, representatives of the nobility zealously reasserted the right of the Estates to vote taxes, a right the Swedish armies of occupation had simply ignored. Yet first in Brandenburg in 1653 and then in Prussia between 1661 and 1663, the Great Elector eventually had his way.

To pay for the permanent standing army he first established in 1660, Frederick William forced the Estates to accept the introduction of permanent taxation without consent. Moreover, the soldiers doubled as tax collectors and policemen, becoming the core of the rapidly expanding state bureaucracy. The power of the Estates declined rapidly thereafter, for the Great Elector had both financial independence and superior force. He turned the screws of taxation: the state's total revenue tripled during his reign. The size of the army leaped about tenfold. In 1688 a population of one million was supporting a peacetime standing army of thirty thousand. Many of the soldiers were French Huguenot immigrants, whom the Great Elector welcomed as the talented, hard-working subjects they were.

In accounting for the Great Elector's fateful triumph, two factors appear central. First, as in the formation of every absolutist state, war was a decisive factor. The ongoing struggle between Sweden and Poland for control of the Baltic after 1648 and the wars of Louis XIV in western Europe created an atmosphere of permanent crisis. The wild Tartars of the Crimea in southern Russia swept through Prussia in the winter of 1656 to 1657, killing and carrying off as slaves more than fifty

Molding the Prussian Spirit   Discipline was strict and punishment brutal in the Prussian army. This scene, from an eighteenth-century book used to teach schoolchildren in Prussia, shows one soldier being flogged while another is being beaten with canes as he walks between rows of troops. The officer on horseback proudly commands. *(University of Illinois Library, Champaign)*

thousand people, according to an old estimate. This invasion softened up the Estates and strengthened the urgency of the elector's demands for more money for more soldiers.

Second, the nobility had long dominated the government through the Estates, but only for its own narrow self-interest. When the crunch came, Prussian nobles proved unwilling to join the representatives of the towns in a consistent common front against royal pretensions. The nobility was all too concerned with its own rights and privileges, especially its freedom from taxation and its unlimited control over the peasants. When, therefore, the Great Elector reconfirmed these privileges in 1653 and after, even while reducing the political power of the Estates, the nobility growled but did not bite. It accepted a compromise whereby the bulk of the new taxes fell on towns and royal authority stopped at the landlords' gates. The elector could and did use naked force to break the liberties of the towns. The main leader of the urban opposition in the key city of Königsberg, for example, was simply arrested and imprisoned for life without trial.

The Consolidation of Prussian Absolutism

By the time of his death in 1688, the Great Elector had created a single state out of scattered principalities. But his new creation was still small and fragile. All the leading states of Europe had many more people—France with 20 million was fully twenty times as populous—and strong monarchy was still a novelty. Moreover, the Great Elector's successor, Elector Frederick III, "the Ostentatious" (r. 1688–1713), was weak of body and mind, and he focused on imitating the style of Louis XIV, building an expensive palace and cultivating the arts. His main political accomplishment was winning a prestigious royal title and being crowned King Frederick I in 1701 as a reward for aiding the Holy Roman emperor in the War of the Spanish Succession.

This tendency toward luxury-loving, petty tyranny was completely reversed by Frederick William I, "the Soldiers' King" (r. 1713–1740). A crude, dangerous psychoneurotic, Frederick William I was nevertheless the most talented reformer ever produced by the Hohenzollern family. It was he who truly established Prussian absolutism and gave it a unique character. It was he who created the best army in Europe, for its size, and it was he who infused strict military values into a whole society. In the words of an outstanding historian of Prussia:

For a whole generation, the Hohenzollern subjects were victimized by a royal bully, imbued with an obsessive bent for military organization and military scales of value. This left a deep mark upon the institutions of Prussiandom and upon the molding of the "Prussian spirit."[3]

Frederick William's attachment to the army and military life was intensely emotional. He had, for example, a bizarre, almost pathological love for tall soldiers, whom he credited with superior strength and endurance. Austere and always faithful to his wife, he nevertheless confided to the French ambassador, "The most beautiful girl or woman in the world would be a matter of indifference to me, but tall soldiers—they are my weakness." Like some fanatical modern-day basketball coach in search of a championship team, he sent his agents throughout Prussia and all of Europe to trick, buy, and kidnap top recruits. Neighboring princes sent him their giants as gifts to win his gratitude. Prussian mothers told their sons, "Stop growing or the recruiting agents will get you."[4]

Profoundly military in temperament, Frederick William always wore an army uniform, and he lived the highly disciplined life of the professional soldier. He began his work by five or six in the morning; at ten he almost always went to the parade ground to drill or inspect his troops. A man of violent temper, Frederick William personally punished the most minor infractions on the spot: a missing button off a soldier's coat quickly provoked a savage beating with a heavy walking stick.

Frederick William's love of the army was also based on a hardheaded conception of the struggle for power and a dog-eat-dog view of international politics. Even before ascending the throne, he bitterly criticized his father's ministers: "They say that they will obtain land and power for the king with the pen; but I say it can be done only with the sword." Years later he summed up his life's philosophy in his instructions to his son: "A formidable army and a war chest large enough to make this army mobile in times of need can create great respect for you in the world, so that you can speak a word like the other powers."[5] This unshakable belief that the welfare of king and state depended on the army above all else reinforced Frederick William's passion for the soldier's life.

The cult of military power provided the rationale for a great expansion of royal absolutism. As the ruthless king himself put it: "I must be served with life and limb, with house and wealth, with honour and conscience, everything must be committed except eternal salvation—that belongs to God, but all else is mine."[6] To make good these extraordinary demands, Frederick William created a strong centralized bureaucracy. More commoners probably rose to top positions in the civil government than at any other time in Prussia's history. Meanwhile the last traces of the parliamentary Estates and local self-government vanished.

The king's grab for power brought him into considerable conflict with the noble landowners, the Junkers. In his early years, he even threatened to destroy them; yet, in the end, the Prussian nobility was not destroyed but enlisted—into the army. Responding to a combination of threats and opportunities, the Junkers became the officer caste. By 1739 all but 5 of 245 officers with the rank of major or above were aristocrats, and most of them were native Prussians. A new compromise had been worked out whereby the proud nobility imperiously commanded the peasantry in the army as well as on the estates.

Coarse and crude, penny-pinching and hard-working, Frederick William achieved results. Above all, he built a first-rate army, although he had only third-rate resources. The standing army increased from thirty-eight thousand to eighty-three thousand during his reign. Prussia, twelfth in Europe in population, had the fourth largest army by 1740. Only the much more populous states of France, Russia, and Austria had larger forces, and even France's army was only twice as large as Prussia's. Moreover, soldier for soldier, the Prussian army became the best in Europe, astonishing foreign observers with its precision, skill, and discipline. For the next two hundred years, Prussia and then Prussianized Germany would usually win the crucial military battles.

Frederick William and his ministers also built an exceptionally honest and conscientious bureaucracy, which not only administered the country but also tried with some success to develop the country economically. Finally, like the miser he was known to be, living very frugally off the income of his own landholdings, the king loved his "blue boys" so much that he hated to "spend" them. This most militaristic of kings was, paradoxically, almost always at peace.

Nevertheless, the Prussian people paid a heavy and lasting price for the obsessions of their royal drillmaster. Civil society became rigid and highly disciplined. Prussia became the "Sparta of the North"; unquestioning obedience was the highest virtue. As a Prussian minister later summed up, "To keep quiet is the first civic duty."[7] Thus the policies of Frederick William I combined with harsh peasant bondage and Junker tyranny to lay the foundations for probably the most militaristic country of modern times.

A Prussian Giant Grenadier   Frederick William I wanted tall, handsome soldiers. He dressed them in tight bright uniforms to distinguish them from the peasant population from which most soldiers came. He also ordered several portraits of his favorites from his court painter, J. C. Merk. Grenadiers wore the miter cap instead of an ordinary hat so that they could hurl their heavy grenades unimpeded by a broad brim. *(The Royal Collection © Her Majesty Queen Elizabeth II)*

THE DEVELOPMENT OF RUSSIA

One of the favorite parlor games of nineteenth-century Russian (and non-Russian) intellectuals was debating whether Russia was a Western, European or a non-Western, Asiatic society. This question was particularly fascinating because it was unanswerable. To this day Russia differs fundamentally from the West in some basic ways, though Russian history has paralleled that of the West in other aspects.

Certainly Russian developments in the early medieval period had important parallels with those in the West. Both the conversion of the eastern Slavs to Christianity (of the Eastern Orthodox variety) and the loose but real political unification of the eastern Slavic territories under a single prince and a single dynasty in the eleventh century were in the mainstream of European medieval civilization. So, too, was the typical feudal division of the land-based society into a boyard nobility and a commoner peasantry. After the death of Great Prince Iaroslav the Wise (r. 1019–1054), the powerful Kievan principality in present-day Ukraine disintegrated into competing political units. But similar fragmentations of central authority occurred in many European kingdoms at various points in the Middle Ages, and a strong native ruler might have emerged in Russia eventually to resume the centralizing work of earlier Kievan monarchs.

Such was not the case, however. Brutally conquered and subjugated by a foreign invader, Russia created a system of rule that was virtually unknown in the West. Thus the differences between Russia and the West became striking and profound in the long period from about 1250 until 1700. And when absolute monarchy triumphed under the rough guidance of Peter the Great in the early eighteenth century, it was a quite different type of absolute monarchy from that of France or even Prussia.

The Mongol Yoke and the Rise of Moscow

Like the Germans and the Italians, the eastern Slavs might have emerged from the Middle Ages weak and politically divided had it not been for the Mongol conquest of the Kievan. Nomadic tribes from present-day Mongolia, the Mongols were temporarily unified in the thirteenth century by Jenghiz Khan (1162–1227), one of history's greatest conquerors. In five years his armies subdued all of China. His successors then turned westward, smashing everything in their path and reaching

the plains of Hungary victorious before they pulled back in 1242. The Mongol army—the Golden Horde—was savage in the extreme, often slaughtering entire populations of cities before burning them to the ground. En route to Mongolia in 1245, Archbishop John of Plano Carpini, the papal ambassador to Mongolia, passed through Kiev, which the Mongols had sacked in 1242, and wrote an unforgettable eyewitness account:

The Mongols went against Russia and enacted a great massacre in the Russian land. They destroyed towns and fortresses and killed people. They besieged Kiev, which had been the capital of Russia, and after a long siege they took it and killed the inhabitants of the city. For this reason, when we passed through that land, we found lying in the field countless heads and bones of dead people; for this city had been extremely large and very populous, whereas now it has been reduced to nothing: barely two hundred houses stand there, and those people are held in the harshest slavery.[8]

Having devastated and conquered, the Mongols ruled the eastern Slavs for more than two hundred years. They built their capital of Saray on the lower Volga (Map 17.3). They forced all the bickering Slavic princes to submit to their rule and to give them tribute and slaves. If the conquered peoples rebelled, the Mongols were quick to punish with death and destruction. Thus the Mongols unified the eastern Slavs, for the Mongol khan was acknowledged by all as the supreme ruler.

The Mongol unification completely changed the internal political situation. Although the Mongols conquered, they were quite willing to use local princes as obedient servants and tax collectors. Therefore, they did not abolish the title of "great prince," bestowing it instead on the prince who served them best and paid them most handsomely.

Beginning with Alexander Nevsky in 1252, the previously insignificant princes of Moscow became particularly adept at serving the Mongols. They loyally put down popular uprisings and collected the khan's harsh taxes. By way of reward, the princes of Moscow emerged as hereditary great princes. Eventually the

MAP 17.3 The Expansion of Russia to 1725   After the disintegration of the Kievan state and the Mongol conquest, the princes of Moscow and their descendants gradually extended their rule over an enormous territory. Ivan the Terrible acquired more territory than Peter the Great.

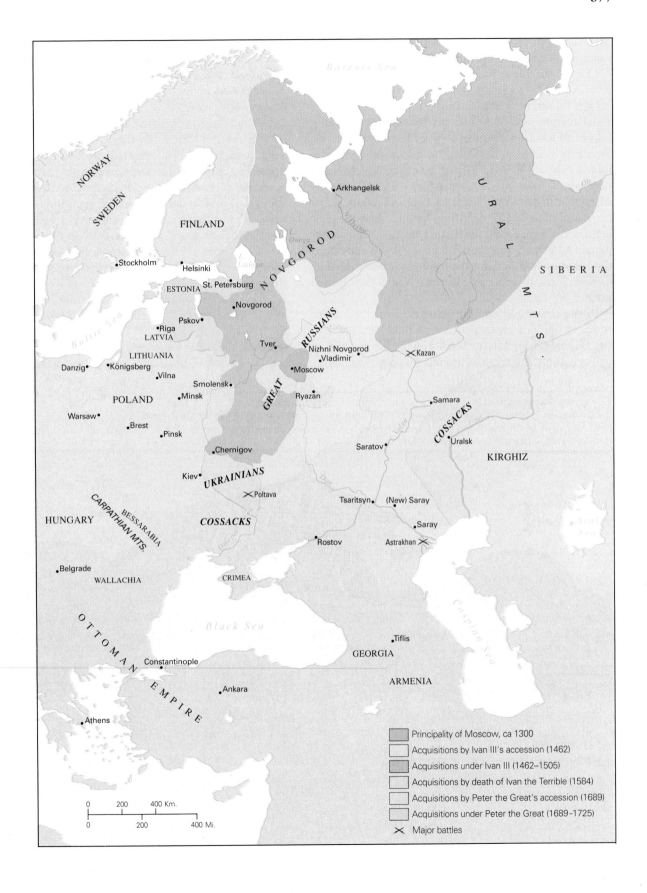

NORWAY

SWEDEN

FINLAND

•Stockholm

•Helsinki

ESTONIA

St. Petersburg

•Novgorod

Pskov•

•Riga

LATVIA

LITHUANIA

Danzig• •Königsberg

•Vilna

Smolensk•

POLAND   •Minsk

Warsaw•

•Brest

•Pinsk

•Chernigov

Kiev• UKRAINIANS

HUNGARY

CARPATHIAN MTS.

BESSARABIA

COSSACKS

•Belgrade

WALLACHIA

CRIMEA

OTTOMAN EMPIRE

Constantinople•

•Ankara

•Athens

Barents Sea

•Arkhangelsk

U R A L   M T S.

SIBERIA

N O V G O R O D

L. Onega

L. Ladoga

Tver•

RUSSIANS

Nizhni Novgorod

•Vladimir

✕Kazan

•Moscow

GREAT

•Ryazan

•Samara

COSSACKS

•Saratov

Uralsk•

KIRGHIZ

✕Poltava

Tsaritsyn•   (New) Saray

•Saray

•Rostov   Astrakhan✕

Black Sea

•Tiflis

GEORGIA

ARMENIA

Caspian Sea

Aral Sea

	Principality of Moscow, ca 1300
	Acquisitions by Ivan III's accession (1462)
	Acquisitions under Ivan III (1462–1505)
	Acquisitions by death of Ivan the Terrible (1584)
	Acquisitions by Peter the Great's accession (1689)
	Acquisitions under Peter the Great (1689–1725)
✕	Major battles

0   200   400 Km.

0   200   400 Mi.

Muscovite princes were able to destroy their princely rivals and even replace the khan as supreme ruler.

One of the more important Muscovite princes was Ivan I (r. 1328–1341), popularly known as "Ivan Moneybags." Extremely stingy, Ivan I built up a large personal fortune and increased his influence by loaning money to less frugal princes to pay their Mongol taxes. Ivan's most serious rival was the prince of Tver, who joined his people in 1327 in a revolt against Mongol oppression. Appointed commander of a large Russian-Mongol army, Ivan laid waste to Tver and its lands. For this proof of devotion, the Mongols made Ivan the general tax collector for all the Slavic lands they had subjugated and named him great prince. Ivan also convinced the metropolitan of Kiev, the leading churchman of all eastern Slavs, to settle in Moscow. Ivan I thus gained greater prestige.

In the next hundred-odd years, the great princes of Moscow significantly increased their holdings. Then, in the reign of Ivan III (r. 1462–1505), the process of gathering in the territories around Moscow was largely completed. Of the principalities that Ivan III purchased and conquered, the large, rich merchant republic of Novgorod was most crucial (see Map 17.3). Thus the princes of Moscow defeated all rivals to win complete princely authority.

Not only was the prince of Moscow the *unique* ruler, he was the *absolute* ruler, the autocrat, the *tsar*—the Slavic contraction for "caesar," with all its connotations. This imperious conception of absolute power was powerfully reinforced by two developments. First, about 1480 Ivan III felt strong enough to stop acknowledging the khan as his supreme ruler. There is good evidence to suggest that Ivan and his successor saw themselves as khans. Certainly they assimilated the Mongol concept of kingship as the exercise of unrestrained and unpredictable power.

Second, after the fall of Constantinople to the Turks in 1453, the tsars saw themselves as the heirs of both the caesars and Orthodox Christianity, the one true faith. All the other kings of Europe were heretics; only the tsars were rightful and holy rulers. The idea was

Collecting Taxes in Russia   Ivan I, known as Ivan Moneybags and pictured here at the center, zealously served his Mongol masters. This work by an unknown artist shows the great prince's agents beating peasants into paying the heavy Mongol tax, a portion of which Ivan skimmed off to increase his own wealth and power. *(Novosti)*

promoted by Orthodox churchmen, who spoke of "holy Russia" as the "Third Rome." As the monk Pilotheus stated, "Two Romes have fallen, but the third stands, and a fourth there will not be."[9] Ivan's marriage to the daughter of the last Byzantine emperor further enhanced the aura of an imperial inheritance of Moscow. Worthy successor to the mighty khan and the true Christian emperor, the Muscovite tsar was a king claiming unrestricted power as his God-given right. The Mongol inheritance weighed heavily on Russia.

As peasants had begun losing their freedom of movement in the fifteenth century, so had the noble boyars begun losing power and influence. For example, when Ivan III conquered the principality of Novgorod in the 1480s, he confiscated fully 80 percent of the land, executing the previous owners or resettling them nearer Moscow. He then kept more than half of the confiscated land for himself and distributed the remainder to members of a newly emerging service nobility, who held the tsar's land on the explicit condition that they serve in the tsar's army. Moreover, Ivan III began to re-quire boyars outside Novgorod to serve him if they wished to retain their lands. Since there were no competing princes to turn to, the boyars had to yield.

Tsar and People to 1689

The rise of the new service nobility accelerated under Ivan IV (r. 1533–1584), the famous Ivan the Terrible. Having ascended the throne at age three, Ivan suffered insults and neglect at the hands of the haughty boyars after his mother mysteriously died, possibly poisoned, when he was just eight. At age sixteen he suddenly pushed aside his hated boyar advisers. In an awe-inspiring ceremony complete with gold coins pouring down on his head, he majestically crowned himself and officially took the august title of tsar for the first time.

Selecting the beautiful and kind Anastasia of the popular Romanov family for his wife and queen, the young tsar soon declared war on the remnants of Mongol power. He defeated the faltering khanates of Kazan and

Ivan the Terrible   Ivan IV, the first to take the title Tsar of Russia, executed many Muscovite boyars and their peasants and servants. His ownership of all the land, trade, and industry restricted economic development. *(National Museum, Copenhagen, Denmark)*

Astrakhan between 1552 and 1556, adding vast new territories to Russia. In the course of these wars, Ivan virtually abolished the old distinction between hereditary boyar private property and land granted temporarily for service. All nobles, old and new, had to serve the tsar in order to hold any land.

The process of transforming the entire nobility into a service nobility was completed in the second part of Ivan the Terrible's reign. In 1557 Ivan turned westward, and for the next twenty-five years Muscovy waged an exhausting, unsuccessful war primarily against the large Polish-Lithuanian state, which joined Poland with much of Ukraine in the sixteenth century. Quarreling with the boyars over the war and blaming them for the sudden death of his beloved Anastasia in 1560, the increasingly cruel and demented Ivan turned to strike down all who stood in his way.

Above all, he struck down the ancient Muscovite boyars with a reign of terror. Leading boyars, their relatives, and even their peasants and servants were executed en masse by a special corps of unquestioning servants. Dressed in black and riding black horses, they were forerunners of the modern dictator's secret police. Large estates were confiscated, broken up, and reapportioned to the lower service nobility. The great boyar families were severely reduced. The newer, poorer, more nearly equal service nobility, still less than 0.5 percent of the total population, was totally dependent on the autocrat.

Ivan also took giant strides toward making all commoners servants of the tsar. His endless wars and demonic purges left much of central Russia depopulated. It grew increasingly difficult for the lower service nobles to squeeze a living for themselves out of the peasants left on their landholdings. As the service nobles demanded more from the remaining peasants, more and more peasants fled toward the wild, recently conquered territories to the east and south. There they formed free groups and outlaw armies known as "Cossacks." The Cossacks maintained their independence beyond the reach of the oppressive landholders and the tsar's hated officials. The solution to the problem of peasant flight was to complete the tying of the peasants to the land, making them serfs perpetually bound to serve the noble landholders, who were bound in turn to serve the tsar.

In the time of Ivan the Terrible, urban traders and artisans were also bound to their towns and jobs so that the tsar could tax them more heavily. Ivan assumed that the tsar owned Russia's trade and industry, just as he owned all the land. In the course of the sixteenth and seventeenth centuries, the tsars therefore took over the mines and industries and monopolized the country's important commercial activities. The urban classes had no security in their work or property, and even the wealthiest merchants were basically dependent agents of the tsar. If a new commercial activity became profitable, it was often taken over by the tsar and made a royal monopoly. This royal monopolization was in sharp contrast to developments in western Europe, where the capitalist middle classes were gaining strength and security in their private property. The tsar's service obligations checked the growth of the Russian middle classes and impoverished the urban lower classes, just as they led to pressure on the boyars, the rise of the lower nobility, and the final enserfment of the peasants.

Ivan the Terrible's system of autocracy and compulsory service struck foreign observers forcibly. Sigismund Herberstein, a German traveler to Russia, wrote in 1571: "All the people consider themselves to be *kholops,* that is, slaves of their Prince." At the same time, Jean Bodin, the French thinker who did so much to develop the modern concept of sovereignty, concluded that Russia's political system was fundamentally different from those of all other European monarchies and comparable only to that of the Ottoman Empire. In both the Ottoman Empire and Russia, as in other parts of Asia and Africa, "the prince is become lord of the goods and persons of his subjects . . . governing them as a master of a family does his slaves."[10] The Mongol inheritance weighed heavily on Russia.

As has so often occurred in Russia, the death of an iron-fisted tyrant—in this case, Ivan the Terrible in 1584—ushered in an era of confusion and violent struggles for power. Events were particularly chaotic after Ivan's son, Theodore, died in 1598 without an heir. The years 1598 to 1613 were aptly called the "Time of Troubles."

The close relatives of the deceased tsar intrigued against and murdered each other, alternately fighting and welcoming the invading Swedes and Poles, who even occupied Moscow. Most serious for the cause of autocracy, there was a great social upheaval. Cossack bands, led by a former slave named Ivan Bolotnikov, marched northward, rallying peasants and slaughtering nobles and officials. The mass of Cossacks and peasants called for the "true tsar," who would restore their freedom of movement and allow them to farm for whomever they pleased, who would reduce their heavy taxes and lighten the yoke imposed by the landlords.

This social explosion from below, which combined with a belated surge of patriotic opposition to Polish invaders, brought the nobles, big and small, to their senses. They put aside their quarrels and finally crushed

Palm Sunday in Moscow   Noble boyars celebrate in Red Square outside the walled Kremlin; St. Basil's Cathedral stands on the left, with its onion-shaped domes reflecting strong Byzantine influences. The boyars wear their traditional beards and long gowns, which Peter the Great would ban in his efforts to establish Western practices in Russia. Note the absence of women. *(British Museum/Fotomas Index)*

the Cossack rebellion at the gates of Moscow. In 1613 the nobles elected Ivan the Terrible's sixteen-year-old grandnephew, Michael Romanov, the new hereditary tsar. Then they rallied around him in the face of common internal and external threats. Michael's election was a real restoration, and his reign saw the gradual reestablishment of tsarist autocracy. (See the feature "Listening to the Past: A Foreign Traveler in Russia" on pages 590–591.) Michael was understandably more kindly disposed toward the supportive nobility than toward the sullen peasants. Thus while peasants were completely enserfed in 1649, Ivan's heavy military obligations on the nobility were relaxed considerably.

In the long reign of Michael's successor, the pious Alexis (r. 1645–1676), this asymmetry of obligations was accentuated. The nobility gained more exemptions from military service, while the peasants were further ground down.

The result was a second round of mass upheaval and protest. In the later seventeenth century, the unity of the Russian Orthodox church was torn apart by a great split. The initiating event was the religious reforms introduced in 1652 by the patriarch Nikon, a dogmatic purist who wished to bring "corrupted" Russian practices of worship into line with the Greek Orthodox model. The self-serving church hierarchy quickly went along, but the intensely religious common people resisted. They saw Nikon as the Antichrist, who was stripping them of the only thing they had—the true religion of "holy Russia."

Great numbers left the church and formed illegal communities of "Old Believers," who were hunted down and persecuted. As many as twenty thousand people burned themselves alive, singing the "hallelujah" in their chants three times rather than twice, as Nikon had demanded, and crossing themselves in the old style, with two rather than three fingers, as they went down in flames. After the great split, the Russian masses were alienated from the established church, which became dependent on the state for its authority.

Again the Cossacks revolted against the state, which was doggedly trying to catch up with them on the frontiers and reduce them to serfdom. Under Stenka Razin they moved up the Volga River in 1670 and 1671, attracting a great army of urban poor and peasants, killing landlords and government officials, and proclaiming freedom from oppression. This rebellion to overthrow the established order was finally defeated by the government. (See the feature "Individuals in Society: Stenka Razin, Russian Rebel.") In response, the thoroughly scared upper classes tightened the screws of serfdom even further. Holding down the peasants, and thereby maintaining the tsar, became almost the principal obligation of the nobility until 1689.

The Reforms of Peter the Great

It is now possible to understand the reforms of Peter the Great (r. 1682–1725) and his kind of monarchial absolutism. Contrary to some historians' assertions, Peter was interested primarily in military power, not in some grandiose westernization plan. A giant for his time, at six feet seven inches, and possessing enormous energy and willpower, Peter was determined to redress the defeats the tsar's armies had occasionally suffered in their wars with Poland and Sweden since the time of Ivan the Terrible.

Peter was equally determined to continue the tsarist tradition of territorial expansion. After a long war, Russia had gained a large mass of Ukraine from weak and decentralized Poland in 1667 (see Map 17.3). And tsarist forces had completed the conquest of the primitive tribes of all Siberia in the seventeenth century. After the seventeen-year-old Peter overturned the regency in 1689, the thirty-six years of his personal rule knew only one year of peace.

When Peter took control in 1689, the heart of his army still consisted of cavalry made up of boyars and service nobility. Foot soldiers played a secondary role, and the whole army served on a part-time basis. The Russian army was lagging behind the professional standing armies being formed in Europe in the seventeenth century. The core of such armies was a highly disciplined infantry that fired and refired rifles as it fearlessly advanced, until it charged with bayonets fixed. Such a large, permanent army was enormously expensive and could be created only with time and at the cost of great sacrifice. Thus Peter's military moves were cautious in the 1690s.

Maintaining an existing Russian alliance with Austria and Poland against the Ottoman Empire, Peter campaigned first against Turkish forts and Tartar vassals on the Black Sea. Learning from early mistakes, he conquered Azov in 1696. Fascinated by weapons and foreign technology, the confident tsar then led a group of 250 Russian officials and young nobles on an eighteen-month tour of western European capitals. Traveling unofficially as an ordinary Russian to avoid formal ceremonies, Peter worked with his hands at various crafts and met with foreign kings and experts. He was particularly impressed with the growing power of the Dutch and the English and considered how Russia could profit from their example.

Returning to Russia, Peter made a fateful decision that would shape his reign and bring massive reforms. He entered into a secret alliance with Denmark and the elector of Saxony, who was also the elected king of Poland, to wage a sudden war of aggression against Sweden. Sweden was then a leading power in northern Europe. Despite the country's small population and limited agricultural resources, Swedish rulers in the seventeenth century had developed a strong absolutist state and built an excellent standing army. Expanding beyond Sweden, they held substantial territory in northern Germany, Finland, and Estonia. Yet these possessions were scattered and appeared vulnerable. Above all, Peter and his allies believed that their combined forces could win easy victories because Sweden was in the hands of a new and inexperienced king. They were mistaken.

Eighteen-year-old Charles XII (1697–1718) surprised Peter when he showed daring military genius. Defeating Denmark quickly in 1700 and forcing it to make peace, Charles turned on Russia. In a blinding snowstorm, his well-trained professional army attacked and routed unsuspecting Russians besieging the Swedish fortress of Navra on the Baltic coast. Peter and the survivors fled in panic to Moscow. It was, for the Russians, a grim beginning to the long and brutal Great Northern War, which lasted from 1700 to 1721.

Individuals in Society

Stenka Razin, Russian Rebel

The Don Cossack Stenka Razin led the largest peasant rebellion in Europe in the seventeenth century, a century rich in peasant revolt. Who was this Cossack leader who challenged Moscow, this outlaw who grew into a social revolutionary?

Descended from fugitives who fled to the turbulent southern frontier in search of freedom, Razin epitomized the old Cossack spirit of liberty and self-rule. Sharing the Cossack love of fighting and adventure, Razin also felt great sympathy for northern "have-nots" who had lost out and could not escape their fate. Why this was so remains a mystery. His family belonged to the Cossack establishment, which had settled the lower Don Valley long ago and received annual payments from the tsar in return for friendship and defense. One folk story tells of a hatred kindled by a Russian prince who unjustly hanged an older brother leading a Cossack detachment in Poland. True or not, rebel leaders like Razin have often come from comfortable backgrounds. As Paul Avrich notes, "Seldom have the oppressed themselves led the way, but rather those who have been aroused by their suffering and degradation."[1]

Whatever his motivation, Stenka Razin was a born leader. A striking personality with violent emotions, he was also shrewd and generous. He understood the lower classes and how to move them. The crowds called him a magician—a magician who hated the privileged and whom they felt compelled to follow.

Razin was a seasoned warrior of about forty years of age when in 1667 he led his first campaign. With an armed band of poor and rootless Cossacks, recent fugitives living upstream from the well-settled Cossacks, Razin sailed down the Volga River and seized a rich convoy of Russian merchant ships. He reportedly told survivors they were free to go or join him as free Cossacks. "I have come to fight only the boyars and the wealthy lords. As for the poor and the plain folk, I shall treat them as brothers."[2] Moving on to plunder Persian commerce on the Caspian Sea, Razin's forces returned home loaded with booty, which they divided equally according to Cossack custom. Gaining immense popularity and responding to threats from Moscow, Razin and his movement changed. The gang of outlaws became a rebel army.

Stenka Razin in Cossack dress, from a contemporary engraving. *(Novosti)*

In early 1670, Razin marched north with seven thousand Don Cossacks. His leaflets proclaimed that he was entering Russia "to establish the Cossack way, so that all men will be equal." Shrewdly blaming treacherous nobles and officials, and not the divinely appointed tsar, for the exploitation of the people, Razin's agents infiltrated the fortified towns along the Volga. Some towns resisted, but many threw open their gates, as the urban poor rose up against the "traitors and bloodsuckers." Peasants joined the revolt, killing lords and burning manor houses.

Frightened but unified, Russia's tiny elite mobilized all its strength. In late 1670, crack cavalry units of service nobility finally repulsed the swollen, ill-equipped army of the poor at Simbirsk on the upper Volga. The insurgents had to retreat. Fighting until the end, Razin was captured, hideously tortured, and chopped into pieces on the execution block. His followers and sympathizers were slaughtered with ferocious cruelty.

A fearless leader in the struggle against tsarist absolutism, Stenka Razin nurtured a myth of rebellion that would inspire future generations with dreams of freedom. He became Russia's most celebrated folk hero. He lived in story and song, an immortal superman who would someday ride out of the forest and deliver the people from oppression.

Questions for Analysis

1. What did Stenka Razin do? Why did his rebellion inspire future generations?

2. How would you interpret Razin? Was he a great hero, a common criminal, or something else?

---

1. Paul Avrich, *Russian Rebels, 1600–1800* (New York: Schocken Books, 1972), p. 67. This account is based on Avrich's masterful study.

2. Quoted ibid., p. 70.

Peter the Great This painting by Louis Karavack celebrates the power and determination of Russia's famous ruler. Most appropriately, it shows him imperiously leading his armies into battle. Peter waged war almost continually throughout his long reign, and the desire to build a large modern army motivated many of his reforms. *(Hermitage, Leningrad/Novosti)*

Suffering defeat and faced with a military crisis, the energetic Peter responded with a long series of practical but far-reaching measures designed to increase state power, strengthen his armies, and gain victory. In essence, Peter's solution was to tighten up Muscovy's old service system and really make it work. He put the nobility back in harness with a vengeance. Every nobleman, great or small, was once again required to serve in the army or in the civil administration—for life. Since a more modern army and government required skilled technicians and experts, Peter created schools and even universities to produce them. One of his most hated reforms required five years of compulsory education away from home for every young nobleman. Peter established an interlocking military-civilian bureaucracy with fourteen ranks, and he decreed that all had to start at the bottom and work toward the top. Some people of non-noble origins rose to high positions in this embryonic meritocracy. Drawing on his experience abroad, Peter searched out talented foreigners and placed them

in his service. These measures gradually combined to make the army and government more powerful and efficient.

Peter also greatly increased the service requirements of the commoners. In the wake of the disaster at Navra, he established a regular standing army of more than 200,000 soldiers, made up mainly of peasants commanded by officers from the nobility. In addition, special forces of Cossacks and foreigners numbered more than 100,000. The departure of a drafted peasant boy was celebrated by his family and village almost like a funeral, as indeed it was, since the recruit was drafted for life. The peasantry also served with its taxes, which increased threefold during Peter's reign, as people—"souls"—replaced land as the primary unit of taxation. Serfs were also arbitrarily assigned to work in the growing number of factories and mines. Most of these industrial enterprises were directly or indirectly owned by the state, and they were worked almost exclusively for the military. In general, Russian serfdom became more oppressive under the reforming tsar.

The constant warfare of Peter's reign consumed 80 to 85 percent of all revenues and brought only modest territorial expansion. Yet the Great Northern War with Sweden was crowned in the end by Russian victory. Mobilizing superior resources and a much larger population, Peter's new war machine crushed the smaller army of Sweden's Charles XII in Ukraine at Poltava in 1709, one of the most significant battles in Russian history. The war dragged on until 1721, but Sweden never really regained the offensive, and Russia eventually annexed Estonia and much of present-day Latvia (see Map 17.3), lands that had never before been under Russian rule. Russia became the dominant power on the Baltic Sea and very much a European Great Power. If victory or defeat is the ultimate historical criterion, Peter's reforms were a success.

There were other important consequences of Peter's reign. Because of his feverish desire to use modern technology to strengthen the army, many Westerners and Western ideas flowed into Russia for the first time. A new class of educated Russians began to emerge. At the same time, vast numbers of Russians, especially among the poor and weak, hated Peter's massive changes. The split between the enserfed peasantry and the educated nobility thus widened, even though all were caught up in the endless demands of the sovereign.

A new idea of state interest, as distinct from the tsar's personal interests, began to take hold. Peter himself fostered this conception of the public interest by claiming time and again to be serving the common good. For the first time, a Russian tsar attached explanations to his decrees in an attempt to gain the confidence and enthusiastic support of the populace. Yet as before, the tsar alone decided what the common good was. Here was a source of future tension between tsar and people.

Thus Peter built on the service obligations of old Muscovy. His monarchial absolutism was truly the culmination of the long development of a unique Russian civilization. Yet the creation of a more modern army and state introduced much that was new and Western to that civilization. This development paved the way for Russia to move much closer to the European mainstream in its thought and institutions during the Enlightenment, especially under Catherine the Great.

 ## ABSOLUTISM AND THE BAROQUE

The rise of royal absolutism in eastern Europe had many consequences. Nobles served their powerful rulers in new ways, while the great inferiority of the urban middle classes and the peasants was reconfirmed. Armies became larger and more professional, while taxes rose and authoritarian traditions were strengthened. Nor was this all. Royal absolutism also interacted with baroque culture and art, baroque music and literature. Inspired in part by Louis XIV of France, the great and not-so-great rulers called on the artistic talent of the age to glorify their power and magnificence. This exaltation of despotic rule was particularly striking in the lavish masterpieces of architecture.

Palaces and Power

Baroque culture and art grew out of the revitalized Catholic church of the later sixteenth century. The papacy and the Jesuits especially encouraged an emotional, exuberant art, which appealed to the senses of churchgoers and proclaimed the confidence and power of the Catholic Reformation. The baroque style then spread throughout Europe in the seventeenth century, for dramatic baroque palaces symbolized the age of absolutist power, as soaring Gothic cathedrals had expressed the idealized spirit of the High Middle Ages.

By 1700 palace building had become a veritable obsession for the rulers of central and eastern Europe. Their baroque palaces were clearly intended to overawe the people with the monarch's strength. The great palaces were also visual declarations of equality with Louis XIV and were therefore modeled after Versailles to a greater or lesser extent. One such palace was

Schönbrunn, an enormous Viennese Versailles begun in 1695 by Emperor Leopold to celebrate Austrian military victories and Habsburg might. Charles XI of Sweden, having reduced the power of the aristocracy, ordered the construction in 1693 of his Royal Palace, which dominates the center of Stockholm to this day. Frederick I of Prussia began his imposing new royal residence in Berlin in 1701, the same year he attained the title of king.

Petty princes in the German lands also contributed mightily to the palace-building mania. Frederick the Great of Prussia noted that every descendent of a princely family "imagines himself to be something like Louis XIV. He builds his Versailles, has his mistresses, and maintains his army."[11] The not-very-important elector-archbishop of Mainz, the ruling prince of that city, confessed apologetically that "building is a craze which costs much, but every fool likes his own hat."[12] The archbishop of Mainz's own "hat" was an architectural gem, like that of another churchly ruler, the prince-bishop of Würzburg.

In central and eastern Europe, the favorite noble servants of royalty became extremely rich and powerful, and they, too, built grandiose palaces in the capital cities. These palaces were in part an extension of the monarch, for they surpassed the buildings of less favored nobles and showed all the high road to fame and fortune. Take, for example, the palaces of Prince Eugene of Savoy. A French nobleman by birth and education, Prince Eugene entered the service of Emperor Leopold I with the relief of the besieged Vienna in 1683 and became Austria's most famous military hero. It was Eugene who led the Austrian army, smashed the Turks, fought Louis XIV to a standstill, and generally guided the triumph of absolutism in Austria. Rewarded with great wealth by his grateful royal employer, Eugene called on the leading architects of the day, J. B. Fischer von Erlach and Johann Lukas von Hildebrandt, to consecrate his glory in stone and fresco. Fischer built Eugene's Winter (or Town) Palace in Vienna, and he and Hildebrandt collaborated on the prince's Summer Palace on the city's outskirts.

The Summer Palace was actually two enormous buildings, the Lower Belvedere and the Upper Belvedere, completed in 1713 and 1722 respectively and joined by one of the most exquisite gardens in Europe. The Upper Belvedere, Hildebrandt's masterpiece, stood gracefully, even playfully, behind a great sheet of water. One entered through magnificent iron gates into a hall where sculptured crouching giants served as pillars; then one moved on to a great staircase of dazzling whiteness and ornamentation. Even today the emotional impact of this building is great: here art and beauty create a sense of immense power and wealth.

Palaces like the Upper Belvedere were magnificent examples of the baroque style. They expressed the baroque delight in bold, sweeping statements, which were intended to provide a dramatic emotional experience. To create this experience, baroque masters dissolved the traditional artistic frontiers: the architect permitted the painter and the artisan to cover a building's undulating surfaces with wildly colorful paintings, graceful sculptures, and fanciful carvings. Space was used in a highly original way to blend everything together in a total environment. These techniques shone in all their glory in the churches of southern Ger-

many and in the colossal halls of royal palaces. Artistic achievement and political statement reinforced each other.

Royal Cities

Absolute monarchs and baroque architects were not content with fashioning ostentatious palaces. They remodeled existing capital cities, or even built new ones, to reflect royal magnificence and the centralization of political power. Karlsruhe, founded in 1715 as the capital city of a small German principality, is one extreme example. There broad, straight avenues radiated out from the palace so that all roads—like all power—were

Würzburg, the Prince-Bishop's Palace   The baroque style brought architects, painters, and sculptors together in harmonious, even playful partnership. This magnificent monumental staircase, designed by Johann Balthasar Neumann in 1735, merges into the vibrant ceiling frescos by Giovanni Battista Tiepolo. A man is stepping out of the picture, and a painted dog resembles a marble statue. *(Erich Lessing/Art Resource, NY)*

focused on the ruler. More typically, the monarch's architects added new urban areas alongside the old city; these areas then became the real heart of the expanding capital.

The distinctive features of these new additions were their broad avenues, their imposing government buildings, and their rigorous mathematical layout. Along these major thoroughfares nobles built elaborate baroque townhouses; stables and servants' quarters were built on the alleys behind. Wide avenues also facilitated the rapid movement of soldiers through the city to quell any disturbance (the king's planners had the needs of the military constantly in mind). Under the arcades along the avenues appeared smart and very expensive shops, the first department stores, with plate-glass windows and fancy displays.

The new avenues brought reckless speed to European cities all across the continent. Whereas everyone had walked through the narrow, twisting streets of the medieval town, the high and mighty now raced down the broad boulevards in their elegant carriages. A social gap opened between the wealthy riders and the gaping, dodging pedestrians. "Mind the carriages!" wrote one eighteenth-century observer in Paris:

Here comes the black-coated physician in his chariot, the dancing master in his coach, the fencing master in his surrey—and the Prince behind six horses at the gallop as if he were in the open country. . . . The threatening wheels of the overbearing rich drive as rapidly as ever over stones stained with the blood of their unhappy victims.[13]

Speeding carriages on broad avenues, an endless parade of power and position: here were the symbols and substance of the baroque city.

The Growth of St. Petersburg

No city illustrated better than St. Petersburg the close ties among politics, architecture, and urban development in this period. In 1700, when the Great Northern War between Russia and Sweden began, the city did not exist. There was only a small Swedish fortress on one of the waterlogged islands at the mouth of the Neva River, where it flows into the Baltic Sea. In 1702 Peter the Great's armies seized this desolate outpost. Within a year the reforming tsar had decided to build a new city there and to make it, rather than ancient Moscow, his capital.

Since the first step was to secure the Baltic coast, military construction was the main concern for the next eight years. A mighty fortress was built on Peter Island,

and a port and shipyards were built across the river on the mainland as a Russian navy came into being. The land was swampy and uninhabited, the climate damp and unpleasant. But Peter cared not at all: for him the inhospitable northern marshland was a future metropolis, gloriously bearing his name.

After the decisive Russian victory at Poltava in 1709 greatly reduced the threat of Swedish armies, Peter moved into high gear. In one imperious decree after another, he ordered his people to build a city that would equal any in the world. Such a city had to be Western and baroque, just as Peter's army had to be Western and permanent. From such a new city, his "window on Europe," Peter also believed it would be easier to reform the country militarily and administratively.

These general political goals matched Peter's architectural ideas, which had been influenced by his travels in western Europe. First, Peter wanted a comfortable, "modern" city. Modernity meant broad, straight, stone-paved avenues; houses built in a uniform line and not haphazardly set back from the street; large parks; canals for drainage; stone bridges; and street lighting. Second, all building had to conform strictly to detailed architectural regulations set down by the government. Finally, each social group—the nobility, the merchants, the artisans, and so on—was to live in a certain section of town. In short, the city and its population were to conform to a carefully defined urban plan of the baroque type.

Peter used the traditional but reinforced methods of Russian autocracy to build his modern capital. The creation of St. Petersburg was just one of the heavy obligations he dictatorially imposed on all social groups in Russia. The peasants bore the heaviest burdens. Just as the government drafted peasants for the army, it also drafted twenty-five thousand to forty thousand men each summer to labor in St. Petersburg for three months without pay. Every ten to fifteen peasant households had to furnish one such worker each summer and then pay a special tax in order to feed that worker in St. Petersburg.

Peasants hated this forced labor in the capital, and each year one-fourth to one-third of those sent risked brutal punishment and ran away. Many peasant construction workers died each summer from hunger, sickness, and accidents. Many also died because peasant villages tended to elect old men or young boys to labor in St. Petersburg since strong and able-bodied men were desperately needed on the farm in the busy summer months. Thus beautiful St. Petersburg was built on the shoveling, carting, and paving of a mass of conscripted serfs.

St. Petersburg, ca 1760   Rastrelli's remodeled Winter Palace, which housed the royal family until the Russian Revolution of 1917, stands on the left along the Neva River. The Navy Office with its famous golden spire and other government office buildings are nearby and across the river. Russia became a naval power and St. Petersburg a great port. *(Michael Holford)*

Peter also drafted more privileged groups to his city, but on a permanent basis. Nobles were summarily ordered to build costly stone houses and palaces in St. Petersburg and to live in them most of the year. The more serfs a noble possessed, the bigger his dwelling had to be. Merchants and artisans were also commanded to settle and build in St. Petersburg. These nobles and merchants were then required to pay for the city's avenues, parks, canals, embankments, pilings, and bridges, all of which were very costly in terms of both money and lives because they were built on a swamp. The building of St. Petersburg was, in truth, an enormous direct tax levied on the wealthy, which in turn forced the peasantry to do most of the work. The only immediate beneficiaries were the foreign architects and urban planners. No wonder so many Russians hated Peter's new city.

Yet the tsar had his way. By the time of his death in 1725, there were at least six thousand houses and nu-

merous impressive government buildings in St. Petersburg. Under the remarkable women who ruled Russia throughout most of the eighteenth century, St. Petersburg blossomed fully as a majestic and well-organized city, at least in its wealthy showpiece sections. Peter's youngest daughter, the quick-witted Elizabeth (r. 1741–1762), named as her chief architect Bartolomeo Rastrelli, who had come to Russia from Italy as a boy of fifteen in 1715. Combining Italian and Russian traditions into a unique, wildly colorful St. Petersburg style, Rastrelli built many palaces for the nobility and all the larger government buildings erected during Elizabeth's reign. He also rebuilt the Winter Palace as an enormous, aqua-colored royal residence, now the Hermitage Museum. There Elizabeth established a flashy, luxury-loving, and slightly crude court, which Catherine the Great in turn made truly imperial. All the while St. Petersburg grew rapidly, and its almost 300,000 inhabitants in 1782 made it one of the world's largest cities. Peter and his successors had created out of nothing a magnificent and harmonious royal city, which unmistakably proclaimed the power of Russia's rulers and the creative potential of the absolutist state.

SUMMARY

From about 1400 to 1650, social and economic developments in eastern Europe increasingly diverged from those in western Europe. In the east, peasants and townspeople lost precious freedoms, while the nobility increased its power and prestige. It was within this framework of resurgent serfdom and entrenched nobility that Austrian and Prussian monarchs fashioned absolutist states in the seventeenth and early eighteenth centuries. These monarchs won absolutist control over standing armies, permanent taxes, and legislative bodies. But they did not question underlying social and economic relationships. Indeed, they enhanced the privileges of the nobility, which furnished the leading servitors for enlarged armies and growing state bureaucracies.

In Russia the social and economic trends were similar, but the timing of political absolutism was different. Mongol conquest and rule were a crucial experience, and a harsh, indigenous tsarist autocracy was firmly in place by the reign of Ivan the Terrible in the sixteenth century. More than a century later, Peter the Great succeeded in tightening up Russia's traditional absolutism and modernizing it by reforming the army, the bureaucracy, and the defense industry. In Russia and throughout eastern Europe, war and the needs of the state in time of war weighed heavily in the triumph of absolutism.

Triumphant absolutism interacted spectacularly with the arts. Baroque art, which had grown out of the Catholic Reformation's desire to move the faithful and exalt the true faith, admirably suited the secular aspirations of eastern European rulers. They built grandiose baroque palaces, monumental public squares, and even whole cities to glorify their power and majesty. Thus baroque art attained magnificent heights in eastern Europe, symbolizing the ideal and harmonizing with the reality of imperious royal absolutism.

NOTES

1. Quoted in F. L. Carsten, *The Origins of Prussia* (Oxford: Clarendon Press, 1954), p. 152.
2. Ibid., p. 175.
3. H. Rosenberg, *Bureaucracy, Aristocracy, and Autocracy: The Prussian Experience, 1660–1815* (Boston: Beacon Press, 1966), p. 38.
4. Quoted in R. Ergang, *The Potsdam Fuhrer: Frederick William I, Father of Prussian Militarism* (New York: Octagon Books, 1972), pp. 85, 87.
5. Ibid., pp. 6–7, 43.
6. Quoted in R. A. Dorwart, *The Administrative Reforms of Frederick William I of Prussia* (Cambridge, Mass.: Harvard University Press, 1953), p. 226.
7. Quoted in Rosenberg, *Bureaucracy, Aristocracy, and Autocracy,* p. 40.
8. Quoted in N. V. Riasanovsky, *A History of Russia* (New York: Oxford University Press, 1963), p. 79.
9. Quoted in I. Grey, *Ivan III and the Unification of Russia* (New York: Collier Books, 1967), p. 42.
10. Both quoted in R. Pipes, *Russia Under the Old Regime* (New York: Charles Scribner's Sons, 1974), pp. 65, 85.
11. Quoted in Ergang, *The Potsdam Fuhrer,* p. 13.
12. Quoted in J. Summerson, in *The Eighteenth Century: Europe in the Age of Enlightenment,* ed. A. Cobban (New York: McGraw-Hill, 1969), p. 80.
13. Quoted in L. Mumford, *The Culture of Cities* (New York: Harcourt Brace Jovanovich, 1938), p. 97.

SUGGESTED READING

All of the books cited in the Notes are recommended. Carsten's is the best study on early Prussian history, and Rosenberg's is a masterful analysis of the social context of Prussian absolutism. In addition to Ergang's work, an exciting and critical biography of ramrod Frederick William I, there is G. Ritter, *Frederick the Great* (1968), a more sympathetic study of the talented son by one of Germany's most famous conservative historians. G. Craig, *The Politics of the Prussian Army, 1640–1945* (1964), expertly traces the great influence of the military on the Prussian state over three hundred years. A good general account is provided in D. McKay and H. Scott, *The Rise of the Great Powers, 1648–1815* (1983). J. Gagliardo, *Germany Under the Old Regime, 1600–1790* (1991), is an impressive survey of developments in all the German states and provides an excellent bibliography. M. Hughes, *Early Modern Germany, 1477–1802* (1992), is also recommended. R. J. Evans, *The Making of the Habsburg Empire, 1550–1700* (1979), is an impressive achievement. C. Ingrao, *The Habsburg Monarchy, 1618–1815* (1994), is a superior synthesis with an up-to-date bibliography. J. Stoye, *The Siege of Vienna* (1964), is a fascinating account of the last great Ottoman offensive, which is also treated in the interesting study by P. Coles, *The Ottoman Impact on Europe, 1350–1699* (1968).

The Austro-Ottoman conflict is a theme of L. S. Stavrianos, *The Balkans Since 1453* (1977), and D. McKay's fine biography, *Prince Eugene of Savoy* (1978). On the Balkans,

(continued on page 592)

LISTENING TO THE
PAST

A Foreign Traveler in Russia

Russia in the seventeenth century remained a remote and mysterious land for western and even central Europeans, who had few direct contacts with the tsar's dominion. Knowledge of Russia came mainly from occasional travelers who had visited Muscovy and sometimes wrote accounts of what they had seen.

The most famous of these accounts was by the German Adam Olearius (ca 1599–1671), who was sent to Moscow by the duke of Holstein on three diplomatic missions in the 1630s. These missions ultimately proved unsuccessful, but they provided Olearius with a rich store of information for his Travels in Moscovy, *from which the following excerpts are taken. Published in German in 1647 and soon translated into several languages (but not Russian), Olearius's unflattering but well-informed study played a major role in shaping European ideas about Russia.*

The government of the Russians is what political theorists call a "dominating and despotic monarchy," where the sovereign, that is, the tsar or the grand prince who has obtained the crown by right of succession, rules the entire land alone, and all the people are his subjects, and where the nobles and princes no less than the common folk—townspeople and peasants—are his serfs and slaves, whom he rules and treats as a master treats his servants. . . .

If the Russians be considered in respect to their character, customs, and way of life, they are justly to be counted among the barbarians. . . . The vice of drunkenness is so common in this nation, among people of every station, clergy and laity, high and low, men and women, old and young, that when they are seen now and then lying about in the streets, wallowing in the mud, no attention is paid to it, as something habitual. If a cart driver comes upon such a drunken pig whom he happens to know, he shoves him onto his cart and drives him home, where he is paid his fare. No one ever refuses an opportunity to drink and to get drunk,

at any time and in any place, and usually it is done with vodka. . . .

The Russians being naturally tough and born, as it were, for slavery, they must be kept under a harsh and strict yoke and must be driven to do their work with clubs and whips, which they suffer without impatience, because such is their station, and they are accustomed to it. Young and half-grown fellows sometimes come together on certain days and train themselves in fisticuffs, to accustom themselves to receiving blows, and, since habit is second nature, this makes blows given as punishment easier to bear. Each and all, they are slaves and serfs. . . .

Because of slavery and their rough and hard life, the Russians accept war readily and are well suited to it. On certain occasions, if need be, they reveal themselves as courageous and daring soldiers. . . .

Although the Russians, especially the common populace, living as slaves under a harsh yoke, can bear and endure a great deal out of love for their masters, yet if the pressure is beyond measure, then it can be said of them: "Patience, often wounded, finally turned into fury." A dangerous indignation results, turned not so much against their sovereign as against the lower authorities, especially if the people have been much oppressed by them and by their supporters and have not been protected by the higher authorities. And once they are aroused and enraged, it is not easy to appease them. Then, disregarding all dangers that may ensue, they resort to every kind of violence and behave like madmen. . . . They own little; most of them have no feather beds; they lie on cushions, straw, mats, or their clothes; they sleep on benches and, in winter, like the non-Germans [i.e., natives] in Livonia, upon the oven, which serves them for cooking and is flat on the top; here husband, wife, children, servants, and maids huddle together. In some houses in the countryside we saw chickens and pigs under the benches and the ovens. . . .

Russians are not used to delicate food and dainties; their daily food consists of porridge, turnips, cabbage, and cucumbers, fresh and pickled, and in Moscow mostly of big salt fish which stink badly, because of the thrifty use of salt, yet are eaten with relish. . . .

The Russians can endure extreme heat. In the bathhouse they stretch out on benches and let themselves be beaten and rubbed with bunches of birch twigs and wisps of bast (which I could not stand); and when they are hot and red all over and so exhausted that they can bear it no longer in the bathhouse, men and women rush outdoors naked and pour cold water over their bodies; in winter they even wallow in the snow and rub their skin with it as if it were soap; then they go back into the hot bathhouse. And since bathhouses are usually near rivers and brooks, they can throw themselves straight from the hot into the cold bath. . . .

Generally noble families, even the small nobility, rear their daughters in secluded chambers, keeping them hidden from outsiders; and a bridegroom is not allowed to have a look at his bride until he receives her in the bridal chamber. Therefore some happen to be deceived, being given a misshapen and sickly one instead of a fair one, and sometimes a kinswoman or even a maidservant instead of a daughter; of which there have been examples even among the highborn. No wonder therefore that often they live together like cats and dogs and that wife-beating is so common among Russians. . . .

In the Kremlin and in the city there are a great many churches, chapels, and monasteries, both within and without the city walls, over two thousand in all. This is so because every nobleman who has some fortune has a chapel built for himself, and most of them are of stone. The stone churches are round and vaulted inside. . . . They allow neither organs nor any other musical instruments in their churches, saying: Instruments that have neither souls nor life cannot praise God. . . .

In their churches there hang many bells, sometimes five or six, the largest not over two hundredweights. They ring these bells to summon people to church, and also when the priest during mass raises the chalice. In Moscow, because of the multitude of churches and chapels, there are several thousand bells, which during the divine service cre-

❖ A school in Moscow: A seventeenth-century illustration from a children's reader shows the fruits of rebellion and obedience. *(Novosti/Sovfoto)*

ate such a clang and din that one unaccustomed to it listens in amazement.

Questions for Analysis

1. In what ways were all social groups in Russia similar, according to Olearius?

2. How did Olearius characterize the Russians in general? What supporting evidence did he offer for his judgment?

3. Does Olearius's account help explain Stenka Razin's rebellion? In what ways?

4. On the basis of these representative passages, why do you think Olearius's book was so popular and influential in central and western Europe?

Source: G. Vernadsky and R. T. Fisher, Jr., eds., *A Source Book for Russian History.* Copyright © 1972 by Yale University Press. Reprinted by permission.

also see T. Stoianovich, *Balkan Worlds: The First and Last Europe* (1994); and the innovative study M. Todorova, *Imaging the Balkans* (1997). M. Pinson, ed., *The Muslims of Bosnia-Herzegovina: Their Historic Development from the Middle Ages to the Dissolution of Yugoslavia* (1993), is a good introduction.

On eastern European peasants and serfdom, D. Chirot, ed., *The Origins of Backwardness in Eastern Europe: Economics and Politics from the Middle Ages Until the Twentieth Century* (1989), is a wide-ranging introduction, which may be compared with J. Blum, "The Rise of Serfdom in Eastern Europe," *American Historical Review* 62 (July 1957): 807–836. E. Levin, *Sex and Society in the World of the Orthodox Slavs, 900–1700* (1989), carries family history to eastern Europe. R. Mousnier, *Peasant Uprisings in Seventeenth-Century France, Russia, and China* (1970), is a fine comparative study. Another valuable comparative study, analyzing the political struggle between rulers and nobles in Poland, Hungary, Latvia, Moldavia, and Ukraine, is O. Subtelny, *Domination in Eastern Europe* (1986). Also see L. and M. Frey, *Societies in Upheaval: Insurrections in France, Hungary and Spain in the Early Eighteenth Century* (1989). J. Blum, *Lord and Peasant in Russia from the Ninth to the Nineteenth Century* (1961), provides a good look at conditions in rural Russia, and P. Avrich, *Russian Rebels, 1600–1800* (1972), treats some of the violent peasant upheavals those conditions produced. R. Hellie, *Enserfment and Military Change in Muscovy* (1971), is out-standing, as is A. Yanov's provocative *Origins of Autocracy: Ivan the Terrible in Russian History* (1981). In addition to the fine surveys by Pipes and Riasanovsky cited in the Notes, J. Billington, *The Icon and the Axe* (1970), is a stimulating history of early Russian intellectual and cultural developments, such as the great split in the church. M. Raeff, *Origins of the Russian Intelligentsia* (1966), skillfully probes the mind of the Russian nobility in the eighteenth century. James Cracraft, ed., *Peter the Great Transforms Russia,* 3d ed. (1991), groups interpretive essays by leading scholars, and B. H. Sumner, *Peter the Great and the Emergence of Russia* (1962), is a fine brief introduction. These works may be compared with the brilliant biography by Russia's greatest prerevolutionary historian, V. Klyuchevsky, *Peter the Great* (English trans., 1958), and with N. Riasanovsky, *The Image of Peter the Great in Russian History and Thought* (1985). G. Vernadsky and R. Fisher, eds., *A Source Book of Russian History from Early Times to 1917,* 3 vols. (1972), is an invaluable, highly recommended collection of documents and contemporary writings. S. Baron, ed., *The Travels of Olearius in Seventeenth-Century Russia* (1967), is also highly recommended.

Three good books on art and architecture are E. Hempel, *Baroque Art and Architecture in Central Europe* (1965); G. Hamilton, *The Art and Architecture of Russia* (1954); and N. Pevsner, *An Outline of European Architecture,* 6th ed. (1960).

18 Toward a New World-view

Most people are not philosophers, but they nevertheless have a basic outlook on life, a more or less coherent world-view. At the risk of oversimplification, one may say that the world-view of medieval and early modern Europe was primarily religious and theological. Not only did Christian or Jewish teachings form the core of people's spiritual and philosophical beliefs, but religious teachings also permeated all the rest of human thought and activity. Political theory relied on the divine right of kings, for example, and activities ranging from marriage and divorce to business and eating habits were regulated by churches and religious doctrines.

In the course of the eighteenth century, this religious and theological world-view underwent a fundamental transformation among the European upper and comfortable classes. Economically secure and increasingly well educated, these privileged groups of preindustrial Europe interacted with talented writers and as a result often came to see the world primarily in secular and scientific terms. And while few individuals abandoned religious beliefs altogether, the role of churches and religious thinking in earthly affairs and in the pursuit of knowledge was substantially reduced. Among many in the aristocracy and solid middle classes, a new critical, scientific, and very "modern" world-view took shape.

- Why did this momentous change occur?
- How did this new world-view affect the way people thought about society and human relations?
- What impact did this new way of thinking have on political developments and monarchial absolutism?

This chapter will focus on these questions.

✤ THE SCIENTIFIC REVOLUTION

The foremost cause of the change in world-view was the scientific revolution. Modern science—precise knowledge of the physical world based on the union of experimental observations with sophisticated mathematics—crystallized in the seventeenth century. Whereas science had been secondary and subordinate in medieval intellectual life, it became independent and even primary for many educated people in the eighteenth century.

The emergence of modern science was a development of tremendous long-term significance. A noted historian has even said that the scientific revolution of the late sixteenth and seventeenth centuries "outshines everything since the rise of Christianity and reduces the Renaissance and Reformation to the rank of mere episodes, mere internal displacements, within the system of medieval Christendom." The scientific revolution was "the real origin both of the modern world and the modern mentality."[1] This statement is an exaggeration, but not much of one. Of all the great civilizations, only that of the West developed modern science. With the scientific revolution Western society began to acquire its most distinctive traits.

Though historians agree that the scientific revolution was enormously important, they approach it in quite different ways. Some scholars believe that the history of scientific achievement in this period had its own basic "internal" logic and that "nonscientific" factors had quite limited significance. These scholars write brilliant, often highly technical, intellectual studies, but they neglect the broader historical context. Other historians stress "external" economic, social, and religious factors, brushing over the scientific developments themselves. Historians of science now realize that these two approaches need to be brought together. Therefore, let us examine the milestones on the fateful march toward modern science first and then search for the nonscientific influences along the route.

Scientific Thought in 1500

Since developments in astronomy and physics were at the heart of the scientific revolution, one must begin with the traditional European conception of the universe and movement within it. In the early 1500s, traditional European ideas about the universe were still based primarily on the ideas of Aristotle, the great Greek philosopher of the fourth century B.C. These ideas had gradually been recovered during the Middle Ages and then brought into harmony with Christian doctrines by medieval theologians. According to this revised Aristotelian view, a motionless earth was fixed at the center of the universe. Around it moved ten separate transparent crystal spheres. In the first eight spheres were embedded, in turn, the moon, the sun, the five known planets, and the fixed stars. Then followed two spheres added during the Middle Ages to account for slight changes in the positions of the stars over the centuries. Beyond the tenth sphere was heaven, with the throne of God and the souls of the saved. Angels kept the spheres moving in perfect circles.

Aristotle's views, suitably revised by medieval philosophers, also dominated thinking about physics and motion on earth. Aristotle had distinguished sharply between the world of the celestial spheres and that of the earth—the sublunar world. The spheres consisted of a perfect, incorruptible "quintessence," or fifth essence. The sublunar world, however, was made up of four imperfect, changeable elements. The "light" elements (air and fire) naturally moved upward, while the "heavy" elements (water and earth) naturally moved downward. These natural directions of motion did not always prevail, however, for elements were often mixed together and could be affected by an outside force such as a human being. Aristotle and his followers also believed that a uniform force moved an object at a constant speed and that the object would stop as soon as that force was removed.

Aristotle's ideas about astronomy and physics were accepted with minor revisions for two thousand years, and with good reason. First, they offered an understandable, commonsense explanation for what the eye actually saw. Second, Aristotle's science as interpreted by Christian theologians fit neatly with Christian doctrines. It established a home for God and a place for Christian souls. It put human beings at the center of the universe and made them the critical link in a "great chain of being" that stretched from the throne of God to the most lowly insect on earth. Thus science was primarily a branch of theology, and it reinforced religious thought. At the same time, medieval "scientists" were already providing closely reasoned explanations of the universe, explanations they felt were worthy of God's perfect creation.

The Copernican Hypothesis

The desire to explain and thereby glorify God's handiwork led to the first great departure from the medieval system. This departure was the work of the Polish clergyman and astronomer Nicolaus Copernicus (1473–1543). As a young man, Copernicus studied church law and astronomy in various European universities. He saw how professional astronomers still depended for their most accurate calculations on the work of Ptolemy, the last great ancient astronomer, who had lived in Alexandria in the second century A.D. Ptolemy's achievement had been to work out complicated rules to explain the minor irregularities in the movement of the planets. These rules enabled stargazers and astrologers to track the planets with greater precision. Many people

then (and now) believed that the changing relationships between planets and stars influenced and even determined the future.

The young Copernicus was uninterested in astrology and felt that Ptolemy's cumbersome and occasionally inaccurate rules detracted from the majesty of a perfect Creator. He preferred an old Greek idea being discussed in Renaissance Italy: that the sun, rather than the earth, was at the center of the universe. Finishing his university studies and returning to a church position in east Prussia, Copernicus worked on his hypothesis from 1506 to 1530. Never questioning the Aristotelian belief in crystal spheres or the idea that circular motion was most perfect and divine, Copernicus theorized that the stars and planets, including the earth, revolved around a fixed sun. Yet Copernicus was a cautious man. Fearing the ridicule of other astronomers, he did not publish his *On the Revolutions of the Heavenly Spheres* until 1543, the year of his death.

Copernicus's theory had enormous scientific and religious implications, many of which the conservative Copernicus did not anticipate. First, it put the stars at rest, their apparent nightly movement simply a result of the earth's rotation. Thus it destroyed the main reason for believing in crystal spheres capable of moving the stars around the earth. Second, Copernicus's theory suggested a universe of staggering size. If in the course of a year the earth moved around the sun and yet the stars appeared to remain in the same place, then the universe was unthinkably large or even infinite. Finally, by characterizing the earth as just another planet, Copernicus destroyed the basic idea of Aristotelian physics—that the earthly world was quite different from the heavenly one. Where, then, was the realm of perfection? Where were heaven and the throne of God?

The Copernican theory quickly brought sharp attacks from religious leaders, especially Protestants. Hearing of Copernicus's work even before it was published, Martin Luther spoke of him as the "new astrologer who wants to prove that the earth moves and goes round. . . . The fool wants to turn the whole art of astronomy upside down." Luther noted that "as the Holy Scripture tells us, so did Joshua bid the sun stand still and not the earth." John Calvin also condemned Copernicus, citing as evidence the first verse of Psalm 93: "The world also is established that it cannot be moved." "Who," asked Calvin, "will venture to place the authority of Copernicus above that of the Holy Spirit?"[2] Catholic reaction was milder at first. The Catholic church had never been hypnotized by literal interpretations of the Bible, and not until 1616 did it officially declare the Copernican theory false.

The Geometry Room at Cracow
The young Copernicus sat in this classroom at the University of Cracow, where he first studied astronomy and mathematics and began to ponder the universe. Diagrams illustrating principles of Euclidean geometry were permanently painted on the walls. *(Erich Lessing/Art Resource, NY)*

This slow reaction also reflected the slow progress of Copernicus's theory for many years. Other events were almost as influential in creating doubts about traditional astronomical ideas. In 1572 a new star appeared and shone very brightly for almost two years. The new star, which was actually a distant exploding star, made an enormous impression on people. It seemed to contradict the idea that the heavenly spheres were unchanging and therefore perfect. In 1577 a new comet suddenly moved through the sky, cutting a straight path across the supposedly impenetrable crystal spheres. It was time, as a typical scientific writer put it, for "the radical renovation of astronomy."[3]

From Brahe to Galileo

One astronomer who agreed was Tycho Brahe (1546–1601). Born into a leading Danish noble family and earmarked for a career in government, Brahe was at an early age tremendously impressed when a partial eclipse of the sun occurred exactly as expected. It seemed to him "something divine that men could know the motions of the stars so accurately that they were able a long time beforehand to predict their places and relative positions."[4] Completing his studies abroad and returning to Denmark, Brahe established himself as Europe's leading astronomer with his detailed observations of the new star of 1572. Aided by generous grants from the king of Denmark, Brahe built the most sophisti-

cated observatory of his day. For twenty years he meticulously observed the stars and planets with the naked eye. An imposing man who had lost a piece of his nose in a duel and replaced it with a special bridge of gold and silver alloy, a noble who exploited his peasants arrogantly and approached the heavens humbly, Brahe's great contribution was his mass of data. His limited understanding of mathematics prevented him, however, from making much sense out of his data. Part Ptolemaic, part Copernican, he believed that all the planets revolved around the sun and that the entire group of sun and planets revolved in turn around the earth-moon system.

It was left to Brahe's brilliant young assistant, Johannes Kepler (1571–1630), to go much further. Kepler was a medieval figure in many ways. Coming from a minor German noble family and trained for the Lutheran ministry, he long believed that the universe was built on mystical mathematical relationships and a musical harmony of the heavenly bodies. Working and reworking Brahe's mountain of observations in a staggering sustained effort after the Dane's death, this brilliant mathematician eventually went beyond mystical intuitions.

Kepler formulated three famous laws of planetary motion. First, building on Copernican theory, he demonstrated in 1609 that the orbits of the planets around the sun are elliptical rather than circular. Second, he demonstrated that the planets do not move at a uniform speed in their orbits. Third, in 1619 he showed that the time a planet takes to make its complete orbit is precisely related to its distance from the sun. Kepler's contribution was monumental. Whereas Copernicus had speculated, Kepler proved mathematically the precise relations of a sun-centered (solar) system. His work demolished the old system of Aristotle and Ptolemy, and in his third law he came close to formulating the idea of universal gravitation.

While Kepler was unraveling planetary motion, a young Florentine named Galileo Galilei (1564–1642) was challenging all the old ideas about motion. Like so many early scientists, Galileo was a poor nobleman first marked for a religious career. However, he soon became fascinated by mathematics. A brilliant student, Galileo became a professor of mathematics in 1589 at age twenty-five. He proceeded to examine motion and mechanics in a new way. Indeed, his great achievement was the elaboration and consolidation of the modern experimental method. That is, rather than speculate about what might or should happen, Galileo conducted controlled experiments to find out what actually *did* happen.

In his famous acceleration experiment, he showed that a uniform force—in this case, gravity—produced a uniform acceleration. Here is how Galileo described his pathbreaking method and conclusion in his *Two New Sciences*:

A piece of wooden moulding . . . was taken; on its edge was cut a channel a little more than one finger in breadth. Having made this groove very straight, smooth and polished, and having lined it with parchment, also as smooth and polished as possible, we rolled along it a hard, smooth and very round bronze ball. . . . Noting . . . the time required to make the descent . . . we now rolled the ball only one-quarter the length of the channel; and having measured the time of its descent, we found it precisely one-half of the former. . . . In such experiments [over many distances], repeated a full hundred times, we always found that the spaces traversed were to each other as the squares of the times, and that this was true for all inclinations of the plane.[5]

With this and other experiments, Galileo also formulated the law of inertia. Rest was not the natural state of objects. Rather, an object continues in motion forever unless stopped by some external force. Aristotelian physics was in a shambles.

In the tradition of Brahe, Galileo also applied the experimental method to astronomy. His astronomical discoveries had a great impact on scientific development. On hearing details about the invention of the telescope

in Holland, Galileo made one for himself and trained it on the heavens. He quickly discovered the first four moons of Jupiter, which clearly suggested that Jupiter could not possibly be embedded in any impenetrable crystal sphere. This discovery provided new evidence for the Copernican theory, in which Galileo already believed.

Galileo then pointed his telescope at the moon. He wrote in 1610 in *Siderus Nuncius*:

I feel sure that the moon is not perfectly smooth, free from inequalities, and exactly spherical, as a large school of philosophers considers with regard to the moon and the other heavenly bodies. On the contrary, it is full of inequalities, uneven, full of hollows and protuberances, just like the surface of the earth itself, which is varied. . . . The next object which I have observed is the essence or substance of the Milky Way. By the aid of a telescope anyone may behold this in a manner which so distinctly appeals to the senses that all the disputes which have tormented philosophers through so many ages are exploded by the irrefutable evidence of our eyes, and we are freed from wordy disputes upon the subject. For the galaxy is nothing else but a mass of innumerable stars planted together in clusters.[6]

Reading these famous lines, one feels a crucial corner in Western civilization being turned. The traditional religious and theological world-view, which rested on determining and accepting the proper established authority, was beginning to give way in certain fields to a critical, scientific method. This new method of learning and investigating was the greatest accomplishment of the entire scientific revolution, for it proved capable of great extension. A historian investigating documents of the past, for example, is not so different from a Galileo studying stars and rolling balls.

Galileo was employed in Florence by the Medici grand dukes of Tuscany, and his work eventually aroused the ire of some theologians. The issue was presented in 1624 to Pope Urban VIII, who permitted Galileo to write about different possible systems of the world as long as he did not presume to judge which one actually existed. After the publication in Italian of his widely read *Dialogue on the Two Chief Systems of the World* in 1632, which openly lampooned the traditional views of Aristotle and Ptolemy and defended those of Copernicus, Galileo was tried for heresy by the papal Inquisition. Imprisoned and threatened with torture, the aging Galileo recanted, "renouncing and cursing" his Copernican errors. Of minor importance in the development of science, Galileo's trial later became for some writers the perfect symbol of the inherent conflict between religious belief and scientific knowledge.

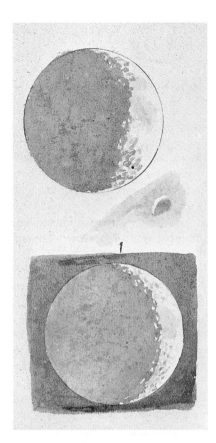
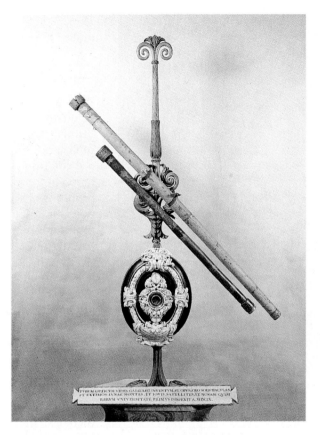

Galileo's Paintings of the Moon   When Galileo published the results of his telescopic observations of the moon, he added these paintings to illustrate the marvels he had seen. Galileo made two telescopes, which are shown here. The larger one magnifies 14 times, the smaller 20 times. *(Biblioteca Nazionale Centrale, Florence; Museum of Science, Florence/Scala/Art Resource, NY)*

Newton's Synthesis

The accomplishments of Kepler, Galileo, and other scientists had taken effect by about 1640. The old astronomy and physics were in ruins, and several fundamental breakthroughs had been made. The new findings had not, however, been fused together in a new synthesis, a single explanatory system that would comprehend motion both on earth and in the skies. That synthesis, which prevailed until the twentieth century, was the work of Isaac Newton (1642–1727).

Newton was born into lower English gentry and attended Cambridge University. A genius who spectacularly united the experimental and theoretical-mathematical sides of modern science, Newton was also fascinated by alchemy. He sought the elixir of life and a way to change base metals into gold and silver. Not without reason did the twentieth-century economist John Maynard Keynes call Newton the "last of the magicians." Newton was also intensely religious. He was

far from being the perfect rationalist so endlessly eulogized by writers in the eighteenth and nineteenth centuries.

Of his intellectual genius and incredible powers of concentration there can be no doubt, however. Arriving at some of his most basic ideas about physics in 1666 at age twenty-four, but unable to prove these theories mathematically, he attained a professorship and studied optics for many years. In 1684 Newton returned to physics for eighteen extraordinarily intensive months. For weeks on end he seldom left his room except to read his lectures. His meals were sent up, but he usually forgot to eat them, his mind fastened like a vise on the laws of the universe. He opened the third book of his immortal *Mathematical Principles of Natural Philosophy*, published in Latin in 1687 and generally known as the *Principia*, with these lines:

In the preceding books I have laid down the principles of philosophy [that is, science]. . . . These principles are the

Isaac Newton   This portrait suggests the depth and complexity of the great genius. Is the powerful mind behind those piercing eyes thinking of science or of religion, or perhaps of both? *(Scala/Art Resource, NY)*

laws of certain motions, and powers or forces, which chiefly have respect to philosophy. . . . It remains that from the same principles I now demonstrate the frame of the System of the World.

Newton made good his grandiose claim. His towering accomplishment was to integrate in a single explanatory system the astronomy of Copernicus, as corrected by Kepler's laws, with the physics of Galileo and his predecessors. Newton did this by means of a set of mathematical laws that explain motion and mechanics. These laws of dynamics are complex, and it took scientists and engineers two hundred years to work out all their implications. Nevertheless, the key feature of the Newtonian synthesis was the law of universal gravitation. According to this law, every body in the universe attracts every other body in the universe in a precise mathematical relationship, whereby the force of attraction is proportional to the quantity of matter of the objects and inversely proportional to the square of the distance between them. The whole universe—from

Kepler's elliptical orbits to Galileo's rolling balls—was unified in one majestic system.

Causes of the Scientific Revolution

With a charming combination of modesty and self-congratulation, Newton once wrote, "If I have seen further [than others], it is by standing on the shoulders of Giants."[7] Surely the path from Copernicus to Newton confirms the "internal" view of the scientific revolution as a product of towering individual genius. The problems of science were inherently exciting, and solution of those problems was its own reward for inquisitive, high-powered minds. Yet there were certainly broader causes as well.

First, the long-term contribution of medieval intellectual life and medieval universities to the scientific revolution was much more considerable than historians unsympathetic to the Middle Ages once believed. By the thirteenth century, permanent universities with professors and large student bodies had been established in western Europe. These universities were supported by society because they trained the lawyers, doctors, and church leaders that society required. By 1300 philosophy had taken its place alongside law, medicine, and theology. Medieval philosophers developed a limited but real independence from theologians and a sense of free inquiry. They nobly pursued a body of knowledge and tried to arrange it meaningfully by means of abstract theories.

Within this framework, science was able to emerge as a minor but distinct branch of philosophy. In the fourteenth and fifteenth centuries, first in Italy and then elsewhere in Europe, leading universities established new professorships of mathematics, astronomy, and physics (natural philosophy) within their faculties of philosophy. Although the prestige of the new fields was low among both professors and students, the pattern of academic science, which grew out of the medieval commitment to philosophy and did not change substantially until the late eighteenth century, undoubtedly promoted scientific development. Rational, critical thinking was applied to scientific problems by a permanent community of scholars. And an outlet existed for the talents of a Galileo or a Newton: all the great pathfinders either studied or taught at universities.

Second, the Renaissance also stimulated scientific progress. One of the great deficiencies of medieval science was its rather rudimentary mathematics. The recovery of the finest works of Greek mathematics—a byproduct of Renaissance humanism's ceaseless search for the knowledge of antiquity—greatly improved European mathematics well into the early seventeenth century. The recovery of more texts also showed that classical mathematicians had their differences; Europeans were thus forced to resolve, if possible, these ancient controversies by means of their own efforts. Finally, the Renaissance pattern of patronage, especially in Italy, was often scientific as well as artistic and humanistic. Various rulers and wealthy business people supported scientific investigations, as the Medicis of Florence supported those of Galileo.

The navigational problems of long sea voyages in the age of overseas expansion were a third factor in the scientific revolution. Ship captains on distant shores needed to be able to chart their positions as accurately as possible so that reliable maps could be drawn and the risks of international trade reduced. As early as 1484, the king of Portugal appointed a commission of mathematicians to perfect tables to help seamen find their latitude. This resulted in the first European navigation manual.

The problem of fixing longitude was much more difficult. In England the government and the great capitalistic trading companies turned to science and scientific education in an attempt to solve this pressing practical problem. When the famous Elizabethan financier Sir Thomas Gresham left a large amount of money to establish Gresham College in London, he stipulated that three of the college's seven professors had to concern themselves exclusively with scientific subjects. The professor of astronomy was directed to teach courses on the science of navigation. A seventeenth-century popular ballad took note of the new college's calling:

This college will the whole world measure
Which most impossible conclude,
And navigation make a pleasure
By finding out the longitude.[8]

At Gresham College scientists had, for the first time in history, an important, honored role in society. They enjoyed close ties with top officials of the Royal Navy and with leading merchants and shipbuilders. Gresham College became the main center of scientific activity in England in the first half of the seventeenth century. The close tie between practical men and scientists also led to the establishment in 1662 of the Royal Society of London, which published scientific papers and sponsored scientific meetings.

Navigational problems were also critical in the development of many new scientific instruments, such as the telescope, barometer, thermometer, pendulum clock, microscope, and air pump. Better instruments, which permitted more accurate observations, often led to

The Observatory at Nuremberg   The quest for scientific knowledge in the seventeenth century was already an expensive undertaking that required teamwork and government support, as this encyclopedic illustration suggests. Nuremberg was a historic center of commerce and culture in southern Germany, and its observatory played a pioneering role in early astronomical advance. *(Kunstsammlungen der Veste Coburg)*

important new knowledge. Galileo with his telescope was by no means unique.

Better instruments were part of a fourth factor in the scientific revolution, the development of better ways of obtaining knowledge about the world. Two important thinkers, Francis Bacon (1561–1626) and René Descartes (1596–1650), represented key aspects of this improvement in scientific methodology.

The English politician and writer Francis Bacon was the greatest early propagandist for the new experimental method, as Galileo was its greatest early practitioner. Rejecting the Aristotelian and medieval method of using speculative reasoning to build general theories, Bacon argued that new knowledge had to be pursued through empirical, experimental research. That is, the researcher who wants to learn more about leaves or rocks should not speculate about the subject but rather collect a multitude of specimens and then compare and analyze them. Thus freed from sterile medieval speculation, the facts will speak for themselves, and important general principles will then emerge. Knowledge will increase. Bacon's contribution was to formalize the empirical method, which had already been used by Brahe and Galileo, into the general theory of inductive reasoning known as *empiricism*.

Bacon claimed that the empirical method would result not only in more knowledge but also in highly practical, useful knowledge. According to Bacon, scientific discoveries like those so avidly sought at Gresham College would bring about much greater control over the physical environment and make people rich and nations powerful. Thus Bacon helped provide a radically new and effective justification for private and public support of scientific inquiry.

The French philosopher René Descartes was a true genius who made his first great discovery in mathematics. As a twenty-three-year-old soldier serving in the Thirty Years' War, he experienced on a single night in 1619 a life-changing intellectual vision. Descartes saw that there was a perfect correspondence between geometry and algebra and that geometrical, spatial figures could be expressed as algebraic equations and vice versa. A major step forward in the history of mathematics, Descartes's discovery of analytic geometry provided scientists with an important new tool. Spending much of his adult life in the Netherlands, Descartes also made contributions to the science of optics. But his greatest achievement was to develop his initial vision into a whole philosophy of knowledge and science.

Like Bacon, Descartes scorned traditional science and had great faith in the powers of the human mind.

Yet Descartes was much more systematic and mathematical than Bacon. He decided it was necessary to doubt everything that could reasonably be doubted and then, as in geometry, to use deductive reasoning from self-evident principles to ascertain scientific laws. Descartes's reasoning ultimately reduced all substances to "matter" and "mind"—that is, to the physical and the spiritual. His view of the world as consisting of two fundamental entities is known as *Cartesian dualism*. Descartes was a profoundly original and extremely influential thinker.

Bacon's inductive experimentalism and Descartes's deductive, mathematical rationalism are combined in the modern scientific method, which began to crystallize in the late seventeenth century. Neither man's extreme approach was sufficient by itself. Bacon's inability to appreciate the importance of mathematics and his obsession with practical results clearly showed the limitations of antitheoretical empiricism. Likewise, some of Descartes's positions—he believed, for example, that it was possible to deduce the whole science of medicine from first principles—aptly demonstrated the inadequacy of rigid, dogmatic rationalism. Thus the modern scientific method has joined precise observations and experimentalism with the search for general laws that may be expressed in rigorously logical, mathematical language.

Finally, there is the question of the role of religion in the development of science. Just as some historians have argued that Protestantism led to the rise of capitalism, others have concluded that Protestantism was a fundamental factor in the rise of modern science. Protestantism, particularly in its Calvinist varieties, supposedly made scientific inquiry a question of individual conscience and not of religious doctrine. The Catholic church, in contrast, supposedly suppressed scientific theories that conflicted with its teachings and thus discouraged scientific progress.

The truth of the matter is more complicated. *All* religious authorities—Catholic, Protestant, and Jewish—opposed the Copernican system to a greater or lesser extent until about 1630, by which time the scientific revolution was definitely in progress. The Catholic church was initially less hostile than Protestant and Jewish religious leaders. This early Catholic toleration and the scientific interests of Renaissance Italy helped account for the undeniable fact that Italian scientists played a crucial role in scientific progress right up to the trial of Galileo in 1633. Thereafter, the Counter-Reformation church became more hostile to science, a change that helped account for the decline of science in

Descartes in Sweden   Queen Christina of Sweden encouraged art and science, and she invited many foreign artists and scholars to visit her court. She speaks here with French mathematician and philosopher René Descartes in 1649. The daughter of Protestant hero Gustavus Adolphus, Christina rejected marriage, abdicated in 1654, converted to Catholicism, and died in Rome. *(Versailles/Bulloz)*

Italy (but not in Catholic France) after 1640. At the same time, Protestant countries such as the Netherlands and Denmark became quite "proscience," especially if the country lacked a strong religious authority capable of imposing religious orthodoxy on scientific questions.

This was certainly the case with Protestant England after 1630. English religious conflicts became so intense that the authorities could not impose religious unity on anything, including science. Significantly, the forerunners of the Royal Society agreed to discuss only "neutral" scientific questions so as not to come to blows over closely related religious and political disputes. The work of Bacon's many followers during Oliver Cromwell's commonwealth helped solidify the neutrality and independence of science. Bacon advocated the experimental approach precisely because it was open-minded and independent of any preconceived religious or philosophical ideas. Neutral and useful, science became an accepted part of life and developed rapidly in England after about 1640.

Some Consequences of the Scientific Revolution

The rise of modern science had many consequences, some of which are still unfolding. First, it went hand in hand with the rise of a new and expanding social group—the international scientific community. Members of this community were linked together by common interests and shared values as well as by journals and the learned scientific societies founded in many countries in the later seventeenth and the eighteenth centuries. Expansion of knowledge was the primary goal of this community, and scientists' material and psychological rewards depended on their success in this endeavor. Thus science became quite competitive, and even more scientific advance was inevitable.

Second, the scientific revolution introduced not only new knowledge about nature but also a new and revolutionary way of obtaining such knowledge—the modern scientific method. In addition to being both theoretical and experimental, this method was highly critical, and it differed profoundly from the old way of getting knowledge about nature. It refused to base its conclusions on tradition and established sources, on ancient authorities and sacred texts.

The scientific revolution had few consequences for economic life and the living standards of the masses until the late eighteenth century at the very earliest. True, improvements in the techniques of navigation facilitated overseas trade and helped enrich leading merchants. But science had relatively few practical economic applications, and the hopes of the early Baconians were frustrated. The close link between theoretical, or pure, science and applied technology, which we take for granted today, simply did not exist in the eighteenth century. Thus the scientific revolution of the seventeenth century was first and foremost an intellectual revolution. It is not surprising that for more than a hundred years its greatest impact was on how people thought and believed.

✠ THE ENLIGHTENMENT

The scientific revolution was the single most important factor in the creation of the new world-view of the eighteenth-century Enlightenment. This world-view, which has played a large role in shaping the modern mind, grew out of a rich mix of ideas. These ideas were diverse and often conflicting, for the talented (and not-so-talented) writers who espoused them competed vigorously for the attention of a growing public of well-educated but fickle readers, who remained a small minority of the population. Despite this diversity, three central concepts stand at the core of Enlightenment thinking.

The most important and original idea of the Enlightenment was that the methods of natural science could and should be used to examine and understand all aspects of life. This was what intellectuals meant by *reason,* a favorite word of Enlightenment thinkers. Nothing was to be accepted on faith. Everything was to be submitted to the rational, critical, scientific way of thinking. This approach often brought the Enlightenment into a head-on conflict with established churches, which rested their beliefs on the special authority of the Bible and Christian theology. A second important Enlightenment concept was that the scientific method was capable of discovering the laws of human society as well as those of nature. Thus was social science born. Its birth led to the third key idea, that of progress. Armed with the proper method of discovering the laws of human existence, Enlightenment thinkers believed that it was at least possible for human beings to create better societies and better people. Their belief was strengthened by some modest improvements in economic and social life during the eighteenth century.

The Enlightenment was therefore profoundly secular. It revived and expanded the Renaissance concentration on worldly explanations. In the course of the eighteenth century, the Enlightenment had a profound impact on the thought and culture of the urban middle classes and the aristocracy. It did not, however, have much appeal for the urban poor and the peasants, who were preoccupied with the struggle for survival and who often resented the Enlightenment attack on traditional popular beliefs (see Chapters 19 and 20).

The Emergence of the Enlightenment

Loosely united by certain key ideas, the European Enlightenment was a broad intellectual and cultural movement that gained strength gradually and did not reach its maturity until about 1750. Yet it was the generation that came of age between the publication of Newton's *Principia* in 1687 and the death of Louis XIV in 1715 that tied the crucial knot between the scientific revolution and a new outlook on life.

Talented writers of that generation popularized hard-to-understand scientific achievements for the educated elite. The most famous and influential popularizer was a versatile French man of letters, Bernard de Fontenelle (1657–1757). He set out to make science witty and entertaining for a broad nonscientific audience, as easy to read as a novel. This was a tall order, but Fontenelle largely succeeded.

His most famous work, *Conversations on the Plurality of Worlds* (1686), begins with two elegant figures walking in the gathering shadows of a large park. One is a woman, a sophisticated aristocrat, and the other is her friend, perhaps even her lover. They gaze at the stars, and their talk turns to a passionate discussion of . . . astronomy! He confides that "each star may well be a different world," then gently stresses how error is giving way to truth. At one point he explains:

There came on the scene . . . one Copernicus, who made short work of all those various circles, all those solid skies, which the ancients had pictured to themselves. . . . Fired with the noble zeal of a true astronomer, he took the earth and spun it very far away from the center of the universe, where it had been installed, and in that center he put the sun, which had a far better title to the honor.[9]

Rather than despair at this dismissal of traditional understanding, Fontenelle's lady rejoices in the knowledge that the human mind is capable of making great progress.

This idea of progress was essentially a creation of the later seventeenth century. Medieval and Reformation thinkers had been concerned primarily with sin and salvation. The humanists of the Renaissance had emphasized worldly matters, but they had looked backward. They had believed it might be possible to equal the magnificent accomplishments of the ancients, but they did not ask for more. Fontenelle and like-minded writers had come to believe that at least in science and mathematics, their era had gone far beyond antiquity. Progress, at least intellectual progress, was very possible.

Popularizing Science   The frontispiece illustration of Fontenelle's *Conversations on the Plurality of Worlds* invites the reader to share the pleasures of astronomy with an elegant lady and an entertaining teacher. The drawing shows the planets revolving around the sun. *(By permission of the Syndics of Cambridge University Library)*

Fontenelle and other writers of his generation were also instrumental in bringing science into conflict with religion. This was a major innovation because many seventeenth-century scientists, both Catholic and Protestant, believed that their work exalted God. They did not draw antireligious implications from their scientific findings. The greatest scientist of them all, Isaac Newton, was a devout, if unorthodox, Christian who saw all of his studies as directed toward explaining God's message.

Fontenelle, in contrast, was skeptical about absolute truth and cynical about the claims of organized religion. Since such unorthodox views could not be stated openly in an absolute monarchy like Louis XIV's France, Fontenelle made his point through subtle editorializing about science. His depiction of the cautious Copernicus as a self-conscious revolutionary was typical. In *Eulogies of Scientists,* Fontenelle exploited with endless variations the fundamental theme of rational, progressive scientists versus prejudiced, reactionary priests.

The progressive and antireligious implications that writers such as Fontenelle drew from the scientific revolution reflected a very real crisis in European thought at the end of the seventeenth century. This crisis had its roots in several intellectual uncertainties and dissatisfactions, of which the demolition of Aristotelian-medieval science was only one.

A second uncertainty involved the whole question of religious truth. The destructive wars of religion that culminated in the Thirty Years' War (1618–1648) had been fought, in part, because religious freedom was an intolerable idea in Europe in the early seventeenth century. Both Catholics and Protestants had believed that religious truth was absolute and therefore worth fighting and dying for. Most Catholics and Protestants also believed that a strong state required unity in religious faith. Yet the disastrous results of the many attempts to impose such religious unity, such as Louis XIV's brutal expulsion of the French Huguenots in 1685, led some people to ask if ideological conformity in religious matters was really necessary. Others skeptically asked if religious truth could ever be known with absolute certainty and concluded that it could not.

The most famous of these skeptics was Pierre Bayle (1647–1706), a French Huguenot who despised Louis XIV and found refuge in the Netherlands. A teacher by profession and a crusading journalist by inclination, Bayle took full advantage of the toleration and intellectual freedom of his adopted land. He critically examined the religious beliefs and persecutions of the past in his *Historical and Critical Dictionary,* written in French and published in the Netherlands in 1697. Demonstrating that human beliefs had been extremely varied and very often mistaken, Bayle concluded that nothing can ever be known beyond all doubt. In religion as in philosophy, humanity's best hope was open-minded toleration. Bayle's skeptical views were very influential. Many eighteenth-century writers mined his inexhaustible vein of critical skepticism for ammunition in their attacks on superstition and theology. Reprinted frequently in the Netherlands and in England, Bayle's four-volume *Dictionary* was found in more private libraries of eighteenth-century France than any other book.

The rapidly growing travel literature on non-European lands and cultures was a third cause of uncertainty. In the wake of the great discoveries, Europeans were learning that the peoples of China, India, Africa, and the Americas all had their own very different beliefs and customs. Europeans shaved their faces and let their hair grow. Turks shaved their heads and let their beards grow. In Europe a man bowed before a woman to show respect. In Siam a man turned his back on a woman when he met her because it was disrespectful to look directly at her. Countless similar examples discussed in the travel accounts helped change the perspective of educated Europeans. They began to look at truth and morality in relative, rather than absolute, terms. If anything was possible, who could say what was right or wrong?

A fourth cause and manifestation of European intellectual turmoil was John Locke's epoch-making *Essay Concerning Human Understanding.* Published in 1690—the same year Locke published his famous *Second Treatise of Civil Government* (see page 554)—Locke's essay brilliantly set forth a new theory about how human beings learn and form their ideas. In doing so, he rejected the prevailing view of Descartes, who had held that all people are born with certain basic ideas and ways of thinking. Locke insisted that all ideas are derived from experience. The human mind at birth is like a blank tablet *(tabula rasa)* on which the environment writes the individual's understanding and beliefs. Human development is therefore determined by education and social institutions, for good or for evil. Locke's *Essay Concerning Human Understanding* passed through many editions and translations. It was, along with Newton's *Principia,* one of the dominant intellectual inspirations of the Enlightenment.

The Philosophes and the Public

By the time Louis XIV died in 1715, many of the ideas that would soon coalesce into the new world-view had been assembled. Yet Christian Europe was still strongly attached to its traditional beliefs, as witnessed by the powerful revival of religious orthodoxy in the first half of the eighteenth century (see pages 681–683). By the outbreak of the American Revolution in 1775, however, a large portion of western Europe's educated elite had embraced many of the new ideas. This acceptance was the work of one of history's most influential groups of intellectuals, the *philosophes*. It was the philosophes who proudly and effectively proclaimed that they, at long last, were bringing the light of knowledge to their ignorant fellow creatures in an Age of Enlightenment.

Philosophe is the French word for "philosopher," and it was in France that the Enlightenment reached its highest development. There were at least three reasons for this. First, French was the international language of the educated classes in the eighteenth century, and the education of the rich and the powerful across Europe often lay in the hands of French tutors espousing Enlightenment ideas. France's cultural leadership was reinforced by the fact that it was still the wealthiest and most populous country in Europe.

Second, after the death of Louis XIV, French absolutism and religious orthodoxy remained strong, but not too strong. Critical books were often banned by the censors, and their authors were sometimes jailed or exiled—but not tortured or burned. Intellectual radicals battled against powerful opposition in France, but they did not face the overwhelming restraints generally found in eastern and east-central Europe. French thinkers were not, however, fighting for widely accepted liberties, as was the case in the Netherlands and in England (to a lesser extent).

Third, the French philosophes were indeed philosophers, asking fundamental philosophical questions about the meaning of life, God, human nature, good and evil, and cause and effect. But in the tradition of Bayle and Fontenelle, they were not content with abstract arguments or ivory-tower speculations. They were determined to reach and influence all the French (and European) economic and social elites, many of which were joined together in the eighteenth-century concept of the educated or enlightened public, or simply the "public."

As a wealth of recent scholarship has shown, the public was quite different from the great majority of the population, which was known as the common people, or simply the "people." French philosophe Jean le Rond d'Alembert (1717–1783) characteristically made a sharp distinction between "the truly enlightened public" and "the blind and noisy multitude."[10] A leading scholar has even concluded that the differences between the upper and comfortable middling groups that made up the French public were "insignificant" in comparison with the great gulf between the public and the common people.[11] Above all, the philosophes believed that the great majority of the common people were doomed to superstition and confusion because they lacked the money and leisure to look beyond their bitter struggle with grinding poverty (see pages 629–631).

Suspicious of the people but intensely committed to reason, reform, and slow, difficult progress, the great philosophes and their imitators were not free to write as they wished, since it was illegal in France to criticize openly either church or state. Their most radical works had to circulate in manuscript form. Knowing that direct attacks would probably be banned or burned, the philosophes wrote novels and plays, histories and philosophies, dictionaries and encyclopedias, all filled with satire and double meanings to spread their message to the public.

One of the greatest philosophes, the baron de Montesquieu (1689–1755), brilliantly pioneered this approach in *The Persian Letters,* an extremely influential social satire published in 1721. Montesquieu's work consisted of amusing letters supposedly written by Persian travelers, who see European customs in unique ways and thereby cleverly criticize existing practices and beliefs.

Having gained fame by using wit as a weapon against cruelty and superstition, Montesquieu settled down on his family estate to study history and politics. His interest was partly personal, for, like many members of the high French nobility, he was dismayed that royal absolutism had triumphed in France under Louis XIV. But Montesquieu was also inspired by the example of the physical sciences, and he set out to apply the critical method to the problem of government in *The Spirit of Laws* (1748). The result was a complex comparative study of republics, monarchies, and despotisms—a great pioneering inquiry in the emerging social sciences.

Showing that forms of government were shaped by history, geography, and customs, Montesquieu focused on the conditions that would promote liberty and prevent tyranny. He argued that despotism could be avoided if political power was divided and shared by a variety of classes and legal orders holding unequal rights and privileges. A strong, independent upper class was especially important, according to Montesquieu, because in order to prevent the abuse of power, "it is necessary that by the arrangement of things, power checks power." Admiring greatly the English balance of power among the king, the houses of Parliament, and the independent courts, Montesquieu believed that in France the thirteen high courts—the *parlements*—were front-line defenders of liberty against royal despotism. Apprehensive about the uneducated poor, Montesquieu was clearly no democrat, but his theory of separation of powers had a great impact on France's wealthy, well-educated elite. The constitutions of the young United States in 1789 and of France in 1791 were based in large part on this theory.

The most famous and in many ways most representative philosophe was François Marie Arouet, who was

Madame du Châtelet was fascinated by the new world system of Isaac Newton. She helped to spread Newton's ideas in France by translating his *Principia* and by influencing Voltaire, her companion for fifteen years until her death. *(Private Collection/Bulloz)*

known by the pen name Voltaire (1694–1778). In his long career, this son of a comfortable middle-class family wrote more than seventy witty volumes, hobnobbed with kings and queens, and died a millionaire because of shrewd business speculations. His early career, however, was turbulent. In 1717 Voltaire was imprisoned for eleven months in the Bastille in Paris for insulting the regent of France. In 1726 a barb from his sharp tongue led a great French nobleman to have him beaten and arrested. This experience made a deep impression on Voltaire. All his life he struggled against legal injustice and unequal treatment before the law. Released from prison after promising to leave the country, Voltaire lived in England for three years and came to share Montesquieu's enthusiasm for English institutions.

Returning to France and soon threatened again with prison in Paris, Voltaire had the great fortune of meeting Gabrielle-Emilie Le Tonnelier de Breteuil, marquise du Châtelet (1706–1749), an intellectually gifted woman from the high aristocracy with a passion for science. Inviting Voltaire to live in her country house at Cirey in Lorraine and becoming his long-time companion (under the eyes of her tolerant husband), Madame du Châtelet studied physics and mathematics and published scientific articles and translations.

Perhaps the finest representative of a small number of elite Frenchwomen and their scientific accomplishments during the Enlightenment, Madame du Châtelet suffered nonetheless because of her gender. Excluded on principle from the Royal Academy of Sciences and from stimulating interchange with other scientists because she was a woman, she depended on private tutors for instruction and became uncertain of her ability to make important scientific discoveries. Madame du Châtelet therefore concentrated on spreading the ideas of others, and her translation with an accompanying commentary of Newton's *Principia* into French for the first (and only) time was her greatest work. But she, who had patiently explained Newton's complex mathematical proofs to Europe's foremost philosophe, had no doubt that women's limited scientific contributions in the past were due to limited and unequal education. She once wrote that if she were a ruler, "I would reform an abuse which cuts off, so to speak, half the human race. I would make women participate in all the rights of humankind, and above all in those of the intellect."[12]

While living at Cirey, Voltaire wrote various works praising England and popularizing English scientific progress. Newton, he wrote, was history's greatest man, for he had used his genius for the benefit of humanity. "It is," wrote Voltaire, "the man who sways our minds by the prevalence of reason and the native force of truth, not they who reduce mankind to a state of slavery by force and downright violence . . . that claims our reverence and admiration."[13] In the true style of the Enlightenment, Voltaire mixed the glorification of science and reason with an appeal for better individuals and institutions.

Yet like almost all of the philosophes, Voltaire was a reformer, not a revolutionary, in social and political matters. He was eventually appointed royal historian in 1743, and his *Age of Louis XIV* portrayed Louis as the dignified leader of his age. Voltaire also began a long correspondence with Frederick the Great and, after the death of his beloved Emilie, accepted Frederick's invitation to come brighten up the Prussian court in Berlin. The two men later quarreled, but Voltaire always admired Frederick as a free thinker and an enlightened monarch.

Unlike Montesquieu, Voltaire pessimistically concluded that the best one could hope for in the way of government was a good monarch, since human beings "are very rarely worthy to govern themselves." Nor did he believe in social and economic equality in human affairs. The idea of making servants equal to their masters was "absurd and impossible." The only realizable equality, Voltaire thought, was that "by which the citizen only depends on the laws which protect the freedom of the feeble against the ambitions of the strong."[14]

Voltaire's philosophical and religious positions were much more radical. In the tradition of Bayle, Voltaire's voluminous writings challenged, often indirectly, the Catholic church and Christian theology at almost every point. Though he was considered by many devout Christians to be a shallow blasphemer, Voltaire's religious views were influential and quite typical of the mature Enlightenment. Voltaire clearly believed in a God, but his was a distant, deistic God, a great Clockmaker who built an orderly universe and then stepped aside and let it run. Above all, Voltaire and most of the philosophes hated all forms of religious intolerance, which they believed often led to fanaticism and savage, inhuman action. Simple piety and human kindness—as embodied in Christ's great commandments to "love God and your neighbor as yourself"—were religion enough, even Christianity enough, as may be seen in Voltaire's famous essay on religion. (See the feature "Listening to the Past: Voltaire on Religion" on pages 626–627.)

The ultimate strength of the French philosophes lay in their number, dedication, and organization. The philosophes felt keenly that they were engaged in a common undertaking that transcended individuals. Their greatest and most representative intellectual achievement was, quite fittingly, a group effort—the seventeen-volume *Encyclopedia: The Rational Dictionary of the Sciences, the Arts, and the Crafts,* edited by Denis Diderot (1713–1784) and Jean le Rond d'Alembert. Diderot and d'Alembert made a curious pair. Diderot began his career as a hack writer, first attracting attention with a skeptical tract on religion that was quickly burned by the judges of Paris. D'Alembert was one of Europe's leading scientists and mathematicians, the orphaned and illegitimate son of celebrated aristocrats. From different circles and with different interests, the two men set out to find coauthors who would examine the rapidly expanding whole of human knowledge. Even more fundamentally, they set out to teach people how to think critically and objectively about all matters. As Diderot said, he wanted the *Encyclopedia* to "change the general way of thinking."[15]

The editors of the *Encyclopedia* had to conquer innumerable obstacles. After the appearance in 1751 of the first volume, which dealt with such controversial subjects as atheism, the soul, and blind people (all words beginning with *a* in French), the government temporarily banned publication. The pope later placed the work on the Catholic church's index of forbidden works and pronounced excommunication on all who read or bought it. The timid publisher watered down some of the articles in the last ten volumes without the editors' consent in an attempt to appease the authorities. Yet Diderot's unwavering belief in the importance of his mission held the encyclopedists together for fifteen years, and the enormous work was completed in 1765. Hundreds of thousands of articles by leading scientists, famous writers, skilled workers, and progressive priests treated every aspect of life and knowledge.

Not every article was daring or original, but the overall effect was little short of revolutionary. Science and the industrial arts were exalted, religion and immortality questioned. Intolerance, legal injustice, and out-of-date social institutions were openly criticized. More generally, the writers of the *Encyclopedia* showed that human beings could use the process of reasoning to expand human knowledge. The encyclopedists were convinced that greater knowledge would result in greater human happiness, for knowledge was useful and made possible economic, social, and political progress. The *Encyclopedia* was widely read, especially in less expensive reprint editions published in Switzerland, and it was extremely influential in France and throughout

Voltaire   leans forward at left to exchange ideas with King Frederick the Great in the center of the picture, as Prussian officials look on. As this painting suggests, Voltaire's radicalism was mainly intellectual and philosophical, not social or political. The men and women of the Enlightenment prized witty, spirited conversation. *(Bildarchiv Preussischer Kulturbesitz)*

---

western Europe as well. It summed up the new world-view of the Enlightenment.

The Later Enlightenment

After about 1770, the harmonious unity of the philosophes and their thought began to break down. As the new world-view became increasingly accepted by the educated public, some thinkers sought originality by exaggerating certain Enlightenment ideas to the exclusion of others. These latter-day philosophes often built rigid, dogmatic systems.

In his *System of Nature* (1770) and other works, the wealthy German-born but French-educated Baron Paul d'Holbach (1723–1789) argued that human beings were machines completely determined by outside forces. Free will, God, and immortality of the soul were foolish myths. D'Holbach's aggressive atheism and determinism, which were coupled with deep hostility toward Christianity and all other religions, dealt the unity of the Enlightenment movement a severe blow. Deists such as Voltaire, who believed in God but not in established churches, were repelled by the inflexible atheism they found in the *System of Nature*. They saw in it the same dogmatic intolerance they had been fighting all their lives.

D'Holbach published his philosophically radical works anonymously in the Netherlands to avoid possible prosecution in France, and in his lifetime he was best known to the public as the generous patron and witty host of writers and intellectuals. At his twice-weekly dinner parties, an inner circle of regulars who knew the baron's secret exchanged ideas with aspiring philosophes and distinguished visitors. One of the most important was Scottish philosopher David Hume (1711–1776), whose carefully argued skepticism had a powerful long-term influence.

Building on Locke's teachings on learning, Hume argued that the human mind is really nothing but a bundle of impressions. These impressions originate only in sense experiences and our habits of joining these experiences together. Since our ideas ultimately reflect only our sense experiences, our reason cannot tell us anything about questions that cannot be verified by sense experience (in the form of controlled experiments or mathematics), such as the origin of the universe or the existence of God. Paradoxically, Hume's rationalistic inquiry ended up undermining the Enlightenment's faith in the power of reason.

Another French aristocrat, Marie-Jean Caritat, the marquis de Condorcet (1743–1794), transformed the Enlightenment belief in gradual, hard-won progress into fanciful utopianism. In his *Progress of the Human Mind,* written in 1793 during the French Revolution (see Chapter 21), Condorcet hypothesized and tracked nine stages of human progress that had already occurred and predicted that the tenth would bring perfection. Ironically, Condorcet wrote this work while fleeing for his life. Caught and condemned by revolutionary extremists, he preferred death by his own hand to the blade of the guillotine.

Other thinkers and writers after about 1770 began to attack the Enlightenment's faith in reason, progress, and moderation. The most famous of these was the Swiss Jean-Jacques Rousseau (1712–1778), a brilliant and difficult thinker, an appealing but neurotic individual. Born into a poor family of watchmakers in Geneva, Rousseau went to Paris and was greatly influenced by Diderot and Voltaire. Always extraordinarily sensitive and suspicious, Rousseau came to believe that his philosophe friends and the women of the Parisian salons were plotting against him. In the mid-1750s, he broke with them personally and intellectually, living thereafter as a lonely outsider with his uneducated common-law wife and going in his own highly original direction.

Like other Enlightenment thinkers, Rousseau was passionately committed to individual freedom. Unlike them, however, he attacked rationalism and civilization as destroying, rather than liberating, the individual. Warm, spontaneous feeling had to complement and correct cold intellect. Moreover, the basic goodness of the individual and the unspoiled child had to be protected from the cruel refinements of civilization. These ideas greatly influenced the early romantic movement (see pages 766–772), which rebelled against the culture of the Enlightenment in the late eighteenth century. They also had a powerful impact on the development of child psychology and modern education. (See the feature "Listening to the Past: A New Way to Educate Children" on pages 686–687.)

Rousseau's contribution to political theory in *The Social Contract* (1762) was equally significant. His contribution was based on two fundamental concepts: the general will and popular sovereignty. According to Rousseau, the general will is sacred and absolute, reflecting the common interests of all the people, who have displaced the monarch as the holder of sovereign power. The general will is not necessarily the will of the majority, however. At times the general will may be the authentic, long-term needs of the people as correctly interpreted by a farseeing minority. Little noticed before the French Revolution, Rousseau's concept of the general will appealed greatly to democrats and nationalists after 1789. The concept has also been used since 1789 by many dictators claiming that they, rather than some momentary majority of the voters, represent the general will and thus the true interests of democracy and the sovereign masses.

Urban Culture and Public Opinion

The writings and press campaigns of the philosophes were part of a profound cultural transformation. The object of impressive ongoing research and scholarly debate in recent years, this transformation had several interrelated aspects.

Of great importance, the European market for books grew dramatically in the eighteenth century. In Germany the number of new titles appearing annually grew substantially and at an accelerating rate, from roughly six hundred new titles in 1700 to about eleven hundred in 1764 and about twenty-six hundred in 1780. Well-studied France, which was indicative of general European trends, witnessed an explosive growth in book consumption. A modest increase in literacy was partly responsible, as the popular classes bought more penny tracts and escapist stories (see pages 668–670). Yet the solid and upper middle classes, the clergy, and the aristocracy accounted for most of the change. The number of books in the hands of these privileged groups increased eightfold to tenfold between the 1690s and the 1780s, when the private library of the typical noble contained more than three hundred volumes. Moreover, a much more avid French reader purchased a totally transformed product. The number of religious and devotional books published legally in Paris declined precipitously, from one-half of the total in the 1690s to one-tenth of the total in the 1780s. History and law held constant, while the proportion of legally published books treating the arts and sciences surged.

Even these figures understate the shift in French taste because France's unpredictable but pervasive censorship caused many books to be printed abroad and then smuggled back into the country for "under-the-cloak" sale. Experts believe that perhaps the majority of French books produced between 1750 and 1789 came from publishing companies located outside France. These publishers, located primarily in the Netherlands and Switzerland but also in England and a few small west German principalities, also smuggled forbidden books in French and other languages into the absolutist states of central, southern, and eastern Europe. The recently discovered catalogues of some of these foreign publishers reveal a massive presence of the famous French philosophes, reaffirming the philosophes' central role in the spread of critical secular attitudes.

The illegal book trade in France also featured an astonishing growth of scandalmongering denunciations of high political figures and frankly pornographic works. These literary forms frequently came together in scathing pornographic accounts of the moral and sexual depravity of the French court, allegedly mired in luxury, perversion, and adultery. A favorite theme was the way that some beautiful but immoral aristocratic women used their sexual charms to gain power over weak rulers and high officials, thereby corrupting the process of government. Spurred by repeated royal directives, the French police did its best to stamp out this underground literature, but new slanders kept cropping up, like the wild tabloid fantasies at checkout counters in today's supermarkets.

Reading more books on many more subjects, the educated public in France and throughout Europe increasingly approached reading in a new way. The result was what some German scholars have called a "reading revolution." The old style of reading in Europe had been centered on sacred texts, full of authority, inspiring reverence and teaching earthly duty and obedience to God. Reading had been patriarchal and communal, with the father of the family slowly reading the text aloud and the audience savoring each word. Now reading involved many texts, which were constantly changing and commanded no special respect. Reading became individual, silent, and rapid. The well-educated classes were reading insatiably, skeptically, and carelessly. Subtle but profound, the reading revolution was closely linked to the rise of a critical world-view.

As the reading public developed, it joined forces with the philosophes to call for the autonomy of the printed word. Immanuel Kant (1724–1804), a professor in East Prussia and the greatest German philosopher of the age, argued in 1784 that if serious thinkers were granted the freedom to exercise their reason publicly in print, then enlightenment would almost surely follow. Kant suggested that Prussia's Frederick the Great was an enlightened monarch precisely because he permitted such freedom of the press.

Outside of Prussia, the Netherlands, and Great Britain, however, the philosophes and the public resorted to discussion and social interchange in order to circumvent censorship and create an autonomous cultural sphere. Indeed, sparkling conversation in private homes spread Enlightenment ideas to Europe's upper middle class and aristocracy. Paris set the example, and other French and European cities followed. In Paris a number of talented and often rich women presided over regular social gatherings of the great and near-great in their elegant drawing rooms, or *salons*. There they encouraged a d'Alembert and a Fontenelle to exchange witty, uncensored observations on literature, science, and philosophy with great aristocrats, wealthy middle-class financiers, high-ranking officials, and noteworthy foreigners. Thus talented hostesses brought the various French elites together and mediated the public's free-wheeling examination of Enlightenment thought.

Elite women also exercised an unprecedented feminine influence on artistic taste. Soft pastels, ornate interiors, sentimental portraits, and starry-eyed lovers protected by hovering cupids were all hallmarks of the style they favored. This style, known as rococo, was popular throughout Europe in the eighteenth century. It has been argued that feminine influence in the drawing room went hand in hand with the emergence of polite society and the general attempt to civilize a rough military nobility. Similarly, some philosophes championed greater rights and expanded education for women, claiming that the position and treatment of women

Enlightenment Culture   was elegant, intellectual, and international. This painting shows the seven-year-old Austrian child prodigy, Wolfgang Amadeus Mozart (1756–1791), playing his own composition at an "English tea" given by the Princess de Conti near Paris. Mozart's phenomenal creative powers lasted a lifetime and he produced a vast range of symphonies, operas, and chamber music. *(Versailles/Bulloz)*

were the best indicators of a society's level of civilization and decency.[16] To be sure, for these male philosophes greater rights for women did not mean equal rights, and the philosophes were not particularly disturbed by the fact that elite women remained legally subordinate to men in economic and political affairs. Elite women lacked many rights, but so did most men.

One of the most famous salons was that of Madame Geoffrin, the unofficial godmother of the *Encyclopedia.* Having lost her parents at an early age, the future Madame Geoffrin was married at fifteen by her well-meaning grandmother to a rich and boring businessman of forty-eight. After dutifully raising her children, Madame Geoffrin broke out of her gilded cage. With

the aid of an aristocratic neighbor and in spite of her husband's loud protests, she developed a twice-weekly salon that counted Fontenelle and Montesquieu among its regular guests. Inheriting a large fortune after her husband's death, Madame Geoffrin gave the encyclopedists generous financial aid and helped save their enterprise from collapse. Corresponding with the king of Sweden and Catherine the Great of Russia, Madame Geoffrin remained her own woman, a practicing Christian who would not tolerate attacks on the church in her house.

The salons seem to have functioned as informal schools where established hostesses bonded with younger women and passed skills on to them. One talented young woman who received such help was Julie de Lespinasse. Eventually forming her own highly informal salon and attracting the keenest minds in France and Europe, Lespinasse epitomized the skills of the Enlightenment hostess. As one philosophe wrote:

She could unite the different types, even the most antago- nistic, sustaining the conversation by a well-aimed phrase, animating and guiding it at will. . . . Politics, religion, phi- losophy, news: nothing was excluded. Her circle met daily from five to nine. There one found men of all ranks in the State, the Church, and the Court, soldiers and foreigners, and the leading writers of the day.[17]

As this passage suggests, the salons created an inde- pendent cultural realm freed from religious dogma and political censorship. There a diverse but educated pub- lic could debate issues and form its own ideas, its own *public opinion.* And all who were educated and civilized had equal rights in the elaboration of this new and pow- erful force. Thus the salons graciously united members of the intellectual, economic, and social elites. In such an atmosphere, the philosophes, the French nobility, and the prosperous middle classes intermingled and in- creasingly influenced one another. Thinking critically about almost any question became fashionable and flourished alongside hopes for human progress through greater knowledge and enlightened public opinion.

 ## THE ENLIGHTENMENT AND ABSOLUTISM

How did the Enlightenment influence political devel- opments? To this important question there is no easy answer. On the one hand, the French philosophes and kindred spirits in most continental countries were pri- marily interested in converting people to critical, scien- tific thinking and were not particularly concerned with politics. On the other hand, such thinking naturally led to political criticism and interest in political reform. The educated public came to regard political change as both possible and desirable. A further problem is that En- lightenment thinkers had different views on politics. Some, led by the nobleman Montesquieu, argued for curbs on monarchial power in order to promote liberty, and some French judges applied such theories in practi- cal questions.

Until the American Revolution, however, most En- lightenment thinkers outside of England and the Nether- lands, especially in central and eastern Europe, believed

that political change could best come from above— from the ruler—rather than from below. There were several reasons for this essentially moderate belief. First, royal absolutism was a fact of life, and the kings and queens of Europe's leading states clearly had no inten- tion of giving up their great powers. Therefore, the philosophes and their sympathizers realistically con- cluded that a benevolent absolutism offered the best opportunities for improving society. Critical thinking was turning the art of good government into an exact science. It was necessary only to educate and "en- lighten" the monarch, who could then make good laws and promote human happiness. Second, Enlighten- ment thinkers turned toward rulers because rulers seemed to be listening, treating them with respect and seeking their advice. Finally, the philosophes distrusted "the people." They believed that the common people were deluded by superstitions and driven by violent pas- sions, little children in need of firm parental guidance.

Encouraged and instructed by the philosophes, many absolutist rulers of the later eighteenth century tried to govern in an "enlightened" manner. Yet because Euro- pean monarchs had long been locked in an intense in- ternational competition, a more enlightened state often meant in practice a more effective state, a state capable of defending itself and defeating its enemies. Moreover, reforms from above had to be grafted onto previous historical developments and existing social structures. Little wonder, then, that the actual programs and ac- complishments of these rulers varied greatly. Let us therefore examine the evolution of monarchial abso- lutism at close range before trying to form any overall judgment regarding the meaning of what historians have often called the "enlightened absolutism" of the later eighteenth century.

Absolutism in Central and Eastern Europe

Enlightenment teachings inspired European rulers in small as well as large states in the second half of the eighteenth century. Absolutist princes and monarchs in several west German and Italian states, as well as in Scandinavia, Spain, and Portugal, proclaimed them- selves more enlightened. A few smaller states were actu- ally the most successful in making reforms, perhaps because their rulers were not overwhelmed by the size and complexity of their realms. Denmark, for example, carried out an extensive and progressive land reform in the 1780s that practically abolished serfdom and gave Danish peasants secure tenure on their farms. Yet by far the most influential of the new-style monarchs were in

Prussia, Russia, and Austria, and they deserve primary attention.

Frederick the Great of Prussia Frederick II (r. 1740–1786), commonly known as Frederick the Great, built masterfully on the work of his father, Frederick William I (see pages 478–479). This was somewhat surprising, for, like many children with tyrannical parents, he rebelled against his family's wishes in his early years. Rejecting the crude life of the barracks, Frederick embraced culture and literature, even writing poetry and fine prose in French, a language his father detested. He threw off his father's dour Calvinism and dabbled with atheism. After trying unsuccessfully to run away in 1730 at age eighteen, he was virtually imprisoned and even compelled to watch his companion in flight beheaded at his father's command. Yet like many other rebellious youths, Frederick eventually reached a reconciliation with his father, and by the time he came to the throne ten years later, Frederick was determined to use the splendid army that his father had left him.

Therefore, when the ruler of Austria, Charles VI, also died in 1740 and his young and charismatic daughter, Maria Theresa, inherited the Habsburg dominions, Frederick suddenly and without warning invaded her rich, mainly German province of Silesia. This action defied solemn Prussian promises to respect the Pragmatic Sanction, which guaranteed Maria Theresa's succession—but no matter. For Frederick it was the opportunity of a lifetime to expand the size and power of Prussia. Although Maria Theresa succeeded in dramatically rallying the normally quarrelsome Hungarian nobility, her ethnically diverse army was no match for Prussian precision. In 1742, as other greedy powers were falling on her lands in the general European War of the Austrian Succession (1740–1748), which also expanded into a world war for empire between France and Britain, she was forced to cede almost all of Silesia to Prussia (see Map 17.2 on page 571). In one stroke Prussia doubled its population to six million people. Now Prussia unquestionably towered above all the other German states and stood as a European Great Power.

Though successful in 1742, Frederick had to spend much of his reign fighting against great odds to save Prussia from total destruction. Maria Theresa was determined to regain Silesia, and when the ongoing competition between Britain and France for colonial empire brought another great conflict in 1756 (see page 647), her able chief minister, Count Wenzel Anton Kaunitz (1711–1794), fashioned an aggressive alliance with France and Russia. During the Seven Years' War (1756–1763), the aim of the alliance was to conquer Prussia and divide up its territory, just as Frederick II and other monarchs had so recently sought to partition the Austrian Empire. Frederick led his army brilliantly, striking repeatedly at vastly superior forces invading from all sides. At times he believed all was lost, but he fought on with stoic courage. In the end, he was miraculously saved: Peter III came to the Russian throne in 1762 and called off the attack against Frederick, whom he greatly admired.

In the early years of his reign, Frederick II had kept his enthusiasm for Enlightenment culture strictly separated from a brutal concept of international politics. He wrote:

Of all States, from the smallest to the biggest, one can safely say that the fundamental rule of government is the principle of extending their territories. . . . The passions of rulers have no other curb but the limits of their power. Those are the fixed laws of European politics to which every politician submits.[18]

But the terrible struggle of the Seven Years' War tempered Frederick and brought him to consider how more humane policies for his subjects might also strengthen the state.

Thus Frederick went beyond a superficial commitment to Enlightenment culture for himself and his circle. He tolerantly allowed his subjects to believe as they wished in religious and philosophical matters. He promoted the advancement of knowledge, improving his country's schools and permitting scholars to publish their findings. Moreover, Frederick tried to improve the lives of his subjects more directly. As he wrote his friend Voltaire, "I must enlighten my people, cultivate their manners and morals, and make them as happy as human beings can be, or as happy as the means at my disposal permit." The legal system and the bureaucracy were Frederick's primary tools. Prussia's laws were simplified, torture of prisoners was abolished, and judges decided cases quickly and impartially. Prussian officials became famous for their hard work and honesty. After the Seven Years' War ended in 1763, Frederick's government also energetically promoted the reconstruction of agriculture and industry in his war-torn country. In all this Frederick set a good example. He worked hard and lived modestly, claiming that he was "only the first servant of the state." Thus Frederick justified monarchy in terms of practical results and said nothing of the divine right of kings.

Frederick's dedication to high-minded government went only so far, however. He never tried to change Prussia's existing social structure. True, he condemned serfdom in the abstract, but he accepted it in practice and did not even free the serfs on his own estates. He accepted and extended the privileges of the nobility, which he saw as his primary ally in the defense and extension of his realm. It became practically impossible for a middle-class person to gain a top position in the government. The Junker nobility remained the backbone of the army and the entire Prussian state.

Nor did Frederick listen to thinkers like Moses Mendelssohn (1729–1786), who urged that Jews be given freedom and civil rights. (See the feature "Individuals in Society: Moses Mendelssohn and the Jewish Enlightenment.") As in other German states, Jews in Prussia remained an oppressed group. The vast majority were confined to tiny, overcrowded ghettos, were excluded by law from most business and professional activities, and could be ordered out of the kingdom at a moment's notice. A very few Jews in Prussia did manage to succeed and obtain the right of permanent settlement, usually by performing some special service for the state. But they were the exception, and Frederick firmly opposed any general emancipation for the Jews, as he did for the serfs.

Catherine the Great of Russia Catherine the Great of Russia (r. 1762–1796) was one of the most remarkable rulers who ever lived, and the French philosophes adored her. Catherine was a German princess from Anhalt-Zerbst, a totally insignificant principality sandwiched between Prussia and Saxony. Her father commanded a regiment of the Prussian army, but her mother was related to the Romanovs of Russia, and that proved to be Catherine's chance.

Peter the Great had abolished the hereditary succession of tsars so that he could name his successor and thus preserve his policies. This move opened a period of palace intrigue and a rapid turnover of rulers until Peter's youngest daughter, Elizabeth, came to the Russian throne in 1741. A shrewd but crude woman—one of her official lovers was an illiterate shepherd boy—Elizabeth named her nephew Peter heir to the throne and chose Catherine to be his wife in 1744. It was a mismatch from the beginning. The fifteen-year-old Catherine was intelligent and attractive; her husband was stupid and ugly, his face badly scarred by smallpox. Ignored by her childish husband, Catherine carefully studied Russian, endlessly read writers such as Bayle and Voltaire, and made friends at court. Soon she knew what she wanted. "I did not care about Peter," she wrote in her *Memoirs,* "but I did care about the crown."[19]

As the old empress Elizabeth approached death, Catherine plotted against her unpopular husband. She selected as her new lover a tall, dashing young officer named Gregory Orlov, who with his four officer brothers commanded considerable support among the soldiers stationed in St. Petersburg. When Peter came to the throne in 1762, his decision to withdraw Russian troops from the coalition against Prussia alienated the army. Nor did Peter III's attempt to gain support from the Russian nobility by freeing it from compulsory state service succeed. At the end of six months, Catherine and her military conspirators deposed Peter III in a palace revolution. Then the Orlov brothers murdered him. The German princess became empress of Russia.

Catherine had drunk deeply at the Enlightenment well. Never questioning the common assumption that absolute monarchy was the best form of government, she set out to rule in an enlightened manner. She had three main goals. First, she worked hard to bring the sophisticated culture of western Europe to backward Russia. To do so, she imported Western architects, sculptors, musicians, and intellectuals. She bought masterpieces of Western art in wholesale lots and patronized the philosophes. An enthusiastic letter writer, she corresponded extensively with Voltaire and praised him as the "champion of the human race." When the French government banned the *Encyclopedia,* she offered to publish it in St. Petersburg. She sent money to Diderot when he needed it. With these and countless similar actions, Catherine won good press in the West for herself and for her country. Moreover, this intellectual ruler, who wrote plays and loved good talk, set the tone for the entire Russian nobility. Peter the Great westernized Russian armies, but it was Catherine who westernized the thinking of the Russian nobility.

Catherine's second goal was domestic reform, and she began her reign with sincere and ambitious projects. Better laws were a major concern. In 1767 she drew up enlightened instructions for the special legislative commission she had appointed to prepare a new law code. No new unified code was ever produced, but Catherine did restrict the practice of torture and allowed limited religious toleration. She also tried to improve education and strengthen local government. The philosophes applauded these measures and hoped more would follow.

Such was not the case. In 1773 a common Cossack soldier named Emelian Pugachev sparked a gigantic uprising of serfs, very much as Stenka Razin had done a century earlier (see page 583). Proclaiming himself the true tsar, Pugachev issued "decrees" abolishing serfdom, taxes, and army service. Thousands joined his cause, slaughtering landlords and officials over a vast area of southwestern Russia. Pugachev's untrained hordes eventually proved no match for Catherine's noble-led regular army. Betrayed by his own company, Pugachev was captured and savagely executed.

Pugachev's rebellion was a decisive turning point in Catherine's domestic policy. On coming to the throne, she had condemned serfdom in theory, but she had been smart enough to realize that any changes would have to be very gradual, or else she would quickly follow her departed husband. Pugachev's rebellion put an end to any illusions she might have had about reform-

ing serfdom. The peasants were clearly dangerous, and her empire rested on the support of the nobility. After 1775 Catherine gave the nobles absolute control of their serfs. She extended serfdom into new areas, such as Ukraine. In 1785 she formalized the nobility's privileged position, freeing nobles forever from taxes and state service. She also confiscated the lands of the Russian Orthodox church and gave them to favorite officials. Under Catherine the Russian nobility attained its most exalted position, and serfdom entered its most oppressive phase.

Catherine's third goal was territorial expansion, and in this respect she was extremely successful. Her armies subjugated the last descendants of the Mongols, the Crimean Tartars, and began the conquest of the Caucasus. Her greatest coup by far was the partitioning of

Pugachev and Catherine This haunting portrait of Pugachev has been painted over an existing portrait of empress Catherine the Great, who seems to be peeking over the rebel leader's head. Painting from life in 1773, the artist may have wanted to represent Pugachev's legitimacy as Catherine's rightful successor. *(From* Pamiatniki Kul'tury, *No. 32, 1961)*

Individuals in Society

Moses Mendelssohn and the Jewish Enlightenment ✛

Lavater (on the right) attempts to convert Mendelssohn, in a painting by Moritz Oppenheim of an imaginary encounter. *(Collection of the Judah L. Magnes Museum, Berkeley)*

In 1743 a small, humpbacked Jewish boy with a stammer left his poor parents in Dessau in central Germany and walked eighty miles to Berlin, the capital of Frederick the Great's Prussia. According to one story, when the boy reached the Rosenthaler Gate, the only one through which Jews could pass, he told the inquiring watchman that his name was Moses, and that he had come to Berlin "to learn." The watchman laughed and waved him through. "Go Moses, the sea has opened before you."[1] Embracing the Enlightenment and seeking a revitalization of Jewish religious thought, Moses Mendelssohn did point his people in a new and uncharted direction.

Turning in Berlin to a learned rabbi he had previously known in Dessau, the young Mendelssohn studied Jewish law and eked out a living copying Hebrew manuscripts in a beautiful hand. But he was soon fascinated by an intellectual world that had been closed to him in the Dessau ghetto. There, like most Jews throughout central Europe, he had spoken Yiddish—a mixture of German, Polish, and Hebrew. Now, working mainly on his own, he mastered German; learned Latin, Greek, French, and English; and studied mathematics and Enlightenment philosophy. Word of his exceptional abilities spread in Berlin's Jewish community, (1,500 of the city's 100,000 inhabitants). He began tutoring the children of a wealthy Jewish silk merchant, and he soon became the merchant's clerk and later his partner. But his great passion remained the life of the mind and the spirit, which he avidly pursued in his off hours.

Gentle and unassuming in his personal life, Mendelssohn was a bold thinker. Reading eagerly in Western philosophy since antiquity, he was, as a pious Jew, soon convinced that Enlightenment teachings need not be opposed to Jewish thought and religion. Indeed, he concluded that reason could complement and strengthen religion, although each would retain its integrity as a separate sphere.[2] Developing his idea in his first great work, "On the Immortality of the Soul" (1767), Mendelssohn used the neutral setting of a philosophical dialogue between Socrates and his followers in ancient Greece to argue that the human soul lived forever. In refusing to bring religion and critical thinking into conflict, he was strongly influenced by contemporary German philosophers who argued similarly on behalf of Christianity. He reflected the way the German Enlightenment generally supported established religion, while the French Enlightenment attacked it. This was the most important difference in Enlightenment thinking between the two countries.

Mendelssohn's treatise on the human soul captivated the educated German public, which marveled that a Jew could have written a philosophical masterpiece. In the excitement, a Christian zealot named Lavater challenged Mendelssohn in a pamphlet to accept Christianity or to demonstrate how the Christian faith was not "reasonable." Replying politely but passionately, the Jewish philosopher affirmed that all his studies had only strengthened him in the faith of his fathers, although he certainly did not seek to convert anyone not born into Judaism. Rather, he urged toleration in religious matters. He spoke up courageously for his fellow Jews and decried the oppression they endured, and he continued to do so for the rest of his life.

Orthodox Jew and German philosophe, Moses Mendelssohn serenely combined two very different worlds. He built a bridge from the ghetto to the dominant culture over which many Jews would pass, including his novelist daughter Dorothea and his famous grandson, the composer Felix Mendelssohn.

Questions for Analysis

1. How did Mendelssohn seek to influence Jewish religious thought in his time?

2. How do Mendelssohn's ideas compare with those of the French Enlightenment?

1. H. Kupferberg, *The Mendelssohns: Three Generations of Genius* (New York: Charles Scribner's Sons, 1972), p. 3.

2. D. Sorkin, *Moses Mendelssohn and the Religious Enlightenment* (Berkeley: University of California Press, 1996), pp. 8ff.

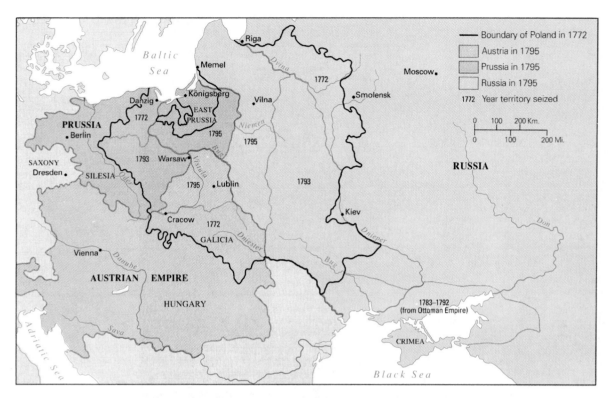

MAP 18.1 The Partition of Poland and Russia's Expansion, 1772–1795   Though all three of the great eastern absolutist states profited from the division of large but weak Poland, Catherine's Russia gained the most. Russia's European border moved far to the west, and the Russian empire became a leading actor in European politics.

Poland (Map 18.1). By 1700 Poland had become a weak and decentralized republic with an elected king (page 572), and Poland's fate in the late eighteenth century demonstrated the dangers of failing to build a strong absolutist state. All important decisions continued to require the unanimous agreement of all nobles elected to the Polish diet, which meant that nothing could ever be done to strengthen the state. When, between 1768 and 1772, Catherine's armies scored unprecedented victories against the Turks and thereby threatened to disturb the balance of power between Russia and Austria in eastern Europe, Frederick of Prussia obligingly came forward with a deal. He proposed that Turkey be let off easily and that Prussia, Austria, and Russia each compensate itself by taking a gigantic slice of Polish territory. Catherine jumped at the chance. The first partition of Poland took place in 1772. Two more partitions, in 1793 and 1795, gave all three powers more Polish territory, and the ancient republic of Poland simply vanished from the map.

Expansion helped Catherine keep the nobility happy, for it provided her with vast new lands to give to her faithful servants and her many lovers. On all the official royal favorites she lavished large estates with many serfs, as if to make sure there were no hard feelings when her interest cooled. Until the end this remarkable woman—who always believed that, in spite of her domestic setbacks, she was slowly civilizing Russia—kept her zest for life. Fascinated by a new twenty-two-year-old flame when she was a roly-poly grandmother in her sixties, she happily reported her good fortune to a favorite former lover: "I have come back to life like a frozen fly; I am gay and well."[20]

The Austrian Habsburgs   In Austria two talented rulers did manage to introduce major reforms, although traditional power politics was more important than Enlightenment teachings. One was Joseph II (r. 1780–1790), a fascinating individual. For an earlier generation of historians, he was the "revolutionary

Maria Theresa   and her husband pose with eleven of their sixteen children at Schönbrunn palace in this family portrait by court painter Martin Meytens (1695–1770). Joseph, the heir to the throne, stands at the center of the star pattern. Wealthy women often had very large families, in part because they seldom nursed their babies as poor women usually did. (*Kunsthistorisches Museum, Vienna*)

emperor," a tragic hero whose lofty reforms were undone by the landowning nobility he dared to challenge. More recent scholarship has revised this romantic interpretation and stressed how Joseph II continued the state-building work of his mother, the empress Maria Theresa, a remarkable but old-fashioned absolutist.

Maria Theresa's long reign (1740–1780) began with her neighbors, led by Frederick II of Prussia, invading her lands and trying to dismember them. Emerging from the long War of the Austrian Succession in 1748

with only the serious loss of Silesia, Maria Theresa and her closest ministers were determined to introduce reforms that would make the state stronger and more efficient. Three aspects of these reforms were most important. First, Maria Theresa introduced measures to bring relations between church and state under government control. Like some medieval rulers, the most devout and very Catholic Maria Theresa aimed at limiting the papacy's political influence in her realm. Second, a whole series of administrative reforms strengthened the central bureaucracy, smoothed out some provincial differences, and revamped the tax system, taxing even the lands of nobles without special exemptions. Third, the government sought to improve the lot of the agricultural population, cautiously reducing the power of lords over their hereditary serfs and their partially free peasant tenants.

Coregent with his mother from 1765 onward and a strong supporter of change, Joseph II moved forward rapidly when he came to the throne in 1780. He controlled the established Catholic church even more closely in an attempt to ensure that it produced better citizens. He granted religious toleration and civic rights to Protestants and Jews—a radical innovation that impressed his contemporaries. In even more spectacular peasant reforms, Joseph abolished serfdom in 1781, and in 1789 he decreed that all peasant labor obligations be converted into cash payments. This ill-conceived measure was violently rejected not only by the nobility but also by the peasants it was intended to help since their primitive barter economy was woefully lacking in money. When a disillusioned Joseph died prematurely at forty-nine, the entire Habsburg empire was in turmoil. His brother Leopold II (r. 1790–1792) was forced to cancel Joseph's radical edicts in order to re-establish order. Peasants lost most of their recent gains, and once again they were required to do forced labor for their lords, as in the 1770s under Maria Theresa.

Absolutism in France

The Enlightenment's influence on political developments in France was complex. The monarchy maintained its absolutist claims, and some philosophes, such as Voltaire, believed that the king was still the best source of needed reform. At the same time, discontented nobles and learned judges drew on thinkers such as Montesquieu for liberal arguments. They sought with some success to limit the king's power, as France diverged from the absolutist states just considered.

In building French absolutism, Louis XIV had successfully drawn on the middle class to curb the political power of the nobility. As long as the Grand Monarch lived, the nobility could only grumble and, like the duke of Saint-Simon in his *Memoirs,* scornfully lament the rise of "the vile bourgeoisie." But when Louis XIV finally died in 1715, to be succeeded by his five-year-old great-grandson, Louis XV (r. 1715–1774), the Sun King's elaborate system of absolutist rule was challenged in a general reaction. Favored by the duke of

Orléans (1674–1723), a licentious rake and nephew of Louis XIV who governed as regent until 1723, the nobility made a strong comeback.

Most important, in 1715 the duke, in return for recognition of his desire to become the sole regent, restored to the high courts of France—the parlements—the ancient right to evaluate royal decrees publicly in writing before they were registered and given the force of law. The restoration of this right to evaluate, or "remonstrate," which had been suspended under Louis XIV, was a fateful step. The high court judges, of which those at the Parlement of Paris were the most important and influential, had originally come from the middle class, and their high position reflected the way that Louis XIV (and earlier French monarchs) had chosen to use that class to build the royal bureaucracy so necessary for an absolutist state. By the eighteenth century, however, these middle-class judges had risen to become hereditary nobles. Moreover, although Louis XIV had curbed the political power of the nobility, he had never challenged its enormous social prestige. Thus high position in the government continued to bestow the noble status that middle-class officials wanted, either right away or after three generations of continual service. The judges of Paris and the provincial high courts, like many high-ranking officials, actually owned their government jobs and freely passed them on as private property from father to son. By allowing this well-entrenched and increasingly aristocratic group to evaluate the king's decrees before they became law, the duke of Orléans sanctioned a counterweight to absolute power.

These implications became clear when the heavy expenses of the War of the Austrian Succession plunged France into financial crisis. In 1748 Louis XV appointed a finance minister who decreed a 5 percent income tax on every individual regardless of social status. Exemption from most taxation had long been a hallowed privilege of the nobility, and other important groups—the clergy, the large towns, and some wealthy bourgeoisie—had also gained special tax advantages over time. The result was a vigorous protest from many sides. Leading the attack, the Parlement of Paris denounced the proposed tax law and rallied public opinion against it. The monarchy retreated; the new tax was dropped.

Following the disastrously expensive Seven Years' War, the conflict re-emerged. The government tried to maintain emergency taxes after the war ended. The Parlement of Paris protested and even challenged the basis of royal authority, claiming that the king's power had to be limited to protect liberty. Once again the government caved in and withdrew the wartime taxes in 1764. Emboldened by this striking victory and widespread support from France's educated elite, the judicial opposition in Paris and the provinces pressed its demands. In a barrage of pamphlets and legal briefs, it asserted that the king could not levy taxes without the consent of the Parlement of Paris acting as the representative of the entire nation.

Indolent and sensual by nature, more interested in his many mistresses than in affairs of state, Louis XV finally roused himself for a determined defense of his absolutist inheritance. "The magistrates," he angrily told the Parlement of Paris in a famous face-to-face confrontation, "are my officers. . . . In my person only does the sovereign power rest."[21] In 1768 Louis appointed a tough career official named René de Maupeou as chancellor and ordered him to crush the judicial opposition.

Maupeou abolished the existing parlements and exiled the vociferous members of the Parlement of Paris to isolated backwaters in the provinces. He created a new and docile parlement of royal officials, and he began once again to tax the privileged groups. A few philosophes applauded these measures: the sovereign was using his power to introduce badly needed reforms that had been blocked by a self-serving aristocratic elite. Most philosophes and educated public opinion as a whole sided with the old parlements, however, and there was widespread criticism of "royal despotism." The illegal stream of scandalmongering, pornographic attacks on the king and his court, became a torrent, and some scholars now believe these lurid denunciations ate away at the foundations of royal authority, especially among the common people in turbulent Paris. The king was being stripped of the sacred aura of God's anointed on earth and was being reinvented in the popular imagination as a loathsome degenerate. Yet the monarchy's power was still great enough for Maupeou simply to ride over the opposition, and Louis XV would probably have prevailed—if he had lived to a very ripe old age.

But Louis XV died in 1774. The new king, Louis XVI (r. 1774–1792), was a shy twenty-year-old with good intentions. Taking the throne, he is reported to have said, "What I should like most is to be loved."[22] The eager-to-please monarch decided to yield in the face of such strong criticism from so much of France's educated elite. He dismissed Maupeou and repudiated the strong-willed minister's work. All the old parlements were reinstated, as enlightened public opinion cheered and anticipated moves toward more represen-

tative government. But such moves were not forthcoming. Instead, a weakened but unreformed monarchy faced a judicial opposition that claimed to speak for the entire French nation. Increasingly locked in stalemate, the country was drifting toward renewed financial crisis and political upheaval.

The Overall Influence of the Enlightenment

Having examined the evolution of monarchial absolutism in four leading states, we can begin to look for meaningful generalizations and evaluate the overall influence of Enlightenment thought on politics. That thought was clustered in two distinct schools: the liberal critique of unregulated monarchy promoted by Montesquieu and the defenders of royal absolutism led by Voltaire.

France clearly diverged from its eastern neighbors in its political development in the eighteenth century. Although neither the French monarchy nor the eastern rulers abandoned the absolutist claims and institutions they had inherited, the monarch's capacity to govern in a truly absolutist manner declined substantially in France. This was not the case in eastern Europe. The immediate cause of this divergence was the political resurgence of the French nobility after 1715 and the growth of judicial opposition, led by the Parlement of Paris. More fundamentally, however, the judicial and aristocratic opposition in France achieved its still rather modest successes because it received major support from educated public opinion, which increasingly made the liberal critique of unregulated royal authority its own. In France, then, the proponents of absolute monarchy were increasingly on the defensive, as was the French monarchy.

The situation in eastern and east-central Europe was different. The liberal critique of absolute monarchy remained an intellectual curiosity, and proponents of reform from above held sway. Moreover, despite differences, the leading eastern European monarchs of the later eighteenth century all claimed that they were acting on the principles of the Enlightenment. The philosophes generally agreed with this assessment and cheered them on. Beginning in the mid-nineteenth century, historians developed the idea of a common "enlightened despotism" or "enlightened absolutism," and they canonized Frederick, Catherine, and Joseph as its most outstanding examples. More recent research has raised doubts about this old interpretation and has led to a fundamental reevaluation.

There is general agreement that these absolutists, especially Catherine and Frederick, did encourage and spread the cultural values of the Enlightenment. Perhaps this was their greatest achievement. Skeptical in religion and intensely secular in basic orientation, they unabashedly accepted the here and now and sought their happiness in the enjoyment of it. At the same time, they were proud of their intellectual accomplishments and good taste, and they supported knowledge, education, and the arts. No wonder the philosophes felt these monarchs were kindred spirits.

Historians also agree that the absolutists believed in change from above and tried to enact needed reforms. Yet the results of these efforts brought only very modest improvements, and the life of the peasantry remained very hard in the eighteenth century. Thus some historians have concluded that these monarchs were not really sincere in their reform efforts. Others disagree, arguing that powerful nobilities blocked the absolutists' genuine commitment to reform. (The old interpretation of Joseph II as the tragic revolutionary emperor forms part of this argument.)

The emerging answer to this controversy is that the later eastern absolutists were indeed committed to reform but that humanitarian objectives were of quite secondary importance. Above all, the absolutists wanted reforms that would strengthen the state and allow them to compete militarily with their neighbors. Modern scholarship has therefore stressed how Catherine, Frederick, and Joseph were in many ways simply continuing the state building of their predecessors, reorganizing armies and expanding bureaucracies to raise more taxes and troops. The reason for this continuation was simple. The international political struggle was brutal, and the stakes were high. First Austria under Maria Theresa and then Prussia under Frederick the Great had to engage in bitter fighting to escape dismemberment, while decentralized Poland was coldly divided and eventually liquidated.

Yet in this drive for more state power, the later absolutists were also innovators, and the idea of an era of enlightened absolutism retains a certain validity. Sharing the Enlightenment faith in critical thinking and believing that knowledge meant power, these absolutists really were more enlightened than their predecessors because they put state-building reforms in a new, broader perspective. Above all, the later absolutists considered how more humane laws and practices could help their populations become more productive and satisfied and thus able to contribute more substantially to the welfare of the state. It was from this perspective that they introduced many of their most progressive reforms, tolerating religious minorities, simplifying legal codes, and promoting practical education.

The primacy of state over individual interests also helps explain some puzzling variations in social policies. For example, Catherine the Great took measures that worsened the peasants' condition because she looked increasingly to the nobility as her natural ally and sought to strengthen it. Frederick the Great basically favored the status quo, limiting only the counterproductive excesses of his trusted nobility against its peasants. Joseph II believed that greater freedom for peasants was the means to strengthen his realm, and he acted accordingly. Each enlightened absolutist sought greater state power, but each believed a different policy would attain it.

The eastern European absolutists of the later eighteenth century combined old-fashioned state building with the culture and critical thinking of the Enlightenment. In doing so, they succeeded in expanding the role of the state in the life of society. Unlike the successors of Louis XIV, they perfected bureaucratic machines that were to prove surprisingly adaptive and capable of enduring into the twentieth century.

SUMMARY

This chapter has focused on the complex development of a new world-view in Western civilization. This new view was essentially critical and secular, drawing its inspiration from the scientific revolution and crystallizing in the Enlightenment.

Decisive breakthroughs in astronomy and physics in the seventeenth century, which demolished the imposing medieval synthesis of Aristotelian philosophy and Christian theology, had only limited practical consequences despite the expectations of scientific enthusiasts. Yet the impact of new scientific knowledge on intellectual life became great. Interpreting scientific findings and Newtonian laws in an antitraditional, antireligious manner, the French philosophes of the Enlightenment extolled the superiority of rational, critical thinking. This new method, they believed, promised not just increased knowledge but even the discovery of the fundamental laws of human society. Although they reached different conclusions when they turned to social and political realities, they did stimulate absolute monarchs to apply reason to statecraft and the search for useful reforms. Above all, the philosophes succeeded in shaping an emerging public opinion and spreading their radically new world-view. These were momentous accomplishments.

NOTES

1. H. Butterfield, *The Origins of Modern Science* (New York: Macmillan, 1951), p. viii.

2. Quoted in A. G. R. Smith, *Science and Society in the Sixteenth and Seventeenth Centuries* (New York: Harcourt Brace Jovanovich, 1972), p. 97.

3. Quoted in Butterfield, *The Origins of Modern Science*, p. 47.

4. Quoted in Smith, *Science and Society*, p. 100.

5. Ibid., pp. 115–116.

6. Ibid., p. 120.

7. A. R. Hall, *From Galileo to Newton, 1630–1720* (New York: Harper & Row, 1963), p. 290.

8. Quoted in R. K. Merton, *Science, Technology and Society in Seventeenth-Century England*, rev. ed. (New York: Harper & Row, 1970), p. 164.

9. Quoted in P. Hazard, *The European Mind, 1680–1715* (Cleveland: Meridian Books, 1963), pp. 304–305.

10. Quoted in R. Chartier, *The Cultural Origins of the French Revolution* (Durham, N.C.: Duke University Press, 1991), p. 27.

11. J. Bosher, *The French Revolution* (New York: W. W. Norton, 1988), p. 31.

12. L. Schiebinger, *The Mind Has No Sex? Women in the Origins of Modern Science* (Cambridge, Mass.: Harvard University Press, 1989), p. 64.

13. Quoted in L. M. Marsak, ed., *The Enlightenment* (New York: John Wiley & Sons, 1972), p. 56.

14. Quoted in G. L. Mosse et al., eds., *Europe in Review* (Chicago: Rand McNally, 1964), p. 156.

15. Quoted in P. Gay, "The Unity of the Enlightenment," *History* 3 (1960): 25.

16. See E. Fox-Genovese, "Women in the Enlightenment," in *Becoming Visible: Women in European History*, 2d ed., ed. R. Bridenthal, C. Koonz, and S. Stuard (Boston: Houghton Mifflin, 1987), esp. pp. 252–259, 263–265.

17. Quoted in G. P. Gooch, *Catherine the Great and Other Studies* (Hamden, Conn.: Archon Books, 1966), p. 149.

18. Quoted in L. Krieger, *Kings and Philosophers, 1689–1789* (New York: W. W. Norton, 1970), p. 257.

19. Quoted in Gooch, *Catherine the Great*, p. 15.

20. Ibid., p. 53.

21. Quoted in R. R. Palmer, *The Age of Democratic Revolution*, vol. 1 (Princeton, N.J.: Princeton University Press, 1959), pp. 95–96.

22. Quoted in G. Wright, *France in Modern Times*, 4th ed. (New York: W. W. Norton, 1987), p. 34.

SUGGESTED READING

The first three authors cited in the Notes—Butterfield, Smith, and Hall—have written excellent general interpretations of the scientific revolution. These may be compared with an outstanding work by M. Jacob, *The Cultural Meaning of the Scientific Revolution* (1988), which has a useful bibliography. The older study of England by Merton, mentioned in the Notes, also analyzes ties between science and the larger community. Schiebinger, cited in the Notes, provides a brilliant analysis of how the new science gradually excluded women interested in science, a question completely neglected in older studies. A. Debus, *Man and Nature in the Renaissance* (1978), is good on the Copernican revolution. M. Boas, *The Scientific Renaissance, 1450–1630* (1966), is especially insightful about the influence of magic on science. S. Drake, *Galileo* (1980), is a good short biography. T. Kuhn, *The Structure of Scientific Revolutions* (1962), is a challenging, much-discussed attempt to understand major breakthroughs in scientific thought over time. E. Andrade, *Sir Isaac Newton* (1958), is a good brief biography, which may be compared with R. Westfall, *Never at Rest: A Biography of Isaac Newton* (1993); and F. Manuel, *The Religion of Isaac Newton* (1974).

Hazard, listed in the Notes, is a classic study of the formative years of Enlightenment thought, and his *European Thought in the Eighteenth Century* (1954) is also recommended. Important recent studies from the cultural perspective include D. Goodman, *The Republic of Letters: A Cultural History of the Enlightenment* (1994); and A. Farge, *Subversive Worlds: Public Opinion in Eighteenth Century France* (1994). P. Gay has written several major studies on the Enlightenment: *Voltaire's Politics* (1959) and *The Party of Humanity* (1971) are two of the best. J. Sklar, *Montesquieu* (1987), is an engaging biography. I. Wade, *The Structure and Form of the French Enlightenment* (1977), is a major synthesis. F. Baumer, *Religion and the Rise of Skepticism* (1969); H. Payne, *The Philosophes and the People* (1976); and H. Chisick, *The Limits of Reform in the Enlightenment: Attitudes Toward the Education of the Lower Classes in Eighteenth-Century France* (1981), are interesting studies of important aspects of Enlightenment thought. D. Van Kley, *The Religious Origins of the French Revolution* (1996), is a stimulating reinterpretation. The changing attitudes of the educated public are imaginatively analyzed by R. Chartier, *The Cultural Origins of the French Revolution* (1991) and *French Historical Studies* (Fall 1992). R. Danton, *The Literary Underground of the Old Regime* (1982), provides a fascinating glimpse of low-life publishing. On women, see the stimulating study by Fox-Genovese cited in the Notes, as well as E. Goldsmith and

D. Goodman, eds., *Going Public: Women and Publishing in Early Modern France* (1995); S. Spencer, ed., *French Women and the Age of Enlightenment* (1984); and K. Rogers, *Feminism in Eighteenth-Century England* (1982). J. Landes, *Women and the Public Sphere in the Age of the French Revolution* (1988), is a fascinating and controversial study of women and politics. L. Wolff, *Inventing Eastern Europe: The Map of Civilization on the Mind of the Enlightenment* (1994), argues that the philosophes were the first to divide Europe into a backward east and an advanced west. Above all, one should read some of the philosophes and let them speak for themselves. Two good anthologies are C. Brinton, ed., *The Portable Age of Reason* (1956); and F. Manuel, ed., *The Enlightenment* (1951). Voltaire's most famous and very amusing novel, *Candide,* is highly recommended, as is S. Gendzier, ed., *Denis Diderot: The Encyclopedia: Selections* (1967). A. Wilson's biography, *Diderot* (1972), is long but rewarding.

In addition to the works mentioned in the Suggested Reading for Chapters 16 and 17, the monarchies of Europe are carefully analyzed in H. Scott, *Enlightened Absolutism* (1990); C. Tilly, ed., *The Formation of National States in Western Europe* (1975); and J. Gagliardo, *Enlightened Despotism* (1967), all of which have useful bibliographies. M. Anderson, *Historians and Eighteenth-Century Europe* (1979), is a valuable introduction to modern scholarship, and C. Behrens, *Society, Government, and the Enlightenment: The Experience of Eighteenth-Century France and Prussia* (1985), is a stimulating comparative study. E. Le Roy Ladurie, *The Ancien Régime* (1996), is an impressive synthesis by a leading French historian. J. Lynch, *Bourbon Spain, 1700–1808* (1989); and R. Herr, *The Eighteenth-Century Revolution in Spain* (1958), skillfully analyze the impact of Enlightenment thought in Spain. Important works on Austria include C. Macartney, *Maria Theresa and the House of Austria* (1970); D. Beales, *Joseph II* (1987); and T. Blanning, *Joseph II and Enlightened Absolutism* (1970). There are several fine works on Russia. J. Alexander, *Catherine the Great: Life and Legend* (1989), is the best biography of the famous ruler, which may be compared with the empress's own story, *The Memoirs of Catherine the Great,* ed. D. Maroger (1961). I. de Madariaga, *Russia in the Age of Catherine the Great* (1981); and P. Dukes, *The Making of Russian Absolutism, 1613–1801* (1982), are strongly recommended. The ambitious reader should also look at A. N. Radishchev, *A Journey from St. Petersburg to Moscow* (English trans., 1958), a famous 1790 attack on Russian serfdom and an appeal to Catherine the Great to free the serfs, for which Radishchev was exiled to Siberia. Two excellent works on Moses Mendelssohn are the brilliant study by D. Sorkin, *Moses Mendelssohn and the Religious Enlightenment* (1996), and the popular biography of the family by H. Kupferberg, *The Mendelssohns: Three Generations of Genius* (1972).

The musical and artistic culture of the time may be approached through A. Cobban, ed., *The Eighteenth Century* (1969), a richly illustrated work with excellent essays; and C. B. Behrens, *The Ancien Régime* (1967). T. Crow, *Painters and Public Life in Eighteenth-Century Paris* (1985), examines artists and cultural politics. C. Rosen, *The Classical Style: Haydn, Mozart, Beethoven* (1972), brilliantly synthesizes music and society, as did Mozart himself in his great opera *The Marriage of Figaro,* where the count is the buffoon and his servant the hero.

LISTENING TO THE
PAST

Voltaire on Religion

Voltaire was the most renowned and probably the most influential of the French philosophes. His biting, satirical novel Candide *(1759) is still widely assigned in college courses, and his witty yet serious* Philosophical Dictionary *remains a source of pleasure and stimulation. The* Dictionary *consists of a series of essays on topics ranging from Adam to Zoroaster, from certainty to circumcision. The following passage is taken from the essay on religion.*

Voltaire began writing the Philosophical Dictionary *in 1752, at the age of fifty-eight, after arriving at the Prussian court in Berlin. Frederick the Great applauded Voltaire's efforts, but Voltaire put the project aside after leaving Berlin, and the first of several revised editions was published anonymously in 1764. It was an immediate, controversial success. Snapped up by an "enlightened" public, it was denounced by religious leaders as a threat to the Christian community and was burned in Geneva and Paris.*

I meditated last night; I was absorbed in the contemplation of nature; I admired the immensity, the course, the harmony of those infinite globes which the vulgar do not know how to admire.

I admired still more the intelligence which directs these vast forces. I said to myself: "One must be blind not to be dazzled by this spectacle; one must be stupid not to recognize its author; one must be mad not to worship the Supreme Being. What tribute of worship should I render Him? Should not this tribute be the same in the whole of space, since it is the same Supreme Power which reigns equally in all space?

"Should not a thinking being who dwells on a star in the Milky Way offer Him the same homage as a thinking being on this little globe of ours? Light is the same for the star Sirius as for us; moral philosophy must also be the same. If a feeling, thinking animal on Sirius is born of a tender father and mother who have been occupied with his happiness, he owes them as much love and care as we owe to our parents. If someone in the Milky Way sees a needy cripple, and if he can aid him and does not do so, then he is guilty toward all the globes.

"Everywhere the heart has the same duties: on the steps of the throne of God, if He has a throne; and in the depths of the abyss, if there is an abyss."

I was deep in these ideas when one of those genii who fill the spaces between the worlds came down to me. I recognized the same aerial creature who had appeared to me on another occasion to teach me that the judgments of God are different from our own, and how a good action is preferable to a controversy.

The genie transported me into a desert all covered with piles of bones. . . . He began with the first pile. "These," he said, "are the twenty-three thousand Jews who danced before a calf, together with the twenty-four thousand who were killed while fornicating with Midianitish women. The number of those massacred for such errors and offences amounts to nearly three hundred thousand.

"In the other piles are the bones of the Christians slaughtered by each other because of metaphysical disputes. They are divided into several heaps of four centuries each. One heap would have mounted right to the sky; they had to be divided."

"What!" I cried, "brothers have treated their brothers like this, and I have the misfortune to be of this brotherhood!"

"Here," said the spirit, "are the twelve million native Americans killed in their own land because they had not been baptized."

"My God! . . . Why assemble here all these abominable monuments to barbarism and fanaticism?"

"To instruct you. . . . Follow me now." [The genie takes Voltaire to the "heroes of humanity, who tried to banish violence and plunder from the world," and tells Voltaire to question them.]

[At last] I saw a man with a gentle, simple face, who seemed to me to be about thirty-five years old. From afar he looked with compassion upon those piles of whitened bones, through which I had been led to reach the sage's dwelling place. I was astonished to find his feet swollen and bleeding, his hands likewise, his side pierced, and his ribs laid bare by the cut of the lash. "Good God!" I said to him, "is it possible for a just man, a sage, to be in this state? I have just seen one who was treated in a very hateful way, but there is no comparison between his torture and yours. Wicked priests and wicked judges poisoned him; is it by priests and judges that you were so cruelly assassinated?"

With great courtesy he answered, "Yes."

"And who were these monsters?"

"They were hypocrites."

"Ah! that says everything; I understand by that one word that they would have condemned you to the cruelest punishment. Had you then proved to them, as Socrates did, that the Moon was not a goddess, and that Mercury was not a god?"

"No, it was not a question of planets. My countrymen did not even know what a planet was; they were all arrant ignoramuses. Their superstitions were quite different from those of the Greeks."

"Then you wanted to teach them a new religion?"

"Not at all; I told them simply: 'Love God with all your heart and your neighbor as yourself, for that is the whole of mankind's duty.' Judge yourself if this precept is not as old as the universe; judge yourself if I brought them a new religion." . . .

"But did you say nothing, do nothing that could serve them as a pretext?"

"To the wicked everything serves as pretext."

"Did you not say once that you were come not to bring peace, but a sword?"

"It was a scribe's error; I told them that I brought peace and not a sword. I never wrote anything; what I said can have been changed without evil intention."

"You did not then contribute in any way by your teaching, either badly reported or badly interpreted, to those frightful piles of bones which I saw on my way to consult with you?"

"I have only looked with horror upon those who have made themselves guilty of all these murders."

. . . [Finally] I asked him to tell me in what true religion consisted.

"Have I not already told you? Love God and your neighbor as yourself."

"Is it necessary for me to take sides either for the Greek Orthodox Church or the Roman Catholic?"

"When I was in the world I never made any difference between the Jew and the Samaritan."

"Well, if that is so, I take you for my only master." Then he made a sign with his head that filled

❖ An impish Voltaire, by the French sculptor Houdon. *(Courtesy of Board of Trustees of the Victoria & Albert Museum)*

me with peace. The vision disappeared, and I was left with a clear conscience.

Questions for Analysis

1. Why did Voltaire believe in a Supreme Being? Does this passage reflect the influence of Isaac Newton's scientific system?

2. Was Voltaire trying to entertain or teach or both? Was he effective? Why or why not?

3. If Voltaire was trying to convey serious ideas about religion and morality, what were those ideas? What was he attacking?

4. If a person today thought and wrote like Voltaire, would that person be called a defender or a destroyer of Christianity? Why?

Source: F. M. Arouet de Voltaire, *Oeuvres completes*, vol. 8, trans. J. McKay (Paris: Firmin-Didot, 1875), pp. 188–190.

19

The Expansion of Europe in the Eighteenth Century

Port of Dieppe (detail), by Joseph Vernet. *(Musée de la Marine, Paris/Bridgeman Art Library, London/ New York)*

The world of absolutism and aristocracy, a combination of raw power and elegant refinement, was a world apart from that of the common people. For the overwhelming majority of the population in the eighteenth century, life remained a struggle with poverty and uncertainty, with the landlord and the tax collector. In 1700 peasants on the land and artisans in their shops lived little better than had their ancestors in the Middle Ages. Only in science and thought, and there only among a few intellectual elites and their followers, had Western society succeeded in going beyond the great achievements of the High Middle Ages, achievements that in turn owed so much to Greece and Rome.

Everyday life was a struggle because European societies, despite their best efforts, still could not produce very much by modern standards. Ordinary men and women might work like their beasts in the fields, and they often did, but there was seldom enough good food, warm clothing, and decent housing. Life went on; history went on. The wars of religion ravaged Germany in the seventeenth century; Russia rose to become a Great Power; the state of Poland simply disappeared; monarchs and nobles continually jockeyed for power and wealth. In 1700 or even 1750, the idea of progress, of substantial improvement in the lives of great numbers of people, was still only the dream of a small elite in fashionable salons.

Yet the economic basis of European life was beginning to change. In the course of the eighteenth century, the European economy emerged from the long crisis of the seventeenth century, responded to challenges, and began to expand once again. Population resumed its growth, while colonial empires developed and colonial elites prospered. Some areas were more fortunate than others. The rising Atlantic powers—Holland, France, and, above all, England—and their colonies led the way. The expansion of agriculture and industry, trade and population, marked the beginning of a surge comparable to that of the eleventh- and twelfth-century springtime of European civilization. But this time, broadly based expansion was not cut short. This time the response to new challenges led toward one of the most influential developments in human history, the Industrial Revolution, considered in Chapter 22.

- What were the causes of this renewed surge?
- Why were the fundamental economic underpinnings of European society beginning to change and what were the dimensions of these changes?

- How did these changes affect people and their work?

These are the questions this chapter will address.

AGRICULTURE AND THE LAND

At the end of the seventeenth century, the economy of Europe was agrarian, as it had been for several hundred years. With the possible exception of Holland, at least 80 percent of the people of all western European countries drew their livelihoods from agriculture. In eastern Europe the percentage was considerably higher.

Men and women lavished their attention on the land, plowing fields and sowing seed, reaping harvests and storing grain. The land repaid these efforts, year after year yielding up the food and most of the raw materials for industry that made life possible. Yet the land was stingy. Even in a rich agricultural region such as the Po Valley in northern Italy, every bushel of wheat sown yielded on average only five or six bushels of grain at harvest during the seventeenth century. The average French yield in the same period was somewhat less. Such yields were barely more than those attained in fertile, well-watered areas in the thirteenth century or in ancient Greece. By modern standards, output was distressingly low. (For each bushel of wheat seed sown today on fertile land with good rainfall, an American or French farmer can expect roughly forty bushels of produce.) In 1700 European agriculture was much more ancient and medieval than it was modern.

If the land was stingy, it was also capricious. In most regions of Europe in the sixteenth and seventeenth centuries, harvests were poor, or even failed completely, every eight or nine years. The vast majority of the population, which lived off the land, might survive a single bad harvest by eating less and drawing on their reserves of grain. But when the land's caprices combined with persistent bad weather—too much rain rotting the seed or drought withering the young stalks—the result was catastrophic. Meager grain reserves were soon exhausted, and the price of grain soared. Provisions from other areas with better harvests were hard to obtain.

In such crisis years, which periodically stalked Europe in the seventeenth and even into the early eighteenth century, a terrible tightening knot in the belly forced people to use substitutes—the "famine foods" of a desperate population. People gathered chestnuts and stripped bark in the forests, they cut dandelions and grass, and they ate these substitutes to escape starvation. In one community in Norway in the early 1700s, people were forced to wash dung from the straw in old manure piles in order to bake a pathetic substitute for bread. Even cannibalism occurred in the seventeenth century.

Such unbalanced and inadequate food in famine years made people weak and extremely susceptible to illness and epidemics. Eating material unfit for human consumption, such as bark or grass, resulted in dysentery and intestinal ailments of many kinds. Influenza and smallpox preyed with particular savagery on populations weakened by famine. In famine years the number of deaths soared far above normal. A third of a village's population might disappear in a year or two. Indeed, the 1690s were as dismal as many of the worst periods of earlier times. One county in Finland, probably typical of the entire country, lost fully 28 percent of its inhabitants in 1696 and 1697. Certain well-studied villages in the Beauvais region of northern France suffered a similar fate. In preindustrial Europe the harvest

was the real king, and the king was seldom generous and often cruel.

To understand why Europeans produced barely enough food in good years and occasionally agonized through years of famine throughout the later seventeenth century, one must follow the plowman, his wife, and his children into the fields to observe their battle for food and life. There the ingenious pattern of farming that Europe had developed in the Middle Ages, a pattern that allowed fairly large numbers of people to survive but could never produce material abundance, was still dominant.

The Open-Field System

The greatest accomplishment of medieval agriculture was the open-field system of village farming developed by European peasants. That system divided the land to be cultivated by the peasants of a given village into several large fields, which were in turn cut up into long, narrow strips. The fields were open, and the strips were not enclosed into small plots by fences or hedges. An individual peasant family—if it was fortunate—held a

Farming the Land   Agricultural methods in Europe changed very slowly from the Middle Ages to the early eighteenth century. This realistic picture from Diderot's *Encyclopedia* has striking similarities with agricultural scenes found in medieval manuscripts. *(University of Illinois Library, Champaign)*

number of strips scattered throughout the various large fields. The land of those who owned but did not till, primarily the nobility, the clergy, and wealthy townspeople, was also in scattered strips. Peasants farmed each large field as a community, with each family following the same pattern of plowing, sowing, and harvesting in accordance with tradition and the village leaders.

The ever-present problem was exhaustion of the soil. When the community planted wheat year after year in a field, the nitrogen in the soil was soon depleted, and crop failure was certain. Since the supply of manure for fertilizer was limited, the only way for the land to recover its life-giving fertility was for a field to lie fallow for a period of time. In the early Middle Ages, a year of fallow was alternated with a year of cropping, so that half the land stood idle in a given year. With time, three-year rotations were introduced, especially on more fertile lands. This system permitted a year of wheat or rye to be followed by a year of oats or beans and only then by a year of fallow. Even so, only awareness of the tragic consequences of continuous cropping forced undernourished populations to let a third (or half) of their cropland lie idle, especially when the fallow still had to be plowed two or three times a year to keep down the weeds.

Traditional village rights reinforced the traditional pattern of farming. In addition to rotating field crops in a uniform way, villages maintained open meadows for hay and natural pasture. These lands were "common" lands, set aside primarily for the draft horses and oxen so necessary in the fields, but open to the cows and pigs of the village community as well. After the harvest, the men and women of the village also pastured their animals on the wheat or rye stubble. In many places such pasturing followed a brief period, also established by tradition, for the gleaning of grain. Poor women would go through the fields picking up the few single grains that had fallen to the ground in the course of the harvest. The subject of a great nineteenth-century painting, *The Gleaners* by Jean François Millet (page 632), this backbreaking work by hard-working but impoverished women meant quite literally the slender margin of survival for some people in the winter months.

In the age of absolutism and nobility, state and landlord continued to levy heavy taxes and high rents as a matter of course. In so doing, they stripped the peasants of much of their meager earnings. The level of exploitation varied.

Generally speaking, the peasants of eastern Europe were worst off. As we saw in Chapter 17, they were serfs bound to their lords in hereditary service. Though serfdom in eastern Europe in the eighteenth century had much in common with medieval serfdom in central and western Europe, it was, if anything, harsher and more oppressive. In much of eastern Europe, there were few limitations on the amount of forced labor the lord could require, and five or six days of unpaid work per week on the lord's land were not uncommon. Well into the nineteenth century, individual Russian serfs and serf families were regularly sold with and without land.

Social conditions were better in western Europe. Peasants were generally free from serfdom. In France, western Germany, and the Low Countries, they owned land and could pass it on to their children. Yet life in the village was unquestionably hard, and poverty was the great reality for most people. For the Beauvais region of France at the beginning of the eighteenth century, it has been carefully estimated that in good years and bad only a tenth of the peasants could live satisfactorily off the fruits of their landholdings. Owning considerably less than half of the land, the peasants of this region had to pay heavy royal taxes, the church's tithe, and dues to the lord, as well as set aside seed for the next season. Left with only half of their crop for their own use, these peasants had to toil and till for others and seek work for wages in a variety of jobs. It was a constant scramble for a meager living. And this was in a rich agricultural region in a country where peasants were comparatively well-off. The privileges of Europe's ruling elites weighed heavily on the people of the land.

Agricultural Revolution

One possible way for European peasants to improve their difficult position was to take land from those who owned but did not labor. Yet the social and political conditions that enabled the ruling elites to squeeze the peasants were ancient and deeply rooted, and powerful forces stood ready to crush any protest. Only with the coming of the French Revolution were European peasants, mainly in France, able to improve their position by means of radical mass action.

Technological progress offered another possibility. The great need was for new farming methods that would enable Europeans to produce more and eat more. Uncultivated fields were the heart of the matter. If peasants (and their noble landlords) could replace the idle fallow with crops, they could increase the land under cultivation by 50 percent. So remarkable were the possibilities and the results that historians have often spoken of the progressive elimination of the fallow, which occurred slowly throughout Europe from the mid-seventeenth century on, as an agricultural revolution.

Millet: The Gleaners   Poor French peasant women search for grains and stalks that the harvesters (in the background) have missed. The open-field system seen here could still be found in parts of Europe in 1857, when this picture was painted. Millet is known for his great paintings expressing social themes. *(Louvre © Photo R.M.N.)*

This agricultural revolution, which took longer than historians used to believe, was a great milestone in human development. The famous French scholar Marc Bloch, who gave his life in the resistance to the Nazis in World War II, summed it up well: "The history of the conquest of the fallow by new crops, a fresh triumph of man over the earth that is just as moving as the great land clearing of the Middle Ages, [is] one of the noblest stories that can be told."[1]

Because grain crops exhaust the soil and make fallowing necessary, the secret to eliminating the fallow lies in alternating grain with certain nitrogen-storing crops. Such crops not only rejuvenate the soil even better than fallowing but also give more produce. The most impor-

tant of these land-reviving crops are peas and beans, root crops such as turnips and potatoes, and clovers and grasses. In the eighteenth century, peas and beans were old standbys; turnips, potatoes, and clover were newcomers to the fields. As the eighteenth century went on, the number of crops that were systematically rotated grew. New patterns of organization allowed some farmers to develop increasingly sophisticated patterns of rotation to suit different kinds of soils. For example, farmers in French Flanders near Lille in the late eighteenth century used a ten-year rotation, alternating a number of grain, root, and hay crops in a given field on a ten-year schedule. Continual experimentation led to more scientific farming.

Improvements in farming had multiple effects. The new crops made ideal feed for animals. Because peasants and larger farmers had more fodder, hay, and root crops for the winter months, they could build up their small herds of cattle and sheep. More animals meant more meat and better diets for the people. More animals also meant more manure for fertilizer and therefore more grain for bread and porridge. The vicious cycle in which few animals meant inadequate manure, which meant little grain and less fodder, which led to fewer animals, and so on, could certainly be broken.

Advocates of the new rotations, who included an emerging group of experimental scientists, some government officials, and a few big landowners, believed that new methods were scarcely possible within the traditional framework of open fields and common rights. A farmer who wanted to experiment with new methods would have to get all the landholders in a village to agree to the plan, and advocates of improvement maintained that this would be difficult, if not impossible, given peasant caution and the force of tradition. Therefore, they argued that innovating agriculturalists needed to enclose and consolidate their scattered holdings into compact, fenced-in fields in order to farm more effectively. In doing so, the innovators also needed to enclose their individual shares of the natural pasture, the common. According to this view, a revolution in village life and organization was the necessary price of technical progress.

That price seemed too high to many rural people. Above all, the village poor believed that they were being asked to pay an unfair and disproportionate share of the bill. With land distributed very unequally all across Europe by 1700, large groups of village poor held small, inadequate holdings or very little land at all. Common rights were precious to these poor peasants. The rights to glean and to graze a cow on the common, to gather firewood in the lord's forest and pick berries in the marsh, were vital because they helped poor peasants retain a modicum of independence and status and avoid falling into the growing group of landless, "proletarian" wage workers. Thus when the small landholders and the village poor could effectively oppose the enclosure of the open fields and the common pasture, they did so. Moreover, in many countries they usually found allies among the larger, predominately noble landowners, who were also wary of enclosure because it required large investments and posed risks for them as well. Only powerful social and political pressures could overcome such combined opposition.

The old system of unenclosed open fields and the new system of continuous rotation coexisted in Europe for a very long time. In large parts of central Russia, for example, the old system did not disappear until after the Bolshevik Revolution in 1917. It could also be found in much of France and Germany in the early years of the nineteenth century because peasants there had successfully opposed efforts to introduce the new techniques in the late eighteenth century. Indeed, until the end of the eighteenth century, the promise of the new system was extensively realized only in the Low Countries and in England.

The Leadership of the Low Countries and England

The new methods of the agricultural revolution originated in the Low Countries. The vibrant, dynamic, middle-class society of seventeenth-century republican Holland was the most advanced in Europe in many areas of human endeavor (pages 554–559). In shipbuilding and navigation, in commerce and banking, in drainage and agriculture, the people of the Low Countries, especially the Dutch, provided models the jealous English and French sought to copy or to cripple.

By the middle of the seventeenth century, intensive farming was well established throughout much of the Low Countries. Enclosed fields, continuous rotation, heavy manuring, and a wide variety of crops—all these innovations were present. Agriculture was highly specialized and commercialized. The same skills that grew turnips produced flax to be spun into linen for clothes and tulip bulbs to lighten the heart with their beauty. The fat cattle of Holland, so beloved by Dutch painters, gave the most milk in Europe. Dutch cheeses were already world renowned.

The reasons for early Dutch leadership in farming were basically twofold. In the first place, since the end of the Middle Ages the Low Countries had been one of the most densely populated areas in Europe. Thus in order to feed themselves and provide employment, the Dutch were forced at an early date to seek maximum yields from their land and to increase the cultivated area through the steady draining of marshes and swamps. Even so, they had to import wheat from Poland and eastern Germany.

The pressure of population was connected with the second cause, the growth of towns and cities in the Low Countries. Stimulated by commerce and overseas trade, Amsterdam grew from 30,000 inhabitants to 200,000 in its golden seventeenth century. The growth of urban population provided Dutch peasants with good markets for all they could produce and allowed each region to specialize in what it did best. Thus the Dutch could

Hendrick Sorgh: Vegetable Market, 1662 The wealth and well-being of the industrious, capitalistic Dutch shine forth in this winsome market scene. The market woman's baskets are filled with delicious fresh produce that ordinary citizens can afford—eloquent testimony to the responsive, enterprising character of Dutch agriculture. *(Historisch Museum, Rotterdam)*

develop their potential, and the Low Countries became "the Mecca of foreign agricultural experts who came . . . to see Flemish agriculture with their own eyes, to write about it and to propagate its methods in their home lands."[2]

The English were the best students. Drainage and water control were one subject in which they received instruction. Large parts of seventeenth-century Holland had once been sea and sea marsh, and the efforts of centuries had made the Dutch the world's leaders in the skills of drainage. In the first half of the seventeenth century, Dutch experts made a great contribution to draining the extensive marshes, or fens, of wet and rainy England.

The most famous of these Dutch engineers, Cornelius Vermuyden, directed one large drainage project in Yorkshire and another in Cambridgeshire. In the Cambridge fens, Vermuyden and his Dutch workers eventually reclaimed forty thousand acres, which were then farmed intensively in the Dutch manner. Although all these efforts were disrupted in the turbulent 1640s

by the English civil war, Vermuyden and his countrymen largely succeeded. Swampy wilderness was converted into thousands of acres of some of the best land in England. On such new land, where traditions and common rights were not yet firmly established, farmers introduced new crops and new rotations fairly easily.

Dutch experience was also important to Viscount Charles Townsend (1674–1738), one of the pioneers of English agricultural improvement. This lord from the upper reaches of the English aristocracy learned about turnips and clover while serving as English ambassador to Holland. In the 1710s, he was using these crops in the sandy soil of his large estates in Norfolk in eastern England, already one of the most innovative agricultural areas in the country. When Lord Charles retired from politics in 1730 and returned to Norfolk, it was said that he spoke of turnips, turnips, and nothing but turnips. This led some wit to nickname his lordship "Turnip" Townsend. But Townsend had the last laugh. Draining extensively, manuring heavily, and sowing crops in regular rotation without fallowing, the farmers who leased Townsend's lands produced larger crops. They and he earned higher incomes. Those who had scoffed reconsidered. By 1740 agricultural improvement in various forms had become something of a craze among the English aristocracy.

Jethro Tull (1674–1741), part crank and part genius, was another important English innovator. A true son of the early Enlightenment, Tull adopted a critical attitude toward accepted ideas about farming and tried to develop better methods through empirical research. He was especially enthusiastic about using horses, rather than slower-moving oxen, for plowing. He also advocated sowing seed with drilling equipment rather than scattering it by hand. Drilling distributed seed in an even manner and at the proper depth. There were also improvements in livestock, inspired in part by the earlier successes of English country gentlemen in breeding ever-faster horses for the races and fox hunts that were their passions. Selective breeding of ordinary livestock was a marked improvement over the old pattern, which has been graphically described as little more than "the

haphazard union of nobody's son with everybody's daughter."

By the mid-eighteenth century, English agriculture was in the process of a long but radical transformation. The eventual result was that by 1870 English farmers were producing 300 percent more food than they had produced in 1700, although the number of people working the land had increased by only 14 percent. This great surge of agricultural production provided food for England's rapidly growing urban population. It was a tremendous achievement.

The Cost of Enclosure

What was the cost of technical progress in England, and to what extent did its payment result in social injustice? Scholars agree that the impetus for enclosing the fields came mainly from the powerful ruling class, the English aristocracy. Owning large estates, the aristocracy benefited directly from higher yields that could support

Selective Breeding   meant bigger livestock and more meat on English tables. This gigantic champion, one of the new improved shorthorn breed, was known as the Newbus Ox. Such great fat beasts were pictured in the press and praised by poets. *(Institute of Agricultural History and Museum of English Rural Life, University of Reading)*

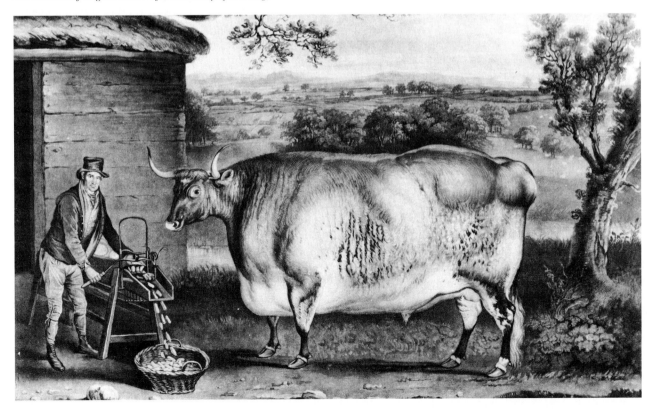

higher rents, and it was able and ready to make expensive investments in the new technology. Beyond these certainties, there are important differences of interpretation among historians.

Many historians stress the initiative and enterprise of the big English landowners, which they contrast with the inertia and conservatism of continental landowners, big and small. These historians also assert that the open fields were enclosed fairly, with both large and small owners receiving their fair share after the strips had been surveyed and consolidated.

Other historians argue that fairness was more apparent than real. The large landowners controlled Parliament, which made the laws. They had Parliament pass hundreds of "enclosure acts," each of which authorized the fencing of open fields in a given village and the division of the common in proportion to one's property in the open fields. The heavy legal and surveying costs of enclosure were also divided among the landowners. This meant that many peasants who had small holdings had to sell out to pay their share of the expenses. Similarly, landless cottagers lost their age-old access to the common pasture without any compensation whatsoever. This dealt landless families a serious blow because it deprived women of the means to raise animals for market and earn vital income. In the spirited words of one critical historian, "Enclosure (when all the sophistications are allowed for) was a plain enough case of class robbery, played according to the fair rules of property and law laid down by a Parliament of property owners and lawyers."[3]

In assessing these conflicting interpretations, one must put eighteenth-century developments in a longer historical perspective. In the first place, as much as half of English farmland was already enclosed by 1750. A great wave of enclosure of English open fields into sheep pastures had already occurred in the sixteenth and early seventeenth centuries and had already dispossessed many English peasants in order to produce wool for the growing textile industry. In the later seventeenth and early eighteenth centuries, many open fields were enclosed fairly harmoniously by mutual agreement among all classes of landowners in English villages. Thus parliamentary enclosure, the great bulk of which occurred after 1760 and particularly during the Napoleonic wars early in the nineteenth century, only completed a process that was in full swing. Nor did an army of landless cottagers and farm laborers appear only in the last years of the eighteenth century. Much earlier, and certainly by 1700 because of the early enclosures for sheep runs, there were perhaps two landless agricultural workers in England for every independent farmer. In 1830, after the enclosures were complete, the proportion of landless laborers was not substantially greater.

By 1700 a highly distinctive pattern of landowner-ship and production existed in England. At one extreme were a few large landowners; at the other, a large mass of landless cottagers who labored mainly for wages and who could graze only a pig or a cow on the village common. In between stood two other groups: small, independent peasant farmers who owned their own land and strong, prosperous tenant farmers who rented land from the big landowners, hired wage laborers, and sold their output on a cash market. Yet the small, independent English peasant farmers had been declining in number since the sixteenth-century enclosures (and even before), and they continued to do so in the eighteenth century. They could not compete with the rising group of profit-minded, market-oriented tenant farmers.

These tenant farmers, many of whom had formerly been independent owners, were the key to mastering the new methods of farming. Well financed by the large landowners, the tenant farmers fenced fields, built drains, and improved the soil with fertilizers. Such improvements actually increased employment opportunities for wage workers in some areas. So did new methods of farming, for land was farmed more intensively without the fallow, and new crops such as turnips required more care and effort. Thus enclosure did not force people off the land and into the towns by eliminating jobs, as has sometimes been claimed.

At the same time, by eliminating common rights and greatly reducing the access of poor men and women to the land, the eighteenth-century enclosure movement marked the completion of two major historical developments in England—the rise of market-oriented estate agriculture and the emergence of a landless rural proletariat. By 1815 a tiny minority of wealthy English (and Scottish) landowners held most of the land and pursued profits aggressively, leasing their holdings through agents at competitive prices to middle-size farmers. These farmers produced mainly for cash markets and relied on landless laborers for their workforce. These landless laborers may have lived as well in 1800 as their predecessors had in 1700 in strictly economic terms. But they had lost that bit of independence and self-respect that common rights had provided. They had become completely dependent on cash wages earned in agriculture or in rural industry for their survival. In no other European country had this "proletarianization"—this transformation of large numbers of small peasant farmers into landless rural wage earners—gone so far as it had in England by the late eighteenth century. And as in the earlier English enclosure movement, the village poor found the cost of economic change and technical progress heavy and unjust.

 ## THE BEGINNING OF THE POPULATION EXPLOSION

Another factor that affected the existing order of life and forced economic changes in the eighteenth century was the remarkable growth of European population, the beginning of the "population explosion." This explosion continued in Europe until the twentieth century, by which time it was affecting nonwestern areas of the globe. What caused the growth of population, and what did the challenge of more mouths to feed and more hands to employ do to the European economy?

Limitations on Population Growth

Many commonly held ideas about population in the past are wrong. One such mistaken idea is that people always married young and had large families. A related error is the belief that past societies were so ignorant that they could do nothing to control their numbers and that population was always growing too fast. On the contrary, until 1700 the total population of Europe grew slowly much of the time, and it followed an irregular cyclical pattern (Figure 19.1).

The cyclical pattern of European population growth had a great influence on many aspects of social and economic life over time, although striking local and regional differences often make generalization difficult. As we have seen, the terrible ravages of the Black Death caused a sharp drop in population and prices after 1350 and also created a labor shortage throughout Europe (see page 566). Lords in eastern Europe responded to this labor shortage by reversing the trend toward personal freedom and gradually reinstituting serfdom. This landlord reaction failed in western Europe, however, where serf obligations had declined or even disappeared by 1500. Moreover, the era of labor shortages and low food prices after the Black Death resulted in an increased standard of living for peasants and artisans. Some economic historians calculate that for those common people in western Europe who managed to steer clear of warfare and of power struggles within the ruling class, the later Middle Ages was an era of exceptional well-being.

But peasant and artisan well-being was eroded in the course of the sixteenth century. The second great surge

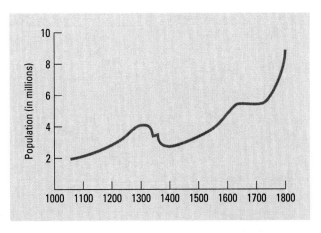

FIGURE 19.1 The Growth of Population in England, 1000–1800   England is a good example of both the uneven increase of European population before 1700 and the third great surge of growth, which began in the eighteenth century. *(Source: E. A. Wrigley,* Population and History. *Copyright © 1969 by McGraw-Hill. Reprinted by permission.)*

of population growth (see Figure 19.1) outstripped the growth of agricultural production after about 1500. There was less food per person, and food prices rose more rapidly than wages, a development intensified by the inflow of precious metals from the Americas and a general, if uneven, European price revolution. The result was a substantial decline in living standards for the great majority of people throughout Europe. This decline especially aggravated the plight of both the urban and the rural poor. By 1600 the pressure of population on resources was severe in much of Europe, and widespread poverty was an undeniable reality.

For this reason, population growth slowed and stopped in seventeenth-century Europe. Births and deaths, fertility and mortality, were in a crude but effective balance. The birthrate—annual births as a proportion of the population—was fairly high but was far lower than it would have been if all women between ages fifteen and forty-five had been having as many children as biologically possible. The death rate in normal years was also high, though somewhat lower than the birthrate. As a result, the population grew modestly in normal years at a rate of perhaps 0.5 to 1 percent, or enough to double the population in 70 to 140 years. This is, of course, a generalization encompassing many different patterns. In areas such as Russia and colonial New England, where there was a great deal of frontier to be settled, the annual rate of natural increase, not counting in-migration, might well have exceeded 1 percent. In a country such as France, where the land had

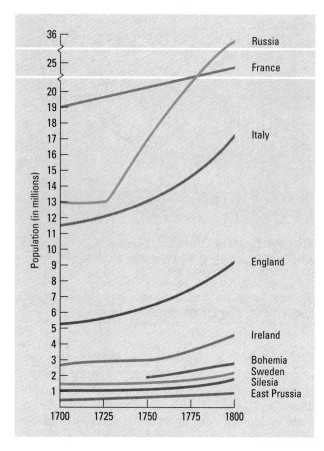

FIGURE 19.2 The Increase of Population in Europe in the Eighteenth Century France's large population continued to support French political and intellectual leadership. Russia emerged as Europe's most populous state because natural increase was complemented by growth from territorial expansion.

long been densely settled, the rate of increase might have been less than 0.5 percent.

Although population growth of even 1 percent per year is fairly modest by the standards of many African and Latin American countries today—some of which are growing at about 3 percent annually—it will produce a very large increase over a long period. An annual increase of even 1 percent will result in sixteen times as many people in three hundred years. Such gigantic increases simply did not occur in agrarian Europe before the eighteenth century. In certain abnormal years and tragic periods—the Black Death was only the most extreme and extensive example—many more people died than were born. Total population fell sharply, even catastrophically. A number of years of modest growth would then be necessary to make up for those who had died in an abnormal year. Such savage increases in

deaths occurred periodically in the seventeenth century on a local and regional scale, and these demographic crises combined with birthrates far below the biological potential to check the growth of population until after 1700.

The grim reapers of demographic crisis were famine, epidemic disease, and war. Famine, the inevitable result of poor farming methods and periodic crop failures, was particularly murderous because it was accompanied by disease. With a brutal one-two punch, famine stunned and weakened a population, and disease finished it off. Disease, as the example of the Black Death illustrates, could also ravage the population independently of famine.

War was another scourge. The indirect effects were more harmful than the organized killing. War spread disease. Soldiers and camp followers passed venereal disease throughout the countryside to scar and kill. Armies requisitioned scarce food supplies for their own use and disrupted the agricultural cycle. The Thirty Years' War witnessed all possible combinations of distress. In the German states, the number of inhabitants declined by more than *two-thirds* in some large areas and by at least one-third almost everywhere else.

The New Pattern of the Eighteenth Century

In the eighteenth century, the population of Europe began to grow markedly. This increase in numbers occurred in all areas of Europe, western and eastern, northern and southern, dynamic and stagnant. Growth was especially dramatic after about 1750 (Figure 19.2).

Although it is certain that Europe's population grew greatly, it is less clear why. Painstaking and innovative research in population history has shown that, because population grew everywhere, it is best to look first for general factors rather than focus on those limited to individual countries or to certain levels of social and economic development. What, then, caused fewer people to die or, possibly, more babies to be born? In some areas some women did have more babies than before because new opportunities for employment in rural industry allowed them to marry at an earlier age, as we shall see (see pages 661–665). But the basic cause for Europe as a whole was a decline in mortality—fewer deaths.

The bubonic plague mysteriously disappeared. Following the Black Death in the fourteenth century, plagues had remained a part of the European experience, striking again and again with savage force, particularly in towns. As late as 1721, a ship from Syria and the Levant, where plague was ever present, brought the

Bubonic Plague in Marseilles, 1721 In this gruesome scene, people are trying to flee the plague-ridden port by ship, but most are prevented from doing so by measures to quarantine the disease. The wharf is littered with the bodies of the dead and dying. Ominous black clouds represent the stench of the polluted air. *(Courtesy of the Trustees of the British Museum)*

monstrous disease to Marseilles. In a few weeks, forty thousand of the city's ninety thousand inhabitants died. The epidemic swept southern France, killing one-third, one-half, even three-fourths of those in the larger towns. Once again an awful fear swept across Europe. But the epidemic passed, and that was the last time plague fell on western and central Europe. The final disappearance of plague was due in part to stricter measures of quarantine in Mediterranean ports and along the Austrian border with Turkey. Human carriers of plague were carefully isolated. Chance and plain good luck were more important, however.

It is now understood that bubonic plague is, above all, a disease of rats. More precisely, it is the black rat that spreads major epidemics, for the black rat's flea is the principal carrier of the plague bacillus. After 1600, for reasons unknown, a new rat of Asiatic origin—the brown, or wander, rat—began to drive out and eventually eliminate its black competitor. In the words of a noted authority, "This revolution in the animal kingdom must have gone far to break the lethal link between rat and man."[4] Although the brown rat also contracts the plague, another kind of flea is its main parasite. That flea carries the plague poorly and, for good measure, has little taste for human blood.

Advances in medical knowledge did not contribute much to reducing the death rate in the eighteenth century. The most important advance in preventive medicine in this period was inoculation against smallpox. This great improvement was long confined mainly to England and probably did little to reduce deaths throughout Europe until the latter part of the century. However, improvements in the water supply and sewerage, which were frequently promoted by strong absolutist monarchies, resulted in somewhat better public health and helped reduce such diseases as typhoid and typhus in some urban areas of western Europe. Eighteenth-century improvements in water supply and in the drainage of swamps and marshes also reduced Europe's large and dangerous insect population. Filthy flies and mosquitoes played a major role in spreading serious epidemics and also in transmitting common diseases, especially those striking children and young adults. Thus early public health measures were probably more important than historians have previously believed, and they helped the decline in mortality that began with the disappearance of plague to continue into the early nineteenth century.

Human beings also became more successful in their efforts to safeguard the supply of food and protect against famine. The eighteenth century was a time of considerable canal and road building in western Europe. These advances in transportation, which were also among the more positive aspects of strong absolutist states, lessened the impact of local crop failure and famine. Emergency supplies could be brought in. The age-old spectacle of localized starvation became less frequent. Wars became more gentlemanly and less destructive than in the seventeenth century and spread fewer epidemics. New foods, particularly the potato from South America, were introduced. Potatoes served as an important alternative source of vitamins A and C for the poor, especially when the grain crops were skimpy or had failed. In short, population grew in the eighteenth century primarily because years of abnormal death rates were less catastrophic. Famines, epidemics, and wars continued to occur, but their severity moderated.

The growth of population in the eighteenth century cannot be interpreted as a sign of human progress, however. As we have seen, serious population pressures on resources were in existence by 1600 and continued throughout the seventeenth century. Thus renewed population growth in the eighteenth century maintained or even increased the imbalance between the number of people and the economic opportunities available to them. There was only so much land available, and tradition slowed the adoption of better farming methods. Therefore, agriculture could not provide enough work for the rapidly growing labor force, and poor people in the countryside had to look for new ways to make a living.

THE GROWTH OF COTTAGE INDUSTRY

The growth of population increased the number of rural workers with little or no land, and this in turn contributed to the development of industry in rural areas. The poor in the countryside increasingly needed to supplement their earnings from agriculture with other types of work, and capitalists from the city were eager to employ them, often at lower wages than urban workers usually commanded. Manufacturing with hand tools in peasant cottages and work sheds grew markedly in the eighteenth century. Rural industry became a crucial feature of the European economy.

To be sure, peasant communities had always made some clothing, processed some food, and constructed some housing for their own use. But in the High Mid-

dle Ages, peasants did not produce manufactured goods on a large scale for sale in a market. Industry in the Middle Ages was dominated and organized by urban craft guilds and urban merchants, who jealously regulated handicraft production and sought to maintain it as an urban monopoly. By the eighteenth century, however, the pressures of rural poverty and the need to employ landless proletarians were overwhelming the efforts of urban artisans to maintain their traditional control over industrial production. A new system was expanding lustily.

The new system has had many names. It has often been called "cottage industry" or "domestic industry" to distinguish it from the factory industry that came later. In recent years, some scholars have preferred to speak of "protoindustrialization," by which they usually mean a stage of rural industrial development with wage workers and hand tools that necessarily preceded the emergence of large-scale factory industry. The focus on protoindustrialization has been quite valuable because it has sparked renewed interest in Europe's early industrial development and shown again that the mechanized factories grew out of a vibrant industrial tradition. However, the evolving concept of protoindustrialization also has different versions, some of which are rigid and unduly deterministic. Thus the phrase *putting-out system,* widely used by contemporaries to describe the key features of eighteenth-century rural industry, still seems a more appropriate term for the new form of industrial production.

The Putting-Out System

The two main participants in the putting-out system were the merchant capitalist and the rural worker. The merchant loaned, or "put out," raw materials to several cottage workers, who processed the raw materials in their own homes and returned the finished product to the merchant. For example, a merchant would provide raw wool, and the workers would spin and weave the wool into cloth. The merchant then paid the outworkers for their work by the piece and proceeded to sell the finished product. There were endless variations on this basic relationship. Sometimes rural workers would buy their own materials and work as independent producers before they sold to the merchant. Sometimes several workers toiled together to perform a complicated process in a workshop. The relative importance of earnings from the land and from industry varied greatly for handicraft workers, although industrial wages usually became more important for a given family with time. In

Rural Industry in Action   This French engraving suggests just how many things could be made in the countryside with simple tools. The workers in this outdoor workshop are making inexpensive but long-lasting wooden shoes, which were widely worn by the poor. *(University of Illinois Library, Champaign)*

all cases, however, the putting-out system was a kind of capitalism. Merchants needed large amounts of capital, which they held in the form of goods being worked up and sold in distant markets. They sought to make profits and increase the capital in their businesses.

The putting-out system grew because it had competitive advantages. Underemployed labor was abundant, and poor peasants and landless laborers would work for low wages. Since production in the countryside was unregulated, workers and merchants could change procedures and experiment as they saw fit. Because they did not need to meet rigid guild standards, which maintained quality but discouraged the development of new methods, cottage industry became capable of producing many kinds of goods. Textiles; all manner of knives, forks, and housewares; buttons and gloves; clocks; and musical instruments could be produced quite satisfactorily in the countryside. Luxury goods for the rich, such as exquisite tapestries and fine porcelain, demanded special training, close supervision, and centralized workshops. Yet such goods were as exceptional as those who

used them. The skills of rural industry were sufficient for everyday articles.

Rural manufacturing did not spread across Europe at an even rate. It appeared first in England and developed most successfully there, particularly for the spinning and weaving of woolen cloth. By 1500 half of England's textiles were being produced in the countryside. By 1700 English industry was generally more rural than urban and heavily reliant on the putting-out system. Continental countries developed rural industry more slowly.

In France at the time of Louis XIV, Colbert had revived the urban guilds and used them as a means to control the cities and collect taxes (see page 540). But the pressure of rural poverty proved too great. In 1762 the special privileges of urban manufacturing were severely restricted in France, and the already developing rural industries were given free rein from then on. The royal government in France had come to believe that the best way to help the poor in the countryside was to encourage the growth of cottage manufacturing. Thus

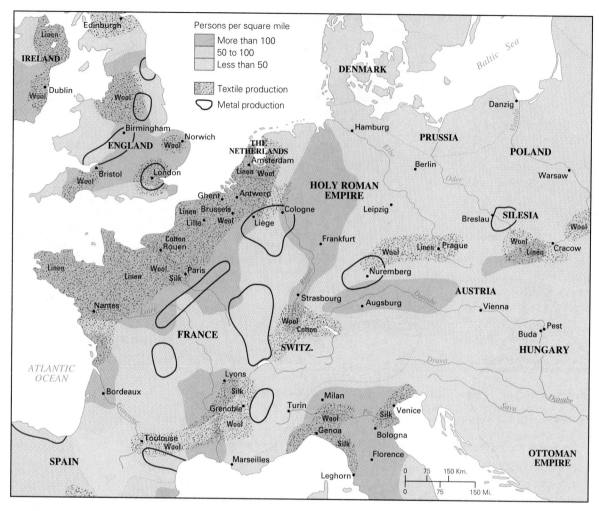

MAP 19.1 Industry and Population in Eighteenth-Century Europe   The growth of cottage manufacturing in rural areas helped country people to increase their income and contributed to increases in the population. This putting-out system began in England, and much of the work was in the textile industry. Cottage industry was also strong in the Low Countries—modern-day Belgium and Holland.

in France, as in Germany and other areas, the later part of the eighteenth century witnessed a remarkable expansion of rural industry in certain densely populated regions (Map 19.1). The pattern established in England was spreading to the continent.

The Textile Industry

Throughout most of history until at least the nineteenth century, the industry that has employed the most people has been textiles. The making of linen, woolen, and, eventually, cotton cloth was the typical activity of cottage workers engaged in the putting-out system. A look inside the cottage of the English rural textile worker illustrates a way of life as well as an economic system.

The rural worker lived in a small cottage with tiny windows and little space. Indeed, the worker's cottage was often a single room that served as workshop, kitchen, and bedroom. There were only a few pieces of furniture, of which the weaver's loom was by far the largest and most important. That loom had changed somewhat in the early eighteenth century, when John Kay's invention of the flying shuttle enabled the weaver to throw the shuttle back and forth between the threads with one hand. Aside from that improvement, however, the loom was as it had been for much of history. In the cottage there were also spinning wheels, tubs for dyeing cloth and washing raw wool, and carding pieces to comb and prepare the raw material.

These different pieces of equipment were necessary because cottage industry was first and foremost a family enterprise. All the members of the family helped in the work, so that "every person from seven to eighty (who retained their sight and who could move their hands) could earn their bread," as one eighteenth-century English observer put it.[5] While the women and children prepared the raw material and spun the thread, the man of the house wove the cloth. There was work for everyone, even the youngest, which encouraged cottage workers to marry early and have large families. After the dirt was beaten out of the raw cotton, it had to be thoroughly cleaned with strong soap in a tub, where tiny feet functioned like the agitator in a washing machine. George Crompton, the son of Samuel Crompton, who in 1784 invented the mule for cotton spinning, recalled

that "soon after I was able to walk I was employed in the cotton manufacture. . . . My mother tucked up my petticoats about my waist, and put me into the tub to tread upon the cotton at the bottom."[6] Slightly older children and aged relatives carded and combed the cotton or wool so that the mother and the older daughter she had taught could spin it into thread. Each member had a task. The very young and very old worked in the family unit as a matter of course.

There was always a serious imbalance in this family enterprise: the work of four or five spinners was needed to keep one weaver steadily employed. Therefore, the wife and the husband had to constantly find more thread and more spinners. Widows and unmarried women—those "spinsters" who spun for their living—were recruited by the wife. Or perhaps the weaver's son went off on horseback to seek thread. The need for more thread might even lead the weaver and his wife to become

The Weaver's Repose   This painting by Decker Cornelis Gerritz (1594–1637) captures the pleasure of release from long hours of toil in cottage industry. The loom realistically dominates the cramped living space and the family's modest possessions. (*Musées Royaux des Beaux-Arts, Brussels. Copyright A.C.I.*)

small capitalist employers. At the end of the week when they received the raw wool or cotton from the merchant manufacturer, they would put out some of this raw material to other cottages. The following week they would return to pick up the thread and pay for the spinning, which would help keep the weaver busy for a week until the merchant came for the finished cloth.

Relations between workers and employers were often marked by sharp conflict. An English popular song written about 1700, called "The Clothier's Delight, or the Rich Men's Joy and the Poor Men's Sorrow," has the merchant boasting of the countless tricks he uses to "beat down wages":

We heapeth up riches and treasure great store
Which we get by griping and grinding the poor.
And this is a way for to fill up our purse
Although we do get it with many a curse.[7]

There were constant disputes over the weights of materials and the quality of the cloth. Merchants accused workers of stealing raw materials, and weavers complained that merchants delivered underweight bales. Suspicions abounded.

There was another problem, at least from the merchant capitalist's point of view. Rural labor was cheap, scattered, and poorly organized. For these reasons it was hard to control. Cottage workers tended to work in spurts. After they got paid on Saturday afternoon, the men in particular tended to drink and relax for two or three days. Indeed, Monday was called "holy Monday" because inactivity was so religiously observed. By the end of the week, the weaver was probably working feverishly to make his quota. But if he did not succeed, there was little the merchant could do. When times were good and the merchant could easily sell everything produced, the weaver and his family did fairly well and were particularly inclined to loaf—to the dismay of the capitalist. Thus the putting-out system in the textile industry had definite shortcomings from the employer's point of view. Ambitious merchant capitalists therefore intensified their search for ways to produce more efficiently and to squeeze still more work out of "undisciplined" cottage workers.

✣ BUILDING THE ATLANTIC ECONOMY

In addition to agricultural improvement, population pressure, and growing cottage industry, the expansion of Europe in the eighteenth century was characterized by the growth of world trade. Spain and Portugal revitalized their empires and began drawing more wealth from renewed development. Yet once again the countries of northwestern Europe—the Netherlands, France, and, above all, Great Britain—benefited most. Great Britain, which was formed in 1707 by the union of England and Scotland in a single kingdom, gradually became the leading maritime power. In the eighteenth century, British ships and merchants succeeded in dominating long-distance trade, particularly the fast-growing intercontinental trade across the Atlantic Ocean. The British played the critical role in building a fairly unified Atlantic economy, which offered remarkable opportunities for them and their colonists.

Mercantilism and Colonial Wars

Britain's commercial leadership in the eighteenth century had its origins in the mercantilism of the seventeenth century (see page 539). European mercantilism was a system of economic regulations aimed at increasing the power of the state. As practiced by a leading advocate such as Colbert under Louis XIV, mercantilism aimed particularly at creating a favorable balance of foreign trade in order to increase a country's stock of gold. A country's gold holdings served as an all-important treasure chest, to be opened periodically to pay for war in a violent age.

Early English mercantilists shared these views. What distinguished English mercantilism was the unusual idea that government economic regulations could and should serve the private interest of individuals and groups as well as the public needs of the state. As Josiah Child, a very wealthy brewer and director of the East India Company, put it, in the ideal economy "Profit and Power ought jointly to be considered."[8] By contrast, in France and other continental countries, seventeenth-century mercantilists generally put the needs of the state far above those of business people and workers. And they seldom saw a possible union of public and private interests for a common good.

The result of the English desire to increase both military power and private wealth was the mercantile system of the Navigation Acts. Oliver Cromwell established the first of these laws in 1651, and the restored monarchy of Charles II extended them further in 1660 and 1663; these Navigation Acts were not seriously modified until 1786. The acts required that most goods imported from Europe into England and Scotland be carried on British-owned ships with British crews or on ships of the country producing the article. Moreover, these laws gave British merchants and shipowners a

COLONIAL COMPETITION AND WAR, 1651–1763

1651–1663	British Navigation Acts create the mercantile system, which is not seriously modified until 1786.
1652–1674	Three Anglo-Dutch wars damage Dutch shipping and commerce.
1664	New Amsterdam is seized and renamed New York.
1701–1713	War of the Spanish Succession is fought.
1713	Peace of Utrecht: Britain wins parts of Canada from France and control of the western African slave trade from Spain.
1740–1748	War of the Austrian Succession results in no change in territorial holdings in North America.
1756–1763	Seven Years' War (known in North America as the French and Indian War) ends in a decisive victory for Britain.
1763	Treaty of Paris: Britain receives all French territory on the North American mainland and achieves dominance in India.

virtual monopoly on trade with British colonies. The colonists were required to ship their products—sugar, tobacco, and cotton—on British (or American) ships and to buy almost all of their European goods from Britain. It was believed that these economic regulations would provide British merchants and workers with profits and employment and provide colonial plantation owners and farmers with a guaranteed market for their products. And the emerging British Empire would develop a shipping industry with a large number of tough, experienced, deep-water seamen, who could be drafted when necessary into the Royal Navy to protect the island nation and its colonial possessions.

The Navigation Acts were a form of economic warfare. Their initial target was the Dutch, who were far ahead of the English in shipping and foreign trade in the mid-seventeenth century (page 554). The Navigation Acts, in conjunction with three Anglo-Dutch wars between 1652 and 1674, did seriously damage Dutch shipping and commerce. The thriving Dutch colony of New Amsterdam was seized in 1664 and renamed "New York." By the late seventeenth century, when the Dutch and the English became allies to stop the expansion of France's Louis XIV, the Netherlands was falling behind England in shipping, trade, and colonies.

Once the Netherlands followed Spain into relative decline, France stood clearly as England's most serious rival in the competition for overseas empire. Rich in natural resources and endowed with a population three or four times that of England, continental Europe's leading military power was already building a powerful fleet and a worldwide system of rigidly monopolized colonial trade. And France, aware that Great Britain coveted large parts of Spain's American empire, was determined to revitalize its Spanish ally. Thus from 1701 to 1763, Britain and France were locked in a series of wars to decide, in part, which nation would become the leading maritime power and claim the lion's share of the profits of Europe's overseas expansion (Map 19.2).

The first round was the War of the Spanish Succession (see page 545), which started when Louis XIV declared his willingness to accept the Spanish crown willed to his grandson. Besides upsetting the continental balance of power, a union of France and Spain threatened to destroy the British colonies in North America. The thin ribbon of British settlements along the Atlantic seaboard from Massachusetts to the Carolinas would be surrounded by a great arc of Franco-Spanish power stretching from French Canada south to Florida and from the Ohio and Mississippi Valleys west to the Rocky Mountains (see Map 19.2). Defeated by a great coalition of states after twelve years of fighting, Louis XIV was forced in the Peace of Utrecht (1713) to cede Newfoundland, Nova Scotia, and the Hudson Bay

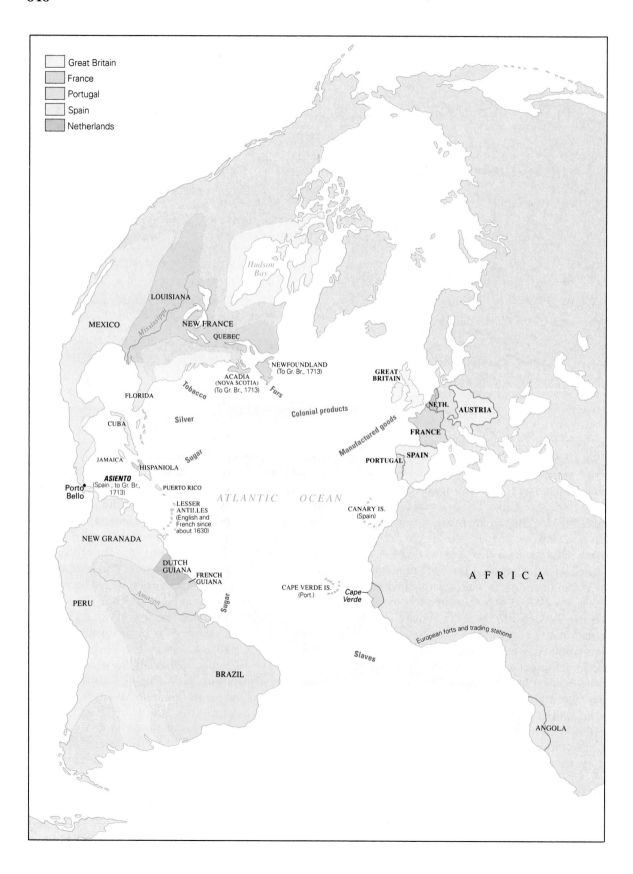

Great Britain
France
Portugal
Spain
Netherlands

Hudson Bay

LOUISIANA

MEXICO

NEW FRANCE

QUEBEC

NEWFOUNDLAND
(To Gr. Br., 1713)

ACADIA
(NOVA SCOTIA)
(To Gr. Br., 1713)

GREAT
BRITAIN

Tobacco

FLORIDA

Furs

Colonial products

NETH.

AUSTRIA

CUBA

Silver

FRANCE

JAMAICA

Sugar

HISPANIOLA

PORTUGAL

SPAIN

Manufactured goods

ASIENTO
(Spain ; to Gr. Br.,
1713)

Porto
Bello

PUERTO RICO

ATLANTIC   OCEAN

CANARY IS.
(Spain)

LESSER
ANTILLES
(English and
French since
about 1630)

NEW GRANADA

DUTCH
GUIANA

AFRICA

FRENCH
GUIANA

CAPE VERDE IS.
(Port.)

Cape-
Verde

PERU

Amazon

Sugar

European forts and trading stations

Slaves

BRAZIL

ANGOLA

territory to Britain. Spain was compelled to give Britain control of the lucrative West African slave trade—the so-called *asiento*—and to let Britain send one ship of merchandise into the Spanish colonies annually, through Porto Bello on the Isthmus of Panama.

France was still a mighty competitor. The War of the Austrian Succession (1740–1748), which started when Frederick the Great of Prussia seized Silesia from Austria's Maria Theresa (see page 615), gradually became a world war that included Anglo-French conflicts in India and North America. Indeed, it was the seizure of French territory in Canada by New England colonists in 1745 that led France to sue for peace in 1748 and to accept a return to the territorial situation existing in North America at the beginning of the war. France's Bourbon ally, Spain, defended itself surprisingly well, and Spain's empire remained intact.

This inconclusive standoff helped set the stage for the Seven Years' War (1756–1763). In central Europe, Austria's Maria Theresa sought to win back Silesia and crush Prussia, thereby re-establishing the Habsburgs' traditional leadership in German affairs. She almost succeeded (see page 615), skillfully winning both France—the Habsburgs' long-standing enemy—and Russia to her cause. Yet Prussia survived, impoverished and exhausted but with its boundaries intact.

Inconclusive in Europe, the Seven Years' War was the decisive round in the Franco-British competition for colonial empire. The fighting began in North America. The population of New France was centered in Quebec and along the St. Lawrence River. But French soldiers and Canadian fur traders had also built forts and trading posts along the Great Lakes, through the Ohio country, and down the Mississippi to New Orleans (Map 19.3). New France was successfully allied with many native American tribes in the territories the French claimed. Thus when Pennsylvania traders and Virginia land speculators began to move across the Appalachian Mountains, officials in Paris and settlers in Canada saw the intrusion as a threat to the very existence of France's far-flung fur-trade empire. In 1753 they built more forts in what is now western Pennsylvania to protect their claims. The following year, a Virginia force, led by twenty-one-year-old George Washington, attacked a small group of French soldiers. Washington was defeated shortly thereafter and forced to surrender. The war to conquer Canada was on.

Although the inhabitants of New France were greatly outnumbered—Canada counted 55,000 inhabitants, as opposed to 1.2 million in the thirteen English colonies—French and Canadian forces under the experienced marquis de Montcalm fought well and scored major victories until 1758. Then, led by their new chief minister, William Pitt, whose grandfather had made a fortune in India, the British diverted men and money from the war in Europe, which remained nevertheless the main focus for the French court at Versailles. The British concentrated instead on the struggle for empire, using superior sea power to destroy the French fleet and choke off French commerce around the world. In 1759 a combined British naval and land force laid siege to fortress Quebec. After four long months, they finally defeated Montcalm's army in a dramatic battle that sealed the fate of France in North America. (See the feature "Individuals in Society: Montcalm and the Fall of New France.")

British victory on all colonial fronts was ratified in the Treaty of Paris (1763). France lost all its possessions on the mainland of North America. Canada and all French territory east of the Mississippi River passed to Britain, and France ceded Louisiana to Spain as compensation for Spain's loss of Florida to Britain. France also gave up most of its holdings in India, opening the way to British dominance on the subcontinent. By 1763 British naval power, built in large part on the rapid growth of the British shipping industry after the passage of the Navigation Acts, had triumphed decisively. Britain had realized its goal of monopolizing a vast trading and colonial empire for its exclusive benefit.

Land and Wealth in British America

Of all Britain's colonies, those on the North American mainland proved most valuable in the long run. The settlements along the Atlantic coast provided an important outlet for surplus population, so that migration abroad limited poverty in England, Scotland, and northern Ireland. The settlers also benefited. In the mainland colonies, they shared in the rights of European conquest and had privileged access to virtually free and unlimited land.

The possibility of having one's own farm was particularly attractive to ordinary men and women from the British Isles. Land in England was already highly concentrated in the hands of the nobility and gentry in

---

MAP 19.2 The Economy of the Atlantic Basin in 1701 The growth of trade encouraged both economic development and military conflict in the Atlantic basin. Four continents were linked together by the exchange of goods and slaves.

Individuals in Society

Montcalm and the Fall of New France

Wars are cruel and wasteful, but they can decide the fate of states and entire peoples. So it was for New France and its Canadian settlers. "The war that resulted in the capitulation of Canada in 1760 . . . is the most important event in Canadian history. When the war broke out there were two Americas, one French and the other English. When it ended, with the defeat of Canada, the first of these Americas had disappeared."[1]

Hopes for France in America rested in large part on Marquis Louis Joseph de Montcalm (1712–1759). A seasoned general when he arrived in Quebec in 1756, Montcalm was winsome, hot-tempered, and vain. Within a year, he and his nominal superior, the equally egotistical marquis de Vaudreuil, governor of New France, had quarreled, and they came to detest each other. Above all, the Canadian-born Vaudreuil loved Canada and feared that France would abandon it. Montcalm was a loyal French soldier, but he cared little for Canada or its settlers. Believing the French position was hopeless, he spent much of his time blaming Vaudreuil and the Canadians for the defeats he anticipated.[2]

Vaudreuil's strategy was to use Canadians and native American allies with French regulars for guerrilla attacks that would tie down British troops far from Quebec. In 1756 and 1757, Montcalm won stunning victories in upper New York, but he refused to follow up and attack Albany as Vaudreuil had ordered. The quarrel of the competing leaders exploded. In the end, Versailles sided with Montcalm, making him supreme commander and ordering the defense strategy he championed.

Quebec sits atop bluffs on the north side of the St. Lawrence River. When in 1759 a British fleet carrying a large army arrived to strike a death blow, Montcalm dug in to the east of Quebec and waited. Laying siege from the south shore, the British pounded Quebec all summer and terrorized the countryside. Still Montcalm refused to come out for the open-field battle the British desired.

By early September, the British general James Wolfe was frantic. Soon a freezing river would force a withdrawal. Deciding on a daring and dangerous plan, British ships floated silently past Quebec at night and

Lieutenant-General the Marquis de Montcalm, French commander in North America. *(National Archives of Canada)*

landed soldiers two miles west of the city, at the base of the steep embankment. The French lookouts were caught napping, and the desperate gamble succeeded. By daybreak on September 13, 1759, forty-four hundred British soldiers stood on the plain outside the city walls. Yet all was not lost. The British were outnumbered and completely exposed to snipers. Above all, Montcalm could afford to wait. He could defend fortress Quebec with his six thousand men, bring up three thousand more positioned nearby, and make Wolfe attack.

Instead, the proud but cautious Montcalm, with his disdain for frontier fighters and hit-and-run tactics, surrendered suddenly to his European training. Marching back to the city from his position to the east, he foolishly ordered an immediate attack. The Canadian militiamen in the French lines had never endured the hell of point-blank firing by battle-hardened troops. When only thirty yards separated the advancing lines, the British unloaded a murderous general salvo and charged with fixed bayonets. The Canadians and French crumbled and fled in defeat. Montcalm and Wolfe were fatally wounded. The war sputtered on for a year, but New France really died with Montcalm and his disastrous attack.

Questions for Analysis

1. How did Montcalm and Vaudreuil differ, and why did they quarrel?
2. Why did Montcalm and his forces lose at Quebec? What were the consequences of defeat?

1. G. Frégault, *Canada: The War of the Conquest* (Toronto: Oxford University Press, 1969), p. ix.
2. W. J. Eccles, *France in America,* rev. ed. (East Lansing: Michigan State University Press, 1990), pp. 199–200, pp. 201–222.

MAP 19.3 European Claims in North America Before and After the Seven Years' War (1756–1763) France lost its vast claims in North America, though the British government then prohibited colonists from settling west of the Appalachian Mountains in 1763. The British wanted to avoid costly wars with Indians living in the newly conquered territory.

1700 and became more so with agricultural improvement and enclosures in the eighteenth century. White settlers who came to the colonies as free men and women, as indentured servants pledged to work seven years for their passage, or as prisoners and convicts could obtain their own farms on easy terms as soon as they had their personal freedom. Life in the mainland colonies was hard, but the settlers succeeded in paying little or no rent to grasping landlords, and taxes were very low. Unlike the great majority of European peasants, who had to accept high rents and taxes as part of the order of things, American farmers could keep most of what they produced.

The availability of land made labor expensive in the colonies. This basic fact, rather than any repressive aspects of the Navigation Acts, limited the growth of industry in the colonies. The advantage for colonists was in farming, and farm they did.

Cheap land and scarce labor were also critical factors in the growth of slavery in the southern colonies. The Spanish and the Portuguese had introduced slavery into the Americas in the sixteenth century. In the seventeenth century, the Dutch aggressively followed their example and transported thousands of Africans to Brazil and the Caribbean. There they worked on sugar plantations that normally earned large profits for plantation owners and European traders. (See the feature "Listening to the Past: An Insight into Slavery" on pages 658–659.) Most slaves came from Africa because native Americans were not accustomed to any form of forced labor and died in large numbers when enslaved.

As England adopted mercantilist policies in the seventeenth century, it also established valuable sugar plantations in the Caribbean and brought slave laborers from Africa. By 1700 the pattern of plantations based on slave exploitation had spread to the Virginia

The Taking of Quebec City   The French successfully defended their capital from British attack in 1690 and again in 1711. But in 1759 British troops landed, scaled the cliffs in the dead of the night, and defeated the French on the Plains of Abraham above Quebec, as this print shows. The battle gave Britain a decisive victory in the long struggle for empire in North America. *(Courtesy of the Royal Ontario Museum, Toronto, Canada)*

lowlands, which British indentured servants were carefully avoiding, and by 1730 the large plantations there were worked entirely by black slaves. The exploitation of slave labor permitted an astonishing tenfold increase in tobacco production between 1700 and 1774 and created a wealthy aristocratic planter class in Maryland and Virginia. Large numbers of African blacks poured into British North America. In 1790, when the U.S. population was approaching 4 million, blacks accounted for almost 20 percent of the total.

Slavery was uncommon in New England and the middle colonies, and in the course of the eighteenth century, the farmers in these areas began to produce more food than they needed. They exported ever more foodstuffs, primarily to the West Indies. There the owners of the sugar plantations came to depend on the mainland colonies for grain and dried fish to feed their slaves. The plantation owners, whether they grew tobacco in Virginia and Maryland or sugar in the West Indies, had the exclusive privilege of supplying the British Isles with their products. The English could not buy cheaper sugar from Brazil, nor were they allowed to grow tobacco in the home islands. Thus white colonists, too, had their place in the protective mercantile system of the Navigation Acts. The American shipping industry grew rapidly in the eighteenth century, for example, because colonial shippers enjoyed the same advantages as did citizens in Britain.

The abundance of almost free land resulted in a rapid increase in the colonial population in the eighteenth century. In a mere three-quarters of a century after 1700, the white population of the mainland colonies multiplied a staggering ten times, as immigrants arrived and colonial couples raised large families.

Rapid population growth did not reduce the white settlers to poverty. On the contrary, agricultural development resulted in fairly high standards of living, in eighteenth-century terms, for mainland colonists.

There was also an unusual degree of economic equality by European standards. Few people were extremely rich, and few were extremely poor. Remarkably, on the eve of the American Revolution, white men and women in the mainland British colonies probably had the highest average income and standard of living in the world.[9] Thus it is clear just how much the colonists benefited from hard work and the mercantile system created by the Navigation Acts.

The Growth of Foreign Trade

Britain and especially England, its most important part, also profited greatly from the mercantile system, as contemporary observers like novelist Daniel Defoe (1659–1731) proudly proclaimed. Above all, the rapidly growing and increasingly wealthy agricultural populations of the mainland colonies provided an expanding market for English manufactured goods. This situation was extremely fortunate, for England in the eighteenth century was gradually losing, or only slowly expanding, its sales to many of its traditional European markets. However, rising demand for manufactured goods in North America as well as in the West Indies, Africa, and Latin America allowed English cottage industry to continue growing and diversifying. Merchant capitalists and manufacturers found new and exciting opportunities for profit and wealth.

Since the late Middle Ages, England had relied very heavily on the sale of woolen cloth in foreign markets. Indeed, as late as 1700, woolen cloth was the only important manufactured good exported from England, and fully 90 percent of it was sold to Europeans. In the course of the eighteenth century, the states of continental Europe were trying to develop their own cottage textile industries in an effort to deal with rural poverty and overpopulation. Like England earlier, these states adopted protectionist, mercantilist policies. They tried by means of tariffs and other measures to exclude competing goods from abroad, whether English woolens or the cheap but beautiful cotton calicoes that the English East India Company brought from India and sold in Europe.

France had already closed its markets to the English in the seventeenth century. In the eighteenth century, German states purchased much less woolen cloth from

A Sugar Mill in Brazil, 1640   European settlers first brought African slaves to the Americas to grow sugar, because Europe's sweet tooth promised quick wealth to planters who succeeded. The slaves' work was extremely demanding and disagreeable, long days under a brutal sun, with dangerous round-the-clock pressing and boiling when the crop came in. *(Musées Royaux des Beaux-Arts de Belgique)*

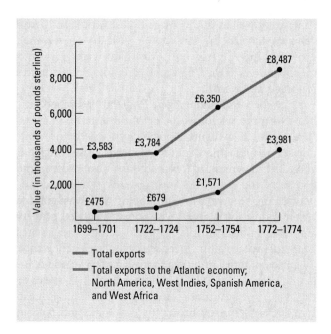

FIGURE 19.3 Exports of English Manufactured Goods, 1700–1774 While trade between England and Europe stagnated after 1700, English exports to Africa and the Americas boomed and greatly stimulated English economic development. *(Source: R. Davis, "English Foreign Trade, 1700–1774," Economic History Review, 2d ser., 15 (1962): 302–303.)*

England and encouraged cottage production of coarse, cheap linens, which became a feared competitor in all of central and southern Europe. By 1773 England was selling only about two-thirds as much woolen cloth to northern and western Europe as it had in 1700. Stagnation or decline in many markets on the continent meant that the English economy badly needed new markets and new products in order to develop and prosper.

Protected colonial markets came to the rescue, more than offsetting stagnating trade with Europe. The markets of the Atlantic economy led the way (Figure 19.3). English exports of manufactured goods to continental Europe increased very modestly, from roughly £2.9 million in 1700 to only £3.3 million in 1773. Meanwhile, sales of manufactured products to the Atlantic economy—primarily the mainland colonies of North America and the West Indian sugar islands, with an important assist from West Africa and Latin America—soared from £500,000 to £4.0 million. Sales to other colonies—Ireland and India—also rose substantially in the eighteenth century.

English exports became much more balanced and diversified. To America and Africa went large quantities of metal items—axes to frontier settlers, firearms, chains

to slaveowners. There were also clocks and coaches, buttons and saddles, china and furniture, musical instruments and scientific equipment, and a host of other things. By 1750 half the nails made in England were going to the colonies. Foreign trade became the bread and butter of some industries.

Thus the mercantilist system formed in the seventeenth century to attack the Dutch and to win power and profit for England achieved remarkable success in the eighteenth century. The English concentrated in their hands much of the trade flowing through the growing Atlantic economy. Of great importance, the pressure of demand from three continents on the cottage industry of one medium-size country heightened the efforts of English merchant capitalists to find new and improved ways to produce more goods. By the 1770s England stood on the threshold of the epoch-making industrial changes that will be described in Chapter 22.

Revival in Colonial Latin America

When the last Spanish Habsburg, the feeble-minded Charles II, died in 1700 (see page 545), Spain's vast empire lay ready for dismemberment. Yet in one of those striking reversals with which history is replete, Spain revived. The empire held together and even prospered, while a European-oriented landowning aristocracy enhanced its position in colonial society.

Spain recovered in part because of better leadership. Louis XIV's grandson, who took the throne as Philip V (r. 1700–1746), brought new men and fresh ideas with him from France and rallied the Spanish people to his Bourbon dynasty in the long War of the Spanish Succession. When peace was restored, a series of reforming ministers reasserted royal authority, overhauling state finances and strengthening defense.

Revitalization in Madrid had positive results in the colonies. They succeeded in defending themselves from numerous British attacks and even increased in size. Spain received Louisiana from France in 1763, and missionaries and ranchers extended Spanish influence all the way to northern California.

Political success was matched by economic improvement. After declining markedly in the seventeenth century, silver mining recovered greatly, and in 1800 Spanish America accounted for half of world silver production. Silver mining also encouraged food production for large mining camps and gave the *Creoles*—people of Spanish blood born in America—the means to purchase more and more European luxuries and manufactured goods. A class of wealthy Creole mer-

The East India Dock, London   This painting by Samuel Scott captures the spirit and excitement of British maritime expansion. Great sailing ships line the quay, bringing profit and romance from far-off India. London grew in population from 350,000 in 1650 to 900,000 in 1800, when it was twice as big as Paris, its nearest rival. *(Courtesy of Board of Trustees of the Victoria & Albert Museum)*

chants arose to handle this flourishing trade, which often relied on smuggled goods from Great Britain.

The Creole elite came to rival the top government officials dispatched from Spain to govern the colonies. Creole estate owners controlled much of the land, and they strove to become a genuine European aristocracy. Estate owners believed that work in the fields was the proper occupation of an impoverished peasantry. The defenseless Indians suited their needs. As the indigenous population recovered in numbers, slavery and periodic forced labor gave way to widespread debt peonage from 1600 on. Under this system, a planter or rancher would keep the estate's Christianized, increasingly Hispanicized Indians in perpetual debt bondage by periodically advancing food, shelter, and a little money. Debt peonage was a form of serfdom.

The large middle group in Spanish colonies consisted of racially mixed *mestizos,* the offspring of Spanish men and Indian women. The most talented mestizos realistically aspired to join the Creoles, for enough wealth and power could make one considered white. Thus by the end of the colonial era, roughly 20 percent of the population was classified as white and about 30 percent as mestizo. Pure-blooded Indians accounted for most of the remainder, but some black slaves were found in every part of Spanish America. Great numbers of blacks went in chains to work the enormous sugar plantations of Portuguese Brazil, and about half the Brazilian population in the early nineteenth century was of African origin. The people of Brazil intermingled sexually and culturally, and the population grew to include every color in the racial rainbow. Thus in the eighteenth century, Spanish and Portuguese colonies developed a growing commerce in silver, sugar, and slaves as well as in manufactured goods for a Europeanized elite. South America occupied an important place in the expanding Atlantic economy.

Adam Smith and Economic Liberalism

Although mercantilist policies strengthened both the Spanish and British colonial empires in the eighteenth

Forming the Mexican People   This painting by an unknown eighteenth-century artist presents a naive but sympathetic view of interracial unions and marriages in colonial Mexico. On the left, the union of a Spanish man and a native American woman has produced a racially mixed mestizo. The handsome group on the right features a mestizo woman and a Spaniard with their little daughter. *(Private Collection/Banco Nacional de Mexico)*

century, a strong reaction against mercantilism ultimately set in. Creole merchants chafed at regulations imposed from Madrid. Small English merchants complained loudly about the injustice of handing over exclusive trading rights to great trading combines such as the East India Company. Wanting a bigger position in overseas commerce, independent merchants in many countries began campaigning against "monopolies" and calling for "free trade."

The general idea of freedom of enterprise in foreign trade was persuasively developed by Scottish professor of philosophy Adam Smith (1723–1790). Smith, whose *Inquiry into the Nature and Causes of the Wealth of Nations* (1776) established the basis for modern economics, was highly critical of eighteenth-century mercantilism. Mercantilism, he said, meant a combination of stifling government regulations and unfair privileges for state-approved monopolies and government favorites. Far preferable was free competition, which would best protect consumers from price gouging and give all citizens a fair and equal right to do what they did best. In keeping with the "system of natural liberty" that he advocated, Smith argued that government should limit itself to "only three duties." It should provide a defense against foreign invasion, maintain civil order with courts and police protection, and sponsor certain indispensable public works and institutions that could never adequately profit private investors.

Often lampooned in the nineteenth and twentieth centuries as a mouthpiece for business interests, Smith was one of the Enlightenment's most original and characteristic thinkers. He relied on the power of reason to unlock the secrets of the secular world, and he believed that he spoke for truth, not for special interests. Thus unlike many disgruntled merchant capitalists, Smith applauded the modest rise in real wages of British workers in the eighteenth century and went on to say, "No society can surely be flourishing and happy, of which the far greater part of the members are poor and miserable." Discussing bargaining between employers and workers over wages, Smith was brutally realistic:

We rarely hear, it has been said, of the combinations of masters; though frequently of those of workmen. But whoever imagines, upon this account, that masters rarely combine, is as ignorant of the world as of the subject. Masters are always and everywhere in a sort of tacit, but constant and uniform combination, not to raise the wages of labour above their actual rate. . . . Masters too sometimes enter into particular combinations to sink the wages even below this rate. These are always conducted with the utmost silence and secrecy, till the moment of execution.[10]

Adam Smith   Appointed professor at Glasgow University at age twenty-seven, Smith established an international reputation with his first book. He then became the well-paid tutor of a rich young lord and traveled widely before publishing *The Wealth of Nations,* the point of departure for modern economics. *(Special Collections/Glasgow University Library)*

Believing, then, that employers as well as workers and consumers were motivated primarily by narrow self-interest, Smith did not call for more laws and more police power to force people to behave properly toward each other in economic affairs. Instead, he made the pursuit of self-interest in a competitive market the source of an underlying and previously unrecognized harmony, a harmony that would result in gradual progress.

According to Smith:

[Every individual generally] neither intends to promote the public interest, nor knows how much he is promoting it. . . .

He is in this case, as in many cases, led by an invisible hand to promote an end which was no part of his intention. Nor is it always the worse for society that it was not part of it. I have never known much good done by those who affected to trade for the public good.[11]

The "invisible hand" of free competition for one and for all disciplined the greed of selfish individuals and provided the most effective means of increasing the wealth of both rich and poor.

Smith's provocative work had a great international impact. Going through eight editions in English and translated into several languages within twenty years, it quickly emerged as the classic argument for economic liberalism and unregulated capitalism.

SUMMARY

While some European intellectual elites and parts of the educated public were developing a new view of the world in the eighteenth century, Europe as a whole was experiencing a gradual but far-reaching expansion. As agriculture began showing signs of modest improvement across the continent, first the Low Countries and then England launched changes that gradually revolutionized agriculture. Plague disappeared, and the populations of all countries grew significantly, thereby encouraging the growth of wage labor, cottage industry, and merchant capitalism.

Europeans also continued their overseas expansion, fighting for empire and profit and, in particular, consolidating their hold on the Americas. A revived Spain and its Latin American colonies participated fully in this expansion. As in agriculture and cottage industry, however, England and its empire proved most successful. The English concentrated much of the growing Atlantic trade in their hands, a development that challenged and enriched English industry and intensified interest in new methods of production and in an emerging economic liberalism. Thus by the 1770s, England was approaching an economic breakthrough fully as significant as the great political upheaval destined to develop shortly in neighboring France.

NOTES

1. M. Bloch, *Les caractères originaux de l'histoire rurale française*, vol. 1 (Paris: Librarie Armand Colin, 1960), pp. 244–245.

2. B. H. Slicher van Bath, *The Agrarian History of Western Europe, A.D. 500–1850* (New York: St. Martin's Press, 1963), p. 240.

3. E. P. Thompson, *The Making of the English Working Class* (New York: Vintage Books, 1966), p. 218.

4. Quoted in E. E. Rich and C. H. Wilson, eds., *The Cambridge Economic History of Europe,* vol. 4 (Cambridge: Cambridge University Press, 1967), p. 85.

5. Quoted in I. Pinchbeck, *Women Workers and the Industrial Revolution, 1750–1850* (New York: F. S. Crofts, 1930), p. 113.

6. Quoted in S. Chapman, *The Lancashire Cotton Industry* (Manchester, England: Manchester University Press, 1903), p. 13.

7. Quoted in P. Mantoux, *The Industrial Revolution in the Eighteenth Century* (New York: Harper & Row, 1961), p. 75.

8. Quoted in C. Wilson, *England's Apprenticeship, 1603–1763* (London: Longmans, Green, 1965), p. 169.

9. G. Taylor, "America's Growth Before 1840," *Journal of Economic History* 24 (December 1970): 427–444.

10. R. Heilbroner, ed., *The Essential Adam Smith* (New York: W. W. Norton, 1986), p. 196.

11. Ibid., p. 265.

SUGGESTED READING

The works by Slicher van Bath and Bloch listed in the Notes are wide-ranging general introductions to the gradual transformation of European agriculture. Bloch's classic has been translated as *French Rural History* (1966). J. Blum, *The End of the Old Order in Rural Europe* (1978), is an impressive comparative study. J. de Vries, *The Dutch Rural Economy in the Golden Age, 1500–1700* (1974), skillfully examines the causes of early Dutch leadership in farming. M. Overton, *Agricultural Revolution in England* (1996), and A. Kussmaul, *A General View of the Rural Economy of England, 1538–1840* (1989), chart the path of agricultural progress in England. J. Neeson, *Commoners: Common Right, Enclosure and Social Change, 1700–1820* (1993), stresses popular resistance to enclosure and the losses it brought for the common people. J. Gargliardo, *From Pariah to Patriot: The Changing Image of the German Peasant, 1770–1840* (1969), examines the development of reforms designed to improve the lot of the peasantry in Germany. R. Forster, *The Nobility of Toulouse in the Eighteenth Century* (1960), and A. Goodwin, ed., *The European Nobility in the Eighteenth Century* (1967), are excellent studies on aristocrats in different countries. E. Le Roy Ladurie, *The Peasants of Languedoc* (1976), a brilliant and challenging study of rural life in southern France for several centuries, complements J. Goody et al., eds., *Family and Inheritance: Rural Society in Western Europe, 1200–1800*

(1976). J. Brewer and R. Porter, eds., *Consumption and the World of Goods* (1993), is a fascinating collection of studies and reflects the growing historical interest in consumption as well as production. O. Hufton deals vividly and sympathetically with rural migration, work, women, and much more in *The Poor in Eighteenth-Century France* (1974).

S. Ogilvie and M. Cerman, eds., *European Proto-industrialization* (1996), is a stimulating, up-to-date survey of several countries by leading scholars. An ambitious re-examination with extensive bibliographical references, M. Gutman, *Toward the Modern Economy: Early Modern Industry in Europe, 1500–1800* (1988), highlights the creativity of rural industry, as does J. Goodman and K. Honeyman, *Gainful Pursuits: The Making of Industrial Europe, 1600–1914* (1988). D. Landes, *The Unbound Prometheus* (1969), places more emphasis on the growing limitations of cottage production. G. Gullickson, *Spinners and Weavers of Auffay: Rural Industry and the Sexual Division of Labor in a French Village, 1750–1850* (1986), and M. Sonenscher, *The Hatters of Eighteenth-Century France* (1987), are valuable studies.

Two excellent multivolume series, one edited by Rich and Wilson and mentioned in the Notes, and the other edited by C. Cipolla, *The Fontana Economic History of Europe,* cover the sweep of economic developments from the Middle Ages to the present and have extensive bibliographies. So does R. Cameron, *A Concise Economic History of the World* (1989), which deals mainly with Europe. F. Braudel, *Civilization and Capitalism, Fifteenth–Eighteenth Centuries* (1981, 1984), is a monumental and highly recommended three-volume synthesis. In the area of trade and colonial competition, V. Barbour, *Capitalism in Amsterdam* (1963), and C. R. Boxer, *The Dutch Seaborne Empire* (1970), are very interesting on Holland. R. Herr, *The Eighteenth-Century Revolution in Spain* (1958), studies economic policy and colonial revival. J. Brewer, *The Sinews of Power: War, Money, and the English State, 1688–1783* (1989), looks at English victories, whereas G. Parker, *The Military Revolution: Military Technology in the Rise of the West* (1988), a masterful, beautifully illustrated work, explores the roots of European power and conquest. J. Black, *Cambridge Illustrated Atlas of Warfare: Renaissance to Revolution, 1492–1792* (1996), surveys war in a global perspective with dramatic pictures and outstanding maps. D. K. Fieldhouse, *The Colonial Empires* (1971), and R. Davies, *The Rise of Atlantic Economies* (1973), are all valuable works on the struggle for empire. W. J. Eccles, *France in America,* rev. ed. (1990), is outstanding and supersedes F. Parkman, *France and England in North America,* a multivolume classic and a famous example of nineteenth-century romantic history.

An Insight into Slavery

Born in Benin, West Africa, Olaudah Equiano (1745?– 1797) was captured when he was about eleven and sold into slavery. He soon found himself on a slave ship bound for the West Indies. He went on to learn English and served a lieutenant in the British navy and a Quaker merchant. Granted his freedom in his twenties, he became a clerk in Britain's growing oceanic trade. Equiano adopted Christianity. His own experiences of slavery combined with his religious beliefs to propel him into the British abolitionist movement. He traveled the British Isles lecturing against slavery and wrote his remarkable memoir, The Interesting Narrative of Olaudah Equiano. *First published in 1789, the book saw eight editions. This selection details Equiano's capture and experiences in the brutal Middle Passage.*

Generally when the grown people in the neighborhood were gone far in the fields to labor, the children assembled together in some of the neighbors' premises to play, and commonly some of us used to get up a tree to look out for any assailant or kidnapper that might come upon us, for they sometimes took those opportunities of our parents' absence to attack and carry off as many as they could seize. . . . One day, when all our people were gone out to their work as usual and only I and my dear sister were left to mind the house, two men and a woman got over our walls, and in a moment seized us both, and without giving us time to cry out or make resistance they stopped our mouths and ran off with us into the nearest wood. . . .

For a long time we had kept to the woods, but at last we came into a road which I believed I knew. I had now some hopes of being delivered, for we had advanced but a little way before I discovered some people at a distance, on which I began to cry out for their assistance: but my cries had no other effect than to make them tie me faster and stop my mouth, and then they put me into a large sack. They also stopped my sister's mouth and tied her hands, and in this manner we proceeded till we were out of the sight of these people. . . . The next

day proved a day of greater sorrow than I had yet experienced, for my sister and I were then separated while we lay clasped in each other's arms. It was in vain that we besought them not to part us; she was torn from me and immediately carried away, while I was left in a state of distraction not to be described. I cried and grieved continually, and for several days I did not eat anything but what they forced into my mouth. At length, after many days' traveling, during which I had often changed masters, I got into the hands of a chieftain in a very pleasant country. This man had two wives and some children, and they all used me extremely well and did all they could to comfort me, particularly the first wife, who was something like my mother. . . .

I did not long remain after my sister [departed]. I was again sold and carried through a number of places till, after traveling a considerable time, I came to a town called Tinmah in the most beautiful country I had yet seen in Africa. . . . I was sold here . . . by a merchant who lived and brought me there. I had been about two or three days at his house when a wealthy widow, a neighbor of his, came there one evening, and brought with her an only son, a young gentleman about my own age and size. Here they saw me; and, having taken a fancy to me, I was bought of the merchant, and went home with them. . . . The next day I was washed and perfumed, and when meal-time came I was led into the presence of my mistress, and ate and drank before her with her son. This filled me with astonishment; and I could scarce help expressing my surprise that the young gentleman should suffer me, who was bound, to eat with him who was free; and not only so, but that he would not at any time either eat or drink till I had taken first, because I was the eldest, which was agreeable to our custom. Indeed everything here, and all their treatment of me, made me forget that I was a slave. . . . In this resemblance to my former happy state I passed about two months; and I now began to think I was to be adopted into the family, and was beginning to be reconciled to my situation, and to forget by degrees my misfortunes, when all at once the delusion vanished; for without the least previous knowledge, one morning early, while my dear master and companion was still asleep, I was wakened out of my reverie to fresh sorrow, and hurried away. . . .

Thus I continued to travel, sometimes by land, sometimes by water, through different countries and various nations, till at the end of six or seven months after I had been kidnapped I arrived at the sea coast.

The first object which saluted my eyes when I arrived on the coast was the sea, and a slave ship which was then riding at anchor and waiting for its cargo. These filled me with astonishment, which was soon converted into terror when I was carried on board. . . .

I was soon put down under the decks, and there I received such a salutation in my nostrils as I had never experienced in my life: so that with the loathsomeness of the stench and crying together, I became so sick and low that I was not able to eat, nor had I the least desire to taste anything. I now wished for the last friend, death, to relieve me; but soon, to my grief, two of the white men offered me eatables, and on my refusing to eat, one of them held me fast by the hands and laid me across I think the windlass, and tied my feet while the other flogged me severely. . . . The white people looked and acted, as I thought, in so savage a manner; for I had never seen among my people such instances of brutal cruelty, and this not only shown towards us blacks but also to some of the whites themselves. . . .

One day, when we had a smooth sea and moderate wind, two of my wearied countrymen who were chained together (I was near them at the time), preferring death to such a life of misery, somehow made through the nettings and jumped into the sea: immediately another quite dejected fellow, who on account of his illness was suffered to be out of irons, also followed their example; and I believe many more would very soon have done the same if they had not been prevented by the ship's crew. . . .

At last we came in sight of the island of Barbados, at which the whites on board gave a great shout and made many signs of joy to us. We did not know what to think of this, but as the vessel drew nearer we plainly saw the harbor and other ships of different kinds and sizes, and we soon anchored amongst them off Bridgetown. . . .

We were not many days in the merchant's custody before we were sold after their usual manner, which is this: On a signal given, (as the beat of a drum) the buyers rush at once into the yard where

❖ Olaudah Equiano, in an engraving from his autobiography, *The Interesting Narrative of . . . Olaudah Equiano* (London, 1789). *(National Portrait Gallery, Smithsonian Institution)*

the slaves are confined, and make choice of that parcel they like best. . . . In this manner, without scruple, are relations and friends separated, most of them never to see each other again. I remember in the vessel in which I was brought over, in the men's apartment there were several brothers who, in the sale, were sold in different lots; and it was very moving on this occasion to see and hear their cries at parting. O, ye nominal Christians! might not an African ask you, learned you this from your God who says unto you, Do unto all men as you would men should do unto you?

Questions for Analysis

1. How did Equiano view the Africans who captured people for slavery and the whites who bought and sold them?

2. How did Equiano and others respond to their enslavement?

3. How do Equiano's religious beliefs show through in the passages reprinted here?

Source: Paul Edwards, ed. and trans., *Equiano's Travels* (Oxford: Heinemann Educational Books, 1967), pp. 25–42.

20

The Changing Life of the People

Market in Piazza San Carlo, Turin (detail), by Michele Graneri (1736–1778). *(Museo Civico, Turin/Madeline Grimaldi)*

The discussion of agriculture and industry in the last chapter showed the common people at work, straining to make ends meet within the larger context of population growth, gradual economic expansion, and ferocious political competition. Yet the world of work was only part of life. That life was embedded in a rich complex of family organization, community practices, everyday experiences, and collective attitudes.

In recent years, historians have intensively studied all these aspects of popular life. The challenge has been formidable because regional variations abounded and the common people left few written records. Yet despite many ongoing debates among specialists, imaginative research has resulted in major findings and much greater knowledge. It is now possible to follow the common people beyond the world of work and ask, "What about the rest of the human experience?"

- What changes occurred in marriage and the family in the course of the eighteenth century?
- What was life like for children, and how did attitudes toward children evolve?
- What did people eat, and how did changes in diet and medical care affect people's lives?
- What were the patterns of popular religion and culture? How did these patterns come into contact—and conflict—with the critical world-view of the educated public and thereby widen the cultural divide between rich and poor in the era of the Enlightenment?

Such questions help us better understand how the peasant masses and urban poor really lived in western Europe before the age of revolution opened at the end of the eighteenth century. These questions will be the focus of this chapter.

❖ MARRIAGE AND THE FAMILY

The basic unit of social organization is the family. It is within the structure of the family that human beings love, mate, and reproduce themselves. It is primarily the family that teaches the child, imparting values and customs that condition an individual's behavior for a lifetime. The family is also an institution woven into the web of history. It evolves and changes, assuming different forms in different times and places.

Extended and Nuclear Families

In many traditional Asian and African societies, the typical family has often been an extended family. A newly married couple, instead of establishing a home, will go to live with either the bride's or the groom's family. The wife and husband raise their children while living under the same roof with their own brothers and sisters, who may also be married. The family is a big, three- or four-generation clan, headed by a patriarch or perhaps a matriarch, and encompassing everyone from the youngest infant to the oldest grandparent.

Extended families, it is often said, provide security for adults and children in traditional agrarian peasant economies. Everyone has a place within the extended family, from cradle to grave. Sociologists frequently assume that the extended family gives way to the conjugal, or nuclear, family with the advent of industrialization and urbanization. In a society characterized by nuclear families, couples establish their own households when they marry, and they raise their children apart from their parents. A similar process has indeed been occurring in much of Asia and Africa today. And since Europe was once agrarian and preindustrial, it has often been believed that the extended family must also have prevailed in Europe before being destroyed by the Industrial Revolution.

In recent years, innovative historians, analyzing previously neglected parish registers of births, deaths, and marriages, have greatly increased knowledge about the details of family life for the great majority of people before the nineteenth century. It seems clear that the extended, three-generation family was a great rarity in western and central Europe by 1700. Indeed, the extended family may never have been common in Europe, although it is hard to know about the early Middle Ages because fewer records survive. When young European couples married, they normally established their own households and lived apart from their parents. When a three-generation household came into existence, it was usually a parent who moved in with a married child rather than a newly married couple moving in with either set of parents.

Most people did not marry young in the seventeenth and early eighteenth centuries. The average person, who was neither rich nor aristocratic, married surprisingly late, many years after reaching adulthood and many more after beginning to work. In one well-studied, apparently typical English village, both men and women married for the first time at an average age of twenty-seven or older in the seventeenth and eighteenth centuries. A similar pattern existed in early-eighteenth-century France. Moreover, a substantial portion of men and women never married at all.

The custom of late marriage combined with a nuclear-family household was a distinctive characteristic of European society. It seems likely that the aggressive dynamism and creativity that have characterized European society were due in large part to the pattern of marriage and family. This pattern fostered and required self-reliance and independence. In preindustrial western Europe in the sixteenth through eighteenth centuries, marriage normally joined a mature man and a mature woman—two adults who had already experienced a great deal of life and could transmit self-reliance and real skills to the next generation.

Chardin: The Kitchen Maid Lost in thought as she pauses in her work, perhaps this young servant is thinking about her village and loved ones there. Chardin was one of eighteenth-century France's greatest painters, and his scenes from everyday life provide valuable evidence for the historian. *(National Gallery of Art, Washington, D.C. Samuel H. Kress Collection)*

Why was marriage delayed? The main reason was that couples normally could not marry until they could support themselves economically. The land was still the main source of income. The peasant son often needed to wait until his father's death to inherit the family farm and marry his sweetheart. Similarly, the peasant daughter and her family needed to accumulate a small dowry to help her fiancé buy land or build a house.

There were also laws and community controls to temper impetuous love and physical attraction. In some areas, couples needed the legal permission or tacit approval of the local lord or landowner in order to marry. In Austria and Germany, there were legal restrictions on marriage, and well into the nineteenth century poor couples had particular difficulty securing the approval of local officials. These officials believed that freedom to marry for the lower classes would mean more landless paupers, more abandoned children, and more money for welfare. Village elders often agreed. Thus prudence, law, and custom combined to postpone the march to the altar. This pattern helped society maintain some kind of balance between the number of people and the available economic resources.

Work Away from Home

Many young people worked within their families until they could start their own households. Boys plowed and wove; girls spun and tended the cows. Many others left home temporarily to work elsewhere. In the towns, a lad might be apprenticed to a craftsman for seven or fourteen years to learn a trade. During that time, he would not be permitted to marry. In most trades, he earned little and worked hard, but if he was lucky, he might eventually be admitted to a guild and establish his economic independence. More often, the young man would drift from one tough job to another: hired hand for a small farmer, wage laborer on a new road, carrier of water in a nearby town. He was always subject to economic fluctuations, and unemployment was a constant threat.

Girls also temporarily left their families to work, at an early age and in large numbers. The range of opportunities open to them was more limited, however. Service in another family's household was by far the most common job, and even middle-class families often sent their daughters into service. Thus a few years away from home as a servant were often a normal part of growing up.

The legions of young servant girls worked hard but had little real independence. Sometimes the employer paid the girl's wages directly to her parents. Constantly under the eye of her mistress, the servant girl found her tasks were many—cleaning, shopping, cooking, caring for the baby. Often the work was endless, for there were no laws to limit exploitation. Rarely were girls so brutalized that they snapped under the strain of such treatment like Varka—the Russian servant girl in Chekhov's chilling story "Sleepy"—who, driven beyond exhaustion, finally quieted her mistress's screaming child by strangling it in its cradle. But court records are full of complaints by servant girls of physical mistreatment by their mistresses. There were many others like the fifteen-year-old English girl in the early eighteenth century who told the judge that her mistress had not only called her "very opprobrious names, as Bitch, Whore and the like," but also "beat her without provocation and beyond measure."[1]

There was also the pressure of seducers and sexual attack. In theory, domestic service offered protection and security within a new family for a young girl leaving home. But in practice, she was often the easy prey of a lecherous master or his sons or friends. Indeed, "the evidence suggests that in all European countries, from Britain to Russia, the upper classes felt perfectly free to exploit sexually girls who were at their mercy."[2] If the girl became pregnant, she was quickly fired and thrown out in disgrace to make her own way. Prostitution and petty thievery were often the harsh consequences of unwanted pregnancy. "What are we?" exclaimed a bitter Parisian prostitute. "Most of us are unfortunate women, without origins, without education, servants and maids for the most part."[3]

Premarital Sex and Community Controls

Did the plight of some former servant girls mean that late marriage in preindustrial Europe went hand in hand with premarital sex and many illegitimate children? For most of western and central Europe until at least 1750, the answer seems to have been no. English parish registers seldom listed more than one bastard out of every twenty children baptized. Some French parishes in the seventeenth century had extraordinarily low rates of illegitimacy, with less than 1 percent of the babies born out of wedlock. Illegitimate babies were apparently a rarity, at least as far as the official church records are concerned.

At the same time, premarital sex was clearly commonplace. In one well-studied English village, 33 percent of all first children were conceived before the couple was married, and many were born within three months of the marriage ceremony. In the mid-eighteenth century, 20 percent of the women in the French village of Auffay, in Normandy, were pregnant when they got married, although only 2 percent of all babies in the village were born to unwed mothers. No doubt many of these French and English couples were already betrothed, or at least "going steady," before they entered into an intimate relationship, and pregnancy simply set the marriage date once and for all.

But the combination of very low rates of illegitimate birth with large numbers of pregnant brides also reflected the powerful social controls of the traditional village, particularly the open-field village, with its pattern of cooperation and common action. That spirit of common action was rapidly mobilized by the prospect of an unwed (and therefore poor) mother with an illegitimate child, a condition inevitably viewed as a grave threat to the economic, social, and moral stability of the closely knit community. Irate parents and anxious village elders, indignant priests and authoritative landlords, all combined to pressure any young people who wavered about marriage in the face of unexpected pregnancy. These controls meant in the countryside that premarital sex was not entered into lightly and that it was generally limited to those contemplating marriage.

The concerns of the village and the family weighed heavily on most aspects of a couple's life, both before and after marriage. One leading authority describes the traditional French peasant household in these terms:

The individuality of the couple, or rather, its tendency towards individuality, was crushed by the family institutions, and also by the social pressures exercised by the village community as a whole, and by the neighborhood in particular. Anything that might endanger the [couple's] household might also prejudice the village community, and the community reacted, occasionally violently, to punish those who contravened the rules. The intrusion of the community into every aspect of family life was very noticeable.[4]

Whereas uninvolved individuals today are inclined to ignore the domestic disputes and marital scandals of others, the people in peasant communities gave such affairs the loudest and most unfavorable publicity, either at the time of the event or during the Carnival season (see page 683). Relying on degrading public rituals, the young men of the village would typically gang up on the person they wanted to punish and force him or her to sit astride a donkey facing backward and holding up the donkey's tail. They would parade the overly brutal spouse-beating husband (or wife), or the couple whose adultery had been discovered, all around the village, loudly proclaiming the offender's misdeeds with scorn and ridicule. The donkey ride and similar colorful humiliations ranging from rotten vegetables splattered on the doorstep to obscene and insulting midnight serenades were common punishments throughout much of Europe. They epitomized the community's far-reaching effort to police personal behavior and maintain community standards.

Community controls did not extend to family planning, however. Once a couple married, it generally had several children. Birth control within marriage was not unknown in western and central Europe before the nineteenth century, but it was primitive and quite undependable. The most common method was *coitus interruptus*—withdrawal by the male before ejaculation. The French, who were apparently early leaders in contraception, were using this method extensively to limit family size by the end of the eighteenth century.

Mechanical and other means of contraception were also used in the eighteenth century, but mainly by certain sectors of the urban population. The "fast set" of London used the "sheath" regularly, although primarily to protect against venereal disease, not pregnancy. Prostitutes used various contraceptive techniques to prevent pregnancy, and such information was available in large towns if a person really sought it.

New Patterns of Marriage and Illegitimacy

In the second half of the eighteenth century, the pattern of late marriage and few births out of wedlock began to change and break down. The number of illegitimate births soared between about 1750 and 1850 as much of Europe experienced an "illegitimacy explosion." In Frankfurt, Germany, for example, illegitimate births rose steadily from about 2 percent of all births in the early 1700s to a peak of about 25 percent around 1850. In Bordeaux, France, 36 percent of all babies were being born out of wedlock by 1840. Small towns and villages experienced less startling climbs, but increases from a range of 1 to 3 percent initially to 10 to 20 percent between 1750 and 1850 were commonplace. Fewer young women were abstaining from premarital intercourse, and, more important, fewer young men were marrying the women they got pregnant. Thus a profound sexual and cultural transformation took place.

Historians are still debating the meaning of this transformation, but two interrelated ideas dominate most interpretations. First, the growth of cottage industry created new opportunities for earning a living, opportunities not tied to the land. Cottage industry tended to develop in areas where the land was poor in quality and divided into small, inadequate holdings. As cottage industry took hold in such areas, population grew rapidly because young people attained greater independence and did not have to wait to inherit a farm in order to get married and have children. A scrap of ground for a garden and a cottage for the loom and spinning wheel could be quite enough for a modest living. A contemporary observer of an area of rapidly growing cottage industry in Switzerland at the end of the eighteenth century described these changes:

The increased and sure income offered by the combination of cottage manufacture with farming hastened and multiplied marriages and encouraged the division of landholdings, while enhancing their value; it also promoted the expansion and embellishment of houses and villages.[5]

Cottage workers married not only at an earlier age but also for different reasons. Nothing could be so businesslike, so calculating, as a peasant marriage that was often dictated by the needs of the couple's families. After 1750, however, courtship became more extensive and freer as cottage industry grew. It was easier to yield to the attraction of the opposite sex and fall in love. Members of the older generation were often highly critical of the lack of responsibility they saw in the early marriages of the poor, the union of "people with only two spinning wheels and not even a bed." But such scolding did not stop cottage workers from marrying for love rather than for economic considerations as they blazed a path that factory workers would follow in the nineteenth century.

Second, the needs of a growing population sent many young villagers to towns and cities in search of temporary or permanent employment. Mobility in turn encouraged new sexual and marital relationships, which were less subject to village tradition and resulted in more illegitimate births. Yet most young women in urban areas found work only as servants or textile workers. Poorly paid, insecure, and with little possibility of truly independent, "liberated" lives, they looked mainly to marriage and family life as an escape from hard work and as the foundation of a satisfying life.

Promises of marriage from a man of the working girl's own class led naturally enough to sex, which was widely viewed as part of serious courtship. In one medium-size French city in 1787 to 1788, the great majority of unwed mothers stated that sexual intimacy had followed promises of marriage. Their sisters in rural Normandy reported again and again that they had been "seduced in anticipation of marriage."[6] Many soldiers, day laborers, and male servants were no doubt sincere in their proposals. But their lives were also insecure, and many hesitated to take on the heavy economic burdens of wife and child.

David Allan: The Penny Wedding (1795) The spirited merry-making of a peasant wedding was a popular theme of European artists. In rural Scotland "penny weddings" like this one were common: guests paid a fee for the food and fun; the money left over went to the newlyweds to help them get started. Music, dancing, feasting, and drinking characterized these community parties, which led the Presbyterian church to oppose them and hasten their decline. *(National Galleries of Scotland)*

Thus it became increasingly difficult for a woman to convert pregnancy into marriage, and in a growing number of cases the intended marriage did not take place. The romantic, yet practical dreams and aspirations of many young workingmen and workingwomen in towns and villages were frustrated by low wages, inequality, and changing economic and social conditions. Old patterns of marriage and family were breaking down among the common people. Only in the late nineteenth century would more stable patterns reappear.

 ## CHILDREN AND EDUCATION

In the traditional framework of agrarian Europe, women married late but then began bearing children rapidly. If a woman married before she was thirty, and if both she and her husband lived to forty-five, the chances were roughly one in two that she would give birth to six or more children. The newborn child entered a dangerous world. Infant mortality was high. One in five was sure to die, and one in three was quite likely to in the poorer areas. Newborn children were very likely to catch mysterious infectious diseases of the chest and stomach, and many babies died of dehydration brought about by a bad bout of ordinary diarrhea. Even in rich families, lit-

tle could be done for an ailing child. Childhood itself was dangerous because of adult indifference, neglect, and even abuse.

Schools and formal education played only a modest role in the lives of ordinary children, and many boys and many more girls never learned to read. Nevertheless, basic literacy was growing among the popular classes, whose reading habits have been intensively studied in recent years. Attempting to peer into the collective attitudes of the common people and compare them with those of the book-hungry cultivated public, historians have produced some fascinating insights.

Child Care and Nursing

Women of the lower classes generally breast-fed their infants and for a much longer period than is customary today. Breast-feeding decreases the likelihood of pregnancy for the average woman by delaying the resumption of ovulation. By nursing their babies, women limited their fertility and spaced their children—from two to three years apart. If a newborn baby died, nursing stopped and a new life could be created. Nursing also saved lives: the breast-fed infant received precious immunity-producing substances with its mother's milk and was more likely to survive than when it was given any artificial food. In many areas of Russia, where the common practice was to give a new child a sweetened (and germ-laden) rag to suck on for its subsistence, half the babies did not survive the first year.

In contrast to the laboring poor, the women of the aristocracy and upper middle class seldom nursed their own children. The upper-class woman felt that breast-feeding was crude, common, and undignified. Instead, she hired a wet nurse to suckle her child. The urban mother of more modest means—the wife of a shop-keeper or an artisan—also commonly used a wet nurse in order to facilitate full-time work in the shop.

Wet-nursing was a very widespread and flourishing business in the eighteenth century, a dismal business within the framework of the putting-out system. The traffic was in babies rather than in wool and cloth, and two or three years often passed before the wet-nurse worker finished her task. The great French historian Jules Michelet described with compassion the plight of the wet nurse, who was still going to the homes of the rich in early-nineteenth-century France:

People do not know how much these poor women are exploited and abused, first by the vehicles which transport them (often barely out of their confinement), and afterward by the employment offices which place them. Taken as nurses on the spot, they must send their own child away, and consequently it often dies. They have no contact with the family that hires them, and they may be dismissed at the first caprice of the mother or doctor. If the change of air and place should dry up their milk, they are discharged without any compensation. If they stay here [in the city] they pick up the habits of the easy life, and they suffer enormously when they are forced to return to their life of [rural] poverty. A good number become servants in order to stay in the town. They never rejoin their husbands, and the family is broken.[7]

Other observers noted the flaws of wet-nursing. It was a common belief that with her milk a nurse passed her bad traits to a baby. When the child turned out poorly, it was assumed that "the nurse had changed it." Many observers charged that nurses were often negligent and greedy. They claimed that there were large numbers of "killing nurses" with whom no child ever survived. The nurse let the child die quickly so that she could take another child and another fee.

Foundlings and Infanticide

In the ancient world it was not uncommon to allow or force newborn babies, particularly girl babies, to die when there were too many mouths to feed. To its great and eternal credit, the early medieval church, strongly influenced by Jewish law, denounced infanticide as a pagan practice and insisted that every human life was sacred. The willful destruction of newborn children became a crime punishable by death. And yet, as the previous reference to killing nurses suggests, direct and indirect methods of eliminating unwanted babies did not disappear. There were, for example, many cases of "overlaying"—parents rolling over and suffocating the child placed between them in their bed. Such parents claimed they had been drunk and had acted unintentionally. In Austria in 1784, suspicious authorities made it illegal for parents to take children under five into bed with them. Severe poverty, on the one hand, and increasing illegitimacy, on the other, conspired to force the very poor to thin their own ranks.

The young girl—very likely a servant—who could not provide for her child had few choices. If she would not have an abortion or employ the services of a killing nurse, she could bundle up her baby and leave it on the doorstep of a church. In the late seventeenth century, Saint Vincent de Paul was so distressed by the number of babies brought to the steps of Notre Dame in Paris that he established a home for foundlings. Others followed his example. In England the government acted on a petition calling for a foundling hospital "to prevent the frequent murders of poor, miserable infants at birth" and "to suppress the inhuman custom of exposing newborn children to perish in the streets."

In much of Europe in the eighteenth century, foundling homes emerged as a favorite charity of the rich and powerful. Great sums were spent on them. The foundling home in St. Petersburg, perhaps the most elaborate and lavish of its kind, occupied the former palaces of two members of the high nobility. In the early nineteenth century it had twenty-five thousand children in its care and was receiving five thousand new babies a year. At their best, foundling homes in the eighteenth century were a good example of Christian charity and social concern in an age of great poverty and inequality.

Yet the foundling home was no panacea. By the 1770s, one-third of all babies born in Paris were being immediately abandoned to the foundling home by their mothers. Fully one-third of all those foundlings were abandoned by married couples, a powerful commentary on the standard of living among the working poor, for whom an additional mouth to feed often meant tragedy.

Furthermore, great numbers of babies entered the foundling homes, but few left. Even in the best of these homes, 50 percent of the babies normally died within a year. In the worst, fully 90 percent did not survive. They succumbed to long journeys over rough roads, the intentional and unintentional neglect of their wet nurses, and the customary childhood illnesses. So great was the carnage that some contemporaries called the foundling hospitals "legalized infanticide."

Attitudes Toward Children

What were the more typical circumstances of children's lives? Did the treatment of foundlings reflect the attitudes of normal parents? Although some scholars argue otherwise, it seems that the young child was often of minor concern to its parents and to society in the eighteenth century. This indifference toward children was found in all classes; rich children were by no means exempt. The practice of using wet nurses, who were casually selected and often negligent, is one example of how even the rich and the prosperous put the child out of sight and out of mind. One French moralist, writing in 1756 about how to improve humanity, observed that "one blushes to think of loving one's children." It has been said that the English gentleman of the period "had more interest in the diseases of his horses than of his children."[8]

Feelings toward children were greatly influenced by the terrible frequency of death among children of all classes. Doctors and clergymen urged parents not to become too emotionally involved with their children, who were so unlikely to survive. Mothers especially did not always heed such warnings, but the risk of emotional devastation was very real for them. The great eighteenth-century English historian Edward Gibbon (1737–1794) wrote that "the death of a new born child before that of its parents may seem unnatural but it is a strictly probable event, since of any given number the greater part are extinguished before the ninth year, before they possess the faculties of the mind and the body." Gibbon's father named all his boys Edward after himself, hoping that at least one of them would survive to carry his name. His prudence was not misplaced. Edward the future historian and eldest survived. Five brothers and sisters who followed him all died in infancy.

The medical establishment was seldom interested in the care of children. One contemporary observer quoted a famous doctor as saying that "he never wished to be called to a young child because he was really at a loss to know what to offer for it." There were "physicians of note who make no scruple to assert that there is nothing to be done for children when they are ill." The best hope for children was often treatment by women healers and midwives, who helped many women deliver their babies and provided advice on child care. Nevertheless, children were still caught in a vicious circle:

Abandoned Children At this French foundlings' home a desperate, secretive mother could give up her baby without any questions, day or night. She placed her child on the revolving table and the nun on duty took it in. Similar practices existed in many countries. *(Jean-Loup Charmet)*

they were neglected because they were very likely to die, and they were likely to die because they were neglected.

Emotional detachment from children often shaded off into abuse. When parents and other adults did turn toward children, it was normally to discipline and control them. The novelist Daniel Defoe (1659–1731), always delighted when he saw very young children working hard in cottage industry, coined the axiom "Spare the rod and spoil the child." He meant it. So did Susannah Wesley (1669–1742), mother of John Wesley, the founder of Methodism. According to her, the first task of a parent toward her children was "to conquer the will, and bring them to an obedient temper." She reported that her babies were "taught to fear the rod, and to cry softly; by which means they escaped the abundance of correction they might otherwise have had, and that most odious noise of the crying of children was rarely heard in the house."[9]

It was hardly surprising that when English parish officials dumped their paupers into the first factories late in the eighteenth century, the children were beaten and brutalized (see pages 744–745). That was part of the child-rearing pattern—considerable indifference, on the one hand, and strict physical discipline, on the other—that prevailed throughout most of the eighteenth century.

From the middle of the century, this pattern came under increasing attack and began to change. Critics, led by Jean-Jacques Rousseau in his famous treatise *Emile* (see the feature "Listening to the Past: A New Way to Educate Children" on pages 686–687), called for greater love, tenderness, and understanding toward children. In addition to supporting foundling homes to discourage infanticide and urging wealthy women to nurse their own babies, these new voices ridiculed the practice of swaddling: wrapping youngsters in tight-fitting clothes and blankets was generally believed to form babies properly by "straightening them out." By the end of the eighteenth century, small children were often being dressed in simpler, more comfortable clothing, allowing much greater freedom of movement. More parents expressed a delight in the love and intimacy of the child and found real pleasure in raising their offspring. These changes were part of the general growth of humanitarianism and cautious optimism about human potential that characterized the eighteenth-century Enlightenment.

Schools and Popular Literature

The role of schools and formal education outside the home was also growing more important. The aristocracy and the rich had led the way in the sixteenth century with special colleges, often run by Jesuits. But schools charged specifically with elementary education of the children of the common people usually did not appear until the seventeenth century. Unlike medieval schools, which mingled all age groups, these elementary schools specialized in boys and girls from seven to twelve, who were taught basic literacy and religion.

Scholars generally agree that the religious struggle unleashed by the Protestant and Catholic Reformations served as the catalyst in promoting popular literacy between 1500 and 1800. Both Protestant and Catholic reformers pushed reading as a means of instilling their

Cultivating the Joy of Discovery
This English painting by Joseph Wright of Derby (1734–1797) reflects new attitudes toward child development and education, which advocated greater freedom and direct experience. The children rapturously watch a planetarium, which illustrates the movements and positions of the planets in the solar system. Wise teachers stand by, letting the children learn at their own pace. *(Derby Museum & Art Gallery/Bridgeman Art Library, London/New York)*

teachings more effectively. Thus literacy was often highest in border areas, such as eastern France, which were open to outside influences and to competition for believers from different churches. The growth of popular education quickened in the eighteenth century, but there was no revolutionary acceleration, and many common people received no formal education.

Prussia led the way in the development of universal education, inspired by the old Protestant idea that every believer should be able to read and study the Bible in the quest for personal salvation and by the new idea of a population capable of effectively serving the state. As early as 1717, Prussia made attendance at elementary schools compulsory, and more Protestant German states, such as Saxony and Württemberg, followed in the eighteenth century. Religious motives were also extremely important elsewhere. From the middle of the seventeenth century, Presbyterian Scotland was convinced that the path to salvation lay in careful study of the Scriptures, and it established an effective network of parish schools for rich and poor alike. The Church of England and the dissenting congregations established "charity schools" to instruct the children of the poor, and in 1682 France began setting up Christian schools to teach the catechism and prayers as well as reading and writing. France did less well than the Habsburg state, the only Catholic land to promote elementary education enthusiastically in the eighteenth century. In 1774 Maria Theresa established a general system of elementary education that called for compulsory education and a school in every community. Some elementary education was becoming a reality for European peoples, and schools were of growing significance in the life of the child.

The result of these efforts was a remarkable growth in basic literacy between 1600 and 1800. Whereas in 1600 only one male in six was barely literate in France and Scotland, and one in four in England, by 1800 almost nine out of ten Scottish males, two out of three French males (Map 20.1), and more than half of English males were literate. In all three countries, the bulk of the jump occurred in the eighteenth century. Women were also increasingly literate, although they lagged behind men in most countries.

The growth in literacy promoted a growth in reading, and historians have carefully examined what the common people read in an attempt to discern what they were thinking. One thing seems certain: the major philosophical works of the Enlightenment had little impact on peasants and workers, who could neither afford nor understand those favorites of the book-hungry educated public.

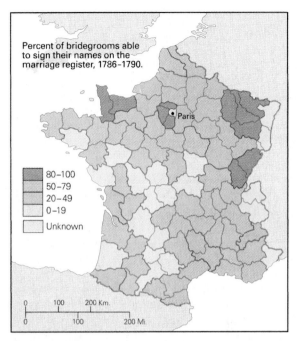

Percent of bridegrooms able to sign their names on the marriage register, 1786–1790.

80–100
50–79
20–49
0–19
Unknown

MAP 20.1 Literacy in France on the Eve of the French Revolution   Literacy rates increased but still varied widely between and within states in eighteenth-century Europe. Northern France was clearly ahead of southern France.

Although the Bible remained the overwhelming favorite, especially in Protestant countries, the staple of popular literature was short pamphlets known as chapbooks. Printed on the cheapest paper available, many chapbooks dealt with religious subjects. They featured Bible stories, prayers, devotions, and the lives of saints and exemplary Christians. Promising happiness after death, devotional literature was also intensely practical. It gave the believer moral teachings and a confidence in God that helped in daily living.

Entertaining, often humorous stories formed a second element of popular literature. Fairy tales, medieval romances, fictionalized history, and fantastic adventures—these were some of the delights that filled the peddler's pack as he approached a village. Both heroes and villains possessed superhuman powers in this make-believe world, a world of danger and magic, of fairy godmothers and evil trolls. But the good fairies always triumphed over the evil ones in the story's marvelous resolution.

The significance of these entertaining stories for the peasant reader is debated. Many scholars see them reflecting a desire for pure escapism and a temporary

A Peasant Family Reading the Bible   Praised by the philosophe Diderot for its moralistic message, this engraving of a painting by Jean-Baptiste Greuze (1725–1805) does capture the power of sacred texts and the spoken word. The peasant patriarch reads aloud from the massive family Bible and the close-knit circle of absorbed listeners concentrates on every word. Only the baby is distracted. *(Bibliothèque Nationale/Giraudon/Art Resource, NY)*

flight from harsh everyday reality. Others see these tales reflecting ancient folk wisdom and counseling prudence in a world full of danger and evil, where wolves dress up like grandmothers and eat Little Red Riding Hoods.

Finally, some popular literature was highly practical, dealing with rural crafts, household repairs, useful plants, and similar matters. Much of such lore was stored in almanacs. With calendars listing secular, religious, and astrological events mixed in with agricultural schedules, bizarre bits of information, and jokes, the almanac was universal, noncontroversial, and highly appreciated, even by many in the comfortable classes. "Anyone who could would read an almanac."[10]

In general, however, the reading of the common people had few similarities with that of educated elites. Popular literature was simple and practical, both as devotional self-help and as how-to instruction. It was also highly escapist, not unlike the mass of inexpensive paperbacks sold in drugstores today. Neither the practical nor the escapist elements challenged the established order. Rather, the common people were apparently con-

tent with works that reinforced traditional values and did not foster social or religious criticism. These results fit well with the modest educational objectives of rulers and educated elites. They believed that carefully limited instruction stressing religion and morals was useful to the masses but that too much study would only disorient them and foster discontent.

 FOOD AND MEDICAL PRACTICE

As we saw in Chapter 19, the European population increased rapidly in the eighteenth century. Plague and starvation gradually disappeared, and Europeans lived longer. What were the characteristics of diets and nutrition in this era of improving health and longevity? Although medical practice played only a small part, what was it like in the eighteenth century? What does a comparison of rich and poor reveal?

Diets and Nutrition

At the beginning of the eighteenth century, ordinary men and women depended on grain as fully as they had in the past. Bread was quite literally the staff of life. Peasants in the Beauvais region of France ate two pounds of bread a day, washing it down with water, green wine, beer, or a little skim milk. Their dark bread was made from a mixture of roughly ground wheat and rye—the standard flour of the common people. The poor also ate grains in soup and gruel. In rocky northern Scotland, for example, people depended on oatmeal, which they often ate half-cooked so that it would swell in their stomachs and make them feel full.

Little wonder, then, that an adequate supply of grain and an affordable price of bread loomed large in the popular imagination. Even peasants normally needed to buy some grain for food, and, in full accord with landless laborers and urban workers, they believed in the old medieval idea of the "just price." That is, they believed that prices should be "fair," protecting both consumers and producers and imposed by government decree if necessary.

In the later eighteenth century, this traditional, moral view of prices and the economy clashed repeatedly with the emerging free-market philosophy of unregulated supply and demand, which was increasingly favored by government officials, large landowners, and economists led by Adam Smith (see page 654). In years of poor harvests and soaring prices, this clash often resulted in food riots and popular disturbances. Peasants and workers would try to stop wagons loaded with grain from leaving their region, or they would seize grain held by speculators and big merchants accused of hoarding and rigging the market. (Usually the tumultuous crowd paid what it considered to be a fair price for what it took.) Governments were keenly aware of the problem of adequate grain supplies, and they would sometimes try to control prices to prevent unrest in crisis years.

Although breadstuffs were all important for the rural and urban poor, they also ate a fair quantity of vegetables. Indeed, vegetables were considered "poor people's food." Peas and beans were probably the most common; grown as field crops in much of Europe since the Middle Ages, they were eaten fresh in late spring and summer. Dried, they became the basic ingredients in the soups and stews of the long winter months. In most regions, other vegetables appeared in season on the tables of the poor, primarily cabbages, carrots, and wild greens. Fruit was uncommon and limited to the summer months.

The common people of Europe loved meat and eggs, but they seldom ate their fill. Indeed, the poor ate less meat in 1700 than in 1500 because their general standard of living had declined as the population surged in the sixteenth century (see page 637) and meat became more expensive. In the eighteenth century, the beginnings of agricultural transformation (see pages 631–

Le Nain: Peasant Family A little wine and a great deal of dark bread: the traditional food of the poor French peasantry accentuates the poetic dignity of this masterpiece, painted about 1640 by Louis Le Nain. *(Louvre © Photo R.M.N.—G. Blot/J. Schor)*

633) increased per capita meat consumption only in Britain and the Low Countries. Moreover, in most European countries harsh game laws deprived the poor of the right to hunt and eat game such as rabbits, deer, and partridges. Only nobles and large landowners could legally kill game. Few laws were more bitterly resented—or more frequently broken—by ordinary people than those governing hunting. When the poor did eat meat—on a religious holiday or at a wedding or other festive occasion—it was most likely lamb or mutton. Sheep could survive on rocky soils and did not compete directly with humans for the slender resources of grain.

Milk was rarely drunk. Perhaps because some individuals do suffer seriously from dairy allergies, it was widely believed that milk caused sore eyes, headaches, and a variety of ills, except among the very young and very old. Milk was used primarily to make cheese and butter, which did not spoil as milk did and which the poor liked but could afford only occasionally. Medical and popular opinion considered whey, the watery liquid left after milk was churned, "an excellent temperate drink."

The diet of the rich—aristocrats, officials, and the comfortable bourgeoisie—was traditionally quite different from that of the poor. The men and women of the upper classes were rapacious carnivores. A truly elegant dinner among the great and powerful consisted of one rich meat after another: a chicken pie, a leg of lamb, a grilled steak, for example. Three separate meat courses might be followed by three fish courses laced with piquant sauces and complemented with sweets, cheeses, and nuts of all kinds. Fruits and vegetables were not often found on the tables of the rich.

There was also an enormous amount of overdrinking among the rich. The English squire, for example, who loved to hunt with his hounds, loved to drink with a similar passion. He became famous as the "four-bottle man." With his dinner he drank red wine from France or white wine from the Rhineland, and with his dessert he took sweet but strong port or Madeira from Portugal. Sometimes he ended the evening under the table in a drunken stupor, but very often he did not. The wine and the meat were consumed together in long hours of sustained excess, permitting the gentleman and his guests to drink enormous quantities without getting stupefyingly drunk.

The diet of small traders, master craftsmen, minor bureaucrats—the people of the towns and cities—was generally less monotonous than that of the peasantry. The markets, stocked by market gardens on the outskirts, provided a substantial variety of meats, vegetables, and fruits, although bread and beans still formed the bulk of such families' diets.

There were also regional dietary differences in 1700. Generally speaking, northern, Atlantic Europe ate better than southern, Mediterranean Europe. The poor of England probably ate best of all. Contemporaries on both sides of the Channel often contrasted the English citizen's consumption of meat with the French peasants' greater dependence on bread and vegetables. The Dutch were also considerably better fed than the average European, in large part because of their advanced agriculture and diversified gardens.

The Impact of Diet on Health

How were the poor and the rich served by their quite different diets? At first glance, the diet of the laboring poor, relying as it did on grains and vegetables, might seem low in protein. However, the whole-grain wheat or rye flour used in eighteenth-century bread retained most of the bran—the ground-up husk—and the all-important wheat germ, which contains higher proportions of some minerals, vitamins, and good-quality proteins than does the rest of the grain. In addition, the field peas and beans eaten by poor people since the early Middle Ages contained protein that complemented the proteins in whole-grain bread. The proteins in whey, cheese, and eggs, which the poor ate at least occasionally, also supplemented the bread and vegetables.

The basic bread-and-vegetables diet of the poor *in normal times* was adequate. But a key dietary problem in some seasons, particularly in the late winter and early spring, was probably getting enough green vegetables (or milk) to ensure adequate supplies of vitamins A and C. A severe deficiency of vitamin C produces scurvy, a disease that leads to rotting gums, swelling of the limbs, and great weakness. Before the season's first vegetables, many people experienced shortages of vitamin C and suffered from mild cases of scurvy. (Scurvy was an acute problem for sailors on long voyages and by the end of the sixteenth century was being controlled on ships by a daily ration of lime juice.)

The practice of gorging on meat, sweets, and spirits caused the rich their own nutritional problems. Because of their great disdain for fresh vegetables, they, too, were very often deficient in vitamins A and C. Gout was a common affliction of the overfed and underexercised rich. No wonder they were often caricatured as dragging their flabby limbs and bulging bellies to the table to stuff their swollen cheeks and poison their livers. People of moderate means, who could afford some

Royal Interest in the Potato Frederick the Great of Prussia, shown here supervising cultivation of the potato, used his influence and position to promote the new food on his estates and throughout Prussia. Peasants could grow potatoes with the simplest hand tools, but it was backbreaking labor, as this painting by R. Warthmüller suggests. *(Private Collection, Hamburg/AKG London)*

meat and dairy products with fair regularity but who had not abandoned the bread and vegetables of the poor, were best off from a nutritional standpoint.

Patterns of food consumption changed rather markedly as the century progressed. More varied diets associated with new methods of farming were confined largely to the Low Countries and England, but a new food—the potato—came to the aid of the poor everywhere. Introduced into Europe from the Americas—along with corn, squash, tomatoes, and many other useful plants—the humble potato is actually an excellent food. Containing a good supply of carbohydrates, calories, and vitamins A and C (especially if it is not overcooked and the skin is eaten), the potato offset the lack of vitamins from green vegetables in the poor person's winter and early-spring diet, and it provided a much higher caloric yield than grain for a given piece of land.

For some desperately poor peasants who needed to get every possible calorie from a tiny plot of land, the potato replaced grain as the primary food in the eighteenth century. This happened first in Ireland, where English (Protestant) repression and exploitation forced large numbers of poor (Catholic) peasants to live off tiny scraps of rented ground. Elsewhere in Europe, potatoes took hold more slowly because many people did not like them. Thus, potatoes were first fed to pigs and livestock, and there was even debate over whether they were fit for humans. In Germany the severe famines caused by the Seven Years' War settled the matter: potatoes were edible and not just "famine food." By the end of the century, the potato had become an important dietary supplement in much of Europe.

There was also a general growth of market gardening, and a greater variety of vegetables appeared in towns and cities. In the course of the eighteenth century, the large towns and cities of maritime Europe began to receive semitropical fruits, such as oranges and lemons, from Portugal and the West Indies, although they were not cheap.

Not all changes in the eighteenth century were for the better, however. Bread began to change, most noticeably for the English and for the comfortable groups on the European continent. Rising incomes and new tastes led to a shift from whole-grain black or brown bread to "bread as white as snow" and started a decline in bread's nutritional value. The high-roughage bran and some of the dark but high-vitamin germ were increasingly sifted out by millers. This foretold further "improvements" in the nineteenth century, which would leave bread perfectly white and greatly reduced in nutritional value.

Another sign of nutritional decline was the growing consumption of sugar. Initially a luxury, sugar dropped rapidly in price as slave-based production increased in the Americas and the sweetener was much more widely used in the eighteenth century. This development probably led to an increase in cavities and to other ailments as well, although the greater or lesser poverty of the laboring poor still protected most of them from the sugar-tooth virus of the rich and well-to-do.

Medical Practitioners

Although sickness, pain, and disease—intractable challenges built into the human condition—permeated the European experience in the eighteenth century, medical science played a very small part in improving the health of most people. Yet the Enlightenment's growing focus on discovering the laws of nature and on human problems did give rise to a great deal of research and experimentation. The century also saw a remarkable rise in the number of medical practitioners. Therefore, when significant breakthroughs in knowledge came in the middle and late nineteenth century, they could be rapidly evaluated and diffused.

Care of the sick in the eighteenth century was the domain of several competing groups: faith healers, apothecaries (or pharmacists), physicians, surgeons, and midwives. Both men and women were prominent in the healing arts, as had been the case since the Middle Ages. But by 1700 the range of medical activities open to women was severely restricted, because women were generally denied admission to medical colleges and lacked the diplomas necessary for practice as physicians and surgeons. In the course of the eighteenth century, women encountered growing criticism and discrimination from competing male practitioners and the medical schools they dominated. The position of women as midwives and healers further eroded, pointing toward the virtual exclusion of women from "scientific medicine" in the early nineteenth century.

Faith healers, one of the most important kinds of healers in medieval Europe, remained active. They and their patients believed that demons and evil spirits caused disease by lodging in people and that the proper treatment was to exorcise, or drive out, the offending devil. This demonic view of disease was strongest in the countryside, where popular belief placed great faith in the healing power of religious relics, prayer, and the laying on of hands. Faith healing was particularly effective in the treatment of mental disorders such as hysteria and depression, where the link between attitude and illness is most direct.

In the larger towns and cities, apothecaries sold a vast number of herbs, drugs, and patent medicines for every conceivable "temperament and distemper." Their prescriptions were incredibly complex—a hundred or more drugs might be included in a single prescription—and often very expensive. Some of the drugs and herbs undoubtedly worked. For example, strong laxatives were given to the rich for their constipated bowels. Indeed, the medical profession continued to believe that regular "purging" of the bowels was essential for good health and the treatment of illness. Much purging was harmful, however, and only bloodletting for the treatment of disease was more effective in speeding patients to their graves. In the countryside, people often turned to midwives and women healers for herbs and folk remedies.

Physicians, who were invariably men, were apprenticed in their teens to a practicing physician for several years of on-the-job training. This training was then rounded out with hospital work or some university courses. Because such prolonged training was expensive, physicians continued to come mainly from prosperous families, and they usually concentrated on urban patients from similar social backgrounds. They had little contact with urban workers and less with peasants.

To their credit, physicians in the eighteenth century were increasingly willing to experiment with new methods, but time-honored practices lay heavily on them. Physicians, like apothecaries, laid great stress on purging. And bloodletting was still considered a medical cure-all. It was the way "bad blood," the cause of illness, was removed and the balance of humors necessary for good health was restored. According to a physician practicing medicine in Philadelphia in 1799, bleeding was proper at the onset of all inflammatory fevers, in all inflammations, and for "asthma, sciatic pains, coughs, head-aches, rheumatisms, the apoplexy, epilepsy, and bloody fluxes."[11] It was also necessary after all falls, blows, and bruises.

Surgeons, in contrast to physicians, made considerable medical and social progress in the eighteenth century. Long considered as ordinary male artisans comparable to butchers and barbers, surgeons began studying anatomy seriously and improved their art. With endless opportunities to practice, army surgeons on gory battlefields led the way. They learned that a soldier with an extensive wound, such as a shattered leg or arm, could perhaps be saved if the surgeon could obtain above the wound a flat surface that could be cauterized with fire. Thus if a soldier (or a civilian) had a broken limb and the bone stuck out, the surgeon amputated so that the remaining stump could be cauterized and the likelihood of death reduced.

The eighteenth-century surgeon (and patient) labored in the face of incredible difficulties. Almost all operations were performed without any painkiller, for the anesthesias of the day were hard to control and were believed too dangerous for general use. The terrible screams of people whose limbs were being sawed off echoed across battlefields and through hospitals. Many patients died from the agony and shock of such operations. Surgery was also performed in the midst of filth and dirt, for there simply was no knowledge of bacteriology and the nature of infection. The simplest wound treated by a surgeon could fester and lead to death.

Midwives, who were a special object of suspicion and persecution in the witch-hunt craze of the sixteenth and seventeenth centuries, continued to deliver the overwhelming majority of babies throughout the eighteenth century. The typical midwife was an older, often widowed woman of modest social origins and long professional experience. Trained initially by another woman practitioner, the midwife primarily assisted in labor and delivering babies. But the midwife also treated female problems, such as irregular menstrual cycles, breast-feeding difficulties, sterility, and venereal disease, and she ministered to small children. (See the feature "Individuals in Society: Martha Ballard, American Midwife.")

The midwife orchestrated labor and birth in a woman's world, where friends and relatives offered the pregnant woman assistance and encouragement in the familiar surroundings of her own home. Excluded by tradition and modesty, the male surgeon (and the husband) rarely entered this world, because most births, then as now, were normal and spontaneous. In seventeenth-century England, for example, a surgeon was called only if the child died without having been born and instruments were needed to deliver the dead baby. Following the invention of the forceps, which might help in an exceptionally difficult birth, surgeon-physicians used their monopoly over this and other instruments to seek lucrative new business. Attacking midwives as ignorant and dangerous, they persuaded growing numbers of wealthy women of the superiority of their services and sought to undermine faith in midwives.

Recent research suggests that women practitioners successfully defended much but not all of their practice in the eighteenth century. In France one enterprising Parisian midwife, Madame du Coudray, skillfully secured royal financing to teach better techniques, which she claimed would lower infant deaths. She then traveled all over France to promote her widely used midwifery textbook and to give hands-on instruction with life-size mannequins and doll-babies to roughly ten thousand women. In northern Italy, state and church

Teaching Midwives   This plate from Madame du Coudray's manual for midwives, *The Art of Childbirth*, illustrates "another incorrect method of delivery." The caption tells the midwife that she should have rotated the baby within the womb to face the mother's back, so that the chin does not catch on the pubis bone and dislocate the jaw. *(Rare Books Division, Countway [Francis A.] Library of Medicine)*

Cette Planche représente encore une fausse manœuvre en préférant de tirer l'enfant la face en devant plutôt que de lui avoir tourné par derrière, ce qui donne lieu au menton de l'enfant de s'accrocher sur les os Pubis et en continuant de le tirer dans cette position la tête se renversant en arrière la machoire peut se luxer, d'ailleurs l'occiput par ce renversement appuyant sur los Sacrum, il est impossible de faire passer la tête dans le détroit du petit bassin, il faut donc en repoussant l'enfant un peu en haut lui retourner la face en arrière.

Individuals in Society

Martha Ballard, American Midwife

The journal of Martha Ballard. *(Maine State Archives)*

In the cold spring of 1789, Martha Ballard delivered fourteen babies in two months of high drama and unsung heroism. An American midwife in a small town on the Kennebec River in central Maine, Ballard attended women on both sides of the icy flooding river, paddling back and forth and braving the harsh and erratic weather. On her way to one patient, she and her terrified horse were caught in a violent rainstorm and almost struck by a falling tree. She recorded the outcome in her diary, which she kept for twenty-seven years: "Assisted by the same allmighty power I got safe thru and arrived unhurt. Mrs Hewins safe delivered at ten hours evening of a daughter."[1] Ballard had persevered and triumphed.

Exceptional in her meticulous record keeping, Ballard embodied many characteristics of the midwife in the eighteenth-century Western world. A mature woman of fifty when her diary opened in 1785, she had learned her trade on the job, assisting other midwives delivering the babies of friends and relatives. She had also learned birthing practices and compassion from her own experience, for she gave birth to nine children between 1756 and 1779. Ballard worked as she was trained, assisted by other women in each patient's own home. She received payment for services in money or in goods, such as food and cloth. In the 1790s, the arrival of a young and inexperienced male doctor brought some competition, but the midwife continued to preside over the vast majority of births in the town.

The great adventures in Ballard's diary were her journeys to expectant mothers and her struggles with the elements. The deliveries themselves were described simply, in matter-of-fact terms. Ballard's women were "unwell," and their "illness" only increased as they passed into labor. Complications were rarely noted, and then only briefly in nontechnical language. Indeed, birthing tragedies hardly appeared in her everyday record. How, the modern reader may ask, can this be?

Part of the answer lies in Ballard's strength of constitution and character, her accepting nature, and her faith in God. Perhaps more lies in her skill, justifiable self-confidence, and enviable record of success. She attended more than eight hundred deliveries and lost not a single mother in birthing, although five died in the recovery period. Moreover, only nineteen babies died stillborn or within an hour or two of birth. These levels of maternal and infant death were not surpassed until 1930 in the United States. Ballard's success shows that if a woman had adequate nutrition (as in New England) and the care of an experienced midwife, childbirth at home was a natural physical process that normally ended well.

Tough and tender, Ballard also practiced as a nurse, physician, mortician, and pharmacist, relying on herbal medicines. For example, she administered mandrake and pinkroot as powerful laxatives and emetics to cause the expulsion of children's intestinal worms, which were contracted by playing in soil infected by human feces and which could grow up to fourteen inches in length.

A large portion of Ballard's time was occupied with laborious housecleaning, gardening, sewing, and bearing, nursing, raising, and teaching her children. Nursing for pay and simply helping her neighbors overlapped. In later life, she endured the disasters of an alcoholic son and her husband's indifference to her fatigue and stomach pain. Unlike the women she delivered, she found relief from these trials only with death at age seventy-seven in 1812.

Questions for Analysis

1. Describe Martha Ballard. What kind of a person was she?

2. What challenges did Ballard face as a midwife? How successfully did she meet them?

1. L. Ulrich, *A Midwife's Tale: The Life of Martha Ballard, Based on Her Diary, 1785–1812* (New York: Alfred A. Knopf, 1990), p. 6. This section draws on Ulrich's pioneering study, a masterpiece of the biographer's art. Abbreviations have been spelled out.

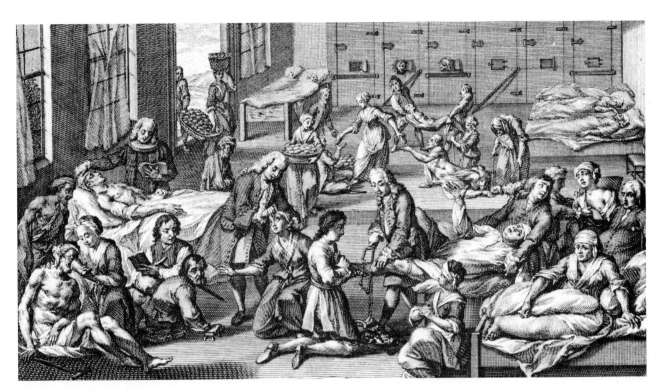

Hospital Life   Patients crowded into hospitals like this one in Hamburg in 1746 had little chance of recovery. A priest by the window administers last rites, while in the center a surgeon coolly saws off the leg of a man who has received no anesthesia. *(Germanisches Nationalmuseum, Nuremberg)*

pressures led to major changes in midwife training and certification, but women remained dominant in the birthing trade. It appears that midwives generally lost no more babies than male doctors, who were still summoned to treat nonelite women only when a life-threatening situation required surgery.

While ordinary physicians were bleeding, apothecaries purging, surgeons sawing, faith healers praying, and midwives assisting, the leading medical thinkers were attempting to pull together and assimilate all the information and misinformation they had been accumulating. The attempt was ambitious: to systematize medicine around simple, basic principles, as Newton had done in physics. But the schools of thought resulting from such speculation and theorizing did little to improve medical care.

Hospitals and Medical Experiments

Hospitals were terrible places throughout most of the eighteenth century. There was no isolation of patients. Operations were performed in a patient's bed. Nurses were old, ignorant, greedy, and often drunk women.

Fresh air was considered harmful, and infections of every kind were rampant. Diderot's article in the *Encyclopedia* on the Hôtel-Dieu in Paris, the "richest and most terrifying of all French hospitals," vividly describes normal conditions of the 1770s:

Imagine a long series of communicating wards filled with sufferers of every kind of disease who are sometimes packed three, four, five or even six into a bed, the living alongside the dead and dying, the air polluted by this mass of unhealthy bodies, passing pestilential germs of their afflictions from one to the other, and the spectacle of suffering and agony on every hand. That is the Hôtel-Dieu.

The result is that many of these poor wretches come out with diseases they did not have when they went in, and often pass them on to the people they go back to live with. Others are half-cured and spend the rest of their days in an invalidism as hard to bear as the illness itself; and the rest perish, except for the fortunate few whose strong constitutions enable them to survive.[12]

No wonder the poor of Paris hated hospitals and often saw confinement there as a plot to kill paupers.

In the last years of the century, the humanitarian concern already reflected in Diderot's description of the Hôtel-Dieu led to a movement for hospital reform throughout western Europe. Efforts were made to improve ventilation and eliminate filth on the grounds that bad air caused disease. The theory was wrong, but the results were beneficial, since the spread of infection was somewhat reduced.

Mental hospitals, too, were incredibly savage institutions. The customary treatment for mental illness was bleeding and cold water, administered more to maintain discipline than to effect a cure. Violent persons were chained to the wall and forgotten. A breakthrough of sorts occurred in the 1790s when William Tuke founded the first humane sanatorium in England. In Paris an innovative warden, Philippe Pinel, took the chains off the mentally disturbed in 1793 and tried to treat them as patients rather than as prisoners.

In the eighteenth century, all sorts of wildly erroneous ideas about mental illness circulated. One was that moonlight caused madness, a belief reflected in the word *lunatic*—someone harmed by lunar light. Another mid-eighteenth-century theory, which lasted until at least 1914, was that masturbation caused madness, not to mention acne, epilepsy, and premature ejaculation. Thus parents, religious institutions, and schools waged relentless war on masturbation by males, although they were curiously uninterested in female masturbation.

In the second half of the eighteenth century, medicine in general turned in a more practical and experimental direction. Some of the experimentation was creative quackery involving the recently discovered phenomenon of electricity. One magnificent quack in London promoted sleep on a cure-all Celestial Bed, which was lavishly decorated with magnets and electrical devices. A single night on the bed cost a small fortune. The rich could buy expensive treatments, but the prevalence of quacks and the general lack of knowledge meant they often got little for their money. Because so many treatments were harmful, the common people were probably much less deprived by their reliance on faith healers and folk medicine than one might think.

Experimentation and the intensified search for solutions to human problems led to some real advances in medicine after 1750, however. The eighteenth century's greatest medical triumph was the conquest of smallpox. With the progressive decline of bubonic plague, smallpox became the most terrible of the infectious diseases. In the words of historian Thomas Macaulay, "Smallpox was always present, filling the churchyard with corpses, tormenting with constant fears all whom it had not stricken." In the seventeenth century, 25 percent of the deaths in the British Isles were due to smallpox, and it is estimated that 60 million Europeans died of it in the eighteenth century. Fully 80 percent of the population was stricken at some point in life, and 25 percent of the total population was left permanently scarred. If ever a human problem cried out for a solution, it was smallpox.

The first step in the conquest of this killer came in the early eighteenth century. An English aristocrat whose great beauty had been marred by the pox, Lady Mary Wortley Montagu, learned about the practice of inoculation in the Ottoman Empire while her husband was serving as British ambassador there. She had her own son successfully inoculated in Constantinople and was instrumental in spreading the practice in England after her return in 1722.

Inoculation against smallpox had long been practiced in the Muslim lands of western Asia. The skin was deliberately broken, and a small amount of matter taken from the pustule of a smallpox victim was applied. The person thus contracted a mild case of smallpox that gave lasting protection against further attack. Inoculation was risky, however, and about one person in fifty died from it. In addition, people who had been inoculated were infectious and often spread the disease, leading to widespread condemnation of inoculation against smallpox in the 1730s.

Success in reducing the risks of inoculation in British colonies and a successful search for cheaper methods led to something approaching mass inoculation in England in the 1760s. Both the danger and the cost had been reduced, and deadly smallpox struck all classes less frequently. On the continent, the well-to-do were also inoculated, beginning with royal families such as those of Maria Theresa and Catherine the Great. The practice then spread to the middle classes. By the later years of the century, smallpox inoculation was playing some part in the decline of the death rate and the general increase in European population.

The final breakthrough against smallpox came at the end of the century. Edward Jenner (1749–1823), a talented country doctor, noted that in the English countryside there was a long-standing belief that dairy maids who had contracted cowpox did not get smallpox. Cowpox produces sores on the cow's udder and on the hands of the milker. The sores resemble those of smallpox, but the disease is mild and not contagious.

For eighteen years Jenner practiced a kind of Baconian science, carefully collecting data on protection against smallpox by cowpox. Finally, in 1796 he performed his first vaccination on a young boy using matter taken from a milkmaid with cowpox. In the next two years, he performed twenty-three successful vaccinations, and in 1798 Jenner published his findings. After Austrian medical authorities replicated Jenner's results, the new method of treatment spread rapidly. Smallpox soon declined to the point of disappearance in Europe and then throughout the world. Jenner eventually received prizes totaling £30,000 from the British government for his great discovery, a fitting recompense for a man who gave an enormous gift to humanity and helped lay the foundation for the science of immunology in the nineteenth century.

 ## RELIGION AND POPULAR CULTURE

Though the critical spirit of the Enlightenment spread among the educated elite in the eighteenth century, the majority of ordinary men and women remained firmly committed to the Christian religion, especially in rural areas. Religious faith promised salvation and eternal life, and it gave comfort and courage in the face of sorrow and death. Religion also remained strong because it was usually embedded in local traditions, everyday social experience, and popular culture.

Yet the popular religion of village Europe was everywhere enmeshed in a larger world of church hierarchies and state power. These powerful outside forces sought to regulate religious life at the local level. Their efforts created tensions that helped set the scene for a vigorous religious revival in Germany and England. Similar tensions arose in Catholic countries, where powerful elites criticized and attacked popular religious practices that their increasingly rationalistic minds deemed foolish and superstitious.

The Institutional Church

As in the Middle Ages, the local parish church remained the basic religious unit all across Europe. Still largely coinciding with the agricultural village, the parish fulfilled many needs. The parish church was the focal point of religious devotion, which went far beyond sermons and Holy Communion. The parish church organized colorful processions and pilgrimages to local shrines. Even in Protestant countries, where such activities were severely restricted, congregations gossiped and swapped stories after services, and neighbors came together in church for baptisms, marriages, funerals, and

A Religious Festival in Urban France   This vibrant painting suggests how religious life interacted with powerful institutions in Catholic Europe. Moving past crowds and through the city, this procession is celebrating the Blessed Sacrament on the Feast of Corpus Christi (the Body of Christ). Church dignitaries are grouped in the center; the colorful nobility is on the left; and the middle orders, with their sober black suits, are on the right. Both participation and hierarchical inequality are the rule. *(Bibliothèque des Arts Décoratifs/Jean-Loup Charmet)*

special events. Thus the parish church was woven into the very fabric of community life.

Moreover, the local church had important administrative tasks. Priests and parsons were truly the bookkeepers of agrarian Europe, and it is because parish registers were so complete that historians have learned so much about population and family life. Parishes also normally distributed charity to the destitute, looked after orphans, and provided whatever primary education was available for the common people.

The many tasks of the local church were usually the responsibility of a resident priest or pastor, a full-time professional working with assistants and lay volunteers. All clerics—whether Roman Catholic, Protestant, Greek Orthodox, or Russian Orthodox—also shared the fate of middlemen in a complicated institutional system. Charged most often with ministering to poor peasants, the priest or parson was the last link in a powerful church-state hierarchy that was everywhere determined to control religion down to the grassroots. However, the regulatory framework of belief, which went back at least to the fourth century when Christianity became the official religion of the Roman Empire, had undergone important changes since 1500.

The Protestant Reformation had burst forth as a culmination of medieval religiosity and a desire to purify Christian belief. Martin Luther, the most influential of the early reformers, preached that all men and women were saved from their sins and God's damnation only by personal faith in Jesus Christ. The individual could reach God directly, without need of priestly intermediaries. This was the revolutionary meaning of Luther's "priesthood of all believers," which broke forever the monopoly of the priestly class over medieval Europe's most priceless treasure—eternal salvation.

As the Reformation gathered force, with peasant upheaval and doctrinal competition, German princes and monarchs in northern Europe put themselves at the head of official churches in their territories. Protestant authorities, with generous assistance from state-certified theologians like Luther, then proceeded to regulate their "territorial churches" strictly, selecting personnel and imposing detailed rules. They joined with Catholics to crush the Anabaptists, who, with their belief in freedom of conscience and separation of church and state, had become the real revolutionaries. Thus the Reformation, initially so radical in its rejection of Rome and its stress on individual religious experience, eventually resulted in a bureaucratization of the church and local religious life in Protestant Europe.

The Reformation era also increased the practical power of Catholic rulers over "their" churches, but it was only in the eighteenth century that some Catholic monarchs began to impose striking reforms. These reforms, which had their counterparts in Orthodox Russia, had a very "Protestant" aspect. They increased state control over the Catholic church, making it less subject to papal influence.

Spain provides a graphic illustration of changing church-state relations in Catholic lands. A deeply Catholic country with devout rulers, Spain nevertheless took firm control of ecclesiastical appointments. Papal proclamations could not even be read in Spanish churches without prior approval from the government. Spain also asserted state control over the Spanish Inquisition, which had been ruthlessly pursuing heresy as an independent agency under Rome's direction for two hundred years. Spain went far toward creating a "national" Catholic church, as France had done earlier.

A more striking indication of state power and papal weakness was the fate of the Society of Jesus. As the most successful of the Catholic Reformation's new religious orders, the well-educated Jesuits were extraordinary teachers, missionaries, and agents of the papacy. In many Catholic countries, the Jesuits exercised tremendous political influence, since individual members held high government positions and Jesuit colleges formed the minds of Europe's Catholic nobility. Yet by playing politics so effectively, the Jesuits eventually elicited a broad coalition of enemies. Especially bitter controversies over the Jesuits rocked the entire Catholic hierarchy in France. Following the earlier example of Portugal, the French king ordered the Jesuits out of France in 1763 and confiscated their property. France and Spain then pressured Rome to dissolve the Jesuits completely. In 1773 a reluctant pope caved in, although the order was revived after the French Revolution.

Some Catholic rulers also turned their reforming efforts on monasteries and convents, believing that the large monastic clergy should make a more practical contribution to social and religious life. Austria, a leader in controlling the church (see page 620) and promoting primary education, showed how far the process could go. Whereas Maria Theresa sharply restricted entry into "unproductive" orders, Joseph II recalled the radical initiatives of the Protestant Reformation. In his Edict on Idle Institutions, Joseph abolished contemplative orders, henceforth permitting only orders that were engaged in teaching, nursing, or other practical work. The number of monks plunged from sixty-five thousand to twenty-seven thousand. The state also expropriated the dissolved monasteries and used their great wealth for charitable purposes and higher salaries for ordinary priests.

Protestant Revival

In their attempt to recapture the vital core of the Christian religion, the Protestant reformers had rigorously suppressed all the medieval practices that they considered nonessential or erroneous. For example, they had taken very seriously the commandment "Thou shalt not make any graven image" (Exodus 20:4), and their radical reforms had reordered church interiors. Relics and crucifixes had been permanently removed from crypt and altar, while stained-glass windows had been smashed and walls and murals covered with whitewash. Processions and pilgrimages, saints and shrines—all such practices had been eliminated because they were not founded on Scripture. Such revolutionary changes had often troubled ordinary churchgoers, but by the late seventeenth century the vast reforms of the Reformation had been completed and thoroughly routinized in most Protestant churches.

Indeed, official Protestant churches had generally settled into a smug complacency. In the Reformation heartland, one concerned German minister wrote that the Lutheran church "had become paralyzed in forms of dead doctrinal conformity" and badly needed a return to its original inspiration.[13] This voice was one of many that would prepare and then guide a powerful Protestant revival, which was largely successful because it answered the intense but increasingly unsatisfied needs of common people.

The Protestant revival began in Germany. It was known as "Pietism," and three aspects helped explain its powerful appeal. First, Pietism called for a warm, emotional religion that everyone could experience. Enthusiasm—in prayer, in worship, in preaching, in life itself—was the key concept. "Just as a drunkard becomes full of wine, so must the congregation become filled with spirit," declared one exuberant writer. Another said simply, "The heart must burn."[14]

Second, Pietism reasserted the earlier radical stress on the priesthood of all believers, thereby reducing the large gulf between the official clergy and the Lutheran laity. Bible reading and study were enthusiastically extended to all classes, and this provided a powerful spur for popular education as well as individual religious development (see page 669). Finally, Pietists believed in the practical power of Christian rebirth in everyday affairs. Reborn Christians were expected to lead good, moral lives and come from all social classes.

Pietism had a major impact on John Wesley (1703–1791), who served as the catalyst for popular religious revival in England. Wesley came from a long line of ministers, and when he went to Oxford University to prepare for the clergy, he mapped a fanatically earnest "scheme of religion." Like some students during final-

A Midsummer Afternoon with a Methodist Preacher   This detail from a painting by de Louterbourg suggests in a humorous manner how Wesley and his followers took their optimistic Christianity to the people of England. Methodist ministers championed open-air preaching and week-long revivals. *(National Gallery of Canada, Ottawa)*

exam period, he organized every waking moment. After becoming a teaching fellow at Oxford, he organized a Holy Club for similarly minded students, who were soon known contemptuously as "Methodists" because they were so methodical in their devotion. Yet like the young Luther, Wesley remained intensely troubled about his own salvation, even after his ordination as an Anglican priest in 1728.

Wesley's anxieties related to grave problems of the faith in England. The Church of England was shamelessly used by the government to provide favorites with high-paying jobs and sinecures. Building of churches practically stopped while the population grew, and in many parishes there was a grave shortage of pews. Services and sermons had settled into an uninspiring routine. That the properly purified religion had been separated from local customs and social life was symbolized by church doors that were customarily locked on weekdays. Moreover, the skepticism of the Enlightenment was making inroads among the educated classes, and deism was becoming popular. Some bishops and church leaders acted as if they believed that doctrines such as the Virgin Birth or the Ascension were little more than particularly elegant superstitions.

Spiritual counseling from a sympathetic Pietist minister from Germany prepared Wesley for a mystical, emotional "conversion" in 1738. He described this critical turning point in his *Journal:*

In the evening I went to a [Christian] society in Aldersgate Street where one was reading Luther's preface to the Epistle to the Romans. About a quarter before nine, while he was describing the change which God works in the heart through faith in Christ, I felt my heart strangely warmed. I felt I did trust in Christ, Christ alone for salvation; and an assurance was given me that he had taken away my sins, even mine, and saved me from the law of sin and death.[15]

Wesley's emotional experience resolved his intellectual doubts. Moreover, he was convinced that any person, no matter how poor or uneducated, might have a similarly heartfelt conversion and gain the same blessed assurance.

Wesley took the good news to the people, traveling some 225,000 miles by horseback and preaching more than forty thousand sermons in fifty years. Since existing churches were often overcrowded and the church-state establishment was hostile, Wesley preached in open fields. People came in large numbers. Of critical importance was Wesley's rejection of Calvinist predestination—the doctrine of salvation granted only to a select few. Expanding on earlier Dutch theologians' views, he preached that *all* men and women who

earnestly sought salvation might be saved. It was a message of hope and joy, of free will and universal salvation.

Wesley's ministry won converts, formed Methodist cells, and eventually resulted in a new denomination. And as Wesley had been inspired by Pietist revival in Germany, so evangelicals in the Church of England and the old dissenting groups now followed Wesley's example, giving impetus to an even broader awakening among the lower classes. In Protestant countries, religion remained a vital force in the lives of the people.

Catholic Piety

Religion also flourished in Catholic Europe around 1700, but there were important differences with Protestant practice. First of all, the visual contrast was striking; baroque art had lavished rich and emotionally exhilarating figures and images on Catholic churches, just as Protestants had removed theirs. From almost every indication, people in Catholic Europe remained intensely religious. More than 95 percent of the population probably attended church for Easter Communion, the climax of the Catholic church year.

The tremendous popular strength of religion in Catholic countries reflected religion's integral role in community life and popular culture. Thus although Catholics reluctantly confessed their sins to priests, they enthusiastically joined together in religious festivals to celebrate the passage of the liturgical year. In addition to the great processional days—such as Palm Sunday, the joyful re-enactment of Jesus' triumphal entry into Jerusalem, or the chanted supplications and penances for three Rogation days before the bodily ascent of Jesus into heaven on Ascension Day—each parish had its own saints' days, processions, and pilgrimages. Led by its priest, a congregation might march around the village or across the countryside to a local shrine or chapel. Before each procession or feast day, the priest explained its religious significance to kindle group piety. But processions were also folklore and tradition, an escape from work, and a form of recreation. A holiday atmosphere sometimes reigned on longer processions, with drinking and dancing and couples disappearing into the woods.

Indeed, devout Catholics held many religious beliefs that were marginal to the Christian faith, often of obscure or even pagan origin. On the Feast of Saint Anthony, for example, priests were expected to bless salt and bread for farm animals to protect them from disease. One saint's relics could help cure a child of fear, and there were healing springs for many ailments. The ordinary person combined a strong Christian faith with a wealth of time-honored superstitions.

Inspired initially by the fervor of the Catholic Counter-Reformation and then to some extent by the critical rationalism of the Enlightenment, parish priests and Catholic hierarchies sought increasingly to "purify" popular religious practice and to detach that purified religion from everyday life in the eighteenth century. Thus one parish priest in France lashed out at his parishioners, claiming that they were "more superstitious than devout . . . and sometimes appear as baptized idolators."[16] Another priest tried to abolish pilgrimages to a local sacred spring of Our Lady reputed to revive dead babies long enough for a proper baptism. French priests particularly denounced the "various remnants of paganism" found in popular bonfire ceremonies during Lent, in which young men, "yelling and screaming like madmen," tried to jump over the bonfires in order to help the crops grow and protect themselves from illness. One priest saw rational Christians regressing into pagan animals—"the triumph of Hell and the shame of Christianity."[17]

In contrast with Protestant reformers, who had already used the power of the territorial state to crush such practices, many Catholic priests and hierarchies preferred a compromise between theological purity and the people's piety, perhaps realizing that the line between divine truth and mere superstition is not easily drawn. Thus the severity of the attack on popular Catholicism varied widely by country and region. Where authorities pursued purification vigorously, as in Austria under Joseph II, pious peasants saw only an incomprehensible attack on the true faith and drew back in anger. Their reaction dramatized the growing tension between the attitudes of educated elites and the common people.

Leisure and Recreation

The combination of religious celebration and popular recreation seen in festivals and processions was most strikingly displayed at Carnival, a time of reveling and excess in Catholic and Mediterranean Europe. Carnival preceded Lent—the forty days of fasting and penitence before Easter—and for a few exceptional days in January or February, a wild release of drinking, masquerading, and dancing reigned. Moreover, a combination of plays, processions, and rowdy spectacles turned the established order upside down. Peasants became nobles, fools turned into philosophers, and the rich were humbled. These once-a-year rituals gave people a much-appreciated chance to release their pent-up frustrations and aggressions before life returned to the usual pattern of leisure and recreation.

That pattern featured socializing in groups, for despite the spread of literacy, the culture of the common people was largely oral rather than written. In the cold, dark winter months, families gathered around the fireplace to talk, sing, tell stories, do craftwork, and keep warm. In some parts of Europe, women would gather together in groups in someone's cottage to chat, sew, spin, and laugh. Sometimes a few young men would be invited so that the daughters (and mothers) could size up potential suitors in a supervised atmosphere. A favorite recreation of men was drinking and talking with buddies in public places, and it was a sorry village that had no tavern. In addition to old favorites such as beer and wine, the common people turned with gusto toward cheap and potent hard liquor, which fell in price because of improved techniques for distilling grain in the eighteenth century.

Towns and cities offered a wide range of amusements. Many of these had to be paid for because the eighteenth century saw a sharp increase in the commercialization of leisure-time activities—a trend that continues to this day. Urban fairs featured prepared foods, acrobats, freak shows, open-air performances, optical illusions, and the like. Such entertainments attracted a variety of social classes. So did the growing number of commercial, profit-oriented spectator sports. These ranged from traveling circuses and horse races to boxing matches and bullfights. Modern sports heroes, such as brain-bashing heavyweight champions and haughty matadors, made their appearance on the historical scene.

"Blood sports," such as bullbaiting and cockfighting, remained popular with the masses. In bullbaiting the bull, usually staked on a chain in the courtyard of an inn, was attacked by ferocious dogs for the amusement of the innkeeper's clients. Eventually the maimed and tortured animal was slaughtered by a butcher and sold as meat. In cockfighting two roosters, carefully trained by their owners and armed with razor-sharp steel spurs, slashed and clawed each other in a small ring until the victor won—and the loser died. An added attraction of cockfighting was that the screaming spectators could bet on the lightning-fast combat and its uncertain outcome.

In trying to place the vibrant popular culture of the common people in broad perspective, historians have stressed the growing criticism levied against it by the educated elites in the second half of the eighteenth century. These elites, which had previously shared the popular enthusiasm for religious festivals, Carnival, drinking in taverns, blood sports, and the like, now

Cockfighting in England This engraving by William Hogarth (1697–1764) satirizes the popular taste for blood sports, which Hogarth despised and lampooned in his famous *Four Stages of Cruelty.* The central figure in the wildly excited gathering is a blind nobleman, who actually existed and seldom missed a fight. Note the steel spurs on the birds' legs. *(Courtesy of Trustees of the British Museum)*

tended to see only superstition, sin, disorder, and vulgarity.[18] The resulting attack on popular culture, which had its more distant origins in the Protestant clergy's efforts to eliminate frivolity and superstition, was intensified as educated elites embraced the critical world-view of the Enlightenment. This shift in cultural attitudes drove a wedge between the common people and the educated public. The mutual hostility that this separation engendered played an important role in the emergence of sharp class conflict in the era of the French and the Industrial Revolutions.

SUMMARY

In recent years, imaginative research has greatly increased the specialist's understanding of ordinary life

and social patterns in the past. The human experience as recounted by historians has become richer and more meaningful, and many mistaken ideas have fallen by the wayside. This has been particularly true of eighteenth-century, predominantly agrarian Europe, which combined a fascinating mixture of continuity and change.

To summarize, the life of the people remained primarily rural and oriented toward the local community. Tradition, routine, and well-established codes of behavior framed much of the everyday experience of the typical villager. Thus just as the three-field agricultural cycle and its pattern of communal rights had determined traditional patterns of grain production, so did community values in the countryside strongly encourage a late age of marriage, a low rate of illegitimate births, and a strict attitude toward children. Patterns of recreation and leisure, from churchgoing and religious festivals to sewing and drinking in groups within an oral culture, also reflected and reinforced community ties and values. Many long-standing ideas and beliefs, ranging from obscure religious customs to support for fair prices, remained strong forces and sustained continuity in popular life.

Yet powerful forces also worked for change. Many of these came from outside and above, from the aggressive capitalists, educated elites, and government officials discussed in the last two chapters. Closely knit villages began to lose control over families and marital practices, as could be seen in the earlier, more romantic marriages of cottage workers and in the beginning of the explosion in illegitimate births. Although the new, less rigorous attitudes toward children that were emerging in elite culture did not reach the people, the elite belief in the usefulness of some education did result in growing popular literacy. The grain-based diet became more varied with the grudging acceptance of the potato, and the benefits of the spectacular conquest of smallpox began to reach the common people in the late eighteenth century. Finally, the common people found that their beliefs and customs were being increasingly attacked by educated elites, who thought they knew better. The popular reaction to these attacks generally remained muted in the eighteenth century, but the common people and their advocates would offer vigorous responses and counterattacks in the revolutionary era.

NOTES

1. Quoted in J. M. Beattie, "The Criminality of Women in Eighteenth-Century England," *Journal of Social History* 8 (Summer 1975): 86.

2. W. L. Langer, "Infanticide: A Historical Survey," *History of Childhood Quarterly* 1 (Winter 1974): 357.

3. Quoted in R. Cobb, *The Police and the People: French Popular Protest, 1789–1820* (Oxford: Clarendon Press, 1970), p. 238.

4. M. Segalen, *Love and Power in the Peasant Family: Rural France in the Nineteenth Century* (New York: Basil Blackwell, 1983), p. 41. The passage as cited here has been edited to the past tense.

5. Quoted in D. S. Landes, ed., *The Rise of Capitalism* (New York: Macmillan, 1966), pp. 56–57.

6. G. Gullickson, *Spinners and Weavers of Auffay: Rural Industry and the Sexual Division of Labor in a French Village, 1750–1850* (Cambridge: Cambridge University Press, 1986), p. 186. See also L. A. Tilly, J. W. Scott, and M. Cohen, "Women's Work and European Fertility Patterns," *Journal of Interdisciplinary History* 6 (Winter 1976): 447–476.

7. J. Michelet, *The People,* trans. with an introduction by J. P. McKay (Urbana: University of Illinois Press, 1973; original publication, 1846), pp. 38–39.

8. Quoted in B. W. Lorence, "Parents and Children in Eighteenth-Century Europe," *History of Childhood Quarterly* 2 (Summer 1974): 1–2.

9. Ibid., pp. 13, 16.

10. E. Kennedy, *A Cultural History of the French Revolution* (New Haven, Conn.: Yale University Press, 1989), p. 47.

11. Quoted in L. S. King, *The Medical World of the Eighteenth Century* (Chicago: University of Chicago Press, 1958), p. 320.

12. Quoted in R. Sand, *The Advance to Social Medicine* (London: Staples Press, 1952), pp. 86–87.

13. Quoted in K. Pinson, *Pietism as a Factor in the Rise of German Nationalism* (New York: Columbia University Press, 1934), p. 13.

14. Ibid., pp. 43–44.

15. Quoted in S. Andrews, *Methodism and Society* (London: Longmans, Green, 1970), p. 327.

16. Quoted in I. Woloch, *Eighteenth-Century Europe: Tradition and Progress, 1715–1789* (New York: W. W. Norton, 1982), p. 292.

17. Quoted in T. Tackett, *Priest and Parish in Eighteenth-Century France* (Princeton, N.J.: Princeton University Press, 1977), p. 214.

18. Woloch, *Eighteenth-Century Europe,* pp. 220–221; see also pp. 214–220 for this section.

SUGGESTED READING

Social topics of the kind considered in this chapter have come into their own in recent years, and the reader is strongly advised to take time to look through recent volumes of some leading journals: *Journal of Social History, Past and Present,* and *Journal of Interdisciplinary History.* In addition, the number of book-length studies continues to expand rapidly. Several of these studies are mentioned in the Notes.

Among general introductions to the history of the family, women, and children, J. Casey, *The History of the Family* (1989), is recommended. A. Imhof, *Lost Worlds: How Our European Ancestors Coped with Everyday Life and Why Life Is So Hard Today* (1996), sheds new light on family ties and attitudes toward death, which may be compared with P. Laslett, *The World We Have Lost* (1965), a pioneering investigation of England before the Industrial Revolution. L. Stone, *The Family, Sex and Marriage in England, 1500–1800* (1977), is a provocative general interpretation, and L. Tilly and J. Scott, *Women, Work and Family* (1978), remains an excellent introduction. Two valuable works on women, both with good bibliographies, are M. Boxer and J. Quataert, eds., *Connecting Spheres: Women in the Western* *(continued on page 688)*

A New Way to Educate Children

Emile, by Jean-Jacques Rousseau, is one of history's most original books. Sometimes called a declaration of rights for children, Emile *challenged existing patterns of child rearing and pleaded for humane treatment of children.*

Rousseau's work also had a powerful impact on theories of education. As the following passage suggests, Emile *argued that education must shield the unspoiled child from the corrupting influences of civilization and allow the child to develop naturally and spontaneously. It is eloquent testimony to Rousseau's troubled life that he neglected his own children and placed all five of them in orphanages.*

Rousseau believed that the sexes were by nature intended for different occupations. Thus Emile *might eventually tackle difficult academic subjects, but Sophie, his future wife in the book, needed to learn only how to manage the home and be a good mother and an obedient wife. The idea that girls and boys should be educated to operate in "separate spheres" was to gain wide acceptance in the nineteenth century.*

A man must know many things which seem useless to a child, but need the child learn, or can he indeed learn, all that the man must know? Try to teach the child what is of use to a child and you will find that it takes all his time. Why urge him to the studies of an age he may never reach, to the neglect of those studies which meet his present needs? "But," you ask, "will it not be too late to learn what he ought to know when the time comes to use it?" I cannot tell; but this I do know, it is impossible to teach it sooner, for our real teachers are experience and emotion, and man will never learn what befits a man except under its own conditions. A child knows he must become a man; all the ideas he may have as to man's place in life are so many opportunities for his instruction, but he should remain in complete ignorance of those ideas which are beyond his grasp. My whole book is one continued argument in support of this fundamental principle of education.

As soon as we have contrived to give our pupil [Emile] an idea of the word "useful," we have got an additional means of controlling him, for this word makes a great impression on him, provided that its meaning for him is a meaning relative to his own age, and provided he clearly sees its relation to his own well-being. . . . "What is the use of that?" In the future this is the sacred formula, the formula by which he and I test every action of our lives. . . .

I do not like verbal explanations. Young people pay little heed to them, nor do they remember them. Things! Things! I cannot repeat it too often. We lay too much stress upon words; we teachers babble, and our students follow our example.

Suppose we are studying the course of the sun and the way to find our bearings, when all at once Emile interrupts me with the question, "What is the use of that?" What a fine lecture I might give [going on and on]! . . . When I have finished I shall have shown myself a regular pedant, I shall have made a great display of learning, and not one single idea has he understood. . . .

But Emile is educated in a simpler fashion. We take so much pains to teach him a difficult idea that he will have heard nothing of all this. At the first word he does not understand, he will run away, he will prance about the room, and leave me to speechify by myself. Let us seek a more commonplace explanation; my scientific learning is of no use to him.

We were observing the position of the forest to the north of Montmorency when he interrupted me with the usual question, "What is the use of that?" "You are right," I said. "Let us take time to think it over, and if we find it is no use we will drop it, for we only want useful games." We find something else to do and geography is put aside for the day.

Next morning I suggest a walk; there is nothing he would like better; children are always ready to run about, and he is a good walker. We climb up to the forest, we wander through its clearings and lose ourselves. . . . At last we [are exhausted and] sit down to rest and to consider our position. I assume that Emile has been educated like an ordinary child. He does not think, he begins to cry; he has no idea we are close to Montmorency, which is hidden from our view by a mere thicket. . . .

Jean-Jacques. "My dear Emile, what shall we do to get out?"

Emile. "I am sure I do not know. I am tired, I am hungry, I am thirsty, I cannot go any further."

Jean-Jacques. "Do you suppose I am any better off? I would cry too if I could make my lunch off tears. Crying is no use, we must look about us. What time is it?"

Emile. "It is noon and I am so hungry!"

Jean-Jacques. "I am so hungry too. . . . Unluckily my dinner won't come to find me. It is twelve o'clock. This time yesterday we were observing the position of the forest from Montmorency. If only we could see the position of Montmorency from the forest—"

Emile. "But yesterday we could see the forest, and here we cannot see the town."

Jean-Jacques. "That is just it. If we could only find it without seeing it. . . . Did not we say the forest was—"

Emile. "North of Montmorency."

Jean-Jacques. "Then Montmorency must lie—"

Emile. "South of the forest."

Jean-Jacques. "We know how to find the north at midday."

Emile. "Yes, by the direction of the shadows."

Jean-Jacques. "But the south?"

Emile. "What shall we do?"

Jean-Jacques. "The south is opposite the north."

Emile. "That is true; we need only find the opposite of the shadows. That is the south! That is the south! Montmorency must be over there! Let us look for it there!"

Jean-Jacques. "Perhaps you are right; let us follow this path through the wood."

Emile. (Clapping his hands.) "Oh, I can see Montmorency! there it is, quite plain, just in front of us! Come to lunch, come to dinner, make haste! Astronomy is some use after all."

Be sure that he thinks this if he does not say it; no matter which, provided I do not say it myself. He will certainly never forget this day's lesson as long as he lives, while if I had only led him to think of all this at home, my lecture would have been forgotten the next day. Teach by doing whenever you can, and only fall back upon words when doing is out of the question.

❖ Jean-Jacques Rousseau (1712–1778), portrayed as a gentle teacher and a pensive philosopher in this contemporary illustration. (*The Granger Collection, New York*)

Questions for Analysis

1. What criticism did Rousseau direct at the social and educational practices of his time?

2. How did Rousseau propose to educate his pupil?

3. Do you think Rousseau's plan appealed to peasants and urban workers in the eighteenth century? Why or why not?

4. In what ways did Rousseau's plan of education and his assumptions on human nature reflect some major ideas of the Enlightenment?

Source: Slightly adapted from J.-J. Rousseau, *Emile, or Education*, trans. B. Foxley (New York: E. P. Dutton, 1911), pp. 141–144.

World, 1500 to the Present (1987); and R. Bridenthal, C. Koonz, and S. Stuard, eds., *Becoming Visible: Women in European History,* 2d ed. (1987). P. Aries, *Centuries of Childhood: A Social History of Family Life* (1962), is another stimulating study. E. Shorter, *The Making of the Modern Family* (1975), is a lively, controversial interpretation, which should be compared with the excellent study by M. Segalen, *Love and Power in the Peasant Family: Rural France in the Nineteenth Century* (1983). A. MacFarlane, *The Family Life of Ralph Josselin* (1970), is a brilliant re-creation of the intimate family circle of a seventeenth-century English clergyman who kept a detailed diary; MacFarlane's *Origins of English Individualism: The Family, Property and Social Transition* (1978) is a major work. L. Pollack, *Forgotten Children: Parent-Child Relations from 1500 to 1900* (1983), is a general introduction. B. Lorence-Kot, *Child-Rearing and Reform: A Study of Nobility in Eighteenth-Century Poland* (1985), stresses the harshness of parental discipline. Various aspects of sexual relationships are treated imaginatively by M. Foucault, *The History of Sexuality* (1981), and R. Wheaton and T. Hareven, eds., *Family and Sexuality in French History* (1980).

L. Moch, *Moving Europeans: Migration in Western Europe Since 1650* (1992), offers a rich, human, and highly recommended account of the movements of millions of ordinary people. J. Burnett, *A History of the Cost of Living* (1969), has a great deal of interesting information about what people spent their money on in the past. J. C. Drummond and A. Wilbraham, *The Englishman's Food: A History of Five Centuries of English Diet,* 2d ed. (1958), remains a valuable and fascinating introduction. J. Knyveton, *Diary of a Surgeon in the Year 1751–1752* (1937), gives a contemporary's unforgettable picture of both eighteenth-century medicine and social customs, as does M. Romsey, *Professional and Popular Medicine in France, 1770–1830: The Social World of Medical Practice* (1988). Good introductions to the evolution of medical practices are B. Ingles, *History of Medicine* (1965); Roy Porter, ed., *The Cambridge Illustrated History of Medicine* (1996); and A. Digby, *Making a Medical Living: Doctors and Patients in the English Market*

for Medicine, 1720–1991 (1994). M. Lindemann, *Health and Healing in Eighteenth-Century Germany* (1996), is a wide-ranging synthesis. H. Marland, ed., *The Art of Midwifery: Early Modern Midwives in Europe* (1993), discusses developments in several countries and complements L. Ulrich, *A Midwife's Tale: The Life of Martha Ballard, Based on Her Diary, 1785–1812* (1990), a superb reconstruction. W. Boyd, *History of Western Education* (1966), is a standard survey, whereas R. Houston, *Literacy in Early Modern Europe: Culture and Education, 1500–1800* (1988), is brief and engaging.

The study of popular culture is expanding. Among older studies, M. George, *London Life in the Eighteenth Century* (1965), is a delight, whereas D. Roche, *The People of Paris: An Essay in Popular Culture in the Eighteenth Century* (1987), presents an unforgettable portrait of the Paris poor. I. Woloch, *Eighteenth-Century Europe: Tradition and Progress, 1715–1789* (1982), includes a survey of popular culture and a good bibliography; E. Kennedy, *A Cultural History of the French Revolution* (1989), beautifully captures rural and urban attitudes in France before and during the French Revolution. R. Malcolmson, *Popular Recreation in English Society, 1700–1850* (1973), provides a colorful account of boxers, bettors, bullbaiting, and more. L. Hunt, *The New Cultural History* (1989), provides an engaging discussion of conceptual issues. G. Rude, *The Crowd in History, 1730–1848* (1964), is an influential effort to see politics and popular protest from below. An important series edited by R. Forster and O. Ranuum considers neglected social questions such as diet, abandoned children, and deviants, as does P. Burke's excellent study, *Popular Culture in Early Modern Europe* (1978). J. Gillis, *For Better, for Worse: Marriage in Britain Since 1500* (1985), and R. Philips, *Untying the Knot: A Short History of Divorce* (1991), are good introductions to institutional changes.

Good works on religious life include J. Delumeau, *Catholicism Between Luther and Voltaire: A New View of the Counter-Reformation* (1977); B. Semmel, *The Methodist Revolution* (1973); and J. Bettey, *Church and Community: The Parish Church in English Life* (1979).

The Revolution in Politics, 1775–1815

The Planting of a Liberty Tree, by Pierre Antoine Leseur. *(Giraudon/Art Resource, NY)*

The last years of the eighteenth century were a time of great upheaval. A series of revolutions and revolutionary wars challenged the old order of monarchs and aristocrats. The ideas of freedom and equality, ideas that have not stopped shaping the world since that era, flourished and spread. The revolutionary era began in North America in 1775. Then in 1789 France, the most influential country in Europe, became the leading revolutionary nation. It established first a constitutional monarchy, then a radical republic, and finally a new empire under Napoleon. The armies of France also joined forces with patriots and radicals abroad in an effort to establish new governments based on new principles throughout much of Europe. The world of modern domestic and international politics was born.

- What caused this era of revolution?
- What were the ideas and objectives of the men and women who rose up violently to undo the established system?
- What were the gains and losses for privileged groups and for ordinary people in a generation of war and upheaval?

These are the questions underlying this chapter's examination of the revolutionary era.

✦ LIBERTY AND EQUALITY

Two ideas fueled the revolutionary period in both America and Europe: liberty and equality. What did eighteenth-century politicians and other people mean by liberty and equality, and why were those ideas so radical and revolutionary in their day?

The call for liberty was first of all a call for individual human rights. Even the most enlightened monarchs customarily claimed that it was their duty to regulate what people wrote and believed. Liberals of the revolutionary era protested such controls from on high. They demanded freedom to worship according to the dictates of their consciences, an end to censorship, and freedom from arbitrary laws and from judges who simply obeyed orders from the government. The Declaration of the Rights of Man, issued at the beginning of the French Revolution, proclaimed, "Liberty consists in being able to do anything that does not harm another person." In theory, therefore, a citizen's rights had "no

limits except those which assure to the other members of society the enjoyment of these same rights." In the context of the monarchial and absolutist forms of government then dominating Europe, this was a truly radical idea.

The call for liberty was also a call for a new kind of government. Revolutionary liberals believed that the people were sovereign—that is, that the people alone had the authority to make laws limiting an individual's freedom of action. In practice, this system of government meant choosing legislators who represented the people and were accountable to them.

Equality was a more ambiguous idea. Eighteenth-century liberals argued that, in theory, all citizens should have identical rights and civil liberties and that the nobility had no right to special privileges based on the accident of birth. However, liberals accepted some well-established distinctions.

First, most eighteenth-century liberals were *men* of their times, and they generally shared with other men the belief that equality between men and women was neither practical nor desirable. Women played an important political role in the French Revolution at several points, but the men of the French Revolution limited formal political rights—the right to vote, to run for office, to participate in government—to men.

Second, liberals never believed that everyone should be equal economically. Quite the contrary. As Thomas Jefferson wrote in an early draft of the American Declaration of Independence (before he changed "property" to the more noble-sounding "happiness"), everyone was equal in "the pursuit of property." Jefferson and other liberals certainly did not expect equal success in that pursuit. Great differences in wealth and income between rich and poor were perfectly acceptable to liberals. The essential point was that everyone should legally have an equal chance.

In eighteenth-century Europe, however, such equality of opportunity was a truly revolutionary idea. Society was still legally divided into groups with special privileges, such as the nobility and the clergy, and groups with special burdens, such as the peasantry. And in most countries, various middle-class groups—professionals, business people, townspeople, and craftsmen—enjoyed privileges that allowed them to monopolize all sorts of economic activity. Liberals criticized not economic inequality itself but this kind of economic inequality based on artificial legal distinctions.

The ideas of liberty and equality—the central ideas of classical liberalism—had deep roots in Western history. The classical Greeks and the Judeo-Christian traditions had affirmed for hundreds of years the sanctity and value of the individual human being, as well as personal responsibility on the part of both common folk and exalted rulers. The hounded and persecuted Protestant radicals of the later sixteenth century had died for the revolutionary idea that individuals were entitled to their own religious beliefs.

Although the liberal creed was rooted in the Western tradition, classical liberalism first crystallized at the end of the seventeenth century and during the Enlightenment of the eighteenth century. Liberal ideas reflected the Enlightenment's stress on human dignity and human happiness on earth and its faith in science, rationality, and progress. Almost all the writers of the Enlightenment were passionately committed to greater personal liberty and equal treatment before the law.

Certain English and French thinkers were mainly responsible for joining the Enlightenment's concern for personal freedom and legal equality to a theoretical justification of liberal self-government. The two most important were John Locke and the baron de Montesquieu. Locke maintained that England's long political tradition rested on "the rights of Englishmen" and on representative government through Parliament. He admired especially the great Whig nobles who had deposed James II and made the bloodless revolution of 1688–1689, and he argued that if a government oversteps its proper function of protecting the natural rights of life, liberty, and private property, it becomes a tyranny. Montesquieu was also inspired by English constitutional history. He, too, believed that powerful "intermediary groups"—such as the judicial nobility of which he was a proud member—offered the best defense of liberty against despotism.

The belief that representative institutions could defend their liberty and interests appealed powerfully to well-educated, prosperous groups, which historians have traditionally labeled as the bourgeoisie. Yet liberal ideas about individual rights and political freedom also appealed to much of the hereditary nobility, at least in western Europe and as formulated by Montesquieu. Representative government did not mean democracy, which liberal thinkers tended to equate with mob rule. Rather, they envisioned voting for representatives as being restricted to those who owned property—those with "a stake in society." England had shown the way. After 1688 it had combined a parliamentary system and considerable individual liberty with a restricted franchise and unquestionable aristocratic pre-eminence. In the course of the eighteenth century, many leading French nobles, led by high-ranking noble judges, who were inspired by the doctrines of Montesquieu, were increasingly eager to follow the English example. Thus eighteenth-century liberalism found broad support among the prosperous, well-educated elites in western Europe.

What liberalism lacked from the beginning was strong popular support. At least two reasons account for the people's wary attitude. First, for common people, the great questions were theoretical and political but immediate and economic; getting enough to eat was a crucial challenge. Second, some of the traditional practices and institutions that liberals wanted to abolish were dear to peasants and urban workers. Comfortable elites had already come into conflict with the people in the eighteenth century over the enclosure of common lands and the regulation of food prices. This conflict would sharpen in the revolutionary era as differences in outlook and well-being led to many misunderstandings and disappointments for both groups.

✤ THE AMERICAN REVOLUTION, 1775–1789

The era of liberal political revolution began in the New World. The thirteen mainland colonies of British North America revolted against their home country and then succeeded in establishing a new unified government.

Americans have long debated the meaning of their revolution. Some have even questioned whether it was a real revolution, as opposed to a war for independence. According to some scholars, the Revolution was conservative and defensive in that its demands were for the traditional liberties of English citizens; Americans were united against the British, but otherwise they were a satisfied people, not torn by internal conflict. Other scholars have argued that, on the contrary, the American Revolution was quite radical. It split families between patriots and Loyalists and divided the country. It achieved goals that were fully as advanced as those obtained by the French in their great revolution a few years later.

How does one reconcile these positions? Both contain large elements of truth. The American revolutionaries did believe that they were demanding only the traditional rights of English men and women. But those traditional rights were liberal rights, and in the American context they had very strong democratic and popular overtones. Thus the American Revolution was fought in the name of established ideals that were still quite radical in the context of the times. And in founding a government firmly based on liberal principles, the Americans set an example that had a forceful impact on Europe and sped up political development there.

The Origins of the Revolution

The American Revolution had its immediate origins in a squabble over increased taxes. The British government had fought and decisively won the Seven Years' War (see page 647) on the strength of its professional army and navy. The American colonists had furnished little real aid. The high cost of the war to the British, however, had led to a doubling of the British national debt. Anticipating further expense defending its recently conquered western lands from native American uprisings, the British government in London set about reorganizing the empire with a series of bold, largely unprecedented measures. Breaking with tradition, the British decided to maintain a large army in North America after peace was restored in 1763. Moreover, they sought to exercise strict control over their newly conquered western lands and to tax the colonies directly. In 1765 the government pushed through Parliament the Stamp Act, which levied taxes on a long list of commercial and legal documents, diplomas, pamphlets, newspapers, almanacs, dice, and playing cards. A stamp glued to each article indicated the tax had been paid.

This effort to increase taxes as part of a tightening up of the empire seemed perfectly reasonable to the British. Heavier stamp taxes had been collected in Great Britain for two generations, and Americans were being asked only to pay a share of their own defense costs. Moreover, Americans had been paying only very low local taxes. The Stamp Act would have doubled taxes to about 2 shillings per person per year. No other people in the European or colonial world (except the Poles) paid so little. Meanwhile, the British paid the highest taxes in the Western world—26 shillings per person. It is not surprising that taxes per person in the newly independent American nation were much higher in 1785 than in 1765, when the British no longer subsidized American defense. The colonists protested the Stamp Act vigorously and violently, however, and after their rioting and boycotts against British goods, Parliament reluctantly repealed the new tax.

As the fury over the Stamp Act revealed, much more was involved than taxes. The key questions were political. To what extent could the home government refashion the empire and reassert its power while limiting the authority of colonial legislatures and their elected representatives? Accordingly, who should represent the colonies, and who had the right to make laws for Americans? While a troubled majority of Americans searched hard for a compromise, some radicals began to proclaim that "taxation without representation is tyranny." The British government replied that Americans were represented in Parliament, albeit indirectly (like most English people themselves), and that the absolute supremacy of Parliament throughout the empire could not be questioned. Many Americans felt otherwise. As John Adams put it, "A Parliament of Great Britain can have no more rights to tax the colonies than a Parliament of Paris." Thus imperial reorganization and parliamentary supremacy came to appear as grave threats to Americans' existing liberties and time-honored institutions.

Americans had long exercised a great deal of independence and gone their own way. In British North America, unlike England and Europe, no powerful established church existed, and personal freedom in questions of religion was taken for granted. The colonial assemblies made the important laws, which were seldom overturned by the home government. The right to vote was much more widespread than in England. In many parts of colonial Massachusetts, for example, as many as 95 percent of the adult males could vote.

Moreover, greater political equality was matched by greater social and economic equality. Neither a hereditary nobility nor a hereditary serf population existed, although the slavery of the Americas consigned blacks to a legally oppressed caste. Independent farmers were the largest group in the country and set much of its tone. In short, the colonial experience had slowly formed a people who felt themselves separate and distinct from the home country. The controversies over taxation intensified those feelings of distinctiveness and separation and brought them to the fore.

In 1773 the dispute over taxes and representation flared up again. The British government had permitted the financially hard-pressed East India Company to ship its tea from China directly to its agents in the colonies rather than through London middlemen who sold to independent merchants in the colonies. Thus the company secured a vital monopoly on the tea trade, and colonial merchants were suddenly excluded from a lucrative business. The colonists were quick to protest.

In Boston men disguised as Indians had a rowdy "tea party" and threw the company's tea into the harbor. This led to extreme measures. The so-called Coercive Acts closed the port of Boston, curtailed local elections and town meetings, and greatly expanded the royal governor's power. County conventions in Massachusetts protested vehemently and urged that the acts be

Toward Revolution in Boston The Boston Tea Party was only one of many angry confrontations between British officials and Boston patriots. On January 27, 1774, an angry crowd seized a British customs collector and then tarred and feathered him. This French engraving of 1784 commemorates the defiant and provocative action. *(The Granger Collection, New York)*

"rejected as the attempts of a wicked administration to enslave America." Other colonial assemblies joined in the denunciations. In September 1774, the First Continental Congress met in Philadelphia, where the more radical members argued successfully against concessions to the Crown. Compromise was also rejected by the British Parliament, and in April 1775 fighting began at Lexington and Concord.

Independence

The fighting spread, and the colonists moved slowly but inevitably toward open rebellion and a declaration of independence. The uncompromising attitude of the British government and its use of German mercenaries went a long way toward dissolving long-standing loyalties to the home country and rivalries among the sepa-

rate colonies. *Common Sense* (1775), a brilliant attack by the recently arrived English radical Thomas Paine (1737–1809), also mobilized public opinion in favor of independence. A runaway bestseller with sales of 120,000 copies in a few months, Paine's tract ridiculed the idea of a small island ruling a great continent. In his call for freedom and republican government, Paine expressed Americans' growing sense of separateness and moral superiority.

On July 4, 1776, the Second Continental Congress adopted the Declaration of Independence. Written by Thomas Jefferson, the Declaration of Independence boldly listed the tyrannical acts committed by George III (r. 1760–1820) and confidently proclaimed the natural rights of mankind and the sovereignty of the American states. Sometimes called the world's greatest political editorial, the Declaration of Independence in effect universalized the traditional rights of English people and made them the rights of all mankind. It stated that "all men are created equal. . . . They are endowed by their Creator with certain unalienable rights. . . . Among these are life, liberty, and the pursuit of happiness." No other American political document has ever caused such excitement, either at home or abroad.

Many American families remained loyal to Britain; many others divided bitterly. After the Declaration of Independence, the conflict often took the form of a civil war pitting patriot against Loyalist. The Loyalists tended to be wealthy and politically moderate. Many patriots, too, were wealthy—individuals such as John Hancock and George Washington—but willingly allied themselves with farmers and artisans in a broad coalition. This coalition harassed the Loyalists and confiscated their property to help pay for the American war effort. The broad social base of the revolutionaries tended to make the liberal revolution democratic. State governments extended the right to vote to many more men (but not to any women) in the course of the war and re-established themselves as republics.

On the international scene, the French sympathized with the rebels from the beginning. They wanted revenge for the humiliating defeats of the Seven Years' War. Officially neutral until 1778, they supplied the great bulk of guns and gunpowder used by the American revolutionaries, very much as foreign great powers have supplied weapons for "wars of national liberation" in our time. By 1777 French volunteers were arriving in Virginia, and a dashing young nobleman, the marquis de Lafayette (1757–1834), quickly became one of Washington's most trusted generals. In 1778 the French government offered a formal alliance to the

American ambassador in Paris, Benjamin Franklin, and in 1779 and 1780 the Spanish and Dutch declared war on Britain. Catherine the Great of Russia helped organize the League of Armed Neutrality in order to protect neutral shipping rights, which Britain refused to recognize.

Thus by 1780 Great Britain was engaged in an imperial war against most of Europe as well as the thirteen colonies. In these circumstances, and in the face of severe reverses in India, the West Indies, and at Yorktown in Virginia, a new British government decided to cut its losses. American negotiators in Paris were receptive. They feared that France wanted a treaty that would bottle up the new United States east of the Allegheny Mountains and give British holdings west of the Alleghenies to France's ally, Spain. Thus the American negotiators deserted their French allies and accepted the extraordinarily favorable terms Britain offered.

By the Treaty of Paris of 1783, Britain recognized the independence of the thirteen colonies and ceded all its territory between the Allegheny Mountains and the Mississippi River to the Americans. Out of the bitter rivalries of the Old World, the Americans snatched dominion over a vast territory.

Framing the Constitution

The liberal program of the American Revolution was consolidated by the federal Constitution, the Bill of Rights, and the creation of a national republic. Assembling in Philadelphia in the summer of 1787, the delegates to the Constitutional Convention were determined to end the period of economic depression, social uncertainty, and very weak central government that had followed independence. The delegates thus decided to grant the federal, or central, government important powers: regulation of domestic and foreign trade, the right to tax, and the means to enforce its laws.

Strong rule would be placed squarely in the context of representative self-government. Senators and congressmen would be the lawmaking delegates of the voters, and the president of the republic would be an elected official. The central government would operate in Montesquieu's framework of checks and balances.

The Signing of the Declaration of Independence, July 4, 1776   John Trumbull's famous painting shows the dignity and determination of America's revolutionary leaders. An extraordinarily talented group, they succeeded in rallying popular support without losing power to more radical forces in the process. *(Yale University Art Gallery)*

The executive, legislative, and judicial branches would systematically balance one another. The power of the federal government would in turn be checked by the powers of the individual states.

When the results of the secret deliberations of the Constitutional Convention were presented to the states for ratification, a great public debate began. The opponents of the proposed constitution—the Antifederalists—charged that the framers of the new document had taken too much power from the individual states and made the federal government too strong. Moreover, many Antifederalists feared for the personal liberties and individual freedoms for which they had just fought. In order to overcome these objections, the Federalists solemnly promised to spell out these basic freedoms as soon as the new constitution was adopted. The result was the first ten amendments to the Constitution, which the first Congress passed shortly after it met in New York in March 1789. These amendments formed an effective bill of rights to safeguard the individual. Most of them—trial by jury, due process of law, right to assemble, freedom from unreasonable search—had their origins in English law and the English Bill of Rights of 1689. Others—the freedoms of speech, the press, and religion—reflected natural-law theory and the American experience.

The American Constitution and the Bill of Rights exemplified the great strengths and the limits of what came to be called "classical liberalism." Liberty meant individual freedoms and political safeguards. Liberty also meant representative government but did not necessarily mean democracy, with its principle of one person, one vote.

Equality—slaves excepted—meant equality before the law, not equality of political participation or wealth. Indeed, economic inequality was resolutely defended by the elite that framed the Constitution. The right to own property was guaranteed by the Fifth Amendment, and if the government took private property, the owner was to receive "just compensation." The radicalism of liberal revolution in America was primarily legal and political, *not* economic or social.

The Revolution's Impact on Europe

Hundreds of books, pamphlets, and articles analyzed and romanticized the American upheaval. Thoughtful Europeans noted, first of all, its enormous long-term implications for international politics. A secret report by the Venetian ambassador to Paris in 1783 stated what many felt: "If only the union of the Provinces is preserved, it is reasonable to expect that, with the fa-

vorable effects of time, and of European arts and sciences, it will become the most formidable power in the world."[1] More generally, American independence fired the imaginations of those aristocrats who were uneasy with their hereditary privileges and those commoners who yearned for equality. Many Europeans believed that the world was advancing and that America was leading the way. As one French writer put it in 1789, "This vast continent which the seas surround will soon change Europe and the universe."

Europeans who dreamed of a new era were fascinated by the political lessons of the American Revolution. The Americans had begun with a revolutionary defense against tyrannical oppression, and they had been victorious. They had then shown how rational beings could assemble together to exercise sovereignty and write a permanent constitution—a new social contract. All this gave greater reality to the concepts of individual liberty and representative government and reinforced one of the primary ideas of the Enlightenment: that a better world was possible.

THE FRENCH REVOLUTION, 1789–1791

No country felt the consequences of the American Revolution more directly than France. Hundreds of French officers served in America and were inspired by the experience. The most famous of these, the young and impressionable marquis de Lafayette, left home as a great aristocrat determined only to fight France's traditional foe, England. He returned with a love of liberty and firm republican convictions. French intellectuals and publicists engaged in passionate analysis of the federal Constitution as well as the constitutions of the various states of the new United States. The American Revolution undeniably hastened upheaval in France.

Yet the French Revolution did not mirror the American example. It was more radical and more complex, more influential and more controversial, more loved and more hated. For Europeans and most of the rest of the world, it was the great revolution of the eighteenth century, *the* revolution that opened the modern era in politics.

The Breakdown of the Old Order

Like the American Revolution, the French Revolution had its immediate origins in the financial difficulties of the government. The efforts of Louis XV's ministers to raise taxes had been thwarted by the high courts, led by

The Extravagance of the French Court   This painting idealizes a party given at the intimate playtime retreat that Queen Marie-Antoinette had built at Versailles. Torches softly light the summer evening as guests talk and enter the artificial caves on the left. Widespread criticism of royal excess undermined support for the monarchy, although Louis XVI was a modest spender compared to Louis XIV. *(Versailles/Photo Bulloz)*

the Parlement of Paris, which was strengthened in its opposition by widespread popular support (see pages 621–622). When renewed efforts to reform the tax system met a similar fate in 1776, the government was forced to finance all of its enormous expenditures during the American war with borrowed money. As a result, the national debt and the annual budget deficit soared. By the 1780s, fully 50 percent of France's annual budget went for ever-increasing interest payments on the ever-increasing debt. Another 25 percent went to maintain the military, while 6 percent was absorbed by the costly and extravagant king and his court at Versailles. Less than 20 percent of the entire national budget was available for the productive functions of the state, such as transportation and general administration. This was an impossible financial situation.

One way out would have been for the government to declare partial bankruptcy, forcing its creditors to ac-

cept greatly reduced payments on the debt. The powerful Spanish monarchy had regularly repudiated large portions of its debt in earlier times, and France had done likewise after an attempt to establish a French national bank had ended in financial disaster in 1720. Yet by the 1780s, the French debt was being held by an army of aristocratic and bourgeois creditors, and the French monarchy, though absolute in theory, had become too weak for such a drastic and unpopular action.

Nor could the king and his ministers, unlike modern governments, print money and create inflation to cover their deficits. Unlike England and Holland, which had far larger national debts relative to their populations, France had no central bank, no paper currency, and no means of creating credit. French money was good gold coin. Therefore, when a depressed economy and a lack of public confidence made it increasingly difficult for the government to obtain new gold loans in 1786, it had no alternative but to try increasing taxes. And since France's tax system was unfair and out-of-date, increased revenues were possible only through fundamental reforms. Such reforms, which would affect all groups in France's complex and fragmented society, opened a Pandora's box of social and political demands. Thus historians have usually looked to social forces and social relationships in their efforts to understand the Revolution, as we shall now see.

Legal Orders and Social Realities

As in the Middle Ages, France's 25 million inhabitants were still legally divided into three orders, or "estates"—the clergy, the nobility, and everyone else. As the nation's first estate, the clergy numbered about 100,000 and had important privileges. It owned about 10 percent of the land and paid only a "voluntary gift," rather than regular taxes, to the government every five years. Moreover, the church levied a tax (the tithe) on landowners, which averaged somewhat less than 10

percent. Much of the church's income was actually drained away from local parishes by political appointees and worldly aristocrats at the top of the church hierarchy—to the intense dissatisfaction of the poor parish priests.

The second legally defined estate consisted of some 400,000 noblemen and noblewomen—the descendants of "those who had fought" in the Middle Ages. The nobles owned outright about 25 percent of the land in France, and they, too, were taxed very lightly. Moreover, nobles continued to enjoy certain manorial rights, or privileges of lordship, that dated back to medieval times and allowed them to tax the peasantry for their own profit. This was done by means of exclusive rights to hunt and fish, village monopolies on baking bread and pressing grapes for wine, fees for justice, and a host of other "useful privileges." In addition, nobles had "honorific privileges," such as the right to precedence on public occasions and the right to wear a sword. These rights conspicuously proclaimed the nobility's legal superiority and exalted social position.

Everyone else was a commoner, legally a member of the third estate. A few commoners—prosperous merchants or lawyers and officials—were well educated and rich, and might even buy up manorial rights as profitable investments. Many more commoners were urban artisans and unskilled day laborers. The vast majority of the third estate consisted of the peasants and agricultural workers in the countryside. Thus the third estate was a conglomeration of vastly different social groups united only by their shared legal status as distinct from the nobility and clergy.

In discussing the long-term origins of the French Revolution, historians have long focused on growing tensions between the nobility and the comfortable members of the third estate, usually known as the *bourgeoisie,* or middle class. A dominant historical interpretation, which has held sway for at least two generations, maintains that the bourgeoisie was basically united by economic position and class interest. Aided by the general economic expansion discussed in Chapter 19, the middle class grew rapidly in the eighteenth century, tripling to about 2.3 million persons, or about 8 percent of France's population. Increasing in size, wealth, culture, and self-confidence, this rising bourgeoisie became progressively exasperated by archaic "feudal" laws restraining the economy and by the growing pretensions of a reactionary nobility, which was closing ranks against middle-class needs and aspirations. As a result, the French bourgeoisie eventually rose up to lead the entire third estate in a great social revolution, a revolution that destroyed feudal privileges and established a

The Three Estates In this political cartoon from 1789 a woman of the third estate struggles under the burden of a nun and an aristocrat. The third estate is being represented in a new way as the true nation, oppressed by the parasitic clergy and nobility. *(Musée Carnavalet/Photo Bulloz)*

capitalist order based on individualism and a market economy.

In recent years, a flood of new research has challenged these accepted views, and once again the French Revolution is a subject of heated scholarly debate. Above all, revisionist historians have questioned the existence of a growing social conflict between a progressive capitalistic bourgeoisie and a reactionary feudal nobility in eighteenth-century France. Instead, these historians see both bourgeoisie and nobility as highly fragmented, riddled with internal rivalries. The great nobility, for example, was profoundly separated from the lesser nobility by differences in wealth, education, and world-view. Differences within the bourgeoisie—between wealthy financiers and local lawyers, for example—were no less profound. Rather than standing as unified blocs against each other, nobility and bourgeoisie formed two parallel social ladders increasingly linked together at the top by wealth, marriage, and Enlightenment culture.

Revisionist historians stress three developments in particular. First, the nobility remained a fluid and relatively open order. Throughout the eighteenth century, substantial numbers of successful commoners continued to seek and obtain noble status through government service and purchase of expensive positions conferring nobility. Thus the nobility of the robe continued to attract the wealthiest members of the middle class and to permit social mobility. Second, key sections of the nobility and the prosperous bourgeoisie formed together the core of the book-hungry Enlightenment public discussed in Chapter 18. Both groups saw themselves as forming part of the educated elite and standing well above the common people—the peasants and the urban poor. Both groups were also equally liberal until revolution actually began, and they generally supported the judicial opposition to the government led by the Parlement of Paris. Third, the nobility and the bourgeoisie were not really at odds in the economic sphere. Both looked to investment in land and government service as their preferred activities, and the ideal of the merchant capitalist was to gain enough wealth to retire from trade, purchase estates, and live nobly as a large landowner. At the same time, wealthy nobles often acted as aggressive capitalists, investing especially in mining, metallurgy, and foreign trade.

The revisionists have clearly shaken the belief that the bourgeoisie and the nobility were inevitably locked in growing conflict before the Revolution. But in stressing the similarities between the two groups, especially at the top, revisionists have also reinforced the view, long maintained by historians, that the Old Regime had ceased to correspond with social reality by the 1780s. Legally, society was still based on rigid orders inherited from the Middle Ages. In reality, France had already moved far toward being a society based on wealth and education, where an emerging elite that included both aristocratic and bourgeois notables was frustrated by a bureaucratic monarchy that continued to claim the right to absolute power.

The Formation of the National Assembly

The Revolution was under way by 1787, though no one could have realized what was to follow. Spurred by a depressed economy and falling tax receipts, Louis XVI's minister of finance revived old proposals to impose a general tax on all landed property as well as to form provincial assemblies to help administer the tax, and he convinced the king to call an assembly of notables to gain support for the idea. The assembled notables, who were mainly important noblemen and high-ranking clergy, were not in favor of it. In return for their support, they demanded that control over all government spending be given to the provincial assemblies. When the government refused, the notables responded that such sweeping tax changes required the approval of the Estates General, the representative body of all three estates, which had not met since 1614.

Facing imminent bankruptcy, the king tried to reassert his authority. He dismissed the notables and established new taxes by decree. In stirring language, the judges of the Parlement of Paris promptly declared the royal initiative null and void. The Parlement went so far as to specify some of the "fundamental laws" against which no king could transgress, such as national consent to taxation and freedom from arbitrary arrest and imprisonment. When the king tried to exile the judges, a tremendous wave of protest swept the country. Frightened investors also refused to advance more loans to the state. Finally in July 1788, a beaten Louis XVI bowed to public opinion and held a spring session of the Estates General. Absolute monarchy was collapsing.

What would replace it? Throughout the unprecedented election campaign of 1788 and 1789, that question excited France. All across the country, clergy, nobles, and commoners came together in their respective orders to draft petitions for change and to elect their respective delegates to the Estates General. The local assemblies of the clergy showed considerable dissatisfaction with the church hierarchy, and two-thirds of the delegates were chosen from among the poorer parish priests, who were commoners by birth. The nobles, already badly split by wealth and education, remained politically divided. A conservative majority was drawn from the poorer and more numerous provincial nobility, but fully one-third of the nobility's representatives were liberals committed to major changes.

As for the third estate, there was great popular participation in the elections. Almost all male commoners twenty-five years of age or older had the right to vote. However, voting required two stages, which meant that most of the representatives finally selected by the third estate were well-educated, prosperous members of the middle class. Most of them were not businessmen but lawyers and government officials. Social status and prestige were matters of particular concern to this economic elite. There were no delegates elected from the great mass of laboring poor, an exclusion that would encourage the peasants and especially the urban artisans to intervene directly and dramatically at numerous points in the Revolution, as we shall see.

The petitions for change coming from the three estates showed a surprising degree of consensus on most issues, as recent research has clearly revealed. There was general agreement that royal absolutism should give way to constitutional monarchy, in which laws and taxes would require the consent of the Estates General meeting regularly. All agreed that in the future individual liberties would have to be guaranteed by law and that the economic position of the parish clergy would have to be improved. It was generally acknowledged that economic development required reforms, such as the abolition of internal trade barriers. The striking similarities in the grievance petitions of the clergy, nobility, and third estate reflected the broad commitment of France's educated elite to liberalism.

Yet an increasingly bitter quarrel undermined this consensus during the intense electoral campaign: *how* would the Estates General vote, and precisely *who* would lead in the political reorganization that was generally desired? The Estates General of 1614 had sat as three separate houses. Any action had required the agreement of at least two branches, a requirement that had virtually guaranteed control by the nobility and the clergy. Immediately after the victory over the king, the aristocratic Parlement of Paris, mainly out of respect for tradition but partly out of a desire to enhance the nobility's political position, ruled that the Estates General should once again sit separately. The ruling was quickly denounced by certain middle-class intellectuals and some liberal nobles. They demanded instead a single assembly dominated by representatives of the third estate to ensure fundamental reforms. Reflecting increased political competition and a growing hostility toward aristocratic aspirations, the abbé Emmanuel Joseph

Sieyès argued in 1789 in his famous pamphlet *What Is the Third Estate?* that the nobility was a tiny, overprivileged minority and that the neglected third estate constituted the true strength of the French nation. When the government agreed that the third estate should have as many delegates as the clergy and the nobility combined, but then rendered this act meaningless by upholding voting by separate order, middle-class leaders saw fresh evidence of an aristocratic conspiracy.

In May 1789, the twelve hundred delegates of the three estates paraded in medieval pageantry through the streets of Versailles to an opening session resplendent with feudal magnificence. The estates were almost immediately deadlocked. Delegates of the third estate refused to transact any business until the king ordered the clergy and nobility to sit with them in a single body. Finally, after a six-week war of nerves, a few parish priests began to go over to the third estate, which on June 17 voted to call itself the "National Assembly." On June 20, the delegates of the third estate, excluded from their hall because of "repairs," moved to a large indoor tennis court. There they swore the famous Oath of the Tennis Court, pledging not to disband until they had written a new constitution.

The king's actions were then somewhat contradictory. On June 23, he made a conciliatory speech urging reforms to a joint session, and four days later he ordered the three estates to meet together. At the same time, the vacillating and indecisive monarch apparently followed the advice of relatives and court nobles, who urged him to dissolve the Estates General by force. The king called an army of eighteen thousand troops toward Versailles, and on July 11 he dismissed his finance minister and his other more liberal ministers. Faced with growing opposition since 1787, Louis XVI had resigned himself to bankruptcy. Now he belatedly sought to reassert his historic "divine right" to rule. The middle-class delegates and their allies from the liberal nobility had done their best, but they were resigned to being disbanded at bayonet point. One third-estate delegate reassured a worried colleague, "You won't hang—you'll only have to go back home."[2]

The Revolt of the Poor and the Oppressed

While the educated delegates of the third estate pressed for symbolic equality with the nobility and clergy in a single legislative body at Versailles, economic hardship gripped the common people of France in a tightening vise. Grain was the basis of the diet of ordinary people in the eighteenth century, and in 1788 the harvest had been extremely poor. The price of bread, which had

The Oath of the Tennis Court   This painting, based on an unfinished work by Jacques-Louis David (1748–1825), enthusiastically celebrates the revolutionary rupture of June 20, 1789. Locked out of their assembly hall at Versailles and joined by some sympathetic priests, the delegates of the third estate have moved to an indoor tennis court and are swearing never to disband until they have written a new constitution and put France on a firm foundation. *(Musée Carnavalet/Photo Bulloz)*

been rising gradually since 1785, began to soar. By July 1789, it had climbed as high as 8 sous per pound in the provinces. In Paris, where bread was regularly subsidized by the government in an attempt to prevent popular unrest, the price rose to 4 sous. The poor could scarcely afford to pay 2 sous per pound, for even at that price a laborer with a wife and three children had to spend half of his wages to buy the family's bread.

Harvest failure and high bread prices unleashed a classic economic depression of the preindustrial age. With food so expensive and with so much uncertainty, the demand for manufactured goods collapsed. Thousands of artisans and small traders were thrown out of work. By the end of 1789, almost half of the French people would be in need of relief. One person in eight was a pauper living in extreme want. In Paris the situation was so desperate in July 1789 that perhaps 150,000 of the city's 600,000 people were without work.

Against this background of dire poverty and excitement generated by the political crisis, the people of Paris entered decisively onto the revolutionary stage. They believed in a general, though ill-defined, way that the economic distress had human causes. They believed that they should have steady work and enough bread at fair prices to survive. Specifically, they feared that the dismissal of the king's moderate finance minister would put them at the mercy of aristocratic landowners and grain speculators. Stories like that quoting the wealthy financier Joseph François Foulon as saying that the poor "should eat grass, like my horses" and rumors that the king's troops would sack the city began to fill the air. Angry crowds formed, and passionate voices urged action. On July 13, the people began to seize arms for

Storming the Bastille This representation by an untrained contemporary artist shows civilians and members of the Paris militia—the "conquerors of the Bastille"—on the attack. This successful action had enormous practical and symbolic significance, and July 14 has long been France's most important national holiday. *(Musée Carnavalet/Photo Hubert Josse)*

the defense of the city as the king's armies moved toward Paris, and on July 14 several hundred of the most determined people marched to the Bastille to search for weapons and gunpowder.

A medieval fortress with walls ten feet thick and eight great towers each one hundred feet high, the Bastille had long been used as a prison. It was guarded by eighty retired soldiers and thirty Swiss mercenaries. The governor of the fortress-prison refused to hand over the powder, panicked, and ordered his men to fire, killing ninety-eight people attempting to enter. Cannon were brought to batter the main gate, and fighting continued until the prison surrendered. The governor of the prison was later hacked to death, and his head and that of the mayor of Paris, who had been slow to give the crowd arms, were stuck on pikes and paraded through the streets. The next day a committee of citizens appointed the marquis de Lafayette commander of the city's armed forces. Paris was lost to the king, who was

forced to recall the finance minister and disperse his troops. The popular uprising had broken the power monopoly of the royal army and thereby saved the National Assembly.

As the delegates resumed their long-winded and inconclusive debates at Versailles, the countryside sent them a radical and unmistakable message. Throughout France, peasants began to rise in spontaneous, violent, and effective insurrection against their lords, ransacking manor houses and burning feudal documents that recorded the peasants' obligations. Neither middle-class landowners, who often owned manors and village monopolies, nor the larger, more prosperous farmers were spared. In some areas, peasants reinstated traditional village practices, undoing recent enclosures and reoccupying old common lands. Peasants seized forests, and taxes went unpaid. Fear of vagabonds and outlaws—called the Great Fear by contemporaries—seized the countryside and fanned the flames of rebellion. The long-suffering peasants were doing their best to free themselves from manorial rights and exploitation.

Faced with chaos, yet afraid to call on the king to restore order, some liberal nobles and middle-class delegates at Versailles responded to peasant demands with a surprise maneuver on the night of August 4, 1789. The duke of Aiguillon, also notably one of France's greatest noble landowners, declared that

in several provinces the whole people forms a kind of league for the destruction of the manor houses, the ravaging of the lands, and especially for the seizure of the archives where the title deeds to feudal properties are kept. It seeks to throw off at last a yoke that has for many centuries weighted it down.[3]

He urged equality in taxation and the elimination of feudal dues. In the end, all the old exactions imposed on the peasants—serfdom where it still existed, exclusive hunting rights for nobles, fees for justice, village monopolies, the right to make peasants work on the roads, and a host of other dues—were abolished, generally without compensation. Though a clarifying law passed a week later was less generous, the peasants ignored the "fine print." They never paid feudal dues again. Thus the French peasantry, which already owned about 30 percent of all the land, achieved a great and unprecedented victory in the early days of revolutionary upheaval. Henceforth, the French peasants would seek mainly to protect and consolidate their revolutionary triumph. As the Great Fear subsided in the countryside, they became a force for order and stability.

A Limited Monarchy

The National Assembly moved forward. On August 27, 1789, it issued the Declaration of the Rights of Man, which stated, "Men are born and remain free and equal in rights." The declaration also maintained that mankind's natural rights are "liberty, property, security, and resistance to oppression" and that "every man is presumed innocent until he is proven guilty." As for law, "it is an expression of the general will; all citizens have the right to concur personally or through their representatives in its formation. . . . Free expression of thoughts and opinions is one of the most precious rights of mankind: every citizen may therefore speak, write, and publish freely." In short, this clarion call of the liberal revolutionary ideal guaranteed equality before the law, representative government for a sovereign people, and individual freedom. This revolutionary credo, only two pages long, was propagandized throughout France and Europe and around the world.

Moving beyond general principles to draft a constitution proved difficult. The questions of how much power the king should retain and whether he could permanently veto legislation led to another deadlock. Once again the decisive answer came from the poor—in this instance, the poor women of Paris.

Women customarily bought the food and managed the poor family's slender resources. In Paris great numbers of women also worked for wages, often within the putting-out system, making garments and beautiful luxury items destined for an aristocratic and international clientele. Immediately after the fall of the Bastille, many of France's great court nobles began to leave Versailles for foreign lands so that a plummeting demand for luxuries intensified the general economic crisis; international markets also declined. The church was no longer able to give its traditional grants of food and money to the poor. Increasing unemployment and hunger put tremendous pressure on household managers, and the result was another popular explosion.

On October 5 some seven thousand desperate women marched the twelve miles from Paris to Versailles to demand action. A middle-class deputy looking out from the Assembly saw "multitudes arriving from Paris including fishwives and bullies from the market, and these people wanted nothing but bread." This great crowd invaded the Assembly, "armed with scythes, sticks and pikes." One tough old woman directing a large group of younger women defiantly shouted into the debate, "Who's that talking down there? Make the chatterbox shut up. That's not the point: the point is that we want bread."[4] Hers was the genuine voice of the people, essential to any understanding of the French Revolution.

The women invaded the royal apartments, slaughtered some of the royal bodyguards, and furiously searched for the queen, Marie Antoinette, who was widely despised for her frivolous and supposedly immoral behavior. "We are going to cut off her head, tear out her heart, fry her liver, and that won't be the end of it," they shouted, surging through the palace in a frenzy. It seems likely that only the intervention of Lafayette and the National Guard saved the royal family. But the only way to calm the disorder was for the king to go and live in Paris, as the crowd demanded.

The next day, the king, the queen, and their son left for Paris in the midst of a strange procession. The heads of two aristocrats, stuck on pikes, led the way. They were followed by the remaining members of the royal bodyguard, unarmed and surrounded and mocked by fierce men holding sabers and pikes. A mixed and victorious multitude surrounded the carriage of the captured royal family, hurling crude insults at the queen. There was drinking and eating among the women, who had clearly emerged as a major and enduring element in the Parisian revolutionary crowd.[5]

The National Assembly followed the king to Paris, and the next two years, until September 1791, saw the consolidation of the liberal revolution. Under middle-class leadership, the National Assembly abolished the French nobility as a legal order and pushed forward with the creation of a constitutional monarchy, which Louis XVI reluctantly agreed to accept in July 1790. In the final constitution, the king remained the head of state, but all lawmaking power was placed in the hands of the National Assembly, elected by the economic upper half of French males.

New laws broadened women's rights to seek divorce, to inherit property, and to obtain financial support from fathers for illegitimate children. But women were not allowed to vote or hold political office for at least two reasons. First, the great majority of comfortable, well-educated males in the National Assembly believed that women should be limited to child rearing and domestic duties and should leave politics and most public activities to men. This was, of course, a hoary idea, but it had been dressed up and re-energized by Rousseau in his influential *Emile* (see page 668). Second, the delegates to the National Assembly were convinced that political life in absolutist France had been profoundly corrupt and that a prime example of this corruption was the way that some talented but immoral aristocratic women had used their sexual charms to manipulate weak rulers and their ministers. Delegates therefore believed that excluding women from politics would help create the civic virtue that had been missing: the political system would be freed from the harmful effects of sexual favors; and pure, home-focused wives would raise the high-minded sons needed to govern the nation.

The National Assembly replaced the complicated patchwork of historic provinces with eighty-three departments of approximately equal size. The jumble of weights and measures that varied from province to province was reformed, leading to the introduction of the simple, rational metric system in 1793. The National Assembly promoted the liberal concept of economic freedom. Monopolies, guilds, and workers combinations were prohibited, and barriers to trade within France were abolished in the name of economic liberty. Thus the National Assembly applied the critical spirit of the Enlightenment to reform France's laws and institutions completely.

The Assembly also imposed a radical reorganization on the country's religious life. It granted religious freedom to the tiny minority of French Jews and Protestants. Of greater impact, it then nationalized the Catholic church's property and abolished monasteries as useless relics of a distant past. The government used all former church property as collateral to guarantee a new paper currency, the *assignats,* and then sold these properties in an attempt to put the state's finances on a solid footing. Although the church's land was sold in large blocks, a procedure that favored nimble speculators and the rich, peasants eventually purchased much of this land when it was subdivided. These purchases strengthened their attachment to the new revolutionary order in the countryside.

The most unfortunate aspect of the religious reorganization of France was that it brought the new government into conflict with the Catholic church and many sincere Christians, especially in the countryside. Many delegates to the National Assembly, imbued with the rationalism and skepticism of the eighteenth-century philosophes, harbored a deep distrust of popular piety and "superstitious religion." They were interested in the church only to the extent that they could seize its land and use the church to strengthen the new state. Thus they established a national church, with priests chosen by voters. In the face of widespread resistance, the National Assembly then required the clergy to take a loyalty oath to the new government. The Catholic clergy became just so many more employees of the state. The pope formally condemned this attempt to subjugate the church, and only half the priests of France took the oath of allegiance. The result was a deep division within both the country and the clergy on the religious question; confusion and hostility among French Catholics were pervasive. The attempt to remake the Catholic church, like the Assembly's abolition of guilds and workers combinations, sharpened the conflict between the educated classes and the common people that had been emerging in the eighteenth century. This policy toward the church was the revolutionary government's first important failure.

✤ WORLD WAR AND REPUBLICAN FRANCE, 1791–1799

When Louis XVI accepted the final version of the completed constitution in September 1791, a young and still obscure provincial lawyer and member of the National Assembly named Maximilien Robespierre (1758–1794) evaluated the work of two years and concluded, "The Revolution is over." Robespierre was both right and wrong. He was right in the sense that the most constructive and lasting reforms were in place. Nothing substantial in the way of liberty and useful reform would be gained in the next generation. He was wrong in the sense that a much more radical stage lay ahead. New heroes and new ideologies were to emerge in revolutionary wars and international conflict.

Foreign Reactions and the Beginning of War

The outbreak and progress of revolution in France produced great excitement and a sharp division of opinion in Europe and the United States. Liberals and radicals saw a mighty triumph of liberty over despotism. In Great Britain especially, they hoped that the French example would lead to a fundamental reordering of the political system. That system, which had been consolidated in the revolution of 1688 to 1689, placed Parliament in the hands of the aristocracy and a few wealthy merchants; the great majority of people had very little say in the government. After the French Revolution began, conservative leaders such as Edmund Burke (1729–1797) were deeply troubled by the aroused spirit of reform. In 1790 Burke published *Reflections on the Revolution in France,* one of the great intellectual defenses of European conservatism. He defended inherited privileges in general and those of the English monarchy and aristocracy. He glorified the unrepresentative Parliament and predicted that thoroughgoing reform like that occurring in France would lead only to chaos and tyranny. Burke's work sparked much debate.

One passionate rebuttal came from a young writer in London, Mary Wollstonecraft (1759–1797). Born into the middle class, Wollstonecraft was schooled in adversity by a mean-spirited father who beat his wife and squandered his inherited fortune. Determined to be independent in a society that generally expected women of her class to become homebodies and obedient wives, she struggled for years to earn her living as a governess and teacher—practically the only acceptable careers for single, educated women—before attaining success as a translator and author. Interested in politics and believing that "a desperate disease requires a powerful remedy" in Great Britain as well as France, Wollstonecraft was incensed by Burke's book. She immediately wrote a blistering, widely read attack, *A Vindication of the Rights of Man* (1790).

Then, fired up on controversy and commitment, she made a daring intellectual leap. She developed for the first time the logical implications of natural-law philosophy in her masterpiece, *A Vindication of the Rights of Woman* (1792). To fulfill the still-unrealized potential of the French Revolution and to eliminate the sexual

Mary Wollstonecraft   Painted by an unknown artist when Mary Wollstonecraft was thirty-two and writing her revolutionary *Vindication of the Rights of Woman,* this portrait highlights the remarkable strength of character that energized Wollstonecraft's brilliant intellect. *(The Board of Trustees of the National Museums and Galleries on Merseyside, Walker Art Gallery)*

inequality she had felt so keenly, she demanded that

the Rights of Women be respected . . . [and] JUSTICE for one-half of the human race. . . . It is time to effect a revolution in female manners, time to restore to them their lost dignity, and make them, as part of the human species, labor, by reforming themselves, to reform the world.

Setting high standards for women—"I wish to persuade women to endeavor to acquire strength, both of mind and body"—Wollstonecraft broke with those who had a low opinion of women's intellectual potential. She advocated rigorous coeducation, which would make women better wives and mothers, good citizens, and even economically independent people. Women could manage businesses and enter politics if only men would give them the chance. Men themselves would benefit from women's rights, for Wollstonecraft believed that "the two sexes mutually corrupt and improve each other."[6] Wollstonecraft's analysis testified to the power of the Revolution to excite and inspire outside of France. Paralleling ideas put forth independently in France by Olympe de Gouges (1748–1793), a self-taught writer and woman of the people (see the feature "Listening to the Past: Revolution and Women's Rights" on pages 722–723), Wollstonecraft's work marked the birth of the modern women's movement for equal rights, and it was ultimately very influential.

The kings and nobles of continental Europe, who had at first welcomed the revolution in France as weakening a competing power, began to feel no less threatened than Burke and his supporters. At their courts, they listened to the diatribes of great court nobles who had fled France and were urging intervention in France's affairs. When Louis XVI and Marie Antoinette were arrested and returned to Paris after trying unsuccessfully to slip out of France in June 1791, the monarchs of Austria and Prussia issued the Declaration of Pillnitz. This carefully worded statement declared their willingness to intervene in France in certain circumstances and was expected to have a sobering effect on revolutionary France without causing war.

But the crowned heads of Europe misjudged the revolutionary spirit in France. When the National Assembly disbanded, it sought popular support by decreeing that none of its members would be eligible for election to the new Legislative Assembly. This meant that when the new representative body convened in October 1791, it had a different character. The great majority of the legislators were still prosperous, well-educated, middle-class men, but they were younger and less cautious than their predecessors. Many of the deputies were loosely allied and called "Jacobins," after the name of their political club.

The new representatives to the Assembly were passionately committed to liberal revolution and distrustful of monarchy after Louis's attempted flight. They increasingly lumped "useless aristocrats" and "despotic monarchs" together, and they easily whipped themselves into a patriotic fury with bombastic oratory. If the courts of Europe were attempting to incite a war of kings against France, then "we will incite a war of people against kings. . . . Ten million Frenchmen, kindled by the fire of liberty, armed with the sword, with reason, with eloquence would be able to change the face of the world and make the tyrants tremble on their thrones."[7] Only Robespierre and a very few others argued that people would not welcome liberation at the point of a gun. Such warnings were brushed aside. France would "rise to the full height of her mission," as one deputy urged. In April 1792, France declared war on Francis II, the Habsburg monarch.

France's crusade against tyranny went poorly at first. Prussia joined Austria in the Austrian Netherlands (present-day Belgium), and French forces broke and fled at their first encounter with armies of this First Coalition. The road to Paris lay open, and it is possible that only conflict between the eastern monarchs over the division of Poland saved France from defeat.

Military reversals and Austro-Prussian threats caused a wave of patriotic fervor to sweep France. The Legislative Assembly declared the country in danger. Volunteer armies from the provinces streamed through Paris, fraternizing with the people and singing patriotic songs like the stirring "Marseillaise," later the French national anthem.

In this supercharged wartime atmosphere, rumors of treason by the king and queen spread in Paris. Once again, as in the storming of the Bastille, the common people of Paris acted decisively. On August 10, 1792, a revolutionary crowd attacked the royal palace at the Tuileries, capturing it after heavy fighting with the Swiss Guards. The king and his family fled for their lives to the nearby Legislative Assembly, which suspended the king from all his functions, imprisoned him, and called for a new National Convention to be elected by universal male suffrage. Monarchy in France was on its deathbed, mortally wounded by war and popular upheaval.

The Second Revolution

The fall of the monarchy marked a rapid radicalization of the Revolution, a phase that historians often call the "second revolution." Louis's imprisonment was followed by the September Massacres. Wild stories seized the city that imprisoned counter-revolutionary aristocrats and priests were plotting with the allied invaders. As a result, angry crowds invaded the prisons of Paris and summarily slaughtered half the men and women they found. In late September 1792, the new, popularly elected National Convention proclaimed France a republic.

The republic sought to create a new popular culture to ensure its future and fashioned compelling symbols that broke with the past and glorified the new order. It adopted a brand-new revolutionary calendar, which eliminated saints' days and renamed the days and the months after the seasons of the year. Citizens were expected to address each other with the friendly "thou" of the people rather than with the formal "you" of the rich and powerful. The republic energetically promoted broad, open-air, democratic festivals. These spectacles brought the entire population together and sought to redirect the people's traditional enthusiasm for Catholic religious celebrations to secular holidays instilling republican virtue and a love of nation. These spectacles were less successful in villages than in cities, where popular interest in politics was greater and Catholicism was weaker.

All of the members of the National Convention were republicans, and at the beginning almost all belonged to the Jacobin club of Paris. The great majority also continued to come from the well-educated middle class. But control of the Convention was increasingly contested by two bitterly competitive groups—the Girondists, named after a department in southwestern France, and the Mountain, led by Robespierre and another young lawyer, Georges Jacques Danton. The Mountain was so called because its members sat on the uppermost left-hand benches of the assembly hall. A majority of the indecisive Convention members, seated in the "Plain" below, floated back and forth between the rival factions.

This division was clearly apparent after the National Convention overwhelmingly convicted Louis XVI of treason. By a narrow majority, the Convention then sentenced him to death in January 1793. Louis died with tranquil dignity on the newly invented guillotine. One of his last statements was "I am innocent and shall die without fear. I would that my death might bring happiness to the French, and ward off the dangers which I foresee."[8]

Both the Girondists and the Mountain were determined to continue the "war against tyranny." The Prussians had been stopped at the Battle of Valmy on September 20, 1792, one day before the republic was proclaimed. Saving the nascent republic with their victory, the armies of revolutionary France then successfully invaded Savoy and captured Nice. A second army corps invaded the German Rhineland and took the city of Frankfurt. To the north, the revolutionary armies won their first major battle at Jemappes and by November 1792 were occupying the entire Austrian Netherlands. Everywhere they went, French armies of occupation chased the princes, "abolished feudalism," and found support among some peasants and middle-class people.

But the French armies also lived off the land, requisitioning food and supplies and plundering local treasures. The liberators looked increasingly like foreign invaders. International tensions mounted. In February 1793, the National Convention, at war with Austria and Prussia, declared war on Britain, Holland, and Spain as well. Republican France was now at war with almost all of Europe, a great war that would last almost without interruption until 1815.

As the forces of the First Coalition drove the French from the Austrian Netherlands, peasants in western France revolted against being drafted into the army. They were supported and encouraged in their resistance by devout Catholics, royalists, and foreign agents.

In Paris the quarrelsome National Convention found itself locked in a life-and-death political struggle between the Girondists and the Mountain. The two groups were in general agreement on questions of policy. Sincere republicans, they hated privilege and wanted to temper economic liberalism with social concern. Yet personal hatreds ran deep. The Girondists feared a bloody dictatorship by the Mountain, and the Mountain was no less convinced that the more moderate Girondists would turn to conservatives and even royalists in order to retain power. With the middle-class delegates so bitterly divided, the laboring poor of Paris emerged as the decisive political factor.

The laboring men and women of Paris always constituted—along with the peasantry in the summer of 1789—the elemental force that drove the Revolution

The End of Louis XVI (detail)   The executioner holds up the severed head of the dead king for the soldiers and the crowd to see in the large, central square of Paris, which is now known as the Place de la Concorde. The execution of the king was a victory for the radicals in Paris, but it horrified Europe's monarchs and conservatives and strengthened their opposition to the French Revolution. *(Musée Carnavalet/ Laurie Platt Winfrey, Inc.)*

forward. It was the artisans, day laborers, market women, and garment workers who had stormed the Bastille, marched on Versailles, driven the king from the Tuileries, and carried out the September Massacres. The petty traders and laboring poor were often known as the *sans-culottes,* "without breeches," because sans-culottes men wore trousers instead of the knee breeches of the aristocracy and the solid middle class. The immediate interests of the sans-culottes were mainly economic, and in the spring of 1793 the economic situation was as bad as the military situation. Rapid inflation, unemployment, and food shortages were again weighing heavily on poor families.

Moreover, by the spring of 1793, the sans-culottes had become keenly interested in politics. Encouraged by the so-called angry men, such as the passionate young ex-priest and journalist Jacques Roux, sans-culottes men and women were demanding radical political action to guarantee them their daily bread. At first the Mountain joined the Girondists in violently rejecting these demands. But in the face of military defeat, peasant revolt, and hatred of the Girondists, the Mountain and especially Robespierre became more sympathetic. The Mountain joined with sans-culottes activists in the city government to engineer a popular uprising, which forced the Convention to arrest thirty-one Girondist deputies for treason on June 2. All power passed to the Mountain.

Robespierre and others from the Mountain joined the recently formed Committee of Public Safety, to which the Convention had given dictatorial power to deal with the national emergency. These developments in Paris triggered revolt in leading provincial cities, such as Lyons and Marseilles, where moderates denounced Paris and demanded a decentralized government. The peasant revolt spread, and the republic's armies were driven back on all fronts. By July 1793, only the areas around Paris and on the eastern frontier were firmly held by the central government. Defeat seemed imminent.

Total War and the Terror

A year later, in July 1794, the Austrian Netherlands and the Rhineland were once again in the hands of conquering French armies, and the First Coalition was falling apart. This remarkable change of fortune was due to the revolutionary government's success in harnessing, for perhaps the first time in history, the explosive forces of a planned economy, revolutionary terror, and modern nationalism in a total war effort.

Robespierre and the Committee of Public Safety advanced with implacable resolution on several fronts in

1793 and 1794. First, in an effort to save revolutionary France, they collaborated with the fiercely patriotic and democratic sans-culottes, who retained the common people's traditional faith in fair prices and a moral economic order and who distrusted most wealthy capitalists and all aristocrats. Thus Robespierre and his coworkers established, as best they could, a planned economy with egalitarian social overtones. Rather than let supply and demand determine prices, the government decreed the maximum allowable prices for a host of key products. Though the state was too weak to enforce all its price regulations, it did fix the price of bread in Paris at levels the poor could afford. Rationing was introduced, and quality was also controlled. Bakers were permitted to make only the "bread of equality"—a brown bread made of a mixture of all available flours. White bread and pastries were outlawed as luxuries. The poor of Paris may not have eaten well, but at least they ate.

They also worked, mainly to produce arms and munitions for the war effort. Craftsmen and small manufacturers were told what to produce and when to deliver. The government nationalized many small workshops and requisitioned raw materials and grain from the peasants. Sometimes planning and control did not go beyond orders to meet the latest emergency: "Ten thousand soldiers lack shoes. You will take the shoes of all the aristocrats in Strasbourg and deliver them ready for transport to headquarters at 10 A.M. tomorrow." Failures to control and coordinate were failures of means and not of desire: seldom if ever before had a government attempted to manage an economy so thoroughly. The second revolution and the ascendancy of the sans-culottes had produced an embryonic emergency socialism, which thoroughly frightened Europe's propertied classes and had great influence on the subsequent development of socialist ideology.

Second, while radical economic measures supplied the poor with bread and the armies with weapons, the Reign of Terror (1793–1794) was solidifying the home front. Special revolutionary courts responsible only to Robespierre's Committee of Public Safety tried rebels and "enemies of the nation" for political crimes. Drawing on popular, sans-culottes support centered in the local Jacobin clubs, these local courts ignored normal legal procedures and judged severely. Some 40,000 French men and women were executed or died in prison. Another 300,000 suspects crowded the prisons and often brushed close to death in a revolutionary court.

Robespierre's Reign of Terror was one of the most controversial phases of the French Revolution. Most historians now believe that the Reign of Terror was not

The Last Roll Call   Prisoners sentenced to death by revolutionary courts listen to an official solemnly reading the names of those selected for immediate execution. After being bound, the prisoners will ride standing up in a small cart through the streets of Paris to the nearby guillotine. As this painting highlights, both women and men were executed for political crimes under the Terror. *(Mansell/Time Inc.)*

directed against any single class. Rather, it was a political weapon directed impartially against all who might oppose the revolutionary government. For many Europeans of the time, however, the Reign of Terror represented a terrifying perversion of the generous ideals that had existed in 1789. It strengthened the belief that France had foolishly replaced a weak king with a bloody dictatorship.

The third and perhaps most decisive element in the French republic's victory over the First Coalition was its ability to continue drawing on the explosive power of patriotic dedication to a national state and a national mission. This is the essence of modern nationalism, and it was something new in history. With a common language and a common tradition newly reinforced by the ideas of popular sovereignty and democracy, the French people were stirred by a common loyalty. The shared danger of foreign foes and internal rebels unified all classes in a heroic defense of the nation.

In such circumstances, war was no longer the gentlemanly game of the eighteenth century, but rather total war, a life-and-death struggle between good and evil. Everyone had to participate in the national effort. According to a famous decree of August 23, 1793:

The young men shall go to battle and the married men shall forge arms. The women shall make tents and clothes, and shall serve in the hospitals; children shall tear rags into lint. The old men will be guided to the public places of the cities to kindle the courage of the young warriors and to preach the unity of the Republic and the hatred of kings.

Like the wars of religion, war in 1793 was a crusade. This war, however, was fought for a secular, rather than a religious, ideology.

The all-out mobilization of French resources under the Terror combined with the fervor of modern nationalism to create an awesome fighting machine. After August 1793, all unmarried young men were subject to the draft, and by January 1794 the French had about 800,000 soldiers on active duty in fourteen armies. A force of this size was unprecedented in the history of European warfare, and recent research concludes that the French armed forces outnumbered their enemies almost four to one.[9] Well trained, well equipped, and constantly indoctrinated, the enormous armies of the republic were led by young, impetuous generals. These generals often had risen from the ranks, and they personified the opportunities the Revolution seemed to offer gifted sons of the people. Following orders from the Committee of Public Safety in Paris to attack relentlessly, French generals used mass assaults at bayonet point to overwhelm the enemy. "No maneuvering, nothing elaborate," declared the fearless General Hoche. "Just cold steel, passion and patriotism."[10] By the spring of 1794, French armies were victorious on all fronts. The republic was saved.

The Thermidorian Reaction and the Directory, 1794–1799

The success of the French armies led Robespierre and the Committee of Public Safety to relax the emergency economic controls, but they extended the political Reign of Terror. Their lofty goal was increasingly an ideal democratic republic where justice would reign and there would be neither rich nor poor. Their lowly means were unrestrained despotism and the guillotine, which struck down any who might seriously question the new order. In March 1794, to the horror of many sans-culottes, Robespierre's Terror wiped out many of the angry men who had been criticizing Robespierre for being soft on the wealthy and who were led by the radical social democrat Jacques Hébert. Two weeks later, several of Robespierre's long-standing collaborators, led by the famous orator Danton, marched up the steps to the guillotine. A strange assortment of radicals and moderates in the Convention, knowing that they might be next, organized a conspiracy. They howled down Robespierre when he tried to speak to the National Convention on 9 Thermidor (July 27, 1794). On the following day, it was Robespierre's turn to be shaved by the revolutionary razor.

As Robespierre's closest supporters followed their leader, France unexpectedly experienced a thorough reaction to the despotism of the Reign of Terror. In a general way, this "Thermidorian reaction" recalled the early days of the Revolution. The respectable middle-class lawyers and professionals who had led the liberal revolution of 1789 reasserted their authority, drawing support from their own class, the provincial cities, and the better-off peasants. The National Convention abolished many economic controls, printed more paper currency, and let prices rise sharply. It severely restricted the local political organizations where the sans-culottes had their strength. And all the while, wealthy bankers and newly rich speculators celebrated the sudden end of the Terror with an orgy of self-indulgence and ostentatious luxury, an orgy symbolized by the shockingly low-cut gowns that quickly became the rage among their wives and mistresses.

The collapse of economic controls, coupled with runaway inflation, hit the working poor very hard. The gaudy extravagance of the rich wounded their pride. The sans-culottes accepted private property, but they believed passionately in small business, decent wages, and economic justice. Increasingly disorganized after Robespierre purged radical leaders, the common people of Paris finally revolted against the emerging new order in early 1795. The Convention quickly used the army to suppress these insurrections. For the first time since the fall of the Bastille, bread riots and uprisings by Parisians living on the edge of starvation were effectively put down by a government that made no concessions to the poor. In the face of all these catastrophes, the revolutionary fervor of the laboring poor in Paris finally subsided. Excluded and disillusioned by the triumphant return of the comfortable educated classes, the urban poor would have little interest in and influence on politics until 1830.

In villages and small towns there arose a great cry for peace and a turning toward religion, especially from women, who had seldom experienced the political radicalization of sans-culottes women in the big cities. Instead, these women had frequently and tenaciously defended their culture and religious beliefs against the often heavy-handed attacks of antireligious revolutionary officials after 1789. As the frustrated government began to retreat on the religious question from 1796 to 1801, the women of rural France brought back the Catholic church and the open worship of God. In the words of a leading historian, these women worked constructively and effectively for a return to a normal and structured lifestyle:

Peacefully but purposefully, they sought to re-establish a pattern of life punctuated by a pealing bell and one in which the rites of passage—birth, marriage, and death— were respected and hallowed. The state had intruded too far and women entered the public arena to push it back and won. It was one of the most resounding political statements made by the populace in the entire history of the Revolution.[11]

As for the middle-class members of the National Convention, in 1795 they wrote yet another constitution, which they believed would guarantee their economic position and political supremacy. As in previous elections, the mass of the population voted only for electors, whose number was cut back to men of substantial means. Electors then elected the members of a reorganized legislative assembly, as well as key officials throughout France. The new assembly also chose a five-man executive—the Directory.

May 5, 1789	Estates General convene at Versailles.
June 17, 1789	Third estate declares itself the National Assembly.
June 20, 1789	Oath of the Tennis Court is sworn.
July 14, 1789	Storming of the Bastille occurs.
July–August 1789	Great Fear ravages the countryside.
August 4, 1789	National Assembly abolishes feudal privileges.
August 27, 1789	National Assembly issues Declaration of the Rights of Man.
October 5, 1789	Women march on Versailles and force royal family to return to Paris.
November 1789	National Assembly confiscates church lands.
July 1790	Civil Constitution of the Clergy establishes a national church. Louis XVI reluctantly agrees to accept a constitutional monarchy.
June 1791	Royal family is arrested while attempting to flee France.
August 1791	Austria and Prussia issue the Declaration of Pillnitz.
April 1792	France declares war on Austria.
August 1792	Parisian mob attacks the palace and takes Louis XVI prisoner.
September 1792	September Massacres occur. National Convention declares France a republic and abolishes monarchy.
January 1793	Louis XVI is executed.
February 1793	France declares war on Britain, Holland, and Spain. Revolts take place in some provincial cities.
March 1793	Bitter struggle occurs in the National Convention between Girondists and the Mountain.
April–June 1793	Robespierre and the Mountain organize the Committee of Public Safety and arrest Girondist leaders.
September 1793	Price controls are instituted to aid the sans-culottes and mobilize the war effort.
1793–1794	Reign of Terror darkens Paris and the provinces.
Spring 1794	French armies are victorious on all fronts.
July 1794	Robespierre is executed. Thermidorian reaction begins.
1795–1799	Directory rules.
1795	Economic controls are abolished, and suppression of the sans-culottes begins.
1797	Napoleon defeats Austrian armies in Italy and returns triumphant to Paris.
1798	Austria, Great Britain, and Russia form the Second Coalition against France.
1799	Napoleon overthrows the Directory and seizes power.

The Directory continued to support French military expansion abroad. War was no longer so much a crusade as a means to meet ever-present, ever-unsolved economic problems. Large, victorious French armies reduced unemployment at home and were able to live off the territories they conquered and plundered.

The unprincipled action of the Directory reinforced widespread disgust with war and starvation. This general dissatisfaction revealed itself clearly in the national elections of 1797, which returned a large number of conservative and even monarchist deputies who favored peace at almost any price. The members of the Directory, fearing for their skins, used the army to nullify the elections and began to govern dictatorially. Two years later, Napoleon Bonaparte ended the Directory in a *coup d'état* and substituted a strong dictatorship for a weak one. The effort to establish stable representative government had failed.

 # THE NAPOLEONIC ERA, 1799–1815

For almost fifteen years, from 1799 to 1814, France was in the hands of a keen-minded military dictator of exceptional ability. One of history's most fascinating leaders, Napoleon Bonaparte (1769–1821) realized the need to put an end to civil strife in France, in order to create unity and consolidate his rule. And he did. But Napoleon saw himself as a man of destiny, and the glory of war and the dream of universal empire proved irresistible. For years he spiraled from victory to victory, but in the end he was destroyed by a mighty coalition united in fear of his restless ambition.

Napoleon's Rule of France

In 1799 when he seized power, young General Napoleon Bonaparte was a national hero. Born in Corsica into an impoverished noble family in 1769, Napoleon left home and became a lieutenant in the French artillery in 1785. After a brief and unsuccessful adventure fighting for Corsican independence in 1789, he returned to France as a French patriot and a dedicated revolutionary. Rising rapidly in the new army, Napoleon was placed in command of French forces in Italy and won brilliant victories there in 1796 and 1797. His next campaign, in Egypt, was a failure, but Napoleon made his way back to France before the fiasco was generally known. His reputation remained intact.

Napoleon soon learned that some prominent members of the legislature were plotting against the Direc-

tory. The dissatisfaction of these plotters stemmed not so much from the fact that the Directory was a dictatorship as from the fact that it was a weak dictatorship. Ten years of upheaval and uncertainty had made firm rule much more appealing than liberty and popular politics to these disillusioned revolutionaries. The abbé Sieyès personified this evolution in thinking. In 1789 he had written that the nobility was grossly overprivileged and that the entire people should rule the French nation. Now Sieyès's motto was "Confidence from below, authority from above."

Like the other members of his group, Sieyès wanted a strong military ruler. The flamboyant thirty-year-old Napoleon was ideal. Thus the conspirators and Napoleon organized a takeover. On November 9, 1799, they ousted the Directors, and the following day soldiers disbanded the legislature at bayonet point. Napoleon was named first consul of the republic, and a new constitution consolidating his position was overwhelmingly approved in a plebiscite in December 1799. Republican appearances were maintained, but Napoleon was already the real ruler of France.

The essence of Napoleon's domestic policy was to use his great and highly personal powers to maintain order and put an end to civil strife. He did so by working out unwritten agreements with powerful groups in France whereby these groups received favors in return for loyal service. Napoleon's bargain with the solid middle class was codified in the famous Civil Code of 1804, which reasserted two of the fundamental principles of the liberal and essentially moderate revolution of 1789: equality of all male citizens before the law and absolute security of wealth and private property. Napoleon and the leading bankers of Paris established the privately owned Bank of France, which loyally served the interests of both the state and the financial oligarchy. Napoleon's defense of the new economic order also appealed successfully to the peasants, who had gained both land and status from the revolutionary changes. Thus Napoleon reconfirmed the gains of the peasantry and reassured the solid middle class, which had already lost a large number of its revolutionary illusions in the face of social upheaval.

At the same time, Napoleon accepted and strengthened the position of the French bureaucracy. Building on the solid foundations that revolutionary governments had inherited from the Old Regime, he perfected a thoroughly centralized state. A network of prefects, subprefects, and centrally appointed mayors depended on Napoleon and served him well. Nor were members of the old nobility slighted. In 1800 and again in 1802, Napoleon granted amnesty to 100,000 émigrés on the condition that they return to France and take a loyalty oath. Members of this returning elite soon ably occupied many high posts in the expanding centralized state. Only one thousand die-hard monarchists were exempted and remained abroad. Napoleon also created a new imperial nobility in order to reward his most talented generals and officials.

Napoleon's great skill in gaining support from important and potentially hostile groups is illustrated by his treatment of the Catholic church in France. In 1800 the French clergy was still divided into two groups: those who had taken an oath of allegiance to the revolutionary government and those in exile or hiding who had refused to do so. Personally uninterested in religion, Napoleon wanted to heal the religious division so that a united Catholic church in France could serve as a bulwark of order and social peace. After long and arduous negotiations, Napoleon and Pope Pius VII

(1800–1823) signed the Concordat of 1801. The pope gained for French Catholics the precious right to practice their religion freely, but Napoleon gained political power: his government now nominated bishops, paid the clergy, and exerted great influence over the church in France.

The domestic reforms of Napoleon's early years were his greatest achievement. Much of his legal and administrative reorganization has survived in France to this day. More generally, Napoleon's domestic initiatives gave the great majority of French people a welcome sense of order and stability. And when Napoleon added the glory of military victory, he rekindled a spirit of national unity that would elude France throughout most of the nineteenth century.

Order and unity had their price: Napoleon's authoritarian rule. Women, who had often participated in revolutionary politics without having legal equality, lost

The Coronation of Napoleon, 1804 (detail)   In this grandiose painting by Jacques-Louis David, Napoleon prepares to crown his beautiful wife, Josephine, in an elaborate ceremony in Notre Dame Cathedral. Napoleon, the ultimate upstart, also crowned himself. Pope Pius VII, seated glumly behind the emperor, is reduced to being a spectator. *(Louvre © Photo R.M.N.)*

THE NAPOLEONIC ERA

November 1799	Napoleon overthrows the Directory.
December 1799	French voters overwhelmingly approve Napoleon's new constitution.
1800	Napoleon founds the Bank of France.
1801	France defeats Austria and acquires Italian and German territories in the Treaty of Lunéville. Napoleon signs the Concordat with the pope.
1802	France signs the Treaty of Amiens with Britain.
December 1804	Napoleon crowns himself emperor.
October 1805	Britain defeats the French and Spanish fleet at the Battle of Trafalgar.
December 1805	Napoleon defeats Austria and Russia at the Battle of Austerlitz.
1807	Napoleon redraws the map of Europe in the treaties of Tilsit.
1810	The Grand Empire is at its height.
June 1812	Napoleon invades Russia with 600,000 men.
Fall–Winter 1812	Napoleon makes a disastrous retreat from Russia.
March 1814	Russia, Prussia, Austria, and Britain form the Quadruple Alliance to defeat France.
April 1814	Napoleon abdicates and is exiled to Elba.
February–June 1815	Napoleon escapes from Elba and rules France until he is defeated at the Battle of Waterloo.

many of the gains they had made in the 1790s. Under the law of the new Napoleonic Code, women were dependents, of either their fathers or their husbands, and they could not make contracts or even have bank accounts in their own names. Indeed, Napoleon and his advisers aimed at re-establishing a "family monarch," where the power of the husband and father was as absolute over the wife and the children as that of Napoleon was over his subjects.

Free speech and freedom of the press—fundamental rights of the liberal revolution enshrined in the Declaration of the Rights of Man—were continually violated. Napoleon constantly reduced the number of newspapers in Paris. By 1811 only four were left, and they were little more than organs of government propaganda.

The occasional elections were a farce. Later laws prescribed harsh penalties for political offenses.

These changes in the law were part of the creation of a police state in France. Since Napoleon was usually busy making war, this task was largely left to Joseph Fouché, an unscrupulous opportunist who had earned a reputation for brutality during the Reign of Terror. As minister of police, Fouché organized a ruthlessly efficient spy system, which kept thousands of citizens under continual police surveillance. People suspected of subversive activities were arbitrarily detained, placed under house arrest, or consigned to insane asylums. After 1810 political suspects were held in state prisons, as they had been during the Terror. There were about twenty-five hundred such political prisoners in 1814.

Napoleon's Wars and Foreign Policy

Napoleon was above all a military man, and a great one. After coming to power in 1799, he sent peace feelers to Austria and Great Britain, the two remaining members of the Second Coalition, which had been formed against France in 1798. When these overtures were rejected, French armies led by Napoleon decisively defeated the Austrians. In the Treaty of Lunéville (1801), Austria accepted the loss of almost all its Italian possessions, and German territory on the west bank of the Rhine was incorporated into France. Once more, as in 1797, the British were alone, and war-weary, like the French.

Still seeking to consolidate his regime domestically, Napoleon concluded the Treaty of Amiens with Great Britain in 1802. France remained in control of Holland, the Austrian Netherlands, the west bank of the Rhine, and most of the Italian peninsula. Napoleon was free to reshape the German states as he wished. The Treaty of Amiens was clearly a diplomatic triumph for Napoleon, and peace with honor and profit increased his popularity at home.

In 1802 Napoleon was secure but unsatisfied. Ever a romantic gambler as well as a brilliant administrator, he could not contain his power drive. Aggressively redrawing the map of Germany so as to weaken Austria and attract the secondary states of southwestern Germany toward France, Napoleon threatened British interests in the eastern Mediterranean and tried to restrict British trade with all of Europe. Deciding to renew war with Britain in May 1803, Napoleon concentrated his armies in the French ports on the Channel in the fall of 1803 and began making preparations to invade England. Yet Great Britain remained dominant on the seas. When Napoleon tried to bring his Mediterranean fleet around Gibraltar to northern France, a combined French and Spanish fleet was, after a series of mishaps, virtually annihilated by Lord Nelson at the Battle of Trafalgar on October 21, 1805. Invasion of England was henceforth impossible. Renewed fighting had its advantages, however, for the first consul used the wartime atmosphere to have himself proclaimed emperor in late 1804.

Austria, Russia, and Sweden joined with Britain to form the Third Coalition against France shortly before the Battle of Trafalgar. Actions such as Napoleon's assumption of the Italian crown had convinced both Alexander I of Russia and Francis II of Austria that Napoleon was a threat to their interests and to the European balance of power. Yet the Austrians and the Russians were no match for Napoleon, who scored a brilliant victory over them at the Battle of Austerlitz in

December 1805. Alexander I decided to pull back, and Austria accepted large territorial losses in return for peace as the Third Coalition collapsed.

Victorious at Austerlitz, Napoleon proceeded to reorganize the German states to his liking. In 1806 he abolished many of the tiny German states as well as the ancient Holy Roman Empire, whose emperor had traditionally been the ruler of Austria. Napoleon established by decree the German Confederation of the Rhine, a union of fifteen German states minus Austria, Prussia, and Saxony. Naming himself "protector" of the confederation, Napoleon firmly controlled western Germany.

Napoleon's intervention in German affairs alarmed the Prussians, who mobilized their armies after more than a decade of peace with France. Napoleon attacked and won two more brilliant victories in October 1806 at Jena and Auerstädt, where the Prussians were outnumbered two to one. The war with Prussia, now joined by Russia, continued into the following spring, and after Napoleon's larger armies won another victory, Alexander I of Russia wanted peace.

For several days in June 1807, the young tsar and the French emperor negotiated face to face on a raft anchored in the middle of the Niemen River. All the while, the helpless Frederick William III of Prussia rode back and forth on the shore anxiously awaiting the results. As the German poet Heinrich Heine said later, Napoleon had but to whistle and Prussia would have ceased to exist. In the subsequent treaties of Tilsit, Prussia lost half of its population, while Russia accepted Napoleon's reorganization of western and central Europe. Alexander also promised to enforce Napoleon's recently decreed economic blockade against British goods.

After the victory at Austerlitz and even more after the treaties of Tilsit, Napoleon saw himself as the emperor of Europe and not just of France. The so-called Grand Empire he built had three parts. The core, or first part, was an ever-expanding France, which by 1810 included Belgium, Holland, parts of northern Italy, and much German territory on the east bank of the Rhine. Beyond French borders Napoleon established the second part: a number of dependent satellite kingdoms, on the thrones of which he placed (and replaced) the members of his large family. The third part comprised the independent but allied states of Austria, Prussia, and Russia. Both satellites and allies were expected after 1806 to support Napoleon's continental system and cease trade with Britain.

The impact of the Grand Empire on the peoples of Europe was considerable. In the areas incorporated into

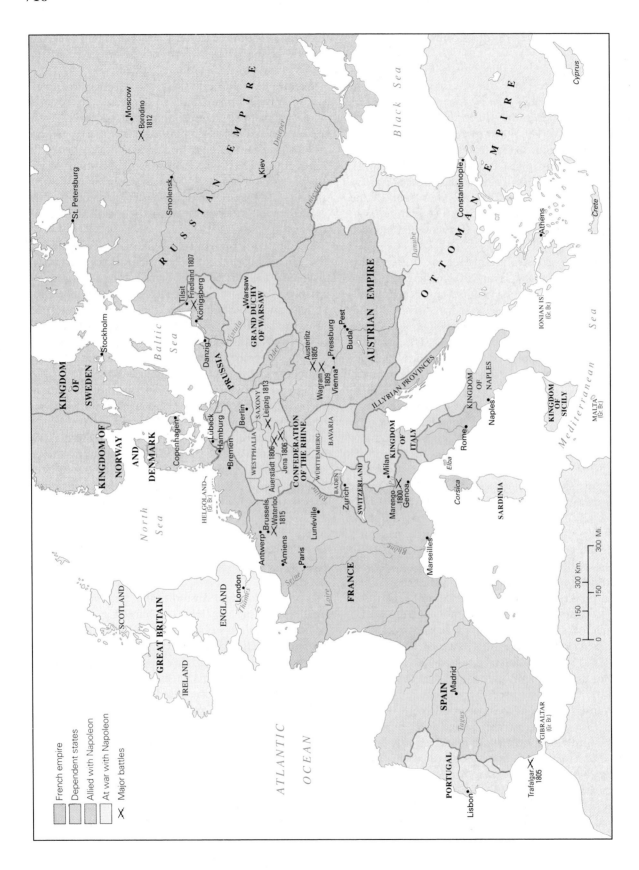

Moscow
Borodino 1812
St. Petersburg
Smolensk
RUSSIAN EMPIRE
Kiev
Dnieper
Dniester
Black Sea
OTTOMAN EMPIRE
Constantinople
Athens
Cyprus
Crete
KINGDOM OF SWEDEN
Stockholm
Baltic Sea
Danzig
Tilsit
Friedland 1807
Königsberg
Warsaw
GRAND DUCHY OF WARSAW
PRUSSIA
Vistula
Oder
Danube
AUSTRIAN EMPIRE
Pest
Buda
Pressburg
Vienna
Austerlitz 1805
Wagram 1809
IONIAN IS. (Gr. Br.)
Mediterranean Sea
KINGDOM OF NORWAY AND DENMARK
Copenhagen
Lübeck
Hamburg
Bremen
Berlin
SAXONY
Leipzig 1813
WESTPHALIA
Auerstädt 1806
Jena 1806
CONFEDERATION OF THE RHINE
WÜRTTEMBERG
BAVARIA
BADEN
Zürich
SWITZERLAND
Rhine
ILLYRIAN PROVINCES
KINGDOM OF ITALY
Milan
Marengo 1800
Genoa
Elba
Rome
KINGDOM OF NAPLES
Naples
KINGDOM OF SICILY
MALTA (Gr. Br.)
Corsica
SARDINIA
North Sea
HELGOLAND (Gr. Br.)
Brussels
Waterloo 1815
Antwerp
Amiens
Paris
Lunéville
Seine
Loire
Rhône
Marseilles
ATLANTIC OCEAN
SCOTLAND
GREAT BRITAIN
ENGLAND
London
Thames
IRELAND
SPAIN
Madrid
Tagus
PORTUGAL
Lisbon
GIBRALTAR (Gr. Br.)
Trafalgar 1805

French empire
Dependent states
Allied with Napoleon
At war with Napoleon
✕ Major battles

0   150   300 Km.
0   150   300 Mi.

Goya: The Third of May, 1808   This great painting screams in outrage at the horrors of war, which Goya witnessed in Spain. Spanish rebels, focused around the Christ-like figure at the center, are gunned down by anonymous French soldiers, grim forerunners of modern death squads and their atrocities. *(Museo del Prado, Madrid)*

France and in the satellites (Map 21.1), Napoleon introduced many French laws, abolishing feudal dues and serfdom where French revolutionary armies had not already done so. Some of the peasants and middle class benefited from these reforms. Yet while he extended progressive measures to his cosmopolitan empire, Napoleon had to put the prosperity and special interests

MAP 21.1 Napoleonic Europe in 1810   Only Great Britain remained at war with Napoleon at the height of the Grand Empire. Many British goods were smuggled through Helgoland, a tiny but strategic British possession off the German coast.

of France first in order to safeguard his power base. Levying heavy taxes in money and men for his armies, Napoleon came to be regarded more as a conquering tyrant than as an enlightened liberator.

The first great revolt occurred in Spain. In 1808 a coalition of Catholics, monarchists, and patriots rebelled against Napoleon's attempts to make Spain a French satellite with a Bonaparte as its king. French armies occupied Madrid, but the foes of Napoleon fled to the hills and waged uncompromising guerrilla warfare. Spain was a clear warning: resistance to French imperialism was growing.

Yet Napoleon pushed on, determined to hold his complex and far-flung empire together. In 1810, when the Grand Empire was at its height, Britain still re-mained at war with France, helping the guerrillas in Spain and Portugal. The continental system, organized to exclude British goods from the continent and force that "nation of shopkeepers" to its knees, was a failure. Instead, it was France that suffered from Britain's counter-blockade, which created hard times for French artisans and the middle class. Perhaps looking for a scapegoat, Napoleon turned on Alexander I of Russia, who in 1811 openly repudiated Napoleon's war of pro-hibitions against British goods.

Napoleon's invasion of Russia began in June 1812 with a force that eventually numbered 600,000, proba-bly the largest force yet assembled in a single army. Only one-third of this Great Army was French, how-ever; nationals of all the satellites and allies were drafted into the operation. (See the feature "Individuals in So-ciety: Jakob Walter, German Draftee with Napoleon.") Originally planning to winter in the Russian city of Smolensk if Alexander did not sue for peace, Napoleon reached Smolensk and recklessly pressed on toward Moscow. The great Battle of Borodino that followed was a draw, and the Russians retreated in good order. Alexander ordered the evacuation of Moscow, which then burned in part, and he refused to negotiate. Fi-nally, after five weeks in the abandoned city, Napoleon ordered a retreat. That retreat was one of the great mil-itary disasters in history. The Russian army, the Russian winter, and starvation cut Napoleon's army to pieces. When the frozen remnants staggered into Poland and Prussia in December, 370,000 men had died and an-other 200,000 had been taken prisoner.[12]

Leaving his troops to their fate, Napoleon raced to Paris to raise yet another army. Possibly he might still have saved his throne if he had been willing to accept a France reduced to its historical size—the proposal of-fered by Austria's foreign minister, Prince Klemens von Metternich. But Napoleon refused. Austria and Prussia deserted Napoleon and joined Russia and Great Britain in the Fourth Coalition. All across Europe, patriots called for a "war of liberation" against Napoleon's op-pression, and the well-disciplined regular armies of Napoleon's enemies closed in for the kill. This time the coalition held together, cemented by the Treaty of Chaumont, which created a Quadruple Alliance in-tended to last for twenty years. Less than a month later, on April 4, 1814, a defeated, abandoned Napoleon ab-dicated his throne. After this unconditional abdication, the victorious allies granted Napoleon the island of Elba off the coast of Italy as his own tiny state. Napoleon was even allowed to keep his imperial title, and France was required to pay him a yearly income of 2 million francs.

The allies also agreed to the restoration of the Bour-bon dynasty, in part because demonstrations led by a few dedicated French monarchists indicated some sup-port among the French people for that course of action. The new monarch, Louis XVIII (r. 1814–1824), tried to consolidate that support by issuing the Consti-tutional Charter, which accepted many of France's revolutionary changes and guaranteed civil liberties. Indeed, the Charter gave France a constitutional monarchy roughly similar to that established in 1791, although far fewer people had the right to vote for rep-resentatives to the resurrected Chamber of Deputies. Moreover, in an attempt to strengthen popular support for Louis XVIII's new government, France was treated leniently by the allies, which agreed to meet in Vienna to work out a general peace settlement.

Yet Louis XVIII—old, ugly, and crippled by gout—totally lacked the glory and magic of Napoleon. Hear-ing of political unrest in France and diplomatic tensions in Vienna, Napoleon staged a daring escape from Elba in February 1815. Landing in France, he issued appeals for support and marched on Paris with a small band of followers. French officers and soldiers who had fought so long for their emperor responded to the call. Louis XVIII fled, and once more Napoleon took command. But Napoleon's gamble was a desperate long shot, for the allies were united against him. At the end of a fran-tic period known as the Hundred Days, they crushed his forces at Waterloo on June 18, 1815, and impris-oned him on the rocky island of St. Helena, far off the western coast of Africa. Old Louis XVIII returned again—this time "in the baggage of the allies," as his detractors scornfully put it—and recommenced his reign. The allies now dealt more harshly with the ap-parently incorrigible French. And Napoleon, doomed to suffer crude insults at the hands of English jailers on distant St. Helena, could take revenge only by writing his memoirs, skillfully nurturing the myth that he had been Europe's revolutionary liberator, a romantic hero whose lofty work had been undone by oppressive reac-tionaries. An era had ended.

SUMMARY

The French Revolution left a compelling and many-sided political legacy. This legacy included, most notably, liberalism, assertive nationalism, radical democratic re-publicanism, embryonic socialism, and self-conscious conservatism. It also left a rich and turbulent history of electoral competition, legislative assemblies, and even mass politics. Thus the French Revolution and conflict-

Individuals in Society

Jakob Walter, German Draftee with Napoleon ❖

In January 1812, a young German named Jakob Walter (1788–1864) was recalled to active duty in the army of Württemberg, a Napoleonic satellite in the Confederation of the Rhine. Stonemason and common draftee, Walter later wrote a rare enlisted man's account of the Russian campaign, a personal history that testified to the terrible price paid by the common people for a generation of war.

Napoleon's invasion of Russia was a desperate gamble from the beginning. French armies were accustomed to living off well-developed local economies, but this strategy did not work well in poor, sparsely populated eastern Europe. Scrounging for food dominated Walter's recollection of earlier fighting in Poland, and now, in 1812, the food situation was much worse. Crossing into Russia, Walter and his buddies found the nearby villages half-burned and stripped of food. Running down an occasional hog, they greedily tore it to pieces and ate it raw. Strangled by dust and thirst and then pelted for days by cold rain, the Great Army raced to catch the retreating Russians and force them into battle. When the famished troops stopped, the desperate search for food began.

In mid-August Walter's company helped storm the city of Smolensk in heavy fighting. From there onward, the road was littered with men, horses, and wagons, and all the towns and villages had been burned by the Russians to deprive the enemy of supplies. Surrounded by all these horrors, Walter almost lost his nerve, but he drew on his Catholic faith and found the courage "to go on trustingly to meet my fate."[1] Fighting at the great Battle of Borodino, "where the death cries and the shattering gunfire seemed a hell," he and the allied troops entered a deserted and fire-damaged Moscow in mid-September. But food, liquor, and fancy silks were there for the taking, and the weather was warm.

On October 18, the reprieve was over, and the retreating allied infantrymen re-entered hell. Yet Walter, "still alert and spirited," was asked by an officer to be his attendant and received for his services a horse to ride. The horse proved a lifesaver. It allowed Walter to forage for food farther off the highway, to flee from approaching Cossacks, and to conserve his strength as

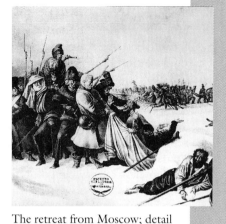

The retreat from Moscow; detail of engraving by G. Küstler. Soldiers strip the sick of their blankets and boots, leaving them to die in the cold. *(New York Public Library, Slavonic Division)*

vicious freezing winter weather set in. Yet food found at great peril could be quickly lost. Once Walter fought off some French soldiers with the help of some nearby Germans, who then robbed him of his bread. But what, he reflected later, could one expect? The starving men had simply lost their humanity. "I myself could look cold-bloodedly into the lamenting faces of the wounded, the freezing, and the burned," he wrote. When his horse was stolen as he slept, he silently stole someone else's. Struggling on in this brutal every-man-for-himself environment, Walter reached Poland in late December and hobbled home, a rare survivor. He went on to recover, marry, and have ten children.

Why did Jakob Walter survive? Pure chance surely played a large part. So did his robust constitution and street smarts. His faith in God also provided strength to meet each day's challenges. The beautiful vision of returning home and seeing his family offered equal encouragement. Finally, he lacked hatred and animosity, whether toward the Russians, the French, or whomever. He accepted the things he could not change and concentrated on those he could.

Questions for Analysis

1. Why was obtaining food such a problem for Jakob Walter and his fellow soldiers?

2. What impresses you most about Walter's account of the Russian campaign?

---

1. Jakob Walter, *The Diary of a Napoleonic Foot Soldier,* ed. with an introduction by M. Raeff (New York: Penguin Books, 1993), p. 53. Also pp. 54, 66.

ing interpretations of its significance presented a whole range of political options and alternative visions of the future. For this reason, it was truly the revolution in modern European politics.

The revolution that began in America and spread to France was a liberal revolution. Revolutionaries on both sides of the Atlantic wanted to establish civil liberties and equality before the law within the framework of representative government, and they succeeded. In France liberal nobles and an increasingly class-conscious middle class overwhelmed declining monarchial absolutism and feudal privilege, thanks to the intervention of the common people—the sans-culottes and the peasants. Featuring electoral competition and civil equality, the government established by the Declaration of the Rights of Man and the French constitution of 1791 was remarkably similar to that created in America by the federal Constitution and the Bill of Rights. France's new political system reflected a social structure based increasingly on wealth and achievement rather than on tradition and legal privileges.

After the establishment of the republic, the radical phase of the Revolution during the Terror, and the fall of Robespierre, the educated elites and the solid middle class reasserted themselves under the Directory. And though Napoleon sharply curtailed representative institutions and individual rights, he effectively promoted the reconciliation of old and new, of centralized bureaucracy and careers open to talent, of noble and bourgeois in a restructured property-owning elite. Louis XVIII had to accept the commanding position of this restructured elite, and in granting representative government and civil liberties to facilitate his restoration to the throne in 1814, he submitted to the rest of the liberal triumph of 1789 to 1791. The liberal core of the French Revolution had successfully survived a generation of war and dictatorship.

Revolution in France, as opposed to in the United States, also left a multiplicity of legacies that extended well beyond the triumphant liberalism of 1789. Indeed, the lived experience of the French Revolution and the wars that went with it exercised a pervasive influence on politics and the political imagination in the nineteenth century, not only in France but throughout Europe and even the rest of the world. First, there was the radical legacy of the embattled republic of 1793 and 1794, with its sans-culottes democratic republicanism and its egalitarian ideology and embryonic socialism. This legacy would inspire republicans, democrats, and early socialists. Second, there was the legacy of a powerful and continuing reaction to the French Revolution and to

aggressive French nationalism. Monarchists and traditionalists now believed that 1789 had been a tragic mistake. They concluded that democratic republicanism and sans-culottes activism led only to war, class conflict, and savage dictatorship. And even though revolutionary upheaval encouraged generations of radicals to believe that political revolution might remake society and even create a new humanity, conservatives and many comfortable moderates were profoundly disillusioned by the revolutionary era. They looked with nostalgia toward the supposedly ordered world of benevolent monarchy, firm government, and respectful common people.

Notes

1. Quoted in R. R. Palmer, *The Age of the Democratic Revolution,* vol. 1 (Princeton, N.J.: Princeton University Press, 1959), p. 239.
2. G. Lefebvre, *The Coming of the French Revolution* (New York: Vintage Books, 1947), p. 81.
3. P. H. Beik, ed., *The French Revolution* (New York: Walker, 1970), p. 89.
4. G. Pernoud and S. Flaisser, eds., *The French Revolution* (Greenwich, Conn.: Fawcett, 1960), p. 61.
5. O. Hufton, *Women and the Limits of Citizenship in the French Revolution* (Toronto: University of Toronto Press, 1992), pp. 3–22.
6. Quotations from Wollstonecraft are drawn from E. W. Sunstein, *A Different Face: The Life of Mary Wollstonecraft* (New York: Harper & Row, 1975), pp. 208, 211; and H. R. James, *Mary Wollstonecraft: A Sketch* (London: Oxford University Press, 1932), pp. 60, 62, 69.
7. Quoted in L. Gershoy, *The Era of the French Revolution, 1789–1799* (New York: Van Nostrand, 1957), p. 150.
8. Pernoud and Flaisser, *The French Revolution,* pp. 193–194.
9. T. Blanning, *The French Revolutionary Wars, 1787–1802* (London: Arnold, 1996), pp. 116–128.
10. Quoted ibid., p. 123.
11. Hufton, *Women and the Limits of Citizenship,* p. 130.
12. D. Sutherland, *France, 1789–1815: Revolution and Counterrevolution* (New York: Oxford University Press, 1986), p. 420.

Suggested Reading

For fascinating eyewitness reports on the French Revolution, see the edited works by Beik and by Pernoud and Flaisser mentioned in the Notes. In addition, A. Young, *Travels in France During the Years 1787, 1788 and 1789*

(1969), offers an engrossing contemporary description of France and Paris on the eve of revolution. E. Burke, *Reflections on the Revolution in France,* first published in 1790, is the classic conservative indictment. The intense passions the French Revolution has generated may be seen in nineteenth-century French historians, notably the enthusiastic J. Michelet, *History of the French Revolution;* the hostile H. Taine; and the judicious A. de Tocqueville, whose masterpiece, *The Old Regime and the French Revolution,* was first published in 1856. Important general studies on the entire period include the work by Palmer, cited in the Notes, which paints a comparative international picture; E. J. Hobsbawm, *The Age of Revolution, 1789–1848* (1962); and O. Connelly, *French Revolution—Napoleonic Era* (1979). P. Schroeder, *The Transformation of European Politics, 1763–1848* (1994), is a masterful synthesis and reinterpretation, which may be compared with L. Dehio, *The Precarious Balance: Four Centuries of the European Power Struggle* (1962).

Revisionist scholarship has created a wealth of new scholarship and interpretation. A. Cobban, *The Social Interpretation of the French Revolution* (1964), and F. Furet, *Interpreting the French Revolution* (1981), are major reassessments of long-dominant ideas, which are admirably presented in N. Hampson, *A Social History of the French Revolution* (1963), and in the volume by Lefebvre listed in the Notes. E. Kennedy, *A Cultural History of the French Revolution* (1989), beautifully written and handsomely illustrated, and W. Doyle, *Origins of the French Revolution,* 3d ed. (1988), are excellent on long-term developments. Among valuable studies, which generally are often quite critical of revolutionary developments, several are noteworthy: J. Bosher, *The French Revolution* (1988); S. Schama, *Citizens: A Chronicle of the French Revolution* (1989); W. Doyle, *The Oxford History of the French Revolution* (1989); and D. Sutherland, *France, 1789–1815: Revolution and Counterrevolution* (1986).

Two excellent anthologies concisely presenting a range of interpretations are F. Kafker and J. Laux, eds., *The French Revolutions: Conflicting Interpretations,* 4th ed. (1989); and G. Best, ed., *The Permanent Revolution: The French Revolution and Its Legacy, 1789–1989* (1988). G. Rudé makes the men and women of the great days of upheaval come alive in his *The Crowd in the French Revolution* (1959), whereas R. R. Palmer studies sympathetically the leaders of the Terror in *Twelve Who Ruled* (1941). Four other particularly interesting, detailed works are B. Shapiro, *Revolutionary Justice in Paris, 1789–1790* (1993); D. Jordan, *The Revolutionary Career of Maximilien Robespierre* (1985); J. P. Bertaud, *The Army of the French Revolution:* *From Citizen-Soldier to Instrument of Power* (1988); and C. L. R. James, *The Black Jacobins* (1938, 1980), on black slave revolt in Haiti. Other significant studies on aspects of revolutionary France include P. Jones's pathbreaking *The Peasantry in the French Revolution* (1988); W. Sewell, Jr.'s imaginative *Work and Revolution in France: The Language of Labor from the Old Regime to 1848* (1980); and L. Hunt's innovative *The Family Romance of the French Revolution* (1992). Two major studies on the era's continuous wars are Blanning, cited in the Notes, and O. Connelly, *Blundering to Glory: Napoleon's Military Campaigns* (1987).

An ongoing explosion of studies on women in the French Revolution is increasing knowledge and also raising conflicting interpretations. This may be seen by comparing two particularly important works: J. Landes, *Women and the Public Sphere in the Age of the French Revolution* (1988); and Hufton, listed in the Notes. D. Outram, *The Body and the French Revolution: Sex, Class and Political Culture* (1989), and L. Hunt, *The Family Romance of the French Revolution* (1992), provide innovative analyses of the gender-related aspects of revolutionary politics and are highly recommended. H. Applewhite and D. Levy, eds., *Women and Politics in the Age of Democratic Revolution* (1990), compares developments in leading countries. Mary Wollstonecraft's dramatic life is the subject of several good biographies, including those by Sunstein and James, cited in the Notes.

Two important works placing political developments in a comparative perspective are P. Higonnet, *Sister Republics: The Origins of French and American Republicanism* (1988); and E. Morgan, *Inventing the People: The Rise of Popular Sovereignty in England and America* (1988). B. Bailyn, *The Ideological Origins of the American Revolution* (1967), is also noteworthy.

The best synthesis on Napoleonic France is L. Bergeron, *France Under Napoleon* (1981). E. Arnold, Jr., ed., *A Documentary Survey of Napoleonic France* (1994), includes political and cultural selections. K. Kafker and J. Laux, eds., *Napoleon and His Times: Selected Interpretations* (1989), is an interesting collection of articles, which may be compared with R. Jones, *Napoleon: Man and Myth* (1977). Good biographies are J. Thompson, *Napoleon Bonaparte: His Rise and Fall* (1952); F. Markham, *Napoleon* (1964); and V. Cronin, *Napoleon Bonaparte* (1972). Wonderful novels inspired by the period include Raphael Sabatini's *Scaramouche,* a swashbuckler of revolutionary intrigue with accurate historical details; Charles Dickens's fanciful *A Tale of Two Cities;* and Leo Tolstoy's monumental saga of Napoleon's invasion of Russia (and much more), *War and Peace.*

Revolution and Women's Rights

The 1789 Declaration of the Rights of Man was a revolutionary call for legal equality, representative government, and individual freedom. But the new rights were strictly limited to men; Napoleon tightened further the subordination of French women.

Among those who saw the contradiction in granting supposedly universal rights to only half the population was Marie Gouze (1748–1793), known to history as Olympe de Gouges. The daughter of a provincial butcher and peddler, she pursued a literary career in Paris after the death of her husband. Between 1790 and 1793, she wrote more than two dozen political pamphlets under her new name. De Gouges's great work was her "Declaration of the Rights of Woman" (1791). Excerpted here, de Gouges's manifesto went beyond the 1789 Rights of Man. It called on males to end their oppression of women and give women equal rights. A radical on women's issues, de Gouges sympathized with the monarchy and criticized Robespierre in print. Convicted of sedition, she was guillotined in November 1793.

. . . Man, are you capable of being just? . . . Tell me, what gives you sovereign empire to oppress my sex? Your strength? Your talents? Observe the Creator in his wisdom . . . and give me, if you dare, an example of this tyrannical empire. Go back to animals, consult the elements, study plants . . . and distinguish, if you can, the sexes in the administration of nature. Everywhere you will find them mingled; everywhere they cooperate in harmonious togetherness in this immortal masterpiece.

Man alone has raised his exceptional circumstances to a principle. . . . [H]e wants to command as a despot a sex which is in full possession of its intellectual faculties; he pretends to enjoy the Revolution and to claim his rights to equality in order to say nothing more about it.

DECLARATION OF THE RIGHTS OF WOMAN AND THE FEMALE CITIZEN

For the National Assembly to decree in its last sessions, or in those of the next legislature:

Preamble

Mothers, daughters, sisters and representatives of the nation demand to be constituted into a national assembly. Believing that ignorance, omission, or scorn for the rights of woman are the only causes of public misfortunes and of the corruption of governments, [the women] have resolved to set forth in a solemn declaration the natural, inalienable, and sacred rights of woman. . . .

. . . the sex that is as superior in beauty as it is in courage during the sufferings of maternity recognizes and declares in the presence and under the auspices of the Supreme Being, the following Rights of Woman and of Female Citizens:

I. Woman is born free and lives equal to man in her rights. Social distinctions can be based only on the common utility.

II. The purpose of any political association is the conservation of the natural and imprescriptible rights of woman and man; these rights are liberty, property, security, and especially resistance to oppression.

III. The principle of all sovereignty rests essentially with the nation, which is nothing but the union of woman and man. . . .

IV. Liberty and justice consist of restoring all that belongs to others; thus, the only limits on the exercise of the natural rights of woman are perpetual male tyranny; these limits are to be reformed by the laws of nature and reason.

V. Laws of nature and reason proscribe all acts harmful to society. . . .

VI. The law must be the expression of the general will; all female and male citizens must contribute either personally or through their representatives to its formation; it must be the same for all: male and female citizens, being equal in the eyes of the law, must be equally admitted to all honors, positions, and public employment according to their capacity and without other distinctions besides those of their virtues and talents.

VII. No woman is an exception; she is accused, arrested, and detained in cases determined by law. Women, like men, obey this rigorous law.

VIII. The law must establish only those penalties that are strictly and obviously necessary. . . .

IX. Once any woman is declared guilty, complete rigor is [to be] exercised by the law.

X. No one is to be disquieted for his very basic opinions; woman has the right to mount the scaffold; she must equally have the right to mount the rostrum, provided that her demonstrations do not disturb the legally established public order.

XI. The free communication of thoughts and opinions is one of the most precious rights of woman, since that liberty assures the recognition of children by their fathers. Any female citizen thus may say freely, I am the mother of a child which belongs to you, without being forced by a barbarous prejudice to hide the truth. . . .

XIII. For the support of the public force and the expenses of administration, the contributions of woman and man are equal; she shares all the duties . . . and all the painful tasks; therefore, she must have the same share in the distribution of positions, employment, offices, honors, and jobs. . . .

XIV. Female and male citizens have the right to verify, either by themselves or through their representatives, the necessity of the public contribution. This can only apply to women if they are granted an equal share, not only of wealth, but also of public administration. . . .

XV. The collectivity of women, joined for tax purposes to the aggregate of men, has the right to demand an accounting of his administration from any public agent.

XVI. No society has a constitution without the guarantee of rights and the separation of powers; the constitution is null if the majority of individuals comprising the nation have not cooperated in drafting it.

XVII. Property belongs to both sexes whether united or separate; for each it is an inviolable and sacred right. . . .

Postscript

Women, wake up. . . . Discover your rights. . . . Oh, women, women! When will you cease to be

❖ The late-eighteenth-century French painting *La Liberté*. *(Bibliothèque Nationale/Giraudon/Art Resource, NY)*

blind? What advantage have you received from the Revolution? A more pronounced scorn, a more marked disdain. . . . [If men persist in contradicting their revolutionary principles,] courageously oppose the force of reason to the empty pretensions of superiority . . . and you will soon see these haughty men, not groveling at your feet as servile adorers, but proud to share with you the treasure of the Supreme Being. Regardless of what barriers confront you; it is in your power to free yourselves; you have only to want to. . . .

Questions for Analysis

1. On what basis did de Gouges argue for gender equality? Did she believe in natural law?

2. What consequences did "scorn for the rights of woman" have for France, according to de Gouges?

3. Did de Gouges stress political rights at the expense of social and economic rights? If so, why?

Source: Olympe de Gouges, "Declaration of the Rights of Woman," in Darline G. Levy, Harriet B. Applewhite, and Mary D. Johnson, eds., *Women in Revolutionary Paris, 1789–1795* (Urbana: University of Illinois Press, 1979), pp. 87–96. Copyright © 1979 by the Board of Trustees, University of Illinois. Used with permission.

22

The Revolution in Energy and Industry

A colored engraving by
J. C. Bourne of the
Great Western Railway
emerging from a tunnel.
*(Science & Society Picture
Library, London)*

While the revolution in France was opening a new political era, another revolution was beginning to transform economic and social life. This was the Industrial Revolution, which began in Great Britain around the 1780s and started to influence continental Europe after 1815. Because the Industrial Revolution was less dramatic than the French Revolution, some historians see industrial development as basically moderate and evolutionary. But from a longer perspective, it was rapid and brought about numerous radical changes. Quite possibly only the development of agriculture during Neolithic times had a comparable impact and significance.

The Industrial Revolution profoundly modified much of human experience. It changed patterns of work, transformed the social class structure and the way people thought about class, and eventually even altered the international balance of political power. The Industrial Revolution also helped ordinary people gain a higher standard of living as the widespread poverty of the preindustrial world was gradually reduced.

Unfortunately, the improvement in the European standard of living was quite limited until about 1850 for at least two reasons. First, even in Britain, only a few key industries experienced a technological revolution. Many more industries continued to use old methods, especially on the continent, and this held down the increase in total production. Second, the increase in total population, which began in the eighteenth century (see page 638), continued all across Europe as the era of the Industrial Revolution unfolded. As a result, the rapid growth in population threatened to eat up the growth in production and to leave most individuals poorer than ever. As a consequence, rapid population growth provided a somber background for European industrialization and made the wrenching transformation all the more difficult.

- What, then, characterized the Industrial Revolution?
- What were its origins, and how did it develop?
- How did the changes it brought affect people and society in an era of continued rapid population growth?

These are some of the questions this chapter will seek to answer.

 ## THE INDUSTRIAL REVOLUTION IN BRITAIN

The Industrial Revolution began in Great Britain, that historic union of Scotland, Wales, and England—the wealthiest and the dominant part of the country. It was something new in history, and it was quite unplanned. With no models to copy and no idea of what to expect, Britain had to pioneer not only in industrial technology but also in social relations and urban living. Between 1793 and 1815, these formidable tasks were complicated by almost constant war with France. As the trailblazer in economic development, as France was in political change, Britain must command special attention.

Eighteenth-Century Origins

Although many aspects of the British Industrial Revolution are still matters for scholarly debate, it is generally agreed that the industrial changes that did occur grew out of a long process of development. First, the expanding Atlantic economy of the eighteenth century served mercantilist Britain remarkably well. The colonial empire that Britain aggressively built, augmented by a strong position in Latin America and in the African slave trade, provided a growing market for British manufactured goods. So did the domestic market. In an age when it was much cheaper to ship goods by water than by land, no part of England was more than twenty miles from navigable water. Beginning in the 1770s, a canal-building boom greatly enhanced this natural advantage (Map 22.1). Rivers and canals provided easy movement of England's and Wales's enormous deposits of iron and coal, resources that would be critical raw materials in Europe's early industrial age. Nor were there any tariffs within the country to hinder trade, as there were in France before 1789 and in politically fragmented Germany.

Second, agriculture played a central role in bringing about the Industrial Revolution in Britain. English farmers in particular were second only to the Dutch in productivity in 1700, and they were continually adopting new methods of farming as the century went on. The result, especially before 1760, was a period of bountiful crops and low food prices. The ordinary English family did not have to spend almost everything it

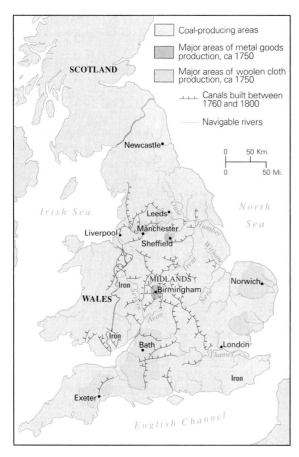

MAP 22.1 Cottage Industry and Transportation in Eighteenth-Century England England had an unusually good system of navigable waterways even before river-linking canals made it better.

earned just to buy bread. It could spend more on, for example, manufactured goods—leather shoes or a razor for the man, a bonnet or a shawl for the woman, toy soldiers for the son, and a doll for the daughter. Thus demand for goods within the country complemented the demand from the colonies.

Third, Britain had other assets that helped give rise to industrial leadership. Unlike eighteenth-century France, Britain had an effective central bank and well-developed credit markets. The monarchy and the aristocratic oligarchy, which had jointly ruled the country since 1688, provided stable and predictable government. At the same time, the government let the domestic economy operate with few controls, encouraging personal initiative, technical change, and a free market. Finally, Britain had long had a large class of hired agricultural laborers, rural proletarians whose numbers were further increased

by the second great round of enclosures in the late eighteenth century. These rural wage earners were relatively mobile—compared to village-bound peasants in France and western Germany, for example—and along with cottage workers they formed a potential industrial labor force for capitalist entrepreneurs.

All these factors combined to initiate the Industrial Revolution, a term first coined by awed contemporaries in the 1830s to describe the burst of major inventions and technical changes they had witnessed in certain industries. This technical revolution went hand in hand with an impressive quickening in the annual rate of industrial growth in Britain. Whereas industry had grown at only 0.7 percent between 1700 and 1760 (before the Industrial Revolution), it grew at the much higher rate of 3 percent between 1801 and 1831 (when industrial transformation was in full swing).[1] The decisive quickening of growth probably came in the 1780s, after the American War of Independence and just before the French Revolution.

Therefore, the great economic and political revolutions that shaped the modern world occurred almost simultaneously, though they began in different countries. The Industrial Revolution was, however, a longer process than the political upheavals. It was not complete in Britain until 1850, and it had no real impact on continental countries until after 1815.

The First Factories

The pressure to produce more goods for a growing market was directly related to the first decisive breakthrough of the Industrial Revolution—the creation of the world's first large factories in the British cotton textile industry. Technological innovations in the manufacture of cotton cloth led to a new system of production and social relationships. Since no other industry experienced such a rapid or complete transformation before 1830, these trailblazing developments deserve special consideration.

Although the putting-out system of merchant capitalism (see pages 640–642) was expanding all across Europe in the eighteenth century, this pattern of rural industry was most fully developed in Britain. There, under the pressure of growing demand, the system's limitations began to outweigh its advantages for the first time. This was especially true in the British textile industry after about 1760.

A constant shortage of thread in the textile industry focused attention on ways of improving spinning. Many a tinkering worker knew that a better spinning wheel promised rich rewards. It proved hard to spin the traditional raw materials—wool and flax—with improved machines, but cotton was different. Cotton textiles had first been imported into Britain from India by the East India Company, and by 1760 there was a tiny domestic industry in northern England. After many experiments over a generation, a gifted carpenter and jack-of-all-trades, James Hargreaves, invented his cotton-spinning jenny about 1765. At almost the same moment, a barber-turned-manufacturer named Richard Arkwright invented (or possibly pirated) another kind of spinning machine, the water frame. These breakthroughs produced an explosion in the infant cotton textile industry in the 1780s, when it was increasing the value of its output at an unprecedented rate of about 13 percent each year. By 1790 the new machines were producing ten times as much cotton yarn as had been made in 1770.

Hargreaves's jenny was simple and inexpensive. It was also hand-operated. In early models, from six to twenty-four spindles were mounted on a sliding carriage, and each spindle spun a fine, slender thread. The woman moved the carriage back and forth with one hand and turned a wheel to supply power with the other. Now it was the male weaver who could not keep up with the vastly more efficient female spinner.

Arkwright's water frame employed a different principle. It quickly acquired a capacity of several hundred spindles and demanded much more power—waterpower. The water frame thus required large specialized mills, factories that employed as many as one thousand workers from the very beginning. The water frame could spin only coarse, strong thread, which was then put out for respinning on hand-powered cottage jennies. Around 1790 an alternative technique invented by Samuel Crompton also began to require more power than the human arm could supply. After that time, all cotton spinning was gradually concentrated in factories.

The first consequences of these revolutionary developments were more beneficial than is generally believed. Cotton goods became much cheaper, and they were bought and treasured by all classes. In the past, only the wealthy could afford the comfort and cleanliness of underwear, which was called "body linen" because it was made from expensive linen cloth. Now millions of poor people, who had earlier worn nothing underneath their coarse, filthy outergarments, could afford to wear cotton slips and underpants as well as cotton dresses and shirts.

Families using cotton in cottage industry were freed from their constant search for adequate yarn from scattered, part-time spinners, since all the thread needed

Hargreave's Spinning Jenny   The loose cotton strands on the slanted bobbins passed up to the sliding carriage and then on to the spindles in back for fine spinning. The worker, almost always a woman, regulated the sliding carriage with one hand and with the other she turned the crank on the wheel to supply power. By 1783 one woman could spin by hand a hundred threads at a time on an improved model. (*Science Museum, London/Michael Holford*)

could be spun in the cottage on the jenny or obtained from a nearby factory. The wages of weavers, now hard-pressed to keep up with the spinners, rose markedly until about 1792. Weavers were among the best-paid workers in England. They were known to walk proudly through the streets with 5-pound notes stuck in their hatbands, and they dressed like the middle class.

One result of this unprecedented prosperity was that large numbers of agricultural laborers became handloom weavers. The growth of handloom cotton weaving was an outstanding example of how breakthroughs in factory production normally stimulated complementary increases in handicraft output. It was also an example of how further mechanization threatened certain groups of handicraft workers, for mechanics and capitalists soon sought to invent a power loom to save on labor costs. This Edmund Cartwright achieved in 1785. But the power looms of the factories worked poorly at first, and handloom weavers continued to receive good wages until at least 1800.

Working conditions in the early factories were less satisfactory than those of cottage weavers and spinners. But until the late 1780s, most British factories were in rural areas, where they had access to waterpower. These factories employed a relatively small percentage of all cotton textile workers. People were reluctant to work in them, partly because they resembled the poorhouses where destitute inmates had to labor for very little pay. Therefore, factory owners turned to young children as a source of labor. More precisely, they turned to children who had been abandoned by their parents and put in the care of local parishes. Parish officers often "apprenticed" such unfortunate foundlings to factory owners. The parish thus saved money, and the factory owners gained workers over whom they exercised almost the authority of slaveowners.

Apprenticed as young as five or six years of age, boy and girl workers were forced by law to labor for their "master" for as many as fourteen years. Housed, fed, and locked up nightly in factory dormitories, the young workers received little or no pay. Hours were appalling—commonly thirteen or fourteen hours a day, six days a week. Harsh physical punishment maintained brutal discipline. To be sure, poor children typically worked long hours from an early age in the eighteenth century and frequently outside the home for a brutal master. But the wholesale coercion of orphans as factory apprentices constituted exploitation on a truly unprecedented scale. This exploitation ultimately piqued the conscience of reformers and reinforced humanitarian attitudes toward children and their labor in the early nineteenth century.

The creation of the world's first modern factories in the British cotton textile industry in the 1770s and 1780s, which grew out of the putting-out system of cottage production, was a major historical development. Both symbolically and substantially, the big new cotton mills marked the beginning of the Industrial Revolution in Britain. By 1831 the largely mechanized cotton textile industry towered above all others, accounting for fully 22 percent of the country's entire industrial production.

The Problem of Energy

The growth of the cotton textile industry might have been stunted or cut short, however, if water from rivers and streams had remained the primary source of power for the new factories. But this did not occur. Instead, an epoch-making solution was found to the age-old problem of energy and power. It was this solution to the energy problem (a problem that reappeared in recent times) that permitted continued rapid development in cotton textiles, the gradual generalization of the factory system, and the triumph of the Industrial Revolution in Britain.

Human beings, like all living organisms, require energy. Adult men and women need two thousand to four thousand calories (units of energy) daily simply to fuel their bodies, work, and survive. Prehistoric people relied on plants and plant-eating animals as their sources of energy. With the development of agriculture, early civilizations were able to increase the number of useful plants and thus the supply of energy. Some plants could be fed to domesticated animals, such as the horse. Stronger than human beings, these animals converted the energy in the plants into work.

Human beings have long used their toolmaking abilities to construct machines that convert one form of energy into another for their own benefit. In the medieval period, people began to develop water mills to grind their grain and windmills to pump water and drain swamps. More efficient use of water and wind in the sixteenth and seventeenth centuries enabled human beings to accomplish more; intercontinental sailing ships were a prime example. Nevertheless, even into the eighteenth century, society continued to rely for energy mainly on plants, and human beings and animals continued to perform most work. This dependence meant that Western civilization remained poor in energy and power.

Lack of power lay at the heart of the poverty that afflicted the large majority of people. The man behind the plow and the woman at the spinning wheel could employ only horsepower and human muscle in their labor. No matter how hard they worked, they could not produce very much. What people needed were new sources of energy and more power at their disposal.

Where was more energy to be found? Almost all energy came directly or indirectly from plants and therefore from the land: grain for people, hay for animals, and wood for heat. The land was also the principal source of raw materials needed for industrial production: wool and flax for clothing, leather for shoes, wood for housing, tools, and ironmaking. And though swamps could be drained and marshes reclaimed from the sea, it was difficult to expand greatly the amount of land available. True, its yield could be increased, as by the elimination of fallow; nonetheless, there were definite limits to such improvements.

The shortage of energy had become particularly severe in Britain by the eighteenth century. Because of the growth of population, most of the great forests of medieval Britain had long ago been replaced by fields of grain and hay. Wood was in ever-shorter supply, yet it remained tremendously important. It served as the primary source of heat for all homes and industries and as a basic raw material. Processed wood (charcoal) was the fuel that was mixed with iron ore in the blast furnace to produce pig iron. The iron industry's appetite for wood was enormous, and by 1740 the British iron industry was stagnating. Vast forests enabled Russia to become the world's leading producer of iron, much of which was exported to Britain. But Russia's potential for growth was limited, too, and in a few decades Russia would reach the barrier of inadequate energy that was already holding England back.

The Steam Engine Breakthrough

As this early energy crisis grew worse, Britain looked toward its abundant and widely scattered reserves of coal as an alternative to its vanishing wood. Coal was first used in Britain in the late Middle Ages as a source of heat. By 1640 most homes in London were heated with it, and it also provided heat for making beer, glass, soap, and other products. Coal was not used, however, to produce mechanical energy or to power machinery. It was there that coal's potential was enormous, as a simple example shows.

One pound of good bituminous coal contains about 3,500 calories of heat energy. A hard-working miner can dig out 500 pounds of coal a day using hand tools. Even an extremely inefficient converter, which transforms only 1 percent of the heat energy in coal into mechanical energy, will produce 27 horsepower-hours of work from the 500 pounds of coal the miner cut out of the earth. The miner, by contrast, produces only about 1 horsepower-hour in the course of a day.

Early steam engines were just such inefficient converters. As more coal was produced, mines were dug deeper and deeper and were constantly filling with water. Mechanical pumps, usually powered by animals walking in circles at the surface, had to be installed. At one mine, fully five hundred horses were used in pumping. Such power was expensive and bothersome. In an attempt to overcome these disadvantages, Thomas Savery in 1698 and Thomas Newcomen in 1705 invented the first primitive steam engines.

Both engines were extremely inefficient. Both burned coal to produce steam, which was then injected into a cylinder or reservoir. In Newcomen's engine, the steam in the cylinder was cooled, creating a partial vacuum in the cylinder. This vacuum allowed the pressure of the earth's atmosphere to push the piston in the cylinder down and operate a pump. By the early 1770s, many of the Savery engines and hundreds of the Newcomen engines were operating successfully, though inefficiently, in English and Scottish mines.

In the early 1760s, a gifted young Scot named James Watt (1736–1819) was drawn to a critical study of the steam engine. Watt was employed at the time by the University of Glasgow as a skilled craftsman making scientific instruments. The Scottish universities were pioneers in practical technical education, and in 1763 Watt was called on to repair a Newcomen engine being used in a physics course. After a series of observations, Watt

Watt's First Steam Engine, 1774 Watt's early engines, like those of Newcomen, were used mainly to pump water from coal mines, as this nineteenth-century photograph suggests. The development of industrial archaeology has led to many open-air reconstructions and industrial museums. *(Hulton-Getty/Tony Stone Images)*

saw why the Newcomen engine wasted so much energy: the cylinder was being heated and cooled for every single stroke of the piston. To remedy this problem, Watt added a separate condenser where the steam could be condensed without cooling the cylinder. This splendid invention greatly increased the efficiency of the steam engine.

To invent something in a laboratory is one thing; to make it a practical success is quite another. Watt needed skilled workers, precision parts, and capital, and the relatively advanced nature of the British economy proved essential. A partnership with a wealthy English toy-maker provided risk capital and a manufacturing plant. In the craft tradition of locksmiths, tinsmiths, and mill-wrights, Watt found skilled mechanics who could install, regulate, and repair his sophisticated engines. From ingenious manufacturers such as the cannon-maker John Wilkinson, who learned to bore cylinders

with a fair degree of accuracy, Watt was gradually able to purchase precision parts. This support allowed him to create an effective vacuum and regulate a complex engine. In more than twenty years of constant effort, Watt made many further improvements. By the late 1780s, the steam engine had become a practical and commercial success in Britain.

The steam engine of Watt and his followers was the Industrial Revolution's most fundamental advance in technology. For the first time in history, humanity had, at least for a few generations, almost unlimited power at its disposal. For the first time, inventors and engineers could devise and implement all kinds of power equipment to aid people in their work. For the first time, abundance was at least a possibility for ordinary men and women.

The steam engine was quickly put to use in several industries in Britain. It drained mines and made possible

James Nasmyth's Mighty Steam Hammer   Nasmyth's invention was the forerunner of the modern pile driver, and its successful introduction in 1832 epitomized the rapid development of steam power technology in Britain. In this painting by the inventor himself, workers manipulate a massive iron shaft being hammered into shape at Nasmyth's foundry near Manchester. *(Science & Society Picture Library, London)*

the production of ever more coal to feed steam engines elsewhere. The steam-power plant began to replace waterpower in the cotton-spinning mills during the 1780s, contributing greatly to that industry's phenomenal rise. Steam also took the place of waterpower in flour mills, in the malt mills used in breweries, in the flint mills supplying the china industry, and in the mills exported by Britain to the West Indies to crush sugar cane.

Steam power promoted important breakthroughs in other industries. The British iron industry was radically transformed. The use of powerful, steam-driven bellows in blast furnaces helped ironmakers switch over rapidly from limited charcoal to unlimited coke (which is made from coal) in the smelting of pig iron after 1770. In the 1780s, Henry Cort developed the puddling furnace, which allowed pig iron to be refined in turn with coke. Strong, skilled ironworkers—the puddlers—"cooked" molten pig iron in a great vat, raking off globs of refined iron for further processing. Cort also developed heavy-duty, steam-powered rolling mills, which were capable of spewing out finished iron in every shape and form.

The economic consequence of these technical innovations was a great boom in the British iron industry. In 1740 annual British iron production was only 17,000 tons. With the spread of coke smelting and the first impact of Cort's inventions, production reached 68,000 tons in 1788, 125,000 tons in 1796, and 260,000 tons in 1806. In 1844 Britain produced 3 million tons of iron. This was a truly amazing expansion. Once scarce and expensive, iron became the cheap, basic, indispensable building block of the economy.

The Coming of the Railroads

The second half of the eighteenth century saw extensive construction of hard and relatively smooth roads, particularly in France before the Revolution. Yet it was passenger traffic that benefited most from this construction. Overland shipment of freight, relying solely on horsepower, was still quite limited and frightfully expensive; shippers used rivers and canals for heavy freight whenever possible. It was logical, therefore, that inventors would try to use steam power.

As early as 1800, an American ran a "steamer on wheels" through city streets. Other experiments followed. In the 1820s, English engineers created steam cars capable of carrying fourteen passengers at ten miles an hour—as fast as the mail coach. But the noisy, heavy steam automobiles frightened passing horses and damaged themselves as well as the roads with their vibra-

tions. For the rest of the century, horses continued to reign on highways and city streets.

The coal industry had long been using plank roads and rails to move coal wagons within mines and at the surface. Rails reduced friction and allowed a horse or a human being to pull a heavier load. Thus once a rail capable of supporting a heavy locomotive was developed in 1816, all sorts of experiments with steam engines on rails went forward. In 1825 after ten years of work, George Stephenson built an effective locomotive. In 1830 his *Rocket* sped down the track of the just-completed Liverpool and Manchester Railway at sixteen miles per hour. This was the world's first important railroad, fittingly steaming in the heart of industrial England.

The line from Liverpool to Manchester was a financial as well as a technical success, and many private companies were quickly organized to build more rail lines. These companies had to get permission for their projects from Parliament and pay for the rights of way they needed; otherwise, their freedom was great. Within twenty years, they had completed the main trunk lines of Great Britain. Other countries were quick to follow.

The significance of the railroad was tremendous. The railroad dramatically reduced the cost and uncertainty of shipping freight overland. This advance had many economic consequences. Previously, markets had tended to be small and local; as the barrier of high transportation costs was lowered, markets became larger and even nationwide. Larger markets encouraged larger factories with more sophisticated machinery in a growing number of industries. Such factories could make goods more cheaply and gradually subjected most cottage workers and many urban artisans to severe competitive pressures.

In all countries, the construction of railroads contributed to the growth of a class of urban workers. Cottage workers, farm laborers, and small peasants did not generally leave their jobs and homes to go directly to work in factories. However, the building of railroads created a strong demand for labor, especially unskilled labor, throughout a country. Hard work on construction gangs was done in the open air with animals and hand tools. Many landless farm laborers and poor peasants, long accustomed to leaving their villages for temporary employment, went to build railroads. By the time the work was finished, life back home in the village often seemed dull and unappealing, and many men drifted to towns in search of work—with the railroad companies, in construction, in factories. By the time they sent for their wives and sweethearts to join them, they had become urban workers.

Railroad Construction presented innumerable challenges, such as the building of bridges to span rivers and gorges. Civil engineers responded with impressive feats and their profession bounded ahead. This painting captures the inauguration of I. K. Brunel's Saltash Bridge, which crosses the Tamar River into Cornwall in southwest England. The high spans allow large ships to pass underneath. *(Elton Collection, Ironbridge Gorge Museum Trust)*

The railroad changed the outlook and values of the entire society. The last and culminating invention of the Industrial Revolution, the railroad dramatically revealed the power and increased the speed of the new age. Racing down a track at sixteen miles per hour or, by 1850, at a phenomenal fifty miles per hour was a new and awesome experience. As a French economist put it after a ride on the Liverpool and Manchester in 1833, "There are certain impressions that one cannot put into words!"

Some great painters, notably Joseph M. W. Turner (1775–1851) and Claude Monet (1840–1926), succeeded in expressing this sense of power and awe. So did the massive new train stations, the cathedrals of the industrial age. Leading railway engineers such as Isambard Kingdom Brunel and Thomas Brassey, whose tunnels pierced mountains and whose bridges spanned valleys, became public idols—the astronauts of their day. Everyday speech absorbed the images of railroading. After you got up a "full head of steam," you "highballed" along. And if you didn't "go off the track," you

might "toot your own whistle." The railroad fired the imagination.

Industry and Population

In 1851 London was the site of a famous industrial fair. This Great Exposition was held in the newly built Crystal Palace, an architectural masterpiece made entirely of glass and iron, both of which were now cheap and abundant. For the millions who visited, one fact stood out: the little island of Britain was the "workshop of the world." It alone produced two-thirds of the world's coal and more than one-half of its iron and cotton cloth. More generally, it has been carefully estimated that in 1860 Britain produced a truly remarkable 20 percent of the entire world's output of industrial goods, whereas it had produced only about 2 percent of the world total in 1750.[2] Experiencing revolutionary industrial change, Britain became the first industrial nation (Map 22.2).

As the British economy significantly increased its production of manufactured goods, the gross national product (GNP) rose roughly fourfold at constant prices between 1780 and 1851. In other words, the British people as a whole increased their wealth and their national income dramatically. At the same time, the population of Britain boomed, growing from about 9 million in 1780 to almost 21 million in 1851. Thus growing numbers consumed much of the increase in total production. According to one important study, average consumption per person increased by only 75 percent between 1780 and 1851, as the growth in the total population ate up a large part of the fourfold increase in GNP in those years.[3]

Although the question is still debated, many economic historians now believe that rapid population growth in Great Britain was not harmful because it facilitated industrial expansion. More people meant a more mobile labor force, with a wealth of young workers in need of employment and ready to go where the jobs were. Contemporaries were much less optimistic. In his famous and influential *Essay on the Principle of Population* (1798), Thomas Malthus (1766–1834) argued that population would always tend to grow faster than the food supply. In Malthus's opinion, the only hope of warding off such "positive checks" to population growth as war, famine, and disease was "prudential restraint." That is, young men and women had to limit the growth of population by the old tried-and-true means of marrying late in life. But Malthus was not optimistic about this possibility. The powerful attraction of the sexes would cause most people to marry early and have many children.

Wealthy English stockbroker and leading economist David Ricardo (1772–1823) coldly spelled out the pessimistic implications of Malthus's thought. Ricardo's depressing "iron law of wages" posited that because of the pressure of population growth, wages would always

---

The Crystal Palace   The Great Exhibition of 1851 attracted more than six million visitors, many of whom journeyed to London on the newly built railroads. Companies and countries displayed their products and juries awarded prizes in the strikingly modern Crystal Palace. Are today's malls really different? *(Courtesy of the Trustees of the British Museum)*

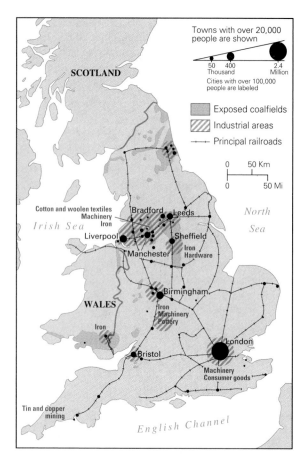

Towns with over 20,000
people are shown

50 400 2.4
Thousand Million

Cities with over 100,000
people are labeled

Exposed coalfields

Industrial areas

Principal railroads

0   50 Km

0   50 Mi

SCOTLAND

Irish Sea

Cotton and woolen textiles
Machinery
Iron

Bradford Leeds

Liverpool

Sheffield

Manchester

Iron
Hardware

North Sea

WALES

Birmingham

Iron
Machinery
Pottery

Iron

London

Bristol

Machinery
Consumer goods

Tin and copper
mining

English Channel

MAP 22.2 The Industrial Revolution in England, ca 1850 Industry concentrated in the rapidly growing cities of the north and the Midlands, where rich coal and iron deposits were in close proximity.

sink to subsistence level. That is, wages would be just high enough to keep workers from starving. With Malthus and Ricardo setting the tone, economics was soon dubbed "the dismal science."

Malthus, Ricardo, and their many followers were proved wrong—in the long run. However, as the great economist John Maynard Keynes quipped during the Great Depression of the 1930s, "we are all dead in the long run." Those who lived through the Industrial Revolution could not see the long run in advance. As modern quantitative studies show, until the 1820s, or even the 1840s, contemporary observers might reasonably have concluded that the economy and the total population were racing neck and neck, with the outcome very much in doubt. The closeness of the race added to the difficulties inherent in the unprecedented journey toward industrial civilization.

There was another problem as well. Perhaps workers, farmers, and ordinary people did not get their rightful share of the new wealth. Perhaps only the rich got richer, while the poor got poorer or made no progress. We will turn to this great issue after looking at the process of industrialization in continental countries in the nineteenth century.

INDUSTRIALIZATION IN CONTINENTAL EUROPE

The new technologies developed in the British Industrial Revolution were adopted rather slowly by businesses in continental Europe. Yet by the end of the nineteenth century, several European countries as well as the United States had also industrialized their economies to a considerable but variable degree. This meant that the process of Western industrialization proceeded gradually, with uneven jerks and national (and regional) variations.

Scholars are still struggling to explain these variations, especially since good answers may offer valuable lessons in our own time for poor countries seeking to improve their material condition through industrialization and economic development. The latest findings on the Western experience are encouraging. They suggest that there were alternative paths to the industrial world in the nineteenth century and that, today as then, there was no need to follow a rigid, predetermined British model.

National Variations

European industrialization, like most economic developments, requires some statistical analysis as part of the effort to understand it. Comparative data on industrial production in different countries over time help give us an overview of what happened. One set of data, the work of a Swiss scholar, compares the level of industrialization on a per capita basis in several countries from 1750 to 1913. These data are far from perfect because there are gaps in the underlying records. But they reflect basic trends and are presented in Table 22.1 for closer study.

As the heading of Table 22.1 makes clear, this is a per capita comparison of levels of industrialization—a comparison of how much industrial product was available, on average, to each person in a given country in a given year. Therefore, all the numbers in Table 22.1 are expressed in terms of a single index number of 100, which

TABLE 22.1   PER CAPITA LEVELS OF INDUSTRIALIZATION, 1750–1913

	1750	1800	1830	1860	1880	1900	1913
Great Britain	10	16	25	64	87	100	115
Belgium	9	10	14	28	43	56	88
United States	4	9	14	21	38	69	126
France	9	9	12	20	28	39	59
Germany	8	8	9	15	25	52	85
Austria-Hungary	7	7	8	11	15	23	32
Italy	8	8	8	10	12	17	26
Russia	6	6	7	8	10	15	20
China	8	6	6	4	4	3	3
India	7	6	6	3	2	1	2

Note: All entries are based on an index value of 100, equal to the per capita level of industrialization in Great Britain in 1900.

Source: P. Bairoch, "International Industrialization Levels from 1750 to 1980," *Journal of European Economic History* 11 (Fall 1982): 294. Data for Great Britain are actually for the United Kingdom, thereby including Ireland with England, Wales, and Scotland. Reprinted with permission.

equals the per capita level of industrial goods in Great Britain (and Ireland) in 1900. Every number is thus a percentage of the 1900 level in Britain and is directly comparable. The countries are listed in roughly the order that they began to use large-scale, power-driven technology.

What does this overview of European industrialization tell us? First, and very significantly, one sees that in 1750 all countries were fairly close together and that Britain was only slightly ahead of its archenemy, France. Second, Britain had opened up a noticeable lead over all continental countries by 1800, and that gap progressively widened as the British Industrial Revolution accelerated to 1830 and reached full maturity by 1860. The British level of per capita industrialization was twice the French level in 1830, for example, and more than three times the French level in 1860. All other large countries (except the United States) had fallen even further behind Britain than France had at both dates. Sophisticated quantitative history confirms the

primacy and relative rapidity of Britain's Industrial Revolution.

Third, variations in the timing and in the extent of industrialization in the continental powers and the United States are also apparent. Belgium, independent in 1831 and rich in iron and coal, led in adopting Britain's new technology. France developed factory production more gradually, and most historians now detect no burst in French mechanization and no acceleration in the growth of overall industrial output that may accurately be called revolutionary. They stress instead France's relatively good pattern of early industrial growth, which was unjustly tarnished by the spectacular rise of Germany and the United States after 1860. By 1913 Germany was rapidly closing in on Britain, while the United States had already passed the first industrial nation in per capita production.

Finally, all European states (as well as the United States, Canada, and Japan) managed to raise per capita industrial levels in the nineteenth century. These continent-wide increases stood in stark contrast to the large and tragic decreases that occurred at the same time in most non-Western countries, most notably in China and India. European countries industrialized to a greater or lesser extent even as most of the non-Western world *de*-industrialized. Thus differential rates of wealth- and power-creating industrial development, which heightened disparities within Europe, also greatly magnified existing inequalities between Europe and the rest of the world. We shall return to this momentous change in Chapter 26.

The Challenge of Industrialization

The different patterns of industrial development suggest that the process of industrialization was far from automatic. Indeed, building modern industry was an awesome challenge. To be sure, throughout Europe the eighteenth century was an era of agricultural improvement, population increase, expanding foreign trade, and growing cottage industry. Great Britain led in these developments, but other countries participated in the general trend. Thus when the pace of British industry began to accelerate in the 1780s, continental businesses began to adopt the new methods as they proved their profitability. British industry enjoyed clear superiority, but at first the continent was close behind.

By 1815, however, the situation was quite different. In spite of wartime difficulties, British industry maintained the momentum of the 1780s and continued to grow and improve between 1789 and 1815. On the continent, the unending political and economic upheavals that began with the French Revolution had another effect: they disrupted trade, created runaway inflation, and fostered social anxiety. War severed normal communications between Britain and the continent, severely handicapping continental efforts to use new British machinery and technology. Moreover, the years from 1789 to 1815 were, even for the privileged French economy receiving special favors from Napoleon, a time of "national catastrophe"—in the graphic words of a leading French scholar.[4] Thus whatever the French Revolution and the Napoleonic era meant politically, economically and industrially they meant that France and the rest of Europe were further behind Britain in 1815 than in 1789.

This widening gap made it more difficult, if not impossible, for other countries to follow the British pattern in energy and industry after peace was restored in 1815. Above all, in the newly mechanized industries, British goods were being produced very economically, and these goods had come to dominate world markets

completely while the continental states were absorbed in war between 1792 and 1815. Continental firms had little hope of competing with mass-produced British goods in foreign markets for a long time. In addition, British technology had become so advanced and complicated that very few engineers or skilled technicians outside England understood it. Moreover, the technology of steam power had grown much more expensive. It involved large investments in the iron and coal industries and, after 1830, required the existence of railroads, which were very costly. Continental business people had great difficulty finding the large sums of money the new methods demanded, and there was a shortage of laborers accustomed to working in factories. Landowners and government officials were often so suspicious of the new form of industry and the changes it brought that they did little at first to encourage it. All these disadvantages slowed the spread of modern industry (Map 22.3).

After 1815, however, when continental countries began to face up to the British challenge, they had at least three important advantages. First, most continental countries had a rich tradition of putting-out enterprise, merchant capitalists, and skilled urban artisans. Such a tradition gave continental firms the ability to adapt and survive in the face of new market conditions. Second, continental capitalists did not need to develop, ever so slowly and expensively, their own advanced technology. Instead, they could simply "borrow" the new methods developed in Great Britain as well as engineers and some of the financial resources these countries lacked. European countries such as France and Russia also had a third asset that many non-Western areas lacked in the nineteenth century. They had strong independent governments, which did not fall under foreign political control. These governments could fashion economic policies to serve their own interests, as they proceeded to do. They would eventually use the power of the state to promote industry and catch up with Britain.

Agents of Industrialization

The British realized the great value of their technical discoveries and tried to keep their secrets to themselves. Until 1825 it was illegal for artisans and skilled mechanics to leave Britain; until 1843 the export of textile machinery and other equipment was forbidden. Many talented, ambitious workers, however, slipped out of the country illegally and introduced the new methods abroad.

One such man was William Cockerill, a Lancashire carpenter. He and his sons began building cotton-

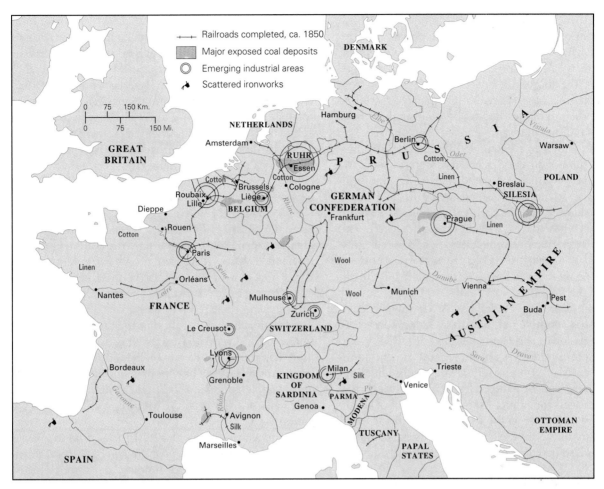

MAP 22.3 Continental Industrialization, ca 1850 Although continental countries were beginning to make progress by 1850, they still lagged far behind Britain. For example, continental railroad building was still in an early stage, whereas the British rail system was essentially complete.

spinning equipment in French-occupied Belgium in 1799. In 1817 the most famous son, John Cockerill, purchased the old summer palace of the deposed bishops of Liège in southern Belgium. Cockerill converted the palace into a large industrial enterprise, which produced machinery, steam engines, and then railway locomotives. He also established modern ironworks and coal mines.

Cockerill's plants in the Liège area became an industrial nerve center, continually gathering new information and transmitting it across Europe. Many skilled British workers came illegally to work for Cockerill, and some went on to found their own companies throughout Europe. Newcomers brought the latest plans and secrets, so Cockerill could boast that ten days after an industrial advance occurred in Britain, he knew all

about it in Belgium. Thus British technicians and skilled workers were a powerful force in the spread of early industrialization.

A second agent of industrialization were talented entrepreneurs such as Fritz Harkort, a business pioneer in the German machinery industry. Serving in England as a Prussian army officer during the Napoleonic wars, Harkort was impressed and enchanted with what he saw. He concluded that Germany had to match all these English achievements as quickly as possible. Setting up shop in an abandoned castle in the still-tranquil Ruhr Valley, Harkort felt an almost religious calling to build steam engines and become the "Watt of Germany."

Harkort's basic idea was simple, but it was enormously difficult to carry out. Lacking skilled laborers to do the job, Harkort turned to England for experienced, though expensive, mechanics. He could not be choosy, and he longed for the day when he could afford to replace the haughty foreigners with his fellow Germans. Getting materials also posed a great problem. He had to import the thick iron boilers that he needed from England at great cost. Moreover, German roads were so bad that steam engines had to be built at the works, completely dismantled and shipped piece by piece to the buyer, and then reassembled by Harkort's technicians. In spite of all these problems, Harkort built and sold engines, winning fame and praise. His ambitious efforts over sixteen years also resulted in large financial losses for himself and his partners, and in 1832 he was forced out of his company by his financial backers, who cut back operations to reduce losses. His career illustrates both the great efforts of a few important business leaders to duplicate the British achievement and the difficulty of the task.

Entrepreneurs like Harkort were obviously exceptional. Most continental businesses adopted factory technology slowly, and handicraft methods lived on. Indeed, as recent research on France has shown, continental industrialization usually brought substantial but uneven expansion of handicraft industry in both rural and urban areas for a time. Artisan production of luxury items grew in France as the rising income of the international middle class created foreign demand for silk scarfs, embroidered needlework, perfumes, and fine wines.

A third force for industrialization was government, which often helped business people in continental countries to overcome some of their difficulties. Tariff protection was one such support. For example, after Napoleon's wars ended in 1815, France was suddenly flooded with cheaper and better British goods. The French government responded by laying high tariffs on many British imports in order to protect the French economy. After 1815 continental governments bore the cost of building roads and canals to improve transportation.

They also bore to a significant extent the cost of building railroads. Belgium led the way in the 1830s and 1840s. In an effort to tie the newly independent nation together, the Belgian government decided to construct a state-owned system. Built rapidly as a unified network, Belgium's state-owned railroads stimulated the development of heavy industry and made the country an early industrial leader. Several of the smaller German states also built state systems.

The Prussian government provided another kind of invaluable support. It guaranteed that the state treasury would pay the interest and principal on railroad bonds if the closely regulated private companies in Prussia were unable to do so. Thus railroad investors in Prussia ran little risk, and capital was quickly raised. In France the state shouldered all the expense of acquiring and laying roadbed, including bridges and tunnels. Finished roadbed was leased to a carefully supervised private company, which usually benefited from a state guarantee of its debts and which needed to provide only the rails, cars, and management. In short, governments helped pay for railroads, the all-important leading sector in continental industrialization.

The career of German journalist and thinker Friedrich List (1789–1846) reflects government's greater role in industrialization on the continent than in England. List considered the growth of modern industry of the utmost importance because manufacturing was a primary means of increasing people's well-being and relieving their poverty. Moreover, List was a dedicated nationalist. He wrote that the "wider the gap between the backward and advanced nations becomes, the more dangerous it is to remain behind." For an agricultural nation was not only poor but also weak, increasingly unable to defend itself and maintain its political independence. To promote industry was to defend the nation.

The practical policies that List focused on in articles and in his influential *National System of Political Economy* (1841) were railroad building and the tariff. List supported the formation of a customs union, or *Zollverein,* among the separate German states. Such a tariff union came into being in 1834. Building on the successful elimination of all internal tariffs in Prussia in 1818, the new customs union allowed goods to move between the German member states without tariffs, and a single uniform tariff was erected against all other nations. List wanted a high protective tariff, which would encourage infant industries, allowing them to develop and eventually hold their own against their more advanced British counterparts. List denounced the British doctrine of free trade as little more than Britain's attempt "to make the rest of the world, like the Hindus, its serfs in all industrial and commercial relations." By the 1840s List's economic nationalism had become increasingly popular in Germany and elsewhere.

Finally, banks, like governments, also played a larger and more creative role on the continent than in England. Previously, almost all banks in Europe had been private, organized as secretive partnerships. All the active partners were liable for all the debts of the firm, which meant that in the event of a disastrous bank-

A German Ironworks, 1850   This big business enterprise has mastered the new British method of smelting iron with coke. Germany, and especially the state of Prussia, was well endowed with both iron and coal, and the rapid exploitation of these resources after 1840 transformed a poor agricultural country into an industrial powerhouse. *(Deutsches Museum Munich)*

ruptcy, each partner could lose all of his or her personal wealth in addition to all the money invested in the partnership. Because of the possibility of unlimited financial loss, the partners of private banks tended to be quite conservative and were content to deal with a few rich clients and a few big merchants. They generally avoided industrial investment as being too risky.

In the 1830s, two important Belgian banks pioneered in a new direction. They received permission from the growth-oriented government to establish themselves as corporations enjoying limited liability. That is, a stockholder could lose only his or her original investment in the bank's common stock and could not be assessed for any additional losses. Publicizing the risk-reducing advantage of limited liability, these Belgian banks were able to attract many shareholders, large and small. They mobilized impressive resources for investment in big industrial companies, became industrial banks, and successfully promoted industrial development.

Similar corporate banks became important in France and Germany in the 1850s and 1860s. Usually working in collaboration with governments, they established and developed many railroads and many companies working in heavy industry, which were increasingly organized as limited liability corporations. The most famous such bank was the Crédit Mobilier of Paris, founded by Isaac and Emile Pereire, two young Jewish journalists from Bordeaux. The Crédit Mobilier advertised extensively. It used the savings of thousands of small investors as well as the resources of big ones. The activities of the bank were far-reaching; it built railroads all over France and Europe. As Emile Pereire had said in 1835, "It is not enough to outline gigantic programs on paper. I must write my ideas on the earth."

The combined efforts of skilled workers, entrepreneurs, governments, and industrial banks meshed successfully between 1850 and the financial crash of 1873. This was a period of unprecedentedly rapid economic growth on the continent. In Belgium, Germany, and

France, key indicators of modern industrial development—such as railway mileage, iron and coal production, and steam-engine capacity—increased at average annual rates of 5 to 10 percent compounded. As a result, rail networks were completed in western and much of central Europe, and the leading continental countries mastered the industrial technologies that had first been developed in Great Britain. In the early 1870s, Britain was still Europe's most industrial nation, but a select handful of countries were closing the gap that had been opened up by the Industrial Revolution.

 ## CAPITAL AND LABOR

Industrial development brought new social relations and intensified long-standing problems between capital and labor in both urban workshops and cottage industry (see pages 640–644). A new group of factory owners and industrial capitalists arose. These men and women and their families strengthened the wealth and size of the middle class, which had previously been made up mainly of merchants and professional people. The nineteenth century became the golden age of the middle class. Modern industry also created a much larger group, the factory workers. For the first time, large numbers of men, women, and children came together under one roof to work with complicated machinery for a single owner or a few partners in large companies.

The growth of new occupational groups in industry stimulated new thinking about social relations. Often combined with reflections on the French Revolution, this thinking led to the development of a new overarching interpretation—a new paradigm—regarding social relationships (see Chapter 23). Briefly, this paradigm argued, with considerable success, that individuals were members of economically determined classes, which had conflicting interests. Accordingly, the comfortable, well-educated "public" of the eighteenth century came increasingly to see itself as the backbone of the middle class (or the middle classes), and the "people" gradually transformed themselves into the modern working class (or working classes). And if the new class interpretation was more of a deceptive simplification than a fundamental truth for some critics, it appealed to many because it seemed to explain what was happening. Therefore, conflicting classes existed, in part, because many individuals came to believe they existed and developed an appropriate sense of class feeling—what Marxists call "class consciousness."

What, then, was the relationship between capital and labor in the early Industrial Revolution? Did the new industrial middle class ruthlessly exploit the workers, as Karl Marx and others have charged?

The New Class of Factory Owners

Early industrialists operated in a highly competitive economic system. As the careers of Watt and Harkort illustrate, there were countless production problems, and success and large profits were by no means certain. Manufacturers therefore waged a constant battle to cut their production costs and stay afloat. Much of the profit had to go back into the business for new and better machinery. "Dragged on by the frenzy of this terrible life," according to one of the dismayed critics, the struggling manufacturer had "no time for niceties. He must conquer or die, make a fortune or drown himself."[5]

Most early industrialists drew upon their families and friends for labor and capital, but they came from a variety of backgrounds. Many, such as Harkort, were from well-established merchant families, which provided a rich network of contacts and support. Others, such as Watt and Cockerill, were of modest means, especially in the early days. Artisans and skilled workers of exceptional ability had unparalleled opportunities. Members of ethnic and religious groups who had been discriminated against in the traditional occupations controlled by the landed aristocracy jumped at the new chances and often helped each other. Scots, Quakers, and other Protestant dissenters were tremendously important in Britain; Protestants and Jews dominated banking in Catholic France. Many of the industrialists were newly rich, and, not surprisingly, they were very proud and self-satisfied.

As factories and firms grew larger, opportunities declined, at least in well-developed industries. It became considerably harder for a gifted but poor young mechanic to start a small enterprise and end up as a wealthy manufacturer. Formal education (for sons and males) became more important as a means of success and advancement, and formal education at the advanced level was expensive. In Britain by 1830 and in France and Germany by 1860, leading industrialists were more likely to have inherited their well-established enterprises, and they were financially much more secure than their struggling fathers and mothers had been. They also had a greater sense of class consciousness, fully aware that ongoing industrial development had widened the gap between themselves and their workers.

The Third-Class Carriage   The French artist Honoré Daumier was fascinated by the railroad and its human significance. This great painting focuses on the peasant grandmother, absorbed in memories. The nursing mother represents love and creativity, the sleeping boy innocence. *(The Metropolitan Museum of Art. Bequest of Mrs. H. O. Havemeyer, 1929. The H. O. Havemeyer Collection [29.100.129])*

The wives and daughters of successful businessmen also found fewer opportunities for active participation in Europe's increasingly complex business world. Rather than contributing as vital partners in a family-owned enterprise, as so many middle-class women such as Elizabeth Strutt had done (see the feature "Individuals in Society: The Strutts: Family Enterprise in Action"), these women were increasingly valued for their ladylike gentility. By 1850 some influential women writers and most businessmen assumed that middle-class wives and daughters should steer clear of undignified work in offices and factories. Rather, a middle-class lady should protect and enhance her femininity. She should concentrate on her proper role as wife and mother, preferably in an elegant residential area far removed from ruthless commerce and the volatile working class.

The New Factory Workers

The social consequences of the Industrial Revolution have long been hotly debated. The condition of British workers during the transformation has always generated the most controversy among historians because Britain was the first country to industrialize and because the social consequences seemed harshest there. Before 1850 other countries had not proceeded very far with industrialization, and almost everyone agrees that the eco-

Individuals in Society

The Strutts: Family Enterprise in Action

For centuries economic life in Europe revolved around hundreds of thousands of small family enterprises. These family enterprises worked farms, crafted products, and traded goods. They built and operated the firms and factories of the early industrialization era, with the notable exceptions of the capital-hungry railroads and a few big banks. Indeed, until late in the nineteenth century, close-knit family groups continued to control most successful businesses, including those organized as corporations.

One successful and fairly well-documented family enterprise began with the marriage of Jedediah Strutt (1726–1797) and Elizabeth Woollat (1729–1774) in Derbyshire in northern England in 1755. The son of a farmer, Jedediah fell in love with Elizabeth when he was apprenticed away from home as a wheelwright and lodged with her parents. Both young people grew up in the close-knit dissenting Protestant community, which did not accept the doctrines of the state-sponsored Church of England, and the well-educated Elizabeth worked in a local school for dissenters and then for a dissenter minister in London. Indecisive and self-absorbed, Jedediah inherited in 1754 a small stock of animals from an uncle and finally married Elizabeth the following year.

Aided by Elizabeth, who was "obviously a very capable woman" and who supplied some of the drive her husband had previously lacked, Jedediah embarked on a new career.[1] He invented a machine to make handsome, neat-fitting ribbed silk stockings, which had previously been made by hand. He secured a patent, despite strong opposition from competitors, and went into production. Elizabeth helped constantly in the enterprise, which was nothing less than an informal partnership between husband and wife.[2]

In 1757, for example, when Jedediah was fighting to uphold his patent in the local court, Elizabeth left her son of nine months and journeyed to London to seek a badly needed loan from her former employer. She also canvassed her London relatives and dissenter friends for orders for stockings and looked for sales agents and sources of capital. Elizabeth's letters reveal a detailed knowledge of ribbed stockings and the prices and quality of different kinds of thread. The family biographers, old-line economic historians writing without a trace of feminist concerns, conclude that her husband "owed much of his success to her energy and counsel." Elizabeth was always "active in the business—a partner in herself."[3] Historians have often overlooked such invaluable contributions from wives like Elizabeth, partly because the legal rights and consequences of partnership were denied to married women in Britain and Europe in the eighteenth and nineteenth centuries.

Jedediah Strutt; painting ca 1790 by Joseph Wright of Derby. *(Derby Museum & Art Gallery/The Bridgeman Art Library, London/New York)*

The Strutt enterprise grew and gradually prospered, but it always retained its family character. The firm built a large silk mill and then went into cotton spinning in partnership with Richard Arkwright, the inventor of the water frame (see page 727). The brothers of both Jedediah and Elizabeth worked for the firm, and their eldest daughter worked long hours in the warehouse. Bearing three sons, Elizabeth fulfilled yet another vital task because the typical family firm looked to its own members for managers and continued success. All three sons entered the business and became cotton textile magnates. Elizabeth never saw these triumphs. The loyal and talented wife in the family partnership died suddenly at age forty-five while in London with Jedediah on a business trip.

Questions for Analysis

1. How and why did the Strutts succeed?
2. What does Elizabeth's life tell us about the role of British women in the early Industrial Revolution?

1. R. Fitton and A. Wadsworth, *The Strutts and the Arkwrights, 1758–1830: A Study of the Early Factory System* (Manchester, England: Manchester University Press, 1958), p. 23.
2. See the excellent discussion by C. Hall, "Strains in the 'Firm of Wife, Children and Friends'? Middle-Class Women and Employment in Early Nineteenth-Century England," in P. Hudson and W. Lee, eds., *Women's Work and the Family Economy in Historical Perspective* (Manchester, England: Manchester University Press, 1990), pp. 106–132.
3. Fitton and Wadsworth, *The Strutts*, pp. 110–111.

nomic conditions of European workers improved after 1850. The countries that followed Britain were able to benefit from British experience in social as well as technical matters. Thus the experience of British workers to about 1850 deserves special attention. (Industrial growth also promoted rapid urbanization, with its own awesome problems, as will be shown in Chapter 24.)

From the beginning, the Industrial Revolution in Britain had its critics. Among the first were the romantic poets. William Blake (1757–1827) called the early factories "satanic mills" and protested against the hard life of the London poor. William Wordsworth (1770–1850) lamented the destruction of the rural way of life and the pollution of the land and water. Some handicraft workers—notably the Luddites, who attacked whole factories in northern England in 1812 and after—smashed the new machines, which they believed were putting them out of work. Doctors and reformers wrote eloquently of problems in the factories and new towns, while Malthus and Ricardo concluded that workers would earn only enough to stay alive.

This pessimistic view was accepted and reinforced by Friedrich Engels (1820–1895), the future revolutionary and colleague of Karl Marx. After studying conditions in northern England, this young middle-class German published in 1844 *The Condition of the Working Class in England,* a blistering indictment of the middle classes. "At the bar of world opinion," he wrote, "I charge the English middle classes with mass murder, wholesale robbery, and all the other crimes in the calendar."[6] The new poverty of industrial workers was worse than the old poverty of cottage workers and agricultural laborers, according to Engels. The culprit was industrial capitalism, with its relentless competition and constant technical change. Engels's extremely influential charge of middle-class exploitation and increasing worker poverty was embellished by Marx and later socialists.

Meanwhile, other observers believed that conditions were improving for the working people. Andrew Ure wrote in 1835 in his study of the cotton industry that conditions in most factories were not harsh and were even quite good. Edwin Chadwick, a great and conscientious government official well acquainted with the problems of the working population, concluded that the "whole mass of the laboring community" was increasingly able "to buy more of the necessities and minor luxuries of life."[7] Nevertheless, if all the contemporary assessments had been counted up, those who thought conditions were getting worse for working people would probably have been the majority.

In an attempt to go beyond the contradictory judgments of contemporaries, some historians have looked at different kinds of sources. Statistical evidence is one such source. If working people suffered a great economic decline, as Engels and later socialists asserted, then they must have bought less and less food, clothing, and other necessities as time went on. The purchasing power of the working person's wages must have declined drastically.

Scholarly statistical studies, which continue to multiply rapidly in an age of easy calculations with computer technology, have weakened the idea that the condition of the working class got much worse with industrialization. But the most recent studies also confirm the view that the early years of the Industrial Revolution were hard ones for British workers. There was little or no increase in the purchasing power of the average British worker from about 1780 to about 1820. The years from 1792 to 1815, a period of almost constant warfare with France, were particularly difficult. Food prices rose faster than wages, and the living conditions of the laboring poor declined. Only after 1820, and especially after 1840, did real wages rise substantially, so that the average worker earned and consumed roughly 50 percent more in real terms in 1850 than in 1770.[8] In short, there was considerable economic improvement for workers throughout Great Britain by 1850, but that improvement was hard won and slow in coming.

This important conclusion must be qualified, however. Increased purchasing power meant more goods, but not necessarily greater happiness. More goods may have provided meager compensation for work that was dangerous and monotonous, for example. Also, statistical studies do not say anything about how the level of unemployment may have risen for the simple reason that there are no good unemployment statistics from this period. Furthermore, the hours in the average workweek increased; to an unknown extent, workers earned more simply because they worked more. Finally, the wartime decline was of great importance. The war years were formative years for the new factory labor force. They were also some of the hardest yet experienced. They colored the early experience of modern industrial life in somber tones.

Another way to consider the workers' standard of living is to look at the goods that they purchased. Again the evidence is somewhat contradictory. Speaking generally, workers ate somewhat more food of higher nutritional quality as the Industrial Revolution progressed, except during wartime. Diets became more varied; people ate more potatoes, dairy products, fruits, and vegetables. Clothing improved, but housing for working people probably deteriorated somewhat. In short, per capita use of specific goods supports the position that the standard of living of the working classes rose, at least moderately, after the long wars with France.

Conditions of Work

What about working conditions? Did workers eventually earn more only at the cost of working longer and harder? Were workers exploited harshly by the new factory owners?

The first factories were cotton mills, which began functioning along rivers and streams in the 1770s. Cottage workers, accustomed to the putting-out system, were reluctant to work in factories even when they received relatively good wages because factory work was different from what they were used to and was unappealing. In the factory, workers had to keep up with the machine and follow its tempo. They had to show up every day and work long, monotonous hours. Factory workers had to adjust their daily lives to the shrill call of the factory whistle.

Cottage workers were not used to that kind of life and discipline. All members of the family worked hard and long, but in spurts, setting their own pace. They could interrupt their work when they wanted to. Women and children could break up their long hours of spinning with other tasks. On Saturday afternoon the head of the family delivered the week's work to the merchant manufacturer and got paid. Saturday night was a time of relaxation and drinking, especially for the men. Recovering from his hangover on Tuesday, the weaver bent to his task on Wednesday and then worked frantically to meet his deadline on Saturday. Like some students today, he might "pull an all-nighter" on Thursday or Friday in order to get his work in.

Also, early factories resembled English poorhouses, where totally destitute people went to live on welfare. Some poorhouses were industrial prisons, where the inmates had to work in order to receive their food and lodging. The similarity between large brick factories and large stone poorhouses increased the cottage workers' fear of factories and their hatred of factory discipline.

It was cottage workers' reluctance to work in factories that prompted the early cotton mill owners to turn to abandoned and pauper children for their labor. As we have seen, these owners contracted with local officials to employ large numbers of these children, who had no say in the matter. Pauper children were often badly treated and terribly overworked in the mills, as they were when they were apprenticed as chimney sweeps, market girls, shoemakers, and so forth. In the eighteenth century, semiforced child labor seemed necessary and was socially accepted. From our modern point of view, it was cruel exploitation and a blot on the record of the new industrial system.

By 1790 the early pattern was rapidly changing. The use of pauper apprentices was in decline, and in 1802 it was forbidden by Parliament. Many more factories were being built, mainly in urban areas, where they could use steam power rather than waterpower and attract a workforce more easily than in the countryside. The need for workers was great. Indeed, people came from near and far to work in the cities, both as factory workers and as laborers, builders, and domestic servants. Yet as they took these new jobs, working people did not simply give in to a system of labor that had formerly repelled them. Rather, they helped modify the system by carrying over old, familiar working traditions.

For one thing, they often came to the mills and the mines as family units. This was how they had worked on farms and in the putting-out system. The mill or mine owner bargained with the head of the family and paid him or her for the work of the whole family. In the cotton mills, children worked for their mothers or fathers, collecting wastes and "piecing" broken threads together. In the mines, children sorted coal and worked the ventilation equipment. Their mothers hauled coal in the tunnels below the surface, while their fathers hewed with pick and shovel at the face of the seam.

The preservation of the family as an economic unit in the factories from the 1790s on made the new surroundings more tolerable, both in Great Britain and in other countries, during the early stages of industrialization. Parents disciplined their children, making firm measures socially acceptable, and directed their upbringing. The presence of the whole family meant that children and adults worked the same long hours (twelve-hour shifts were normal in cotton mills in 1800). In the early years, some very young children were employed solely to keep the family together. Jedediah Strutt, for example, believed children should be at least ten years old to work in his mills, but he reluctantly employed seven-year-olds to satisfy their parents. Adult workers were not particularly interested in limiting the minimum working age or hours of their children as long as family members worked side by side. Only when technical changes threatened to place control and discipline in the hands of impersonal managers and foremen did adult workers protest against inhuman conditions in the name of their children.

Some enlightened employers and social reformers in Parliament definitely felt otherwise. They argued that more humane standards were necessary, and they used widely circulated parliamentary reports to influence

Cotton Mill Workers   Family members often worked side by side in early British factories, and the child on the left is quite possibly the daughter of the woman nearby. They are combing raw cotton and drawing it into loose strands called rovings, which will be spun into fine thread on the machines to the right. *(Mary Evans Picture Library)*

public opinion. (See the feature "Listening to the Past: The Testimony of Young Mining Workers" on pages 752–753) For example, Robert Owen (1771–1858), a very successful manufacturer in Scotland, testified in 1816 before an investigating committee on the basis of his experience. He stated that "very strong facts" demonstrated that employing children under ten years of age as factory workers was "injurious to the children, and not beneficial to the proprietors." The parliamentary committee asked him to explain, and the testimony proceeded as follows:

"Seventeen years ago, a number of individuals, with myself, purchased the New Lanark establishment from the late Mr Dale, of Glasgow. At that period I find that there were 500 children, who had been taken from poor-houses, chiefly in Edinburgh. . . . The hours of work at that time were thirteen, inclusive of meal times, and an hour and a half was allowed for meals. I very soon discovered that although those children were very well fed, well clothed, well

lodged, and very great care taken of them when out of the mills, their growth and their minds were materially injured by being employed at those ages within the cotton mills for eleven and a half hours per day. . . . Their limbs were generally deformed, their growth was stunted, and although one of the best school-masters upon the old plan was engaged to instruct those children every night, in general they made but a very slow progress, even in learning the common alphabet. . . ."

"Do you think the age of ten the best period for the admission of children into full and constant employment for ten or eleven hours per day, within woollen, cotton, and other mills or manufactories?"

"I do not."

"What other period would you recommend for their full admission to full work?"

"Twelve years."[9]

Owen's testimony rang true because he had already raised the age of employment in his mills and was promoting education for young children. Workers also provided graphic testimony at such hearings as the reformers pressed Parliament to pass corrective laws. They scored some important successes.

Their most significant early accomplishment was the Factory Act of 1833. It limited the factory workday for children between nine and thirteen to eight hours and that of adolescents between fourteen and eighteen to twelve hours, although the act made no effort to regulate the hours of work for children at home or in small businesses. The law also prohibited the factory employment of children under nine; they were to be enrolled in the elementary schools that factory owners were required to establish. The employment of children declined rapidly. Thus the Factory Act broke the pattern of whole families working together in the factory because efficiency required standardized shifts for all workers.

Ties of blood and kinship were important in other ways in Great Britain in the formative years between about 1790 and 1840. Many manufacturers and builders hired workers through subcontractors. They paid the subcontractors on the basis of what the subcontractors and their crews produced—for smelting so many tons of pig iron or moving so much dirt or gravel for a canal or roadbed. Subcontractors in turn hired and fired their own workers, many of whom were friends and relations. The subcontractor might be as harsh as the greediest capitalist, but the relationship between subcontractor and work crew was close and personal. This kind of personal relationship had traditionally existed in cottage industry and in urban crafts, and it was more acceptable to many workers than impersonal factory discipline. This system also provided people with an easy way to find a job. Even today, a friend or relative who is a supervisor is frequently worth a hundred formal application forms.

Ties of kinship were particularly important for newcomers, who often traveled great distances to find work. Many urban workers in Great Britain were from Ireland. Forced out of rural Ireland by population growth and deteriorating economic conditions from 1817 on, Irish in search of jobs could not be choosy; they took what they could get. As early as 1824, most of the workers in the Glasgow cotton mills were Irish; in 1851 one-sixth of the population of Liverpool was Irish. Even when Irish workers were not related directly by blood, they were held together by ethnic and religious ties. Like other immigrant groups elsewhere, they worked together, formed their own neighborhoods, and not only survived but also thrived.

The Sexual Division of Labor

The era of the Industrial Revolution witnessed major changes in the sexual division of labor. In preindustrial Europe most people generally worked in family units. By tradition, certain jobs were defined by sex—women and girls for milking and spinning, men and boys for plowing and weaving. But many tasks might go to either sex because particular circumstances dictated a family's response in its battle for economic survival. This pattern of family employment carried over into early factories and subcontracting, but it collapsed as child labor was restricted and new attitudes emerged. A different sexual division of labor gradually arose to take its place. The man emerged as the family's primary wage earner, while the woman found only limited job opportunities. Generally denied good jobs at good wages in the growing urban economy, women were expected to concentrate on unpaid housework, child care, and craftwork at home.

This new pattern of "separate spheres" had several aspects. First, all studies agree that married women from the working classes were much less likely to work full-time for wages outside the house after the first child arrived, although they often earned small amounts doing putting-out handicrafts at home and taking in boarders. Second, when married women did work for wages outside the house, they usually came from the poorest, most desperate families, where the husbands were poorly paid, sick, unemployed, or missing. Third, these poor married (or widowed) women were joined by legions of young unmarried women, who worked full-time but only in certain jobs. Fourth, all women were generally confined to low-paying, dead-end jobs. Virtually no occupation open to women paid a wage sufficient for a person to live independently. Men predominated in the better-paying, more promising employments. Evolving gradually as family labor declined, but largely in place in the urban sector of the British economy by 1850, the new sexual division of labor constituted a major development in the history of women and of the family.

If the reorganization of paid work along gender lines is widely recognized, there is as yet no agreement on its causes. One school of scholars sees little connection with industrialization and finds the answer in the deeply ingrained sexist attitudes of a "patriarchal tradition," which predated the economic transformation. These scholars stress the role of male-dominated craft unions in denying workingwomen access to good jobs and in reducing them to unpaid maids dependent on their husbands. Other scholars, believing that the gender roles of women and men can vary enormously with time and culture, look more to a combination of economic and biological factors in order to explain why the mass of women were either unwilling or unable to halt the emergence of a sex-segregated division of labor.

Three ideas stand out in this more recent interpretation. First, the new and unfamiliar discipline of the clock and the machine was especially hard on married women of the laboring classes. Above all, relentless factory discipline conflicted with child care in a way that labor on the farm or in the cottage had not. A woman operating earsplitting spinning machinery could mind a child of seven or eight working beside her (until such work was outlawed), but she could no longer pace herself through pregnancy, even though overwork during pregnancy heightened the already high risks of childbirth. Nor could a woman breast-feed her baby on the job, although breast-feeding extended the life span of the child. Thus a working-class woman had strong incentives to concentrate on child care within her home if her family could afford it.

Second, running a household in conditions of primitive urban poverty was an extremely demanding job in its own right. There were no supermarkets or discount department stores, no running water or public transportation. Everything had to be done on foot. As in the poor sections of many inner cities today, shopping and feeding the family constituted a never-ending challenge. The woman marched from one tiny shop to another, dragging her tired children (for who was to watch them?) and struggling valiantly with heavy sacks, tricky shopkeepers, and walkup apartments. Yet another brutal job outside the house—a "second shift"—had limited appeal for the average married woman. Thus women might well have accepted the emerging division of labor as the best available strategy for family survival in the industrializing society.[10]

Third, why were the women who did work for wages outside the home segregated and confined to certain "women's jobs"? No doubt the desire of males to monopolize the best opportunities and hold women down provides part of the answer. Yet as some feminist scholars have argued, sex-segregated employment was also a collective response to the new industrial system. Previously, at least in theory, young people worked under a watchful parental eye. The growth of factories and mines brought unheard-of opportunities for girls and boys to mix on the job, free of familial supervision. Continuing to mix after work, they were "more likely to form liaisons, initiate courtships, and respond to ad-

vances."[11] Such intimacy also led to more unplanned pregnancies and fueled the illegitimacy explosion that had begun in the late eighteenth century and that gathered force until at least 1850 (see pages 664–665). Thus segregation of jobs by gender was partly an effort by older people to help control the sexuality of working-class youths.

Investigations into the British coal industry before 1842 provide a graphic example of this concern. (See the feature "Listening to the Past: The Testimony of Young Mining Workers" on pages 752–753.) The middle-class men leading the inquiry, who expected their daughters and wives to pursue ladylike activities, often failed to appreciate the physical effort of the girls and women who dragged with belt and chain the unwheeled carts of coal along narrow underground passages. But they professed horror at the sight of girls and women working without shirts, which was a common practice because of the heat, and they quickly assumed the prevalence of licentious sex with the male miners, who also wore very little clothing. In fact, most girls and married women worked for related males in a family unit that provided considerable protection and restraint. Yet many witnesses from the working class believed that "blackguardism and debauchery" were common and that "they are best out of the pits, the lasses." Some miners stressed particularly the sexual danger of letting girls work past puberty. As one explained:

I consider it a scandal for girls to work in the pits. Till they are 12 or 14 they may work very well but after that it's an abomination. . . . The work of the pit does not hurt them, it is the effect on their morals that I complain of, and after 14 they should not be allowed to go. . . . After that age it is dreadful for them.[12]

The Mines Act of 1842 prohibited underground work for all women as well as for boys under ten.

Some women who had to support themselves protested against being excluded from coal mining, which paid higher wages than most other jobs open to working-class women. But provided they were part of families that could manage economically, the girls and the women who had worked underground were generally pleased with the law. In explaining her satisfaction in 1844, one mother of four provided a real insight into why many women accepted the emerging sexual division of labor:

While working in the pit I was worth to my [miner] husband seven shillings a week, out of which we had to pay 2 1/2 shillings to a woman for looking after the younger children. I used to take them to her house at 4 o'clock in the morning, out of their own beds, to put them into hers. Then there was one shilling a week for washing; besides, there was mending to pay for, and other things. The house was not guided. The other children broke things; they did not go to school when they were sent; they would be playing about, and get ill-used by other children, and their clothes torn. Then when I came home in the evening, everything was to do after the day's labor, and I was so tired I had no heart for it; no fire lit, nothing cooked, no water fetched, the house dirty, and nothing comfortable for my husband. It is all far better now, and I wouldn't go down again.[13]

The Early Labor Movement in Britain

Many kinds of employment changed slowly during and after the Industrial Revolution in Great Britain. In 1850 more British people still worked on farms than in any other occupation. The second-largest occupation was domestic service, with more than one million household servants, 90 percent of whom were women. Thus many old, familiar jobs outside industry lived on and provided alternatives for individual workers. This helped ease the transition to industrial civilization.

Within industry itself, the pattern of small-scale production with handicraft skills remained unchanged in many trades, even as some others were revolutionized by technological change. For example, as in the case of cotton and coal, the British iron industry was completely dominated by large-scale capitalist firms by 1850. One iron magnate in Wales employed six thousand workers in his plant, and many large ironworks had more than one thousand people on their payrolls. Yet the firms that fashioned iron into small metal goods, such as tools, tableware, and toys, employed on average fewer than ten wage workers, who used time-honored handicraft skills. Only gradually after 1850 did some owners find ways to reorganize some handicraft industries with new machines and new patterns of work. The survival of small workshops gave many workers an alternative to factory employment.

Working-class solidarity and class-consciousness developed in small workshops as well as in large factories, however. In the northern factory districts, where thousands of "hired hands" looked across at a tiny minority of managers and owners, anticapitalist sentiments were frequent by the 1820s. Commenting in 1825 on a strike in the woollen center of Bradford and the support it had gathered from other regions, one paper claimed with pride that "it is all the workers of England against a few masters of Bradford."[14] Modern technology had created a few versus a many.

The transformation of some traditional trades by organizational changes, rather than technological innova-

Girl Dragging Coal Wagons   Published by reformers in Parliament as part of a multivolume investigation into child labor in coal mines (see pages 752–753), this picture was one of several that shocked public opinion and contributed to the Mines Act of 1842. Stripped to the waist and harnessed to the wagon with belt and chain, this underground worker is "hurrying" coal from the face of the seam to the mine shaft. *(The British Library)*

tions, could also create ill will and class feeling. The liberal concept of economic freedom, which by 1760 in Great Britain had already broken down many old guild restrictions on wages and cottage industry, gathered strength in the late eighteenth and early nineteenth centuries. As in France during the French Revolution, the British government attacked monopolies, guilds, and workers combinations in the name of individual liberty. In 1799 Parliament passed the Combination Acts, which outlawed unions and strikes. In 1813 to 1814, Parliament repealed the old and often disregarded law of 1563 regulating the wages of artisans and the conditions of apprenticeship. As a result of these and other measures, certain skilled artisan workers, such as bootmakers and high-quality tailors, found aggressive capitalists ignoring traditional work rules and flooding their trades with unorganized women workers and children to beat down wages.

The liberal capitalist attack on artisan guilds and work rules was bitterly resented by many craftworkers, who subsequently played an important part in Great Britain and in other countries in gradually building a modern labor movement to improve working conditions and to serve worker needs. The Combination Acts were widely disregarded by workers. Printers, papermakers, carpenters, tailors, and other such craftsmen continued to take collective action, and societies of skilled factory workers also organized unions. Unions sought to control the number of skilled workers, limit apprenticeship to members' own children, and bargain with owners over wages. They were not afraid to strike; there was, for example, a general strike of adult cotton spinners in Manchester in 1810. In the face of widespread union activity, Parliament repealed the Combination Acts in 1824, and unions were tolerated, though not fully accepted, after 1825.

The next stage in the development of the British trade-union movement was the attempt to create a single large national union. This effort was led not so much by working people as by social reformers such as Robert Owen. Owen, a self-made cotton manufacturer (see page 745), had pioneered in industrial relations by combining firm discipline with concern for the health, safety, and hours of his workers. After 1815 he experimented with cooperative and socialist communities, including one at New Harmony, Indiana. Then in 1834 Owen organized one of the largest and most visionary of the early national unions, the Grand National Consolidated Trades Union. When this and other grandiose schemes collapsed, the British labor movement moved once again after 1851 in the direction of craft unions

(see Chapter 23). The most famous of these "new model unions" was the Amalgamated Society of Engineers. These unions won real benefits for members by fairly conservative means and thus became an accepted part of the industrial scene.

British workers also engaged in direct political activity in defense of their own interests. After the collapse of Owen's national trade union, a great deal of the energy of working people went into the Chartist movement, whose goal was political democracy. The key Chartist demand—that all men be given the right to vote—became the great hope of millions of aroused people. Workers were also active in campaigns to limit the workday in factories to ten hours and to permit duty-free importation of wheat into Great Britain to secure cheap bread. Thus working people developed a sense of their own identity and played an active role in shaping the new industrial system. Clearly, they were neither helpless victims nor passive beneficiaries.

SUMMARY

Western society's industrial breakthrough grew out of a long process of economic and social change in which the rise of capitalism, overseas expansion, and the growth of rural industry stood out as critical preparatory developments. Eventually taking the lead in all of these developments, and also profiting from stable government, abundant natural resources, and a flexible labor force, Britain experienced between the 1780s and the 1850s an epoch-making transformation, one that is still aptly termed the Industrial Revolution.

Building on technical breakthroughs, power-driven equipment, and large-scale enterprise, the Industrial Revolution in England greatly increased output in certain radically altered industries, stimulated the large handicraft and commercial sectors, and speeded up overall economic growth. Rugged Scotland industrialized at least as fast as England, and Great Britain became the first industrial nation. By 1850 the level of British per capita industrial production was surpassing continental levels by a growing margin, and Britain savored a near monopoly in world markets for mass-produced goods.

Continental countries inevitably took rather different paths to the urban industrial society. They relied more on handicraft production in both towns and villages. Only in the 1840s did railroad construction begin to create the strong demand for iron, coal, and railway equipment that speeded up the process of industrialization in the 1850s and 1860s.

The rise of modern industry had a profound impact on people and their lives. In the early stages, Britain again led the way, experiencing in a striking manner the long-term social changes accompanying the economic transformation. Factory discipline and Britain's stern capitalist economy weighed heavily on working people, who, however, actively fashioned their destinies, refusing to be passive victims. Improvements in the standard of living came slowly, although they were substantial by 1850. The era of industrialization fostered new attitudes toward child labor, encouraged protective factory legislation, and called forth a new sense of class feeling and an assertive labor movement. It also promoted a more rigid division of roles and responsibilities within the family that was detrimental to women, another gradual but profound change of revolutionary proportions.

NOTES

1. N. F. R. Crafts, *British Economic Growth During the Industrial Revolution* (Oxford: Oxford University Press, 1985), p. 32.
2. P. Bairoch, "International Industrialization Levels from 1750 to 1980," *Journal of European Economic History* 11 (Spring 1982): 269–333.
3. Crafts, *British Economic Growth*, pp. 45, 95–102.
4. M. Lévy-Leboyer, *Les banques européennes et l'industrialisation dans la première moitié du XIXe siècle* (Paris: Presses Universitaires de France, 1964), p. 29.
5. J. Michelet, *The People,* trans. with an introduction by J. P. McKay (Urbana: University of Illinois Press, 1973; original publication, 1846), p. 64.
6. F. Engels, *The Condition of the Working Class in England,* trans. and ed. W. O. Henderson and W. H. Chaloner (Stanford, Calif.: Stanford University Press, 1968), p. xxiii.
7. Quoted in W. A. Hayek, ed., *Capitalism and the Historians* (Chicago: University of Chicago Press, 1954), p. 126.
8. Crafts, *British Economic Growth*, p. 95.
9. Quoted in E. R. Pike, *"Hard Times": Human Documents of the Industrial Revolution* (New York: Praeger, 1966), p. 109.
10. See especially J. Brenner and M. Rama, "Rethinking Women's Oppression," *New Left Review* 144 (March–April 1984): 33–71, and sources cited there.
11. J. Humphries, ". . . 'The Most Free from Objection' . . . : The Sexual Division of Labor and Women's Work in Nineteenth-Century England," *Journal of Economic History* 47 (December 1987): 948.
12. Ibid., p. 941; Pike, *"Hard Times,"* p. 266.
13. Pike, *"Hard Times,"* p. 208.
14. Quoted in D. Geary, ed., *Labour and Socialist Movements in Europe Before 1914* (Oxford: Berg, 1989), p. 29.

SUGGESTED READING

There is a vast and exciting literature on the Industrial Revolution. R. Cameron, *A Concise Economic History of the World* (1989), provides an introduction to the issues and has a carefully annotated bibliography. J. Goodman and K. Honeyman, *Gainful Pursuits: The Making of Industrial Europe, 1600–1914* (1988), D. S. Landes, *The Unbound Prometheus: Technological Change and Industrial Development in Western Europe from 1750 to the Present* (1969), and S. Pollard, *Peaceful Conquest: The Industrialization of Europe* (1981), are excellent general treatments of European industrial growth. These studies also suggest the range of issues and interpretations. R. Sylla and G. Toniolo, eds., *Patterns of European Industrialization* (1991), is an important collection by specialists. T. Kemp, *Industrialization in Europe,* 2d ed. (1985), is also useful. P. Hudson, *The Industrial Revolution* (1992), M. Berg, *The Age of Manufactures: Industry, Innovation and Work in Britain, 1700–1820* (1985), and P. Mathias, *The First Industrial Nation: An Economic History of Britain, 1700–1914* (1969), admirably discuss the various aspects of the British breakthrough and offer good bibliographies, as does the work by Crafts mentioned in the Notes. W. Rostow, *The Stages of Economic Growth: A Non-Communist Manifesto* (1960), has been a popular, provocative study.

W. Walton, *France and the Crystal Palace: Bourgeois Taste and Artisan Manufacture in the 19th Century* (1992), and H. Kirsh, *From Domestic Manufacturing to Industrial Revolution: The Case of the Rhineland Textile Districts* (1989), examine the gradual transformation of handicraft techniques and their persistent importance in the international economy. R. Cameron, *France and the Economic Development of Europe, 1800–1914* (1961), traces the spread of railroads and industry across Europe. A. S. Milward and S. B. Saul, *The Economic Development of Continental Europe, 1780–1870* (1973) and *The Development of the Economies of Continental Europe, 1850–1914* (1977), may be compared with J. Clapham's old-fashioned classic, *Economic Development of France and Germany* (1963). P. O'Brien, "Path Dependency, or Why Britain Became an Industrialized and Urbanized National Economy Long Before France," *Economic History Review* 49 (May 1966): 213–249, is a stimulating comparative essay, and C. Heywood, *The Economic Development of France, 1750–1914* (1992), introduces the main issues and provides an up-to-date bibliography. Other important works on industrial developments are C. Tilly and E. Shorter, *Strikes in France, 1830–1848* (1974); D. Ringrose, *Transportation and Economic Stagnation in Spain, 1750–1850* (1970); L. Schofer, *The Formation of a Modern Labor Force* (1975), which focuses on the Silesian part of Germany; and W. Blackwell, *The Industrialization of Russia,* 2d ed. (1982). L. Moch, *Paths to the City: Regional Migration in Nineteenth-Century France* (1983), and W. Schivelbusch, *Disenchanted Night: The Industrialization of Light in the Nineteenth Century* (1983), imaginatively analyze quite different aspects of industrialization's many consequences.

The debate between "optimists" and "pessimists" about the consequences of industrialization in Britain goes on. Two excellent studies with a gender perspective revitalize the debate: D. Valenze, *The First Industrial Woman* (1995); and P. Hudson and W. Lee, eds., *Women's Work and the Family Economy in Historical Perspective* (1990). P. Taylor, ed., *The Industrial Revolution: Triumph or Disaster?* (1970), is a useful introduction to older studies. Hayek's collection of essays, cited in the Notes, stresses positive aspects. It is also fascinating to compare Engels's classic condemnation, cited in the Notes, with Andrew Ure's optimistic defense, *The Philosophy of Manufactures,* first published in 1835 and reprinted recently. J. Rule, *The Labouring Classes in Early Industrial England, 1750–1850* (1987), is a recommended synthesis. E. P. Thompson continues and enriches the En-gels tradition in *The Making of the English Working Class* (1963), an exciting book rich in detail and early working-class lore. Pike's documentary collection, cited in the Notes, provides fascinating insights into the lives of working people. An unorthodox but moving account of a doomed group is D. Bythell, *The Handloom Weavers* (1969). L. Davidoff and C. Hall, *Family Fortunes: Men and Women of the English Middle Class, 1750–1850* (1987), examines both economic activities and cultural beliefs with great skill. F. Klingender, *Art and the Industrial Revolution,* rev. ed. (1968), is justly famous, and M. Ignatieff, *A Just Measure of Pain* (1980), is an engrossing study of prisons during British industrialization. D. S. Landes, *Revolution in Time: Clocks and the Making of the Modern World* (1983), is a brilliant integration of industrial and cultural history.

Among general studies, G. S. R. Kitson Clark, *The Making of Victorian England* (1967), is particularly imaginative. A. Briggs, *Victorian People* (1955), provides an engrossing series of brief biographies. H. Ausubel discusses a major reformer in *John Bright* (1966), and B. Harrison skillfully illuminates the problem of heavy drinking in *Drink and the Victorians* (1971). The most famous contemporary novel dealing with the new industrial society is Charles Dickens's *Hard Times,* an entertaining but exaggerated story. *Mary Barton* and *North and South* by Elizabeth Gaskell are more realistic portrayals, and both are highly recommended.

LISTENING TO THE PAST

The Testimony of Young Mining Workers

The use of child labor in British industrialization quickly attracted the attention of humanitarians and social reformers. This interest led to investigations by parliamentary commissions, which resulted in laws limiting the hours and the ages of children working in large factories. Designed to build a case for remedial legislation, parliamentary inquiries gave large numbers of workers a rare chance to speak directly to contemporaries and to historians.

The moving passages that follow are taken from testimony gathered in 1841 and 1842 by the Ashley Mines Commission. Interviewing employers and many male and female workers, the commissioners focused on the physical condition of the youth and on the sexual behavior of workers far underground. The subsequent Mines Act of 1842 sought to reduce immoral behavior and sexual bullying by prohibiting underground work for all women (and for boys younger than ten).

Mr. Payne, coal master:

That children are employed generally at nine years old in the coal pits and sometimes at eight. In fact, the smaller the vein of coal is in height, the younger and smaller are the children required; the work occupies from six to seven hours per day in the pits; they are not ill-used or worked beyond their strength; a good deal of depravity exists but they are certainly not worse in morals than in other branches of the Sheffield trade, but upon the whole superior; the morals of this district are materially improving; Mr. Bruce, the clergyman, has been zealous and active in endeavoring to ameliorate their moral and religious education. . . .

Ann Eggley, hurrier, 18 years old:

I'm sure I don't know how to spell my name. We go at four in the morning, and sometimes at half-past four. We begin to work as soon as we get down. We get out after four, sometimes at five, in the evening. We work the whole time except an hour for dinner, and sometimes we haven't time to eat. I hurry [move coal wagons underground] by myself, and have done so for long. I know the corves [small coal wagons] are very heavy, they are the biggest corves anywhere about. The work is far too hard for me; the sweat runs off me all over sometimes. I am very tired at night. Sometimes when we get home at night we have not power to wash us, and then we go to bed. Sometimes we fall asleep in the chair. Father said last night it was both a shame and a disgrace for girls to work as we do, but there was naught else for us to do. I began to hurry when I was seven and I have been hurrying ever since. I have been 11 years in the pits. The girls are always tired. I was poorly twice this winter; it was with headache. I hurry for Robert Wiggins; he is not akin to me. . . . We don't always get enough to eat and drink, but we get a good supper. I have known my father go at two in the morning to work . . . and he didn't come out till four. I am quite sure that we work constantly 12 hours except on Saturdays. We wear trousers and our shifts in the pit and great big shoes clinkered and nailed. The girls never work naked to the waist in our pit. The men don't insult us in the pit. The conduct of the girls in the pit is good enough sometimes and sometimes bad enough. I never went to a day-school. I went a little to a Sunday-school, but I soon gave it over. I thought it too bad to be confined both Sundays and week-days. I walk about and get the fresh air on Sundays. I have not learnt to read. I don't know my letters. I never learnt naught. I never go to church or chapel; there is no church or chapel at Gawber, there is none nearer than a mile. . . . I have never heard that a good man came into the world who was God's son to save sinners. I never heard of Christ at all. Nobody has ever told me about him, nor have my father and mother ever taught me to pray. I know no prayer; I never pray.

Patience Kershaw, aged 17:

My father has been dead about a year; my mother is living and has ten children, five lads and five lasses; the oldest is about thirty, the youngest is four; three lasses go to mill; all the lads are colliers, two getters and three hurriers; one lives at home and does nothing; mother does nought but look after home.

All my sisters have been hurriers, but three went to the mill. Alice went because her legs swelled from hurrying in cold water when she was hot. I never went to day-school; I go to Sunday-school, but I cannot read or write; I go to pit at five o'clock in the morning and come out at five in the evening; I get my breakfast of porridge and milk first; I take my dinner with me, a cake, and eat it as I go; I do not stop or rest any time for the purpose; I get nothing else until I get home, and then have potatoes and meat, not every day meat. I hurry in the clothes I have now got on, trousers and ragged jacket; the bald place upon my head is made by thrusting the corves; my legs have never swelled, but sisters' did when they went to mill; I hurry the corves a mile and more under ground and back; they weigh 300; I hurry 11 a day; I wear a belt and chain at the workings to get the corves out; the putters [miners] that I work for are *naked* except their caps; they pull off all their clothes; I see them at work when I go up; sometimes they beat me, if I am not quick enough, with their hands; they strike me upon my back; the boys take liberties with me, sometimes, they pull me about; I am the only girl in the pit; there are about 20 boys and 15 men; all the men are naked; I would rather work in mill than in coal-pit.

Isabel Wilson, 38 years old, coal putter:

When women have children thick [fast] they are compelled to take them down early. I have been married 19 years and have had 10 bairns [children]; seven are in life. When on Sir John's work was a carrier of coals, which caused me to miscarry five times from the strains, and was gai [very] ill after each. Putting is no so oppressive; last child was born on Saturday morning, and I was at work on the Friday night.

Once met with an accident; a coal brake my cheek-bone, which kept me idle some weeks.

I have wrought below 30 years, and so has the guid man; he is getting touched in the breath now.

None of the children read, as the work is no regular. I did read once, but no able to attend to it

❖ Female mine worker, from a parliamentary report, 1842. (*Mary Evans Picture Library*)

now; when I go below lassie 10 years of age keeps house and makes the broth or stir-about.

Questions for Analysis

1. To what extent are the testimonies of Ann Eggley and Patience Kershaw in harmony with that of Payne?

2. Describe the work of Eggley and Kershaw. What do you think of their work? Why?

3. What strikes you most about the lives of these workers?

4. The witnesses were responding to questions from middle-class commissioners. What did the commissioners seem interested in? Why?

Source: J. Bowditch and C. Ramsland, eds., *Voices of the Industrial Revolution.* Copyright © 1961, 1989 by the University of Michigan. Reprinted by permission.

23 Ideologies and Upheavals, 1815–1850

Revolutionaries in Transylvania. Ana Ipatescu, of the first group of revolutionaries in Transylvania against Russia, 1848. *(National Historical Museum, Bucharest/E.T. Archive)*

The momentous economic and political transformation of modern times began in the late eighteenth century with the Industrial Revolution in England and then the French Revolution. Until about 1815, these economic and political revolutions were separate, involving different countries and activities and proceeding at very different paces. The Industrial Revolution created the factory system and new groups of capitalists and industrial workers in northern England, but almost continual warfare with France checked the spread of that revolution to continental Europe. Meanwhile, England's ruling aristocracy suppressed all forms of political radicalism at home and joined with crowned heads abroad to oppose and eventually defeat revolutionary and Napoleonic France. The economic and political revolutions worked at cross-purposes and even neutralized each other.

After peace returned in 1815, the situation changed. Economic and political changes tended to fuse, reinforcing each other and bringing about what historian Eric Hobsbawm has incisively called the "dual revolution." For instance, the growth of the industrial middle class encouraged the drive for representative government, and the demands of the French sans-culottes in 1793 and 1794 inspired many socialist thinkers. Gathering strength, the dual revolution rushed on to alter completely first Europe and then the rest of the world. Much of world history in the past two centuries can be seen as the progressive unfolding of the dual revolution.

In Europe in the nineteenth century, as in Asia and Africa in more recent times, the interrelated economic and political transformation was built on complicated histories, strong traditions, and highly diverse cultures. Radical change was eventually a constant, but the particular results varied enormously. In central and eastern Europe especially, the traditional elites—the monarchs, noble landowners, and bureaucrats—proved capable of defending their privileges and eventually using nationalism as a way to respond to the dual revolution and to serve their interests, as we shall see in Chapter 25.

The dual revolution also posed a tremendous intellectual challenge. The meanings of the economic, political, and social changes that were occurring, as well as the ways they would be shaped by human action, were anything but clear. These changes fascinated observers and stimulated the growth of new ideas and powerful ideologies. The most important of these were conservatism, liberalism, nationalism, and socialism.

- How did thinkers develop these ideas to describe and shape the transformation going on before their eyes?
- How did the artists and writers of the romantic movement also reflect and influence changes in this era?
- How did the political revolution, derailed in France and resisted by European monarchs, eventually break out again after 1815?
- Why did the revolutionary surge triumph briefly in 1848 and then fail almost completely?

These are the questions this chapter will explore.

 ## THE PEACE SETTLEMENT

The eventual triumph of revolutionary economic and political forces was by no means certain as the Napoleonic era ended. Quite the contrary. The conservative, aristocratic monarchies of Russia, Prussia, Austria, and Great Britain had finally defeated France and reaffirmed their determination to hold France in line. But many other international questions were outstanding, and the allies agreed to meet at the Congress of Vienna to fashion a general peace settlement.

Most people felt a profound longing for peace. The great challenge for political leaders in 1814 was to construct a settlement that would last and not sow the seeds of another war. Their efforts were largely successful and contributed to a century unmarred by destructive, generalized war (Map 23.1).

The European Balance of Power

The allied powers were concerned first and foremost with the defeated enemy, France. Agreeing to the restoration of the Bourbon dynasty (see page 718), the allies were quite lenient toward France after Napoleon's abdication. France was given the boundaries it possessed in 1792, which were larger than those of 1789, and France did not have to pay any war reparations. Thus the victorious powers did not foment a spirit of injustice and revenge in the defeated country.

When the four allies of the Quadruple Alliance met together at the Congress of Vienna, assisted in a minor way by a host of delegates from the smaller European

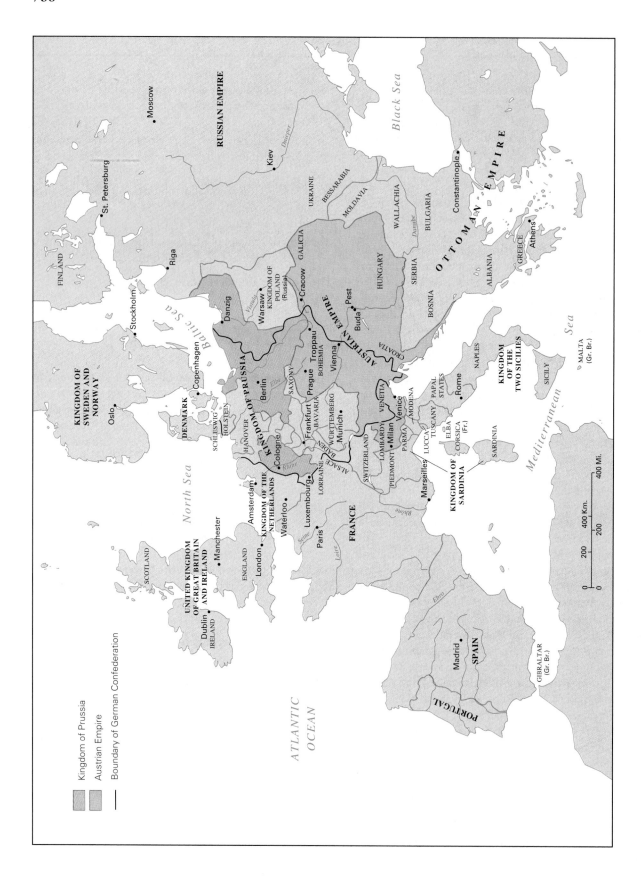

Kingdom of Prussia

Austrian Empire

Boundary of German Confederation

RUSSIAN EMPIRE

Moscow

St. Petersburg

Kiev

FINLAND

Riga

UKRAINE

BESSARABIA

MOLDAVIA

WALLACHIA

BULGARIA

Black Sea

Constantinople

OTTOMAN EMPIRE

Stockholm

Baltic Sea

GALICIA

KINGDOM OF POLAND (Russia)

Warsaw

Cracow

HUNGARY

SERBIA

BOSNIA

ALBANIA

GREECE

Athens

Mediterranean Sea

KINGDOM OF SWEDEN AND NORWAY

Oslo

Copenhagen

DENMARK

SCHLESWIG

HOLSTEIN

Danzig

Vistula

KINGDOM OF PRUSSIA

Berlin

SAXONY

Elbe

Prague

BOHEMIA

Troppau

AUSTRIAN EMPIRE

Vienna

Buda

Pest

CROATIA

Danube

MALTA (Gr. Br.)

HANOVER

Frankfurt

BAVARIA

Munich

WÜRTTEMBERG

VENETIA

Venice

Milan

LOMBARDY

MODENA

PARMA

NAPLES

KINGDOM OF THE TWO SICILIES

SICILY

Rome

PAPAL STATES

TUSCANY

LUCCA

ELBA

CORSICA (Fr.)

SARDINIA

North Sea

Amsterdam

KINGDOM OF THE NETHERLANDS

Cologne

Rhine

BADEN

SWITZERLAND

ALSACE

PIEDMONT

KINGDOM OF SARDINIA

Marseilles

Rhône

Manchester

UNITED KINGDOM OF GREAT BRITAIN AND IRELAND

ENGLAND

London

SCOTLAND

Dublin

IRELAND

Waterloo

Luxembourg

LORRAINE

Paris

Seine

FRANCE

Loire

ATLANTIC OCEAN

Ebro

Madrid

SPAIN

GIBRALTAR (Gr. Br.)

PORTUGAL

400 Mi.

400 Km.

200

200

0

0

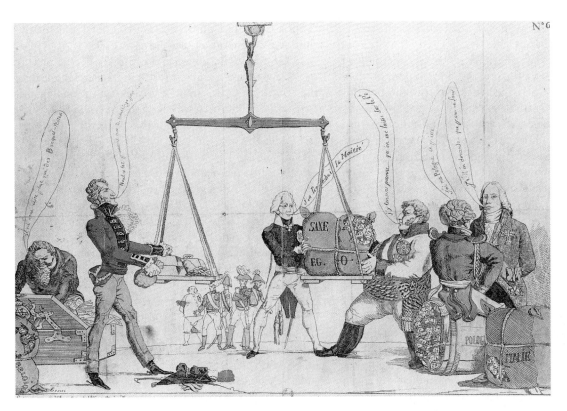

Adjusting the Balance   The Englishman on the left uses his money to counterbalance the people that the Prussian and the fat Metternich are gaining in Saxony and Italy. Alexander I sits happily on his prize, Poland. This cartoon captures the essence of how most people thought about balance-of-power diplomacy at the Congress of Vienna. *(Bibliothèque Nationale, Paris)*

states, they also agreed to raise a number of formidable barriers against renewed French aggression. The Low Countries—Belgium and Holland—were united under an enlarged Dutch monarchy capable of opposing France more effectively. Above all, Prussia received considerably more territory on France's eastern border so as to stand as the "sentinel on the Rhine" against France. In these ways, the Quadruple Alliance combined leniency toward France with strong defensive measures.

In their moderation toward France, the allies were motivated by self-interest and traditional ideas about the balance of power. To Klemens von Metternich and Robert Castlereagh, the foreign ministers of Austria

MAP 23.1 Europe in 1815   Europe's leaders re-established a balance of political power after the defeat of Napoleon. Prussia gained territory on the Rhine and in Saxony and consolidated its position as a Great Power.

and Great Britain, respectively, as well as their French counterpart, Charles Talleyrand, the balance of power meant an international equilibrium of political and military forces that would discourage aggression by any combination of states or, worse, the domination of Europe by any single state.

The Great Powers—Austria, Britain, Prussia, Russia, and France—used the balance of power to settle their own dangerous disputes at the Congress of Vienna. There was general agreement among the victors that each of them should receive compensation in the form of territory for their successful struggle against the French. Great Britain had already won colonies and strategic outposts during the long wars. Metternich's Austria gave up territories in Belgium and southern Germany but expanded greatly elsewhere, taking the rich provinces of Venetia and Lombardy in northern Italy as well as former Polish possessions and new lands on the eastern coast of the Adriatic (see Map 23.1). There was also agreement that Prussia and Russia should be compensated. But where and to what extent?

That was the ticklish question that almost led to renewed war in January 1815.

The vaguely progressive, impetuous Tsar Alexander I of Russia wanted to restore the ancient kingdom of Poland, on which he expected to bestow the benefits of his rule. The Prussians agreed, provided they could swallow up the large and wealthy kingdom of Saxony, their German neighbor to the south. These demands were too much for Castlereagh and Metternich, who feared an unbalancing of forces in central Europe. In an astonishing about-face, they turned for diplomatic support to the wily Talleyrand and the defeated France he represented, signing a secret alliance directed against Russia and Prussia. War seemed imminent.

But the threat of war caused the rulers of Russia and Prussia to moderate their demands. Russia accepted a small Polish kingdom, and Prussia took only part of Saxony (see Map 23.1). This compromise was very much within the framework of balance-of-power ideology. And it enabled France to regain its Great Power status and end its diplomatic isolation.

Unfortunately for France, Napoleon suddenly escaped from his "comic kingdom" on the island of Elba. Yet the peace concluded after Napoleon's final defeat at Waterloo was still relatively moderate toward France. Fat old Louis XVIII was restored to his throne for a second time. France lost only a little territory, had to pay an indemnity of 700 million francs, and had to support a large army of occupation for five years.

The rest of the settlement already concluded at the Congress of Vienna was left intact. The members of the Quadruple Alliance, however, did agree to meet periodically to discuss their common interests and to consider appropriate measures for the maintenance of peace in Europe. This agreement marked the beginning of the European "congress system," which lasted long into the nineteenth century and settled many international crises through international conferences and balance-of-power diplomacy.

Intervention and Repression

There was also a domestic political side to the re-establishment of peace. Within their own countries, the leaders of the victorious states were much less flexible. In 1815 under Metternich's leadership, Austria, Prussia, and Russia embarked on a crusade against the ideas and politics of the dual revolution. This crusade lasted until 1848. The first step was the Holy Alliance, formed by Austria, Prussia, and Russia in September 1815. First proposed by Russia's Alexander I, the alliance soon became a symbol of the repression of liberal and revolutionary movements all over Europe.

In 1820 revolutionaries succeeded in forcing the monarchs of Spain and the southern Italian kingdom of the Two Sicilies to grant liberal constitutions against their wills. Metternich was horrified: revolution was rising once again. Calling a conference at Troppau in Austria under the provisions of the Quadruple Alliance, he and Alexander I proclaimed the principle of active intervention to maintain all autocratic regimes whenever they were threatened. Austrian forces then marched into Naples in 1821 and restored Ferdinand I to the throne of the Two Sicilies, while French armies likewise restored the Spanish regime.

In the following years, Metternich continued to battle against liberal political change. Sometimes he could do little, as in the case of the new Latin American republics that broke away from Spain. Nor could he undo the dynastic changes of 1830 and 1831 in France and Belgium. Nonetheless, until 1848 Metternich's system proved quite effective in central Europe, where his power was the greatest.

Metternich's policies dominated not only Austria and the Italian peninsula but also the entire German Confederation, which the peace settlement of Vienna had called into being. The confederation was composed of thirty-eight independent German states, including Prussia and Austria. These states met in complicated assemblies dominated by Austria, with Prussia a willing junior partner in the execution of repressive measures.

It was through the German Confederation that Metternich had the infamous Carlsbad Decrees issued in 1819. These decrees required the thirty-eight German member states to root out subversive ideas in their universities and newspapers. The decrees also established a permanent committee with spies and informers to investigate and punish any liberal or radical organizations. Metternich's ruthless imposition of repressive internal policies on the governments of central Europe contrasted with the intelligent moderation he had displayed in the general peace settlement of 1815.

Metternich and Conservatism

Metternich's determined defense of the status quo made him a villain in the eyes of most progressive, optimistic historians of the nineteenth century. Yet rather than denounce the man, we can try to understand him and the general conservatism he represented.

Born into the middle ranks of the landed nobility of the Rhineland, Prince Klemens von Metternich (1773–

1859) was an internationally oriented aristocrat who made a brilliant diplomatic career in Austria. Austrian foreign minister from 1809 to 1848, the cosmopolitan Metternich always remained loyal to his class and jealously defended its rights and privileges to the day he died. Like most other conservatives of his time, he did so with a clear conscience. The nobility was one of Europe's most ancient institutions, and conservatives regarded tradition as the basic source of human institutions. In their view, the proper state and society remained those of pre-1789 Europe, which rested on a judicious blend of monarchy, bureaucracy, aristocracy, and respectful commoners.

Metternich firmly believed that liberalism, as embodied in revolutionary America and France, had been responsible for a generation of war with untold bloodshed and suffering. Liberal demands for representative government and civil liberties had unfortunately captured the imaginations of some middle-class lawyers, business people, and intellectuals, who were engaged in a vast conspiracy to impose their beliefs on society and destroy the existing order. Like many other conservatives then and since, Metternich blamed liberal revolutionaries for stirring up the lower classes, which he believed desired nothing more than peace and quiet.

The threat of liberalism appeared doubly dangerous to Metternich because it generally went with national aspirations. Liberals believed that each people, each national group, had a right to establish its own independent government and seek to fulfill its own destiny. The idea of national self-determination was repellent to Metternich. It not only threatened the existence of the aristocracy but also threatened to destroy the Austrian Empire and revolutionize central Europe.

The vast Austrian Empire of the Habsburgs was a great dynastic state. Formed over centuries by war, marriage, and luck, it was made up of many peoples (Map 23.2). The Germans had long dominated the empire, yet they accounted for only one-fourth of the population. The Magyars (Hungarians), a substantially smaller group, dominated the kingdom of Hungary, though they did not account for a majority of the population in that part of the Austrian Empire.

The Czechs, the third major group, were concentrated in Bohemia and Moravia. There were also large numbers of Italians, Poles, and Ukrainians as well as smaller groups of Slovenes, Croats, Serbs, Ruthenians, and Romanians. The various Slavic peoples, together with the Italians and the Romanians, represented a widely scattered and completely divided majority in an empire dominated by Germans and Hungarians. Differ-

Metternich   This portrait by Sir Thomas Lawrence reveals much about Metternich the man. Handsome, refined, and intelligent, Metternich was a great aristocrat who was passionately devoted to the defense of his class and its interests. *(The Royal Collection © Her Majesty Queen Elizabeth II)*

ent ethnic groups often lived in the same provinces and even in the same villages. Thus the different parts and provinces of the empire differed in languages, customs, and institutions.

The multinational state Metternich served was both strong and weak. It was strong because of its large population and vast territories; it was weak because of its many and potentially dissatisfied nationalities. In these circumstances, Metternich virtually had to oppose liberalism and nationalism, for Austria was simply unable to accommodate these ideologies, which had gathered strength in the French Revolution and were part of its enduring legacy. Other conservatives supported Austria because they could imagine no better fate for the jumble of small nationalities wedged precariously between masses of Germans and hordes of Russians in east-central Europe. Metternich's repressive conservatism had understandable roots in the dilemma of rising nationalism.

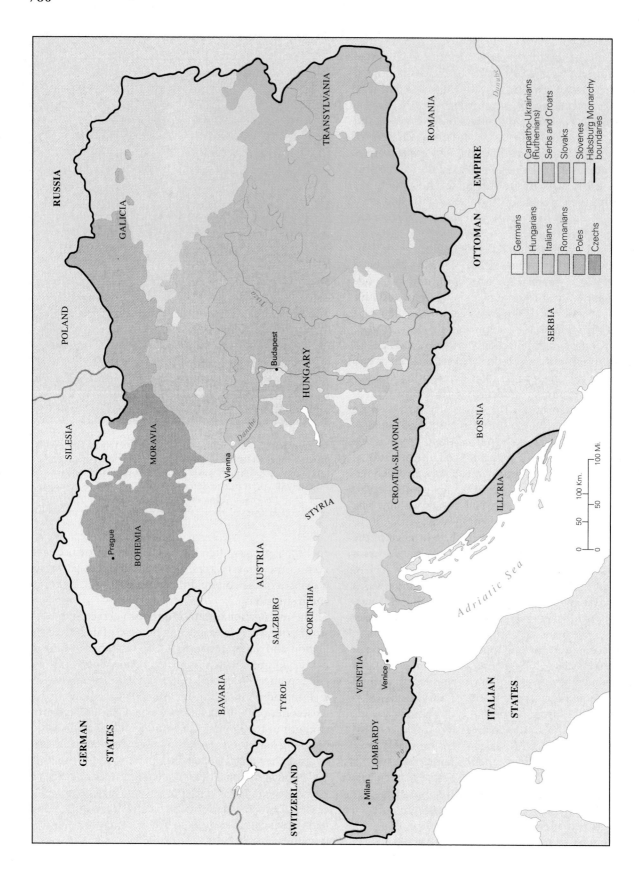

RUSSIA

POLAND

GALICIA

SILESIA

MORAVIA

Prague
BOHEMIA

GERMAN
STATES

BAVARIA

TYROL

SWITZERLAND

Vienna

SALZBURG

CORINTHIA

AUSTRIA

STYRIA

Milan
LOMBARDY

VENETIA

Venice

TRANSYLVANIA

ROMANIA

Budapest
HUNGARY

Tisza

Danube

Po

CROATIA-SLAVONIA

ILLYRIA

Adriatic Sea

ITALIAN
STATES

OTTOMAN
EMPIRE

SERBIA

BOSNIA

Danube

Germans
Hungarians
Italians
Romanians
Poles
Czechs

Carpatho-Ukrainians
(Ruthenians)
Serbs and Croats
Slovaks
Slovenes
Habsburg Monarchy
boundaries

0   50   100 Km.

0   50   100 Mi.

✤ RADICAL IDEAS AND EARLY SOCIALISM

The years following the peace settlement of 1815 were years of profound intellectual activity. Intellectuals and social observers were seeking to understand the revolutionary changes that had occurred and were still taking place. These efforts led to ideas that still motivate the world.

Almost all of these basic ideas were radical. In one way or another, they opposed the old, deeply felt conservatism that Metternich exemplified so well. Revived conservatism, with its stress on tradition, a hereditary monarchy, a strong and privileged landowning aristocracy, and an official church, was rejected by radicals. Instead, they developed and refined alternative visions—alternative ideologies—and tried to convince society to act on them. With time, they were very successful.

Liberalism

The principal ideas of liberalism—liberty and equality—were by no means defeated in 1815. First realized successfully in the American Revolution and then achieved in part in the French Revolution, this political and social philosophy continued to pose a radical challenge to revived conservatism. Liberalism demanded representative government as opposed to autocratic monarchy, equality before the law as opposed to legally separate classes. The idea of liberty also continued to mean specific individual freedoms: freedom of the press, freedom of speech, freedom of assembly, and freedom from arbitrary arrest. In Europe only France with Louis XVIII's Constitutional Charter and Great Britain with its Parliament and historic rights of English men and women had realized much of the liberal program in 1815. Even in those countries, liberalism had not fully succeeded; elsewhere, liberal demands were a call for freedom and revolutionary change.

Although liberalism retained its cutting edge, it was seen by many as being a somewhat duller tool than it had been. The reasons for this were that liberalism faced more radical ideological competitors in the early nineteenth century and that liberalism resolutely opposed government intervention in social and economic affairs,

even if the need for action seemed great to social critics and reformers. This form of liberalism is often called "classical" liberalism in the United States in order to distinguish it sharply from modern American liberalism, which usually favors more government programs to meet social needs and to regulate the economy. Opponents of classical liberalism especially criticized its economic principles, which called for unrestricted private enterprise and no government interference in the economy. This philosophy was popularly known as the doctrine of laissez faire.

The idea of a free economy had first been persuasively formulated by Scottish philosophy professor Adam Smith, whose *Inquiry into the Nature and Causes of the Wealth of Nations* (1776) founded modern economics. Smith was highly critical of eighteenth-century mercantilism and its attempt to regulate trade and economic activity. Far preferable were free competition and the "invisible hand" of the self-regulating market, which would give all citizens a fair and equal opportunity to do what they did best. Smith argued effectively that freely competitive private enterprise would result in greater income for everyone, not just the rich. He was a spokesman for general economic development, not narrow business interests.

In the early nineteenth century, the British economy was progressively liberalized as old restrictions on trade and industry were relaxed or eliminated. This liberalization promoted continued economic growth in the Industrial Revolution. At the same time, however, economic liberalism and laissez-faire economic thought were embraced most enthusiastically by business groups and became a doctrine associated with business interests. Businessmen used the doctrine to defend their right to do exactly as they wished in their factories. Labor unions were outlawed because they supposedly restricted free competition and the individual's "right to work."

The teachings of Thomas Malthus and David Ricardo especially helped make economic liberalism an ideology of business interests in many people's minds. As we have seen (page 733), Malthus argued that population would always tend to grow faster than the supply of food. This led Ricardo to formulate his iron law of wages, which said that because of the pressure of population growth, wages would be just high enough to keep workers from starving. Malthus and Ricardo thought of themselves as objective social scientists. Yet their teachings were often used by industrial and middle-class interests in England, the continent, and the United States to justify opposing any kind of

MAP 23.2 **Peoples of the Habsburg Monarchy, 1815**
The old dynastic state was a patchwork of nationalities. Note the widely scattered pockets of Germans and Hungarians.

government action to protect or improve the lot of workers: if workers were poor, it was their own fault, the result of their breeding like rabbits.

In the early nineteenth century, liberal political ideals also became more closely associated with narrow class interests. Early-nineteenth-century liberals favored representative government, but they generally wanted property qualifications attached to the right to vote. In practice, this meant limiting the vote to well-to-do aristocratic landowners, substantial businessmen, and successful members of the professions. Workers and peasants as well as the lower middle class of shopkeepers, clerks, and artisans did not own the necessary property and thus could not vote.

As liberalism became increasingly identified with the middle class after 1815, some intellectuals and foes of conservatism felt that liberalism did not go nearly far enough. Inspired by memories of the French Revolution and the contemporary example of exuberant Jacksonian democracy in the young American republic, they called for an end to property ownership as a qualification for voting, at least for males. Giving all men the vote, they felt, would allow the masses to join in government and would lead to democracy.

Many people who believed in democracy also believed in the republican form of government. They detested the power of the monarchy, the privileges of the aristocracy, and the great wealth of the upper middle class. These democrats and republicans were more radical than the liberals. Taking for granted much of the liberal program, they sought to go beyond it. Democrats and republicans were also more willing than most liberals to endorse violent upheaval to achieve goals. All of this meant that liberals and radical, democratic republicans could join forces against conservatives only up to a point.

Nationalism

Nationalism was a second radical idea in the years after 1815, an idea destined to have an enormous influence in the modern world. In this complex ideology, three points stand out. First, nationalism has normally evolved from a real or imagined *cultural* unity, manifesting itself especially in a common language, history, and territory. Second, nationalists have usually sought to turn this cultural unity into *political* reality so that the territory of each people coincides with its state boundaries. It was this goal that made nationalism so potentially explosive in central and eastern Europe after 1815, when there were either too few states (Austria, Russia, and the Ottoman Empire) or too many (the Italian penin-

sula and the German Confederation) and when different peoples overlapped and intermingled. Third, modern nationalism had its immediate origins in the French Revolution and the Napoleonic wars. Nationalism was effectively harnessed by the French republic during the Reign of Terror to help repel foreign foes, and all across Europe patriots tried to kindle nationalist flames in the war against Napoleon. Thus by 1815 there were already hints of nationalism's remarkable ability to spread and develop.

Between 1815 and 1850, most people who believed in nationalism also believed in either liberalism or radical, democratic republicanism. In more recent times, however, many governments have been very nationalistic without favoring liberty and democracy. Why, then, was love of liberty almost synonymous with love of nation in the early nineteenth century?

A common faith in the creativity and nobility of the people was perhaps the single most important reason for the linking of these two concepts. Liberals and especially democrats saw the people as the ultimate source of all government. The people (or some of them) elected their officials and governed themselves within a framework of personal liberty. Yet such self-government would be possible only if the people were united by common traditions and common loyalties. In practice, common loyalties rested above all on a common language. Thus liberals and nationalists agreed that a shared language forged the basic unity of a people, a unity that transcended local or provincial interests and even class differences.

Early nationalists usually believed that every nation, like every citizen, had the right to exist in freedom and to develop its character and spirit. They were confident that the independence and freedom of other nations, as in the case of other citizens within a nation, would not lessen the freedom of their own country. Rather, the symphony of nations would promote the harmony and ultimate unity of all peoples. As French historian Jules Michelet put it in *The People* in 1846, each citizen "learns to recognize his country . . . as a note in the grand concert; through it he himself participates and loves the world." Similarly, the great Italian patriot Giuseppe Mazzini believed that "in laboring according to the true principles of our country we are laboring for Humanity." (See the feature "Listening to the Past: Faith in Democratic Nationalism" on pages 786–787.) Thus the liberty of the individual and the love of a free nation overlapped greatly in the early nineteenth century.

Nationalism also had a negative side. Even as early nationalists talked of serving the cause of humanity,

Carbonari Going to Jail, 1821
Emerging out of a guild of charcoal burners, the Carbonari became a secret society opposed to Napoleonic rule. After 1815, the Carbonari pressed for an Italian republic and led unsuccessful uprisings against the Austrian occupiers. National ideals appealed especially to the middle class, as these prisoners with their top hats suggest. *(© Fabbri/Artephot)*

they stressed the differences among peoples. German pastor and philosopher Johann Herder (1744–1803) had argued that every people has its own particular spirit and genius, which it expresses through culture and language. Yet Herder (and others after him) could not define the uniqueness of the French, German, and Slavic peoples without comparing and contrasting one people with another. Thus even early nationalism developed a strong sense of "we" and "they."

"They" were often the enemy. The leader of the Czech cultural revival, the passionate democrat and nationalist historian Francis Palacký, is a good example of this tendency. In his histories, he lauded the Czech people's achievements, which he characterized as a long struggle against brutal German domination. To this "we-they" outlook, it was all too easy for nationalists to add two other highly volatile ingredients: a sense of national mission and a sense of national superiority. As Mazzini characteristically wrote, "Peoples never stop before they have achieved the ultimate aim of their existence, before having fulfilled their mission." Even Michelet, so alive to the aspirations of other peoples,

could not help speaking in 1846 of the "superiority of France"; the principles espoused in the French Revolution had made France the "salvation of mankind."

German and Spanish nationalists had a very different opinion of France. To them, the French often seemed as oppressive as the Germans seemed to the Czechs, as hateful as the Russians seemed to the Poles. The despised enemy's mission might seem as oppressive as the American national mission seemed to the Mexicans after the U.S. annexation of Texas. In 1845 American journalist and strident nationalist John Louis O'Sullivan wrote that taking land from an "imbecile and distracted Mexico" was a laudable step in the "fulfillment of our manifest destiny to overspread the continent allotted by Providence for the free development of our yearly multiplying millions."[1]

Early nationalism was thus ambiguous. Its main thrust was liberal and democratic. But below the surface lurked ideas of national superiority and national mission, which could lead to aggressive crusades and counter-crusades, as had happened in the French Revolution and in the "wars of liberation" against Napoleon.

French Utopian Socialism

Socialism was the new radical doctrine after 1815, and to understand it one must begin with France. Despite the fact that France lagged far behind Great Britain in developing modern industry, almost all the early socialists were French. Although they differed on many specific points, these French thinkers were acutely aware that the political revolution in France and the rise of modern industry in England had begun a transformation of society. Yet they were disturbed by what they saw. Liberal practices in politics, such as competition for votes, and in economics, such as free markets and the end of guild regulation, appeared to be fomenting selfish individualism and splitting the community into isolated fragments. There was, they believed, an urgent need for a further reorganization of society to establish cooperation and a new sense of community. Starting from this shared outlook, individual French thinkers went in many different directions. They searched the past, analyzed existing conditions, and fashioned luxurious utopias. Yet certain ideas tied their critiques and visions together.

Early French socialists believed in economic planning. Inspired by the emergency measures of 1793 and 1794 in France, they argued that the government should rationally organize the economy and not depend on destructive competition to do the job. Early socialists also shared an intense desire to help the poor and protect them from the rich. With passionate moral fervor, they preached that the rich and the poor should be more nearly equal economically. Finally, socialists believed that private property should be strictly regulated by the government or that it should be abolished and replaced by state or community ownership. Planning, greater economic equality, and state regulation of property—these were the key ideas of early French socialism and of all socialism since.

One of the most influential early socialist thinkers was a nobleman, Count Henri de Saint-Simon (1760–1825). A curious combination of radical thinker and successful land speculator, Saint-Simon optimistically proclaimed the tremendous possibilities of industrial development: "The age of gold is before us!" The key to progress was proper social organization. Such an arrangement of society required the "parasites"—the court, the aristocracy, lawyers, churchmen—to give way, once and for all, to the "doers"—the leading scientists, engineers, and industrialists. The doers would carefully plan the economy and guide it forward by undertaking vast public works projects and establishing investment banks. Saint-Simon also stressed in highly moralistic terms that every social institution ought to have as its main goal improved conditions for the poor. Saint-Simon's stress on industry and science inspired middle-class industrialists and bankers such as the Pereire brothers, founders of the Crédit Mobilier (see page 739).

After 1830 the socialist critique of capitalism became sharper. Charles Fourier (1772–1837), a lonely, saintly man with a tenuous hold on reality, described a socialist utopia in lavish mathematical detail. Hating the urban wage system, Fourier envisaged self-sufficient communities of 1,620 people living communally on 5,000 acres devoted to a combination of agriculture and industry. Although Fourier waited in vain each day at noon in his apartment for a wealthy philanthropist to endow his visionary schemes, he was very influential. Several utopian communities were founded along the lines he prescribed. The majority were founded in the United States.

Fourier was also an early proponent of the total emancipation of women. Extremely critical of middle-class family life, Fourier believed that most marriages were only another kind of prostitution. According to Fourier, young single women were shamelessly "sold" to their future husbands for dowries and other financial considerations. Therefore, Fourier called for the abolition of marriage, free unions based only on love, and sexual freedom. Many middle-class men and women found these ideas, which were shared and even practiced by some followers of Saint-Simon, shocking and immoral. The socialist program for the liberation of women as well as workers appeared to them as doubly dangerous and revolutionary.

Louis Blanc (1811–1882), a sharp-eyed, intelligent journalist, was much more practical. In his *Organization of Work* (1839), he urged workers to agitate for universal voting rights and to take control of the state peacefully. Blanc believed that the full power of the state should be directed at setting up government-backed workshops and factories to guarantee full employment. The right to work had to become as sacred as any other right.

Finally, there was Pierre Joseph Proudhon (1809–1865), a self-educated printer who wrote a pamphlet in 1840 titled *What Is Property?* His answer was that it was nothing but theft. Property was profit that was stolen from the worker, who was the source of all wealth. Unlike most socialists, Proudhon feared the power of the state and was often considered an anarchist.

Of great importance, the message of French utopian socialists interacted with the experiences of French urban workers, as recent research stresses. In Paris especially, workers cherished the memory of the radical phase of the French Revolution and its efforts to regulate economic life and protect the poor. Skilled artisans, with a long tradition of guilds, apprenticeship, and control of quality and wage rates, became violently opposed to laissez-faire laws that denied workers the right to organize and promoted brutal, unrestrained competition instead. Trying to maintain some control of their trades and conditions of work and developing a sense of class in the process, workers favored collective action and government intervention in economic life. Thus the aspirations of workers and utopian theorists reinforced each other, and a genuine socialist movement emerged in Paris in the 1830s and 1840s.

French utopian ideas had some influence outside France. But the economic arguments of the French utopians were weak, and their specific programs often seemed too fanciful to be taken seriously. To Karl Marx was left the task of establishing firm foundations for modern socialism.

The Birth of Marxian Socialism

In 1848 the thirty-year-old Karl Marx (1818–1883) and the twenty-eight-year-old Friedrich Engels (1820–1895) published *The Communist Manifesto,* which became the bible of socialism. The son of a Jewish lawyer who had converted to Christianity, the atheistic young Marx had studied philosophy at the University of Berlin before turning to journalism and economics. He read widely in French socialist thought and was influenced by it. He shared Fourier's view of middle-class marriage as legalized prostitution, and he, too, looked forward to the emancipation of women and the abolition of the family. But by the time Marx was twenty-five, he was developing his own socialist ideas.

Early French socialists often appealed to the middle class and the state to help the poor. Marx ridiculed such appeals as naive. He argued that the interests of the middle class and those of the industrial working class were inevitably opposed to each other. Indeed, according to the *Manifesto,* the "history of all previously existing society is the history of class struggles." In Marx's view, one class had always exploited the other, and with the advent of modern industry, society was split more clearly than ever before: between the middle class (the bourgeoisie) and the modern working class (the proletariat). The bourgeoisie had reduced everything to a matter of money and "naked self-interest." "In a word, for exploitation, veiled by religious and political illusions, the bourgeoisie had substituted naked, shameless, direct brutal exploitation."

Just as the bourgeoisie had triumphed over the feudal aristocracy, Marx predicted, the proletariat would conquer the bourgeoisie in a violent revolution. While a tiny minority owned the means of production and grew richer, the ever-poorer proletariat was constantly growing in size and in class-consciousness. In this process, the proletariat was aided, according to Marx, by a portion of the bourgeoisie who had gone over to the proletariat and who (like Marx and Engels) "had raised themselves to the level of comprehending theoretically the historical moment." And the critical moment was very near. "Let the ruling classes tremble at a Communist revolution. The proletarians have nothing to lose but their chains. They have a world to win. WORKING MEN OF ALL COUNTRIES, UNITE!" So ends *The Communist Manifesto.*

Karl Marx   Active in the revolution of 1848, Marx fled from Germany in 1849 and settled in London. There he wrote *Capital,* the weighty exposition of his socialist theories, and worked to organize the working class. Marx earned a modest living as a journalist, supplemented by financial support from his coauthor, Friedrich Engels. *(Istar-Tass/Sovfoto)*

In brief outline, Marx's ideas may seem to differ only slightly from the wild and improbable ideas of the utopians of his day. Yet Marx must be taken seriously because his ideas—practically unknown in 1848—became very influential in the later nineteenth century. He appeared to unite sociology, economics, and all human history in a vast and imposing edifice. In doing so, he synthesized in his socialism not only French utopian schemes but also English classical economics and German philosophy—the major intellectual currents of his day. Moreover, after the young Marx fled to England as a penniless political refugee following the revolutions of 1848, he continued to show a rare flair for combining complex theorization with both lively popular writing and practical organizational ability. This combination of theoretical and practical skills contributed greatly to the subsequent diffusion of Marx's socialist synthesis after 1860, as will be shown in Chapter 25.

Marx's debt to England was great. He was the last of the classical economists. Following David Ricardo, who had taught that labor was the source of all value, Marx went on to argue that profits were really wages stolen from the workers. Moreover, Marx incorporated Engels's charges of terrible oppression of the new class of factory workers in England; thus Marx's doctrines seemed to be based on hard facts.

Marx's theory of historical evolution was built on the philosophy of the German Georg Hegel (1770–1831). Hegel believed that history is "ideas in motion": each age is characterized by a dominant set of ideas, which produces opposing ideas and eventually a new synthesis. The idea of being had been dominant initially, for example, and it had produced its antithesis, the idea of nonbeing. This idea in turn had resulted in the synthesis of becoming. Thus history has pattern and purpose.

Marx retained Hegel's view of history as a dialectic process of change but made economic relationships between classes the driving force. This dialectic explained the decline of agrarian feudalism and the rise of industrial capitalism. And Marx stressed again and again that the "bourgeoisie, historically, has played a most revolutionary part. . . . During its rule of scarcely one hundred years the bourgeoisie has created more massive and more colossal productive forces than have all preceding generations together." Here was a convincing explanation for people trying to make sense of the dual revolution. Marx's next idea, that it was now the bourgeoisie's turn to give way to the socialism of revolutionary workers, appeared to many the irrefutable capstone of a brilliant interpretation of humanity's long development. Thus Marx pulled together powerful ideas and insights to create one of the great secular religions out of the intellectual ferment of the early nineteenth century.

 ## THE ROMANTIC MOVEMENT

Radical concepts of politics and society were accompanied by comparable changes in literature and other arts during the dual revolution. The early nineteenth century marked the acme of the romantic movement, which profoundly influenced the arts and enriched European culture immeasurably.

The romantic movement was in part a revolt against classicism and the Enlightenment. Classicism was essentially a set of artistic rules and standards that went hand in glove with the Enlightenment's belief in rationality, order, and restraint. The classicists believed that the ancient Greeks and Romans had discovered eternally valid aesthetic rules and that playwrights and painters should continue to follow them. Classicists could enforce these rules in the eighteenth century because they dominated the courts and academies for which artists worked.

Forerunners of the romantic movement appeared from about 1750 on. Of these, Rousseau (see page 611)—the passionate advocate of feeling, freedom, and natural goodness—was the most influential. Romanticism then crystallized fully in the 1790s, primarily in England and Germany. The French Revolution kindled the belief that radical reconstruction was also possible in cultural and artistic life (even though many early English and German romantics became disillusioned with events in France and turned from liberalism to conservatism in politics). Romanticism gained strength until the 1840s.

Romanticism's Tenets

Romanticism was characterized by a belief in emotional exuberance, unrestrained imagination, and spontaneity in both art and personal life. In Germany early romantics of the 1770s and 1780s called themselves the "Storm and Stress" (*Sturm und Drang*) group, and many romantic artists of the early nineteenth century lived lives of tremendous emotional intensity. Suicide, duels to the death, madness, and strange illnesses were not uncommon among leading romantics. Romantic artists typically led bohemian lives, wearing their hair long and uncombed in preference to powdered wigs and living in cold garrets rather than frequenting stiff drawing rooms. They rejected materialism and sought to escape to lofty spiritual heights through their art. Great individualists, the romantics believed the full development of one's

Nature and the Meaning of Life Caspar David Friedrich (1774–1840) was Germany's greatest romantic painter, and his *Traveler Looking over a Sea of Fog* (1815) is a representative masterpiece. Friedrich's paintings often focus on dark silhouetted figures, silently contemplating an eerie landscape. Friedrich came to believe that humans were only an insignificant part of an all-embracing higher unity. *(Hamburger Kunsthalle)*

unique human potential to be the supreme purpose in life. The romantics were driven by a sense of an unlimited universe and by a yearning for the unattained, the unknown, the unknowable.

Nowhere was the break with classicism more apparent than in romanticism's general conception of nature. Classicism was not particularly interested in nature. In the words of eighteenth-century English author Samuel Johnson, "A blade of grass is always a blade of grass; men and women are my subjects of inquiry." Nature was portrayed by classicists as beautiful and chaste, like an eighteenth-century formal garden. The romantics, in contrast, were enchanted by nature. Sometimes they found it awesome and tempestuous, as in Théodore

Géricault's painting *The Raft of the Medusa,* which shows the survivors of a shipwreck adrift in a turbulent sea. Others saw nature as a source of spiritual inspiration. As the great English landscape artist John Constable declared, "Nature is Spirit visible."

Most romantics saw the growth of modern industry as an ugly, brutal attack on their beloved nature and on the human personality. They sought escape—in the unspoiled Lake District of northern England, in exotic North Africa, in an idealized Middle Ages. Yet some romantics found a vast, awesome, terribly moving power in the new industrial landscape. In ironworks and cotton mills, they saw the flames of hell and the evil genius of Satan himself.

Fascinated by color and diversity, the romantic imagination turned toward the study and writing of history with a passion. For romantics, history was not a minor branch of philosophy from which philosophers picked suitable examples to illustrate their teachings. History was beautiful, exciting, and important in its own right. It was the art of change over time—the key to a universe that was now perceived to be organic and dynamic. It was no longer perceived to be mechanical and static, as it had to the philosophes of the eighteenth-century Enlightenment.

Historical studies supported the development of national aspirations and encouraged entire peoples to seek in the past their special destinies. This trend was especially strong in Germany and other eastern European countries. As the famous English historian Lord Acton put it, the growth of historical thinking associated with the romantic movement was a most fateful step in the story of European thought.

Literature

Britain was the first country where romanticism flowered fully in poetry and prose, and the British romantic writers were among the most prominent in Europe. Wordsworth, Coleridge, and Scott were all active by 1800, to be followed shortly by Byron, Shelley, and Keats. All were poets: romanticism found its distinctive voice in poetry, as the Enlightenment had in prose.

A towering leader of English romanticism, William Wordsworth (1770–1850) traveled in France after his graduation from Cambridge. There he fell passionately in love with a Frenchwoman, who bore him a daughter. He was deeply influenced by the philosophy of Rousseau and the spirit of the early French Revolution. Back in England, prevented by war and the Terror from returning to France, Wordsworth settled in the countryside with his sister, Dorothy, and Samuel Taylor Coleridge (1772–1834).

In 1798 the two poets published their *Lyrical Ballads,* one of the most influential literary works in the history of the English language. In defiance of classical rules, Wordsworth and Coleridge abandoned flowery poetic conventions for the language of ordinary speech, simultaneously endowing simple subjects with the loftiest majesty. This twofold rejection of classical practice was at first ignored and then harshly criticized, but by 1830 Wordsworth had triumphed.

One of the best examples of Wordsworth's romantic credo and genius is "Daffodils":

I wandered lonely as a cloud
That floats on high o'er vales and hills,
When all at once I saw a crowd,
A host, of golden daffodils;
Beside the lake, beneath the trees,
Fluttering and dancing in the breeze.

. . . .

The waves beside them danced, but they
Out-did the sparkling waves in glee:
A poet could not but be gay,
In such a jocund company:
I gazed—and gazed—but little thought
What wealth the show to me had brought:

For oft, when on my couch I lie
In vacant or in pensive mood,
They flash upon that inward eye
Which is the bliss of solitude;
And then my heart with pleasure fills,
And dances with the daffodils.

Here indeed are simplicity and love of nature in commonplace forms, which could be appreciated, very democratically, by everyone and not just by an intellectual elite. Here, too, is Wordsworth's romantic conviction that nature has the power to elevate and instruct. Wordsworth's conception of poetry as the "spontaneous overflow of powerful feeling recollected in tranquility" is well illustrated by the last stanza.

Born in Edinburgh, Walter Scott (1771–1832) personified the romantic movement's fascination with history. Raised on his grandfather's farm, Scott fell under the spell of the old ballads and tales of the Scottish border. He was also deeply influenced by German romanticism, particularly by the immortal poet and dramatist Johann Wolfgang von Goethe (1749–1832). Scott translated Goethe's famous *Gotz von Berlichingen,* a play about a sixteenth-century knight who revolted against centralized authority and championed individual freedom—at least in Goethe's romantic drama. A natural storyteller, Scott then composed long narrative poems and a series of historical novels. Scott excelled in faithfully re-creating the spirit of bygone ages and great historical events, especially those of Scotland.

Classicism remained strong in France under Napoleon and inhibited the growth of romanticism there. In 1813 Germaine de Staël (1766–1817), a Franco-Swiss writer living in exile, urged the French to throw away their worn-out classical models. Her study *On Germany* (1810) extolled the spontaneity and enthusiasm of German writers and thinkers, and it had a powerful impact on the post-1815 generation in France. (See the feature

"Individuals in Society: Germaine de Staël, Romantic Genius.") Between 1820 and 1850, the romantic impulse broke through in the poetry and prose of Lamartine, de Vigny, Hugo, Dumas, and Sand. Of these, Victor Hugo (1802–1885) was the greatest in both poetry and prose.

Son of a Napoleonic general, Hugo achieved an amazing range of rhythm, language, and image in his lyric poetry. His powerful novels exemplified the romantic fascination with fantastic characters, strange settings, and human emotions. The hero of Hugo's famous *Hunchback of Notre Dame* (1831) is the great cathedral's deformed bellringer, a "human gargoyle" overlooking the teeming life of fifteenth-century Paris. A great admirer of William Shakespeare, whom classical critics had derided as undisciplined and excessive, Hugo also championed romanticism in drama. His play *Hernani* (1830) consciously broke all the old rules, as Hugo renounced his early conservatism and equated freedom in literature with liberty in politics and society. Hugo's political evolution was thus exactly the opposite of Wordsworth's, in whom youthful radicalism gave way to middle-aged caution. As the contrast between the two artists suggests, romanticism was a cultural movement compatible with many political beliefs.

Amandine Aurore Lucie Dupin (1804–1876), a strong-willed and gifted woman generally known by her pen name, George Sand, defied the narrow conventions of her time in an unending search for self-fulfillment. After eight years of unhappy marriage in the provinces, she abandoned her dullard of a husband and took her two children to Paris to pursue a career as a writer. There Sand soon achieved fame and wealth, eventually writing over eighty novels on a variety of romantic and social themes. All were shot through with a typically romantic love of nature and moral idealism. George Sand's striking individualism went far beyond her flamboyant preference for men's clothing and cigars and her notorious affairs with poet Alfred de Musset and composer Frédéric Chopin, among others. Her semi-autobiographical novel *Lélia* was shockingly modern, delving deeply into her tortuous quest for sexual and personal freedom.

In central and eastern Europe, literary romanticism and early nationalism often reinforced each other. Seeking a unique greatness in every people, well-educated romantics plumbed their own histories and cultures. Like modern anthropologists, they turned their attention to peasant life and transcribed the folksongs, tales, and proverbs that the cosmopolitan Enlightenment had disdained. The brothers Jacob and Wilhelm Grimm were particularly successful at rescuing German fairy tales from oblivion. In the Slavic lands, romantics played a decisive role in converting spoken peasant languages into modern written languages. The greatest of all Russian poets, Aleksander Pushkin (1799–1837), rejecting eighteenth-century attempts to force Russian poetry into a classical straitjacket, used his lyric genius to mold the modern literary language.

Art and Music

The greatest and most moving romantic painter in France was Eugène Delacroix (1798–1863), probably the illegitimate son of French foreign minister Talleyrand. Delacroix was a master of dramatic, colorful scenes that stirred the emotions. He was fascinated with remote and exotic subjects, whether lion hunts in Morocco or the languishing, sensuous women of a sultan's harem. Yet he was also a passionate spokesman for freedom. His masterpiece, *Liberty Leading the People,* celebrated the nobility of popular revolution in general and revolution in France in particular.

In England the most notable romantic painters were Joseph M. W. Turner (1775–1851) and John Constable (1776–1837). Both were fascinated by nature, but their interpretations of it contrasted sharply, aptly symbolizing the tremendous emotional range of the romantic movement. Turner depicted nature's power and terror; wild storms and sinking ships were favorite subjects. Constable painted gentle Wordsworthian landscapes in which human beings were at one with their environment, the comforting countryside of unspoiled rural England.

It was in music that romanticism realized most fully and permanently its goals of free expression and emotional intensity. Whereas the composers of the eighteenth century had remained true to well-defined structures, such as the classical symphony, the great romantics used a great range of forms to create a thousand musical landscapes and evoke a host of powerful emotions. Romantic composers also transformed the small classical orchestra, tripling its size by adding wind instruments, percussion, and more brass and strings. The crashing chords evoking the surge of the masses in Chopin's Revolutionary Etude, the bottomless despair of the funeral march in Beethoven's Third Symphony, the solemn majesty of a great religious event in Schumann's Rhenish Symphony—such were the modern orchestra's musical paintings that plumbed the depths of human feeling.

Individuals in Society

Germaine de Staël, Romantic Genius

Germaine de Staël, by J.-B. Isabey. *(© Photo R.M.N.–J. G. Berizzi)*

Rich, intellectual, passionate, and assertive, Germaine Necker de Staël (1766–1817) astonished contemporaries and still fascinates historians. She was strongly influenced by her parents, poor Swiss Protestants who soared to the top of prerevolutionary Parisian society. Her brilliant but rigid mother filled Germaine's head with knowledge, and each week the precocious child listened, wide-eyed and attentive, to illustrious writers and philosophers performing at her mother's salon. At age twelve, she suffered a physical and mental breakdown. Only then was she allowed to have a playmate and romp and run on the family estate. Her adoring father was Jacques Necker, a banker who made an enormous fortune and became France's reform-minded minister of finance before the Revolution. Worshiping her father in adolescence, Germaine also came to love politics.

Accepting at nineteen an arranged marriage with Baron de Staël-Holstein, a womanizing Swedish diplomat bewitched by her dowry, Germaine began her life's work. She opened an intellectual salon and began to write and publish. Her wit and exuberance attracted foreigners and liberal French aristocrats, one of whom became the first of many lovers as her marriage soured and she searched unsuccessfully for the happiness of her parents' union. Fleeing Paris in 1792 and returning after the Thermidorian reaction, she subsequently angered Napoleon by criticizing his dictatorial rule. In 1803 he permanently banished her from Paris.

Retiring again to her isolated estate in Switzerland and skillfully managing her inherited wealth, Staël fought insomnia with opium and boredom with parties that attracted luminaries from all over Europe. Always seeking stimulation for her restless mind, she traveled widely in Italy and Germany and drew upon these experiences in her novel *Corinne* (1807) and her study *On Germany* (1810). Both works summed up her romantic faith and enjoyed enormous success.

Staël urged creative individuals to abandon traditional rules and classical models. She encouraged them to embrace experimentation, emotion, and enthusiasm. Enthusiasm, which she had in abundance, was the key, the royal road to creativity, personal fulfillment, and human improvement. Thrilling to music, for example, she felt that only an enthusiastic person could really appreciate this gift of God, this wordless message that "unifies our dual nature and blends senses and spirit in a common rapture."[1]

Yet a profound sadness runs through her writing. This sadness, so characteristic of the romantic temperament, grew in part out of disappointments in love and prolonged exile. But it also grew out of the insoluble predicament of being an enormously gifted woman in an age of intense male chauvinism. Little wonder that uneasy male competitors and literary critics took delight in ridiculing and defaming her as a neurotic and masculine woman, a mediocre and unnatural talent who had foolishly dared to enter the male world of serious thought and action. Even her supporters could not accept her for what she was. The admiring poet Lord Byron recognized her genius and called her "the most eminent woman author of this, or perhaps of any century." But he quickly added that "she should have been born a man."[2]

Buffeted and saddened by scorn and condescension because of her gender, Staël advocated equal rights for women throughout her life. Only with equal rights and duties—in education and careers, in love and marital relations—could an exceptional woman like herself, or indeed any woman, ever hope to realize her intellectual and emotional potential. Practicing what she preached as best she could, Germaine de Staël was a trailblazer in the struggle for women's rights.

Questions for Analysis

1. In what ways did Germaine de Staël's life and thought reflect basic elements of the romantic movement?
2. Why did male critics often attack Staël? What do these criticisms tell us about gender relations in the early nineteenth century?

1. Quoted in G. R. Besser, *Germaine de Staël Revisited* (New York: Twayne Publishers, 1994), p. 106. Enhanced by a feminist perspective, this is the best recent study.
2. Quoted ibid., p. 139.

Heroes of Romanticism   Observed by a portrait of Byron and bust of Beethoven, Liszt plays for friends in this painting by Josef Danhauser. From left to right sit Alexander Dumas, George Sand (characteristically wearing men's garb), and Marie d'Agoult, Liszt's mistress. Standing are Victor Hugo, Paganini, and Rossini. In fact, this gathering of geniuses was imaginary, part of an advertising campaign by a German piano manufacturer to sell pianos to the comfortable middle class. *(Bildarchiv Preussischer Kulturbesitz)*

This range and intensity gave music and musicians much greater prestige than in the past. Music no longer simply complemented a church service or helped a nobleman digest his dinner. Music became a sublime end in itself. It became for many the greatest of the arts, precisely because it achieved the most ecstatic effect and most perfectly realized the endless yearning of the soul. It was worthy of great concert halls and the most dedicated sacrifice. The unbelievable one-in-a-million performer—the great virtuoso who could transport the listener to ecstasy and hysteria—became a cultural hero. The composer Franz Liszt (1811–1886) vowed to do for the piano what Nicolo Paganini (1784–1840) had done for the violin, and he was lionized as the greatest pianist of his age. People swooned for Liszt as they scream for rock stars today.

Though romanticism dominated music until late in the nineteenth century, no composer ever surpassed its first great master, Ludwig van Beethoven (1770–1827). Extending and breaking open classical forms, Beethoven used contrasting themes and tones to produce dramatic conflict and inspiring resolutions. As the contemporary German novelist Ernst Hoffmann (1776–1822) wrote, "Beethoven's music sets in motion the lever of fear, of awe, of horror, of suffering, and awakens just that infinite longing which is the essence of Romanticism." Beethoven's range was tremendous; his output included symphonies, chamber music, sonatas for violin and piano, Masses, an opera, and a great many songs.

At the peak of his fame, in constant demand as a composer and recognized as the leading concert pianist of his day, Beethoven began to lose his hearing. He considered suicide but eventually overcame despair: "I will take fate by the throat; it will not bend me completely to its will."[2] Beethoven continued to pour out immortal music. Among other achievements, he fully exploited for the first time the richness and beauty of the piano. Beethoven never heard much of his later work, including the unforgettable choral finale to the Ninth Symphony, for his last years were silent, spent in total deafness.

 ## REFORMS AND REVOLUTIONS

While the romantic movement was developing, liberal, national, and socialist forces battered against the conservatism of 1815. In some countries, change occurred gradually and peacefully. Elsewhere, pressure built up like steam in a pressure cooker without a safety valve and eventually caused an explosion in 1848. Three important countries—Greece, Great Britain, and France—experienced variations on this basic theme.

National Liberation in Greece

National, liberal revolution, frustrated in Italy and Spain by conservative statesmen, succeeded first after 1815 in Greece. Since the fifteenth century, the Greeks had been living under the domination of the Ottoman Turks. In spite of centuries of foreign rule, the Greeks had survived as a people, united by their language and the Greek Orthodox religion. It was perfectly natural that the general growth of national aspirations and a desire for independence would inspire some Greeks in the early nineteenth century. This rising national movement led to the formation of secret societies and then to revolt in 1821, led by Alexander Ypsilanti, a Greek patriot and a general in the Russian army.

The Great Powers, particularly Metternich, were opposed to all revolution, even revolution against the Islamic Turks. They refused to back Ypsilanti and supported the Ottoman Empire. Yet for many Europeans, the Greek cause became a holy one. Educated Americans and Europeans were in love with the culture of classical Greece; Russians were stirred by the piety of their Orthodox brethren. Writers and artists, moved by the romantic impulse, responded enthusiastically to the Greek struggle.

The Greeks, though often quarreling among themselves, battled on against the Turks and hoped for the eventual support of European governments. In 1827 Great Britain, France, and Russia responded to popular demands at home and directed Turkey to accept an armistice. When the Turks refused, the navies of these three powers trapped the Turkish fleet at Navarino and destroyed it. Russia then declared another of its periodic wars of expansion against the Turks. This led to the establishment of a Russian protectorate over much of present-day Romania, which had also been under Turkish rule. Great Britain, France, and Russia finally declared Greece independent in 1830 and installed a German prince as king of the new country in 1832. In the end, the Greeks had won: a small nation had gained its independence in a heroic war against a foreign empire.

Liberal Reform in Great Britain

Eighteenth-century British society had been both flexible and remarkably stable. It was dominated by the landowning aristocracy, but that class was neither closed nor rigidly defined. Successful business and professional people could buy land and become gentlefolk, while the common people had more than the usual opportunities of the preindustrial world. Basic civil rights for all were balanced by a tradition of deference to one's social superiors. Parliament was manipulated by the king and was thoroughly undemocratic. Only about 8 percent of the population could vote for representatives to Parliament, and by the 1780s there was growing interest in some kind of political reform.

But the French Revolution threw the British aristocracy into a panic for a generation, making it extremely hostile to any attempts to change the status quo. The Tory party, completely controlled by the landed aristocracy, was particularly fearful of radical movements at home and abroad. Castlereagh initially worked closely with Metternich to restrain France and restore a conservative balance in central Europe. This same intense conservatism motivated the Tory government at home. After 1815 the aristocracy defended its ruling position by repressing every kind of popular protest.

The first step in this direction began with revision of the Corn Laws in 1815. Corn Laws to regulate the foreign grain trade had long existed, but they were not needed during a generation of war with France because the British had been unable to import cheap grain from eastern Europe. As shortages occurred and agricultural prices skyrocketed, a great deal of marginal land had been brought under cultivation. This development had been a bonanza for the landed aristocracy, whose fat rent rolls became even fatter. Peace meant that grain could be imported again and that the price of wheat and bread would go down. To almost everyone except the aristocracy, lower prices seemed highly desirable.

The aristocracy, however, rammed far-reaching changes in the Corn Laws through Parliament. The new regulation prohibited the importation of foreign grain unless the price at home rose above 80 shillings per quarter ton—a level reached only in time of harvest disaster before 1790. Seldom has a class legislated more selfishly for its own narrow economic advantage or done more to promote a class-based view of political action.

Delacroix: Massacre at Chios   The Greek struggle for freedom and independence won the enthusiastic support of liberals, nationalists, and romantics. The Ottoman Turks were portrayed as cruel oppressors who were holding back the course of history, as in this moving masterpiece by Delacroix. *(Louvre © Photo R.M.N.)*

THE PRELUDE TO 1848

March 1814	Russia, Prussia, Austria, and Britain form the Quadruple Alliance to defeat France.
April 1814	Napoleon abdicates.
May–June 1814	Bourbon monarchy is restored; Louis XVIII issues the Constitutional Charter providing for civil liberties and representative government. First Peace of Paris: allies combine leniency with a defensive posture toward France.
October 1814– June 1815	Congress of Vienna peace settlement establishes balance-of-power principle and creates the German Confederation.
February 1815	Napoleon escapes from Elba and marches on Paris.
June 1815	Battle of Waterloo is fought.
September 1815	Austria, Prussia, and Russia form the Holy Alliance to repress liberal and revolutionary movements.
November 1815	Second Peace of Paris and renewal of Quadruple Alliance punish France and establish the European "congress system."
1819	In Carlsbad Decrees, Metternich imposes harsh measures throughout the German Confederation.
1820	Revolution occurs in Spain and the kingdom of the Two Sicilies. At the Congress of Troppau, Metternich and Alexander I of Russia proclaim the principle of intervention to maintain autocratic regimes.
1821	Austria crushes a liberal revolution in Naples and restores the Sicilian autocracy. Greeks revolt against the Ottoman Turks.
1823	French armies restore the Spanish regime. United States proclaims the Monroe Doctrine.
1824	Reactionary Charles X succeeds Louis XVIII in France.
1830	Charles X repudiates the Constitutional Charter; insurrection and collapse of the government follow. Louis Philippe succeeds to the throne and maintains a narrowly liberal regime until 1848. Greece wins independence from the Ottoman Empire.
1832	Reform Bill expands British electorate and encourages the middle class.
1839	Louis Blanc publishes *Organization of Work*.
1840	Pierre Joseph Proudhon publishes *What Is Property?*
1846	Jules Michelet publishes *The People*.
1848	Karl Marx and Friedrich Engels publish *The Communist Manifesto*.

Hayter: The House of Commons, 1833   This collective portrait of the first parliament elected after the Reform Bill of 1832 was painted over several years. The arrangement of the members reflects Britain's historic two-party system, with the majority on one side and the "loyal opposition" on the other. Most European countries developed multiparty systems and coalition politics, with competing groups seated in a large half circle. *(Trustees of the National Portrait Gallery, London)*

The change in the Corn Laws, coming as it did at a time of widespread unemployment and postwar economic distress, resulted in protests and demonstrations by urban laborers. The laborers were supported by radical intellectuals, who campaigned for a reformed House of Commons that would serve the nation and not just the aristocracy. In 1817 the Tory government responded by temporarily suspending the traditional rights of peaceable assembly and habeas corpus. Two years later, Parliament passed the infamous Six Acts, which, among other things, placed controls on a heavily taxed press and practically eliminated all mass meetings. These acts followed an enormous but orderly protest, at Saint Peter's Fields in Manchester, that had been savagely broken up by armed cavalry. Nicknamed the "Battle of Peterloo," in scornful reference to the British victory at Waterloo, this incident demonstrated the government's determination to repress and stand fast.

Ongoing industrial development was not only creating urban and social problems but also strengthening the upper middle classes. The new manufacturing and commercial groups insisted on a place for their new wealth alongside the landed wealth of the aristocracy in the framework of political power and social prestige. They called for many kinds of liberal reform: reform of town government, organization of a new police force, more rights for Catholics and dissenters, and reform of the Poor Laws that provided aid to some low-paid workers. In the 1820s, a less frightened Tory government moved in the direction of better urban administration, greater economic liberalism, and civil equality for Catholics. The prohibition on imports of foreign grain was replaced by a heavy tariff. These actions encouraged the middle classes to press on for reform of Parliament so they could have a larger say in government and perhaps repeal the latest revision of the Corn Laws, that symbol of aristocratic domination.

The Whig party, though led like the Tories by great aristocrats, had by tradition been more responsive to commercial and manufacturing interests. In 1830 a Whig ministry introduced "an act to amend the representation of the people of England and Wales." Defeated, then passed by the House of Commons, this reform bill was rejected by the House of Lords. But when in 1832 the Whigs got the king to promise to create enough new peers to pass the law, the House of Lords reluctantly gave in rather than see its snug little club ruined by upstart manufacturers and plutocrats. A mighty surge of popular protest had helped the king and lords make up their minds.

The Reform Bill of 1832 had profound significance. The House of Commons had emerged as the all-important legislative body. In the future, an obstructionist House of Lords could always be brought into line by the threat of creating new peers. The new industrial areas of the country gained representation in the Commons, and many old "rotten boroughs"—electoral districts that had very few voters and that the landed aristocracy had bought and sold—were eliminated.

The redistribution of seats reflected the shift in population to the northern manufacturing counties and the gradual emergence of an urban society. As a result of the Reform Bill of 1832, the number of voters increased by about 50 percent, giving about 12 percent of the total population the right to vote. Comfortable middle-class groups in the urban population, as well as some substantial farmers who leased their land, received the vote. Thus the pressures building in Great Britain were successfully—though only temporarily—released. A major reform had been achieved peacefully, without revolution or civil war. More radical reforms within the system appeared difficult but not impossible. Legislation could solve problems and improve social conditions.

The principal radical program was embodied in the "People's Charter" of 1838 and the Chartist movement (see page 749). Partly inspired by the economic distress of the working class in the 1830s and 1840s, the Chartists' core demand was universal male (but not female) suffrage. They saw complete political democracy and rule by the common people as the means to a good and just society. Hundreds of thousands of people signed gigantic petitions calling on Parliament to grant all men the right to vote, first and most seriously in 1839, again in 1842, and yet again in 1848. Parliament rejected all three petitions. In the short run, the working poor failed with their Chartist demands, but they learned a valuable lesson in mass politics.

While calling for universal male suffrage, many working-class people joined with middle-class manufacturers in the Anti–Corn Law League, founded in Manchester in 1839. Mass participation made possible a popular crusade against the tariff on imported grain and against the landed aristocracy. People were fired up by dramatic popular orators such as John Bright and Richard Cobden. These fighting liberals argued that lower food prices and more jobs in industry depended on repeal of the Corn Laws. Much of the working class agreed. The climax of the movement came in 1845. In that year, Ireland's potato crop failed, and rapidly rising food prices marked the beginning of the Irish famine. Famine prices for food and even famine itself also seemed likely in England. To avert the impending catastrophe, Tory prime minister Robert Peel joined with the Whigs and a minority of his own party to repeal the Corn Laws in 1846 and allow free imports of grain. England escaped famine. Thereafter, the liberal doctrine of free trade became almost sacred dogma in Great Britain.

The following year, the Tories passed a bill designed to help the working classes, but in a different way. This was the Ten Hours Act of 1847, which limited the workday for women and young people in factories to ten hours. Tory aristocrats continued to champion legislation regulating factory conditions. They were competing vigorously with the middle class for the support of the working class. This healthy competition between a still-vigorous aristocracy and a strong middle class was a crucial factor in Great Britain's peaceful evolution. The working classes could make temporary alliances with either competitor to better their own conditions.

The people of Ireland did not benefit from this political competition. Long ruled as a conquered people, the great mass of the population (outside the northern counties of Ulster, which were partly Presbyterian) were Irish Catholic peasants who rented their land from a tiny minority of Church of England Protestants, many of whom lived in England (see Chapter 20). Ruthlessly exploited and growing rapidly in numbers, Irish peasants had come to depend on the potato crop, the size of which varied substantially from year to year. Potato failures could not be detected in time to plant other crops, nor could potatoes be stored for more than a year. Moreover, Ireland's precarious potato economy was a subsistence economy, which therefore lacked a well-developed network of roads and trade capable of distributing other foods in time of disaster. When the crop failed in 1845, the Irish were very vulnerable.

In 1846, 1848, and 1851, the potato crop failed again in Ireland and throughout much of Europe. The

Evictions of Irish Peasants who could not pay their rent continued for decades after the Great Famine. Surrounded by a few meager possessions, this family has been turned out of its cottage in the 1880s. The door is nailed shut to prevent their return. *(Lawrence Collection, National Library of Ireland, Dublin)*

general result was high food prices, widespread suffering, and, frequently, social upheaval. In Ireland the result was unmitigated disaster—the Great Famine. Blight attacked the young plants, and the tubers rotted. Widespread starvation and mass fever epidemics followed. Total losses of population were staggering. Fully 1 million emigrants fled the famine between 1845 and 1851, going primarily to the United States and Great Britain, and at least 1.5 million people died or were not born because of the disaster. The British government's efforts at famine relief were too little, too late. Moreover, the government energetically supported heartless landowner demands with armed force. Tenants who could not pay their rents were evicted and their homes broken up or burned. Famine or no, Ireland remained a conquered province, a poor agricultural land that had gained little from the liberal reforms and the industrial developments that were transforming Britain.

The Revolution of 1830 in France

Louis XVIII's Constitutional Charter of 1814—theoretically a gift from the king but actually a response to political pressures—was basically a liberal constitution (see page 720). The economic and social gains made by sections of the middle class and the peasantry in the French Revolution were fully protected, great intellectual and artistic freedom was permitted, and a real parliament with upper and lower houses was created. Immediately after Napoleon's abortive Hundred Days, the moderate, worldly king refused to bow to the wishes of die-hard aristocrats such as his brother Charles, who wished to sweep away all the revolutionary changes and return to a bygone age of royal absolutism and aristocratic pretension. Instead, Louis appointed as his ministers moderate royalists, who sought and obtained the support of a majority of the representatives elected to the lower Chamber of Deputies between 1816 and Louis's death in 1824.

Louis XVIII's charter was anything but democratic. Only about 100,000 of the wealthiest people out of a total population of 30 million had the right to vote for the deputies who, with the king and his ministers, made the laws of the nation. Nonetheless, the "notable people" who did vote came from very different backgrounds. There were wealthy businessmen, war profiteers, successful professionals, ex-revolutionaries, large landowners from the old aristocracy and the middle class, Bourbons, and Bonapartists.

The old aristocracy, with its pre-1789 mentality, was a minority within the voting population. It was this situation that Louis's successor, Charles X (r. 1824–1830), could not abide. Crowned in a lavish, utterly medieval, five-hour ceremony in the cathedral of Reims in 1824, Charles was a true reactionary. He wanted to re-establish the old order in France. Increasingly blocked by the opposition of the deputies, Charles finally repudiated the Constitutional Charter in an attempted coup in July 1830. He issued decrees stripping much of the wealthy middle class of its voting rights, and he censored the press. The immediate reaction, encouraged by journalists and lawyers, was an insurrection in the capital by printers, other artisans, and small traders. In "three glorious days," the government collapsed. Paris boiled with revolutionary excitement, and Charles fled. Then the upper middle class, which had fomented the revolt, skillfully seated Charles's cousin, Louis Philippe, duke of Orléans, on the vacant throne.

Louis Philippe (r. 1830–1848) accepted the Constitutional Charter of 1814; adopted the red, white, and blue flag of the French Revolution; and admitted that he was merely the "king of the French people." In spite of such symbolic actions, the situation in France remained fundamentally unchanged. Casimir Périer, a wealthy banker and Louis Philippe's new chief minister, bluntly told a deputy who complained when the vote was extended only from 100,000 to 170,000 citizens, "The trouble with this country is that there are too many people like you who imagine that there has been a revolution in France."[3] The wealthy notable elite actually tightened its control as the old aristocracy retreated to the provinces to sulk harmlessly. For the upper middle class, there had been a change in dynasty in order to protect the status quo and the narrowly liberal institutions of 1815. Republicans, democrats, social reformers, and the poor of Paris were bitterly disappointed. They had made a revolution, but it seemed for naught.

 ## THE REVOLUTIONS OF 1848

In 1848 revolutionary political and social ideologies combined with severe economic crisis and the romantic impulse to produce a vast upheaval across Europe. Only the most advanced and the most backward major countries—reforming Great Britain and immobile Russia—escaped untouched. Governments toppled; monarchs and ministers bowed or fled. National independence, liberal-democratic constitutions, and social reform: the lofty aspirations of a generation seemed at hand. Yet in the end, the revolutions failed. Why was this so?

A Democratic Republic in France

The late 1840s in Europe were hard economically and tense politically. The potato famine in Ireland in 1845 and in 1846 had echoes on the continent. Bad harvests jacked up food prices and caused misery and unemployment in the cities. "Prerevolutionary" outbreaks occurred all across Europe: an abortive Polish revolution in the northern part of Austria in 1846, a civil war between radicals and conservatives in Switzerland in 1847, and an armed uprising in Naples, Italy, in January 1848. Revolution was almost universally expected, but it took revolution in Paris—once again—to turn expectations into realities.

Louis Philippe's "bourgeois monarchy" had been characterized by stubborn inaction and complacency. There was a glaring lack of social legislation, and politics was dominated by corruption and selfish special interests. With only the rich voting for deputies, many of the deputies were docile government bureaucrats.

The government's stubborn refusal to consider electoral reform heightened a sense of class injustice among middle-class shopkeepers, skilled artisans, and unskilled working people, and it eventually touched off a popular revolt in Paris. Barricades went up on the night of February 22, 1848, and by February 24 Louis Philippe had abdicated in favor of his grandson. But the common people in arms would tolerate no more monarchy. This refusal led to the proclamation of a provisional republic, headed by a ten-man executive committee and certified by cries of approval from the revolutionary crowd.

A generation of historians and journalists had praised the First French Republic, and their work had borne fruit: the revolutionaries were firmly committed to a republic (as opposed to any form of constitutional monarchy), and they immediately set about drafting a constitution for France's Second Republic. Moreover, they wanted a truly popular and democratic republic so that the healthy, life-giving forces of the common people—the peasants, the artisans, and the unskilled workers—could reform society with wise legislation. In practice, building such a republic meant giving the right to vote to every adult male, and this was quickly done. Revolutionary compassion and sympathy for freedom were expressed in the freeing of all slaves in French colonies, the abolition of the death penalty, and the establishment of a ten-hour workday for Paris.

Yet there were profound differences within the revolutionary coalition in Paris. On the one hand, there were the moderate, liberal republicans of the middle class. They viewed universal male suffrage as the ultimate concession to be made to popular forces, and they strongly opposed any further radical social measures. On the other hand, there were radical republicans and hard-pressed artisans. Influenced by a generation of utopian socialists, and appalled by the poverty and misery of the urban poor, the radical republicans were

Delacroix: Liberty Leading the People   This famous romantic painting glorifies the July Revolution in Paris in 1830. Raising high the revolutionary tricolor, Liberty unites the worker, bourgeois, and street child in a righteous crusade against privilege and oppression. The revolution of 1848 began as a similar crusade, but class warfare in Paris soon shattered the hope of rich and poor joined together for freedom. *(Louvre © Photo R.M.N)*

THE REVOLUTIONS OF 1848

February	Revolt against Louis Philippe's "bourgeois monarchy" takes place in Paris; Louis Philippe abdicates; a provisional republic is proclaimed.
February–June	Establishment and rapid growth of government-sponsored workshops occur in France.
March 3	Hungarians under Kossuth demand autonomy from the Austrian Empire.
March 13	Uprising of students and workers occurs in Vienna; Metternich flees to London.
March 19–21	Frederick William IV of Prussia is forced to salute the bodies of slain revolutionaries in Berlin and agrees to a liberal constitution and merger into a new German state.
March 20	Ferdinand I of Austria abolishes serfdom and promises reforms.
March 26	Workers in Berlin issue a series of socialist demands.
April 22	French voters favor moderate republicans over radicals 5 to 1.
May 15	Parisian socialist workers invade the Constitutional Assembly and unsuccessfully proclaim a new revolutionary state.
May 18	Frankfurt Assembly begins writing a new German constitution.
June 17	Austrian army crushes a working-class revolt in Prague.
June 22–26	French government abolishes the national workshops, provoking an uprising. June Days: republican army defeats the rebellious Parisian working class.
October	Austrian army besieges and retakes Vienna from students and working-class radicals.
December	Conservatives force Ferdinand I of Austria to abdicate in favor of young Francis Joseph. Frederick William IV disbands the Prussian Constituent Assembly and grants Prussia a conservative constitution. Louis Napoleon wins a landslide victory in the French presidential elections.
March 1849	Frankfurt Assembly elects Frederick William IV of Prussia emperor of the new German state; Frederick William refuses and reasserts his royal authority in Prussia.
June–August 1849	Habsburg and Russian forces defeat the Hungarian independence movement.

committed to some kind of socialism. So were many artisans, who hated the unrestrained competition of cutthroat capitalism and who advocated a combination of strong craft unions and worker-owned businesses.

Worsening depression and rising unemployment brought these conflicting goals to the fore in 1848. Louis Blanc, who along with a worker named Albert represented the republican socialists in the provisional government, pressed for recognition of a socialist right to work. Blanc asserted that permanent government-sponsored cooperative workshops should be established for workers. Such workshops would be an alternative to capitalist employment and a decisive step toward a new, noncompetitive social order.

The moderate republicans wanted no such thing. They were willing to provide only temporary relief. The resulting compromise set up national workshops—soon to become little more than a vast program of pick-and-shovel public works—and established a special commission under Blanc to "study the question." This satisfied no one. The national workshops were, however, better than nothing. An army of desperate poor from the French provinces and even from foreign countries streamed into Paris to sign up. As the economic crisis worsened, the number enrolled in the workshops soared from 10,000 in March to 120,000 by June, and another 80,000 were trying unsuccessfully to join.

While the workshops in Paris grew, the French masses went to the election polls in late April. Voting in most cases for the first time, the people of France elected to the new Constituent Assembly about five hundred moderate republicans, three hundred monarchists, and one hundred radicals who professed various brands of socialism. One of the moderate republicans was the author of *Democracy in America,* Alexis de Tocqueville (1805–1859), who had predicted the overthrow of Louis Philippe's government. To this brilliant observer, socialism was the most characteristic aspect of the revolution in Paris.

This socialist revolution was evoking a violent reaction not only among the frightened middle and upper classes but also among the bulk of the population—the peasants. The French peasants owned land, and according to Tocqueville, "private property had become with all those who owned it a sort of bond of fraternity."[4] The countryside, Tocqueville wrote, had been seized with a universal hatred of radical Paris. Returning from Normandy to take his seat in the new Constituent Assembly, Tocqueville saw that a majority of the members were firmly committed to the republic and strongly opposed to the socialists and their artisan allies, and he shared their sentiments.

This clash of ideologies—of liberal capitalism and socialism—became a clash of classes and arms after the elections. The new government's executive committee dropped Blanc and thereafter included no representative of the Parisian working class. Fearing that their socialist hopes were about to be dashed, artisans and unskilled workers invaded the Constituent Assembly on May 15 and tried to proclaim a new revolutionary state. But the government was ready and used the middle-class National Guard to squelch this uprising. As the workshops continued to fill and grow more radical, the fearful but powerful propertied classes in the Assembly took the offensive. On June 22, the government dissolved the national workshops in Paris, giving the workers the choice of joining the army or going to workshops in the provinces.

The result was a spontaneous and violent uprising. Frustrated in attempts to create a socialist society, masses of desperate people were now losing even their life-sustaining relief. As a voice from the crowd cried out when the famous astronomer François Arago counseled patience, "Ah, Monsieur Arago, you have never been hungry!"[5] Barricades sprang up in the narrow streets of Paris, and a terrible class war began. Working people fought with the courage of utter desperation, but the government had the army and the support of peasant France. After three terrible "June Days" and the death or injury of more than ten thousand people, the republican army under General Louis Cavaignac stood triumphant in a sea of working-class blood and hatred.

The revolution in France thus ended in spectacular failure. The February coalition of the middle and working classes had in four short months become locked in mortal combat. In place of a generous democratic republic, the Constituent Assembly completed a constitution featuring a strong executive. This allowed Louis Napoleon, nephew of Napoleon Bonaparte, to win a landslide victory in the election of December 1848. The appeal of his great name as well as the desire of the propertied classes for order at any cost had produced a semi-authoritarian regime.

The Austrian Empire in 1848

Throughout central Europe, the first news of the upheaval in France evoked feverish excitement and eventually revolution. Liberals demanded written constitutions, representative government, and greater civil liberties from authoritarian regimes. When governments hesitated, popular revolts followed. Urban workers and students served as the shock troops, but they were allied with middle-class liberals and peasants. In the face of this united front, monarchs collapsed and granted almost everything. The popular revolutionary coalition, having secured great and easy victories, then broke down as it had in France. The traditional forces—the monarchy, the aristocracy, and the regular army—recovered their nerve, reasserted their authority, and took back many, though not all, of the concessions. Reaction was everywhere victorious.

The revolution in the Austrian Empire began in Hungary, where nationalistic Hungarians demanded national autonomy, full civil liberties, and universal suffrage. When the monarchy in Vienna hesitated, Viennese students and workers took to the streets, and peasant disorders broke out in parts of the empire. The Habsburg emperor Ferdinand I (r. 1835–1848) capitulated and promised reforms and a liberal constitution. Metternich fled in disguise toward London. The old absolutist order seemed to be collapsing with unbelievable rapidity.

The coalition of revolutionaries was not stable, however. The Austrian Empire was overwhelmingly agricultural, and serfdom still existed. On March 20, as part of its capitulation before upheaval, the monarchy abolished serfdom, with its degrading forced labor and feudal services. Feeling they had won a victory reminiscent of that in France in 1789, newly free men and women of the land then lost interest in the political and social questions agitating the cities. Meanwhile, the coalition of urban revolutionaries also broke down. When artisan workers and the urban poor rose in arms and presented their own demands for socialist workshops and universal voting rights for men, the prosperous middle classes recoiled in alarm.

The coalition of March was also weakened, and ultimately destroyed, by conflicting national aspirations. In March the Hungarian revolutionary leaders pushed through an extremely liberal, almost democratic, constitution. But the Hungarian revolutionaries also sought to transform the mosaic of provinces and peoples that was the kingdom of Hungary into a unified, centralized, Hungarian nation. To the minority groups that formed half of the population—the Croats, Serbs, and Romanians—such unification was completely unacceptable. Each felt entitled to political autonomy and cultural independence. The Habsburg monarchy in Vienna exploited the fears of the minority groups, and they were soon locked in armed combat with the new Hungarian government. In a somewhat similar way, Czech nationalists based in Bohemia and the city of Prague came into conflict with German nationalists. Thus the national aspirations within the Austrian Empire enabled the monarchy to play off one group against the other.

Finally, the conservative aristocratic forces gathered around Emperor Ferdinand I regained their nerve and reasserted their great strength. The archduchess Sophia, a conservative but intelligent and courageous Bavarian princess married to the emperor's brother, provided a rallying point. Deeply ashamed of the emperor's collapse before a "mess of students," she insisted that Ferdinand, who had no heir, abdicate in favor of her son, Francis Joseph.[6] Powerful nobles who held high positions in the government, the army, and the church agreed completely. They organized around Sophia in a secret conspiracy to reverse and crush the revolution.

Their first breakthrough came when the army bombarded Prague and savagely crushed a working-class revolt there on June 17. Other Austrian officials and nobles began to lead the minority nationalities of Hungary against the revolutionary government proclaimed by the Hungarian patriots. At the end of October, the well-equipped, predominantly peasant troops of the regular Austrian army attacked the student and working-class radicals in Vienna and retook the city at the cost of more than four thousand casualties. Thus the determination of the Austrian aristocracy and the loyalty of its army were the final ingredients in the triumph of reaction and the defeat of revolution.

When Francis Joseph (r. 1848–1916) was crowned emperor of Austria immediately after his eighteenth birthday in December 1848, only Hungary had yet to be brought under control. But another determined conservative, Nicholas I of Russia (r. 1825–1855), obligingly lent his iron hand. On June 6, 1849, 130,000 Russian troops poured into Hungary and subdued the country after bitter fighting. For a number of years, the Habsburgs ruled Hungary as a conquered territory.

Prussia and the Frankfurt Assembly

After Austria, Prussia was the largest and most influential German kingdom. Prior to 1848, the goal of middle-class Prussian liberals had been to transform absolutist Prussia into a liberal constitutional monarchy, which would lead the thirty-eight states of the German Confederation into the liberal, unified nation desired by liberals throughout the German states. The agitation following the fall of Louis Philippe encouraged Prussian liberals to press their demands. When the artisans and factory workers in Berlin exploded in March and joined temporarily with the middle-class liberals in the struggle against the monarchy, the autocratic yet paternalistic Frederick William IV (r. 1840–1861) vacillated and finally caved in. On March 21, he promised to grant Prussia a liberal constitution and to merge Prussia into a new national German state that was to be created. But urban workers wanted much more and the Prussian aristocracy wanted much less than the moderate constitutional liberalism the king conceded. The workers issued a series of democratic and vaguely socialist demands that troubled their middle-class allies, and the conservative clique gathered around the king to urge counter-revolution.

As an elected Prussian Constituent Assembly met in Berlin to write a constitution for the Prussian state, a self-appointed committee of liberals from various German states successfully called for a national assembly to

Street Fighting in Frankfurt, 1848   Workers and students could tear up the cobblestones, barricade a street, and make it into a fortress. But urban revolutionaries were untrained and poorly armed. They were no match for professional soldiers led by tough officers who were sent against them after frightened rulers had recovered their nerve. *(The Granger Collection, New York)*

begin writing a federal constitution for a unified German state. Meeting in Frankfurt in May, the National Assembly was a curious revolutionary body. It was a really serious middle-class body of lawyers, professors, doctors, officials, and businessmen.

Convened to write a constitution, the learned body was soon absorbed in a battle with Denmark over the provinces of Schleswig and Holstein, an extremely complicated issue from a legal point of view. The provinces were inhabited primarily by Germans but were ruled by the king of Denmark, although Holstein was a member

of the German Confederation. When Frederick VII, the new nationalistic king of Denmark, tried to integrate both provinces into the rest of his state, the Germans in these provinces revolted. Hypnotized by this conflict, the National Assembly at Frankfurt debated ponderously and finally called on the Prussian army to oppose Denmark in the name of the German nation. Prussia responded and began war with Denmark. As the Schleswig-Holstein issue demonstrated, the national ideal was a crucial factor motivating the German middle classes in 1848.

In March 1849, the National Assembly finally completed its drafting of a liberal constitution and elected King Frederick William of Prussia emperor of the new German national state (minus Austria and Schleswig-Holstein). By early 1849, however, reaction had been successful almost everywhere. Frederick William had reasserted his royal authority, disbanded the Prussian Constituent Assembly, and granted his subjects a limited, essentially conservative constitution. Reasserting that he ruled by divine right, Frederick William contemptuously refused to accept the "crown from the gutter." Bogged down by their preoccupation with nationalist issues, the reluctant revolutionaries in Frankfurt had waited too long and acted too timidly.

When Frederick William, who really wanted to be emperor but only on his own authoritarian terms, tried to get the small monarchs of Germany to elect him emperor, Austria balked. Supported by Russia, Austria forced Prussia to renounce all its schemes of unification in late 1850. The German Confederation was reestablished. Attempts to unite the Germans—first in a liberal national state and then in a conservative Prussian empire—had failed completely.

SUMMARY

In 1814 the victorious allied powers sought to restore peace and stability in Europe. Dealing moderately with France and wisely settling their own differences, the allies laid the foundations for beneficial international cooperation throughout much of the nineteenth century. Led by Metternich, the conservative powers also sought to prevent the spread of subversive ideas and radical changes in domestic politics. Yet European thought has seldom been more powerfully creative than after 1815, and ideologies of liberalism, nationalism, and socialism all developed to challenge the existing order in this period of early industrialization and rapid population growth. The romantic movement, breaking decisively with the dictates of classicism, reinforced the spirit of change and revolutionary anticipation.

All of these forces culminated in the liberal and nationalistic revolutions of 1848. Political, economic, and social pressures that had been building since 1815 exploded dramatically, but the upheavals of 1848 were abortive, and very few revolutionary goals were realized. The moderate, nationalistic middle classes were unable to consolidate their initial victories in France or elsewhere in Europe. Instead, they drew back when artisans, factory workers, and radical socialists rose up to present their own much more revolutionary demands. This retreat facilitated the efforts of dedicated aristocrats in central Europe and made possible the crushing of Parisian workers by a coalition of solid bourgeoisie and landowning peasantry in France. A host of fears, a sea of blood, and a torrent of disillusion had drowned the lofty ideals and utopian visions of a generation. The age of romantic revolution was over.

NOTES

1. Quoted in H. Kohn, *Nationalism* (New York: Van Nostrand, 1955), pp. 141–142.
2. Quoted in F. B. Artz, *From the Renaissance to Romanticism: Trends in Style in Art, Literature, and Music, 1300–1830* (Chicago: University of Chicago Press, 1962), pp. 276, 278.
3. Quoted in G. Wright, *France in Modern Times,* 4th ed. (Chicago: Rand McNally, 1987), p. 145.
4. A. de Tocqueville, *Recollections* (New York: Columbia University Press, 1949), p. 94.
5. M. Agulhon, *1848* (Paris: Éditions du Seuil, 1973), pp. 68–69.
6. W. L. Langer, *Political and Social Upheaval, 1832–1852* (New York: Harper & Row, 1969), p. 361.

SUGGESTED READING

The works cited in the Notes are highly recommended. Wright's work is a lively introduction to French history with stimulating biographical discussions; Langer's is a balanced synthesis with an excellent bibliography. Among general studies, R. Gildea, *Barricades and Borders: Europe, 1800–1914,* 2d ed. (1996), is recommended. C. Morazé, *The Triumph of the Middle Classes* (1968), a wide-ranging procapitalist interpretation, may be compared with E. J. Hobsbawm's flexible Marxism in *The Age of Revolution, 1789–1848* (1962). For English history, E. Thompson, *The Rise of Respectable Society, 1830–1900* (1986), A. Briggs's socially oriented *The Making of Modern England, 1784–1867* (1967), and D. Thomson, *England in the Nineteenth Century, 1815–1914* (1951), are excellent. Restoration France is sympathetically portrayed by G. de Bertier de Sauvigny in *The Bourbon Restoration* (1967). R. Price, *A Social History of Nineteenth-Century France* (1987), is a fine synthesis. T. Hamerow studies the social implications of the dual revolution in Germany in *Restoration, Revolution, Reaction, 1815–1871* (1966), which may be compared with H. Treitschke's bombastic, pro-Prussian *History of Germany in the Nineteenth Century* (1915–1919), a classic of nationalistic history. H. James, *A German Identity, 1770–1990* (1989), and J. Sheehan, *Germany, 1770–1866* (1989), are stimulating general histories that skillfully incorporate recent research. Two important reconsiderations of nationalism are B. Anderson, *Imagined Communities,* 2d ed. (1991); and E. Hobsbawm and T. Ranger, *The Invention of Tradition* (1990). R. Brubaker, *Citizenship and Nationhood in France and Germany* (1992), is an important comparative study. E. Kedourie, *Nationalism* (1960), is an influential historical critique of the new faith. H. Kissinger, *A World Restored* (1957), offers not only a provocative interpretation of the Congress of Vienna but also insights into the mind of Richard Nixon's famous secretary of state. Compare that volume with H. Nicolson's entertaining *The Congress of Vienna* (1946). On 1848, J. Sperber, *The European Revolutions, 1848–1851* (1993), is a solid recent synthesis. M. Agulhon, *The Republican Experiment, 1848–1852* (1983), and P. Stearns, *The Revolutionary Tide in Europe* (1974), are outstanding older works. I. Deak, *The Lawful Revolution: Louis Kossuth and the Hungarians, 1848–49* (1979), is a noteworthy study of an interesting figure.

On early socialism and Marxism, see A. Lindemann's stimulating survey, *A History of European Socialism* (1983), and W. Sewell, Jr., *Work and Revolution in France: The Language of Labor from the Old Regime to 1848* (1980), as well as G. Lichtheim's high-powered *Marxism* (1961) and his *Short History of Socialism* (1970). J. Seigel, *Marx's Fate: The Shape of a Life* (1978), is a major biography. Fourier is treated sympathetically in J. Beecher, *Charles Fourier* (1986). J. Schumpeter, *Capitalism, Socialism and Democracy* (1947), is magnificent but difficult, a real mind-stretcher. Also highly recommended is B. Taylor, *Eve and the New Jerusalem: Socialism and Feminism in the Nineteenth Century* (1983), which explores fascinating English attempts to emancipate workers and women at the same time. On liberalism, see R. Heilbroner's entertaining *The Worldly Philosophers* (1967) and G. de Ruggiero's classic *History of European Liberalism* (1959). J. Barzun, *Classic, Romantic and Modern* (1961), skillfully discusses the emergence of romanticism, and J. Seigel, *Bohemian Paris: Culture, Politics, and the Boundaries of Bourgeois Life* (1986), imaginatively places romantic aspirations in a broad cultural framework. R. Stromberg, *An Intellectual History of Modern Europe,* 3d ed. (1981), and F. Baumer, *Modern European Thought: Continuity and Change in Ideas, 1600–1950* (1970), are valuable surveys. The important place of religion in nineteenth-century thought is considered from different perspectives in H. McLeod, *Religion and the People of Western Europe* (1981); and O. Chadwick, *The Secularization of the European Mind in the Nineteenth Century* (1976). Two good church histories with useful bibliographies are J. Altholz, *The Churches in the Nineteenth Century* (1967); and A. Vidler, *The Church in an Age of Revolution: 1789 to the Present Day* (1961).

The thoughtful reader is strongly advised to delve into the incredibly rich writing of contemporaries. J. Bowditch and C. Ramsland, eds., *Voices of the Industrial Revolution* (1961), is an excellent starting point, with well-chosen selections from leading economic thinkers and early socialists. H. Hugo, ed., *The Romantic Reader,* is another fine anthology. Mary Shelley's *Frankenstein,* a great romantic novel, draws an almost lovable picture of the famous monster and is highly recommended. Jules Michelet's compassionate masterpiece *The People,* a famous historian's anguished examination of French social divisions on the eve of 1848, draws one into the heart of the period and is highly recommended. Alexis de Tocqueville covers some of the same ground less romantically in his *Recollections,* which may be compared with Karl Marx's white-hot "instant history," *Class Struggles in France, 1848–1850.* Great novels that accurately portray aspects of the times are Victor Hugo, *Les Misérables,* an exciting story of crime and passion among France's poor; Honoré de Balzac, *La Cousine Bette* and *Le Père Goriot;* and Thomas Mann, *Buddenbrooks,* a wonderful historical novel that traces the rise and fall of a prosperous German family over three generations during the nineteenth century.

Faith in Democratic Nationalism

Early advocates of the national ideal usually believed that progress for one people would also contribute to the progress of all humanity. They believed that a Europe of independent nation-states would provide the proper framework for securing freedom, democracy, social justice, and even international peace.

This optimistic faith guided Joseph Mazzini (1805–1872), the leading prophet of Italian nationalism and unification. Banished from Italy in 1830, the exiled Mazzini founded a secret society called Young Italy to fight for Italian unification and a democratic republic. Mazzini's group inspired numerous local insurrections and then led Italy's radicals in the unsuccessful revolutions of 1848. Italy was united a decade later, but by other means.

Mazzini's best-known work was The Duties of Man, *a collection of essays. The following famous selection, titled "Duties Towards Your Country," was written in 1858 and addressed to Italian workingmen.*

Your first Duties . . . are to Humanity. . . . But what can each of you, with his isolated powers, do for the moral improvement, for the progress of Humanity? . . .

God gave you the means of multiplying your forces and your powers of action indefinitely when he gave you a Country, when, like a wise overseer of labor, who distributes the different parts of the work according to the capacity of the workmen, he divided Humanity into distinct groups upon the face of our globe, and thus planted the seeds of nations. Evil governments have disfigured the design of God, which you may see clearly marked out, as far, at least, as regards Europe, by the courses of the great rivers, by the lines of the lofty mountains, and by other geographical conditions; they have disfigured it by conquest, by greed, by jealousy of the just sovereignty of others; disfigured it so much that today there is perhaps no nation except England and France whose confines correspond to this design.

[These evil governments] did not, and they do not, recognize any country except their own families and dynasties, the egoism of caste. But the divine design will infallibly be fulfilled. Natural divisions, the innate spontaneous tendencies of the peoples will replace the arbitrary divisions sanctioned by evil governments. The map of Europe will be remade. The Countries of the People will rise, defined by the voice of the free, upon the ruins of the Countries of Kings and privileged castes. Between these Countries there will be harmony and brotherhood. And then the work of Humanity for the general amelioration, for the discovery and application of the real law of life, carried on in association and distributed according to local capacities, will be accomplished by peaceful and progressive development.

Then each of you, strong in the affections and in the aid of many millions of men speaking the same language, endowed with the same tendencies, and educated by the same historic tradition, may hope by your personal effort to benefit the whole of Humanity.

Without Country you have neither name, voice, nor rights, no admission as brothers into the fellowship of the Peoples. You are the bastards of Humanity. Soldiers without a banner, . . . you will find neither faith nor protection. . . . Do not beguile yourselves with the hope of emancipation from unjust social conditions if you do not first conquer a Country for yourselves; where there is no Country there is no common agreement to which you can appeal; the egoism of self-interest rules alone, and he who has the upper hand keeps it, since there is no common safeguard for the interests of all. . . .

O my Brothers! love your Country. Our Country is our home, the home which God has given us, placing therein a numerous family which we love and are loved by. . . . In labouring according to true principles for our Country we are labouring for Humanity; our Country is the fulcrum of the lever which we have to wield for the common good. If we give up this fulcrum we run the risk of becoming useless to our Country and to Humanity. . . .

There is no true Country without a uniform law. There is no true Country where the uniformity of that law is violated by the existence of caste, privilege, and inequality, where the powers and faculties of a large number of individuals are suppressed or dormant, where there is no common principle accepted, recognized, and developed by all. In such a state of things there can be no Nation, no People, but only a multitude, a fortuitous agglomeration of men whom circumstances have brought together and different circumstances will separate. In the name of your love for your Country you must combat without truce the existence of every privilege, every inequality, upon the soil which has given you birth. . . .

Your Country should be your Temple. God at the summit, a People of equals at the base. Do not accept any other formula, any other moral law, if you do not want to dishonour your Country and yourselves. Let the secondary laws for the gradual regulation of your existence be the progressive application of this supreme law.

And in order that they should be so, it is necessary that *all* should contribute to the making of them. The laws made by one fraction of the citizens only can never by the nature of things and men do otherwise than reflect the thoughts and aspirations and desires of that fraction; they represent, not the whole country, but a third, a fourth part, a class, a zone of the country. The law must express the general aspiration, promote the good of all, respond to a beat of the nation's heart. The whole nation therefore should be, directly or indirectly, the legislator. By yielding this mission to a few men, you put the egoism of one class in the place of the Country, which is the union of *all* the classes.

A Country is not a mere territory; the particular territory is only its foundation. The Country is the idea which rises upon that foundation; it is the sentiment of love, the sense of fellowship which binds together all the sons of that territory.

So long as a single one of your brothers is not represented by his own vote in the development of the national life—so long as a single one vegetates uneducated among the educated—so long as a single one able and willing to work languishes in

❖ Portrait of Giuseppe Mazzini, from the Museo del Risorgimento, Milan. *(Museo del Risorgimento/ Scala/Art Resource, NY)*

poverty for want of work—you have not got a Country such as it ought to be, the Country of all and for all.

Votes, education, work are the three main pillars of the nation; do not rest until your hands have solidly erected them.

Questions for Analysis

1. What did Mazzini mean by "evil governments"? Why are they evil?

2. What are the characteristics of the "true Country"?

3. What form of government is best? Why?

4. Why, according to Mazzini, should poor workingmen have been interested in the political unification of Italy?

5. How might a woman today criticize Mazzini's program? Debate how Mazzini might respond to such criticism.

Source: Slightly adapted from J. Mazzini, *The Duties of Man and Other Essays* (London: J. M. Dent and Sons, 1907), pp. 51–57.

24 Life in the Emerging Urban Society

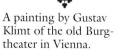

A painting by Gustav Klimt of the old Burgtheater in Vienna. *(Museen der Stadt Wien)*

The era of intellectual and political upheaval that culminated in the revolutions of 1848 was also an era of rapid urbanization. After 1848 Western political development veered off in a novel and uncharted direction, but the growth of towns and cities rushed forward with undiminished force. Thus Western society was urban and industrial in 1900 as surely as it had been rural and agrarian in 1800. The urbanization of society was both a result of the Industrial Revolution and a reflection of its enormous long-term impact.

- What was life like in the cities, and how did it change?
- What did the emergence of urban industrial society mean for rich and poor and those in between?
- How did families change as they coped with the challenges and the opportunities of the developing urban civilization?
- What changes in science and thought reflected and influenced this new civilization?

These are the questions this chapter will investigate.

⚜ TAMING THE CITY

The growth of industry posed enormous challenges for all elements of Western society, from young factory workers confronting relentless discipline to aristocratic elites maneuvering to retain political power. As we saw in Chapter 22, the early consequences of economic transformation were mixed and far-reaching and by no means wholly negative. By 1850 at the latest, working conditions were improving and real wages were rising for the mass of the population, and they continued to do so until 1914. Thus given the poverty and uncertainty of preindustrial life, some historians maintain that the history of industrialization in the nineteenth century is probably better written in terms of increasing opportunities than in terms of greater hardships.

Critics of this relatively optimistic view of industrialization claim that it neglects the quality of life in urban areas. They stress that the new industrial towns and cities were awful places where people, especially poor people, suffered from bad housing, lack of sanitation, and a sense of hopelessness. They ask if these drawbacks did not more than cancel out higher wages and greater

opportunity. An examination of the development of cities in the nineteenth century provides some answers to this complex question.

Industry and the Growth of Cities

Since the Middle Ages, European cities had been centers of government, culture, and large-scale commerce. They had also been congested, dirty, and unhealthy. People were packed together almost as tightly as possible within the city limits. The typical city was a "walking city": for all but the wealthiest classes, walking was the only available form of transportation.

Infectious disease spread with deadly speed in cities, and people were always more likely to die in the city than in the countryside. In the larger towns, more people died each year than were born, on average, and urban populations were able to maintain their numbers only because newcomers were continually arriving from rural areas. Little could be done to improve these conditions. Given the pervasive poverty, absence of urban transportation, and lack of medical knowledge, the deadly and overcrowded conditions could only be accepted fatalistically. They were the urban equivalents of bad weather and poor crops, the price of urban excitement and opportunity.

Clearly, deplorable urban conditions did not originate with the Industrial Revolution. What the Industrial Revolution did was to reveal those conditions more nakedly than ever before. The steam engine freed industrialists from dependence on the energy of fast-flowing streams and rivers so that by 1800 there was every incentive to build new factories in urban areas. Cities had better shipping facilities than the countryside and thus better supplies of coal and raw materials. There were also many hands wanting work in the cities, for cities drew people like a magnet. And it was a great advantage for a manufacturer to have other factories nearby to supply the business's needs and buy its products. Therefore, as industry grew, there was also a rapid expansion of already overcrowded and unhealthy cities.

The challenge of the urban environment was felt first and most acutely in Great Britain. The number of people living in cities of 20,000 or more in England and Wales jumped from 1.5 million in 1801 to 6.3 million in 1851 and reached 15.6 million in 1891. Such cities accounted for 17 percent of the total English population in 1801, 35 percent as early as 1851, and fully 54

MAP 24.1 European Cities of 100,000 or More, 1800 and 1900 There were more large cities in Great Britain in 1900 than in all of Europe in 1800. Northwestern Europe was the most urbanized area.

percent in 1891. Other countries duplicated the English pattern as they industrialized (Map 24.1). An American observer was hardly exaggerating when he wrote in 1899 that "the most remarkable social phenomenon of the present century is the concentration of population in cities."[1]

In the 1820s and 1830s, people in Britain and France began to worry about the condition of their cities. In those years, the populations of a number of British cities were increasing by 40 to 70 percent each decade. With urban areas expanding at such previously undreamed-of rates, people's fatalistic acceptance of overcrowded, unsanitary urban living conditions began to give way to active concern. Something urgently needed to be done.

On one point everyone could agree: except on the outskirts, each town or city was using every scrap of land to the fullest extent. Parks and open areas were almost nonexistent. A British parliamentary committee reported in 1833 that "with a rapidly increasing population, lodged for the most part in narrow courts and confined streets, the means of occasional exercise and recreation in fresh air are every day lessened, as inclosures [of vacant areas] take place and buildings spread themselves on every side."[2] Buildings were erected on the smallest possible lots in order to pack the maximum number of people into a given space. Narrow houses were built wall to wall in long rows. These row houses

had neither front nor back yards, and only a narrow alley in back separated one row from the next. Or buildings were built around tiny courtyards completely enclosed on all four sides. Many people lived in extremely small, often overcrowded cellars or attics. "Six, eight, and even ten occupying one room is anything but uncommon," wrote a doctor from Aberdeen in Scotland for a government investigation in 1842.

These highly concentrated urban populations lived in extremely unsanitary and unhealthy conditions. Open drains and sewers flowed alongside or down the middle of unpaved streets. Because of poor construction and an absence of running water, the sewers often filled with garbage and excrement. Toilet facilities were primitive in the extreme. In parts of Manchester, as many as two hundred people shared a single outhouse. Such privies filled up rapidly, and since they were infrequently emptied, sewage often overflowed and seeped into cellar dwellings.

The extent to which filth lay underfoot and the smell of excrement filled the air is hard to believe; yet it was abundantly documented between 1830 and 1850. One London construction engineer found, for example, that the cellars of two large houses on a major road were "full of night-soil [human excrement], to the depth of three feet, which had been permitted for years to accumulate from the overflow of the cesspools." Moreover, some courtyards in poorer neighborhoods became dunghills, collecting excrement that was sometimes sold as fertilizer. By the 1840s there was among the better-off classes a growing, shocking "realization that, to put it as mildly as possible, millions of English men, women, and children were living in shit."[3]

Who or what was responsible for these awful conditions? The crucial factors were the tremendous pressure of more people and the *total* absence of public transportation. People simply had to jam themselves together if they were to be able to walk to shops and factories. Another factor was that government in Great Britain, both local and national, was slow to provide sanitary facilities and establish adequate building codes. This slow pace was probably attributable more to a need to explore and identify what precisely should be done than to rigid middle-class opposition to government action. Certainly, Great Britain had no monopoly on overcrowded and unhealthy urban conditions; many continental cities with stronger traditions of municipal regulation were every bit as bad.

Most responsible of all was the sad legacy of rural housing conditions in preindustrial society combined with appalling ignorance. As one authority concludes, there "were rural slums of a horror not surpassed by the rookeries of London. . . . The evidence shows that the decent cottage was the exception, the hovel the rule."[4] Thus housing was far down on the newcomer's list of priorities, and it is not surprising that many people carried the filth of the mud floor and the dung of the barnyard with them to the city.

Indeed, ordinary people generally took dirt and filth for granted. One English miner told an investigator, "I do not think it usual for the lasses [in the coal mines] to wash their bodies; my sisters never wash themselves." As for the men, "their legs and bodies are as black as your hat."[5]

Filth and Disease   This 1852 drawing from *Punch* tells volumes about the unhealthy living conditions of the urban poor. In the foreground children play with a dead rat and a woman scavenges a dungheap. Cheap rooming houses provide shelter for the frightfully overcrowded population. *(The British Library)*

A COURT FOR KING CHOLERA.

Public Health and the Bacterial Revolution

Although cleanliness was not next to godliness in most people's eyes, it was becoming so for some reformers. The most famous of these was Edwin Chadwick, one of the commissioners charged with the administration of relief to paupers under Britain's revised Poor Law of 1834. Chadwick was a good *Benthamite*—that is, a follower of radical philosopher Jeremy Bentham (1748–1832). Bentham had taught that public problems ought to be dealt with on a rational, scientific basis and according to the "greatest good for the greatest number." Applying these principles, Chadwick soon became convinced that disease and death actually caused poverty simply because a sick worker was an unemployed worker and orphaned children were poor children. Most important, Chadwick believed that disease could be prevented by cleaning up the urban environment. That was his "sanitary idea."

Building on a growing number of medical and sociological studies, Chadwick collected detailed reports from local Poor Law officials on the "sanitary conditions of the laboring population" and published his hard-hitting findings in 1842. This mass of widely publicized evidence proved that disease was related to filthy environmental conditions, which were in turn caused largely by lack of drainage, sewers, and garbage collection. Putrefying, smelly excrement was worse than just revolting. It polluted the atmosphere and caused disease.

Chadwick correctly believed that the stinking excrement of communal outhouses could be dependably carried off by water through sewers at less than one-twentieth the cost of removing it by hand. The cheap iron pipes and tile drains of the industrial age would provide running water and sewerage for all sections of town, not just the wealthy ones. In 1848, with the cause strengthened by the cholera epidemic of 1846, Chadwick's report became the basis of Great Britain's first public health law, which created a national health board and gave cities broad authority to build modern sanitary systems.

The public health movement won dedicated supporters in the United States, France, and Germany from the 1840s on. Governments accepted at least limited responsibility for the health of all citizens, and their programs broke decisively with the age-old fatalism of urban populations in the face of shockingly high mortality. By the 1860s and 1870s, European cities were making real progress toward adequate water supplies and sewerage systems, and city dwellers were beginning to reap the reward of better health.

Still, effective control of communicable disease required a great leap forward in medical knowledge and biological theory. Early reformers such as Chadwick were seriously handicapped by the prevailing *miasmatic theory* of disease—the belief that people contract disease when they breathe the bad odors of decay and putrefying excrement—in short, the theory that smells cause disease. The miasmatic theory was a reasonable deduction from empirical observations: cleaning up filth did produce laudable results. Yet the theory was very incomplete. Keen observation by doctors and public health officials in the 1840s and 1850s pinpointed the role of bad drinking water in the transmission of disease and suggested that contagion was *spread through* filth and not caused by it, thus weakening the miasmatic idea.

The breakthrough was the development of the *germ theory* of disease by Louis Pasteur (1822–1895), a French chemist who began studying fermentation in 1854 at the request of brewers. Using his microscope to develop a simple test that brewers could use to monitor the fermentation process and avoid spoilage, Pasteur

Louis Pasteur   Shown here working in his laboratory, Pasteur made fundamental discoveries in biology and chemistry. A symbol of scientific achievement, he was—and is—greatly revered by all classes in France. *(Institut Pasteur)*

found that fermentation depended on the growth of living organisms and that the activity of these organisms could be suppressed by heating the beverage—by "pasteurizing" it. The breathtaking implication was that specific diseases were caused by specific living organisms—germs—and that those organisms could be controlled in people as well as in beer, wine, and milk.

By 1870 the work of Pasteur and others had demonstrated the general connection between germs and disease. When, in the middle of the 1870s, German country doctor Robert Koch and his coworkers developed pure cultures of harmful bacteria and described their life cycles, the dam broke. Over the next twenty years, researchers—mainly Germans—identified the organisms responsible for disease after disease. These discoveries led to the development of a number of effective vaccines.

Acceptance of the germ theory brought about dramatic improvements in the deadly environment of hospitals and surgery. In 1865, when Pasteur showed that the air was full of bacteria, English surgeon Joseph Lister (1827–1912) immediately grasped the connection between aerial bacteria and the problem of wound infection. He reasoned that a chemical disinfectant applied to a wound dressing would "destroy the life of the floating particles." Lister's "antiseptic principle" worked wonders. In the 1880s, German surgeons developed the more sophisticated practice of sterilizing not only the wound but also everything—hands, instruments, clothing—that entered the operating room.

The achievements of the bacterial revolution coupled with the ever more sophisticated public health movement saved millions of lives, particularly after about 1880. Mortality rates began to decline dramatically in European countries (Figure 24.1) as the awful death sentences of the past—diphtheria, typhoid, typhus, cholera, yellow fever—became vanishing diseases. City dwellers benefited especially from these developments. By 1910 a great silent revolution had occurred: the death rates for people of all ages in urban areas were generally no greater than those for people in rural areas, and sometimes they were less.

Urban Planning and Public Transportation

If public health was greatly improved in the course of the nineteenth century, that was only part of the urban challenge. Overcrowding, bad housing, and lack of transportation could not be solved by sewers and better medicine; yet in these areas, too, important transformations significantly improved the quality of urban life after midcentury.

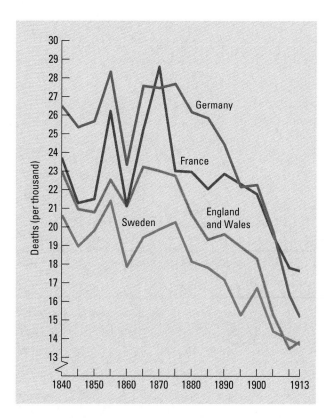

FIGURE 24.1 The Decline of Death Rates in England and Wales, Germany, France, and Sweden, 1840–1913 A rising standard of living, improvements in public health, and better medical knowledge all contributed to the dramatic decline of death rates in the nineteenth century.

More effective urban planning was one of the keys to improvement. Urban planning was in decline by the early nineteenth century, but after 1850 its practice was revived and extended. France took the lead during the rule of Napoleon III (r. 1848–1870), who sought to stand above class conflict and promote the welfare of all his subjects through government action. He believed that rebuilding much of Paris would provide employment, improve living conditions, and testify to the power and glory of his empire. In the baron Georges Haussmann (1809–1884), an aggressive, impatient Alsatian whom he placed in charge of Paris, Napoleon III found an authoritarian planner capable of bulldozing both buildings and opposition. In twenty years, Paris was transformed (Map 24.2).

The Paris of 1850 was a labyrinth of narrow, dark streets, the results of desperate overcrowding. In a central city not twice the size of New York's Central Park lived more than one-third of the city's 1 million inhabitants. Terrible slum conditions and extremely

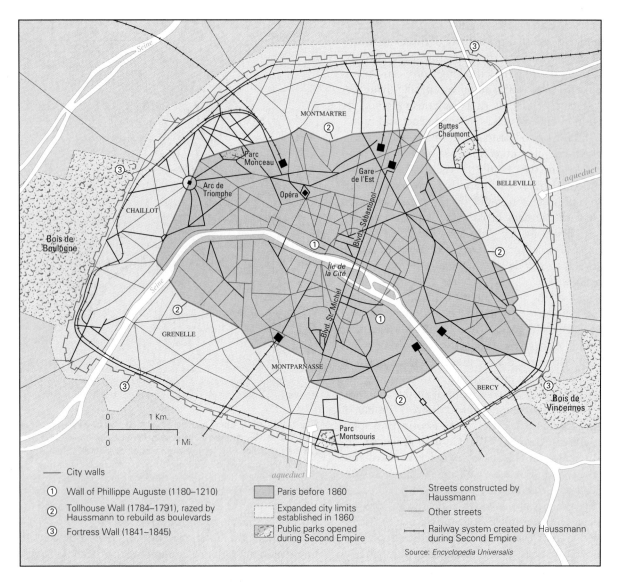

MAP 24.2 The Modernization of Paris, ca 1850–1870 Broad boulevards, large parks, and grandiose train stations transformed Paris. The cutting of the new north-south axis—known as the Boulevard Saint-Michel—was one of Haussmann's most controversial projects. It razed much of Paris's medieval core and filled the Île de la Cité with massive government buildings.

high death rates were facts of life. There were few open spaces and only two public parks for the entire metropolis. Public transportation played a very small role in this enormous walking city.

Haussmann and his fellow planners proceeded on many interrelated fronts. With a bold energy that often shocked their contemporaries, they razed old buildings in order to cut broad, straight, tree-lined boulevards through the center of the city as well as in new quarters on the outskirts. These boulevards, designed in part to prevent the easy construction and defense of barricades

by revolutionary crowds, permitted traffic to flow freely. Their creation also demolished some of the worst slums. New streets stimulated the construction of better housing, especially for the middle classes. Small neighborhood parks and open spaces were created throughout the city, and two very large parks suitable for all kinds of holiday activities were developed—one on the wealthy west side and one on the poor east side of the city. The city also improved its sewers, and a system of aqueducts more than doubled the city's supply of good fresh water.

Apartment Living in Paris   This drawing shows how different social classes lived together in European cities about 1850. Passing the middle-class family on the first (American second) floor, the economic condition of the tenants declined until one reached abject poverty in the garret. (*Bibliothèque Nationale, Paris*)

Haussmann and Napoleon III tried to make Paris a more beautiful city, and to a large extent they succeeded. The broad, straight boulevards, such as those radiating out like the spokes of a wheel from the Arch of Triumph and those centering on the new Opera House, afforded impressive vistas. If for most people Paris remains one of the world's most beautiful and enchanting cities, it is in part because of the transformations of Napoleon III's Second Empire.

Rebuilding Paris provided a new model for urban planning and stimulated modern urbanism throughout Europe, particularly after 1870. In city after city, public authorities mounted a coordinated attack on many of the interrelated problems of the urban environment. As in Paris, improvements in public health through better water supply and waste disposal often went hand in hand with new boulevard construction. Cities such as Vienna and Cologne followed the Parisian example of tearing

The Urban Landscape: Madrid in 1900 This wistful painting of a Spanish square on a rainy day, by Enrique Martinez Cubells y Ruiz (1874–1917), includes a revealing commentary on public transportation. Coachmen wait atop their expensive hackney cabs for a wealthy clientele, while modern electric streetcars that carry the masses converge on the square from all directions. *(Museo Municipal, Madrid/The Bridgeman Art Library, London/New York)*

down old walled fortifications and replacing them with broad, circular boulevards on which office buildings, town halls, theaters, opera houses, and museums were erected. These ring roads and the new boulevards that radiated out from them toward the outskirts eased movement and encouraged urban expansion (see Map 24.2). Zoning expropriation laws, which allowed a majority of the owners of land in a given quarter of the city to impose major street or sanitation improvements on a reluctant minority, were an important mechanism of the new urbanism.

The development of mass public transportation was also of great importance in the improvement of urban living conditions. Such transportation came late, but in a powerful rush. In the 1870s, many European cities authorized private companies to operate horse-drawn streetcars, which had been developed in the United States, to carry riders along the growing number of major thoroughfares. Then in the 1890s, the real revolution occurred: European countries adopted another American transit innovation, the electric streetcar.

Electric streetcars were cheaper, faster, more dependable, and more comfortable than their horse-drawn counterparts. Service improved dramatically. Millions of Europeans—workers, shoppers, schoolchildren—hopped on board during the workweek. And on weekends and holidays, streetcars carried millions on happy outings to parks and countryside, racetracks and music halls. In 1886 the horse-drawn streetcars of Austria-Hungary, France, Germany, and Great Britain were carrying about 900 million riders. By 1910 electric streetcar systems in the four countries were carrying 6.7 billion riders.[6] Each man, woman, and child was using public transportation four times as often in 1910 as in 1886.

Good mass transit helped greatly in the struggle for decent housing. The new boulevards and horse-drawn streetcars had facilitated a middle-class move to better housing in the 1860s and 1870s; similarly, after 1890 electric streetcars gave people of modest means access to new, improved housing. The still-crowded city was able to expand and become less congested. In England in 1901, only 9 percent of the urban population was "overcrowded" in terms of the official definition of more than two persons per room. On the continent, many city governments in the early twentieth century were building electric streetcar systems that provided transportation to new public and private housing developments in outlying areas of the city for the working classes. Poor, overcrowded housing, long one of the blackest blots on the urban landscape, was in retreat—

another example of the gradual taming of the urban environment.

RICH AND POOR AND THOSE IN BETWEEN

General improvements in health and in the urban environment had beneficial consequences for all kinds of people. Yet differences in living conditions among social classes remained gigantic.

Social Structure

How much did the almost-completed journey to an urban, industrialized world change the social framework of rich and poor and those in between? The first great change was a substantial and undeniable increase in the standard of living for the average person. The real wages of British workers, for example, which had already risen by 1850, almost doubled between 1850 and 1906. Similar increases occurred in continental countries as industrial development quickened after 1850. Ordinary people took a major step forward in the centuries-old battle against poverty, reinforcing efforts to improve many aspects of human existence.

There is another side to the income coin, however, and it must be stressed as well. Greater economic rewards for the average person did *not* eliminate hardship and poverty, nor did they make the wealth and income of the rich and the poor significantly more equal. In almost every advanced country around 1900, the richest 5 percent of all households in the population received 33 percent of all national income. The richest 20 percent of households received anywhere from 50 to 60 percent of all national income, while the entire bottom 80 percent received only 40 to 50 percent. Moreover, the bottom 30 percent of households received 10 percent or less of all income. These enormous differences are illustrated in Figure 24.2.

The middle classes, smaller than they are today, accounted for less than 20 percent of the population; thus the statistics show that the upper and middle classes alone received more than 50 percent of all income. The poorest 80 percent—the working classes, including peasants and agricultural laborers—received less altogether than the two richest classes. Moreover, income taxes on the wealthy were light or nonexistent. Thus the gap between rich and poor remained enormous at the beginning of the twentieth century. It was probably almost as

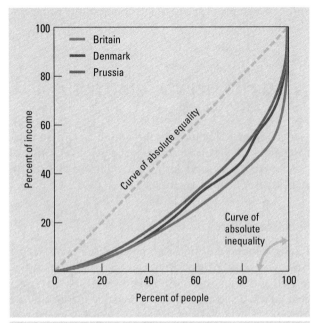

Distribution of Income

	Richest 5%	Richest 10%	Richest 20%	Poorest 60%
Britain	43%		59%	
Denmark	30%	39%	55%	31%
Prussia	30%		50%	33%

FIGURE 24.2 The Distribution of Income in Britain, Denmark, and Prussia in 1913 The so-called Lorenz curve is useful for showing the degree of economic inequality in a given society. The closer the actual distribution of income lies to the (theoretical) curve of absolute equality, where each 20 percent of the population receives 20 percent of all income, the more incomes are nearly equal. European society was very far from any such equality before World War I. Notice that incomes in Prussia were somewhat more equal than those in Britain. (Source: S. Kuznets, Modern Economic Growth, Yale University Press, New Haven, 1966, pp. 208–209. Reprinted by permission.)

stroyed. There developed an almost unlimited range of jobs, skills, and earnings; one group or subclass shaded off into another in a complex, confusing hierarchy. Thus the tiny elite of the very rich and the sizable mass of the dreadfully poor were separated from each other by a range of subclasses, each filled with individuals struggling to rise or at least to hold their own in the social order. In this atmosphere of competition and hierarchy, neither the middle classes nor the working classes acted as a unified force. This social and occupational hierarchy developed enormous variations, but the age-old pattern of great economic inequality remained firmly intact.

The Middle Classes

By the beginning of the twentieth century, the diversity and range within the urban middle class were striking. Indeed, it is more meaningful to think of a confederation of middle classes loosely united by occupations requiring mental, rather than physical, skill. At the top stood the upper middle class, composed mainly of the most successful business families from banking, industry, and large-scale commerce. These families were the prime beneficiaries of modern industry and scientific progress. As people in the upper middle class gained in income and progressively lost all traces of radicalism after the trauma of 1848, they were almost irresistibly drawn toward the aristocratic lifestyle. And although the genuine hereditary aristocracy constituted only a tiny minority in every European country, it retained imposing wealth, unrivaled social prestige, and substantial political influence. This was especially true in central and eastern Europe, where the monarch—the highest-ranking noble of them all—continued to hold great political power.

As the aristocracy had long divided the year between palatial country estates and lavish townhouses during "the season," so the upper middle class purchased country places or built beach houses for weekend and summer use. The number of servants was an important indicator of wealth and standing for the middle class, as it had always been for the aristocracy. Private coaches and carriages, ever-expensive items in the city, were also signs of rising social status. More generally, the rich businessman and certainly his son devoted less time to business and more to "culture" and easy living than was the case in less wealthy or well-established commercial families.

The topmost reaches of the upper middle class tended to shade off into the old aristocracy to form a new upper class. This was the 5 percent of the population that,

great as it had been in the age of agriculture and aristocracy before the Industrial Revolution.

The great gap between rich and poor endured, in part, because industrial and urban development made society more diverse and less unified. By no means did society split into two sharply defined opposing classes, as Marx had predicted. Instead, economic specialization enabled society to produce more effectively and in the process created more new social groups than it de-as we have seen, received roughly 33 percent of the national income in European countries before 1914. Much of the aristocracy welcomed this development. Having experienced a sharp decline in its relative income in the course of industrialization, the landed aristocracy had met big business coming up the staircase and was often delighted to trade titles, country homes, and snobbish elegance for good hard cash. Some of the best bargains were made through marriages to American heiresses. Correspondingly, wealthy aristocrats tended increasingly to exploit their agricultural and mineral resources as if they were business people. Bismarck was not the only proud nobleman to make a fortune distilling brandy on his estates.

Below the wealthy upper middle class were much larger, much less wealthy, and increasingly diversified middle-class groups. Here one found the moderately successful industrialists and merchants as well as professionals in law and medicine. This was the middle middle class, solid and quite comfortable but lacking great wealth. Below it were independent shopkeepers, small traders, and tiny manufacturers—the lower middle class. Both of these traditional elements of the middle class expanded modestly in size with economic development.

Meanwhile, the traditional middle class was gaining two particularly important additions. The expansion of industry and technology created a growing demand for experts with specialized knowledge. The most valuable of the specialties became solid middle-class professions. Engineering, for example, emerged from the world of skilled labor as a full-fledged profession of great importance, considerable prestige, and many branches. Architects, chemists, accountants, and surveyors, to name only a few, first achieved professional standing in this period. They established criteria for advanced training and certification and banded together in organizations to promote and defend their interests.

Management of large public and private institutions also emerged as a kind of profession as governments provided more services and as very large corporations such as railroads came into being. Government officials and many private executives were not capitalists in the sense that they owned business enterprises. But public and private managers did have specialized knowledge and the capacity to earn a good living. And they shared most of the values of the business-owning entrepreneurs and the older professionals.

Industrialization also expanded and diversified the lower middle class. The number of independent, property-owning shopkeepers and small business people grew, and so did the number of white-collar employees—a mixed group of traveling salesmen, book-keepers, store managers, and clerks who staffed the offices and branch stores of large corporations. White-collar employees were propertyless and often earned no more than the better-paid skilled or semiskilled workers did. Yet white-collar workers were fiercely committed to the middle class and to the ideal of moving up in society. In the Balkans, for example, clerks let their fingernails grow very long to distinguish themselves from people who worked with their hands. The tie, the suit, and soft, clean hands were no-less-subtle marks of class distinction than wages.

Relatively well educated but without complex technical skills, many white-collar groups aimed at achieving professional standing and the accompanying middle-class status. Elementary school teachers largely succeeded in this effort. From being miserably paid part-time workers in the early nineteenth century, teachers rode the wave of mass education to respectable middle-class status and income. Nurses also rose from the lower ranks of unskilled labor to precarious middle-class standing. Dentistry was taken out of the hands of working-class barbers and placed in the hands of highly trained (and middle-class) professionals.

In spite of growing occupational diversity and conflicting interests, the middle classes were loosely united by a certain style of life. Food was the largest item in the household budget, for middle-class people liked to eat very well. In France and Italy, the middle classes' love of good eating meant that even in large cities, activity ground almost to a halt between half past twelve and half past two on weekdays as husbands and schoolchildren returned home for the midday meal. The European middle classes consumed meat in abundance, and a well-off family might spend 10 percent of its substantial earnings on meat and fully 25 percent of its income on food and drink.

Spending on food was also great because the dinner party was this class's favored social occasion. A wealthy family might give a lavish party for eight to twelve almost every week, whereas more modest households would settle for once a month. Throughout middle-class Europe, such dinners were served in the "French manner": eight or nine separate courses, from appetizers at the beginning to coffee and liqueurs at the end. An ordinary middle-class meal normally consisted of only four courses—soup, fish, meat, and dessert.

The middle-class wife could cope with this endless procession of meals, courses, and dishes because she had both servants and money at her disposal. Indeed, the employment of at least one enormously helpful full-time maid to cook and clean was the best single sign that a family had crossed the cultural divide separating

A Snack for the Upper Middle Class Stylish French women, strolling along the famous Champs-Elysées in Paris, have stopped off for a bite to eat at this classy pastry shop in an 1889 painting by Jean Béraud. Few children are present, emblematic of small families and widespread birth control in France. *(Musée Carnavalet/Photo Bulloz)*

the working classes from what some contemporary observers called the "servant-keeping classes." The greater a family's income, the greater the number of servants it employed. A really prosperous English family in 1900 might employ a hierarchy of ten servants: a manservant, a cook, a kitchen maid, two housemaids, a serving maid, a governess, a gardener, a coachman, and a stable boy. Food and servants together absorbed about 50 percent of income at all levels of the middle class.

Well fed and well served, the middle classes were also well housed by 1900. Many quite prosperous families rented, rather than owned, their homes. Apartment living, complete with tiny rooms for servants under the eaves of the top floor, was commonplace, and wealthy investors and speculative builders found good profits in middle-class housing. By 1900 the middle classes were

also quite clothes-conscious. The factory, the sewing machine, and the department store had all helped reduce the cost and expand the variety of clothing. Middle-class women were particularly attentive to the fickle dictates of fashion.

Education was another growing expense, as middle-class parents tried to provide their children with ever more crucial advanced education. The keystones of culture and leisure were books, music, and travel. The long realistic novel, the heroics of composers Wagner and Verdi, the diligent striving of the dutiful daughter at the piano, and the packaged tour to a foreign country were all sources of middle-class pleasure.

Finally, the middle classes were loosely united by a shared code of expected behavior and morality. This code was strict and demanding. It laid great stress on hard work, self-discipline, and personal achievement. Men and women who fell into crime or poverty were generally assumed to be responsible for their own circumstances. Traditional Christian morality was reaffirmed by this code and was preached tirelessly by middle-class people. Drunkenness and gambling were denounced as vices; sexual purity and fidelity were celebrated as virtues. In short, the middle-class person was supposed to know right from wrong and was expected to act accordingly.

The Working Classes

About four out of five people belonged to the working classes at the turn of the century. Many members of the working classes—that is, people whose livelihoods depended on physical labor and who did not employ domestic servants—were still small landowning peasants and hired farm hands. This was especially true in eastern Europe. In western and central Europe, however, the typical worker had left the land. In Great Britain, less than 8 percent of the people worked in agriculture, and in rapidly industrializing Germany only 25 percent were employed in agriculture and forestry. Even in less industrialized France, less than 50 percent of the people depended on the land in 1900.

The urban working classes were even less unified and homogeneous than the middle classes. In the first place, economic development and increased specialization expanded the traditional range of working-class skills, earnings, and experiences. Meanwhile, the old sharp distinction between highly skilled artisans and unskilled manual workers gradually broke down. To be sure, highly skilled printers and masons as well as unskilled dockworkers and common laborers continued to exist. But between these extremes there appeared ever more semiskilled groups, many of which were composed of factory workers and machine tenders (Figure 24.3).

In the second place, skilled, semiskilled, and unskilled workers developed widely divergent lifestyles and cultural values, and their differences contributed to a keen sense of social status and hierarchy within the working classes. The result was great variety and limited class unity.

Highly skilled workers, who made up about 15 percent of the working classes, became a real "labor aristocracy." These workers earned only about two-thirds of the income of the bottom ranks of the servant-keeping classes, but that was fully twice as much as the earnings of unskilled workers. The most "aristocratic" of the highly skilled workers were construction bosses and factory foremen, men who had risen from the ranks and were fiercely proud of their achievement. The labor aristocracy also included members of the traditional highly skilled handicraft trades that had not been mechanized or placed in factories, like cabinetmakers, jewelers, and printers. This group as a whole was under constant long-term pressure. Irregularly but inexorably, factory methods were being extended to more crafts, and many skilled artisans were being replaced by lower-paid semiskilled factory workers. In the later nineteenth century, traditional woodcarvers and watchmakers virtually disappeared, for example, as the making of furniture and timepieces now took place in the factory.

At the same time, the labor aristocracy was consistently being enlarged by new kinds of skilled workers such as shipbuilders and railway locomotive engineers. Thus the labor elite remained in a state of flux as individuals and whole crafts moved in and out of it.

To maintain this precarious standing, the upper working class adopted distinctive values and strait-laced, almost puritanical behavior. Like the middle classes, the labor aristocracy was strongly committed to the family and to economic improvement. Families in the upper working class saved money regularly, worried about their children's education, and valued good housing. Despite these similarities, skilled workers viewed themselves not as aspirants to the middle class but as the pacesetters and natural leaders of all the working

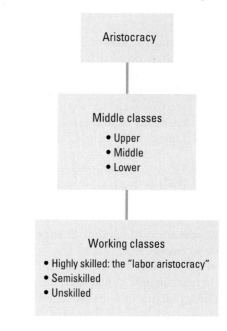

FIGURE 24.3 The Urban Social Hierarchy

classes. Well aware of the degradation not so far below them, they practiced self-discipline and stern morality.

The upper working class in general frowned on heavy drinking and sexual permissiveness. An organized temperance movement was strong in the countries of northern Europe, such as Great Britain, where a generation advocated tea as the "cup that cheers but does not inebriate." As one German labor aristocrat somberly warned, "The path to the brothel leads through the tavern" and from there quite possibly to drastic decline or total ruin for person and family.[7]

Men and women of the labor aristocracy were quick to find fault with those below them who failed to meet their standards. In 1868 William Lovett, an English labor aristocrat if ever there was one, denounced "this ignorant recklessness and improvidence that produce the swarms of half-starved, neglected, and ignorant children we see in all directions; who mostly grow up to become the burdens and often the pests of society, which the industrious and frugal have to support."[8] Finally, many members of the labor aristocracy had definite political and philosophical beliefs, whether Christian or socialist or both. Such beliefs further strengthened the firm moral code of the upper working class.

Below the labor aristocracy stood semiskilled and unskilled urban workers. The enormous complexity of this sector of the world of labor is not easily summarized. Workers in the established crafts—carpenters, bricklayers, pipe fitters—stood near the top of the semiskilled hierarchy, often flirting with (or sliding back from) the labor elite. A large number of the semiskilled were factory workers who earned highly variable but relatively good wages and whose relative importance in the labor force was increasing.

Below the semiskilled workers was a larger group of unskilled workers that included day laborers such as longshoremen, wagon-driving teamsters, teenagers, and every kind of "helper." Many of these people had real skills and performed valuable services, but they were unorganized and divided, united only by the common fate of meager earnings. The same lack of unity characterized street vendors and market people—self-employed workers who competed savagely with each other and with the established shopkeepers of the lower middle class.

One of the largest components of the unskilled group was domestic servants, whose numbers grew steadily in the nineteenth century. In advanced Great Britain, for example, one out of every seven employed persons was a domestic servant in 1911. The great majority were women; indeed, one out of every three girls in Britain between the ages of fifteen and twenty was a domestic servant. Throughout Europe and America, a great many female domestics in the cities were recent migrants from rural areas. As in earlier times, domestic service was still hard work at low pay with limited personal independence and the danger of sexual exploitation. For the full-time general maid in a lower-middle-class family, there was an unending routine of baby-sitting, shopping, cooking, and cleaning. In the great households, the girl was at the bottom of a rigid hierarchy of status-conscious butlers and housekeepers.

Nonetheless, domestic service had real attractions for "rough country girls" with strong hands and few specialized skills. Marriage prospects were better, or at least more varied, in the city. And though wages were low, they were higher and more regular than in hard agricultural work. Finally, as one London observer noted, young girls and other migrants were drawn to the city by

the contagion of numbers, the sense of something going on, the theaters and the music halls, the brightly lighted streets and busy crowds—all, in short, that makes the difference between the Mile End fair on a Saturday night, and a dark and muddy country lane, with no glimmer of gas and with nothing to do.[9]

Many young domestics from the countryside made a successful transition to working-class wife and mother. Yet with an unskilled or unemployed husband and a growing family, such a woman often had to join the broad ranks of workingwomen in the "sweated industries." These industries flowered after 1850 and resembled the old putting-out and cottage industries of earlier times. The women normally worked at home, paid by the piece and not by the hour. They and their young daughters, for whom organization and collective action were virtually impossible, earned pitiful wages and lacked any job security.

Some women did hand-decorating of every conceivable kind of object; the majority, however, made clothing, especially after the advent of the sewing machine. Foot-powered sewing machines allowed the poorest wife or widow in the foulest dwelling to rival and eventually supplant the most highly skilled male tailor. By 1900 only a few such tailors lingered on in high-priced "tailor-made" shops. An army of poor women accounted for the bulk of the inexpensive "ready-made" clothes displayed on department store racks and in tiny shops.

Notwithstanding the rise and fall of groups and individuals, the urban working classes sought fun and recreation, and they found both. Across the face of Europe,

A School for Servants   Although domestic service was poorly paid, there was always plenty of competition for the available jobs. Schools sprang up to teach young women the manners and the household skills that employers in the "servant-keeping classes" demanded. *(Greater London Council Photograph Library)*

drinking remained unquestionably the favorite leisure-time activity of working people. For many middle-class moralists as well as moralizing historians since, love of drink has been a curse of the modern age—a sign of social dislocation and popular suffering. Certainly, drinking was deadly serious business. One English slum dweller recalled that "drunkenness was by far the commonest cause of dispute and misery in working class homes. On account of it one saw many a decent family drift down through poverty into total want."[10]

Generally, however, heavy "problem" drinking declined in the late nineteenth century as it became less and less socially acceptable. This decline reflected in part the moral leadership of the upper working class. At the same time, drinking became more public and social. Cafés and pubs became increasingly bright, friendly places. Working-class political activities, both moderate and radical, were also concentrated in taverns and pubs. Moreover, social drinking in public places by married

couples and sweethearts became an accepted and widespread practice for the first time. This greater participation by women undoubtedly helped civilize the world of drink and hard liquor.

The two other leisure-time passions of the working classes were sports and music halls. A great decline in "cruel sports," such as bullbaiting and cockfighting, had occurred throughout Europe by the late nineteenth century. Their place was filled by modern spectator sports, of which racing and soccer were the most popular. There was a great deal of gambling on sports events, and for many a working person a desire to decipher racing forms provided a powerful incentive toward literacy. Music halls and vaudeville theaters, the working-class counterparts of middle-class opera and classical theater, were enormously popular throughout Europe. In 1900 there were more than fifty such halls and theaters in London alone. Music hall audiences were thoroughly mixed, which may account for the fact that drunkenness, sexual intercourse and pregnancy before marriage, marital difficulties, and problems with mothers-in-law were favorite themes of broad jokes and bittersweet songs.

In more serious moments, religion and Christian churches continued to provide working people with solace and meaning. The eighteenth-century vitality of popular religion in Catholic countries and the Protestant rejuvenation exemplified by German Pietism and English Methodism (see pages 681–682) carried over into the nineteenth century. Indeed, many historians see the early nineteenth century as an age of religious revival. Yet historians also recognize that by the last two or three decades of the nineteenth century, a considerable decline in both church attendance and church do-

nations was occurring in most European countries. And it seems clear that this decline was greater for the urban working classes than for their rural counterparts or for the middle classes.

What did the decline in working-class church attendance really mean? Some have argued that it accurately reflected a general decline in faith and religious belief. Others disagree, noting correctly that most working-class families still baptized their children and considered themselves Christians. Although more research is necessary, it appears that the urban working classes in Europe did become more secular and less religious in the late nineteenth and early twentieth centuries. They rarely repudiated the Christian religion, but it tended to play a diminishing role in their daily lives.

Working-Class Entertainment, Seville, Spain Music and dancing add to the appeal of drinking and talking in this popular "singing café." The absence of women in the audience may mean that this café has a dubious reputation. *(Conway Picture Library)*

Part of the reason for this change was that the construction of churches failed to keep up with the rapid growth of urban population, especially in new working-class neighborhoods. Thus the vibrant, materialistic urban environment undermined popular religious impulses, which were poorly served in the cities. Equally important, however, was the fact that throughout the nineteenth century both Catholic and Protestant churches were normally seen as they saw themselves— as conservative institutions defending social order and custom. Therefore, as the European working classes became more politically conscious, they tended to see the established (or quasi-established) "territorial church" as defending what they wished to change and as allied with their political opponents. Especially the men of the urban working classes developed vaguely antichurch attitudes, even though they remained neutral or positive toward religion. They tended to regard regular church attendance as "not our kind of thing"—not part of urban working-class culture.

The pattern was different in the United States. There, most churches also preached social conservatism in the nineteenth century. But because church and state had always been separate and because there was always a host of competing denominations and even different religions, working people identified churches much less with the political and social status quo. Instead, individual churches in the United States were often closely identified with an ethnic group rather than with a social class; and churches thrived, in part, as a means of asserting ethnic identity. This same process did occur in Europe if the church or synagogue had never been linked to the state and served as a focus for ethnic cohesion. Irish Catholic churches in Protestant Britain and Jewish synagogues in Russia were outstanding examples.

❖ THE CHANGING FAMILY

Urban life wrought many fundamental changes in the family. Although much is still unknown, it seems clear that in the second half of the nineteenth century the family had stabilized considerably after the disruption of the late eighteenth and early nineteenth centuries. The home became more important for both men and women. The role of women and attitudes toward children underwent substantial change, and adolescence emerged as a distinct stage of life. These are but a few of the transformations that affected all social classes in varying degrees.

Premarital Sex and Marriage

By 1850 the preindustrial pattern of lengthy courtship and mercenary marriage was pretty well dead among the working classes. In its place, the ideal of romantic love had triumphed. Couples were ever more likely to come from different, even distant, towns and to be more nearly the same age, further indicating that romantic sentiment was replacing tradition and financial considerations.

Economic considerations in marriage remained more important to the middle classes than to the working classes after 1850. In France dowries and elaborate legal marriage contracts were common practice among the middle classes in the later nineteenth century, and marriage was for many families one of life's most crucial financial transactions. A popular author advised young Frenchmen that "marriage is in general a means of increasing one's credit and one's fortune and of insuring one's success in the world."[11] This preoccupation with money led many middle-class men in France and elsewhere to marry late, after they had been established economically, and to choose women considerably younger and less sexually experienced than themselves. These differences between husband and wife became a source of tension in many middle-class marriages.

A young woman of the middle class found her romantic life carefully supervised by her well-meaning mother, who schemed for a proper marriage and guarded her daughter's virginity like the family's credit. (See the feature "Listening to the Past: Middle-Class Youth and Sexuality" on pages 820–821.) After marriage, middle-class morality sternly demanded fidelity.

Middle-class boys were watched, too, but not as vigilantly. By the time they reached late adolescence, they had usually attained considerable sexual experience with maids or prostitutes. With marriage a distant, uncertain possibility, it was all too easy for the young man of the middle classes to turn to the urban underworld of prostitution and sexual exploitation to satisfy his desires.

In the early nineteenth century, sexual experimentation before marriage also triumphed, as did illegitimacy. There was an "illegitimacy explosion" between 1750 and 1850 (see page 664). By the 1840s, as many as one birth in three was occurring outside of wedlock in many large cities. Although poverty and economic uncertainty undoubtedly prevented many lovers from marrying, there were also many among the poor and propertyless who saw little wrong with having illegitimate offspring. One young Bavarian woman answered happily when asked why she kept having illegitimate children, "It's O.K. to make babies. . . . The king has o.k.'d it!"[12] Thus the pattern of romantic ideals, premarital sexual activity, and widespread illegitimacy was firmly established by midcentury among the urban working classes.

It is hard to know how European couples managed sex, pregnancy, and marriage after 1850 because such questions were considered improper both in polite conversation and in public opinion polls. Yet there are many telltale clues. In the second half of the century, the rising rate of illegitimacy was reversed: more babies were born to married mothers. Some observers have argued that this shift reflected the growth of puritanism and a lessening of sexual permissiveness among the unmarried. This explanation, however, is unconvincing.

The percentage of brides who were pregnant continued to be high and showed little or no tendency to decline after 1850. In many parts of urban Europe around 1900, as many as one woman in three was going to the altar an expectant mother. Moreover, unmarried people almost certainly used the cheap condoms and diaphragms the industrial age had made available to prevent pregnancy, at least in predominately Protestant countries.

Thus unmarried young people were probably engaging in just as much sexual activity as their parents and grandparents who had created the illegitimacy explosion of 1750 to 1850. But in the later nineteenth century, pregnancy for a young single woman led increasingly to marriage and the establishment of a two-parent household. This important development reflected the growing respectability of the working classes as well as their gradual economic improvement. Skipping out was less acceptable, and marriage was less of an economic challenge. Thus the urban working-class couple became more stable, and that stability strengthened the family as an institution.

Prostitution

In Paris alone, 155,000 women were registered as prostitutes between 1871 and 1903, and 750,000 others were suspected of prostitution in the same years. Men of all classes visited prostitutes, but the middle and upper classes supplied much of the motivating cash. Thus, though many middle-class men abided by the publicly professed code of stern puritanical morality, others indulged their appetites for prostitutes and sexual promiscuity.

My Secret Life, the anonymous eleven-volume autobiography of an English sexual adventurer from the servant-keeping classes, provides a remarkable picture of such a man. Beginning at an early age with a maid, the author becomes progressively obsessed with sex and devotes his life to living his sexual fantasies. In almost every one of his innumerable encounters all across Europe, this man of wealth simply buys his pleasure. Usually meetings are arranged in a businesslike manner: regular and part-time prostitutes quote their prices; working-class girls are corrupted by hot meals and baths.

At one point, he offers a young girl a sixpence for a kiss and gets it. Learning that the pretty, unskilled working girl earns nine pence a day, he offers her the equivalent of a week's salary for a few moments of fondling. When she finally agrees, he savagely exults that "*her* want was my opportunity." Later he offers more money for more gratification, and when she refuses, he tries unsuccessfully to rape her in a hackney cab. On another occasion he takes a farm worker by force: "Her tears ran down. If I had not committed a rape, it looked uncommonly like one." He then forces his victim to take money to prevent a threatened lawsuit, while the foreman advises the girl to keep quiet and realize that "you be in luck if he likes you."[13]

Obviously atypical in its excesses, *My Secret Life,* in its encyclopedic thoroughness, does reveal the dark side of sex and class in urban society. Frequently thinking of their wives largely in terms of money, family, and social position, the men of the comfortable classes often purchased sex and even affection from poor girls both before and after marriage. Moreover, the great continuing differences between rich and poor made for every kind of debauchery and sexual exploitation, including the brisk trade in poor virgins that the author of *My Secret Life* particularly relishes. Brutal sexist behavior was part of life—a part the sternly moral women (and men) of the upper working class detested and tried to shield their daughters from. For many poor young women, prostitution, like domestic service, was a stage of life and not a permanent employment. Having chosen it for two or three years in their twenties, they went on to marry (or live with) men of their own class and establish homes and families.

Kinship Ties

Within working-class homes, ties to relatives after marriage—kinship ties—were in general much stronger than many social observers have recognized. Most newlyweds tried to live near their parents, though not in the same house. Indeed, for many married couples in later-nineteenth-century cities, ties to mothers and fathers, uncles and aunts, were more important than ties to nonrelated acquaintances.

Toulouse-Lautrec: A la Mie   Wealthy nobleman by birth and tragically disabled by accident, Henri de Toulouse-Lautrec (1864–1901) was irresistibly drawn to the bizarre individuals who made Paris night life the scandal of Europe. This painting portrays an aging prostitute and her reptile-like companion, a powerful study in degradation. *(S. A. Denio Collection and General Income. Courtesy of Museum of Fine Arts, Boston)*

People turned to their families for help in coping with sickness, unemployment, death, and old age. Although governments were generally providing more welfare services by 1900, the average couple and its children inevitably faced crises. Funerals, for example, brought sudden demands, requiring a large outlay for special clothes, carriages, and burial services. Unexpected death or desertion could leave the bereaved or abandoned, especially widows and orphans, in need of financial aid or perhaps a foster home. Relatives responded hastily to such cries, knowing full well that their own time of need and repayment would undoubtedly come.

Relatives were also valuable at less tragic moments. If a couple was very poor, an aged relation often moved in to cook and mind the children so that the wife could earn badly needed income outside the home. Sunday dinners were often shared, as were outgrown clothing and useful information. Often the members of a large family group all lived in the same neighborhood.

Gender Roles and Family Life

Industrialization and the growth of modern cities brought great changes to the lives of European women. These changes were particularly consequential for married women, and most women did marry in the nineteenth century.

After 1850 the work of most wives became increasingly distinct and separate from that of their husbands. Husbands became wage earners in factories and offices, while wives tended to stay home and manage households and care for children. The preindustrial pattern among both peasants and cottage workers, in which husbands and wives worked together and divided up household duties and child rearing, declined. Only in a few occupations, such as retail trade, did married couples live where they worked and struggle together to make their mom-and-pop operations a success. Factory employment for married women also declined as the early practice of hiring entire families in the factory disappeared.

As economic conditions improved, most men expected married women to work outside the home only in poor families. One old English worker recalled that "the boy wanted to get into a position that would enable him to keep a wife and family, as it was considered a thoroughly unsatisfactory state of affairs if the wife had to work to help maintain the home."[14] The ideal became a strict division of labor by gender: the wife as mother and homemaker, the husband as wage earner.

This rigid gender division of labor meant that married women faced great injustice when they needed—or wanted—to move into the man's world of employment outside the home. Husbands were unsympathetic or hostile. Well-paying jobs were off-limits to women, and a woman's wage was almost always less than a man's, even for the same work.

Moreover, married women were subordinated to their husbands by law and lacked many basic legal rights. In England the situation in the early nineteenth century was summed up in a famous line from jurist William Blackstone: "In law husband and wife are one person, and the husband is that person." Thus a wife in England had no legal identity and hence no right to own property in her own name. Even the wages she might earn belonged to her husband. In France the Napoleonic Code (see pages 712–713) also enshrined the principle of female subordination and gave the wife few legal rights regarding property, divorce, and custody of the children. Legal inferiority for women permeated Western society.

With all women facing discrimination in education and employment and with middle-class women suffering especially from a lack of legal rights, there is little wonder that some women rebelled and began the long-continuing fight for equality of the sexes and the rights of women. Their struggle proceeded on two main fronts. First, following in the steps of women such as Mary Wollstonecraft (see page 705), organizations founded by middle-class feminists campaigned for equal legal rights for women as well as access to higher education and professional employment. These middle-class feminists argued that unmarried women and middle-class widows with inadequate incomes simply had to have more opportunities to support themselves. Middle-class feminists also recognized that paid (as opposed to unpaid) work could relieve the monotony that some women found in their sheltered middle-class existence and put greater meaning into their lives.

In the later nineteenth century, these organizations scored some significant victories, such as the 1882 law giving English married women full property rights. But progress was always slow and hard won. For example, in Germany before 1900, women were not admitted as fully registered students at a single university, and it was virtually impossible for a woman to receive certification and practice as a lawyer or doctor. (See the feature "Individuals in Society: Franziska Tiburtius, Pioneering Professional.") In the years before 1914, middle-class feminists increasingly shifted their attention to political action and fought for the right to vote for women.

Women inspired by utopian and especially Marxian socialism blazed a second path. Often scorning the programs of middle-class feminists, socialist women leaders argued that the liberation of (working-class) women would come only with the liberation of the entire working class through revolution. In the meantime, they championed the cause of workingwomen and won some practical improvements, especially in Germany, where the socialist movement was most effectively organized. In a general way, these different approaches to women's issues reflected the diversity of classes in urban society.

If the ideology and practice of rigidly separate roles undoubtedly narrowed women's horizons and caused some women to rebel, there was a brighter side to the same coin. As home and children became the typical wife's main concerns in the late nineteenth century, her control and influence there apparently became increasingly strong throughout Europe. Among the English working classes, it was the wife who generally determined how the family's money was spent. In many families, the husband gave all his earnings to his wife to manage, whatever the law might read. She returned to him only a small allowance for carfare, beer, tobacco, and union dues. All the major domestic decisions, from the children's schooling and religious instruction to the

Individuals in Society

Franziska Tiburtius, Pioneering Professional

Franziska Tiburtius, pioneering woman physician in Berlin. *(Ullstein Bilderdienst)*

Why did a small number of women in the late nineteenth century brave great odds and embark on a professional career? And how did a few of those manage to reach their objectives? The career and personal reflections of Franziska Tiburtius, a pioneer in German medicine, suggests that talent, determination, and economic necessity were critical ingredients.[1]

Like many women of her time who would study and pursue a professional career, Franziska Tiburtius (1843–1927) was born into a property-owning family of modest means. The youngest of nine children on a small estate in northeastern Germany, the sensitive child wilted with a harsh governess but flowered with a caring teacher and became an excellent student.

Graduating at sixteen and needing to support herself, Tiburtius had few opportunities. A young woman from a "proper" background could work as a governess or a teacher without losing her respectability and spoiling her matrimonial prospects, but that was about it. She tried both avenues. Working for six years as a governess in a noble family and no doubt learning that poverty was often one's fate in this genteel profession, she then turned to teaching. Called home from her studies in Britain in 1871 to care for her brother, who had contracted typhus as a field doctor in the Franco-Prussian War, she found her calling. She decided to become a medical doctor.

Supported by her family, Tiburtius's decision was truly audacious. In all Europe, only the University of Zurich in republican Switzerland accepted female students. Moreover, if it became known that she had studied medicine and failed, she would never get a job as a teacher. No parent would entrust a daughter to an "emancipated" radical who had carved up dead bodies!

Although the male students at the university sometimes harassed the women with crude pranks, Tiburtius thrived. The revolution of the microscope and the discovery of microorganisms was rocking Zurich, and she was fascinated by her studies. She became close friends with a fellow female medical student from Germany, Emilie Lehmus, with whom she would form a lifelong partnership in medicine. She did her internship with families of cottage workers around Zurich and loved her work.

Graduating at age thirty-three in 1876, Tiburtius went to stay with her brother the doctor in Berlin. Well qualified to practice, she ran into pervasive discrimination. She was not even permitted to take the state medical exams and could practice only as an unregulated (and unprofessional) "natural healer." But after persistent fighting with the bureaucrats, she was able to display her diploma and practice as "Franziska Tiburtius, M.D. University of Zurich." She and Lehmus were in business.

Soon the two women realized their dream and opened a clinic, subsidized by a wealthy industrialist, for women factory workers. The clinic filled a great need and was soon treating many patients. A room with beds for extremely sick women was later expanded into a second clinic.

Tiburtius and Lehmus became famous. For fifteen years, they were the only women doctors in all Berlin. An inspiration for a new generation of women, they added the wealthy to their thriving practice. But Tiburtius's clinics always concentrated on the poor, providing them with subsidized and up-to-date treatment. Talented, determined, and working with her partner, Tiburtius experienced the joys of personal achievement and useful service, joys that women and men share in equal measure.

Questions for Analysis

1. How does Franziska Tiburtius's life reflect both the challenges and the changing roles of middle-class women in the later nineteenth century?
2. In what ways was Tiburtius's career related to improvements in health in urban society and to the expansion of the professions?

1. This portrait draws on Conradine Lück, *Frauen: Neun Lebensschicksale* (Reutlingen: Ensslin & Laiblin, n.d.), pp. 153–185.

selection of new furniture or a new apartment, were hers. In France women had even greater power in their assigned domain. One English feminist noted in 1908 that "though legally women occupy a much inferior status than men [in France], in practice they constitute the superior sex. They are the power behind the throne."[15]

Women ruled at home partly because running the urban household was a complicated, demanding, and valuable task. Twice-a-day food shopping, penny-pinching, economizing, and the growing crusade against dirt—not to mention child rearing—were a full-time occupation. Nor were there any laborsaving appliances to help, and even when servants were present, they had to be carefully watched and supervised. Working yet another job for wages outside the home had limited appeal for most married women unless such earnings were essential for family survival. Many married women in the working classes did make a monetary contribution to family income by taking in boarders or doing piece-work at home in the sweated industries (see page 802).

The wife also guided the home because a good deal of her effort was directed toward pampering her husband as he expected. In countless humble households, she saw that he had meat while she ate bread, that he relaxed by the fire while she did the dishes.

The woman's guidance of the household went hand in hand with the increased emotional importance of home and family. The home she ran was idealized as a warm shelter in a hard and impersonal urban world. For a child of the English slums in the early 1900s,

home, however poor, was the focus of all love and interests, a sure fortress against a hostile world. Songs about its beauties were ever on people's lips. "Home, sweet home," first heard in the 1870s, had become "almost a second national anthem." Few walls in lower-working-class houses lacked "mottoes"—colored strips of paper, about nine inches wide and eighteen inches in length, attesting to domestic joys: EAST, WEST, HOME'S BEST; BLESS OUR HOME; GOD IS MASTER OF THIS HOUSE; HOME IS THE NEST WHERE ALL IS BEST.[16]

By 1900 home and family were what life was all about for millions of people of all classes.

Married couples also developed stronger emotional ties to each other. Even in the comfortable classes, marriages in the late nineteenth century were based more on sentiment and sexual attraction than they had been earlier in the century, as money and financial calculation declined in importance. Affection and eroticism became more central to the couple after marriage. Gustave Droz, whose bestseller *Mr., Mrs., and Baby* went through 121 editions between 1866 and 1884, saw

love within marriage as the key to human happiness. He condemned men who made marriage sound dull and practical, men who were exhausted by prostitutes and rheumatism and who wanted their young wives to be little angels. He urged women to follow their hearts and marry a man more nearly their own age:

A husband who is stately and a little bald is all right, but a young husband who loves you and who drinks out of your glass without ceremony, is better. Let him, if he ruffles your dress a little and places a kiss on your neck as he passes. Let him, if he undresses you after the ball, laughing like a fool. You have fine spiritual qualities, it is true, but your little body is not bad either and when one loves, one loves completely. Behind these follies lies happiness.[17]

Many French marriage manuals of the late 1800s stressed that women had legitimate sexual needs, such as the "right to orgasm." Perhaps the French were a bit more enlightened in these matters than other nationalities. But the rise of public socializing by couples in cafés and music halls as well as franker affection within the family suggests a more erotic, pleasurable intimate life for women throughout Western society. This, too, helped make the woman's role as mother and homemaker acceptable and even satisfying.

Child Rearing

One striking sign of deepening emotional ties within the family was the growing love and concern that mothers gave their tiny infants. Because so many babies died so early in life, mothers in preindustrial Western society often avoided making a strong emotional commitment to a newborn in order to shield themselves from recurrent heartbreak. Early emotional bonding and a willingness to make real sacrifices for the welfare of the infant were beginning to spread among the comfortable classes by the end of the eighteenth century, but the ordinary mother of modest means adopted new attitudes only as the nineteenth century progressed. The baby became more important, and women became better mothers.

Mothers increasingly breast-fed their infants, for example, rather than paying wet nurses to do so. Breast-feeding involved sacrifice—a temporary loss of freedom, if nothing else. Yet in an age when there was no good alternative to mother's milk, it saved lives. This surge of maternal feeling also gave rise to a wave of specialized books on child rearing and infant hygiene, such as Droz's phenomenally successful book. Droz urged fathers to get into the act and pitied those "who do not know how to roll around on the carpet, play at being a horse and a great wolf, and undress their baby."[18] Another sign, from France, of increased affection is that fewer illegitimate babies were abandoned as foundlings after about 1850. Moreover, the practice of swaddling disappeared completely. Instead, ordinary mothers allowed their babies freedom of movement and delighted in their spontaneity.

The loving care lavished on infants was matched by greater concern for older children and adolescents. They, too, were wrapped in the strong emotional ties of a more intimate and protective family. For one thing, European women began to limit the number of children they bore in order to care adequately for those they had. It was evident by the end of the nineteenth century that the birthrate was declining across Europe, as Figure 24.4 shows, and it continued to do so until after World War II. The Englishwoman who married in the 1860s, for example, had an average of about six children; her daughter marrying in the 1890s had only four; and her granddaughter marrying in the 1920s had only two or possibly three.

The most important reason for this revolutionary reduction in family size, in which the comfortable and well-educated classes took the lead, was parents' desire to improve their economic and social position and that of their children. Children were no longer an economic asset in the later nineteenth century. By having fewer youngsters, parents could give those they had valuable advantages, from music lessons and summer vacations to long, expensive university educations and suitable dowries. A young German skilled worker with only one child spoke for many in his class when he said, "We want to get ahead, and our daughter should have things better than my wife and sisters did."[19] Thus the growing tendency of couples in the late nineteenth century to use a variety of contraceptive methods—rhythm method, withdrawal method, and mechanical devices—certainly reflected increased concern for children.

Indeed, many parents, especially in the middle classes, probably became *too* concerned about their children, unwittingly subjecting them to an emotional pressure cooker of almost unbearable intensity. The result was that many children and especially adolescents came to feel trapped and in need of greater independence.

Prevailing biological and medical theories led parents to believe in the possibility that their own emotional characteristics were passed on to their offspring and that they were thus directly responsible for any abnormality in a child. The moment the child was conceived was thought to be of enormous importance. "Never run the risk of conception when you are sick or overtired or unhappy," wrote one influential American

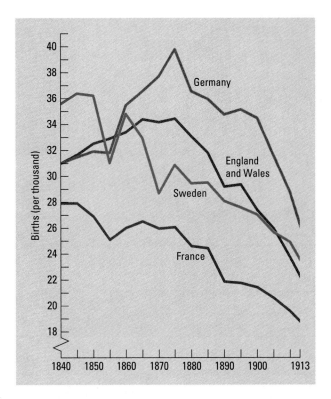

FIGURE 24.4 The Decline of Birthrates in England and Wales, France, Germany, and Sweden, 1840–1913 Women had fewer babies for a variety of reasons, including the fact that their children were increasingly less likely to die before reaching adulthood. Compare with Figure 24.1 on page 793.

woman. "For the bodily condition of the child, its vigor and magnetic qualities, are much affected by conditions ruling this great moment."[20] So might the youthful "sexual excess" of the father curse future generations. Although this was true in the case of syphilis, which could be transmitted to unborn children, the rigid determinism of such views left little scope for the child's individual development.

Another area of excessive parental concern was the sexual behavior of the child. Masturbation was viewed with horror, for it represented an act of independence and even defiance. Diet, clothing, games, and sleeping were carefully regulated. Girls were discouraged from riding horses and bicycling because rhythmic friction simulated masturbation. Boys were dressed in trousers with shallow and widely separated pockets. Between 1850 and 1880, there were surgical operations for children who persisted in masturbating. Thereafter until about 1905, various restraining apparatuses were more often used.

A Working-Class Home, 1875   Emotional ties within ordinary families grew stronger in the nineteenth century. Parents gave their children more love and better care. *(Illustrated London News, LXVI, 1875. Photo courtesy of Boston Public Library)*

These and less blatant attempts to repress the child's sexuality were a source of unhealthy tension, often made worse by the rigid division of gender roles within the family. It was widely believed that mother and child loved each other easily but that relations between father and child were necessarily difficult and often tragic. The father was a stranger; his world of business was far removed from the maternal world of spontaneous affection. Moreover, the father was demanding, often expecting the child to succeed where he himself had failed and making his love conditional on achievement. Little wonder that the imaginative literature of the late nineteenth century came to deal with the emotional and destructive elements of father-son relationships. In the Russian Feodor Dostoevski's great novel *The Brothers Karamazov* (1880–1881), for example, four sons work knowingly or unknowingly to destroy their father. Later at the murder trial, one of the brothers claims to speak for all mankind and screams out, "Who doesn't wish his father dead?"

Sigmund Freud (1856–1939), the Viennese founder of psychoanalysis, formulated the most striking analysis of the explosive dynamics of the family, particularly the middle-class family in the late nineteenth century. A physician by training, Freud began his career treating mentally ill patients. He noted that the hysteria of his patients appeared to originate in bitter early-childhood experiences wherein the child had been obliged to repress strong feelings. When these painful experiences were recalled and reproduced under hypnosis or through the patient's free association of ideas, the patient could be brought to understand his or her unhappiness and eventually deal with it.

One of Freud's most influential ideas concerned the Oedipal tensions resulting from the son's instinctive competition with the father for the mother's love and affection. More generally, Freud postulated that much of human behavior is motivated by unconscious emotional needs whose nature and origins are kept from conscious awareness by various mental devices he called "defense mechanisms." Freud concluded that much unconscious psychological energy is sexual energy, which is repressed and precariously controlled by rational thinking and moral rules. If Freud exaggerated the sexual and familial roots of adult behavior, that exaggeration was itself a reflection of the tremendous emotional intensity of family life in the late nineteenth century.

The working classes probably had more avenues of escape from such tensions than did the middle classes. Unlike their middle-class counterparts, who remained economically dependent on their families until a long education was finished or a proper marriage secured, working-class boys and girls went to work when they reached adolescence. Earning wages on their own, they could bargain with their parents for greater independence within the household by the time they were sixteen or seventeen. If they were unsuccessful, they could and did leave home to live cheaply as paying lodgers in other working-class homes. Thus the young person from the working classes broke away from the family more easily when emotional ties became oppressive. In the twentieth century, middle-class youths would follow this lead.

 ## SCIENCE AND THOUGHT

Major changes in Western science and thought accompanied the emergence of urban society. Two aspects of these complex intellectual developments stand out as especially significant. First, scientific knowledge expanded rapidly, influencing the Western world-view even more profoundly than ever before and spurring the creation of new products and whole industries. Second, between about the 1840s and the 1890s, European literature underwent a shift from soaring romanticism to tough-minded realism.

The Triumph of Science

As the pace of scientific advance quickened and as theoretical advances resulted in great practical benefits, science exercised growing influence on human thought. The intellectual achievements of the scientific revolution had resulted in few such benefits, and theoretical knowledge had also played a relatively small role in the Industrial Revolution in England. But breakthroughs in industrial technology enormously stimulated basic scientific inquiry, as researchers sought to explain theoretically how such things as steam engines and blast furnaces actually worked. The result was an explosive growth of fundamental scientific discoveries from the 1830s onward. And in contrast to earlier periods, these theoretical discoveries were increasingly transformed into material improvements for the general population.

A perfect example of the translation of better scientific knowledge into practical human benefits was the work of Louis Pasteur and his followers in biology and the medical sciences. Another was the development of the branch of physics known as *thermodynamics*. Building on Isaac Newton's laws of mechanics and on studies of steam engines, thermodynamics investigated the relationship between heat and mechanical energy. By midcentury, physicists had formulated the fundamental laws of thermodynamics, which were then applied to mechanical engineering, chemical processes, and many other fields. The *law of conservation of energy* held that different forms of energy—such as heat, electricity, and magnetism—could be converted but neither created nor destroyed. Nineteenth-century thermodynamics demonstrated that the physical world was governed by firm, unchanging laws.

Chemistry and electricity were two other fields characterized by extremely rapid scientific progress. And in both fields, "science was put in the service of industry," as the influential economist Alfred Marshall (1842–1924) argued at the time.

Chemists devised ways of measuring the atomic weight of different elements, and in 1869 the Russian chemist Dmitri Mendeleev (1834–1907) codified the rules of chemistry in the periodic law and the periodic table. Chemistry was subdivided into many specialized branches, such as *organic chemistry*—the study of the compounds of carbon. Applying theoretical insights gleaned from this new field, researchers in large German chemical companies discovered ways of transforming the dirty, useless coal tar that accumulated in coke ovens into beautiful, expensive synthetic dyes for the world of fashion. The basic discoveries of Michael Faraday (1791–1867) on electromagnetism in the 1830s and 1840s resulted in the first dynamo (generator) and opened the way for the subsequent development of the telegraph, electric motors, electric lights, and electric streetcars. The successful application of scientific research in the fast-growing electrical and organic chemical industries promoted solid economic growth between 1880 and 1913 and provided a model for other industries. Systematic "R & D"—research and development—was born in the late nineteenth century.

The triumph of science and technology had at least three more significant consequences. First, though ordinary citizens continued to lack detailed scientific knowledge, everyday experience and innumerable popularizers impressed the importance of science on the popular mind.

Second, as science became more prominent in popular thinking, the philosophical implications of science formulated in the Enlightenment spread to broad sections of the population. Natural processes appeared to be determined by rigid laws, leaving little room for either divine intervention or human will. Yet scientific and technical advances had also fed the Enlightenment's optimistic faith in human progress, which now appeared endless and automatic to many middle-class minds.

Third, the methods of science acquired unrivaled prestige after 1850. For many, the union of careful experiment and abstract theory was the only reliable route to truth and objective reality. The "unscientific" intuitions of poets and the revelations of saints seemed hopelessly inferior.

Social Science and Evolution

From the 1830s onward, many thinkers tried to apply the objective methods of science to the study of society. In some ways, these efforts simply perpetuated the critical thinking of the philosophes. Yet there were important differences. The new "social scientists" had access to the massive sets of numerical data that governments had begun to collect on everything from children to crime, from population to prostitution. In response, social scientists developed new statistical methods to analyze these facts "scientifically" and supposedly to test their theories. And the systems of the leading nineteenth-century social scientists were more unified, all-encompassing, and dogmatic than those of the philosophes. Marx was a prime example (see pages 765–766).

Another extremely influential system builder was French philosopher Auguste Comte (1798–1857). Initially a disciple of the utopian socialist Saint-Simon (see pages 764–765), Comte wrote the six-volume *System of Positive Philosophy* (1830–1842), which was largely overlooked during the romantic era. But when the political failures of 1848 completed the swing to realism, Comte's philosophy came into its own. Its influence has remained great to this day.

Comte postulated that all intellectual activity progresses through predictable stages:

The great fundamental law . . . is this:—that each of our leading conceptions—each branch of our knowledge— passes successively through three different theoretical conditions: the Theological, or fictitious; the Metaphysical, or abstract; and the Scientific, or positive. . . . The first is the necessary point of departure of human understanding, and the third is the fixed and definitive state. The second is merely a transition.[21]

By way of example, Comte noted that the prevailing explanation of cosmic patterns had shifted, as knowledge of astronomy developed, from the will of God (the theological) to the will of an orderly nature (the metaphysical) to the rule of unchanging laws (the scientific). Later, this same intellectual progression took place in increasingly complex fields—physics, chemistry,

and, finally, the study of society. By applying the scientific, or *positivist,* method, Comte believed, his new discipline of sociology would soon discover the eternal laws of human relations. This colossal achievement would in turn enable expert social scientists to impose a disciplined harmony and well-being on less enlightened citizens. Dismissing the "fictions" of traditional religions, Comte became the chief priest of the religion of science and rule by experts.

Comte's stages of knowledge exemplify the nineteenth-century fascination with the idea of evolution and dynamic development. Thinkers in many fields, such as the romantic historians and "scientific" Marxists, shared and applied this basic concept. In geology, Charles Lyell (1797–1875) effectively discredited the long-standing view that the earth's surface had been formed by short-lived cataclysms, such as biblical floods and earthquakes. Instead, according to Lyell's principle of uniformitarianism, the same geological processes that are at work today slowly formed the earth's surface over an immensely long time. The evolutionary view of biological development, first proposed by the Greek Anaximander in the sixth century B.C., re-emerged in a more modern form in the work of Jean Baptiste Lamarck (1744–1829). Lamarck asserted that all forms of life had arisen through a long process of continuous adjustment to the environment.

Lamarck's work was flawed—he believed that the characteristics parents acquired in the course of their lives could be inherited by their children—and was not accepted, but it helped prepare the way for Charles Darwin (1809–1882), the most influential of all nineteenth-century evolutionary thinkers. As the official naturalist on a five-year scientific cruise to Latin America and the South Pacific beginning in 1831, Darwin carefully collected specimens of the different animal species he encountered on the voyage. Back in England, convinced by fossil evidence and by his friend Lyell that the earth and life on it were immensely ancient, Darwin came to doubt the general belief in a special divine creation of each species of animal. Instead, he concluded, all life had gradually evolved from a common ancestral origin in an unending "struggle for survival." After long hesitation, Darwin published his research, which immediately attracted wide attention.

Darwin's great originality lay in suggesting precisely *how* biological evolution might have occurred. His theory is summarized in the title of his work *On the Origin of Species by the Means of Natural Selection* (1859). Decisively influenced by Thomas Malthus's gloomy theory that populations naturally grow faster than their food supplies (see page 733), Darwin argued that chance differences among the members of a given species help some survive while others die. Thus the variations that prove useful in the struggle for survival are selected naturally and gradually spread to the entire species through reproduction. Darwin did not explain why such variations occurred in the first place, and not until the early twentieth century did the study of genetics and the concept of mutation provide some answers.

As the capstone of already-widespread evolutionary thinking, Darwin's theory had a powerful and many-sided influence on European thought and the European middle classes. Darwin was hailed as the great scientist par excellence, the "Newton of biology," who had revealed once again the powers of objective science. Darwin's findings also reinforced the teachings of secularists such as Comte and Marx, who scornfully dismissed religious belief in favor of agnostic or atheistic materialism. In the great cities especially, religion was on the defensive. Finally, many writers applied the theory of biological evolution to human affairs. Herbert Spencer (1820–1903), an English disciple of Auguste Comte, saw the human race as driven forward to ever-greater specialization and progress by the brutal economic struggle. According to Spencer, this unending struggle efficiently determined the "survival of the fittest." The poor were the ill-fated weak; the prosperous were the chosen strong. Understandably, Spencer and other Social Darwinists were especially popular with the upper middle class.

Realism in Literature

In 1868 Emile Zola (1840–1902), the giant of the realist movement in literature, defended his violently criticized first novel against charges of pornography and corruption of morals. Such accusations were meaningless, Zola claimed: he was only a purely objective scientist using

the modern method, the universal instrument of inquiry of which this age makes such ardent use to open up the future. . . . I chose characters completely dominated by their nerves and their blood, deprived of free-will, pushed to each action of their lives by the fatality of their flesh. . . . I have simply done on living bodies the work of analysis which surgeons perform on corpses.[22]

Zola's literary manifesto articulated the key themes of realism, which had emerged in the 1840s and continued to dominate Western culture and style until the 1890s. Realist writers believed that literature should de-

Attracting Females was an integral part of the struggle for survival, according to Darwin. He theorized that those males who were most attractive to females would have the most offspring, like this type of monkey that had developed ornamental hair, giving him devastating sex appeal. Darwin used this illustration in *The Descent of Man* (1871). *(Library of Congress)*

pict life exactly as it was. Forsaking poetry for prose and the personal, emotional viewpoint of the romantics for strict, scientific objectivity, the realists simply observed and recorded—content to let the facts speak for themselves.

The major realist writers focused their extraordinary powers of observation on contemporary everyday life. Emphatically rejecting the romantic search for the exotic and the sublime, they energetically pursued the typical and the commonplace. Beginning with a dissection of the middle classes, from which most of them sprang, many realists eventually focused on the working classes, especially the urban working classes, which had been neglected in imaginative literature before this time. The realists put a microscope to many unexplored

"Life Is Everywhere"   The simple but profound joys of everyday life infuse this outstanding example of Russia's powerful realist tradition. Painted in 1888 by N. A. Yaroshenko, this representation of the mother and child and adoring men also draws on the classic theme of the infant Jesus and the holy family. *(Sovfoto)*

and taboo subjects—sex, strikes, violence, alcoholism—and hastened to report that slums and factories teemed with savage behavior. Many shocked middle-class critics denounced realism as ugly sensationalism wrapped provocatively in pseudoscientific declarations and crude language.

The realists' claims of objectivity did not prevent the elaboration of a definite world-view. Unlike the romantics, who had gloried in individual freedom and an unlimited universe, realists such as Zola were strict determinists. Human beings, like atoms, were components of the physical world, and all human actions were caused by unalterable natural laws. Heredity and environment determined human behavior; good and evil were merely social conventions.

The realist movement began in France, where romanticism had never been completely dominant, and three of its greatest practitioners—Balzac, Flaubert, and Zola—were French. Honoré de Balzac (1799–1850) spent thirty years writing a vastly ambitious panorama of postrevolutionary French life. Known collectively as *The Human Comedy,* this series of nearly one hundred books vividly portrays more than two thousand characters from virtually all sectors of French society. Balzac pictures urban society as grasping, amoral, and brutal, characterized by a Darwinian struggle for wealth and power. In *Le Père Goriot* (1835), the hero, a poor student from the provinces, eventually surrenders his idealistic integrity to feverish ambition and society's pervasive greed.

Madame Bovary (1857), the masterpiece of Gustave Flaubert (1821–1880), is far narrower in scope than Balzac's work but unparalleled in its depth and accuracy of psychological insight. Unsuccessfully prosecuted as an outrage against public morality and religion, Flaubert's carefully crafted novel tells the ordinary, even banal, story of a frustrated middle-class housewife who has an adulterous love affair and is betrayed by her lover. Without moralizing, Flaubert portrays the provincial middle class as petty, smug, and hypocritical.

Zola was most famous for his seamy, animalistic view of working-class life. But he also wrote gripping, carefully researched stories featuring the stock exchange, the big department store, and the army, as well as urban slums and bloody coal strikes. Like many later realists, Zola sympathized with socialism, a sympathy evident in his overpowering *Germinal* (1885).

Realism quickly spread beyond France. In England, Mary Ann Evans (1819–1880), who wrote under the pen name George Eliot, brilliantly achieved a more deeply felt, less sensational kind of realism. "It is the habit of my imagination," George Eliot wrote, "to strive after as full a vision of the medium in which a character moves as one of the character itself." Her great novel *Middlemarch: A Study of Provincial Life* (1871–1872) examines masterfully the ways in which people are shaped by their social medium as well as their own inner strivings, conflicts, and moral choices. Thomas Hardy (1840–1928) was more in the Zola tradition. His novels, such as *Tess of the D'Urbervilles* (1891) and *The Return of the Native* (1878), depict men and women frustrated and crushed by fate and bad luck.

The greatest Russian realist, Count Leo Tolstoy (1828–1910), combined realism in description and character development with an atypical moralizing, which came to dominate his later work. Tolstoy's greatest work is *War and Peace* (1864–1869), a monumental novel set against the historical background of Napoleon's invasion of Russia in 1812. Tolstoy probed deeply into the lives of a multitude of unforgettable characters, such as the ill-fated Prince Andrei; the shy, fumbling Pierre; and the enchanting, level-headed Natasha. Tolstoy went to great pains to develop his fatalistic theory of history, which regards free will as an illusion and the achievements of even the greatest leaders as only the channeling of historical necessity. Yet Tolstoy's central message is one that most of the people discussed in this chapter would have readily accepted: human love, trust, and everyday family ties are life's enduring values.

Thoroughgoing realism (or "naturalism," as it was often called) arrived late in the United States, most arrestingly in the work of Theodore Dreiser (1871–1945). His first novel, *Sister Carrie* (1900), a story of an ordinary farm girl who does well going wrong in Chicago, so outraged conventional morality that the publisher withdrew the book. The United States subsequently became a bastion of literary realism in the twentieth century after the movement had faded away in Europe.

and provided themselves with other badly needed urban services. Gradually they tamed the ferocious savagery of the traditional city.

As urban civilization emerged, there were major changes in family life. Especially among the working classes, family life became more stable, more loving, and less mercenary. These improvements had a price, however. Gender roles for men and women became sharply defined and rigidly separate. Women especially tended to be locked into a subordinate and stereotypical role. Nonetheless, on balance, the quality of family life improved for all family members. Better, more stable family relations reinforced the benefits for the masses of higher real wages, increased social security, political participation, and education.

While the quality of urban and family life improved, the class structure became more complex and diversified than before. Urban society featured many distinct social groups, which existed in a state of constant flux and competition. The gap between rich and poor remained enormous and really quite traditional in mature urban society, although there were countless gradations between the extremes. Large numbers of poor women in particular continued to labor as workers in sweated industries, as domestic servants, and as prostitutes in order to satisfy the demands of their masters in the servant-keeping classes. Urban society in the late nineteenth century represented a long step forward for humanity, but it remained very unequal.

Inequality was a favorite theme of realist novelists such as Balzac and Zola. More generally, literary realism reflected Western society's growing faith in science, material progress, and evolutionary thinking. The emergence of urban, industrial civilization accelerated the secularization of the Western world-view.

SUMMARY

The revolution in industry had a decisive influence on the urban environment. The populations of towns and cities grew rapidly because it was economically advantageous to locate factories and offices in urban areas. This rapid growth worsened long-standing overcrowding and unhealthy living conditions and posed a frightening challenge for society. Eventually government leaders, city planners, reformers, scientists, and ordinary citizens responded. They took effective action in public health

NOTES

1. A. Weber, *The Growth of Cities in the Nineteenth Century* (New York: Columbia University Press, 1899), p. 1.
2. Quoted in W. Ashworth, *The Genesis of Modern British Town Planning* (London: Routledge & Kegan Paul, 1954), p. 17.
3. S. Marcus, "Reading the Illegible," in *The Victorian City: Images and Realities,* ed. H. J. Dyos and Michael Wolff, vol. 1 (London: Routledge & Kegan Paul, 1973), p. 266.
4. E. Gauldie, *Cruel Habitations: A History of Working-Class Housing, 1780–1918* (London: George Allen & Unwin, 1974), p. 21.

5. Quoted in E. Chadwick, *Report on the Sanitary Condition of the Labouring Population of Great Britain,* ed. M. W. Flinn (Edinburgh: University of Edinburgh Press, 1965; original publication, 1842), pp. 315–316.

6. J. P. McKay, *Tramways and Trolleys: The Rise of Urban Mass Transport in Europe* (Princeton, N.J.: Princeton University Press, 1976), p. 81.

7. Quoted in R. P. Neuman, "The Sexual Question and Social Democracy in Imperial Germany," *Journal of Social History* 7 (Winter 1974): 276.

8. Quoted in B. Harrison, "Underneath the Victorians," *Victorian Studies* 10 (March 1967): 260.

9. Quoted in J. A. Banks, "The Contagion of Numbers," in *The Victorian City: Images and Realities,* ed. H. J. Dyos and Michael Wolff, vol. 1 (London: Routledge & Kegan Paul, 1973), p. 112.

10. Quoted in R. Roberts, *The Classic Slum: Salford Life in the First Quarter of the Century* (Manchester, England: University of Manchester Press, 1971), p. 95.

11. Quoted in T. Zeldin, *France, 1848–1945,* vol. 1 (Oxford: Clarendon Press, 1973), p. 288.

12. Quoted in J. M. Phayer, "Lower-Class Morality: The Case of Bavaria," *Journal of Social History* 8 (Fall 1974): 89.

13. Quoted in S. Marcus, *The Other Victorians: A Study of Sexuality and Pornography in Mid-Nineteenth-Century England* (New York: Basic Books, 1966), p. 142.

14. Quoted in G. S. Jones, "Working-Class Culture and Working-Class Politics in London, 1870–1900: Notes on the Remaking of a Working Class," *Journal of Social History* 7 (Summer 1974): 486.

15. Quoted in Zeldin, *France,* p. 346.

16. Roberts, *The Classic Slum,* p. 35.

17. Quoted in Zeldin, *France,* p. 295.

18. Quoted ibid., p. 328.

19. Quoted in Neuman, "The Sexual Question," p. 281.

20. Quoted in S. Kern, "Explosive Intimacy: Psychodynamics of the Victorian Family," *History of Childhood Quarterly* 1 (Winter 1974): 439.

21. A. Comte, *The Positive Philosophy of Auguste Comte,* trans. H. Martineau, vol. 1 (London: J. Chapman, 1853), pp. 1–2.

22. Quoted in G. J. Becker, ed., *Documents of Modern Literary Realism* (Princeton, N.J.: Princeton University Press, 1963), p. 159.

SUGGESTED READING

All of the books and articles cited in the Notes are highly recommended. T. Zeldin, *France, 1848–1945,* 2 vols. (1973, 1977), is a pioneering social history that opens many doors, as is the ambitious synthesis by T. Hamerow, *The Birth of a New Europe: State and Society in the Nineteenth Century* (1983). F. Thompson, *The Rise of Respectable Society: A Social History of Victorian Britain, 1830–1900* (1986), is a laudable survey.

On the European city, D. Harvey, *Consciousness and the Urban Experience* (1985), is provocative. D. Silverman, *Art Nouveau in Fin-de-Siècle France: Politics, Psychology, and Style* (1989), and D. Pickney, *Napoleon III and the Rebuilding of Paris* (1972), are major studies. Also recommended are P. Fritzsche, *Reading Berlin in 1900* (1996), an imaginative cultural investigation; O. Olsen, *The City as a Work of Art: London, Paris, and Vienna* (1986), an architectural feast; and M. Hamm, ed., *The City in Russian History* (1976), which still has no equal. D. Grew, *Town in the Ruhr: A Social History of Bochum, 1860–1914* (1979), is an influential study. T. Clark, *The Painting of Modern Life: Paris in the Age of Manet and His Followers* (1985), and J. Merriman, *Margins of City Life: Explorations on the French Urban Frontier* (1991), are important works on France. The outstanding study by J. Schmiechen, *Sweated Industries and Sweated Labor: The London Clothing Trades* (1984), complements H. Mayhew's wonderful contemporary study, *London Labour and the Labouring Poor* (1861), reprinted recently. Michael Crichton's realistic historical novel on organized crime, *The Great Train Robbery* (1976), is excellent. E. Johnson, *Urbanization and Crime: Germany, 1871–1914* (1995), presents a portrait of a police state zealously defending property rights. J. P. Goubert, *The Conquest of Water: The Advent of Health in the Industrial Age* (1989), and A. Corbin, *The Foul and the Fragrant: Odor and the French Social Imagination of Public Health* (1986), are excellent introductions to sanitary developments and attitudes toward smells. For society as a whole, J. Burnett, *History of the Cost of Living* (1969), cleverly shows how different classes spent their money, and B. Tuchman, *The Proud Tower* (1966), draws an unforgettable portrait of people and classes before 1914. B. Gottlieb, *The Family in the Western World* (1993), is a wide-ranging recent synthesis. L. Pollock, *Forgotten Children: Parent-Child Relations from 1500 to 1900* (1983), explores long-term changes and patterns. J. Laver's handsomely illustrated *Manners and Morals in the Age of Optimism, 1848–1914* (1966) investigates the urban underworld and relations between the sexes. Sexual attitudes are also examined in J. Walkowitz, *Prostitution and Victorian Society: Women, Class and State* (1980); and L. Engelstein, *The Key to Happiness: Sex and the Search for Modernity in Fin-de-Siècle Russia* (1992). G. Alter, *Family and Female Life Course: The Women of Verviers, Belgium, 1849–1880* (1988), and A. McLaren, *Sexuality and Social Order: Birth Control in Nineteenth-Century France* (1982), explore attitudes toward family planning.

Studies on women continue to expand rapidly. In addition to the general works by Shorter, Wrigley, Stone, and Tilly and Scott cited in Chapter 20, recommended recent surveys include U. Frevert, *Women in German History: From Bourgeois Emancipation to Sexual Liberation* (1990); and M. Perrot, ed., *A History of Private Life* (1990), a fascinating book. Eye-opening specialized investigations include L. Davidoff, *The Best Circles* (1973), and P. Jalland, *Women, Marriage and Politics, 1860–1914* (1986), on upper-class society types; B. Engel, *Between the Fields and the City: Women, Work and Family in Russia, 1861–1914* (1994); and P. Smith, *Feminism in the Third Republic* (1996). M. J. Peterson, *Love and Work in the Lives of Victorian Gentlewomen* (1989), J. Coffin, *The Politics of Women's Work: The Paris Garment Trades, 1750–1914* (1996), and M. Vicinus, *Independent Women: Work and Community for Single Women, 1850–1920* (1985), examine women at work. M. Vicinus, ed., *Suffer and Be Still* (1972) and *A Widening Sphere* (1981), are far-ranging collections of essays on women's history, as is R. Bridenthal, C. Koonz, and S. Stuard, eds., *Becoming Visible: Women in European History,* 2d ed. (1987). Feminism is treated perceptively in R. Evans, *The Feminists: Women's Emancipation in Europe, America, and Australia* (1979), and C. Moses, *French Feminism in the Nineteenth Century* (1984). L. Tickner, *The Spectacle of Women: Imagery of the Suffrage Campaign, 1907–1914* (1988), perceptively discusses Britain. J. Gillis, *Youth and History* (1974), is a good introduction. J. Donzelot, *The Policing of Families* (1979), stresses the loss of family control of all aspects of life to government agencies.

Among studies on the working classes, M. Maynes, *Taking the Hard Road: Life Course in French and German Workers' Biographies in the Era of Industrialization* (1995), provides fascinating stories and shows how workers saw themselves. Everyday life in a great city comes wonderfully alive in W. S. Haine, *The World of the Paris Café: Sociability Among the French Working Class, 1789–1914* (1996). J. Wegs, *Growing Up Working Class: Continuity and Change Among Viennese Youth, 1890–1938* (1989), is recommended.

Two recommended studies on the middle classes are P. Pillbeam, *The Middle Classes in Europe, 1789–1914: France, Germany, Italy, and Russia* (1990), a stimulating introduction, and J. Kocka and A. Mitchell, eds., *Bourgeois Society in the Nineteenth Society* (1993), an up-to-date collection by leading specialists. Two fine recent studies on the professions are A. Digby, *Making a Medical Living: Doctors and Patients in the English Market for Medicine, 1720–1922* (1994); and A. Quartaro, *Women Teachers and Popular Education in Nineteenth-Century France* (1995). Servants and their employers receive excellent treatment in T. McBride, *The Domestic Revolution: The Modernization of Household Service in England and France, 1820–1912* (1976); and B. Smith, *Ladies of the Leisure Class: The Bourgeoises of Northern France in the Nineteenth Century* (1981), which may be compared with the innovative study by M. Miller, *The Bon Marché: Bourgeois Culture and the Department Store, 1869–1920* (1981).

On Darwin, M. Ruse, *The Darwinian Revolution* (1979), is a good starting point, as are P. Bowler, *Evolution: The History of an Idea,* rev. ed. (1989); and G. Himmelfarb, *Darwin and the Darwinian Revolution* (1968). O. Chadwick, *The Secularization of the European Mind in the Nineteenth Century* (1976), analyzes the impact of science (and other factors) on religious belief. M. Teich and R. Porter, eds., *Fin de Siècle and Its Legacy* (1990), is a fascinating collection of essays, ranging widely from industry and cars to sports and painting. The masterpieces of the great realist social novelists remain among the best and most memorable introductions to nineteenth-century culture and thought. In addition to the novels discussed in this chapter and those cited in the Suggested Reading for Chapters 22 and 23, Ivan Turgenev's *Fathers and Sons* and Emile Zola's *The Dram-Shop* are especially recommended.

Middle-Class Youth and Sexuality

Growing up in Vienna in a prosperous Jewish family, Stephan Zweig (1881–1942) became an influential voice calling for humanitarian values and international culture in early-twentieth-century Europe. Passionately opposed to the First World War, Zweig wrote poetry, plays, and novels. But he was most famous for many outstanding biographies, which featured shrewd psychological portraits of intriguing historical figures such as Magellan and Marie Antoinette. After Hitler came to power in Germany in 1933, Zweig lived in exile until his death in 1942.

Zweig's last work was The World of Yesterday *(1943), one of the truly fascinating autobiographies of the twentieth century. In the following passage taken from that work, Zweig recalls and also interprets the romantic experiences and the sexual frustrations of middle-class youth before the First World War.*

During the eight years of our higher schooling [beyond grade school], something had occurred which was of great importance to each one of us: we ten-year-olds had grown into virile young men of sixteen, seventeen, and eighteen, and Nature began to assert its rights. . . . It did not take us long to discover that those authorities in whom we had previously confided—school, family, and public morals—manifested an astonishing insincerity in this matter of sex. But what is more, they also demanded secrecy and reserve from us in this connection. . . .

This "social morality," which on the one hand privately presupposed the existence of sexuality and its natural course, but on the other would not recognize it openly at any price, was doubly deceitful. While it winked one eye at a young man and even encouraged him with the other "to sow his wild oats," as the kindly language of the home put it, in the case of a woman it studiously shut both eyes and acted as if it were blind. That a man could experience desires, and was permitted to experience them, was silently admitted by custom. But to admit frankly that a woman could be subject to similar desires, or that creation for its eternal purposes also required a female polarity, would have transgressed the conception of the "sanctity of womanhood." In the pre-Freudian era, therefore, the axiom was agreed upon that a female person could have no physical desires as long as they had not been awakened by man, and that, obviously, was officially permitted only in marriage. But even in those moral times, in Vienna in particular, the air was full of dangerous erotic infection, and a girl of good family had to live in a completely sterilized atmosphere, from the day of her birth until the day when she left the altar on her husband's arm. In order to protect young girls, they were not left alone for a single moment. . . . They had to practise the piano, learn singing and drawing, foreign languages, and the history of literature and art. They were educated and overeducated. But while the aim was to make them as educated and as socially correct as possible, at the same time society anxiously took great pains that they should remain innocent of all natural things to a degree unthinkable today. . . .

What possibilities actually existed for a young man of the middle-class world? In all the others, in the so-called lower classes, the problem was no problem at all. . . . In most of our Alpine villages the number of natural children greatly exceeded the legitimate ones. Among the proletariat, the worker, before he could get married, lived with another worker in free love. . . . It was only in our middle-class society that such a remedy as an early marriage was scorned. . . . And so there was an artificial interval of six, eight, or ten years between actual manhood and manhood as society accepted it; and in this interval the young man had to take care of his own "affairs" or adventures.

Those days did not give him too many opportunities. Only a very few particularly rich young men could afford the luxury of keeping a mistress, that is, taking an apartment and paying her expenses. And only a very few fortunate young men achieved the literary ideal of love of the times—the only one which it was permitted to describe in novels—an affair with a married woman. The others helped themselves for the most part with shopgirls and waitresses, and this offered little inner satisfaction. . . . But, generally speaking, prostitution was still the foundation of the erotic life outside of marriage; in a certain sense it constituted a dark underground vault over which rose the gorgeous structure of middle-class society with its faultless, radiant façade.

The present generation has hardly any idea of the gigantic extent of prostitution in Europe before the [First] World War. Whereas today it is as rare to meet a prostitute on the streets of a big city as it is to meet a wagon in the road, then the sidewalks were so sprinkled with women for sale that it was more difficult to avoid than to find them. To this was added the countless number of "closed houses," the night clubs, the cabarets, the dance parlours with their dancers and singers, and the bars with their "come-on" girls. At that time female wares were offered for sale at every hour and at every price. . . . The same world that so pathetically defended the purity of womanhood allowed this cruel sale of women, organized it, and even profited thereby.

❖ Nineteenth-century illustration depicting socializing in Vienna. (*Österreichische Nationalbibliothek*)

Questions for Analysis

1. According to Zweig, how did the sex lives of young middle-class women and young middle-class men differ?

2. What accounted for these differences?

3. Was there nonetheless a basic underlying unity in the way society treated both the young men and the young women of the comfortable middle class? If so, what was that unity?

4. Zweig ends his chapter with a value judgment: "It was a bad time for youth." Do you agree or disagree? Why?

Source: The World of Yesterday by Stephan Zweig, translated by Helmut Ripperger. Translation copyright 1943 by the Viking Press, Inc. Used with permission of Viking Penguin, a division of Penguin Putnam Inc.; Williams Verlag AG, Zurich; and Atrium Press Ltd., London.

25

The Age of Nationalism, 1850–1914

France's Napoleon III and Empress Eugénie greet Britain's Queen Victoria and Prince Albert in a dazzling ceremony in Paris in 1855. *(The Royal Collection © Her Majesty Queen Elizabeth II)*

The revolutions of 1848 closed one era and opened another. Urban industrial society began to take a strong hold on the continent and in the young United States, as it already had in Great Britain. Internationally, the repressive peace and diplomatic stability of Metternich's time were replaced by a period of war and rapid change. In thought and culture, exuberant romanticism gave way to hardheaded realism. In the Atlantic economy, the hard years of the 1840s were followed by good times and prosperity throughout most of the 1850s and 1860s. Perhaps most important of all, Western society progressively found, for better or worse, a new and effective organizing principle capable of coping with the many-sided challenge of the dual revolution and the emerging urban civilization. That principle was nationalism—dedication to an identification with the nation-state.

The triumph of nationalism is an enormously significant historical development that was by no means completely predictable. After all, nationalism had been a powerful force since at least 1789. Yet it had repeatedly failed to realize its goals, most spectacularly so in 1848.

- Why, then, did nationalism become in one way or another an almost universal faith in Europe and in the United States between 1850 and 1914?
- More specifically, how did nationalism evolve so that it appealed not only to predominately middle-class liberals but also to the broad masses of society?

These are the questions this chapter will seek to answer.

 NAPOLEON III IN FRANCE

Early nationalism was generally liberal and idealistic and often democratic and radical as well. The ideas of nationhood and popular sovereignty posed a fearful revolutionary threat to conservatives like Metternich. Yet from the vantage point of the twentieth century, it is clear that nationalism wears many masks: it may be narrowly liberal or democratic and radical, as it was for Mazzini and Michelet, but it can also flourish in dictatorial states, which may be conservative, fascist, or communist. Napoleon I's France had already combined national devotion with authoritarian rule. Significantly, it was Napoleon's nephew, Louis Napoleon, who revived and extended this merger. He showed how governments could reconcile popular and conservative forces in an authoritarian nationalism. In doing so, he provided a model for political leaders elsewhere.

The Second Republic and Louis Napoleon

Although Louis Napoleon Bonaparte had played no part in French politics before 1848, universal male suffrage gave him three times as many votes as the four other presidential candidates combined in the French presidential election of December 1848. This outcome occurred for several reasons. First, Louis Napoleon had the great name of his uncle, whom romantics had transformed from a dictator into a demigod as they created a Napoleonic legend after 1820. Second, as Karl Marx stressed at the time, middle-class and peasant property owners feared the socialist challenge of urban workers, and they wanted a tough ruler to provide protection. Third, in late 1848 Louis Napoleon had a positive "program" for France, which was to guide him through most of his long reign. This program had been elaborated earlier in two pamphlets, *Napoleonic Ideas* and *The Elimination of Poverty,* which he had written while imprisoned for an attempt to overthrow Louis Philippe's government. Prior to the presidential election, these pamphlets had been widely circulated.

Above all, Louis Napoleon believed that the government should represent the people and that it should try hard to help them economically. But how were these tasks to be done? Parliaments and political parties were not the answer, according to Louis Napoleon. French politicians represented special-interest groups, particularly middle-class ones. When they ran a parliamentary government, they stirred up class hatred because they were not interested in helping the poor. The answer was a strong, even authoritarian, national leader, like the first Napoleon, who would serve all the people, rich and poor. This leader would be linked to the people by direct democracy, his sovereignty uncorrupted by politicians and legislative bodies. These political ideas went hand in hand with Louis Napoleon's vision of national unity and social progress. Rather than doing nothing or providing only temporary relief for the awful poverty of the poor, the state and its leader had a sacred duty to provide jobs and stimulate the economy. All classes would benefit by such action.

Louis Napoleon's political and social ideas were at least vaguely understood by large numbers of French

Rebuilding Paris   Cutting new boulevards through Paris was like smashing superhighways through inner cities after World War II. Expensive and time-consuming, it brought massive demolitions, protests that the old city was being ruined, and big new buildings, such as the lavish opera house seen in the distance. Napoleon believed that boulevards would be harder for revolutionaries to barricade than narrow streets. *(Photo Bulloz)*

peasants and workers in December 1848. To many common people, he appeared to be a strong man *and* a forward-looking champion of their interests, and that is why they voted for him.

Elected to a four-year term, President Louis Napoleon had to share power with a conservative National Assembly. With some misgivings, he signed a bill to increase greatly the role of the Catholic church in primary and secondary education. In France, as elsewhere in Europe after 1848, the anxious well-to-do saw religion as a bulwark against radicalism. As one leader of the church in France put it, "There is only one recipe for making those who own nothing believe in property-rights: that is to make them believe in God, who dictated the Ten Commandments and who promises eternal punishment to those who steal."[1] Very reluctantly, Louis Napoleon also signed another law depriving many poor people of the right to vote. He took

these conservative measures for two main reasons: he wanted the Assembly to vote funds to pay his personal debts, and he wanted it to change the constitution so he could run for a second term.

The Assembly did neither. Thus in 1851 Louis Napoleon began to conspire with key army officers. On December 2, 1851, he illegally dismissed the Assembly and seized power in a *coup d'état*. There was some armed resistance in Paris and widespread insurrection in the countryside in southern France, but these protests were crushed by the army. Restoring universal male suffrage, Louis Napoleon called on the French people, as his uncle had done, to legalize his actions. They did: 92 percent voted to make him president for ten years. A year later, 97 percent in a plebiscite made him hereditary emperor; for the third time, and by the greatest margin yet, the authoritarian Louis Napoleon was overwhelmingly elected to lead the French nation.

Napoleon III's Second Empire

Louis Napoleon—now proclaimed Emperor Napoleon III—experienced both success and failure between 1852 and 1870. His greatest success was with the economy, particularly in the 1850s. His government encouraged the new investment banks and massive railroad construction that were at the heart of the Industrial Revolution on the continent. The government also fostered general economic expansion through an ambitious program of public works, which included the rebuilding of Paris to improve the urban environment (see pages 793–797). The profits of business people soared with prosperity, and the working classes did not fare poorly either. Their wages more than kept up with inflation, and jobs were much easier to find.

Louis Napoleon always hoped that economic progress would reduce social and political tensions. This hope was at least partially realized. Until the mid-1860s, there was little active opposition and there was even considerable support for his government from France's most dissatisfied group, the urban workers. Napoleon III's regulation of pawnshops and his support of credit unions and better housing for the working classes were evidence of positive concern in the 1850s. In the 1860s, he granted workers the right to form unions and the right to strike—important economic rights denied by earlier governments.

At first, political power remained in the hands of the emperor. He alone chose his ministers, and they had great freedom of action. At the same time, Napoleon III restricted but did not abolish the Assembly. Members were elected by universal male suffrage every six years, and Louis Napoleon and his government took the parliamentary elections very seriously. They tried to entice notable people, even those who had opposed the regime, to stand as government candidates in order to expand the base of support. Moreover, the government used its officials and appointed mayors to spread the word that the election of the government's candidates—and the defeat of the opposition—was the key to roads, tax rebates, and a thousand other local concerns.

In 1857 and again in 1863, Louis Napoleon's system worked brilliantly and produced overwhelming electoral victories. Yet in the 1860s, Napoleon III's electoral system gradually disintegrated. A sincere nationalist, Napoleon had wanted to reorganize Europe on the principle of nationality and gain influence and territory for France and himself in the process. Instead, problems in Italy and the rising power of Prussia led to increasing criticism at home from his Catholic and nationalist supporters. With increasing effectiveness, the middle-class liberals who had always wanted a less authoritarian regime continued to denounce his rule.

Napoleon was always sensitive to the public mood. Public opinion, he once said, always wins the last victory. Thus in the 1860s, he progressively liberalized his empire. He gave the Assembly greater powers and the opposition candidates greater freedom, which they used to good advantage. In 1869 the opposition, consisting of republicans, monarchists, and liberals, polled almost 45 percent of the vote.

The next year, a sick and weary Louis Napoleon again granted France a new constitution, which combined a basically parliamentary regime with a hereditary emperor as chief of state. In a final great plebiscite on the eve of the disastrous war with Prussia, 7.5 million Frenchmen voted in favor of the new constitution, and only 1.5 million opposed it. Napoleon III's attempt to reconcile a strong national state with universal male suffrage was still evolving and was doing so in a democratic direction.

NATION BUILDING IN ITALY AND GERMANY

Louis Napoleon's triumph in 1848 and his authoritarian rule in the 1850s provided the old ruling classes of Europe with a new model in politics. To what extent might the expanding urban middle classes and even portions of the growing working classes rally to a strong and essentially conservative national state? This was one of the great political questions in the 1850s and 1860s. In central Europe, a resounding answer came with the national unification of Italy and Germany.

Italy to 1850

Italy had never been united prior to 1850. Part of Rome's great empire in ancient times, the Italian peninsula was divided in the Middle Ages into competing city-states, which led the commercial and cultural revival of the West with amazing creativity. A battleground for great powers after 1494, Italy was reorganized in 1815 at the Congress of Vienna. The rich northern provinces of Lombardy and Venetia were taken by Metternich's Austria. Sardinia and Piedmont were under the rule of an Italian monarch, and Tuscany, with its famous capital Florence, shared north-central Italy with several smaller states. Central Italy and Rome were ruled by the papacy, which had always considered an independent political existence necessary to fulfill its spiritual mission. Naples and Sicily were ruled, as they had been for almost a hundred years, by a branch of the Bourbons. Metternich was not wrong in dismissing Italy as "a geographical expression" (Map 25.1).

Between 1815 and 1848, the goal of a unified Italian nation captured the imaginations of many Italians. There were three basic approaches. The first was the radical program of the idealistic patriot Giuseppe Mazzini, who preached a centralized democratic republic based on universal male suffrage and the will of the people (see page 762). The second was that of Vincenzo Gioberti, a Catholic priest who called for a federation of existing states under the presidency of a progressive pope. The third was the program of those who looked for leadership to the autocratic kingdom of Sardinia-Piedmont, much as many Germans looked to Prussia.

The third alternative was strengthened by the failures of 1848, when Austria smashed Mazzini's republicanism. Almost by accident, Sardinia's monarch, Victor Emmanuel, retained the liberal constitution granted under duress in March 1848. This constitution provided for a fair degree of civil liberties and real parliamentary government, with deputies elected on the basis of a narrow franchise limited to the nobility and the comfortable middle class. To the Italian middle classes, Sardinia appeared to be a liberal, progressive state ideally suited to achieve the goal of national unification. By contrast, the middle-class elite and its allies in the liberal aristocracy distrusted Mazzini's vision of democratic republicanism. They feared it might lead to renewed upheaval, social revolution, and intervention by France or Austria. Nationalists in the lower middle class and on the left usually continued to support a republican Italy.

As for the papacy, the initial cautious support by Pius IX (r. 1846–1878) for unification had given way to fear and hostility after he was temporarily driven from Rome during the upheavals of 1848. For a long generation, the papacy would stand resolutely opposed not only to national unification but also to most modern trends. In 1864 in the *Syllabus of Errors,* Pius IX strongly denounced rationalism, socialism, separation of church and state, and religious liberty, denying that "the Roman pontiff can and ought to reconcile and align himself with progress, liberalism, and modern civilization."

Cavour and Garibaldi in Italy

Sardinia had the good fortune of being led by a brilliant statesman, Count Camillo Benso di Cavour, the dominant figure in the Sardinian government from 1850 until his death in 1861. Indicative of the coming tacit alliance between the aristocracy and the solid middle class under the banner of the strong nation-state, Cavour came from a noble family and embraced the economic doctrines and business activities associated with the prosperous middle class. Before entering politics, he made a substantial fortune in sugar mills, steamships, banks, and railroads. Cavour's national goals were limited and realistic. Until 1859 he sought unity only for the states of northern and perhaps central Italy in a greatly expanded kingdom of Sardinia. He did not seek to incorporate the Papal States or the kingdom of the Two Sicilies, with their very different cultures and governments, into an Italy of all the Italians.

In the 1850s, Cavour worked to consolidate Sardinia as a liberal constitutional state capable of leading northern Italy. His program of highways and railroads, of civil liberties and opposition to clerical privilege, increased support for Sardinia throughout northern Italy. Yet Cavour realized that Sardinia could not drive Austria out of Lombardy and Venetia and unify northern Italy under Victor Emmanuel without the help of a powerful ally. He sought that ally in the person of Napoleon III, who believed in national consolidation, especially if it could be combined with modest expansion for France.

In a complicated series of diplomatic maneuvers, Cavour worked for a secret diplomatic alliance with Napoleon III against Austria. Finally, in July 1858 he succeeded and goaded Austria into attacking Sardinia in 1859. Napoleon III came to Sardinia's defense. Then after the victory of the combined Franco-Sardinian forces, Napoleon III did a sudden about-face. Deciding it was not in his interest to have too strong a state on his southern border and criticized by French Catholics for supporting the pope's declared enemy, Napoleon III abandoned Cavour. He made a compromise peace with the Austrians at Villafranca in July 1859. Sardinia would receive only Lombardy, the area around Milan. The rest of the map of Italy would remain essentially unchanged. Cavour resigned in a rage.

Yet Cavour's plans were salvaged by the skillful maneuvers of his allies in the moderate nationalist movement. While the war against Austria had raged in the north, pro-Sardinian nationalists in central Italy had fanned revolts and driven out their easily toppled princes. Large crowds demonstrated, singing "Foreigners, get out of Italy!" and passionately chanting, "Italy and Victor Emmanuel!" Using and controlling the popular enthusiasm, the middle-class nationalist leaders in central Italy ignored the compromise peace of Villafranca and called for fusion with Sardinia.

This was not at all what France and the other Great Powers wanted, but the nationalists held firm. Cavour

MAP 25.1 The Unification of Italy, 1859–1870   The leadership of Sardinia-Piedmont and nationalist fervor were decisive factors in the unification of Italy.

returned to power in early 1860 to work out a deal with Napoleon III. Sardinia had to cede Savoy and Nice to France, but for this price Napoleon III dropped his objections. The people of central Italy then voted overwhelmingly to join a greatly enlarged kingdom of Sardinia. Cavour had achieved his original goal of a northern Italian state (see Map 25.1).

For superpatriots such as Giuseppe Garibaldi (1807–1882), the job of unification was still only half done. The son of a poor sailor, Garibaldi had long personified the romantic, revolutionary nationalism of Mazzini and 1848. (See the feature "Individuals in Society: Garibaldi, Hero of the People.") All his life, he had fought and plotted wars of national liberation. In the early

Individuals in Society

Garibaldi, Hero of the People

When Giuseppe Garibaldi (1807–1882) visited England in 1864, he received the most triumphant welcome ever given to any foreigner. Honored and feted by politicians and high society, he also captivated the masses. An unprecedented crowd of a half million people cheered his carriage through the streets of London. These ovations were no fluke. In his time, Garibaldi was probably the most famous and most beloved figure in the world.[1] How could this be?

A rare combination of wild adventure and extraordinary achievement partly accounted for his demigod status. Born in Nice, Garibaldi went to sea at fifteen and sailed the Mediterranean for twelve years. At seventeen his travels took him to Rome, and he was converted in an almost religious experience to the "New Italy, the Italy of all the Italians." As he later wrote in his best-selling *Autobiography,* "The Rome that I beheld with the eyes of youthful imagination was the Rome of the future—the dominant thought of my whole life."

Sentenced to death in 1834 for his part in a revolutionary uprising in Genoa, Garibaldi barely escaped to South America. For twelve years, he led a guerrilla band in Uruguay's struggle for independence from Argentina. "Shipwrecked, ambushed, shot through the neck," he found in a tough young woman, Anna da Silva, a mate and companion in arms. Their first children nearly starved in the jungle while Garibaldi, clad in his long red shirt, fashioned a legend as a fearless freedom fighter.

Returning to Italy in 1848, the campaigns of his patriotic volunteers against the Austrians in 1848 and 1859 mobilized democratic nationalists. The stage was set for his volunteer army to liberate Sicily against enormous odds, astonishing the world and creating a large Italian state. Garibaldi's achievement matched his legend.

A brilliant fighter, the handsome and inspiring leader was an uncompromising idealist of absolute integrity. He never drew any personal profit from his exploits, continuing to milk his goats and rarely possessing more than one change of clothing. When Victor Emmanuel offered him lands and titles after his

Giuseppe Garibaldi, the charismatic leader, shown in an 1856 engraving based on a photograph. *(Corbis-Bettmann)*

great victory in 1861, even as the left-leaning volunteers were disbanded and humiliated, Garibaldi declined, saying he could not be bought off. Returning to his farm on a tiny rocky island, he denounced the government without hesitation when he concluded that it was betraying the dream of unification with its ruthless rule in the south. Yet even after a duplicitous Italian government caused two later attacks on Rome to fail, his faith in the generative power of national unity never wavered. Garibaldi showed that ideas and ideals count in history.

Above all, millions of ordinary men and women identified with Garibaldi because they believed that he was fighting for them. They recognized him as one of their own and saw that he remained true to them in spite of his triumphs, thereby ennobling their own lives and aspirations. Welcoming runaway slaves as equals in Latin America, advocating the emancipation of women, introducing social reforms in the south, and pressing for free education and a broader suffrage in the new Italy, Garibaldi the national hero fought for freedom and human dignity. The common people understood, and loved him for it.

Questions for Analysis

1. Why was Garibaldi so famous and popular?

2. Nationalism evolved and developed in the nineteenth century. How did Garibaldi fit into this evolution? What kind of a nationalist was he?

1. Denis Mack Smith, *Garibaldi: A Great Life in Brief* (New York: Alfred A. Knopf, 1956), pp. 136–147; and Denis Mack Smith, "Giuseppe Garibaldi," *History Today,* August 1991, pp. 20–26.

1860s Garibaldi, ever a radical man of action, devised a bold plan to use a private army of patriotic volunteers to "liberate" the kingdom of the Two Sicilies. Cavour opposed the invasion, but he dared not stop it because of Garibaldi's enormous popular appeal. Slipping out of Genoa and landing on the shores of Sicily in May 1860, Garibaldi's guerrilla band of a thousand "Red Shirts" captured the imagination of the Sicilian peasantry. Outwitting the twenty-thousand-man royal army, the guerrilla leader won battles, gained volunteers, and took Palermo. Then he and his men crossed to the mainland, marched triumphantly toward Naples, and prepared to attack Rome and the pope.

Expecting and probably hoping at first that Garibaldi would fail, the wily Cavour now moved quickly to profit from his victories. He sent Sardinian forces to occupy most of the Papal States (but not Rome) and to intercept Garibaldi. Knowing that an attack on Rome might bring about war with France, Cavour feared Garibaldi's radicalism above all. As temporary ruler of Sicily and Naples, Garibaldi had already introduced free education and tentative social reforms and had disbanded the Jesuits and nationalized their property. Therefore, Cavour immediately organized a plebiscite in the conquered territories. Despite the urging of some more radical supporters, the patriotic Garibaldi did not oppose Cavour, and the people of the south voted to join Sardinia. When Garibaldi and Victor Emmanuel rode through Naples to cheering crowds, they symbolically sealed the union of north and south, of monarch and nation-state.

Garibaldi and Victor Emmanuel   The historic meeting in Naples between the leader of Italy's revolutionary nationalists and the king of Sardinia sealed the unification of northern and southern Italy in a unitary state. With only the sleeve of his red shirt showing, Garibaldi offers his hand—and his conquests—to the uniformed king and his moderate monarchical government. *(Fabio Lensini/Madeline Grimoldi)*

Cavour had succeeded. He had controlled Garibaldi and had turned popular nationalism in a conservative direction. The new kingdom of Italy, which expanded to include Venice in 1866 and Rome in 1870, mainly because of Prussian victories over Austria and then France in those years, was neither radical nor democratic. Italy was a parliamentary monarchy under Victor Emmanuel, but in accordance with the liberal Sardinian constitution of 1848, only a small minority of Italian males had the right to vote. The properted classes and the common people were divided.

Moreover, a great gap separated the progressive, industrializing north from the stagnant, agrarian south. This gap would actually increase in the new Italian state. Harsh administrators from Sardinia immediately canceled Garibaldi's wartime reforms, and they often ruled Sicily and Naples like a conquered territory, dashing the hopes "liberation" had raised and leading to disillusionment and widespread banditry. The peasant industries of the south also declined precipitously, increasing the weight of existing poverty and sending millions abroad in search of a better life. The new Italy was united on paper, but profound divisions remained.

Germany Before Bismarck

In the aftermath of 1848, while Louis Napoleon consolidated his rule and Cavour schemed, the German states were locked in a political stalemate. With Russian diplomatic support, Austria had blocked the half-hearted attempt of Frederick William IV of Prussia (r. 1840–1861) to unify Germany "from above." This action contributed to a growing tension between Austria and Prussia as each power sought to block the other within the reorganized German Confederation, made up of thirty-eight sovereign states after 1815 (see pages 758 and 782–784). Stalemate also prevailed in the domestic politics of the individual states as Austria, Prussia, and the smaller German kingdoms entered a period of reaction and immobility in the 1850s.

At the same time, powerful economic forces were undermining the political status quo. As we have seen, modern industry grew rapidly in Europe throughout the 1850s. Nowhere was this growth more rapid than within the German customs union (Zollverein). Developing gradually under Prussian leadership after 1818 and founded officially in 1834 to stimulate trade and increase the revenues of member states, the Zollverein had not included Austria. After 1848 this exclusion became a crucial factor in the Austro-Prussian rivalry.

The Zollverein's tariff duties were substantially reduced so that Austria's highly protected industry could

not bear to join. In retaliation, Austria tried to destroy the Zollverein by inducing the south German states to leave it, but without success. Indeed, by the end of 1853 all the German states except Austria had joined the customs union. A new Germany excluding Austria was becoming an economic reality. Middle-class and business groups in the Zollverein were enriching themselves and finding solid economic reasons to bolster their idealistic support of national unification. The growing economic integration of the states within the Zollverein gave Prussia a valuable advantage in its struggle against Austria's supremacy in German political affairs.

The national uprising in Italy in 1859 made a profound impression in the German states. In Prussia great political change and war—perhaps with Austria, perhaps with France—seemed quite possible. Along with his top military advisers, the tough-minded William I of Prussia (r. 1861–1888), who had replaced the unstable Frederick William IV as regent in 1858 and become king himself in 1861, was convinced of the need for major army reforms. William I wanted to double the size of the highly disciplined regular army. He also wanted to reduce the importance of the reserve militia, a semipopular force created during the Napoleonic wars. Army reforms meant a bigger defense budget and higher taxes.

Prussia had emerged from 1848 with a parliament of sorts, which was in the hands of the liberal middle class by 1859. The wealthy middle class, like the landed aristocracy, was greatly overrepresented by the Prussian electoral system, and it wanted society to be less, not more, militaristic. Above all, middle-class representatives wanted to establish once and for all that the parliament, not the king, had the ultimate political power. They also wanted to ensure that the army was responsible to Prussia's elected representatives and was not a "state within a state." These demands were popular. The parliament rejected the military budget in 1862, and the liberals triumphed completely in new elections. King William then called on Count Otto von Bismarck to head a new ministry and defy the parliament. This was a momentous choice.

Bismarck Takes Command

The most important figure in German history between Luther and Hitler, Otto von Bismarck (1815–1898) has been the object of enormous interest and debate. A great hero to some, a great villain to others, Bismarck was above all a master of politics. Born into the Prussian landowning aristocracy, the young Bismarck was a wild and tempestuous student given to duels and drinking. Proud of his Junker heritage and always devoted to his Prussian sovereign, Bismarck had a strong personality and an unbounded desire for power. Yet in his drive to secure power for himself and for Prussia, Bismarck was extraordinarily flexible and pragmatic. "One must always have two irons in the fire," he once said. He kept his options open, pursuing one policy and then another as he moved with skill and cunning toward his goal.

Bismarck first honed his political skills as a diplomat. Acquiring a reputation as an ultraconservative in the Prussian assembly in 1848, he fought against Austria as the Prussian ambassador to the German Confederation from 1851 to 1859. Transferred next to St. Petersburg and then to Paris, he worked toward a basic goal that was well-known by 1862—to build up Prussia's strength and consolidate Prussia's precarious Great Power status.

To achieve this goal, Bismarck was convinced that Prussia had to control completely the northern, predominately Protestant part of the German Confederation. He saw three possible paths open before him. He might work with Austria to divide up the smaller German states lying between them. Or he might combine with foreign powers—France and Italy or even Russia—in a war against Austria. Or he might ally with the forces of German nationalism to defeat and expel Austria from German affairs. He explored each possibility in many complicated diplomatic maneuvers, but in the end the last path was the one Bismarck took.

That Bismarck would join with the forces of German nationalism to increase Prussia's power seemed unlikely when he took office as chief minister in 1862. Bismarck's appointment made a strong but unfavorable impression. His speeches were a sensation and a scandal. Declaring that the government would rule without parliamentary consent, Bismarck lashed out at the middle-class opposition: "The great questions of the day will not be decided by speeches and resolutions—that was the blunder of 1848 and 1849—but by blood and iron." Denounced for this view that "might makes right," Bismarck had the Prussian bureaucracy go right on collecting taxes, even though the parliament refused to approve the budget. Bismarck reorganized the army. And for four years, from 1862 to 1866, the voters of Prussia continued to express their opposition by sending large liberal majorities to the parliament.

The Austro-Prussian War, 1866

Opposition at home spurred the search for success abroad. The ever-knotty question of Schleswig-Holstein provided a welcome opportunity. In 1864, when the Danish king tried again, as in 1848, to bring

Otto von Bismarck   The commanding presence and the haughty pride of the Prussian statesman are clearly evident in this photo taken shortly before he came to power. Dressed in formal diplomatic attire as Prussia's ambassador in Paris, Bismarck is perhaps on his way to see Emperor Louis Napoleon and size up his future adversary once again. *(Archiv Für Kunst und Geschichte, London)*

the provinces into a more centralized Danish state against the will of the German Confederation, Prussia joined Austria in a short and successful war against Denmark. However, Bismarck was convinced that Prussia had to control completely the northern, predominately Protestant part of the German Confederation, which meant expelling Austria from German affairs. After the victory over Denmark, Bismarck's skillful maneuvering had Prussia in a position to force Austria out by war, if necessary.

Bismarck knew that a war with Austria would have to be a localized one that would not provoke a mighty alliance against Prussia. Russia was no problem because Bismarck had already gained Alexander II's gratitude by supporting Russia's repression of a Polish uprising in 1863. Napoleon III—the "sphinx without a riddle," according to Bismarck—was charmed into neutrality with vague promises of more territory along the Rhine. Thus when Austria proved unwilling to give up its historic role in German affairs, Bismarck was in a position to engage in a war of his own making.

The Austro-Prussian War of 1866 lasted only seven weeks. Utilizing railroads to mass troops and the new breechloading needle gun to achieve maximum firepower, the reorganized Prussian army overran northern Germany and defeated Austria decisively at the Battle of Sadowa in Bohemia. Anticipating Prussia's future needs, Bismarck offered Austria realistic, even generous, peace terms. Austria paid no reparations and lost no territory to Prussia, although Venice was ceded to Italy. But the German Confederation was dissolved, and Austria agreed to withdraw from German affairs. The states north of the Main River were grouped in the new North German Confederation, led by an expanded Prussia. The mainly Catholic states of the south remained independent while forming alliances with Prussia. Bismarck's fundamental goal of Prussian expansion was being realized (Map 25.2).

The Taming of the Parliament

Bismarck had long been convinced that the old order he so ardently defended should make peace, on its own terms, with the liberal middle class and the nationalist movement. He realized that nationalism was not necessarily hostile to conservative, authoritarian government. Moreover, Bismarck believed that because of the events of 1848, the German middle class could be led to prefer the reality of national unity under conservative leadership to a long, uncertain battle for truly liberal institutions. During the constitutional struggle over army reform and parliamentary authority, he had delayed but not abandoned this goal. Thus during the attack on Austria in 1866, he increasingly identified Prussia's fate with the "national development of Germany."

In the aftermath of victory, Bismarck fashioned a federal constitution for the new North German Confederation. Each state retained its own local government, but the king of Prussia became president of the confederation and the chancellor—Bismarck—was responsible only to the president. The federal government—William I and Bismarck—controlled the army and foreign affairs. There was also a legislature consisting of two houses that shared equally in the making of laws. Delegates to the upper house were appointed by the different states, but members of the lower house were elected by universal, single-class, male suffrage. With this radical innovation, Bismarck opened the door to popular participation and the possibility of going over the head of the middle class directly to the people, much as Napoleon III had done in France. All the while, however, ultimate power rested as securely as ever in the hands of Prussia and its king and army.

In Prussia itself, Bismarck held out an olive branch to the parliamentary opposition. Marshaling all his diplomatic skill, Bismarck asked the parliament to pass a special indemnity bill to approve after the fact all the government's spending between 1862 and 1866. Most of the liberals jumped at the chance to cooperate. For four long years, they had opposed and criticized Bismarck's "illegal" measures. Yet Bismarck, the king, and the army with its aristocratic leadership had succeeded beyond the wildest dreams of the liberal middle class. In 1866 German unity was in sight, and the people were to be allowed to participate actively in the new state.

Many liberals repented their "sins," and none repented more ardently than Hermann Baumgarten, a thoroughly decent history professor and member of the liberal opposition. In his essay "A Self-Criticism of German Liberalism," he confessed in 1866: "We thought that by agitation we could transform Germany. . . . Yet we have experienced a miracle almost without parallel. The victory of our principles would have brought us misery, whereas the defeat of our principles has brought boundless salvation."[2] The constitutional struggle was over. The German middle class was bowing respectfully before Bismarck and the monarchial authority and aristocratic superiority he represented. In the years before 1914, the virtues of the aristocratic Prussian army officer increasingly replaced those of the middle-class liberal in public esteem and set the social standard.[3]

The Franco-Prussian War, 1870–1871

The rest of the story of German unification is anticlimactic. In 1867 Bismarck formed an alliance with four south German states and transformed the Zollverein into a customs parliament. But the south Germans were reluctant to go further because of their different religious and political traditions. Bismarck realized that a patriotic war with France would drive the south German states into his arms. The French obligingly played their part. The apparent issue—whether a distant relative of Prussia's William I (and France's

MAP 25.2 The Unification of Germany, 1866–1871   This map deserves careful study. Note how Prussian expansion, Austrian expulsion from the old German Confederation, and the creation of a new German empire went hand in hand. Austria lost no territory, but Prussia's neighbors in the north suffered grievously or simply disappeared. The annexation of Alsace-Lorraine turned France into a lasting enemy of Germany before 1914.

Napoleon III) might become king of Spain—was only a diplomatic pretext. By 1870 the French leaders of the Second Empire, goaded by Bismarck and alarmed by their powerful new neighbor on the Rhine, had decided on a war to teach Prussia a lesson.

As soon as war against France began in 1870, Bismarck had the wholehearted support of the south German states. With other governments standing still—Bismarck's generosity to Austria in 1866 was paying big dividends—German forces under Prussian leadership decisively defeated the main French army at Sedan on September 1, 1870. Louis Napoleon himself was captured and humiliated. Three days later, French patriots in Paris proclaimed yet another French republic and vowed to continue fighting. But after five months, in January 1871, a starving Paris surrendered, and France went on to accept Bismarck's harsh peace terms. By this time, the south German states had agreed to join a new German empire. The victorious William I was proclaimed emperor of Germany in the Hall of Mirrors in the palace of Versailles. Europe had a nineteenth-century German "sun king." As in the 1866 constitution, the king of Prussia and his ministers had ultimate power in the new German Empire, and the lower house of the legislature was elected by universal male suffrage.

Bismarck and the new German Empire imposed a harsh peace on France. Despite the desperate pleas of French leaders, France was forced to pay a colossal indemnity of 5 billion francs and to cede the rich eastern province of Alsace and part of Lorraine to Germany. The German general staff asserted that this annexation would enhance military security, and German nationalists claimed that the Alsacians, who spoke a German dialect as well as French, wanted to rejoin the fatherland after more than two hundred years. But both cases were weak, and revenge for France's real and imagined aggression in the past was probably the decisive factor. In any event, French men and women of all classes viewed the seizure of Alsace and Lorraine as a terrible crime. They could never forget and never forgive, and thus relations between France and Germany after 1871 were tragically poisoned.

The Franco-Prussian War, which Europeans generally saw as a test of nations in a pitiless Darwinian struggle for existence, released an enormous surge of patriotic feeling in Germany. Bismarck's genius, the invincible Prussian army, the solidarity of king and people in a unified nation—these and similar themes were trumpeted endlessly during and after the war. The weakest of the Great Powers in 1862 (after Austria, Britain, France, and Russia), Prussia had become, with fortification by the other German states, the most powerful state in Europe in less than a decade. Most Germans were enormously proud, enormously relieved. And they were somewhat drunk with success, blissfully imagining themselves the fittest and best of the European species. Semi-authoritarian nationalism and a "new conservatism," which was based on an alliance of the propertied classes and sought the active support of the working classes, had triumphed in Germany. Only a few critics remained dedicated to the liberal ideal of truly responsible parliamentary government.

 ## NATION BUILDING IN THE UNITED STATES

Closely linked to European developments in the nineteenth century, the United States experienced the full drama of nation building and felt the power of nationalism to refashion politics and remake states. Yet competing national aspirations served first to divide rather than unite the nation.

Slavery and Territorial Expansion

The "United" States was divided by slavery from its birth, and its early growth continued this separation. The purchase of France's Louisiana Territory in 1803 opened an enormous area for settlement and set the stage for growing regional tensions as economic development carried free and slaveholding states in very different directions.

Northerners extended family farms to western regions and began building English-model factories in the Northeast. By 1850 an industrializing, urbanizing North was also building a system of canals and railroads and attracting most of the rising tide of European immigrants. In the South, industry and cities did not develop, and newcomers avoided the region. And even though three-quarters of all Southern white families were small farmers and owned no slaves in 1850, plantation owners holding twenty or more slaves dominated the economy and the society. These profit-minded slaveowners used gangs of black slaves to claim a vast new kingdom across the Deep South where cotton was king (Map 25.3). By 1850, this kingdom was producing 5 million bales a year (as opposed to only 4,000 bales in 1791) and satisfied an apparently insatiable demand from cotton mills in Great Britain, other European countries, and New England.

The rise of the cotton empire had momentous consequences. First, it revitalized slave-based agriculture and created great wealth—and not just for rich Southern slaveholders. Cotton accounted for two-thirds of the value of all American exports by the 1850s, and many economic historians believe it ignited rapid U.S. economic growth. Second, the large profits flowing from cotton led influential Southerners to defend slavery. Southern whites saw themselves as a closely knit "we" distinct from a Northern "they." At the same time, Northern whites came to see their free-labor system as being no less economically and morally superior. Thus regional antagonisms intensified.

These antagonisms came to a climax after 1848 when Mexico, defeated in war, ceded to the United States half

Slavery and Cotton The intense activity and the systematic exploitation of slave labor on large cotton plantations come alive in this contemporary painting. Slaves of both sexes and of all ages pick the cotton and transport it to smoke-belching worksheds, shown in the background, for later processing in cotton gins. *(The Collection of Jay P. Altmayer)*

a million square miles of territory stretching from west Texas to the Pacific Ocean. Whether and to what extent Congress should permit slavery in this new territory became an absorbing and divisive political issue. Attitudes hardened on both sides, and outbreaks of violence multiplied. In Abraham Lincoln's famous words, the United States was a "house divided."

Civil War and Reunification

Lincoln's election as president in 1860 gave Southern "fire-eaters" the chance they had been waiting for. Eventually eleven states left the Union, determined to win their own independence and forming a government they called the Confederate States of America. When Southern troops fired on a Union fort in South Carolina's Charleston harbor, war began.

The long Civil War (1861–1865) was the bloodiest conflict in all of American history, but in the end the South was decisively defeated and the Union preserved. The vastly superior population, industry, and transportation of the North placed the South at a great, probably fatal, disadvantage. Less obvious factors tied to morale and national purpose contributed to the outcome. The enormous gap between the slave-owning elite and the poor whites made it impossible for the South to build effectively on the patriotism of 1861. As the war ground on, many ordinary whites felt that the burden of war was falling mainly on their shoulders because big planters resisted taxation and used loopholes to avoid the draft. Desertions from Southern armies mounted rapidly from the summer of 1863 on as soldiers became disillusioned.

Slavery itself weakened the South's war effort. Although blacks were used on the home front in countless

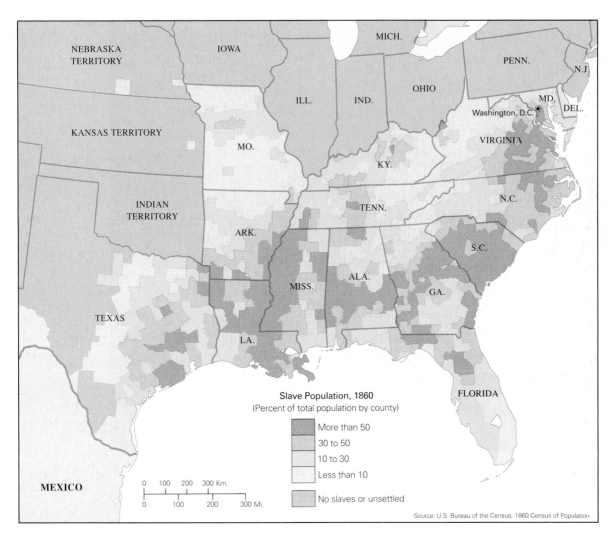

MAP 25.3 Slavery in the United States, 1860   This map illustrates the nation on the eve of the Civil War. Although many issues contributed to the developing opposition between North and South, slavery was the fundamental, enduring force that underlay all others. Lincoln's prediction, "I believe this government cannot endure permanently half slave and half free," tragically proved correct.

ways, owners generally kept them on the plantations for fear of their running away or starting a slave rebellion. Nevertheless, tens of thousands escaped to Union armies, supplying many of the 200,000 black soldiers who served in those armies.

In the North, by contrast, many people prospered during the war years. Enthusiasm remained high, and certain dominant characteristics of American life and national culture took shape. Powerful business corporations emerged, steadfastly supported by the Republican party during and after the war. The Homestead Act of 1862, which gave western land to those who would settle it, and the Thirteenth Amendment of 1865, which

ended slavery, reinforced the concept of free labor taking its chances in a market economy. Finally, the success of Lincoln and the North in holding the Union together seemed to confirm that the "manifest destiny" of the United States was indeed to straddle a continent as a great world power. Thus a new American nationalism grew out of the war aimed at preventing Southern nationhood.

Northern victory also led to a "national" policy of sorts toward American blacks. Congress at first guaranteed the legal freedom of blacks, but Northern whites lost interest in continued sectional struggle, and Southern whites regained control of the state governments.

Antietam: Critical Turning Point   Building on recent victories, Confederate General Robert E. Lee entered Maryland in 1862 and threatened Washington, D.C., engaging Union forces at Antietam Creek on September 17, 1862. The ensuing twelve-hour battle claimed 23,000 dead and wounded and ended in a murderous draw. This dramatic painting, by a northern officer who survived the battle, shows Union soldiers storming a key bridge under withering Confederate fire in the battle's late afternoon climax. Lee retreated and European support for the South waned. President Lincoln issued the preliminary Emancipation Proclamation, which made the war more of a crusade against slavery. *(National Park Service Collection)*

In addition, Northern efforts to "reconstruct" the South did not include land reform. Freed blacks were generally forced to continue laboring for white landowners in the unfair arrangement called sharecropping. Thus as a result of war and reunification, the life of blacks in the Southern states moved much closer to that of the small number of blacks in the North, who had long been free but unequal citizens.

 ## THE MODERNIZATION OF RUSSIA

Russia also experienced a profound midcentury crisis of nation building. This crisis was unlike those occurring in Italy and Germany, for Russia had no need to build a single state out of a jumble of principalities. The Russian empire was already an enormous multinational state that contained all the ethnic Russians and many other nationalities as well. Rather, as in the United States, the long-term challenge facing the government was to hold the existing state together, either by means of political compromise or by military force. Thus Russia's rulers saw national self-determination as a subversive ideology in the early nineteenth century, and they tried with some success to limit its development among their non-Russian subjects.

Yet old autocratic Russia found itself in serious trouble after 1853. It became clear to Russia's leaders that the country had to embrace the process of *modernization*. A vague and often overworked term, modernization is a great umbrella under which some writers place most of the major developments of the last two hundred or even five hundred years. Yet defined narrowly— as changes that enable a country to compete effectively with the leading countries at a given time—modernization can be a useful concept. It fits Russia after the Crimean War particularly well.

The "Great Reforms"

In the 1850s, Russia was a poor agrarian society. Industry was little developed, and almost 90 percent of the population lived on the land. Agricultural techniques were backward: the ancient open-field system reigned supreme. Serfdom was still the basic social institution. Bound to the lord on a hereditary basis, the peasant serf was little more than a slave. Individual serfs and serf families were regularly sold, with and without land, in the early nineteenth century. Serfs were obliged to furnish labor services or money payments as the lord saw fit. Moreover, the lord could choose freely among the serfs for army recruits, who had to serve for twenty-five years, and he could punish a serf with deportation to Siberia. Sexual exploitation of female serfs by their lords was common.

Serfdom had become the great moral and political issue for the government by the 1840s, but it might still have lasted many more years had the Crimean War of 1853 to 1856 not occurred. The war began as a dispute with France over who should protect certain Christian shrines in the Ottoman Empire. Because the fighting was concentrated in the Crimean peninsula on the Black Sea, Russia's transportation network of rivers and wagons failed to supply the distant Russian armies adequately. France and Great Britain, aided by Sardinia and the Ottoman Empire, inflicted a humiliating defeat on Russia.

This military defeat marked a turning point in Russian history. The Russian state had been built on the military, and Russia had not lost a major war for a century and a half. This defeat demonstrated that Russia had fallen behind the rapidly industrializing nations of western Europe in many areas. At the very least, Russia needed railroads, better armaments, and reorganization of the army if it was to maintain its international position. Moreover, the disastrous war had caused hardship and raised the specter of massive peasant rebellion. Reform of serfdom was imperative. And as the new tsar, Alexander II (r. 1855–1881), told the serf owners, it would be better if reform came from above. Military disaster thus forced Alexander II and his ministers along the path of rapid social change and general modernization.

The first and greatest of the reforms was the freeing of the serfs in 1861. Human bondage was abolished forever, and the emancipated peasants received, on average, about half of the land. Yet they had to pay fairly high prices for their land, and because the land was owned collectively, each peasant village was jointly responsible for the payments of all the families in the village. The government hoped that collective responsibility would strengthen the peasant village as a social unit and prevent the development of a class of landless peasants. In practice, collective ownership and responsibility made it very difficult for individual peasants to improve agricultural methods or leave their villages. Thus the effects of the reform were limited, for it did not encourage peasants to change their old habits and attitudes.

Most of the later reforms were also halfway measures. In 1864 the government established a new institution of local government, the *zemstvo*. Members of this local assembly were elected by a three-class system of towns, peasant villages, and noble landowners. A zemstvo executive council dealt with local problems. The establishment of the zemstvos marked a significant step toward popular participation, and Russian liberals hoped it would lead to an elected national parliament. They were soon disappointed. The local zemstvo remained subordinate to the traditional bureaucracy and the local nobility, which were heavily favored by the property-based voting system. More successful was reform of the legal system, which established independent courts and equality before the law. Education was also liberalized somewhat, and censorship was relaxed but not removed.

The Industrialization of Russia

Until the twentieth century, Russia's greatest strides toward modernization were economic rather than political. Industry and transport, both so vital to the military, were transformed in two industrial surges. The first of these came after 1860. The government encouraged and subsidized private railway companies, and construction boomed. In 1860 the empire had only about 1,250 miles of railroads; by 1880 it had about 15,500 miles. The railroads enabled agricultural Russia to export grain and thus earn money for further industrialization. Domestic manufacturing was stimulated, and by the end of the 1870s Russia had a well-developed railway-equipment industry. Industrial suburbs grew up around Moscow and St. Petersburg, and a class of modern factory workers began to take shape.

Industrial development strengthened Russia's military forces and gave rise to territorial expansion to the south and east. Imperial expansion greatly excited many ardent Russian nationalists and superpatriots, who became some of the government's most enthusiastic supporters. Industrial development also contributed

Freeing the Peasants in 1861   A noble landowner reads the emancipation decree to his serfs, dutifully assembled in front of his mansion on Prozorov estate. As this photograph suggests, the gap between the peasants and their former owners would remain enormous after 1861, in part because the government feared that complete freedom would lead to anarchy and upheaval. *(Novosti)*

mightily to the spread of Marxian thought and the transformation of the Russian revolutionary movement after 1890.

In 1881 Alexander II was assassinated by a small group of terrorists. The era of reform came to an abrupt end, for the new tsar, Alexander III (r. 1881–1894), was a determined reactionary. Russia, and indeed all of Europe, experienced hard times economically in the 1880s. Political modernization remained frozen until 1905, but economic modernization sped forward in the massive industrial surge of the 1890s. Nationalism played a decisive role, as it had after the Crimean War. The key leader was Sergei Witte, the tough, competent minister of finance from 1892 to 1903. Early in his career, Witte found in the writings of Friedrich List (see page 738) an analysis and a program for action. List had stressed the peril for Germany of remaining behind

England in the 1830s and 1840s. Witte saw the same threat of industrial backwardness threatening Russia's power and greatness.

Witte moved forward on several fronts. A railroad manager by training, he believed that railroads were "a very powerful weapon . . . for the direction of the economic development of the country."[4] Therefore, the government built state-owned railroads rapidly, doubling the network to thirty-five thousand miles by the end of the century. The gigantic trans-Siberian line connecting Moscow with Vladivostok on the Pacific Ocean five thousand miles away was Witte's pride, and it was largely completed during his term of office. Following List's advice, Witte established high protective tariffs to build Russian industry, and he put the country on the gold standard of the "civilized world" in order to strengthen Russian finances.

Witte's greatest innovation, however, was to use the West to catch up with the West. He aggressively encouraged foreigners to use their abundant capital and advanced technology to build great factories in backward Russia. As he told the tsar, "The inflow of foreign capital is . . . the only way by which our industry will be able to supply our country quickly with abundant and cheap products."[5] This policy was brilliantly successful, especially in southern Russia. There, in eastern Ukraine, foreign capitalists and their engineers built an enormous and very modern steel and coal industry almost from scratch in little more than a decade. By 1900 only the United States, Germany, and Great Britain were producing more steel than Russia. The Russian petroleum industry had even pulled up alongside that of the United States and was producing and refining half the world's oil.

Witte knew how to keep foreigners in line. Once a leading foreign businessman came to him and angrily demanded that the Russian government fulfill a contract it had signed and pay certain debts immediately. Witte asked to see the contract. He read it and then carefully tore it to pieces and threw it in the wastepaper basket without a word of explanation. It was just such a fiercely autocratic and independent Russia that was catching up with the advanced nations of the West.

The Revolution of 1905

Catching up partly meant vigorous territorial expansion, for this was the age of Western imperialism. By 1903 Russia had established a sphere of influence in Chinese Manchuria and was casting greedy eyes on northern Korea. When the diplomatic protests of equally imperialistic Japan were ignored, the Japanese launched a surprise attack in February 1904. To the amazement of self-confident Europeans, Asian Japan scored repeated victories, and Russia was forced in September 1905 to accept a humiliating defeat.

As is often the case, military disaster abroad brought political upheaval at home. The business and professional classes had long wanted to match economic with political modernization. Their minimal goal was to turn the last of Europe's absolutist monarchies into a liberal, representative regime. Factory workers, strategically concentrated in the large cities, had all the grievances of early industrialization and were organized in a radical and still illegal labor movement. Peasants had gained little from the era of reforms and were suffering from poverty and overpopulation. At the same time, nationalist sentiment was emerging among the empire's minorities. The politically and culturally dominant ethnic Russians were only about 45 percent of the population, and by 1900 some intellectuals among the subject nationalities were calling for self-rule and autonomy. Separatist nationalism was strongest among the Poles and Ukrainians. With the army pinned down in Manchuria, all these currents of discontent converged in the revolution of 1905.

The beginning of the revolution pointed up the incompetence of the government. On a Sunday in January 1905, a massive crowd of workers and their families converged peacefully on the Winter Palace in St. Petersburg to present a petition to the tsar. The workers were led by a trade-unionist priest named Father Gapon, who had been secretly supported by the police as a preferable alternative to more radical unions. Carrying icons and respectfully singing "God save the tsar," the workers did not know Nicholas II had fled the city. Sud-

Bloody Sunday This print from a contemporary French newspaper shows the tragic conclusion of the effort to present a petition to the tsar on January 22, 1905. Soldiers on the left fire directly into the crowd of unarmed workers led by Father Gapon, who holds the petition and an upraised cross. A Cossack brigade charges another group of peaceful demonstrators on the bridge. *(Jean-Loup Charmet)*

denly troops opened fire, killing and wounding hundreds. The "Bloody Sunday" massacre turned ordinary workers against the tsar and produced a wave of general indignation.

Outlawed political parties came out into the open, and by the summer of 1905 strikes, peasant uprisings, revolts among minority nationalities, and troop mutinies were sweeping the country. The revolutionary surge culminated in October 1905 in a great paralyzing general strike, which forced the government to capitulate. The tsar issued the October Manifesto, which granted full civil rights and promised a popularly elected duma (parliament) with real legislative power. The manifesto split the opposition. It satisfied most moderate and liberal demands, but the Social Democrats rejected it and led a bloody workers' uprising in Moscow in December 1905. Frightened middle-class leaders helped the government repress the uprising and survive as a constitutional monarchy.

On the eve of the opening of the first Duma in May 1906, the government issued the new constitution, the Fundamental Laws. The tsar retained great powers. The Duma, elected indirectly by universal male suffrage, and a largely appointive upper house could debate and pass laws, but the tsar had an absolute veto. As in Bismarck's Germany, the emperor appointed his ministers, who did not need to command a majority in the Duma.

The disappointed, predominately middle-class liberals, the largest group in the newly elected Duma, saw the Fundamental Laws as a step backward. Efforts to cooperate with the tsar's ministers soon broke down. The tsar then dismissed the Duma, only to find that a more hostile and radical opposition was elected in 1907. After three months of deadlock, the tsar dismissed the second Duma. Thereupon he and his reactionary advisers unilaterally rewrote the electoral law so as to increase greatly the weight of the propertied classes at the expense of workers, peasants, and national minorities.

The new law did have the intended effect. With landowners assured half the seats in the Duma, the government secured a loyal majority in 1907 and again in 1912. Thus armed, the tough, energetic chief minister, Peter Stolypin, pushed through important agrarian reforms that were designed to break down collective village ownership of land and to encourage the more enterprising peasants—a strategy known as the "wager on the strong." On the eve of the First World War, Russia was partially modernized, a conservative constitutional monarchy with a peasant-based but industrializing economy.

 ## THE RESPONSIVE NATIONAL STATE, 1871-1914

For central and western Europe, the unification of Italy and Germany by "blood and iron" marked the end of a dramatic period of nation building. After 1871 the heartland of Europe was organized into strong national states. Only on the borders of Europe—in Ireland and Russia, in Austria-Hungary and the Balkans—did subject peoples still strive for political unity and independence. Despite national differences, European domestic politics after 1871 had a common framework, the firmly established national state. The common themes within that framework were the emergence of mass politics and growing mass loyalty toward the national state.

For good reason, ordinary people—the masses of an industrializing, urbanizing society—felt increasing loyalty to their governments. More people could vote. By 1914 universal male suffrage had become the rule rather than the exception. This development had as much psychological as political significance. Ordinary men were no longer denied the right to vote because they lacked wealth or education. They felt that they counted; they could influence the government to some extent. They were becoming "part of the system."

Women also began to demand the right to vote. The women's suffrage movement achieved its first success in the western United States, and by 1913 women could vote in twelve states. Europe, too, moved slowly in this direction. In 1914 Norway gave the vote to most women. Elsewhere, women such as the English Emmeline Pankhurst were very militant in their demands. They heckled politicians and held public demonstrations. These efforts generally failed before 1914, but they prepared the way for the triumph of the women's suffrage movement immediately after World War I.

As the right to vote spread, politicians and parties in national parliaments represented the people more responsively. The multiparty system prevailing in most countries meant that parliamentary majorities were built on shifting coalitions of different parties, and this gave individual parties leverage to obtain benefits for their supporters. Governments also passed laws to alleviate general problems, thereby acquiring greater legitimacy and appearing more worthy of support.

There was a less positive side to building support for strong nation-states after 1871. Governments, often led by conservatives inspired by the examples of Cavour and Bismarck, found that they could manipulate national feeling to create a sense of unity and to divert attention away from underlying class conflicts. For example, conservative and moderate leaders who despised socialism found that workers who voted socialist would still rally around the flag in a diplomatic crisis or that they would cheer enthusiastically when distant territory of doubtful value was seized in Africa or Asia (see Chapter 26). Therefore, governing elites frequently channeled national sentiment in an antiliberal and militaristic direction after 1871. This policy helped manage domestic conflicts, but only at the expense of increasing the international tensions that erupted in 1914 in cataclysmic war and revolution (see Chapter 27).

The German Empire

Politics in Germany after 1871 reflected many of the general developments. The new German Empire was a federal union of Prussia and twenty-four smaller states. Much of the everyday business of government was conducted by the separate states, but there was a strong national government with a chancellor—until 1890, Bismarck—and a popularly elected lower house, called the *Reichstag*. Although Bismarck refused to be bound by a parliamentary majority, he tried nonetheless to maintain one. This situation gave the political parties opportunities. Until 1878 Bismarck relied mainly on the National Liberals, who had rallied to him after 1866. They supported legislation useful for further economic and legal unification of the country.

Less wisely, they backed Bismarck's attack on the Catholic church, the so-called *Kulturkampf*, or "struggle for civilization." Like Bismarck, the middle-class National Liberals were particularly alarmed by Pius IX's declaration of papal infallibility in 1870. That dogma seemed to ask German Catholics to put loyalty to their church above loyalty to their nation. Only in Protestant Prussia did the Kulturkampf have even limited success. Catholics throughout the country generally voted for the Catholic Center party, which blocked passage of national laws hostile to the church. Finally, in 1878 Bismarck abandoned his attack. Indeed, he and the Catholic Center party entered into an uneasy but mutually advantageous alliance. Their reasons for doing so were largely economic.

After a worldwide financial bust in 1873, European agriculture was in an increasingly difficult position. Wheat prices plummeted as cheap grain poured in from the United States, Canada, and Russia. New lands were opening up in North America and Russia, and the combination of railroads and technical improvements in shipping cut freight rates for grain drastically. European peasants, with their smaller, less efficient farms, could not compete in cereal production, especially in western

and southern Germany. The peasantry there was largely Catholic, and the Catholic Center party was thus converted to higher tariffs to protect the economic interests of its supporters.

The same competitive pressures caused the Protestant Junkers, who owned large estates in eastern Germany, to embrace the cause of higher tariffs. These noble landowners were joined by some of the iron and steel magnates of the Prussian Rhineland and Westphalia who had previously favored free trade. With three such influential groups lobbying energetically, Bismarck was happy to go along with a new protective tariff in 1879. In doing so, he won new supporters in the Reichstag—the Center party of the Catholics and the Conservative party of the Prussian landowners—and he held on to most of the National Liberals.

Bismarck had been looking for a way to increase taxes and raise more money for the government. The solution he chose was higher tariffs. Many other governments acted similarly. The 1880s and 1890s saw a widespread return to protectionism. France, in particular, established very high tariffs to protect agriculture and industry, peasants and manufacturers, from foreign competition. Thus the German government and other governments responded effectively to a major economic problem and won greater loyalty. The general rise of protectionism in the late nineteenth century was also an outstanding example of the dangers of self-centered nationalism: high tariffs led to international name-calling and nasty trade wars.

As for socialism, Bismarck tried to stop its growth in Germany because he genuinely feared its revolutionary language and allegiance to a movement transcending the nation-state. In 1878, after two attempts on the life of William I by radicals (though not socialists), Bismarck used a carefully orchestrated national outcry to ram through the Reichstag a law that strictly controlled socialist meetings and publications and outlawed the Social Democratic party, which was thereby driven underground. However, German socialists displayed a discipline and organization worthy of the Prussian army itself. Bismarck decided to try another tack.

Thus Bismarck's essentially conservative nation-state pioneered with social measures designed to win the support of working-class people. In 1883 he pushed through the Reichstag the first of several modern social security laws to help wage earners. The laws of 1883 and 1884 established national sickness and accident insurance; the law of 1889 established old-age pensions and retirement benefits. Henceforth sick, injured, and retired workers could look forward to some regular benefits from the state. This national social security system, paid for through compulsory contributions by wage earners and employers as well as grants from the state, was the first of its kind anywhere. (The United States would not take similar measures for fifty years.) Bismarck's social security system did not wean workers from voting socialist, but it did give them a small stake in the system and protect them from some of the uncertainties of the complex urban industrial world. This enormously significant development was a product of political competition and government efforts to win popular support.

Increasingly, the great issues in German domestic politics were socialism and the Marxian Social Demo-cratic party. In 1890 the new emperor, the young, idealistic, and unstable William II (r. 1888–1918), opposed Bismarck's attempt to renew the law outlawing the Social Democratic party. Eager to rule in his own right and to earn the support of the workers, William II forced Bismarck to resign. After the "dropping of the pilot," German foreign policy changed profoundly and mostly for the worse, but the government did pass new laws to aid workers and to legalize socialist political activity.

Yet William II was no more successful than Bismarck in getting workers to renounce socialism. Indeed, socialist ideas spread rapidly, and more and more Social

The Need for Social Security   This dramatic painting of busy workers in an iron-rolling mill in Berlin highlights the many dangers of the industrial workplace. Industrial accidents that killed or maimed were a fact of life, as were work-related illnesses and periodic unemployment. Germany's pioneering social security laws were an influential response to these challenges. *(Alte Nationalgalerie, Berlin/AKG London)*

Democrats were elected to the Reichstag in the 1890s. After opposing a colonial war in German Southwest Africa in 1906 that led to important losses in the general elections of 1907, the German Social Democratic party broadened its base and adopted a more patriotic tone. In the elections of 1912, the party scored a great victory, becoming the largest single party in the Reichstag. This victory shocked aristocrats and their wealthy conservative middle-class allies, heightening the fears of an impending socialist upheaval in both groups. Yet the "revolutionary" socialists were actually becoming less and less revolutionary in Germany. In the years before World War I, the strength of socialist opposition to greater military spending and imperialist expansion declined substantially, for example. German socialists identified increasingly with the German state, and they concentrated on gradual social and political reform.

Republican France

Although Napoleon III's reign made some progress in reducing antagonisms between classes, the war with Prussia undid these efforts, and in 1871 France seemed hopelessly divided once again. The patriotic republicans who proclaimed the Third Republic in Paris after the military disaster at Sedan refused to admit defeat. They defended Paris with great heroism for weeks, living off rats and zoo animals until they were starved into submission by German armies in January 1871. When national elections then sent a large majority of conservatives and monarchists to the National Assembly and France's new leaders decided they had no choice but to surrender Alsace and Lorraine to Germany, the traumatized Parisians exploded in patriotic frustration and proclaimed the Paris Commune in March 1871. Vaguely radical, the leaders of the Commune wanted to govern Paris without interference from the conservative French countryside. The National Assembly, led by aging politician Adolphe Thiers, would hear none of it. The Assembly ordered the French army into Paris and brutally crushed the Commune. Twenty thousand people died in the fighting. As in June 1848, it was Paris against the provinces, French against French.

Out of this tragedy, France slowly formed a new national unity, achieving considerable stability before 1914. How is one to account for this? Luck played a part. Until 1875 the monarchists in the "republican" National Assembly had a majority but could not agree who should be king. The compromise Bourbon candidate refused to rule except under the white flag of his ancestors—a completely unacceptable condition. In the meantime, Thiers's destruction of the radical Commune and his other firm measures showed the fearful provinces and the middle class that the Third Republic might be moderate and socially conservative, escaping the excesses that many still associated with the republican government of Robespierre and the Terror (see pages 704–706). France therefore retained the republic, though reluctantly. As President Thiers cautiously said, this was "the government which divides us least."

Another stabilizing factor was the skill and determination of the moderate republican leaders in the early years. The most famous of these was Léon Gambetta, the son of an Italian grocer, a warm, easygoing, unsuccessful lawyer who had turned professional politician. A master of emerging mass politics, Gambetta combined eloquence with the personal touch as he preached a republic of truly equal opportunity. Gambetta was also instrumental in establishing absolute parliamentary supremacy between 1877 and 1879, when the deputies challenged Marshall MacMahon and forced the somewhat autocratic president of the republic to resign. By 1879 the great majority of members of both the upper and the lower houses of the National Assembly were republicans. Although these republicans were split among many parliamentary groups and later among several parties—a situation that led to constant coalition politics and the rapid turnover of ministers—the Third Republic had firm foundations after almost a decade.

The moderate republicans sought to preserve their creation by winning the hearts and minds of the next generation. Trade unions were fully legalized, and France acquired a colonial empire. More important, under the leadership of Jules Ferry, the moderate republicans of small towns and villages passed a series of laws between 1879 and 1886 establishing free compulsory elementary education for both girls and boys. At the same time, they greatly expanded the state system of public tax-supported schools. Thus France shared fully in the general expansion of public education, which served as a critical nation-building tool throughout the Western world in the late nineteenth century.

In France most elementary and much secondary education had traditionally been in the parochial schools of the Catholic church, which had long been hostile to republics and to much of secular life. Free compulsory elementary education in France became secular republican education. The pledge of allegiance and the national anthem replaced the catechism and the "Ave Maria." Militant young male and female teachers carried the ideology of patriotic republicanism into every corner of France. In their classes, these women and men

Captain Alfred Dreyfus Leaving an 1899 reconsideration of his original court martial, Dreyfus receives an insulting "guard of dishonor" from soldiers whose backs are turned. Top army leaders were determined to brand Dreyfus as a traitor. *(Bibliothèque Nationale, Paris)*

sought to win the loyalty of the young citizens to the republic so that France would never again vote en masse for dictators like the two Napoleons.

Unlike most Western countries (including the United States), which insisted on the total "purity" of their female elementary teachers and would not hire married women, the Third Republic actively encouraged young teachers to marry and guaranteed that both partners would teach in the same location. There were three main reasons for this unusual policy. First, married female (and male) teachers with their own children provided a vivid contrast to celibate nuns (and priests), who had for generations stood for most primary education in the popular mind. Second, the republican leaders believed that married women (and men) would better cope with the potential loneliness and social isolation of unfamiliar towns and villages, especially where the local Catholic school was strong. Third, French politicians and opinion leaders worried continually about France's very low birthrate after 1870, and they believed that women combining teaching careers and motherhood would provide the country with a good example. Hiring married schoolteachers was part of an

effort to create a whole new culture of universal, secular, and republican education. This illustrates a larger truth—that truly lasting political change must usually be supported by changes in the underlying culture.

Although the educational reforms of the 1880s disturbed French Catholics, many of them rallied to the republic in the 1890s. The limited acceptance of the modern world by the more liberal Pope Leo XIII (1878–1903) eased tensions between church and state. Unfortunately, the Dreyfus affair changed all that.

Alfred Dreyfus, a Jewish captain in the French army, was falsely accused and convicted of treason. His family never doubted his innocence and fought to reopen the case, enlisting the support of prominent republicans and intellectuals such as novelist Emile Zola. In 1898 and 1899, the case split France apart. On one side was the army, which had manufactured evidence against Dreyfus, joined by anti-Semites and most of the Catholic establishment. On the other side stood the civil libertarians and most of the more radical republicans.

This battle, which eventually led to Dreyfus's being declared innocent, revived republican feeling against the church. Between 1901 and 1905, the government severed all ties between the state and the Catholic church after centuries of close relations. The salaries of priests and bishops were no longer paid by the government, and all churches were given to local committees of lay Catholics. Catholic schools were put completely on their own financially, and in a short time they lost a third of their students. The state school system's power of indoctrination was greatly strengthened. In France only the growing socialist movement, with its very different and thoroughly secular ideology, stood in opposition to patriotic, republican nationalism.

Great Britain and Ireland

Britain in the late nineteenth century has often been seen as a shining example of peaceful and successful political evolution. Germany was stuck with a manipulated parliament that gave an irresponsible emperor too much power; France had a quarrelsome parliament that gave its presidents too little power. Great Britain, in contrast, seemed to enjoy an effective two-party parliament that skillfully guided the country from classical liberalism to full-fledged democracy with hardly a misstep.

This view of Great Britain is not so much wrong as it is incomplete. After the right to vote was granted to males of the solid middle class in 1832, opinion leaders and politicians wrestled with the uncertainties of a further expansion of the franchise. In his famous essay *On Liberty,* published in 1859, philosopher John Stuart Mill (1806–1873), the leading heir to the Benthamite tradition (see page 792), probed the problem of how to protect the rights of individuals and minorities in the emerging age of mass electoral participation. Mill pleaded eloquently for the practical and moral value inherent in safeguarding individual differences and unpopular opinions. In 1867 Benjamin Disraeli and the Conservatives extended the vote to all middle-class males and the best-paid workers. The son of a Jewish stockbroker and himself a novelist and urban dandy, the ever-fascinating Disraeli (1804–1881) was willing to risk this "leap in the dark" in order to gain new supporters. The Conservative party, he believed, needed to broaden its traditional base of aristocratic and landed support if it was to survive. After 1867 English political parties and electoral campaigns became more modern, and the "lower orders" appeared to vote as responsibly as their "betters." Hence the Third Reform Bill of 1884 gave the vote to almost every adult male.

While the House of Commons was drifting toward democracy, the House of Lords was content to slumber nobly. Between 1901 and 1910, however, that bastion of aristocratic conservatism tried to reassert itself. Acting as supreme court of the land, it ruled against labor unions in two important decisions. And after the Liberal party came to power in 1906, the Lords vetoed several measures passed by the Commons, including the so-called People's Budget. The Lords finally capitulated, as they had done in 1832, when the king threatened to create enough new peers to pass the bill.

Aristocratic conservatism yielded to popular democracy once and for all. The result was that extensive social welfare measures, slow to come to Great Britain, were passed in a spectacular rush between 1906 and 1914. During those years, the Liberal party, inspired by the fiery Welshman David Lloyd George (1863–1945), substantially raised taxes on the rich as part of the People's Budget. This income helped the government pay for national health insurance, unemployment benefits, old-age pensions, and a host of other social measures. The state was integrating the urban masses socially as well as politically.

This record of accomplishment was only part of the story, however. On the eve of World War I, the ever-emotional, ever-unanswered question of Ireland brought Great Britain to the brink of civil war. In the 1840s, Ireland had been decimated by famine, which fueled an Irish revolutionary movement. Thereafter, the English slowly granted concessions, such as the abolition of the privileges of the Anglican church and rights for Irish peasants. Liberal prime minister William Gladstone (1809–1898), who had proclaimed twenty years earlier that "my mission is to pacify Ireland," introduced bills to give Ireland self-government in 1886 and in 1893. They failed to pass. After two decades of relative quiet, Irish nationalists in the British Parliament saw their chance. They supported the Liberals in their battle for the People's Budget and received a home-rule bill for Ireland in return.

Thus Ireland, the emerald isle, was on the brink of achieving self-government. Yet Ireland was (and is) composed of two peoples. As much as the Irish Catholic majority in the southern counties wanted home rule, precisely that much did the Irish Protestants of the northern counties of Ulster come to oppose it. Motivated by the accumulated fears and hostilities of generations, the Protestants of Ulster refused to submerge themselves in a Catholic Ireland, just as Irish Catholics had refused to submit to a Protestant Britain.

The Ulsterites vowed to resist home rule in northern Ireland. By December 1913 they had raised 100,000 armed volunteers, and they were supported by much of English public opinion. Thus in 1914 the Liberals in the House of Lords introduced a compromise home-rule bill that did not apply to the northern counties. This bill, which openly betrayed promises made to Irish nationalists, was rejected, and in September the original home-rule bill was passed but simultaneously suspended for the duration of the hostilities—the momentous Irish question had been overtaken by an earth-shattering world war in August 1914.

Irish developments illustrated once again the power of national feeling and national movements in the nineteenth century. Moreover, they were proof that governments could not elicit greater loyalty unless they could capture and control that elemental current of national feeling. Though Great Britain had much going for it—power, Parliament, prosperity—none of these availed in the face of the conflicting nationalisms espoused by Catholics and Protestants in northern Ireland. Similarly, progressive Sweden was powerless to stop the growth of the Norwegian national movement, which culminated in Norway's breaking away from Sweden and becoming a fully independent nation in 1905. In this light, one can also see how hopeless was the case of the Ottoman Empire in Europe in the later nineteenth century. It was only a matter of time before the Serbs, Bulgarians, and Romanians would break away, and they did.

"No Home Rule"   Posters like this one helped to foment pro-British, anti-Catholic sentiment in the northern Irish counties of Ulster before the First World War. The rifle raised defiantly and the accompanying rhyme are a thinly veiled threat of armed rebellion and civil war. *(Courtesy, Ulster Museum, Belfast)*

The Austro-Hungarian Empire

The dilemma of conflicting nationalisms in Ireland also helps one appreciate how desperate the situation in the Austro-Hungarian Empire had become by the early twentieth century. In 1849 Magyar nationalism had driven Hungarian patriots to declare an independent Hungarian republic, which was savagely crushed by Russian and Austrian armies (see pages 781–782). Throughout the 1850s, Hungary was ruled as a conquered territory, and Emperor Francis Joseph and his bureaucracy tried hard to centralize the state and Germanize the language and culture of the different nationalities.

Then in the wake of defeat by Prussia in 1866, a weakened Austria was forced to strike a compromise and establish the so-called dual monarchy. The empire was divided in two, and the nationalistic Magyars gained virtual independence for Hungary. Henceforth each half of the empire agreed to deal with its own "barbarians"—its own minorities—as it saw fit. The two states were joined only by a shared monarch and common ministries for finance, defense, and foreign affairs. The popular mayor of Vienna from 1897 to 1910, Dr. Karl Lueger, combined anti-Semitic rhetoric with calls for "Christian socialism" and municipal ownership of basic services. Lueger appealed especially to the

The Language Ordinances of 1897,   which were intended to satisfy the Czechs by establishing equality between German and the local language in non-German districts of Austria, produced a powerful backlash among Germans. This wood engraving shows troops dispersing German protesters of the new law before the parliament building. *(Österreichische Nationalbibliothek)*

German lower middle class—and to an unsuccessful young artist named Adolf Hitler.

In Hungary the Magyar nobility in 1867 restored the constitution of 1848 and used it to dominate both the Magyar peasantry and the minority populations until 1914. Only the wealthiest one-fourth of adult males had the right to vote, making the parliament the creature of the Magyar elite. Laws promoting the use of the Magyar (Hungarian) language in schools and government were rammed through and bitterly resented, especially by the Croatians and Romanians. While Magyar extremists campaigned loudly for total separation from Austria, the radical leaders of the subject nationalities dreamed in turn of independence from Hungary. Unlike most major countries, which harnessed nationalism to strengthen the state after 1871, the Austro-

Hungarian Empire was progressively weakened and destroyed by it.

✥ MARXISM AND THE SOCIALIST MOVEMENT

Nationalism served, for better or worse, as a new unifying principle. But what about socialism? Did the rapid growth of socialist parties, which were generally Marxian parties dedicated to an international proletarian revolution, mean that national states had failed to gain the support of workers? Certainly, many prosperous and conservative citizens were greatly troubled by the socialist movement. And numerous historians have portrayed the years before 1914 as a time of increasing conflict between revolutionary socialism, on the one hand, and a nationalist alliance of the conservative aristocracy and the prosperous middle class, on the other. This question requires close examination.

The Socialist International

Socialism appealed to large numbers of workingmen and workingwomen in the late nineteenth century, and the growth of socialist parties after 1871 was phenomenal. (See the feature "Listening to the Past: The Making of a Socialist" on pages 854–855.) Neither Bismarck's antisocialist laws nor his extensive social security system checked the growth of the German Social Democratic party, which espoused the Marxian ideology. By 1912 it had millions of followers and was the largest party in the Reichstag. Socialist parties also grew in other countries, though nowhere else with such success. In 1883 Russian exiles in Switzerland founded the Russian Social Democratic party, which grew rapidly after 1890 despite internal disputes. In France various socialist parties re-emerged in the 1880s after the carnage of the Paris Commune. They were finally unified in 1905 in an increasingly powerful Marxian party called the French Section of the Workers International. Belgium and Austria-Hungary also had strong socialist parties.

As the name of the French party suggests, Marxian socialist parties were eventually linked together in an international organization. As early as 1848, Marx had laid out his intellectual system in *The Communist Manifesto* (see pages 765–766). He had declared that "the working men have no country," and he had urged proletarians of all nations to unite against their governments. Joining the flood of radicals and republicans who fled continental Europe for England and America after the unsuccessful revolutions of 1848, Marx settled in London. Poor and depressed, he lived on his meager earnings as a journalist and on the gifts of his friend Friedrich Engels. Marx never stopped thinking of revolution. Digging deeply into economics and history, he concluded that revolution follows economic crisis and tried to prove this position in *Critique of Political Economy* (1859) and in his greatest theoretical work, *Capital* (1867).

The bookish Marx also excelled as a practical organizer. In 1864 he played an important role in founding the First International of socialists—the International Working Men's Association. In the following years, he battled successfully to control the organization and used its annual meetings as a means of spreading his realistic, "scientific" doctrines of inevitable socialist revolution. Then Marx enthusiastically embraced the passionate, vaguely radical patriotism of the Paris Commune and its terrible conflict with the French National Assembly as a giant step toward socialist revolution. This impetuous action frightened many of his early supporters, especially the more moderate British labor leaders. The First International collapsed.

Yet international proletarian solidarity remained an important objective for Marxists. In 1889, as the individual parties in different countries grew stronger, socialist leaders came together to form the Second International, which lasted until 1914. The International was only a federation of national socialist parties, but it had a great psychological impact. Every three years, delegates from the different parties met to interpret Marxian doctrines and plan coordinated action. May 1 (May Day) was declared an annual international one-day strike, a day of marches and demonstrations. A permanent executive for the International was established. Many feared and many others rejoiced in the growing power of socialism and the Second International.

Unions and Revisionism

Was socialism really radical and revolutionary in these years? On the whole, it was not. Indeed, as socialist parties grew and attracted large numbers of members, they looked more and more toward gradual change and steady improvement for the working class and less and less toward revolution. The mainstream of European socialism became militantly moderate; that is, socialists increasingly combined radical rhetoric with sober action.

Workers themselves were progressively less inclined to follow radical programs. There were several reasons for this. As workers gained the right to vote and to participate politically in the nation-state, they focused their attention more on elections than on revolutions. And as workers won real, tangible benefits, this furthered the process. Workers were also not immune to patriotic education and indoctrination during military service, and many responded positively to drum-beating parades and aggressive foreign policy as they loyally voted for socialists. Nor were workers a unified social group.

Perhaps most important of all, workers' standard of living rose gradually but substantially after 1850 as the promise of the Industrial Revolution was at least

"Greetings from the May Day Festival"　Workers participated enthusiastically in the
annual one-day strike on May 1 to honor internationalist socialist solidarity, as this postcard
from a happy woman visitor to her cousin suggests. Speeches, picnics, and parades were the
order of the day, and workers celebrated their respectability and independent culture. Picture
postcards developed with railroads and mass travel. *(AKG London)*

partially realized. In Great Britain, for example, workers
could buy almost twice as much with their wages in
1906 as in 1850, and most of the increase came after
1870. Workers experienced similar gradual increases in
most continental countries after 1850, though much
less strikingly in late-developing Russia. Improvement
in the standard of living was much more than merely a
matter of higher wages. The quality of life improved
dramatically in urban areas. For all these reasons, workers tended more and more to become militantly moderate: they demanded gains, but they were less likely to
take to the barricades in pursuit of them.

The growth of labor unions reinforced this trend toward moderation. In the early stages of industrialization, modern unions were generally prohibited by law.
A famous law of the French Revolution had declared all
guilds and unions illegal in the name of "liberty" in
1791. In Great Britain, attempts by workers to unite

were considered criminal conspiracies after 1799. Other
countries had similar laws, and these obviously hampered union development. In France, for example,
about two hundred workers were imprisoned each year
between 1825 and 1847 for taking part in illegal combinations. Unions were considered subversive bodies,
only to be hounded and crushed.

From this sad position workers struggled to escape.
Great Britain led the way in 1824 and 1825 when
unions won the right to exist but (generally) not the
right to strike. After the collapse of Robert Owen's attempt to form one big union in the 1830s (see page
749), new and more practical kinds of unions appeared.
Limited primarily to highly skilled workers such as ma-
chinists and carpenters, the "new model unions"
avoided both radical politics and costly strikes. Instead,
their sober, respectable leaders concentrated on winning better wages and hours for their members through

collective bargaining and compromise. This approach helped pave the way to full acceptance in Britain in the 1870s, when unions won the right to strike without being held legally liable for the financial damage inflicted on employers. After 1890 unions for unskilled workers developed, and between 1901 and 1906 the legal position of British unions was further strengthened.

Germany was the most industrialized, socialized, and unionized continental country by 1914. German unions were not granted important rights until 1869, and until the antisocialist law was repealed in 1890, they were frequently harassed by the government as socialist fronts. Nor were socialist leaders particularly interested in union activity, believing as they did in the iron law of low wages and the need for political revolution. The result was that as late as 1895, there were only about 270,000 union members in a male industrial workforce of nearly 8 million. Then with German industrialization still storming ahead and almost all legal harassment eliminated, union membership skyrocketed, reaching roughly 3 million in 1912.

This great expansion both reflected and influenced the changing character of German unions. Increasingly, unions in Germany focused on bread-and-butter issues—wages, hours, working conditions—rather than on the dissemination of pure socialist doctrine. Genuine collective bargaining, long opposed by socialist intellectuals as a "sellout," was officially recognized as desirable by the German Trade Union Congress in 1899. When employers proved unwilling to bargain, a series of strikes forced them to change their minds.

Between 1906 and 1913, successful collective bargaining gained a prominent place in German industrial relations. In 1913 alone, over ten thousand collective bargaining agreements affecting 1.25 million workers were signed. Gradual improvement, not revolution, was becoming the primary goal of the German trade-union movement.

The German trade unions and their leaders were in fact, if not in name, thoroughgoing revisionists. *Revisionism*—that most awful of sins in the eyes of militant Marxists in the twentieth century—was an effort by various socialists to update Marxian doctrines to reflect the realities of the time. Thus the socialist Edward Bernstein (1850–1932) argued in 1899 in his *Evolutionary Socialism* that Marx's predictions of ever-greater poverty for workers and ever-greater concentration of wealth in ever-fewer hands had been proved false. Therefore, Bernstein suggested, socialists should reform their doctrines and tactics. They should combine with other progressive forces to win gradual evolutionary gains for workers through legislation, unions, and further economic development. These views were denounced as heresy by the German Social Democratic party and later by the entire Second International. Yet the revisionist, gradualist approach continued to gain the tacit acceptance of many German socialists, particularly in the trade unions.

Moderation found followers elsewhere. In France the great socialist leader Jean Jaurès (1859–1914) formally repudiated revisionist doctrines in order to establish a unified socialist party, but he remained at heart a gradualist and optimistic secular humanist. Questions of revolution split Russian Marxists.

Socialist parties before 1914 had clear-cut national characteristics. Russians and socialists in the Austro-Hungarian Empire tended to be the most radical. The German party talked revolution and practiced reformism, greatly influenced by its enormous trade-union movement. The French party talked revolution and tried to practice it, unrestrained by a trade-union movement that was both very weak and very radical. In England the socialist but non-Marxian Labour party, reflecting the well-established union movement, was formally committed to gradual reform. In Spain and Italy, Marxian socialism was very weak. There anarchism, seeking to smash the state rather than the bourgeoisie, dominated radical thought and action.

In short, socialist policies and doctrines varied from country to country. Socialism itself was to a large extent "nationalized" behind the imposing façade of international unity. This helps explain why when war came in 1914, almost all socialist leaders supported their governments.

SUMMARY

From the mid-nineteenth century on, Western society became nationalistic as well as urban and industrial. Nation-states and strong-minded national leaders gradually enlisted widespread support and gave men and women a greater sense of belonging. Even socialism became increasingly national in orientation, gathering strength as a champion of working-class interests in domestic politics. Yet even though nationalism served to unite peoples, it also drove them apart. Though most obvious in the United States before the Civil War and in Austria-Hungary and Ireland, this was in a real sense true for all of Western civilization. The universal national faith, which reduced social tensions within states, promoted a bitter, brutal competition between states and thus threatened the progress and unity it had helped to build.

NOTES

1. Quoted in G. Wright, *France in Modern Times,* 4th ed. (New York: W. W. Norton, 1987), p. 138.
2. Quoted in H. Kohn, *The Mind of Germany: The Education of a Nation* (New York: Charles Scribner's Sons/Macmillan, 1960), p. 159.
3. H. Schulze, *States, Nations and Nationalism: From the Middle Ages to the Present* (Oxford: Blackwell, 1994), pp. 222–223, 246–247.
4. Quoted in T. von Laue, *Sergei Witte and the Industrialization of Russia* (New York: Columbia University Press, 1963), p. 78.
5. Quoted in J. McKay, *Pioneers for Profit: Foreign Entrepreneurship and Russian Industrialization, 1885–1913* (Chicago: University of Chicago Press, 1970), p. 11.

SUGGESTED READING

In addition to the general works mentioned in the Suggested Reading for Chapter 23, R. Gildea, *Barricades and Borders: Europe, 1800–1914,* 2d ed. (1996), and T. Blanning, *The Cambridge Illustrated History of Europe* (1996), provide useful and up-to-date surveys of the entire nineteenth century. G. Craig, *Germany, 1866–1945* (1980), and B. Moore, *Social Origins of Dictatorship and Democracy* (1966), are outstanding.

R. Tombs, *France, 1814–1914* (1996), is an impressive recent survey with an up-to-date bibliography, and R. Anderson, *France, 1870–1914* (1977), provides a clear introduction. D. Harvey, *Napoleon III and His Comic Empire* (1988), brings the world of Louis Napoleon vibrantly alive, whereas K. Marx, *The Eighteenth Brumaire of Louis Napoleon,* is a famous denunciation of the coup d'état. E. Weber, *France, Fin de Siècle* (1986), captures the spirit of Paris at the end of the century. G. Gullickson, *Unruly Women of Paris: Images of the Commune* (1996), is an exciting portrait of contested images of radical women in the Paris Commune, and E. Accampo, R. Fuchs, and M. Stewart, *Gender and the Politics of Social Reform in France, 1870–1914* (1995), shows how views of women influenced social legislation. E. Weber, *Peasants into Frenchmen* (1976), stresses the role of education and modern communications in the transformation of rural France after 1870. E. Cahm, *The Dreyfus Affair in French Society and Politics* (1996), and G. Chapman, *The Dreyfus Case: A Re-*

assessment (1955), are careful examinations of the famous case. In *Jean Barois,* Nobel Prize winner Roger Du Gard accurately re-creates in novel form the Dreyfus affair, and Emile Zola's novel *The Debacle* treats the Franco-Prussian War realistically.

The resurgence of European nationalism since the fall of communism has led to important new studies; particularly recommended are H. Schulze, *States, Nations and Nationalism: From the Middle Ages to the Present* (1996), and R. Brubaker, *Citizenship and Nationhood in France and Germany* (1992). D. M. Smith has written widely on Italy, and his *Garibaldi* (1956) and *Mazzini* (1994) are engaging biographies. In addition to the study on Germany by Kohn cited in the Notes, see O. Pflanze, *Bismarck and the Development in Germany: The Period of Unification, 1815–1871* (1963); D. Williamson, *Bismarck and Germany, 1862–1890* (1994); and E. Eyck, *Bismarck and the German Empire* (1964). H. Wehler, *The German Empire, 1871–1918* (1985), stresses the strength of the landed nobility and the weakness of the middle class in an influential synthesis, which is challenged by D. Blackbourn and G. Eley, *The Peculiarities of German History: Bourgeois Society and Politics in Nineteenth-Century Germany* (1984). M. Kitchen, *The Cambridge Illustrated History of Germany* (1996), features handsome pictures and a readable text. F. Stern, *Gold and Iron* (1977), is a fascinating examination of relations between Bismarck and his financial adviser, the Jewish banker Bleichröder. L. Cecil, *Wilhelm II: Prince and Emperor, 1859–1900* (1989), probes the character and politics of Germany's ruler. K. McAleer, *Dueling: The Cult of Honor in Fin-de-Siècle Germany* (1994), K. D. Barkin, *The Controversy over German Industrialization, 1890–1902* (1970), and E. Spencer, *Management and Labor in Imperial Germany: Ruhr Industrialists as Employers* (1984), are valuable in-depth investigations. H. Glasser, ed., *The German Mind in the Nineteenth Century* (1981), is an outstanding anthology, as are R. E. Joeres and M. Maynes, eds., *German Women in the Eighteenth and Nineteenth Centuries* (1986); and P. Mendes-Flohr, ed., *The Jew in the Modern World: A Documentary History* (1980). C. Schorske, *Fin de Siècle Vienna: Politics and Culture* (1980), and P. Gay, *Freud, Jews, and Other Germans* (1978), are brilliant on aspects of modern culture. A. Sked, *The Decline and Fall of the Habsburg Empire, 1815–1918* (1989), and R. Kann, *The Multinational Empire,* 2 vols. (1950, 1964), probe the intricacies of the nationality problem in Austria-Hungary. Southern nationalism in the United States has been interpreted from different perspectives by P. Escott, *After Secession: Jefferson Davis and the Failure of Confederate Nationalism* (1974); and D. Faust, *The Creation of Confederate Nationalism* (1988). E. Foner, *A Short History of Reconstruction* (1989), is recommended.

In addition to the studies on Russian industrial development by von Laue and McKay cited in the Notes,

P. Gatrell, *The Tsarist Economy, 1850–1917* (1986), and A. Rieber, *Merchants and Entrepreneurs in Imperial Russia* (1982), are recommended. Among fine studies on Russian development, see especially H. Rogger, *Russia in the Age of Modernization and Revolution, 1881–1917* (1983), which has an excellent bibliography; T. Emmons, *The Russian Landed Gentry and the Peasant Emancipation of 1861* (1968); and H. Troyat, *Daily Life in Russia Under the Last Tsar* (1962). T. Friedgut, *Iuzovka and Revolution: Life and Work in Russia's Donbass, 1869–1924* (1989), R. Zelnik, *Labor and Society in Tsarist Russia, 1855–1870* (1971), and R. Johnson, *Peasant and Proletarian: The Working Class of Moscow at the End of the Nineteenth Century* (1979), skillfully treat different aspects of working-class life and politics. W. E. Mosse, *Alexander II and the Modernization of Russia* (1958), discusses midcentury reforms, whereas A. Geifman, *Thou Shalt Kill: Revolutionary Terrorism in Russia* (1993), probes the politics of violence in a pioneering study. J. Le Donne, *The Russian Empire and the World, 1700–1917: The Geopolitics of Expansion and Containment* (1996), reconsiders Russian foreign affairs.

G. Dangerfield, *The Strange Death of Liberal England* (1961), brilliantly examines social tensions in Ireland as well as English women's struggle for the vote before 1914. P. Gurney, *Co-operative Culture and the Politics of Consumption in England, 1870–1930* (1996), breaks new ground and is recommended. D. Boyce, *Nationalism in Ireland*, 2d ed. (1991), provides an excellent account of the Irish struggle for nationhood. The theme of aristocratic strength and survival is expanded in A. Mayer's provocative *Persistence of the Old Regime: Europe to the Great War* (1981). J. Seigel, *Marx's Fate: The Shape of a Life* (1978), is an outstanding biography. C. Schorske, *German Social Democracy, 1905–1917* (1955), is a modern classic. V. Lidtke, *The Alternative Culture: Socialist Labor in Imperial Germany* (1985), and J. Quataert, *Reluctant Feminists in German Social Democracy, 1885–1917* (1979), are also recommended for the study of the German socialists. H. Goldberg, *The Life of Jean Jaurès* (1962), is a sympathetic account of the great French socialist leader. Two excellent collections by specialists are L. Berlanstein, ed., *Rethinking Labor History* (1993); and D. Geary, ed., *Labour and Socialist Movements in Europe Before 1914* (1989), which examines several different countries and has up-to-date references.

The Making of a Socialist

Nationalism and socialism appeared locked in bitter competition in Europe before 1914, but they actually complemented each other in many ways. Both faiths were secular as opposed to religious, and both fostered political awareness. A working person who became interested in politics and developed nationalist beliefs might well convert to socialism at a later date.

This was the case for Adelheid Popp (1869–1939), a self-taught workingwoman who became an influential socialist leader. Born into a desperately poor working-class family in Vienna and remembering only a "hard and gloomy childhood," she was forced by her parents to quit school at age ten to begin full-time work. She struggled with low-paying piecework for years before she landed a solid factory job, as she recounts in the following selection from her widely read autobiography.

Always an avid reader, Popp became the editor of a major socialist newspaper for German workingwomen. She then told her life story so that all workingwomen might share her truth: "Socialism could change and strengthen others, as it did me."

[Finally] I found work again; I took everything that was offered me in order to show my willingness to work, and I passed through much. But at last things became better. [At age fifteen] I was recommended to a great factory which stood in the best repute. Three hundred girls and about fifty men were employed. I was put in a big room where sixty women and girls were at work. Against the windows stood twelve tables, and at each sat four girls. We had to sort the goods which had been manufactured, others had to count them, and a third set had to brand on them the mark of the firm. We worked from 7 A.M. to 7 P.M. We had an hour's rest at noon, half-an-hour in the afternoon. . . . I had never yet been paid so much. . . .

I seemed to myself to be almost rich. . . . [Yet] from the women of this factory one can judge how sad and full of deprivation is the lot of a factory worker. In none of the neighbouring factories were the wages so high; we were envied everywhere. Parents considered themselves fortunate if they could get their daughters of fourteen in there on leaving school. . . . And even here, in this paradise, all were badly nourished. Those who stayed at the factory for the dinner hour would buy themselves for a few pennies a sausage or the leavings of a cheese shop. . . . In spite of all the diligence and economy, every one was poor, and trembled at the thought of losing her work. All humbled themselves, and suffered the worst injustice from the foremen, not to risk losing this good work, not to be without food. . . .

I did not only read novels and tales; I had begun . . . to read the classics and other good books. I also began to take an interest in public events. . . . I was not democratically inclined. I was full of enthusiasm then for emperors, and kings and highly placed personages played no small part in my fancies. . . . I bought myself a strict Catholic paper, that criticised very adversely the workers' movement, which was attracting notice. Its aim was to educate in a patriotic and religious direction. . . . I took the warmest interest in the events that occurred in the royal families, and I took the death of the Crown Prince of Austria so much to heart that I wept a whole day. . . . Political events [also] held me in suspense. The possibility of a war with Russia roused my patriotic enthusiasm. I saw my brother already returning from the battlefield covered with glory. . . .

When a particularly strong anti-Semitic feeling was noticeable in political life, I sympathised with it for a time. A broad sheet, "How Israel Attained Power and Sovereignty over all the Nations of the Earth," fascinated me. . . .

About this time an Anarchist group was active. Some mysterious murders which had taken place were ascribed to the Anarchists, and the police made use of them to oppress the rising workmen's movement. . . . I followed the trial of the Anarchists with passionate sympathy. I read all the speeches, and because, as always happens, Social Democrats, whom the authorities really wanted to attack, were among the accused, I learned their views. I became full of enthusiasm. Every single Social Democrat . . . seemed to me a hero. . . .

There was unrest among the workers . . . and demonstrations of protest followed. When these were repeated the military entered the "threatened" streets. . . . In the evenings I rushed in the greatest excitement from the factory to the scene of the disturbance. The military did not frighten me; I only left the place when it was "cleared."

Later on my mother and I lived with one of my brothers who had married. Friends came to him, among them some intelligent workmen. One of these workmen was particularly intelligent, and . . . could talk on many subjects. He was the first Social Democrat I knew. He brought me many books, and explained to me the difference between Anarchism and Socialism. I heard from him, also for the first time, what a republic was, and in spite of my former enthusiasm for royal dynasties, I also declared myself in favour of a republican form of government. I saw everything so near and so clearly, that I actually counted the weeks which must still elapse before the revolution of state and society would take place.

From this workman I received the first Social Democratic party organ. . . . I first learned from it to understand and judge of my own lot. I learned to see that all I had suffered was the result not of a divine ordinance, but of an unjust organization of society. . . .

In the factory I became another woman. . . . I told my [female] comrades all that I had read of the workers' movement. Formerly I had often told stories when they had begged me for them. But instead of narrating . . . the fate of some queen, I now held forth on oppression and exploitation. I told of accumulated wealth in the hands of a few, and introduced as a contrast the shoemakers who had no shoes and the tailors who had no clothes. On breaks I read aloud the articles in the Social Democratic paper and explained what Socialism was as far as I understood it. . . . [While I was read-

❖ 1890 engraving of a meeting of workers in Berlin. *(Bildarchiv Preussischer Kulturbesitz)*

ing] it often happened that one of the clerks passing by shook his head and said to another clerk: "The girl speaks like a man."

Questions for Analysis

1. How did Popp describe and interpret work in the factory?

2. To what extent did her socialist interpretation of factory life fit the facts she described?

3. What were Popp's political interests before she became a socialist?

4. How and why did she become a Social Democrat?

5. Was this account likely to lead other working-women to socialism? Why or why not?

Source: Slightly adapted from A. Popp, *The Autobiography of a Working Woman,* trans. E. C. Harvey (Chicago: F. G. Browne, 1913), pp. 29, 34–35, 39, 66–69, 71, 74, 82–90.

26

The West and the World

The Emigrant Ship by the British painter Charles J. Staniland, 1898. *(Bradford Art Galleries and Museums/Bridgeman Art Library, London/New York)*

While industrialization and nationalism were transforming urban life and Western society, Western society itself was reshaping the world. At the peak of its power and pride, the West entered the third and most dynamic phase of the aggressive expansion that had begun with the Crusades and continued with the great discoveries and the rise of seaborne colonial empires. An ever-growing stream of products, people, and ideas flowed out of Europe in the nineteenth century. Hardly any corner of the globe was left untouched. The most spectacular manifestations of Western expansion came in the late nineteenth century when the leading European nations established or enlarged their far-flung political empires. The political annexation of territory in the 1880s—the "new imperialism," as it is often called by historians—was the capstone of a profound underlying economic and technological process.

- How and why did this many-sided, epoch-making expansion occur in the nineteenth century?
- What were some of its consequences for the West?
- How did Western expansion affect the rest of the world?

These are the questions this chapter will examine.

 ## INDUSTRIALIZATION AND THE WORLD ECONOMY

The Industrial Revolution created, first in Great Britain and then in continental Europe and North America, a growing and tremendously dynamic economic system. In the course of the nineteenth century, that system was extended across the face of the earth. Some of this extension into non-Western areas was peaceful and beneficial for all concerned, for the West had many products and techniques the rest of the world desired. If peaceful methods failed, however, Europeans did not stand on ceremony. They used their superior military power to force non-Western nations to open their doors to Western economic interests. In general, Westerners fashioned the global economic system so that the largest share of the ever-increasing gains from trade, technology, and migration flowed to the West and its propertied classes.

The Rise of Global Inequality

The Industrial Revolution in Europe marked a momentous turning point in human history. Indeed, it is only by placing Europe's economic breakthrough in a global perspective that one can truly appreciate its revolutionary implications and consequences.

From such a global perspective, the ultimate significance of the Industrial Revolution was that it allowed those regions of the world that industrialized in the nineteenth century to increase their wealth and power enormously in comparison to those that did not. As a result, a gap between the industrializing regions (mainly Europe and North America) and the nonindustrializing ones (mainly Africa, Asia, and Latin America) opened up and grew steadily throughout the nineteenth century. Moreover, this pattern of uneven global development became institutionalized, or built into the structure of the world economy. Thus we evolved a "lopsided world," a world of rich lands and poor.

Historians have long been aware of this gap, but it is only recently that historical economists have begun to chart its long-term evolution with some precision. Their findings are extremely revealing, although one must understand that they contain a margin of error and other limitations as well. The findings of one such study are summarized in Figure 26.1. This figure compares the long-term evolution of average income per person in today's "developed" (or industrialized) regions—defined as western and eastern Europe, North America, and Japan—with that found in the "Third World," a term that is now widely used by international organizations and by scholars to group Africa, Asia, and Latin America into a single unit. To get these individual income figures, researchers estimate a country's gross national product (GNP) at different points in time, convert those estimates to some common currency, and divide by the total population.

Figure 26.1 highlights three main points. First, in 1750 the average standard of living was no higher in Europe as a whole than in the rest of the world. In 1750 Europe was still a poor agricultural society. Moreover, the average per-person income in the wealthiest European country (Great Britain) was less than twice that in the poorest non-Western land. By 1970, however, the average person in the wealthiest countries had an income fully twenty-five times as great as that received by

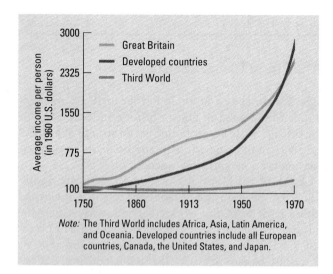

FIGURE 26.1 The Growth of Average Income per Person in the Third World, Developed Countries, and Great Britain, 1750–1970, in 1960 U.S. dollars and prices. *(Source: P. Bairoch and M. Lévy-Leboyer, eds.,* Disparities in Economic Development Since the Industrial Revolution. *Copyright © 1981 by P. Bairoch and M. Lévy-Leboyer. Reprinted with permission of St. Martin's Press, Inc., and Macmillan Ltd.)*

the average person in the poorest countries of Africa and Asia.

Second, it was industrialization that opened the gaps in average wealth and well-being among countries and regions. One sees that Great Britain had jumped well above the European average by 1830, when the first industrial nation was well in advance of its continental competitors. One also sees how Great Britain's lead gradually narrowed as other European countries and the United States successfully industrialized in the course of the nineteenth century.

Third, income per person stagnated in the Third World before 1913, in striking contrast to the industrializing regions. Only after 1945, in the era of political independence and decolonization, did Third World countries finally make some real economic progress, beginning in their turn the critical process of industrialization.

The rise of these enormous income disparities, which are poignant indicators of equal disparities in food and clothing, health and education, life expectancy and general material well-being, has generated a great deal of debate. One school of interpretation stresses that the West used science, technology, capitalist organization, and even its critical world-view to create its wealth and

greater physical well-being. Another school argues that the West used its political and economic power to steal much of its riches, continuing in the nineteenth (and twentieth) century the rapacious colonialism born of the era of expansion.

These issues are complex, and there are few simple answers. As noted in Chapter 22, the wealth-creating potential of technological improvement and more intensive capitalist organization was indeed great. At the same time, those breakthroughs rested, in part, on Great Britain's having already used political force to dominate the world economy in the nineteenth century. Wealth—unprecedented wealth—was indeed created, but the lion's share of that new wealth flowed to the West and its propertied classes.

The World Market

Commerce between nations has always been a powerful stimulus to economic development. Never was this more true than in the nineteenth century, when world trade grew prodigiously. World trade grew modestly until about 1840, and then it took off. After a slowdown in the last years of the century, another surge lasted until World War I. In 1913 the value of world trade was roughly $38 billion, or about *twenty-five* times what it had been in 1800. (This amount actually understates the growth since average prices of both manufactured goods and raw materials were lower in 1913 than in 1800.) In a general way, the enormous increase in international commerce summed up the growth of an interlocking world economy centered in and directed by Europe.

Great Britain played a key role in using trade to tie the world together economically. In 1815 Britain already had a colonial empire, for India, Canada, Australia, and other scattered areas remained British possessions after American independence. The technological breakthroughs of the Industrial Revolution allowed Britain to manufacture cotton textiles, iron, and other goods more cheaply and to far outstrip domestic demand for such products. Thus British manufacturers sought export markets first in Europe and then around the world.

Take the case of cotton textiles. By 1820 Britain was exporting 50 percent of its production. Europe bought 50 percent of these cotton textile exports, while India bought only 6 percent. Then as European nations and the United States erected protective tariff barriers and promoted domestic industry, British cotton textile manufacturers aggressively sought and found other foreign markets in non-Western areas. By 1850 India was buying 25 percent and Europe only 16 percent of a much larger total. As a British colony, India could not raise tariffs to protect its ancient cotton textile industry, and thousands of Indian weavers lost their livelihoods.

After the repeal of the Corn Laws in 1846 (see page 775), Britain also became the world's single best market. The decisive argument in the battle against tariffs on imported grain had been, "We must give if we mean honestly to receive, and we must buy as well as sell." Until 1914 Britain thus remained the world's emporium, where not only agricultural products and raw materials but also manufactured goods entered freely. Free access to Britain's enormous market stimulated the development of mines and plantations in many non-Western areas.

The growth of trade was facilitated by the conquest of distance. The earliest railroad construction occurred in Europe (including Russia) and in America north of the Rio Grande; other parts of the globe saw the building of rail lines after 1860. By 1920 more than one-quarter of the world's railroads were in Latin America, Asia, Africa, and Australia. Wherever railroads were built, they drastically reduced transportation costs, opened new economic opportunities, and called forth new skills and attitudes. Moreover, in the areas of massive European settlement—North America and Australia—they were built in advance of the population and provided a means of settling the land.

The power of steam revolutionized transportation by sea as well as by land. In 1807 inhabitants of the Hudson Valley in New York saw the "Devil on the way to Albany in a saw-mill," as Robert Fulton's steamship *Clermont* traveled 150 miles upstream in thirty-two hours. Steam power, long used to drive paddle wheelers on rivers, particularly in Russia and North America, finally began to supplant sails on the oceans of the world in the late 1860s. Lighter, stronger, cheaper steel replaced iron, which had replaced wood. Screw propellers superseded paddle wheels, while mighty compound steam engines cut fuel consumption by half. Passenger and freight rates tumbled, and the intercontinental shipment of low-priced raw materials became feasible. In addition to the large passenger liners and freighters of the great shipping companies, there were innumerable independent tramp steamers searching endlessly for cargo around the world.

An account of an actual voyage by a typical tramp freighter highlights nineteenth-century developments in global trade. The ship left England in 1910 carrying rails and general freight to western Australia. From there it carried lumber to Melbourne in southeastern Australia, where it took on harvester combines for Argentina. In Buenos Aires it loaded wheat for Calcutta, and in Calcutta it took on jute for New York. From New York it carried a variety of industrial products to Australia before returning to England with lead, wool, and wheat after a voyage of approximately seventy-two thousand miles to six continents in seventeen months.

The revolution in land and sea transportation helped European pioneers open up vast new territories and produce agricultural products and raw materials there for sale in Europe. Moreover, the development of refrigerated railway cars and, from the 1880s, refrigerator ships enabled first Argentina and then the United States, Australia, and New Zealand to ship mountains of chilled or frozen beef and mutton to European (mainly British) consumers. From Asia, Africa, and Latin America came not only the traditional tropical products—spices, tea, sugar, coffee—but also new raw materials for industry, such as jute, rubber, cotton, and coconut oil.

Intercontinental trade was enormously facilitated by the Suez and Panama Canals. Of great importance, too, was large and continual investment in modern port facilities, which made loading and unloading cheaper, faster, and more dependable. Finally, transoceanic telegraph cables inaugurated rapid communications among the financial centers of the world. While a British tramp freighter steamed from Calcutta to New York, a broker in London was arranging by telegram for it to carry an American cargo to Australia. World commodity prices were also instantaneously conveyed by the same network of communications.

The growth of trade and the conquest of distance encouraged the expanding European economy to make massive foreign investments. Beginning about 1840, European capitalists started to invest large sums in foreign lands. They did not stop until the outbreak of World War I in 1914. By that year, Europeans had invested more than $40 billion abroad. Great Britain, France, and Germany were the principal investing countries, although by 1913 the United States was emerging as a substantial foreign investor. The sums involved were enormous (Map 26.1). In the decade before 1914, Great Britain was investing 7 percent of its annual national income abroad, or slightly more than it was investing in its entire domestic economy. The great gap between rich and poor within Europe meant that the wealthy and moderately well-to-do could and did send great sums abroad in search of interest and dividends.

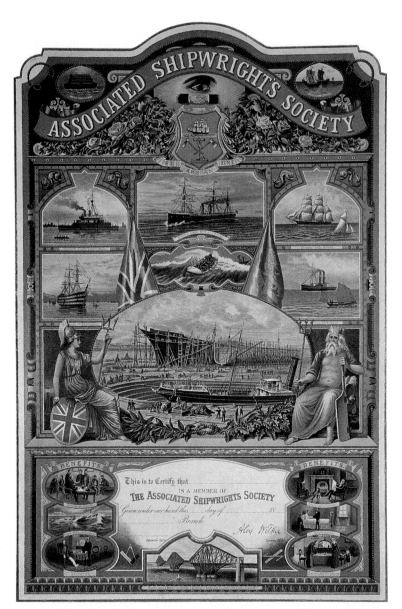

British Ships and Shipbuilders continued to dominate international trade before the First World War. This handsome membership certificate of the British shipbuilders union features the vessels that drew the world together and were Britain's pride. Britain's thriving shipbuilding industry was concentrated in southern Scotland along the Clyde. *(Trade Union Congress, London/Bridgeman Art Library, London/New York)*

Most of the capital exported did not go to European colonies or protectorates in Asia and Africa. About three-quarters of total European investment went to other European countries, the United States and Canada, Australia and New Zealand, and Latin America. Europe found its most profitable opportunities for investment in construction of the railroads, ports, and utilities that were necessary to settle and develop the almost-vacant lands in such places as Australia and the Americas. By lending money for a railroad in Argentina or in Canada's prairie provinces, for example, Europeans not only collected interest but also enabled white settlers to buy European rails and locomotives, developed sources of cheap wheat, and opened still more territory for European settlement. Much of this investment—such as in American railroads, fully a third of whose capital in 1890 was European, or in Russian railroads, which drew heavily on loans from France—was peaceful and mutually beneficial for lenders and borrowers. The victims were native American Indians and Australian aborigines, who were decimated by the diseases, liquor, and weapons of an aggressively expanding Western society.

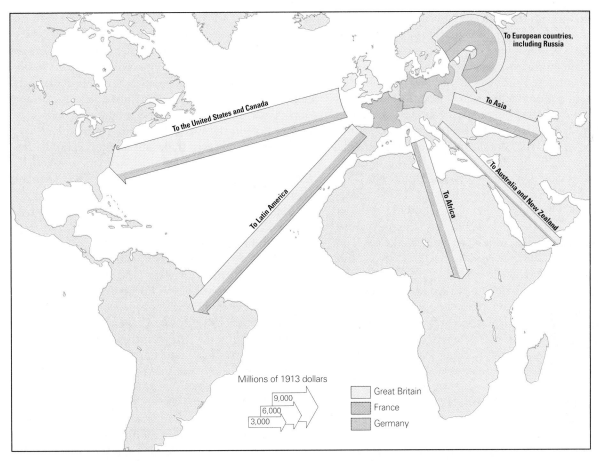

To European countries, including Russia

To Asia

To the United States and Canada

To Latin America

To Africa

To Australia and New Zealand

Millions of 1913 dollars

9,000
6,000
3,000

Great Britain
France
Germany

MAP 26.1 European Investment to 1914 Foreign investment grew rapidly after 1850, and Britain, France, and Germany were the major investing nations. As this map suggests, most European investment was not directed to the African and Asian areas seized by the "new imperialism" after 1880.

The Opening of China and Japan

Europe's relatively peaceful development of robust offshoots in sparsely populated North America, Australia, and much of Latin America absorbed huge quantities of goods, investments, and migrants. From a Western point of view, that was the most important aspect of Europe's global thrust. Yet Europe's economic and cultural penetration of old, densely populated civilizations was also profoundly significant, especially for the non-European peoples affected by it. With such civilizations Europeans also increased their trade and profit. Moreover, as had been the case ever since Vasco da Gama and Christopher Columbus, the expanding Western society was prepared to use force, if necessary, to attain its de-

sires. This was what happened in China and Japan, two crucial examples of the general pattern of intrusion into non-Western lands.

Traditional Chinese civilization was self-sufficient. For centuries China had sent more goods and inventions to Europe than it had received, and this was still the case in the eighteenth century. Europeans and the English in particular had developed a taste for Chinese tea, but they had to pay for it with hard silver since China was supremely uninterested in European wares. Trade with Europe was carefully regulated by the Chinese imperial government—the Manchu Dynasty—which was more interested in isolating and controlling the strange "sea barbarians" than in pursuing commercial exchange. The imperial government refused to establish diplomatic relations with the "inferior" European states, and it required all foreign merchants to live in the southern city of Canton and to buy from and sell to only the local merchant monopoly. Practices considered harmful to Chinese interests, such as the sale of opium and the export of silver from China, were strictly forbidden.

For years the little community of foreign merchants in Canton had to accept the Chinese system. By the 1820s, however, the dominant group, the British, were flexing their muscles. Moreover, in the smoking of opium—that "destructive and ensnaring vice" denounced by Chinese decrees—they had found something the Chinese really wanted. Grown legally in British-occupied India, opium was smuggled into China by means of fast ships and bribed officials. The more this rich trade developed, the greedier British merchants became, and the more they resented the patriotic attempts of the Chinese government to stem the tide of drug addiction. By 1836 the aggressive goal of the British merchants in Canton was an independent British colony in China and "safe and unrestricted liberty" in trade. Spurred on by economic motives, they pressured the British government to take decisive action and enlisted the support of British manufacturers with visions of vast Chinese markets to be opened.

At the same time, the Manchu government decided that the opium trade had to be stamped out. It was ruining the people and stripping the empire of its silver, which was going to British merchants to pay for the opium. The government began to prosecute Chinese drug dealers vigorously and in 1839 sent special envoy Lin Tse-hsü to Canton. Lin Tse-hsü ordered the foreign merchants to obey China's laws, "for our great unified Manchu Empire regards itself as responsible for the habits and morals of its subjects and cannot rest content to see any of them become victims of a deadly poison."[1] The British merchants refused and were expelled, whereupon war soon broke out.

Using troops from India and being in control of the seas, the British occupied several coastal cities and forced China to surrender. In the Treaty of Nanking in 1842, the imperial government was forced to cede the island of Hong Kong to Britain forever, pay an indemnity of $100 million, and open up four large cities to foreign trade with low tariffs.

Thereafter the opium trade flourished, and Hong Kong developed rapidly as an Anglo-Chinese enclave. China continued to nurture illusions of superiority and isolation, however, and refused to accept foreign diplomats in Peking, the imperial capital. Finally, there was a second round of foreign attack between 1856 and 1860, culminating in the occupation of Peking by seventeen thousand British and French troops and the intentional burning of the emperor's summer palace. Another round of harsh treaties gave European merchants and missionaries greater privileges and protection. Thus did Europeans use military aggression to blow a hole in the wall of Chinese seclusion and open the country to foreign trade and foreign ideas. Blasting away at Chinese sovereignty as well, they forced the Chinese to accept trade and investment on unfavorable terms for the foreseeable future.

China's neighbor Japan had its own highly distinctive civilization and even less use for Westerners. European traders and missionaries first arrived in Japan in the sixteenth century. By 1640 Japan had reacted quite negatively to their presence. The government decided to seal off the country from all European influences in order to preserve traditional Japanese culture and society. Officials ruthlessly persecuted Japanese Christians and expelled all but a few Dutch merchants, who were virtually imprisoned in a single port and rigidly controlled. When American and British whaling ships began to appear off Japanese coasts almost two hundred years later, the policy of exclusion was still in effect. An order of 1825 commanded Japanese officials to "drive away foreign vessels without second thought."[2]

Japan's unbending isolation seemed hostile and barbaric to the West, particularly to the United States. It complicated the practical problems of shipwrecked American sailors and the provisioning of whaling ships and China traders sailing in the eastern Pacific. It also thwarted the hope of trade and profit. Moreover, Americans shared the self-confidence and dynamism of expanding Western society. They had taken California from Mexico in 1848, and Americans felt destined to play a great role in the Pacific. It seemed, therefore, the duty of the United States to force the Japanese to share their ports and behave as a "civilized" nation.

After several unsuccessful American attempts to establish commercial relations with Japan, Commodore Matthew Perry steamed into Edo (now Tokyo) Bay in 1853 and demanded diplomatic negotiations with the emperor. Japan entered a grave crisis. Some Japanese warriors urged resistance, but senior officials realized how defenseless their cities were against naval bombardment. Shocked and humiliated, they reluctantly signed a treaty with the United States that opened two ports and permitted trade. Over the next five years, more treaties spelled out the rights and privileges of the

East Meets West   This painting gives a Japanese view of the first audience of the American Consul and his staff with the shogun, Japan's hereditary military governor, in 1859. The Americans appear strange and ill at ease. *(Laurie Platt Winfrey, Inc.)*

Western nations and their merchants in Japan. Japan was "opened." What the British had done in China with war, the Americans had done in Japan with only the threat of war.

Western Penetration of Egypt

Egypt's experience illustrates not only the explosive power of the expanding European economy and society but also their seductive appeal in non-Western lands. European involvement in Egypt also led to a new model of formal political control, which European powers applied widely in Africa and Asia after 1882.

Of great importance in African and Middle Eastern history, the ancient land of the pharaohs had since 525 B.C. been ruled by a succession of foreigners, most recently by the Ottoman Turks. In 1798 French armies under young General Napoleon Bonaparte invaded the Egyptian part of the Ottoman Empire and occupied the territory for three years. Into the power vacuum left by the French withdrawal stepped an extraordinary Albanian-born Turkish general, Muhammad Ali (1769–1849).

First appointed governor of Egypt by the Turkish sultan, Muhammad Ali soon disposed of his political rivals and set out to build his own state on the strength of a large, powerful army organized along European lines. He drafted for the first time the illiterate, despised peasant masses of Egypt, and he hired French and Italian army officers to train these raw recruits and their Turkish officers. The government was also reformed, new lands were cultivated, and communications were improved. By the time of his death in 1849, Muhammad Ali had established a strong and virtually independent Egyptian state, to be ruled by his family on a hereditary basis within the Turkish empire.

Muhammad Ali's policies of modernization attracted large numbers of Europeans to the banks of the Nile. As one Arab sheik of the Ottoman Empire remarked in the 1830s, "Englishmen are like ants; if one finds a bit of meat, hundreds follow."[3] The port city of Alexandria had more than fifty thousand Europeans by 1864, most of them Italian, Greek, French, or English. Europeans served not only as army officers but also as engineers, doctors, government officials, and police officers. Others found their "meat" in trade, finance, and shipping.

To pay for a modern army as well as for European services and manufactured goods, Muhammad Ali encouraged the development of commercial agriculture geared to the European market. This development had profound implications. Egyptian peasants had been poor but largely self-sufficient, growing food for their own consumption on state-owned lands allotted to them by tradition. Faced with the possibility of export agriculture, high-ranking officials and members of Muhammad Ali's family began carving large private landholdings out of the state domain. The new landlords made the peasants their tenants and forced them to grow cash crops for European markets. Borrowing money from European lenders at high rates and still making good profits, Egyptian landowners "modernized" agriculture, but to the detriment of peasant well-being.

These trends continued under Muhammad Ali's grandson Ismail, who in 1863 began his sixteen-year rule as Egypt's *khedive,* or prince. Educated at France's leading military academy, Ismail was a westernizing autocrat. He dreamed of using European technology and capital to modernize Egypt quickly and build a vast empire in northeast Africa. The large irrigation networks

---

A Western Hotel in Cairo This photo suggests both the reality and the limits of modernization in Ismail's Egypt. An expensive hotel, complete with terrace cafe and gaslight, now adorns the Egyptian capital. But the hotel is for foreigners, and the native Egyptians are servants and outsiders. *(Popperfoto/Archive Photos)*

he promoted caused cotton production and exports to Europe to boom. Ismail also borrowed large sums to install modern communications, and with his support the Suez Canal was completed by a French company in 1869. The Arabic of the masses, rather than the Turkish of the conquerors, became the official language, and young Egyptians educated in Europe helped spread new skills and new ideas in the bureaucracy. Cairo acquired modern boulevards, Western hotels, and an opera house. As Ismail proudly declared, "My country is no longer in Africa, we now form part of Europe."[4]

Yet Ismail was too impatient and too reckless. His projects were enormously expensive, and the sale of his stock in the Suez Canal to the British government did not relieve the situation. By 1876 Egypt owed foreign bondholders a colossal $450 million and could not pay the interest on its debt. Rather than let Egypt go bankrupt and repudiate its loans, as had some Latin American countries and U.S. state governments in the early nineteenth century, the governments of France and Great Britain intervened politically to protect the European bankers who held the Egyptian bonds. They forced Ismail to appoint French and British commissioners to oversee Egyptian finances so that the Egyptian debt would be paid in full. This was a momentous decision. It implied direct European political control and was a sharp break with the previous pattern of trade and investment. Throughout most of the nineteenth century, Europeans had used naked military might and political force primarily to make sure that non-Western lands would accept European trade and investment. Now Europeans were going to determine the state budget and effectively rule Egypt.

Foreign financial control evoked a violent nationalistic reaction among Egyptian religious leaders, young intellectuals, and army officers. In 1879, under the leadership of Colonel Ahmed Arabi, they formed the Egyptian Nationalist party. Continuing diplomatic pressure, which forced Ismail to abdicate in favor of his weak son, Tewfiq (r. 1879–1892), resulted in bloody anti-European riots in Alexandria in 1882. A number of Europeans were killed, and Tewfiq and his court had to flee to British ships for safety. When the British fleet bombarded Alexandria, more riots swept the country, and Colonel Arabi declared that "an irreconcilable war existed between the Egyptians and the English." But a British expeditionary force decimated Arabi's forces and as a result occupied all of Egypt.

The British said their occupation was temporary, but British armies remained in Egypt until 1956. They maintained the façade of the khedive's government as an autonomous province of the Ottoman Empire, but the khedive was a mere puppet. The able British consul, General Evelyn Baring, later Lord Cromer, ruled the country after 1883. Once a vocal opponent of involvement in Egypt, Baring was a paternalistic reformer who had come to believe that "without European interference and initiative reform is impossible here." Baring's rule did result in tax reforms and better conditions for peasants, while foreign bondholders tranquilly collected the interest on their investments and Egyptian nationalists nursed their injured pride.

In Egypt Baring and the British reluctantly but spectacularly provided a new model for European expansion in densely populated lands. Such expansion was based on military force, political domination, and a self-justifying ideology of beneficial reform. This model was to predominate until 1914. Thus did Europe's Industrial Revolution lead to tremendous political as well as economic expansion throughout the world.

 ## THE GREAT MIGRATION

A poignant human drama was interwoven with economic expansion: millions of people pulled up stakes and left their ancestral lands in the course of history's greatest migration. To millions of ordinary people, for whom the opening of China and the interest on the Egyptian debt had not the slightest significance, this great movement was the central experience in the saga of Western expansion. It was, in part, because of this great migration that the West's impact on the world in the nineteenth century was so powerful and many-sided.

The Pressure of Population

In the early eighteenth century, the growth of European population entered its third and decisive stage, which continued unabated until the twentieth century (see Chapter 19). Birthrates eventually declined in the nineteenth century, but so did death rates, mainly because of the rising standard of living and secondarily because of the medical revolution. Thus the population of Europe (including Asiatic Russia) more than doubled, from approximately 188 million in 1800 to roughly 432 million in 1900.

These figures actually understate Europe's population explosion, for between 1815 and 1932 more than

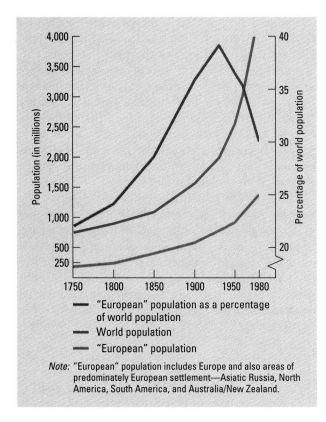

FIGURE 26.2 The Increase of European and World Populations, 1750–1980 *(Sources: W. Woodruff,* Impact of Western Man: A Study of Europe's Role in the World Economy. *St. Martin's Press, New York, 1967, p. 103; United Nations,* Statistical Yearbook, 1982, *1985, pp. 2–3.)*

60 million people left Europe. These migrants went primarily to the "areas of European settlement"—North and South America, Australia, New Zealand, and Siberia—where they contributed to a rapid growth in numbers. The population of North America (the United States and Canada) alone grew from 6 million to 81 million between 1800 and 1900 because of continual immigration and high fertility rates. Since population grew more slowly in Africa and Asia than in Europe, as Figure 26.2 shows, Europeans and people of European origin jumped from about 22 percent of the world's total to about 38 percent on the eve of World War I.

The growing number of Europeans provided further impetus for Western expansion. It was a driving force behind emigration. As in the eighteenth century, the rapid increase in numbers put pressure on the land

and led to land hunger and relative overpopulation in area after area. In most countries, migration increased twenty years after a rapid growth in population, as many children of the baby boom grew up, saw little available land and few opportunities, and migrated. This pattern was especially prevalent when rapid population increase predated extensive industrial development, which offered the best long-term hope of creating jobs within the country and reducing poverty. Thus millions of country folk went abroad as well as to nearby cities in search of work and economic opportunity. The case of the Irish, who left in large numbers for Britain during the Industrial Revolution and for the United States after the potato famine, was extreme but not unique.

Before looking at the people who migrated, let us consider three facts. First, the number of men and women who left Europe increased rapidly before World War I. As Figure 26.3 shows, more than 11 million left in the first decade of the twentieth century, over five times the number departing in the 1850s. The outflow of migrants was clearly an enduring characteristic of European society for the entire period.

Second, different countries had very different patterns of movement. As Figure 26.3 also shows, people left Britain and Ireland (which are not distinguished in the British figures) in large numbers from the 1840s on. This emigration reflected not only rural poverty but also the movement of skilled, industrial technicians and the preferences shown to British migrants in the British Empire. Ultimately, about one-third of all European migrants between 1840 and 1920 came from the British Isles. German migration was quite different. It grew irregularly after about 1830, reaching a first peak in the early 1850s and another in the early 1880s. Thereafter it declined rapidly, for Germany's rapid industrialization was providing adequate jobs at home. This pattern contrasted sharply with that of Italy. More and more Italians left the country right up to 1914, reflecting severe problems in Italian villages and relatively slow industrial growth. Thus, migration patterns mirrored social and economic conditions in the various European countries and provinces.

Third, although the United States absorbed the largest number of European migrants, less than half of all migrants went to the United States. Asiatic Russia, Canada, Argentina, Brazil, Australia, and New Zealand also attracted large numbers, as Figure 26.4 shows. Moreover, migrants accounted for a larger proportion of the total population in Argentina, Brazil, and Canada than in the United States. Between 1900 and 1910,

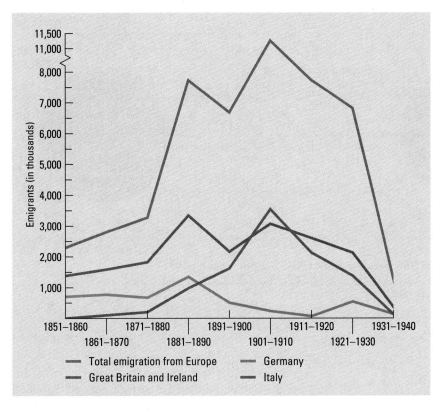

FIGURE 26.3 Emigration from Europe by Decades, 1851–1940   *(Source: W. Woodruff, ed.,* Impact of Western Man: A Study of Europe's Role in the World Economy. *Copyright © 1967 by W. Woodruff. Reprinted by permission of St. Martin's Press, Inc.)*

for example, new arrivals represented 3 percent of Argentina's population each year, as opposed to only 1 percent for the United States. The common American assumption that European migration meant migration to the United States is quite inaccurate.

European Migrants

What kind of people left Europe, and what were their reasons for doing so? Most were poor people from rural areas, though seldom from the poorest classes. Indeed, the European migrant was most often a small peasant landowner or a village craftsman whose traditional way of life was threatened by too little land, estate agriculture, and cheap, factory-made goods. German peasants who left the Rhineland and southwestern Germany between 1830 and 1854, for example, felt trapped by what Friedrich List called the "dwarf economy," with

its tiny landholdings and declining craft industries. Selling out and moving to buy much cheaper land in the American Midwest became a common response. Contrary to what is often said, the European migrant was generally not a desperately impoverished landless peasant or urban proletarian, but an energetic small farmer or skilled artisan trying hard to stay ahead of poverty.

Determined to maintain or improve their status, migrants were a great asset to the countries that received them. This was doubly so because the vast majority were young and very often unmarried. Fully 67 percent of those admitted to the United States were under thirty-one years of age, and 90 percent were under forty. They came in the prime of life and were ready to work hard in the new land, at least for a time. Many Europeans moved but remained within Europe, settling temporarily or permanently in another European country. Jews from eastern Europe and peasants from Ireland migrated to Great Britain, Russians and Poles

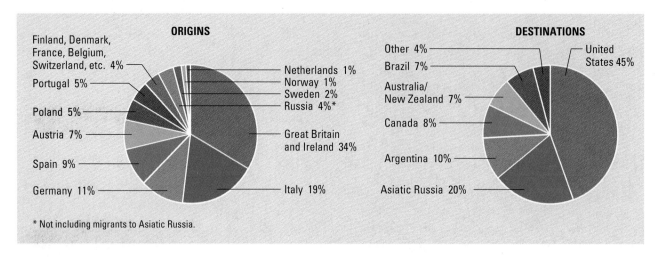

FIGURE 26.4 Origin and Destination of European Emigrants, 1851–1960 *(Source: W. Woodruff,* Impact of Western Man: A Study of Europe's Role in the World Economy. *St. Martin's Press, New York, 1967, pp. 108–109 and references cited therein. Reprinted with permission of St. Martin's Press, Inc.)*

sought work in Germany, and Latin peoples from Spain, Portugal, and Italy entered France.

Even in the New World, many Europeans, especially by the end of the nineteenth century, were truly migrants as opposed to immigrants—that is, they returned home after some time abroad. One in two migrants to Argentina and probably one in three to the United States eventually returned to their native land. The likelihood of repatriation varied greatly by nationality. Seven out of eight people who migrated from the Balkans to the United States in the late nineteenth century returned to their countries. At the other extreme, only one person in ten from Ireland and only one in twenty among eastern European Jews returned to their country of origin.

Once again, the possibility of buying land in the old country was of central importance. Land in Ireland (as well as in England and Scotland) was tightly held by large, often absentee landowners, and little land was available for purchase. In Russia Jews were left in relative peace until the assassination of Alexander II by non-Jewish terrorists in 1881 brought a new tsar and an official policy of pogroms and savage discrimination. Russia's 5 million Jews were already confined to the market towns and small cities of the so-called Pale of Settlement, where they worked as artisans and petty traders. Most land was held by non-Jews. Therefore, when Russian Jewish artisans began in the 1880s to es-

cape both factory competition and oppression by migrating—a migration that eventually totaled 2 million people—this was basically a once-and-for-all departure. Non-Jewish migrants from Russia, who constituted a majority of those leaving the tsar's empire after 1905, had access to land and thus returned much more frequently to their peasant villages in central Russia, Poland, and Ukraine.

The mass movement of Italians illustrates many of the characteristics of European migration. As late as the 1880s, which was for Italians, as for Russian Jews, the first decade of substantial exodus, three in every four Italians depended on agriculture. With the influx of cheap North American wheat, the long-standing problems of the Italian village became more acute. And since industry was not advancing fast enough to provide jobs for the rapidly growing population, many Italians began to leave their country for economic reasons. Most Italian migrants were not landless laborers from areas dominated by large estates; such people tended to stay in Italy and turned increasingly toward radical politics. Instead, most migrants were small landowning peasants whose standard of living was falling because of rural overpopulation and agricultural depression. Migration provided them with an escape valve and possible income to buy more land.

Many Italians went to the United States, but before 1900 more went to Argentina and Brazil; indeed, two out of three migrants to both countries came from Italy. In Brazil the large coffee planters, faced with the collapse of black slavery, attracted Italians to their plantations with subsidized travel and promises of relatively high wages.

Many Italians had no intention of settling abroad permanently. Some called themselves "swallows": after harvesting their own wheat and flax in Italy, they "flew" to Argentina to harvest wheat between December and April. Returning to Italy for the spring planting, they repeated this exhausting process. This was a very hard life, but a frugal worker could save $250 to $300 in the course of a season. A one-way passage from Latin America to Italy usually cost only $25 to $30 and sometimes as little as $8. Italian migrants also dominated the building trades and the architectural profession in Latin America and succeeded in giving a thoroughly Italian character to many Latin American cities.

Other Italians migrated to other European countries. France was a favorite destination. In 1911 the Italian-born population of France was roughly a third as large as that in the United States.

Ties of family and friendship played a crucial role in the movement of peoples. Many people from a given province or village settled together in rural enclaves or tightly knit urban neighborhoods thousands of miles away. Very often a strong individual—a businessman, a religious leader—would blaze the way and others would follow, in a pattern called "chain migration."

Many landless young European men and women were spurred to leave by a spirit of revolt and independence. In Sweden and in Norway, in Jewish Russia and

The Jewish Market   on New York's Lower East Side was a bustling center of economic and social life in 1900. Jewish immigrants could usually find work with Jewish employers, and New York's Jewish population soared from 73,000 in 1880 to 1.1 million in 1910. *(The Granger Collection, New York)*

in Italy, these young people felt frustrated by the small privileged classes, which often controlled both church and government and resisted demands for change and greater opportunity. Many a young Norwegian seconded the passionate cry of Norway's national poet, Martinius Bjørnson: "Forth will I! Forth! I will be crushed and consumed if I stay."[5]

Many young Jews wholeheartedly agreed with a spokesman of Kiev's Jewish community in 1882, who declared, "Our human dignity is being trampled upon, our wives and daughters are being dishonored, we are looted and pillaged: either we get decent human rights or else let us go wherever our eyes may lead us."[6] Thus for many, migration was a radical way to "get out from under." Migration slowed down when the people won basic political and social reforms, such as the right to vote and social security.

Asian Migrants

Not all migration was from Europe. A substantial number of Chinese, Japanese, Indians, and Filipinos—to name only four key groups—responded to rural hardship with temporary or permanent migration. At least 3 million Asians (as opposed to more than 60 million Europeans) moved abroad before 1920. Most went as indentured laborers to work under incredibly difficult conditions on the plantations or in the gold mines of Latin America, southern Asia, Africa, California, Hawaii, and Australia. White estate owners very often used Asians to replace or supplement blacks after the suppression of the slave trade.

In the 1840s, for example, there was a strong demand for field hands in Cuba, and the Spanish government actively recruited Chinese laborers. They came

Chinese Laborers Arriving in South Africa In the early twentieth century many black Africans refused to work in the harsh conditions that prevailed in South Africa's rapidly expanding gold mines. Thus capitalists turned to Chinese migrants on strict three-year contracts for additional labor power. The Chinese were limited to unskilled jobs and could not settle or own property in South Africa. *(Courtesy, Dr. Oscar Norwich)*

under eight-year contracts, were paid about 25 cents a day, and were fed potatoes and salted beef. Between 1853 and 1873, when such migration was stopped, more than 130,000 Chinese laborers went to Cuba. The majority spent their lives as virtual slaves. The great landlords of Peru also brought in more than 100,000 workers from China in the nineteenth century, and there were similar movements of Asians elsewhere.

Such migration from Asia would undoubtedly have grown to much greater proportions if planters and mine owners in search of cheap labor had been able to hire as many Asian workers as they wished. But they could not. Asians fled the plantations and gold mines as soon as possible, seeking greater opportunities in trade and towns. There they came into conflict with local populations, whether in Malaya, East Africa, or areas settled by Europeans.

These European settlers demanded a halt to Asian migration. One Australian brutally summed up the typical view: "The Chinaman knows nothing about Caucasian civilization. . . . It would be less objectionable to drive a flock of sheep to the poll than to allow Chinamen to vote. The sheep at all events would be harmless."[7] By the 1880s, Americans and Australians were building "great white walls"—discriminatory laws designed to keep Asians out. Thus a final, crucial factor in the migrations before 1914 was the general policy of "whites only" in the open lands of possible permanent settlement. This, too, was part of Western dominance in the increasingly lopsided world. Largely successful in monopolizing the best overseas opportunities, Europeans and people of European ancestry reaped the main benefits from the great migration. By 1913 people in Australia, Canada, and the United States all had higher average incomes than people in Great Britain, still Europe's wealthiest nation.

WESTERN IMPERIALISM

The expansion of Western society reached its apex between about 1880 and 1914. In those years, the leading European nations not only continued to send massive streams of migrants, money, and manufactured goods around the world, but also rushed to create or enlarge vast *political* empires abroad. This political empire building contrasted sharply with the economic penetration of non-Western territories between 1816 and 1880, which had left a China or a Japan "opened" but politically independent. By contrast, the empires of the late nineteenth century recalled the old European colonial empires of the seventeenth and eighteenth centuries and led contemporaries to speak of the new imperialism.

Characterized by a frantic rush to plant the flag over as many people and as much territory as possible, the new imperialism had momentous consequences. It resulted in new tensions among competing European states, and it led to wars and rumors of war with non-European powers. The new imperialism was aimed primarily at Africa and Asia. It put millions of black, brown, and yellow peoples directly under the rule of whites. How and why did whites come to rule these peoples?

The Scramble for Africa

The most spectacular manifestation of the new imperialism was the seizure of Africa, which broke sharply with previous patterns and fascinated contemporary Europeans and Americans. As late as 1880, European nations controlled only 10 percent of the African continent, and their possessions were hardly increasing. The French had begun conquering Algeria in 1830, and within fifty years substantial numbers of French, Italian, and Spanish colonists had settled among the overwhelming Arab majority.

At the other end of the continent, in South Africa, the British had taken possession of the Dutch settlements at Cape Town during the wars with Napoleon I. This takeover had led disgruntled Dutch cattle ranchers and farmers in 1835 to make their so-called Great Trek into the interior, where they fought the Zulu and Xhosa peoples for land. After 1853, while British colonies such as Canada and Australia were beginning to evolve toward self-government, the Boers, or Afrikaners (as the descendants of the Dutch in the Cape Colony were beginning to call themselves), proclaimed their political independence and defended it against British armies. By 1880 Afrikaner and British settlers, who detested each other, had wrested control of much of South Africa from the Zulu, Xhosa, and other African peoples.

European trading posts and forts dating back to the Age of Discovery and the slave trade dotted the coast of West Africa. The Portuguese proudly but ineffectively held their old possessions in Angola and Mozambique. Elsewhere over the great mass of the continent, Europeans did not rule.

Between 1880 and 1900, the situation changed drastically. Britain, France, Germany, and Italy scrambled for African possessions as if their national livelihoods depended on it. By 1900 nearly the whole continent

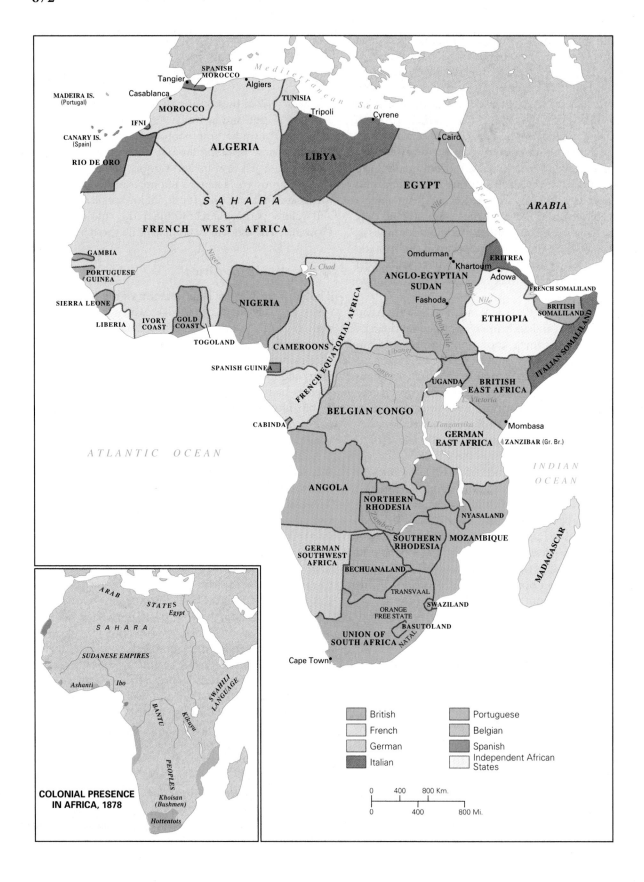

SPANISH MOROCCO

MADEIRA IS.
(Portugal)

Tangier
Casablanca
MOROCCO
IFNI
CANARY IS.
(Spain)
RIO DE ORO

Algiers
TUNISIA
Tripoli
Cyrene
Cairo

Mediterranean Sea

ALGERIA
LIBYA
EGYPT
ARABIA

SAHARA

FRENCH WEST AFRICA

GAMBIA
PORTUGUESE GUINEA
SIERRA LEONE
LIBERIA
IVORY COAST
GOLD COAST
TOGOLAND
NIGERIA
Niger
L. Chad
Nile
Red Sea

Omdurman
Khartoum
ERITREA
Adowa
ANGLO-EGYPTIAN SUDAN
Fashoda
White Nile
ETHIOPIA
FRENCH SOMALILAND
BRITISH SOMALILAND
ITALIAN SOMALILAND

CAMEROONS
SPANISH GUINEA
FRENCH EQUATORIAL AFRICA
Ubangi
Congo

CABINDA
BELGIAN CONGO
UGANDA
BRITISH EAST AFRICA
L. Victoria
GERMAN EAST AFRICA
L. Tanganyika
Mombasa
ZANZIBAR (Gr. Br.)

ATLANTIC OCEAN

INDIAN OCEAN

ANGOLA
NORTHERN RHODESIA
NYASALAND
Zambezi
GERMAN SOUTHWEST AFRICA
SOUTHERN RHODESIA
MOZAMBIQUE
MADAGASCAR
BECHUANALAND
TRANSVAAL
SWAZILAND
ORANGE FREE STATE
BASUTOLAND
UNION OF SOUTH AFRICA
NATAL
Cape Town

COLONIAL PRESENCE IN AFRICA, 1878

ARAB STATES
Egypt
SAHARA
SUDANESE EMPIRES
Ashanti
Ibo
SWAHILI LANGUAGE
BANTU
Kikuyu
PEOPLES
Khoisan (Bushmen)
Hottentots

British
French
German
Italian

Portuguese
Belgian
Spanish
Independent African States

0   400   800 Km.

0   400   800 Mi.

had been carved up and placed under European rule: only Ethiopia in northeast Africa, which repulsed Italian invaders, and Liberia on the West African coast remained independent. In the years before 1914, the European powers tightened their control and established colonial governments to rule their gigantic empires (Map 26.2).

The Dutch settler republics also succumbed to imperialism, but the final outcome was quite different. The British, led by Cecil Rhodes in the Cape Colony, leapfrogged over the Afrikaner states in the early 1890s and established protectorates over Bechuanaland (now Botswana) and Rhodesia (now Zimbabwe and Zambia), named in honor of its freelance imperial founder. Trying unsuccessfully to undermine the stubborn Afrikaners in the Transvaal, where English-speaking capitalists like Rhodes were developing fabulously rich gold mines, the British conquered their white rivals in the bloody Boer War (1899–1902). In 1910 their territories were united with the old Cape Colony and the eastern province of Natal in a new Union of South Africa, established—unlike any other territory in Africa—as a largely "self-governing" colony. This enabled the defeated Afrikaners to use their numerical superiority over the British settlers to gradually take political power, as even the most educated nonwhites lost the right to vote outside the Cape Colony. (See the feature "Individuals in Society: Cecil Rhodes: Empire Building in Southern Africa.")

In the complexity of the European seizure of Africa, certain events and individuals stand out. Of enormous importance was the British occupation of Egypt, which established the new model of formal political control. There was also the role of Leopold II of Belgium (r. 1865–1909), an energetic, strong-willed monarch with a lust for distant territory. "The sea bathes our coast, the world lies before us," he had exclaimed in 1861. "Steam and electricity have annihilated distance, and all the non-appropriated lands on the surface of the globe can become the field of our operations and of our success."[8] By 1876 Leopold was focusing on central Africa. Subsequently, he formed a financial syndicate under his personal control to send Henry M. Stanley, a sensation-seeking journalist and part-time explorer, to the Congo basin. Stanley was able to establish trading stations, sign "treaties" with African chiefs, and plant Leopold's flag. Leopold's actions alarmed the French, who quickly sent out an expedition under Pierre de Brazza. In 1880 de Brazza signed a treaty of protection with the chief of the large Teke tribe and began to establish a French protectorate on the north bank of the Congo River.

Leopold's buccaneering intrusion into the Congo area raised the question of the political fate of Africa. By 1882, when the British successfully invaded and occupied Egypt, the richest and most developed land in Africa, Europe had caught "African fever." There was a gold rush mentality, and the race for territory was on.

To lay down some basic rules for this new and dangerous game of imperialist competition in sub-Saharan Africa, Jules Ferry of France and Otto von Bismarck of Germany arranged an international conference on Africa in Berlin in 1884 and 1885. The conference established the principle that European claims to African territory had to rest on "effective occupation" in order to be recognized by other states. This principle was very important. It meant that Europeans would push relentlessly into interior regions from all sides and that no single European power would be able to claim the entire continent. The conference recognized Leopold's personal rule over a neutral Congo free state and declared all of the Congo basin a free-trade zone. The conference also agreed to work to stop slavery and the slave trade in Africa.

The Berlin conference coincided with Germany's sudden emergence as an imperial power. Prior to about 1880, Bismarck, like many other European leaders at the time, had seen little value in colonies. Colonies reminded him, he said, of a poor but proud nobleman who wore a fur coat when he could not afford a shirt underneath. Then in 1884 and 1885, as political agitation for expansion increased, Bismarck did an abrupt about-face, and Germany established protectorates over a number of small African kingdoms and tribes in Togo, Cameroons, southwest Africa, and, later, East Africa. In acquiring colonies, Bismarck cooperated against the British with France's Ferry, who was as ardent for empire as he was for education. With Bismarck's tacit approval, the French pressed vigorously southward from Algeria, eastward from their old forts on the Senegal coast, and northward from de Brazza's newly formed protectorate on the Congo River. The object of these three thrusts was Lake Chad, a malaria-infested swamp on the edge of the Sahara Desert.

Meanwhile, the British began enlarging their West African enclaves and impatiently pushing northward from the Cape Colony and westward from Zanzibar.

MAP 26.2 The Partition of Africa   European nations carved up Africa after 1880 and built vast political empires. What African states remained independent?

Individuals in Society

Cecil Rhodes: Empire Building in Southern Africa ✛

Cecil Rhodes (1853–1902) epitomized the dynamism and the ruthlessness of the new imperialism. He built a corporate monopoly, claimed vast tracts in Africa, and established the famous Rhodes scholarships to develop colonial (and American) leaders who would love and strengthen the British Empire. But to Africans, he left a bitter legacy.

Rhodes came from a large middle-class family and at seventeen went to southern Africa to seek his fortune. He soon turned to diamonds, newly discovered at Kimberley, picked good partners, and was wealthy by 1876. But Rhodes, often called a dreamer, wanted more. He entered Oxford University, while returning periodically to Africa, and his musings crystallized in a belief in progress through racial competition and territorial expansion. "I contend," he wrote, "that we [English] are the finest race in the world and the more of the world we inhabit the better it is for the human race."[1]

Rhodes's belief in British expansion never wavered. In 1880 he formed the De Beers Mining Company, and by 1888 his firm monopolized southern Africa's diamond production and earned fabulous profits. Rhodes also entered the Cape Colony's legislature and became the all-powerful prime minister from 1890 to 1896. His main objective was to dominate the Afrikaner republics and to impose British rule on as much land as possible beyond their northern borders. Working through a state-approved private company financed in part by De Beers, Rhodes's agents forced and cajoled African kings to accept British "protection," then put down rebellions with Maxim machine guns. Britain thus obtained a great swath of empire on the cheap.

But Rhodes, like many high achievers obsessed with power and personal aggrandizement, went too far. He backed, and then in 1896 failed to call back, a failed invasion of the Transvaal, which was designed to topple the Dutch-speaking republic. Repudiated by top British leaders who had encouraged his plan, Rhodes had to resign as prime minister. In declining health, he continued to agitate against the Afrikaner republics. He died at age forty-nine as the Boer War (1899–1902) ended.

Cecil Rhodes, after crushing the last African revolt in Rhodesia in 1896. *(Brown Brothers)*

In accounting for Rhodes's remarkable but flawed achievements, both sympathetic and critical biographers stress his imposing size, enormous energy, and powerful personality. His ideas were commonplace, but he believed in them passionately, and he could persuade and inspire others to follow his lead. Rhodes the idealist was nonetheless a born negotiator, a crafty dealmaker who believed that everyone could be had for a price. According to his best biographer, Rhodes's homosexuality—discreet, partially repressed, and undeniable—was also "a major component of his magnetism and his success."[2] Never comfortable with women, he loved male companionship. He drew together a "band of brothers," both gay and straight, to share in the pursuit of power.

Rhodes cared nothing for the rights of blacks. Ever a combination of visionary and opportunist, he looked forward to an eventual reconciliation of Afrikaners and British in a united white front. Therefore, as prime minister of the Cape Colony, he broke with the colony's liberal tradition and supported Afrikaner demands to reduce drastically the number of black voters and limit black freedoms. This helped lay the foundation for the Union of South Africa's brutal policy of racial segregation known as *apartheid* after 1948.

Questions for Analysis

1. How did Rhodes relate to Afrikaners and to black Africans? How do you account for the differences and the similarities?

2. In what ways does Rhodes's career throw additional light on the debate over the causes of the new imperialism?

1. Robert Rotberg, *The Founder: Cecil Rhodes and the Pursuit of Power* (New York: Oxford University Press, 1988), p. 150.
2. Ibid., p. 408.

Omdurman, 1898 European machine guns cut down the charging Muslim tribesmen again and again. "It was not a battle but an execution," said one witness. Thus the Sudan was conquered and one million square miles were added to the British Empire. *(E.T. Archive)*

Their thrust southward from Egypt was blocked in the Sudan by fiercely independent Muslims, who massacred a British force at Khartoum in 1885.

A decade later, another British force, under General Horatio H. Kitchener, moved cautiously and more successfully up the Nile River, building a railroad to supply arms and reinforcements as it went. Finally, in 1898 these British troops met their foe at Omdurman (see Map 26.2), where Muslim tribesmen armed with spears charged time and time again only to be cut down by the recently invented machine gun. For one smug participant, the young British officer Winston Churchill, it was "like a pantomime scene" in a play. "These extraordinary foreign figures . . . march up one by one from the darkness of Barbarism to the footlights of civilization . . . and their conquerors, taking their possessions, forget even their names. Nor will history record such

trash." For another, more somber English observer, "It was not a battle but an execution. The bodies were not in heaps . . . but they spread evenly over acres and acres."[9] In the end, eleven thousand brave but poorly armed Muslim tribesmen lay dead, while only twenty-eight Britons had been killed.

Continuing up the Nile after the Battle of Omdurman, Kitchener's armies found that a small French force had already occupied the village of Fashoda. Locked in imperial competition with Britain ever since the British occupation of Egypt, France had tried to beat the British to one of Africa's last unclaimed areas—the upper reaches of the Nile. The result was a serious diplomatic crisis and even the threat of war. Eventually, wracked by the Dreyfus affair (see page 845) and unwilling to fight, France backed down and withdrew its forces, allowing the British to take over.

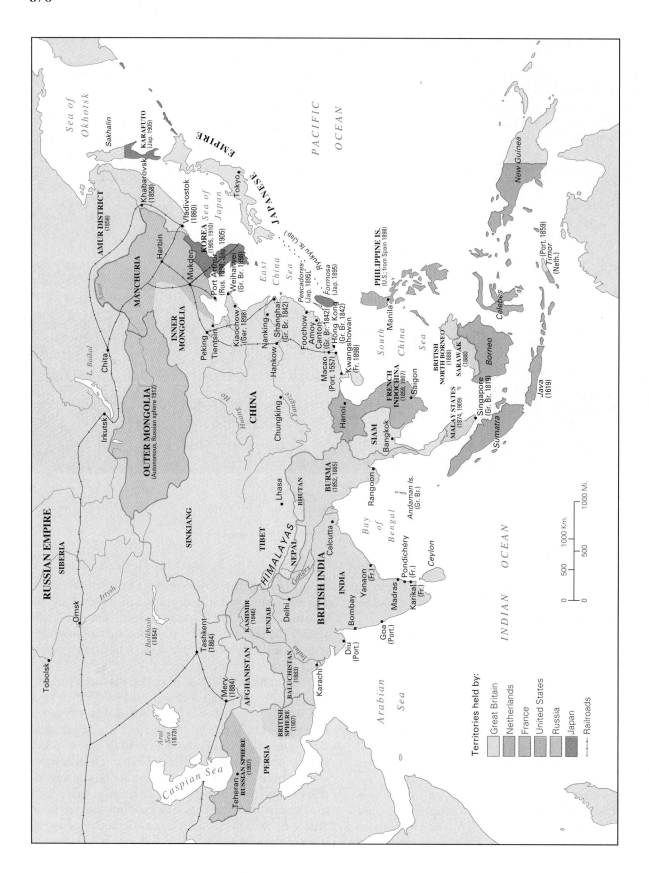

RUSSIAN EMPIRE

SIBERIA

Sea of Okhotsk

Sakhalin

KARAFUTO (Jap. 1905)

JAPANESE EMPIRE

Khabarovsk (1858)

AMUR DISTRICT (1858)

Vladivostok (1860)

Tokyo

Sea of Japan

Harbin

MANCHURIA

Mukden

KOREA (1905, 1910)

Port Arthur (Rus. 1898–Jap. 1905)

Weihaiwei (Gr. Br. 1898)

Ryukyu Is. (Jap.)

Chita

L. Baikal

INNER MONGOLIA

Peking

Tientsin

Kiaochow (Ger. 1898)

Nanking

Shanghai (Gr. Br. 1842)

Pescadores (Jap. 1895)

Formosa (Jap. 1895)

East China Sea

PHILIPPINE IS. (U.S. from Spain 1898)

Manila

Irkutsk

OUTER MONGOLIA (Autonomous, Russian sphere 1912)

Hankow

Foochow (Gr. Br. 1842)

Amoy (Gr. Br. 1842)

Canton (Gr. Br. 1842)

Hong Kong (Gr. Br. 1842)

Kwangshowan (Fr. 1898)

South China Sea

BRITISH NORTH BORNEO (1888)

SARAWAK (1888)

Borneo

Celebes

New Guinea

(Port. 1859) *Timor* (Neth.)

CHINA

Chungking

Huang Ho

Yangtze

Macao (Port. 1557)

Omsk

Tobolsk

L. Balkhash (1854)

Irtysh

SINKIANG

Tashkent (1864)

Lhasa

TIBET

BHUTAN

BURMA (1852, 1885)

Rangoon

Andaman Is. (Gr. Br.)

Bay of Bengal

FRENCH INDOCHINA (1859, 1907)

Hanoi

Saigon

SIAM

Bangkok

MALAY STATES (1874, 1909)

Singapore (Gr. Br. 1819)

Sumatra

Java (1619)

Merv (1884)

AFGHANISTAN

KASHMIR (1846)

PUNJAB

Delhi

NEPAL

HIMALAYAS

Ganges

Indus

BALUCHISTAN (1883)

BRITISH SPHERE (1907)

Karachi

BRITISH INDIA

Calcutta

INDIA

Bombay

Yanaon (Fr.)

Pondichéry (Fr.)

Madras

Karikal (Fr.)

Goa (Port.)

Diu (Port.)

Ceylon

Aral Sea (1873)

RUSSIAN SPHERE (1907)

PERSIA

Teheran

Caspian Sea

Arabian Sea

INDIAN OCEAN

PACIFIC OCEAN

Territories held by:

Great Britain

Netherlands

France

United States

Russia

Japan

Railroads

1000 Mi.

1000 Km.

500

500

0

0

The British conquest of the Sudan exemplifies the general process of empire building in Africa. The fate of the Muslim force at Omdurman was eventually inflicted on all native peoples who resisted European rule: they were blown away by vastly superior military force. But however much the European powers squabbled for territory and privilege around the world, they always had the sense to stop short of actually fighting each other. Imperial ambitions were not worth a great European war.

Imperialism in Asia

Although the sudden division of Africa was more spectacular, Europeans also extended their political control in Asia. In 1815 the Dutch ruled little more than the island of Java in the East Indies. Thereafter they gradually brought almost all of the three-thousand-mile archipelago under their political authority, though—in good imperialist fashion—they had to share some of the spoils with Britain and Germany. In the critical decade of the 1880s, the French under the leadership of Ferry took Indochina. India, Japan, and China also experienced a profound imperialist impact (Map 26.3).

Two other great imperialist powers, Russia and the United States, also acquired rich territories in Asia. Russia, whose history since the later Middle Ages had been marked by almost continual expansion, moved steadily forward on two fronts throughout the nineteenth century. Russians conquered Muslim areas to the south in the Caucasus and in central Asia and also proceeded to nibble greedily on China's outlying provinces in the Far East, especially in the 1890s.

The United States' great conquest was the Philippines, taken from Spain in 1898 after the Spanish-American War. When it quickly became clear that the United States had no intention of granting independence, Philippine patriots rose in revolt and were suppressed only after long, bitter fighting. (Not until 1934 was a timetable for independence established.) Some Americans protested the taking of the Philippines, but to no avail. Thus another great Western power joined the imperialist ranks in Asia.

MAP 26.3 Asia in 1914 India remained under British rule, while China precariously preserved its political independence. The Dutch empire in modern-day Indonesia was old, but French control of Indochina was a product of the new imperialism.

Causes of the New Imperialism

Many factors contributed to the late-nineteenth-century rush for territory and empire, which was in turn one aspect of Western society's generalized expansion in the age of industry and nationalism. It is little wonder that controversies have raged over interpretation of the new imperialism, especially since authors of every persuasion have often exaggerated particular aspects in an attempt to prove their own theories. Yet despite complexity and controversy, basic causes are clearly identifiable.

Economic motives played an important role in the extension of political empires, especially the British Empire. By the late 1870s, France, Germany, and the United States were industrializing rapidly behind rising tariff barriers. Great Britain was losing its early lead and facing increasingly tough competition in foreign markets. In this new economic situation, Britain came to value old possessions, such as India and Canada, more highly. The days when a leading free-trader such as Richard Cobden could denounce the "bloodstained fetish of Empire" and statesman Benjamin Disraeli could call colonies a "millstone round our necks" came to an abrupt end. When continental powers began to grab any and all unclaimed territory in the 1880s, the British followed suit immediately. They feared that France and Germany would seal off their empires with high tariffs and restrictions and that future economic opportunities would be lost forever.

Actually, the overall economic gains of the new imperialism proved quite limited before 1914. The new colonies were simply too poor to buy much, and they offered few immediately profitable investments. Nonetheless, even the poorest, most barren desert was jealously prized, and no territory was ever abandoned. Colonies became important for political and diplomatic reasons. Each leading country saw colonies as crucial to national security, military power, and international prestige. For instance, safeguarding the Suez Canal played a key role in the British occupation of Egypt, and protecting Egypt in turn led to the bloody conquest of the Sudan. National security was a major factor in the U.S. decision to establish firm control over the Panama Canal Zone in 1903. Far-flung possessions guaranteed ever-growing navies the safe havens and the dependable coaling stations they needed in time of crisis or war.

Many people were convinced that colonies were essential to great nations. "There has never been a great power without great colonies," wrote one French publicist in 1877. "Every virile people has established colonial power," echoed the famous nationalist historian of Germany, Heinrich von Treitschke. "All great nations in the fullness of their strength have desired to set their mark upon barbarian lands and those who fail to participate in this great rivalry will play a pitiable role in time to come."[10]

Treitschke's harsh statement reflects not only the increasing aggressiveness of European nationalism after Bismarck's wars of German unification but also Social Darwinian theories of brutal competition among races. As one prominent English economist argued, the "strongest nation has always been conquering the weaker . . . and the strongest tend to be best." Thus European nations, which were seen as racially distinct parts of the dominant white race, had to seize colonies to show they were strong and virile. Moreover, since racial struggle was nature's inescapable law, the conquest of inferior peoples was just. "The path of progress is strewn with the wreck . . . of inferior races," wrote one professor in 1900. "Yet these dead peoples are, in very truth, the stepping stones on which mankind has risen to the higher intellectual and deeper emotional life of today."[11] Social Darwinism and harsh racial doctrines fostered imperialist expansion.

So did the industrial world's unprecedented technological and military superiority. Three aspects were crucial. First, the rapidly firing machine gun, so lethal at Omdurman in the Sudan, was an ultimate weapon in many another unequal battle. Second, newly discovered quinine proved no less effective in controlling attacks of malaria, which had previously decimated whites in the tropics whenever they left breezy coastal enclaves and dared to venture into mosquito-infested interiors. Third, the combination of the steamship and the international telegraph permitted Western powers to quickly concentrate their firepower in a given area when it was needed. Never before—and never again after 1914—would the technological gap between the West and non-Western regions of the world be so great.

Social tensions and domestic political conflicts also contributed mightily to overseas expansion, according to a prominent interpretation of recent years. Certainly in Germany, in Russia, and in other countries to a lesser extent, contemporary critics of imperialism charged conservative political leaders with manipulating colonial issues in order to divert popular attention from the class struggle at home and to create a false sense of national unity. Therefore, imperial propagandists relentlessly stressed that colonies benefited workers as well as capitalists, providing jobs and cheap raw materials that raised workers' standard of living. Government leaders and their allies in the tabloid press successfully encouraged the masses to savor foreign triumphs and glory in the supposed increase in national prestige. In short, conservative leaders defined imperialist development as a national necessity, and then they used the realization of that necessity to justify the status quo and their continued hold on power.

Finally, certain special-interest groups in each country were powerful agents of expansion. Shipping companies wanted lucrative subsidies. White settlers on dangerous, turbulent frontiers constantly demanded more land and greater protection. Missionaries and humanitarians wanted to spread religion and stop the slave trade. Explorers and adventurers sought knowledge and excitement. Military men and colonial officials, whose role has often been overlooked by those who write on imperialism, foresaw rapid advancement and high-paid positions in growing empires. The actions of such groups and the determined individuals who led them thrust the course of empire forward.

Western society did not rest the case for empire solely on naked conquest and a Darwinian racial struggle or on power politics and the need for naval bases on every ocean. Imperialists developed additional arguments in order to satisfy their consciences and answer their critics.

A favorite idea was that Europeans could and should "civilize" more primitive, nonwhite peoples. According to this view, nonwhites would eventually receive the benefits of modern economies, cities, advanced medicine, and higher standards of living. In time, they might be ready for self-government and Western democracy. Thus the French spoke of their sacred "civilizing mission." Rudyard Kipling (1865–1936), who wrote masterfully of Anglo-Indian life and was perhaps the most influential British writer of the 1890s, exhorted Europeans (and Americans in the United States) to unselfish service in distant lands:

Take up the White Man's Burden—
  Send forth the best ye breed—
Go bind your sons to exile
  To serve your captives' need,
To wait in heavy harness,
  On fluttered folk and wild—
Your new-caught, sullen peoples
  Half-devil and half-child.[12]

Many Americans accepted the ideology of the white man's burden. It was an important factor in the decision to rule, rather than liberate, the Philippines after the Spanish-American War. Like their European counterparts, these Americans sincerely believed that their civilization had reached unprecedented heights and that they had unique benefits to bestow on all "less advanced" peoples. Another argument was that imperial government protected natives from tribal warfare as well as cruder forms of exploitation by white settlers and business people.

Peace and stability under European control also permitted the spread of Christianity—the "true" religion. In Africa Catholic and Protestant missionaries com-

peted with Islam south of the Sahara, seeking converts and building schools to spread the Gospel. Many Africans' first real contact with whites was in mission schools. As late as 1942, for example, 97 percent of Nigeria's student population was in mission schools. Some peoples, such as the Ibo in Nigeria, became highly Christianized.

Such occasional successes in black Africa contrasted with the general failure of missionary efforts in India, China, and the Islamic world. There Christians often

A Missionary School   A Swahili schoolboy leads his classmates in a reading lesson in Dar es Salaam in German East Africa before 1914, as portraits of Emperor William II and his wife look down on the classroom. Europeans argued that they were spreading the benefits of a superior civilization with schools like this one, which is unusually solid because of its strategic location in the capital city. *(Ullstein Bilderdienst)*

preached in vain to peoples with ancient, complex religious beliefs. Yet the number of Christian believers around the world did increase substantially in the nineteenth century, and missionary groups kept trying. Unfortunately, "many missionaries had drunk at the well of European racism," and this probably prevented them from doing better.[13]

Critics of Imperialism

The expansion of empire aroused sharp, even bitter, critics. A forceful attack was delivered in 1902, after the unpopular Boer War, by radical English economist J. A. Hobson (1858–1940) in his *Imperialism,* a work that influenced Lenin and others. Hobson contended that the rush to acquire colonies was due to the economic needs of unregulated capitalism, particularly the need of the rich to find outlets for their surplus capital. Yet, Hobson argued, imperial possessions did not pay off economically for the country as a whole. Only unscrupulous special-interest groups profited from them, at the expense of both the European taxpayer and the natives. Moreover, Hobson argued that the quest for empire diverted popular attention away from domestic reform and the need to reduce the great gap between rich and poor. These and similar arguments were not very persuasive, however. Most people then (and now) were sold on the idea that imperialism was economically profitable for the homeland, and a broad and genuine enthusiasm for empire developed among the masses.

Hobson and many other critics struck home, however, with their moral condemnation of whites imperiously ruling nonwhites. They rebelled against crude Social Darwinian thought. "O Evolution, what crimes are committed in thy name!" cried one foe. Another sardonically coined a new beatitude: "Blessed are the strong, for they shall prey on the weak."[14] Kipling and his kind were lampooned as racist bullies whose rule rested on brutality, racial contempt, and the Maxim machine gun. Henry Labouchère, a member of Parliament and prominent spokesman for this position, mocked Kipling's famous poem:

Pile on the Brown Man's burden!
And if ye rouse his hate,
Meet his old-fashioned reasons
With Maxims up to date,
With shells and Dum-Dum bullets
A hundred times plain
The Brown Man's loss must never
Imply the White Man's gain.[15]

Similarly, in *Heart of Darkness* Polish-born novelist Joseph Conrad (1857–1924) castigated the "pure selfishness" of Europeans in "civilizing" Africa; the main character, once a liberal scholar, turns into a savage brute.

Critics charged Europeans with applying a degrading double standard and failing to live up to their own noble ideals. At home Europeans had won or were winning representative government, individual liberties, and a certain equality of opportunity. In their empires, Europeans imposed military dictatorships on Africans and Asians; forced them to work involuntarily, almost like slaves; and discriminated against them shamelessly. Only by renouncing imperialism, its critics insisted, and giving captive peoples the freedoms Western society had struggled for since the French Revolution would Europeans be worthy of their traditions. Europeans who denounced the imperialist tide provided colonial peoples with a Western ideology of liberation.

 ## RESPONSES TO WESTERN IMPERIALISM

To peoples in Africa and Asia, Western expansion represented a profoundly disruptive assault. Everywhere it threatened traditional ruling classes, traditional economies, and traditional ways of life. Christian missionaries and European secular ideologies challenged established beliefs and values. Non-Western peoples experienced a crisis of identity, one made all the more painful by the power and arrogance of the white intruders.

The initial response of African and Asian rulers was to try driving the unwelcome foreigners away. This was the case in China, Japan, and the upper Sudan, as we have seen. Violent antiforeign reactions exploded elsewhere again and again, but the superior military technology of the industrialized West almost invariably prevailed. Beaten in battle, many Africans and Asians concentrated on preserving their cultural traditions at all costs. Others found themselves forced to reconsider their initial hostility. Some (such as Ismail of Egypt) concluded that the West was indeed superior in some ways and that it was therefore necessary to reform their societies and copy European achievements. Thus it is possible to think of responses to the Western impact as a spectrum, with "traditionalists" at one end, "westernizers" or "modernizers" at the other, and many shades of opinion in between. Both before and after European domination, the struggle among these groups was often intense. With time, however, the modernizers tended to gain the upper hand.

When the power of both the traditionalists and the modernizers was thoroughly shattered by superior force, the great majority of Asians and Africans accepted imperial rule. Political participation in non-Western lands was historically limited to small elites, and the masses were used to doing what their rulers told them. In these circumstances Europeans, clothed in power and convinced of their righteousness, governed smoothly and effectively. They received considerable support from both traditionalists (local chiefs, landowners, religious leaders) and modernizers (Western-educated professional classes and civil servants).

Nevertheless, imperial rule was in many ways an imposing edifice built on sand. Support for European rule among the conforming and accepting millions was shallow and weak. Thus the conforming masses followed with greater or lesser enthusiasm a few determined personalities who came to oppose the Europeans. Such leaders always arose, both when Europeans ruled directly and when they manipulated native governments, for at least two basic reasons.

First, the nonconformists—the eventual anti-imperialist leaders—developed a burning desire for human dignity. They came to feel that such dignity was incompatible with foreign rule, with its smirks and smiles, its paternalism and condescension. Second, potential leaders found in the Western world the ideologies and justification for their protest. They discovered liberalism, with its credo of civil liberty and political self-determination. They echoed the demands of anti-imperialists in Europe and America that the West live up to its own ideals. Above all, they found themselves attracted to modern nationalism, which asserted that every people had the right to control its own destiny. After 1917 anti-imperialist revolt would find another weapon in Lenin's version of Marxian socialism. Thus the anti-imperialist search for dignity drew strength from Western culture, as is apparent in the development of three major Asian countries—India, Japan, and China.

Empire in India

India was the jewel of the British Empire, and no colonial area experienced a more profound British impact. Unlike Japan and China, which maintained a real or precarious independence, and unlike African territories, which were annexed by Europeans only at the end of the nineteenth century, India was ruled more or less absolutely by Britain for a very long time.

Arriving in India on the heels of the Portuguese in the seventeenth century, the British East India Company had conquered the last independent native state by 1848. The last "traditional" response to European rule—the attempt by the established ruling classes to drive the white man out by military force—was broken in India in 1857 and 1858. Those were the years of the Great Rebellion (which the British called a "mutiny"), when an insurrection by Muslim and Hindu mercenaries in the British army spread throughout northern and central India before it was finally crushed, primarily by loyal native troops from southern India. Thereafter Britain ruled India directly. India illustrates, therefore, for better and for worse, what generations of European domination might produce.

After 1858 India was ruled by the British Parliament in London and administered by a tiny, all-white civil service in India. In 1900 this elite consisted of fewer than 3,500 top officials, for a population of 300 million. The white elite, backed by white officers and native troops, was competent and generally well-disposed toward the welfare of the Indian peasant masses. Yet it practiced strict job discrimination and social segregation, and most of its members quite frankly considered the jumble of Indian peoples and castes to be racially inferior. As Lord Kitchener, one of the most distinguished top military commanders in India, stated:

It is this consciousness of the inherent superiority of the European which has won for us India. However well educated and clever a native may be, and however brave he may prove himself, I believe that no rank we can bestow on him would cause him to be considered an equal of the British officer.[16]

When, for example, the British Parliament in 1883 was considering a major bill to allow Indian judges to try white Europeans in India, the British community rose in protest and defeated the measure. The idea of being judged by Indians was inconceivable to the Europeans, for it was clear to them that the empire in India rested squarely on racial inequality.

In spite of (or perhaps even because of) their strong feelings of racial and cultural superiority, the British acted energetically and introduced many desirable changes to India. Realizing that they needed well-educated Indians to serve as skilled subordinates in the government and army, the British established a modern system of progressive secondary education in which all instruction was in English. Thus through education and

Imperial Complexities in India   Britain permitted many native princes to continue their rule, if they accepted British domination. This photo shows a road-building project designed to facilitate famine relief in a southern native state. Officials of the local Muslim prince and their British "advisers" watch over workers drawn from the Hindu majority. *(Nizam's Good Works Project-Famine Relief: Road Building, Aurangabad 1895–1902, from Judith Mara Gutman,* Through Indian Eyes. *Courtesy, Private Collection)*

government service, the British offered some Indians excellent opportunities for both economic and social advancement. High-caste Hindus, particularly quick to respond, emerged as skillful intermediaries between the British rulers and the Indian people, and soon they formed a new elite profoundly influenced by Western thought and culture.

This new bureaucratic elite played a crucial role in modern economic development, which was a second result of British rule. Irrigation projects for agriculture, the world's third-largest railroad network for good communications, and large tea and jute plantations geared to the world economy were all developed. Unfortunately, the lot of the Indian masses improved little, for the increase in production was eaten up by population increase.

Finally, with a well-educated, English-speaking Indian bureaucracy and modern communications, the British created a unified, powerful state. They placed under the same general system of law and administration the different Hindu and Muslim peoples and the vanquished kingdoms of the entire subcontinent—groups that had fought each other for centuries during the Middle Ages and had been repeatedly conquered by

Muslim and Mongol invaders. It was as if Europe, with its many states and varieties of Christianity, had been conquered and united in a single great empire.

In spite of these achievements, the decisive reaction to European rule was the rise of nationalism among the Indian elite. No matter how anglicized and necessary a member of the educated classes became, he or she could never become the white ruler's equal. The top jobs, the best clubs, the modern hotels, and even certain railroad compartments were sealed off to brown-skinned men and women. The peasant masses might accept such inequality as the latest version of age-old oppression, but the well-educated, English-speaking elite eventually could not. For the elite, racial discrimination meant not only injured pride but also bitter injustice. It flagrantly contradicted those cherished Western concepts of human rights and equality. Moreover, it was based on dictatorship, no matter how benign.

By 1885, when educated Indians came together to found the predominately Hindu Indian National Congress, demands were increasing for the equality and self-government Britain enjoyed and had already granted white-settler colonies, such as Canada and Australia. By 1907, emboldened in part by Japan's success (see the next section), the radicals in the Indian National Congress were calling for complete independence. Even the moderates were demanding home rule for India through an elected parliament. Although there were sharp divisions between Hindus and Muslims, Indians were finding an answer to the foreign challenge. The common heritage of British rule and Western ideals, along with the reform and revitalization of the Hindu religion, had created a genuine movement for national independence.

The Example of Japan

When Commodore Matthew Perry arrived in Japan in 1853 with his crude but effective gunboat diplomacy, Japan was a complex feudal society. At the top stood a figurehead emperor; but for more than two hundred years, real power had been in the hands of a hereditary military governor, the *shogun*. With the help of a warrior nobility known as *samurai*, the shogun governed a country of hard-working, productive peasants and city dwellers. Often poor and restless, the intensely proud samurai were humiliated by the sudden American intrusion and the unequal treaties with Western countries.

When foreign diplomats and merchants began to settle in Yokohama, radical samurai reacted with a wave of antiforeign terrorism and antigovernment assassinations between 1858 and 1863. The imperialist response was swift and unambiguous. An allied fleet of American, British, Dutch, and French warships demolished key forts, further weakening the power and prestige of the shogun's government. Then in 1867, a coalition led by patriotic samurai seized control of the government with hardly any bloodshed and restored the political power of the emperor. This was the Meiji Restoration, a great turning point in Japanese development.

The immediate, all-important goal of the new government was to meet the foreign threat. The battle cry of the Meiji reformers was "Enrich the state and strengthen the armed forces." Yet how were these tasks to be done? In an about-face that was one of history's most remarkable chapters, the young but well-trained, idealistic but flexible leaders of Meiji Japan dropped their antiforeign attacks. Convinced that Western civilization was indeed superior in its military and industrial aspects, they initiated from above a series of measures to reform Japan along modern lines. They were convinced that "Japan must be reborn with America its mother and France its father."[17] In the broadest sense, the Meiji leaders tried to harness the power inherent in Europe's dual revolution in order to protect their country and catch up with the West.

In 1871 the new leaders abolished the old feudal structure of aristocratic, decentralized government and formed a strong unified state. Following the example of the French Revolution, they dismantled the four-class legal system and declared social equality. They decreed freedom of movement in a country where traveling abroad had been a most serious crime. They created a free, competitive, government-stimulated economy. Japan began to build railroads and modern factories. Thus the new generation adopted many principles of a free, liberal society, and, as in Europe, such freedom resulted in a tremendously creative release of human energy.

Yet the overriding concern of Japan's political leadership was always a powerful state, and to achieve this, more than liberalism was borrowed from the West. A powerful modern navy was created, and the army was completely reorganized along French and German lines, with three-year military service for all males and a professional officer corps. (See the feature "Listening to the Past: A Japanese Plan for a Modern Army" on pages 888–889.) This army of draftees effectively put down disturbances in the countryside, and in 1877 it was used to crush a major rebellion by feudal elements protesting the loss of their privileges. Japan also borrowed rapidly and adapted skillfully the West's science and modern technology, particularly in industry, medicine, and education. Many Japanese were encouraged to study abroad, and the government paid large salaries to attract foreign experts. These experts were always carefully controlled, however, and replaced by trained Japanese as soon as possible.

By 1890, when the new state was firmly established, the wholesale borrowing of the early restoration had given way to more selective emphasis on those things foreign that were in keeping with Japanese tradition. Following the model of the German Empire, Japan established an authoritarian constitution and rejected democracy. The power of the emperor and his ministers was vast; that of the legislature, limited.

Japan successfully copied the imperialism of Western society. Expansion not only proved that Japan was strong; it also cemented the nation together in a great mission. Having "opened" Korea with the gunboat diplomacy of imperialism in 1876, Japan decisively defeated China in a war over Korea in 1894 to 1895 and took Formosa (modern-day Taiwan). In the next years, Japan competed aggressively with the leading European powers for influence and territory in China, particularly Manchuria. There Japanese and Russian imperialism met and collided. In 1904 Japan attacked Russia without warning, and after a bloody war, Japan emerged with a valuable foothold in China, Russia's former protectorate over Port Arthur (see Map 26.3). By 1910, with the annexation of Korea, Japan had become a major imperialist power, continually expanding its influence in China in spite of sharp protests from its distant Pacific neighbor, the United States.

Japan became the first non-Western country to use an ancient love of country to transform itself and thereby meet the many-sided challenge of Western expansion. Moreover, Japan demonstrated convincingly that a modern Asian nation could defeat and humble a great Western power. Many Chinese nationalists were fascinated by Japan's achievement. A group of patriots in French-ruled southern Vietnam sent Vietnamese students to Japan to learn the island empire's secret of success. Japan provided patriots throughout Asia and Africa with an inspiring example of national recovery and liberation.

Japanese Industrialization   The famous Tomioka silk-reeling factory pioneered with mass-production techniques and women factory workers in the 1870s. The combination of European technology and native dress seen here symbolizes Japan's successful integration of Western practices into the traditional culture of its society. *(Laurie Platt Winfrey, Inc.)*

The Empress Dowager Tzu Hsi (1835–1908) drew on conservative forces, like the court eunuchs surrounding her here, to maintain her power. Three years after her death in 1908, a revolution broke out and forced the last Chinese emperor, a boy of six, to abdicate. *(Freer Gallery of Art and Arthur M. Sackler Gallery Archives, Smithsonian Institution. Photographer: Hsun-ling. Negative no. 261)*

Toward Revolution in China

In 1860 the two-hundred-year-old Manchu Dynasty in China appeared on the verge of collapse. Efforts to repel foreigners had failed, and rebellion and chaos wracked the country. Yet the government drew on its traditional strengths and made a surprising comeback that lasted more than thirty years.

Two factors were crucial in this reversal. First, the traditional ruling groups temporarily produced new and effective leadership. Loyal scholar-statesmen and generals quelled disturbances such as the great Tai Ping rebellion. The empress dowager Tzu Hsi, a truly remarkable woman, governed in the name of her young son and combined shrewd insight with vigorous action to revitalize the bureaucracy.

Second, destructive foreign aggression lessened, for the Europeans had obtained their primary goal of commercial and diplomatic relations. Indeed, some Europeans contributed to the dynasty's recovery. A talented Irishman effectively reorganized China's customs office and increased the government tax receipts, while a sympathetic American diplomat represented China in foreign lands and helped strengthen the central government. Such efforts dovetailed with the dynasty's efforts to adopt some aspects of Western government and technology while maintaining traditional Chinese values and beliefs.

The parallel movement toward domestic reform and limited cooperation with the West collapsed under the blows of Japanese imperialism. The Sino-Japanese War of 1894 to 1895 and the subsequent harsh peace treaty revealed China's helplessness in the face of aggression, triggering a rush for foreign concessions and protectorates in China. At the high point of this rush in 1898, it appeared that the European powers might actually divide China among themselves, as they had recently divided Africa. Probably only the jealousy each nation felt toward its imperialist competitors saved China from partition, although the U.S. Open Door policy, which opposed formal annexation of Chinese territory, may have helped tip the balance. In any event, the tempo of foreign encroachment greatly accelerated after 1894.

So, too, did the intensity and radicalism of the Chinese reaction. Like the leaders of the Meiji Restoration, some modernizers saw salvation in Western institutions.

In 1898 the government launched a desperate "hundred days of reform" in an attempt to meet the foreign challenge. More radical reformers, such as the revolutionary Sun Yat-sen (1866–1925), who came from the peasantry and was educated in Hawaii by Christian missionaries, sought to overthrow the dynasty altogether and establish a republic.

On the other side, some traditionalists turned back toward ancient practices, political conservatism, and fanatical hatred of the "foreign devils." "Protect the country, destroy the foreigner" was their simple motto. Such conservative, antiforeign patriots had often clashed with foreign missionaries, whom they charged with undermining reverence for ancestors and thereby threatening the Chinese family and the entire society. In the agony of defeat and unwanted reforms, secret societies such as the Boxers rebelled. In northeastern China, more than two hundred foreign missionaries and several thousand Chinese Christians were killed. Once again the imperialist response was swift and harsh. Peking was occupied and plundered by foreign armies. A heavy indemnity was imposed.

The years after the Boxer Rebellion (1900–1903) were ever more troubled. Anarchy and foreign influence spread as the power and prestige of the Manchu Dynasty declined still further. Antiforeign, antigovernment revolutionary groups agitated and plotted. Finally in 1912, a spontaneous uprising toppled the Manchu Dynasty. After thousands of years of emperors and empires, a loose coalition of revolutionaries proclaimed a Western-style republic and called for an elected parliament. The transformation of China under the impact of expanding Western society entered a new phase, and the end was not in sight.

SUMMARY

In the nineteenth century, the industrializing West entered the third and most dynamic phase of its centuries-old expansion into non-Western lands. In so doing, Western nations profitably subordinated those lands to their economic interests, sent forth millions of emigrants, and established political influence in Asia and vast political empires in Africa. The reasons for this culminating surge were many, but the economic thrust of robust industrial capitalism, an ever-growing lead in technology, and the competitive pressures of European nationalism were particularly important.

Western expansion had far-reaching consequences. For the first time in human history, the world became in many ways a single unit. Moreover, European expansion diffused the ideas and techniques of a highly developed civilization. Yet the West relied on force to conquer and rule, and it treated non-Western peoples as racial inferiors. Thus non-Western elites, often armed with Western doctrines, gradually responded to the Western challenge. They launched a national, anti-imperialist struggle for dignity, genuine independence, and modernization. This struggle would emerge as a central drama of world history after the great European civil war of 1914 to 1918, which reduced the West's technological advantage and shattered its self-confidence and complacent moral superiority.

NOTES

1. Quoted in A. Waley, *The Opium War Through Chinese Eyes* (New York: Macmillan, 1958), p. 29.
2. Quoted in J. W. Hall, *Japan, from Prehistory to Modern Times* (New York: Delacorte Press, 1970), p. 250.
3. Quoted in R. Hallett, *Africa to 1875* (Ann Arbor: University of Michigan Press, 1970), p. 109.
4. Quoted in Earl of Cromer, *Modern Egypt* (London, 1911), p. 48.
5. Quoted in T. Blegen, *Norwegian Migration to America,* vol. 2 (Northfield, Minn.: Norwegian-American Historical Association, 1940), p. 468.
6. Quoted in I. Howe, *World of Our Fathers* (New York: Harcourt Brace Jovanovich, 1976), p. 25.
7. Quoted in C. A. Price, *The Great White Walls Are Built: Restrictive Immigration to North America and Australia, 1836–1888* (Canberra: Australian National University Press, 1974), p. 175.
8. Quoted in W. L. Langer, *European Alliances and Alignments, 1871–1890* (New York: Vintage Books, 1931), p. 290.
9. Quoted in J. Ellis, *The Social History of the Machine Gun* (New York: Pantheon Books, 1975), pp. 86, 101.
10. Quoted in G. H. Nadel and P. Curtis, eds., *Imperialism and Colonialism* (New York: Macmillan, 1964), p. 94.
11. Quoted in W. L. Langer, *The Diplomacy of Imperialism,* 2d ed. (New York: Alfred A. Knopf, 1951), pp. 86, 88.
12. Rudyard Kipling, *The Five Nations* (London, 1903).
13. E. H. Berman, "African Responses to Christian Mission Education," *African Studies Review* 17 (1974): 530.
14. Quoted in Langer, *The Diplomacy of Imperialism,* p. 88.
15. Quoted in Ellis, *The Social History of the Machine Gun,* pp. 99–100.
16. Quoted in K. M. Panikkar, *Asia and Western Dominance: A Survey of the Vasco da Gama Epoch of Asian History* (London: George Allen & Unwin, 1959), p. 116.
17. Quoted in Hall, *Japan,* p. 289.

SUGGESTED READING

General surveys of European expansion in a broad perspective include R. Betts, *Europe Overseas* (1968); A. Thornton, *Imperialism in the Twentieth Century* (1977); T. Smith, *The Patterns of Imperialism* (1981); and W. Woodruff, *Impact of Western Man* (1967), which has an extensive bibliography. D. K. Fieldhouse has written two fine surveys, *Economics and Empire, 1830–1914* (1970) and *Colonialism, 1870–1945* (1981). J. A. Hobson's classic *Imperialism* (1902) is readily available, and the Marxist-Leninist case is effectively presented in V. G. Kieran, *Marxism and Imperialism* (1975). Among the growing number of cultural studies probing the minds of imperialists and non-Europeans, E. Said, *Orientalism* (1978), is an influential and controversial interpretation, and B. Cohn, *Colonialism and Its Form of Knowledge: The British in India* (1966), is a culminating work by a leading anthropologist.

Britain's leading position in European imperialism is examined in a lively way by B. Porter, *The Lion's Share* (1976); P. Cain and A. Hopkins, *British Imperialism: Innovation and Expansion, 1688–1914* (1993); and J. Morris, *Pax Britannica* (1968). P. Marshall, ed., *Cambridge Illustrated History of the British Empire* (1996), and D. Judd, *The Victorian Empire* (1970), are stunning pictorial histories. G. Stocking, *Victorian Anthropology* (1987), is a brilliant analysis of the cultural and racial implications of Western expansion. R. Robinson and J. Gallagher, *Africa and the Victorians: The Climax of Imperialism* (1961), is an influential interpretation. R. Aldrich, *Greater France: A History of French Overseas Expansion* (1996), and W. Baumgart, *Imperialism: The Idea and Reality of British and French Colonial Expansion* (1982), are well-balanced studies. H. Brunschwig, *French Colonialism, 1871–1914* (1966), is a classic short study. A. Moorehead, *The White Nile* (1971), tells the fascinating story of the European exploration of the mysterious Upper Nile. R. Rotberg, *The Founder: Cecil Rhodes and the Pursuit of Power* (1988), examines the imperialist's mind and times with great skill, and B. Roberts, *Cecil Rhodes: Flawed Colossus* (1987), is engaging and entertaining. A Blunt, *Travel, Gender, and Imperialism: Mary Kingsley and West Africa* (1994), analyzes a complicated woman whose travels made her into a powerful critic of British expansion. Volumes 5 and 6 of K. Latourette, *History of the Expansion of Christianity,* 7 vols. (1937–1945), examine the powerful impulse for missionary work in non-European areas. D. Headrick looks at the diffusion of Western technology in *The Tentacles of Progress: Technology Transfer in the Age of Imperialism, 1850–1940* (1988), and P. Curtin, *Death by Migration: Europe's Encounter with the Tropical World in the Nineteenth Century* (1989), ably charts the medical revolution in the tropics. C. Erikson, *Emigration from Europe, 1815–1914* (1976), R. Vecoli and S. Sinke, eds., *A Century of European Migrations, 1830–1930* (1991), and L. Moch, *Moving Europeans: Migration in Europe Since 1650* (1993), are valuable general studies.

Howe and Blegen, cited in the Notes, provide dramatic accounts of Jewish and Norwegian migration to the United States. Most other migrant groups have also found their historians: M. Walker, *Germany and the Emigration, 1816–1885* (1964), and W. Adams, *Ireland and Irish Emigration to the New World* (reissued 1967), are outstanding. Ellis's well-illustrated study of the machine gun is fascinating, as is Price on the restriction of Asian migration to Australia. Both works are cited in the Notes.

E. Wolf, *Europe and the People Without History* (1982), considers, with skill and compassion, the impact of imperialism on non-Western peoples. Two classic studies on personal relations between European rulers and non-European subjects are D. Mannoni, *Prospero and Caliban: The Psychology of Colonialization* (1964); and F. Fanon, *Wretched of the Earth* (1965), a bitter attack on white racism by a black psychologist active in the Algerian revolution. B. Smith, *European Vision and the South Pacific* (1988), is an original and influential work combining art history and intellectual development. V. Ware, *Beyond the Pale: White Women, Racism and History* (1992), examines the complex role of European women in imperialism. Novels also bring the psychological and human dimensions of imperialism alive. H. Rider Haggard, *King Solomon's Mines,* portrays the powerful appeal of adventure in exotic lands; Rudyard Kipling, the greatest writer of European expansion, is at his stirring best in *Kim* and *Soldiers Three.* Joseph Conrad unforgettably probes European motives in *Heart of Darkness,* whereas André Gide, *The Immoralist,* closely examines European moral corruption in North Africa. William Boyd, *An Ice-Cream War,* a good story of British and Germans fighting each other in Africa during the First World War, is a favorite with students.

P. Ebrey, *The Cambridge Illustrated History of China* (1996), is a lively and beautiful work by a leading specialist. J. Spence, *The Search for Modern China* (1990), is also recommended. I. Hsü, *The Rise of Modern China,* 5th ed. (1995), is a fine history with many suggestions for further reading. E. Reischauer's topical survey, *Japan: The Story of a Nation* (1981), is recommended, as are T. Huber, *The Revolutionary Origins of Modern Japan* (1981); and Y. Fukuzawa, *Autobiography* (1966), the account of a leading intellectual who saw the birth of modern Japan.

G. Perry, *The Middle East: Fourteen Islamic Centuries* (1983), concisely surveys nineteenth-century developments. B. Lewis, *The Middle East and the West* (1963), is a penetrating analysis of the impact of Western ideas on Middle Eastern thought. P. Curtin et al., *African History: From Earliest Times to Independence,* 2d ed. (1995), and R. July, *A History of the African People,* 4th ed. (1992), contain excellent brief introductions to Africa in the age of imperialism. J. D. Fage, *A History of Africa,* 3d ed. (1995), is also recommended. A classic study of Western expansion from an Indian viewpoint is Panikkar's volume mentioned in the Notes. S. Wolpert, *A New History of India,* 5th ed. (1997), incorporates recent scholarship in a wide-ranging study that is highly recommended.

LISTENING TO THE
PAST

A Japanese Plan for a Modern Army

Japan responded to the challenge posed by the imperialist West by adapting the methods and technologies of the West, and Yamagata Aritomo (1838–1922) contributed significantly to that approach and its successes. Born into the military nobility known as samurai, Yamagata joined in the movement to restore the power of the emperor. To him fell the task of strengthening the armed forces. He traveled in Europe for about a year and a half, studying Europe's armies and navies. On his return in 1872, he wrote the memorandum reprinted here, "Opinion on Military Affairs and Conscription." The next year, he helped overturn traditional Japanese society by writing a law calling for a Japanese army drafted from the whole male population, on the Western pattern. No longer would fighting be the province of samurai alone.

A military force is required to defend the country and protect its people. Previous laws of this country inculcated in the minds of the samurai these basic functions, and there was no separation between the civilian and military affairs. Nowadays civilian officials and military officials have separate functions, and the practice of having the samurai serve both functions has been abandoned. It is now necessary to select and train those who can serve the military functions, and herein lies the change in our military system. . . .

The status of our armed forces today is as follows: We have the so-called Imperial Guards whose functions are nothing more than to protect the sacred person of His Majesty and to guard the Imperial Palace. We have altogether more than twenty battalions manning the four military garrisons who are deployed to maintain domestic tranquility, and are not equipped to fight against any foreign threat. As to our navy, we have a few battleships yet to be completed. How can they be sufficient to counteract foreign threats? . . .

The first concern of the Ministry of Military Affairs is to set up a system to defend our homeland. For this purpose two categories of soldiers are required: a standing army and those on the reserve list. The number of troops differ from country to country. Of the major countries, Russia maintains the largest number of troops and the United States the smallest. The reason for this discrepancy comes from the fact that the governmental system differs from one country to another. Consequently the regulations governing each of the countries also differ. The Netherlands and Belgium are among the smallest countries, but they are located between large countries, and in order to avoid contempt and scorn from their neighbors, they diligently go about the business of defending their countries. Even though one of these countries has a total area not exceeding one-third of the area of our country, it maintains a standing army numbering not less than forty to fifty thousand. . . .

. . . The creation of a standing army for our country is a task which cannot be delayed. It is recommended that a certain number of strong and courageous young men be selected from each of the prefectures in accordance with the size of the prefectures, and that such young men be trained in the Western-type military science and placed under rigorous drills, so that they may be deployed as occasion demands.

The so-called reservists do not normally remain within the military barracks. During peacetime they remain in their homes, and in an emergency they are called to service. All of the countries in Europe have reservists, and amongst them Prussia has most of them. There is not a single able-bodied man in Prussia who is not trained in military affairs. Recently Prussia and France fought each other and the former won handily. . . .

It is recommended that our country adopt a system under which any able-bodied man twenty years of age be drafted into military service, unless his absence from home will create undue hardship for his family. There shall be no distinction made between the common man and those who are of the samurai class. They shall all be formed into ranks, and after completion of a period of service, they shall be returned to their homes. In this way every man will become a soldier, and not a single region in the country will be without defense. Thus our defense will become complete.

The second concern of the Ministry is coastal defense. This includes building of warships and constructing coastal batteries. Actually, battleships are movable batteries. Our country has thousands of miles of coastline, and any mobile corner of our country can become the advance post of our enemy. . . .

The third concern of the Military is to create resources for the navy and the army. There are three items under consideration, namely military academies, a bureau of military supplies, and a bureau of munitions depots. It is not difficult to have one million soldiers in a short time, but it is difficult to gain one good officer during the same span of time. Military academies are intended to train officers for these two services. If we pay little attention to this need today, we shall not be able to have the services of capable officers for another day. Therefore, without delay military academies must be created and be allowed to prosper. . . . The bureau of military supplies shall be in charge of procuring military provisions and manufacturing weapons of war for the two services. The bureau of munitions depots shall store such provisions and munitions. If we lack military provisions and weapons and our munitions depots are empty, what good will the million soldiers in the army or thousands of warships do? . . .

Some people may argue that while they are aware of the urgency in the need for the Ministry of Military Affairs, they cannot permit the entire national resources to be committed to the need of one ministry alone. They further aver that from the larger perspective of the imperial government, there are so many other projects covering a wide range of things which require governmental attention. . . . This argument fails to discern the fundamental issues. The recommendations herein presented by the Ministry of Military Affairs in no way asks for the stoppage of all governmental activities or for the monopolization of all government revenues. But in a national emergency, a new set of priorities must be established. Those of us who are given the task of governing must learn from the past, discern the present, and weigh all matters carefully. . . .

Those of us who govern must first of all discern the conditions prevailing in the world, set up priorities and take appropriate measures. In our opinion Russia has been acting very arrogantly. Previously, contrary to the provisions of the Treaty of Sevastopol, she placed her warships in the Black Sea. Southward, she has shown her aggressive intent to-

❖ The new Japanese army, with Western uniforms, ca 1870. (*Tsuneo Tamba Collection, Yokohama, Japan/Laurie Platt Winfrey, Inc.*)

ward Muslim countries and toward India. Westward, she has crossed the borders of Manchuria and has been navigating the Amur River. Her intents being thus, it is inevitable that she will move eastward sooner or later by sending troops to Hokkaido, and then taking advantage of the seasonal wind move to the warmer areas.

At a time like this it is very clear where the priority of this country must lie. We must now have a well-trained standing army supplemented by a large number of reservists. We must build warships and construct batteries. We must train officers and soldiers. We must manufacture and store weapons and ammunitions. The nation may consider that it cannot bear the expenses. However, even if we wish to ignore it, this important matter cannot disappear from us. Even if we prefer to enter into this type of defense undertaking, we cannot do without our defense for a single day.

Questions for Analysis

1. What aspects of military modernization are highlighted here? What goals was Aritomo trying to achieve with each proposal?

2. How does Aritomo use the examples of European countries to reach conclusions?

3. How does Aritomo anticipate criticism and explain the need for prompt action?

Source: David John Lu, *Japan: A Documentary History* (Armonk, N.Y.: M. E. Sharpe, 1997), pp. 315–318. Excerpted with permission.

27

The Great Break:
War and Revolution

❖
John Singer Sargent's
World War I painting
*Gassed. (By courtesy of the
Trustees of the Imperial
War Museum)*

In the summer of 1914, the nations of Europe went willingly to war. They believed they had no other choice. Moreover, both peoples and governments confidently expected a short war leading to a decisive victory. Such a war, they believed, would "clear the air," and European society would be able to go on as before.

These expectations were almost totally mistaken. The First World War was long, indecisive, and tremendously destructive. To the shell-shocked generation of survivors, it was known simply as the Great War: the war of unprecedented scope and intensity. From today's perspective, it is clear that the First World War marked a great break in the course of Western historical development since the French and Industrial Revolutions. A noted British political scientist has gone so far as to say that even in victorious and relatively fortunate Great Britain, the First World War was *the* great turning point in government and society, "as in everything else in modern British history. . . . There's a much greater difference between the Britain of 1914 and, say, 1920, than between the Britain of 1920 and today."[1] This strong statement contains a great amount of truth, for all of Europe as well as for Britain.

- What caused the Great War?
- How did the war lead to revolution and the fall of empires?
- How and why did war and revolution have such enormous and destructive consequences?
- How did the years of trauma and bloodshed form elements of today's world, many of which people now accept and even cherish?

These are the questions this chapter will address and try to answer.

 THE FIRST WORLD WAR

The First World War was so long and destructive because it involved all the Great Powers and because it quickly degenerated into a senseless military stalemate. Like evenly matched boxers in a championship bout, the two sides tried to wear each other down. But there was no referee to call a draw, only the blind hammering of a life-or-death struggle. What were the roots of this terrible ordeal?

The Bismarckian System of Alliances

The Franco-Prussian War and the founding of the German Empire opened a new era in international relations. France was decisively defeated in 1871 and forced to pay a large war indemnity and give up Alsace-Lorraine. In ten short years, from 1862 to 1871, Bismarck had made Prussia-Germany—traditionally the weakest of the Great Powers—the most powerful nation in Europe (see pages 830–834). Had Bismarck been a Napoleon or a Hitler, for whom no gain was ever sufficient, continued expansion would no doubt sooner or later have raised a powerful coalition against the new German Empire. Yet he was not. As Bismarck never tired of repeating after 1871, Germany was a "satisfied" power. Within Europe, Germany had no territorial ambitions and wanted only peace.

But how was peace to be preserved? Bismarck's first concern was to keep an embittered France diplomatically isolated and without military allies. His second concern was the threat to peace posed from the east, from Austria-Hungary and from Russia. Those two enormous multinational empires had many conflicting interests, particularly in the Balkans, where the Ottoman Empire—the "sick man of Europe"—was ebbing fast. There was a real threat that Germany might be dragged into a great war between the two rival empires. Bismarck's solution was a system of alliances (Figure 27.1) to restrain both Russia and Austria-Hungary, to prevent conflict between them, and to isolate a hostile France, which could never forget the loss of Alsace-Lorraine.

A first step was the creation in 1873 of the conservative Three Emperors' League, which linked the monarchs of Austria-Hungary, Germany, and Russia in an alliance against radical movements. In 1877 and 1878, when Russia's victories in a war with the Ottoman Empire threatened the balance of Austrian and Russian interests in the Balkans and the balance of British and Russian interests in the Middle East, Bismarck played the role of sincere peacemaker. At the Congress of Berlin in 1878, he saw that Austria obtained the right to "occupy and administer" the Ottoman provinces of Bosnia and Herzegovina to counterbalance Russian gains; at the same time, independent Balkan states were carved from the disintegrating Ottoman Empire.

Bismarck's balancing efforts at the congress infuriated Russian nationalists, and this led Bismarck to con-

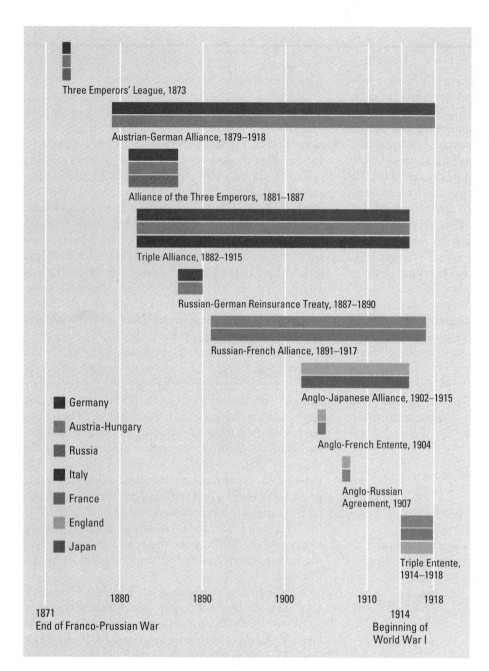

FIGURE 27.1 The Alliance System After 1871   Bismarck's subtle diplomacy maintained reasonably good relations among the eastern monarchies—Germany, Russia, and Austria-Hungary—and kept France isolated. The situation changed dramatically in 1891, when the Russian-French Alliance divided the Great Powers into two fairly equal military blocs.

clude a defensive military alliance with Austria against Russia in 1879. Motivated by tensions with France, Italy joined Germany and Austria in 1882, thereby forming what became known as the Triple Alliance.

Bismarck continued to work for peace in eastern Europe, seeking to neutralize tensions between Austria-Hungary and Russia. In 1881 he capitalized on their mutual fears and cajoled them both into a secret alliance with Germany. This Alliance of the Three Emperors lasted until 1887. It established the principle of cooperation among all three powers in any further division of the Ottoman Empire, while each state pledged friendly neutrality in case one of the three found itself at war with a fourth power (except the Ottoman Empire).

Bismarck also maintained good relations with Britain and Italy, while encouraging France in Africa but keeping France isolated in Europe. In 1887 Russia declined to renew the Alliance of the Three Emperors because of new tensions in the Balkans. Bismarck craftily substituted the Russian-German Reinsurance Treaty, by which both states promised neutrality if the other was attacked.

Bismarck's accomplishments in foreign policy after 1871 were great. For almost a generation, he maintained German leadership in international affairs, and he worked successfully for peace by managing conflicts and by restraining Austria-Hungary and Russia with defensive alliances.

The Rival Blocs

In 1890 the young, impetuous Emperor William II dismissed Bismarck, in part because of the chancellor's friendly policy toward Russia since the 1870s. William then adamantly refused to renew the Russian-German Reinsurance Treaty, in spite of Russian willingness to do so. This fateful departure in foreign affairs prompted long-isolated republican France to court absolutist Russia, offering loans, arms, and friendship. In both countries, there were enthusiastic public demonstrations, and in 1891 in St. Petersburg harbor, the autocratic Alexander III stood bareheaded on a French battleship while a band played the "Marseillaise," the hymn of the Revolution. A preliminary agreement between the two countries was reached in 1891, and in early 1894 France and Russia became military allies. This alliance (see Figure 27.1) was to remain in effect as long as the Triple Alliance of Austria, Germany, and Italy existed. As a result, continental Europe was dangerously divided into two rival blocs.

Great Britain's foreign policy became increasingly crucial. Long content with "splendid isolation" and no permanent alliances, Britain after 1891 was the only uncommitted Great Power. Could Britain afford to remain isolated, or would it feel compelled to take sides? Alliance with France or Russia certainly seemed highly unlikely. With a vast and rapidly expanding empire, Britain was often in serious conflict with these countries around the world.

Britain also squabbled with Germany: Emperor William II was a master of tactless public statements, and Britain found Germany's pursuit of greater world power after about 1897 disquieting. Nevertheless, many Germans and some Britons believed that their leaders would eventually formalize the "natural alliance" they felt already united the advanced, racially related Germanic and Anglo-Saxon peoples. Alas, such an understanding never materialized. Instead, the generally good relations that had prevailed between Prussia and Great Britain ever since the mid-eighteenth century, and certainly under Bismarck, gave way to a bitter Anglo-German rivalry.

There were several reasons for this tragic development. Commercial rivalry in world markets between Germany and Great Britain increased sharply in the 1890s. Above all, Germany's decision in 1900 to expand greatly its battle fleet posed a challenge to Britain's long-standing naval supremacy. This decision coincided with the hard-fought Boer War (1899–1902) between the British and the tiny Dutch republics of southern Africa, which had a major impact on British policy. British political leaders saw that Britain was overextended around the world. The Boer War also brought into the open widespread anti-British feeling, as editorial writers in many nations denounced this latest manifestation of British imperialism. There was even talk of Germany, Austria, France, and Russia forming a grand alliance against the bloated but insatiable British Empire. Therefore, British leaders prudently set about shoring up their exposed position with alliances and agreements.

Britain improved its often-strained relations with the United States and in 1902 concluded a formal alliance with Japan (see Figure 27.1). Britain then responded favorably to the advances of France's skillful foreign minister, Théophile Delcassé, who wanted better relations with Britain and was willing to accept British rule in Egypt in return for British support of French plans to dominate Morocco. The resulting Anglo-French Entente of 1904 settled all outstanding colonial disputes between Britain and France.

Frustrated by Britain's turn toward France in 1904 and wanting a diplomatic victory to gain greater popularity at home, Germany's leaders decided to test the strength of the entente and drive a wedge between Britain and France. First Germany threatened and bullied France into dismissing Delcassé. However, rather than accept the typical territorial payoff of imperial competition—a slice of French jungle somewhere in Africa or a port in Morocco—in return for French

German Warships Under Full Steam As these impressive ships engaged in battle exercises in 1907 suggest, Germany did succeed in building a large modern navy. But Britain was equally determined to maintain its naval superiority, and the spiraling arms race helped poison relations between the two countries. *(Bibliothèque des Arts Décoratifs/Jean-Loup Charmet)*

primacy in Morocco, the Germans foolishly rattled their swords by insisting in 1905 on an international conference on the whole Moroccan question; nor did the Germans present precise or reasonable demands. Germany's crude bullying forced France and Britain closer together, and Germany left the resulting Algeciras Conference of 1906 empty-handed and isolated (except for Austria-Hungary).

The result of the Moroccan crisis and the Algeciras Conference was something of a diplomatic revolution. Britain, France, Russia, and even the United States began to see Germany as a potential threat, a would-be intimidator that might seek to dominate all Europe. At the same time, German leaders began to see sinister plots to "encircle" Germany and block its development as a world power. In 1907 Russia, battered by its disastrous war with Japan and the revolution of 1905, agreed to settle its quarrels with Great Britain in Persia

and central Asia with the Anglo-Russian Agreement (see Figure 27.1). As a result of that agreement, Germany's blustering paranoia increased, as did Britain's thinly disguised hostility.

Germany's decision to add a large, enormously expensive fleet of big-gun battleships to its already expanding navy also heightened tensions after 1907. German nationalists, led by the extremely persuasive Admiral Alfred von Tirpitz, saw a large navy as the legitimate mark of a great world power and as a source of pride and patriotic unity. But British leaders such as David Lloyd George saw it as a detestable military challenge, which forced them to spend the "People's Budget" (see page 846) on battleships rather than social welfare. Ongoing economic rivalry also contributed to distrust and hostility between the two nations. Unscrupulous journalists and special-interest groups in both countries portrayed healthy competition in foreign trade and investment as a form of economic warfare.

Many educated shapers of public opinion and ordinary people in Britain and Germany were increasingly locked in a fateful "love-hate" relationship between the two countries. Proud nationalists in both countries simultaneously admired and feared the power and accomplishments of their nearly equal rival. In 1909 the mass-circulation London *Daily Mail* hysterically informed its readers in a series of reports that "Germany is deliberately preparing to destroy the British Empire."[2] By then Britain was psychologically, if not officially, in the Franco-Russian camp. The leading nations of Europe were divided into two hostile blocs, both ill-prepared to deal with upheaval on Europe's southeastern frontier.

The Outbreak of War

In the early years of this century, war in the Balkans was as inevitable as anything can be in human history. The reason was simple: nationalism was destroying the Ottoman Empire and threatening to break up the Austro-Hungarian Empire. The only questions were what kinds of wars would occur and where they would lead.

Greece had long before led the struggle for national liberation, winning its independence in 1832. In 1875 widespread nationalist rebellion in the Ottoman Empire had resulted in Turkish repression, Russian intervention, and Great Power tensions. Bismarck had helped resolve this crisis at the 1878 Congress of Berlin, which worked out the partial division of Turkish possessions in Europe. Austria-Hungary obtained the right to "occupy and administer" Bosnia and Herzegovina. Serbia and Romania won independence, and a part of Bulgaria won local autonomy. The Ottoman Empire retained important Balkan holdings, for Austria-Hungary and Russia each feared the other's domination of totally independent states in the area (Map 27.1).

After 1878 the siren call of imperialism lured European energies, particularly Russian energies, away from the Balkans. This diversion helped preserve the fragile balance of interests in southeastern Europe. By 1903, however, Balkan nationalism was on the rise once again. Serbia led the way, becoming openly hostile toward both Austria-Hungary and the Ottoman Empire. The Serbs, a Slavic people, looked to Slavic Russia for support of their national aspirations. To block Serbian expansion and to take advantage of Russia's weakness after the revolution of 1905, Austria in 1908 formally annexed Bosnia and Herzegovina, with their large Serbian, Croatian, and Muslim populations. The kingdom of Serbia erupted in rage but could do nothing without Russian support.

Then in 1912, in the First Balkan War, Serbia turned southward. With Greece and Bulgaria, it took Macedonia from the Ottoman Empire and then quarreled with Bulgaria over the spoils of victory—a dispute that led in 1913 to the Second Balkan War. Austria intervened in 1913 and forced Serbia to give up Albania. After centuries, nationalism had finally destroyed the Ottoman Empire in Europe (Map 27.2). This sudden but long-awaited event elated the Balkan nationalists and dismayed the leaders of multinational Austria-Hungary. The former hoped and the latter feared that Austria might be next to be broken apart.

Within this tense context, Archduke Francis Ferdinand, heir to the Austrian and Hungarian thrones, and his wife, Sophie, were assassinated by Serbian revolutionaries living in Bosnia on June 28, 1914, during a state visit to the Bosnian capital of Sarajevo. The assassins were closely connected to the ultranationalist Serbian society the Black Hand. This revolutionary group was secretly supported by members of the Serbian government and was dedicated to uniting all Serbians in a single state. Although the leaders of Austria-Hungary did not and could not know all the details of Serbia's involvement in the assassination plot, they concluded after some hesitation that Serbia had to be severely punished once and for all. After nearly a month of maneuvering, on July 23 Austria-Hungary presented Serbia with an unconditional ultimatum.

The Serbian government had just forty-eight hours in which to agree to cease all subversion in Austria and all anti-Austrian propaganda in Serbia. Moreover, a thorough investigation of all aspects of the assassination at Sarajevo was to be undertaken in Serbia by a joint commission of Serbian and Austrian officials. These demands amounted to control of the Serbian state. When Serbia replied moderately but evasively, Austria began to mobilize and then declared war on Serbia on July 28. Thus a desperate multinational Austria-Hungary deliberately chose war in a last-ditch attempt to stem the rising tide of hostile nationalism within its borders and save the existing state. The "Third Balkan War" had begun.

Of prime importance in Austria-Hungary's fateful decision was Germany's unconditional support. Emperor William II and his chancellor, Theobald von

MAP 27.1 The Balkans After the Congress of Berlin, 1878   The Ottoman Empire suffered large territorial losses but remained a power in the Balkans.

MAP 27.2 The Balkans in 1914   Ethnic boundaries did not follow political boundaries, and Serbian national aspirations threatened Austria-Hungary.

Bethmann-Hollweg, gave Austria-Hungary a "blank check" and urged aggressive measures in early July, even though they realized that war between Austria and Russia was the most probable result. They knew Russian pan-Slavs saw Russia not only as the protector but also as the eventual liberator of southern Slavs. As one pan-Slav had said much earlier, "Austria can hold her part of the Slavonian mass as long as Turkey holds hers and vice versa."[3] At the very least, a resurgent Russia could not stand by, as in the Bosnian crisis, and simply watch the Serbs be crushed. Yet Bethmann-Hollweg apparently hoped that while Russia (and therefore France) would go to war, Great Britain would remain neutral, unwilling to fight for "Russian aggression" in the distant Balkans. After all, Britain had reached only "friendly understandings" with France and Russia on

colonial questions and had no alliance with either power.

In fact, the diplomatic situation was already out of control. Military plans and timetables began to dictate policy. Russia, a vast country, would require much longer to mobilize its armies than Germany and Austria-Hungary. On July 28, as Austrian armies bombarded Belgrade, Tsar Nicholas II ordered a partial mobilization against Austria-Hungary. Almost immediately he found that this was impossible. All the complicated mobilization plans of the Russian general staff had assumed a war with both Austria and Germany: Russia could not mobilize against one without mobilizing against the other. Therefore, on July 29 Russia ordered full mobilization and in effect declared general war. For, as French general Boisdeffre had said to the agreeing

Russian tsar when the Franco-Russian military convention was being negotiated in 1892, "mobilization is a declaration of war."[4]

The same tragic subordination of political considerations to military strategy descended on Germany. The German general staff had also thought only in terms of a two-front war. The staff's plan for war—the Schlieffen plan, the work of Count Alfred von Schlieffen, chief of the German general staff from 1891 to 1906 and a professional military man—called for knocking out France first with a lightning attack through neutral Belgium before turning on Russia.

Thus on August 2, 1914, General Helmuth von Moltke, "acting under a dictate of self-preservation," demanded that Belgium permit German armies to pass through its territory. Belgium, whose neutrality had been solemnly guaranteed in 1839 by all the great states including Prussia, refused. Germany attacked. Thus Germany's terrible, politically disastrous response to a war in the Balkans was an all-out invasion of France by way of the plains of neutral Belgium on August 3. In the face of this act of aggression, Great Britain joined France and declared war on Germany the following day. The First World War had begun.

Nationalist Opposition in the Balkans   This band of well-armed and determined guerrillas from northern Albania was typical of groups fighting against Ottoman rule in the Balkans. Balkan nationalists succeeded in driving the Ottoman Turks out of most of Europe, but their victory increased tensions with Austria-Hungary and among the Great Powers. *(Roger-Viollet)*

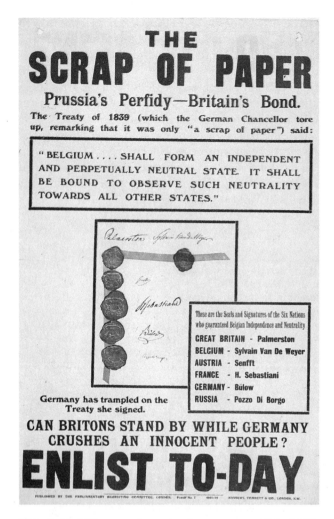

This British Poster shows the signature page of the 1839 treaty guaranteeing the neutrality of Belgium. When German armies invaded Belgium in 1914, Chancellor Bethmann-Hollweg cynically dismissed the treaty as a "scrap of paper"—a perfect line for anti-German propaganda. *(By courtesy of the Trustees of the Imperial War Museum)*

Reflections on the Origins of the War

Although few events in history have aroused such interest and controversy as the coming of the First World War, the question of immediate causes and responsibilities can be answered with considerable certainty. Austria-Hungary deliberately started the Third Balkan War. A war for the right to survive was Austria-Hungary's desperate, although understandable, response to the aggressive, yet understandable, revolutionary drive of Serbian nationalists to unify their people in a single state. Moreover, in spite of Russian intervention in the quarrel, it is clear that from the beginning of the crisis, Germany not only pushed and goaded Austria-Hungary but also was responsible for turning a little war into the Great War by means of a sledgehammer attack on Belgium and France. Why Germany was so aggressive in 1914 is less certain.

Diplomatic historians stress that German leaders lost control of the international system after Bismarck's resignation in 1890. They felt increasingly that Germany's status as a world power was declining, while that of Britain, France, Russia, and the United States was growing. Indeed, the powers of what officially became in August 1914 the Triple Entente—Great Britain, France, and Russia—were checking Germany's vague but real aspirations as well as working to strangle Austria-Hungary, Germany's only real ally. Germany's aggression in 1914 reflected the failure of all European leaders, not just those in Germany, to incorporate Bismarck's mighty empire permanently and peacefully into the international system.

Another more controversial interpretation, which has been developed by anticonservative German historians in recent years, argues that domestic conflicts and social tensions lay at the root of Germany's increasingly belligerent foreign policy from the late 1890s onward. Germany industrialized and urbanized rapidly after 1870 and established a popularly elected parliament. But German society was not democratized, and ultimate political power remained concentrated in the hands of the monarchy, the army, and the Prussian nobility. Determined to hold on to power and increasingly frightened by the rising socialist movement and in 1914 by a powerful new wave of strikes and grassroots working-class militancy, which was encouraged but never controlled by a few radical socialist intellectuals such as the fiery Rosa Luxemburg (see page 918), the German ruling class was willing to take chances. It was willing to gamble on diplomatic victory and even on war as the means of rallying the masses to its side and preserving its privileged position. Historians have also discerned similar, if less clear-cut, behavior in Great Britain, where leaders faced civil war in northern Ireland, and in Russia, where the revolution of 1905 had brought tsardom to its knees.

This stimulating debate over social tensions and domestic political factors correctly suggests that the triumph of nationalism was a crucial underlying precondition of the Great War. Nationalism was at the heart of the Balkan wars, in the form of Serbian aspirations and the grandiose pan-German versus pan-Slavic racism of some fanatics. Nationalism also drove the spiraling arms race. Broad popular commitment to "my country right or wrong" weakened groups that thought in terms of international communities and consequences. Thus the big international bankers, who were frightened by the prospect of war in July 1914, and the extreme-left socialists, who believed that the enemy was at home and not abroad, were equally out of step with national feeling. In each country, the great majority of the population enthusiastically embraced the outbreak of war in August 1914. In each country, people believed that their country had been wronged, and they rallied to defend it. Patriotic nationalism brought unity in the short run.

Nonetheless, the wealthy governing classes certainly underestimated the risk of war to themselves in 1914. They had forgotten that great wars and great social revolutions very often go hand in hand. Metternich's alliance of conservative forces in support of international peace and the social status quo had become only a distant memory.

The First Battle of the Marne

When the Germans invaded Belgium in August 1914, they and everyone else believed that the war would be short, for urban society rested on the food and raw materials of the world economy: "The boys will be home by Christmas." The Belgian army heroically defended its homeland, however, and fell back in good order to join a rapidly landed British army corps near the Franco-Belgian border. This action complicated the original Schlieffen plan of concentrating German armies on the right wing and boldly capturing Paris in a vast encircling movement. Moreover, the German left wing in Lorraine failed to retreat, thwarting the plan to suck French armies into Germany and then annihilate them. Instead, by the end of August, dead-tired German soldiers were advancing along an enormous front in the scorching summer heat. The neatly designed prewar plan to surround Paris from the north and west had been thrown into confusion.

French armies totaling 1 million, reinforced by more than 100,000 British troops, had retreated in orderly fashion before Germany's 1.5 million men in the field. Under the leadership of the steel-nerved General Joseph Joffre, the French attacked a gap in the German line at the Battle of the Marne on September 6. For three days, France threw everything into the attack. At one point, the French government desperately requisitioned all the taxis of Paris to rush reserves to the troops at the front. Finally, the Germans fell back. Paris and France had been miraculously saved.

Stalemate and Slaughter

The attempts of French and British armies to turn the German retreat into a rout were unsuccessful, however, and so were moves by both sides to outflank each other in northern France. As a result, both sides began to dig trenches to protect themselves from machine-gun fire. By November 1914, an unbroken line of trenches extended from the Belgian ports through northern France, past the fortress of Verdun, and on to the Swiss frontier.

In the face of this unexpected stalemate, slaughter on the western front began in earnest. The defenders on both sides dug in behind rows of trenches, mines, and barbed wire. For days and even weeks, ceaseless shelling by heavy artillery supposedly "softened up" the enemy in a given area (and also signaled the coming attack). Then young draftees and their junior officers went "over the top" of the trenches in frontal attacks on the enemy's line.

The cost in lives was staggering, the gains in territory minuscule. The massive French and British offensives during 1915 never gained more than 3 miles of blood-soaked earth from the enemy. In the Battle of the Somme in the summer of 1916, the British and French gained an insignificant 125 square miles at the cost of 600,000 dead or wounded, while the Germans lost 500,000 men. That same year, the unsuccessful German campaign against Verdun cost 700,000 lives on both sides. British poet Siegfried Sassoon (1886–1967) wrote of the Somme offensive, "I am staring at a sunlit picture of Hell."

Terrible 1917 saw General Robert Nivelle's French army almost destroyed in a grand spring attack at Champagne. At Passchendaele in the fall, the British traded 400,000 casualties for 50 square miles of Belgian Flanders. The hero of Erich Remarque's great novel *All Quiet on the Western Front* (1929) describes one attack:

We see men living with their skulls blown open; we see soldiers run with their two feet cut off. . . . Still the little piece of convulsed earth in which we lie is held. We have yielded no more than a few hundred yards of it as a prize to the enemy. But on every yard there lies a dead man.

Such was war on the western front.

The Tragic Absurdity of Trench Warfare　Soldiers charge across a scarred battlefield and overrun an enemy trench. The dead defender on the right will fire no more. But this is only another futile charge that will yield much blood and little land. A whole generation is being decimated by the slaughter. *(By courtesy of the Trustees of the Imperial War Museum)*

The war of the trenches shattered an entire generation of young men. Millions who could have provided political creativity and leadership after the war were forever missing. Moreover, those who lived through the slaughter were maimed, shell-shocked, embittered, and profoundly disillusioned. The young soldiers went to war believing in the world of their leaders and elders, the pre-1914 world of order, progress, and patriotism.

Then, in Remarque's words, the "first bombardment showed us our mistake, and under it the world as they had taught it to us broke in pieces." For many, the sacrifice and comradeship of the battlefield became life's crucial experience, which "soft" civilians could never understand. A chasm opened up between veterans and civilians, making the hard postwar reconstruction all the more difficult.

Otto Dix: War   Returning to Germany after the war, Dix was haunted by the horrors he had seen. This vivid expressionist masterpiece, part of a triptych painted in 1929–1932, probes the tormented memory of endless days in muddy trenches and dugouts, living with rats and lice and the constant danger of exploding shells, snipers, and all-out attack. Many who escaped death or dismemberment were mentally wounded forever by their experiences. *(Staatliche Kunstsammlungen Dresden)*

The Widening War

On the eastern front, slaughter did not degenerate into suicidal trench warfare. With the outbreak of the war, the "Russian steamroller" immediately moved into eastern Germany. Very badly damaged by the Germans under Generals Paul von Hindenburg and Erich Ludendorff at the Battles of Tannenberg and the Masurian Lakes in August and September 1914, Russia never threatened Germany again. On the Austrian front, enormous armies seesawed back and forth, suffering enormous losses. Austro-Hungarian armies were repulsed twice by Serbia in bitter fighting. But with the help of German forces, they reversed the Russian advances of 1914 and forced the Russians to retreat deep into their own territory in the eastern campaign of

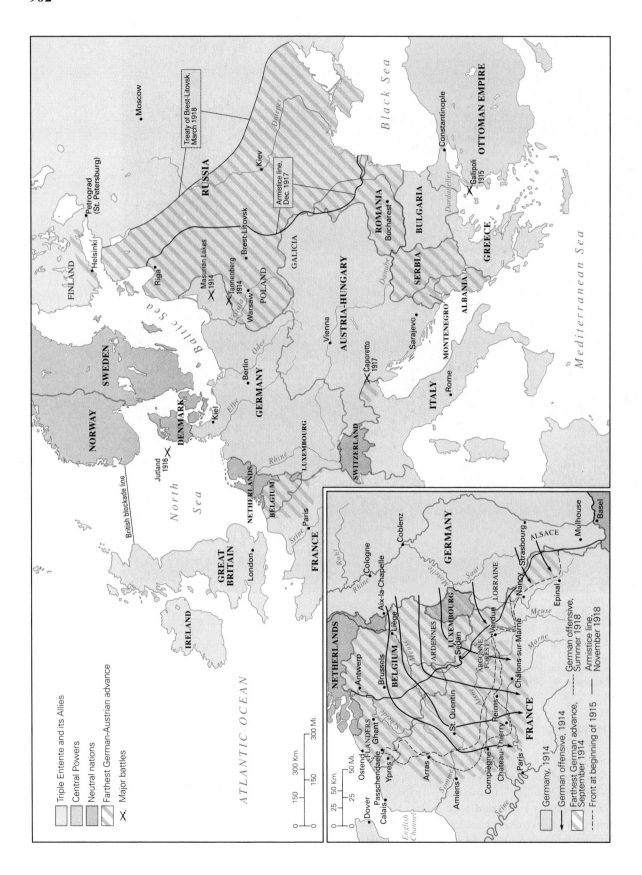

Triple Entente and its Allies
Central Powers
Neutral nations
Farthest German-Austrian advance
X Major battles

MOSCOW

FINLAND
Helsinki
Petrograd (St. Petersburg)

Treaty of Brest-Litovsk, March 1918

RUSSIA
Kiev

Armistice line, Dec. 1917

Black Sea

OTTOMAN EMPIRE
Constantinople
Gallipoli 1915
Dardanelles

ROMANIA
Bucharest

BULGARIA

SERBIA

GREECE

ALBANIA

MONTENEGRO

Riga
Masurian Lakes 1914
Tannenberg 1914
Brest-Litovsk
Vistula
Warsaw
POLAND
GALICIA

Danube

Mediterranean Sea

SWEDEN

Baltic Sea

AUSTRIA-HUNGARY
Vienna
Sarajevo

Oder

NORWAY

DENMARK
Kiel
Elbe
Berlin
GERMANY

Caporetto 1917

ITALY
Rome

Jutland 1916

North Sea

Rhine

LUXEMBOURG

SWITZERLAND

British blockade line

NETHERLANDS
BELGIUM
Paris
FRANCE
Seine

GREAT BRITAIN
London

IRELAND

ATLANTIC OCEAN

300 Mi.
150
0
300 Km.
150
0

Germany, 1914
German offensive, 1914
Farthest German advance, September 1914
Front at beginning of 1915
German offensive, Summer 1918
Armistice line, November 1918

NETHERLANDS
Antwerp
Brussels
BELGIUM
Liège
Aix-la-Chapelle
Cologne
Rhine
Coblenz
Ruhr
GERMANY
Moselle
Saar
Mulhouse
Basel
ALSACE
Strasbourg
Nancy
LORRAINE
Epinal
Meuse
Verdun
LUXEMBOURG
Sedan
ARDENNES
ARGONNE FOREST
Châlons-sur-Marne
Marne
Château-Thierry
Reims
Meuse
St. Quentin
Aisne
Compiègne
FRANCE
Paris
Seine
Amiens
Arras
Somme
Ypres
Ghent
FLANDERS
Ostend
Passchendaele
Dover
Calais
English Channel

50 Mi.
25
0
50 Km.
25
0

Indian Soldiers from the so-called warrior castes had long been a critical factor in imperial Britain's global power. These Indian troops, preparing for the Battle of the Somme in 1916, ironically appear to be out for a pleasant bicycling excursion. Dispatched to France in October 1914, most Indian soldiers were moved to western Asia in 1915 to fight against the Ottoman Empire. *(By courtesy of the Trustees of the Imperial War Museum)*

1915. A staggering 2.5 million Russians were killed, wounded, or taken prisoner that year.

These changing tides of victory and defeat brought neutral countries into the war (Map 27.3). Italy, a member of the Triple Alliance since 1882, had declared its neutrality in 1914 on the grounds that Austria had launched a war of aggression. Then in May 1915, Italy joined the Triple Entente of Great Britain, France, and Russia in return for promises of Austrian territory. Bulgaria allied with Austria and Germany, now known as the Central Powers, in September 1915 in order to settle old scores with Serbia.

MAP 27.3 The First World War in Europe The trench war on the western front was concentrated in Belgium and northern France, while the war in the east encompassed an enormous territory.

The entry of Italy and Bulgaria in 1915 was part of a general widening of the war. The Balkans, with the exception of Greece, came to be occupied by the Central Powers, and British forces were badly defeated in 1915 trying to take the Dardanelles from Turkey, Germany's ally. More successful was the entente's attempt to incite Arab nationalists against their Turkish overlords. An enigmatic British colonel, soon known to millions as Lawrence of Arabia, aroused the Arab princes to revolt in early 1917. In 1918 British armies from Egypt smashed the Ottoman Empire once and for all. In the Middle East campaign, the British drew on forces from Australia, New Zealand, and India. Contrary to German hopes, the colonial subjects of the British (and French) did not revolt but loyally supported their foreign masters. The European war extended around the globe as Great Britain, France, and Japan seized Germany's colonies.

A crucial development in the expanding conflict came in April 1917, when the United States declared war on Germany. American intervention grew out of the war at sea, sympathy for the Triple Entente, and the increasing desperation of total war. At the beginning of the war, Britain and France had established a total naval blockade to strangle the Central Powers and prevent deliveries of food and raw materials from overseas. No neutral ship was permitted to sail to Germany with any cargo. The blockade annoyed Americans, but effective propaganda about German atrocities in occupied Belgium as well as lush profits from selling war supplies to Britain and France blunted American indignation.

Moreover, in early 1915 Germany launched a counter-blockade using the murderously effective submarine, a new weapon that violated traditional niceties of fair warning under international law. In May 1915, after sinking about ninety ships in the British war zone, a German submarine sank the British passenger liner *Lusitania,* which was also carrying arms and munitions. More than 1,000 lives, among them 139 Americans, were lost. President Woodrow Wilson protested vigorously. Germany was forced to relax its submarine warfare for almost two years; the alternative was almost certain war with the United States.

Early in 1917, the German military command—confident that improved submarines could starve Britain into submission before the United States could come to its rescue—resumed unrestricted submarine warfare. Like the invasion of Belgium, this was a reckless gamble. British shipping losses reached staggering proportions, though by late 1917 naval strategists had come up with an effective response: the convoy system for safe transatlantic shipping. In the meantime, an embattled President Wilson had told a sympathetic Congress and people that the "German submarine warfare against commerce is a warfare against mankind." Thus the last uncommitted great nation, as fresh and enthusiastic as Europe had been in 1914, entered the world war in April 1917, almost three years after it began. Eventually the United States was to tip the balance in favor of the Triple Entente and its allies.

✣ THE HOME FRONT

Before looking at the last year of the Great War, let us turn our attention to the people on the home front. They were tremendously involved in the titanic struggle. War's impact on them was no less massive than on the men crouched in the trenches. (See the feature "Listening to the Past: The Experience of War" on pages 924–925.)

Mobilizing for Total War

In August 1914, most people had greeted the outbreak of hostilities enthusiastically. In every country, the masses believed that their nation was in the right and defending itself from aggression. With the exception of a few extreme left-wingers, even socialists supported the war. Tough standby plans to imprison socialist leaders and break general strikes protesting the war proved quite unnecessary in 1914. In Germany, for example, the trade unions voted not to strike, and socialists in the Reichstag voted money for war credits in order to counter the threat of Russian despotism. A German socialist volunteered for the front, explaining to fellow members of the Reichstag that "to shed one's blood for the fatherland is not difficult: it is enveloped in romantic heroism."[5] Everywhere the support of the masses and working class contributed to national unity and an energetic war effort.

By mid-October generals and politicians had begun to realize that more than patriotism would be needed to win the war, whose end was not in sight. Each country experienced a relentless, desperate demand for men and weapons. In France, for example, the generals found themselves needing 100,000 heavy artillery shells a day, as opposed to the 12,000 they had anticipated using. This enormous quantity had to come from a French steel industry that had lost three-fourths of its iron resources in the first days of the war, when Germany seized the mines of French Lorraine. Each belligerent quickly faced countless shortages, for prewar Europe had depended on foreign trade and a great international division of labor. In each country, economic life and organization had to change and change fast to keep the war machine from sputtering to a stop. And change they did.

In each country, a government of national unity began to plan and control economic and social life in order to wage "total war." Free-market capitalism was abandoned, at least "for the duration." Instead, government planning boards established priorities and decided what was to be produced and consumed. Rationing, price and wage controls, and even restrictions on workers' freedom of movement were imposed by government. Only through such regimentation could a country make the greatest possible military effort.

Thus, though there were national variations, the great nations all moved toward planned economies commanded by the established political leadership.

This revolutionary development would burn deeply into the twentieth-century consciousness. The planned economy of total war released the tremendous energies first harnessed by the French under Robespierre during the French Revolution. Total war, however, was based on tremendously productive industrial economies not confined to a single nation. The result was an effective—and therefore destructive—war effort on all sides.

Moreover, the economy of total war blurred the old distinction between soldiers on the battlefield and civilians at home. As President Wilson told Americans shortly after the United States entered the war, there were no armies in the traditional sense. Rather, "there are entire nations armed. Thus the men [and women] who remain to till the soil and man the factories are not less a part of the army than the men beneath the battle flags."[6] The war was a war of whole peoples and entire populations, and the loser would be the society that cracked first.

Finally, however awful the war was, the ability of governments to manage and control highly complicated economies strengthened the cause of socialism. With the First World War, state socialism became for the first time a realistic economic blueprint rather than a utopian program.

Germany illustrates the general trend. It also went furthest in developing a planned economy to wage total war. As soon as war began, Walter Rathenau, the talented, foresighted Jewish industrialist in charge of Germany's largest electrical company, convinced the government to set up the War Raw Materials Board to ration and distribute raw materials. Under Rathenau's direction, every useful material from foreign oil to barnyard manure was inventoried and rationed. Moreover, the board launched successful attempts to produce substitutes, such as synthetic rubber and synthetic nitrates. Without the spectacular double achievement

Waging Total War   A British war plant strains to meet the insatiable demand for trench-smashing heavy artillery shells. Quite typically, many of these defense workers are women. *(By courtesy of the Trustees of the Imperial War Museum)*

of discovering a way to "fix" nitrogen present in the air and then producing synthetic nitrates in enormous quantity to make explosives, the blockaded German war machine would have stalled in a matter of months.

Food was also rationed in accordance with physical need. Men and women doing hard manual work were given extra rations. During the last two years of the war, only children and expectant mothers received milk rations. Sometimes mistakes were made that would have been funny if they had not been tragic. In early 1915, German authorities calculated that greedy pigs were eating food that hungry people needed, and they ordered a "hog massacre," only to discover later that too few pigs remained to eat an abundant potato crop. Germany also failed to tax the war profits of private firms heavily enough. This contributed to massive deficit financing, inflation, the growth of a black market, and the eventual re-emergence of class conflict.

Following the terrible Battles of Verdun and the Somme in 1916, Chancellor Bethmann-Hollweg was driven from office in 1917 by military leaders Hindenburg and Ludendorff, who became the real rulers of Germany. They decreed the ultimate mobilization for total war. Germany, said Hindenburg, could win only "if all the treasures of our soil that agriculture and industry can produce are used exclusively for the conduct of War. . . . All other considerations must come second."[7] This goal, they believed, required that every German man, woman, and child be drafted into the service of the war. Thus in December 1916, military leaders rammed through the Reichstag the Auxiliary Service Law, which required all males between seventeen and sixty to work only at jobs considered critical to the war effort.

Although women and children were not specifically mentioned, this forced-labor law was also aimed at them. Many women already worked in war factories, mines, and steel mills, where they labored, like men, at the heaviest and most dangerous jobs. With the passage of the Auxiliary Service Law, many more women followed. Children were organized by their teachers into garbage brigades to collect every scrap of useful materials: grease strained from dishwater, coffee grounds, wastepaper, tin cans, metal door knockers, bottles, rags, hair, bones, and so forth as well as acorns, chestnuts, pine cones, and rotting leaves. Potatoes gave way to turnips, and people averaged little more than one thousand calories a day. Thus in Germany total war led to the establishment of history's first "totalitarian" society, and war production increased while some people starved to death.

Great Britain mobilized for total war less rapidly and less completely than Germany, for it could import materials from its empire and from the United States. By 1915, however, a serious shortage of shells had led to the establishment of the Ministry of Munitions under David Lloyd George. The ministry organized private industry to produce for the war, controlled profits, allocated labor, fixed wage rates, and settled labor disputes. By December 1916, when Lloyd George became prime minister, the British economy was largely planned and regulated. More than two hundred factories and 90 percent of all imports were bought and allocated directly by the state. Subsequently, even food was strictly rationed, while war production continued to soar. Great Britain had followed successfully in Germany's footsteps.

The Social Impact

The social impact of total war was no less profound than the economic impact, though again there were important national variations. The millions of men at the front and the insatiable needs of the military created a tremendous demand for workers. Jobs were available for everyone. This situation had seldom, if ever, been seen before 1914, when unemployment and poverty had been facts of urban life. This exceptional demand for labor brought about momentous changes.

One such change was greater power and prestige for labor unions. Having proved their loyalty in August 1914, labor unions became an indispensable partner of government and private industry in the planned war economy. Unions cooperated with war governments on work rules, wages, and production schedules in return for real participation in important decisions. This entry of labor leaders and unions into policy-making councils paralleled the entry of socialist leaders into the war governments.

The role of women changed dramatically. In every country, large numbers of women left home and domestic service to work in industry, transportation, and offices. By 1917 women formed fully 43 percent of the labor force in Russia. The number of women driving buses and streetcars increased tenfold in Great Britain. Moreover, women became highly visible—not only as munitions workers but as bank tellers, mail carriers, even police officers.

At first, the male-dominated unions were hostile to women moving into new occupations, believing that their presence would lower wages and change work rules. But government pressure and the principle of equal pay for equal work (at least until the end of the war) overcame these objections. Women also served as nurses and doctors at the front. In general, the war greatly expanded the range of women's activities and changed attitudes toward women. As a direct result of women's many-sided war effort, Britain, Germany, and Austria granted women the right to vote immediately after the war. Women also showed a growing spirit of independence during the war, as they started to bob their hair, shorten their skirts, and smoke in public.

War also promoted greater social equality, blurring class distinctions and lessening the gap between rich and poor. This blurring was most apparent in Great Britain, where wartime hardship was never extreme. In fact, the bottom third of the population generally lived *better* than they ever had, for the poorest gained most from the severe shortage of labor. English writer Robert Roberts recalled how his parents' tiny grocery store in the slums of Manchester thrived during the war as never before when people who had scrimped to buy bread and soup bones were able to afford fancy cakes and thick steaks. In 1924 a British government study revealed that the distribution of income had indeed shifted in favor of the poorest; only half as many families lived in severe poverty as in 1911, even though total production of goods had not increased. In continental countries, greater equality was reflected in full employment, rationing according to physical needs, and a sharing of hardships. There, too, society became more uniform and more egalitarian, in spite of some war profiteering.

Finally, death itself had no respect for traditional social distinctions. It savagely decimated the young aristocratic officers who led the charge, and it fell heavily on the mass of drafted peasants and unskilled workers who followed. Yet death often spared the aristocrats of labor, the skilled workers and foremen. Their lives were too valuable to squander at the front, for they were needed to train the newly recruited women and older unskilled men laboring valiantly in war plants at home.

Growing Political Tensions

During the first two years of war, most soldiers and civilians supported their governments. Even in Austria-Hungary—the most vulnerable of the belligerents, with its competing nationalities—loyalty to the state and monarchy remained astonishingly strong through 1916. Belief in a just cause, patriotic nationalism, the planned economy, and a sharing of burdens united peoples behind their various national leaders. Furthermore,

each government did its best to control public opinion in order to bolster morale. Newspapers, letters, and public addresses were rigorously censored. Good news was overstated; bad news was repressed or distorted.

Each government used both crude and subtle propaganda to maintain popular support. German propaganda hysterically pictured black soldiers from France's African empire raping German women, while German atrocities in Belgium and elsewhere were ceaselessly recounted and exaggerated by the French and British. Patriotic posters and slogans, slanted news, and biased editorials inflamed national hatreds and helped sustain superhuman efforts.

By the spring of 1916, however, people were beginning to crack under the strain of total war. In April 1916, Irish nationalists in Dublin tried to take advantage of this situation and rose up against British rule in their great Easter Rebellion. A week of bitter fighting passed before the rebels were crushed and their leaders executed. On May 1, 1916, several thousand demonstrators in Berlin heard the radical socialist leader Karl Liebknecht (1871–1919) shout, "Down with the government! Down with the war!" Liebkneckt was immediately arrested and imprisoned, but his daring action electrified Europe's far left. Strikes and protest marches over inadequate food began to flare up on every home front.

Soldiers' morale also began to decline. Italian troops mutinied. Numerous French units refused to fight after General Nivelle's disastrous offensive of May 1917. Only tough military justice for leaders and a tacit agreement with the troops that there would be no more grand offensives enabled the new general in chief, Henri Philippe Pétain, to restore order. A rising tide of war-weariness and defeatism also swept France's civilian population before Georges Clemenceau emerged as a ruthless and effective wartime leader in November 1917. Clemenceau (1841–1929) established a virtual dictatorship, pouncing on strikers and jailing without trial journalists and politicians who dared to suggest a compromise peace with Germany.

The strains were worse for the Central Powers. In October 1916, the chief minister of Austria was assassinated by a young socialist crying, "Down with Absolutism! We want peace!"[8] The following month, when feeble old Emperor Francis Joseph died sixty-eight years after his mother, Sophia, had pushed him onto the throne in 1848 (see page 782), a symbol of unity disappeared. In spite of absolute censorship, political dissatisfaction and conflicts among nationalities grew. In April 1917, Austria's chief minister summed up the sit-

Irish Nationalists Organized in 1913 to press for home rule in Ireland, the unofficial Irish Citizen Army was committed to complete independence from Great Britain. Shown here beneath a defiant pro-republican banner, it fought with other militant groups in the Easter Rebellion. *(Lawrence Collection, National Library of Ireland, Dublin)*

uation in the gloomiest possible terms. The country and army were exhausted. Another winter of war would bring revolution and disintegration. "If the monarchs of the Central Powers cannot make peace in the coming months," he wrote, "it will be made for them by their peoples."[9] Both Czech and Yugoslav leaders demanded autonomous democratic states for their peoples. The British blockade kept tightening; people were starving.

The strain of total war and of the Auxiliary Service Law was also evident in Germany. In the winter of 1916 to 1917, Germany's military position appeared increasingly desperate. Stalemates and losses in the west were matched by temporary Russian advances in the east: hence the military's insistence on an all-or-nothing gamble of unrestricted submarine warfare when the Triple Entente refused in December 1916 to consider peace on terms favorable to the Central Powers.

Also, the national political unity of the first two years of war was collapsing as the social conflict of prewar Germany re-emerged. A growing minority of moderate socialists in the Reichstag began to vote against war credits. With little taste for violent upheaval and civil war, they called for a compromise "peace without annexations or reparations." In July 1917, a coalition of socialists and Catholics passed a resolution in the Reichstag to that effect. Such a peace was unthinkable for conservatives and military leaders. So also was the surge in revolutionary agitation and strikes by war-weary workers that occurred in early 1917. When the bread ration was further reduced in April, more than 200,000 workers struck and demonstrated for a week in Berlin, returning to work only under the threat of prison and military discipline. Thus militaristic Germany, like its ally Austria-Hungary (and its enemy France), was beginning to crack in 1917. Yet it was Russia that collapsed first and saved the Central Powers—for a time.

 ## THE RUSSIAN REVOLUTION

The Russian Revolution of 1917 was one of modern history's most momentous events. Directly related to the growing tensions of World War I, it had a significance far beyond the wartime agonies of a single European nation. The Russian Revolution opened a new era. For some, it was Marx's socialist vision come true; for others, it was the triumph of dictatorship. To all, it presented a radically new prototype of state and society.

The Fall of Imperial Russia

Like its allies and its enemies, Russia embraced war with patriotic enthusiasm in 1914. At the Winter Palace, while throngs of people knelt and sang, "God save the tsar," Tsar Nicholas II (r. 1894–1917) repeated the oath Alexander I had sworn in 1812 and vowed never to make peace as long as the enemy stood on Russian soil. Russia's lower house, the Duma, voted war credits. Conservatives anticipated expansion in the Balkans, while liberals and most socialists believed alliance with Britain and France would bring democratic reforms. For a moment, Russia was united.

Soon the strains of war began to take their toll. Unprecedented artillery barrages used up Russia's supplies of shells and ammunition, and better-equipped German armies inflicted terrible losses. In 1915 substantial numbers of Russian soldiers were sent to the front without rifles; they were told to find their arms among the dead. There were 2 million Russian casualties in 1915 alone. Despite declining morale among soldiers and civilians, most of Russia's battered peasant army did not collapse but continued to fight courageously until early 1917.

Under the shock of defeat, Russia moved toward full mobilization on the home front. The Duma and organs of local government took the lead, setting up special committees to coordinate defense, industry, transportation, and agriculture. These efforts improved the military situation, and Russian factories produced more than twice as many shells in 1916 as in 1915. Yet there were many failures, and Russia mobilized less effectively for total war than the other warring nations.

The great problem was leadership. Under the constitution resulting from the revolution of 1905 (see pages 840–841), the tsar had retained complete control over the bureaucracy and the army. Legislation proposed by the Duma, which was weighted in favor of the wealthy and conservative classes, was subject to the tsar's veto. Moreover, Nicholas II fervently wished to maintain the sacred inheritance of supreme royal power, which, with the Orthodox church, was for him the key to Russia's greatness. A kindly, slightly stupid man, of whom a friend said he "would have been an ideal country gentleman, devoting his life to wife and children, his farms and his sport," Nicholas failed to form a close partnership with his citizens in order to fight the war more effectively. He came to rely instead on the old bureaucratic apparatus, distrusting the moderate Duma, rejecting popular involvement, and resisting calls to share power.

As a result, the Duma, the educated middle classes, and the masses became increasingly critical of the tsar's leadership. Following Nicholas's belated dismissal of the incompetent minister of war, demands for more democratic and responsive government exploded in the Duma in the summer of 1915. "From the beginning of the war," declared one young liberal, "public opinion has understood the character and magnitude of the struggle; it has understood that short of organizing the whole country for war, victory is impossible. But the Government has rejected every offer of help with disdain."[10] In September parties ranging from conservative to moderate socialist formed the Progressive bloc, which called for a completely new government responsible to the Duma instead of the tsar. In answer, Nicholas temporarily adjourned the Duma and announced that he was traveling to the front in order to lead and rally Russia's armies.

His departure was a fatal turning point. With the tsar in the field with the troops, control of the government was taken over by the hysterical empress, Tsarina Alexandra, and a debauched adventurer and self-proclaimed holy man, Rasputin. A minor German princess and granddaughter of England's Queen Victoria, Nicholas's wife was a devoted mother with a sick child, a strong-willed woman with a hatred of parliaments. Having constantly urged her husband to rule absolutely, Alexandra tried to do so herself in his absence. She seated and unseated the top ministers. Her most trusted adviser was "our Friend Grigori," an uneducated Siberian preacher who was appropriately nicknamed "Rasputin"—the "Degenerate."

Rasputin began his career with a sect noted for mixing sexual orgies with religious ecstasies, and his influence rested on mysterious healing powers. Alexis, Alexandra's fifth child and heir to the throne, suffered from the rare blood disease hemophilia. The tiniest cut meant uncontrollable bleeding, terrible pain, and possible death. Medical science could do nothing. Only Rasputin could miraculously stop the bleeding, perhaps through hypnosis. The empress's faith in Rasputin was limitless. "Believe more in our Friend," she wrote her husband in 1916. "He lives for you and Russia." In this atmosphere of unreality, the government slid steadily toward revolution.

In a desperate attempt to right the situation and end unfounded rumors that Rasputin was the empress's lover, three members of the high aristocracy murdered Rasputin in December 1916. The empress went into semipermanent shock, her mind haunted by the dead

Family Portrait   With husband Nicholas II standing behind her, the beautiful but tense Alexandra shows one of her daughters, who could not inherit the throne, to her grandmother, Queen Victoria of Britain, and Victoria's son, the future Edward VII. European monarchs were closely related by blood and breeding before 1914. (*Nicholas A. de Basily Collection, Hoover Institution*)

man's prophecy: "If I die or you desert me, in six months you will lose your son and your throne."[11] Food shortages in the cities worsened; morale declined. On March 8, women calling for bread in Petrograd (formerly St. Petersburg) started riots, which spontaneously spread to the factories and then elsewhere throughout the city. From the front, the tsar ordered troops to restore order, but discipline broke down, and the soldiers joined the revolutionary crowd. The Duma responded by declaring a provisional government on March 12, 1917. Three days later, Nicholas abdicated.

The Provisional Government

The March revolution was the result of an unplanned uprising of hungry, angry people in the capital, but it was joyfully accepted throughout the country. The patriotic upper and middle classes rejoiced at the prospect of a more determined and effective war effort, while workers happily anticipated better wages and more food. All classes and political parties called for liberty and democracy. They were not disappointed. As Lenin said, Russia became the freest country in the world. After generations of arbitrary authoritarianism, the provisional government quickly established equality before the law; freedom of religion, speech, and assembly; the right of unions to organize and strike; and the rest of the classic liberal program.

Yet both the liberal and moderate socialist leaders of the provisional government rejected social revolution. The reorganized government formed in May 1917, which included the fiery agrarian socialist Alexander Kerensky, refused to confiscate large landholdings and give them to peasants, fearing that such drastic action in the countryside would only complete the disintegration of Russia's peasant army. For the patriotic Kerensky, as for other moderate socialists, the continuation of war was still the all-important national duty. There would be plenty of time for land reform later, and thus all the government's efforts were directed toward a last offensive in July. Human suffering and war-weariness grew, sapping the limited strength of the provisional government.

From its first day, the provisional government had to share power with a formidable rival—the Petrograd Soviet (or council) of Workers' and Soldiers' Deputies. Modeled on the revolutionary soviets of 1905, the Petrograd Soviet was a huge, fluctuating mass meeting of two thousand to three thousand workers, soldiers, and socialist intellectuals. Seeing itself as a true grassroots revolutionary democracy, this counter- or half-government suspiciously watched the provisional government and issued its own radical orders, further weakening the provisional government. Most famous of these was Army Order No. 1, issued to all Russian military forces as the provisional government was forming.

Order No. 1 stripped officers of their authority and placed power in the hands of elected committees of common soldiers. Designed primarily to protect the revolution from some counter-revolutionary Bonaparte on horseback, Army Order No. 1 instead led to a total collapse of army discipline. Many an officer was hanged for his sins. Meanwhile, following the foolhardy summer offensive, masses of peasant soldiers began "voting with their feet," to use Lenin's graphic phrase. That is, they began returning to their villages to help their families get a share of the land, which peasants were simply seizing as they settled old scores in a great agrarian upheaval. All across the country, liberty was turning into anarchy in the summer of 1917. It was an unparalleled

THE RUSSIAN REVOLUTION

1914	Russia enthusiastically enters the First World War.
1915	Russia suffers 2 million casualties. Progressive bloc calls for a new government responsible to the Duma rather than to the tsar. Tsar Nicholas adjourns the Duma and departs for the front; Alexandra and Rasputin exert a strong influence on the government.
December 1916	Rasputin is murdered.
March 8, 1917	Bread riots take place in Petrograd (St. Petersburg).
March 12, 1917	Duma declares a provisional government.
March 15, 1917	Tsar Nicholas abdicates without protest.
April 3, 1917	Lenin returns from exile and denounces the provisional government.
May 1917	Reorganized provisional government, including Kerensky, continues the war. Petrograd Soviet issues Army Order No. 1, granting military power to committees of common soldiers.
Summer 1917	Agrarian upheavals: peasants seize estates; peasant soldiers desert the army to participate.
October 1917	Bolsheviks gain a majority in the Petrograd Soviet.
November 6, 1917	Bolsheviks seize power; Lenin heads the new "provisional workers' and peasants' government."
November 1917	Lenin accepts peasant seizure of land and worker control of factories; all banks are nationalized.
January 1918	Lenin permanently disbands the Constituent Assembly.
February 1918	Lenin convinces the Bolshevik Central Committee to accept a humiliating peace with Germany in order to safeguard the revolution.
March 1918	Treaty of Brest-Litovsk: Russia loses one-third of its population. Trotsky as war commissar begins to rebuild the Russian army. Government moves from Petrograd to Moscow.
1918–1920	Great civil war takes place.
Summer 1918	Eighteen regional governments compete for power. White armies oppose the Bolshevik Revolution.
1919	White armies are on the offensive but divided politically; they receive little benefit from Allied intervention.
1920	Lenin and the Red Army are victorious, retaking Belorussia and Ukraine.

opportunity for the most radical and most talented of Russia's many socialist leaders, Vladimir Ilyich Lenin (1870–1924).

Lenin and the Bolshevik Revolution

From his youth, Lenin's whole life had been dedicated to the cause of revolution. Born into the middle class, Lenin became an implacable enemy of imperial Russia when his older brother was executed for plotting to kill the tsar in 1887. As a law student, Lenin began searching for a revolutionary faith. He found it in Marxian socialism, which began to win converts among radical intellectuals as industrialization surged forward in Russia in the 1890s. Exiled to Siberia for three years because of socialist agitation, Lenin studied Marxian doctrines with religious intensity. After his release, this young priest of socialism joined fellow believers in western Europe. There he lived for seventeen years and developed his own revolutionary interpretations of the body of Marxian thought.

Three interrelated ideas were central for Lenin. First, like other eastern European radical socialists after 1900, he turned to the early fire-breathing Marx of 1848 and *The Communist Manifesto* for inspiration. Thus Lenin stressed that capitalism could be destroyed only by violent revolution. He tirelessly denounced all revisionist theories of a peaceful evolution to socialism as betraying Marx's message of unending class conflict. Lenin's second, more original idea was that under certain conditions a socialist revolution was possible even in a relatively backward country like Russia. Though capitalism was not fully developed there and the industrial

Mass Demonstrations in Petrograd   in June 1917 showed a surge of working-class support for the Bolsheviks. In this photo a few banners of the Mensheviks and other moderate socialists are drowned in a sea of Bolshevik slogans. *(Sovfoto)*

working class was small, the peasants were poor and thus potential revolutionaries.

Lenin believed that at a given moment revolution was determined more by human leadership than by vast historical laws. Thus was born his third basic idea: the necessity of a highly disciplined workers' party, strictly controlled by a dedicated elite of intellectuals and full-time revolutionaries like Lenin himself. Unlike ordinary workers and trade-union officials, this elite would never be seduced by short-term gains. It would not stop until revolution brought it to power.

Lenin's theories and methods did not go unchallenged by other Russian Marxists. At meetings of the Russian Social Democratic Labor party in London in 1903, matters came to a head. Lenin demanded a small, disciplined, elitist party, while his opponents wanted a more democratic party with mass membership. The Russian party of Marxian socialism promptly split into two rival factions. Lenin's camp was called *Bolsheviks,* or "majority group"; his opponents were *Mensheviks,* or "minority group." Lenin's majority did not last, but Lenin did not care. He kept the fine-sounding name Bolshevik and developed the party he wanted: tough, disciplined, revolutionary.

Unlike most other socialists, Lenin did not rally round the national flag in 1914. Observing events from neutral Switzerland, he saw the war as a product of imperialistic rivalries and as a marvelous opportunity for class war and socialist upheaval. The March revolution was, Lenin felt, a step in that direction. Since propaganda and internal subversion were accepted weapons of total war, the German government graciously provided the impatient Lenin, his wife, and about twenty trusted colleagues with safe passage across Germany and back into Russia in April 1917. The Germans hoped that Lenin would undermine the sagging war effort of the world's freest society. They were not disappointed.

Arriving triumphantly at Petrograd's Finland Station on April 3, Lenin attacked at once. To the great astonishment of the local Bolsheviks, he rejected all cooperation with the "bourgeois" provisional government of the liberals and moderate socialists. His slogans were radical in the extreme: "All power to the soviets"; "All land to the peasants"; "Stop the war now." Never a slave to Marxian determinism, the brilliant but not unduly intellectual Lenin was a superb tactician. The moment was now.

Yet Lenin almost overplayed his hand. An attempt by the Bolsheviks to seize power in July collapsed, and Lenin fled and went into hiding. He was charged with being a German agent, and indeed he and the Bolsheviks were getting money from Germany.[12] But no matter. Intrigue between Kerensky, who became prime minister in July, and his commander in chief, General Lavr Kornilov, a popular war hero "with the heart of a lion and the brains of a sheep," resulted in Kornilov's leading a feeble attack against the provisional government in September. In the face of this rightist "counter-revolutionary" threat, the Bolsheviks were rearmed and redeemed. Kornilov's forces disintegrated, but Kerensky lost all credit with the army, the only force that might have saved him and democratic government in Russia.

Trotsky and the Seizure of Power

Throughout the summer, the Bolsheviks had appealed very effectively to the workers and soldiers of Petrograd, markedly increasing their popular support. Party membership had soared from 50,000 to 240,000, and in October the Bolsheviks gained a fragile majority in the Petrograd Soviet. Moreover, Lenin had found a strong right arm—Leon Trotsky, the second most important person in the Russian Revolution.

A spellbinding revolutionary orator and independent radical Marxist, Trotsky (1879–1940) supported Lenin wholeheartedly in 1917. It was Trotsky who brilliantly executed the Bolshevik seizure of power. Painting a vivid but untruthful picture of German and counter-revolutionary plots, Trotsky first convinced the Petrograd Soviet to form a special military-revolutionary committee in October and make him its leader. Military power in the capital passed into Bolshevik hands. Trotsky's second master stroke was to insist that the Bolsheviks reduce opposition to their coup by taking power in the name not of the Bolsheviks, but of the more popular and democratic soviets, which were meeting in Petrograd from all over Russia in early November. On the night of November 6, militants from Trotsky's committee joined with trusty Bolshevik soldiers to seize government buildings and pounce on members of the provisional government. Then they went on to the congress of soviets. There a Bolshevik majority—roughly 390 of 650 turbulent delegates—declared that all power had passed to the soviets and named Lenin head of the new government.

The Bolsheviks came to power for three key reasons. First, by late 1917 democracy had given way to anarchy: power was there for those who would take it. Second, in Lenin and Trotsky the Bolsheviks had an utterly determined and truly superior leadership, which both the tsarist government and the provisional government lacked. Third, in 1917 the Bolsheviks succeeded in appealing to many soldiers and urban workers, people who were exhausted by war and eager for socialism. With time, many workers would become bitterly disappointed, but for the moment they had good reason to believe that they had won what they wanted.

Dictatorship and Civil War

History is full of short-lived coups and unsuccessful revolutions. The truly monumental accomplishment of Lenin, Trotsky, and the rest of the Bolsheviks was not taking power but keeping it. In the next four years, the Bolsheviks went on to conquer the chaos they had helped create, and they began to build their kind of dictatorial socialist society. The conspirators became conquerors. How was this done?

Lenin had the genius to profit from developments over which he and the Bolsheviks had no control. Since summer, a peasant revolution had been sweeping across Russia as the tillers of the soil invaded and divided among themselves the great and not-so-great estates of the landlords and the church. Peasant seizure of the land—a Russian 1789—was not very Marxian, but it was quite unstoppable in 1917. Thus Lenin's first law, which supposedly gave land to the peasants, actually merely approved what peasants were already doing. Urban workers' great demand in November was direct control of individual factories by local workers committees. This, too, Lenin ratified with a decree in November.

Unlike many of his colleagues, Lenin acknowledged that Russia had lost the war with Germany, that the Russian army had ceased to exist, and that the only realistic goal was peace at any price. That price was very high. Germany demanded in December 1917 that the Soviet government give up all its western territories. These areas were inhabited by Poles, Finns, Lithuanians, and other non-Russians—all those people who had been conquered by the tsars over three centuries and put into the "prisonhouse of nationalities," as Lenin had earlier called the Russian empire.

At first, Lenin's fellow Bolsheviks would not accept such great territorial losses. But when German armies resumed their unopposed march into Russia in February 1918, Lenin had his way in a very close vote in the Central Committee of the party. "Not even his greatest enemy can deny that at this moment Lenin towered like a giant over his Bolshevik colleagues."[13] A third of old Russia's population was sliced away by the German meat ax in the Treaty of Brest-Litovsk in March 1918. With peace, Lenin had escaped the certain disaster of

continued war and could pursue his goal of absolute political power for the Bolsheviks—now renamed Communists—within Russia.

In November 1917, the Bolsheviks had cleverly proclaimed their regime only a "provisional workers' and peasants' government," promising that a freely elected Constituent Assembly would draw up a new constitution. But free elections produced a stunning setback for the Bolsheviks, who won less than one-fourth of the elected delegates. The Socialist Revolutionaries—the peasants' party—had a clear majority. The Constituent Assembly met for only one day, on January 18, 1918. It was then permanently disbanded by Bolshevik soldiers acting under Lenin's orders. Thus even before the peace with Germany, Lenin was forming a one-party government.

The destruction of the democratically elected Constituent Assembly helped feed the flames of civil war. People who had risen up for self-rule in November saw that once again they were getting dictatorship from the capital. For the next three years, "Long live the [democratic] soviets; down with the Bolsheviks" was to be a popular slogan. The officers of the old army took the lead in organizing the so-called White opposition to the Bolsheviks in southern Russia, Ukraine, Siberia, and west of Petrograd. The Whites came from many social groups and were united only by their hatred of the Bolsheviks—the Reds.

By the summer of 1918, fully eighteen self-proclaimed regional governments—several of which represented minority nationalities—were competing with Lenin's Bolsheviks in Moscow. By the end of the year, White armies were on the attack. In October 1919, it appeared they might triumph, as they closed in on Lenin's government from three sides. Yet they did not. By the spring of 1920, the White armies had been almost completely defeated, and the Bolshevik Red Army had retaken Belorussia and Ukraine. The following year, the Communists also reconquered the independent nationalist governments of the Caucasus. The civil war was over; Lenin had won.

Lenin and the Bolsheviks won for several reasons. Strategically, they controlled the center, while the Whites were always on the fringes and disunited. Moreover, the poorly defined political program of the Whites was vaguely conservative, and it did not unite all the foes of the Bolsheviks under a progressive, democratic banner. For example, the most gifted of the White generals, the nationalistic General Anton Denikin, refused to call for a democratic republic and a federation of nationalities, although he knew that doing so would help his cause. Most important, the Communists quickly developed a better army, an army for which the divided Whites were no match.

Once again, Trotsky's leadership was decisive. The Bolsheviks had preached democracy in the army and elected officers in 1917. But beginning in March 1918, Trotsky as war commissar reestablished the draft and the most drastic discipline for the newly formed Red Army. Soldiers deserting or disobeying an order were summarily shot. Moreover, Trotsky made effective use of former tsarist army officers, who were actively recruited and given unprecedented powers of discipline over their troops. In short, Trotsky formed a disciplined and effective fighting force.

The Bolsheviks also mobilized the home front. Establishing "war communism"—the application of the total war concept to a civil conflict—they seized grain from peasants, introduced rationing, nationalized all banks and industry, and required everyone to work. Although these measures contributed to a breakdown of normal economic activity, they also served to maintain labor discipline and to keep the Red Army supplied.

"Revolutionary terror" also contributed to the Communist victory. The old tsarist secret police was reestablished as the Cheka, which hunted down and executed thousands of real or supposed foes, such as the tsar and his family and other "class enemies." At one point shortly after the government moved from Petrograd to Moscow in March 1918, a circus clown in Moscow was making fun of the Bolsheviks to an appreciative audience. Chekists in the crowd quickly pulled out their guns and shot several laughing people. Moreover, people were shot or threatened with being shot for minor nonpolitical failures. The terror caused by the secret police became a tool of the government. The Cheka sowed fear, and fear silenced opposition.

Finally, foreign military intervention in the civil war ended up helping the Communists. After Lenin made peace with Germany, the Allies (the Americans, British, and Japanese) sent troops to Archangel and Vladivostok to prevent war materiel they had sent the provisional government from being captured by the Germans. After the Soviet government nationalized all foreign-owned factories without compensation and refused to pay all of Russia's foreign debts, Western governments, particularly that of France, began to support White armies in the south and west. Yet these efforts were small and halfhearted. In 1919 Western peoples were sick of war, and few Western politicians believed in a military crusade against the Bolsheviks. Thus Allied intervention in the civil war did not aid the Whites effec-

Lenin Rallies Worker and Soldier Delegates   at a midnight meeting of the Petrograd Soviet, as the Bolsheviks rise up and seize power on November 6, 1917. This painting from the 1940s idealizes Lenin, but his great talents as a revolutionary leader are undeniable. In this re-creation Stalin, who actually played only a small role in the uprising, is standing behind Lenin, already his trusty right-hand man. *(Sovfoto)*

tively, though it did permit the Communists to appeal to the patriotic nationalism of ethnic Russians, in particular former tsarist army officers. Allied intervention was both too little and too much.

Together, the Russian Revolution and the Bolshevik triumph were one of the reasons the First World War was such a great turning point in modern history. A radically new government, based on socialism and one-party dictatorship, came to power in a great European state, maintained power, and eagerly encouraged worldwide revolution. Although halfheartedly constitutional monarchy in Russia was undoubtedly headed for some kind of political crisis before 1914, it is hard to imagine the triumph of the most radical proponents of change and reform except in a situation of total collapse. That was precisely what happened to Russia in the First World War.

 THE PEACE SETTLEMENT

Victory over revolutionary Russia boosted sagging German morale, and in the spring of 1918 the Germans launched their last major attack against France. Yet this offensive failed, just as those before it had. With breathtaking rapidity, the United States, Great Britain, and France decisively defeated Germany militarily. The guns of world war finally fell silent. Then as civil war spread in Russia and as chaos engulfed much of eastern Europe, the victorious Western Allies came together in Paris to establish a lasting peace.

Expectations were high; optimism was almost unlimited. The Allies labored intensively and soon worked out terms for peace with Germany and for the creation of the peacekeeping League of Nations. Nevertheless, the hopes of peoples and politicians were soon disappointed, for the peace settlement of 1919 turned out to be a failure. Rather than creating conditions for peace, it sowed the seeds of another war. Surely this was the ultimate tragedy of the Great War, a war that directly and indirectly cost $332 billion and left 10 million dead and another 20 million wounded. How did this tragedy happen? Why was the peace settlement unsuccessful?

The End of the War

In early 1917, the strain of total war was showing everywhere. After the Russian Revolution in March, there were major strikes in Germany. In July a coalition of moderates passed a "peace resolution" in the Reichstag, calling for peace without territorial annexations. To counter this moderation born of war-weariness, the German military established a virtual dictatorship. The military also aggressively exploited the collapse of Russian armies after the Bolshevik Revolution. Advancing almost unopposed on the eastern front in early 1918, the German high command won great concessions from Lenin in the Treaty of Brest-Litovsk in March 1918.

With victory in the east quieting German moderates, General Ludendorff and company fell on France once more in the great spring offensive of 1918. For a time, German armies pushed forward, coming within 35 miles of Paris. But Ludendorff's exhausted, overex-

tended forces never broke through. They were decisively stopped in July at the second Battle of the Marne, where 140,000 fresh American soldiers saw action. Adding 2 million men in arms to the war effort by August, the late but massive American intervention decisively tipped the scales in favor of Allied victory.

By September British, French, and American armies were advancing steadily on all fronts, and a panicky General Ludendorff realized that Germany had lost the war. Yet he insolently insisted that moderate politicians shoulder the shame of defeat, and on October 4 the emperor formed a new, more liberal German government to sue for peace. As negotiations over an armistice dragged on, an angry and frustrated German people finally rose up. On November 3, sailors in Kiel mutinied, and throughout northern Germany soldiers and workers began to establish revolutionary councils on the Russian soviet model. The same day, Austria-Hungary surrendered to the Allies and began breaking apart. Revolution broke out in Germany, and masses of workers demonstrated for peace in Berlin. With army discipline collapsing, the emperor abdicated and fled to Holland. Socialist leaders in Berlin proclaimed a German republic on November 9 and simultaneously agreed to tough Allied terms of surrender. The armistice went into effect on November 11, 1918. The war was over.

Revolution in Germany

Military defeat brought political revolution to Germany and Austria-Hungary, as it had to Russia. In Austria-Hungary the revolution was primarily nationalistic and republican in character. Having started the war to preserve an antinationalistic dynastic state, the Habsburg empire had perished in the attempt. In its place, independent Austrian, Hungarian, and Czechoslovakian republics were proclaimed, while a greatly expanded Serbian monarchy united the South Slavs and took the name of Yugoslavia. The prospect of firmly establishing the new national states overrode class considerations for most people in east-central Europe.

The German Revolution of November 1918 resembled the Russian Revolution of March 1917. In both cases, a genuine popular uprising welled up from below, toppled an authoritarian monarchy, and brought the establishment of a liberal provisional republic. In both countries, liberals and moderate socialists took control of the central government, while workers' and soldiers' councils formed a counter-government. In Germany, however, the moderate socialists and their liberal allies won, and the Lenin-like radical revolutionaries in the councils lost. In communist terms, the liberal, republican revolution in Germany in 1918 was only half a revolution: a bourgeois political revolution without a communist second installment. It was Russia without Lenin's Bolshevik triumph.

There were several reasons for the German outcome. The great majority of Marxian socialist leaders in the Social Democratic party were, as before the war, really pink and not red. They wanted to establish real political democracy and civil liberties, and they favored the gradual elimination of capitalism. They were also German nationalists, appalled by the prospect of civil war and revolutionary terror. Moreover, there was less popular support among workers and soldiers for the extreme radicals than in Russia. Nor did the German peasantry, which already had most of the land, at least in western Germany, provide the elemental force that has driven all great modern revolutions, from the French to the Chinese.

Of crucial importance was the fact that the moderate German Social Democrats, unlike Kerensky and company, accepted defeat and ended the war the day they took power. This act ended the decline in morale among soldiers and prevented the regular army, with its conservative officer corps, from disintegrating. When radicals headed by Karl Liebknecht and Rosa Luxemburg and their supporters in the councils tried to seize control of the government in Berlin in January, the moderate socialists called on the army to crush the uprising. Liebknecht and Luxemburg were arrested and then brutally murdered by army leaders. Their murders, widely believed to have had government support, caused many working-class activists in the Social Democratic party to break away in anger and join the pro-Lenin German Communist party that Liebknecht's group had just founded. Finally, even if the moderate socialists had followed Liebknecht and Luxemburg on the Leninist path, it is very unlikely they would have succeeded. Civil war in Germany would certainly have followed. And the Allies, who were already occupying western Germany according to the terms of the armistice, would have marched on to Berlin and ruled Germany directly. Historians have often been unduly hard on Germany's moderate socialists. (See the feature "Individuals in Society: Rosa Luxemburg, Revolutionary Socialist.")

The Treaty of Versailles

The peace conference opened in Paris in January 1919 with seventy delegates representing twenty-seven victorious nations. There were great expectations. A young British diplomat later wrote that the victors "were convinced that they would never commit the blunders and iniquities of the Congress of Vienna [of 1815]." Then the "misguided, reactionary, pathetic aristocrats" had cynically shuffled populations; now "we believed in nationalism, we believed in the self-determination of peoples." Indeed, "we were journeying to Paris . . . to found a new order in Europe. We were preparing not Peace only, but Eternal Peace."[14] This general optimism and idealism had been greatly strengthened by President Wilson's January 1918 peace proposal, the Fourteen Points, which stressed national self-determination and the rights of small countries.

The real powers at the conference were the United States, Great Britain, and France, for Germany was not allowed to participate and Russia was locked in civil war and did not attend. Italy was considered part of the Big Four, but its role was quite limited. Almost immediately the three great Allies began to quarrel. President Wilson, who was wildly cheered by European crowds as the spokesman for a new idealistic and democratic international cooperation, was almost obsessed with creating the League of Nations. Wilson insisted that this question come first, for he passionately believed that only a permanent international organization could protect member states from aggression and avert future wars. Wilson had his way, although Lloyd George of Great Britain and especially Clemenceau of France were unenthusiastic. They were primarily concerned with punishing Germany.

Playing on British nationalism, Lloyd George had already won a smashing electoral victory in December on the popular platform of making Germany pay for the war. "We shall," he promised, "squeeze the orange until the pips squeak." Personally inclined to make a somewhat moderate peace with Germany, Lloyd George was to a considerable extent a captive of demands for a total victory worthy of the sacrifices of total war against a totally depraved enemy. As Kipling summed up the general British feeling at the end of the war, the Germans were "a people with the heart of beasts."[15]

France's Georges Clemenceau, "the Tiger" who had broken wartime defeatism and led his country to victory, wholeheartedly agreed. Like most French people, Clemenceau wanted old-fashioned revenge. He also wanted lasting security for France. This, he believed, required the creation of a buffer state between France and Germany, the permanent demilitarization of Germany, and vast German reparations. He feared that sooner or later Germany with its 60 million people would attack France with its 40 million unless the Germans were

Individuals in Society

Rosa Luxemburg, Revolutionary Socialist

Rosa Luxemburg, addressing a meeting of the Socialist International in 1907. *(AKG London)*

When Rosa Luxemburg (1870–1919) was arrested and then clubbed down and murdered by soldiers while being taken to jail, the left wing of European socialism lost a leading thinker and a passionate activist. But it gained an icon, a revolutionary saint.

Luxemburg grew up in Warsaw, the fifth child in a loving, nonreligious Jewish family. Speaking Polish and German at home, the mature Luxemburg identified "indignantly with Polish victims of linguistic oppression far more easily than with her fellow Jews."[1] But recent research also suggests that she was profoundly affected by the 1881 anti-Jewish riots and massacres in Russia and tsarist Poland, when middle-class Jewish families like hers huddled in terror until the Russian government decided the riots had gone far enough. These pogroms of 1881 led many Jewish intellectuals to turn to socialism. So it was with Luxemburg. She found in Marxism the promise of liberation for *all* oppressed groups and thus an end to terrible ethnic hatreds.

Smuggled out of Poland in 1889 and studying economics and socialism in Zurich with like-minded Polish exiles, one of whom became her lover and lifelong companion in revolution, Luxemburg settled in 1898 in Germany, the heartland of Marxian socialism. Small, foreign-born, and walking with a limp because of a childhood accident, she relentlessly attacked all revisions of Marxism (see page 851) and emerged in Germany as the "most prominent and influential of the party's radicals." She denounced any compromise with capitalism and stressed the absolute necessity of revolution.

Luxemburg also played a leading role in the outlawed Polish Socialist party. She thrilled to the revolution of 1905 in the tsarist empire and worked feverishly for the cause in Warsaw—"the happiest months of my life." Strengthened in her revolutionary convictions, she fought to radicalize Germany's socialists. When senior party and trade-union leaders opposed her ideas and tried to marginalize her, she went over their heads to the rank and file. A popular speaker who lectured tirelessly to enthusiastic working-class audiences, "Red Rosa" even challenged army discipline and the emperor as she condemned militarism as well as capitalism. In 1913 she told a large meeting, "If they think we are going to lift the weapons of murder against our French and other brethren, then we shall shout: 'We will not do it!'"[2] Arrested and tried for sedition, she was sentenced to prison.

The outbreak of war put existing trends in fast-forward. Luxemburg was heartbroken when the Second International stood by impotently in all countries and Germany's Social Democrats rallied to the government. From prison she denounced her former coworkers as working-class traitors and cheered on Karl Liebknecht's tiny group of radical socialists (see page 917). After her release in November 1918, she embraced the Bolshevik Revolution and worked with heart and soul for a replay of radical revolution in Germany until her martyr's death two months later.

Rosa Luxemburg's legacy is complex, but two points seem clear. First, she personified brilliantly the resurgent radical minority in Marxian socialism after 1905, which eventually triumphed in Russia and was rejected in Germany. Second, brave and ever multinational, Luxemburg embodied the strongest element in prewar socialism's hostility toward militarism and national hatreds, an idealistic vision tragically shattered in the great break of World War I.

Questions for Analysis

1. In what ways did Rosa Luxemburg's career reflect tensions and divisions in the Marxian socialist movement in Germany and throughout Europe before and during the First World War?

2. Evaluate Luxemburg's life. Was she a success or a failure? Or was she both? Defend your conclusions in a class debate.

1. Richard Abraham, *Rosa Luxemburg: A Life for the International* (Oxford and New York: Berg, 1989), p. 20; also pp. 75, 80. This brief study is excellent.
2. J. P. Nettl, *Rosa Luxemburg,* abr. ed. (New York: Schocken Books, 1969), p. 321.

Versailles, June 28, 1919   This group portrait by William Orpen features the three principal Allied leaders, seated in the center, who have finally reached an agreement. The scholarly Wilson is third from the left, next to the old tiger, Clemenceau of France, who is turned toward the strong-willed Lloyd George of Britain. *(Courtesy of the Trustees of the Imperial War Museum)*

permanently weakened. Moreover, France had no English Channel (or Atlantic Ocean) as a reassuring barrier against German aggression. Wilson, supported by Lloyd George, would hear none of this. Clemenceau's demands seemed vindictive, violating morality and the principle of national self-determination. By April the countries attending the conference were deadlocked on the German question, and Wilson packed his bags to go home.

Clemenceau's obsession with security reflected his anxiety about France's long-term weakness. In the end, convinced that France should not break with its allies because France could not afford to face Germany alone in the future, he agreed to a compromise. He gave up the French demand for a Rhineland buffer state in return for a formal defensive alliance with the United States and Great Britain. Under the terms of this alliance, both Wilson and Lloyd George promised that their countries would come to France's aid in the event of a German attack. Thus Clemenceau appeared to win his goal of French security, as Wilson had won his of a permanent international organization. The Allies moved quickly to finish the settlement, believing that any adjustments would later be possible within the dual framework of a strong Western alliance and the League of Nations (Map 27.4).

The Treaty of Versailles between the Allies and Germany was the key to the settlement, and the terms were not unreasonable as a first step toward re-establishing international order. (Had Germany won, it seems certain that France and Belgium would have been treated with greater severity, as Russia had been at Brest-

MAP 27.4 Shattered Empires and Territorial Changes After World War I The Great War brought tremendous changes in eastern Europe. New nations were established, and a dangerous power vacuum was created between Germany and Soviet Russia.

Litovsk.) Germany's colonies were given to France, Britain, and Japan as League of Nations mandates. Germany's territorial losses within Europe were minor, thanks to Wilson. Alsace-Lorraine was returned to France. Parts of Germany inhabited primarily by Poles were ceded to the new Polish state, in keeping with the principle of national self-determination. Predominately German Danzig was also placed within the Polish tariff lines, but as a self-governing city under League of Nations protection. Germany had to limit its army to 100,000 men and agree to build no military fortifications in the Rhineland.

More harshly, the Allies declared that Germany (with Austria) was responsible for the war and had therefore to pay reparations equal to all civilian damages caused by the war. This unfortunate and much-criticized clause expressed inescapable popular demands for German blood, but the actual figure was not set, and there was the clear possibility that reparations might be set at a reasonable level in the future when tempers had cooled.

When presented with the treaty, the German government protested vigorously. But there was no alternative, especially considering that Germany was still starving because the Allies had not yet lifted their naval blockade. On June 28, 1919, German representatives of the ruling moderate Social Democrats and the Catholic party signed the treaty in the Sun King's Hall of Mirrors at Versailles, where Bismarck's empire had been joyously proclaimed almost fifty years before.

Separate peace treaties were concluded with the other defeated powers—Austria, Hungary, Bulgaria, and Turkey. For the most part, these treaties merely ratified the existing situation in east-central Europe following the breakup of the Austro-Hungarian Empire. Like Austria, Hungary was a particularly big loser, as its "captive" nationalities (and some interspersed Hungarians) were ceded to Romania, Czechoslovakia, Poland, and Yugoslavia. Italy got some Austrian territory. The Turkish empire was broken up. France received Lebanon and Syria, while Britain took Iraq and Palestine, which was to include a Jewish national home first promised by Britain in 1917. Officially League of Nations mandates, these acquisitions of the Western powers were one of the more imperialistic elements of the peace settlement. Another was mandating Germany's holdings in China to Japan. The age of Western imperialism lived on. National self-determination remained a reality only for Europeans and their offspring.

American Rejection of the Versailles Treaty

The rapidly concluded peace settlement of early 1919 was not perfect, but within the context of war-shattered Europe it was an acceptable beginning. The principle of national self-determination, which had played such a large role in starting the war, was accepted and served as an organizing framework. Germany had been punished but not dismembered. A new world organization complemented a traditional defensive alliance of satisfied powers. The serious remaining problems could be worked out in the future. Moreover, Allied leaders had seen speed as essential for another reason: they detested Lenin and feared that his Bolshevik Revolution might spread. They realized that their best answer to Lenin's unending calls for worldwide upheaval was peace and tranquillity for war-weary peoples.

There were, however, two great interrelated obstacles to such peace: Germany and the United States. Plagued by communist uprisings, reactionary plots, and popular disillusionment with losing the war at the last minute, Germany's moderate socialists and their liberal and Catholic supporters faced an enormous challenge. Like French republicans after 1871, they needed time (and luck) if they were to establish firmly a peaceful and democratic republic. Progress in this direction required understanding, yet firm treatment of Germany by the victorious Western Allies, particularly by the United States.

However, the U.S. Senate and, to a lesser extent, the American people rejected Wilson's handiwork. Republican senators led by Henry Cabot Lodge refused to ratify the Treaty of Versailles without changes in the articles creating the League of Nations. The key issue was the League's power—more apparent than real—to require member states to take collective action against aggression.

Lodge and others believed that this requirement gave away Congress's constitutional right to declare war. No doubt Wilson would have been wise to accept some reservations. But in failing health, Wilson, with narrow-minded self-righteousness, rejected all attempts at compromise. He instructed loyal Democratic senators to vote against any reservations whatsoever to the Treaty of Versailles. In doing so, Wilson ensured that the treaty would never be ratified by the United States in any form and that the United States would never join the League of Nations. Moreover, the Senate refused to ratify Wilson's treaties forming a defensive alliance with France and Great Britain. America turned its back on Europe.

Perhaps understandable in the light of American traditions and the volatility of mass politics, the Wilson-Lodge fiasco and the newfound gospel of isolationism nevertheless represented a tragic and cowardly renunciation of America's responsibility. Using America's action as an excuse, Great Britain, too, refused to ratify its defensive alliance with France. Bitterly betrayed by its allies, France stood alone. Very shortly France was to take actions against Germany that would feed the fires of German resentment and seriously undermine democratic forces in the new republic. The great hopes of early 1919 had turned to ashes by the end of the year. The Western alliance had collapsed, and a grandiose plan for permanent peace had given way to a fragile truce. For this and for what came later, the United States must share a large part of the guilt.

SUMMARY

Why did World War I have such revolutionary consequences? Why was it such a great break with the past? World War I was, first of all, a war of committed peoples. In France, Britain, and Germany in particular, governments drew on genuine popular support. This support reflected not only the diplomatic origins of the war but also the way western European society had been unified under the nationalist banner in the later nineteenth century, despite the fears that the growing socialist movement aroused in conservatives. The relentlessness of total war helps explain why so many died, why so many were crippled physically and psychologically, and why Western civilization would in so many ways never be the same again. More concretely, the war swept away monarchs and multinational empires. National self-determination apparently triumphed across Europe, not only in Austria-Hungary but also in many of Russia's western borderlands. Except in Ireland and parts of Soviet Russia, the revolutionary dream of national unity, born of the French Revolution, had finally come true.

Two other revolutions were products of the war. In Russia the Bolsheviks established a radical regime, smashed existing capitalist institutions, and stayed in power with a new kind of authoritarian rule. Whether the new Russian regime was truly Marxian or socialist was questionable, but it indisputably posed a powerful, ongoing revolutionary challenge to Europe and its colonial empires.

More subtle but quite universal in its impact was an administrative revolution. This revolution, born of the need to mobilize entire societies and economies for total war, greatly increased the power of government. And after the guns grew still, government planning and wholesale involvement in economic and social life did not disappear in Europe. Liberal market capitalism and a well-integrated world economy were among the many casualties of the administrative revolution, and greater social equality was everywhere one of its results. Thus even in European countries where a communist takeover never came close to occurring, society still experienced a great revolution.

Finally, the "war to end war" did not bring peace—only a fragile truce. In the West, the Allies failed to maintain their wartime solidarity. Germany remained unrepentant and would soon have more grievances to nurse. Moreover, the victory of national self-determination in eastern Europe created small, weak states and thus a power vacuum between a still-powerful Germany and a potentially mighty communist Russia. A vast area lay open to military aggression from two sides.

NOTES

1. M. Beloff, quoted in *U.S. News & World Report,* March 8, 1976, p. 53.
2. Quoted in J. Remak, *The Origins of World War I* (New York: Holt, Rinehart & Winston, 1967), p. 84.
3. Quoted in W. E. Mosse, *Alexander II and the Modernization of Russia* (New York: Collier Books, 1962), pp. 125–126.
4. Quoted in Remak, *The Origins of World War I,* p. 123.
5. Quoted in J. E. Rodes, *The Quest for Unity: Modern Germany, 1848–1970* (New York: Holt, Rinehart & Winston, 1971), p. 178.
6. Quoted in F. P. Chambers, *The War Behind the War, 1914–1918* (London: Faber & Faber, 1939), p. 444.
7. Quoted ibid., p. 168.
8. Quoted in R. O. Paxton, *Europe in the Twentieth Century* (New York: Harcourt Brace Jovanovich, 1975), p. 109.
9. Quoted in Chambers, *The War Behind the War,* p. 378.
10. Quoted ibid., p. 110.
11. Quoted ibid., pp. 302, 304.
12. A. B. Ulam, *The Bolsheviks* (New York: Collier Books, 1968), p. 349.
13. Ibid., p. 405.
14. H. Nicolson, *Peacemaking 1919* (New York: Grosset & Dunlap Universal Library, 1965), pp. 8, 31–32.
15. Quoted ibid., p. 24.

SUGGESTED READING

E. Hobsbawm, *The Age of Extremes: A History of the World, 1914–1991* (1996), is a recent and provocative interpretation by a famous historian, with a good discussion of war and revolution. O. Hale, *The Great Illusion, 1900–1914* (1971), is a thorough account of the prewar era. Remak's volume cited in the Notes, J. Joll, *The Origins of the First World War* (1992), and L. Lafore, *The Long Fuse* (1971), are recommended studies of the causes of the First World War. V. Steiner, *Britain and the Origins of the First World War* (1978), and G. Kennan, *The Decline of Bismarck's European Order: Franco-Russian Relations, 1875–1890* (1979), are also major contributions. K. Jarausch, *The Enigmatic Chancellor* (1973), is an important study on Bethmann-Hollweg and German policy in 1914. M. Gilbert, *The First World War: A Complete History* (1994), is comprehensive and up-to-date, while C. Falls, *The Great War* (1961), is a fine brief introduction to military aspects of the war. B. Tuchman, *The Guns of August* (1962), is a marvelous account of the dramatic first month of the war and the beginning of military stalemate. J. Winter, *The Experience of World War I* (1988), is a strikingly illustrated history of the war, and A. Horne, *The Price of Glory: Verdun 1916* (1979), is a moving account of the famous siege. J. Ellis, *Eye-Deep in Hell* (1976), is a vivid account of trench warfare, whereas J. Keegan's fascinating *Face of Battle* (1976) examines soldiers and warfare in a long-term perspective. V. Brittain's *Testament of Youth* (1933), the moving autobiography of an English nurse in wartime, shows lives buffeted by new ideas and personal tragedies, and D. Gorham, *Vera Brittain: A Feminist Life* (1996), is a major study of Brittain's life. A. Marwick, *War and Change in Twentieth-Century Europe* (1990), is a useful synthesis.

F. L. Carsten, *War Against War* (1982), considers radical movements in Britain and Germany. The comprehensive and exciting study by Chambers mentioned in the Notes is still very useful. M. Higonnet, J. Jensen, and M. Weitz, eds., *Behind the Lines: Gender and the Two World Wars* (1987), examines the changes that the war brought for women and for relations between the sexes. S. Hynes, *A War Imagined: The First World War and English Culture* (1990), examines intellectual and cultural reactions. Two important recent studies on France are M. Hanna, *The Mobilization of Intellect: French Scholars and Writers in the Great War* (1996); and J. Keiger, *Raymond Poincaré* (1997), an excellent reconsideration of one of France's most important leaders before, during, and after the First World War. G. Feldman, *Army, Industry, and Labor in Germany, 1914–1918* (1966), shows the impact of total war and military dictatorship on Germany. Two excellent collections of essays, R. Wall and J. Winter, eds., *The Upheaval of War: Family, Work, and Welfare in Europe, 1914–1918* (1988), and J. Roth, ed., *World War I* (1967), probe the enormous consequences of the war for people and society. In addition to F. Fischer's influential interpretation, *Germany's Aims in the First World War* (1967), the debate over Germany's guilt and aggression may be approached through G. Feldman, ed., *German Imperialism, 1914–1918* (1972), and A. Hillgruber, *Germany and the Two World Wars* (1981). Two excellent biographies on Rosa Luxemburg, R. Abraham, *Rosa Luxemburg: A Life for the International* (1989), an excellent introduction, and J. Nettl, *Rosa Luxemburg* (2 vols., 1966; abr. ed., 1966), a pioneering and sympathetic study, also discuss the splits between radical and moderate socialists during the conflict. In addition to Erich Maria Remarque's great novel *All Quiet on the Western Front* (1928), Henri Barbusse, *Under Fire* (1917), and Jules Romains, *Verdun* (1939), are highly recommended for their fictional yet realistic re-creations of the war. P. Fussell, *The Great War and Modern Memory* (1975), probes all the powerful literature inspired by the war. M. Ecksteins, *Rites of Spring: The Great War and the Birth of the Modern Age* (1989), is an imaginative cultural investigation that has won critical acclaim.

C. Read, *From Tsar to Soviets: The Russian People and Their Revolution, 1917–1921* (1996), is recent and highly recommended. S. Fitzpatrick, *The Russian Revolution* (1982), is an older provocative interpretation. R. Suny and A. Adams, eds., *The Russian Revolution and Bolshevik Victory* (1990), presents a wide range of old and new interpretations. Ulam's work cited in the Notes, which focuses on Lenin, is a classic introduction to the Russian Revolution, whereas D. Volkogonov, *Lenin: A New Biography* (1994), is a lively study with some new revelations by a well-known post-Communist Russian historian. B. Wolfe, *Three Who Made a Revolution* (1955), an old but good collective biography of Lenin, Trotsky, and Stalin, and R. Conquest, *V. I. Lenin* (1972), are recommended. L. Trotsky himself wrote the colorful and exciting *History of the Russian Revolution* (1932), which may be compared with the classic eyewitness account of the young, pro-Bolshevik American J. Reed, *Ten Days That Shook the World* (1919). A. Geifman, *Thou Shalt Kill: Revolutionary Terrorism in Russia, 1894–1917* (1994), is an important pioneering work on the cultural impact of political assassination. R. Pipes, *The Formation of the Soviet Union* (1968), is recommended for its excellent treatment of the nationality problem during the revolution. D. Koenker, W. Rosenberg, and R. Suny, eds., *Party, State and Society in the Russian Civil War* (1989), probes the social foundations of Bolshevik victory. A. Wildman, *The End of the Russian Imperial Army* (1980), is a fine account of the soldiers' revolt, and G. Leggett, *The Cheka: Lenin's Secret Police* (1981), shows revolutionary terror in action. S. Volkov, *St. Petersburg: A Cultural History* (1997), is particularly moving on the great city's tragic moments in the twentieth century. Boris Pasternak's justly celebrated *Doctor Zhivago* is a great historical novel of the revolutionary era. R. Massie, *Nicholas and Alexandra* (1971), is a moving popular biography of Russia's last royal family and the terrible health problem of the heir to the throne. Nicolson's study listed in the Notes captures the spirit of the Versailles settlement. T. Bailey, *Woodrow Wilson and the Lost Peace* (1963), and W. Widenor, *Henry Cabot Lodge and the Search for an American Foreign Policy* (1981), are also recommended. A. Mayer, *The Politics and Diplomacy of Peacemaking* (1969), stresses the influence of domestic social tensions and widespread fear of further communist revolt.

LISTENING TO THE
PAST

The Experience of War

World War I was a "total" war: it enlisted the efforts of men, women, adults, and children, both at home and on the battlefield. It was a terrifying and painful experience for all those involved. To be sure, it was not the romantic endeavor it was purported to be. The documents below offer two different wartime experiences. The first excerpt is from a letter written by a German soldier fighting in the trenches. The second is from the diary of a Viennese woman. As you read both passages, think about the different ways war and its consequences were made real for these two people.

A German Soldier Writes from the Trenches, March 1915
Souchez, March 11th, 1915

"So fare you well, for we must now be parting," so run the first lines of a soldier-song which we often sang through the streets of the capital. These words are truer than ever now, and these lines are to bid farewell to you, to all my nearest and dearest, to all who wish me well or ill, and to all that I value and prize.

Our regiment has been transferred to this dangerous spot, Souchez. No end of blood has already flowed down this hill. A week ago the 142nd attacked and took four trenches from the French. It is to hold these trenches that we have been brought here. There is something uncanny about this hill-position. Already, times without number, other battalions of our regiment have been ordered here in support, and each time the company came back with a loss of twenty, thirty or more men. In the days when we had to stick it out here before, we had 22 killed and 27 wounded. Shells roar, bullets whistle; no dug-outs, or very bad ones; mud, clay, filth, shell-holes so deep that one could bathe in them.

This letter has been interrupted no end of times. Shells began to pitch close to us—great English 12-inch ones—and we had to take refuge in a cellar. One such shell struck the next house and buried four men, who were got out from the ruins horribly mutilated. I saw them and it was ghastly!

Everybody must be prepared now for death in some form or other. Two cemeteries have been made up here, the losses have been so great. I ought not to write that to you, but I do so all the same, because the newspapers have probably given you quite a different impression. They tell only of our gains and say nothing about the blood that has been shed, of the cries of agony that never cease. The newspaper doesn't give any description either of *how* the "heroes" are laid to rest, though it talks about "heroes' graves" and writes poems and such-like about them. Certainly in Lens I have attended funeral-parades where a number of dead were buried in one large grave with pomp and circumstance. But up here it is pitiful the way one throws the dead bodies out of the trench and lets them lie there, or scatters dirt over the remains of those which have been torn to pieces by shells.

I look upon death and call upon life. I have not accomplished much in my short life, which has been chiefly occupied with study. I have commended my soul to the Lord God. It bears His seal and is altogether His. Now I am free to dare anything. My future life belongs to God, my present one to the Fatherland, and I myself still possess happiness and strength.

A Viennese Woman Remembers Home Front Life

Ten dekagrammes [3½ ounces] of horse-flesh per head are to be given out to-day for the week. The cavalry horses held in reserve by the military authorities are being slaughtered for lack of fodder, and the people of Vienna are for a change to get a few mouthfuls of meat of which they have so long been deprived. Horse-flesh! I should like to know whether my instinctive repugnance to horse-flesh as food is personal, or whether my dislike is shared by many other housewives. My loathing of it is based, I believe, not on a physical but on a psychological prejudice.

I overcame my repugnance, rebuked myself for being sentimental, and left the house. A soft, steady rain was falling, from which I tried to protect myself with galoshes, waterproof, and umbrella. As I left the house before seven o'clock and the meat distribution did not begin until nine o'clock, I hoped to get well to the front of the queue.

No sooner had I reached the neighbourhood of the big market hall than I was instructed by the police to take a certain direction. I estimated the crowd waiting here for a meagre midday meal at two thousand at least. Hundreds of women had spent the night here in order to be among the first and make sure of getting their bit of meat. Many had brought with them improvised seats—a little box or a bucket turned upside down. No one seemed to mind the rain, although many were already wet through. They passed the time chattering, and the theme was the familiar one: What have you had to eat? What are you going to eat? One could scent an atmosphere of mistrust in these conversations: they were all careful not to say too much or to betray anything that might get them into trouble.

At length the sale began. Slowly, infinitely slowly, we moved forward. The most determined, who had spent the night outside the gates of the hall, displayed their booty to the waiting crowd: a ragged, quite freshly slaughtered piece of meat with the characteristic yellow fat. [Others] alarmed those standing at the back by telling them that there was only a very small supply of meat and that not half the people waiting would get a share of it. The crowd became very uneasy and impatient, and before the police on guard could prevent it, those standing in front organized an attack on the hall which the salesmen inside were powerless to repel. Everyone seized whatever he could lay his hands on, and in a few moments all the eatables had vanished. In the confusion stands were overturned, and the police forced back the aggressors and closed the gates. The crowds waiting outside, many of whom had been there all night and were soaked through, angrily demanded their due, whereupon the mounted police made a little charge, provoking a wild panic and much screaming and cursing. At length I reached home, depressed and disgusted, with a broken umbrella and only one galosh.

We housewives have during the last four years grown accustomed to standing in queues; we have also grown accustomed to being obliged to go home with empty hands and still emptier stomachs. Only very rarely do those who are sent away disappointed give cause for police intervention. On the other hand, it happens more and more frequently

❖ Germans wait in line for their meager rations in Berlin in 1916. *(Corbis-Bettmann)*

that one of the pale, tired women who have been waiting for hours collapses from exhaustion. The turbulent scenes which occurred to-day inside and outside the large market hall seemed to me perfectly natural. In my dejected mood the patient apathy with which we housewives endure seemed to me blameworthy and incomprehensible.

Questions for Analysis

1. How did the soldier see the war he was in? Was it a grand patriotic effort? Or was it a story of senseless bloodshed and loss of life?

2. How did the soldiers cope with the reality of war in the trenches?

3. How did the experience of the Viennese woman differ from the soldier's?

4. Were the women who pillaged the food hall "blameworthy" or "reprehensible," as the Viennese woman says?

Sources: Alfons Ankenbrand, in *German Students' War Letters,* ed. A. F. Wedd (London: Methuen, 1929), pp. 72–73; *Blockade: The Diary of an Austrian Middle-Class Woman, 1914–1924,* trans. Winifred Ray (New York: Ray Long & Richard Smith, 1932), pp. 63–68.

28 The Age of Anxiety

Dust, a painting of the Great Depression by the American painter Ben Shahn. *(Courtesy, Kennedy Galleries, New York. © Vaga)*

When Allied diplomats met in Paris in early 1919 with their optimistic plans for building a lasting peace, most people looked forward to happier times. They hoped that life would return to normal after the terrible trauma of total war. They hoped that once again life would make sense in the familiar prewar terms of peace, prosperity, and progress. These hopes were in vain. The Great Break—the First World War and the Russian Revolution—had mangled too many things beyond repair. Life would no longer fit neatly into the old molds.

Instead, great numbers of men and women felt themselves increasingly adrift in a strange, uncertain, and uncontrollable world. They saw themselves living in an age of anxiety, an age of continual crisis (this age lasted until at least the early 1950s). In almost every area of human experience, people went searching for ways to put meaning back into life.

- What did such doubts and searching mean for Western thought, art, and culture?
- How did leaders deal with the political dimensions of uncertainty and try to re-establish real peace and prosperity between 1919 and 1939?
- Why did those leaders fail?

These are the questions this chapter will explore.

✤ UNCERTAINTY IN MODERN THOUGHT

A complex revolution in thought and ideas was under way before the First World War, but only small, unusual groups were aware of it. After the war, new and upsetting ideas began to spread through the entire population. Western society began to question and even abandon many cherished values and beliefs that had guided it since the eighteenth-century Enlightenment and the nineteenth-century triumph of industrial development, scientific advances, and evolutionary thought.

Before 1914 most people still believed in progress, reason, and the rights of the individual. Progress was a daily reality, apparent in the rising standard of living, the taming of the city, and the steady increase in popular education. Such developments also encouraged the comforting belief in the logical universe of Newtonian physics as well as faith in the ability of a rational human mind to understand that universe through intellectual investigation. And just as there were laws of science, so were there laws of society that rational human beings could discover and then wisely act on. At the same time, the rights of the individual were not just taken for granted; they were actually increasing. Well-established political rights were gradually spreading to women and workers, and new "social rights," such as old-age pensions, were emerging. In short, before World War I most Europeans had a moderately optimistic view of the world, and with good reason.

Nevertheless, since the 1880s, a small band of serious thinkers and creative writers had been attacking these well-worn optimistic ideas. These critics rejected the general faith in progress and the power of the rational human mind. An expanding chorus of thinkers echoed and enlarged their views after the experience of history's most destructive war—a war that suggested to many that human beings were a pack of violent, irrational animals quite capable of tearing the individual and his or her rights to shreds. Disorientation and pessimism were particularly acute in the 1930s, when the rapid rise of harsh dictatorships and the Great Depression transformed old certainties into bitter illusions.

No one expressed this state of uncertainty better than French poet and critic Paul Valéry (1871–1945) in the early 1920s. Speaking of the "crisis of the mind," Valéry noted that Europe was looking at its future with dark foreboding:

The storm has died away, and still we are restless, uneasy, as if the storm were about to break. Almost all the affairs of men remain in a terrible uncertainty. We think of what has disappeared, and we are almost destroyed by what has been destroyed; we do not know what will be born, and we fear the future, not without reason. . . . Doubt and disorder are in us and with us. There is no thinking man, however shrewd or learned he may be, who can hope to dominate this anxiety, to escape from this impression of darkness.[1]

In the midst of economic, political, and social disruptions, Valéry saw the "cruelly injured mind," besieged by doubts and suffering from anxieties. This was the general intellectual crisis of the twentieth century, which touched almost every field of thought. The implications of new ideas and discoveries in philosophy, physics, psychology, and literature played a central role in this crisis, disturbing "thinking people" everywhere.

"The War, as I Saw It"   This was the title of a series of grotesque drawings that appeared in 1920 in *Simplicissimus,* Germany's leading satirical magazine. Nothing shows better the terrible impact of World War I than this profoundly disturbing example of expressionist art. (*Caroline Buckler*)

Modern Philosophy

Among those thinkers in the late nineteenth century who challenged the belief in progress and the general faith in the rational human mind, German philosopher Friedrich Nietzsche (1844–1900) was particularly influential. The son of a Lutheran minister, Nietzsche rejected Christianity and became a professor of classical languages until ill health forced him to retire at an early age. Never a systematic philosopher, Nietzsche wrote as a prophet in a provocative and poetic style. His first great work in 1872 argued that ever since classical Athens, the West had overemphasized rationality and stifled the passion and animal instinct that drive human activity and true creativity. Nietzsche went on to ques-

tion all values. He claimed that Christianity embodied a "slave morality," which glorified weakness, envy, and mediocrity. In Nietzsche's most famous line, a wise fool proclaims that "God is dead," dead because He has been murdered by lackadaisical modern Christians who no longer really believe in Him. Nietzsche viewed the pillars of conventional morality—reason, democracy, progress, respectability—as outworn social and psychological constructs whose influence was suffocating self-realization and excellence.

Nietzsche painted a dark world, foreshadowing perhaps his loss of sanity in 1889. The West was in decline; false values had triumphed. The death of God left people disoriented and depressed. The only hope for the individual was to accept the meaninglessness of human existence and then make that very meaninglessness a source of self-defined personal integrity and hence liberation. This would at least be possible for a few superior individuals, who could free themselves from the humdrum thinking of the masses and become true heroes. Little read during his active years, Nietzsche attracted growing attention in the early twentieth century, especially from German radicals who found inspiration in Nietzsche's ferocious assault on the conventions of pre-1914 imperial Germany. Subsequent generations have each discovered new Nietzsches, and his influence remains enormous to this day.

This growing dissatisfaction with established ideas before 1914 was apparent in other important thinkers. In the 1890s, French philosophy professor Henri Bergson (1859–1941) convinced many young people through his writing that immediate experience and intuition were as important as rational and scientific thinking for understanding reality. Indeed, according to Bergson, a religious experience or a mystical poem was often more accessible to human comprehension than a scientific law or a mathematical equation.

Another thinker who agreed about the limits of rational thinking was French socialist Georges Sorel (1847–1922). Sorel frankly characterized Marxian socialism as an inspiring but unprovable religion rather than a rational scientific truth. Socialism would come to power, he believed, through a great, violent strike of all working people, which would miraculously shatter capitalist society. Sorel rejected democracy and believed that the masses of the new socialist society would have to be tightly controlled by a small revolutionary elite.

The First World War accelerated the revolt against established certainties in philosophy, but that revolt went in two very different directions. In English-speaking countries, the main development was the acceptance of logical empiricism (or logical positivism) in university circles. In continental countries, where esoteric and remote logical empiricism did not win many converts, the primary development in philosophy was existentialism.

Logical empiricism was truly revolutionary. It quite simply rejected most of the concerns of traditional philosophy, from the existence of God to the meaning of happiness, as nonsense and hot air. This outlook began primarily with Austrian philosopher Ludwig Wittgenstein (1889–1951), who later immigrated to England, where he trained numerous disciples.

Wittgenstein argued in his pugnacious *Tractatus Logico-Philosophicus* (Essay on Logical Philosophy) in 1922 that philosophy is only the logical clarification of thoughts, and therefore it becomes the study of language, which expresses thoughts. The great philosoph-

ical issues of the ages—God, freedom, morality, and so on—are quite literally senseless, a great waste of time, for statements about them can be neither tested by scientific experiments nor demonstrated by the logic of mathematics. Statements about such matters reflect only the personal preferences of a given individual. As Wittgenstein put it in the famous last sentence of his work, "Of what one cannot speak, of that one must keep silent." Logical empiricism, which has remained dominant in England and the United States to this day, drastically reduced the scope of philosophical inquiry. Anxious people could find few, if any, answers in this direction.

Some looked for answers in *existentialism*. Highly diverse and even contradictory, existential thinkers were loosely united in a courageous search for moral values

Friedrich Nietzsche This colored photograph of the German philosopher was taken in 1882, when he was at the height of his creative powers. A brilliant iconoclast, Nietzsche debunked European values and challenged the optimistic faith in human rationality before World War I. (*AKG London*)

in a world of terror and uncertainty. Theirs were true voices of the age of anxiety.

Most existential thinkers in the twentieth century were atheists. Often inspired by Nietzsche, who had already proclaimed the death of God and called for new values, they did not believe a supreme being had established humanity's fundamental nature and given life its meaning. In the words of the famous French existentialist Jean-Paul Sartre (1905–1980), human beings simply exist: "They turn up, appear on the scene." Only after they "turn up" do they seek to define themselves. Honest human beings are terribly alone, for there is no God to help them. They are hounded by despair and the meaninglessness of life. The crisis of the existential thinker epitomized the modern intellectual crisis—the shattering of beliefs in God, reason, and progress.

Existentialists did recognize that human beings, unless they kill themselves, must act. Indeed, in the words of Sartre, "man is condemned to be free." There is therefore the possibility—indeed, the necessity—of giving meaning to life through actions, of defining oneself through choices. To do so, individuals must become "engaged" and choose their own actions courageously and consistently and in full awareness of their inescapable responsibility for their own behavior. In the end, existentialists argued, human beings can overcome life's absurdity.

Modern existentialism first attained prominence in Germany in the 1920s when philosophers Martin Heidegger and Karl Jaspers found a sympathetic audience among disillusioned postwar university students. But it was in France during and immediately after World War II that existentialism came of age. The terrible conditions of the war reinforced the existential view of and approach to life. On the one hand, the armies of the German dictator Hitler had conquered most of Europe and unleashed a hideous reign of barbarism. On the other, men and women had more than ever to define themselves by their actions. Specifically, each individual had to choose whether to join the resistance against Hitler or accept and even abet tyranny. The writings of Sartre, who along with Albert Camus (1913–1960) was the leading French existentialist, became enormously influential. Himself active in the French resistance, Sartre and his colleagues offered a powerful answer to profound moral issues and the contemporary crisis.

The Revival of Christianity

The loss of faith in human reason and in continual progress also led to a renewed interest in the Christian view of the world. Christianity and religion in general had been on the defensive in intellectual circles since the Enlightenment. In the years before 1914, some theologians, especially Protestant ones, had felt the need to interpret Christian doctrine and the Bible so that they did not seem to contradict science, evolution, and common sense. Christ was therefore seen primarily as the greatest moral teacher, and the "supernatural" aspects of his divinity were strenuously played down. Indeed, some modern theologians were embarrassed by the miraculous, unscientific aspects of Christianity and turned away from them.

Especially after World War I, a number of thinkers and theologians began to revitalize the fundamentals of Christianity. Sometimes described as Christian existentialists because they shared the loneliness and despair of atheistic existentialists, they stressed human beings' sinful nature, the need for faith, and the mystery of God's forgiveness. The revival of fundamental Christian belief after World War I was fed by rediscovery of the work of nineteenth-century Danish religious philosopher Søren Kierkegaard (1813–1855), whose ideas became extremely influential. Having rejected formalistic religion, Kierkegaard had eventually resolved his personal anguish over his imperfect nature by making a total religious commitment to a remote and majestic God.

Similar ideas were brilliantly developed by Swiss Protestant theologian Karl Barth (1886–1968), whose many influential writings after 1920 sought to re-create the religious intensity of the Reformation. For Barth, the basic fact about human beings is that they are imperfect, sinful creatures whose reason and will are hopelessly flawed. Religious truth is therefore made known to human beings only through God's grace. People have to accept God's word and the supernatural revelation of Jesus Christ with awe, trust, and obedience. Lowly mortals should not expect to "reason out" God and his ways.

Among Catholics, the leading existential Christian thinker was Gabriel Marcel (1887–1973). Born into a cultivated French family, where his atheistic father was "gratefully aware of all that . . . art owed to Catholicism but regarded Catholic thought itself as obsolete and tainted with absurd superstitions,"[2] Marcel found in the Catholic church an answer to what he called the postwar "broken world." Catholicism and religious belief provided the hope, humanity, honesty, and piety for which he hungered. Flexible and gentle, Marcel and his countryman Jacques Maritain (1882–1973) denounced anti-Semitism and supported closer ties with non-Catholics.

After 1914 religion became much more relevant and meaningful to thinking people than it had been before the war. In addition to Marcel and Maritain, many other illustrious individuals turned to religion between about 1920 and 1950. Poets T. S. Eliot and W. H. Auden, novelists Evelyn Waugh and Aldous Huxley, historian Arnold Toynbee, Oxford professor C. S. Lewis, psychoanalyst Karl Stern, physicist Max Planck, and philosopher Cyril Joad were all either converted to religion or attracted to it for the first time. (See the feature "Listening to the Past: A Christian View of Evil" on pages 954–955.) Religion, often of a despairing, existential variety, was one meaningful answer to terror and anxiety. In the words of another famous Roman Catholic convert, English novelist Graham Greene, "One began to believe in heaven because one believed in hell."[3]

The New Physics

Ever since the scientific revolution of the seventeenth century, scientific advances and their implications had greatly influenced the beliefs of thinking people. By the late nineteenth century, science was one of the main pillars supporting Western society's optimistic and rationalistic view of the world. The Darwinian concept of evolution had been accepted and assimilated in most intellectual circles. Progressive minds believed that science, unlike religion and philosophical speculation, was based on hard facts and controlled experiments. Science seemed to have achieved an unerring and almost complete picture of reality. Unchanging natural laws seemed to determine physical processes and permit useful

Unlocking the Power of the Atom Many of the fanciful visions of science fiction came true in the twentieth century, although not exactly as first imagined. This 1927 cartoon satirizes a professor who has split the atom and unwittingly destroyed his building and neighborhood in the process. In the Second World War the professors harnessed the atom in bombs and decimated faraway cities and foreign civilians. *(Mary Evans Picture Library)*

solutions to more and more problems. All this was comforting, especially to people who were no longer committed to traditional religious beliefs. And all this was challenged by the new physics.

An important first step toward the new physics was the discovery at the end of the nineteenth century that atoms were not like hard, permanent little billiard balls. They were actually composed of many far-smaller, fast-moving particles, such as electrons and protons. Polish-born physicist Marie Curie (1867–1934) and her French husband discovered that radium constantly emits subatomic particles and thus does not have a constant atomic weight. Building on this and other work in radiation, German physicist Max Planck (1858–1947) showed in 1900 that subatomic energy is emitted in uneven little spurts, which Planck called "quanta," and not in a steady stream, as previously believed. Planck's discovery called into question the old sharp distinction between matter and energy; the implication was that matter and energy might be different forms of the same thing. The old view of atoms as the stable, basic building blocks of nature, with a different kind of unbreakable atom for each of the ninety-two chemical elements, was badly shaken.

In 1905 German-born Jewish genius Albert Einstein (1879–1955) went further than the Curies and Planck in undermining Newtonian physics. His famous theory of special relativity postulated that time and space are relative to the viewpoint of the observer and that only the speed of light is constant for all frames of reference in the universe. In order to make his revolutionary and paradoxical idea somewhat comprehensible to the nonmathematical layperson, Einstein later used analogies involving moving trains. For example, if a woman in the middle of a moving car got up and walked forward to the door, she had gone, relative to the train, a half car length. But relative to an observer on the embankment, she had gone farther. The closed framework of Newtonian physics was quite limited compared to that of Einsteinian physics, which unified an apparently infinite universe with the incredibly small, fast-moving subatomic world. Moreover, Einstein's theory stated clearly that matter and energy are interchangeable and that even a particle of matter contains enormous levels of potential energy.

The 1920s opened the "heroic age of physics," in the apt words of one of its leading pioneers, Ernest Rutherford (1871–1937). Breakthrough followed breakthrough. In 1919 Rutherford showed that the atom could be split. By 1944 seven subatomic particles had been identified, of which the most important was the neutron. The neutron's capacity to pass through other atoms allowed for even more intense experimental bombardment of matter, leading to chain reactions of unbelievable force. This was the road to the atomic bomb.

Although few nonscientists understood this revolution in physics, the implications of the new theories and discoveries, as presented by newspapers and popular writers, were disturbing to millions of men and women in the 1920s and 1930s. The new universe was strange and troubling. It lacked any absolute objective reality. Everything was "relative," that is, dependent on the observer's frame of reference. Moreover, the universe was uncertain and undetermined, without stable building blocks. In 1927 German physicist Werner Heisenberg (1901–1976) formulated the "principle of uncertainty," which postulates that because it is impossible to know the position and speed of an individual electron, it is therefore impossible to predict its behavior. Instead of Newton's dependable, rational laws, there seemed to be only tendencies and probabilities in an extraordinarily complex and uncertain universe.

Moreover, a universe described by abstract mathematical symbols seemed to have little to do with human experience and human problems. When, for example, Planck was asked what science could contribute to resolving conflicts of values, his response was simple: "Science is not qualified to speak to this question." Physics, the queen of the sciences, no longer provided people easy, optimistic answers—for that matter, it did not provide any answers at all.

Freudian Psychology

With physics presenting an uncertain universe so unrelated to ordinary human experience, questions regarding the power and potential of the human mind assumed special significance. The findings and speculations of leading psychologist Sigmund Freud (see page 812) were particularly disturbing.

Before Freud, poets and mystics had probed the unconscious and irrational aspects of human behavior. But most professional, "scientific" psychologists assumed that a single, unified conscious mind processed sense experiences in a rational and logical way. Human behavior in turn was the result of rational calculation—of "thinking"—by the conscious mind. Basing his insights on the analysis of dreams and of hysteria, Freud developed a very different view of the human psyche beginning in the late 1880s.

Munch: The Dance of Life   Like his contemporary Sigmund Freud, the expressionist painter Edvard Munch studied the turmoil and fragility of human thought and action. Solitary figures struggling with fear and uncertainty dominate his work. Here the girl in white represents innocence, the tense woman in black stands for mourning and rejection, and the woman in red evokes the joy of passing pleasure. *(© Munch-museet, Oslo kommunes kunstsamlinger. Photo: Jacques Lathion, Nasjongalleriet, Oslo)*

According to Freud, human behavior is basically irrational. The key to understanding the mind is the primitive, irrational unconscious, which he called the *id*. The unconscious is driven by sexual, aggressive, and pleasure-seeking desires and is locked in a constant battle with the other parts of the mind: the rationalizing conscious (the *ego*), which mediates what a person *can* do, and ingrained moral values (the *superego*), which specify what a person *should* do. Human behavior is a product of a fragile compromise between instinctual drives and the controls of rational thinking and moral values. Since the instinctual drives are extremely powerful, the ever-present danger for individuals and whole societies is that unacknowledged drives will overwhelm the control mechanisms in a violent, distorted way. Yet Freud also agreed with Nietzsche that the mechanisms of rational thinking and traditional moral values can be too strong. They can repress sexual desires too effectively, crippling individuals and entire peoples with guilt and neurotic fears.

Freudian psychology and clinical psychiatry had become an international movement by 1910, but only after 1918 did they receive popular attention, especially in the Protestant countries of northern Europe and in the United States. Many opponents and even some enthusiasts interpreted Freud as saying that the first requirement for mental health is an uninhibited sex life. Thus after the First World War, the popular interpretation of Freud reflected and encouraged growing sexual experimentation, particularly among middle-class women. For more serious students, the psychology of Freud and his followers drastically undermined the old, easy optimism about the rational and progressive nature of the human mind.

Twentieth-Century Literature

The general intellectual climate of pessimism, relativism, and alienation was also articulated in literature. Novelists developed new techniques to express new realities. The great nineteenth-century novelists had typically written as all-knowing narrators, describing realistic characters and their relationship to an understandable, if sometimes harsh, society. In the twentieth century, most major writers adopted the limited, often confused viewpoint of a single individual. Like Freud, these novelists focused their attention on the complexity and irrationality of the human mind, where feelings, memories, and desires are forever scrambled. The great French novelist Marcel Proust (1871–1922), in his semi-autobiographical *Remembrance of Things Past*

Virginia Woolf   Her novels captured sensations like impressionist paintings, and her home attracted a circle of artists and writers known as the Bloomsbury Group. Many of Woolf's essays dealt with women's issues and urged greater opportunity for women's creativity. *(Gisèle Freund/Photo Researchers, Inc.)*

(1913–1927), recalled bittersweet memories of childhood and youthful love and tried to discover their innermost meaning. To do so, Proust lived like a hermit in a soundproof Paris apartment for ten years, withdrawing from the present to dwell on the past.

Serious novelists also used the "stream-of-consciousness" technique to explore the psyche. In *Jacob's Room* (1922), Virginia Woolf (1882–1941) created a novel made up of a series of internal monologues, in which ideas and emotions from different periods of time bubble up as randomly as from a patient on a psychoanalyst's couch. William Faulkner (1897–1962), perhaps America's greatest twentieth-century novelist, used the same technique in *The Sound and the Fury* (1922), much of whose intense drama is confusedly seen through the eyes of an idiot. The most famous stream-of-consciousness novel—and surely the most disturbing novel of its generation—is *Ulysses,* which Irish novelist James Joyce (1882–1941) published in 1922. Into an account of an ordinary day in the life of an ordinary man, Joyce weaves an extended ironic parallel between his hero's aimless wanderings through the streets and pubs of Dublin and the adventures of Homer's hero Ulysses on his way home from Troy. Abandoning conventional grammar and blending foreign words, puns, bits of knowledge, and scraps of memory together in bewildering confusion, the language of Ulysses is intended to mirror modern life itself: a gigantic riddle waiting to be unraveled.

As creative writers turned their attention from society to the individual and from realism to psychological relativity, they rejected the idea of progress. Some even described "anti-utopias," nightmare visions of things to come. In 1918 an obscure German high school teacher named Oswald Spengler (1880–1936) published *The Decline of the West,* which quickly became an international sensation. According to Spengler, every culture experiences a life cycle of growth and decline. Western civilization, in Spengler's opinion, was in its old age, and death was approaching in the form of conquest by the yellow race. T. S. Eliot (1888–1965), in his famous poem *The Waste Land* (1922), depicts a world of growing desolation, although after his conversion to Anglo-Catholicism in 1927, Eliot came to hope cautiously for humanity's salvation. No such hope appears in the work of Franz Kafka (1883–1924), whose novels *The Trial* (1925) and *The Castle* (1926), as well as several of his greatest short stories, portray helpless individuals crushed by inexplicably hostile forces. The German-Jewish Kafka died young, at forty-one, and so did not see the world of his nightmares materialize in the Nazi state.

Englishman George Orwell (1903–1950), however, had seen both that reality and its Stalinist counterpart by 1949, when he wrote perhaps the ultimate in anti-utopian literature: *1984*. Orwell set the action in the future, in 1984. Big Brother—the dictator—and his totalitarian state use a new kind of language, sophisticated technology, and psychological terror to strip a weak individual of his last shred of human dignity. The supremely self-confident chief of the Thought Police tells the tortured, broken, and framed Winston Smith, "If you want a picture of the future, imagine a boot stamping on a human face—forever."[4] A phenomenal bestseller, *1984* spoke to millions of people in the closing years of the age of anxiety.

MODERN ART AND MUSIC

Throughout the twentieth century, there has been considerable unity in the arts. The "modernism" of the immediate prewar years and the 1920s is still strikingly modern. Like the scientists and creative artists who were partaking of the same culture, creative artists rejected old forms and old values. Modernism in art and music meant constant experimentation and a search for new kinds of expression. And though many people find the many and varied modern visions of the arts strange, disturbing, and even ugly, the twentieth century, so dismal in many respects, will probably stand as one of Western civilization's great artistic eras.

Architecture and Design

Modernism in the arts was loosely unified by a revolution in architecture. This revolution intended nothing less than a transformation of the physical framework of urban society according to a new principle: *functionalism*. Buildings, like industrial products, should be useful and "functional"—that is, they should serve, as well as possible, the purpose for which they were made. Thus architects and designers had to work with engineers, town planners, and even santitation experts. Moreover, they had to throw away useless ornamentation and find beauty and aesthetic pleasure in the clean lines of practical constructions and efficient machinery. Franco-Swiss genius Le Corbusier (1887–1965) insisted that "a house is a machine for living in."[5]

The United States, with its rapid urban growth and lack of rigid building traditions, pioneered in the new architecture. In the 1890s, the Chicago school of architects, led by Louis H. Sullivan (1856–1924), used cheap steel, reinforced concrete, and electric elevators to build skyscrapers and office buildings lacking almost any exterior ornamentation. In the first decade of the twentieth century, Sullivan's student Frank Lloyd Wright (1869–1959) built a series of radically new and truly modern houses featuring low lines, open interiors, and mass-produced building materials. Europeans were inspired by these and other American examples of functional construction, like the massive, unadorned grain elevators of the Midwest.

In Europe architectural leadership centered in German-speaking countries until Hitler took power in 1933. In 1911 twenty-eight-year-old Walter Gropius (1883–1969) broke sharply with the past in his design of the Fagus shoe factory at Alfeld, Germany—a clean, light, elegant building of glass and iron. After the First World War, Gropius merged the schools of fine and applied arts at Weimar into a single, interdisciplinary school, the Bauhaus. The Bauhaus brought together many leading modern architects, designers, and theatrical innovators. Working as an effective, inspired team, they combined the study of fine art, such as painting and sculpture, with the study of applied art in the crafts of printing, weaving, and furniture making. Throughout the 1920s, the Bauhaus, with its stress on functionalism and good design for everyday life, attracted enthusiastic students from all over the world. It had a great and continuing impact.

Another leader in the "international" style, Ludwig Mies van der Rohe (1886–1969), followed Gropius as director of the Bauhaus in 1930 and immigrated to the United States in 1937. His classic Lake Shore Apartments in Chicago, built between 1948 and 1951, symbolized the triumph of steel-frame and glass-wall modern architecture in the great building boom after the Second World War.

Modern Painting

Modern painting grew out of a revolt against French impressionism. The *impressionism* of such French painters as Claude Monet (1840–1926), Pierre Auguste Renoir (1841–1919), and Camille Pissarro (1830–1903) was, in part, a kind of "superrealism." Leaving exact copying of objects to photography, these artists sought to capture the momentary overall feeling, or impression, of light falling on a real-life scene before their eyes. By 1890, when impressionism was finally established, a few artists known as *postimpressionists,* or sometimes as *expressionists,* were already striking out in new directions. After 1905 art increasingly took on a

Frank Lloyd Wright: The "Falling Water" House   Often considered Wright's master-piece, Falling Water combines modern architectural concepts with close attention to a spectacular site. Anchored to a high rock ledge by means of reinforced concrete, the house soars out over a cascading waterfall at Bear Run in western Pennsylvania. Built in 1937 for a Pittsburgh businessman, Falling Water is now open to the public and attracts 70,000 visitors each year. *(Western Pennsylvania Conservancy/Art Resource, NY)*

nonrepresentational, abstract character, a development that reached its high point after World War II.

Though individualistic in their styles, postimpressionists were united in their desire to know and depict worlds other than the visible world of fact. Like the early-nineteenth-century romantics, they wanted to portray unseen, inner worlds of emotion and imagination. Like modern novelists, they wanted to express a complicated psychological view of reality as well as an

overwhelming emotional intensity. In *The Starry Night* (1889), for example, the great Dutch expressionist Vincent van Gogh (1853–1890) painted the vision of his mind's eye. Flaming cypress trees, exploding stars, and a cometlike Milky Way swirl together in one great cosmic rhythm. Paul Gauguin (1848–1903), the French stockbroker-turned-painter, pioneered in expressionist techniques, though he used them to infuse his work with tranquillity and mysticism. In 1891 he fled to the

South Pacific in search of unspoiled beauty and a primitive way of life. Gauguin believed that the form and design of a picture were important in themselves and that the painter need not try to represent objects on canvas as the eye actually saw them.

Fascination with form, as opposed to light, was characteristic of postimpressionism and expressionism. Paul Cézanne (1839–1906), who had a profound influence on twentieth-century painting, was particularly committed to form and ordered design. He told a young painter, "You must see in nature the cylinder, the sphere, and the cone."[6] As Cézanne's later work became increasingly abstract and nonrepresentational, it also moved away from the traditional three-dimensional perspective toward the two-dimensional plane, which has characterized so much of modern art. The expressionism of a group of painters led by Henri Matisse (1869–1954) was so extreme that an exhibition of their work in Paris in 1905 prompted shocked critics to call them *les fauves*—"the wild beasts." Matisse and his followers still painted real objects, but their primary concern was the arrangement of color, line, and form as an end in itself.

In 1907 a young Spaniard in Paris, Pablo Picasso (1881–1973), founded another movement—*cubism*.

Cubism concentrated on a complex geometry of zigzagging lines and sharply angled, overlapping planes. About three years later came the ultimate stage in the development of abstract, nonrepresentational art. Artists such as the Russian-born Wassily Kandinsky (1866–1944) turned away from nature completely. "The observer," said Kandinsky, "must learn to look at [my] pictures . . . as form and color combinations . . . as a representation of mood and not as a representation of *objects*."[7] On the eve of the First World War, extreme expressionism and abstract painting were developing rapidly not only in Paris but also in Russia and Germany. Modern art had become international.

In the 1920s and 1930s, the artistic movements of the prewar years were extended and consolidated. The most notable new developments were *dadaism* and *surrealism*. Dadaism attacked all accepted standards of art and behavior, delighting in outrageous conduct. Its name, from the French word *dada,* meaning "hobbyhorse," is deliberately nonsensical. A famous example of dadaism is a reproduction of Leonardo da Vinci's *Mona Lisa* in which the famous woman with the mysterious smile sports a mustache and is ridiculed with an obscene inscription. After 1924 many dadaists were attracted to surrealism, which became very influential in art in the

Picasso: Guernica   In this rich, complex work a shrieking woman falls from a burning house on the far right. On the left a woman holds a dead child, while toward the center are fragments of a warrior and a screaming horse pierced by a spear. Picasso has used only the mournful colors of black, white, and gray. *(© Copyright ARS, NY. Museo Nacional Centro de Arte Reina Sofia, Madrid, Spain)*

late 1920s and 1930s. Surrealists painted a fantastic world of wild dreams and complex symbols, where watches melted and giant metronomes beat time in precisely drawn but impossible alien landscapes.

Refusing to depict ordinary visual reality, surrealist painters made powerful statements about the age of anxiety. Picasso's twenty-six-foot-long mural *Guernica* (1937) masterfully unites several powerful strands in twentieth-century art. Inspired by the Spanish civil war, the painting commemorates the bombing of the ancient Spanish town of Guernica by fascist planes, an attack that took the lives of a thousand people—one out of every eight inhabitants—in a single night of terror. Combining the free distortion of expressionism, the overlapping planes of cubism, and the surrealist fascination with grotesque subject matter, *Guernica* is what Picasso meant it to be: an unforgettable attack on "brutality and darkness."

Modern Music

Developments in modern music were strikingly parallel to those in painting. Composers, too, were attracted by the emotional intensity of expressionism. The ballet *The Rite of Spring* by composer Igor Stravinsky (1882–1971) practically caused a riot when it was first performed in Paris in 1913 by Sergei Diaghilev's famous Russian dance company. The combination of pulsating, dissonant rhythms from the orchestra pit and an earthy representation of lovemaking by the dancers on the stage seemed a shocking, almost pornographic enactment of a primitive fertility rite.

After the experience of the First World War, when irrationality and violence seemed to pervade the human experience, expressionism in opera and ballet flourished. One of the most famous and powerful examples was the opera *Wozzeck*, by Alban Berg (1885–1935), first performed in Berlin in 1925. Blending a half-sung, half-spoken kind of dialogue with harsh, atonal music, *Wozzeck* is a gruesome tale of a soldier driven by Kafka-like inner terrors and vague suspicions of unfaithfulness to murder his mistress.

Some composers turned their backs on long-established musical conventions. As abstract painters arranged lines and color but did not draw identifiable objects, so modern composers arranged sounds without creating recognizable harmonies. Led by Viennese composer Arnold Schönberg (1874–1951), they abandoned traditional harmony and tonality. The musical notes in a given piece were no longer united and organized by a key; instead they were independent and unrelated. Schönberg's twelve-tone music of the 1920s

arranged all twelve notes of the scale in an abstract, mathematical pattern, or "tone row." This pattern sounded like no pattern at all to the ordinary listener and could be detected only by a highly trained eye studying the musical score. Accustomed to the harmonies of classical and romantic music, audiences generally resisted modern atonal music. Only after the Second World War did it begin to win acceptance.

MOVIES AND RADIO

Until after World War II at the earliest, these revolutionary changes in art and music appealed mainly to a minority of "highbrows" and not to the general public. That public was primarily and enthusiastically wrapped up in movies and radio. The long-declining traditional arts and amusements of people in villages and small towns almost vanished, replaced by standardized, commercial entertainment.

Moving pictures were first shown as a popular novelty in naughty peepshows—"What the Butler Saw"—and penny arcades in the 1890s, especially in Paris. The first movie houses date from an experiment in Los Angeles in 1902. They quickly attracted large audiences and led to the production of short, silent action films such as the eight-minute *Great Train Robbery* of 1903. American directors and business people then set up "movie factories," at first in the New York area and then after 1910 in Los Angeles. These factories churned out two short films each week. On the eve of the First World War, full-length feature films such as the Italian *Quo Vadis* and the American *Birth of a Nation,* coupled with improvements in the quality of pictures, suggested the screen's vast possibilities.

During the First World War, the United States became the dominant force in the rapidly expanding silent-film industry. In the 1920s, Mack Sennett (1884–1960) and his zany Keystone Kops specialized in short, slapstick comedies noted for frantic automobile chases, custard-pie battles, and gorgeous bathing beauties. Screen stars such as Mary Pickford and Lillian Gish, Douglas Fairbanks and Rudolf Valentino, became household names, with their own "fan clubs." Yet Charlie Chaplin (1889–1978), a funny little Englishman working in Hollywood, was unquestionably the king of the "silver screen" in the 1920s. In his enormously popular role as a lonely tramp, complete with baggy trousers, battered derby, and an awkward, shuffling walk, Chaplin symbolized the "gay spirit of laughter in a cruel, crazy world."[8] Chaplin also demonstrated that in the hands of a genius, the new medium could combine mass entertainment and artistic accomplishment.

The early 1920s were also the great age of German films. Protected and developed during the war, the large German studios excelled in bizarre expressionist dramas, beginning with *The Cabinet of Dr. Caligari* in 1919. Unfortunately, their period of creativity was short-lived. By 1926 American money was drawing the leading German talents to Hollywood and consolidating America's international domination. Film making was big business, and European theater owners were forced to book whole blocks of American films to get the few pictures they really wanted. This system put European producers at a great disadvantage until "talkies" permitted a revival of national film industries in the 1930s, particularly in France.

Whether foreign or domestic, motion pictures became the main entertainment of the masses until after the Second World War. In Great Britain one in every four adults went to the movies twice a week in the late 1930s, and two in five went at least once a week. Continental countries had similar figures. The greatest appeal of motion pictures was that they offered ordinary people a temporary escape from the hard realities of everyday life. For an hour or two, the moviegoer could flee the world of international tensions, uncertainty, unemployment, and personal frustrations. The appeal of escapist entertainment was especially strong during the Great Depression. Millions flocked to musical comedies featuring glittering stars such as Ginger Rogers and Fred Astaire and to the fanciful cartoons of Mickey Mouse and his friends.

Radio became possible with the transatlantic "wireless" communication of Guglielmo Marconi (1874–1937) in 1901 and the development of the vacuum tube in 1904, which permitted the transmission of speech and music. But only in 1920 were the first major public broadcasts of special events made in Great Britain and the United States. Lord Northcliffe, who had pioneered in journalism with the inexpensive, mass-circulation *Daily Mail,* sponsored a broadcast of "only one artist . . . the world's very best, the soprano Nellie Melba."[9] Singing from London in English, Italian, and French, Melba was heard simultaneously all over Europe on June 16, 1920. This historic event captured the public's imagination. The meteoric career of radio was launched.

Every major country quickly established national broadcasting networks. In the United States such networks were privately owned and financed by advertising. In Great Britain Parliament set up an independent,

The Great Dictator   In 1940 the renowned actor and director Charlie Chaplin abandoned the little tramp to satirize the "great dictator," Adolf Hitler. Chaplin had strong political views and made a number of films with political themes as the escapist fare of the Great Depression gave way to the reality of the Second World War. *(The Museum of Modern Art/Still Film Archives)*

public corporation, the British Broadcasting Corporation (BBC), supported by licensing fees. Elsewhere in Europe the typical pattern was direct control by the government.

Whatever the institutional framework, radio became popular and influential. By the late 1930s, more than three out of every four households in both democratic Great Britain and dictatorial Germany had at least one cheap, mass-produced radio. In other European countries, radio ownership was not quite so widespread, but the new medium was no less important.

Radio in unscrupulous hands was particularly well suited for political propaganda. Dictators such as Mussolini and Hitler controlled the airwaves and could reach enormous national audiences with their frequent, dramatic speeches. In democratic countries, politicians such as President Franklin Roosevelt and Prime

Minister Stanley Baldwin effectively used informal "fireside chats" to bolster their support.

Motion pictures also became powerful tools of indoctrination, especially in countries with dictatorial regimes. Lenin himself encouraged the development of Soviet film making, believing that the new medium was essential to the social and ideological transformation of the country. Beginning in the mid-1920s, a series of epic films, the most famous of which were directed by Sergei Eisenstein (1898–1948), brilliantly dramatized the communist view of Russian history.

In Germany Hitler turned to a young and immensely talented woman film maker, Leni Riefenstahl (b. 1902), for a masterpiece of documentary propaganda, *The Triumph of the Will,* based on the Nazi party rally at Nuremberg in 1934. Riefenstahl combined stunning aerial photography, joyful crowds welcoming Hitler, and mass processions of young Nazi fanatics. Her film was a brilliant and all-too-powerful documentary of Germany's "Nazi rebirth." The new media of mass culture were potentially dangerous instruments of political manipulation.

✦ THE SEARCH FOR PEACE AND POLITICAL STABILITY

As established patterns of thought and culture were challenged and mangled by the ferocious impact of World War I, so also was the political fabric stretched and torn by the consequences of the great conflict. The Versailles settlement had established a shaky truce, not a solid peace. Thus national leaders faced a gigantic task as they struggled with uncertainty and sought to create a stable international order within the general context of intellectual crisis and revolutionary artistic experimentation.

The pursuit of real and lasting peace proved difficult for many reasons. Germany hated the Treaty of Versailles. France was fearful and isolated. Britain was undependable, and the United States had turned its back on European problems. Eastern Europe was in ferment, and no one could predict the future of communist Russia. Moreover, the international economic situation was poor and greatly complicated by war debts and disrupted patterns of trade. Yet for a time, from 1925 to late 1929, it appeared that peace and stability were within reach. When the subsequent collapse of the 1930s mocked these hopes, the disillusionment of liberals in the democracies was intensified.

Germany and the Western Powers

Germany was the key to lasting peace. Yet to Germans of all political parties, the Treaty of Versailles represented a harsh, dictated peace, to be revised or repudiated as soon as possible. The treaty had neither broken nor reduced Germany, which was potentially still the strongest country in Europe. Thus the treaty had fallen between two stools: too harsh for a peace of reconciliation, too soft for a peace of conquest.

Moreover, with ominous implications for the future, France and Great Britain did not see eye to eye on Germany. By the end of 1919, France wanted to stress the harsh elements in the Treaty of Versailles. Most of the war in the west had been fought on French soil, and the expected costs of reconstruction, as well as repaying war debts to the United States, were staggering. Thus French politicians believed that massive reparations from Germany were a vital economic necessity. Also, having compromised with President Wilson only to be betrayed by America's failure to ratify the treaty, many French leaders saw strict implementation of all provisions of the Treaty of Versailles as France's last best hope. Large reparation payments could hold Germany down indefinitely, and France would realize its goal of security.

The British soon felt differently. Prewar Germany had been Great Britain's second-best market in the entire world, and after the war a healthy, prosperous Germany appeared to be essential to the British economy. Indeed, many English people agreed with the analysis of the young English economist John Maynard Keynes (1883–1946), who eloquently denounced the Treaty of Versailles in his famous *Economic Consequences of the Peace* (1919). According to Keynes's interpretation, astronomical reparations and harsh economic measures would indeed reduce Germany to the position of an impoverished second-rate power, but such impoverishment would increase economic hardship in all countries. Only a complete revision of the foolish treaty could save Germany—and Europe. Keynes's attack exploded like a bombshell and became very influential. It stirred deep guilt feelings about Germany in the English-speaking world, feelings that often paralyzed English and American leaders in their relations with Germany and its leaders between the First and the Second World Wars.

The British were also suspicious of France's army—momentarily the largest in Europe—and France's foreign policy. Ever since 1890, France had looked to Russia as a powerful ally against Germany. But with

Russia hostile and socialist, and with Britain and the United States unwilling to make any firm commitments, France turned to the newly formed states of eastern Europe for diplomatic support. In 1921 France signed a mutual defense pact with Poland and associated itself closely with the so-called Little Entente, an alliance that joined Czechoslovakia, Romania, and Yugoslavia against defeated and bitter Hungary. The British and the French were also on cool terms because of conflicts relating to their League of Nations mandates in the Middle East.

While French and British leaders drifted in different directions, the Allied reparations commission completed its work. In April 1921, it announced that Germany had to pay the enormous sum of 132 billion gold marks ($33 billion) in annual installments of 2.5 billion gold marks. Facing possible occupation of more of its territory, the young German republic, which had been founded in Weimar but moved back to Berlin, made its first payment in 1921. Then in 1922, wracked by rapid inflation and political assassinations and motivated by hostility and arrogance as well, the Weimar Republic announced its inability to pay more. It proposed a moratorium on reparations for three years, with the clear implication that thereafter reparations would be either drastically reduced or eliminated entirely.

The British were willing to accept a moratorium on reparations, but the French were not. Led by their tough-minded, legalistic prime minister, Raymond Poincaré (1860–1934), they decided they had to either call Germany's bluff or see the entire peace settlement dissolve to France's great disadvantage. So, despite strong British protests, in early January 1923, armies of France and its ally Belgium began to occupy the Ruhr district, the heartland of industrial Germany, creating the most serious international crisis of the 1920s. If forcible collection proved impossible, France would use occupation to paralyze Germany and force it to accept the Treaty of Versailles.

Strengthened by a wave of patriotism, the German government ordered the people of the Ruhr to stop working and start passively resisting the French occupation. The coal mines and steel mills of the Ruhr grew silent, leaving 10 percent of Germany's total population in need of relief. The French answer to passive resistance was to seal off not only the Ruhr but also the entire Rhineland from the rest of Germany, letting in only enough food to prevent starvation. The French also revived plans for a separate state in the Rhineland.

By the summer of 1923, France and Germany were engaged in a great test of wills. French armies could not collect reparations from striking workers at gunpoint. But French occupation was indeed paralyzing Germany and its economy and had turned rapid German inflation into runaway inflation. Faced with the need to support the striking Ruhr workers and their employers, the German government began to print money to pay its bills. Prices soared. People went to the store with a big bag of paper money; they returned home with a handful of groceries. German money rapidly lost all value, and so did anything else with a stated fixed value.

Runaway inflation brought about a social revolution. The accumulated savings of many retired and middle-

"Hands Off the Ruhr"   The French occupation of the Ruhr to collect reparations payments raised a storm of patriotic protest in Germany. This anti-French poster of 1923 turns Marianne, the personification of French republican virtue, into a vicious harpy. *(International Instituut voor Sociale Geschiedenis)*

Hände weg vom Ruhrgebiet!

class people were wiped out. Catastrophic inflation cruelly mocked the old middle-class virtues of thrift, caution, and self-reliance. Many Germans felt betrayed. They hated and blamed the Western governments, their own government, big business, the Jews, the workers, and the communists for their misfortune. They were psychologically prepared to follow radical leaders in a crisis.

In August 1923, as the mark fell and political unrest grew throughout Germany, Gustav Stresemann (1878–1929) assumed leadership of the government. Stresemann adopted a compromising attitude. He called off passive resistance in the Ruhr and in October agreed in principle to pay reparations but asked for a re-examination of Germany's ability to pay. Poincaré accepted. His hard line was becoming increasingly unpopular with French citizens, and it was hated in Britain and the United States.

More generally, in both Germany and France, power was finally passing to the moderates, who realized that continued confrontation was a destructive, no-win situation. Thus after five long years of hostility and tension, culminating in a kind of undeclared war in the Ruhr in 1923, Germany and France decided to give compromise and cooperation a try. The British, and even the Americans, were willing to help. The first step was a reasonable compromise on the reparations question.

Hope in Foreign Affairs, 1924–1929

The reparations commission appointed an international committee of financial experts headed by American banker Charles G. Dawes to re-examine reparations from a broad perspective. The resulting Dawes Plan (1924) was accepted by France, Germany, and Britain. Germany's yearly reparations were reduced and depended on the level of German economic prosperity. Germany would also receive large loans from the United States to promote German recovery. In short, Germany would get private loans from the United States and pay reparations to France and Britain, thus enabling those countries to repay the large sums they owed the United States.

This circular flow of international payments was complicated and risky, but for a while it worked. The German republic experienced a spectacular economic recovery. By 1929 Germany's wealth and income were 50 percent greater than in 1913. With prosperity and large, continual inflows of American capital, Germany easily paid about $1.3 billion in reparations in 1927 and 1928, enabling France and Britain to pay the United States. In this way the Americans, who did not have armies but who did have money, belatedly played a part in the general economic settlement that, though far from ideal, facilitated the worldwide recovery of the late 1920s.

This economic settlement was matched by a political settlement. In 1925 the leaders of Europe signed a number of agreements at Locarno, Switzerland. Germany and France solemnly pledged to accept their common border, and both Britain and Italy agreed to fight either France or Germany if one invaded the other. Stresemann also agreed to settle boundary disputes with Poland and Czechoslovakia by peaceful means, and France promised those countries military aid if Germany attacked them. For years, a "spirit of Locarno" gave Europeans a sense of growing security and stability in international affairs.

Other developments also strengthened hopes. In 1926 Germany joined the League of Nations, where Stresemann continued his "peace offensive." In 1928 fifteen countries signed the Kellogg-Briand Pact, initiated by French prime minister Aristide Briand and U.S. secretary of state Frank B. Kellogg. This multinational pact "condemned and renounced war as an instrument of national policy." The signing states agreed to settle international disputes peacefully. Often seen as idealistic nonsense because it made no provisions for action in case war actually occurred, the pact was still a positive step. It fostered the cautious optimism of the late 1920s and also encouraged the hope that the United States would accept its responsibilities as a great world power and contribute to European stability.

Hope in Democratic Government

Domestic politics also offered reason to hope. During the occupation of the Ruhr and the great inflation, republican government in Germany had appeared on the verge of collapse. In 1923 communists momentarily entered provincial governments, and in November an obscure nobody named Adolf Hitler leaped onto a table in a beer hall in Munich and proclaimed a "national socialist revolution." But Hitler's plot to seize control of the government was poorly organized and easily crushed, and Hitler was sentenced to prison, where he outlined his theories and program in his book *Mein Kampf* (My Struggle). Throughout the 1920s, Hitler's National Socialist party attracted support only from a few fanatical anti-Semites, ultranationalists, and disgruntled ex-servicemen. In 1928 his party had an insignificant twelve seats in the Reichstag. Indeed, after

An American in Paris   The young Josephine Baker suddenly became a star when she brought an exotic African eroticism to French music halls in 1925. American blacks and Africans had a powerful impact on entertainment in Europe in the 1920s and 1930s. *(Hulton-Getty/Tony Stone Images)*

1923 democracy seemed to take root in Weimar Germany. A new currency was established, and the economy boomed.

The moderate businessmen who tended to dominate the various German coalition governments were convinced that economic prosperity demanded good relations with the Western powers, and they supported parliamentary government at home. Stresemann himself was a man of this class, and he was the key figure in every government until his death in 1929. Elections were held regularly, and republican democracy appeared to have growing support among a majority of the Germans.

There were, however, sharp political divisions in the country. Many unrepentant nationalists and monarchists populated the right and the army. Members of Germany's recently formed Communist party were noisy and active on the left. The Communists, directed from Moscow, reserved their greatest hatred and sharpest barbs for their cousins the Social Democrats, whom they endlessly accused of betraying the revolution. The working classes were divided politically, but a majority supported the nonrevolutionary but socialist Social Democrats.

The situation in France had numerous similarities to that in Germany. Communists and Socialists battled for the support of the workers. After 1924 the democratically elected government rested mainly in the hands of coalitions of moderates, and business interests were well represented. France's great accomplishment was rapid rebuilding of its war-torn northern region. The expense of this undertaking led, however, to a large deficit and substantial inflation. By early 1926, the franc had fallen to 10 percent of its prewar value, causing a severe crisis. Poincaré was recalled to office, while Briand remained minister for foreign affairs. The Poincaré government proceeded to slash spending and raise taxes, restoring confidence in the economy. The franc was "saved," stabilized at about one-fifth of its prewar value. Good times prevailed until 1930.

Despite political shortcomings, France attracted artists and writers from all over the world in the 1920s. Much of the intellectual and artistic ferment of the times flourished in Paris. As writer Gertrude Stein (1874–1946), a leader of the large colony of American expatriates living in Paris, later recalled, "Paris was where the twentieth century was."[10] More generally, France appealed to foreigners and the French as a harmonious combination of small businesses and family farms, of bold innovation and solid traditions.

Britain, too, faced challenges after 1920. The wartime trend toward greater social equality continued, however, helping maintain social harmony. The great problem was unemployment. Many of Britain's best markets had been lost during the war. In June 1921, almost 2.2 million people—23 percent of the labor force—were out of work, and throughout the 1920s unemployment hovered around 12 percent. Yet the state provided unemployment benefits of equal size to all those without jobs and supplemented those payments with subsidized housing, medical aid, and increased old-age pensions. These and other measures kept living standards from seriously declining, defused class tensions, and pointed the way toward the welfare state Britain established after World War II.

Relative social harmony was accompanied by the rise of the Labour party as a determined champion of the working classes and of greater social equality. Committed to the kind of moderate, "revisionist" socialism that had emerged before World War I (see page 849), the Labour party replaced the Liberal party as the main opposition to the Conservatives. The new prominence of the Labour party reflected the decline of old liberal ideals of competitive capitalism, limited government control, and individual responsibility. In 1924 and 1929, the Labour party under Ramsay MacDonald (1866–1937) governed the country with the support of the smaller Liberal party. Yet Labour moved toward socialism gradually and democratically, so that the middle classes were not overly frightened as the working classes won new benefits.

The Conservatives under Stanley Baldwin (1867–1947) showed the same compromising spirit on social issues. The last line of Baldwin's greatest speech in March 1925 summarized his international and domestic programs: "Give us peace in our time, O Lord." In spite of such conflicts as the 1926 strike by hard-pressed coal miners, which ended in an unsuccessful general strike, social unrest in Britain was limited in the 1920s and in the 1930s as well. In 1922 Britain granted southern, Catholic Ireland full autonomy after a bitter guerrilla war, thereby removing another source of prewar friction. Thus developments in both international relations and the domestic politics of the leading democracies gave cause for optimism in the late 1920s.

 ## THE GREAT DEPRESSION, 1929–1939

Like the Great War, the Great Depression must be spelled with capital letters. Economic depression was nothing new. Depressions occurred throughout the nineteenth century with predictable regularity, as they recur in the form of recessions and slumps to this day. What was new about this depression was its severity and duration. It struck the entire world with ever-greater intensity from 1929 to 1933, and recovery was uneven and slow. Only with the Second World War did the depression disappear in much of the world.

The social and political consequences of prolonged economic collapse were enormous. The depression shattered the fragile optimism of political leaders in the late 1920s. Mass unemployment and failing farms made insecurity a reality for millions of ordinary people, who had paid little attention to the intellectual crisis or to new directions in art and ideas (Map 28.1). In desperation, people looked for leaders who would "do something." They were willing to support radical attempts to deal with the crisis by both democratic leaders and dictators.

The Economic Crisis

There is no agreement among historians and economists about why the Great Depression was so deep and lasted so long. Thus it is best to trace the course of the great collapse before trying to identify what caused it.

Though economic activity was already declining moderately in many countries by early 1929, the crash of the stock market in the United States in October of that year triggered the collapse into the Great Depression. The American economy had prospered in the late 1920s, but there were large inequalities in income and a serious imbalance between "real" investment and stock market speculation. Thus net investment—in factories, farms, equipment, and the like—actually fell from $3.5 billion in 1925 to $3.2 billion in 1929. In the same years, as money flooded into stocks, the value of shares traded on the exchanges soared from $27 billion to $87 billion. As a financial historian concludes in an important new study, "It should have been clear to everybody concerned that a crash was inevitable under such conditions."[11] Of course it was not. Irving Fisher,

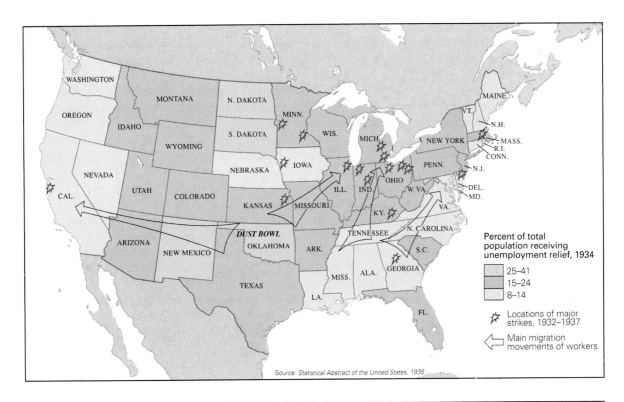

Percent of total
population receiving
unemployment relief, 1934

- 25–41
- 15–24
- 8–14

☆ Locations of major
strikes, 1932–1937

⇐ Main migration
movements of workers

Source: *Statistical Abstract of the United States, 1935*

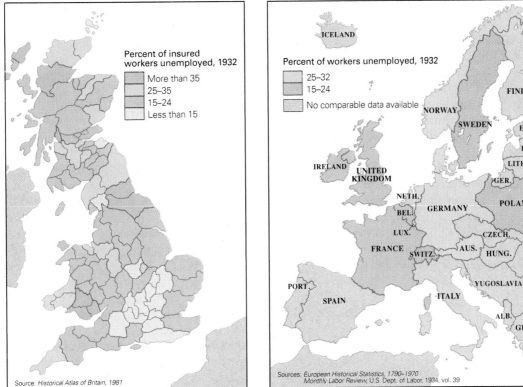

Percent of insured
workers unemployed, 1932

- More than 35
- 25–35
- 15–24
- Less than 15

Source: *Historical Atlas of Britain, 1981*

Percent of workers unemployed, 1932

- 25–32
- 15–24
- No comparable data available

Sources: *European Historical Statistics, 1790–1970*
Monthly Labor Review, U.S. Dept. of Labor, 1934, vol. 39

MAP 28.1 The Great Depression in the United States, Britain, and Europe National
and regional differences were substantial. Germany, industrial northern Britain, and the
American Midwest were particularly hard hit.

one of America's most brilliant economists, was highly optimistic in 1929 and fully invested in stocks. He then lost his entire fortune and would have been forced from his house if his university had not bought it and rented it to him.

The American stock market boom was built on borrowed money. Many wealthy investors, speculators, and people of modest means had bought stocks by paying only a small fraction of the total purchase price and borrowing the remainder from their stockbrokers. Such buying "on margin" was extremely dangerous. When prices started falling, the hard-pressed margin buyers either had to put up more money, which was often impossible, or sell their shares to pay off their brokers. Thus thousands of people started selling all at once. The result was a financial panic. Countless investors and speculators were wiped out in a matter of days or weeks.

The general economic consequences were swift and severe. Stripped of wealth and confidence, battered investors and their fellow citizens started buying fewer goods. Prices fell, production began to slow down, and unemployment began to rise. Soon the entire American economy was caught in a vicious, spiraling decline.

The financial panic in the United States triggered a worldwide financial crisis, and that crisis resulted in a drastic decline in production in country after country. Throughout the 1920s, American bankers and investors had lent large amounts of capital to many countries. Many of these loans were short-term, and once panic broke, New York bankers began recalling them. Gold reserves thus began to flow out of European countries, particularly Germany and Austria, toward the United States. It became very hard for European business people to borrow money, and the panicky public began to withdraw its savings from the banks. These banking problems eventually led to the crash of the largest bank in Austria in 1931 and then to general financial chaos. The recall of private loans by American bankers also accelerated the collapse in world prices, as business people around the world dumped industrial goods and agricultural commodities in a frantic attempt to get cash to pay what they owed.

The financial crisis led to a general crisis of production: between 1929 and 1933, world output of goods fell by an estimated 38 percent. As this happened, each country turned inward and tried to go it alone. In 1931, for example, Britain went off the gold standard, refusing to convert bank notes into gold, and reduced the value of its money. Britain's goal was to make its goods cheaper and therefore more salable in the world market. But because more than twenty nations, including the United States in 1934, also went off the gold standard, few countries gained a real advantage. Similarly, country after country followed the example of the United States when in 1930 it raised protective tariffs to their highest levels ever and tried to seal off shrinking national markets for American producers only. Within this context of fragmented and destructive economic nationalism, recovery finally began in 1933.

Although opinions differ, two factors probably best explain the relentless slide to the bottom from 1929 to early 1933. First, the international economy lacked a leadership able to maintain stability when the crisis came. Specifically, as a noted American economic historian concludes, the seriously weakened British, the traditional leaders of the world economy, "couldn't and the United States wouldn't" stabilize the international economic system in 1929.[12] The United States, which had momentarily played a positive role after the occupation of the Ruhr, cut back its international lending and erected high tariffs.

The second factor was poor national economic policy in almost every country. Governments generally cut their budgets and reduced spending when they should have run large deficits in an attempt to stimulate their economies. After World War II, such a "counter-cyclical policy," advocated by John Maynard Keynes, became a well-established weapon against downturn and depression. But in the 1930s, Keynes's prescription was generally regarded with horror by orthodox economists.

Mass Unemployment

The need for large-scale government spending was tied to mass unemployment. As the financial crisis led to cuts in production, workers lost their jobs and had little money to buy goods. In Britain unemployment had averaged 12 percent in the 1920s; between 1930 and 1935, it averaged more than 18 percent. Far worse was the case of the United States, where unemployment had averaged only 5 percent in the 1920s. In 1932 unemployment soared to about 33 percent of the entire labor force: 14 million people were out of work (see Map 28.1). Only by pumping new money into the economy could the government increase demand and break the vicious cycle of decline.

Along with economic effects, mass unemployment posed a great social problem that mere numbers cannot adequately express. Millions of people lost their spirit and dignity in an apparently hopeless search for work. Homes and ways of life were disrupted in millions of personal tragedies. Young people postponed marriages

Isaac Soyer: Employment Agency (1937)   The frustration and agony of looking for work against long odds are painfully evident in this American masterpiece. The time-killing, pensive resignation, and dejection seen in the three figures are only aspects of the larger problem. One of three talented brothers born in Russia and trained as artists in New York, Isaac Soyer worked in the tradition of American realism and concentrated on people and the influence of their environment. *(Oil on canvas, 34¼ × 45 in. Collection of Whitney Museum of American Art, Purchase 37.44)*

they could not afford, and birthrates fell sharply. There was an increase in suicide and mental illness. Poverty or the threat of poverty became a grinding reality. In 1932 the workers of Manchester, England, appealed to their city officials—a typical appeal echoed throughout the Western world:

We tell you that thousands of people . . . are in desperate straits. We tell you that men, women, and children are going hungry. . . . We tell you that great numbers are being rendered distraught through the stress and worry of trying to exist without work. . . .

If you do not do this—if you do not provide useful work for the unemployed—what, we ask, is your alternative? Do not imagine that this colossal tragedy of unemployment is going on endlessly without some fateful catastrophe. Hungry men are angry men.[13]

Mass unemployment was a terrible time bomb preparing to explode.

The New Deal in the United States

Of all the major industrial countries, only Germany was harder hit by the Great Depression, or reacted more radically to it, than the United States. Depression was so traumatic in the United States because the 1920s had been a period of complacent optimism. The Great Depression and the response to it marked a major turning point in American history.

President Herbert Hoover (1895–1972) and his administration initially reacted to the stock market crash and economic decline with dogged optimism and limited action. But when the full force of the financial crisis struck Europe in the summer of 1931 and boomeranged back to the United States, people's worst fears became reality. Banks failed; unemployment soared. Between 1929 and 1932, industrial production fell by about 50 percent, and net income from the average American farm plunged by two-thirds.

In these tragic circumstances, Franklin Delano Roosevelt (1882–1945), the most important American leader in the twentieth century, came to the fore. As a rich, winsome, almost frivolous young man, Roosevelt had zoomed to early political success. But in 1921 he was stricken by polio and never really regained the use of his legs. Strengthened and humanized by his struggle with tragedy, he re-entered politics in 1928 and became governor of New York. Full of charm and confidence in 1932, he won a landslide electoral victory with grand but vague promises of a "New Deal for the forgotten man."

Roosevelt's basic goal was to reform capitalism in order to preserve it. In his words, "A frank examination of the profit system in the spring of 1933 showed it to be in collapse; but substantially everybody in the United States, in public office and out of public office, from the very rich to the very poor, was as determined as was my Administration to save it."[14] Roosevelt rejected socialism and government ownership of industry in 1933. To right the situation, he chose forceful government intervention in the economy.

In this choice, Roosevelt and his advisers were greatly influenced by American experience in World War I. During the wartime emergency, the American economy had been thoroughly planned and regulated. Roosevelt and his "brain trust" of advisers adopted similar policies to restore prosperity and reduce social inequality. Roosevelt was flexible, pragmatic, and willing to experiment. Government intervention and experimentation were combined in some of the New Deal's most significant measures.

Innovative programs promoted agricultural recovery, a top priority. Almost half of the American population still lived in rural areas, and Roosevelt's greatest support came from farmers, who desperately needed higher prices to save their farms. Roosevelt's bold decision to leave the gold standard and reduce the value of the dollar was designed precisely to raise American prices and rescue farmers. The Agricultural Adjustment Act of 1933 also aimed at raising prices and farm income by carefully restricting the acreage farmers could cultivate and then paying them cash for the set-asides. These planning measures worked, at least for a while, and farmers enthusiastically repaid Roosevelt in 1936 with overwhelming support.

The most ambitious attempt to control and plan the economy was the National Recovery Administration (NRA), established by Congress right after Roosevelt took office. The key idea behind the NRA was to reduce competition and fix prices and wages for everyone's benefit, along with sponsoring enough public works projects to ensure recovery. The NRA's goal required government, business, and labor to hammer out detailed regulations for each industry. Because the NRA broke with the cherished American tradition of free competition and aroused conflicts among business people, consumers, and bureaucrats, it did not work well. By the time the NRA was declared unconstitutional in 1935, Roosevelt and the New Deal were already moving away from government efforts to plan and control the entire economy.

Instead, Roosevelt and his advisers attacked the key problem of mass unemployment directly. The federal government accepted the responsibility of employing directly as many people as financially possible, something Hoover had consistently rejected. Thus when it became clear in late 1933 that the initial program of public works was too small, new agencies were created to undertake a vast range of projects.

The most famous of these was the Works Progress Administration (WPA), set up in 1935. At its peak in late 1938, this government agency employed more than 3 million individuals. One-fifth of the entire labor force worked for the WPA at some point in the 1930s. To this day, thousands of public buildings, bridges, and highways built by the WPA stand as monuments to energetic government efforts to provide people with meaningful work. The WPA was enormously popular in a nation long schooled in self-reliance and the work ethic.

Relief programs like the WPA were part of the New Deal's most fundamental commitment, the commitment to use the federal government to provide for the welfare of all Americans. This commitment realized the progressive agenda of social reformers, and it marked a profound shift from the traditional stress on family support and community responsibility. Embraced by a large majority in the 1930s, this shift in attitudes proved to be one of the New Deal's most enduring legacies. The programs would change, but the belief in a welfare state would dominate for almost four decades.

Eleanor Roosevelt, the president's wife, worked tirelessly to create and mobilize support for enlightened government action. She was quite effective. In 1935 she proudly summed up progress made at one of her influential and totally unprecedented press conferences, which were limited to women reporters: "The big achievement of the last two years is the great change in the thinking of the country. Imperceptibly we have come to realize that government has a responsibility to defend the weak."[15] Scarred by her own griefs, this extraordinary First Lady radiated genuine warmth and heartfelt compassion in endless travels, talks, columns, and photos. She humanized New Deal programs for millions of struggling Americans. No distant bureaucrat, she was a friend, someone who really cared. (See the feature "Individuals in Society: Eleanor Roosevelt: Pain, Compassion, Self-Realization.")

Going beyond efforts to promote economic recovery, many New Deal initiatives sought to meet social needs. Following the path blazed by Germany's Bismarck in the 1880s, the U.S. government in 1935 established a national social security system, with old-age pensions and unemployment benefits, to protect many workers against some of life's uncertainties. The National Labor Relations Act of 1935 gave union organizers the green light by declaring collective bargaining to be the policy of the United States. Following some bitter strikes, such as a sit-down strike at General Motors in early 1937, union membership more than doubled, from 4 million in 1935 to 9 million in 1940. In general, between 1935 and 1938 government rulings and social reforms chipped away at the privileges of the wealthy and tried to help ordinary people.

Yet despite undeniable accomplishments in social reform, the New Deal was only partly successful as a response to the Great Depression. At the height of the recovery in May 1937, 7 million workers were still unemployed. The economic situation then worsened seriously in the recession of 1937 and 1938. Production fell sharply, and although unemployment never again reached the 15 million mark of 1933, it hit 11 million in 1938 and was still a staggering 10 million when war broke out in Europe in September 1939.

The New Deal never did pull the United States out of the depression. This failure frustrated Americans then, and it is still puzzling today. Perhaps, as some have claimed, Roosevelt should have used his enormous popularity and prestige in 1933 to nationalize the banks, the railroads, and some heavy industry so that national economic planning could have been successful. Even though Roosevelt's sharp attack on big business

and the wealthy after 1935 had popular appeal, it also damaged business confidence and made the great capitalists uncooperative. Given the low level of profit and the underutilization of many factories, however, it is questionable whether business would have behaved much differently even if the New Deal had catered to it.

It is often argued that the New Deal did not put enough money into the economy through deficit financing. Like his predecessors in the White House, Roosevelt was attached to the ideal of the balanced budget. His largest deficit was only $4.4 billion in 1936. Compare this figure with deficits of $21.5 billion in 1942 and $57.4 billion in 1943, when the nation was fully engaged in total war and unemployment had vanished. By 1945 many economists were concluding that the New Deal's deficit-financed public works had been too small a step in the right direction. These Keynesian views were to be very influential in economic policy in Western countries after the Second World War.

The Scandinavian Response to the Depression

Of all the Western democracies, the Scandinavian countries under Social Democratic leadership responded most successfully to the challenge of the Great Depression. Having grown steadily in number in the late nineteenth century, the Social Democrats became the largest political party in Sweden and then in Norway after the First World War. In the 1920s, they passed important social reform legislation for both peasants and workers, gained practical administrative experience, and developed a unique kind of socialism. Flexible and nonrevolutionary, Scandinavian socialism grew out of a strong tradition of cooperative community action. Even before 1900, Scandinavian agricultural cooperatives had shown how individual peasant families could join together for everyone's benefit. Labor leaders and capitalists were also inclined to work together.

When the economic crisis struck in 1929, socialist governments in Scandinavia built on this pattern of cooperative social action. Sweden in particular pioneered in the use of large-scale deficits to finance public works and thereby maintain production and employment. Scandinavian governments also increased social welfare benefits, from old-age pensions and unemployment insurance to subsidized housing and maternity allowances. All this spending required a large bureaucracy and high taxes, first on the rich and then on practically everyone. Yet both private and cooperative enterprise thrived, as did democracy. Some observers saw Scandinavia's welfare socialism as an appealing "middle way"

Individuals in Society

Eleanor Roosevelt: Pain, Compassion, Self-Realization ✤

Eleanor Roosevelt in 1932, serving food to needy women in the kitchen of a New York restaurant. *(Corbis-Bettmann)*

Few individuals in the twentieth century have been as admired or as influential as Eleanor Roosevelt (1884–1962). Yet her strengths were not inborn; rather they emerged slowly out of suffering, crisis, and personal growth.

Born into New York's gilded upper class, Eleanor experienced much sorrow as a child. Her beautiful socialite mother mocked her as unattractive and dreary, while her father spiraled downward into alcoholism and self-destruction. Orphaned at ten and assigned to an austere grandmother, she blossomed briefly in her late teens. Though drawn to social work, she followed convention and "entered society." Still shy and lacking in self-esteem, she fell in love with Franklin Roosevelt, a handsome distant cousin. They were married in a lavish wedding when Eleanor was twenty-one. Her uncle Theodore Roosevelt, president of the United States, gave her away.

Eleanor Roosevelt made a total commitment to marriage and her husband's career. Flanked by nurses and servants, she bore six children in ten years. As a politician's wife and young matron, she also hosted innumerable social functions. Relishing occasional volunteer service, she became, as she later reflected, a "completely dependent person." Ever serious and not very romantic, she and her insensitive, fun-loving husband drifted apart.

In 1918, when she was thirty-four, she discovered by accident that Franklin had been having a four-year love affair with her personal secretary. She felt totally betrayed. As she recalled later, "The bottom dropped out of my own particular world, and I faced myself, my surroundings, my world, honestly for the first time."[1] Taking stock and "really growing up," she told her husband that he could either have a divorce or break off the affair forever. As Franklin reluctantly turned away from divorce and passionate love to save his political future, a tried-in-the-fire Eleanor gradually went her own way, developing her own interests. Nursing Franklin with total devotion in 1921 when he was struck by polio, she transformed their failed marriage into a professional partnership.

Grief enlarged Eleanor's power to love and serve, and in the 1920s she developed her potential and honed her skills.[2] She formed deep friendships with leading women social reformers and made their cause her own. And she matured as a savvy politician within the New York Democratic party, pressing her issues and keeping the Roosevelt name alive.

Eleanor subsequently used the White House as a stage for her exceptional abilities. First, she worked effectively from inside, forming her own entourage and helping women and political allies get key government jobs. Second, blessed with wonderful health and unfailing energy, she sold the New Deal to the American people. Traveling widely as the immobilized president's "eyes and ears," she pressed her husband in public and private to act more energetically for "people programs" and black civil rights. When in the 1930s blacks shifted massively and for good from the "party of Lincoln" to the "party of Roosevelt" (and southern segregation), even though they made little progress toward full civil rights, they did so in part because they knew that *Mrs.* Roosevelt supported their cause.

Eleanor Roosevelt grew to be a great humanitarian and an inspiring public figure. While Franklin mobilized politicians, she galvanized social reformers. And in their joint creation of a new kind of government, the idols of millions rekindled a bit of their early affection.

Questions for Analysis

1. How did Eleanor Roosevelt grow as a person and a public figure? How do you explain this growth?
2. What kind of programs and New Deal policies did she favor? Was she a moderate or a radical?

1. Joseph Lash, *Eleanor and Franklin* (New York: W. W. Norton, 1971), p. 226.
2. Lois Scharf, *Eleanor Roosevelt: First Lady of American Liberalism* (Boston: Twayne, 1987), pp. 57–82; also see pp. 82–112, 135–145.

between sick capitalism and cruel communism or fascism.

Recovery and Reform in Britain and France

In Britain MacDonald's Labour government and then, after 1931, the Conservative-dominated coalition government followed orthodox economic theory. The budget was balanced, but unemployed workers received barely enough welfare to live. Despite government lethargy, the economy recovered considerably after 1932. By 1937 total production was about 20 percent higher than in 1929. In fact, for Britain the years after 1932 were actually somewhat better than the 1920s had been, quite the opposite of the situation in the United States and France.

This good but by no means brilliant performance reflected the gradual reorientation of the British economy. After going off the gold standard in 1931 and establishing protective tariffs in 1932, Britain concentrated increasingly on the national, rather than the international, market. The old export industries of the Industrial Revolution, such as textiles and coal, continued to decline, but new industries, such as automobiles and electrical appliances, grew in response to British home demand. Moreover, low interest rates encouraged a housing boom. By the end of the decade, there were highly visible differences between the old, depressed industrial areas of the north and the new, growing areas of the south. These developments encouraged Britain to look inward and avoid unpleasant foreign questions.

Because France was relatively less industrialized and more isolated from the world economy, the Great Depression came late. But once the depression hit France, it stayed and stayed. Decline was steady until 1935, and a short-lived recovery never brought production or employment back up to predepression levels. Economic stagnation both reflected and heightened an ongoing political crisis. There was no stability in government. As before 1914, the French parliament was made up of many political parties, which could never cooperate for very long. In 1933, for example, five coalition cabinets formed and fell in rapid succession.

The French lost the underlying unity that had made government instability bearable before 1914. Fascist-type organizations agitated against parliamentary democracy and looked to Mussolini's Italy and Hitler's Germany for inspiration. In February 1934, French fascists and semifascists rioted and threatened to overturn the republic. At the same time, the Communist party and many workers opposed to the existing system were

Scandinavian Socialism   championed cooperation and practical welfare measures, playing down strident rhetoric and theories of class conflict. The Oslo Breakfast, depicted in the lower part of this poster, exemplified the Scandinavian approach. It provided every schoolchild in the Norwegian capital with a good breakfast free of charge. (*Universitets-biblioteket i Oslo*)

looking to Stalin's Russia for guidance. The vital center of moderate republicanism was sapped from both sides.

Frightened by the growing strength of the fascists at home and abroad, the Communists, the Socialists, and the Radicals formed an alliance—the Popular Front—for the national elections of May 1936. Their clear victory reflected the trend toward polarization. The number of Communists in the parliament jumped dramatically from 10 to 72, while the Socialists, led by Léon Blum, became the strongest party in France, with 146 seats. The really quite moderate Radicals slipped badly, and the conservatives lost ground to the semifascists.

In the next few months, Blum's Popular Front government made the first and only real attempt to deal with the social and economic problems of the 1930s in France. Inspired by Roosevelt's New Deal, the Popular Front encouraged the union movement and launched a far-reaching program of social reform, complete with paid vacations and a forty-hour workweek. Popular with workers and the lower middle class, these measures were quickly sabotaged by rapid inflation and cries of revolution from fascists and frightened conservatives. Wealthy people sneaked their money out of the country, labor unrest grew, and France entered a severe financial crisis. Blum was forced to announce a "breathing spell" in social reform.

The fires of political dissension were also fanned by civil war in Spain. Communists demanded that France support the Spanish republicans, while many French conservatives would gladly have joined Hitler and Mussolini in aiding the attack of Spanish fascists. Extremism grew, and France itself was within sight of civil war. Blum was forced to resign in June 1937, and the Popular Front quickly collapsed. An anxious and divided France drifted aimlessly once again, preoccupied by Hitler and German rearmament.

SUMMARY

After the First World War, Western society entered a complex and difficult era—truly an age of anxiety. Intellectual life underwent a crisis marked by pessimism, uncertainty, and fascination with irrational forces. Ceaseless experimentation and rejection of old forms characterized art and music, while motion pictures and radio provided a new, standardized entertainment for the masses. Intellectual and artistic developments that had been confined to small avant-garde groups before 1914, along with the insecure state of mind they expressed, gained wider currency.

Politics and economics were similarly disrupted. In the 1920s, political leaders groped to create an enduring peace and rebuild the prewar prosperity, and for a brief period late in the decade, they even seemed to have succeeded. Then the Great Depression shattered that fragile stability. Uncertainty returned with redoubled force in the 1930s. The international economy collapsed, and unemployment struck millions worldwide. The democracies turned inward as they sought to cope with massive domestic problems and widespread disillusionment. Generally speaking, they were not very successful, although relief measures and social concern eased distress and prevented revolutions in the leading Western nations. The old liberal ideals of individual rights and responsibilities, elected government, and economic freedom declined and seemed outmoded to many. And in many countries of central and eastern Europe, these ideas were abandoned completely, as we shall see in the next chapter.

NOTES

1. P. Valéry, *Variety,* trans. M. Cowley (New York: Harcourt Brace, 1927), pp. 27–28.
2. Quoted in S. Hughes, *The Obstructed Path: French Social Thought in the Years of Desperation, 1930–1960* (New York: Harper & Row, 1967), p. 82.
3. G. Greene, *Another Mexico* (New York: Viking Press, 1939), p. 3.
4. G. Orwell, *1984* (New York: New American Library, 1950), p. 220.
5. C. E. Jeanneret-Gris (Le Corbusier), *Towards a New Architecture* (London: J. Rodker, 1931), p. 15.
6. Quoted in A. H. Barr, Jr., *What Is Modern Painting?* 9th ed. (New York: Museum of Modern Art, 1966), p. 27.
7. Quoted ibid., p. 25.
8. R. Graves and A. Hodge, *The Long Week End: A Social History of Great Britain, 1918–1939* (New York: Macmillan, 1941), p. 131.
9. Quoted in A. Briggs, *The Birth of Broadcasting,* vol. 1 (London: Oxford University Press, 1961), p. 47.
10. Quoted in R. J. Sontag, *A Broken World, 1919–1939* (New York: Harper & Row, 1971), p. 129.
11. Dietmar Rothermund, *The Global Impact of the Great Depression, 1929–1939* (London and New York: Routledge, 1996), p. 50.
12. C. P. Kindleberger, *The World in Depression, 1929–1939* (Berkeley and Los Angeles: University of California Press, 1973), p. 292.
13. Quoted in S. B. Clough et al., eds., *Economic History of Europe: Twentieth Century* (New York: Harper & Row, 1968), pp. 243–245.
14. Quoted in D. Dillard, *Economic Development of the North Atlantic Community* (Englewood Cliffs, N.J.: Prentice-Hall, 1967), p. 591.
15. Quoted in Lois Scharf, *Eleanor Roosevelt: First Lady of American Liberalism* (Boston: Twayne, 1987), p. 110.

SUGGESTED READING

A. Bullock, ed., *The Twentieth Century* (1971), is particularly noteworthy because it is a lavish visual feast combined with penetrating essays on major developments. Two excellent accounts of contemporary history—one with a liberal and the other with a conservative point of view—are R. Paxton, *Europe in the Twentieth Century,* 3d ed. (1997), and P. Johnson, *Modern Times: The World from the Twenties* to the Eighties (1983). R. Clark, *Hope and Glory: Britain, 1900–1990* (1996), and J. McMillan, *Twentieth-Century France: Politics and Society, 1898–1991* (1992), are two recommended national surveys. Crucial changes in thought before and after World War I are discussed in three rewarding intellectual histories: S. Kern, *The Culture of Time and Space, 1880–1918* (1983); M. Berman, *All That Is Solid Melts into Air: The Experience of Modernity* (1982); and G. Masur, *Prophets of Yesterday* (1961). H. S. Hughes, *Consciousness and Society* (1956), and M. Biddiss, *Age of the Masses: Ideas and Society Since 1870* (1977), are stimulating and useful. R. Stromberg, *European Intellectual History Since 1789* (1986), is a clear general account. W. Kaufmann, *Nietzsche* (1974), is a sympathetic and justly famous older study, and S. Aschheim, *The Nietzsche Legacy in Germany, 1890–1990* (1992), considers the range of responses to the pioneering philosopher. W. Barrett, *Irrational Man: A Study in Existential Philosophy* (1958), is still useful.

N. Cantor, *The American Century: Varieties of Culture in Modern Times* (1997), is a pugnacious and stimulating survey. J. Rewald, *The History of Impressionism* (1961), and R. Golan, *Modernity and Nostalgia: Art and Politics in France Between the Wars* (1995), are excellent and also reflect changing tastes in art history. Barr, cited in the Notes, is helpful. P. Collaer, *A History of Modern Music* (1961), and H. R. Hitchcock, *Architecture: Nineteenth and Twentieth Centuries* (1958), are good introductions, whereas T. Wolfe, *From Bauhaus to My House* (1981), is a lively critique of modern architecture. L. Barnett, *The Universe and Dr. Einstein* (1952), is a fascinating study of the new physics. A. Storr, *Freud* (1989), and P. Rieff, *Freud* (1956), consider the man and how his theories have stood the test of time. S. Freud, *Civilization and Its Discontents* (1930), which is highly recommended, explores Freud's theory of instinct and repression, arguing that society's necessary repression of instinctual drives will always leave people unhappy. M. White, ed., *The Age of Analysis* (1955), opens up basic questions of twentieth-century psychology and philosophy. H. Liebersohn, *Fate and Utopia in German Sociology* (1988), analyzes developments in German social science. J. Willett, *The New Sobriety: Art and Politics in the Weimar Period, 1917–1933* (1978), considers the artistic renaissance and the political culture in Germany in the 1920s. M. Marrus, ed., *Emergence of Leisure* (1974), is a pioneering inquiry into an important aspect of mass culture. H. Daniels-Rops, *A Fight for God*, 2 vols. (1966), is a sympathetic history of the Catholic church between 1870 and 1939.

G. Ambrosius and W. Hibbard, *A Social and Economic History of Twentieth-Century Europe* (1989), and F. Tipton

and R. Aldrich, *An Economic and Social History of Europe, 1890–1939* (1987), are recommended and interesting to compare. P. Fritzsche, *Rehearsals for Fascism: Populism and Political Mobilization in Weimar Germany* (1990), R. Wohl, *The Generation of 1914* (1979), and R. Kuisel, *Capital and State in Modern France: Renovation and Economic Management* (1982), are three important studies on aspects of the postwar challenge. S. Reynolds, *France Between the Wars: Gender and Politics* (1996), and J. Keiger, *Raymond Poincaré* (1996), are major reconsiderations of French politics from different perspectives. H. James, *The German Slump: Politics and Economics, 1924–1936* (1986), is an excellent analysis of economic recovery and subsequent collapse. M. Childs, *Sweden: The Middle Way* (1961), applauds Sweden's efforts at social reform. L. Scharf, *Eleanor Roosevelt: First Lady of American Liberalism* (1987), is a pioneering interpretation, and J. Youngs, *Eleanor Roosevelt: A Personal and Public Life* (1985), is exceptionally well written. Both are highly recommended, as is Eleanor Roosevelt's own moving account, *This Is My Story* (1937). O. and L. Handlin, *Liberty in America Since 1600*, vol. 4 (1994), argues that the United States has erred in moving from equality of opportunity to equality of results since 1920. In addition to the contemporary works discussed in the text, the crisis of the interwar period comes alive in R. Crossman, ed., *The God That Failed* (1950), in which famous Western writers tell why they were attracted to and later repelled by communism; J. Ortega y Gasset's renowned *The Revolt of the Masses* (1932); and F. A. Hayek's *The Road to Serfdom* (1944), a famous warning of the dangers to democratic freedoms.

In addition to Rothermund's and Kindleberger's excellent studies of the Great Depression cited in the Notes, P. Temin, *Lessons from the Great Depression* (1987), is a judicious evaluation by an outstanding economic historian. J. Garraty, *Unemployment in History* (1978), is noteworthy, though novels best portray the human tragedy of economic decline. W. Holtby, *South Riding* (1936), and W. Greenwood, *Love on the Dole* (1933), are moving stories of the Great Depression in England. Hans Fallada, *Little Man, What Now?* (1932), is the classic counterpart for Germany. Also highly recommended as commentaries on English life between the wars are N. Gray, *The Worst of Times: An Oral History of the Great Depression in Britain* (1985); and George Orwell, *The Road to Wigan Pier* (1972). Among French novelists, André Gide painstakingly examines the French middle class and its values in *The Counterfeiters*; Albert Camus, the greatest of the existential novelists, is at his unforgettable best in *The Stranger* (1942) and *The Plague* (1947).

LISTENING TO THE PAST

A Christian View of Evil

The English philosopher C. E. M. Joad (1891–1953) stands out among intellectuals who turned toward religion in the age of anxiety. As a university student, he shed his faith and became a militant rationalist who was "frequently in demand for lectures and articles which adopted an attitude hostile to revealed religion in general, and to the Christian Church in particular." Only after intense reflection did Joad retrace his steps and come to reaccept Christianity. Ever the serious intellectual, he described and analyzed his "spiritual odyssey" in closely reasoned and influential writings.

The following selection is taken from God and Evil, *published in 1942 when Hitler's empire posed the problem of human depravity in the starkest terms. Reconsidering the modern secular faith in the primacy of environmental influences and in the perfectibility of humankind, Joad found these beliefs wanting. He reaffirmed the Christian focus on sin and the need for God's grace to escape from evil and find salvation.*

There is, we are told, a revival of interest in religious matters. . . . In this revival of interest I have shared. . . . As a young man at Oxford, I participated, as was natural to my age and generation, in prolonged and frequent discussions of religion which, finding me a Christian, left me as they did many of my generation, an agnostic, an agnostic who entertained a deep-seated suspicion of all dogmatic creeds. . . .

As an agnostic, I felt convinced of two things: first, . . . within the sphere of religion that we did not and probably could not know the truth; secondly, in regard to the so-called religious truths that I had been taught, as, for example, that God created the world as stated in Genesis [and] . . . sent His Son into it to redeem mankind, that it was improbable that they were true and certain that they could not be *known* to be true. In the confidence of this conviction I proceeded, to all intents

and purposes, to turn my back upon the whole subject. . . .

It was only after the coming of the Nazis that my mind began again to turn in the direction of religion. . . . [With] the outbreak of [the Second World] war the subject leapt straight into the forefront of my consciousness where it has remained ever since. . . .

I take it [my spiritual odyssey] to be not untypical. From conversations and discussions, especially with students, I surmise that the revival of interest in religion is widespread. . . . This topical relevance of religion derives from two sources. [First, there is] the relation between religion and politics. This connection . . . subsists at all times, but in quiet times of peace it usually remains implicit. The peculiar circumstances of the last twenty-five years have, however, combined to thrust it into the foreground of men's consciousness. . . . Thus times of revolutionary political change are also times of religious questioning and discussion.

The other source of the specifically topical interest in religion is . . . the obtrusiveness of evil. [Perhaps] there is no more evil abroad in Western civilization than there was at the end of the last century, but it cannot be denied that what there is of it is more obtrusive. I am not referring to evils arising from the relation between the sexes upon which the Church has laid such exclusive stress. . . . I mean the evils of cruelty, savagery, oppression, violence, egotism, aggrandisement, and lust for power. So pervasive and insistent have these evils become that it is at times difficult to avoid concluding that the Devil has been given a longer rope than usual, . . . [and] it becomes correspondingly more difficult to explain it away by the various methods which have been fashionable during the last twenty years.

There was, for example, the explanation of evil in terms of economic inequality and injustice. Socialist writers had taught my generation that bad conditions were the cause of human wretchedness . . . and also of human wickedness. Poverty . . . was the supreme sin; supreme if only because it was the source of all the others. . . .

And the moral [of this teaching]? That evil is due to bad social conditions. Now you can reform bad social conditions by Act of Parliament, substituting comfort, cleanliness, security, and financial competence for discomfort, dirt, insecurity, and want. Therefore, presumably, you can make men virtuous . . . by Act of Parliament.

There was a later explanation of evil in terms of early psychological maltreatment and consequent psychological maladjustment. Evil, then, according to this view, was the result not of bad social, but of bad psychological conditions; not so much of an imperfect society, as of an imperfect family, an ill-directed nursery, and a wrongly run school. Reform society, said the Socialist, and evil will disappear. Reform the school and the family, the psychoanalysts added, and society will reform itself and, once again, evil will disappear. . . .

The contemporary view of evil is untenable. . . . Evil is not *merely* a by-product of unfavourable circumstances; it is too widespread and too deep-seated to admit of any such explanation; so widespread, so deep-seated that one can only conclude that what the religions have always taught is true, and that evil is endemic in the heart of man. . . . The intellectual blunder [of the comfortable and secure late nineteenth century was] . . . denying what we had traditionally been taught, the doctrine of original sin. . . .

For the simple truth is that one cannot help oneself. . . . For one cannot help but know that one's character is *not* strong enough, one's efforts *not* efficacious, at least, that they are not, if unaided. . . . There are two alternatives [to giving in to evil].

The first, since the world is evil, is to escape from it and to find, first in withdrawal, and, as an ultimate hope, in Nirvana, the true way of life. The second is to face evil and to seek to overcome it. . . . The first is the way of the East, the second of Christianity. My temperament and disposition incline me to the second, but the second I know to be impossible unless I am assisted from without. By the grace of God we are assured, such assistance may be obtained and evil may be overcome; otherwise, there is no resource and no resistance.

❖ The British philosopher Cyril Edwin Mitchinson Joad (1891–1953). *(Hulton-Deutsch/Tony Stone Images)*

Questions for Analysis

1. How did Joad account for a renewed interest in religious matters?

2. Joad concentrated on the problem of evil in human affairs. What did he mean by "evil"? Was it becoming more powerful in his time?

3. What, according to Joad, were the usual explanations for the existence of evil? What was his view of these explanations?

4. In Joad's view, how did the Christian doctrine of original sin relate to the problem of evil? How could the Christian overcome sin and evil?

Source: C. E. M. Joad, *God and Evil* (New York: Harper & Brothers, 1943), pp. 9–20, 103–104. Copyright © 1943 by Harper and Brothers.

29

Dictatorships and the Second World War

Hugo Jager's photograph of a crowd of enthusiastic Hitler supporters. *(Hugo Jager, Life Magazine, © Time Inc.)*

The era of anxiety and economic depression was also a time of growing strength for political dictatorship. Popularly elected governments and basic civil liberties declined drastically in Europe. On the eve of the Second World War, liberal democratic governments were surviving only in Great Britain, France, the Low Countries, the Scandinavian nations, and Switzerland. Elsewhere in Europe, various kinds of "strongmen" ruled. Dictatorship seemed the wave of the future. Thus the decline in liberal political institutions and the intellectual crisis were related elements in the general crisis of European civilization.

The era of dictatorship is a highly disturbing chapter in the history of Western civilization. The key development was not only the resurgence of authoritarian rule but also the rise of a particularly ruthless and dynamic tyranny. This new kind of tyranny reached its full realization in the Soviet Union and Nazi Germany in the 1930s. Stalin and Hitler mobilized their peoples for enormous undertakings and ruled with unprecedented severity. Hitler's mobilization was ultimately directed toward racial aggression and territorial expansion, and his sudden attack on Poland in 1939 started World War II.

Nazi armies were defeated by a great coalition, and today we want to believe that the era of totalitarian dictatorship was a terrible accident, that Stalin's slave-labor camps and Hitler's gas chambers "can't happen again." Yet the cruel truth is that horrible atrocities continue to plague the world in our time. The Khmer Rouge inflicted genocide on its people in Kampuchea, and civil war in Bosnia and in Rwanda led to racially motivated atrocities recalling the horrors of World War II. And there are other examples. Thus it is all the more vital that we understand Europe's era of brutal and aggressive dictatorship in order to guard against the possibility of its recurrence in the future.

- What was the nature of twentieth-century dictatorship and authoritarian rule?
- How did people live in the most extreme states: the Soviet Union and Nazi Germany?
- How did the rise of aggressive dictatorships result in another world war?

These are among the questions this chapter will seek to answer.

 ## AUTHORITARIAN STATES

Both conservative and radical dictatorships swept through Europe in the 1920s and the 1930s. Although these two types of dictatorship shared some characteristics and sometimes overlapped in practice, they were in essence profoundly different. Conservative authoritarian regimes were an old story in Europe. Radical dictatorships were a new and frightening development.

Conservative Authoritarianism

The traditional form of antidemocratic government in European history was conservative authoritarianism. Like Catherine the Great in Russia and Metternich in Austria, the leaders of such governments tried to prevent major changes that would undermine the existing social order. To do so, they relied on obedient bureaucracies, vigilant police departments, and trustworthy armies. Popular participation in government was forbidden or else severely limited to such natural allies as landlords, bureaucrats, and high church officials. Liberals, democrats, and socialists were persecuted as subversive radicals, often finding themselves in jail or exile.

Yet old-fashioned authoritarian governments were limited in their power and in their objectives. Lacking modern technology and communications, they did not have the capacity to control many aspects of their subjects' lives. Nor did they wish to do so. Preoccupied with the goal of mere survival, these governments largely limited their demands to taxes, army recruits, and passive acceptance. As long as the people did not try to change the system, they often had considerable personal independence.

After the First World War, this kind of authoritarian government revived, especially in the less-developed eastern part of Europe. There the parliamentary regimes that had been founded on the wreckage of empires in 1918 fell one by one. By early 1938, only economically and socially advanced Czechoslovakia remained true to liberal political ideals. Conservative dictators also took over in Spain and Portugal.

There were several reasons for this development. These lands lacked a strong tradition of self-government, with its necessary restraint and compromise. Moreover, many of these new states, such as Yugoslavia, were torn by ethnic conflicts that threatened their very existence.

Dictatorship appealed to nationalists and military leaders as a way to repress such tensions and preserve national unity. Large landowners and the church were still powerful forces in these largely agrarian areas, and they often looked to dictators to save them from progressive land reform or communist agrarian upheaval. So did some members of the middle class, which was small and weak in eastern Europe. Finally, though some kind of democracy managed to stagger through the 1920s in Austria, Bulgaria, Romania, Greece, Estonia, and Latvia, the Great Depression delivered the final blow to those countries in 1936.

Although some of the conservative authoritarian regimes adopted certain Hitlerian and fascist characteristics in the 1930s, their general aims were limited. They were concerned more with maintaining the status quo than with forcing society into rapid change or war. This tradition continued into our own time, especially in some of the military dictatorships that ruled in Latin America until the late 1980s.

Hungary was a good example of conservative authoritarianism. In the chaos of collapse in 1919, Béla Kun formed a Lenin-style government, but communism in Hungary was soon crushed by foreign troops, large landowners, and hostile peasants. Thereafter, a combination of great and medium-size landowners instituted a semi-authoritarian regime, which maintained the status quo in the 1920s. Hungary had a parliament, but elections were carefully controlled. The peasants did not have the right to vote, and an upper house representing the landed aristocracy was re-established. There was no land reform or major social change. In the 1930s, the Hungarian government remained conservative and nationalistic. Increasingly, it was opposed by a Nazi-like fascist movement, the Arrow Cross, which demanded radical reform and mobilization of the masses.

Another example of conservative authoritarianism was newly independent Poland, where democratic government was overturned in 1926 when General Joseph Pilsudski (1867–1935) established a military dictatorship. Sandwiched between Russia and Germany, Poland was torn by bitter party politics. Pilsudski silenced opposition and tried to build a strong state. His principal supporters were the army, major industrialists, and dedicated nationalists.

Yet another example of conservative authoritarianism was Portugal, at the westernmost end of the European peninsula. Constantly shaken by military coups and uprisings after a republican revolution in 1910, very poor and underdeveloped Portugal finally got a strong dictator in Antonio de Oliveira Salazar in 1932. A devout Catholic, Salazar gave the church the strongest possible position in the country, while controlling the press and outlawing most political activity. Yet there was no attempt to mobilize the masses or to accomplish great projects. The traditional society was firmly maintained, and that was enough.

Totalitarianism or Fascism?

While conservative authoritarianism predominated in the smaller states of central and eastern Europe by the mid-1930s, radical dictatorships emerged in the Soviet Union, in Germany, and to a lesser extent in Italy. Almost all scholars agree that the leaders of these radical dictatorships violently rejected parliamentary restraint and liberal values. Scholars also agree that these dictatorships exercised unprecedented control over the masses and sought to mobilize them for action. But beyond these certainties, there has always been controversy over the nature of these regimes.

Three main approaches to understanding radical dictatorships concern us here. The first approach relates the radical dictatorships to the rise of modern totalitarianism. The second focuses on the idea of fascism as the unifying impulse. The third stresses the limitations of such broad generalizations and the uniqueness of each regime. Each school has strengths and weaknesses.

The concept of *totalitarianism* emerged in the 1920s and the 1930s, although it is frequently and mistakenly seen as developing only after 1945 as a part of anti-Soviet propaganda during the cold war. In 1924 Mussolini spoke of the "fierce totalitarian will" of his movement in Italy. In the 1930s, more and more British, American, and German exiled writers used the concept of totalitarianism to describe what they saw happening before their eyes. They linked Italian and especially German fascism with Soviet communism in "a 'new kind of state' that could be called totalitarian." With the alliance between Hitler and Stalin in 1939, "all doubts" about the totalitarian nature of both dictatorships "were swept away for most Americans."[1]

Early writers believed that modern totalitarianism burst on the scene with the revolutionary total war effort of 1914 to 1918. The war called forth a tendency to subordinate all institutions and all classes to the state in order to achieve one supreme objective: victory. As French thinker Elie Halévy put it in 1936, the varieties of modern totalitarian tyranny—fascism, Nazism, and communism—could be thought of as "feuding brothers" with a common father: the nature of modern war.[2]

Writers such as Halévy believed that the crucial experience of World War I was carried further by Lenin and

Nazi Mass Rally, 1936   This picture captures the essence of the totalitarian interpretation of dynamic modern dictatorship. The uniformed members of the Nazi party have willingly merged themselves into a single force and await the command of the godlike leader. *(Wide World Photos)*

the Bolsheviks during the Russian civil war. Lenin showed how a dedicated minority could make a total effort and achieve victory over a less-determined majority. Moreover, Lenin demonstrated how institutions and human rights might be subordinated to the needs of a single group—the Communist party—and its leader, Lenin. Lenin also provided a model for single-party dictatorship, and he inspired imitators, including Adolf Hitler. The modern totalitarian state then reached maturity in the 1930s in the Stalinist U.S.S.R. and Nazi Germany.

Embellishing on early insights, numerous Western political scientists and historians argued in the 1950s and the 1960s that the totalitarian state used modern technology and communications to exercise complete political power. But it did not stop there. Increasingly, the state took over and tried to control just as completely the economic, social, intellectual, and cultural aspects of people's lives. Deviation from the norm even

in art or family behavior could become a crime. In theory, nothing was politically neutral; nothing was outside the scope of the state.

This grandiose vision of total state control broke decisively not only with conservative authoritarianism but also with nineteenth-century liberalism and democracy. Indeed, totalitarianism was a radical revolt against liberalism. Classical liberalism, which emerged decisively in the American and French Revolutions, sought to limit the power of the state and protect the rights of the individual. Moreover, liberals stood for rationality, peaceful progress, economic freedom, and a strong middle class. All of that disgusted totalitarians as sentimental slop. They believed in willpower, preached conflict, and worshiped violence. The individual was infinitely less valuable than the state, and there were no lasting rights, only temporary rewards for loyal and effective service.

Unlike old-fashioned authoritarianism, modern totalitarianism was based not on an elite but on people who had already become engaged in the political process, most notably through commitment to nationalism and socialism. Thus according to this interpretation, real totalitarian states built on mass movements and possessed boundless dynamism. Totalitarian societies were fully mobilized societies, moving toward some goal. And as soon as one goal was achieved at the cost of enormous sacrifice, another arose at the leader's command to take its place. Thus totalitarianism was in the end a *permanent* revolution, an *unfinished* revolution, in which rapid, profound change imposed from on high went on forever.

A second group of writers approached radical dictatorships outside the Soviet Union through the concept of *fascism*. A term of pride for Mussolini and Hitler, who used it to describe the supposedly "total" and revolutionary character of their movements, fascism was severely criticized by these writers and linked to reactionary forces, decaying capitalism, and domestic class conflict. Orthodox Marxists first argued that fascism was the way powerful capitalists sought to manipulate a mass movement capable of destroying the revolutionary working class and thus protect the enormous profits to be reaped through war and territorial expansion. Orthodox Marxists also rejected the totalitarian model, discerning at least some elements of the genuine socialism they desired in communist regimes such as that of Stalin.

Scholarly interest in fascism declined in the 1950s but revived thereafter. Comparative studies of fascist movements all across Europe showed that they shared many characteristics, including extreme, often expansionist nationalism; an antisocialism aimed at destroying working-class movements; alliances with powerful capitalists and landowners; mass parties, which appealed especially to the middle class and the peasantry; a dynamic and violent leader; and glorification of war and the military. European fascism remains a product of class conflict, capitalist crisis, and postwar upheaval in these more recent studies, but the basic interpretation has become less dogmatic and more subtle and convincing.

Historians today often adopt a third approach, which emphasizes the uniqueness of developments in each country. This approach has been both reflected and encouraged in recent years by an outpouring of specialized historical studies that stress change over time and challenge overarching interpretations like totalitarianism and fascism as too static and theoretical. This is especially true for Hitler's Germany, and a similar revaluation of Stalin's U.S.S.R. is in progress now that the fall of communism has opened the former Soviet Union's archives to new research. For this third school of historians, differences and changes in historical patterns are often more important than striking but frequently superficial similarities.

Four tentative judgments concerning these debates seem appropriate. First, as is often the case in history, leading schools of interpretation are rather closely linked to the political passions and the ideological commitments of the age. Thus modern Western "bourgeois-liberal" observers and moderate socialists, worried by the dual challenge of the Nazi and Soviet dictatorships, often found the totalitarian framework convincing in the 1930s and in the early cold war. At the same time, communists and orthodox Marxists saw profound structural differences between the continued capitalism in fascist countries and the socialism established in the Soviet Union, and starting in the 1960s New Left writers shared this view.

Second, as a noted scholar has recently concluded, the concept of totalitarianism retains real value for historical understanding. It correctly highlights that both Hitler's Germany and Stalin's Soviet Union made an unprecedented "total claim" on the belief and behavior of their respective citizens.[3] Third, antidemocratic, antisocialist movements sprang up all over Europe, but only in Italy and Germany (and some would say Spain) were they able to take power. Studies of fascist movements seeking power locate common elements, but they do not explain what fascist governments actually did. Fourth, the problem of Europe's radical dictatorships is complex, and there are few easy answers.

STALIN'S SOVIET UNION

Many of Lenin's harshest critics claim that he established the basic outlines of a modern totalitarian dictatorship after the Bolshevik Revolution and during the Russian civil war. If this is so, then Joseph Stalin (1879–1953) certainly finished the job. A master of political infighting, Stalin cautiously consolidated his power and eliminated his enemies in the mid-1920s. Then in 1928, as undisputed leader of the ruling Communist party, he launched the first five-year plan—the "revolution from above," as he so aptly termed it.

The five-year plans were extremely ambitious. Often incorrectly considered a mere set of economic measures to speed up the Soviet Union's industrial development, the five-year plans actually marked the beginning of a renewed attempt to mobilize and transform Soviet society along socialist lines. The ultimate goal of the plans was to generate new attitudes, new loyalties, and a new socialist humanity. The means Stalin and the small Communist party elite chose in order to do so were constant propaganda, enormous sacrifice by the people, and the concentration of all power in party hands. Thus the Soviet Union in the 1930s became a dynamic, modern totalitarian state.

From Lenin to Stalin

By spring 1921, Lenin and the Bolsheviks had won the civil war, but they ruled a shattered and devastated land. Many farms were in ruins, and food supplies were exhausted. In southern Russia, drought combined with the ravages of war to produce the worst famine in generations. By 1920, according to the government, from 50 to 90 percent of the population in seventeen provinces was starving. Industrial production also broke down completely. In 1921, for example, output of steel and cotton textiles was only about 4 percent of what it had been in 1913. The Bolsheviks had destroyed the economy as well as their foes.

In the face of economic disintegration, riots by peasants and workers, and an open rebellion by previously pro-Bolshevik sailors at Kronstadt, the tough but ever-flexible Lenin changed course. In March 1921, he an-

nounced the New Economic Policy (NEP), which re-established limited economic freedom in an attempt to rebuild agriculture and industry. During the civil war, the Bolsheviks had simply seized grain without payment, in accordance with the extreme policies of "war communism." With the NEP, Lenin substituted a grain tax on the country's peasant producers, who were permitted to sell their surpluses in free markets. Peasants were also encouraged to buy as many goods as they could afford from private traders and small handicraft manufacturers, groups that were now allowed to reappear. Heavy industry, railroads, and banks, however, remained wholly nationalized.

The NEP was shrewd and successful both politically and economically. Politically, it was a necessary but temporary compromise with the Soviet Union's overwhelming peasant majority. Flushed with victory after the revolutionary gains of 1917, the peasants would have fought to hold on to their land. Realizing that his government was not strong enough to take land from the peasants and turn them into state workers, Lenin made a deal with the only force capable of overturning his government. Economically, the NEP brought rapid recovery. In 1926 industrial output surpassed the level of 1913, and Soviet peasants were producing almost as

Lenin and Stalin in 1922   Lenin re-established limited economic freedom throughout the Soviet Union in 1921, but he ran the country and the Communist party in an increasingly authoritarian way. Stalin carried the process much further and eventually built a regime based on harsh dictatorship. *(Sovfoto)*

much grain as before the war. Counting shorter hours and increased social benefits, urban workers as well as peasants were living somewhat better than they had in the past.

As the economy recovered and the government partially relaxed its censorship and repression, an intense struggle for power began in the inner circles of the Communist party, for Lenin had left no chosen successor when he died in 1924. The principal contenders were the stolid Stalin and the flamboyant Trotsky.

The son of a shoemaker, Joseph Dzhugashvili—later known as Stalin—studied for the priesthood but was expelled from his theological seminary, probably for rude rebelliousness. By 1903 he had joined the Bolsheviks. In the years before the First World War, he engaged in many revolutionary activities in the southern Transcaucasian area of the multinational Russian empire, including a daring bank robbery to get money for the Bolsheviks. This raid gained Lenin's attention and approval.

Stalin was a good organizer but a poor speaker and writer, with no experience outside of Russia. Trotsky, a great and inspiring leader who had planned the 1917 takeover (see page 913) and then created the victorious Red Army, appeared to have all the advantages. Yet it was Stalin who succeeded Lenin. Stalin won because he was more effective at gaining the all-important support of the party, the only genuine source of power in the one-party state. Rising to general secretary of the party's Central Committee just before Lenin's first stroke in 1922, Stalin used his office to win friends and allies with jobs and promises.

The practical Stalin also won because he appeared better able than the brilliant Trotsky to relate Marxian teaching to Soviet realities in the 1920s. Stalin developed a theory of "socialism in one country" that was more appealing to the majority of communists than Trotsky's doctrine of "permanent revolution." Stalin argued that the Russian-dominated Soviet Union had the ability to build socialism on its own. Trotsky maintained that socialism in the Soviet Union could succeed only if revolution occurred quickly throughout Europe. To many Russian communists, Trotsky's views seemed to sell their country short and to promise risky conflicts with capitalist countries by recklessly encouraging revolutionary movements around the world. Stalin's willingness to break with the NEP and "build socialism" at home appealed to young militants in the party, who detested the capitalist-appearing NEP.

With cunning skill, Stalin gradually achieved supreme power between 1922 and 1927. First, he allied with Trotsky's personal enemies to crush Trotsky, who was expelled from the Soviet Union in 1929 and eventually was murdered in Mexico in 1940, undoubtedly on Stalin's order. Second, Stalin aligned with the moderates, who wanted to go slow at home, to suppress Trotsky's radical followers. Third, having defeated all the radicals, he turned against his allies, the moderates, and destroyed them as well. Stalin's final triumph came at the party congress of December 1927, which condemned all "deviation from the general party line" formulated by Stalin. The dictator and his followers were then ready to launch the revolution from above—the real revolution for millions of ordinary citizens.

The Five-Year Plans

The party congress of 1927, which ratified Stalin's consolidation of power, marked the end of the NEP and the beginning of the era of socialist five-year plans. Building on planning models developed by Soviet economists in the 1920s, the first five-year plan had staggering economic objectives. In just five years, total industrial output was to increase by 250 percent. Heavy industry, the preferred sector, was to grow even faster. Agricultural production was slated to increase by 150 percent, and one-fifth of the peasants in the Soviet Union were scheduled to give up their private plots and join socialist collective farms. By 1930 economic and social change was sweeping the country.

Stalin unleashed his "second revolution" for a variety of interrelated reasons. There were, first of all, ideological considerations. Like Lenin, Stalin and his militant supporters were deeply committed to socialism as they understood it. They feared a gradual restoration of capitalism, and they burned to stamp out the NEP's private traders, independent artisans, and property-owning peasants. Purely economic motivations were also important. Although the economy had recovered, it seemed to have stalled in 1927 and 1928. A new socialist offensive seemed necessary if industry and agriculture were to grow rapidly.

Political considerations were most important. Internationally, there was the old problem, remaining from prerevolutionary times, of catching up with the advanced and presumably hostile capitalist nations of the West. Stalin said in 1931, when he pressed for ever-greater speed and sacrifice, "We are fifty or a hundred years behind the advanced countries. We must make good this distance in ten years. Either we do it, or we shall go under."[4]

Domestically, there was what communist writers of the 1920s called the "cursed problem"—the problem

Life in a Forced-Labor Camp   This rare photo from about 1933 shows the reality of de-ported peasants and other political prisoners building the Stalin–White Sea Canal in far north-ern Russia, with their bare hands and under the most dehumanizing conditions. In books and plays Stalin's followers praised the project as a model for the regeneration of "reactionaries" and "Kulak exploiters" through the joys of socialist work. *(David King Collection)*

of the peasants. For centuries the peasants had wanted to own the land, and finally they had it. Sooner or later, the communists reasoned, the peasants would become conservative little capitalists and pose a threat to the regime. At the same time, the mainly urban commu-nists believed that the feared and despised "class en-emy" in the villages could be squeezed to provide the enormous sums needed for all-out industrialization. Thus Stalin decided on a war against the peasantry in order to bring it under the control of the state and to make it pay the costs of the new socialist offensive.

That war was *collectivization*—the forcible consolida-tion of individual peasant farms into large, state-controlled enterprises. Beginning in 1929, peasants all over the Soviet Union were ordered to give up their land and animals and become members of collective farms, although they continued to live in their own

homes. As for the *kulaks,* the better-off peasants, Stalin instructed party workers to "liquidate them as a class." Stripped of land and livestock, the kulaks were generally not even permitted to join the collective farms. Many starved or were deported to forced-labor camps for "re-education."

Since almost all peasants were in fact poor, the term *kulak* soon meant any peasant who opposed the new system. Whole villages were often attacked. One conscience-stricken colonel in the secret police con-fessed to a foreign journalist,

I am an old Bolshevik. I worked in the underground against the Tsar and then I fought in the Civil War. Did I do all that in order that I should now surround villages with machine guns and order my men to fire indiscriminately into crowds of peasants? Oh, no, no![5]

Forced collectivization of the peasants led to economic and human disaster. Large numbers of peasants slaughtered their animals and burned their crops in sullen, hopeless protest. Between 1929 and 1933, the number of horses, cattle, sheep, and goats in the Soviet Union fell by at least half. Nor were the state-controlled collective farms more productive. The output of grain barely increased between 1928 and 1938, when it was almost identical to that of 1913. Communist economists had expected collectivized agriculture to pay for new factories. Instead, the state had to invest heavily in agriculture, building thousands of tractors to replace slaughtered draft horses. Collectivized agriculture was unable to make any substantial financial contribution to Soviet industrial development in the first five-year plan.

The human dimension of the tragedy was absolutely staggering. As one leading historian writes in outrage, "The number dying in Stalin's war against the peasants was higher than the total deaths of all the countries in World War I." Yet, he notes, in Stalin's war only one side was armed and the other side bore almost all the casualties, many of whom were women, children, and the old.[6] Stalin himself confided to Winston Churchill at Yalta in 1945 that 10 million people had died in the course of collectivization.

In Ukraine the drive against peasants snowballed into a general assault on Ukrainians as reactionary nationalists and enemies of socialism. Thus in 1932, as collectivization and deportations continued, Stalin and his associates set levels of grain deliveries for the Ukrainian collective at excessively high levels, and they refused to relax those quotas or even allow food relief when Ukrainian communist leaders reported that starvation was occurring. The result was a terrible man-made famine in Ukraine in 1932 and 1933, which probably claimed 6 million lives. Stalin denied completely the existence of famine, and for years the party successfully suppressed much of the truth at home and abroad.

Collectivization, justly called the "second serfdom," was a cruel but real victory for communist ideologues. By the end of 1932, fully 60 percent of peasant families had been herded onto collective farms; by 1938, 93 percent. Regimented as employees of the state and dependent on the state-owned tractor stations, the collectivized peasants were no longer even a potential political threat to Stalin and the Communist party. Moreover, the state paid very low prices for grain and was thus assured of low-cost grain for bread for urban workers, who were much more important politically than the peasants.

Yet, as recent research shows, peasants fought back with indirect daily opposition and forced the suppos-

edly all-powerful state to make modest compromises. Peasants secured the right to limit a family's labor on the state-run farms and to cultivate tiny, grudgingly tolerated family plots, which provided them with much of their food. In 1938 these family plots produced 22 percent of all Soviet agricultural produce on only 4 percent of all cultivated land, eloquent testimony to the inefficiency of collectivized agriculture and the quiet resistance of the weak in the countryside.

The industrial side of the five-year plans was more successful—indeed, quite spectacular. The output of industry doubled in the first five-year plan and doubled again in the second. Soviet industry produced about four times as much in 1937 as it had in 1928. No other major country had ever achieved such rapid industrial growth. Heavy industry led the way; consumer industry grew quite slowly. Steel production—a near-obsession with Stalin, whose name fittingly means "man of steel" in Russian—increased roughly 500 percent between 1928 and 1937. A new heavy industrial complex was built almost from scratch in western Siberia. Industrial growth also went hand in hand with urban development. Cities rose where nomadic tribes had grazed their flocks. More than 25 million people migrated to cities during the 1930s.

The great industrialization drive, concentrated between 1928 and 1937, was an awe-inspiring achievement purchased at enormous sacrifice. The sudden creation of dozens of new factories required a great increase in total investment. Although few nations had ever invested more than one-sixth of their yearly net national income, Soviet planners decreed that more than one-third of net income go for investment. This meant that only two-thirds of everything being produced could be consumed by the people *and* the increasingly voracious military. The money for investment was collected from the people by means of heavy, hidden sales taxes.

Two other factors contributed importantly to rapid industrialization: firm labor discipline and foreign engineers. Between 1930 and 1932, trade unions lost most of their power. The government could assign workers to any job anywhere in the country, and individuals could not move without the permission of the police. When factory managers needed more hands, they called on their counterparts on the collective farms, who sent them millions of "unneeded" peasants over the years.

Foreign engineers were hired to plan and construct many of the new factories. Highly skilled American engineers, hungry for work in the depression years, were particularly important until newly trained Soviet experts began to replace them after 1932. The gigantic mills of the new Siberian steel industry were modeled on America's best. Thus Stalin's planners harnessed even the skill and technology of capitalist countries to promote the surge of socialist industry.

Life and Culture in Soviet Society

The aim of Stalin's five-year plans was to create a new kind of society and human personality as well as a strong industrial economy and a powerful army. Stalin and his helpers were good Marxian economic determinists. Once everything was owned by the state, they believed, a socialist society and a new kind of human being would inevitably emerge. Their utopian vision of a new humanity floundered, but they did build a new society, whose broad outlines existed into the mid-1980s. Life in this society had both good and bad aspects.

Because consumption was reduced to pay for investment, there was no improvement in the average standard of living. Indeed, the most careful studies show that the average nonfarm wage apparently purchased only about half as many goods in 1932 as in 1928. After 1932 real wages rose slowly, so that in 1937 workers could buy about 60 percent of what they had bought in 1928 and less than in 1913. Collectivized peasants experienced greater declines.

Life was hard in Stalin's Soviet Union. The masses of people lived primarily on black bread and wore old, shabby clothing. There were constant shortages in the stores, although very heavily taxed vodka was always readily available. A shortage of housing was a particularly serious problem. Millions were moving into the cities, but the government built few new apartments. In 1940 there were approximately 4 people per room in every urban dwelling, as opposed to 2.7 per room in 1926. A relatively lucky family received one room for all its members and shared both a kitchen and a toilet with others on the floor. Less fortunate workers, kulaks, and class enemies built scrap-lumber shacks or underground dugouts in shantytowns.

Life was hard but by no means hopeless. Idealism and ideology had real appeal for many communists, who saw themselves heroically building the world's first socialist society while capitalism crumbled in a worldwide depression and degenerated into fascism in the West. This optimistic belief in the future of the Soviet Union also attracted many disillusioned Westerners to communism in the 1930s.

On a more practical level, Soviet workers did receive some important social benefits, such as old-age pensions, free medical services, free education, and daycare centers for children. Unemployment was almost unknown. Finally, there was the possibility of personal advancement.

The keys to improving one's position were specialized skills and technical education. Rapid industrialization required massive numbers of trained experts, such as skilled workers, engineers, and plant managers. Thus the Stalinist state broke with the egalitarian policies of the 1920s and provided tremendous incentives to those who could serve its needs. It paid the mass of unskilled workers and collective farmers very low wages, but it dangled high salaries and many special privileges before its growing technical and managerial elite. This elite joined with the political and artistic elites in a new upper class, whose members were rich, powerful, and insecure. Thus millions struggled for an education. One young man summed it up: "In Soviet Russia there is no capital except education. If a person does not want to become a collective farmer or just a cleaning woman, the only means you have to get something is through education."[7]

The radical transformation of Soviet society had a profound impact on women's lives. Marxists had traditionally believed that both capitalism and the middle-class husband exploited women. The Russian Revolution of 1917 immediately proclaimed complete equality of rights for women. In the 1920s, divorce and abortion were made easily available, and women were urged to work outside the home and liberate themselves sexually. The most prominent Bolshevik feminist, Alexandra Kollontai, went so far as to declare that the sex act had no more significance than "drinking a glass of water."[8] After Stalin came to power, sexual and familial liberation was played down, and the most lasting changes for women involved work and education.

Young women were constantly told that they had to be fully equal to men, that they could and should do anything men could do. Peasant women in Russia had long experienced the equality of backbreaking physical labor in the countryside, and with the advent of the five-year plans, millions of women also toiled in factories and in heavy construction, building dams, roads, and steel mills in summer heat and winter frost. Many of the opportunities open to men through education were also open to women. Determined women pursued their studies and entered the ranks of the better-paid specialists in industry and science. Medicine practically became a woman's profession. By 1950, 75 percent of all doctors in the Soviet Union were women.

Soviet society gave women great opportunities, but it demanded great sacrifices as well. The vast majority of women simply *had* to work outside the home. Wages

Adult Education Illiteracy, especially among women, was a serious problem after the Russian Revolution. This early photo suggests how many adults successfully learned to read and write throughout the Soviet Union. *(Sovfoto)*

were so low that it was almost impossible for a family or couple to live only on the husband's earnings. Men continued to dominate the very best jobs. Finally, rapid change and economic hardship led to many broken families, creating further physical, emotional, and mental strains for women. In any event, the massive mobilization of women was a striking characteristic of the Soviet state.

Culture lost its autonomy in the 1930s and became thoroughly politicized through constant propaganda and indoctrination. Party activists lectured workers in factories and peasants on collective farms, while newspapers, films, and radio broadcasts endlessly recounted socialist achievements and capitalist plots. Whereas the 1920s had seen considerable experimentation in modern art and theater, intellectuals were ordered by Stalin to become "engineers of human minds." Writers and artists who could effectively combine genuine creativity and political propaganda became the darlings of the regime. It became increasingly important for the successful writer and artist to glorify Russian nationalism. Russian history was rewritten so that early tsars such as Ivan the Terrible and Peter the Great became worthy forerunners of the greatest Russian leader of all—Stalin.

Stalin seldom appeared in public, but his presence was everywhere—in portraits, statues, books, and quotations from his "sacred" writings. Although the gov-

ernment persecuted religion and turned churches into "museums of atheism," the state had both an earthly religion and a high priest—Marxism-Leninism and Joseph Stalin.

Stalinist Terror and the Great Purges

In the mid-1930s, the great offensive to build socialism and a new socialist personality culminated in ruthless police terror and a massive purging of the Communist party. First used by the Bolsheviks in the civil war to maintain their power, terror as state policy was revived in the collectivization drive against the peasants. The top members of the party and government publicly supported Stalin's initiatives, but there was some grumbling in the party. At a small gathering in November 1932, even Stalin's wife complained bitterly about the misery of the people and the horrible famine in Ukraine. Stalin showered her with insults, and she died that same night, apparently by her own hand. In late 1934, Stalin's number-two man, Sergei Kirov, was suddenly and mysteriously murdered. Although Stalin himself probably ordered Kirov's murder, he used the incident to launch a reign of terror.

In August 1936, sixteen prominent Old Bolsheviks confessed to all manner of plots against Stalin in spectacular public trials in Moscow. Then in 1937 the secret police arrested a mass of lesser party officials and newer members, also torturing them and extracting more confessions for more show trials. In addition to the party faithful, union officials, managers, intellectuals, army officers, and countless ordinary citizens were struck down. In all, at least 8 million people were probably arrested, and millions of these were executed or never returned from prisons and forced-labor camps.

Stalin and the remaining party leadership recruited 1.5 million new members to take the place of those purged. Thus more than half of all Communist party members in 1941 had joined since the purges. "These new men were 'thirty-something' products of the Second Revolution of the 1930s, Stalin's upwardly mobile yuppies, so to speak."[9] Often sons (and daughters) of workers, they had usually studied in the new technical schools, and they soon proved capable of managing the government and large-scale production. One of the most important products of the great purges, this new generation of Stalin-formed communists would serve the leader effectively until his death in 1953, and they would govern the Soviet Union until the early 1980s.

Stalin's mass purges remain baffling, for almost all historians believe that those purged posed no threat and confessed to crimes they had not committed. Possibly Stalin believed that the old communists, like the peasants under the NEP, were a potential threat to be wiped out in a preventive attack. Certainly the highly publicized purges sent a warning to the people: no one was secure; everyone had to serve the party and its leader with redoubled devotion. Some Western scholars have also argued that the terror reflected a fully developed totalitarian state, which must always be fighting real or imaginary enemies.

The long-standing Western interpretation that puts the blame for the great purges on Stalin, which became

Factory Workers Endorse the Moscow Trials   Voicing opposition in public was a one-way ticket to a forced-labor camp. Yet revisionist historians also argue that genuine fears of foreign plots and widespread resentment of privileged elites created considerable popular support for the great purges among ordinary Soviet citizens. *(David King Collection)*

popular in Russia with both leading historians and the general public after the fall of communism, has nevertheless been challenged in recent years. Revisionist historians argue that Stalin's fears were exaggerated but real. Moreover, these fears and suspicions were shared by many in the party and in the general population. Bombarded with ideology and political slogans, the population responded energetically to Stalin's directives. Investigations and trials snowballed into a mass hysteria, a new witch-hunt that claimed millions of victims.[10] In short, in this view of the 1930s, a popular but deluded Stalin found large numbers of willing collaborators for crime as well as for achievement.

 ## MUSSOLINI AND FASCISM IN ITALY

Mussolini's movement and his seizure of power in 1922 were important steps in the rise of dictatorships in Europe between the two world wars. Like all the future dictators, the young Mussolini hated liberalism and wanted to destroy it in Italy. But although Mussolini began as a revolutionary socialist, like Stalin, he turned against the working class and successfully sought the support of conservatives. At the same time, Mussolini and his supporters were the first to call themselves "fascists"—revolutionaries determined to create a certain kind of totalitarian state. Yet few scholars today would argue that Mussolini succeeded. His dictatorship was brutal and theatrical, but it remained a halfway house between conservative authoritarianism and dynamic totalitarianism.

The Seizure of Power

In the early twentieth century, Italy was a liberal state with civil rights and a constitutional monarchy. On the eve of the First World War, the parliamentary regime finally granted universal male suffrage, and Italy appeared to be moving toward democracy. But there were serious problems. Much of the Italian population was still poor, and many peasants were more attached to their villages and local interests than to the national state. Moreover, the papacy, many devout Catholics, conservatives, and landowners remained strongly opposed to liberal institutions and to the heirs of Cavour and Garibaldi—the middle-class lawyers and politicians who ran the country largely for their own benefit. Relations between church and state were often tense. Class differences were also extreme, and a powerful revolutionary socialist movement had developed. Only in Italy among the main European countries did the radical left wing of the Socialist party gain the leadership as early as 1912, and only in Italy did the Socialist party unanimously oppose the war from the very beginning.[11]

The war worsened the political situation. Having fought on the side of the Allies almost exclusively for purposes of territorial expansion, the parliamentary government bitterly disappointed Italian nationalists with Italy's modest gains at Versailles. Workers and peasants also felt cheated: to win their support during the war, the government had promised social and land reform, which it did not deliver after the war.

The Russian Revolution inspired and energized Italy's revolutionary socialist movement. The Socialist party quickly lined up with the Bolsheviks, and radical workers and peasants began occupying factories and seizing land in 1920. These actions scared and mobilized the property-owning classes. Moreover, after the war the pope lifted his ban on participation by Catholics in Italian politics, and a strong Catholic party quickly emerged. Thus by 1921 revolutionary socialists, antiliberal conservatives, and frightened property owners were all opposed—though for different reasons—to the liberal parliamentary government.

Into these crosscurrents of unrest and fear stepped the blustering, bullying Benito Mussolini (1883–1945). Son of a village schoolteacher and a poor blacksmith, Mussolini began his political career as a Socialist party leader and radical newspaper editor before World War I. In 1914, powerfully influenced by antidemocratic cults of violent action, the young Mussolini urged that Italy join the Allies, a stand for which he was expelled from the Italian Socialist party. Later Mussolini fought at the front and was wounded in 1917. Returning home, he began organizing bitter war veterans like himself into a band of fascists—from the Italian word for "a union of forces."

At first Mussolini's program was a radical combination of nationalist and socialist demands, including territorial expansion, benefits for workers, and land reform for peasants. As such, it competed directly with the well-organized Socialist party and failed to get off the ground. When Mussolini saw that his violent verbal assaults on rival Socialists won him growing support from conservatives and the frightened middle classes, he shifted gears in 1920. In thought and action, Mussolini was a striking example of the turbulent uncertainty of the age of anxiety.

Mussolini and his growing private army of Black Shirts began to grow violent. Typically, a band of fascist toughs would roar off in trucks at night and swoop down on a few isolated Socialist organizers, beating them up and force-feeding them almost deadly doses of castor oil. Few people were killed, but socialist newspapers, union halls, and local Socialist party headquarters were destroyed. Mussolini's toughs pushed Socialists out of the city governments of northern Italy.

A skillful politician, Mussolini allowed his followers to convince themselves that they were not just opposing the "Reds" but also making a real revolution of their own, forging a strong, dynamic movement that would help the little people against the established interests. With the government breaking down in 1922, largely because of the chaos created by his direct-action bands, Mussolini stepped forward as the savior of order and property. Striking a conservative note in his speeches and gaining the sympathetic neutrality of army leaders, Mussolini demanded the resignation of the existing government and his own appointment by the king. In October 1922, to force matters, a large group of fascists marched on Rome to threaten the king and force him to call on Mussolini. The threat worked. Victor Emmanuel III (r. 1900–1946), who had no love for the old liberal politicians, asked Mussolini to form a new cabinet. Thus, after widespread violence and a threat of armed uprising, Mussolini seized power "legally." He was immediately granted dictatorial authority for one year by the king and the parliament.

The Regime in Action

Mussolini became dictator on the strength of Italians' rejection of parliamentary government coupled with fears of Soviet-style revolution. Yet what he intended to do with his power was by no means clear until 1924. Some of his dedicated supporters pressed for a "second revolution." Mussolini's ministers, however, included old conservatives, moderates, and even two reform-minded Socialists. A new electoral law was passed giving two-thirds of the representatives in the parliament to the party that won the most votes, a change that allowed the Fascist party and its allies to win an overwhelming majority in 1924. Shortly thereafter, five of Mussolini's thugs kidnapped and murdered Giacomo Matteotti, the leader of the Socialists in the parliament. In the face of this outrage, the opposition demanded that Mussolini's armed squads be dissolved and all violence be banned.

Although Mussolini may or may not have ordered Matteotti's murder, he stood at the crossroads of a severe political crisis. After some hesitation, he charged forward. Declaring his desire to "make the nation Fascist," he imposed a series of repressive measures. Freedom of the press was abolished, elections were fixed, and the government ruled by decree. Mussolini ar-

Mussolini   was a charismatic orator with a sure touch for emotional propaganda. He loved settings that linked fascist Italy to the glories of imperial Rome. Poised to address a mass rally in Rome at the time of Matteotti's murder, Mussolini then called for 90,000 more volunteers to join his gun-toting fascist militia. Members of the militia stand as an honor guard in front of the podium. *(Popperfoto/Archive Photos)*

rested his political opponents, disbanded all independent labor unions, and put dedicated Fascists in control of Italy's schools. Moreover, he created a fascist youth movement, fascist labor unions, and many other fascist organizations. Mussolini trumpeted his goal in a famous slogan of 1926: "Everything in the state, nothing outside the state, nothing against the state." By the end of that year, Italy was a one-party dictatorship under Mussolini's unquestioned leadership.

Mussolini, however, did not complete the establishment of a modern totalitarian state. His Fascist party never became all-powerful. It never destroyed the old power structure, as the Communists did in the Soviet Union, or succeeded in dominating it, as the Nazis did in Germany. Membership in the Fascist party was more a sign of an Italian's respectability than a commitment to radical change. Interested primarily in personal power, Mussolini was content to compromise with the old conservative classes that controlled the army, the economy, and the state. He never tried to purge these classes or even move very vigorously against them. He controlled and propagandized labor but left big business to regulate itself, profitably and securely. There was no land reform.

Mussolini also drew increasing support from the Catholic church. In the Lateran Agreement of 1929, he recognized the Vatican as a tiny independent state, and he agreed to give the church heavy financial support. The pope expressed his satisfaction and urged Italians to support Mussolini's government.

Nothing better illustrates Mussolini's unwillingness to harness everyone and everything for dynamic action than his treatment of women. He abolished divorce and told women to stay at home and produce children. To promote that goal, he decreed a special tax on bachelors in 1934. In 1938 women were limited by law to a maximum of 10 percent of the better-paying jobs in industry and government. Italian women appear not to have changed their attitudes or behavior in any important way under fascist rule.

Mussolini's government did not pass racial laws until 1938 and did not persecute Jews savagely until late in the Second World War, when Italy was under Nazi control. Nor did Mussolini establish a truly ruthless police state. Only twenty-three political prisoners were condemned to death between 1926 and 1944. In spite of much pompous posing by the chauvinist leader and in spite of mass meetings, salutes, and a certain copying of Hitler's aggression in foreign policy after 1933, Mussolini's fascist Italy, though repressive and undemocratic, was never really totalitarian.

✤ HITLER AND NAZISM IN GERMANY

The most frightening dictatorship developed in Nazi Germany. A product of Hitler's evil genius as well as of Germany's social and political situation and the general attack on liberalism and rationality in the age of anxiety, the Nazi movement shared some of the characteristics of Mussolini's Italian model and was a form of fascism. The Nazi dictatorship smashed or took over most independent organizations, mobilized the economy, and persecuted the Jewish population. Thus Nazism asserted an unlimited claim over German society and proclaimed that all ultimate power belonged to its endlessly aggressive leader—Adolf Hitler. The aspirations of Nazism were truly totalitarian.

The Roots of Nazism

Nazism grew out of many complex developments, of which the most influential were extreme nationalism and racism. These two ideas captured the mind of the young Hitler, and it was he who dominated Nazism for as long as it lasted.

Born the fourth child of a successful Austrian customs official and an indulgent mother, Adolf Hitler (1889–1945) spent his childhood in small towns in Austria. A good student in grade school, Hitler did poorly on reaching high school and dropped out at age fourteen following the death of his father. After four years of unfocused loafing, Hitler finally left for Vienna, where he lived a comfortable, lazy life on his generous orphan's pension and found most of the perverted beliefs that guided his life.

In Vienna Hitler soaked up extreme German nationalism, which was particularly strong there. Austro-German nationalists, as if to compensate for their declining position in the Austro-Hungarian Empire, believed Germans to be a superior people and the natural rulers of central Europe. They often advocated union with Germany and violent expulsion of "inferior" peoples as the means of maintaining German domination of the Austro-Hungarian Empire.

Hitler was deeply impressed by Vienna's mayor, Karl Lueger (1844–1910). With the help of the Catholic trade unions, he had succeeded in winning the support of the little people of Vienna for an attack on capitalism and liberalism. A master of mass politics in the urban world, Lueger showed Hitler the enormous potential of anticapitalist and antiliberal propaganda.

From Lueger and others, Hitler eagerly absorbed virulent anti-Semitism, racism, and hatred of Slavs. He developed an unshakable belief in the crudest, most exaggerated distortions of the Darwinian theory of survival, the superiority of Germanic races, and the inevitability of racial conflict. Thus anti-Semitism and racism became Hitler's most passionate convictions, his explanation for everything. The Jews, he claimed, directed an international conspiracy of finance capitalism and Marxian socialism against German culture, German

HITLER AND NAZISM IN GERMANY 971

unity, and the German race. Hitler's belief was totally irrational, but he never doubted it.

Although he moved to Munich in 1913 to avoid being drafted in the Austrian army, the lonely Hitler greeted the outbreak of the First World War as a salvation. He later wrote in his autobiography, *Mein Kampf,* that, "overcome by passionate enthusiasm, I fell to my knees and thanked heaven out of an overflowing heart." The struggle and discipline of war gave life meaning, and Hitler served bravely as a dispatch carrier on the western front.

When Germany was suddenly defeated in 1918, Hitler's world was shattered. Not only was he a fanatical nationalist, but war was also his reason for living. Convinced that Jews and Marxists had "stabbed Germany in the back," he vowed to fight on. And in the bitterness and uncertainty of postwar Germany, his wild speeches began to attract attention.

In late 1919, Hitler joined a tiny extremist group in Munich called the German Workers' party. In addition to denouncing Jews, Marxists, and democrats, the German Workers' party promised unity under a uniquely German "national socialism," which would abolish the injustices of capitalism and create a mighty "people's community." By 1921 Hitler had gained absolute control of this small but growing party. He was already a master of mass propaganda and political showmanship. His most effective tool was the mass rally, where he often worked his audience into a frenzy with wild, demagogic attacks on the Versailles treaty, the Jews, the war profiteers, and Germany's Weimar Republic.

Party membership multiplied tenfold after early 1922. In late 1923, the Weimar Republic seemed on the verge of collapse, and Hitler, inspired by Mussolini's recent easy victory, decided on an armed uprising in Munich. Despite the failure of the poorly organized plot and Hitler's arrest, Nazism had been born.

Hitler's Road to Power

At his trial, Hitler violently denounced the Weimar Republic, and he gained enormous publicity and attention. Moreover, he learned from his unsuccessful revolt. Hitler concluded that he had to undermine, rather than overthrow, the government and come to power legally through electoral competition. He forced his more violent supporters to accept his new strategy. He also used his brief prison term to dictate *Mein Kampf.* There he expounded on his basic themes: "race," with a stress on anti-Semitism; "living space," with a sweeping vision of war and conquered territory; and the leader-dictator (*Führer*), with unlimited, arbitrary power.

In the years of prosperity and relative stability between 1924 and 1929, Hitler concentrated on building his National Socialist German Workers' party, or Nazi party. By 1928 the party had 100,000 highly disciplined members under Hitler's absolute control. To appeal to the middle-class voters, Hitler de-emphasized the anticapitalist elements of national socialism and vowed to fight Bolshevism.

Yet the Nazis remained a small splinter group in 1928, when they received only 2.6 percent of the vote in the general elections and twelve seats in the Reichstag. There the Nazi deputies pursued the legal strategy of using democracy to destroy democracy.

The Great Depression, shattering economic prosperity from 1929 on, presented Hitler with a fabulous opportunity. Unemployment jumped from 1.3 million in 1929 to 5 million in 1930; that year Germany had almost as many unemployed as all the other countries of Europe combined. Industrial production fell by one-half between 1929 and 1932. By the end of 1932, an incredible 43 percent of the labor force was unemployed. No factor contributed more to Hitler's success than the economic crisis. Never very interested in economics before, Hitler began promising German voters economic as well as political and international salvation.

Above all, Hitler rejected free-market capitalism and advocated government programs to bring recovery. Nazi economic writers promised "to create a 'third path' between centralized state planning and laissez-faire capitalism." Hitler pitched his speeches especially to middle- and lower-middle-class groups—small business people, officeworkers, artisans, and peasants—as well as to skilled workers striving for middle-class status. Seized by panic as bankruptcies increased, unemployment soared, and the Communists made dramatic election gains, great numbers of middle- and lower-middle-class people "voted their pocketbooks,"[12] as new research argues convincingly, and deserted the conservative and moderate parties for the Nazis.

In the election of 1930, the Nazis won 6.5 million votes and 107 seats, which made them second in strength only to the Social Democrats, the moderate socialists. As the economic and political situation continued to deteriorate, Hitler and the Nazis made more dramatic gains. In July 1932, the Nazis gained 14.5 million votes—38 percent of the total—and became the largest party in the Reichstag.

The appeal to pocketbook interests was particularly effective in the early 1930s because Hitler appeared more mainstream, playing down his anti-Jewish hatred and racist nationalism. A master of mass propaganda and psychology, he had written in *Mein Kampf* that the

Hitler in Opposition Hitler returns the salute of his Brown Shirts in this photograph from the third party day rally in Nuremberg in 1927. The Brown Shirts formed a private army within the Nazi movement, and their uniforms, marches, salutes, and vandalism helped keep Hitler in the public eye in the 1920s. *(Courtesy, Bison Books, London)*

of enthralled listeners, found a sense of belonging as well as hope for better times.

Hitler and the Nazis also appealed strongly to German youth. Indeed, in some ways the Nazi movement was a mass movement of young Germans. Hitler himself was only forty in 1929, and he and most of his top aides were much younger than other leading German politicians. "National Socialism is the organized will of the youth," proclaimed the official Nazi slogan, and the battle cry of Gregor Strasser, a leading Nazi organizer, was "Make way, you old ones."[13] In 1931 almost 40 percent of Nazi party members were under thirty, compared with 20 percent of Social Democrats. National recovery, exciting and rapid change, and personal advancement were the appeals of Nazism to millions of German youths.

Another reason Hitler came to power was that normal democratic government broke down as early as May 1930. Unable to gain the support of a majority in the Reichstag, Chancellor (chief minister) Heinrich Brüning convinced the president, the aging war hero General Hindenburg, to authorize rule by decree. Intending to use this emergency measure indefinitely, Brüning was determined to overcome the economic crisis by cutting back government spending and ruthlessly forcing down prices and wages. Brüning's ultra-orthodox policies not only intensified the economic collapse in Germany but also convinced many voters that the country's republican leaders were stupid and corrupt, thereby adding to Hitler's appeal. After President Hindenburg forced Brüning to resign in May 1932, his successor continued to rule by decree.

The continuation of the struggle between the Social Democrats and the Communists, right up until the moment Hitler took power, was another aspect of the breakdown of democratic government. The Communists refused to cooperate with the Social Democrats, even though the two parties together outnumbered the Nazis in the Reichstag, even after the elections of 1932. German Communists (and the still complacent Stalin) were blinded by hatred of socialists and by ideology: the Communists believed that Hitler's fascism represented the last agonies of monopoly capitalism and that a communist revolution would soon follow his taking power. Socialist leaders pleaded, even at the Soviet Embassy, for at least a temporary alliance with the Communists to block Hitler, but to no avail. Disunity on the left was undoubtedly another nail in the republic's coffin.

Finally, Hitler excelled in the dirty, backroom politics of the decaying Weimar Republic. That, in fact, brought him to power. In complicated infighting in 1932, he

masses were the "driving force of the most important changes in this world" and were themselves driven by fanaticism and not by knowledge. To arouse such hysterical fanaticism, he believed that all propaganda had to be limited to a few simple, endlessly repeated slogans. But now when he harangued vast audiences with wild oratory and simple slogans, he featured "national rebirth" and the "crimes" of the Versailles treaty. And many uncertain individuals, surrounded by thousands cleverly succeeded in gaining additional support from key people in the army and big business. These people thought they could use Hitler for their own advantage to get increased military spending, fat contracts, and tough measures against workers. Many conservative and nationalistic politicians thought similarly. They thus accepted Hitler's demand to join the government only if he became chancellor. There would be only two other National Socialists and nine solid conservatives as ministers, and in such a coalition government, they reasoned, Hitler could be used and controlled. On January 30, 1933, Adolf Hitler, leader of the largest party in Germany, was legally appointed chancellor by Hindenburg.

The Nazi State and Society

Hitler moved rapidly and skillfully to establish an unshakable dictatorship. Continuing to maintain legal appearances, he immediately called for new elections. In the midst of a violent electoral campaign, the Reichstag building was partly destroyed by fire. Although the Nazis themselves may have set the fire, Hitler screamed that the Communist party was responsible. On the strength of this accusation, he convinced President Hindenburg to sign dictatorial emergency acts that practically abolished freedom of speech and assembly as well as most personal liberties.

When the Nazis won only 44 percent of the vote in the elections, Hitler immediately outlawed the Communist party and arrested its parliamentary representatives. Then on March 23, 1933, the Nazis pushed through the Reichstag the so-called Enabling Act, which gave Hitler absolute dictatorial power for four years. Armed with the Enabling Act, Hitler and the Nazis moved to smash or control all independent organizations. Their deceitful stress on legality, coupled with divide-and-conquer techniques, disarmed the opposition until it was too late for effective resistance.

Germany soon became a one-party state. Only the Nazi party was legal. Elections were farces. The Reichstag was jokingly referred to as the most expensive glee club in the country, for its only function was to sing hymns of praise to the Führer. Hitler and the Nazis took over the government bureaucracy intact, installing many Nazis in top positions. At the same time, they created a series of overlapping Nazi party organizations responsible solely to Hitler.

As research in recent years shows, the resulting system of dual government was riddled with rivalries, contradictions, and inefficiencies. Thus the Nazi state lacked the all-compassing unity that its propagandists claimed and was sloppy and often disorganized. Yet this fractured system suited Hitler and his purposes. He could play the established bureaucracy against his private, personal "party government" and maintain his freedom of action. Hitler could concentrate on general principles and the big decisions, which he always made.

In the economic sphere, one big decision outlawed strikes and abolished independent labor unions, which were replaced by the Nazi Labor Front. Professional people—doctors and lawyers, teachers and engineers—also saw their previously independent organizations swallowed up by Nazi associations. Nor did the Nazis neglect cultural and intellectual life. Publishing houses were put under Nazi control, and universities and writers were quickly brought into line. Democratic, socialist, and Jewish literature was put on ever-growing blacklists. Passionate students and pitiful professors burned forbidden books in public squares. Modern art and architecture were ruthlessly prohibited. Life became violently anti-intellectual. As the cynical Joseph Goebbels put it, "When I hear the word 'culture' I reach for my gun."[14] By 1934 a brutal dictatorship characterized by frightening dynamism and obedience to Hitler was already largely in place.

Only the army retained independence, and Hitler moved brutally and skillfully to establish his control there, too. He realized that the army as well as big business was suspicious of the Nazi storm troopers (the SA), the quasi-military band of 3 million toughs in brown shirts who had fought communists and beaten up Jews before the Nazis took power. These unruly storm troopers expected top positions in the army and even talked of a "second revolution" against capitalism. Hitler decided that the SA leaders had to be eliminated. On the night of June 30, 1934, he struck.

Hitler's elite personal guard—the SS—arrested and shot without trial roughly a thousand SA leaders and assorted political enemies. His propagandists then spread lies about SA conspiracies. Shortly thereafter army leaders swore a binding oath of "unquestioning obedience . . . to the Leader of the German State and People, Adolf Hitler." The SS grew rapidly. Under its methodical, inhuman leader, Heinrich Himmler (1900–1945), the SS joined with the political police, the Gestapo, to expand its network of special courts and concentration camps. Nobody was safe.

From the beginning, Jews were a special object of Nazi persecution. By the end of 1934, most Jewish lawyers, doctors, professors, civil servants, and musicians had lost their jobs and the right to practice their

974 **CHAPTER 29** DICTATORSHIPS AND THE SECOND WORLD WAR

professions. In 1935 the infamous Nuremberg Laws classified as Jewish anyone having one or more Jewish grandparents and deprived Jews of all rights of citizenship. By 1938 roughly 150,000 of Germany's half a million Jews had emigrated, sacrificing almost all their property in order to leave Germany.

Following the assassination of a German diplomat in Paris by a young Jewish boy trying desperately to strike out at persecution, the attack on the Jews accelerated. A well-organized wave of violence, known to history as "Kristallnacht," smashed windows, looted shops, and destroyed homes and synagogues. German Jews were then rounded up and made to pay for the damage. Another 150,000 Jews fled Germany. Some Germans privately opposed these outrages, but most went along or looked the other way. This lack of opposition reflected anti-Semitism to a degree still being debated by historians, but it certainly reflected the strong popular support Hitler's government enjoyed.

Hitler's Popularity

Hitler had promised the masses economic recovery— "work and bread"—and he delivered. Breaking with Brüning's do-nothing policies, Hitler launched a large public works program to help pull Germany out of the depression. Work began on superhighways, offices, gigantic sports stadiums, and public housing. Hitler also appointed as Germany's central banker a well-known conservative named Hjalmar Schacht, who skillfully restored credit and business. In 1936 an openly aggressive Hitler broke with Schacht, and Germany turned decisively toward rearmament and preparation for war. As a result of these policies (and plain good luck), unemployment dropped steadily, from 6 million in January 1933 to about 1 million in late 1936. By 1938 there was a shortage of workers, as unemployment fell to 2 percent, and women began to take jobs previously denied them by the antifeminist Nazis. Thus between 1932 and 1938, the standard of living for the average employed worker increased moderately. The profits of business rose sharply. For millions of people, economic recovery was tangible evidence that Nazi promises were more than show and propaganda.

For the masses of ordinary German citizens who were not Jews, Slavs, Gypsies, Jehovah's Witnesses, communists, or homosexuals, Hitler's government meant greater equality and more opportunities. In 1933 the position of the traditional German elites—the landed aristocracy, the wealthy capitalists, and the well-educated professional classes—was still very strong. Barriers between classes were generally high. Hitler's rule introduced changes that lowered these barriers. For example, stiff educational requirements, which favored the well-to-do, were relaxed. The new Nazi elite included many young and poorly educated dropouts, rootless lower-middle-class people like Hitler who rose to the top with breathtaking speed. More generally, the Nazis tolerated privilege and wealth only as long as they served the needs of the party. Even big business was constantly ordered around.

Yet few historians today believe that Hitler and the Nazis brought about a real social revolution, as an earlier generation of scholars often argued. Millions of modest middle-class and lower-middle-class people *felt* that Germany was becoming more open and equal, as Nazi propagandists constantly claimed. But quantitative studies show that the well-educated classes held on to most of their advantages and that only a modest social leveling occurred in the Nazi years. It is significant that the Nazis shared with the Italian fascists the stereotypic view of women as housewives and mothers. Only under the relentless pressure of war did they reluctantly mobilize large numbers of German women for work in offices and factories.

Hitler's rabid nationalism, which had helped him gain power, continued to appeal to Germans after 1933. Ever since the wars against Napoleon, many Germans had believed in a special mission for a superior German nation. The successes of Bismarck had furthered such feelings, and near-victory in World War I made nationalists eager for renewed expansion in the 1920s. Thus when Hitler went from one foreign triumph to another and a great German empire seemed within reach, the majority of the population was delighted and kept praising the Führer's actions well into the war.

Not all Germans supported Hitler, however, and a number of German groups actively resisted him after 1933. Tens of thousands of political enemies were imprisoned, and thousands were executed. But opponents of the Nazis pursued various goals, and they were never unified, a fact that helps account for their ultimate lack of success. In the first years of Hitler's rule, the principal resisters were the communists and the socialists in the trade unions. But the expansion of the SS system of terror after 1935 smashed most of these leftists. A second group of opponents arose in the Catholic and Protestant churches. However, their efforts were directed primarily at preserving genuine religious life, not at overthrowing Hitler. Finally in 1938 (and again in 1942 to 1944), some high-ranking army officers, who feared the consequences of Hitler's reckless aggression, plotted against him, unsuccessfully.

✤ NAZI EXPANSION AND THE SECOND WORLD WAR

Although economic recovery and somewhat greater opportunity for social advancement won Hitler support, they were only byproducts of the Nazi regime. The guiding and unique concepts of Nazism remained space and race—the territorial expansion of the superior German race. As Germany regained its economic strength and as independent organizations were brought under control, Hitler formed alliances with other dictators and began expanding. German expansion was facilitated by the uncertain, divided, pacific Western democracies, which tried to buy off Hitler to avoid war.

Yet war inevitably broke out, in both the West and the East, for Hitler's ambitions were essentially unlimited. On both war fronts, Nazi soldiers scored enormous successes until late 1942, establishing a vast empire of death and destruction. Hitler's reckless aggression also raised a mighty coalition determined to smash the Nazi order. Led by Britain, the United States, and the Soviet Union, the Grand Alliance—to use Winston Churchill's favorite term—functioned quite effectively in military terms. By the summer of 1943, the tide of battle had turned. Two years later, Germany and its allies lay in ruins, utterly defeated. Thus the terrible Nazi empire proved short-lived.

Aggression and Appeasement, 1933–1939

Hitler's tactics in international politics after 1933 strikingly resembled those he had used in domestic politics between 1924 and 1933. When Hitler was weak, he righteously proclaimed that he intended to overturn the "unjust system" established by the Treaties of Versailles and Locarno—but only by legal means. As he grew stronger, and as other leaders showed their willingness to compromise, he increased his demands and finally began attacking his independent neighbors (Map 29.1).

Hitler realized that his aggressive policies had to be carefully camouflaged at first, for Germany's army was limited by the Treaty of Versailles to only 100,000 men. As he told a group of army commanders in February 1933, the early stages of his policy of "conquest of new living space in the East and its ruthless Germanization" had serious dangers. If France had real leaders, Hitler said, it would "not give us time but attack us, presumably with its eastern satellites."[15] To avoid such threats to his plans, Hitler loudly proclaimed his peaceful intentions to all the world. Nevertheless, he felt strong

The Glorification of Gender Difference The Nazi state favored traditional roles for women, believing that they should keep house and raise families, preferably large ones. Thus this propaganda poster starkly informs young women that their job is motherhood. Young men entering the State Labor Service are depicted as happy, self-confident "soldiers of work," bonding together and preparing for battle. *(AKG London)*

enough to walk out of a sixty-nation disarmament conference and withdraw from the League of Nations in October 1933. Gustav Stresemann's policy of peaceful cooperation (see page 942) was dead; the Nazi determination to rearm was out in the open.

Following this action, which met with widespread approval at home, Hitler moved to incorporate independent Austria into a greater Germany. Austrian Nazis climaxed an attempted overthrow by murdering the Austrian chancellor in July 1934. They were unable to take power, however, because a worried Mussolini, who had initially greeted Hitler as a fascist little brother, massed his troops on Brenner Pass and threatened

EVENTS LEADING TO WORLD WAR II

1919	Treaty of Versailles is signed; J. M. Keynes publishes *Economic Consequences of the Peace*.
1919–1920	U.S. Senate rejects the Treaty of Versailles.
1921	Germany is billed $33 billion in reparations.
1922	Mussolini seizes power in Italy; Germany proposes a moratorium on reparations.
January 1923	France and Belgium occupy the Ruhr; Germany orders passive resistance to the occupation.
October 1923	Stresemann agrees to reparations based on Germany's ability to pay.
1924	Dawes Plan: German reparations are reduced and put on a sliding scale. Large U.S. loans to Germany are recommended to promote German recovery; occupation of the Ruhr ends; Adolf Hitler dictates *Mein Kampf*.
1924–1929	Spectacular German economic recovery occurs; circular flow of international funds enables sizable reparations payments.
1925	Treaties of Locarno promote European security and stability.
1926	Germany joins the League of Nations.
1928	Kellogg-Briand Pact renounces war as an instrument of international affairs.
1929	Young Plan further reduces German reparations; U.S. stock market crashes.
1929–1933	Great Depression rages.
1931	Japan invades Manchuria.
1932	Nazis become the largest party in the Reichstag.
January 1933	Hitler is appointed chancellor of Germany.
March 1933	Reichstag passes the Enabling Act, granting Hitler absolute dictatorial power.
October 1933	Germany withdraws from the League of Nations.
July 1934	Nazis murder the Austrian chancellor.
1935	Nuremberg Laws deprive Jews of all rights of citizenship.
March 1935	Hitler announces German rearmament.
June 1935	Anglo-German naval agreement is signed.
October 1935	Mussolini invades Ethiopia and receives Hitler's support.
March 1936	German armies move unopposed into the demilitarized Rhineland.
July 1936	Civil war breaks out in Spain.
1937	Japan invades China; Rome-Berlin Axis in effect.
March 1938	Germany annexes Austria.
September 1938	Munich Conference: Britain and France agree to German seizure of the Sudetenland from Czechoslovakia.
March 1939	Germany occupies the rest of Czechoslovakia; appeasement ends in Britain.
August 1939	Nazi-Soviet nonaggression pact is signed.
September 1, 1939	Germany invades Poland.
September 3, 1939	Britain and France declare war on Germany.

MAP 29.1 The Growth of Nazi Germany, 1933–1939   Until March 1939, Hitler brought ethnic Germans into the Nazi state; then he turned on the Slavic peoples he had always hated. He stripped Czechoslovakia of its independence and prepared for an attack on Poland in September 1939.

to fight. When in March 1935 Hitler established a general military draft and declared the "unequal" disarmament clauses of the Treaty of Versailles null and void, other countries appeared to understand the danger. With France taking the lead, Italy and Great Britain protested strongly and warned against future aggressive actions.

Yet the emerging united front against Hitler quickly collapsed. Of crucial importance, Britain adopted a pol-

icy of appeasement, granting Hitler everything he could reasonably want (and more) in order to avoid war. The first step was an Anglo-German naval agreement in June 1935 that broke Germany's isolation. The second step came in March 1936 when Hitler suddenly marched his armies into the demilitarized Rhineland, brazenly violating the Treaties of Versailles and Locarno. This was the last good chance to stop the Nazis, for Hitler had ordered his troops to retreat if France resisted militarily.

But an uncertain France would not move without British support, and the occupation of German soil by German armies seemed right and just to Britain. With a greatly improved strategic position, Germany handed France a tremendous psychological defeat.

British appeasement, which practically dictated French policy, lasted far into 1939. It was motivated by British feelings of guilt toward Germany and the pacifism of a population still horrified by the memory of the First World War. As in Germany, many powerful conservatives in Britain underestimated Hitler. They believed that Soviet communism was the real danger and that Hitler could be used to stop it. A leading member of Britain's government personally told Hitler in November 1937 that it was his conviction that Hitler "not only had accomplished great things in Germany itself, but that through the total destruction of Communism in his own country . . . Germany rightly had to be considered as a Western bulwark against Communism."[16] Such rigid anticommunist feelings made an alliance between the Western powers and Stalin unlikely.

As Britain and France opted for appeasement and the Soviet Union watched all developments suspiciously, Hitler found powerful allies. In 1935 the bombastic Mussolini decided that imperial expansion was needed to revitalize Italian fascism. From Italian colonies on the east coast of Africa, he attacked the independent African kingdom of Ethiopia. The Western powers and the League of Nations piously condemned Italian aggression without saving Ethiopia from defeat, while Hitler supported Italy energetically and overcame Mussolini's lingering doubts about the Nazis. The result in late 1936 was an agreement on close cooperation between Italy and Germany, the so-called Rome-Berlin Axis. Japan, which had been expanding into Manchuria since 1931, soon joined the Axis alliance.

At the same time, Germany and Italy intervened in the long, complicated Spanish civil war, where their support eventually helped General Francisco Franco's fascist movement defeat republican Spain. Only the Soviet Union gave aid to the leftist government that Franco fought, for public opinion in Britain and especially in France was hopelessly divided on the Spanish question.

In late 1937, while proclaiming peaceful intentions to the British and their gullible prime minister, Neville Chamberlain, Hitler told his generals his real plans. His "unshakable decision" was to crush Austria and Czechoslovakia at the earliest possible moment as the first step in his long-contemplated drive to the east for living space. By threatening Austria with invasion, Hitler forced the Austrian chancellor in March 1938 to put local Nazis in control of the government. The next day, German armies moved in unopposed, and Austria be-

Cartoonist David Low's biting criticism of appeasing leaders appeared shortly after Hitler remilitarized the Rhineland. Appeasement also appealed to millions of ordinary citizens in Britain and France, who wanted to avoid at any cost another great war. *(Reproduced by permission of London Evening/Solo Standard)*

came two more provinces of Greater Germany (see Map 29.1).

Simultaneously, Hitler began demanding that the pro-Nazi, German-speaking minority of western Czechoslovakia—the Sudetenland—be turned over to Germany. Yet democratic Czechoslovakia was prepared to defend itself. Moreover, France had been Czechoslovakia's ally since 1924; and if France fought, the Soviet Union was pledged to help. As war appeared inevitable—for Hitler had already told the leader of the Sudeten Germans that "we must always ask so much we cannot be satisfied"—appeasement triumphed again. In September 1938, Chamberlain flew to Germany three times in fourteen days. In these negotiations, to which the U.S.S.R. was deliberately not invited, Chamberlain and the French agreed with Hitler that the Sudetenland should be ceded to Germany immediately. Returning to London from the Munich Conference, Chamberlain told cheering crowds that he had secured "peace with honor . . . peace for our time." Sold out by the Western powers, Czechoslovakia gave in.

Confirmed once again in his opinion of the Western democracies as weak and racially degenerate, Hitler accelerated his aggression. In a shocking violation of his solemn assurances that the Sudetenland was his last territorial demand, Hitler's armies occupied the Czech lands in March 1939, while Slovakia became a puppet state. The effect on Western public opinion was electrifying. For the first time, there was no possible rationale of self-determination for Nazi aggression since Hitler was seizing Czechs and Slovaks as captive peoples. Thus when Hitler used the question of German minorities in Danzig as a pretext to confront Poland, a suddenly militant Chamberlain declared that Britain and France would fight if Hitler attacked his eastern neighbor. Hitler did not take these warnings seriously and decided to press on.

In an about-face that stunned the world, Hitler offered and Stalin signed a ten-year Nazi-Soviet nonaggression pact in August 1939. Each dictator promised to remain neutral if the other became involved in war. An attached secret protocol, which became known only after the war, ruthlessly divided eastern Europe into German and Soviet zones, "in the event of a political territorial reorganization." The nonaggression pact itself was enough to make Britain and France cry treachery, for they, too, had been negotiating with Stalin. But Stalin had remained distrustful of Western intentions, and Hitler had offered immediate territorial gain.

For Hitler, everything was set. He told his generals on the day of the nonaggression pact, "My only fear is that at the last moment some dirty dog will come up with a mediation plan." On September 1, 1939, German armies and warplanes smashed into Poland from three sides. Two days later, Britain and France, finally true to their word, declared war on Germany. The Second World War had begun.

Hitler's Empire, 1939–1942

Using planes, tanks, and trucks in the first example of a *blitzkrieg*, or "lightning war," Hitler's armies crushed Poland in four weeks. While the Soviet Union quickly took its part of the booty—the eastern half of Poland and the independent Baltic states of Lithuania, Estonia, and Latvia—French and British armies dug in in the west. They expected another war of attrition and economic blockade.

In spring 1940, the lightning war struck again. After occupying Denmark, Norway, and Holland, German motorized columns broke through southern Belgium, split the Franco-British forces, and trapped the entire British army on the beaches of Dunkirk. By heroic efforts, the British withdrew their troops but not their equipment.

France was taken by the Nazis. Aging marshal Henri-Philippe Pétain formed a new French government—the so-called Vichy government—to accept defeat, and German armies occupied most of France. By July 1940, Hitler ruled practically all of western continental Europe; Italy was an ally, and the Soviet Union and Spain were friendly neutrals. Only Britain, led by the uncompromising Winston Churchill (1874–1965), remained unconquered. Churchill proved to be one of history's greatest wartime leaders, rallying the British with stirring speeches, infectious confidence, and bulldog determination.

Germany sought to gain control of the air, the necessary first step toward an amphibious invasion of Britain. In the Battle of Britain, up to a thousand German planes attacked British airfields and key factories in a single day, dueling with British defenders high in the skies. Losses were heavy on both sides. Then in September Hitler angrily and foolishly changed his strategy, turning from military objectives to indiscriminate bombing of British cities in an attempt to break British morale. British aircraft factories increased production, anti-aircraft defense improved with the help of radar, and the heavily bombed people of London defiantly dug in. In September and October 1940, Britain was beating Germany three to one in the air war. There was no possibility of immediate German invasion of Britain.

In these circumstances, the most reasonable German strategy would have been to attack Britain through the

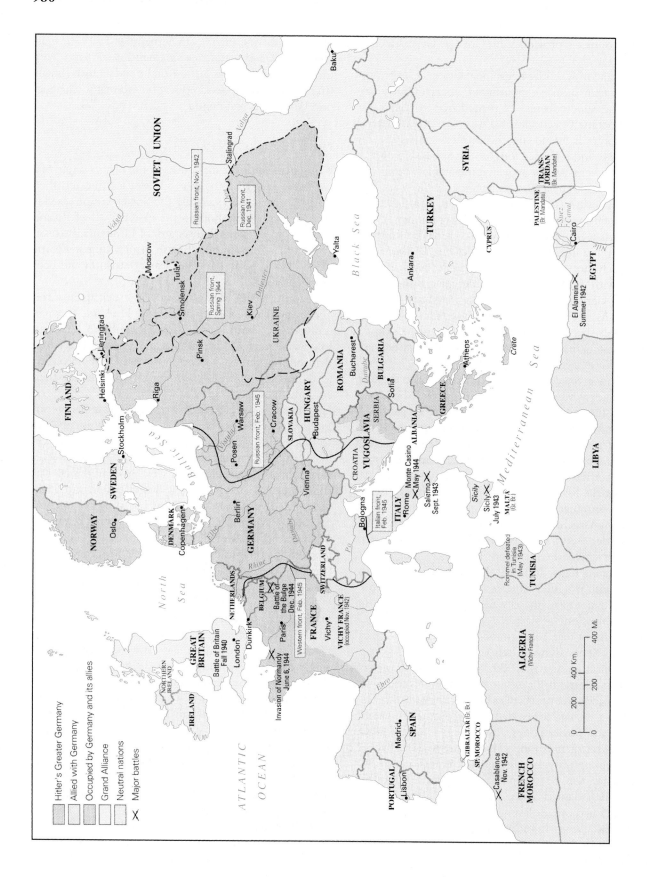

eastern Mediterranean, taking Egypt and the Suez Canal and pinching off Britain's supply of oil. By April 1941, Germany had already moved to the southeast, conquering Greece and Yugoslavia and forcing Hungary, Romania, and Bulgaria into alliances. But Hitler was not a reasonable person. His lifetime obsession with a vast eastern European empire for the "master race" dictated policy. So in June 1941, German armies suddenly attacked the Soviet Union along a vast front (Map 29.2). By October 1941, Leningrad was practically surrounded, Moscow was besieged, and most of Ukraine had been overrun. But with Britain still unconquered, Hitler's decision was a wild, irrational gamble epitomizing the violent, unlimited, and ultimately self-destructive ambitions of Nazism. The Soviets did not collapse, and when a severe winter struck German armies outfitted in summer uniforms, the invaders were stopped.

While Hitler's armies dramatically expanded the war in Europe, his Japanese allies did the same in Asia. Engaged in a general but undeclared war against China since 1937, Japan's rulers had increasingly come into diplomatic conflict with the Pacific basin's other great power, the United States. When the Japanese occupied French Indochina in July 1941, the United States retaliated by cutting off sales of vital rubber, scrap iron, oil, and aviation fuel. Tension mounted further, and on December 7, 1941, Japan attacked the U.S. naval base at Pearl Harbor in Hawaii. Hitler immediately declared war on the United States, and Japanese forces advanced swiftly into Southeast Asia (see Map 29.3 on page 986).

Meanwhile, though stalled in Russia, Hitler ruled over a vast European empire stretching from the outskirts of Moscow to the English Channel. Hitler, the Nazi leadership, and the loyal German army were positioned to greatly accelerate construction of their "New Order" in Europe, and they continued their efforts until their final collapse in 1945. In doing so, they showed what Nazi victory would have meant.

Hitler's New Order was based firmly on the guiding principle of Nazi totalitarianism: racial imperialism. Within this New Order, the Nordic peoples—the Dutch, Norwegians, and Danes—received preferential treatment, for they were racially related to the master race, the Germans. The French, an "inferior" Latin people,

occupied a middle position. They were heavily taxed to support the Nazi war effort but were tolerated as a race. Once Nazi reverses began to mount in late 1942, however, all the occupied territories of western and northern Europe were exploited with increasing intensity. Material shortages and both mental and physical suffering afflicted millions of people.

Slavs in the conquered territories to the east were treated with harsh hatred as "subhumans." At the height of success in 1941 and 1942, Hitler set the tone. He painted for his intimate circle the fantastic vision of a vast eastern colonial empire where Poles, Ukrainians, and Russians would be enslaved and forced to die out, while Germanic peasants resettled the resulting abandoned lands. But he needed countless helpers and many ambitious initiators to turn his dreams into reality. These accomplices came forth.

Himmler and the elite corps of SS volunteers, supported (or condoned) by military commanders and German policemen in the occupied territories, pressed relentlessly to implement this program of destruction even before victory was secured. In western Poland, the SS arrested and evacuated Polish peasants to cleanse the region and create a "mass settlement space" for Germans. Polish workers and Soviet prisoners of war were transported to Germany, where conditions of slave labor were so harsh that four out of five Soviet prisoners did not survive the war.

Finally, the Nazi state condemned all European Jews to extermination, along with many Gypsies, Jehovah's Witnesses, and captured communists. After the fall of Warsaw, the Nazis stepped up their expulsion campaign and began deporting all German Jews to occupied Poland. There they and Jews from all over Europe were concentrated in ghettos, compelled to wear the Jewish star, and turned into slave laborers.

In 1941, as part of the "war of annihilation" in the Soviet Union, expulsion spiraled into extermination. On the Russian front, Himmler's special SS killing squads and also regular army units forced Soviet Jews to dig giant pits, which became mass graves as the victims were lined up on the edge and cut down by machine guns. Then in late 1941, Hitler and the Nazi leadership, in some still-debated combination, ordered the SS to stop all Jewish emigration from Europe and speeded up planning for mass murder. As one German diplomat put it, "The Jewish Question must be resolved in the course of the war, for only so can it be solved without a worldwide outcry."[17] The "final solution of the Jewish question"—the murder of every single Jew—had begun. All over the Nazi empire, Jews were systematically

MAP 29.2 World War II in Europe The map shows the extent of Hitler's empire at its height, before the Battle of Stalingrad in late 1942 and the subsequent advances of the Allies until Germany surrendered on May 7, 1945.

Prelude to Murder This photo captures the terrible inhumanity of Nazi racism. Frightened and bewildered families from the soon-to-be-destroyed Warsaw ghetto are being forced out of their homes by German soldiers for deportation to concentration camps. There they face murder in the gas chambers. *(Roger-Viollet)*

arrested, packed like cattle onto freight trains, and dispatched to extermination camps. Many Jews could hardly imagine the enormity of the crime that lay before them. (See the feature "Listening to the Past: Witness to the Holocaust" on pages 990–991.)

At the camps, the victims were taken by force or deception to "shower rooms," which were actually gas chambers. These gas chambers, first perfected in the quiet, efficient execution of seventy thousand mentally ill Germans between 1938 and 1941, permitted rapid, hideous, and thoroughly bureaucratized mass murder. For fifteen to twenty minutes came the terrible screams and gasping sobs of men, women, and children choking to death on poison gas. Then, only silence. Special camp workers quickly yanked the victims' gold teeth from their jaws, and the bodies were then cremated, or sometimes boiled for oil to make soap. At Auschwitz-Birkenau, the most infamous of the Nazi death factories, as many as twelve thousand human beings were slaughtered each day. The extermination of European Jews was the ultimate monstrosity of Nazi racism and racial imperialism. By 1945, 6 million Jews had been murdered.

Who was responsible for this terrible crime? An older generation of historians usually laid most of the guilt on Hitler and the Nazi leadership. Ordinary Germans had little knowledge of the extermination camps, it was argued, and those who cooperated had no alternative given the brutality of Nazi terror and totalitarian control. But in recent years, many studies have revealed a much broader participation of German people in the Holocaust and popular indifference (or worse) to the fate of the Jews. Yet exactly why so many perpetrated or condoned Nazi crimes has remained unclear.

In a controversial work, the American historian Daniel Goldhagen has reignited discussion of Nazi crimes by arguing that, above all, the extreme anti-Semitism of "ordinary Germans" led them to respond to Hitler and to become his "willing executioners" in World War II.[18] Yet in most occupied countries, local non-German officials also cooperated in the arrest and deportation of Jews to a large extent. As in Germany, only a few exceptional bystanders, like those in the French village of Le Chambon, did not turn a blind eye. (See the feature "Individuals in Society: Le Chambon, a Refuge for the Persecuted.") Thus some scholars have concluded that the key for most Germans (and most people in occupied countries) was that they felt no personal responsibility for Jews, and therefore they were not prepared to help them. This meant that many individuals, conditioned by Nazi racist propaganda but also influenced by peer pressure and brutalizing wartime violence, were psychologically prepared to perpetrate ever-greater crimes. They were ready to plumb the depths of evil and to spiral downward from mistreatment to arrest to mass murder.

The Grand Alliance

While the Nazis built their savage empire, the Allies faced the hard fact that chance, rather than choice, had brought them together. Stalin had been cooperating fully with Hitler between August 1939 and June 1941, and only the Japanese attack on Pearl Harbor in December 1941 and Hitler's immediate declaration of war had overwhelmed powerful isolationism in the United States. The Allies' first task was to overcome their mutual suspicions and build an unshakable alliance on the quicksand of accident. By means of three interrelated policies, they succeeded.

First, President Roosevelt accepted Churchill's contention that the United States should concentrate first on defeating Hitler. Only after victory in Europe was achieved would the United States turn toward the Pacific for an all-out attack on Japan, the lesser threat. The promise of huge military aid under America's policy of "Europe first" helped solidify the anti-Hitler coalition.

Second, within the European framework, the Americans and the British put immediate military needs first. They consistently postponed tough political questions relating to the eventual peace settlement and thereby avoided conflicts that might have split the alliance until after the war.

Third, to further encourage mutual trust, the Allies adopted the principle of the "unconditional surrender" of Germany and Japan. This policy cemented the Grand Alliance because it denied Hitler any hope of dividing his foes. It probably also discouraged Germans and Japanese who might have tried to overthrow their dictators in order to make a compromise peace. Of great importance for the postwar shape of Europe, it meant that Soviet and Anglo-American armies would almost certainly come together to divide all of Germany, and most of the continent, among the victorious allies.

The military resources of the Grand Alliance were awesome. The strengths of the United States were its mighty industry, its large population, and its national unity. Even before Pearl Harbor, President Roosevelt had called America the "arsenal of democracy" and given military aid to Britain and the Soviet Union. Now the United States geared up rapidly for all-out war production and drew heavily on a generally cooperative Latin America for resources. It not only equipped its own armies but also eventually gave its allies about $50 billion in arms and equipment. Britain received by far the most, but about one-fifth of the total went to the Soviet Union in the form of badly needed trucks, planes, and munitions.

Too strong to lose and too weak to win standing alone, Britain continued to make a great contribution as well. The British economy was totally and effectively mobilized, and the sharing of burdens through rationing and heavy taxes on war profits maintained social harmony. Moreover, by early 1943 the Americans and the British were combining small aircraft carriers with radar-guided bombers to rid the Atlantic of German submarines. Britain, the impregnable floating fortress, became a gigantic frontline staging area for the decisive blow to the heart of Germany.

As for the Soviet Union, so great was its strength that it might well have defeated Germany without Western help. In the face of the German advance, whole factories and populations were successfully evacuated to eastern Russia and Siberia. There war production was reorganized and expanded, and the Red Army was increasingly well supplied. The Red Army was also well led, for a new generation of talented military leaders quickly arose to replace those so recently purged. Most important of all, Stalin drew on the massive support and heroic determination of the Soviet people, especially those in the central Russian heartland. Broad-based Russian nationalism, as opposed to narrow communist ideology, became the powerful unifying force in what was appropriately called the "Great Patriotic War of the Fatherland."

Finally, the United States, Britain, and the Soviet Union were not alone. They had the resources of much of the world at their command. And, to a greater or lesser extent, they were aided by a growing resistance movement against the Nazis throughout Europe, even in Germany. Thus although Ukrainian peasants sometimes welcomed the Germans as liberators, the barbaric occupation policies of the Nazis quickly drove them to join and support behind-the-lines guerrilla forces. More generally, after the U.S.S.R. was invaded in June 1941, communists throughout Europe took the lead in the underground resistance, joined by a growing number of patriots and Christians. Anti-Nazi leaders from occu-

Individuals in Society

Le Chambon, a Refuge for the Persecuted ✛

On a cold night in February 1943, French officials arrived in Le Chambon-sur-Lignon in southern France. Known as a "nest of Jews in Protestant country," Le Chambon was a mountainous town of three thousand people that hid Jews and openly said so to the government.[1] Now the officials had finally come to arrest the Protestant minister André Trocmé, the assistant minister Edouard Theis, and the local school principal—the leaders of this defiant cell. Watching silently, the villagers demonstrated their unmistakable solidarity. They lined the streets, sang "A Mighty Fortress Is Our God," and then fell in behind their friends as they passed. As on other occasions, the people of Le Chambon showed the moral courage that would cause others in the region to search their hearts and examine their own conduct toward Jews.

Imprisoned in a camp with communists and resistance fighters, the three men led religious services, discussion groups, and classes that attracted prisoners and even guards. The camp administration, perhaps fearing that its authority was being subverted, offered the three men freedom in return for a signed oath of obedience to the Vichy government, which ruled southern France in collaboration with the Nazi occupiers in the north. Trocmé and his companions refused, but they were mysteriously released the next day. Returning home, Trocmé believed that the village had influential friends in the government.

The strength of the villagers and the quality of their leadership, so clearly evident in these confrontations with the state in early 1943, help explain how Le Chambon became one of the safest places for Jews in Europe in the first two years of the Nazi occupation and how it and the surrounding area successfully sheltered about thirty-five hundred Jewish refugees. Pastors Trocmé and Theis were inspired rebels who wanted to live an active, dangerous Christian love. They conceived of Le Chambon as a city of refuge for the innocent and as a means of overcoming evil with good through nonviolence. Magda Trocmé, André's spirited wife and the mother of four young children, was equally important. Warm and practical, she instinctively aided those in need. She welcomed Jews arriving at the parsonage, housed them, and helped find families to shelter them. She carried on after André himself fled in late 1943 to escape arrest by the Gestapo. Within the village, prayer meetings became conspiracies of goodness. A Jewish refugee printer forged papers and ration cards for the guests, and Theis and the local network helped them escape to Switzerland.

If the how is clear, the why is less so. Certainly a collective memory of persecution helped the Protestants of Le Chambon and nearby villages to identify with the Jews and feel a moral responsibility for their fate. They, too, were a tiny minority in France, the descendants of Protestant refugees who had fled to the mountains and been hounded and executed. But non-Protestants also joined the cause. Above all, the Trocmés, Theis, and the villagers responded because they had a strong moral philosophy rooted in their Christian belief. They believed that they should not obey evil laws but rather abide by God's commandments. They considered it evil to harm anyone, for God had instructed them to love and care for each other. Finally, Le Chambon was broadly representative of other exceptional groups and individuals who worked to help Jews in Nazi Europe. The common experience showed that a sense of moral responsibility was crucial, and that goodness, like evil, is contagious in life-and-death ethical situations.

Questions for Analysis

1. What did the people of Le Chambon-sur-Lignon do? Why did they do it?

2. What is the larger significance of the town's actions in terms of the Holocaust? Debate the idea that "goodness, like evil, is contagious."

André and Magda Trocmé, resistance leaders at Le Chambon, in a family snapshot taken shortly before 1940. *(Papers of André and Magda Trocmé, Swarthmore College Peace Collection)*

1. Philip Hallie, *Lest Innocent Blood Be Shed: The Story of the Village of Le Chambon and How Goodness Happened There* (New York: Harper & Row, 1979), p. 18. In addition to this moving study, see *Weapons of Spirit* (1986), a documentary film by Pierre Sauvage.

pied countries established governments-in-exile in London, like that of the "Free French" under the intensely proud General Charles de Gaulle. These governments gathered valuable secret information from resistance fighters and even organized armies to help defeat Hitler.

The Tide of Battle

Barely halted at the gates of Moscow and Leningrad in 1941, the Germans renewed their offensive against the Soviet Union in July 1942, driving toward the southern city of Stalingrad and occupying most of the city in a month of incredibly savage house-to-house fighting.

Then, in November 1942, Soviet armies counterattacked. They rolled over Romanian and Italian troops to the north and south of Stalingrad, quickly closing the trap and surrounding the entire German Sixth Army of 300,000 men. The surrounded Germans were systematically destroyed, until by the end of January 1943 only 123,000 soldiers were left to surrender. Hitler, who had refused to allow a retreat, had suffered a catastrophic defeat. In the summer of 1943, the larger, better-equipped Soviet armies took the offensive and began moving forward (see Map 29.2).

In late 1942, the tide also turned in the Pacific and in North Africa. By late spring 1942, Japan had established a great empire in East Asia (Map 29.3). Unlike the Nazis, the Japanese made clever appeals to local nationalists, who hated European imperial domination and preferred Japan's so-called Greater Asian Co-prosperity Sphere.

Then in the Battle of the Coral Sea in May 1942, Allied naval and air power stopped the Japanese advance and also relieved Australia from the threat of invasion. This victory was followed by the Battle of Midway Island, in which American pilots sank all four of the attacking Japanese aircraft carriers and established American naval superiority in the Pacific. In August 1942, American marines attacked Guadalcanal in the Solomon Islands. Badly hampered by the policy of "Europe first"—only 15 percent of Allied resources were going to fight the war in the Pacific in early 1943—the Americans and the Australians nevertheless began "island hopping" toward Japan. Japanese forces were on the defensive.

In North Africa the war had been seesawing back and forth since 1940 (see Map 29.2). In May 1942, combined German and Italian armies were finally defeated

The Normandy Invasion, Omaha Beach   Airborne paratroopers landed behind German coastal fortifications around midnight, and American and British forces hit several beaches at daybreak as Allied ships and bombers provided cover. American troops secured full control of Omaha Beach by nightfall, but at a price of three thousand casualties. Allied air power prevented the Germans from bringing up reserves and counterattacking. *(Corbis-Bettmann)*

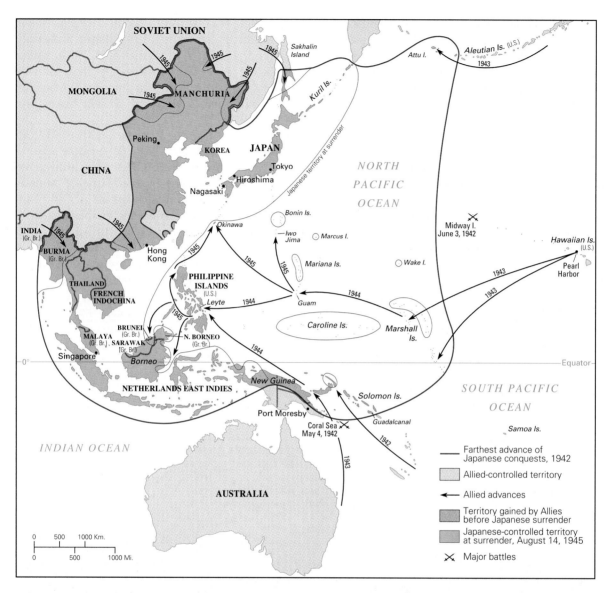

MAP 29.3 World War II in the Pacific Japanese forces overran an enormous amount of territory in 1942, which the Allies slowly recaptured in a long, bitter struggle. As this map shows, Japan still held a large Asian empire in August 1945, when the unprecedented devastation of atomic warfare suddenly forced it to surrender.

by British forces at the Battle of El Alamein, only seventy miles from Alexandria. In October the British counterattacked in Egypt, and almost immediately thereafter an Anglo-American force landed in Morocco and Algeria. These French possessions, which were under the control of Pétain's Vichy government, quickly went over to the side of the Allies.

Having driven the Axis powers from North Africa by the spring of 1943, Allied forces maintained the initiative by invading Sicily and then mainland Italy. Mus-

solini was deposed by a war-weary people, and the new Italian government publicly accepted unconditional surrender in September 1943. Italy, it seemed, was liberated. Yet German commandos rescued Mussolini in a daring raid and put him at the head of a puppet government. German armies seized Rome and all of northern Italy. Fighting continued in Italy.

Indeed, bitter fighting continued in Europe for almost two years. Germany, less fully mobilized for war than Britain in 1941, applied itself to total war in 1942 and enlisted millions of German women and millions of prisoners of war and slave laborers from all across occupied Europe in that effort. Between early 1942 and July 1944, German war production actually tripled. Although British and American bombing raids killed many German civilians, these raids were surprisingly ineffective from a military point of view. Also, German resistance against Hitler failed. After an unsuccessful attempt on Hitler's life in July 1944, SS fanatics brutally liquidated thousands of Germans. Terrorized at home and frightened by the prospect of unconditional surrender, the Germans fought on with suicidal stoicism.

On June 6, 1944, American and British forces under General Dwight Eisenhower landed on the beaches of Normandy, France, in history's greatest naval invasion. In a hundred dramatic days, more than 2 million men and almost half a million vehicles pushed inland and broke through German lines. Rejecting proposals to strike straight at Berlin in a massive attack, Eisenhower moved forward cautiously on a broad front. Not until March 1945 did American troops cross the Rhine and enter Germany.

The Soviets, who had been advancing steadily since July 1943, reached the outskirts of Warsaw by August 1944. For the next six months, they moved southward into Romania, Hungary, and Yugoslavia. In January 1945, the Red Army again moved westward through Poland, and on April 26 it met American forces on the Elbe River. The Allies had closed their vise on Nazi Germany and overrun Europe. As Soviet forces fought their way into Berlin, Hitler committed suicide in his bunker, and on May 7 the remaining German commanders capitulated.

Three months later, the United States dropped atomic bombs on Hiroshima and Nagasaki in Japan. Mass bombing of cities and civilians, one of the terrible new practices of World War II, had ended in the final nightmare—unprecedented human destruction in a single blinding flash. On August 14, 1945, the Japanese announced their surrender. The Second World War, which had claimed the lives of more than 50 million soldiers and civilians, was over.

SUMMARY

The Second World War marked the climax of the tremendous practical and spiritual maladies of the age of anxiety, which led in many lands to the rise of dictatorships. Many of these dictatorships were variations on

A Hiroshima Survivor Remembers   Yasuko Yamagata was seventeen when she saw the brilliant blue-white "lightning flash" that became a fiery orange ball consuming everything that would burn. Thirty years later Yamagata painted this scene, her most unforgettable memory of the atomic attack. An incinerated woman, poised as if running with her baby clutched to her breast, lies near a water tank piled high with charred corpses. *(From a public exhibition assembled by the Japan Broadcasting Corporation)*

conservative authoritarianism, but there was also a fateful innovation—a new kind of dictatorship that was dynamic and theoretically unlimited in its actions.

When apprehensive middle-class liberals in the West faced the rise of these new dictatorships, they often focused on their perceived similarities. Liberals fastened on the violent, profoundly antiliberal, and apparently totalitarian character of these brutal challengers, linking the one-party socialism of Lenin and Stalin with the one-party fascism of Mussolini and Hitler. In contrast, the political left usually insisted on the differences between the revolutionary socialist tradition—triumphing, however imperfectly, in the Bolsheviks' Soviet Union—and the reactionary and capitalist nature of European fascist movements and fascist governments in Italy and Germany. As the dramatic struggles of the 1930s and the Second World War (and early cold war) fall into a longer historical perspective and as more research adds new insights, a growing number of historians are stressing the limitations of both the totalitarian and fascist models and concentrating instead on the uniqueness of developments in each regime.

Hitler's Nazism appears increasingly as a uniquely evil and nihilistic system. Nazism had fascist origins, but German fascism in power ultimately presented only superficial similarities with fascism in Italy. As for Hitler's Germany and Stalin's U.S.S.R., both asserted a total claim on the lives of their citizens, posed ambitious goals, and found enthusiastic supporters. This combination gave both dictatorships their awesome power and dynamism. That dynamism was, however, channeled in quite different directions. Stalin and the Communist party aimed at building their kind of socialism and the new socialist personality at home. Hitler and the Nazi elite aimed at unlimited territorial and racial aggression on behalf of a master race; domestic recovery was only a means to that end.

Nazi racism and unlimited aggression made war inevitable, first with the western European democracies, then with hated eastern neighbors, and finally with the United States. Plunging Europe into the ultimate nightmare, unlimited aggression unwittingly forged a mighty coalition that smashed the racist Nazi empire and its leader. In the words of the ancient Greeks, he whom the gods would destroy, they first make mad.

NOTES

1. A. Gleason, *Totalitarianism: The Inner History of the World War* (New York: Oxford University Press, 1995), p. 50.

2. E. Halévy, *The Era of Tyrannies* (Garden City, N.Y.: Doubleday, 1965), pp. 265–316, esp. p. 300.

3. I. Kershaw, *The Nazi Dictatorship: Problems and Perspectives of Interpretation,* 2d ed. (London: Edward Arnold, 1989), p. 34.

4. Quoted in A. G. Mazour, *Soviet Economic Development: Operation Outstrip, 1921–1965* (Princeton, N.J.: Van Nostrand, 1967), p. 130.

5. Quoted in I. Deutscher, *Stalin: A Political Biography,* 2d ed. (New York: Oxford University Press, 1967), p. 325.

6. R. Conquest, *The Harvest of Sorrow: Soviet Collectivization and the Terror-Famine* (New York: Oxford University Press, 1986), pp. 4, 303.

7. Quoted in H. K. Geiger, *The Family in Soviet Russia* (Cambridge, Mass.: Harvard University Press, 1968), p. 156.

8. Quoted in B. Rosenthal, "Women in the Russian Revolution and After," in *Becoming Visible: Women in European History,* ed. R. Bridenthal and C. Koonz (Boston: Houghton Mifflin, 1976), p. 383.

9. M. Malia, *The Soviet Tragedy: A History of Socialism in Russia* (New York: Free Press, 1994), p. 248.

10. R. Thurston, *Life and Terror in Stalin's Russia, 1934–1941* (New Haven, Conn.: Yale University Press, 1996), esp. pp. 16–106; also Malia, *The Soviet Tragedy,* pp. 227–270.

11. R. Vivarelli, "Interpretations on the Origins of Fascism," *Journal of Modern History* 63 (March 1991): 41.

12. W. Brustein, *The Logic of Evil: The Social Origins of the Nazi Party, 1925–1933* (New Haven, Conn.: Yale University Press, 1996), pp. 52, 182.

13. Quoted in K. D. Bracher, *The German Dictatorship: The Origins, Structure and Effects of National Socialism* (New York: Praeger, 1970), pp. 146–147.

14. Quoted in R. Stromberg, *An Intellectual History of Modern Europe* (New York: Appleton-Century-Crofts, 1966), p. 393.

15. Quoted in Bracher, *The German Dictatorship,* p. 289.

16. Quoted ibid., p. 306.

17. Quoted in M. Marrus, *The Holocaust in History* (Hanover, N.H., and London: University Press of New England, 1987), p. 28.

18. D. Goldhagen, *Hitler's Willing Executioners: Ordinary Germans and the Holocaust* (New York: Vintage Books, 1997).

SUGGESTED READING

The historical literature on fascist and totalitarian dictatorships is rich and fascinating. Kershaw's work, cited in the Notes, provides an excellent survey of this literature, includes extensive bibliographical references, and is highly recommended. P. Brooker, *Twentieth-Century Dictatorships: The Ideological One-Party State* (1995), compares leading examples throughout the world, and Gleason, cited in the Notes, is an important recent study. H. Arendt, *The Origins of Totalitarianism* (1951), is a classic interpretation. F. L. Carsten, *The Rise of Fascism* (1982), and W. Laqueur, ed., *Fascism* (1976), are also recommended. Z. Sternhell, *Neither Right nor Left: Fascist Ideology in France* (1986), is important and stimulating, stressing the antiliberal and antisocialist origins of fascist thinking in France.

Malia's work, cited in the Notes, is a provocative reassessment of Soviet history and an excellent introduction to scholarly debates. It may be compared with the fine synthesis M. Lewin, *The Making of the Soviet System* (1985). R. Stites, *The Women's Liberation Movement in Russia: Feminism, Nihilism, and Bolshevism, 1860–1930* (1978), and the works by Geiger and Deutscher, cited in the Notes, are highly recommended. R. McNeal, *Stalin: Man and Ruler* (1988), is useful. S. Cohen, *Bukharin and the Bolshevik Revolution* (1973), examines the leading spokesman of moderate communism, who was destroyed by Stalin. R. Conquest, *The Great Terror: A Reassessment* (1990), is an excellent account of Stalin's purges of the 1930s, and A. Solzhenitsyn, *The Gulag Archipelago* (1964), passionately condemns Soviet police terror. Three important reconsiderations of Soviet purges, peasants, and urban life are Thurston's revisionist work, cited in the Notes; S. Fitzpatrick, *Stalin's Peasants: Resistance and Survival in the Russian Village After Collectivization* (1994); and S. Kotkin, *Magnetic Mountain: Stalinism as Civilization* (1995). Arthur Koestler, *Darkness at Noon* (1956), is a famous fictional account of Stalin's trials of the Old Bolsheviks. Conquest's work, cited in the Notes, authoritatively recounts Soviet collectivization and the human-made famine. Two other remarkable books are J. Scott, *Behind the Urals* (1973), an eyewitness account of an American steelworker in the Soviet Union in the 1930s; and S. Alliluyeva, *Twenty Letters to a Friend* (1967), the amazing reflections of Stalin's daughter.

A. De Grand, *Italian Fascism: Its Origins and Development* (1989), and A. Lyttelton, *The Seizure of Power: Fascism in Italy, 1919–1929,* 2d ed. (1987), are excellent studies of Italy under Mussolini. D. Mack Smith, *Mussolini* (1982), is authoritative. Ignazio Silone, *Bread and Wine* (1937), is a moving novel by a famous opponent of dictatorship in Italy. E. Morante, *History* (1978), a fictional account of one family's divergent reactions to Mussolini's rule, is recommended. Two excellent books on Spain are H. Thomas, *The Spanish Civil War* (1977); and E. Malefakis, *Agrarian Reform and Peasant Revolution in Spain* (1970). In the area of foreign relations, G. Kennan, *Russia and the West Under Lenin and Stalin* (1961), is justly famous; A. L. Rowse, *Appeasement* (1961), powerfully denounces the policies of the appeasers. R. Paxton, *Vichy France* (1973), tells a controversial story extremely well.

On Germany, F. Stern, *The Politics of Cultural Despair* (1963), and W. Smith, *The Ideological Origins of Nazi Imperialism* (1986), are fine complementary studies on the origins of Nazism. Bracher's work, cited in the Notes, remains an outstanding account of Hitler's Germany. Two major studies by influential German historians are M. Brozat, *The Nazi State* (1981); and H. Mommsen, *From Weimar to Auschwitz* (1991). W. Shirer, *The Rise and Fall of the Third Reich* (1960), is a gripping popular account of an American journalist who experienced Nazi Germany firsthand. J. Fest, *Hitler* (1974), is engrossing, and A. Bullock, *Hitler and Stalin* (1993), is a fascinating comparison by a master biographer. I. Kershaw, *The "Hitler Myth": Image and Reality in the Third Reich* (1987), is a provocative reassessment of the limits of Hitler's power. M. Mayer, *They Thought They Were Free* (1955), probes the minds of ten ordinary Nazis and why they believed that Hitler was their liberator. A. Speer, *Inside the Third Reich* (1970), contains the fascinating recollections of Hitler's wizard of the armaments industry. C. Koonz, *Mothers in the Fatherland: Women, the Family, and Nazi Politics* (1987), and D. Peukert, *Inside Nazi Germany: Conformity, Opposition, and Racism in Everyday Life* (1987), are pioneering forays into the social history of the Nazi era. G. Mosse, *Toward the Final Solution* (1978), is a powerful history of European racism. Moving accounts of the Holocaust include Y. Bauer, *A History of the Holocaust* (1982); M. Gilbert, *The Holocaust: The History of the Jews During the Second World War* (1985); and R. Hilberg, *The Destruction of the European Jews, 1933–1945*, 3 vols., rev. ed. (1985), a monumental scholarly achievement. M. Marrus, *The Holocaust in History* (1987), is an excellent interpretive survey by a leading authority. Goldhagen's widely debated study, cited in the Notes, may be compared with C. Browning, *Ordinary Men: Reserve Police Battalion 101 and the Final Solution in Poland* (1992). E. Staub, *The Roots of Evil: The Origins of Genocide and Other Group Violence* (1989), is a profound study by a noted psychologist with a gift for history. Especially recommended are E. Weisel, *Night* (1961), a brief and compelling autobiographical account of a young Jew in a Nazi concentration camp; and A. Frank, *The Diary of Anne Frank*, is a remarkable personal account of a Jewish girl in hiding during the Nazi occupation of Holland. A. Fraser, *The Gypsies* (1992), considers a misunderstood people decimated by Nazi terror.

J. Campbell, *The Experience of World War II* (1989), is attractively illustrated and captures the drama of global conflict, as does G. Keegan, *The Second World War* (1990). G. Wright, *The Ordeal of Total War, 1939–1945* (1990), and C. Emsley, *World War II and Its Consequences* (1990), are also recommended. B. H. Liddell Hart, *The History of the Second World War* (1971), is an overview of military developments. G. Weinberg, *The Foreign Policy of Hitler*, 2 vols. (1970, 1980), is a thorough account of the diplomatic origins and course of World War II from the German perspective. Two dramatic studies of special aspects of the war are A. Dallin, *German Rule in Russia, 1941–1945* (1981), which analyzes the effects of Nazi occupation policies on the Soviet population; and L. Collins and D. La Pierre, *Is Paris Burning?* (1965), a best-selling account of the liberation of Paris and Hitler's plans to destroy the city.

Witness to the Holocaust

The Second World War brought mass murder to the innocent. The Nazis and their allies slaughtered 6 million Jews in addition to about 5 million Slavs, Gypsies, Jehovah's Witnesses, homosexuals, and mentally ill persons. On the Russian front, some Jews were simply mowed down with machine guns, but most Jews were arrested in their homelands and taken in freight cars to unknown destinations, which were in fact extermination camps. The most infamous camp—really two camps on different sides of a railroad track—was Auschwitz-Birkenau in eastern Poland. There 2 million people were murdered in gas chambers.

The testimony of camp survivors helps us comprehend the unspeakable crime known to history as the Holocaust. One eyewitness was Marco Nahon, a Greek Jew and physician who escaped extermination at Auschwitz-Birkenau along with several thousand other slave laborers in the camp. The following passage is taken from Birkenau: The Camp of Death, *which Nahon wrote in 1945 after his liberation. Conquered by Germany in 1941, Greece was divided into German, Italian, and Bulgarian zones of occupation. The Nahon family lived in Dimotika in the Bulgarian zone.*

Early in March 1943, disturbing news arrives from Salonika [in the German occupation zone]: the Germans are deporting the Jews [of Salonika]. They lock them up in railway cattlecars . . . and send them to an unknown destination—to Poland, it is said. . . . Relatives and friends deliberate. What can be done in the face of this imminent threat? . . . My friend Vitalis Djivré speaks with conviction: "We must flee, cross over into Turkey at once, go to Palestine, Egypt—anywhere at all—but leave immediately.". . . A few friends and I held a completely different opinion. . . . [I say that] I am not going to emigrate. They are going to take us away to Germany or Poland [to work]? If so, I'll work. . . . It is certain that the Allies will be the victors, and once the war is over, we'll go back home. . . .

Until the end we were deaf to all the warnings. . . . [None of the warnings] would be regarded as indicating the seriousness of the drama in preparation. But does not the human mind find inconceivable the total extermination of an innocent population? In this tragic error lay the main cause, the sole cause, of our perdition. . . .

On Monday May 10, 1943, the bugles awaken us at a very early hour. We [have already been arrested and] today we are leaving for Poland. . . . As soon as a freight car has been packed to capacity with people, it is quickly locked up, and immediately the remaining passengers are pushed into the next one. . . .

Every two days the train stops in some meadow in open country. The car doors are flung open, and the whole transport spreads out in the fields. Men and women attend to their natural needs, side by side, without any embarrassment. Necessity and common misfortune have made them part of one and the same family. . . .

We are now in a small station in Austria. Our car door half opens; a Schupo [German police officer] is asking for the doctor. . . . He leads me to the rear of the convoy and shuts me inside the car where the woman is in labor. She is very young; this is her first child. The car, like all the others, is overcrowded. The delivery takes place in deplorable conditions, in front of everybody—men, women, and children. Fortunately, everything turns out well, and a few hours later a baby boy comes into the world. The new mother's family is very happy and passes candy around. Surely no one realizes that two days later the mother and her baby and more than half of the company will pass through the chimney of a crematorium at Birkenau.

It is May 16, 1943. We have reached the end of our journey [and arrived at Auschwitz-Birkenau]. The train stops along a wooden platform. Through the openings of the cars we can see people wearing strange costumes of blue and white stripes [the prisoners who work in the camp]. We immediately notice that they are doing nothing voluntarily but are moving and acting on command. . . . The people in stripes . . . line us up five by five, the women on one side, the men on the other. I lose sight of my wife and little girl in the crowd. I will never see them again.

They make us march, swiftly as always, before a group of [German] officers. One of them, without uttering a word and with the tip of his forefinger, makes a rapid selection. He is, as we know later on, the Lagerarzt, the SS medical doctor of the camp [the notorious Dr. Mengele]. They call him here the "Angel of Death." [Mengele divides the men into two groups: those who are young and sturdy for work in the camp, and those who are old, sick, and children. The women are also divided and only healthy young women without children are assigned to work. All those not selected for work] are immediately loaded on trucks and driven off somewhere. Where? Nobody knows yet. . . .

[After being assigned to a crude windowless barrack,] we must file before the . . . scribes, who are responsible for receiving and registering the transport. Each prisoner must fill out a form in which he relinquishes his identity and becomes a mere number. . . . I am given the number 122274. My son, who is next, gets 122275. This tattoo alarms us terribly. . . . Each one of us now comes to realize in the deepest part of his conscious being, and with a bitter sense of affliction, that from this moment on he is no more than an animal. . . .

After our meal [of watery soup] Léon Yahiel, a veteran among the Lager inmates, . . . gives us this little speech: "My friends, here you must . . . forget your families, your wives, your children. You must live only for yourselves and try to last as long as possible." At these words our spirits plunge into grief and despair. Forget about our families? The hint is unmistakable. Our minds are confused. . . . Our families taken away from us forever? No, it is humanly not conceivable that we should pay such a penalty without having done anything to deserve it, without any provocation.

What miserable wretches we prisoners are! We have no idea that while we entertain these thoughts, our wives, our children, our mothers and our fathers have already ceased to exist. They have arrived at Auschwitz this morning, healthy and full of life. They have now been reduced to smoke and ashes.

❖ Jewish victims of Nazism, on the arrival platform at Auschwitz station. *(AKG London)*

Questions for Analysis

1. How did the Jews of Dimotika react in early 1943 to the news of Jews being deported? Why?

2. Describe the journey to Auschwitz-Birkenau. Did those on the train know what was awaiting them there?

3. How did the Nazis divide the Jews at Auschwitz-Birkenau? Why?

4. What did you learn from Nahon's account? What parts of his testimony made the greatest impression on you?

Source: Slightly adapted from M. Nahon, *Birkenau: The Camp of Death,* trans. J. Bowers (Tuscaloosa: University of Alabama Press, 1989), pp. 21, 23, 33–39. Copyright © 1989 by The University of Alabama Press. Used by permission of the publisher.

30 Cold War Conflicts and Social Transformations, 1945–1985

❖

The reality of the Berlin Wall, grim symbol of postwar division in Europe. *(Sahm Doherty/Liaison)*

The total defeat of the Nazis and their allies in 1945 laid the basis for one of Western civilization's most remarkable recoveries. A battered western Europe dug itself out from under the rubble and fashioned a great renaissance, building strong democracies, vibrant economies, and new societies. The United States also made solid progress, and the Soviet Union became more humane and less dictatorial. Yet there was also a tragic setback. The Grand Alliance against Hitler gave way to an apparently endless cold war in which tension between East and West threatened world peace.

In the late 1960s and early 1970s, the postwar Western renaissance came to an end. First, as cold war competition again turned very hot in Vietnam, postwar certainties such as domestic political stability and social harmony evaporated, and several countries experienced major crises. Second, the astonishing postwar economic advance came to a halt, and this had serious social consequences. Third, new roles for women interacted with a powerful "second wave" of feminist thought and action in the 1970s, resulting in major changes for women and gender relations. Thus the long cold war created an underlying unity for the years 1945 to 1985, but the first half of the cold war era was quite different from the second.

- What were the causes of the cold war?
- How and why, in spite of the cold war, did western Europe recover so successfully from the ravages of war and Nazism?
- To what extent did communist eastern Europe and the United States also experience such a recovery?
- How did political crisis strike many countries from the late 1960s on?
- Why, after a generation, did the economy shift into reverse gear, and what were some of the social consequences of the reversal?
- How did the changing lives of women interact with the second wave of the women's movement?

These are the questions this chapter will seek to answer.

✦ THE DIVISION OF EUROPE

In 1945 triumphant American and Russian soldiers came together and embraced on the banks of the Elbe River in the heart of vanquished Germany. At home, in the United States and in the Soviet Union, the soldiers' loved ones erupted in joyous celebration. Yet victory was flawed. The Allies could not cooperate politically in peacemaking. Motivated by different goals and hounded by misunderstandings, the United States and the Soviet Union soon found themselves at loggerheads. By the end of 1947, Europe was rigidly divided. It was West versus East in a cold war that was waged around the world for forty years.

The Origins of the Cold War

The most powerful allies in the wartime coalition—the Soviet Union and the United States—began to quarrel almost as soon as the unifying threat of Nazi Germany disappeared. A tragic disappointment for millions of people, the hostility between the Eastern and Western superpowers was the sad but logical outgrowth of military developments, wartime agreements, and long-standing political and ideological differences.

In the early phases of the Second World War, the Americans and the British made military victory their highest priority. They consistently avoided discussion of Stalin's war aims and the shape of the eventual peace settlement. For example, when Stalin asked the United States and Britain to agree to the Soviet Union's moving its western border of 1938 farther west at the expense of Poland, in effect ratifying the gains that Stalin had made from his deal with Hitler in 1939, the British and Americans were noncommittal. Stalin received only a military alliance and no postwar commitments. Yet the United States and Britain did not try to take advantage of the Soviet Union's precarious position in 1942, because they feared that hard bargaining would encourage Stalin to consider making a separate peace with Hitler. They focused instead on the policy of unconditional surrender to solidify the alliance.

By late 1943, discussion about the shape of the postwar world could no longer be postponed. The conference that Stalin, Roosevelt, and Churchill held in the Iranian capital of Teheran in November 1943 thus proved of crucial importance in determining subsequent events. There, the "Big Three" jovially reaffirmed their determination to crush Germany and searched for the appropriate military strategy. Churchill, fearful of the military dangers of a direct attack, argued that American and British forces should follow up their Italian campaign with an indirect attack on Germany through the Balkans. Roosevelt, however, agreed with Stalin that an American-British frontal assault through France would be better. This agreement was part of Roosevelt's general effort to meet Stalin's wartime demands whenever possible, and it had momentous political implications. It meant that the Soviet and the American-British armies would come together in defeated Germany along a north-south line and that only Soviet troops would liberate eastern Europe. Thus the basic shape of postwar Europe was emerging even as the fighting continued.

When the Big Three met again in February 1945 at Yalta on the Black Sea in southern Russia, advancing Soviet armies were within a hundred miles of Berlin. The Red Army had occupied not only Poland but also Bulgaria, Romania, Hungary, part of Yugoslavia, and much of Czechoslovakia. The temporarily stalled American-British forces had yet to cross the Rhine into Germany. Moreover, the United States was far from defeating Japan. In short, the Soviet Union's position was strong and America's weak.

There was little the increasingly sick and apprehensive Roosevelt could do but double his bet on Stalin's peaceful intentions. It was agreed at Yalta that Germany would be divided into zones of occupation and would pay heavy reparations to the Soviet Union. At American insistence, Stalin agreed to declare war on Japan after Germany was defeated. As for Poland and eastern Europe—"that Pandora's Box of infinite troubles," according to American secretary of state Cordell Hull—the Big Three struggled to reach an ambiguous compromise at Yalta: eastern European governments were to be freely elected but pro-Russian. As Churchill put it at the time, "The Poles will have their future in their own hands, with the single limitation that they must honestly follow in harmony with their allies, a policy friendly to Russia."[1]

The Yalta compromise over eastern Europe broke down almost immediately. Even before the Yalta Conference, Bulgaria and Poland were controlled by communists who arrived home with the Red Army. Elsewhere in eastern Europe, pro-Soviet "coalition" governments of several parties were formed, but the key ministerial posts were reserved for Moscow-trained communists.

At the postwar Potsdam Conference of July 1945, the long-avoided differences over eastern Europe finally surged to the fore. The compromising Roosevelt had died and been succeeded by the more determined President Harry Truman, who demanded immediate free elections throughout eastern Europe. Stalin refused point-blank. "A freely elected government in any of these East European countries would be anti-Soviet," he admitted simply, "and that we cannot allow."[2]

Here, then, is the key to the much-debated origins of the cold war. American ideals, pumped up by the crusade against Hitler, and American politics, heavily influenced by millions of voters from eastern Europe, demanded free elections in Soviet-occupied eastern Europe. Stalin, who had lived through two enormously destructive German invasions, wanted absolute military security from Germany and its potential Eastern allies, once and for all. Suspicious by nature, he believed that only communist states could be truly dependable allies, and he realized that free elections would result in independent and possibly hostile governments on his western border. Moreover, by the middle of 1945, there was no way short of war that the United States could determine political developments in eastern Europe, and war was out of the question. Stalin was bound to have his way.

West Versus East

The American response to Stalin's exaggerated conception of security was to "get tough." In May 1945, Truman abruptly cut off all aid to the U.S.S.R. In October he declared that the United States would never recognize any government established by force against the free will of its people. In March 1946, former British prime minister Churchill ominously informed an American audience that an "iron curtain" had fallen across the continent, dividing Germany and all of Europe into two antagonistic camps. Emotional, moralistic denunciations of Stalin and communist Russia emerged as part of American political life. Yet the United States also responded to the popular desire to "bring the boys home" and demobilized with great speed. When the war against Japan ended in September 1945, there were 12 million Americans in the armed forces; by 1947 there were only 1.5 million, as opposed to 6 million for the Soviet Union. Some historians have argued that American leaders believed that the atomic bomb gave the United States all the power it needed, but "getting tough" really meant "talking tough."

Stalin's agents quickly reheated what they viewed as the "ideological struggle against capitalist imperialism." The large, well-organized Communist parties of France and Italy obediently started to uncover American plots to take over Europe and challenged their own governments with violent criticisms and large strikes. The Soviet Union also put pressure on Iran, Turkey, and Greece, while a bitter civil war raged in China. By the spring of 1947, it appeared to many Americans that

The Big Three   In 1945 a triumphant Winston Churchill, an ailing Franklin Roosevelt, and a determined Joseph Stalin met at Yalta in southern Russia to plan for peace. Cooperation soon gave way to bitter hostility. *(F.D.R. Library)*

Stalin was determined to export communism by subversion throughout Europe and around the world.

The United States responded to this challenge with the Truman Doctrine, which was aimed at "containing" communism to areas already occupied by the Red Army. Truman told Congress in March 1947, "I believe it must be the policy of the United States to support free people who are resisting attempted subjugation by armed minorities or by outside pressure." To begin, Truman asked Congress for military aid to Greece and Turkey. Then, in June, Secretary of State George C. Marshall offered Europe economic aid—the Marshall Plan—to help it rebuild.

Stalin refused Marshall Plan assistance for all of eastern Europe. He purged the last remaining noncommunist elements from the coalition governments of eastern Europe and established Soviet-style, one-party communist dictatorships. The seizure of power in Czechoslo-

vakia in February 1948 was particularly brutal and antidemocratic, and it greatly strengthened Western fears of limitless communist expansion. Thus, when Stalin blocked all traffic through the Soviet zone of Germany to Berlin, the former capital, which the occupying powers had also divided into sectors at the end of the war, the Western allies acted firmly but not provocatively. Hundreds of planes began flying over the Soviet roadblocks around the clock, supplying provisions to the people of West Berlin and thwarting Soviet efforts to swallow up the West Berliners. After 324 days, the Soviets backed down: containment seemed to work. In 1949, therefore, the United States formed an anti-Soviet military alliance of Western governments: the North Atlantic Treaty Organization (NATO). Stalin countered by tightening his hold on his satellites, later united in the Warsaw Pact. Europe was divided into two hostile blocs.

The Berlin Airlift   Standing in the rubble of their bombed-out city, a German crowd in the American sector awaits the arrival of a U.S. transport plane flying in over the Soviet blockade in 1948. The crisis over Berlin was a dramatic indication of growing tensions among the Allies, which resulted in the division of Europe into two hostile camps. *(Walter Sanders, LIFE MAGAZINE © Time Inc.)*

In late 1949, the communists triumphed in China, frightening and angering many Americans, who saw new evidence of a powerful worldwide communist conspiracy. When the Russian-backed communist forces of northern Korea invaded southern Korea in 1950, President Truman acted swiftly. American-led United Nations armies intervened. The cold war had spread around the world and become very hot.

The rapid descent from victorious Grand Alliance to bitter cold war was intimately connected with the tragic fate of eastern Europe. After 1932, when the eastern European power vacuum invited Nazi racist imperialism, the appeasing Western democracies mistakenly did nothing. They did, however, have one telling insight: how, they asked themselves, could they unite with Stalin to stop Hitler without giving Stalin great gains on his western borders? After Hitler's invasion of the Soviet Union, the Western powers preferred to ignore this question and hope for the best. But when Stalin later began to claim the spoils of victory, the United States began to protest and professed outrage. This belated opposition quite possibly encouraged even more aggressive measures by the always-suspicious Stalin, and it helped explode the quarrel over eastern Europe into

a global confrontation. Thus the Soviet-American confrontation became institutionalized and formed the bedrock of the long cold war era, which lasted until the mid-1980s despite intermittent periods of relaxation.

THE WESTERN RENAISSANCE, 1945–1968

As the cold war divided Europe into two blocs, the future appeared bleak on both sides of the iron curtain. European economic conditions were the worst in generations, and many feared that economic depression would strike the United States. Politically, Europe was weak and divided, a battleground for cold war ambitions. Moreover, western European empires were crumbling in the face of nationalism in Asia and Africa. Yet Europe recovered, and the nations of western Europe led the way. In less than a generation, western Europe achieved unprecedented economic prosperity and peaceful social transformation, while the United States boomed and eventually experienced a wholesome social revolution. It was an amazing rebirth—a true renaissance.

The Postwar Challenge

After the war, economic conditions in western Europe were terrible. Runaway inflation and black markets testified to severe shortages and hardships. Many people believed that Europe was quite simply finished.

Suffering was most intense in defeated Germany. The major territorial change of the war had moved the Soviet Union's border far to the west. Poland was in turn compensated for this loss to the Soviets with land taken from Germany (Map 30.1). To solidify these changes in boundaries, 13 million Germans were driven from their homes in eastern Germany (and other countries in eastern Europe) and forced to resettle in a greatly reduced Germany. The Russians were also seizing factories and equipment as reparations, even tearing up railroad tracks and sending the rails to the Soviet Union.

In 1945 and 1946, conditions were not much better in the Western zones, for the Western allies also treated the German population with great severity at first. Countless Germans sold prized possessions to American soldiers to buy food. By the spring of 1947, refugee-clogged, hungry, prostrate Germany was on the verge of total collapse and threatening to drag down the rest of Europe. Yet western Europe was not finished. The Nazi occupation and the war had discredited old ideas and old leaders. All over Europe, many people were willing to change and experiment, and new groups and new leaders were coming to the fore to guide these aspirations. Progressive Catholics and revitalized Catholic political parties—the Christian Democrats—were particularly influential.

In Italy the Christian Democrats emerged as the leading party in the first postwar elections in 1946, and in early 1948 they won an absolute majority in the parliament in a landslide victory. Their very able leader was Alcide De Gasperi, a courageous antifascist firmly committed to political democracy, economic reconstruction, and moderate social reform. In France, too, the Catholic party also provided some of the best postwar leaders after January 1946, when General Charles de Gaulle, the inspiring wartime leader of the Free French, resigned after having re-established the free and democratic Fourth Republic. As Germany was partitioned by the cold war, a radically purified Federal Republic of Germany (as West Germany was officially known) found new and able leadership among its Catholics. In 1949 Konrad Adenauer, the former mayor of Cologne and a long-time anti-Nazi, began his long, highly successful democratic rule; the Christian Democrats became West Germany's majority party for a generation. In providing effective leadership for their respective countries, the Christian Democrats were inspired and united by a common Christian and European heritage. They steadfastly rejected authoritarianism and narrow nationalism and placed their faith in democracy and cooperation.

The socialists and the communists, active in the resistance against Hitler, also emerged from the war with increased power and prestige, especially in France and Italy. They, too, provided fresh leadership and pushed for social change and economic reform with considerable success. In the immediate postwar years, welfare measures such as family allowances, health insurance, and increased public housing were enacted throughout continental Europe. Britain followed the same trend. The voters threw out Churchill and the Conservatives in 1945, and the victorious socialist Labour party moved toward establishment of a "welfare state." Many industries were nationalized, and the government provided free medical service. Thus all across Europe, social reform complemented political transformation, creating solid foundations for a great European renaissance.

The United States also supplied strong and creative leadership, providing western Europe with both massive economic aid and ongoing military protection. Economic aid was channeled through the Marshall Plan, and military security was provided through NATO, which featured American troops stationed permanently in Europe and the American nuclear umbrella. Thus the United States assumed its international responsibilities after the Second World War, exercising the leadership it had shunned after 1919.

As Marshall Plan aid poured in, the battered economies of western Europe began to turn the corner in 1948. The outbreak of the Korean War in 1950 further stimulated economic activity, and Europe entered a period of rapid economic progress that lasted into the late 1960s. Never before had the European economy grown so fast. There were many reasons for western Europe's brilliant economic performance. American aid helped the process get off to a fast start. Moreover, economic growth became a basic objective of all western European governments, for leaders and voters were determined to avoid a return to the dangerous and demoralizing stagnation of the 1930s. Thus governments generally accepted Keynesian economics (see pages 940 and 946) and sought to stimulate their economies. They also adopted a variety of imaginative and successful strategies.

In postwar West Germany, Minister of Economy Ludwig Erhard, a roly-poly, cigar-smoking former professor, broke decisively with the straitjacketed Nazi

MAP 30.1 Europe After the Second World War Both the Soviet Union and Poland took land from Germany, which the Allies partitioned into occupation zones. Those zones subsequently formed the basis of the East and West German states, as the iron curtain fell to divide both Germany and Europe. Austria was detached from Germany and also divided into four occupation zones, but the Soviets subsequently permitted Austria to be unified as a neutral state.

economy. Erhard bet on the free-market economy while maintaining the extensive social welfare network inherited from the Hitler era. He and his teachers believed not only that capitalism was more efficient but also that political and social freedom could thrive only if there were real economic freedom. Erhard's first step was to reform the currency and abolish rationing and price controls in 1948. He boldly declared, "The only ration coupon is the Mark."[3] West Germany's success renewed respect for free-market capitalism.

The French innovation was a new kind of planning. Under the guidance of Jean Monnet, an economic pragmatist and apostle of European unity, a planning commission set ambitious but flexible goals for the French economy and used the nationalized banks to funnel money into key industries. Thus France combined flexible planning and a "mixed" state and private economy to achieve the most rapid economic development in its long history.

In most countries, there were many people ready to work hard for low wages and the hope of a better future. Moreover, although many consumer products had been invented or perfected since the late 1920s, during the depression and war few Europeans had been able to buy them. In 1945 the electric refrigerator, the washing machine, and the automobile were rare luxuries. There was a great potential demand, which the economic system moved to satisfy. Finally, western European nations abandoned protectionism and gradually created a large unified market known as the "Common Market." This historic action, which certainly stimulated the economy, was part of a larger search for European unity.

Toward European Unity

Western Europe's political recovery was spectacular in the generation after 1945. Republics were re-established in France, West Germany, and Italy. Constitutional monarchs were restored in Belgium, Holland, and Norway. Democratic governments, often within the framework of multiparty politics and shifting parliamentary coalitions, took root again and thrived. National self-determination was accompanied by civil liberties and individual freedom.

A similarly extraordinary achievement was the march toward a united Europe. The Christian Democrats, with their shared Catholic heritage, were particularly committed to "building Europe," and other groups shared their dedication. Many Europeans believed that only unity could forestall European conflict in the future and that only a new "European nation" could reassert western Europe's influence in world affairs dominated by the United States and the Soviet Union.

The close cooperation among European states required by the Americans for Marshall Plan aid led to the creation of both the Organization of European Economic Cooperation (OEEC) and the Council of Europe in 1948. European federalists hoped that the Council of Europe would quickly evolve into a true European parliament with sovereign rights, but this did not happen. Britain, with its empire and its "special relationship" with the United States, consistently opposed giving any real political power—any sovereignty—to the council. Many old-fashioned continental nationalists and communists felt similarly.

Frustrated in the direct political approach, European federalists turned toward economics as a way of working toward genuine unity. Two far-seeing French statesmen, the planner Jean Monnet and Foreign Minister Robert Schuman, took the lead in 1950 and called for a special international organization to control and integrate all European steel and coal production. West Germany, Italy, Belgium, the Netherlands, and Luxembourg accepted the French idea in 1952; the British would have none of it. The immediate economic goal—a single steel and coal market without national tariffs or quotas—was rapidly realized. The more far-reaching political goal was to bind the six member nations so closely together economically that war among them would eventually become unthinkable and virtually impossible.

In 1957 the six nations of the Coal and Steel Community signed the Treaty of Rome, which created the European Economic Community, generally known as the "Common Market" (Map 30.2). The first goal of the treaty was a gradual reduction of all tariffs among the six in order to create a single market almost as large as that of the United States. Other goals included the free movement of capital and labor and common economic policies and institutions. The Common Market was a great success, encouraging companies and regions to specialize in what they did best.

The development of the Common Market fired imaginations and encouraged hopes of rapid progress toward political as well as economic union. In the 1960s, however, these hopes were frustrated by a resurgence of more traditional nationalism. France took the lead. Mired in a bitter colonial war in Algeria, the French turned in 1958 to General de Gaulle, who established the Fifth Republic and ruled as its president until 1969. De Gaulle was at heart a romantic nationalist, and he labored to re-create a powerful, truly independent France. Viewing the United States as the main threat to genuine French (and European) independence, he withdrew all French military forces from the "American-controlled" NATO command as France developed its own nuclear weapons. Within the Common Market, de Gaulle refused to permit the scheduled advent of majority rule. Thus throughout the 1960s, the Common Market thrived economically but remained a union of sovereign states.

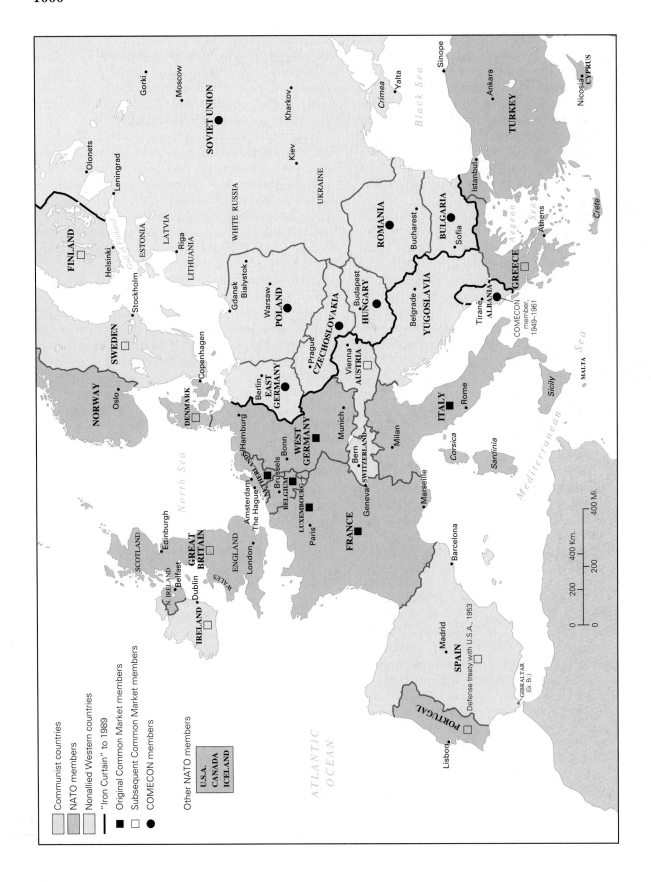

Communist countries
NATO members
Nonallied Western countries
"Iron Curtain" to 1989
Original Common Market members
Subsequent Common Market members
COMECON members

Other NATO members

U.S.A.
CANADA
ICELAND

Decolonization

In the postwar era, Europe's long-standing overseas expansion was dramatically reversed. Future generations will almost certainly see this rolling back of Western expansion as one of world history's great turning points (Map 30.3).

The most basic cause of imperial collapse—what Europeans called "decolonization"—was the rising demand of Asian and African peoples for national self-determination, racial equality, and personal dignity. This demand spread from intellectuals to the masses in virtually every colonial territory after the First World War. As a result, colonial empires had already been shaken by 1939, and the way was prepared for the eventual triumph of independence movements. Yet the new nations of Asia and Africa were deeply influenced by Western ideas and achievements, so that the "westernization" of the world rushed forward even as European empires passed into history.

European empires had been based on an enormous power differential between the rulers and the ruled, a difference that had declined almost to the vanishing point by 1945. Not only was western Europe poor and battered immediately after the war, but most Europeans regarded their empires very differently after 1945 than before 1914, or even before 1939. Empire had rested on self-confidence and self-righteousness; Europeans had believed their superiority to be not only technical and military but also spiritual and moral. The horrors of the Second World War destroyed such complacent arrogance and gave opponents of imperialism much greater influence in Europe. With its political power and moral authority in tatters, Europe could either submit to decolonization or enter into risky wars of reconquest. After 1945 many Europeans were willing to let go of their colonies more or less voluntarily and to concentrate on rebuilding at home.

Indian independence played a key role in decolonization. When the Labour party came to power in Great Britain in 1945, it was determined to leave India. British socialists had always opposed imperialism, and the heavy cost of governing India had become an intol-

African Independence   Britain's Queen Elizabeth II pays an official visit in 1961 to Ghana, the former Gold Coast colony. Accompanying the queen at the colorful welcoming ceremony is Ghana's popular Kwame Nkrumah, who was educated in black colleges in the United States and led Ghana's breakthrough to independence in 1957. *(UPI/Corbis-Bettmann)*

erable burden. Empire in India ended in 1947, and most Asian colonies achieved independence shortly thereafter. Although the French obstinately tried to reestablish colonial rule in Indochina, they were defeated in 1954, and two independent Vietnamese states came into being. The French also fought a long, dirty war to keep Algeria, but Algeria won its independence in 1962 (see Map 30.3).

In much of Africa south of the Sahara, decolonization proceeded much more smoothly. Beginning in 1957, Britain's colonies achieved independence with little or no bloodshed and then entered a very loose association with Britain as members of the British Commonwealth of Nations. In 1958 the clever de Gaulle offered the leaders of French black Africa the choice of a total break with France or immediate independence within a kind of French commonwealth. All but one of

MAP 30.2 European Alliance Systems   After the cold war divided Europe into two hostile military alliances, six western European countries formed the Common Market in 1957. The Common Market grew later to include most of western Europe. The communist states organized their own economic association—COMECON.

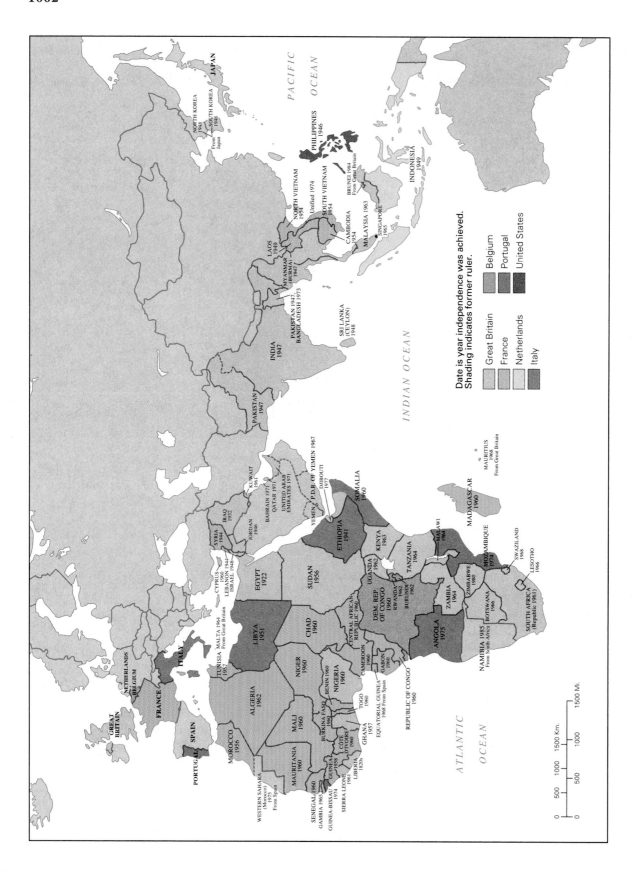

Date is year independence was achieved.
Shading indicates former ruler.

Great Britain
France
Netherlands
Italy
Belgium
Portugal
United States

JAPAN

PACIFIC OCEAN

NORTH KOREA 1948
SOUTH KOREA 1948
From Japan

PHILIPPINES 1946

NORTH VIETNAM 1954
Unified 1974
SOUTH VIETNAM 1954
CAMBODIA 1954
MALAYSIA 1963
SINGAPORE 1965
BRUNEI 1984 From Great Britain
INDONESIA 1949

LAOS 1949
MYANMAR (BURMA) 1947
PAKISTAN 1947
BANGLADESH 1973
SRI LANKA (CEYLON) 1948

INDIA 1947

PAKISTAN 1947

INDIAN OCEAN

KUWAIT 1961
BAHRAIN 1971
QATAR 1971
UNITED ARAB EMIRATES 1971
YEMEN 1918
P.D.R. OF YEMEN 1967
DJIBOUTI 1977
SOMALIA 1960

IRAQ 1932
JORDAN 1946
SYRIA 1944
CYPRUS 1960
LEBANON 1944
ISRAEL 1948

MAURITIUS 1968 From Great Britain

ETHIOPIA 1941
KENYA 1963
UGANDA 1962
TANZANIA 1964
MALAWI 1964
MADAGASCAR 1960
MOZAMBIQUE 1974
SWAZILAND 1968
LESOTHO 1966

EGYPT 1922
SUDAN 1956
DEM. REP. OF CONGO 1960
RWANDA 1962
BURUNDI 1962
ZAMBIA 1964
ZIMBABWE 1980
BOTSWANA 1966
SOUTH AFRICA (Republic 1961)

NETHERLANDS
BELGIUM
FRANCE
ITALY

LIBYA 1951
CHAD 1960
CENTRAL AFRICAN REPUBLIC 1960
NAMIBIA 1985 From South Africa
ANGOLA 1975

TUNISIA 1957
MALTA 1964 From Great Britain

GREAT BRITAIN

PORTUGAL
SPAIN

MOROCCO 1956
ALGERIA 1962
NIGER 1960
NIGERIA 1960
CAMEROON 1960
GABON 1960
REPUBLIC OF CONGO 1960

WESTERN SAHARA (Morocco) 1975 From Spain
MAURITANIA 1960
MALI 1960
BURKINA FASO 1960
BENIN 1960
TOGO 1960
GHANA 1957
EQUATORIAL GUINEA 1968 From Spain

SENEGAL 1960
GAMBIA 1965
GUINEA-BISSAU 1974
GUINEA 1958
SIERRA LEONE 1961
LIBERIA 1820s
CÔTE D'IVOIRE 1960

ATLANTIC OCEAN

0   500   1000   1500 Mi.
0   500   1000   1500 Km.

the new states chose association with France. As in the past, the French and their Common Market partners, who helped foot the bill, saw themselves as continuing their civilizing mission in black Africa. More important, they saw in Africa untapped markets for their industrial goods, raw materials for their factories, outlets for profitable investment, and good temporary jobs for their engineers and teachers. The British acted somewhat similarly.

As a result, western European countries actually managed to increase their economic and cultural ties with their former African colonies in the 1960s and 1970s. Above all, they used the lure of special trading privileges and heavy investment in French- and English-language education to enhance a powerful Western presence in the new African states. This situation led a variety of leaders and scholars to charge that western Europe (and the United States) had imposed a system of neocolonialism on the former colonies. According to this view, *neocolonialism* was a system designed to perpetuate Western economic domination and undermine the promise of political independence, thereby extending to Africa (and much of Asia) the economic subordination that the United States had established in Latin America after the political revolutions of the early nineteenth century. At the very least, enduring influence in black Africa testified to western Europe's resurgent economic and political power in international relations.

America's Civil Rights Revolution

The Second World War cured the depression in the United States and brought about an economic boom. Unemployment practically vanished, and the well-being of Americans increased dramatically. Despite fears that peace would bring renewed depression, conversion to a peacetime economy went smoothly. As in western Europe, the U.S. economy proceeded to advance fairly steadily for a long generation.

Prosperity helps explain why postwar domestic politics consisted largely of modest adjustments to the status quo until the 1960s. Truman's upset victory in 1948 demonstrated that Americans had no interest in undoing Roosevelt's social and economic reforms. The

MAP 30.3 The New States in Africa and Asia   Divided primarily along religious lines into two states, British India led the way to political independence in 1947. Most African territories achieved statehood by the mid-1960s, as European empires passed away, unlamented.

Congress proceeded to increase Social Security benefits, subsidize middle- and lower-class housing, and raise the minimum wage. These and other liberal measures consolidated the New Deal. In 1952 the Republican party and the voters turned to General Dwight D. Eisenhower (1890–1969), a national hero and self-described moderate.

The federal government's only major new undertaking during the Eisenhower years (1953–1961) was the interstate highway system, a suitable symbol of the basic satisfaction of the vast majority. Some Americans feared that the United States was becoming a "blocked society," obsessed with stability and incapable of wholesome change. This feeling contributed in 1960 to the election of the young John F. Kennedy (1917–1963), who promised to "get the country moving again." President Kennedy captured the popular imagination, revitalized the old Roosevelt coalition, and modestly expanded existing liberal legislation before he was struck down by an assassin's bullet in 1963.

Belatedly and reluctantly, complacent postwar America did experience a genuine social revolution. After a long struggle, African Americans (and their white supporters) threw off a deeply entrenched system of segregation, discrimination, and repression. This civil rights movement advanced on several fronts. Eloquent lawyers from the National Association for the Advancement of Colored People (NAACP) challenged school segregation in the courts. In 1954 they won a landmark decision in the Supreme Court, which ruled in *Brown v. Board of Education* that "separate educational facilities are inherently unequal." Blacks effectively challenged institutionalized inequality with bus boycotts, sit-ins, and demonstrations. As civil rights leader Martin Luther King, Jr. (1929–1968), told the white power structure, "We will not hate you, but we will not obey your evil laws."[4]

In key northern states, African Americans used their growing political power to gain the support of the liberal wing of the Democratic party. A liberal landslide elected Lyndon Johnson (1908–1973) president in 1964. The Civil Rights Act of 1964 categorically prohibited discrimination in public services and on the job. In the follow-up Voting Rights Act of 1965, the federal government firmly guaranteed all blacks the right to vote. By the 1970s, substantial numbers of blacks had been elected to public and private office throughout the southern states, proof positive that dramatic changes had occurred in American race relations. The civil rights movement also provided an inspiring model for women and other groups seeking political and social change.

The March on Washington in August 1963 marked a dramatic climax in the civil rights struggle. More than 200,000 people gathered at the Lincoln Memorial to hear the young Martin Luther King, Jr., deliver his greatest address, his "I have a dream" speech. *(Francis Miller,* LIFE MAGAZINE © *Time Warner Inc.)*

African Americans enthusiastically supported new social legislation in the mid-1960s. President Johnson solemnly declared "unconditional war on poverty." Congress and the administration created a host of antipoverty projects, such as a domestic peace corps, free preschools for poor children, and community-action programs. Although these programs were directed to all poor Americans—the majority of whom were white—they were also intended to increase economic equality for blacks. Thus the United States promoted in the mid-1960s the kind of fundamental social reform that western Europe had embraced immediately after the Second World War. The United States became more of a welfare state, as government spending for social benefits rose dramatically and approached European levels.

 ## SOVIET EASTERN EUROPE, 1945–1968

While western Europe surged ahead economically after the Second World War and increased its political power as American influence gradually waned, eastern Europe followed a different path. The Soviet Union first tightened its grip on the "liberated" nations of eastern Europe under Stalin and then refused to let go. Thus postwar economic recovery in eastern Europe proceeded along Soviet lines, and political and social developments were strongly influenced by changes in the Soviet Union. These changes went forward at a slow and uneven pace, and they appeared almost to halt after Leonid Brezhnev came to power.

Stalin's Last Years, 1945–1953

Americans were not the only ones who felt betrayed by Stalin's postwar actions. The "Great Patriotic War of the Fatherland" had fostered Russian nationalism and a relaxation of dictatorial terror. It also had produced a rare but real unity between Soviet rulers and most Russian people. Having made a heroic war effort, the vast majority of the Soviet people hoped in 1945 that a grateful party and government would grant greater freedom and democracy. Such hopes were soon crushed.

Even before the war ended, Stalin was moving his country back toward rigid dictatorship. As early as 1944, the leading members of the Communist party were being given a new motivating slogan: "The war on Fascism ends, the war on capitalism begins."[5] By early 1946, Stalin was publicly singing the old tune that war was inevitable as long as capitalism existed. Stalin's new foreign foe in the West provided an excuse for re-establishing a harsh dictatorship. Many returning soldiers and ordinary citizens were purged in 1945 and 1946, as Stalin revived the terrible forced-labor camps of the 1930s.

Culture and art were also purged in violent campaigns that reimposed rigid anti-Western ideological conformity. Many artists were denounced, including the composers Sergei Prokofiev and Dimitri Shosta-kovich and the outstanding film director Sergei Eisenstein. In 1949 Stalin launched a savage verbal attack on Soviet Jews, accusing them of being pro-Western and antisocialist.

In the political realm, Stalin reasserted the Communist party's complete control of the government and his absolute mastery of the party. Five-year plans were reintroduced to cope with the enormous task of economic reconstruction. Once again, heavy and military industry were given top priority, and consumer goods, housing, and collectivized agriculture were neglected. Everyday life was very hard. In short, it was the 1930s all over again in the Soviet Union, although police terror was less intense.

Stalin's prime postwar innovation was to export the Stalinist system to the countries of eastern Europe. The Communist parties of eastern Europe had established one-party states by 1948, thanks to the help of the Red Army and the Russian secret police. Rigid ideological indoctrination, attacks on religion, and a lack of civil liberties were soon facts of life. Industry was nationalized, and the middle class was stripped of its possessions. Economic life was then faithfully recast in the Stalinist mold. Forced industrialization, with five-year plans and a stress on heavy industry, lurched forward without regard for human costs. The collectivization of agriculture began.

Sergei Eisenstein: Ivan the Terrible Eisenstein's final masterpiece—one of the greatest films ever—was filmed during the Second World War and released in two parts in 1946. In this chilling scene, the crafty paranoid tyrant, who has saved Russia from foreign invaders, invites the unsuspecting Prince Vladimir to a midnight revel that will lead to his murder. The increasingly demonic Ivan seemed to resemble Stalin, and Eisenstein was censored and purged. *(David King Collection)*

Only Josip Broz Tito (1892–1980), the resistance leader and Communist chief of Yugoslavia, was able to resist Soviet domination successfully. Tito stood up to Stalin in 1948, and since there was no Russian army in Yugoslavia, he got away with it. Yugoslavia prospered as a multiethnic state until it began to break apart in the 1980s (see page 1054). Tito's successful proclamation of Communist independence led the infuriated and humiliated Stalin to re-enact the great show trials of the 1930s (see page 966). Popular Communist leaders who, like Tito, had led the resistance against Germany, were purged as Stalin sought to create absolutely obedient instruments of domination in eastern Europe. (See the feature "Individuals in Society: Tito and the Rise of Independent Communism.")

Reform and De-Stalinization, 1953–1964

In 1953 the aging Stalin finally died, and the dictatorship that he had built began to change. Even as Stalin's heirs struggled for power, they realized that reforms were necessary because of the widespread fear and hatred of Stalin's political terrorism. The power of the secret police was curbed, and many of the forced-labor camps were gradually closed. Change was also necessary for economic reasons. Agriculture was in bad shape, and shortages of consumer goods were discouraging hard work and initiative. Moreover, Stalin's belligerent foreign policy had led directly to a strong Western alliance, which isolated the Soviet Union.

On the question of just how much change should be permitted in order to preserve the system, the Communist leadership was badly split. Conservatives wanted to make as few changes as possible. Reformers, who were led by Nikita Khrushchev, argued for major innovations. Khrushchev (1894–1971), who had joined the party as an uneducated coal miner in 1918 at age twenty-four and had been one of the new people rising to a high-level position in the 1930s, emerged as the new ruler in 1955.

To strengthen his position and that of his fellow reformers within the party, Khrushchev launched an all-out attack on Stalin and his crimes at a closed session of the Twentieth Party Congress in 1956. In gory detail, he described to the startled Communist delegates how Stalin had tortured and murdered thousands of loyal Communists, how he had trusted Hitler completely and bungled the country's defense, and how he had "supported the glorification of his own person with all conceivable methods." Khrushchev's "secret speech"

was read at Communist party meetings held throughout the country, and it strengthened the reform movement.

The liberalization—or "de-Stalinization," as it was called in the West—of the Soviet Union was genuine. The Communist party jealously maintained its monopoly on political power, but Khrushchev shook up the party and brought in new members. Some resources were shifted from heavy industry and the military toward consumer goods and agriculture, and Stalinist controls over workers were relaxed. The Soviet Union's very low standard of living finally began to improve and continued to rise substantially throughout the booming 1960s.

De-Stalinization created great ferment among writers and intellectuals who hungered for cultural freedom. The poet Boris Pasternak (1890–1960) finished his great novel *Doctor Zhivago* in 1956. Published in the West but not in Russia, *Doctor Zhivago* is both a literary masterpiece and a powerful challenge to communism. It tells the story of a prerevolutionary intellectual who rejects the violence and brutality of the revolution of 1917 and the Stalinist years. Even as he is destroyed, he triumphs because of his humanity and Christian spirit. Pasternak was denounced—but he was not shot. Other talented writers followed Pasternak's lead, and courageous editors let the sparks fly.

The writer Aleksandr Solzhenitsyn (b. 1918) created a sensation when his *One Day in the Life of Ivan Denisovich* was published in the Soviet Union in 1962. Solzhenitsyn's novel portrays in grim detail life in a Stalinist concentration camp—a life to which Solzhenitsyn himself had been unjustly condemned—and is a damning indictment of the Stalinist past.

Khrushchev also de-Stalinized Soviet foreign policy. "Peaceful coexistence" with capitalism was possible, he argued, and great wars were not inevitable. Khrushchev even made concessions, agreeing in 1955 to real independence for a neutral Austria after ten long years of Allied occupation. Thus there was considerable relaxation of cold war tensions between 1955 and 1957. At the same time, Khrushchev began wooing the new nations of Asia and Africa—even if they were not communist—with promises and aid.

De-Stalinization stimulated rebelliousness in the eastern European satellites. Having suffered in silence under Stalin, communist reformers and the masses were quickly emboldened to seek much greater liberty and national independence. Poland took the lead in 1956, when extensive rioting brought a new government that managed to win greater autonomy.

Hungary experienced a real and tragic revolution. Led by students and workers—the classic urban revolutionaries—the people of Budapest installed a liberal communist reformer as their new chief in October 1956. Soviet troops were forced to leave the country. But after the new government promised free elections and renounced Hungary's military alliance with Moscow, the Russian leaders ordered an invasion and crushed the national and democratic revolution. Fighting was bitter until the end, for the Hungarians hoped that the United States would come to their aid. When this did not occur, most people in eastern Europe concluded that their only hope was to strive for small domestic gains while following Russia obediently in foreign affairs.

The End of Reform

By late 1962, opposition in party circles to Khrushchev's policies was strong, and in 1964 Khrushchev fell in a bloodless palace revolution. Under Leonid Brezhnev (1906–1982), the Soviet Union began a period of stagnation and limited "re-Stalinization." The basic reason for this development was that Khrushchev's Communist colleagues saw de-Stalinization as a dangerous, two-sided threat. How could Khrushchev denounce the dead dictator without eventually denouncing and perhaps even arresting his still-powerful henchmen? Moreover, the widening campaign of de-Stalinization posed a clear threat to the dictatorial authority of the party. It was producing growing, perhaps uncontrollable, criticism of the whole communist system. The party had to tighten up considerably while there was still time. Khrushchev had to go.

Another reason for conservative opposition was that Khrushchev's policy toward the West was erratic and ultimately unsuccessful. In 1958 he ordered the Western allies to evacuate West Berlin within six months. In response, the allies reaffirmed their unity in West Berlin, and Khrushchev backed down. Then in 1961, as relations with communist China deteriorated dramatically, Khrushchev ordered the East Germans to build a wall between East and West Berlin, thereby sealing off West Berlin in clear violation of existing access agreements between the Great Powers. The recently elected U.S. president, John F. Kennedy, acquiesced to the construction of the Berlin Wall. Emboldened and seeing a chance to change the balance of military power decisively, Khrushchev ordered missiles with nuclear warheads installed in Fidel Castro's communist Cuba in

1962. President Kennedy countered with a naval blockade of Cuba. After a tense diplomatic crisis, Khrushchev agreed to remove the Soviet missiles in return for American pledges not to disturb Castro's regime. Khrushchev looked like a bumbling buffoon; his influence, already slipping, declined rapidly after the Cuban fiasco.

After Brezhnev and his supporters took over in 1964, they started talking quietly of Stalin's "good points" and ignoring his crimes. This change informed Soviet citizens that further liberalization could not be expected at home. Soviet leaders, determined never to suffer Khrushchev's humiliation in the face of American nuclear superiority, also launched a massive arms buildup. Yet Brezhnev and company proceeded cautiously in the mid-1960s and avoided direct confrontation with the United States.

In the wake of Khrushchev's reforms, the 1960s brought modest liberalization and more consumer goods to eastern Europe, as well as somewhat greater national autonomy, especially in Poland and Romania. In January 1968, the reform elements in the Czechoslovak Communist party gained a majority and voted out the long-time Stalinist leader in favor of Alexander Dubček (b. 1921), whose new government launched dramatic reforms.

Educated in Moscow, Dubček was a dedicated Communist. But he and his allies believed that they could reconcile genuine socialism with personal freedom and internal party democracy. Thus local decision making by trade unions, managers, and consumers replaced rigid bureaucratic planning, and censorship was relaxed. The reform program proved enormously popular.

Although Dubček remembered the lesson of the Hungarian revolution and constantly proclaimed his loyalty to the Warsaw Pact, the determination of the Czech reformers to build what they called "socialism with a human face" frightened hard-line Communists. These fears were particularly strong in Poland and East Germany, where leaders knew full well that they lacked popular support. Moreover, the Soviet Union feared that a liberalized Czechoslovakia would eventually be drawn to neutrality or even to the democratic West. Thus the Eastern bloc countries launched a concerted campaign of intimidation against the Czech leaders, and in August 1968, 500,000 Russian and allied eastern European troops suddenly occupied Czechoslovakia. The Czechs made no attempt to resist militarily, and the arrested Czech leaders surrendered to Soviet demands. The reform program was abandoned, and the Czechoslovak experiment in humanizing communism came to an end. Shortly after the invasion of Czechoslovakia,

Individuals in Society

Tito and the Rise of Independent Communism   ⟠

Josip Tito (1892–1980) was always a dedicated communist. But after fighting the Nazis and bringing revolution to Yugoslavia, he experienced Stalin's wrath. He then built an independent communist state and achieved remarkable influence as a world leader.

Tito was born into a peasant family of mixed ethnic background in northwest Croatia, in what was then Austria-Hungary. Leaving home as a teenager for work in towns, he became a communist labor organizer in the 1920s. Imprisoned for five years in the 1930s, Tito went to Moscow and in 1937 was charged by the Soviets to reorganize the Communist party of Yugoslavia and then to lead the resistance to Nazi and Italian occupation.

Communist revolution was always Tito's main goal. His guerrilla forces fought as much against the competing noncommunist resistance movement, centered in the Serbian region of Yugoslavia and loyal to the deposed monarchy, as against the Nazis and Italians and their collaborators in Croatia, Bosnia, and Serbia. Yet Tito played down his revolutionary objectives and appealed with some success to all ethnic groups in Yugoslavia. He promised "brotherhood and unity" when the carnage ended. Liberating Yugoslavia in 1945 in coordination with Stalin's Red Army, which moved on in pursuit of the retreating Germans, Tito and his followers quickly established the first Stalinist regime in eastern Europe. Yugoslavia's peasants were exploited to pay for heavy industry. Tito's picture was everywhere, and the Communists held all power.

Yet Stalin grew dissatisfied with his ally. Tito bubbled with revolutionary enthusiasm. He supported the Greek communists in their civil war, called for a communist federation in the Balkans, and enraged U.S. public opinion by shooting down an American "spy plane" over Yugoslavia. Stalin preferred cautious moderation in relations with the West, which would, he hoped, facilitate Soviet consolidation in eastern Europe and encourage a division of the world into spheres of influence. Above all, he demanded absolutely obedient Communist leaders. In 1948 he suddenly denounced Tito as a heretic and called on Yugoslavia's Communist party to oust him. Tito later described the rupture as his most traumatic experi-

Marshal Tito in 1940, planning operations for the liberation of Yugoslavia. *(Corbis-Bettmann)*

ence, but he stayed calm, rallied party stalwarts, and survived.

At first, Tito's independent communism remained strictly Stalinist, imprisoning opponents and proclaiming its Marxist-Leninist orthodoxy. But Tito soon steered a middle course between East and West. He approved the introduction of "workers' self-management" in Yugoslavia, which loosened the state's hold on the economy and was trumpeted internationally as a radical step toward genuine communism. In the 1950s and 1960s, Tito's one-party dictatorship allowed greater personal freedom and presented would-be communist reformers in eastern Europe with an intriguing model.

Yugoslavia's independent, "nonaligned" communism became an influential model in world politics. Tito adroitly negotiated indispensable military commitments from the United States to keep Stalin's armies at bay, and he received massive U.S. aid. But he also re-established generally good relations with the Soviet Union after Stalin's death. Finally, Tito joined with India's Jawaharlal Nehru and Egypt's Gamal Abdel Nasser to lead and inspire the movement of nonaligned, newly independent countries. Pressing his case on many fronts, Tito strengthened the idea that Third World nations should avoid crippling cold war alliances and concentrate instead on building independent socialist states like his.

Questions for Analysis

1. Does the rupture between Tito and Stalin throw light on the origins of the cold war? In what ways?

2. What were the characteristics of Tito's independent communism? How did it enhance his status as a leader?

The End of Reform   In August 1968 Soviet tanks rumbled into Prague to extinguish Czechoslovakian efforts to build a humane socialism. Here people watch the massive invasion from the sidewalks, knowing full well the suicidal danger of armed resistance. *(Joseph Koudelka PP/Magnum)*

Brezhnev declared the so-called Brezhnev Doctrine, according to which the Soviet Union and its allies had the right to intervene in any socialist country whenever they saw the need.

The 1968 invasion of Czechoslovakia was the crucial event of the Brezhnev era, which really lasted beyond the aging leader's death in 1982 until the emergence in 1985 of Mikhail Gorbachev. The invasion demonstrated the determination of the ruling elite to maintain the status quo in the Soviet bloc. In the U.S.S.R. that determination resulted in further repression, but the Soviet Union appeared quite stable in the 1970s and early 1980s.

✦ POSTWAR SOCIAL TRANSFORMATIONS, 1945–1968

While Europe staged its astonishing political and economic recovery from the Nazi nightmare, the patterns of everyday life and the structure of Western society were changing no less rapidly and remarkably. Epoch-making inventions and new technologies profoundly affected human existence. Important groups in society formulated new attitudes and demands, which were closely related to the changing class structure and social reforms. An international youth culture took shape and rose to challenge established lifestyles and even governments.

Science and Technology

Ever since the scientific revolution of the seventeenth century and the Industrial Revolution at the end of the eighteenth century, scientific and technical developments had powerfully influenced attitudes, society, and everyday life. Never was this influence stronger than after about 1940. Science and technology proved so productive and influential because, for the first time in history, "pure theoretical" science and "practical" technology (or "applied" science) were effectively joined together on a massive scale.

With the advent of the Second World War, pure science lost its impractical innocence. Most leading university scientists went to work on top-secret projects to help their governments fight the war. The development by British scientists of radar to detect enemy aircraft was a particularly important outcome of this new kind of sharply focused research. A radically improved radar system played a key role in Britain's victory in the battle for air supremacy in 1940. The air war also greatly stimulated the development of jet aircraft and spurred further research on electronic computers, which calculated the complex mathematical relationships between fast-moving planes and anti-aircraft shells to increase the likelihood of a hit.

The most spectacular result of directed scientific research during the war was the atomic bomb. In August 1939, physicist Albert Einstein wrote to President Franklin Roosevelt that recent work in physics suggested that "it may become possible to set up a nuclear chain reaction in a large mass of uranium" and to construct "extremely powerful bombs of a new type."[6] This letter and ongoing experiments by nuclear physicists led to the top-secret Manhattan Project, which ballooned into a mammoth crash. After three years of intensive effort, the first atomic bomb was successfully tested in July 1945. In August 1945, two bombs were dropped on Hiroshima and Nagasaki, thereby ending the war with Japan.

The atomic bomb showed the world both the awesome power and the heavy moral responsibilities of modern science and its high priests. As one Los Alamos scientist exclaimed as he watched the first mushroom cloud rise over the American desert, "We are all sons-of-bitches now!"[7]

The spectacular results of directed research during World War II inspired a new model for science—"Big Science." By combining theoretical work with sophisticated engineering in a large organization, Big Science could attack extremely difficult problems, from better products for consumers to new and improved weapons for the military. Big Science was extremely expensive, requiring large-scale financing from governments and large corporations.

Populous, victorious, and wealthy, the United States took the lead in Big Science after World War II. Between 1945 and 1965, spending on scientific research and development in the United States grew five times as fast as the national income, and by 1965 such spending took 3 percent of all U.S. income. It was generally accepted that government should finance science heavily in both the "capitalist" United States and the "socialist" Soviet Union.

One reason for the similarity was that science was not demobilized in either country after the war. Scientists remained a critical part of every major military establishment, and a large portion of all postwar scientific research went for "defense." New weapons such as rockets, nuclear submarines, and spy satellites demanded breakthroughs no less remarkable than those of radar and the first atomic bomb. After 1945 roughly one-quarter of all men and women trained in science and engineering in the West—and perhaps more in the Soviet Union—were employed full-time in the production of weapons to kill other humans.

Sophisticated science, lavish government spending, and military needs all came together in the space race of the 1960s. In 1957 the Soviets used long-range rockets developed in their nuclear weapons program to put a satellite in orbit. In 1961 they sent the world's first cosmonaut circling the globe. Embarrassed by Soviet triumphs and breaking with President Eisenhower's opposition to an expensive space program, President Kennedy made an all-out U.S. commitment to catch up with the Soviets and land a crewed spacecraft on the moon "before the decade was out." Harnessing pure science, applied technology, and up to $5 billion a year, the Apollo Program achieved its ambitious objective in 1969. Four more moon landings followed by 1972.

The rapid expansion of government-financed research in the United States attracted many of Europe's best scientists during the 1950s and 1960s. Thoughtful Europeans lamented this "brain drain" and feared that Europe was falling hopelessly behind the United States in science and technology. In fact, a revitalized Europe was already responding to the American challenge, pooling their efforts on such Big Science projects as the *Concorde* supersonic passenger airliner and the peaceful uses of atomic energy.

The rise of Big Science and of close ties between science and technology greatly altered the lives of scientists. The scientific community grew much larger than ever before. There were about four times as many scientists in Europe and North America in 1975 as in 1945. Scientists, technologists, engineers, and medical specialists counted after 1945, in part because there were so many of them.

One consequence of the growth of science was its high degree of specialization, for no one could possibly master a broad field such as physics or medicine. Intense specialization in new disciplines and subdisciplines increased the rates at which both basic knowledge was acquired and practical applications were made.

Highly specialized modern scientists and technologists normally had to work as members of a team, which completely changed the work and lifestyle of modern scientists. A great deal of work therefore went on in large bureaucratic organizations, where the individual was very often a small cog in a great machine. The growth of large scientific bureaucracies in government and private enterprise suggested how scientists and technologists permeated the entire society and many aspects of life.

Modern science became highly, even brutally, competitive. This competitiveness is well depicted in Nobel Prize winner James Watson's fascinating book *The Double Helix,* which tells how in 1953 Watson and an Englishman, Francis Crick, discovered the structure of DNA, the molecule of heredity. A brash young American Ph.D. in his twenties, Watson seemed almost obsessed by the idea that some other research team would find the solution first and thereby deprive him of the fame and fortune he desperately wanted. With so many thousands of like-minded researchers in the wealthy countries of the world, scientific and technical knowledge rushed forward in the postwar era.

The Changing Class Structure

Rapid economic growth went a long way toward creating a new society in Europe after the Second World War. European society became more mobile and more democratic. Old class barriers relaxed, and class distinctions became fuzzier.

Changes in the structure of the middle class were particularly influential in the general drift toward a less rigid class structure. In the nineteenth and early twentieth centuries, the model for the middle class had been the independent, self-employed individual who owned a business or practiced a liberal profession such as law or medicine. Ownership of property—usually inherited property—and strong family ties had often been the keys to wealth and standing within the middle class. After 1945 this pattern declined drastically in western Europe. A new breed of managers and experts replaced traditional property owners as the leaders of the middle class. Ability to serve the needs of a big organization largely replaced inherited property and family connections in determining an individual's social position in the middle and upper middle class. At the same time, the middle class grew massively and became harder to define.

There were several reasons for these developments. Rapid industrial and technological expansion created in large corporations and government agencies a powerful demand for technologists and managers. Moreover, the old propertied middle class lost control of many family-owned businesses, and many small businesses (including family farms) simply passed out of existence as their former owners joined the ranks of salaried employees.

Top managers and ranking civil servants therefore represented the model for a new middle class of salaried specialists. Well paid and highly trained, often with backgrounds in engineering or accounting, these experts increasingly came from all social classes, even the working class. Pragmatic and realistic, they were primarily concerned with efficiency and practical solutions to concrete problems. Everywhere successful managers and technocrats passed on the opportunity for all-important advanced education to their children, but only in rare instances could they pass on the positions

Claes Oldenburg: "Soft" Sculpture Emerging in the 1950s, pop (for *popular*) art recognized the presence and power of exploding technology. This was especially true in sculpture, where artists incorporated new materials and procedures and often offered a humorous view of mass culture. Oldenburg's influential one-man show in 1962 manipulated and confused perceptions of everyday facts, placing such things as this giant vinyl Floor Cake, among other whimsical objects, in a room of furniture. (*© Robert R. McElroy*)

they had attained. Thus the new middle class, which was based largely on specialized skills and high levels of education, was more open, democratic, and insecure than the old propertied middle class.

The structure of the lower classes also became more flexible and open. There was a mass exodus from farms and the countryside, as one of the most traditional and least mobile groups in European society drastically declined. Meanwhile, because of rapid technological change, the industrial working class ceased to expand, and job opportunities for white-collar and service employees grew rapidly. Such employees bore a greater resemblance to the new middle class of salaried specialists than to industrial workers, who were also better educated and more specialized.

European governments were reducing class tensions with a series of social security reforms. Many of these reforms—such as increased unemployment benefits and more extensive old-age pensions—simply strengthened social security measures first pioneered in Bismarck's Germany before the First World War (see pages 842–843). Other programs were new, like comprehensive national health systems directed by the state. Most countries also introduced family allowances—direct government grants to parents to help them raise their children. These allowances helped many poor families make ends meet. Most European governments also gave maternity grants and built inexpensive public housing for low-income families and individuals. These and other social reforms provided a humane floor of well-being. Reforms also promoted greater equality because they were expensive and were paid for in part by higher taxes on the rich.

The rising standard of living and the spread of standardized consumer goods also worked to level Western society, as the percentage of income spent on food and drink declined substantially. For example, the European automobile industry expanded phenomenally after lagging far behind the United States since the 1920s. In 1948 there were only 5 million cars in western Europe, but in 1965 there were 44 million. Car ownership was democratized and came within the range of better-paid workers.

Europeans took great pleasure in the products of the "gadget revolution" as well. Like Americans, Europeans filled their houses and apartments with washing machines, vacuum cleaners, refrigerators, dishwashers, radios, TVs, and stereos. The purchase of consumer goods was greatly facilitated by installment purchasing, which allowed people to buy on credit. Before the Second World War, Europeans had rarely bought "on time." But with the expansion of social security safe-guards, reducing the need to accumulate savings for hard times, ordinary people were increasingly willing to take on debt. This change had far-reaching consequences.

Leisure and recreation occupied an important place in consumer societies. The most astonishing leisure-time development was the blossoming of mass travel and tourism. Before the Second World War, most people had neither the time nor the money for it. But with month-long paid vacations required by law in most European countries and widespread automobile ownership, beaches and ski resorts came within the reach of the middle class and many workers. By the late 1960s, packaged tours with cheap group flights and bargain hotel accommodations had made even distant lands easily accessible. A French company grew rich building imitation Tahitian paradises around the world. At Swedish nudist colonies on secluded West African beaches, officeworkers from Stockholm fleetingly worshiped the sun in the middle of the long northern winter. Truly, consumerism had come of age.

Youth and the Counterculture

Economic prosperity and a more democratic class structure had a powerful impact on youth throughout the Western world. The bulging cohort of youth born after World War II developed a distinctive and very international youth culture. Self-consciously different in the late 1950s, this youth culture became increasingly oppositional in the 1960s, interacting with a revival of leftist thought to create a "counterculture" that rebelled against parents, authority figures, and the status quo.

Young people in the United States took the lead. American college students in the 1950s were docile and often dismissed as the "Silent Generation," but some young people did revolt against the conformity and boredom of middle-class suburbs. These "young rebels" wore tightly pegged pants and idolized singer Elvis Presley and actor James Dean. The "beat" movement of the late 1950s expanded on the theme of revolt, and Jack Kerouac vividly captured the restless motion of the beatniks in his autobiographical novel *On the Road.* People like Kerouac clustered together in certain urban areas, such as the Haight Ashbury district of San Francisco or the Near North Side of Chicago. There the young (and the not-so-young) fashioned a highly publicized subculture that blended radical politics, unbridled personal experimentation (with drugs and communal living, for example), and new artistic styles. This subculture quickly spread to major American and western European cities.

The Beatles   The older generation often saw sexual license and immorality in the group's frank lyrics and suggestive style. But in comparison with all that came after them in the world of pop music, the Beatles were sentimental and wholesome. *(John Zimmerman/Camera Press/Retna Ltd.)*

Rock music helped tie this international subculture together. Rock grew out of the black music culture of rhythm and blues, which was flavored with country and western to make it more accessible to white teenagers. The mid-1950s signaled a breakthrough as Bill Hailey called on record buyers to "Rock Around the Clock" and Elvis Presley warned them to keep off of his "Blue Suede Shoes." In the 1960s, the Beatles thrilled millions of young people, often to their parents' dismay. Like Elvis, the Beatles suggested personal and sexual freedom that many older people found disturbing.

It was Bob Dylan, a young folksinger turned rock poet with an acoustic guitar, who best expressed the radical political as well as cultural aspirations of the "younger generation." In a song that became a rallying cry, Dylan sang that "the times they are a'changing."[8] The song captured the spirit of growing alienation between the generation whose defining experiences had been the Great Depression and World War II and the generation ready to reject the complacency of the 1950s. Increasing discontent with middle-class confor-

mity and the injustices of racism and imperialism fueled the young leaders of social protest and reflected a growing spirit of rebellion.

Certainly the sexual behavior of young people, or at least some young people, appeared to change dramatically in the 1960s and into the 1970s. More young people engaged in sexual intercourse, and they did so at an earlier age. For example, a 1973 study reported that only 4.5 percent of West German youths born in 1945 and 1946 had experienced sexual relations before their seventeenth birthday but that 32 percent of those born in 1953 and 1954 had done so.[9] Perhaps even more significant was the growing tendency of young unmarried people to live together in a separate household on a semipermanent basis, with little thought of getting married or having children. Thus many youths, especially middle-class youths, defied social custom, claiming in effect that the long-standing monopoly of married couples on legitimate sexual unions was dead.

Several factors contributed to the emergence of the international youth culture in the 1960s. First, mass communications and youth travel linked countries and continents together. Second, the postwar baby boom meant that young people became an unusually large part of the population and could therefore exercise exceptional influence on society as a whole. Third, postwar prosperity and greater equality gave young people more purchasing power than ever before. This enabled them to set their own trends and mass fads in everything from music to chemical stimulants. Common patterns of consumption and behavior fostered generational loyalty. Finally, prosperity meant that good jobs were readily available. Students and young job seekers had little need to fear punishment from strait-laced employers for unconventional behavior.

The youth culture practically fused with the counterculture in opposition to the established order in the late 1960s. Student protesters embraced romanticism and revolutionary idealism, dreaming of complete freedom and simpler, purer societies. The materialistic West was hopelessly rotten, but better societies were being built in the newly independent countries of Asia and Africa, or so many young radicals believed. Thus the Vietnam War took on special significance. Many politically active students in the United States and Europe believed that the older generation in general and American leaders in particular were fighting an immoral and imperialistic war against a small and heroic people who wanted only national unity and human dignity. As the war in Vietnam intensified, so did worldwide student opposition to it.

Student protests in western Europe also highlighted more general problems of youth, education, and a society of specialists. In contrast to the United States, high school and university educations in Europe had been limited for centuries to a small elite. Whereas 22 percent of the American population was going on to some form of higher education in 1950, only 3 to 4 percent of western European youths were doing so. Then en-

Student Rebellion in Paris   These rock-throwing students in the Latin Quarter of Paris are trying to force education reforms and even to topple de Gaulle's government. Throughout May 1968 students clashed repeatedly with France's tough riot police in bloody street fighting. De Gaulle remained in power, but a major reform of French education did follow. *(Bruno Barbey/Magnum)*

rollments skyrocketed. By 1960 at least three times as many students were going to some kind of university as had attended before the war, and the number continued to rise sharply until the 1970s. Reflecting the development of a more democratic class structure and a growing awareness that higher education was the key to success, European universities gave more scholarships and opened their doors to more students from the lower middle and lower classes.

The rapid expansion of higher education created problems as well as opportunities for students. Classes were overcrowded, and there was little contact with professors. Competition for grades became intense. Moreover, although more practical areas of study were gradually added, many students felt that they were not getting the kind of education they needed for jobs in the modern world and that basic university reforms were absolutely necessary. At the same time, some reflective students warned of the dangers of narrowly trained experts. They feared that universities would soon do nothing but turn out docile technocrats both to stock and to serve "the establishment."

The many tensions within the exploding university population came to a head in the late 1960s and early 1970s. Following the American example, European university students rose to challenge their university administrations and even their governments. The most far-reaching of these revolts occurred in France in 1968. Students occupied buildings and took over the University of Paris, which led to violent clashes with police. Most students demanded both changes in the curriculum and a real voice in running the university. Some student radicals went further, linking the attack on French universities to New Left critiques of capitalism and appealing to France's industrial workers for help. Rank-and-file workers ignored the advice of their cautious union officials, and a more or less spontaneous general strike spread across France in May 1968. It seemed certain that President de Gaulle's Fifth Republic would collapse.

In fact, de Gaulle stiffened, like an irate father. Declaring that he was in favor of university reforms and higher minimum wages but would oppose the "bedwetting" of undisciplined students and workers, he moved troops toward Paris and called for new elections. Thoroughly frightened by the student-sparked upheaval and fearful that a successful revolution could lead to an eventual communist takeover, the masses of France voted overwhelmingly for de Gaulle's party and a return to law and order. Workers went back to work, and the mini-revolution collapsed. Yet the proud de Gaulle and the postwar European renaissance that he

represented had been shaken, and within a year he resigned. Growing out of the counterculture and youthful idealism, the student rebellion of 1968 signaled the end of an era and the return of conflict and uncertainty in the 1970s and early 1980s.

RENEWED CHALLENGES IN THE LATE COLD WAR, 1968–1985

Similar to but more important than the student upheaval in France and the crushing of socialist reform in Czechoslovakia, the Vietnam War marked the beginning of a new era of challenges and uncertainties in the late 1960s. The Vietnam War and its aftermath divided the people of the United States, shook the ideology of containment, and weakened the Western alliance. A second major challenge appeared when the great postwar economic boom came to a close in 1973 and opened up a long period of economic stagnation, widespread unemployment, and social dislocation.

The United States and Vietnam

President Johnson wanted to go down in history as a master reformer and a healer of old wounds. Instead, he opened new ones with the Vietnam War.

Although many student radicals believed that imperialism was the main cause, American involvement in Vietnam was more clearly a product of the cold war and the ideology of containment (see page 995). From the late 1940s on, most Americans and their leaders viewed the world in terms of a constant struggle to stop the spread of communism. As western Europe began to revive and China established a communist government in 1949, efforts to contain communism shifted to Asia. The bloody Korean War (1950–1953) ended in stalemate, but the United States did succeed in preventing a communist takeover in South Korea. After the defeat of the French in Vietnam in 1954, the Eisenhower administration refused to sign the Geneva Accords that temporarily divided the country into two zones pending national unification by means of free elections. President Eisenhower then acquiesced in the refusal of the anticommunist South Vietnamese government to accept the verdict of elections and provided it with military aid. President Kennedy greatly increased the number of American "military advisers" to sixteen thousand.

After successfully depicting his opponent, Barry Goldwater, as a trigger-happy extremist in a nuclear age and resoundingly winning the 1964 election on a peace platform, President Johnson greatly expanded the American role in the Vietnam conflict. As Johnson explained to his ambassador in Saigon, "I am not going to lose Vietnam. I am not going to be the President who saw Southeast Asia go the way China went."[10] American strategy was to "escalate" the war sufficiently to break the will of the North Vietnamese and their southern allies without resorting to "overkill," which might risk war with the entire Communist bloc. Thus South Vietnam received massive military aid, American forces in the South gradually grew to half a million men, and the United States bombed North Vietnam with ever-greater intensity. But there was no invasion of the North or naval blockade. In the end, the American strategy of limited warfare backfired. It was the Americans themselves who grew weary and the American leadership that cracked.

The undeclared war in Vietnam, fought nightly on American television, eventually divided the nation. Initial support was strong. The politicians, the media, and the population as a whole saw the war as part of a legitimate defense against communist totalitarianism in all poor countries. But an antiwar movement quickly emerged on college campuses, where the prospect of being drafted to fight savage battles in Asian jungles made male stomachs churn. In October 1965, student protesters joined forces with old-line socialists, New Left intellectuals, and pacifists in antiwar demonstrations in fifty American cities. By 1967 a growing number of critics denounced the war as a criminal intrusion into a complex and distant civil war.

Criticism reached a crescendo after the Vietcong Tet Offensive in January 1968. This, the communists' first comprehensive attack with conventional weapons on major cities in South Vietnam, failed militarily: the Vietcong suffered heavy losses, and the attack did not spark a mass uprising. But Washington had been claiming that victory in South Vietnam was in sight, and U.S. critics of the Vietnam War quickly interpreted the bloody combat as a decisive American defeat. America's leaders lost heart. In 1968, after a humiliatingly narrow victory in the New Hampshire primary, President Johnson called for negotiations with North Vietnam and announced that he would not stand for re-election.

Elected by a razor-slim margin in 1968, President Richard Nixon (1913–1994) sought to gradually disengage America from Vietnam and the accompanying national crisis. Intensifying the continuous bombardment of the enemy while simultaneously pursuing peace talks with the North Vietnamese, Nixon suspended the draft, so hated on college campuses, and cut American forces in Vietnam from 550,000 to 24,000 in four years. The cost of the war dropped dramatically. Moreover, President Nixon launched a flank attack in diplomacy. He journeyed to China in 1972 and reached a spectacular if limited reconciliation with the People's Republic of China. In doing so, Nixon took advantage of China's growing fears of the Soviet Union and undermined North Vietnam's position.

Fortified by the overwhelming endorsement of the voters in his 1972 electoral triumph, President Nixon and Secretary of State Henry Kissinger finally reached a peace agreement with North Vietnam. The agreement allowed remaining American forces to complete their withdrawal, and the United States reserved the right to resume bombing if the accords were broken. Fighting

Divisions over the Vietnam War   ran deep in the United States. Antiwar protesters captured the public's attention, but anti-Vietcong demonstrations like this one spoke for many Americans. Opinion polls showed that fewer than 20 percent of Americans supported withdrawal from Vietnam until after the November 1968 elections, by which time the decision to get out gradually had been made. *(Burt Glinn/Magnum)*

declined markedly in South Vietnam, where the South Vietnamese army appeared to hold its own against the Vietcong. The storm of crisis in the United States seemed to have passed.

On the contrary, the country reaped the Watergate whirlwind. Like some other recent American presidents, Nixon authorized spying activities that went beyond the law. Going further than his predecessors, he allowed special units to use various illegal means to stop the leaking of government documents to the press. One such group broke into the Democratic party headquarters in Washington's Watergate complex in June 1972 and was promptly arrested. Nixon and many of his assistants then tried to hush up the bungled job, but the media and the machinery of congressional investigation eventually exposed the administration's web of lies and lawbreaking. In 1974 a beleaguered Nixon was forced to resign in disgrace.

The consequences of renewed political crisis flowing from the Watergate affair were profound. First, Watergate resulted in a major shift of power away from the presidency and toward Congress, especially in foreign affairs. Therefore, as American aid to South Vietnam diminished in 1973 and as an emboldened North Vietnam launched a general invasion against South Vietnamese armies in early 1974, Congress refused to permit any American military response. A second consequence of the U.S. crisis was that after more than thirty-five years of battle, the Vietnamese communists unified their country in 1975 as a harsh dictatorial state. Third, the belated fall of South Vietnam in the wake of Watergate shook America's postwar confidence and left the country divided and uncertain about its proper role in world affairs.

Détente or Cold War?

One alternative to the badly damaged policy of containing communism was the policy of *détente,* or the progressive relaxation of cold war tensions. Thus while the cold war continued to rage outside Europe and generally defined superpower relations between the Soviet Union and the United States, West Germany took a major step toward genuine peace in Europe.

West German chancellor Willy Brandt (1913–1992) took the lead when in December 1970 he flew to Poland for the signing of a historic treaty of reconciliation. In a dramatic moment rich in symbolism, Brandt laid a wreath at the tomb of the Polish unknown soldier and another at the monument commemorating the armed uprising of Warsaw's Jewish ghetto against occupying Nazi armies. Standing before the ghetto memor-

ial, a somber Brandt fell to his knees and knelt as if in prayer. "I wanted," Brandt said later, "to ask pardon in the name of our people for a million-fold crime which was committed in the misused name of the Germans."[11]

Brandt's gesture at the Warsaw ghetto memorial and the treaty with Poland were part of his policy of reconciliation with eastern Europe. Indeed, Brandt aimed at nothing less than a comprehensive peace settlement for central Europe and the two German states established after 1945. The Federal Republic of Germany (West Germany), formed out of the American, British, and French zones of occupation and based on freely expressed popular sovereignty, had long claimed that the communist German Democratic Republic (East Germany) lacked free elections and hence any legal or moral basis. West Germany also refused to accept the loss of German territory taken by Poland and the Soviet Union after 1945. However, Brandt, the popular socialist mayor of West Berlin when the Berlin Wall was built in 1961, believed that the wall showed the painful limitations of West Germany's official hard line toward communist eastern Europe and the need for a new foreign policy.

Winning the chancellorship in 1969, Brandt negotiated treaties with the Soviet Union, Poland, and Czechoslovakia that formally accepted existing state boundaries and the loss of German territory to Poland and the Soviet Union (see Map 30.1) in return for a mutual renunciation of force or the threat of force. Using the imaginative formula of "two German states within one German nation," Brandt's government also broke decisively with the past and entered into direct relations with East Germany, aiming for modest practical improvements rather than reunification, which at that point was completely impractical.

Brandt's bold initiatives encouraged President Nixon to sponsor a broader, American-led framework of reducing East-West tensions in the early 1970s. Thus Nixon's ambiguous policy of phased withdrawal from Vietnam was sold as part of détente, although it was designed mainly to end the conflict over the Vietnam War in the United States. After Nixon was forced to resign, détente reached its high point when all European nations (except isolationist Albania), the United States, and Canada signed the Final Act of the Helsinki Conference in 1975. Thirty-five nations agreed that Europe's existing political frontiers could not be changed by force, and they solemnly accepted numerous provisions guaranteeing the human rights and political freedoms of their citizens.

Optimistic hopes for détente in international relations gradually faded in the later 1970s. Brezhnev's So-

Willy Brandt in Poland, 1970
Chancellor Brandt's gesture at the Warsaw memorial to the Jewish victims of Nazi terrorism was criticized by some West Germans but praised by many more. This picture reached an enormous audience, appearing in hundreds of newspapers in both the East and the West. *(Bilderdienst Süddeutscher Verlag)*

viet Union ignored the human rights provisions of the Helsinki agreement, and East-West political competition remained very much alive outside Europe. Many Americans became convinced that the Soviet Union was taking advantage of détente, steadily building up its military might and pushing for political gains and revolutions in Africa, Asia, and Latin America. The Soviet invasion of Afghanistan in December 1979, which was designed to save an increasingly unpopular Marxist regime, was especially alarming. Many Americans feared that the oil-rich states of the Persian Gulf would be next, and once again they looked to the Atlantic alliance and military might to thwart communist expansion.

President Jimmy Carter (b. 1924), elected in 1976, tried to lead the Atlantic alliance beyond verbal condemnation and urged economic sanctions against the Soviet Union. Yet only Great Britain among the European allies supported the American initiative. The alliance showed the same lack of concerted action when the Solidarity movement rose in Poland. Some observers concluded that the alliance had lost the will to think and act decisively in dealing with the Soviet bloc.

The Atlantic alliance endured, however. The U.S. military buildup launched by Carter in his last years in office was greatly accelerated by President Ronald Reagan (b. 1911), who was swept into office in 1980 by a wave of patriotism and economic discontent. The new American leadership acted as if the military balance had tipped in favor of the Soviet Union, which Reagan anathematized as the "evil empire." Increasing defense spending enormously, the Reagan administration concentrated especially on nuclear arms and an expanded navy as keys to American power in the post-Vietnam age.

The broad swing in the historical pendulum toward greater conservatism in the 1980s gave Reagan invaluable allies in western Europe. In Great Britain a strong-willed Margaret Thatcher worked well with Reagan and was a forceful advocate for a revitalized Atlantic alliance. After a distinctly pro-American Helmut Kohl (b. 1930) came to power with the conservative Christian Democrats in 1982, West Germany and the United States once again effectively coordinated military and political policy toward the Soviet bloc.

Passing in the 1970s and early 1980s from détente to confusion to regeneration, the Atlantic alliance bent, but it did not break. In maintaining the alliance, the Western nations gave indirect support to ongoing efforts to liberalize authoritarian communist eastern Europe and probably helped convince the Soviet Union's Mikhail Gorbachev that endless cold war conflict was foolish and dangerous.

The Troubled Economy

For twenty years after 1945, most Europeans were pre-occupied with the possibilities of economic progress and consumerism. The more democratic class structure also helped to reduce social tension, and ideological conflict went out of style. In the late 1960s, sharp criticism and social conflict re-emerged, however. As we have seen, the anti-Vietnam War movement and the international student rebellion of the late 1960s evidenced the passing of postwar social stability.

Yet it was the reappearance of economic crisis in the early 1970s that brought the most serious challenges for the average person. The postwar international monetary system was based on the American dollar, which foreign governments could exchange for gold at $35 an ounce and which was considered to be "as good as gold." Giving foreign aid and fighting foreign wars, the United States sent billions abroad. By early 1971, it had only $11 billion in gold left, and Europe had accumulated U.S. $50 billion. Foreigners then panicked and raced to exchange their dollars for gold. President Richard Nixon responded by stopping the sale of American gold, the value of the dollar fell sharply, and inflation accelerated worldwide. Fixed rates of exchange were abandoned, and great uncertainty replaced postwar predictability in international trade and finance.

Even more damaging was the dramatic reversal in the price and availability of energy. The great postwar boom was fueled by cheap oil, especially in western Europe. Cheap oil from the Middle East permitted energy-intensive industries—automobiles, chemicals, and electric power—to expand rapidly and lead other sectors of the economy forward. By 1971 the Arab-led Organization of Petroleum Exporting Countries (OPEC) had watched the price of crude oil decline consistently compared with the rising price of manufactured goods. OPEC decided to reverse that trend by presenting a united front against the oil companies. The stage was set for a revolution in energy prices during the fourth Arab-Israeli war in October 1973, when Egypt and Syria launched a surprise attack on Israel. OPEC then declared an embargo on oil shipments to the United States, which supported Israel with an emergency airlift of weapons, and in the course of a year crude oil prices quadrupled. It was widely realized that the rapid price rise was economically destructive, but the world's big powers did nothing. The Soviet Union was a great oil exporter and benefited directly; the United States was immobilized, its attention absorbed by the Watergate crisis in politics (see page 1017). Thus governments, industry, and individuals had no other choice than to deal piecemeal with the so-called oil shock—a "shock" that turned out to be an earthquake.

Coming on the heels of upheaval in the international monetary system, the revolution in energy prices plunged the world into its worst economic decline since the 1930s. The energy-intensive industries that had driven the economy up in the 1950s and 1960s now dragged it down. Unemployment rose; productivity and living standards declined. By 1976 a modest recovery was in progress. But when a fundamentalist Islamic revolution struck Iran and oil production collapsed in that country, the price of crude oil doubled in 1979, and the world economy succumbed to its second oil shock. Unemployment and inflation rose dramatically before another uneven recovery began in 1982. In the summer of 1985, however, the unemployment rate in western Europe rose to its highest level since the Great Depression. Nineteen million people were unemployed.

One telling measure of the troubled economy was the "misery index," first used with considerable effect by candidate Jimmy Carter in the 1976 U.S. presidential debates. The misery index combined rates of inflation and unemployment in a single, powerfully emotional number. Figure 30.1 shows a comparison of misery indexes for the United States, Japan, and the Common Market countries between 1970 and 1986. "Misery" increased on both sides of the Atlantic, but the increase was substantially greater in western Europe, where these hard times were often referred to simply as "the crisis." Japan did better than both Europe and the U.S. in this period.

Throughout the 1970s and 1980s, anxious observers, recalling the disastrous consequences of the Great Depression, worried that the Common Market would disintegrate in the face of severe economic dislocation and that economic nationalism would halt steps toward European unity. Yet the Common Market—now officially known as the European Economic Community—continued to exert a powerful attraction on nonmembers. In 1973 Denmark and Iceland, in addition to Britain, finally joined. Greece joined in 1981, and Portugal and Spain entered in 1986. The nations of the European

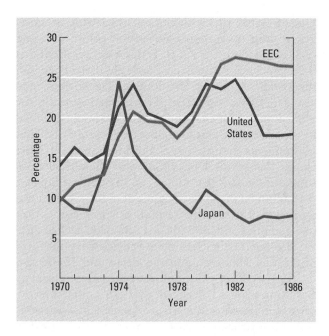

FIGURE 30.1 The Misery Index, 1970–1986   Combining rates of unemployment and inflation provided a simple but effective measure of economic hardship. This particular index represents the sum of two times the unemployment rate plus the inflation rate, reflecting the widespread belief that joblessness causes more suffering than higher prices. EEC = European Economic Community, or Common Market countries. *(Source: OECD data, as given in* The Economist, *June 15, 1985, p. 69.)*

Economic Community also cooperated more closely in international undertakings, and the movement toward unity for western Europe stayed alive.

Society in a Time of Economic Uncertainty

The most pervasive consequences of economic stagnation in the 1970s and early 1980s were probably psychological and attitudinal. Optimism gave way to pessimism; romantic utopianism yielded to sober realism. This drastic change in mood—a complete surprise only to those who had never studied history—affected states, institutions, and individuals in countless ways.

To be sure, there were heartbreaking human tragedies—lost jobs, bankruptcies, homelessness, and mental breakdowns. But on the whole, the welfare system fashioned in the postwar era prevented mass suffering and degradation through extended benefits for the unemployed, pensions for the aged, free medical care and special allowances for the needy, and a host of lesser supports. The responsive, socially concerned national state undoubtedly contributed to the preservation of political stability and democracy in the face of economic

difficulties that might have brought revolution and dictatorship in earlier times.

The energetic response of governments to social needs helps explain the sharp increase in total government spending in most countries during the 1970s and early 1980s. In 1982 western European governments spent an average of more than 50 percent of gross national income, as compared to only 37 percent fifteen years earlier. In all countries, people were much more willing to see their governments increase spending than raise taxes. This imbalance contributed to the rapid growth of budget deficits, national debts, and inflation. By the late 1970s, a powerful reaction against government's ever-increasing role had set in, however, and Western governments were gradually forced to introduce austerity measures to slow the seemingly inexorable growth of public spending and the welfare state.

Part of a broad cultural shift toward greater conservatism, growing voter dissatisfaction with government and government spending helped bring Margaret Thatcher (b. 1925) to power in Britain in 1979. Thatcher had some success in slowing government spending and in "privatizing" industry—that is, in selling off state-owned companies to private investors. Of great social significance, Thatcher's Conservative government encouraged low- and moderate-income renters in state-owned housing projects to buy their apartments at rock-bottom prices. This privatization initiative created a whole new class of property owners, thereby eroding the electoral base of Britain's socialist Labour party.

President Ronald Reagan's success in the United States was more limited. With widespread popular support and the agreement of most congressional Democrats as well as Republicans, Reagan in 1981 pushed through major cuts in income taxes all across the board. But Reagan and Congress failed miserably at cutting government spending, which increased as a percentage of national income in the course of his presidency. Reagan's obsession with the Soviet threat and his massive military buildup were partly responsible, but spending on social programs also grew rapidly. First, the harsh recession of the early 1980s required that the government spend more on unemployment benefits, welfare benefits, and medical treatment for the poor. Second, Reagan's crude antiwelfare rhetoric mobilized the liberal opposition to defend the poor and eventually turned many moderates against him. Thus the budget deficit and the U.S. government debt soared, tripling in a decade.

The striking but temporary exception to the trend toward greater frugality was François Mitterrand (1916–

"The New Poor" Economic crisis and prolonged unemployment in the early 1980s reduced the status of many people from modest affluence to harsh poverty, creating a class of new poor. This photograph captures that human tragedy. After two years of unemployment, this homeless French officeworker (lower right) still dresses up and looks for work. But he must sleep each night in a makeshift shelter for the destitute. *(Dennis Stock/Magnum)*

1996) of France. After his election as president in 1981, Mitterrand led his Socialist party and Communist allies on a lurch to the left, launching a vast program of nationalization and public investment designed to spend France out of economic stagnation. By 1983 this attempt had clearly failed. Mitterrand's Socialist government was then compelled to impose a wide variety of austerity measures and to maintain those policies for the rest of the decade.

When governments were forced to restrain spending, large scientific projects were often singled out for cuts. These reductions reinforced the ongoing computer revolution. That revolution thrived on the diffusion of ever-cheaper computational and informational capacity to small research groups and private businesses, which were both cause and effect of the revolution itself. Big organizations lost some of their advantages as small firms and even individuals became able to link electronically with their region and most of the world.

Individuals felt the impact of austerity at an early date, for unlike governments, they could not pay their bills by printing money and going ever further into debt. The energy crisis of the 1970s forced them to reexamine not only their fuel bills but also the whole pattern of self-indulgent materialism in the postwar years. The result in both Europe and North America was a leaner, tougher lifestyle in the 1970s and early 1980s, featuring more attention to nutrition and a passion for exercise. Correspondingly, there was less blind reliance on medical science for good health and a growing awareness that individuals had to accept a large portion of the responsibility for illness and disease. More people began to realize that they could substantially increase their life spans simply by eating regular meals, sleeping seven or eight hours each night, exercising two or three times a week, maintaining moderate weight, forgoing smoking, and using alcohol only in moderation. For example, a forty-five-year-old American male who practiced three or fewer of these habits in the late 1970s could expect to live to be sixty-seven; one who adhered to five or six could expect to live eleven more years, to age seventy-eight.

Economic troubles also strengthened existing trends within the family. Men and women were encouraged to postpone marriage until they had put their careers on a firm foundation, so the age of marriage rose sharply for both sexes in many Western countries. Indeed, the very real threat of unemployment—or "underemployment" in a dead-end job—seemed to shape the outlook of a whole generation. The students of the 1980s were serious, practical, and often conservative. As one young woman at a French university told a reporter in 1985, "Jobs are the big worry now, so everyone wants to learn something practical."[12] In France as elsewhere, the shift away from the romantic visions and the political activism of the late 1960s was astonishing.

Harder times also meant that ever more women entered or remained in the workforce after they married. Although attitudes related to personal fulfillment were one reason for the continuing increase—especially for well-educated, upper-middle-class women (see the next section)—many wives in poor and middle-class families simply had to work outside the home because of economic necessity. As in preindustrial Europe, the wife's earnings provided the margin of survival for millions of hard-pressed families.

 THE CHANGING LIVES OF WOMEN

A growing emancipation of women in Europe and North America was unquestionably one of the most significant changes of the entire cold war era, and the 1970s and early 1980s were the period of breakthrough. The struggle for women's emancipation had distant roots, going back at least to the French Revolution, which stimulated pioneering feminists to formulate the first systematic demands for women's rights and gender equality. Yet a period of retrogression followed, and only in the later nineteenth century did the first wave of an organized women's movement win some modest rights, mainly for middle-class women (see pages 807–810). World War I also brought some gains for women, but many of those won in the workplace were then lost in the 1920s and 1930s. Nor did the economic expansion after World War II include many measures that were designed specifically to help women.

How then is one to explain the rise of a strong and remarkably effective women's movement in the 1970s and 1980s? Two sets of factors seem most important. First, as we shall see, long-term changes in the basic patterns of motherhood and work outside the home played a critical role because these changes had a major impact on women's life experiences and expectations. Second, a new wave of feminist thinkers and organizers

convincingly interpreted these experiences, demanded gender equality, and mobilized a militant women's movement. This movement first assumed real significance in the late 1960s, gathered strength in the next decade, and won significant victories in the 1970s and 1980s.

Motherhood and Work Outside the Home

Before the Industrial Revolution, most men and women married late, and substantial numbers never married at all. Once a woman was married, however, she very often had children as long as she was fertile, and she bore several children, of whom a third to a half would not survive to adulthood. With the growth of industry and urban society, people began to marry earlier, and fewer remained unmarried. As industrial development led to higher incomes and better diets, more children survived to adulthood, and population grew rapidly in the nineteenth century. By the late nineteenth century, contraception within marriage was spreading.

In the twentieth century, and especially after World War II, these trends continued. In the 1950s and 1960s, the typical woman in the West continued to marry at an earlier age and have her children quickly. Indeed, women in Europe and North America were having about 80 percent of their children before age thirty. As for family size, the postwar baby boom made for larger families and a fairly rapid population growth of 1 to 1.5 percent per year in many European countries. In the 1960s, however, the long-term decline in birthrates resumed, and from the mid-1970s onward total population practically stopped growing or even declined in many European countries. The United States followed the same trend. The rate of population growth from natural increase (that is, excluding immigration) dropped by two-thirds, from 1.5 percent to 0.6 percent per year between the 1950s and the 1970s.

The culmination of the trends toward early marriage, early childbearing, and small family size in wealthy urban societies had revolutionary implications for women. Above all, pregnancy and child care occupied a much smaller portion of a woman's life than at the beginning of this century. By the early 1970s, about half of Western women were having their last baby by the age of twenty-six or twenty-seven. When the youngest child trooped off to kindergarten, the average mother still had more than forty years of life in front of her.

This was a momentous change. Throughout history male-dominated society insisted on defining most married women (and most young unmarried women) as mothers (and potential mothers). And motherhood was very demanding: pregnancy followed pregnancy, and there were many children to nurse, guide, and bury. In the postwar years, however, the period devoted to having babies and caring for young children became a relatively short phase in most women's total life span. Perhaps a good deal of the frustration that many women felt in the late 1960s and 1970s was due to the fact that their role as mothers no longer absorbed the energies of a lifetime, and that new roles in the male-dominated world of work outside the family were limited or simply unavailable.

For centuries before the Industrial Revolution, ordinary women worked hard and long on farms and in home industries while bearing and caring for their large families. With the growth of modern industry and large cities, young women continued to work as wage earners, but poor married women typically struggled instead to earn money at home by practicing some low-paid craft as they looked after their children. In the middle classes, it was a rare and tough-minded woman who worked outside the home for wages, although charity work was socially acceptable.

In the twentieth century and especially after World War II, the ever-greater complexity of the modern economy and its sophisticated technology meant that almost all would-be wage earners had to go outside the home to find cash income. Moreover, because child care took less of married women's lives, it often appeared that the full-time mother-housewife had less economic value for families. At the same time, young Western women shared fully in the postwar education revolution and could take advantage of the need for well-trained people in a more fluid society. The result was a sharp rise across Europe and North America in the number of married women who became full-time and part-time wage earners outside the home.

The trend went the furthest in eastern Europe before the collapse of communism. There women accounted for almost half of all employed persons in the postwar era. In noncommunist western Europe and North America, there was a good deal of variety, with the percentage of married women in the workforce rising from a range for different countries of roughly 20 to 25 percent in 1950 to a range of 40 to 70 percent in the early 1980s.

The rising employment of married women was undoubtedly a powerful force in the drive for women's equality and emancipation. Take the critical matter of the widespread differences between men and women in pay, occupation, and advancement. The young unmarried woman of sixty or a hundred years ago was more inclined to accept such injustices. She was conditioned

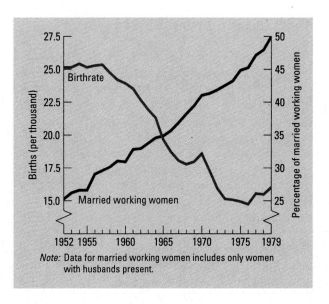

Note: Data for married working women includes only women with husbands present.

FIGURE 30.2 The Decline of the Birthrate and the Increase of Married Working Women in the United States, 1952–1979   The challenge of working away from home encouraged American wives to prefer fewer children and helped to lower the birthrate.

to think of them as temporary nuisances and to look forward to marriage and motherhood for fulfillment. In the postwar era and recent past, a married wage earner in her thirties gradually developed a totally different perspective. She saw employment as a permanent condition within which she, like her male counterpart, sought not only income but also psychological satisfaction. Sexism and discrimination grew loathsome and evoked the sense of injustice that drives revolutions and reforms. When powerful voices arose to challenge the system, they found support among young working-women.

Rising employment for married women was a factor in the decline of the birthrate (Figure 30.2). Women who worked outside the home had significantly fewer children than women of the same age who did not. Moreover, survey research showed that young women who had held jobs and intended to do so again revised downward the number of children they expected to have after the first lovable but time-consuming baby was born. One reason was obvious: raising a family while holding down a full-time job was a tremendous challenge and often resulted in the woman's being grossly overworked. The fatiguing, often frustrating multiple demands of job, motherhood, and marriage simply became more manageable with fewer children.

The Women's Movement

The 1970s marked the birth of a revitalized grassroots, broad-based movement devoted to promoting the interests of women. Three basic reasons accounted for this major development. First, ongoing changes in underlying patterns of motherhood and paid work created novel conditions and new demands, as has just been suggested. Second, a vanguard of feminist intellectuals articulated a powerful critique of gender relations, which stimulated many women to rethink their assumptions and challenge the status quo. Third, taking a lesson from the civil rights movement in the United States and worldwide student protest against the Vietnam War, dissatisfied individuals recognized that they had to band together if they were to influence politics and secure fundamental reforms.

The first and one of the most influential major works produced by the second wave was *The Second Sex* (1949) by the French writer and philosopher Simone de Beauvoir (1908–1986). Characterizing herself as a "dutiful daughter" of the bourgeoisie in childhood, the adolescent Beauvoir came to see her pious and submissive mother as foolishly renouncing any self-expression outside of home and marriage and showing Beauvoir the dangers of a life she did not want. A brilliant university student, Beauvoir began at the Sorbonne a complex and generally fruitful relationship with an equally gifted classmate, future philosopher Jean-Paul Sartre, who became her lifelong intellectual companion and sometime lover.

Beauvoir analyzed the position of women within the framework of existential thought (see pages 928–930). She argued that women—like all human beings—were in essence free but that they had almost always been trapped by particularly inflexible and limiting conditions. (See the feature "Listening to the Past: A Feminist Critique of Marriage" on pages 1028–1029.) Only by means of courageous action and self-assertive creativity could a woman become a completely free person and escape the role of the inferior "other" that men had constructed for her gender. Drawing on history, philosophy, psychology, biology, and literature, Beauvoir's massive investigation inspired a generation of women intellectuals.

One such woman was Betty Friedan (b. 1924), who played a key role in reopening a serious discussion of women's issues in the United States. Unlike Beauvoir, who epitomized French individualism in believing that each woman had to chart her own course, Friedan reflected the American faith in group action and political

solutions. As a working wife and the mother of three small children in the 1950s, Friedan became acutely aware of the conflicting pressures of career and family. Conducting an in-depth survey of her classmates at Smith College fifteen years after their graduation, she concluded that many well-educated women shared her growing dissatisfaction. In her pathbreaking study *The Feminine Mystique* (1963), Friedan identified this dissatisfaction as the "problem that has no name." According to Friedan, the cause of this nameless problem was a crisis of identity. Women were not permitted to become mature adults and genuine human beings. Instead, they were expected to conform to a false, infantile pattern of femininity and live (like Beauvoir's mother) for their husbands and children. In short, women faced what feminists would soon call *sexism,* a pervasive social problem that required drastic reforms.

When long-standing proposals to treat sex discrimination as seriously as race discrimination fell again on deaf ears, Friedan took the lead in 1966 in founding the National Organization for Women (NOW) to press for women's rights. NOW flourished, growing from seven hundred members in 1967 to forty thousand in 1974. Many other women's organizations of varying persuasions rose to follow NOW in Europe and the United States. Throughout the 1970s, a proliferation of publications, conferences, and institutions devoted to women's issues reinforced the emerging international movement.

Although national peculiarities abounded, this movement generally shared the common strategy of entering the political arena and changing laws regarding women. First, advocates of women's rights pushed for new statutes in the workplace: laws against discrimination, "equal pay for equal work," and measures such as maternal leave and affordable daycare designed to help women combine careers and family responsibilities. Second, the movement concentrated on gender and family questions, including the right to divorce (in some Catholic countries), legalized abortion, the needs of single parents (who were usually women), and protection from rape and physical violence. In almost every country, the effort to decriminalize abortion served as a catalyst in mobilizing an effective, self-conscious women's movement (and in creating an opposition to it, as in the United States).

In countries that had long placed women in a subordinate position, the legal changes were little less than revolutionary. In Italy, for example, new laws abolished restrictions on divorce and abortion, which had been strengthened by Mussolini and defended energetically by the Catholic church in the postwar era. By 1988 divorce and abortion were common in Italy, which had the lowest birthrate in Europe. More generally, the sharply focused women's movement of the 1970s won new rights for women. The movement became more diffuse in the 1980s and early 1990s, however, a victim of both its successes and the resurgence of an antifeminist opposition.

The accomplishments of the women's movement encouraged mobilization by many other groups. Homosexual men and lesbian women pressed their own demands, organizing politically and calling for an end to legal discrimination and social harassment. People with physical disabilities joined together to promote their interests. Thus many subordinate groups challenged the dominant majorities, and the expansion and redefinition of human liberty—one of the great themes of modern Western and world history—continued.

SUMMARY

The recovery of western Europe after World War II was one of the most striking chapters in the long, uneven course of Western civilization. Although the dangerous tensions of the cold war frustrated hopes for a truly peaceful international order, the transition from imperialism to decolonization proceeded rapidly, surprisingly smoothly, and without serious damage to western Europe. Genuine political democracy gained unprecedented strength in western Europe, and rapid economic progress marked a generation.

Fundamental social changes accompanied the political recovery and economic expansion after World War II. Pure science combined with applied technology to achieve remarkable success. The triumphs of applied science contributed not only to economic expansion but also to a more fluid, less antagonistic class structure, in which specialized education was the high road to advancement.

Postwar developments in eastern Europe displayed both similarities to and differences from developments in western Europe and North America. Perhaps the biggest difference was that Stalin imposed harsh one-party rule in the lands occupied by his armies, which led to the bitter cold war. Nevertheless, the Soviet Union became less dictatorial under Khrushchev, and the standard of living in the Soviet Union improved markedly in the 1950s and 1960s.

In the late 1960s and early 1970s, Europe and North America entered a time of crisis. Many nations, from

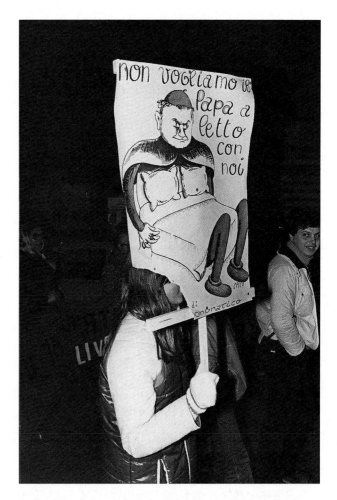

Italian Feminists   demonstrate in Rome in 1981 for the passage of legislation legalizing abortion, which the pope and the Catholic church have steadfastly opposed. This woman's provocative sign says that she does not want the pope in her bed. *(Giansanti/Sygma)*

France to Czechoslovakia to the United States, experienced major political difficulties, as cold war conflicts and ideological battles divided peoples and shook governments. Beginning with the oil shocks of the 1970s, severe economic problems added to the turmoil and brought real hardship to millions of people. Yet in western Europe and North America, the welfare system held firm, and both democracy and the movement toward European unity successfully passed through the storm. The women's movement also mobilized effectively and won expanded rights in the best tradition of Western civilization. Finally, efforts to achieve détente in central Europe while still maintaining a strong Atlantic alliance achieved some success. This modest progress helped lay the foundations for the sudden end of the cold war and the opening of a new era.

NOTES

1. Quoted in N. Graebner, *Cold War Diplomacy, 1945–1960* (Princeton, N.J.: Van Nostrand, 1962), p. 17.
2. Quoted ibid.
3. Quoted in J. Hennessy, *Economic "Miracles"* (London: Andre Deutsch, 1964), p. 5.
4. Quoted in S. E. Morison et al., *A Concise History of the American Republic* (New York: Oxford University Press, 1977), p. 697.
5. Quoted in D. Treadgold, *Twentieth Century Russia,* 5th ed. (Boston: Houghton Mifflin, 1981), p. 442.
6. Quoted in J. Ziman, *The Force of Knowledge: The Scientific Dimension of Society* (Cambridge: Cambridge University Press, 1976), p. 128.
7. Quoted in S. Toulmin, *The Twentieth Century: A Promethean Age,* ed. A. Bullock (London: Thames & Hudson, 1971), p. 294.
8. Quoted in N. Cantor, *Twentieth-Century Culture: Modernism to Deconstruction* (New York: Peter Lang, 1988), p. 252.
9. M. Mitterauer, *The History of Youth* (Oxford: Basil Blackwell, 1992), p. 40.
10. Quoted in Morison et al., *A Concise History,* p. 735.
11. Quoted in Kessing's Research Report, *Germany and East Europe Since 1945: From the Potsdam Agreement to Chancellor Brandt's "Ostpolitik"* (New York: Charles Scribner's Sons, 1973), pp. 284–285.
12. *Wall Street Journal,* June 28, 1985, p. 1.

SUGGESTED READING

Three valuable general studies with extensive bibliographies are W. Laqueur, *Europe in Our Time: A History, 1945–1992* (1992); C. Black, *Rebirth: A History of Europe Since World War II* (1992); and P. Johnson, *Modern Times: The World from the Twenties to the Eighties* (1983). A good introduction to international politics is provided by W. Keylor, *The Twentieth Century: An International History* (1984). Winston Churchill and Charles de Gaulle both wrote histories of the war in the form of memoirs. Other interesting memoirs are those of Dwight Eisenhower, *Crusade in Europe* (1948); and Dean Acheson, *Present at the Creation* (1969), a defense of American foreign policy in the early cold war. K. Sainsbury, *Churchill and Roosevelt at War: The War They Fought and the Peace They Hoped to Make* (1994), is an excellent, very readable introduction. Valuable recent studies on the cold war include P. de Senar-

clens, *From Yalta to the Iron Curtain: The Great Powers and the Origins of the Cold War* (1995); and M. Walker, *The Cold War: A History* (1993).

D. Urwin, *The Community of Europe: A History of European Integration,* 2d ed. (1995), and R. Mayne, *The Recovery of Europe, 1945–1973* (1973), focus on steps toward western European unity. P. Lane, *Europe Since 1945: An Introduction* (1985), is an interesting combination of text and political documents. W. Leuchtenberg, *In the Shadow of FDR: From Harry Truman to Ronald Reagan* (1989), ably discusses developments in the United States. Postwar economic and social developments are analyzed in G. Ambrosius and W. Hibbard, *A Social and Economic History of Twentieth-Century Europe* (1989); and F. Tipton and R. Aldrich, *An Economic and Social History of Europe from 1939 to the Present* (1986).

Two outstanding works on France are J. Ardagh, *The New French Revolution* (1969), which puts the momentous social changes since 1945 in human terms; and S. Bernstein, *The Republic of de Gaulle, 1958–1969* (1993). On postwar West Germany, H. Turner, *The Two Germanies Since 1945: East and West* (1987), and W. Patterson and G. Smith, eds., *The West German Model: Perspectives on a Stable State* (1981), are good introductions. R. Dahrendorf, *Society and Democracy in Germany* (1971), is a classic interpretation. The spiritual dimension of West German recovery is probed by Günter Grass in his world-famous novel *The Tin Drum* (1963), as well as in the novels of Heinrich Böll. A. Marwick, *British Society Since 1945* (1982), and A. H. Halsey, *Change in British Society* (1981), are good on postwar developments. F. Zweig, *The Worker in an Affluent Society* (1961), probes family life and economic circumstances in the British working class on the basis of extensive interviews. R. von Albertini, *Decolonialization* (1971), is still a good history of the decline and fall of European empires, to be compared with T. von Laue, *The World Revolution of Westernization: The Twentieth Century in Global Perspective* (1987), a stimulating interpretation.

Z. Brzezinski, *The Grand Failure: The Birth and Death of Communism in the Twentieth Century* (1989), is a readable overview by a leading American scholar. L. Johnson, *Central Europe: Enemies, Neighbors, Friends* (1996), is an up-to-date synthesis discussing major developments, and H. Seton-Watson, *The East European Revolution* (1965), is a classic history of the communization of eastern Europe. J. Ridley, *Tito* (1994), is lively and learned. P. Zinner, *National Communism and Popular Revolt in Eastern Europe* (1956) and *Revolution in Hungary* (1962), are excellent on the tragic events of 1956. A. Amalrik, *Will the Soviet Union Survive Until 1984?* (1970), is a fascinating and prophetic interpretation of Soviet society and politics in the 1960s by a Russian who paid for his criticism with prison and exile. A. Lee, *Russian Journal* (1981), is a fine journalistic account by a perceptive American observer.

Ziman's volume, cited in the Notes, which has an excellent bibliography, is a penetrating look at science by a leading physicist. A. Bramwell, *Ecology in the Twentieth Century: A History* (1989), examines negative aspects of technical and industrial development. Two more stimulating works on postwar technology are J. J. Servan-Schreiber, *The World Challenge* (1981); and H. Jacoby, *The Bureaucratization of the World* (1973).

In addition to previously mentioned country studies, A. Simpson, *The New Europeans* (1968), provides a good guide to Western society in the 1960s. Mitterauer and Cantor, both cited in the Notes, are excellent on the youth culture and the trends that made it possible. W. Hampton, *Guerrilla Minstrels: John Lennon, Joe Hill, Woodie Guthrie, Bob Dylan* (1986), is highly recommended. L. Wylie, *Village in the Vauclause* (1964), and P. J. Hélias, *The Horse of Pride* (1980), provide fascinating pictures of life in the French village before prosperity arrived. A. Kriegel, *The French Communists* (1972) and *Eurocommunism* (1978), are also recommended. D. Caute, *The Year of the Barricades: A Journey Through 1968* (1988), is a high-energy account that brings the upheavals of 1968 to life, while noted sociologist R. Aron's *The Elusive Revolution* (1969) is highly critical. Two outstanding works on the Vietnam War are N. Sheehan, *A Bright and Shining Lie: John Paul Vann and America in Vietnam* (1988); and A. Short, *The Origins of the Vietnam War* (1989). Among the many books to come out of the Czechoslovak experience in 1968, I. Svitak, *The Czechoslovak Experiment, 1968–1969* (1971), and Z. Zeman, *Prague Spring* (1969), are particularly recommended.

General studies on women include B. Smith, *Changing Lives: Women in European History Since 1700* (1989), which provides a good overview and a current bibliography. E. Sullerot, *Women, Society and Change* (1971), is an outstanding analysis of women's evolving roles after 1945. Two extremely influential books on women and their new awareness are S. de Beauvoir, *The Second Sex* (1962), and B. Friedan, *The Feminine Mystique* (1963). These may be compared with C. Lasch, *Haven in a Heartless World* (1977), and A. Cherlin, *Marriage, Divorce, Remarriage* (1981), which interpret changes in the American family.

On feminism and the women's movement, see N. Cott, *The Grounding of Modern Feminism* (1987). J. Lovenduski, *Women and European Politics: Contemporary Feminism and Public Policy* (1986), provides an extremely useful comparative study of similar developments in different countries. The women's movement in Italy is considered in L. Birnbaum, *Liberazione de la Donna* (1986), which is written in English despite the Italian title. C. Duchen, *Feminism in France: From May '68 to Mitterrand* (1986), is also recommended. L. Appignanesi, *Simone de Beauvoir* (1988), is a readable study of the life and thought of the famous thinker. Good studies on British women include E. Wilson, *Only Halfway to Paradise: Women in Postwar Britain, 1945–1968* (1980), and M. Barrett, *Women's Opposition Today* (1980). U. Frevert, *Women in German History: From Bourgeois Emancipation to Sexual Liberation* (1989), is both learned and engaging. Two good studies on Soviet women before the collapse of communism are F. DuPlessix Gray, *Soviet Women* (1989), and T. Mamonova, ed., *Women and Russia* (1986).

A Feminist Critique of Marriage

Having grown up in Paris in a middle-class family and become a teacher, novelist, and intellectual, Simone de Beauvoir (1908–1986) turned increasingly to feminist concerns after World War II. Her most influential work was The Second Sex *(1949), a massive declaration of independence for contemporary women.*

As an existentialist, de Beauvoir believed that all individuals must accept responsibility for their lives and strive to overcome the tragic dilemmas they face. Studying the experience of woman since antiquity, de Beauvoir argued that man had generally used education and social conditioning to create a dependent "other," a negative nonman who was not permitted to grow and strive for freedom.

Marriage—on the man's terms—was part of this unjust and undesirable process. De Beauvoir's conclusion that some couples could establish free and equal unions was based in part on her experience with philosopher Jean-Paul Sartre, de Beauvoir's encouraging companion and sometime lover.

Every human existence involves transcendence and immanence at the same time; to go forward, each existence must be maintained, for it to expand toward the future it must integrate the past, and while intercommunicating with others it should find self-confirmation. These two elements—maintenance and progression—are implied in any living activity, and for *man* marriage permits precisely a happy synthesis of the two. In his occupation and his political life he encounters change and progress, he senses his extension through time and the universe; and when he is tired of such roaming, he gets himself a home, a fixed location, and an anchorage in the world. At evening he restores his soul in the home, where his wife takes care of his furnishings and children and guards the things of the past that she keeps in store. But she has no other job than to maintain and provide for life in pure and unvarying generality; she perpetuates the species without change, she ensures the even rhythm of the days and the continuity of the home, seeing to it that the doors are locked. But she is allowed no direct influence upon the future nor upon the world; she reaches out beyond herself toward the social group only through her husband as intermediary.

Marriage today still retains, for the most part, this traditional form. . . . The male is called upon for action, his vocation is to produce, fight, create, progress, to transcend himself toward the totality of the universe and the infinity of the future; but traditional marriage does not invite women to transcend herself with him; it confines her in immanence, shuts her up within the circle of herself. She can thus propose to do nothing more than construct a life of stable equilibrium in which the present as a continuance of the past avoids the menaces of tomorrow—that is, construct precisely a life of happiness. . . .

In domestic work, with or without the aid of servants, woman makes her home her own, finds social justification, and provides herself with an occupation, an activity, that deals usefully and satisfyingly with material objects—shining stoves, fresh, clean clothes, bright copper, polished furniture—but provides no escape from immanence and little affirmation of individuality. . . . Few tasks are more like the torture of Sisyphus than housework, with its endless repetition: the clean becomes soiled, the soiled is made clean, over and over, day after day. The housewife wears herself out marking time: she makes nothing, simply perpetuates the present. She never senses conquest of a positive Good, but rather indefinite struggle against negative Evil. . . . Washing, ironing, sweeping, ferreting out rolls of lint from under wardrobes—all this halting of decay is also the denial of life; for time simultaneously creates and destroys, and only its negative aspect concerns the housekeeper. . . .

Thus woman's work within the home gives her no autonomy; it is not directly useful to society, it does not open out on the future, it produces nothing. It takes on meaning and dignity only as it is linked with existent beings who reach out beyond themselves, transcend themselves, toward society in production and action. That is, far from freeing the matron, her occupation makes her dependent upon husband and children; she is justified through them; but in their lives she is only an inessential intermediary. . . .

The tragedy of marriage is not that it fails to assure woman the promised happiness—there is no such thing as assurance in regard to happiness—but that it mutilates her; it dooms her to repetition and routine. The first twenty years of woman's life are extraordinarily rich, as we have seen; she discovers the world and her destiny. At twenty or thereabouts mistress of a home, bound permanently to a man, a child in her arms, she stands with her life virtually finished forever. Real activities, real work, are the prerogative of her man: she has mere things to occupy her which are sometimes tiring but never fully satisfying. . . .

Marriage should be a combining of two whole, independent existences, not a retreat, an annexation, a flight, a remedy. . . . The couple should not be regarded as a unit, a close cell; rather each individual should be integrated as such in society at large, where each (whether male or female) could flourish without aid; then attachments could be formed in pure generosity with another individual equally adapted to the group, attachments that would be founded upon the acknowledgment that both are free.

This balanced couple is not a utopian fancy: such couples do exist, sometimes even within the frame of marriage, most often outside it. Some mates are united by a strong sexual love that leaves them free in their friendships and in their work; others are held together by a friendship that does not preclude sexual liberty; more rare are those who are at once lovers and friends but do not seek in each other their sole reasons for living. Many nuances are possible in the relations between a man and a woman: in comradeship, pleasure, trust, fondness, co-operation, and love, they can be for each other the most abundant source of joy, richness, and power available to human beings.

❖ Simone de Beauvoir at home in Paris, June 1985. *(Gerard Gastand/Sipa Press)*

Questions for Analysis

1. How did de Beauvoir analyze marriage and marriage partners in terms of existential philosophy?

2. To what extent does a married woman benefit from a "traditional" marriage, according to de Beauvoir? Why?

3. What was de Beauvoir's solution to the situation she described? Was her solution desirable? Realistic?

4. What have you learned about the history of women that supports or challenges de Beauvoir's analysis? Include developments since World War II and your own reflections.

Source: Simone de Beauvoir, *The Second Sex,* trans. H. M. Parshley. Copyright © 1952 and renewed 1980 by Alfred A. Knopf, Inc. Reprinted by permission of the publisher.

31

Revolution, Reunification, and Rebuilding: 1985 to the Present

Erzsebet Bridge,
Budapest. *(© Giulo
Veggi/White Star/Photo
Researchers)*

In the late twentieth century, massive changes swept through eastern Europe and opened a new era in human history. Efforts in the late 1980s to reform and revitalize the communist system in the Soviet Union snowballed out of control, and in 1989 revolutions swept away communist rule throughout the entire Soviet bloc. The cold war came to a spectacular end, West Germany absorbed East Germany, and the Soviet Union broke into fifteen independent countries. Thus after forty years of cold war division, Europe reestablished a basic underlying unity, as faith in democratic government and some kind of market economy became the common creed. Indeed, the peoples of Europe (and European settlement) were perhaps more united than at any time since the sixteenth-century Protestant and Catholic Reformations, which had split medieval civilization into opposing camps. In 1991 hopes for peaceful democratic progress were almost universal.

The 1990s saw the realization of some of these hopes, but the new era brought its own problems and even terrible tragedies. The cold war division of Europe had kept a lid on ethnic conflicts and nationalism, which suddenly burst into the open and led to a disastrous civil war in the former Yugoslavia and in parts of the old Soviet Union. Moreover, most western European economies were plagued by high unemployment and struggling to adapt to the extremely competitive global economy, which undermined cherished social benefits and also complicated the task of reconstruction in the former communist states. Thus in eastern Europe, the process of rebuilding shattered societies was much more difficult than optimists had envisioned in the post–cold war euphoria of 1991, and in western Europe, the road toward integration and monetary union proved bumpy.

- Why did efforts to reform the communist system fail and result in successful anticommunist revolutions throughout eastern Europe?
- What were the consequences of these revolutions and the end of the cold war?
- How, in the 1990s, did the different parts of a unifying Europe meet the challenges of postcommunist reconstruction, resurgent nationalism, and economic union?
- What are the prospects for Europe and Western civilization as they enter the third millennium?

These are the fundamental questions that this chapter will address.

 ## THE DECLINE OF COMMUNISM IN EASTERN EUROPE

The Soviet bloc perplexed Western observers in the 1970s and early 1980s, and with good reason. On the one hand, attempts to liberalize the system continued, and the brutality of the Stalinist era was never reestablished after Nikita Khrushchev fell from power in 1964. These changes encouraged Western hopes of gradual liberalization and of a more democratic, less threatening Soviet eastern Europe.

On the other hand, hard facts frequently intervened to undermine these hopes. In addition to periodic threats and military action, the Soviet Union repeatedly demonstrated that it remained a harsh and aggressive dictatorship that paid only lip service to egalitarian ideology and was determined to uphold its rule throughout eastern Europe. Periodic efforts to achieve fundamental political change were doomed to failure sooner or later—or so it seemed to most Western experts into the mid-1980s.

And then Mikhail Gorbachev burst on the scene. The new Soviet leader opened an era of reform that was as sweeping as it was unexpected. Many believed that Gorbachev would soon fall from power and that his reforms would fail in the Soviet Union. As a matter of fact, Gorbachev's reforms rapidly transformed Soviet culture and politics, and they drastically reduced cold war tensions. But communism, which Gorbachev wanted so desperately to revitalize in order to save it, continued to decline as a functioning system throughout the Soviet bloc.

The Soviet Union to 1985

The 1968 invasion of Czechoslovakia (see page 1007) was the crucial event of the Brezhnev era, a period that actually lasted beyond the aging leader's death in 1982 until the emergence in 1985 of Gorbachev. The invasion demonstrated unmistakably the intense conservatism of the Soviet Union's ruling elite and its determination to maintain the status quo in the Soviet bloc.

"What's This? You Have Your Own Opinion?" This cartoon, published in the Soviet Union's enormously popular satirical magazine *The Crocodile,* shows a Soviet manager getting into trouble for drawing a nonstandard doodle at a meeting. Jokes poking fun at communist bosses and human foibles permeated Soviet culture, especially the oral culture, in the Brezhnev era. *(© Vneshtorgizdat, Moscow)*

Indeed, the aftermath of intervention in Czechoslovakia also brought a certain re-Stalinization of the U.S.S.R. But now dictatorship was collective rather than personal, and coercion replaced uncontrolled terror. This compromise seemed to suit the leaders and a majority of the people, and the Soviet Union appeared stable in the 1970s and early 1980s.

A slowly rising standard of living for ordinary people contributed to this stability, although the economic crisis of the 1970s greatly slowed the rate of improvement, and long lines and innumerable shortages persisted. The enduring differences between the life of the elite and the life of ordinary people also reinforced the system. Ambitious individuals had tremendous incentive to do as the state wished in order to gain access to special, well-stocked stores, to attend special schools, and to travel abroad.

Another source of stability was the enduring nationalism of ordinary Great Russians. Party leaders successfully identified themselves with Russian patriotism, stressing their role in saving the country during the Second World War and protecting it now from foreign foes, including eastern European "counter-revolutionaries." Moreover, the politically dominant Great Russians, who were concentrated in the central Russian heartland and in Siberia (which was formally designated as the Russian Federation) and who also held through the Communist party the commanding leadership positions in the non-Russian republics, constituted less than half of the total Soviet population. The Great Russians generally feared that greater freedom and open political competition might result in demands for autonomy and even independence not only by eastern European nationalities but also by the non-Russian nationalities of the smaller republics and the autonomous regions within the Soviet Union itself. Thus liberalism and democracy generally appeared to Great Russians as alien political philosophies designed to undermine the U.S.S.R.'s power and greatness.

The strength of the government was expressed in the re-Stalinization of culture and art. Free expression and open protest disappeared. In 1968, when a small group of dissenters appeared in Moscow's Red Square to protest the invasion of Czechoslovakia, they were arrested before they could unfurl their banners. This proved to be the high point of dissent, for in the 1970s Brezhnev and company made certain that Soviet intellectuals did not engage in public protest. Acts of open nonconformity and protest were severely punished, but with sophisticated, cunning methods.

Most frequently, dissidents were blacklisted and thus rendered unable to find decent jobs since the government was the only employer. This fate was enough to keep most in line. More determined but unrenowned protesters were quietly imprisoned in jails or mental institutions. Celebrated nonconformists such as Aleksandr Solzhenitsyn were permanently expelled from the country. Once again, Jews were persecuted as a "foreign" element, though some were eventually permitted to immigrate to Israel. As the distinguished Russian dissident historian Roy Medvedev explained in the mid-1970s,

The technology of repression has become more refined in recent years. Before, repression always went much further than necessary. Stalin killed millions of people when arresting 1,000 would have enabled him to control the people. Our leaders . . . found out eventually that you don't have to put people in prison or in a psychiatric hospital to silence them. There are other ways.[1]

Eliminating the worst aspects of Stalin's dictatorship strengthened the regime, and almost all Western experts concluded that rule by a self-perpetuating Communist party elite in the Soviet Union appeared to be quite solid in the 1970s and early 1980s.

Yet beneath the dreary immobility of political life in the Brezhnev era, the Soviet Union was actually experiencing profound changes. As a perceptive British journalist put it in 1986, "The country went through a social revolution while Brezhnev slept."[2] Three aspects of this revolution, which was seldom appreciated by Western observers at the time, were particularly significant.

First, the growth of the urban population, which had raced forward at breakneck speed in the Stalin years, continued rapidly in the 1960s and 1970s. In 1985 two-thirds of all Soviet citizens lived in cities, and one-quarter lived in big cities. Of great significance, this expanding urban population lost its old peasant ways, exchanging them for more education, better job skills, and greater sophistication.

Second, the number of highly trained scientists, managers, and specialists expanded prodigiously, increasing fourfold between 1960 and 1985. Thus the class of well-educated, pragmatic, and self-confident experts, which played such an important role in restructuring industrial societies after World War II (see pages 1011–1012), developed rapidly in the Soviet Union. Moreover, leading Soviet scientists and technologists, like their colleagues in the West, sought membership in the international "invisible college" of their disciplines. Correspondingly, they sought the intellectual freedom necessary to do significant work, and they often obtained it because their research had practical (and military) value.

Third, education and freedom for experts in their special areas helped foster the growth of Soviet public opinion, just as the reading revolution of the eighteenth century had encouraged the development of independent public opinion in France. Educated people read, discussed, and formed definite ideas about social questions. And if caution dictated conventional ideas (at least in public), many important issues could be approached and debated in "nonpolitical" terms. Developing definite ideas on such issues as environmental pollution or urban transportation, educated urban people increasingly saw themselves as worthy of having a voice in society's decisions, even its political decisions. This, too, was part of the quiet transformation that set the stage for the Gorbachev era.

Solidarity in Poland

Gorbachev's reforms interacted with a resurgence of popular protest in the Soviet Union's satellite empire. Developments in Poland were most striking and significant. There workers joined together en masse to fight peacefully for freedom and self-determination, while the world watched in amazement. Crushed in the short run but refusing to admit defeat, Polish workers waged a long campaign that inspired and reflected a powerful reform current in eastern Europe.

Poland had been an unruly satellite from the beginning. Stalin said that introducing communism to Poland was like putting a saddle on a cow. Efforts to saddle the cow—really a spirited stallion—led to widespread riots in 1956 (see page 1006). As a result, Polish Communists dropped their efforts to impose Soviet-style collectivization on the peasants and to break the Roman Catholic church. Most agricultural land remained in private hands, and the Catholic church thrived. With an independent peasant agriculture and a vigorous church, the Communists failed to monopolize society.

They also failed to manage the economy effectively. Even the booming 1960s saw little economic improvement. When the government suddenly announced large price increases right before Christmas in 1970, Poland's working class rose again in angry protest. Factories were occupied, and strikers were shot, but a new Communist leader came to power nevertheless. The government then wagered that massive inflows of Western capital and technology, especially from Willy Brandt's rich and now-friendly West Germany (see pages 1017–1019), could produce a Polish "economic miracle" that would win popular support for the regime. Instead, bureaucratic incompetence, coupled with worldwide recession after the first oil shock in 1973, put the economy into a nosedive in the mid-1970s. Workers, intellectuals, and the church became increasingly restive. Then the real Polish miracle occurred: Cardinal Karol Wojtyla, archbishop of Cracow, was elected pope in 1978. In June 1979, he returned from Rome for an astonishing pilgrimage across his native land. Preaching love of Christ and country and the "inalienable rights of man," Pope John Paul II drew enormous crowds and electrified the Polish nation. The economic crisis became a moral and spiritual crisis as well.

In August 1980, as scattered strikes to protest higher meat prices spread, the sixteen thousand workers at the gigantic Lenin Shipyards in Gdansk (formerly known as Danzig) laid down their tools and occupied the showpiece plant. As other workers along the Baltic coast joined "in solidarity," the strikers advanced truly revolutionary demands: the right to form free trade unions, the right to strike, freedom of speech, release of political prisoners, and economic reforms. After eighteen days of shipyard occupation, as families brought food to the gates and priests said Mass daily amid huge overhead cranes, the government gave in and accepted the workers' demands in the Gdansk Agreement. In a state where the Communist party claimed to rule on behalf of the proletariat, a working-class revolt had won an unprecedented victory.

Led by feisty Lenin Shipyards electrician and devout Catholic Lech Walesa (b. 1943), the workers proceeded to organize their free and democratic trade union. They called it "Solidarity." Joined by intellectuals and supported by the Catholic church, Solidarity became the union of a nation. By March 1981 it had a membership of 9.5 million, out of 12.5 million who were theoretically eligible. A full-time staff of 40,000 linked the union members together as Solidarity published its own newspapers and cultural and intellectual freedom blossomed in Poland. Solidarity's leaders had tremendous, well-organized support, and the ever-present threat of calling a nationwide strike gave them real power in ongoing negotiations with the Communist bosses.

But if Solidarity had power, it did not try to take the reins of government in 1981. History, the Brezhnev Doctrine, and virulent attacks from communist neighbors all seemed to guarantee the intervention of the Red Army and a terrible bloodbath if Polish Communists "lost control." Thus the Solidarity revolution remained a "self-limiting revolution" aimed at defending the cultural and trade-union freedoms won in the Gdansk Agreement, and it refused to use force to challenge directly the Communist monopoly of political power. (See the feature "Listening to the Past: A Solidarity Leader Speaks from Prison" on pages 1062–1063.)

Solidarity's combination of strength and moderation postponed a showdown. The Soviet Union, already facing sharp criticism for its European missile policy and condemned worldwide for its invasion of Afghanistan, played a waiting game of threats and pressure. After a crisis in March 1981 that followed police beatings of Solidarity activists, Walesa settled for minor government concessions, and Solidarity again dropped plans for a massive general strike. This marked a turning point. Criticism of Walesa's moderate leadership and calls for local self-government in unions and factories grew. Solidarity lost its cohesiveness. The worsening economic crisis also encouraged grassroots radicalism and frustration: a hunger-march banner proclaimed, "A hungry nation can eat its rulers."[3] With an eye on Western, and especially West German, opinion leaders, who generally preferred tyranny to instability in eastern Europe (although they seldom admitted this fact), the Polish Communist leadership shrewdly denounced Solidarity for promoting economic collapse and provoking Soviet invasion. In December 1981, Communist leader General Wojciech Jaruzelski suddenly struck in the dead of a subfreezing night, proclaiming martial law, cutting all communications, arresting Solidarity's leaders, and "saving" the nation.

Outlawed and driven underground, Solidarity fought successfully to maintain its organization and to voice the aspirations of the Polish masses after 1981. Part of the reason for the union's survival was the government's unwillingness (and probably its inability) to impose full-scale terror. Moreover, in schools and shops, in factories and offices, millions decided to continue acting as if they were free, even though they were not. Therefore, cultural and intellectual life remained extremely vigorous in spite of renewed repression. At the same time, the faltering Polish economy, battered by renewed global recession in the early 1980s and crippled by a disastrous brain drain after 1981, continued to deteriorate. Thus popular support for outlawed Solidarity

Lech Walesa and Solidarity   An inspiration for fellow workers at the Lenin Shipyards in the dramatic and successful strike against the Communist bosses in August 1980, Walesa played a key role in Solidarity before and after it was outlawed. Speaking here to old comrades at the Lenin Shipyards after Solidarity was again legalized in 1988, Walesa personified an enduring opposition to Communist rule in eastern Europe. *(Merrillon/Liaison)*

remained strong and deep under martial law in the 1980s, preparing the way for the union's political rebirth toward the end of the decade.

The rise and survival of Solidarity showed again the fierce desire of millions of eastern Europeans for greater political liberty. The union's strength also demonstrated the enduring appeal of cultural freedom, trade-union rights, patriotic nationalism, and religious feeling. Not least, Solidarity's challenge encouraged fresh thinking in the Soviet Union, ever the key to lasting change in the Eastern bloc.

Gorbachev's Reforms in the Soviet Union

Fundamental change in Russian history has often come in short, intensive spurts, which contrast vividly with long periods of immobility. We have studied four of these spurts: the ambitious "westernization" of Peter the Great in the early eighteenth century (see pages 582–585), the great reforms connected with the freeing of the serfs in the mid-nineteenth century (see pages 837–838), the Russian Revolution of 1917 (see pages 908–916), and Stalin's wrenching "revolution from above" in the 1930s (see pages 961–965). To this select list of decisive transformations, we must now add the era of reform launched by Mikhail Gorbachev in 1985. Gorbachev's initiatives brought political and cultural liberalization to the Soviet Union, and they then permitted democracy and national self-determination to triumph spectacularly in the old satellite empire and eventually in the Soviet Union itself, although this was certainly not Gorbachev's original intention.

As we have seen, the Soviet Union's Communist party elite seemed secure in the early 1980s as far as any challenge from below was concerned. The long-established system of administrative controls continued to stretch downward from the central ministries and state committees to provincial cities, and from there to factories, neighborhoods, and villages. At each level of this massive state bureaucracy, the overlapping hierarchy of the Communist party, with its 17.5 million members, continued to watch over all decisions and manipulate every aspect of national life. Organized opposition was impossible, and average people simply left politics to the bosses.

Yet the massive state and party bureaucracy was a mixed blessing. It safeguarded the elite, but it also pro-

Newly Elected President Mikhail Gorbachev vowed in his acceptance speech before the Supreme Soviet, the U.S.S.R.'s parliament, to assume "all responsibility" for the success or failure of *perestroika*. Previous parliaments were no more than tools of the Communist party, but this one actively debated and even opposed government programs. *(Vlastimir Shone/Liaison)*

moted apathy in the masses. Discouraging personal initiative and economic efficiency, it was ill suited to secure the effective cooperation of the rapidly growing class of well-educated urban experts. Therefore, when the ailing Brezhnev finally died in 1982, his successor, the long-time chief of the secret police, Yuri Andropov (1914–1984), tried to invigorate the system. Andropov introduced modest reforms to improve economic performance and campaigned against worker absenteeism and high-level corruption. Relatively little came of these efforts, but they combined with a sharply worsening economic situation to set the stage for the emergence in 1985 of Mikhail Gorbachev (b. 1931), the most vigorous Soviet leader in a generation.

Trained as a lawyer and working his way up as a Communist party official in the northern Caucasus, where he caught the attention of Andropov and other senior party members, Gorbachev was smart, charming, and tough. As long-time Soviet foreign minister Andrei Gromyko reportedly said, "This man has a nice smile, but he has got iron teeth."[4] Gorbachev believed in communism, but he realized it was failing to keep up with Western capitalism and technology. This was eroding the Soviet Union's status as a superpower. Thus Gorbachev (and his intelligent, influential wife, Raisa, a dedicated professor of Marxist-Leninist thought) wanted to save the Soviet system by revitalizing it with fundamental reforms. Gorbachev was also an idealist. He wanted to improve conditions for ordinary citizens. Understanding full well that the endless waste and expense of the cold war arms race had had a disastrous impact on living conditions in the Soviet Union, which remained much poorer than the United States and western Europe, he realized that improvement at home required better relations with the West.

In his first year in office, Gorbachev attacked corruption and incompetence in the bureaucracy, and he consolidated his power by packing the top level of the party with his supporters. He attacked alcoholism and drunkenness, which were deadly scourges of Soviet society. More basically, he elaborated his ambitious reform program.

The first set of reform policies was designed to transform and restructure the economy, which directed so much output to the military and failed to provide for the real needs of the Soviet population. To accomplish this economic "restructuring," this *perestroika,* Gorbachev and his supporters permitted an easing of government price controls on some goods, more independence for state enterprises, and the setting up of profit-seeking private cooperatives to provide personal services for consumers. These reforms initially produced a few improvements, but shortages then grew as the economy stalled at an intermediate point between central planning and free-market mechanisms. By late 1988, Gorbachev's timid economic initiatives had met with very little success, creating widespread consumer dissatisfaction and posing a serious threat to his leadership and the entire reform program.

Gorbachev's bold and far-reaching campaign "to tell it like it is" was much more successful. Very popular in a country where censorship, dull uniformity, and outright lies had long characterized public discourse, the newfound "openness," or *glasnost,* of the government and the media marked an astonishing break with the past. A disaster such as the Chernobyl nuclear accident in 1986, which devastated part of Ukraine and showered Europe with radioactive fallout, was investigated and reported with honesty and painstaking thoroughness. Long-banned and vilified émigré writers sold millions of copies of their works in new editions, while denunciations of Stalin and his terror became standard fare in plays and movies. Thus initial openness in government pronouncements quickly went much further than Gorbachev intended and led to something approaching free speech and free expression, a veritable cultural revolution.

Democratization was the third element of reform. Beginning as an attack on corruption in the Communist party and as an attempt to bring the class of educated experts into the decision-making process, it led to the first free elections in the Soviet Union since 1917. Gorbachev and the party remained in control, but a minority of critical independents were elected in April 1989 to a revitalized Congress of People's Deputies. Many top-ranking Communists who ran unopposed saw themselves defeated as a majority of angry voters struck their names from the ballot and prevented their election. Millions of Soviets then watched the new congress for hours on television as Gorbachev and his ministers saw their proposals debated and even rejected. Thus millions of Soviet citizens took practical lessons in open discussion, critical thinking, and representative government. The result was a new political culture at odds with the Communist party's monopoly of power and control.

Democratization ignited demands for greater autonomy and even for national independence by non-Russian minorities, especially in the Baltic region and in the Caucasus. These demands certainly went beyond anything that Gorbachev had envisaged. In April 1989, troops with sharpened shovels charged into a rally of Georgian separatists in Tbilisi and left twenty dead. But whereas China's Communist leaders brutally massacred similar prodemocracy demonstrators in Beijing in June 1989 and reimposed rigid authoritarian rule, Gorbachev drew back from repression. Thus nationalist demands continued to grow in the non-Russian Soviet republics.

Finally, the Soviet leader brought "new political thinking" to the field of foreign affairs and acted on it. He withdrew Soviet troops from Afghanistan and sought to reduce East-West tensions. Of enormous importance, he sought to halt the arms race with the United States and convinced President Ronald Reagan of his sincerity. In December 1987, the two leaders agreed in a Washington summit to eliminate all land-based intermediate-range missiles in Europe, setting the stage for more arms reductions. Gorbachev also encouraged reform movements in Poland and Hungary and pledged to respect the political choices of the peoples of eastern Europe. He thereby repudiated the Brezhnev Doctrine, which in 1968 had arrogantly proclaimed the right of the Soviet Union and its allies to intervene at will in eastern Europe. By early 1989, it seemed that if Gorbachev held to his word, the tragic Soviet occupation of eastern Europe might well wither away, taking the long cold war with it once and for all.

THE REVOLUTIONS OF 1989

Instead, history accelerated. In 1989 Gorbachev's plan to reform communism in order to save it snowballed out of control. A series of largely peaceful revolutions swept across eastern Europe (Map 31.1), overturning existing communist regimes and ending the communists' monopoly of power. Revolutionary mass demonstrations led to the formation of provisional governments dedicated to democratic elections, human rights, and national rejuvenation. Watched on television in the Soviet Union and around the world, these stirring events marked the triumph and the transformation of the long-standing opposition to communist rule and foreign domination in eastern Europe.

The revolutions of 1989 had momentous consequences, many of which are still unfolding. First, the peoples of eastern Europe joyfully re-entered the mainstream of contemporary European life and culture, after

MAP 31.1 Democratic Movements in Eastern Europe, 1989   With Gorbachev's repudiation of the Brezhnev Doctrine, the revolutionary drive for freedom and democracy spread throughout eastern Europe. Countries that had been satellites in the orbit of the Soviet Union began to set themselves free to establish their own place in the universe of free nations.

having been been conquered and brutalized by Nazis and communists for almost sixty years. Second, Gorbachev's reforms now boomeranged, and a complicated anticommunist revolution swept through the Soviet Union, as the once mighty multinational empire committed suicide and broke into a large Russia and fourteen other independent states. Third, West Germany quickly absorbed its East German rival and emerged as the most influential country in Europe. Finally, the long cold war came to an abrupt end, and the United States suddenly stood as the world's only superpower.

The Collapse of Communism in Eastern Europe

Solidarity and the Polish people led the way to revolution in eastern Europe. In 1988 widespread labor unrest, raging inflation, and the outlawed Solidarity's refusal to cooperate with the military government had brought Poland to the brink of economic collapse. Profiting from Gorbachev's tolerant attitude and skillfully mobilizing forces, Solidarity pressured Poland's frustrated Communist leaders into another round of negotiations that might work out a sharing of power to resolve the political stalemate and the economic crisis. The subsequent agreement in early 1989 legalized Solidarity again after eight years. The agreement also declared that a large minority of representatives to the Polish parliament would be chosen by free elections in June 1989. The Communist party was still guaranteed a majority, and General Jaruzelski would be president for four years. Expecting to win many of the contested seats, the Communists believed that their rule was guaranteed for four years and that Solidarity would keep the workers in line.

Lacking access to the state-run media, Solidarity succeeded nonetheless in mobilizing the country and winning most of the contested seats in an overwhelming and largely unexpected victory. Moreover, many angry voters crossed off the names of unopposed party candidates, so that the Communist party failed to win the majority they had anticipated. Solidarity members jubilantly entered the Polish parliament as the first freely elected opposition in a communist country, and a dangerous stalemate quickly developed. But Solidarity leader Lech Walesa, a gifted politician who always repudiated violence, adroitly obtained a majority by securing the allegiance of two minor procommunist parties that had been part of the coalition government after World War II. Significantly, at a critical moment, Gorbachev told the Polish Communists again that Moscow would not intervene to save them. In August 1989, the editor of Solidarity's weekly newspaper was sworn in as the first noncommunist leader in eastern Europe since Stalin used Soviet armies to impose his system there after the Second World War.

In its first year and a half, the new Solidarity government cautiously introduced revolutionary political changes. It eliminated the hated secret police, the Communist ministers in the government, and finally Jaruzelski himself, but it did so step by step in order to avoid confrontation with the army or the Soviet Union. However, in economic affairs, the Solidarity-led government was radical from the beginning. Pointing to the disastrous economic condition of the country and its people, the new government applied "shock therapy" designed to make a clean break with state planning and ownership and to move quickly to market mechanisms and private property. Developed in the fall of 1989, the Solidarity government abolished controls on many prices on January 1, 1990, and reformed the monetary system with a "big bang." Showing for the first time how a communist economic system might be dismantled with breathtaking speed, the Polish program provided a model for similar radical action in other postcommunist countries.

Hungary followed Poland. Hungary's Communist party boss, János Kádár, had permitted liberalization of the rigid planned economy after the 1956 uprising in exchange for political obedience and continued Communist control. In May 1988, in an effort to retain power by granting modest political concessions, the party replaced Kádár with a reform communist. But opposition groups rejected piecemeal progress, and in the summer of 1989 the Hungarian Communist party agreed in a bold gamble to renounce one-party rule and to hold free elections in early 1990. Welcoming Western investment and moving rapidly toward multiparty democracy, Hungary's Communists now enjoyed considerable popular support and they believed, quite mistakenly it turned out, that they could defeat the opposition in the upcoming elections. In an effort to strengthen their support at home and also put pressure on East Germany's hard-line Communist regime, the Hungarians opened their border to East Germans and tore down the barbed-wire "iron curtain" with Austria. In doing so, Hungary repudiated its treaty commitment to prevent East Germans from escaping to the West, but Hungary's reform communists claimed that they were only following the United Nations convention on political refugees. Thus tens of thousands of dissatisfied East German "vacationers" began pouring into Hungary, crossed into Austria as refugees, and continued on to immediate resettlement in thriving West Germany.

The flight of East Germans led to the rapid growth of a homegrown protest movement in East Germany. Intellectuals, environmentalists, and Protestant ministers took the lead, organizing huge candlelight demonstrations and arguing that a truly democratic, independent, but still socialist East Germany was both possible and desirable. These "stayers" failed to convince the "leavers," however, who continued to flee the country en masse. In a desperate attempt to stabilize the situation, the East German government opened the Berlin Wall in November 1989, and people danced for joy atop that grim symbol of the prison state. East Germany's aging Communist leaders were swept aside, and a reform government took power, calling for a wide-ranging political dialogue and scheduling general elections for March 1990.

In Czechoslovakia, communism died in December 1989 in an almost good-humored ousting of Communist bosses in ten short days. This so-called Velvet Rev-

East Germans Escaping to the West   After Hungary allowed more than 30,000 "vacationing" East Germans to pass into Austria and on to a tumultuous welcome in West Germany, Czechoslovakia followed suit. Hordes of East Germans, like those shown here, converged on the West German embassy in Prague. Then the East German government gave up, opening the Berlin wall and scheduling free elections. *(BUU/Saussier/Liaison)*

olution grew out of popular demonstrations led by students, intellectuals, and a dissident playwright turned moral revolutionary named Václav Havel. (See the feature "Individuals in Society: Václav Havel: Apostle of Regeneration.") The protesters practically took control of the streets and forced the Communists into a power-sharing arrangement, which quickly resulted in the resignation of the Communist government. As 1989 ended, the Czechoslovak assembly elected Havel president.

Only in Romania was revolution violent and bloody. There iron-fisted Communist dictator Nicolae Ceauşescu (1918–1989) had long combined Stalinist brutality with stubborn independence from Moscow. Faced with mass protests in December, Ceauşescu, alone among eastern European bosses, ordered his ruthless security forces to slaughter thousands, thereby sparking a classic armed uprising. After Ceauşescu's forces

were defeated, the tyrant and his wife were captured and executed by a military court. A coalition government emerged from the fighting, although the legacy of Ceauşescu's oppression left a very troubled country.

The Disintegration of the Soviet Union

As 1990 began, the revolutionary changes that Gorbachev had permitted, and even encouraged, had triumphed in all but two eastern European states—tiny Albania and the vast Soviet Union. The great question now became whether the Soviet Union would follow its former satellites and whether reform communism would give way to a popular anticommunist revolution. Near civil war between Armenians and Azerbaijanis in the Caucasus; assertions of independence in the Baltic States, including Lithuania's bold declaration of

Individuals in Society

Václav Havel: Apostle of Regeneration

Václav Havel, playwright, dissident leader, and the first post-communist president of the Czech Republic. (Chris Niedenthal/Black Star)

On the night of November 24, 1989, the revolution in Czechoslovakia reached its climax. Three hundred thousand people had poured into Prague's historic Wenceslas Square to continue the massive protests that had erupted a week earlier after the police savagely beat student demonstrators. Now all eyes were focused on a high balcony. There an elderly man with a gentle smile and a middle-aged intellectual in jeans and sport jacket stood arm in arm and acknowledged the cheers of the crowd. "Dubček-Havel," the people roared. "Dubček-Havel!" Alexander Dubček, who represented the failed promise of reform communism in the 1960s (see page 1006), was symbolically passing the torch to Václav Havel, who embodied the uncompromising opposition to communism that was sweeping the country. That very evening, the hard-line Communist government resigned, and soon Havel was the unanimous choice to head a new democratic Czechoslovakia. Who was this man to whom the nation turned in 1989?

Born in 1936 into a prosperous, cultured, upper-middle-class family, the young Havel was denied admission to the university because of his class origins. Loving literature and philosophy, he gravitated to the theater, became a stagehand, and emerged in the 1960s as a leading playwright. His plays were set in vague settings, developed existential themes, and poked fun at the absurdities of life and the pretensions of communism. In his private life, Havel thrived on good talk, Prague's lively bar scene, and officially forbidden rock-and-roll.

In 1968 the Soviets rolled into Czechoslovakia, and Havel watched in horror as a tank commander opened fire on a crowd of peaceful protesters in a small town. "That week," he recorded, "was an experience I shall never forget."[1] The free-spirited artist threw himself into the intellectual opposition to communism and became its leading figure for the next twenty years. The costs of defiance were enormous. Purged and blacklisted, Havel lifted barrels in a brewery and wrote bitter satires that could not be staged. In 1977 he and a few other dissidents publicly protested Czechoslovak violations of the Helsinki Accord on human rights, and in 1989 this Charter '77 group became the inspiration for Civic Forum, the democratic coalition that toppled communism. Havel spent five years in prison and was constantly harassed by the police.

Havel's thoughts and actions focused on truth, decency, and moral regeneration. In 1975, in a famous open letter to Czechoslovakia's Communist boss, Havel wrote that the people were indeed quiet, but only because they were "driven by fear. . . . Everyone has something to lose and so everyone has reason to be afraid." Thus Havel saw lies, hypocrisy, and apathy undermining and poisoning all human relations in his country. "Order has been established—at the price of a paralysis of the spirit, a deadening of the heart, and a spiritual and moral crisis in society."[2]

Yet Havel saw a way out of the Communist quagmire. He argued that a profound but peaceful revolution in human values was possible. Such a revolution could lead to the moral reconstruction of Czech and Slovak society, where, in his words, "values like trust, openness, responsibility, solidarity and love" might again flourish and nurture the human spirit. Havel was a voice of hope and humanity, a voice who inspired his compatriots with a lofty vision of a moral postcommunist society. As president of his country, Havel continued to speak eloquently on the great questions of our time.

Questions for Analysis

1. Why did Havel oppose Communist rule? How did his goals differ from those of Dubček and other advocates of reform communism?

2. Havel has been called a "moralist in politics." Is this a good description of him? Why? Can you think of a better one?

---

1. Quoted in M. Simmons, *The Reluctant President: A Political Life of Václav Havel* (London: Methuen, 1991), p. 91.
2. Quoted ibid., p. 110.

national sovereignty; and growing dissatisfaction among the Great Russian masses were all parts of a fluid, unstable political situation. Increasingly, the reform-minded Gorbachev stood as a moderate besieged by both those who wanted revolutionary changes and hard-line Communists who longed to reverse course and clamp down.

In February 1990, as competing Russian politicians noisily presented their programs and nationalists in the non-Russian republics demanded autonomy or independence from the Soviet Union, the Communist party suffered a stunning defeat in local elections throughout the country. As in the eastern European satellites, dem-

ocrats and anticommunists won clear majorities in the leading cities of the Russian Federation. Moreover, in Lithuania the people elected an uncompromising nationalist as president, and the newly chosen parliament declared Lithuania an independent state. Gorbachev responded by placing an economic embargo on Lithuania, but he refused to use the army to crush the separatist government. The result was a tense political stalemate, which undermined popular support for Gorbachev. Separating himself further from Communist hard-liners, a hard-pressed Gorbachev asked Soviet citizens to ratify a new constitution, which formally abolished the Communist party's monopoly of political

Celebrating Victory, August 1991   A Russian soldier flashes the victory sign in front of the Russian parliament, as the last-gasp coup attempt of Communist hard-liners is defeated by Boris Yeltsin and an enthusiastic public. The soldier has cut the hammer and sickle out of the Soviet flag, consigning those famous symbols of proletarian revolution to what Trotsky once called the "garbage can of history." *(Filip Horvat/Saba)*

power and expanded the power of the Congress of People's Deputies. Retaining his post as party secretary, Gorbachev convinced a majority of deputies to elect him president of the Soviet Union.

Gorbachev's eroding power and his unwillingness to risk a universal suffrage election for the presidency strengthened his great rival, Boris Yeltsin (b. 1931). A radical reform communist who had been purged by party conservatives in 1987 and had never forgiven Gorbachev's role in his fall, Yeltsin was a tough and crafty Siberian who had staged a remarkable comeback as the most prominent figure in the democratic movement in the Russian Federation. In May 1990, Yeltsin was elected leader of the Russian parliament. He boldly announced that Russia would declare its independence and put its laws and interests above those of the multinational Soviet Union. Yeltsin's declaration broadened the base of the anticommunist movement, skillfully joining the patriotism of ordinary Russians with the democratic aspirations of big-city intellectuals. Gorbachev countered by trying to save the Soviet Union with a new treaty that would link the member republics in a looser, freely accepted confederation. Nine republics agreed to join, but the three Baltic States (Lithuania, Latvia, and Estonia), as well as Armenia, Georgia, and Moldova, spurned Gorbachev's pleas. Thus the Soviet Union continued to unravel, and the country's economic decline accelerated.

Opposed by democrats and nationalists, Gorbachev was also challenged again by the Communist old guard. Defeated at the Communist party congress in July 1990, a gang of hard-liners kidnapped a vacationing Gorbachev and his family in the Caucasus and tried to seize the Soviet government in August 1991. But the attempted coup collapsed in the face of massive popular resistance, which rallied around Yeltsin, recently elected president of the Russian Federation by universal suffrage. As the world watched spellbound on television, Yeltsin defiantly denounced the rebels from atop a stalled tank in central Moscow and declared the "rebirth of Russia." The army supported Yeltsin, and Gorbachev was rescued and returned to power as head of the Soviet Union.

The leaders of the coup wanted to preserve Communist power, state ownership, and the multinational Soviet Union, but they succeeded only in destroying all three. An anticommunist revolution swept the Russian Federation as Yeltsin and his supporters outlawed the Communist party and confiscated its property. Locked in a personal and political duel with Gorbachev, Yeltsin

and his democratic allies declared Russia independent and withdrew from the Soviet Union. All the other Soviet republics also left. The Soviet Union—and Gorbachev's job—ceased to exist on December 25, 1991 (Map 31.2).

To be sure, the independent republics of the old Soviet Union were bound together by innumerable ties. A loose but indispensable confederation, christened the Commonwealth of Independent States, was established as 1991 ended, but its prospects were anything but clear. Many foreign observers speculated that the new Russia, which was often harking back to nationalistic and prerevolutionary symbols, would eventually seek to reclaim the tsarist inheritance and bring the supposedly independent states of the commonwealth under Moscow's control. However, as 1992 opened, Russian dreams of empire seemed as dead as the Soviet Union. And throughout the rest of the 1990s, the enormous challenges inherent in building a market economy and a democratic society would fully absorb Russian energies.

German Unification and the End of the Cold War

The revolutions of 1989 and the collapse of communism transformed eastern Europe, as people tore down the walls and put in elected officials. The liberation of eastern Europe enhanced the prospect of ending the cold war, rooted above all in Stalin's brutal imposition of Soviet rule in eastern Europe after World War II (see pages 1004–1006). Yet the sudden death of communism in East Germany in 1989 also reopened the potentially dangerous "German question," for Gorbachev's rapidly changing but still powerful Soviet Union still had special rights in Germany, as did the Western allies. Renewed cold war conflict over Germany was still possible.

Taking power in October 1989, East German reform communists, enthusiastically supported by leading East German intellectuals and former dissidents, wanted to preserve socialism by making it genuinely democratic and responsive to the needs of the people. They argued for a "third way," which would go beyond the failed Stalinism they had experienced and the ruthless capitalism they saw in the West. These reformers supported closer ties with West Germany, but they feared unification and they wanted to preserve a distinct East German identity.

These efforts failed, and within a few months East Germany was absorbed into an enlarged West Germany,

MAP 31.2 Russia and the Successor States   After the attempt in August 1991 to depose Gorbachev failed, an anticommunist revolution swept the Soviet Union. Led by Russia and Boris Yeltsin, the republics that formed the Soviet Union declared their sovereignty and independence. Eleven of the fifteen republics then formed a loose confederation called the Commonwealth of Independent States, but the integrated economy of the Soviet Union dissolved into separate national economies, each with its own goals and policies.

much like a faltering smaller company is merged into a larger rival and ceases to exist. Three factors were particularly important in this sudden absorption. First, in the first week after the Berlin Wall was opened, almost 9 million East Germans—roughly one-half of the total population—poured across the border into West Germany. Almost all returned to their homes in the East, but the joy of warm welcomes from long-lost friends and loved ones and the exhilarating experience of shopping in the well-stocked stores of the much wealthier West aroused long-dormant hopes of unity among ordinary citizens.

Second, West German chancellor Helmut Kohl and his closest advisers skillfully exploited the historic opportunity on their doorstep. Sure of support from the

United States, whose leadership he had steadfastly followed, in November 1989 Kohl presented a ten-point plan for a step-by-step unification in cooperation with both East Germany and the international community. Building on his bold call for reunification without fanning fears of a dangerous greater Germany, Kohl then promised the ordinary citizens of a struggling, bankrupt East Germany an immediate economic bonanza— a one-for-one exchange of all East German marks in savings accounts and pensions into much more valuable West German marks. This generous offer helped a well-financed conservative-liberal "Alliance for Germany," which was set up in East Germany and was closely tied to Kohl's West German Christian Democrats, to overwhelm those who argued for the preservation of some kind of independent socialist society in East Germany. In March 1990, the Alliance outdistanced the Socialist party and won almost 50 percent of the votes in an East German parliamentary election. (The Communists ignominiously fell to fringe-party status.) The Alliance for Germany quickly negotiated an economic union on favorable terms with Chancellor Kohl, who wanted to complete the unification of the two Germanies as quickly as he could.

Finally, in the summer of 1990, the complicated international aspect of German unification was successfully resolved. This aspect was critical. Unification would once again make Germany the strongest state in central Europe and would directly affect the security of the Soviet Union and the general European balance of power. But Gorbachev swallowed hard—Western cartoonists delighted in showing Stalin turning over in his grave—and negotiated the best deal he could. In a historic agreement signed by Gorbachev and Kohl in July 1990, a uniting Germany solemnly affirmed its peaceful intentions and pledged never to develop nuclear, biological, or chemical weapons. In deference to Russian pride, Germany allowed the Soviet forces stationed in East Germany to withdraw gradually and with dignity. In side agreements, Germany sweetened the deal for Gorbachev by promising to make enormous loans to the hard-pressed Soviet Union. In doing so, Kohl continued Willy Brandt's strategy of buying favor in eastern Europe with aid and credit, a strategy that had proved highly effective. On October 3, 1990, East Germany merged into West Germany, forming henceforth a single nation under the West German laws and constitution.

The peaceful reunification of Germany accelerated the pace of agreements to reduce armaments and liquidate the cold war. With the Soviet Union's budget deficit rising rapidly in 1990, Gorbachev especially sought arrangements to justify massive cuts in military spending. Thus in November 1990, delegates from twenty-two European countries joined those from the United States and the Soviet Union in Paris and agreed to a scaling down of all their armed forces. The delegates also solemnly affirmed that all existing borders in Europe—from unified Germany to the newly independent Baltic republics—were legal and valid. The Paris Accord was for all practical purposes a general peace treaty, bringing an end to World War II and the cold war that followed.

The establishment of peace in Europe encouraged the United States and the Soviet Union to scrap a significant portion of their nuclear weapons. Having already agreed in 1987 to remove all land-based intermediate-range missiles from Europe, the two great nuclear superpowers pledged in July 1991 a major mutual reduction of intercontinental ballistic missiles with their multiple nuclear warheads in the START I agreement. In September 1991, a confident President George Bush unilaterally declared another major cut in American nuclear weapons. He also canceled the around-the-clock alert status for American bombers outfitted with atomic bombs. A floundering Gorbachev quickly followed suit. For the first time in four decades, Soviet and American nuclear weapons were no longer standing ready to destroy capitalism, communism, and life itself.

As anticommunist revolutions swept eastern Europe and East-West tensions rapidly disappeared, the Soviet Union lost both the will and the means to be a mighty superpower. Yet the United States retained the increased strength resulting from the Reagan arms buildup, as well as its desire to influence political and economic developments on a global scale. Thus the United States, still flanked by many allies, emerged rather suddenly as the world's only surviving superpower.

In 1991 the United States used its military superiority on a grand scale in a quick war with Iraq in western Asia. Emerging in 1988 from an eight-year war with neighboring Iran with a big, tough army equipped by the Soviet bloc, western Europe, and the United States, Iraq's strongman Saddam Hussein (b. 1937) set out to make himself the leader of the entire Arab world. Eyeing the great oil wealth of his tiny southern neighbor, Saddam Hussein suddenly sent his military forces into Kuwait in August 1990 and proclaimed Iraq's annexation of Kuwait.

Reacting vigorously, the United States called on the United Nations to turn back Iraqi aggression and free Kuwait. The five permanent members of the U.N. Security Council—the United States, the Soviet Union, China, the United Kingdom, and France—agreed in August 1990 to impose a strict naval blockade on Iraq. Naval forces, led by the United States but augmented by ships from several nations, then enforced the blockade and halted all trade between Iraq and the rest of the world. Receiving the support of ground units from some Arab states as well as from Great Britain and France, the United States also landed first 200,000, and then a total of 500,000, American soldiers in Saudi Arabia near the border of Kuwait. When a defiant Saddam Hussein refused to withdraw from Kuwait and pay reparations, the Security Council authorized the U.S.-led

"Saddam, Surrender!" So reads the caption under the image of an advancing U.S. soldier on the cover of a leading Italian newsmagazine, which repeatedly featured the crisis over Kuwait and the war with Iraq. This heavy Italian coverage was symptomatic of enormous coverage worldwide. Although U.S. forces provided most of the muscle, twenty-eight countries, including Italy, participated in Operation Desert Storm. (U.S. News & World Report/ PANORAMA/*Mondadori. Courtesy, Madeline Grimoldi*)

military coalition to attack Iraq. The American army and air force then smashed Iraqi forces in a lightning-quick desert campaign, although the United States stopped short of toppling Saddam because it feared a sudden disintegration of Iraq more than Saddam's hanging on to power.

The defeat of Iraqi armies received saturation coverage by the world's media. The spectacularly efficient operation demonstrated the awesome power of the U.S. military, rebuilt and revitalized by the spending and patriotism of the 1980s. It showed with equal clarity the secondary status of a declining Soviet Union,

which did not veto and even endorsed U.S. proposals in the U.N. Security Council. Little wonder that in the flush of yet another victory, President Bush spoke of a "new world order," an order that would apparently feature the United States and a cooperative United Nations working together to impose peace and security throughout the world.

✦ BUILDING A NEW EUROPE IN THE 1990s

The fall of communism, the end of the cold war, and the collapse of the Soviet Union opened a new era in European and world history. Few would disagree with this statement. Yet the dimensions and significance of this new era, opening suddenly and unexpectedly, are far from clear. A constant stream of information and events assails us, but what, we wonder, is truly significant and what is of only momentary importance? We are so close to what is going on that we lack vital perspective. Indeed, it is particularly difficult to interpret intelligently recent events. As the French philosopher Voltaire once said, "People who venture to write contemporary history must expect to be attacked for everything they have said and everything they have not said."[5]

Yet the historian must take a stand and find patterns of development and explanation. Thus we shall concentrate on two main themes of European development in the 1990s. First, considering that Europe has taken giant strides toward a loose unification of fundamental institutions and beliefs, we shall examine broad economic, social, and political trends that operated all across the continent in the 1990s. These trends include national economies increasingly caught up in global capitalism, the defense of social achievements under attack, and a powerful resurgence of nationalism and ethnic conflict. Second, with these common themes providing an organizational framework, we shall examine the course of development in the three overlapping but still distinct regions of contemporary Europe. These are Russia and the western states of the old Soviet Union; previously communist eastern Europe; and western Europe.

Common Patterns and Problems

The end of the cold war and the disintegration of the Soviet Union ended the division of Europe into two opposing camps with two different political and economic systems. Thus, although Europe in the 1990s was a collage of diverse peoples with their own politics, cultures, and histories, the entire continent shared an underlying network of common developments and challenges.

Of great importance, in economic affairs European leaders embraced, or at least accepted, a large part of the neoliberal, free-market vision of capitalist development. This was most strikingly the case in eastern Europe, where states such as Poland and Hungary implemented market reforms and sought to create vibrant capitalist economies. Thus postcommunist governments in eastern Europe freed prices, turned state enterprises over to private owners, and sought to move toward strong currencies and balanced budgets. Milder doses of this same free-market medicine were administered by politicians and big business to the lackluster economies of western Europe. These initiatives and proposals for further changes marked a considerable modification in western Europe's still-dominant welfare capitalism, which had been consolidated in the 1950s and 1960s and which featured a belief in government intervention, high taxes, and high levels of social benefits.

Two factors were particularly important in accounting for this ongoing shift from welfare state activism to tough-minded capitalism, which European socialists and leftist intellectuals regularly denounced as "savage capitalism," a dog-eat-dog throwback to the early industrial era. First, Europeans were only following practices and ideologies revived and enshrined in the 1980s in the United States and Great Britain (see page 1020). Western Europeans especially took American prescriptions more seriously in the 1990s. They did so because U.S. prestige and power were so high after the United States "won the cold war" (as American publicists liked to proclaim) and because the U.S. economy outperformed its western European counterparts in the Clinton years as it had in the Reagan era. Second, the deregulation of markets and the privatization of state-controlled enterprises in different European countries were an integral part of the powerful trend toward a wide-open, wheeler-dealer global economy. The rules of the global economy, which were laid down by powerful Western governments, multinational corporations, and big banks and international financial organizations such as the International Monetary Fund (IMF), called for the free movement of capital and goods and services, as well as low inflation and limited government deficits. Accepting these rules and attempting to follow them was the price of participating in the global economy.

In the 1990s, the ongoing computer and electronics revolution strengthened the move toward a global economy. That revolution thrived on the diffusion of ever-cheaper computational and informational capacity to small research groups and private businesses, which were both cause and effect of the revolution itself. Big organizations found it advantageous to farm out ever more work to small firms and home workers, who became able to link electronically with clients, regions, and most of the world. By the 1990s, an inexpensive personal computer had the power of a 1950s mainframe that filled a room and cost hundreds of thousands of dollars. The computer revolution reduced the costs of distance, speeding up communications and helping businesses tap cheaper labor overseas. Reducing the friction of distance made threats of moving factories abroad ring true and helped hold down wages at home.

The freer global economy, which probably did speed up world economic growth as enthusiasts invariably claimed, had powerful social consequences. Millions of ordinary citizens in western Europe saw global capitalism and freer markets as challenging hard-won social achievements. As in the United States and Great Britain in the 1980s, the public in other countries generally opposed the unemployment that accompanied corporate downsizing, the efforts to reduce the power of labor unions, and, above all, government plans to reduce social benefits. The difficulties with state-financed health care systems, with their costs rising as populations aged and more sophisticated treatments became available, provoked fierce debate and even upheaval. The reaction was particularly intense in France and Germany, where unions remained strong and socialists championed a minimum of change in social policies.

In the 1990s, political developments across the European continent were loosely unified by common patterns and problems. Most obviously, the demise of European communism brought the apparent triumph of liberal democracy everywhere. All countries embraced genuine electoral competition, with elected presidents and legislatures and the outward manifestations of representative liberal governments. With some notable exceptions, such as discrimination against Gypsies and illegal immigrants, countries also guaranteed basic civil liberties. Thus, for the first time since before the French Revolution, almost all of Europe followed the same general political model, although the variations were endless.

Guggenheim Museum, Bilbao, Spain Praised by admirers as the "first great building of the twenty-first century," Bilbao's exotic undulating museum of contemporary art is intended to revitalize the Basque region of northwestern Spain through international prestige, cultural renaissance, and tourism. Selected in a global competition, Frank Gehry's design relies heavily on three-dimensional computer modeling to hold dramatic opposites in delicate balance, as well as to translate complex forms into construction blueprints. *(Jeff Goldberg/Esto. All rights reserved)*

The triumph of the liberal-democratic program in Europe (and large parts of Latin America and Asia) led the American scholar Francis Fukuyama to discern the "end of history" in an influential book by that title. According to Fukuyama, first fascism and Nazism and then communism had been definitively bested by liberal-democratic politics and market economics. Con-versely, as James Cronin perceptively noted, the fall of communism and the end of ideological competition also marked the return of nationalism and national history.[6] The cold war and the superpowers had generally kept their allies and clients in line, either by force or by granting them conditional aid. As soon as the cold war was over, nationalism and ethnic conflict re-emerged, and history, as the story of different peoples, began again.

The resurgence of nationalism in the 1990s led to terrible tragedy and bloodshed in parts of eastern Europe, as it did in several hot spots in Africa and Asia. During the civil war in Yugoslavia, many observers feared that national and ethnic hatreds would spread throughout eastern Europe and infect western Europe in the form of racial hostility toward minorities and immigrants. Yet if nationalist and racist incidents were a recurring European theme, they remained limited in the extent of their damage. Of critical importance in this regard was the fact that all states wished to become or remain full-fledged members of the European society of nations and to join eventually an ever-expanding European Community, renamed the European Union in 1993. States that embraced national hatred and ethnic warfare, most notably Serbia, were branded as outlaws and boycotted and isolated by the international community. The process of checking resurgent nationalism in Europe and generally keeping it from getting out of hand was almost as significant as the resurgence itself.

Recasting Russia

Politics and economics were closely intertwined in Russia after the attempted Communist coup in 1991 and the dissolution of the Soviet Union. President Boris Yeltsin, his democratic supporters, and his economic ministers wanted to create conditions that would prevent forever a return to communism and would also right the faltering economy. Following the example of some postcommunist governments in eastern Europe and agreeing with those Western advisers who argued that private economies were always best, the Russian reformers opted in January 1992 for breakneck liberalization. Their shock therapy freed prices on 90 percent of all Russian goods, with the exception of bread, vodka, oil, and public transportation. The government also launched a rapid privatization of industry and turned thousands of factories and mines over to new private companies. Within a year, 64 percent of the privatized firms were owned by their workers, and each citizen received a voucher worth 10,000 rubles (about $22) to buy stock in private companies. However, control of the privatized companies usually remained in the hands of the old bosses, the managers and government officials who had been running the factories and ministries in the communist era.

President Yeltsin and his economic reformers believed that shock therapy would revive production and bring prosperity after a brief period of hardship. As the president explained, "Everyone will find life harder for approximately six months, then prices will fall and goods will begin to fill the market. By the autumn of 1992 the economy will have stabilized."[7] The results of the reforms were in fact quite different. Prices increased 250 percent on the very first day, and they kept on soaring, increasing twenty-six times in the course of 1992. At the same time, Russian production fell a staggering 20 percent. Nor did the situation stabilize quickly. Throughout 1995 rapid but gradually slowing inflation raged, and output continued to fall. According to most estimates, in 1996 the Russian economy produced at least one-third and possibly as much as one-half less than in 1991. Only in 1997 did the economy stop declining. That year a respected expert concluded that "Russia has suffered a minimum of five years of economic travail. . . . It is necessary to acknowledge that the economic reforms in Russia have not been the success so many insisted they were for so long."[8]

Rapid economic liberalization worked poorly in Russia for several reasons. Perhaps most important, Soviet industry had been highly monopolized and strongly tilted toward military goods. Production of many items had been concentrated in one or two gigantic factories or interconnected combines that supplied the entire economy. With privatization these powerful state monopolies simply became powerful private monopolies. These private monopolies then cut production and raised prices in order to obtain large profits, as in the case of producers of raw materials, or to reduce losses in noncompetitive industries, such as steel and automobiles.

This was not what Yeltsin and the free-market ideologues around him had expected. According to standard economic theory, monopoly prices and profits should have encouraged new firms to enter production, thereby increasing Russian output and pushing down prices through competition. But this desirable process developed very slowly. Powerful managers and bureaucrats forced Yeltsin's government to hand out enormous subsidies and credits to reinforce the positions of big firms and to avoid bankruptcies and the discipline of a free market. The managerial elite also combined with criminal elements, which had already been strong in the late Soviet period, to intimidate would-be rivals and prevent the formation of new businesses. Not that most ordinary Soviet citizens were eager to start businesses.

For decades they had been told that all capitalists were "speculators" and "exploiters," and as Russian business became associated in popular culture with crime, corruption, and national decline, most people had little reason to change their minds. In short, enterprise directors and politicians combined to subvert Yeltsin's unrealistic "radical" liberalization. This group then succeeded in eliminating worker ownership and converted large portions of previously state-owned industry into their own private property.

Runaway inflation and poorly executed privatization brought a profound social revolution to Russia. A new capitalist elite acquired great wealth and power, while large numbers of people fell into abject poverty, and the majority struggled in the midst of decline to make ends meet.

Managers, former officials, and financiers who came out of the privatization process with large shares of the old state monopolies stood at the top of the reorganized elite. The richest plums were found in Russia's enormous oil and natural resources industries, headed in the Soviet era by Viktor Chernomyrdin, who later became Yeltsin's prime minister. In 1992 Chernomyrdin and his allies convinced Yeltsin to keep the price of oil sold in Russia frozen at only 1 percent of the world price. This enabled unscrupulous enterprise directors to divert oil abroad, selling it through Russian front men and dishonestly pocketing enormous gains. The president of one big Russian oil company, who was worth virtually nothing in 1991, was worth $2.4 billion in 1995. From all indications, crime and corruption permeated Russian business big and small. Russian (and foreign) business leaders always moved with their bodyguards, but murders of executives were nonetheless common. The new elite was more highly concentrated in Moscow than ever before, and westerners who visited only the capital had difficulty believing that there was a national economic decline. By 1996 Moscow, with 5 percent of the population, accounted for 35 percent of the country's national income and controlled 80 percent of its capital resources.

At the other extreme, the vast majority saw their savings become practically worthless. Pensions lost much of their value, and whole markets were devoted to people selling off their personal goods to survive. Unemployment rose, and in 1996 35 percent of the population was living in poverty. The quality of public services and health care declined precipitously. Perhaps the most telling statistic, summing up millions of hardships and tragedies, was the truly catastrophic decline in the life expectancy of the average Russian male from sixty-nine years in 1991 to only fifty-eight years in 1996. Only in 1997 did living conditions for ordinary people begin to improve a bit as the economy finally began to grow.

Yeltsin and his supporters proved more successful in politics. Rapid economic decline in 1992 and 1993 increased popular dissatisfaction. This encouraged the Russian parliament, dominated by former Communists elected in 1990, to oppose Yeltsin's plan for constitutional reform. Yeltsin and his coalition of democratic reformers and big business interests pressed for a strong presidential system, while an opposition of communists, nationalists, and populists defended the authority of the parliament. Winning in April 1993 the support of 58 percent of the population in a referendum on his proposed constitution, Yeltsin then brought in tanks to crush a parliamentary mutiny in October 1993 and literally blew away the last vestiges of Soviet power. Although Yeltsin's allies in the reform parties lost ground to the communists and the nationalists in two subsequent elections, in 1996 Yeltsin won re-election as president in an impressive come-from-behind victory.

Yeltsin's victory in 1996 suggested to some observers that free and open elections had become a regular and accepted core of Russian political life. To be sure, political problems remained. The constitution concentrated power in the hands of the president, and parliament was subordinate. Russian political parties were weak, and only Russia's superrich had organized effectively to pursue their interests. Russia still lacked a rule of law and a reorganized court system to deal with crime and corruption. Yet with all politicians looking to the ballot box for legitimacy, there was some reason to hope that a growing tradition of Russian democracy would eventually rise to meet these challenges.

Russia's moderation in relations with foreign countries also provided reasons for guarded optimism as the century came to a close. First, military spending continued to decline under Yeltsin. Second, Russia reluctantly accepted the enlargement of NATO in 1997 to include Poland, Hungary, and the Czech Republic and negotiated a treaty with NATO to provide a framework for cooperation in the future. Third, Russia generally respected the independence of the Soviet successor states, peacefully resolving disputes with Ukraine and the Baltic republics. Moreover, although bitter ethnic conflicts abounded in central Asia and the Caucasus and resulted in outbreaks of civil war in Georgia, Armenia, Azerbaijan, and central Asia, Russia generally played a

Battling to Survive   These impoverished Russian women are selling their clothing and personal possessions in order to buy food for themselves and their families. Today's Russia is a relatively free society with a competitive electoral system, but begging, homelessness, and high crime rates have also taken root. *(Sovfoto)*

moderating role in these conflicts. Seldom did it use its position as dominant regional power to make matters worse.

The notable exception to this pattern was in Chechnya. In 1991 this tiny republic of 1 million Muslims on Russia's southern border with Georgia declared its independence from the Russian Federation (see Map 31.2). After a three-year stalemate, Yeltsin ordered the Russian army to crush the separatists. But Chechnya resisted with ferocious valor, and the unpopular war went poorly for Russia. In 1996 a wily Yeltsin accepted a face-saving truce and withdrew Russian soldiers, which helped him substantially in his close campaign for re-

election. Thus the Russian people spurned military adventure and reinforced popular sovereignty as the ultimate authority in public life.

Progress and Tragedy in Eastern Europe

Developments in eastern Europe shared important similarities with those in Russia, as many of the problems were the same. First, the postcommunist states of the former satellite empire worked to replace state planning and socialism with market mechanisms and private property. Second, Western-style electoral politics took hold, and as in Russia these politics were marked by

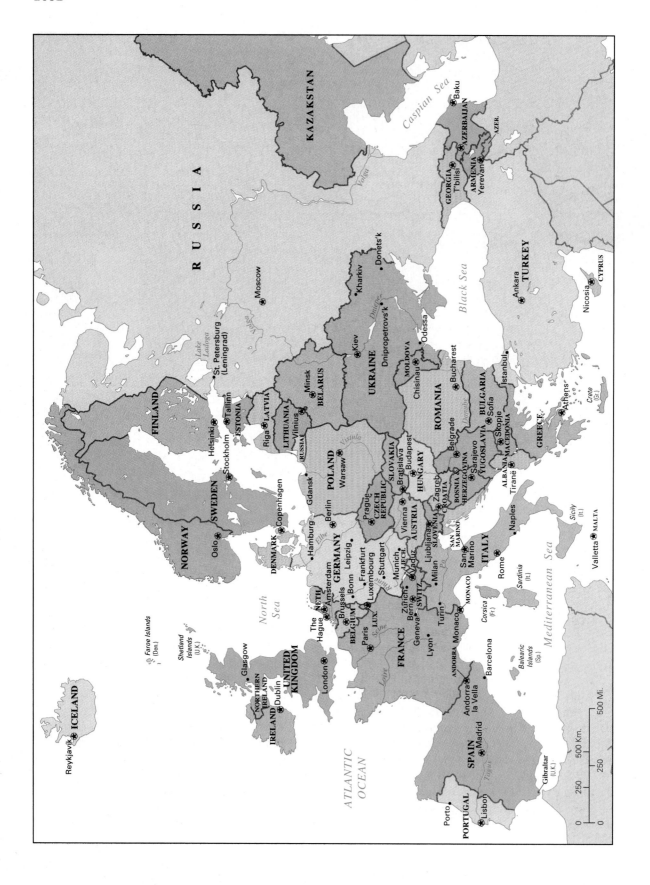

intense battles between presidents and parliaments and by weak political parties. Third, the social consequences of these revolutionary changes were similar to those in Russia. Inequality increased greatly. Ordinary citizens and the elderly were once again the big losers, while the young and the ex-Communists, whose privileges had included superior education and well-connected positions, were the big winners. Inequalities between richer and poorer regions also increased. Capital cities such as Warsaw, Prague, and Budapest concentrated wealth, power, and opportunity as never before, while provincial centers stagnated, and old industrial areas declined. Crime and gangsterism increased in the streets and in the executive suites, for it was frequently associated with big business and politicians.

Yet the 1990s saw more than a difficult transition, with high social costs, to market economies and freely elected governments in eastern Europe. As we have seen, the peoples of eastern Europe never fully accepted communism, which the opposition that triumphed in 1989 increasingly equated with Russian imperialism and the loss of national independence. The joyous crowds that toppled communist regimes in 1989 believed that they were liberating the nation as well as the individual. Thus communism died, and nationalism was reborn.

The surge of nationalism in eastern Europe recalled a similar surge of state creation after World War I. Then, too, authoritarian multinational empires had come crashing down in defeat and revolution, as the Austro-Hungarian Empire had broken apart and Russia's influence had receded. Then, too, peoples with long histories and rich cultures had drawn upon ideologies of popular sovereignty and national self-determination to throw off foreign rule and found new states, which contained ethnic minorities and conflicting nationalities to a greater or lesser extent. In the 1990s, the peoples of eastern Europe had a similar chance to create free, democratic, and peaceful national communities.

The response to this opportunity in the former communist countries was quite varied, but it was on a whole

---

MAP 31.3 Contemporary Europe   No longer divided by ideological competition and the cold war, today's Europe features a large number of independent states. Several of these states were previously part of the Soviet Union and Yugoslavia, both of which broke into many different countries. Czechoslovakia also divided on ethnic lines, while a reunited Germany emerged, once again, as the dominant nation in central Europe.

considerably better than the former Yugoslavia and the war in Bosnia (see page 1054) would suggest. Most observers agreed that Poland, the Czech Republic, and Hungary were the most successful in the 1990s (Map 31.3). Each of these three countries met the critical challenge of economic reconstruction more successfully than Russia. Each could claim to be the economic leader in eastern Europe, depending on the criteria selected. Poland had the fastest economic growth, the Czech Republic privatized the most completely and had the most foreign investment, and Hungary developed the most sophisticated market. The reasons for these successes included considerable experience with limited market reforms before 1989, flexibility and lack of dogmatism in government policy, and an enthusiastic embrace of capitalism by a rapidly rising entrepreneurial class. In the first five years of reform, Poland created twice as many new businesses as Russia, with a total population only one-fourth as large.

The three northern countries in the former Soviet bloc also did far better than Russia in creating new civic institutions, legal systems, and independent broadcasting networks that reinforced political freedom and national revival. Lech Walesa in Poland and Václav Havel in Czechoslovakia were elected presidents of their countries and proved as remarkable in power as in opposition. Continuing to call for ethical and spiritual regeneration after Czechoslovakia's "Velvet Revolution" in 1989, Havel and the Czech parliament accepted a "velvet divorce" in 1993 when Slovakian nationalists, dissatisfied with Czech majority rule and regional inequalities, wanted to break off and form their own state. In this instance, as in others in the 1990s, the three northern states managed to control national and ethnic tensions that might have destroyed their post-communist reconstruction. For all three countries, the horrors of war in the former Yugoslavia exemplified the dangers of playing with aggressive nationalism.

The popular goal of "rejoining the West" also was a powerful force toward moderation. Poles, Hungarians, and Czechs had been an integral part of medieval Christendom, and centuries later their opposition to communist rule was inspired in part by memories of liberal-democratic values in the 1920s. Now these nations wanted to complete the job, hoping to find security in NATO membership and prosperity in western Europe's ever-tighter economic union. Membership required many proofs of character and stability, however. Providing these proofs and endorsed by the Clinton administration, Poland, Hungary, and the Czech Republic were accepted into the NATO alliance in 1997.

Gaining admission to the European Union (EU) promised to be much more difficult. These three states (and others) could aspire to join the EU sometime in the future only if they continued to behave like "good Europeans."

Slovakia, Romania, and Bulgaria were the eastern European laggards in the postcommunist transition. Western traditions were much weaker there, and all three countries were much poorer than their neighbors to the north. In 1993 Bulgaria and Romania had per capita national incomes of $1,140, in contrast to Hungary ($3,830) and the Czech Republic ($2,710). But there was no going back, and progress was eventually made. After a slow start economically and politically, with grisly pictures of AIDS babies in grotesque orphanages and rampaging unpaid miners, the Romanian government claimed strenuously and with considerable justification that it was finally moving toward capitalism, democracy, and eventual integration with the West in NATO and the European Union. Slovakia and Bulgaria seemed to be following suit.

The great postcommunist tragedy was Yugoslavia. Under Josip Tito, Yugoslavia had been a federation of republics and regions under strict communist rule (see page 1008). But after Tito's death in 1980, power passed increasingly to the sister republics. This encouraged a revival of regional and ethnic conflicts, exacerbated by charges of ethnically inspired massacres during World War II and by a one-third decline in the Yugoslav standard of living between 1983 and 1988.

The revolutions of 1989 accelerated the breakup of Yugoslavia. The feuding Communist-turned-nationalist leaders of the different republics could not agree on a new constitution, and in January 1990 they abolished Yugoslavia's formerly all-powerful League of Communists. President Slobodan Milosevic of the Serbian republic speeded up preparations for a "greater Serbia," intending to grab territory from Yugoslavia's other republics and to combine all Serbs in a single state (Map 31.4). Milosevic's threats strengthened the cause of separatism, and in June 1991 Slovenia and Croatia declared their independence. Milosevic and Serbian separatists retaliated with a war of aggression, backed by the powerful Yugoslavian army and its largely Serbian officer corps. The Slovenes repulsed the invaders, but in Croatia the Serbian minority of about 12 percent and Milosevic's army seized about 30 percent of the territory, burning villages and pounding historic towns to pieces.

In 1992 the civil war spread to Bosnia-Herzegovina when it declared its independence. Serbs made up about 30 percent of Bosnia-Herzegovina's complex multiethnic society, and they adamantly refused to live under the Bosnian Muslims, who constituted 43 percent of the population (see Map 31.4). Local Serbian militias seized territory. Serbs, as well as Croats and Muslims to a far lesser extent, also ruthlessly drove "foreign" civilians from their homes with a combination of shelling, killing, raping, concentration camps, and torture. Cynically described as "ethnic cleansing," these atrocities were intended to send local minorities fleeing as traumatized refugees and to make each enclave ethnically homogeneous. The suffering was incalculable. Yugoslavia had been a tolerant and largely successful multiethnic state with groups living side by side and often intermarrying. The Bosnian war resulted in between 80,000 and 250,000 deaths and more than 3 million refugees.

Scenes of cruelty and slaughter on the nightly news shocked the world, but the Western nations had great difficulty formulating an effective response. By late 1994, a series of peace plans had failed and the Serbs controlled 70 percent of Bosnia-Herzegovina and 25 percent of Croatia. But the Muslims, strengthened by an alliance with the Croats and by American military aid, held on. Moreover, an isolated Milosevic wanted to ditch the Bosnian Serbs in order to hang on to power in his country, which had been isolated and impoverished by an effective international embargo.

The turning point came in July 1995, when Bosnian Serbs overran one of the United Nations' "safe areas," the predominately Muslim town of Srebrenica, and killed several thousand civilians. Western public opinion cried out for action, and a previously divided NATO bombed Bosnian Serb military targets as the Croatian army drove all the Serbs from Croatia. Reaffirming U.S. pre-eminence as the only superpower, President Bill Clinton brought the warring sides to Dayton, Ohio, where in November 1995 they reached a complicated accord. The Dayton Accord forced the Bosnian Serbs to remain in a loose federal state, where they administered only 49 percent of the country and the Muslim-Croatian alliance administered the rest. Troops from many NATO countries, including the United States, policed the agreement and maintained peace as 1998 opened. The civil war in Bosnia-Herzegovina was a monument to human cruelty and evil in the worst tradition of the twentieth century. But the belated fragile

Ethnic Majority
- Albanians
- Bulgarians
- Croatians
- Hungarians
- Macedonians
- Montenegrins
- Bosnians or Sandzak Muslims
- Romanians
- Serbs
- Slovenes
- No majority present
- ▬▬ Yugoslavia in 1991
- --- Republic boundaries
- --- Autonomous region boundaries

MAP 31.4 The Ethnic Composition of Yugoslavia, 1991   Yugoslavia had the most ethnically diverse population in eastern Europe. The Republic of Croatia had substantial Serbian and Muslim minorities. Bosnia-Herzegovina had large Muslim, Serbian, and Croatian populations, none of which had a majority. In June 1991, Serbia's brutal effort to seize territory and unite all Serbs in a single state brought a tragic civil war.

peace and ongoing efforts to repatriate refugees and to try alleged war criminals before an international tribunal also testified to the regenerative power of liberal values and human rights as the century drew to a close.

Unity and Identity in Western Europe

The movement toward western European unity, which since the late 1940s had inspired practical politicians seeking economic recovery and idealistic visionaries wanting to construct a genuine European identity that transcends destructive national rivalries, received a powerful second wind in the mid-1980s. The Single

European Act of 1986 laid down a detailed legal framework for establishing a single market, which would add the free movement of labor, capital, and services to the existing free trade in goods. With work proceeding vigorously toward the single market, which went into effect in 1993 as the European Community proudly rechristened itself the European Union (EU), French president François Mitterrand and German chancellor Helmut Kohl took the lead in pushing for a monetary union of EU members. After long negotiations and compromises, designed especially to overcome Britain's long-standing reluctance to cede aspects of sovereignty, in December 1991 the member states reached an agree-

Escape from Srebrenica   A Bosnian Muslim refugee arrives at the United Nations base in Tuzla and with her anguished screams tells the world of the Serbian atrocities. Several thousand civilians were murdered at Srebrenica, and Western public opinion finally demanded decisive action. Efforts continue to arrest those Serbs believed responsible and to try them for crimes against humanity. *(J. Jones/Sygma)*

ment in the Dutch town of Maastricht. The Maastricht treaty set strict financial criteria for joining the proposed monetary union, with its single currency, and set 1999 as the target date for its establishment. The treaty also anticipated the development of common policies on defense and foreign affairs after achieving monetary union.

Western European elites and opinion makers generally supported the decisive step toward economic integration embodied in the Maastricht treaty. They saw monetary union as a means of coping with Europe's ongoing economic problems, imposing financial discipline, cutting costs, and reducing high unemployment. And although European elites seldom stressed the point

in public debates, they saw monetary union as an historic, irreversible step toward a basic political unity. This unity would allow western Europe as a whole to regain its rightful place in world politics and to deal with the United States as an equal. After campaigning effectively in their countries for ratification of the Maastricht treaty, Kohl and his new counterpart in France, President Jacques Chirac, continued to lead an all-European effort to reduce national budget deficits to 3 percent of gross national product (GNP), achieve low inflation, and curb the growth of national debt. Even Italy and Spain, long regarded by international financiers as profligate states, tightened their belts and met the tough Maastricht standards. In early 1998, it appeared very likely that all of the EU's large states, with the exception of still-reluctant Britain, would join the new monetary union on schedule in 1999.

The Maastricht plan for monetary union encountered widespread skepticism and considerable opposition from ordinary people, leftist political parties, and patriotic nationalists. Ratification votes were close, especially when the public rather than the politicians could vote yes or no on the question. French voters ratified the treaty with only 51 percent in favor, and Danish voters rejected it before narrowly approving it in a second referendum.

There were several interrelated reasons for this widespread popular opposition, which remained strong as 1998 opened. First, many people resented the unending flow of rules handed down by the EU's ever-growing bureaucracy in Brussels, which sought to impose common standards on everything from cheese to daycare and undermined national practices and local traditions. Second, the Maastricht treaty, the transnational "Euro" currency it promised, and vague plans for political unification gave still more power to distant bureaucrats and political insiders. Many people feared that these changes would undermine popular sovereignty and democratic control through national politics and electoral competition. Above all, many ordinary citizens feared that the new Europe was being made at their expense. Budget cuts and financial austerity meant reductions in health care and social benefits and apparently did nothing to reduce western Europe's high unemployment rate. Thus the road toward European monetary union was bumpy, as voters, protesters, and concerned citizens contested cuts in spending and defended the social achievements of the postwar welfare state.

Events in France dramatically illustrated these developments. Mitterrand's Socialist government had been forced to adopt conservative financial policies in the 1980s (see pages 1020–1022), and more cuts followed the Maastricht treaty. In early 1993, frustrated French voters elected Jacques Chirac president and gave a coalition of conservatives and moderates an overwhelming victory. The Socialist party suffered total defeat, and the once-powerful Communist party was reduced almost to fringe-party status. With unemployment climbing to a new high of 10.7 percent in the European Union by October 1993, and with industrial production and national income declining, the new French government faced a dilemma. Chirac had won by promising a vigorous attack on unemployment, but

the Maastricht criteria demanded retrenchment. After some hesitation, Chirac's government chose deficit-reducing cuts in health benefits and transportation service. The Socialist opposition, the unions, and the railroad workers responded with massive protest marches and a crippling national strike, which closed down rail traffic throughout France for almost a month. Paris freeways became creeping parking lots as exhausted workers struggled with nightmare commutes. Yet the strike was widely supported by the public, despite the enormous inconvenience. Many ordinary people felt that the strikers were also fighting for them. The government had to back down, although it continued its austerity program with less provocative measures. In 1995 disgruntled French voters gave the Socialists control of the National Assembly. The Socialists quickly passed a controversial new law to reduce the legal workweek to 35 hours, in an attempt to reduce France's stubborn 12 percent unemployment rate without budget-busting spending. More generally, much of the western European public increasingly saw laws to cut the workweek and share the work as a way to reconcile desires for social welfare and a humane market economy with financial discipline and global competition.

Battles over budgets and high unemployment throughout the European Union raised profound questions about the meaning of European unity and identity. Would the European Union remain an exclusive Western club, or would it expand in the foreseeable future to include the postcommunist nations of eastern Europe, which aspired so ardently to EU membership? And if some eastern countries were admitted, how could Muslim Turkey's long-standing application be ignored? Conversely, how could a European Union of twenty-five to thirty countries have any real cohesion and common identity? These questions perplexed western Europeans throughout the 1990s.

The merging of East Germany into the German Federal Republic suggested the enormous difficulties of full East-West integration under the best conditions. After 1991 Helmut Kohl's Germany pumped massive investments into its new eastern provinces, but people in the east still saw factories closed, soaring unemployment, and social dislocation. Germany's generous social benefits cushioned the economic difficulties, but many ordinary citizens felt hurt and humiliated. West German practices weighed especially hard on eastern German women. Before unification, the overwhelming majority of these women had worked outside the home, effectively supported by cheap child care, flexible hours, and

French Commuters, 1995   Individuals and local governments improvised all manner of tactics to cope with the French transportation strike. Left without trains, city buses, and underground Metro service, these workers have been bused in from the suburbs on charter coaches. They are transferring to tourist boats being used to link temporarily a few points on the Seine. Many still face long walks to their jobs. *(Michel Verreault/Liaison)*

the prevailing socialist ideology. Now they faced expensive child care and a variety of pressures to stay at home and let men take the hard-to-find jobs. Many of these women, who had found autonomy and self-esteem in paid work, felt a keen sense of loss.

Instructed by the serious and largely unexpected difficulties of unification in Germany, where rising unemployment reached a postwar high of 12.8 percent in late 1997 and a catastrophic 20 percent in eastern Germany, western Europeans proceeded very cautiously in considering new requests for EU membership. Workers especially feared competition from low-paid but well-educated and hard-working eastern Europeans. Sweden, Finland, and Austria were admitted because they

had strong capitalist economies and because they did not need to maintain the legal neutrality that the Soviet Union had required during the cold war. But of the former communist states, only Poland, the Czech Republic, and Hungary had any foreseeable chance of becoming EU members, and even they would need to wait until some unnamed time in the early twenty-first century. A former dissident in Hungary summed up the situation: the former Eastern bloc countries wanted to establish a road map leading toward integration and full membership, "but all they receive for their pains is mysterious *mañana* [tomorrow]. . . . 'Now! Now! Now!' says the East. 'No! No! No!' says the West."[9] Almost a decade after the revolutions of 1989 and the end of the cold war, a reunifying Europe was moving toward common institutions and groping for a common identity, but the process was far from complete.

 ## ENTERING THE NEW MILLENNIUM

What about the future? For centuries astrologers and scientists, experts and ordinary people, have sought to answer this question. Although it may seem that the study of the past has little to say about the future, the study of history over a long period is actually very useful in this regard. It helps put the future in perspective.

Certainly, history is full of erroneous predictions, a few of which we have mentioned in this book. Yet lack of success has not diminished the age-old desire to look into the future, and, as we enter not only a new century but a new millennium, that desire is stronger than ever. Self-proclaimed experts even pretend that they have created a new science of futurology. With great pomposity, they often act as if their hunches and guesses about future human developments are inescapable realities. Yet the study of history teaches healthy skepticism regarding such predictions, however scientific they may appear. Past results suggest that most such predictions will simply not come true or not in the anticipated way. Thus history provides some psychological protection from the visions of modern prognosticators.

This protection is particularly valuable when we realize that views of the future tend to swing between pessimistic and optimistic extremes from one generation, or even from one decade, to the next. These swings back and forth between optimism and pessimism, which one historian has aptly called "the great seesaw" in the development of the Western world, reflect above all the current situation of the observers.[10] Thus in the economic stagnation and revived cold war of the 1970s and 1980s, many projections into the future were quite pessimistic, just as they were very optimistic in the 1950s and 1960s. Many people in the Western world feared that conditions were going to get worse rather than better. For example, there were fears that trade wars would permanently cripple the world economy, that pollution would destroy the environment, and that the traditional family would disappear. Many experts and politicians predicted that the energy crisis—in the form of skyrocketing oil prices—meant disaster in the form of lower standards of living at best and the collapse of civilization at worst. In fact, oil prices collapsed

in the early 1980s and they stayed low thereafter. It was heartening in that time of pessimism to know that most dire predictions do not prove true, just as the same knowledge of likely error is sobering in times of optimistic expectations.

Perhaps the most frightening source of pessimism and ominous predictions in recent times was the nuclear arms race. Not only did the United States and the Soviet Union accumulate unbelievably destructive nuclear arsenals, but Great Britain, France, China, India, and Israel also unlocked the secret of "the bomb." Other countries became equipped or desired to "go nuclear." Thus in the late 1970s and early 1980s, some gloomy experts predicted that twenty or thirty states might have nuclear weapons by the end of the century. In a world plagued by local wars and ferocious regional conflicts, these experts concluded that nuclear war was almost inevitable and speculated that the human race was an "endangered species."

Yet such predictions and the undeniable seriousness of the arms race jolted Western populations out of their customary fatalism regarding nuclear weapons. Efforts to reduce or even halt the nuclear buildup in the Soviet Union and the NATO alliance made some real progress. Above all, the Gorbachev era in the Soviet Union opened the way to new thinking and genuine superpower cooperation on nuclear arms questions. This cooperation accelerated after the fall of communism in Europe and the end of the cold war. Germany formally promised never to build nuclear arms as part of the price of German unification. Organized efforts to stop maverick states, such as Iraq and North Korea, from getting nuclear weapons made real progress. An optimistic projection from these developments could reasonably conclude that the global political will necessary to control nuclear proliferation will exist in the future.

Indeed, optimistic visions of the future were in the air after the end of the cold war. The pendulum definitely swung, most notably in the United States. Untroubled in the late 1990s by the high unemployment and early stages of corporate downsizing that soured the mood in western Europe, the United States celebrated its dynamic economy, its booming stock market, and the belated return in 1997 of rising real incomes for average workers. U.S. military power, leadership in world affairs, and excellence in advanced technologies also encouraged optimism and rosy projections. Little wonder that the large American contingent was riding high at the prestigious annual World Economic Forum of political leaders and top business executives at Davos, Switzerland, in February 1998. According to reports by journalists, the Americans explained in speeches and meetings that the world's future in the new millennium had already arrived in the United States, and they declared that future excellent. To repeat, just as it is heartening to know that most dire predictions do not prove true in pessimistic times, so is the same knowledge sobering in times of optimistic expectations.

Whatever does or does not happen, the study of history puts the future in perspective in other ways. We have seen that every age has its problems and challenges. Others before us have trod the paths of uncertainty and crisis. This knowledge helps save us from exaggerated self-pity in the face of our own predicaments.

Perhaps our Western heritage may rightly inspire us with pride and measured self-confidence. We stand, momentarily, at the head of the long procession of Western civilization. Sometimes the procession has wandered, or backtracked, or done terrible things. But it has also carried the efforts and sacrifices of generations of toiling, struggling ancestors. Through no effort of our own, we are the beneficiaries of those sacrifices and achievements. Now that it is our turn to carry the torch onward, we may remember these ties with our forebears.

To change the metaphor, we in the West are like a card player who has been dealt many good cards. Some of them are obvious, such as our technical and scientific heritage or our commitments to human rights and the individual. Others are not so obvious, sometimes half-forgotten or even hidden up the sleeve. Think, for example, of the Christian Democrats, the moderate Catholic party that emerged after World War II to play such an important role in the western European renaissance. And in the almost miraculous victory of peaceful revolution in eastern Europe in 1989—in what Czech playwright turned president Václav Havel called "the power of the powerless"—we see again the regenerative strength of the Western ideals of individual rights, representative government, and nationhood in the European homeland. We hold a good hand.

Our study of history, of mighty struggles and fearsome challenges, of shining achievements and tragic failures, gives a sense of what is the essence of life itself: the process of change over time. Again and again we have seen how peoples and societies evolve, influenced by ideas, human passions, and material conditions. As surely as anything is sure, this process of change over time will continue as the future becomes the present and then the past. And students of history are better prepared to make sense of this unfolding process be-

cause they have already observed it. They know how change is rooted in existing historical forces, and their projections will probably be better than many of the trendy speculations of futurologists. Students of history are also prepared for the new and unexpected in human development, for they have already seen great breakthroughs and revolutions. They have an understanding of how things really happen.

NOTES

1. Quoted in H. Smith, *The Russians* (New York: Quadrangle Books/New York Times, 1976), pp. 455–456.
2. M. Walker, *The Waking Giant: Gorbachev's Russia* (New York: Pantheon Books, 1987), p. 175.
3. T. G. Ash, *The Polish Revolution: Solidarity* (New York: Charles Scribner's Sons, 1983), p. 186.
4. Quoted in *Time,* January 6, 1986, p. 66.
5. Quoted in W. Laqueur, *Europe Since Hitler* (Baltimore: Penguin Books, 1972), p. 9. Rephrased slightly.
6. F. Fukuyama, *The End of History and the Last Man* (New York: Free Press, 1992); and J. Cronin, *The War the Cold War Made: Order, Chaos, and Return of History* (New York: Routledge, 1996), pp. 267–281.
7. Quoted in R. Suny, *The Soviet Experiment: Russia, the USSR, and the Successor States* (New York: Oxford University Press, 1998), p. 490.
8. M. Goldman, "Russia's Reform Effort: Is There Growth at the End of the Tunnel?" *Current History* 96 (October 1997): 313.
9. Quoted in L. Johnson, *Central Europe: Enemies, Neighbors, Friends* (New York: Oxford University Press, 1996), p. 286.
10. G. Blainey, *The Great Seesaw: A New View of the Western World* (London: Macmillan, 1988).

SUGGESTED READING

Many of the studies cited in the Suggested Reading for Chapters 29 and 30 are of value for the years since 1985 as well. Among other general works, F. Gilbert, *The End of the European Era: 1890 to the Present* (1991), is particularly helpful with its evenhanded account and extensive bibliography. Journalistic accounts in major newspapers and magazines are also invaluable tools for an understanding of recent developments. *Current History,* which devotes each monthly issue to either a geographical region or a contemporary issue, is especially recommended.

M. Dobbs, *Down with Big Brother: The Fall of the Soviet Empire* (1997), is a superb firsthand account by an inspired journalist who covered events in Russia and eastern Eu-

Britain's Millennium Dome will celebrate the arrival of the next thousand years in spectacular fashion. The lavish, 20-acre structure will offer visitors countless multimedia and interactive events, designed to entertain, thrill, and even stimulate thinking. This is an artist's rendering of "The Body Zone," one of the millennium exhibitions reveling in futuristic fantasies. *(NMEC/Hayes Division)*

rope between 1977 and 1993. On the Soviet Union, in addition to works cited in Chapter 30, the books by Smith and Walker cited in the Notes are fascinating eyewitness accounts of Soviet life in the 1970s and mid-1980s. The comprehensive history by Suny cited in the Notes is excellent on Russia in the 1990s and has up-to-date bibliographies. J. Hough and M. Fainsod, *How the Soviet Union Is Governed* (1979), is representative of Western scholarly thinking about the Soviet Union in the Brezhnev era. M. Lewin, *The Gorbachev Phenomenon: A Historical Interpretation* (1988), is excellent on the origins of the reforms. B. Eklof, *Soviet Briefing: Gorbachev and the Reform Period* (1989), focuses on 1987, a critical year. A. Shevchenko, *Breaking with Moscow* (1985), is the altogether fascinating autobiography of a top Soviet diplomat who defected to the United States. Two valuable studies by leading author-

ities on Russia today are M. Goldman, *Lost Opportunity: What Has Made Economic Reform in Russia So Difficult?* (1996); and M. McFaul, *Russia's 1996 Presidential Election: The End of Polarized Politics* (1996).

The recent work by Johnson cited in the Notes ably interprets developments in eastern Europe before and after the revolutions of 1989. For developments in Poland, M. Kaufman, *Mad Dreams, Saving Graces: Poland, a Nation in Conspiracy* (1989), carries developments through the summer of 1989; R. Leslie, *The History of Poland Since 1863* (1981), provides long-term perspective. T. Ash, *The Magic Lantern: The Revolution of '89 Witnessed in Warsaw, Budapest, Berlin, and Prague* (1990), is exciting instant history. Ash's book on Solidarity, cited in the Notes, is also recommended and may be compared with the less sympa-
(continued on page 1064)

LISTENING TO THE
PAST

A Solidarity Leader Speaks from Prison

Solidarity built a broad-based alliance of intellectuals, workers, and the Catholic church, which was one reason it became such a powerful movement in Poland. Another reason was Solidarity's commitment to social and political change through nonviolent action. This enabled Solidarity to avoid a bloodbath in 1981 and thus maintain its structure after martial law was declared, although at the time foreign observers often criticized Lech Walesa's leadership for being too cautious and unrealistic.

One of Walesa's closest coworkers was Adam Michnik. Walesa was a skilled electrician and a devout Catholic, whereas Michnik was an intellectual and disillusioned Communist. But their faith in nonviolence and gradual change bound them together. Trained as an historian but banned from teaching because of his leadership in student strikes in 1968, Michnik earned his living as a factory worker. In 1977 he joined with others to found the Committee for the Defense of Workers (KOR), which supported workers fired for striking. In December 1981, Michnik was arrested with the rest of Solidarity's leadership. While in prison until July 1994, he wrote his influential Letters from Prison, *from which the following is taken.*

Why did Solidarity renounce violence? This question returned time and again in my conversations with foreign observers. I would like to answer it now. People who claim that the use of force in the struggle for freedom is necessary must first prove that in a given situation it will be effective and that force, when it is used, will not transform the idea of liberty into its opposite.

No one in Poland is able to prove today that violence will help us to dislodge Soviet troops from Poland and to remove the communists from power. The U.S.S.R. has such enormous military power that confrontation is simply unthinkable. In other words, we have no guns. Napoleon, upon hearing a similar reply, gave up asking further questions. However, Napoleon was above all interested in military victories and not building democratic, pluralistic societies. We, by contrast, cannot leave it at that.

In our reasoning, pragmatism is inseparably intertwined with idealism. Taught by history, we suspect that by using force to storm the existing Bastilles we shall unwittingly build new ones. It is true that social change is almost always accompanied by force. But it is not true that social change is merely a result of the violent collision of various forces. Above all, social changes follow from a confrontation of different moralities and visions of social order. Before the violence of rulers clashes with the violence of their subjects, values and systems of ethics clash inside human minds. Only when the old ideas of the rulers lose this moral duel will the subjects reach for force—sometimes. This is what happened in the French Revolution and the Russian Revolution—two examples cited in every debate as proof that revolutionary violence is preceded by a moral breakdown of the old regime. But both examples lose their meaning when they are reduced to such compact notions, in which the Encyclopedists are paired with the destruction of the Bastille, and the success of radical ideologies in Russia is paired with the storming of the Winter Palace. An authentic event is reduced to a sterile scheme.

In order to understand the significance of these revolutions, one must remember Jacobin and Bolshevik terror, the guillotines of the sans-culottes, and the guns of the commissars. Without reflection on the mechanisms in victorious revolutions that gave birth to terror, it is impossible to even pose the fundamental dilemma facing contemporary freedom movements. Historical awareness of the possible consequences of revolutionary violence must be etched into any program of struggle for freedom. The experience of being corrupted by terror must be imprinted upon the consciousness of everyone who belongs to a freedom movement. [Or], as Simone Weil wrote, freedom will again become a refugee from the camp of the victors. . . .

Solidarity's program and ethos are inextricably tied to this strategy. Revolutionary terror has always been justified by a vision of an ideal society. In the name of this vision, Jacobin guillotines and

Bolshevik execution squads carried out their unceasing, gruesome work. The road to God's Kingdom on Earth led through rivers of blood.

Solidarity has never had a vision of an ideal society. It wants to live and let live. Its ideals are closer to the American Revolution than to the French. . . . The ethics of Solidarity, with its consistent rejection of the use of force, has a lot in common with the idea of nonviolence as espoused by Gandhi and Martin Luther King, Jr. But it is not an ethic representative of pacifist movements.

Pacifism as a mass movement aims to avoid suffering; pacifists often say that no cause is worth suffering or dying for. The ethics of Solidarity are based on an opposite premise: that there are causes worth suffering and dying for. Gandhi and King died for the same cause as the miners in Wujek who rejected the belief that it is better to remain a willing slave than to become a victim of murder [and who were shot down by police for striking against the imposition of martial law in 1981]. . . .

But ethics cannot substitute for a political program. We must therefore think about the future of Polish-Russian relations. Our thinking about this key question must be open; it should consider many different possibilities. . . .

The Soviet state has a new leader; he is a symbol of transition from one generation to the next within the Soviet elite. This change may offer an opportunity, since Mikhail Gorbachev has not yet become a prisoner of his own decisions. No one can rule out the possibility that an impulse for reform will spring from the top of the hierarchy of power. This is exactly what happened in the time of Alexander II and, a hundred years later, under Khrushchev. Reform is always possible, even in the face of resistance by the old apparatus. . . .

So what can now happen [in Poland]?

The "fundamentalists" say, no compromises. Talking about compromise, dialogue, or understanding demobilizes public opinion, pulls the wool over the eyes of the public, spreads illusions. Walesa's declarations about readiness for dialogue were often severely criticized from this point of view. I do not share the fundamentalist point of view. . . . The logic of fundamentalism precludes any attempt to find compromise, even in the future. It harbors not only the belief that communists are ineducable but also a certainty that they are unable to behave rationally, even in critical situations—that, in other words, they are condemned to suicidal obstinacy.

This is not so obvious to me. Historical experience shows that communists were sometimes forced by circumstances to behave rationally and to agree

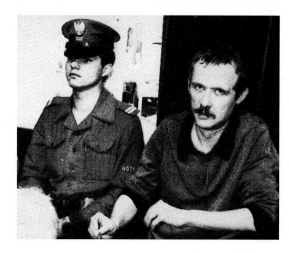

❖ Solidarity activist Adam Michnik in 1984, appearing under police guard in the military court that will sentence him to prison. (*Wide World Photos*)

to compromises. Thus the strategy of understanding must not be cast aside. We should not assume that a bloody confrontation is inevitable and, consequently, rule out the possibility of evolutionary, bloodless change. This should be avoided all the more inasmuch as democracy is rarely born from bloody upheavals. We should be clear in our minds about this: The continuing conflict may transform itself into either a dialogue or an explosion. The TKK [the underground Temporary Coordinating Committee of outlawed Solidarity] and [Lech] Walesa are doing everything in their power to make dialogue possible. Their chances of success will be greater if the level of self-organization of independent Polish society increases. For street lynchings, angry crowds are enough; compromise demands an organized society.

Questions for Analysis

1. What arguments does Michnik present for opposing the government with nonviolent actions? Are his arguments convincing?

2. How did Michnik's study of history influence his thinking? What lessons did he learn?

3. Analyze Michnik's attitudes toward the Soviet Union and Poland's Communist leadership. What policies did he advocate? Why?

Source: Adam Michnik, *Letters from Prison and Other Essays*, trans. Maya Latynski (Berkeley and Los Angeles: University of California Press, 1985), pp. 86–89, 92, 95, by permission of the University of California Press. Copyright © 1985 by The Regents of the University of California.

thetic account by N. Ascherson, *The Polish August: The Self-Limiting Revolution* (1982). A. Bramberg, ed., *Poland: Genesis of a Revolution* (1983), is a valuable collection of documents with extensive commentary. G. Stokes, ed., *From Stalinism to Pluralism: A Documentary History of Eastern Europe Since 1945,* 2d ed. (1996), is another excellent collection. V. Havel, *The Art of the Impossible: Politics as Morality in Practice, Speeches and Writings, 1990–1996* (1997), reflects the hopes and worries of the Czech leader since 1989. Two excellent, judicious studies on the tragedy in Yugoslavia are J. Lampe, *Yugoslavia as History: Twice There Was a Country* (1996); and T. Judah, *The Serbs: History, Myth and the Destruction of Yugoslavia* (1997). M. Pinson, *The Muslims of Bosnia-Herzegovina,* 2d ed, is a useful brief history. T. Rosenberg, *The Haunted Land: Facing Europe's Ghosts After Communism* (1995), is a moving look at people's lives in postcommunist eastern Europe.

The work by Cronin cited in the Notes provides a stimulating view of the late cold war and the massive changes following it. K. Jarausch, *The Rush to Unity* (1994), considers German unification critically from the perspective of domestic politics. P. Zelikow and C. Rice, *Germany Unified and Europe Transformed: A Study in Statecraft* (1995), is an award-winning study of relations between the Great Powers and the peaceful resolution of the German question. P. Katzenstein, ed., *Tamed Power: Germany in Europe* (1997), examines united Germany's integration into the larger European Union. The culture and politics of protest are provocatively analyzed in H. Hughes, *Sophisticated Rebels: The Political Culture of European Dissent, 1968–1987* (1988). G. Rose, *Jacques Delors and European Integration* (1995), analyzes the controversies surrounding the European Union in the 1990s. L. Barzini, *The Europeans* (1983), draws engaging group portraits of the different European peoples, and W. Laqueur, *The Germans* (1985), is a contemporary report by a famous historian doubling as a journalist; both works are recommended. J. Ardagh, *Germany and the Germans: The United Germany in the Mid-*

1990s, is another insightful study. P. Jenkins, *Mrs. Thatcher's Revolution: The End of the Socialist Era* (1988), and D. Singer, *Is Socialism Doomed? The Meaning of Mitterrand* (1988), are provocative studies on Great Britain and France in the 1980s.

The contemporary resurgence of nationalism is analyzed by R. Brubaker, *Nationalism Reframed: Nationhood and the National Question* (1996); and R. Caplan and John Feffer, *Europe's New Nationalism: States and Minorities in Conflict* (1996). D. Gompert and F. Larrabee, eds., *America and Europe: A Partnership in a New Era* (1997), features a number of European views of relations between the United States and Europe. N. Cantor, *The American Century: Varieties of Culture in Modern Times* (1997), is a lively consideration of many cultural developments that includes the 1990s. C. Goldin, *Understanding the Gender Gap: An Economic History of American Women* (1989), provides a provocative economic analysis of women's issues. Three important books on globalization are S. Strange, *The Retreat of the State: The Diffusion of Power in the World Economy* (1996); W. Greider, *One World, Ready or Not: The Manic Logic of Global Capitalism* (1997); and B. Eichengreen, *Globalizing Capital: A History of the International Monetary System* (1996). The November 1997 issue of *Current History,* "The Global Economy," provides an excellent introduction to this hotly debated issue. P. Kennedy, *Preparing for the Twenty-First Century* (1993), is a look into the future by a leading historian of international power politics. The work by Fukuyama cited in the Notes illustrates the widespread euphoria after the collapse of communism, arguing that democratic capitalism has defeated all its competitors. This optimistic projection may be compared with the somber future envisioned a generation ago in the influential and representative works by R. Heilbroner, *An Inquiry into the Human Prospect* (1974), and J. Revel, *The Totalitarian Temptation* (1977). The pathbreaking study of Blainey cited in the Notes examines the cycle of pessimism and optimism in Western history in fascinating detail.

Index

	Government	Society and Economy
3200 B.C.	Dominance of Sumerian cities in Mesopotamia, ca 3200–2340 Unification of Egypt; Archaic Period, ca 3100–2660 Old Kingdom of Egypt, ca 2660–2180 Dominance of Akkadian empire in Mesopotamia, ca 2331–2200 Middle Kingdom in Egypt, ca 2080–1640	Neolithic peoples rely on settled agriculture, while others pursue nomadic life, ca 7000–ca 3000 Development of wheeled transport in Mesopotamia, by ca 3200 Expansion of Mesopotamian trade and culture into modern Turkey, the Middle East, and Iran, ca 2600
2000 B.C.	Babylonian empire, ca 2000–1595 Hyksos invade Egypt, ca 1640–1570 Hittite Empire, ca 1600–1200 Kassites overthrow Babylonians, ca 1595 New Kingdom in Egypt, ca 1570–1075	First wave of Indo-European migrants, by 2000 Extended commerce in Egypt, by ca 2000 Horses introduced into western Asia, by ca 2000
1500 B.C.	Third Intermediate Period in Egypt, ca 1100–700 Unified Hebrew Kingdom under Saul, David, and Solomon, ca 1025–925	Use of iron increases in western Asia, by ca 1300–1100 Second wave of Indo-European migrants, by ca 1200
1000 B.C.	Hebrew Kingdom divided into Israel and Judah, 925 Assyrian Empire, ca 900–612 Phoenicians found Carthage, 813 Kingdom of Kush conquers and reunifies Egypt, 8th c. Medes conquers Persia, 710 Babylon wins independence from Assyria, 626 Dracon issues law code at Athens, 621 Cyrus the Great conquers Medes, founds Persian Empire, 550 Solon's reforms at Athens, ca 549 Persians complete conquest of ancient Near East, 521–464 Reforms of Cleisthenes in Athens, 508	Concentration of landed wealth in Greece, ca 750–600 Greek overseas expansion, ca 750–550 Beginning of coinage in western Asia, ca 640
500 B.C.	Battle of Marathon, 490 Xerxes' invasion of Greece, 480–479 Delian Confederacy, 478/7 Twelve Tables in Rome, 451/0 Valerio-Horatian laws in Rome, 449 Peloponnesian War, 431–404 Rome captures Veii, 396 Gauls sack Rome, 390 Roman expansion in Italy, 390–290 Conquests of Alexander the Great, 334–323 Punic Wars, 264–146 Reforms of the Gracchi, 133–121	Building of the Via Appia begins, 312 Growth of Hellenistic trade and cities, ca 300–100 Beginning of Roman silver coinage, 269 Growth of slavery, decline of small farmers in Rome, ca 250–100 Agrarian reforms of the Gracchi, 133–121

Religion and Philosophy	Science and Technology	Arts and Letters
Growth of anthropomorphic religion in Mesopotamia, ca 3000–2000 Emergence of Egyptian polytheism and belief in personal immortality, ca 2660 Spread of Mesopotamian and Egyptian religious ideas as far north as modern Anatolia and as far south as central Africa, ca 2600	Development of wheeled transport in Mesopotamia, by ca 3200 Use of widespread irrigation in Mesopotamia and Egypt, ca 3000 Construction of the first pyramid in Egypt, ca 2600	Sumerian cuneiform writing, ca 3200 Egyptian hieroglyphic writing, ca 3100
Emergence of Hebrew monotheism, ca 1700 Mixture of Hittite and Near Eastern religious beliefs, ca 1595	Construction of the first ziggurats in Mesopotamia, ca 2000 Widespread use of bronze in the ancient Near East, ca 1900 Babylonian mathematical advances, ca 1800	*Epic of Gilgamesh,* ca 1900 Code of Hammurabi, ca 1790
Exodus of the Hebrews from Egypt into Palestine, 13th c. Religious beliefs of Akhenaten, ca 1367	Hittites introduce iron technology, ca 1400	Phoenicians develop alphabet, ca 1400 Naturalistic art in Egypt under Akhenaten, ca 1367 Egyptian Book of the Dead, ca 1300
Era of the prophets in Israel, ca 1100–500 Intermixture of Etruscan and Roman religious cults, ca 753–509 Growing popularity of local Greek religious cults, ca 700 B.C.–A.D. 337 Babylonian Captivity of the Hebrews, 586–539	Babylonian astronomical advances, ca 750–400	Beginning of the Hebrew Bible, ca 9th c. Traditional beginning of the Olympic Games, 776 Babylonian astronomical advances, ca 750–400 Homer, traditional author of the *Iliad* and *Odyssey,* ca 700 Hesiod, author of the *Theogony* and *Works and Days,* ca 700 Archilochos, lyric poet, 648 Aeschylus, first significant Athenian tragedian, 525/4–456
Pre-Socratic philosophers, 5th c. Socrates, 469–399 Plato, 429–347 Diogenes, leading proponent of cynicism, ca 412–323 Aristotle, 384–322 Epicurus, 340–270 Zeno, founder of Stoic philosophy, 335–262 Emergence of Mithraism, ca 300 Spread of Hellenistic mystery religions, 2nd c. Greek cults brought to Rome, ca 200	Hippocrates, formal founder of medicine ca 430 Theophrastus, founder of botany, ca 372–288 Aristarchos of Samos, advances in astronomy, ca 310–230 Euclid codifies geometry, ca 300 Herophilus, discoveries in medicine, ca 300–250 Archimedes, works on physics and hydrologics, ca 287–212	Sophocles, tragedian who used his plays to explore moral and political problems, ca 496–406 Euripides, the most personal of the Athenian tragedians, ca 480–406 Thucydides, historian of the Peloponnesian War, ca 460–400 Aristophanes, the greatest writer of Old Comedy, ca 457–ca 385 Herodotus, the father of history, ca 450

	Government	Society and Economy
100 B.C.	Dictatorship of Sulla, 88–79 Civil war in Rome, 78–27 Dictatorship of Caesar, 45–44 Principate of Augustus, 31 B.C.–A.D. 14	Reform of the Roman calendar, 46
A.D. 300	Constantine removes capital of Roman Empire to Constantinople, ca 315 Visigoths defeat Roman army at Adrianople (378), signaling massive German invasions into the empire Bishop Ambrose asserts church's independence from the state, 380 Death of emperor Romulus Augustus marks end of Roman Empire in the West, 476 Clovis issues Salic law of the Franks, ca 490	Growth of serfdom in Roman Empire, ca 200–500 Economic contraction in Roman Empire, 3rd c.
500	Law Code of Justinian, 529 Dooms of Ethelbert, king of Kent, ca 604 Spread of Islam across Arabia, the Mediterranean region, Spain, North Africa, and Asia as far as India, ca 630–733	Gallo-Roman aristocracy intermarries with Germanic chieftains Decline of towns and trade, ca 500–700 Agrarian economy predominates in the West, ca 500–1500
700	Charles Martel defeats Muslims at Tours, 733 Pippin III anointed king of the Franks, 754 Charlemagne secures Frankish crown, r. 768–814	Height of Muslim commercial activity, ca 700–1300
800	Imperial coronation of Charlemagne, Christmas 800 Treaty of Verdun, 843 Viking, Magyar, and Muslim invasions, ca 845–900	Byzantine commerce and industry, ca 800–1000 Invasions and unstable conditions lead to increase of serfdom
1000	Seljuk Turks conquer Muslim Baghdad, 1055 Norman conquest of England, 1066 Penance of Henry IV at Canossa, 1077	Agrarian economy predominates in the West, 1000–1500 Decline of Byzantine free peasantry, ca 1025–1100 Growth of towns and trade in the West, ca 1050–1300 Domesday Book, 1086
1100	Henry I of England, r. 1100–1135 Louis VI of France, r. 1108–1137 Frederick I of Germany, r. 1152–1190 Henry II of England, r. 1154–1189 Thomas Becket murdered, 1170 Philip Augustus of France, r. 1180–1223	Henry I of England establishes the Exchequer, 1130 Beginnings of the Hanseatic League, 1159

Religion and Philosophy	Science and Technology	Arts and Letters
Mithraism spreads to Rome, 27 B.C.–A.D. 270 Dedication of the Ara Pacis Augustae, 9 Traditional birth of Jesus, ca 3	Pliny the Elder, student of natural history, 23 B.C.–A.D. 79 Frontinus, engineering advances in Rome, 30 B.C.–A.D. 104	Virgil, 70–19 B.C. Livy, ca 59 B.C.–A.D. 17 Ovid, 43 B.C.–A.D. 17
Constantine legalizes Christianity, 312 Theodosius declares Christianity the official state religion, 380 Donatist heretical movement at its height, ca 400 St. Augustine, *The City of God,* ca 425 Clovis adopts Roman Christianity, 496		St. Jerome publishes the Latin *Vulgate,* late 4th c. St. Augustine, *Confessions,* ca 390 Byzantines preserve Greco-Roman culture, ca 400–1000
Rule of St. Benedict, 529 Monasteries established in Anglo-Saxon England, 7th c. Muhammad preaches reform, ca 610 Publication of the Qu'ran, 651 Synod of Whitby, 664	Using watermills, Benedictine monks exploit energy of fast-flowing rivers and streams Heavy plow and improved harness facilitate use of multiple-ox teams; harrow widely used in northern Europe	Boethius, *The Consolation of Philosophy,* ca 520 Justinian constructs church of Santa Sophia, 532–537 Pope Gregory the Great publishes *Dialogues, Pastoral Care, Moralia,* 590–604
Missionary work of St. Boniface in Germany, ca 710–750 Iconoclastic controversy in Byzantine Empire, 726–843 Pippin III donates Papal States to the papacy, 756	Byzantines successfully use "Greek fire" in naval combat against Arab fleets attacking Constantinople, 673, 717	Lindisfarne Gospel Book, ca 700 Bede, *Ecclesiastical History of the English Nation,* ca 700 *Beowulf,* ca 700 Carolingian Renaissance, ca 780–850
Foundation of abbey of Cluny, 909 Byzantine conversion of Russia, late 10th c.	Stirrup and nailed horseshoes become widespread in shock combat Paper, invented in China ca 2nd c., enters Europe through Muslim Spain in 10th c.	Byzantines develop the Cyrillic script, late 10th c.
Beginning of reformed papacy, 1046 Schism between Roman and Greek Orthodox churches, 1054 Pope Gregory VII, 1073–1085 Peter Abelard, 1079–1142 St. Bernard of Clairvaux, 1090–1153 First Crusade, 1095–1099	Arab conquests bring new irrigation methods, cotton cultivation, and manufacture to Spain, Sicily, southern Italy Avicenna, Arab scientist, d. 1037	Romanesque style in architecture and art, ca 1000–1200 *Song of Roland,* ca 1095 Muslim musicians introduce lute, rebec—stringed instruments and ancestors of violin
Universities begin, ca 1100–1300 Concordat of Worms ends investiture controversy, 1122 Height of Cistercian monasticism, 1125–1175 Aristotle's works translated into Latin, ca 1140–1260 Third Crusade, 1189–1192 Pope Innocent III, 1198–1216	In castle construction Europeans, copying Muslim and Byzantine models, erect rounded towers and crenelated walls Windmill invented, ca 1180 Some monasteries, such as Clairvaux and Canterbury Cathedral Priory, supplied by underground pipes with running water and indoor latrines, elsewhere very rare until 19th c.	*Rubaiyat of Umar Khayyam,* ca 1120 Dedication of abbey church of Saint-Denis launches Gothic style, 1144 Hildegard of Bingen, 1098–1179 Court of troubador poetry, especially that of Chrétien de Troyes, circulates widely

	Government	Society and Economy
1200	Spanish victory over Muslims at Las Navas de Tolosa, 1212 Frederick II of Germany and Sicily, r. 1212–1250 Magna Carta, 1215 Louis IX of France, r. 1226–1270 Mongols end Abbasid caliphate, 1258 Edward I of England, r. 1272–1307 Philip IV (the Fair) of France, r. 1285–1314 England and France at war, 1296	Economic revival, growth of towns, clearing of wasteland contribute to great growth of personal freedom, 13th c. Agricultural expansion leads to population growth, ca 1225–1300
1300	Philip IV orders arrest of Pope Boniface at Anagni, 1303 Hundred Years' War, 1337–1450 Political chaos in Germany, ca 1350–1450 Merchant oligarchies or despots rule Italian city-states	European economic depression, ca 1300–1450 Black Death begins ca 1347; returns intermittently until 18th c. Height of the Hanseatic League, 1350–1450 Peasant and working-class revolts: France, 1358; Florence, 1378; England, 1381
1400	Appearance of Joan of Arc, 1429–1431 Medici domination of Florence begins, 1434 Princes in Germany consolidate power, ca 1450–1500 Ottoman Turks under Mahomet II capture Constantinople, May 1453 Wars of the Roses in England, 1453–1471 Ferdinand and Isabella complete reconquista in Spain, 1492 French invasion of Italy, 1494	Population decline, peasants' revolts, high labor costs contribute to decline of serfdom in western Europe Christopher Columbus reaches the Americas, October 1492 Portuguese gain control of East Indian spice trade, 1498–1511
1500	Charles V, Holy Roman emperor, 1519–1556 Imperial sack of Rome, 1527 Philip II of Spain, r. 1556–1598 Revolt of the Netherlands, 1566–1609 St. Bartholomew's Day massacre, August 24, 1572 Defeat of the Spanish Armada, 1588 Henry IV of France issues Edict of Nantes, 1598	Balboa discovers the Pacific, 1513 Magellan's crew circumnavigates the earth, 1519–1522 Spain gains control of Central and South America, ca 1520–1550 Peasants' Revolt in Germany, 1524–1525 "Times of Troubles" in Russia, 1598–1613
1600	Thirty Years' War, 1618–1648 Richelieu dominates French government, 1624–1643 Frederick William, Elector of Brandenburg, r. 1640–1688 English Civil War, 1642–1649	Chartering of British East India Company, 1600 Famine and taxation lead to widespread revolts, decline of serfdom in western Europe, ca 1600–1650 English Poor Law, 1601

Religion and Philosophy	Science and Technology	Arts and Letters
Crusaders capture Constantinople (Fourth Crusade), 1204 Maimonides, d. 1204 Founding of Franciscan order, 1210 Fourth Lateran Council, 1215 Founding of Dominican order, 1216 Thomas Aquinas (1225–1274) marks height of Scholasticism Pope Boniface VIII, 1294–1303	*Notebooks* of Villard de Honnecourt, a master mason (architect), a major source for Gothic engineering, ca 1250 Development of double-entry bookkeeping in Florence and Genoa, ca 1250–1340 Venetians purchase secrets of glass manufacture from Syria, 1277 Mechanical clock invented, ca 1290	*Parzifal, Roman de la Rose, King Arthur and the Round Table* celebrate virtues of knighthood Height of Gothic style, ca 1225–1300
Babylonian Captivity of the papacy, 1307–1377 John Wyclif, ca 1330–1384 Great Schism in the papacy, 1377–1418	Edward III of England uses cannon in siege of Calais, 1346	Petrarch, 1304–1374 Paintings of Giotto, ca 1305–1337 Dante, *Divine Comedy,* ca 1310 Boccaccio, *The Decameron,* ca 1350 Jan van Eyck, 1366–1441 Brunelleschi, 1377–1446 Chaucer, *Canterbury Tales,* ca 1385–1400
Council of Constance, 1414–1418 Pragmatic Sanction of Bourges, 1438 Expulsion of Jews from Spain, 1492	Water-powered blast furnaces operative in Sweden, Austria, the Rhine Valley, Liège, ca 1400 Leonardo Fibonacci's *Liber Abaci* (1202) popularizes use of Hindu-Arabic numerals, "a major factor in the rise of science in the Western world" Paris and largest Italian cities pave streets, making street cleaning possible Printing and movable type, ca 1450	Masaccio, 1401–1428 Botticelli, 1444–1510 Leonardo da Vinci, 1452–1519 Albrecht Dürer, 1471–1528 Michelangelo, 1475–1564 Raphael, 1483–1520 Rabelais, ca 1490–1553
Lateran Council attempts reforms of church abuses, 1512–1517 Machiavelli, *The Prince,* 1513 Concordat of Bologna, 1516 More, *Utopia,* 1516 Luther, *Ninety-five Theses,* 1517 Henry VIII of England breaks with Rome, 1532–1534 Loyola establishes Society of Jesus, 1540 Calvin establishes theocracy in Geneva, 1541 Merici establishes Ursuline order for education of women, 1544 Council of Trent, 1545–1563 Peace of Augsburg, 1555 Hobbes, 1588–1679 Descartes, 1596–1650	Copernicus, *On the Revolutions of the Heavenly Bodies,* 1543 Galileo, 1564–1642 Kepler, 1571–1630 Harvey, 1578–1657	Erasmus, *The Praise of Folly,* 1509 Castiglione, *The Courtier,* 1528 Cervantes, 1547–1616 Baroque movement in the arts, ca 1550–1725 Shakespeare, 1564–1616 Rubens, 1577–1640 Montaigne, *Essays,* 1598 Velazquez, 1599–1660
Huguenot revolt in France, 1625	Bacon, *The Advancement of Learning,* 1605 Boyle, 1627–1691 Leeuwenhoek, 1632–1723	Rembrandt van Rijn, 1606–1669 Golden Age of Dutch culture, 1625–1675 Vermeer, 1632–1675 Racine, 1639–1699

	Government	Society and Economy
1600 (cont.)	Louis XIV, r. 1643–1715 Peace of Westphalia, 1648 The Fronde in France, 1648–1660	Chartering of Dutch East India Company, 1602 Height of Dutch commercial activity, ca 1630–1665
1650	Protectorate in England, 1653–1658 Leopold I, Habsburg emperor, r. 1658–1705 Treaty of the Pyrenees, 1659 English monarchy restored, 1660 Siege of Vienna, 1683 Glorious Revolution in England, 1688–1689 Peter the Great of Russia, r. 1689–1725	Height of mercantilism in Europe, ca 1650–1750 Principle of peasants' "hereditary subjugation" to their lords affirmed in Prussia, 1653 Colbert's economic reforms in France, ca 1663–1683 Cossack revolt in Russia, 1670–1671
1700	War of the Spanish Succession, 1701–1713 Peace of Utrecht, 1713 Frederick William I of Prussia, r. 1713–1740 Louis XV of France, r. 1715–1774 Maria Theresa of Austria, r. 1740–1780 Frederick the Great of Prussia, r. 1740–1786	Foundation of St. Petersburg, 1701 Last appearance of bubonic plague in western Europe, ca 1720 Enclosure movement in England, ca 1730–1830 Jeremy Bentham, 1748–1823
1750	Seven Years' War, 1756–1763 Catherine the Great of Russia, r. 1762–1796 Partition of Poland, 1772–1795 Louis XVI of France, r. 1774–1792 American Revolution, 1776–1783 Beginning of the French Revolution, 1789	Start of general European population increase, ca 1750 Growth of illegitimate births, ca 1750–1850 Adam Smith, *The Wealth of Nations,* 1776 Thomas Malthus, *Essay of the Principle of Population,* 1798
1800	Napoleonic era, 1799–1815 Congress of Vienna, 1814–1815 "Battle of Peterloo," Great Britain, 1819	European economic imperialism, ca 1816–1880
1825	Greece wins independence, 1830 Revolution in France, 1830 Great Britain: Reform Bill of 1832; Poor Law reform, 1834; Chartists, repeal of Corn Laws, 1838–1848 British complete occupation of India, 1848 Revolutions in Europe, 1848	Height of French utopian socialism, 1830s–1840s German Zollverein founded, 1834 European capitalists begin large-scale foreign investment, 1840s Great Famine in Ireland, 1845–1851 Marx, *Communist Manifesto,* 1848
1850	Second Empire in France, 1852–1870 Crimean War, 1853–1856 Unification of Italy, 1859–1870 Civil War, United States, 1861–1865 Bismarck leads Germany, 1862–1890 Unification of Germany, 1864–1871 Britain's Second Reform Bill, 1867 Third Republic in France, 1870–1940	Crédit Mobilier founded in France, 1852 Japan opened to European influence, 1853 Mill, *On Liberty,* 1859 Russian serfs emancipated, 1861 First Socialist International, 1864–1871 Marx, *Das Capital,* 1867

Religion and Philosophy	Science and Technology	Arts and Letters
Patriarch Nikon's reforms split Russian Orthodox church, 1652 Test Act in England excludes Roman Catholics from public office, 1673 Revocation of Edict of Nantes, 1685 James II tries to restore Catholicism as state religion, 1685–1688 Montesquieu, 1689–1755 Locke, *Second Treatise on Civil Government,* 1690 Pierre Bayle, *Historical and Critical Dictionary,* 1697	Tull (1674–1741) encourages innovation in English agriculture Newton, *Principia Mathematica,* 1687 Newcomen develops steam engine, 1705	Construction of baroque palaces and remodeling of capital cities throughout central and eastern Europe, ca 1650–1725 J. S. Bach, 1685–1750 Fontenelle, *Conversations on the Plurality of Worlds,* 1686 The Enlightenment, ca 1690–1790 Voltaire, 1694–1778
Wesley, 1703–1791 Hume, 1711–1776 Diderot, 1713–1784 Condorcet, 1743–1794		
Ricardo, 1772–1823 Fourier, 1772–1837 Papacy dissolves the Jesuits, 1773 Church reforms of Joseph II in Austria, 1780s Reorganization of the church in France, 1790s	Hargreaves's spinning jenny, ca 1765 Arkwright's water frame, ca 1765 Watt's steam engine promotes industrial breakthroughs, 1780s War widens the gap in technology between Britain and the continent, 1792–1815 Jenner's smallpox vaccine, 1796	*Encyclopedia,* edited by Diderot and d'Alembert, published, 1751–1765 Mozart, 1756–1791 Rousseau, *The Social Contract,* 1762 Beethoven, 1170–1827 Wordsworth, 1770–1850 Romanticism, ca 1790–1850 Wollstonecraft, *A Vindication of the Rights of Women,* 1792
Napoleon signs Concordat with Pope Pius VII regulating Catholic church in France, 1801 Spencer, 1820–1903		
Comte, *System of Positive Philosophy,* 1830–1842 List, *National System of Political Economy,* 1841 Nietzsche, 1844–1900 Sorel, 1847–1922	First railroad, Great Britain, 1825 Faraday studies electromagnetism, 1830–1840s	Balzac, *The Human Comedy,* 1829–1841 Delacroix, *Liberty Leading the People,* 1830 Hugo, *Hunchback of Notre Dame,* 1831
Decline in church attendance among working classes, ca 1850–1914 Pope Pius IX, *Syllabus of Errors,* denounces modern thoughts, 1864 Doctrine of papal infallibility, 1870	Modernization of Paris, ca 1850–1870 Great Exhibition, London, 1851 Darwin, *Origin of Species,* 1859 Pasteur develops germ theory of disease, 1860s Suez Canal opened, 1869 Mendeleev develops the periodic table, 1869	Realism, ca 1850–1870 Freud, 1856–1939 Flaubert, *Madame Bovary,* 1857 Tolstoy, *War and Peace,* 1869 Impressionism in art, ca 1870–1900 Eliot (Mary Ann Evans), *Middlemarch,* 1872

	Government	Society and Economy
1875	Congress of Berlin, 1878 European "scramble for Africa," 1880–1900 Britain's Third Reform Bill, 1884 Berlin conference on Africa, 1884 Dreyfus affair in France, 1894–1899 Spanish-American War, 1898 Boer War, 1899–1902	Full property rights for women, Great Britain, 1882 Social welfare legislation, Germany, 1883–1889 Second Socialist International, 1889–1914 Witte directs modernization of Russian economy, 1892–1899
1900	Russo-Japanese War, 1904–1905 Revolution in Russia, 1905 Balkan wars, 1912–1913	Women's suffrage movement, England, ca 1900–1914 Social welfare legislation, France, 1904, 1910; England, 1906–1914 Agrarian reforms in Russia, 1907–1912
1914	World War I, 1914–1918 Easter Rebellion, 1916 U.S. declares war on Germany, 1917 Bolshevik Revolution, 1917–1918 Treaty of Versailles, 1919	Planned economics in Europe, 1914 Auxiliary Service Law in Germany, 1916 Bread riots in Russia, March 1917
1920	Mussolini seizes power, 1922 Stalin uses forced collectivization, police terror, ca 1929–1939 Hitler gains power, 1933 Rome-Berlin Axis, 1936 Nazi-Soviet Non-Aggression Pact, 1939 World War II, 1939–1945	New Economic Policy in the Soviet Union, 1921 Dawes Plan for reparations and recovery, 1924 The Great Depression, 1929–1939 Rapid industrialization in Soviet Union, 1930s Roosevelt's "New Deal," 1933
1940	United Nations, 1945 Cold war begins, 1947 Fall of colonial empires, 1947–1962 Communist government in China, 1949 Korean War, 1950–1953 "De-Stalinization" in Soviet Union, 1955–1962	The Holocaust, 1941–1945 Marshall Plan, 1947 European economic progress, ca 1950–1969 European Coal and Steel Community, 1952 European Economic Community, 1957
1960	The Berlin Wall goes up, 1961 United States in Vietnam, ca 1961–1973 Student rebellion in France, 1968 Soviet tanks end Prague Spring, 1968 Détente, 1970s Soviets in Afghanistan, 1979	Civil rights movement in United States, 1960s Collapse of postwar monetary system, 1971 OPEC oil price increases, 1973 and 1979 Stagflation, 1970s Women's movement, 1970s
1980	U.S. military buildup, 1980s Solidarity in Poland, 1980 Gorbachev takes power, 1985 Unification of Germany, 1989 Revolutions in eastern Europe, 1989–1990 End of Soviet Union, 1991 War in former Yugoslavia, 1991–1995	Growth of debt, 1980s Economic crisis in Poland, 1988 Maastricht Treaty proposes monetary union, 1990 Conservative economic policies in western Europe, 1990s

Religion and Philosophy	Science and Technology	Arts and Letters
Growth of public education in France, ca 1880–1900 Growth of mission schools in Africa, 1890–1914	Emergence of modern immunology, ca 1875–1900 Trans-Siberian Railroad, 1890s Marie Curie, discovery of radium, 1898 Electrical industry: lighting and streetcars, 1880–1900	Zola, *Germinal,* 1885 Kipling, "The White Man's Burden," 1899
Separation of church and state, France, 1901–1905 Jean-Paul Sartre, 1905–1980	Planck develops quantum theory, ca 1900 First airplane flight, 1903 Einstein develops relativity theory, 1905–1910	"Modernism," ca 1900–1929 Conrad, *Heart of Darkness,* 1902 Cubism in art, ca 1905–1930 Proust, *Remembrance of Things Past,* 1913–1927
Schweitzer, *Quest of the Historical Jesus,* 1906	Submarine warfare, 1915 Ernest Rutherford splits the atom, 1919	Spengler, *The Decline of the West,* 1918
Emergence of modern existentialism, 1920s Wittgenstein, *Essay on Logical Philosophy,* 1922 Revival of Christianity, 1920s and 1930s	"Heroic age of physics," 1920s First major public radio broadcasts in Great Britain and the United States, 1920 Heisenberg, "principle of uncertainty," 1927 Talking movies, 1930 Radar system in England, 1939	Gropius, the Bauhaus, 1920s Dadaism and surrealism, 1920s Woolf, *Jacob's Room,* 1922 Joyce, *Ulysses,* 1922 Eliot, *The Waste Land,* 1922 Remarque, *All Quiet on the Western Front,* 1929 Picasso, *Guernica,* 1937
De Beauvoir, *The Second Sex,* 1949 Communists fail to break Catholic church in Poland, 1950s	Oppenheimer, 1904–1967 "Big Science" in United States, ca 1940–1970 U.S. drops atomic bombs on Japan, 1945 Watson and Crick discover structure of DNA molecule, 1953 Russian satellite in orbit, 1957	Cultural purge in Soviet Union, 1946–1952 Van der Rohe, Lake Shore Apartments, 1948–1951 Orwell, *1984,* 1949 Pasternak, *Doctor Zhivago,* 1956 The "beat" movement in the United States, late 1950s
Catholic church opposes the legalization of divorce and abortion, 1970 to present Pope John Paul II electrifies Poland, 1979	European Council for Nuclear Research (CERN), 1960 Space race, 1960s Russian cosmonaut first to orbit globe, 1961 American astronaut first person on the moon, 1969	The Beatles, 1960s Solzhenitsyn, *One Day in the Life of Ivan Denisovitch,* 1962 Friedan, *The Feminine Mystique,* 1963 Servan-Schreiber, *The American Challenge,* 1967
Revival of religion in Soviet Union, 1985 to present Fukuyama proclaims "end of history," 1991	Reduced spending on Big Science, 1980s Computer revolution continues, 1980s and 1990s	Solzhenitsyn returns to Russia, 1994